Handbook of Insurance

Huebner International Series on Risk, Insurance, and Economic Security

J. David Cummins, Editor
The Wharton School
University of Pennsylvania
Philadelphia, Pennsylvania, USA

Series Advisors:

Dr. Phelim P. Boyle
University of Waterloo, Canada
Dr. Jean Lemaire
University of Pennsylvania, USA
Professor Akihiko Tsuboi
Kagawa University, Japan
Dr. Richard Zeckhauser
Harvard University, USA

Other books in the series:

Cummins, J. David and Derrig, Richard A.: *Classical Insurance Solvency Theory*
Borba, Philip S. and Appel, David: *Benefits, Costs, and Cycles in Workers' Compensation*
Cummins, J. David and Derrig, Richard A.: *Financial Models of Insurance Solvency*
Williams, C. Arthur: *An International Comparison of Workers' Compensation*
Cummins, J. David and Derrig, Richard A.: *Managing the Insolvency Risk of Insurance Companies*
Dionne, Georges: *Contributions to Insurance Economics*
Dionne, Georges and Harrington, Scott E.: *Foundations of Insurance Economics*
Klugman, Stuart A.: *Bayesian Statistics in Actuarial Science*
Durbin, David and Borba, Philip: *Workers' Compensation Insurance: Claim Costs, Prices and Regulation*
Cummins, J. David: *Financial Management of Life Insurance Companies*
Gustavson, Sandra G. and Harrington, Scott E.: *Insurance, Risk Management, and Public Policy*
Lemaire, Jean: *Bonus-Malus Systems in Automobile Insurance*
Dionne, Georges and Laberge-Nadeau, Claire: *Automobile Insurance: Road Safety, New Drivers, Risks, Insurance Fraud and Regulation*
Taylor, Greg: *Loss Reserving: An Actuarial Perspective*

Handbook of Insurance

Edited by

Georges Dionne
Risk Management Chair
HEC-Montréal

KLUWER ACADEMIC PUBLISHERS
Boston / Dordrecht / London

Distributors for North, Central and South America:
Kluwer Academic Publishers
101 Philip Drive
Assinippi Park
Norwell, Massachusetts 02061 USA
Telephone (781) 871-6600
Fax (781) 871-6528
E-Mail <kluwer@wkap.com>

Distributors for all other countries:
Kluwer Academic Publishers Group
Distribution Centre
Post Office Box 322
3300 AH Dordrecht, THE NETHERLANDS
Telephone 31 78 6392 392
Fax 31 78 6546 474
E-Mail <orderdept@wkap.nl>

Electronic Services <http://www.wkap.nl>

Library of Congress Cataloging-in-Publication Data

Handbook of insurance / edited by Georges Dionne.
p. cm. — (Huebner international series on risk, insurance, and economic security; 22)
Includes bibliographical references and index.
ISBN 0-7923-7870-9
1. Insurance—Handbooks, manuals, etc. I. Dionne, Georges. II. Series.

HG8061 .H36 2000
368—dc21

00-031342

Copyright © 2000 by Kluwer Academic Publishers.

All rights reserved. No part of this publication may be reproduced, stored in a retrieval system or transmitted in any form or by any means, mechanical, photocopying, recording, or otherwise, without the prior written permission of the publisher, Kluwer Academic Publishers, 101 Philip Drive, Assinippi Park, Norwell, Massachusetts 02061

Printed on acid-free paper.

Printed in the United States of America

To:

J. David Cummins,
University of Pennsylvania

Robert Lacroix,
Université de Montréal

Pierre Picard,
Université de Paris X-Nanterre

Jean-Marie Toulouse
HEC-Montréal

for providing me significant leverages over the past twenty years.

TABLE OF CONTENTS

CONTRIBUTING AUTHORS

Pierre-André Chiappori
University of Chicago, USA
pchiappo@midway.uchicago.edu

Keith J. Crocker
University of Michigan, USA
kcrocker@umich.edu

J. David Cummins
University of Pennsylvania, USA
cummins@wharton.upenn.edu

Patricia Danzon
University of Pennsylvania, USA
danzon@wharton.upenn.edu

Georges Dionne
École des Hautes Études Commerciales, Canada
georges.dionne@hec.ca

Neil Doherty
University of Pennsylvania, USA
doherty@wharton.upenn.edu

Louis Eeckhoudt
Faculté Universitaire Catholique de Mons, Belgium
eeckhoud@message.fucam.ac.be

Nathalie Fombaron
Université de Paris X-Nanterre, France
nathalie.fombaron@u-paris10.fr

Bernard Fortin
Université Laval, Canada
bfor@ecn.ulaval.ca

James Garven
Louisiana State University, USA
jim@garven.com

Christian Gollier
Université de Toulouse I, France
gollier@cict.fr

Tarek M. Harchaoui
Statistique Canada, Canada
harctar@statcan.ca

Scott Harrington
University of South Carolina, USA
scottnet@darla.badm.sc.edu

Howard Kunreuther
University of Pennsylvania, USA
kunreuther@wharton.upenn.edu

Paul Lanoie
École des Hautes Études Commerciales, Canada
paul.lanoie@hec.ca

Henri Loubergé
Université de Genève, Switzerland
henri.louberge@ecopo.unige.ch

Mark J. Machina
University of California, San Diego, USA
mmachina@weber.ucsd.edu

Richard MacMinn
University of Texas, USA
macminn@mail.utexas.edu

David Mayers
University of California, Riverside, USA
david.mayers@ucr.edu

Olivia S. Mitchell
University of Pennsylvania, USA
mitchelo@wharton.upenn.edu

Greg Niehaus
University of South Carolina
gregn@darla.badm.sc.edu

Jean-François Outreville
Office des Nations Unies, Switzerland
joutreville@unog.ch

Richard D. Phillips
Georgia State University, USA
rphillips@gsu.edu

Pierre Picard
Université de Paris-X Nanterre, France
pierre.picard@u-paris10.fr

Jean Pinquet
Université de Paris-X Nanterre, France
pinquet@u-paris10.fr

Laureen Regan
Temple University, USA
lregan@thunder.ocis.temple.edu

Harris Schlesinger
University of Alabama, USA
hschlesi@cbu.ua.edu

Clifford W. Smith
University of Rochester, USA
smith@simon.rochester.edu

Stephen D. Smith
Georgia State University, USA
sdsmith@gsu.edu

Arthur Snow
University of Georgia, USA
snow@rigel.econ.uga.edu

Sharon Tennyson
Cornell University, USA
st96@cornell.edu

Bertrand Villeneuve
Université de Toulouse 1, France
villeneu@cict.fr

Mary A. Weiss
Temple University, USA
mweiss@thunder.temple.edu

Ralph Winter
University of Toronto, Canada
rwinter@chass.utoronto.ca

Peter Zweifel
Zurich University, Switzerland
pzweifel@sozoec.unizh.ch

REFEREES

D. Arnaud
Université d'Angers, France

R. Arnott
Boston College, USA

M.M. Boyer
École des Hautes Études Commerciales, Canada

P. Boyle
University of Waterloo, Canada

R. Butler
University of Minnesota, USA

B. Caillaud
École Nationale des Ponts et Chaussées, France

P.A. Chiappori
University of Chicago, USA

A.P. Contandriopoulos
Université de Montréal, Canada

K. Crocker
University of Michigan, USA

D. Cummins
University of Pennsylvania, USA

M. Crouhy
CIBC, Canada

K. Dachraoui
École des Hautes Études Commerciales, Canada

R.A. Devlin
University of Ottawa, Canada

G. Dionne
École des Hautes Études Commerciales, Canada

N. Doherty
University of Pennsylvania, USA

L. Eeckhoudt
Université Catholique de Mons, Belgium

C. Fluet
Université du Québec à Montréal, Canada

N. Fombaron
Université de Paris X-Nanterre, France

B. Fortin
Université Laval, Canada

R. Gagné
École des Hautes Études Commerciales, Canada

J. Garven
Louisiana State University, USA

H. Geman
ESSEC, France

C. Gollier
Université de Toulouse I, France

A. Gron
Northwestern University, USA

T. Harchaoui
Statistique Canada, Canada

S. Harrington
University of South Carolina, USA

I. Hendel
Princeton University, USA

M. Huberman
Université de Montréal, Canada

M. Hoy
University of Guelph, Canada

B. Jullien
Université de Toulouse I, France

E. Karni
The Johns Hopkins University, USA

A. Kleffner
University of Calgary, Canada

R. Klein
Georgia State University, USA

H. Loubergé
Université de Genève, Switzerland

M. Machina
University of California, San Diego, USA

D. Mayers
University of California, Riverside, USA

J. Meyer
Michigan State University, USA

O.S. Mitchell
University of Pennsylvania, USA

P. Ouellette
Université du Québec à Montréal, Canada

J.F. Outreville
Office des Nations Unies, Switzerland

M. Pauly
University of Pennsylvania, USA

S. Perelman
Université de Liège, Belgium

J.E. Pesando
University of Toronto, Canada

L. Posey
Penn State University, USA

R. Puelz
Southern Methodist University, USA

B. Salanié
INSEE, France

C. Smith
University of Rochester, USA

S. Spaeter
Université de Strasbourg, France

P.K. Trivedi
Indiana University, USA

B. Venard
ESSCA, France

J.C. Vergnaud
Université de Strasbourg, France

B. Villeneuve
Université de Toulouse I, France

D. Vittas
The World Bank, USA

M. Weiss
Temple University, USA

D. Zajdenweber
Université de Paris X-Nanterre, France

PREFACE

Denis Kessler

President of the Fédération Française des Sociétés d'Assurances

As the new century begins, the question of risk and theories as to how it should be understood and measured are at the forefront. We know that risks evolve, and that today's risks are different from those of the past. The characteristics, frequency, intensity and, above all, the very nature of risks are changing radically.

If risks are becoming increasingly complex, it is because they are related to technological developments, new economic and social activities, and the aggregate effects of multiple factors. At the same time, risks have become more integrated, since a given event may have a series of consequences, giving rise to yet other risks. Risks are often interrelated, and sometimes the combined effect is greater than the sum of the individual parts. Smoking poses a risk, contact with asbestos poses another, and we know that the combined effect of these two risks does not merely increase the threat to health incrementally, but also exponentially.

The risks of today and tomorrow are also becoming more foreseeable as knowledge increases and we upgrade our statistical databases. This trend poses a major challenge to the insurance industry. Advances in genetics and more sophisticated knowledge of weather patterns, for example, have an impact on insurance techniques.

Risks are also becoming more endogenous to the behaviors of economic agents as we improve our understanding of such risks, as well as of the aggravating factors or, conversely, the preventive measures whose efficacy can be measured. A pedestrian who is hit on the head by a falling flowerpot is not responsible for his misfortune. A smoker, on the other hand, engages in behavior that greatly increases his likelihood of contracting a number of health problems. The risk run by the smoker can be quantified and priced.

Finally, the new risks tend to unfold more gradually, are more spread out in time and space, and often surface well after the causal event. This is true of environmental impairment, health risks and long-term care. Some risks are long-lasting or irreversible, making the analysis of appropriate preventive measures a complex matter. This leads us to the now famous "principle of precaution."

Given the changing face of risks, insurance techniques must evolve radically, and a new paradigm of risk and uncertainty must be constructed.

At the end of World War II, the rise of game theory and the first precepts of economic uncertainty theory initiated research in the field, laying the theoretical foundations that will be vital to the practice of insurance tomorrow. In the 1960's and 1970's, theoretical work in these areas made spectacular strides possible, in the form of sophisticated economic risk models and the creation of new financial instruments.

This theoretical body of work, enriched by developments to come, should be applied to the science of risk. Broken down into their smallest component parts, these risks can be hedged by relatively simple instruments, such as the "plain vanilla" options of finance.

New and better-targeted insurance products can be designed to better meet the needs and expectations of economic agents while more effectively dealing with the issues of moral hazard and adverse selection. Consequently, the insurability of risks will expand significantly.

However, this conceptual progress will not translate into better pricing of risks in general, and of previously uninsurable risks in particular, unless practical risk management tools and the means of relaying information are also improved. The issue of access to information needs to be resolved, as does the question of methods used to monitor both insureds and claims.

Naturally, these changes will affect the organization and processes of the insurance industry. We are likely to see broader integration of the various segments of the insurance offer, as the development of new risk management techniques further blurs the lines between various specialties and between insurance products.

In the face of new risks, and given our ability to better understand known risks, the nature of insurance demand is bound to change. It will be more closely aligned with the desire on the part of economic agents for protection against risks, which appears to increase with the level of democracy and wealth.

We can expect a strong rise in the demand for insurance on the part of corporations, which is strongly correlated to their ability to generate lasting profit. Private individuals are expected to demand more personalized products and greater freedom of choice in terms of the insurance products available to them. It is very likely that the days of cumbersome, constraining and uniform offers in health insurance, for example, are over.

This transformation of risks and the attendant demand for insurance will ultimately and necessarily lead to major changes in the insurance industry. This will be seen on the level of product distribution as well as organizational and strategic choices, in particular the relationship with banking services.

But this transformation in the nature of risks and insurance demand will also affect pricing policy and risk management in insurance companies. Here again, the development of new risk management and diversification techniques through reinsurance or direct access to the financial markets should offer insurers more options in terms of portfolio management, which will benefit end customers.

The new generation of derivative products, indexed to meteorological data for example, lays the foundations of the risk management tools that will support this enlarged insurance offer. Not only do such products allow for better coverage of risks whose complexity or magnitude previously rendered them all but uninsurable, they also contribute to optimizing insurance company investments, asset liability management and accounting for underwriting cycles.

The work accomplished by Georges Dionne and the authors who contributed to this project is of vital importance to anyone who is interested in the development of insurance. It lays the foundations of a new knowledge base—practically a new discipline: that of the science of risks, which is likely to lie at the heart of our future.

INTRODUCTION

It was the article "Uncertainty and the Welfare Economics of Medical Care" by Kenneth Arrow (*American Economic Review*, 1963) that first drew my research attention to risk, uncertainty, insurance, and information problems. This article proposed the first theorem showing that full insurance above a deductible is optimal when the premium contains a fixed-percentage loading, provided there are no information problems. It also suggested economic definitions of moral hazard and adverse selection. It generated many doctoral dissertations, my own included.

During the 1970s, different contributions proposed theorems regarding optimal insurance coverage, security design, and equilibrium concepts for situations with imperfect information. The 1980s were characterized by several theoretical developments such as the consideration of more than one period; of many contracting agents; of multiple risks; of non-expected utility; of commitment; and of several information problems simultaneously. Other economic and financial issues such as underwriting cycles, price volatility, insurance distribution, liability insurance crisis, and retention capacity were addressed by academics and practitioners during that period. Hierarchical relationships in firms and organizations and organizational forms were also studied, along with the pricing and design of insurance contracts in the presence of many risks.

The empirical study of information problems became a real issue in the 1990s. These years were also marked by the development of financial derivative products and large losses due to catastrophic events. The last months of 1999 were again catastrophic for South America and Europe. Alternatives to insurance and reinsurance coverages for these losses are now currently being proposed by financial markets.

The aim of this book is to provide a reference work on insurance for professors, researchers, graduate students, regulators, consultants, and practitioners. It proposes an overview of current research with references to the main contributions in different fields. It contains twenty-eight chapters written by thirty-five collaborators who have produced significant research in their respective domains of expertise. It can be considered as a complement to the previous books I edited for the S.S. Huebner Foundation of Insurance Education in 1992: *Foundations of Insurance Economics—Readings in Economics and Finance* (with S. Harrington) and *Contributions to Insurance Economics.*

Each chapter is presented with an abstract and keywords and each can be read independently of the others. They were (with very few exceptions) reviewed by at least two anonymous referees.

HISTORY AND FOUNDATIONS OF INSURANCE THEORY

The first chapter is concerned with history. H. Loubergé relates the evolution of insurance research since 1973. One important message from this contribution is that the significant developments of insurance economics during the last 25 years are exemplified by those in the economics of risk and uncertainty and in financial theory.

We next turn to the foundations of insurance theory in the absence of information problems. M. Machina's chapter investigates whether or not some classical results of insurance theory remain robust despite "departures from the expected utility hypothesis." His analysis covers insurance demand; deductible and co-insurance choices; optimal insurance contracts; multilateral risk-sharing agreements; and self-insurance vs self-protection. The general answer to the above question is positive although other restrictions are necessary since the technique of "generalized expected utility analysis" is broader than that of the classical, linear expected-utility model.

C. Gollier concentrates on comparisons among optimal insurance designs. He shows that three significant results can be obtained without the restriction of linear expected utility: (1) at least one state of the world is without insurance coverage; (2) the indemnity schedule is deterministic; and (3) the optimal contract contains a straight deductible. However, the hypothesis of linear expected utility generates additional results when transaction costs are nonlinear.

The ways in which changes in risk affect optimal-decision variables is a difficult and elusive research topic. The major problem is that risk aversion is not sufficient to predict that a decision-maker will reduce his optimal risky activity (or increase his insurance coverage) if an exogenous increase in risk is made in the portfolio. Usually, strong assumptions are needed regarding the variation of different measures of risk aversion or regarding distribution functions, in order to obtain intuitive comparative static results. C. Gollier and L. Eeckhoudt increase the level of difficulty by adding a background risk to the controllable risk. They propose restrictions on first- and second-order stochastic dominance to obtain the desired results. They also consider restrictions on preferences.

H. Schlesinger has contributed to many articles on market insurance demand, particularly as related to deductible insurance. He first presents the classical results related to changes in optimal coinsurance and deductible insurance with respect to initial wealth, loading (price), and risk aversion. Comparisons with self-protection and self-insurance are given and the basic models are extended to account for default and background risks.

ASYMMETRIC INFORMATION

The book then moves on to asymmetric information problems, which have often been introduced into economics and finance journals through examples of insurance allocation problems. Two sections of the book are devoted to this subject. The first reviews the main results related to ex-ante and ex-post moral hazard (fraud), adverse selection, liability insurance, and risk classification. The second studies the empirical significance of these resource allocation problems.

R. Winter extends his 1992 survey by presenting the development of optimal insurance under moral hazard over the past twenty-five years. He shows how the insurance context manages to introduce some structural devices. For example, optimal insurance contracts vary when effort affects the frequency (deductible) rather than the severity (coinsurance above a deductible) of accidents. The author also discusses dynamic contracts and contract renegotiation.

The chapter by G. Dionne, N. Doherty, and N. Fombaron proposes an extension of Dionne and Doherty (1992). Many new subjects are added to the classical one-period models of Stiglitz (Monopoly) and Rothschild and Stiglitz (Competition). Much more attention is paid to the recent developments of multi-period contracting. A section on the endogenous choice of types before contracting was added and another one treats moral hazard and adverse selection simultaneously. Finally, the last section covers various new subjects related to adverse selection: risk categorization and residual adverse selection; various types of risk aversion; incomplete symmetrical information; principals better informed than agents; *uberrima fides* and adverse selection with multiple risks.

The literature of risk classification was strongly influenced by K. Crocker and A. Snow. Risk classification may increase efficiency when certain conditions are met but it may also introduce adverse equity in some risk classes. The authors revise the theory of risk classification in insurance markets and discuss in detail its implications for efficiency and equity. They show how the adverse equity consequences of risk classification are related to economic efficiency through their treatment of the social cost of risk classification.

S. Harrington and P. Danzon study the basic relationships between liability law, liability insurance, and loss control. They study what implications limited wealth and liability have for the demand for liability insurance and accident deterrence. They discuss many other subjects such as correlated risks and liability insurance markets; liability insurance contract disputes; tort and liability insurance crises in the 1980s; and the efficiency of the U.S. tort liability/liability insurance system.

Insurance fraud is now a significant resource-allocation problem in many countries. It seems that traditional insurance contracts are not efficient to control this problem. In fact, there is a commitment issue involved, since audit costs may become quite substantial for different claims. P. Picard surveys the recent development of two types of models: costly state verification and costly state falsification. In the second type, the insured may use resources to modify the claims, whereas in the first he simply lies. Other subjects include adverse selection; credibility constraints on anti-fraud policies; and collusion between policy-holders and insurers' agents.

The empirical measurement of information problems is a recent research topic. Many issues are considered in the two chapters written by P.A. Chiappori (11) and G. Dionne (12). P.A. Chiappori puts the emphasis on empirical models that test for or evaluate the scope of asymmetric information in the insurance relationship, whereas G. Dionne discusses insurance and other markets such as labour and used cars. P.A. Chiappori suggests that empirical estimation of theoretical models requires precise information on the contract: information available to both parties on performance and transfers. He provides many examples of articles that approximate such conditions. G. Dionne concentrates his review on adverse selection and moral hazard in different markets. He concludes that efficient mechanisms seem to reduce the theoretical distortions due to information problems and even eliminate some residual information problems. However, this conclusion is stronger for adverse selection. One explanation is that adverse selection is related to exogenous characteristics, while moral hazard is due to endogenous actions that may change at any point in time. Finally, he shows how some insurance contract characteristics may induce insurance fraud!

B. Fortin and P. Lanoie review the major contributions on workers compensation, focusing on empirical measurement of the incentive effects of different workers compensation regimes. They also discuss the theoretical issues raised concerning the effects of such insurance on the individual's behaviour. They show how workers compensation can influence the frequency, duration, and nature of claims. They also examine what impact workers compensation has on wages and productivity. Finally, they show how workers compensation can be a substitute for unemployment insurance, a subject on which they have contributed in the literature.

The last paper on the empirical measurement of information problems presents statistical models of experience rating in automobile insurance. J. Pinquet shows how predictions on longitudinal data can be performed via a heterogeneous model. He also offers consistent estimations for numbers and costs of claims distribution. Examples are given for count-data models and empirical results from the portfolios of insurers in France are presented.

RISK MANAGEMENT AND INSURANCE PRICING

Risk management in insurance is now linked to the financial management of different risks. N. Doherty points out that the recent financial innovations in managing catastrophe risk may be interpreted as a response to the problem of insurance and reinsurance capacity brought on by the catastrophes having occurred over the last ten years. His chapter starts by showing why risk is costly to firms. The structure developed shows how reinsurance, financial instruments, insurance policy design, leverage management and organizational structure are linked to managing the different risks.

The role of corporate insurance demand has not received much attention in the literature, although we observe that insurance contracts are regularly purchased by corporations and do have their importance in the management of corporate risk. The model developed by R. MacMinn and J. Garven focuses on the efficiency gains of corporate insurance to reduce bankruptcy costs, agency costs, and tax costs. In fact, insurance is simply another risk management tool much like corporate hedging.

D. Cummins, R. Phillips, and S. Smith survey the finance literature on corporate hedging and financial-risk management and show how it applies to insurance. They also present empirical results on corporate hedging. They then develop a theoretical model to explain why insurers manage risk. They emphasize that the main motivation is to avoid shocks to capital that may trigger liquidations. The chapter by H. Kunreuther examines the role of insurance in managing risks from natural disasters, by linking insurance to cost-effective risk mitigation measures. The author outlines the roles that private markets (financial, institutions, and real estate developers) and municipalities can play in encouraging the adoption of cost-effective risk mitigation measures.

We then attack insurance pricing. Two complementary chapters treat this subject: the first discusses financial-pricing models, while the second introduces underwriting cycles. D. Cummins and R. Phillips propose a comprehensive survey of financial pricing for property-liability insurance and propose some extensions to existing models. Financial-pricing models are based on either the capital-asset pricing model; the intertemporal capital-asset pricing model; arbitrage theory or option pricing. Also presented are approaches using internal rate of return and insurance derivatives such as catastrophic-risk-call-spread and bonds.

After reviewing evidence that market insurance prices follow a second-order autoregressive process, S. Harrington and G. Niehaus present different theories that try to explain the cyclical behaviour of insurance prices. Capital shocks may explain periods of high insurance prices, while moral hazard and/or winners-curse effects can explain periods of low insurance prices. The potential effects of price regulation are also summarized.

INDUSTRIAL ORGANIZATION

The section on the industrial organization of insurance markets starts off with the two researchers who have most influenced this area of research, D. Mayers and C. Smith. They stress the association between the choice of organizational structure and the firm's contracting costs. They analyze the incentives of individuals involved in the three major functions of insurance firms: the executive function, the owner function, and the customer function. They also examine evidence on corporate-policy choices by alternative organizational structures: executive compensation policy; board composition; choice of distribution systems; reinsurance decisions; and use of participating policies. The relative efficiency of different organizational forms are reviewed.

Insurance distribution systems are analyzed by L. Regan and S. Tennyson. Their chapter focuses on three major economic issues: (1) the choice of distributive system(s) by an insurer; (2) the nature of insurer-agent relationships; and (3) the regulation of insurance distribution activities, including regulation of entry and disclosure of information to the consumer. J.F. Outreville studies the retention capacity of insurance markets in developing countries. He analyzes which factors may affect the aggregate-retention capacity of a country and provides statistical results obtained from a data base published by the United States Conference on Trade and Development of the 1988–1990 period.

Measuring the efficiency and productivity of financial firms is very difficult, since the definitions of output are multidimensional. Cummins and Weiss review the basics of modern frontier methodologies; discuss input and output measurement for insurers; and review the significant contributions made on these topics. As pointed out by the authors, modern frontier efficiency and productivity methodologies represent the state of the art in measurement of firm performance. Measures of efficiency and productivity based on these methods are useful in testing economic hypotheses about market structure, corporate governance, organizational form and other important topics. The measurement of efficiency and productivity also is useful in informing regulators about the firm's performance and in comparing performance across countries. So, they hope that more economists will use these methodologies for the insurance industry. The contribution of T. Harchaoui reviews the treatment of the insurance business in the system of national accounts, with a focus on measurement of productivity analysis. He first shows that the macroeconomics approach is very limited in many aspects. A more desaggregated approach allows for better understanding of the delineation of insurers' lines of business; the measurement of their activity; and their interactions with the economy.

LIFE INSURANCE, PENSIONS, AND ECONOMIC SECURITY

The book ends with life insurance, pensions, and economic security. It is well known that pension institutions face difficult years. One development, studied by O. Mitchell, is that defined contribution plans are now very popular, often at the expense of pension benefits. This changes the risk and rewards for participants and for government regulators. The expenses associated with pension management have become an important issue. For the author, reforms will be necessary to restore government social security programs to solvency.

B. Villeneuve analyses the micro-foundations of life insurance markets. He starts with the well-known life-cycle hypothesis and builds on contract theory to highlight the main issues in life insurance design. He shows how the trade-off between flexibility and opportunistic behaviour is an equilibrium outcome of actual life insurance contracts.

P. Zweifel proposes two types of reasons for the existence and growth of social insurance: (1) possible enhancements of efficiency and (2) public choice related to the interests of governments and politicians. Empirical evidence suggests that the second one is significant to explain the choice between private and social insurance. It also shows that individuals in the United States and Germany are subject to excess asset variance. Four proposals to improve the interplay between private and social insurance are formulated.

ACKNOWLEDGEMENTS

I wish to acknowledge all the authors and the referees for their significant contributions. The preparation of this book would not have been possible without the generous collaboration of Claire Boisvert who managed all the correspondence and spent many hours on all stages of the production process. I also thank Rose Antonelli and Jill Strathdee from Kluwer for their efficient collaboration. The preparation of the book was financed by the Huebner Foundation of Insurance Education, HEC-Montreal, the *Fédération Française des Sociétés d'Assurance* (FFSA), FCAR (Quebec), and CRSH (Canada).

Georges Dionne
Risk Management Chair
HEC-Montréal

Part I
History

1 Developments in Risk and Insurance Economics: the Past 25 Years*

Henri Loubergé

University of Geneva

Abstract

The paper reviews the evolution in insurance economics over the past 25 years, by first recalling the situation in 1973, then presenting the developments and new approaches which flourished since then. The paper argues that these developments were only possible because steady advances were made in the economics of risk and uncertainty and in financial theory. Insurance economics has grown in importance to become a central theme in modern economics, providing not only practical examples to illustrate new theories, but also inspiring new ideas of relevance for the general economy.

Keywords: Insurance economics, research, developments, economics of risk and uncertainty, insurance theory.

JEL Classification Numbers: D80, G22.

1.1 INTRODUCTION

In the early seventies, some 25 years ago, the economics of risk and insurance was still embryonic. Indeed, when the International Association for the Study of Insurance Economics (known as the "Geneva Association") was founded in 1973, one of the main goals of its promoters was to foster the development of risk and insurance education in economics curricula. In particular, there existed then a clear need to develop an understanding for risk and insurance issues among the future partners of the insur-

* This survey is based on a previous survey published in The *Geneva Papers on Risk and Insurance—Issues and Practices* in October 1998. The revision was performed on the occasion of a visit to the University of Alabama, Department of economics, finance and legal studies. The support of this university is gratefully acknowledged. I thank Georges Dionne, Louis Eeckhoudt and Harris Schlesinger for their comments on successive versions of this survey. The usual disclaimer applies.

ance industry. It seemed also necessary to attract the attention of economists to risk and insurance as a stimulating and promising research field.

At that time, some attempts to link insurance to general economic theory had already been made, but they were still scarce. The books written by Pfeffer (1956), Mahr (1964), Greene (1971) and Carter (1972), or the one edited by Hammond (1968), tried to bridge the gap. (Corporate) risk management started, at least in the United States, to be considered seriously as a branch of study—see Mehr and Hedges (1963) and Greene (1973) as early references. The main obstacle was obvious: traditional economic theory was based on the assumption of perfect knowledge—with some *ad hoc* departures from this assumption, as in the theory of imperfect competition or in keynesian macroeconomics. In order to witness an integration of risk and insurance issues into general economics, the theory of risk had to develop and to gain a position at the heart of economic theory. The foundations were already at hand: the von Neumann-Morgenstern (1947) and Savage (1954) theory of behavior under uncertainty, the Friedman-Savage (1948) application to risk attitudes, Pratt's (1964) analysis of risk aversion, Rothschild and Stiglitz's (1970) characterization of increases in risk, and the Arrow (1953) and Debreu (1959) model of general equilibrium under uncertainty. These approaches had already started to bring about a first revolution in the study of finance, with the Markowitz (1959) model of portfolio selection and the Sharpe (1964)—Lintner (1965)—Mossin (1966) model of equilibrium capital asset pricing (the CAPM). With the benefit of hindsight, we know now that they did provide the starting point for the accomplishment of one of the Geneva Association's long term objective: the integration of risk and insurance research into the mainstream of economic theory.

The purpose of this chapter is to remind the reader of the situation of insurance economics in 1973 (section 1.2), and to summarize its main development since then (section 1.3). A fourth section introduces a personal bias towards financial economics by focussing on the new approaches which resulted from the growing integration of insurance and finance. The fifth section concludes. Due to limitations in space and time, two important related topics were omitted from this survey: health economics and social security. In addition, life insurance is only partially covered in the fourth section. The discussion is mainly concentrated on risk and insurance economics issues as they relate to property-liability insurance.

1.2 INSURANCE ECONOMICS IN 1973

In 1973, the economic theory of insurance had already begun to develop on the basis of five seminal papers: Borch (1962), Arrow (1963), Mossin (1968), Ehrlich and Becker (1972) and Joskow (1973).[1] All these papers were based on the expected utility

[1] Note that two of these six authors, Kenneth Arrow and Gary Becker, received later the highest distinction for economic research—the Nobel Prize in economics.

paradigm. Following these papers, and more particularly the first two of them, a bunch of important papers were published. They were a signal that the elaboration of an economic theory of risk and insurance was under way.

1.2.1 Borch (1962)

In his 1962 *Econometrica* paper "Equilibrium in Reinsurance Markets", Karl Borch showed how Arrow's (1953) model of general equilibrium under uncertainty could be applied to the problem of risk-sharing among reinsurers. But generations of economists later learned that this insurance application had far-reaching implications for the general economy.[2] In 1953 Arrow had shown that financial markets provide an efficient tool to reach a Pareto-optimal allocation of risks in the economy. Nine years later, Borch's theorem[3] was showing how the mechanism could be organized in practice.

The main argument is the following. In a population of risk-averse individuals, only social risks matter. Individual risks do not really matter, because they can be diversified away using insurance markets (the reinsurance pool of Borch's paper). But social risks—those affecting the economy at large—cannot be diversified: they have to be shared among individuals. Borch's theorem on Pareto-optimal risk exchanges implies that the sharing rule is based on individual risk-tolerances (Wilson, 1968). Each individual (reinsurer) gets a share in the social risk (the reinsurance pool) in proportion to its absolute risk-tolerance, the inverse of absolute risk-aversion. If all individual utility functions belong to a certain class (later known as the HARA[4] class, and including the most widely used utility functions), the sharing rule is linear. The abovementioned CAPM, for long the dominant paradigm in finance theory, represents a special case of this general result.

In my view, Borch's paper provides the corner stone of insurance economics. It may be conveniently used to show how the insurance mechanism of risk-pooling is part of a more global financial mechanism of risk-allocation, and how a distinction may nevertheless be made between insurance institutions and other financial institutions.[5] For this reason, it may be used to clarify ideas on a hotly-debated issue: the links between finance and insurance (see section 1.4 below).

In the years until 1973, Borch's seminal contribution found its main insurance economics extensions in the papers by Arrow (1970) and Kihlstrom and Pauly

[2] See Gollier (1992) for a review of the economic theory of risk exchanges, Drèze (1979) for an application to human capital, and Drèze (1990) for an application to securities *and* labor markets.

[3] Actually, Borch's theorem was already present in Borch (1960), but the latter article was primarily written for actuaries, whereas the 1962 *Econometrica* paper was addressed to economists.

[4] HARA = Hyperbolic Absolute Risk Aversion. As noted by Drèze (1990), the linearity of the sharing rule follows from the linearity of the absolute risk tolerance implied by hyperbolic absolute risk aversion.

[5] The question whether or not "institutions" are needed to allocate risks in the economy was tackled later in the finance literature.

(1971).[6] Arrow (1970) explicitly defined insurance contracts as conditional claims—an exchange of money now against conditional money in the future. Kihlstrom and Pauly (1971) introduced information costs in the risk-sharing model: they argued that economies of scale in the treatment of information explain why insurance companies exist. In 1974, Marshall extended further this analysis by introducing a distinction between two modes of insurance operations: reserves and mutualization. Under the reserve mode, aggregate risk is transferred to external risk-bearers (investors). With mutualization, external transfer does not apply, or cannot apply: aggregate losses are shared among insureds.

1.2.2 Arrow (1963)

The article published in 1963 by Kenneth Arrow in *The American Economic Review* under the title "Uncertainty and the Welfare Economics of Medical Care" represents the second point of departure for risk and insurance economics. This work may be credited with at least three contributions. Firstly, the article provided, for the first time, what has become now the most famous result in the theory of insurance demand: if the insurance premium is loaded, using a fixed-percentage loading above the actuarial value of the policy, then it is optimal for an expected utility maximizing insured to remain partially at risk, i.e., to purchase incomplete insurance coverage. More specifically, Arrow proved that full insurance coverage above a deductible is optimal in this case. Secondly, Arrow also proved that, when the insured and insurer are both risk-averse expected utility maximizers, Borch's theorem applies: the Pareto-optimal contract involves both a deductible and coinsurance of the risk above the deductible—a result later extended by Moffet (1979) and Raviv (1979), and more recently generalized by Gollier and Schlesinger (1996) and by Schlesinger (1997) under the less restrictive assumption of risk aversion.[7] Thirdly, the paper was also seminal in the sense that it introduced asymmetric information into the picture. Arrow noted that transaction costs and risk aversion on the insurer's side were explanations for incomplete risk-transfer, but he also realized that moral hazard and adverse selection represented major obstacles for a smooth running of the insurance mechanism. By attracting the attention of economists to these problems, he paved the way to more focused work by Pauly (1968) and Spence and Zeckhauser (1971)—on moral hazard—and by Akerlof (1970), on adverse selection.

[6] The applications of Borch's theorem in the actuarial literature are reviewed by Lemaire (1990).

[7] More precisely, Schlesinger (1997) considers one version of Arrow's theorem: the case where the insurer is risk neutral and the insured is risk averse (risk aversion being defined by Schlesinger as preferences consistent with second-degree stochastic dominance). In this case a straight deductible policy is optimal whenever the insurer's costs are proportional to the indemnity payment.

1.2.3 Mossin (1968)

The paper by Jan Mossin, "Aspects of Rational Insurance Purchasing", published in 1968 in *The Journal of Political Economy*, is generally considered as the seminal paper on the theory of insurance demand—although some of Mossin's results were also implicit in Arrow (1963) and explicit in another paper on insurance demand published the same year, but earlier, in the same journal (Smith, 1968).[8] Mossin's paper is mainly famous to have shown: 1) that partial insurance coverage is optimal for a risk-averse expected utility maximizer when the insurance premium is such that a positive proportional loading applies to the actuarial value of the policy;[9] and 2) that insurance is an inferior good if the individual has decreasing absolute risk aversion (DARA). It was later pointed out (see below) that these strong results are respectively based on the implicit assumptions that the individual faces only one risk, and that the amount at risk is fixed (unrelated to wealth or income).

1.2.4 Ehrlich and Becker (1972)

In the modern theory of risk management, insurance is only seen as one of the tools available to manage risk. The whole set of tools may be decomposed into subsets according to the different steps of the risk management process. Insurance belongs to the set of risk-transfer tools and represents a very powerful financial mechanism to transfer risk to the market. Another subset corresponds to risk-prevention. Broadly, risk-prevention mechanisms may be classified under two headings: mechanisms intended to modify the probability of an event; and mechanisms intended to mitigate the consequences of an event. Ehrlich and Becker (1972) were the first to propose a rigorous economic analysis of risk prevention. They coined the terms *self-protection* and *self-insurance* to designate the two kinds of mechanisms and studied their relationship to "market insurance". For this reason, their paper may be seen as the first theoretical paper on risk management. Briefly, the paper provides three main results:

1) In the absence of market insurance, a risk averse expected utility maximizer will engage into self-protection and self-insurance activities, but the optimal "investment" in these activities depends on their cost. As usual, marginal benefit (in terms of higher expected utility) has to be weighted against the marginal disutility brought about by additional costs, so that complete elimination of the risk is not optimal in general.

2) Self-insurance and market insurance are substitutes: an increase in the degree of protection provided by the insurer induces a rational individual to reduce his invest-

[8] Optimal insurance coverage using a deductible was also analyzed by Pashigian, Schkade and Menefee (1966) and by Gould (1969).

[9] Incomplete insurance may be obtained using a deductible or coinsurance (or both).

ment into activities (or behavior) aimed at reducing the consequences of the insured event. Of course, this result is also of importance for the theory of moral hazard (see section 3), but Ehrlich and Becker did not assume asymmetric information.

3) Self-protection and market insurance may be complement or substitutes, depending on the sensitivity of the insurance premium to the effects of self protection. Thus, the insurer can give to the insured an incentive to engage into self-protection activities (which reduce the likelihood of a loss) by introducing a link between the premium rate and the observation of such activities. This result is also of importance for the theory of moral hazard, and more generally for agency theory (the theory of relationships between an agent and a principal).

1.2.5 Joskow (1973)

The paper published by Paul Joskow in the *Bell Journal of Economics and Management Science* under the title "Cartels, Competition and Regulation in the Property-Liability Insurance Industry" represents the first successful attempt to submit the insurance sector to an economic evaluation. The paper assesses competition by analyzing market concentration and barriers to entry, it measures returns to scale, and discusses insurance distribution systems and rate regulation. By providing empirical results on these issues, it has provided a reference point for subsequent research on the sector. Briefly, Joskow found that the insurance industry was approximately competitive, that constant returns to scale could not be excluded, and that the direct writer system was more efficient than the independent agency system.

1.3 DEVELOPMENTS

The five seminal contributions presented in the preceding section prepared the ground for numerous developments. These may be grouped under three main headings: the demand for insurance and protection, economic equilibrium under asymmetric information, and insurance market structure. It is striking to realize that many of these developments are not developments in insurance economics per se. They occurred within the wider domain of general economics, insurance providing in some cases an illustration of general results, and in other cases a stimulation to search for general results.[10]

1.3.1 Optimal Insurance and Protection

The observation of economic life shows that individuals generally do not insist to get partial coverage when they subscribe an insurance policy. As the insurance premiums

[10] The survey of developments presented in this section draws on the excellent survey of insurance economics by Dionne and Harrington (1992).

are generally loaded (at least to cover insurance costs), this is however the behavior which would be expected from them, according to Mossin's (1968) results. Moreover, insurance does not seem to be empirically an inferior good. If it was, insurance companies would be flourishing in the poorer nations and would be classified among the declining industries in the richer nations of the world. This is, again, in contradiction with Mossin's analysis (given that absolute risk aversion is, indeed, empirically decreasing). One of the seminal papers at the roots of insurance economics has thus led to two paradoxes, and it is interesting to observe how theory was reconciled with factual observation.

The second paradox (insurance is an inferior good) did not stimulate much research effort. Some scholars tried to dig into the idea by exploring the conditions under which insurance would be not only an inferior good, but also a Giffen good: see Hoy and Robson (1981), and Briys, Dionne and Eeckhoudt (1989). But the interest remained limited. There are probably two reasons for that. Firstly, following Arrow (1970), it was quickly recognized among economists that insurance is a financial claim. Thus it does not seem really appropriate to apply to insurance concepts which were derived to categorize consumption goods. Secondly, it has probably been noticed by most scholars that the condition under which Mossin's result obtains is not generally met in practice. Mossin assumes that the individual's wealth increases, but that the risky component of wealth remains unchanged. In reality, changes in wealth generally imply changes in the portion of wealth exposed to a risk of loss, and this is sufficient to resolve the paradox (see Chesney and Loubergé, 1986).

The first paradox (partial coverage is optimal) has stimulated much more research effort. It has first been noticed that the result is not robust to changes in the pricing assumptions: for example, full insurance is optimal if the loading is a lump sum.[11] Some researchers pointed out that the result was either reinforced, or did not hold, if the behavioral assumptions were modified: see Razin (1976) and Briys and Loubergé (1985), or the nonexpected utility developments mentioned below. But the most interesting breakthrough came from enlarging the scope of the analysis. This was made in the early eighties by deriving the logical conclusion from the observation that insurance is a financial claim. It had been recognized for long (Markowitz, 1959) that the demand for financial assets should take place in a portfolio context, taking into consideration imperfect correlations across random asset returns. The same kind of reasoning was applied to insurance by Mayers and Smith (1983), Doherty and Schlesinger (1983a) (1983b), Turnbull (1983) and Doherty (1984). In this portfolio approach, which was soon accepted as an important improvement, the demand for insurance coverage on one risk should not be analyzed in isolation from the other risks faced by the decision-maker: insurance demand is not separable, even when the

[11] It is obvious that the paradox may be resolved if one introduces differential information. If the insured overestimates the probability (or the amount) of loss, full insurance may be optimal, even when the premium is loaded with a fixed proportional factor.

risks are independent (Eeckhoudt and Kimball, 1992). When considering the insurance demand for one risk, one has to take into account the other risks, their stochastic dependence with the first risk, whether they are insurable or not, and under what conditions, whether some insurance is compulsory or subsidized, whether a riskless asset is traded, etc.: see, e.g., Schlesinger and Doherty (1985), von Schulenburg (1986), Kahane and Kroll (1985), Briys, Kahane and Kroll (1988), and Gollier and Scarmure (1994).[12] Thus, assuming that correlation is a sufficient measure of dependence, it may be optimal to partially insure a risk which is negatively correlated with an other risk, even if the premium is actuarial. Conversely, it may be optimal to fully insure a risk in spite of unfair pricing, if this risk is positively correlated with an other uninsurable risk. In a portfolio context, incomplete markets for insurance provide a rationale for full insurance of the insurable risks. Mossin's paradox can thus be resolved by changing the perspective, instead of changing the analytical model (the expected utility model).[13]

Building on these premises, the current research program is mainly devoted to extend these preliminary results to more general cases of stochastic dependence. Several papers verify the conditions under which optimal insurance demand under background risk has desirable comparative statics properties, such as an increase in optimal insurance coverage when the insured or uninsured risks increase, or whether a deductible policy remains optimal under background risk: see Eeckhoudt and Kimball (1992), Meyer (1992), Dionne and Gollier (1992), Eeckhoudt, Gollier and Schlesinger (1991) (1996), Gollier and Schlesinger (1995), Gollier (1995), Gollier and Pratt (1996), Gollier and Schlee (1997), Tibiletti (1995), Guiso and Jappelli (1998), Meyer and Meyer (1998).

Research integrating joint optimal decisions on consumption, saving and insurance represents a different research program, which was addressed by Moffet (1977) and Dionne and Eeckhoudt (1984). The latter authors have shown that investing in the riskless asset is a substitute to insurance purchasing. This work was generalized by Briys (1988) using a continuous-time model. A related avenue of research concerns the joint determination of insurable asset purchases and optimal insurance coverage: see Meyer and Ormiston (1996) and Eeckhoudt, Meyer and Ormiston (1997) for recent work along this line.

Surprisingly, research on risk prevention (self-protection and self-insurance activities) has not benefited much from progress in the theory of insurance demand. Analysis has remained mainly circumscribed to the framework proposed by Ehrlich and Becker (1972). For example, Boyer and Dionne (1989) have shown that self-

[12] On a related theme, see also Doherty and Schlesinger (1990) for the case where the insurance contract itself is risky, due to a non-zero probability of insurer default. The paper shows that full insurance is not optimal under fair insurance pricing and that the usual comparative statics result from the single risk model do not carry over to the model with default risk.

[13] These theoretical advances closely followed similar advances in the theory of risk premiums under multiple sources of risk: Kihlstrom, Romer and Williams (1981), Ross (1981).

insurance leads to stronger changes in risk than self-protection (see also Chang and Ehrlich, 1985). Dionne and Eeckhoudt (1985) obtained the surprising result that an increase in risk aversion does not necessarily result in higher self-protection, everything else constant (see also Briys and Schlesinger, 1990). Dionne and Eeckhoudt (1988) also investigated the effects of increasing risk on optimal investment in self-protection activities. But in contrast with most other domains of risk and insurance economics, the analysis was not yet replaced in a broader context. A step in that direction was nevertheless made by Briys, Schlesinger and von Schulenburg (1991) with their analysis of "risky risk management".

Other work in the theory of optimal insurance concerns:

1) The specific issues raised by the corporate demand for insurance: these issues will be considered in section 4 below.

2) The extension of the expected utility model to take into account state-dependent utility functions. One can thus introduce into the analysis important observations from reality. For example, the observation that the indemnity paid by the insurer cannot provide complete compensation for a non monetary loss, such as the loss of a child, or the observation that the marginal utility of wealth is different under good health and under disability: see Arrow (1974), Cook and Graham (1977) and Schlesinger (1984) for important papers along this line.

3) The replacement of the expected utility model with recent generalizations, grouped under the heading "nonexpected utility analysis". This research program started recently but it has already produced several interesting results. Using the distinction between risk aversion of order 1 and risk aversion of order 2,[14] Segal and Spivak (1990) have shown that Mossin's (1968) result on the optimality of partial coverage under a loaded insurance premium does not hold necessarily if risk aversion is of order 1 (see also Schlesinger, 1997). Now, risk aversion of order 1 may occur under the expected utility model (if the utility is not differentiable at the endowment point), or under some generalizations of this model, such as Yaari's (1987) dual theory, or Quiggin's (1982) rank-dependent expected utility theory. In particular, using Yaari's model, Doherty and Eeckhoudt (1995) have shown that only full insurance or no insurance (corner solutions) are optimal with proportional insurance, when the premium is loaded.[15] Karni (1992) has shown that Arrow's (1963) result on the optimality of a deductible policy is robust to a change in behavioral assumptions if the modified model satisfy some differentiability conditions, which are met by Yaari's (1987) and Quiggin's (1982) models. Indeed, Schlesinger (1987) has shown that this result is very robust to a change of model. Konrad and Skaperdas (1993) applied Ehrlich and Becker's (1972) analysis of self-insurance and self-protection to the rank-dependent expected utility model. Schlee (1995) confronted the comparative statics of deductible

[14] The orders of risk aversion, as defined by Segal and Spivak (1990), rests on the behavior of the risk premium in the limit, as the risk tends towards zero.

[15] This result is reminiscent of the same result obtained under Hurwicz's model of choice under risk: see Briys and Loubergé (1985).

insurance in the two classes of model. So far, the most comprehensive attempt to submit classical results in insurance economics to a robustness test by shifting from expected utility to nonexpected utility can be found in Machina (1995, 2000). He uses his generalized expected utility analysis (Machina, 1982) and concludes that most of the results are quite robust to dropping the expected utility hypothesis. However, the generality of his conclusion is challenged by Karni (1995) since Segal and Spivak (1990) have shown that Machina's generalized expected utility theory is characterized by risk aversion of order 2.

The demand for insurance under background risk in a nonexpected utility setting was analyzed by Doherty and Eeckhoudt (1995) using Yaari's (1987) dual choice theory. They show that an interior solution (partial insurance) *may* be obtained under proportional coverage and a loaded insurance premium if an independent background risk is present (full insurance remains optimal if the premium is fair). Dropping the independence assumption, they note that the likelihood to get a corner solution increases. But, qualitatively, the effects of introducing positively or negatively correlated background risks are the same as under expected utility. More generally, Schlesinger (1997) has shown that introducing an independent background risk in a decision model with risk aversion does not change the predictions obtained under a single source of risk: full insurance is optimal under a fair premium; partial or full insurance may be optimal under a loaded premium; and a deductible policy remains optimal.

1.3.2 Economic Equilibrium under Asymmetric Information

The Arrow (1953) model shows that a market economy leads to a general and efficient[16] economic equilibrium—even under uncertainty—if the financial market is complete, i.e., provided the traded securities and insurance contracts make possible to cover any future contingency. This is an important result since it extends to the case of uncertainty the classical result on the viability and efficiency of a free market economy.

However, as Arrow himself noticed in his 1963 article (see above), complete coverage is not always available (or even optimal) in insurance markets due to various reasons. Among these reasons, asymmetric information has received much attention in the economic literature and has been generally discussed under two main headings: moral hazard and adverse selection. Moral hazard exists when (1) the contract outcome is partly under the influence of the insured, and (2) the insurer is unable to

[16] An economic equilibrium is efficient if it is Pareto optimal: it is impossible to organize a reallocation of resources which would increase the satisfaction of one individual without hurting at least one other individual. The first theorem of welfare economics states that any competitive equilibrium is Pareto optimal, and the second theorem states that a particular Pareto optimum may be reached by combining lump sum transfers among agents with a competitive economic system. In an efficient equilibrium, market prices reflect social opportunity costs.

observe, without costs, to which extent the reported losses are attributable to the insured's behavior. Adverse selection occurs when (1) the prospective insureds are heterogeneous, and (2) the risk class to which they belong cannot be determined *a priori* by the insurer (at least not without costs), so that every insured is charged the same premium rate. Clearly, asymmetric information is a source of incompleteness in insurance markets: e.g., a student cannot be insured against the risk of failing at an exam; a healthy old person may not find medical insurance coverage at an acceptable premium, etc. For this reason, a free market economy may not be efficient, and this may justify government intervention.

1.3.2.1 Moral Hazard

Economists make a distinction between two kinds of moral hazard, depending on the timing of the insured's action. If the latter occurs before the realization of the insured event, one has *ex ante* moral hazard, while *ex post* moral hazard exists when the insured's action is taken after the insured event.[17]

Ex ante moral hazard was studied by Pauly (1974), Marshall (1976), Holmstrom (1979) and Shavell (1979), among others. They showed that insurance reduces the incentive to take care when the insurer is unable to monitor the insured's action. Dionne (1982) pointed out that moral hazard is also present when the insured event results in non-monetary losses, for example the loss of an irreplaceable commodity. Quite generally, partial provision of insurance is optimal under moral hazard. More specifically it was demonstrated that uniform pricing is not optimal when the insured's behavior affects the probability of a loss. The equilibrium premium *rate* is an increasing function of the amount of coverage purchased (non linear pricing): see Pauly (1974). In addition, under moral hazard in loss reduction, the optimal contract is conceived such as to make the degree of coverage a non-increasing function of the amount of losses, large losses signalling careless behavior by the insured. Small losses are fully covered, but losses exceeding a limit are partially covered (Winter, 1992, proposition 4). Shavell (1982) (1986) extended the study of moral hazard to the case of liability insurance. He showed that making liability insurance compulsory results in less than optimal care.

The existence of long-term (multi-period) contracts does not necessarily mitigate the effect of moral hazard. Under the infinite period case, Rubinstein and Yaari (1983) proved that the insurer can eliminate the moral hazard problem by choosing an appropriate experience rating scheme that provides an incentive to take care. But the result does not, in general, carry over to the finite period case (Winter, 1992). In addition, the possibility for the insured to switch to an other insurer makes a penalty scheme difficult to enforce in truly competitive insurance markets, where insurers do not share information on prospective insureds.

[17] *Ex post* moral hazard is particularly important in medical insurance, where claimed expenses are dependent on decisions made by the patient and the physician once illness has occurred.

Ex post moral hazard was first pointed out by Spence and Zeckhauser (1971), and studied later by Townsend (1979) and Dionne (1984). In this case, the nature of the accident is not observable by the insurer, who has to rely on the insured's report or engage in costly verification (in the limit, the moral hazard problem becomes a fraud problem—see Picard, 1996). Mookerjee and Png (1989) showed that random audits represents the appropriate response by the insurer in this situation.

The consequences of moral hazard for the efficiency of a market economy were studied by Helpman and Laffont (1975), Stiglitz (1983), Arnott and Stiglitz (1990) and Arnott (1992), among others. They showed that a competitive equilibrium may not exist under moral hazard, and that the failure to get complete insurance coverage results at best in sub-efficient equilibrium. This is due to the fact that "moral hazard involves a trade-off between the goal of efficient risk bearing, which is met by allocating the risk to the insurer, and the goal of efficient incentives, which requires leaving the consequences of decisions about care with the decision maker." (Winter, 1992, p. 63). However, government intervention does not necessarily improve welfare in this case. This depends on government information, compared with the information at the disposal of private insurers. Arguments may be put forward in favour of a taxation and subsidization policy providing incentives to avoid and reduce losses, but public provision of insurance does not solve the moral hazard problem (Arnott and Stiglitz, 1990).

Moral hazard has become a popular theme in economics, not only because its presence in insurance markets results in less than optimal functioning of any economic system, but also because it is a widespread phenomenon. As Winter (1992) notes, moral hazard can be defined broadly as a conflict of interests between an individual (behaving rationally) in an organization, and the collective interest of the organization. Insurance markets provide the best illustration for the effect of moral hazard, but the latter is also observed in labour relationships, in finance contracts, and quite generally in all circumstances where the final wealth of a *principal* is both uncertain and partially dependent upon the behavior of an *agent* whose actions are imperfectly observable: for example, in a corporation, the wealth of the firm's owners (stockholders) is partly dependent upon the actions of the manager; in judicial procedure, the final outcome is partly dependent upon the efforts of the lawyers; in a team, the success of the team is partly dependent on the individual effort of the members, etc. All these situations were studied in the economic and financial literature under the headings of *principal-agent relationships* or *agency theory*, with close connections to the literature on moral hazard in insurance: in both cases, the objective is to define the optimal "incentive contract" to mitigate the effect of asymmetric information, and to study the consequences of different arrangements on deviations from efficiency: see Ross (1973), Radner (1981) and Grossman and Hart (1983) for canonical references. Similarly, the consequences for general economic equilibrium of market incompleteness brought about, among other causes, by moral hazard has become a central theme of research in economics: see, e.g., Polemarchakis (1990). On the moral hazard issue, at least, developments in insurance economics were closely related to developments in general economic theory.

1.3.2.2 Adverse Selection

A central development in the study of adverse selection was the paper by Rothschild and Stiglitz (1976). This paper assumed two classes in the insured population: "good risks" and "bad risks". The two classes differ only with respect to their accident probability. The authors showed that a competitive insurance market does not necessarily reach an equilibrium under adverse selection, and that, if it does, the "good risks" suffer a welfare loss. More specifically, under the assumptions of the model, including the assumption of myopic behavior by insurers (pure Cournot-Nash strategy), equilibrium obtains if the proportion of good risks in the economy is not "too large". The equilibrium situation involves the supply of discriminating contracts providing full insurance at a high price to the bad risks and partial coverage at a low price to the good risks.[18] Compared to the symmetric information case, the bad risks get the same expected utility, but the good risks suffer a welfare loss. The policy implication of the model is that, in some circumstances, insurance markets may fail, and monopolistic insurance (under government supervision) may be justified as a second best.[19]

Extensions of the basic Rothschild-Stiglitz model are due to Wilson (1977), Spence (1978) and Riley (1979), who dropped the assumption of myopic behavior by insurers. Then, an equilibrium exists always, either as a separating equilibrium (Riley, Wilson), or as a pooling equilibrium (Wilson). Moreover, Spence showed that this equilibrium is efficient if the discriminating insurance contracts are combined with cross-subsidization among risk classes, the low risks subsidizing the high risks.[20] Other, more recent, extensions concern the case where the individuals face a random loss distribution (Doherty and Jung, 1993; Doherty and Schlesinger, 1995; Landsberger and Meilijson, 1996; Young and Browne, 1997), and the case where they are exposed to multiple risks (Fluet and Pannequin, 1997). Allard, Cresta and Rochet (1997) have also shown that the Rothschild-Stiglitz results are not robust to the introduction of transaction costs: for arbitrary small fixed set-up costs pooling equilibria may exist in a competitive insurance market, and high risk individuals (rather than low risk individuals) are rationed. In addition, it is important to note that a separating equilibrium may be invalidated if insureds have the opportunity to purchase cov-

[18] Insurance contracts are defined in terms of price *and* quantity, instead of price for any quantity. Insureds reveal their class by their choice in the menu of contracts. There is no "pooling" equilibrium, but a "separating" equilibrium.

[19] Stiglitz (1977) studied the monopolistic insurance case. Under asymmetric information, the monopolist insurer maximizes profit by supplying a menu of disciminating contracts. At the equilibrium situation, the high risks get some consumer surplus, but the low risks are restricted to partial insurance and do not get any surplus.

[20] See Crocker and Snow (1985) for a review of these models, and Dionne and Doherty (1992) for a survey of adverse selection.

erage for the same risk from different insurers. For this reason, Hellwig (1988) extended the model to take into account the sharing of information by insurers about the policyholders.

These models were empirically tested by Dahlby (1983, 1992) for the Canadian automobile insurance market, and by Puelz and Snow (1994), who used individual data provided by an automobile insurer in the state of Georgia. Both studies report strong evidence of adverse selection and provide empirical support for the separating equilibrium outcome; in addition, the former study found evidence of cross-subsidization among risk classes, whereas the latter found no such evidence.

Other insurance devices to deal with adverse selection are experience rating and risk categorization. They may be used as substitutes or complements to discriminating contracts. Dionne (1983) and Dionne and Lasserre (1985) on one hand, and Cooper and Hayes (1987) on the other hand, extended Stiglitz's (1977) monopoly model to multi-period contracts, respectively with an infinite horizon and a finite horizon, and with full commitment by the insurer to the terms of the contract.[21] Hosios and Peters (1989) extended the finite horizon case to limited commitment. In this case, contract renegociation becomes relevant, as information on the risk types increases over time. In addition, strategic use of accident underreporting becomes an issue.

Cooper and Hayes (1987) also extended the Rothschild Stiglitz (1976) model to a two-period framework. They were able to demonstrate the beneficial effect of experience rating under full commitment by insurers, even when the insureds have the opportunity to switch to a different insurer in the second period (semi-commitment). At equilibrium, the competitive insurer earns a profit on good risks in the first period, compensated by a loss in the second period on those good risks who do not report an accident. This temporal profit pattern was labelled as "highballing" by D'Arcy and Doherty (1990). A different model, without any commitment, and assuming myopic behavior by insureds, was proposed by Kunreuther and Pauly (1985). The non-enforceability of contracts imply that sequences of one-period contracts are written. Private information by insurers about the accident experience of their customers allow negative expected profits in the first period and positive expected profits on the policies they renew in subsequent periods ("lowballing").[22] More recently, Dionne and Doherty (1994) proposed a model assuming private information by the insurer about the loss experience of their customer and "semi-commitment with renegociation": the insured has the option to renew its contract on prespecified conditions (future premiums are conditional on prior loss experience). This latter assumption seems to come closer to actual practices in insurance markets. They derive an equilibrium with first-period semipooling[23] and second-period separation. Their model predicts "high-

[21] In the monopoly case, insureds cannot switch to an other insurer over time.

[22] In Kunreuther and Pauly (1985), the insurers have no information about the other contracts that their customers might write. For this reason, price-quantity contracts are unavailable. The equilibrium is a pooling equilibrium with partial insurance for the good risks, as in Pauly (1974).

[23] In the first period, insureds may choose either a pooling contract with partial coverage and possible renegociation in the second year, or the Rothschild-Stiglitz contract designed for high risks.

balling", since a positive rent must be paid in the second period to the high risk individuals which experienced no loss in the first period, and this is compensated by a positive expected profit on the pooling contract in the first period.[24] Their empirical test based on data from Californian automobile insurers provides some support to this prediction: they conclude that some (but not all) insurers use semi-commitment strategies to attract portfolio of predominantly low-risk drivers. In contrast, the prediction of "lowballing" had previously received empirical support in D'Arcy and Doherty (1990).

Risk categorization, which uses statistical information on correlations between risk classes and observable variables (such as age, sex, domicile, etc.), was studied by Hoy (1982), Crocker and Snow (1986) and Rea (1992). Their work shows that risk categorization enhances efficiency when classification is costless, but its effect is ambiguous when statistical information is costly (see also Bond and Crocker, 1991). These results are of utmost political importance, given the ethical critics on the use of observable personal attributes, such as sex and race, in insurance rating. The problem of risk categorization is even more acute, when the personal attributes are not observable *a priori* but may be revealed to the insurer and/or the insured after some informational steps have been decided, as in the case of genetic diseases. Rothschild and Stiglitz (1997) point out that this results in a conflict between the social value of insurance and competition among insurers: if valuable information about the probability (or certainty) for the insured to suffer from a particular genetic disease can be made available, insurers will want to get this information. But this will result in less insurance coverage: the insureds who are virtually certain to get the disease will not be able to get insurance, whereas those who are revealed to be immune to the disease will not need insurance any longer.[25] For ethical reason, it is likely that society will prohibit the use of genetic information by insurers to categorize risks (steps were already made in that direction in the USA). But this means that adverse selection problems will be enhanced, at least in medical insurance: as Doherty and Posey (1998) have shown, private testing is encouraged when test results are confidential and there is a treatment option available,[26] but the insurers are unable to charge different prices to different customers with private information about their genetic patrimony.

Like moral hazard, but to a lesser extent, adverse selection is an important problem beyond the domain of insurance. It is mainly encountered in labour markets, where the employers are uninformed about the productivity of the prospective employees, and in financial markets, where banks and finance companies lack information on the reimbursement prospects of different borrowers. The insurance economics lit-

[24] For good risks who do not file a claim in the first period the reward takes the form of additional coverage in the second period.

[25] This is an example of the well-known result that additional public information may have adverse welfare consequences (see, e.g., Arrow, 1978).

[26] In contrast, Doherty and Thistle (1996) find that additional private information has no value if there is no treatment option conditional on this information.

erature on adverse selection reviewed above has thus led to applications to other economic domains: see, e.g., Miyazaki (1977) for an application to the labour market and Stiglitz and Weiss (1981) for an application to credit markets. Note, however, that in these cases, quality signalling by the informed agents represents a feasible strategy to circumvent the asymmetric information problem (Spence, 1973). For example, education and dividend payments find an additional justification in these circumstances. In contrast, signalling does not generally occur in insurance markets: insureds do not engage in specific activities to signal that they are good risks.

1.3.2.3 Moral Hazard and Adverse Selection

As Arnott (1992) notes, only limited progress has been made in analyzing moral hazard and adverse selection together, and this has considerably hindered empirical investigation in the economics of insurance, since both problems combine in actual insurance markets. First attempts were made by Dionne and Lasserre (1987) in the monopoly case and by Eisen (1990) in the competitive case. More recently, Bond and Crocker (1991) pointed out that risk categorization may be endogenous if it is based on information on consumption goods that are statistically correlated with an individual's risk (*correlative products*). Thus, adverse selection and moral hazard becomes related. If individual consumption is not observable, taxation of correlative products by the government may be used to limit moral hazard and reduce the need for self-selection mechanisms as an instrument for dealing with adverse selection. New developments along this line may be expected.

1.3.3 Insurance Market Structure

Numerous studies on the insurance sector have followed the lead provided by Joskow (1973). The availability of data and better incentives to perform economic research explain that most of these studies pertain to the US market.

— Insurance distribution systems were mainly analyzed by Cummins and VanDerhei (1979).[27]

— Returns to scale in the insurance industry were submitted to empirical investigation by numerous authors, e.g., Doherty (1981), and Fecher, Perelman and Pestieau (1991).

The various forms of organizational structure in the insurance industry—stock companies, mutuals, Lloyds' underwriters—were analyzed in an agency theory framework by Mayers and Smith in a series of papers: (1981), (1986) and (1988) among others. They verified that conflicts of interest between owners, managers and policyholders affect the choice of organizational form for different insurance branches (see also Hansmann, 1985).

[27] See, however, Zweifel and Ghermi (1990) for a study using Swiss data.

— The effects of rate and solvency regulation were scrutinized in numerous researches, such as Borch (1974), Ippolito (1979), Munch and Smallwood (1980), Danzon (1983), Finsinger and Pauly (1984), Pauly, Kleindorfer and Kunreuther (1986), Harrington (1984), Cummins and Harrington (1987), D'Arcy (1988). These studies were stimulated by the traditional government regulation of insurance activities, a general trend towards deregulation over the recent decades, and the consumer pressures for re-regulation (mainly in California) since the end of the 1980s. Dionne and Harrington (1992) conclude their survey of research on insurance regulation by noting: firstly, that "not much is presently known about the magnitude of the effects of regulatory monitoring and guaranty funds on default risk" (p. 32); and secondly, that rate regulation seems to have produced a variety of effects. It favored high risk groups, increased market size and encouraged insurers' exits, but nonetheless reduced the ratio of premiums to losses and operating expenses.

A related avenue of research, not considered by Joskow (1973), deals with cycles in the insurance industry. It has been noticed in the seventies that insurance company profits seemed submitted to more or less regular cycles, and that this phenomenon was reflected in cyclical capacity and premium rates. The Geneva Association sponsored one of the first investigations in this area (Mormino, 1979). The most often quoted papers were published later by Venezian (1985), Cummins and Outreville (1987), and Doherty and Kang (1988). The US insurance liability "crisis" of the mid-eighties stimulated research in insurance cycles (see Harrington, 1988). Briefly, this research suggests that delays in the adjustment of premiums to expected claims costs, due to regulation or structural causes, are responsible for cyclical effects. Grace and Hotchkiss (1995) find that external unanticipated economic shocks have little effect on underwriting performance.

The economic analysis of practical problems that the insurance industry has been facing over the past years also attracted the attention of researchers. One of these problems, the insurance of catastrophes, has become a major concern for the industry and the subject of intensive academic research. The major journals in the economics of insurance devoted recently special issues on this topic. Researchers have tended to take a broad view of the subject, so that the term "catastrophe" has been used to encompass different kinds of situations: not only natural catastrophes (like earthquakes, floods and hurricanes) and man-made catastrophes (such as Tchernobyl or Bhopal); but also socio-economic developments that result in catastrophic accumulation of claims to insurers (see, e.g., Zeckhauser, 1995). The prominent example is the liability crisis in the United States, due to the adoption of strict producers' liability and the evolution in the courts' assessments of compensations to victims, as in the cases of asbestos, breast implants, pharmaceuticals, etc. (see Viscusi, 1995). To cope with the financial consequences of catastrophes, traditional insurance and reinsurance is often insufficient (see Kunreuther, 1996). Several researchers have advocated more government involvement (see, e.g., Lewis and Murdock, 1996), but others argue that the government has no comparative advantage to the market in providing coverage for catastrophic losses (Priest, 1996). Alternative solutions may be found in financial innovation, either in the design of insurance contracts (see Doherty and Dionne, 1993, and Doherty and Schlesinger, 1998), or in the design of financial securities (see section 4 below), or both.

Let us mention, finally, a topic which was not covered by Joskow (1973) and which does not seem to have concerned many researchers: the issues raised by international insurance trade. Research on this topic remained relatively limited and concentrated in Europe: see Dickinson (1977) for an early reference and Pita Barros (1993) for a more recent analysis.

1.4 NEW APPROACHES: FINANCE AND INSURANCE

Apart from the tremendous developments summarized in the preceding section, risk and insurance economics has witnessed a major re-orientation in the 1970s and 1980s: insurance has been analyzed more and more in the general framework of financial theory. This change of perspective was implicit in the definition of Arrow (1970): "insurance is an exchange of money for money". It was also foreshadowed by the recognition that insurers were financial intermediaries (Gurley and Shaw, 1960). It became soon impossible to maintain a dichotomy in the analysis of the insurance firm: insurance operations on one hand, financial investment on the other hand. As a result, insurance research became deeply influenced by advances in the theory of finance. The more so that finance underwent a major revolution in the 1970s, with the development of option theory, and that this revolution stressed the similarity between insurance products and new concepts due to financial innovation (e.g., *portfolio insurance*).[28]

1.4.1 Portfolio Theory and the CAPM

The influence of portfolio theory on the analysis of insurance demand was mentioned in the preceding section. But this theory had also a profound influence on the theory of insurance supply. It was soon recognized that financial intermediaries could be analyzed as a joint portfolio of assets and liabilities (Michaelsen and Goshay, 1967), and this global approach was applied to insurance company management. Under this view, insurers have to manage a portfolio of correlated insurance liabilities and investment assets, taking into account balance sheet and solvency constraints, and there is no justification for separating the operations in two distinct domains: what matters is the overall return on equity (see Kahane and Nye, 1975, and Kahane, 1977).[29]

[28] The similarity between option contracts and insurance policies was stressed by Briys and Loubergé (1983).

[29] See also Loubergé (1983) for an application to international reinsurance operations, taking foreign exchange risk into account, and MacMinn and Witt (1987) for a related model.

This way of looking at insurance operations led to a theory of insurance rating, reflecting the move observed a decade earlier in finance from portfolio theory to the capital asset pricing model. Applying this model to insurance, it turns out that equilibrium insurance prices will reflect the undiversifiable risk of insurance operations. If insurance risks are statistically uncorrelated with financial market risk, equilibrium insurance prices are given by the present value of expected claims costs (in the absence of transaction costs). If they are statistically correlated, a positive *or negative* loading is observed in equilibrium. The model was developed by Biger and Kahane (1978), Hill (1979) and Fairley (1979). It was empirically evaluated by Cummins and Harrington (1985). It was also applied to determine the "fair" regulation of insurance rating in Massachussets (Hill and Modigliani, 1986).[30]

1.4.2 Option Pricing Theory

A main limitation of the capital asset pricing model is that it does not take into account non linearities arising from features such as limited liability and asymmetric tax schedules. These aspect are best analyzed using option pricing theory, since it is well known that optional clauses imply non linearities in portfolio returns. Doherty and Garven (1986) and Cummins (1988) analyzed the influence of limited liability and default risk on insurance prices, while Garven and Loubergé (1996) studied the effects of asymmetric taxes on equilibrium insurance prices and reinsurance trade among risk-neutral insurers. A major implication of these studies is that loaded premiums are not only the reflect of transaction costs and asymmetric information, or insurers' risk aversion. They reflect undiversifiable risk arising from institutional features, and they lead to prices implying risk-sharing in equilibrium, even when market participants are risk neutral.

The importance of option theory for the economics of insurance has also been recently observed in the domain of life insurance. This resulted from the fact that competition between insurers and bankers, to attract saving, has led to the inclusion of numerous optional features (hidden options) in life insurance contracts. Advances in option theory are thus currently often used to value life insurance contracts (see, e.g., Brennan and Schwartz, 1976, Ekern and Persson, 1996, and Nielsen and Sandmann, 1996), or to assess the effects of life insurance regulation (Briys and de Varenne, 1994).

1.4.3 Insurance and Corporate Finance

The portfolio approach to insurance demand led to a paradox when applied to corporations. The latter are owned by stockholders who are able to diversify risks in a

[30] Myers and Cohn (1986) extended the model to multi-period cash flows, while Kraus and Ross (1982) considered the application to insurance of the more general arbitrage pricing theory.

stock portfolio. If insurance risks, such as accident and fire, are diversifiable in the economy, the approach leads to the conclusion that corporations should not bother to insure them. They would increase shareholders' wealth by remaining uninsured instead of paying loaded premiums (Mayers and Smith, 1982).[31] The paradox was solved using the modern theory of corporate finance, where the firm is considered as a nexus of contracts between various stakeholders: managers, employees, suppliers, bondholders, banks, stockholders, consumers, etc. Reduction of contracting and bankruptcy costs provides an incentive to manage risk and to purchase insurance, even if the premium is loaded and the shareholders are indifferent to insurance risk: see Main (1982) and Mayers and Smith (1982) (1990). In addition, convex tax schedules arising from progressive tax rates and incomplete loss offset offer another explanation for concern with insurance risk management in widely-held corporations: see Smith, Smithson and Wilford (1990).

However, as Doherty (1997) notes, these considerations have changed the relationship of corporate managers to insurance and risk management. The latter are no longer merely used because risks arise. They must find their justification in the overall objective of value maximization. In addition, the development of financial engineering in the 1980's challenged traditional insurance strategies in corporate risk management.[32] Traditional insurance strategies often involve large transaction costs, and they fail if the risk is not diversifiable, as in the case of the US liability crisis. For this reason, innovative financial procedures, such as finite risk plans and financial reinsurance, represent promising instruments for dealing with corporate risks. Of course, they widen the competitive interface between banks and insurers.

The theory of corporate finance was also used by Garven (1987) to study the capital structure decision of the insurance firm. His paper shows that redundant tax shields, default risk, bankruptcy costs and the above-mentioned agency costs influence the insurer's capital structure decision. But here also, as Doherty (1997) remarks, insurers' management has been deeply influenced by developments in the financial markets. The concept of asset-liability management, which has its roots in the portfolio approach mentioned above, means that insurers are less relying on reinsurance as the natural instrument to hedge their risks. This is all the more important that developments in the financial markets in the 1990's have seen the emergence of derivative products intended to complement traditional reinsurance treaties.

[31] The same kind of argument was used by Doherty and Tinic (1981) to question the motivation of reinsurance demand by insurers.

[32] Note that the term "risk management" has lost the insurance connotation that it had until the 1970's. In the economic and financial literature, it is nowadays more commonly associated with the management of financial exposures, using derivative instruments, than with the management of "pure" risks, using risk prevention and risk transfer instruments such as insurance. When one uses the term "risk management" now, it is often necessary to make clear whether one intends to mean "corporate risk management" or "financial risk management". This distinction will tend to become obsolete with the import of financial risk management strategies in the area of corporate risk management.

1.4.4 Insurance and Financial Markets

In 1973, the insurance/banking interface was a sensitive subject. It was generally not well-considered, in the insurance industry, to state that insurance was a financial claim and that insurers and bankers performed related functions in the economy. Twenty-five years later, and after numerous recent experiences of mergers and agreements between banks and insurers, the question is not whether the two activities are closely related, but where do they differ.

It is easy for an economist of risk and insurance to provide a general answer to this question. The answer is founded on Borch's mutuality principle (see section 2) and on subsequent work on risk-sharing. Insurance and banking, like all financial activities, are concerned with the transfer of money across the two-dimensional space of time and states of nature. Insurance deals mainly—but not exclusively (see life insurance)—with transfers across states that do not necessarily involve a change in social wealth. In contrast, banking and financial markets perform transfers across states which often involve a change in social wealth. In other words, insurance is concerned with diversifiable risk; banks and finance companies (e.g., mutual funds) are concerned with undiversifiable (social) risk.

This kind of distinction has been used before to draw a line between private and public (social) insurance. According to this view, social insurance is called for when the limits of private insurability are reached in the sense that the insured events are positively correlated, so that diversifiability does not obtain: epidemic diseases, losses from natural catastrophes, unemployment, etc.[33] But, in the absence of redistributive concerns or of market incompleteness due to moral hazard, it becomes more and more obvious that financial markets are able to perform social insurance functions, in addition to their traditional function of sharing production risk.

A case in point is the evolution in the natural catastrophes branch of insurance. As a matter of fact, since losses from natural catastrophes are correlated, they should be excluded from the private insurance area. Nonetheless, private insurance companies used to cover this risk because geographical dispersion seemed possible using the international reinsurance market. However, over the last years, the private insurability of this risk has been challenged by various developments: an increased frequency of hurricanes,[34] huge losses, and a concentration of insured values in selected exposed areas of the globe: the USA (mainly California and Florida), Japan and Western Europe (mainly the South). As a result, potential losses have exceeded the financial capacity of the catastrophe reinsurance market (see Kielholz and Durrer, 1987). One possible solution to the insurability problem is the traditional recourse to

[33] Public insurance may also be justified on equity considerations, e.g., in medical insurance.

[34] It remains to be seen whether this increased frequency is due to permanent changes (due to global warming of the atmosphere), or whether it represents a temporary phenomenon (with no departure from randomness in the long run).

government insurance using increased taxation. This is the solution which was adopted in France (Magnan, 1995): a reserve fund financed by specific taxes on property-liability insurance contracts indemnifies victims from natural catastrophes. Another solution is the securitization of the risk using special purpose derivative markets. This is the solution proposed by the Chicago Board of Trade with the catastrophe options and futures contracts launched in December 1992: see D'Arcy and France (1992) and Cummins and Geman (1995) for an analysis of these contracts.[35] A third solution is the securitization of the risk using more familiar securities, such as coupon bonds, issued by a finance company (on behalf of an insurer), or by a public agency (on behalf of the State): see Briys (1997), and Loubergé, Kellezi and Gilli (1999) for a presentation and analysis of insurance-linked bonds. The marketing of these new insurance-based securities is based on the huge pool of financial capacity provided by worldwide capital markets and the prospects for risk diversification made available to investors in these securities. It illustrates the increased integration of insurance and investment banking, both activities performing a fundamental economic function, the transfer of risks.

1.5 CONCLUSION

In the early seventies', it was not clear what would be the development of risk and insurance economics over the years to come. 25 years later, it is comforting to realize that considerable developments have taken place: the length of the reference list below, unconventionally divided in pre-1973 and post-1973 references gives an account of the quantitative aspects of these developments.

As this paper shows, the developments have mainly taken place along three avenues of research:

1. The theory of risk-taking behavior in the presence of multiple risks, which encompasses the theory of optimal insurance coverage, the theory of optimal portfolio investment, and the theory of optimal risk prevention.

2. The issues raised by asymmetric information for contracts design and market equilibrium, a theme which extends beyond insurance economics and concerns all contractual relations in the economy, e.g., on labour markets, products markets and financial markets.

3. The applications of new financial paradigms, such as contingent claims analysis, to the analysis of insurance firms, insurance markets and corporate risk management, a development which links more closely insurance economics to financial economics, and insurance to finance.

[35] The early options and futures on four narrow-based indices of natural catastrophes were replaced in October 1995 by call spreads on nine broad-based indices. Lewis and Murdock (1996) propose to have the same kind of contract supplied by Federal authorities, in order to complete the reinsurance market.

Risk and insurance economics represents nowadays a major theme in general economic theory. This does not mean that risk and insurance education, *per se*, has become a predominant theme—although important developments took place also at this level. But risk and insurance issues have become pervasive in economic education, more particularly in microeconomics. To support this statement, one may verify in the second section of the following list of references that many important papers for the advancement of risk and insurance theory were published in general economic and financial journals, and not only in the leading specialized reviews. Indeed, given that this goal of the seventies' was reached, it may be wondered whether an other objective, the development of specialized risk and insurance education and research, which had been given less importance then, should not be reevaluated today. From the experience with the tremendous research activity we have witnessed in the study of financial markets over the past years, we are allowed to infer that specialized research in insurance economics would receive a major impulse from the creation of complete, reliable and easily accessible insurance data bases.

1.6 REFERENCES

1 Publication Until 1973

Akerlof, J.A. (1970). "The market for 'lemons': quality uncertainty and the market mechanism," *Quarterly Journal of Economics*, 84, 488–500.

Arrow, K.J. (1953). "Le rôle des valeurs boursières pour la répartition la meilleure des risques," in *Econométrie*, CNRS, Paris, 41–47. English version: "The role of securities in the optimal allocation of risk-bearing," *Review of Economic Studies*, 31, 1964, 91–96.

Arrow, K.J. (1963). "Uncertainty and the welfare economics of medical care," *American Economic Review*, 53, 941–969.

Arrow, K.J. (1970). "Insurance, risk and resource allocation," in K.J. Arrow, *Essays in the Theory of Risk Bearing*, North Holland, 134–143.

Borch, K. (1960). "The safety loading of reinsurance premiums," *Skandinavisk Aktuarie tidskrift*, 43, 163–184.

Borch, K. (1962). "Equilibrium in a reinsurance market," *Econometrica*, 30, 424–444.

Carter, R.L. (1972). *Economics and Insurance*. PH Press.

Debreu, G. (1959). *Theory of Value*. John Wiley.

Ehrlich, J. and G. Becker (1972). "Market insurance, self insurance and self protection," *Journal of Political Economy*, 80, 623–648.

Friedman, M. and L.J. Savage (1948). "The utility analysis of choices involving risk," *Journal of Political Economy*, 56, 279–304.

Gould, J.P. (1969). "The expected utility hypothesis and the selection of optimal deductibles for a given insurance policy," *Journal of Business*, 42, 143–151.

Greene, M. (1971). *Risk Aversion, Insurance and the Future*. Indiana University Press.

Greene, M. (1973). *Risk and Insurance*. South Western.

Gurley, J. and Shaw (1960). *Money in a Theory of Finance*, Brookings Institution.

Hammond, J.D. (1968). *Essays in the Theory of Risk and Insurance*. Scott Foresman.

Huebner Foundation for Insurance Education (1972). *Risk and Insurance Instruction in American Colleges and Universities*. University of Pennsylvania.

Joskow, P.J. (1973). "Cartels, competition and regulation in the property-liability insurance industry," *Bell Journal of Economics and Management Science*, 4, 327–427.

Kihlstrom, R.E. and M. Pauly (1971). "The role of insurance in the allocation of risk," *American Economic Review*, 61, 371–379.

Lintner, J. (1965). "Security prices, risk and maximal gain from diversification," *Journal of Finance*, 20, 587–615.

Mahr, W. (1964). *Einführung in die Versicherungswirtschaft*. Duncker & Humblot.

Markowitz, H.M. (1959). *Portfolio Selection—Efficient Diversification of Investments*. John Wiley.

Mehr, R. and B. Hedges (1963). *Risk Management in the Business Enterprise*. Irwin.

Michaelson, J.B. and R.C. Goshay (1967). "Portfolio selection in financial intermediaries: A new approach," *Journal of Financial and Quantitative Analysis*, 2, 166–199.

Mossin, J. (1966). "Equilibrium in a capital asset market," *Econometrica*, 34, 768–783.

Mossin, J. (1968). "Aspects of rational insurance purchasing," *Journal of Political Economy*, 79, 553–568.

Neumann, J. von and O. Morgenstern (1947). *Theory of Games and Economic Behavior*. Princeton University Press.

Pashigian, B., L. Schkade and G. Menefee (1966). "The selection of an optimal deductible for a given insurance policy," *Journal of Business*, 39, 35–44.

Pauly, M. (1968). "The economics of moral hazard: Comment," *American Economic Review*, 58, 531–536.

Pfeffer, I. (1956). *Insurance and Economic Theory*. Irwin.

Pratt, J. (1964). "Risk aversion in the small and in the large," *Econometrica*, 32, 122–136.

Ross, S. (1973). "The economic theory of agency: The principal's problem," *American Economic Review*, 63, 134–139.

Rothschild, M. and J. Stigliz (1970). "Increasing risk: I. A definition," *Journal of Economic Theory*, 2, 225–243.

Savage, L.J. (1954). *Foundation of Statistics*. John Wiley.

Sharpe, W. (1964). "Capital asset prices: A theory of market equilibrium under conditions of risk," *Journal of Finance*, 19, 425–442.

Smith, V. (1968). "Optimal insurance coverage," *Journal of Political Economy*, 79, 68–77.

Spence, M. and R. Zeckhauser (1971). "Insurance, information and individual action," *American Economic Review*, 61, 380–387.

Spence, M. (1973). "Job market signalling," *Quarterly Journal of Economics*, 87, 355–374.

Wilson, R. (1968). "The theory of syndicates," *Econometrica*, 36, 113–132.

2 Publication After 1973

Allard, M., J.P. Cresta and J.C. Rochet (1997). "Pooling and separating equilibria in insurance markets with adverse selection and distribution costs," *Geneva Papers on Risk and Insurance Theory*, 22, 103–120.

Arnott, R. (1992). "Moral hazard and competitive insurance markets," in *Contributions to Insurance Economics*, G. Dionne (ed.), Kluwer Academic Publishers, 325–358.

Arnott, R. and J.E. Stiglitz (1990). "The welfare economics of moral hazard," in *Risk, Information and Insurance: Essays in the Memory of Karl Borch*, H. Loubergé (ed.), Kluwer Academic Publishers, 91–121.

Arrow, K.J. (1974). "Optimal insurance and generalized deductibles," *Scandinavian Actuarial Journal*, 1, 1–42.

Arrow, K.J. (1978). "Risk allocation and information: Some recent theoretical developments," *Geneva Papers on Risk and Insurance*, 8, 5–19.

Borch, K. (1974). "Capital markets and the supervision of insurance companies," *Journal of Risk and Insurance*, 41, 397–405.

Biger, N. and Y. Kahane (1978). "Risk considerations in insurance ratemaking," *Journal of Risk and Insurance*, 45, 121–132.

Bond, E.W. and K.J. Crocker (1991). "Smoking, skydiving and knitting: the endogenous categorization of risks in insurance markets with asymmetric information." *Journal of Political Economy*, 99, 177–200.

Boyer, M. and G. Dionne (1989). "More on insurance, protection and risk," *Canadian Journal of Economics*, 22, 202–205.

Brennan, M.J. and E. Schwartz (1976). "The pricing of equity-linked life insurance policies with an asset value guarantee," *Journal of Financial Economics*, 3, 195–213.

Briys, E. (1988). "On the theory of rational insurance purchasing in a continuous time model," *Geneva Papers on Risk and Insurance*, 13, 165–177.

Briys, E. (1997). "From Genoa to Kobe: Natural hazards, insurance risk and the pricing of insurance-linked bonds," *working paper*, Lehman Brothers International.

Briys, E., G. Dionne and L. Eeckhoudt (1989). "More on insurance as a Giffen good," *Journal of Risk and Uncertainty*, 2, 420–425.

Briys, E., Y. Kahane and Y. Kroll (1988). "Voluntary insurance coverage, compulsory insurance, and risky-riskless portfolio opportunities," *Journal of Risk and Insurance*, 55, 713–722.

Briys, E. and H. Loubergé (1983). "Le contrat d'assurance comme option de vente," *Finance*, 4, 139–153.

Briys, E. and H. Loubergé (1985). "On the theory of rational insurance purchasing," *Journal of Finance*, 40, 577–581.

Briys, E. and H. Schlesinger (1990). "Risk aversion and the propensities for self-insurance and self-protection," *Southern Economic Journal*, 57, 458–467.

Briys, E., H. Schlesinger and M. von Schulenburg (1991). "Reliability of risk management: market insurance, self-insurance and self-protection reconsidered," *Geneva Papers on Risk and Insurance Theory*, 16.

Briys, E. and F. de Varenne (1994). "Life insurance in a contingent claims framework: Pricing and regulatory implications," *Geneva Papers on Risk and Insurance Theory*, 19, 53–72.

Chang, Y.M. and I. Ehrlich (1985). "Insurance, protection from risk and risk bearing," *Canadian Journal of Economics*, 18, 574–587.

Chesney, M. and H. Loubergé (1986). "Risk aversion and the composition of wealth in the demand for full insurance coverage," *Schweizerische Zeitschrift für Volkswirt schaft und Statistik*, 122, 359–370.

Cook, P.J. and D.A. Graham (1977). "The demand for insurance production: The case of irreplaceable commodities," *Quarterly Journal of Economics*, 91, 143–156.

Cooper, R. and B. Hayes (1987). "Multi-period insurance contracts," *International Journal of Industrial Organization*, 5, 211–231.

Crocker, K.J. and A. Snow (1985). "The efficiency of competitive equilibria in insurance markets with adverse selection," *Journal of Public Economics*, 26, 207–219.

Crocker, K.J. and A. Snow (1986). "The efficiency effects of categorical discrimination in the insurance industry," *Journal of Political Economy*, 94, 321–344.

Cummins, J.D. (1988). "Risk-based premiums for insurance guaranty funds," *Journal of Finance*, 43, 823–839.

Cummins, J.D. and H. Geman (1995). "Pricing catastrophe futures and call spreads," *Journal of Fixed Income*, 4, 46–57.

Cummins, J.D. and S.E. Harrington (1985). "Property-liability insurance rate regulation: Estimation of underwriting betas using quarterly profit data," *Journal of Risk and Insurance*, 52, 16–43.

Cummins, J.D. and S.E. Harrington (1987). "The impact of rate regulation on property-liability insurance loss ratios: A cross-sectional analysis with individual firm data," *Geneva Papers on Risk and Insurance*, 12, 50–62.

Cummins, J.D. and J.F. Outreville (1987). "An international analysis of underwriting cycles in property-liability insurance," *Journal of Risk and Insurance*, 54, 246–262.

Cummins, J.D. and J.L. Vanderhei (1979). "A note on the relative efficiency of property-liability insurance distribution systems," *Bell Journal of Economics*, 10, 709–720.

Dahlby, B. (1983). "Adverse selection and statistical discrimination: An analysis of Canadian automobile insurance market," *Journal of Public Economics*, 20, 121–131.

Dahlby, B. (1992). "Testing for asymmetric information in Canadian automobile insurance," in *Contributions to Insurance Economics*, G. Dionne (ed.), Kluwer Academic Publishers, 423–443.

Danzon, P.M. (1983). "Rating bureaus in US property-liability insurance markets: Anti or pro-competitive?" *Geneva Papers on Risk and Insurance*, 8, 371–402.

D'Arcy, S.P. (1988). "Application of economic theories of regulation to the property-liability insurance industry," *Journal of Insurance Regulation*, 7, 19–52.

D'Arcy, S.P. and N. Doherty (1990). "Adverse selection, private information and lowballing in insurance markets," *Journal of Business*, 63, 145–163.

D'Arcy, S.P. and V.G. France (1992). "Catastrophe futures: A better hedge for insurers," *Journal of Risk and Insurance*, 59, 575–601.

Dickinson, G.M. (1977). "International insurance transactions and the balance of payments," *Geneva Papers on Risk and Insurance*, No 6.

Dionne, G. (1982). "Moral hazard and state-dependent utility function," *Journal of Risk and Insurance*, 49, 405–423.

Dionne, G. (1983). "Adverse selection and repeated insurance contracts," *Geneva Papers on Risk and Insurance*, 8, 316–333.

Dionne, G. (1984). "Search and insurance," *International Economic Review*, 25, 357–367.

Dionne, G. and N. Doherty (1992). "Adverse selection in insurance markets: A selective survey," in *Contributions to Insurance Economics*, G. Dionne (ed.), Kluwer Academic Publishers, 97–140.

Dionne, G. and N. Doherty (1994). "Adverse selection, commitment and renegociation: Extension to and evidence from insurance markets," *Journal of Political Economy*, 102, 209–235.

Dionne, G. and L. Eeckhoudt (1984). "Insurance and saving: Some further results," *Insurance: Mathematics and Economics*, 3, 101–110.

Dionne, G. and L. Eeckhoudt (1985). "Self insurance, self protection and increased risk aversion," *Economics Letters*, 17, 39–42.

Dionne, G. and L. Eeckhoudt (1988). "Increasing risk and self-protection activities," *Geneva Papers on Risk and Insurance*, 13, 132–136.

Dionne, G. and C. Gollier (1992). "Comparative statics under multiple sources of risk with applications to insurance demand," *Geneva Papers on Risk and Insurance Theory*, 17, 21–33.

Dionne, G. and P. Lasserre (1985). "Adverse selection, repeated insurance contracts and announcement strategy," *Review of Economic Studies*, 52, 719–723.

Dionne, G. and P. Lasserre (1987). "Dealing with moral hazard and adverse selection simultaneously," working paper, University of Pennsylvania.

Dionne G. and S.E. Harrington (1992). "An introduction to insurance economics," in *Foundations of Insurance Economics*, G. Dionne and S.E. Harrington (eds.), Kluwer Academic Publishers, 1–48.

Doherty, N. (1981). "The measurement of output and economies of scale in property-liability insurance," *Journal of Risk and Insurance*, 48, 390–402.

Doherty, N. (1984). "Portfolio efficient insurance buying strategies," *Journal of Risk and Insurance*, 51, 205–224.

Doherty, N. (1997). "Corporate insurance: Competition from capital markets and financial institutions," *Assurances*, 65, 63–94.

Doherty, N. and G. Dionne (1993). "Insurance with undiversifiable risk: Contract structure and organizational form of insurance firms," *Journal of Risk and Uncertainty*, 6, 187–203.

Doherty, N. and L. Eeckhoudt (1995). "Optimal insurance without expected utility: The dual theory and the linearity of insurance contracts," *Journal of Risk and Uncertainty*, 10, 157–179.

Doherty, N. and J.R. Garven (1986). "Price regulation in property-liability insurance: A contingent claims approach," *Journal of Finance*, 41, 1031–1050.

Doherty, N. and H.J. Jung (1993). "Adverse selection when loss severities differ: first-best and costly equilibria," *Geneva Papers on Risk and Insurance Theory*, 18, 173–182.

Doherty, N. and H.B. Kang (1988). "Price instability for a financial intermediary: interest rates and insurance price cycles," *Journal of Banking and Finance*, 12, 191–214.

Doherty, N. and L. Posey (1998). "On the value of a checkup: Adverse selection, moral hazard and the value of information," *Journal of Risk and Insurance*, 65, 189–211.

Doherty, N. and H. Schlesinger (1983a). "Optimal insurance in incomplete markets," *Journal of Political Economy*, 91, 1045–1054.

Doherty, N. and H. Schlesinger (1983b). "The optimal deductible for an insurance policy when initial wealth is random," *Journal of Business*, 56, 555–565.

Doherty, N. and H. Schlesinger (1990). "Rational insurance purchasing: Considerations of contract nonperformance," *Quarterly Journal of Economics*, 105, 243–253.

Doherty, N. and H. Schlesinger (1995). "Severity risk and the adverse selection of frequency risk," *Journal of Risk and Insurance*, 62, 649–665.

Doherty, N. and H. Schlesinger (1998). "Securitization and insurance contracts," working paper, University of Alabama.

Doherty, N. and P. Thistle (1996). "Adverse selection with endogenous information in insurance markets," *Journal of Public Economics*, 63, 83–102.

Doherty, N. and S. Tinic (1981). "Reinsurance under conditions of capital market equilibrium," *Journal of Finance*, 36, 949–953.

Drèze, J. (1979). "Human capital and risk-bearing," *Geneva Papers on Risk and Insurance*, No 12.

Drèze, J. (1990). "The role of securities and labor contracts in the optimal allocation of risk-bearing," in *Risk, Information and Insurance*, H. Loubergé (ed.), Kluwer Academic Publishers, 41–65.

Eeckhoudt, L., C. Gollier and H. Schlesinger (1991). "Increases in risk and deductible insurance," *Journal of Economic Theory*, 55, 435–440.

Eeckhoudt, L., C. Gollier and H. Schlesinger (1996). "Changes in background risk and risk-taking behavior," *Econometrica*, 64, 683–689.

Eeckhoudt, L. and M. Kimball (1992). "Background risk, prudence, and the demand for insurance," in *Contributions to Insurance Economics*, G. Dionne (ed.), Kluwer Academic Publishers, 239–254.

Eeckhoudt, L., J. Meyer and M.B. Ormiston (1997). "The interactions between the demand for insurance and insurable assets," *Journal of Risk and Uncertainty*, 14, 25–39.

Eisen, R. (1990). "Problems of equilibria in insurance markets with asymmetric information," in *Risk, Information and Insurance*, H. Loubergé (ed.), Kluwer Academic Publishers, 123–141.

Ekern, S. and S.A. Persson (1996). "Exotic unit-linked life insurance contracts," in *Financial Risk and Derivatives*, H. Loubergé and M. Subrahmanyam (eds.), Kluwer Academic Publishers, 35–63.

Fairley, W. (1979). "Investment income and profit margins in property-liability insurance: Theory and empirical results," *Bell Journal of Economics*, 10, 192–210.

Fecher, F., S. Perelman and P. Pestieau (1991). "Scale economies and performance in the French insurance industry," *Geneva Papers on Risk and Insurance—Issues and Practices*, no. 60, 315–326.

Finsinger, J. and M. Pauly (1984). "Reserve levels and reserve requirements for profi-maximizing insurance firms," in *Risk and Capital*, G. Bamberg and K. Spremann (eds.), Springer Verlag, 160–180.

Fluet, C. and F. Pannequin (1997). "Complete versus incomplete insurance contracts under adverse selection with multiple risks," *Geneva Papers on Risk and Insurance Theory*, 22, 81–101.

Garven, J.R. (1987). "On the application of finance theory to the insurance firm," *Journal of Financial Services Research*, 1, 57–76.

Garven, J.R. and H. Loubergé (1996). "Reinsurance, taxes and efficiency: A contingent claims model of insurance market equilibrium," *Journal of Financial Intermediation*, 5, 74–93.

Gollier, C. (1992). "Economic theory of risk exchanges: A review," in *Contributions to Insurance Economics*, G. Dionne (ed.), Kluwer Academic Publishers, 3–23.

Gollier, C. (1995). "The comparative statics of changes in risk revisited," *Journal of Economic Theory*, 66, 522–536.

Gollier, C. and J.W. Pratt (1996). "Risk vulnerability and the tempering effect of background risk," *Econometrica*, 64, 1109–1123.

Gollier, C. and P. Scarmure (1994). "The spillover effect of compulsory insurance," *Geneva Papers on Risk and Insurance Theory*, 19, 23–34.

Gollier, C. and E. Schlee (1997). "Increased risk taking with multiple risks," working paper.

Gollier, C. and H. Schlesinger (1995). "Second best insurance contract design in an incomplete market," *Scandinavian Journal of Economics*, 97, 123–135.

Gollier, C. and H. Schlesinger (1996). "Arrow's theorem on the optimality of deductibles: A stochastic dominance approach," *Economic Theory*, 7, 359–363.

Grace, M.F. and J.L. Hotchkiss (1995). "External impacts on the property-liability insurance cycle," *Journal of Risk and Insurance*, 62, 738–754.

Grossman, S. and O.D. Hart (1983). "An analysis of the principal-agent problem," *Econometrica*, 51, 7–45.

Guiso, L. and T. Jappelli (1998). "Background uncertainty and the demand for insurance against insurable risks," *Geneva Papers on Risk and Insurance Theory*, 23, 7–27.

Hansmann, H. (1985). "The organization of insurance companies: Mutual versus stock," *Journal of Law, Economics and Organization*, 1, 125–153.

Harrington, S.E. (1984). "The impact of rate regulation on prices and underwriting results in the property-liability insurance industry: A survey," *Journal of Risk and Insurance*, 51, 577–617.

Harrington, S.E. (1988). "Prices and profits in the liability insurance market," in *Liability: Perspectives and Policy*, R. Litan and C. Winston (eds.), The Brooking Institution, 42–100.

Hellwig, M. (1988). "A note on the specification of interfirm communication in insurance markets with adverse selection," *Journal of Economic Theory*, 46, 154–163.

Helpman, E. and J.J. Laffont (1975). "On moral hazard in general equilibrium," *Journal of Economic Theory*, 10, 8–23.

Hill, R.D. (1979). "Profit regulation in property-liability insurance," *Bell Journal of Economics*, 10, 172–191.

Hill, R.D. and F. Modigliani (1986). "The Massachussets model of profit regulation in nonlife insurance: Theory and empirical results," in *Fair Rate of Return in Property-Liability Insurance*, J.D. Cummins and S.E. Harrington (eds.), Kluwer Academic Publishers.

Holmstrom, B. (1979). "Moral hazard and observability," *Bell Journal of Economics*, 10, 74–91.

Hosios, A.J. and M. Peters (1989). "Repeated insurance contracts with adverse selection and limited commitment," *Quarterly Journal of Economics*, 104, 229–253.

Hoy, M. (1982). "Categorizing risks in the insurance industry," *Quarterly Journal of Economics*, 97, 321–336.

Hoy, M. and R.J. Robson (1981). "Insurance as a Giffen good," *Economics Letters*, 8, 47–51.

Ippolito, R. (1979). "The effects of price regulation in the automobile insurance industry," *Journal of Law and Economics*, 22, 55–89.

Kahane, Y. (1977). "Capital adequacy and the regulation of financial intermediaries," *Journal of Banking and Finance*, 1, 207–218.

Kahane, Y. and Y. Kroll (1985). "Optimal insurance coverage in situations of pure and speculative risk and the risk-free asset," *Insurance Mathematics and Economics*, 4, 191–199.

Kahane, Y. and D.J. Nye (1975). "A portfolio approach to the property-liability insurance industry," *Journal of Risk and Insurance*, 42, 579–598.

Karni, E. (1992). "Optimal insurance: A nonexpected utility analysis," in *Contributions to Insurance Economics*, G. Dionne (ed.), Kluwer Academic Publishers, 217–238.

Karni, E. (1995). "Non-expected utility and the robustness of the classical insurance paradigm—discussion," in *Non-Expected Utility and Risk Management*, C. Gollier and M. Machina (eds.), Kluwer Academic Publishers, 51–56.

Kielholz, W. and A. Durrer (1997). "Insurance derivatives and securitization: New hedging perspectives for the US cat insurance market," *Geneva Papers on Risk and Insurance—Issues and Practices*, no. 82, 3–16.

Kihlstrom, R.E., D. Romer and S. Williams (1981). "Risk aversion with random initial wealth," *Econometrica*, 49, 911–920.

Konrad, K. and S. Skaperdas (1993). "Self-insurance and self-protection: A non-expected utility analysis," *Geneva Papers on Risk and Insurance Theory*, 18, 131–146.

Kraus, A. and S.A. Ross (1982). "The determinants of fair profits for the property-liability insurance firm," *Journal of Finance*, 37, 1015–1030.

Kunreuther, H. (1996). "Mitigating disaster losses through insurance," *Journal of Risk and Uncertainty*, 12, 171–187.

Kunreuther, H. and M. Pauly (1985). "Market equilibrium with private knowledge: An insurance example," *Journal of Public Economics*, 26, 269–288.

Landsberger, M. and I. Meilijson (1996). "Extraction of surplus under adverse selection: The case of insurance markets," *Journal of Economic Theory*, 69, 234–239.

Lemaire, J. (1990). "Borch's theorem: A historical survey of applications," in *Risk, Information and Insurance*, H. Loubergé (ed.), Kluwer Academic Publishers, 15–37.

Lewis, C.M. and K.C. Murdock (1996). "The role of government contracts in discretionary reinsurance markets for natural disasters," *Journal of Risk and Insurance*, 63, 567–597.

Loubergé, H. (1983). "A portfolio model of international reinsurance operations," *Journal of Risk and Insurance*, 50, 44–60.

Loubergé, H., E. Kellezi and M. Gilli (1999). "Using catastrophe-linked securities to diversify insurance risk: A financial analysis of cat bonds," *Journal of Insurance Issues*, 22, 125–146.

Machina, M. (1982). "Expected utility analysis without the independence axiom," *Econometrica*, 50, 277–323.

Machina, M. (1995). "Non-expected utility and the robustness of the classical insurance paradigm," in *Non-Expected Utility and Risk Management*, C. Gollier and M. Machina (eds.), Kluwer Academic Publishers, 9–50. An expanded version (2000) is published in this book.

MacMinn, R.D. and R.C. Witt (1987). "A financial theory of the insurance firm under uncertainty and regulatory constraints," *Geneva Papers on Risk and Insurance*, 12, 3–20.

Magnan, S. (1995). "Catastrophe insurance system in France," *Geneva Papers on Risk and Insurance*, No 77, 474–480.

Main, B. (1982). "Business insurance and large, widely-held corporations," *Geneva Papers on Risk and insurance*, 7, 237–247.

Marshall, J.M. (1974). "Insurance theory: Reserves versus mutuality," *Economic Inquiry*, 12, 476–492.

Marshall, J.M. (1976). "Moral hazard," *American Economic Review*, 66, 880–890.

Mayers, D. and C.W. Smith (1981). "Contractual provisions, organizational structure, and conflict control in insurance markets," *Journal of Business*, 54, 407–434.

Mayers, D. and C.W. Smith (1982). "On the corporate demand for insurance," *Journal of Business*, 55, 281–296.

Mayers, D. and C.W. Smith (1983). "The interdependence of individual portfolio decisions and the demand for insurance," *Journal of Political Economy*, 91, 304–311.

Mayers, D. and C.W. Smith (1986). "Ownership structure and control: The mutualization of stock life insurance companies," *Journal of Financial Economics*, 16, 73–98.

Mayers, D. and C.W. Smith (1988). "Ownership structure across lines of property-casualty insurance," *Journal of Law and Economics*, 31, 351–378.

Mayers, D. and C.W. Smith (1990). "On the corporate demand for insurance: Evidence from the reinsurance market," *Journal of Business*, 63, 19–40.

Meyer, J. (1992). "Beneficial changes in random variables under multiple sources of risk and their comparative statics," *Geneva Papers on Risk and Insurance Theory*, 17, 7–19.

Meyer, D. and J. Meyer (1998). "Changes in background risk and the demand for insurance," *Geneva Papers on Risk and Insurance Theory*, 23, 29–40.

Meyer, J. and M.B. Ormiston (1996). "Demand for insurance in a portfolio setting," *Geneva Papers on Risk and Insurance Theory*, 20, 203–212.

Miyazaki, H. (1977). "The rat race and internal labor markets," *Bell Journal of Economics*, 8, 394–418.

Moffet, D. (1977). "Optimal deductible and consumption theory," *Journal of Risk and Insurance*, 44, 669–683.

Moffet, D. (1979). "The risk-sharing problem," *Geneva Papers on Risk and Insurance*, 4, 5–13.

Mookherjee, D. and I. Png (1989). "Optimal auditing, insurance and redistribution," *Quarterly Journal of Economics*, 104, 205–228.

Mormino, C.A. (1979). "Insurance cycles: An Italian experience," *Etudes et Dossiers de l'Association de Genève*, No 33.

Munch, P. and D.E. Smallwood (1980). "Solvency regulation in the property-liability insurance industry: Empirical evidence," *Bell Journal of Economics*, 11, 261–282.

Myers, S.C. and R.A. Cohn (1986). "A discounted cash flow approach to property-liability insurance rate regulation," in *Fair Rate of Return in Property-Liability Insurance*, J.D. Cummins and S.E. Harrington (eds.), Kluwer Academic Publishers.

Nielsen, J.A. and K. Sandmann (1996). "Uniqueness of the fair premium for equity-linked life insurance contracts," in *Financial Risk and Derivatives*, H. Loubergé and M. Subrahmanyam (eds.), Kluwer Academic Publishers, 65–102.

Pauly, M. (1974). "Overinsurance and public provision of insurance: The role of moral hazard and adverse selection," *Quarterly Journal of Economics*, 88, 44–62.

Pauly, M., P.R. Kleindorfer and H. Kunreuther (1986). "Regulation and quality competition in the US insurance industry," in *The Economics of Insurance Regulation*, J. Finsinger and M. Pauly (eds.), MacMillan.

Picard, P. (1996). "Auditing claims in insurance markets with fraud: The credibility issue," *Journal of Public Economics*, 63, 27–56.

Pita Barros, P. (1993). "Freedom of services and competition in insurance markets," *Geneva Papers on Risk and Insurance Theory*, 18, 93–101.

Polemarchakis, H. (1990). "Competitive allocation when the asset market is incomplete," *Geneva Papers on Risk and Insurance Theory*, 15, 5–16.

Priest, G.L. (1996). "The government, the market and the problem of catastrophic losses," *Journal of Risk and Uncertainty*, 12, 219–237.

Puelz, R. and A. Snow (1994). "Evidence on adverse selection: Equilibrium signalling and cross-subsidization in the insurance market," *Journal of Political Economy*, 102, 236–257.

Quiggin, J.C. (1982). "A theory of anticipated utility," *Journal of Economic Behavior and Organization*, 3, 323–343.

Radner, R. (1981). "Monitoring cooperative agreements in a repeated principal-agent relationship," *Econometrica*, 49, 1127–1148.

Raviv, A. (1979). "The design of an optimal insurance policy," *American Economic Review*, 69, 84–86.

Razin, A. (1976). "Rational insurance purchasing," *Journal of Finance*, 31, 133–137.

Rea, S.A. (1992). "Insurance classifications and social welfare," in *Contributions to Insurance Economics*, G. Dionne (ed.), Kluwer Academic Publishers, 377–396.

Riley, J.G. (1979). "Informational equilibrium," *Econometrica*, 47, 331–359.

Ross, S. (1981). "Some stronger measures of risk aversion in the small and in the large with applications," *Econometrica* 49, 621–638.

Rothschild, M. and J.E. Stiglitz (1976). "Equilibrium in competitive insurance markets: The economics of markets with imperfect information," *Quarterly Journal of Economics*, 90, 629–650.

Rothschild, M. and J.E. Stiglitz (1997). "Competition and insurance twenty years later," *Geneva Papers on Risk and Insurance Theory*, 22, 73–79.

Rubinstein, A. and M.E. Yaari (1983). "Repeated insurance contracts and moral hazard," *Journal of Economic Theory*, 30, 74–97.

Schlee, E. (1995). "The comparative statics of deductible insurance in expected- and non-expected utility theories," in *Non-Expected Utility and Risk Management*, C. Gollier and M. Machina (eds.), Kluwer Academic Publishers, 57–72.

Schlesinger, H. (1984). "Optimal insurance for irreplaceable commodities," *Journal of Risk and Insurance*, 51, 131–137.

Schlesinger, H. (1997). "Insurance demand without the expected utility paradigm," *Journal of Risk and Insurance*, 64, 19–39.

Schlesinger, H. and N. Doherty (1985). "Incomplete markets for insurance: An overview," *Journal of Risk and Insurance*, 52, 402–423.

Schulenburg, M. von (1986). "Optimal insurance purchasing in the presence of compulsory insurance and insurable risks," *Geneva Papers on Risk and Insurance*, 38, 5–16.

Segal, U. and A. Spivak (1990). "First order versus second order risk aversion," *Journal of Economic Theory*, 51, 111–125.

Shavell, S. (1979). "On moral hazard and insurance," *Quarterly Journal of Economics*, 93, 541–562.

Shavell, S. (1982). "On liability and insurance," *Bell Journal of Economics*, 13, 120–132.

Shavell, S. (1986). "The judgement proof problem," *International Review of Law and Economics*, 6, 45–58.

Smith C., C. Smithson and S. Wilford (1990). "Financial engineering: why hedge ?" in *Handbook of Financial Engineering*, Harper & Row, chap. 5, 126–137.

Spence, M. (1978). "Product differentiation and performance in insurance markets," *Journal of Public Economics*, 10, 427–447.

Stiglitz, J.E. (1977). "Monopoly, non-linear pricing and imperfect information: The insurance market," *Review of Economic Studies*, 44, 407–430.

Stiglitz, J.E. (1983). "Risk, incentives and insurance: The pure theory of moral hazard," *Geneva Papers on Risk and Insurance*, 8, 4–33.

Stiglitz, J.E. and A. Weiss (1981). "Credit rationing in markets with imperfect information," *American Economic Review*, 71, 393–410.

Tibiletti, L. (1995). "Beneficial changes in random variables via copulas: An application to insurance," *Geneva Papers on Risk and Insurance Theory*, 20, 191–202.

Townsend, R. (1979). "Optimal contracts and competitive contracts with costly state verification," *Journal of Economic Theory*, 22, 265–293.

Turnbull, S. (1983). "Additional aspects of rational insurance purchasing," *Journal of Business*, 56, 217–229.

Venezian, E. (1985). "Ratemaking methods and profit cycles in property and liability insurance," *Journal of Risk and Insurance*, 52, 477–500.

Viscusi, W.K. (1995). "Insurance and catastrophes: The changing role of the liability system," *Geneva Papers on Risk and Insurance Theory*, 20, 177–184.

Wilson, C. (1977). "A model of insurance markets with incomplete information," *Journal of Economic Theory*, 12, 167–207.

Winter, R.A. (1992). "Moral hazard and insurance contracts," in *Contributions to Insurance Economics*, G. Dionne (ed.), Kluwer Academic Publishers, 61–96.

Yaari, M. (1987). "The dual theory of choice under risk," *Econometrica*, 55, 95–115.

Young, V.R. and M.J. Browne (1997). "Explaining insurance policy provisions via adverse selection," *Geneva Papers on Risk and Insurance Theory*, 22, 121–134.

Zeckhauser, R. (1995). "Insurance and catastrophes," *Geneva Papers on Risk and Insurance Theory*, 20, 157–175.

Zweifel, P. and P. Ghermi (1990). "Exclusive vs. independent agencies: A comparison of performance," *Geneva Papers on Risk and Insurance Theory*, 15, 171–192.

Part II
Insurance Theory without Information Problems

2 Non-Expected Utility and the Robustness of the Classical Insurance Paradigm*

Mark J. Machina

University of California, San Diago

Abstract
This chapter uses the technique of "generalized expected utility analysis" to explore the robustness of some of the basic results in classical insurance theory to departures from the expected utility hypothesis on agents' risk preferences. The areas explored include individual demand for coinsurance and deductible insurance, the structure of Pareto-efficient bilateral insurance contracts, the structure of Pareto-efficient multilateral risk sharing agreements, and self-insurance vs. self-protection. Most, though not all, of the basic results in this area are found to be quite robust to dropping the expected utility hypothesis.

Keywords: Insurance, risk sharing, non-expected utility, expected utility.
JEL Classification Numbers: D8, G22.

2.1 INTRODUCTION

The purpose of this chapter is to explore what the classical theory of insurance and non-expected utility theory might have to contribute to each other.

For the benefit of readers more familiar with insurance theory than with non-expected utility, we begin by describing what non-expected utility risk preferences are, along with some ways—both algebraic and graphical—to represent and analyze them. The first point to be made is that non-expected utility is *not* an *alternative* to

* This chapter is an expanded version of Machina (1995), which was presented as the Geneva Risk Lecture at the 21st Seminar of the European Group of Risk and Insurance Economists ("Geneva Association"), Toulouse, France, 1994. I have benefited from the comments of Michael Carter, Georges Dionne, Christian Gollier, Peter Hammond, Edi Karni, Mike McCosker, Garey Ramey, Suzanne Scotchmer, Joel Sobel, Alan Woodfield and anonymous reviewers. Support from the National Science Foundation Economics Program and Decision, Risk and Management Science Program (Grants SES 92-09012 and SBR-9870894) is gratefully acknowledged.

expected utility. Rather, it is a *generalization* of it, in the way that CES utility functions over commodity bundles are generalizations of Cobb-Douglas utility functions, or perhaps more aptly, in the way that general quasiconcave functions are generalizations of Cobb-Douglas functions.

To set the stage, the reader is asked to think of the classical expected utility-based theory of insurance as analogous to the situation of someone who has developed the theory of consumer demand using only Cobb-Douglas utility functions. Such a Cobb-Douglas scientist has an easy and tractable model to work with, and he or she is likely to discover and prove many results, such as the Slutsky equation, or that income elasticities are identically unity, or that cross-price elasticities are identically zero. But we know that while the Slutsky equation is a general property of all utility functions over commodity bundles, the two elasticity results are specific to the Cobb-Douglas functional form, and most definitely not true of more general utility functions. It is hard to see how our scientist could have known the robust results from the non-robust results, unless he or she at least took a peek at more general "non-Cobb-Douglas" preferences.

The goal of this chapter is to examine some of the classic theoretical results in individual and market insurance theory from the more general non-expected utility point of view, and determine which of these classic results are robust (like the Slutsky equation) and which are not. As mentioned, this chapter is ultimately about what non-expected utility theory and insurance theory can contribute to each other. The identification of the robust results can contribute to insurance theory, by determining which theorems can be most heavily relied upon for further theoretical implications. The identification of the non-robust results can contribute to non-expected utility theory, by determining which parts of current insurance theory are in effect testable implications of the expected utility hypothesis. Since insurance provides the largest, most systematic, and most intensive set of field data on both individual and market choices under uncertainty, this would provide non-expected utility researchers with a very useful opportunity to apply real-world data to the testing of the expected utility model, and the calibration of more general models of choice under uncertainty.

The results examined in this chapter are selected for breadth rather than depth. This reflects that fact that it is no longer possible to present *all* results in the theory of insurance in a single paper (hence the need for the present volume). It also reflects the fact that the more specific and sophisticated results often require more specialized assumptions (such as convexity of marginal utility, or HARA utility functions), whose natural generalizations to non-expected utility have yet to be fully worked out. But most of all, I also feel we can learn most about robustness by starting out with an examination of the most basic and fundamental results in each of the various branches of insurance theory.

Section 2.2 of this chapter introduces the notion of non-expected utility preferences over lotteries, and describes how they can be represented and analyzed, both graphically and algebraically. The next several sections use these tools to examine the robustness of classic results in insurance theory to these more general risk preferences. Section 2.3 covers the individual's demand for insurance, taking the form of the insurance contract (coinsurance or deductible) as given. Section 2.4 examines the optimal form of insurance contract. Section 2.5 considers general conditions for Pareto efficient risk sharing among many individuals. Section 2.6 examines self-insurance versus self-protection. Section 2.7 explores non-differentiabilities ("kinks") in preferences over payoffs levels. Section 2.8 discusses both extensions and a specific limitation of the approach to robustness presented in this chapter. Finally, Section 2.9 illustrates how the insurability of some risks can actually *induce* non-expected utility preferences over other risks. Section 2.10 concludes.

2.2 NON-EXPECTED UTILITY PREFERENCES AND GENERALIZED EXPECTED UTILITY ANALYSIS

Non-expected utility theory typically works with the same objects of choice as standard insurance theory, namely lotteries over final wealth levels, which can be represented by discrete probability distributions of the form $\mathbf{P} = (x_1, p_1; \ldots; x_n, p_n)$, or in more general analyses, by cumulative distribution functions $F(\cdot)$.[1] Non-expected utility theory also follows the standard approach by assuming—or positing axioms sufficient to imply—that the individual's preference relation $\succcurlyeq$ over such lotteries can be represented by means of a **preference function** $\mathcal{V}(\mathbf{P}) = \mathcal{V}(x_1, p_1; \ldots; x_n, p_n)$. Just as with preferences over commodity bundles, the preference function $\mathcal{V}(\cdot)$ can be analyzed both graphically, by means of its indifference curves, and algebraically.

When examining general non-expected utility preferences, it is useful to keep in mind the "benchmark" special case of expected utility. Recall that under the expected utility hypothesis, $\mathcal{V}(\cdot)$ takes the specific form:

$$\mathcal{V}(x_1, p_1; \ldots; x_n, p_n) \equiv \sum_{i=1}^{n} U(x_i) \cdot p_i \tag{1}$$

for some **von Neumann-Morgenstern utility function** $U(\cdot)$.

The normative appeal of the expected utility axioms is well known. However, in their capacity as *descriptive* economists, non-expected utility theorists wonder whether restricting attention solely to the functional form (1) might not be like the "Cobb-Douglas hypothesis" of the above scientist. They would like to determine which results of classic risk and insurance theory follow *because* of that functional form, and which might follow from the properties of risk aversion and/or first order stochastic dominance preference *in general*, without requiring the functional form (1). To do this, we begin by illustrating how one can analyze general non-expected utility preference functions $\mathcal{V}(x_1, p_1; \ldots; x_n, p_n)$, and compare them to expected utility.

[1] Depending upon the context, the probabilities in these distributions can either be actuarially determined chances, or a decision-maker's subjective probabilities over states of nature or events.

2.2.1 Graphical Depictions of Non-Expected Utility Preferences

Two diagrams can illustrate the key similarities and differences between expected utility and non-expected utility preferences, by depicting how preferences over probability distributions $\mathbf{P} = (x_1, p_1; \ldots; x_n, p_n)$ depend upon (i) changes in the outcomes $\{x_1, \ldots, x_n\}$ for a fixed set of probabilities $\{\bar{p}_1, \ldots, \bar{p}_n\}$, and (ii) changes in the probabilities $\{p_1, \ldots, p_n\}$ for a fixed set of outcomes $\{\bar{x}_1, \ldots, \bar{x}_n\}$.

Preferences over changes in the *outcomes* can be illustrated in the classic "Hirshleifer-Yaari diagram" (Hirshleifer (1965, 1966), Yaari (1965, 1969), Hirshleifer and Riley (1979, 1992)). Assume there are two states of nature, with fixed probabilities $(\bar{p}_1, \bar{p}_2)$ adding to one, so that we restrict attention to probability distributions of the form $(x_1, \bar{p}_1; x_2, \bar{p}_2)$, which can be represented by points in the (x_1, x_2) plane, as in Figure 1. A family of *expected utility* indifference curves in this diagram are the level curves of some expected utility preference function $\mathcal{V}(\mathbf{P}) = U(x_1)\cdot\bar{p}_1 + U(x_2)\cdot\bar{p}_2$, with slope (marginal rate of substitution) given by

$$MRS_{EU}(x_1, x_2) \equiv -\frac{U'(x_1)\cdot\bar{p}_1}{U'(x_2)\cdot\bar{p}_2} \tag{2}$$

Besides indifference curves, Figure 1 also contains two other constructs. The 45° line consists of all sure prospects (x, x), and is accordingly termed the **certainty line**.

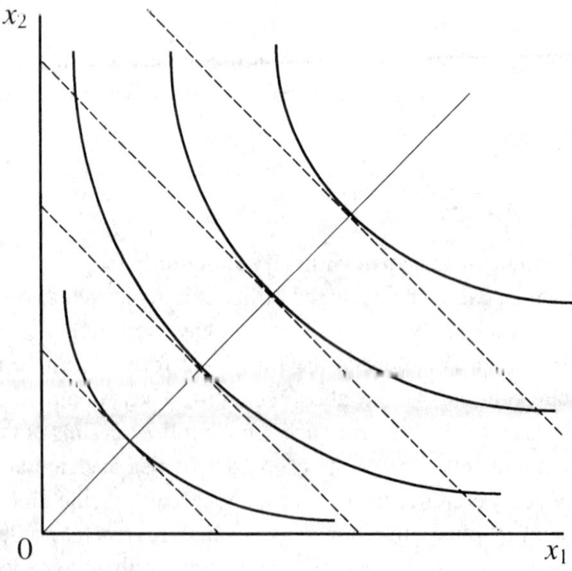

Figure 1 Risk Averse Expected Utility Indifference Curves in the Hirshleifer-Yaari Diagram

The parallel dashed lines are loci of constant *expected value* $x_1 \cdot \bar{p}_1 + x_2 \cdot \bar{p}_2$, with slope accordingly given by (the negative of) the **odds ratio** $\bar{p}_1/\bar{p}_2$. In insurance theory these lines are frequently termed "fair odds lines"—here we shall call them **iso-expected value lines**.

Formula (2) can be shown to imply two very specific properties of expected utility indifference curves in the Hirshleifer-Yaari diagram:

> "***MRS*** **at certainty = odds ratio"**: The *MRS* at every point (x, x) on the 45° line equals (the negative of) the odds ratio $\bar{p}_1/\bar{p}_2$, and
>
> **"rectangle property"**: Given the corner points (x_1^*, x_2^*), (x_1^*, x_2^{**}), (x_1^{**}, x_2^*), (x_1^{**}, x_2^{**}) of any rectangle in the diagram, the products of the *MRS*'s at diagonally opposite pairs are equal[2]

Besides these two properties, the indifference curves in Figure 1 exhibit three other features of risk preferences on the part of the underlying preference function $\mathcal{V}(\cdot)$ that generates them. The first feature is that they are downward sloping. To see what this reflects, note that any north, east or northeast movement in the diagram will, by raising x_1 and/or x_2, lead to a first order stochastically dominating probability distribution. Accordingly, any set of indifference curves that is downward sloping is reflecting **first order stochastic dominance preference** on the part of its underlying preference function $\mathcal{V}(\cdot)$. Of course, under expected utility, this is equivalent to the condition that $U(\cdot)$ is an increasing function of x.

The second feature of these indifference curves is that they are *steeper* than the iso-expected value lines in the region above the 45° line, and *flatter* than the iso-expected value lines in the region below the 45° line. To see what this reflects, note that, starting at any point (x_1, x_2) and moving along its iso-expected value line in a direction *away from the certainty line* serves to further increase the larger outcome of the probability distribution, and further decrease the smaller outcome, and does so in a manner which preserves the expected value of the prospect. This is precisely a mean preserving increase in risk.[3] Thus, indifference curves that are steeper/flatter than the iso-expected values lines in the region above/below the certainty line are made worse off by all such increases in risk, and hence reflect the property of **risk aversion** on the part of their underlying preference function $\mathcal{V}(\cdot)$. Under expected utility, this property is equivalent to the condition that $U(\cdot)$ is a concave function of x.

[2] An interpretive note: The rectangle property is essentially the condition that (smooth) expected utility preferences are separable across mutually exclusive states of nature. Given the rectangle property, the *MRS* at certainty property is equivalent to "state-independent" preferences, a property we shall assume throughout this chapter. For important analyses of *state-dependent* preferences under both expected utility and non-expected utility, see Karni (1985, 1987). For a specific application to insurance theory, see Cook and Graham (1977).

[3] E.g., Rothschild and Stiglitz (1970, 1971).

The third feature of the indifference curves in Figure 1 is that they are "bowed-in" toward the origin. This means that any convex combination $(\lambda \cdot x_1 + (1 - \lambda) \cdot x_1^*, \lambda \cdot x_2 + (1 - \lambda) \cdot x_2^*)$ of any two indifferent points (x_1, x_2) and (x_1^*, x_2^*) will be preferred to these points. Expressed more generally, we term this property **outcome convexity**: namely, for any set of probabilities $\{\bar{p}_1, \ldots, \bar{p}_n\}$:

$$(x_1, \bar{p}_1; \ldots; x_n, \bar{p}_n) \sim (x_1^*, \bar{p}_1; \ldots; x_n^*, \bar{p}_n)$$
$$\Rightarrow (\lambda \cdot x_1 + (1-\lambda) \cdot x_1^*, \bar{p}_1; \ldots; \lambda \cdot x_n + (1-\lambda) \cdot x_n^*, \bar{p}_n) \succcurlyeq (x_1, \bar{p}_1; \ldots; x_n, \bar{p}_n) \quad (3)$$

for all $\lambda \in (0, 1)$.[4] This property of risk preferences has been examined, under various names, by Tobin (1958), Debreu (1959, Ch. 7), Yaari (1965, 1969), Dekel (1989) and Karni (1992). Under expected utility, it is equivalent to the condition that $U(\cdot)$ is concave.

Note what these last two paragraphs imply: Since under expected utility the properties of risk aversion and outcome convexity are *both* equivalent to concavity of $U(\cdot)$, it follows that expected utility indifference curves in the plane—and expected utility preferences in general—will be risk averse *if and only if* they are outcome-convex. We'll see the implications of this below.

A family of *non-expected utility* indifference curves, on the other hand, consists of the level curves of some general preference function $\mathcal{V}(\mathbf{P}) = \mathcal{V}(x_1, \bar{p}_1; x_2, \bar{p}_2)$, with slope therefore given by

$$MRS_{\mathcal{V}}(x_1, x_2) = -\frac{\partial \mathcal{V}(x_1, \bar{p}_1; x_2, \bar{p}_2)/\partial x_1}{\partial \mathcal{V}(x_1, \bar{p}_1; x_2, \bar{p}_2)/\partial x_2} \quad (4)$$

Two such examples, derived from two different preference functions $\mathcal{V}(\cdot)$ and $\mathcal{V}^*(\cdot)$, are illustrated in Figures 2a and 2b. In these figures, just as in Figure 1, the indifference curves are generated by some underlying preference function $\mathcal{V}(\cdot)$ defined over the probability distributions implied by each (x_1, x_2) pair under the well-defined state probabilities $(\bar{p}_1, \bar{p}_2)$—we refer to such preferences over (x_1, x_2) bundles as **probabilistically sophisticated**.

Expected utility and non-expected utility preference functions, and hence their respective indifference maps, have two features in common, and two important differences. Their first common feature is first order stochastic dominance preference. This property is the stochastic analogue of "more money is better," and makes just as much sense under non-expected utility as under expected utility. As we have seen, this translates into downward sloping indifference curves in the Hirshleifer-Yaari diagram, and is reflected in both Figure 2a and 2b.

The second common feature is the "*MRS* at certainty = odds ratio" condition, as seen in Figures 2a and 2b. The non-expected utility version of this property, namely,

[4] An alternative term for property (3) is **quasiconvexity in the outcomes**.

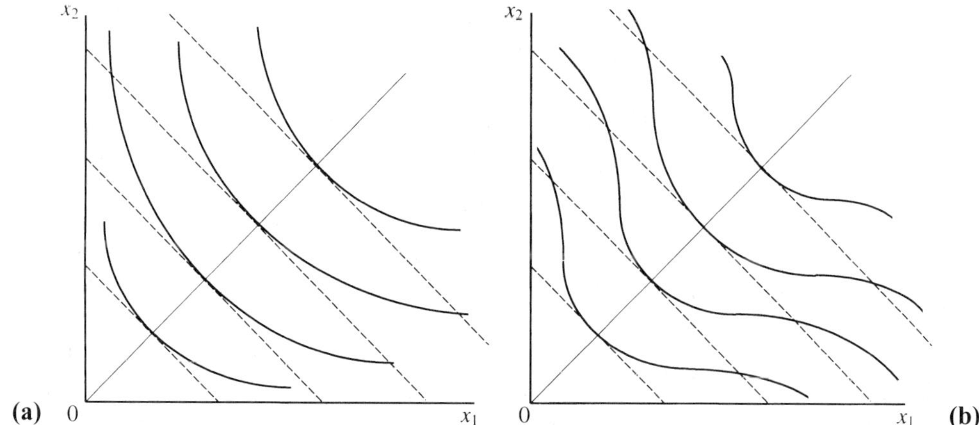

Figures 2a and 2b Risk Averse Non-Expected Utility Indifference Curves (Outcome-Convex and Non-Outcome Convex)

that any sufficiently "smooth" non-expected utility preference function $\mathcal{V}(\cdot)$ must satisfy

$$MRS_{\mathcal{V}}(x,x) \equiv -\left.\frac{\partial \mathcal{V}(x_1,\bar{p}_1;x_2,\bar{p}_2)/\partial x_1}{\partial \mathcal{V}(x_1,\bar{p}_1;x_2,\bar{p}_2)/\partial x_2}\right|_{x_1=x_2=x} = -\frac{\bar{p}_1}{\bar{p}_2} \tag{5}$$

follows from an early result of Samuelson (1960, pp. 34–37, eq. 5). Note that it implies that we can "recover" a non-expected utility (or expected utility) maximizer's subjective *probabilities* from their indifference curves over state-indexed *outcomes* in the Hirshleifer-Yaari diagram.

The first of the two important *differences* between expected utility and non-expected utility should not come as a surprise. Any departure from the additively-separable expected utility form (1) means that the so-called "rectangle property" on *MRS*'s will no longer hold. This is a well-known consequence of indifference curves over any kind of commodities, once we drop the assumption of separability of the preference function that generates them.

We come now to the second important difference between expected utility and non-expected utility indifference curves—the one that will play a very important role in our analysis. Note that while the non-expected utility indifference curves of Figure 2a needn't satisfy the rectangle property for *MRS*'s, they do satisfy both risk aversion[5] and outcome convexity—just like the expected utility indifference curves of Figure 1. However, the non-expected utility indifference curves of Figure 2b are risk averse but *not* outcome convex. In other words, in the absence of the expected utility hypoth-

[5] As before, they satisfy risk aversion since they are steeper/flatter than the iso-expected value lines in the region above/below the 45° line, so mean preserving increases in risk make them worse off.

esis, *risk aversion is no longer equivalent to outcome convexity*, and as Dekel (1989) has formally shown, it is quite possible for a preference function $\mathcal{V}(\cdot)$ (and hence its indifference curves) to be globally risk averse but not outcome-convex.[6]

On the other hand, Dekel has shown that if a non-expected utility $\mathcal{V}(\cdot)$ is outcome-convex then it must be risk averse. Although this is a formal result that applies to preferences over general probability distributions, the graphical intuition can be seen from Figure 2a: Recall that non-expected utility indifference curves must be tangent to the iso-expected value lines. Thus, if they are also outcome-convex, they must be steeper than these lines above the 45° line and flatter than them below the 45° line, which is exactly the condition for risk aversion in the diagram.

Thus, in the absence of the expected utility, risk aversion is seen to be a logically distinct—and weaker—property than outcome convexity. This means that when dropping the expected utility hypothesis and examining the robustness of some insurance result that "only requires risk aversion," we'll have to determine it really was "only risk aversion" that had been driving the result in question, or whether it was risk aversion *plus* outcome convexity that had been doing so.

Let's now illustrate preferences over changes in the *probabilities*, for fixed outcome values. Specifically, pick any three values $\bar{x}_1 < \bar{x}_2 < \bar{x}_3$, and consider the set of all probability distributions of the form $(\bar{x}_1, p_1; \bar{x}_2, p_2; \bar{x}_3, p_3)$. Since we must have $p_2 = 1 - p_1 - p_3$, we can plot each of these distributions as a point (p_1, p_3) plane, as in Figures 3a and 3b. Once again, a family of *expected utility* indifference curves will consist of the level curves of some expected utility preference function $\mathcal{V}(\mathbf{P}) = U(\bar{x}_1)\cdot p_1 + U(\bar{x}_2)\cdot p_2 + U(\bar{x}_3)\cdot p_3$, which, after substituting for p_2, takes the form

$$U(\bar{x}_2)+[U(\bar{x}_3)-U(\bar{x}_2)]\cdot p_3-[U(\bar{x}_2)-U(\bar{x}_1)]\cdot p_1 \tag{6}$$

with *MRS* accordingly given by

$$MRS_{EU}(p_1, p_3) \equiv \frac{U(\bar{x}_2)-U(\bar{x}_1)}{U(\bar{x}_3)-U(\bar{x}_2)} \tag{7}$$

and with the direction of increasing preference indicated by the arrows in the figures.

A family of *non-expected utility* indifference curves in the (p_1, p_3) diagram consist of the level curves of some general preference function $\mathcal{V}(\bar{x}_1, p_1, \bar{x}_2, p_2; \bar{x}_3, p_3)$, again subject to $p_2 = 1 - p_1 - p_3$. Substituting in to obtain the expression $\mathcal{V}(\bar{x}_1, p_1; \bar{x}_2, 1 -$

[6] For an explicit example, based on the proof of Dekel's Proposition 1, let $\mathcal{V}(\mathbf{P}) \equiv [\Sigma\sqrt{x_i}\cdot p_i - 5]^3 + 8\cdot[\Sigma x_i\cdot p_i - 49]^3$. Since the cube function is strictly increasing over all positive *and negative* arguments, this preference function is strictly increasing in each x_i and satisfies strict first order stochastic dominance preference. Since any mean preserving spread lowers the first bracketed term yet preserves the second, $\mathcal{V}(\cdot)$ is also strictly risk averse. Calculation reveals that $\mathcal{V}(\$100, \tfrac{1}{2}; \$0, \tfrac{1}{2}) = \mathcal{V}(\$49, \tfrac{1}{2}; \$49, \tfrac{1}{2}) = 8$ but $\mathcal{V}(\$74.5, \tfrac{1}{2}; \$24.5, \tfrac{1}{2}) \approx 6.74$. But since the latter probability distribution is a 50:50 outcome mixture of the first two, $\mathcal{V}(\cdot)$ is not outcome-convex.

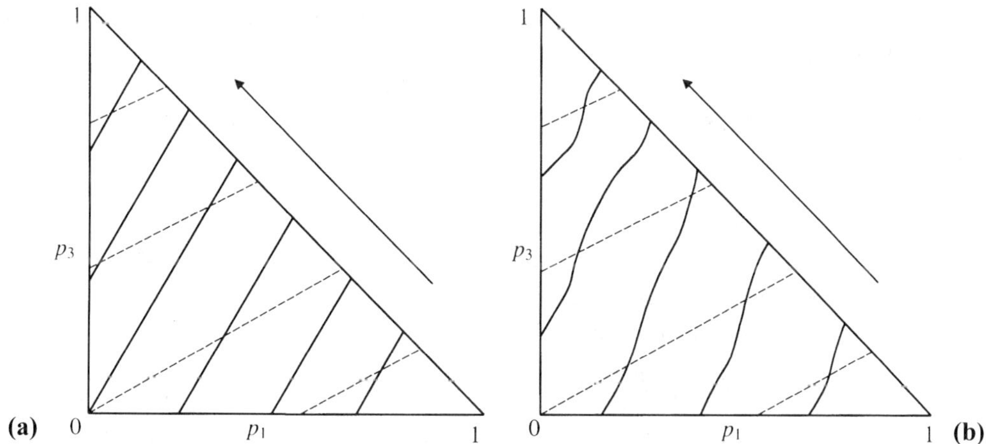

Figures 3a and 3b Risk Averse Indifference Curves in the Probability Triangle Diagram (Expected Utility and Non-Expected Utility)

$p_1 - p_3; \bar{x}_3, p_3)$, we have that the slope of these indifference curves at any point (p_1, p_3) is given by the formula

$$MRS_{\mathcal{V}}(p_1, p_3) \equiv \left. \frac{\dfrac{\partial \mathcal{V}(\mathbf{P})}{\partial p_2} - \dfrac{\partial \mathcal{V}(\mathbf{P})}{\partial p_1}}{\dfrac{\partial \mathcal{V}(\mathbf{P})}{\partial p_3} - \dfrac{\partial \mathcal{V}(\mathbf{P})}{\partial p_2}} \right|_{\mathbf{P}=(\bar{x}_1, p_1; \bar{x}_2, 1-p_1-p_3; \bar{x}_3, p_3)} \tag{8}$$

Figure 3a highlights the single most significant feature of expected utility preferences, namely the property of "linearity in the probabilities." As the level curves of a linear function (formula (1) or (6)), expected utility indifference curves in the probability diagram are parallel straight lines. This is the source of much of the predictive power of the expected utility model, since it implies that knowledge of the indifference curves in the neighborhood of any one point in the triangle implies knowledge of them over the whole triangle.

As we did for the Hirshleifer-Yaari diagram, we can also ask what the properties of first order stochastic dominance preference and risk aversion look like in the probability triangle. A pure *northward* movement in the triangle implies a rise in p_3, along (of course) with a matching drop in p_2. This corresponds to shifting probability from the outcome $\bar{x}_2$ up to the higher outcome $\bar{x}_3$. A *westward* movement implies a drop in p_1 with matching rise in p_2. An exact (45°) *northwestward* movement implies a rise in p_3 with equal drop in p_1 (no change in p_2). All three of these movements shift probability mass from some lower outcome up to some higher outcome, and hence are stochastically dominating shifts. Since the indifference curves in both Figures 3a and 3b are upward sloping, they prefer such shifts, and hence, reflect first order stochastic dominance preference.

The property of risk aversion is once again illustrated by reference to iso-expected value lines. In the probability triangle, they are the (dashed) level curves of the formula

$$\bar{x}_1 \cdot p_1 + \bar{x}_2 \cdot (1 - p_1 - p_3) + \bar{x}_3 \cdot p_3 = \bar{x}_2 + [\bar{x}_3 - \bar{x}_2] \cdot p_3 - [\bar{x}_2 - \bar{x}_1] \cdot p_1 \tag{9}$$

and hence have slope $[\bar{x}_2 - \bar{x}_1]/[\bar{x}_3 - \bar{x}_2]$. Northeast movements along these lines increase both of the outer (i.e., the "tail") probabilities p_1 and p_3 at the expense of the middle probability p_2, in a manner which does not change the expected value, so they represent the mean preserving spreads in the triangle. Since the indifference curves in both Figures 3a and 3b are steeper than these lines, they are made worse off by such increases in risk, and hence are risk averse.

Besides risk aversion *per se*, these diagrams can also illustrate *comparative risk aversion*—i.e., the property that one individual is *more risk averse* than another. Arrow (1965b) and Pratt (1964) have shown that the algebraic condition for comparative risk aversion under expected utility is that a pair of utility functions $U_1(\cdot)$ and $U_2(\cdot)$ satisfy the equivalent conditions:

$$U_1(x) \equiv \varphi(U_2(x)) \quad \text{for some increasing concave } \varphi(\cdot) \tag{10}$$

$$-\frac{U_1''(x)}{U_1'(x)} \geq -\frac{U_2''(x)}{U_2'(x)} \quad \text{for all } x \tag{11}$$

$$\frac{U_1'(x^*)}{U_1'(x)} \leq \frac{U_2'(x^*)}{U_2'(x)} \quad \text{for all } x^* > x \tag{12}$$

Figures 4a and 4b illustrate the implications of these algebraic conditions for indifference curves in the Hirshleifer-Yaari and the triangle diagrams. The indifference curves of the more risk averse utility function $U_1(\cdot)$ are solid; those of $U_2(\cdot)$ are dotted. In the Hirshleifer-Yaari diagram, the *MRS* formula (2) and inequality (12) imply that the indifference curves of the more risk averse $U_1(\cdot)$ are flatter than those of $U_2(\cdot)$ below the 45° line, and steeper than them above it. In the triangle diagram, the *MRS* formula (7) and a bit of calculus applied to either (11) or (12) yields that the indifference curves of the more risk averse $U_1(\cdot)$ are steeper than those of $U_2(\cdot)$.

Comparing Figures 4a and 4b with Figures 1 and 3a reveals that in each case, the relative slope conditions for *comparative* risk aversion are simply a generalization of the slope conditions for risk aversion *per se*. This is such a natural result that we would want to adopt it for *non-expected utility* indifference curves as well. In other words, when we come to determine the *algebraic* condition for comparative risk aversion

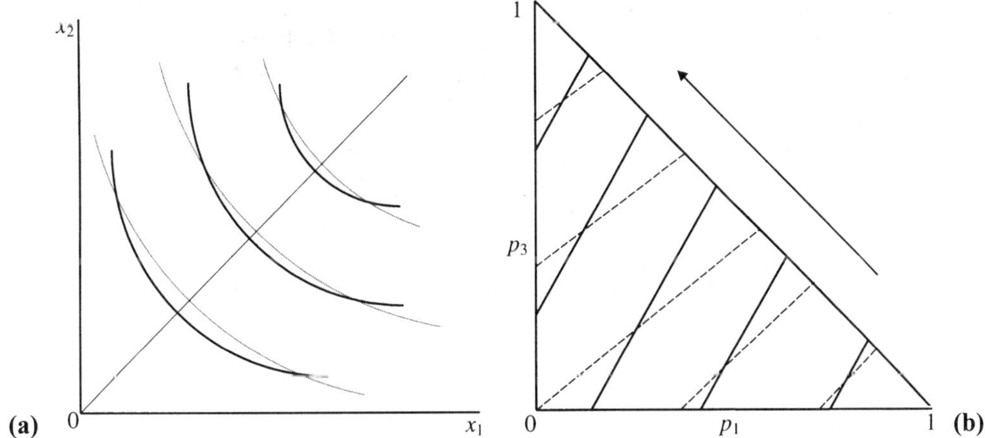

Figures 4a and 4b Comparative Risk Aversion for Expected Utility Indifference Curves

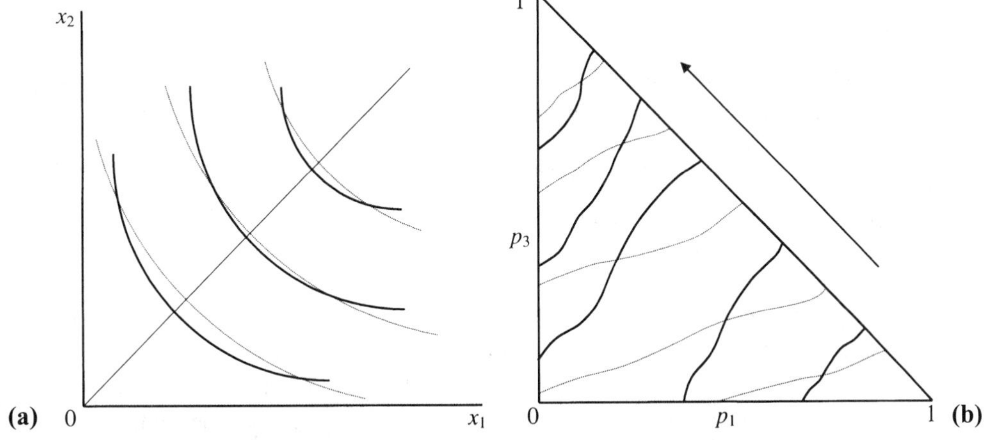

Figures 5a and 5b Comparative Risk Aversion for Non-Expected Utility Indifference Curves

under non-expected utility, we would insist that it imply these same relative slope conditions on indifference curves as in Figures 5a and 5b.

2.2.2 Algebraic Analysis of Non-Expected Utility Preferences

What about algebraic analysis in the absence of expected utility? Consider about how we might reassure our Cobb-Douglas scientist, puzzled at how we could drop

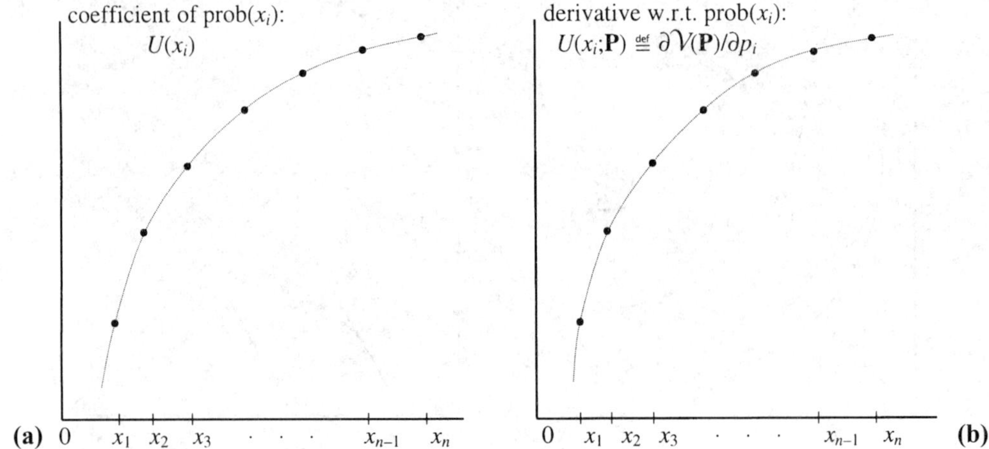

Figures 6a and 6b Expected Utility Probability Coefficients and Non-Expected Utility Probability Derivatives Plotted Against Their Corresponding Outcome Values

the well-structured formula $c_1^{\alpha_1} \ldots c_m^{\alpha_m}$ for a shapeless general preference function $\mathcal{U}(c_1, \ldots, c_m)$. We would say that we conduct our analysis in terms of the *derivatives* $\left\{\frac{\partial \mathcal{U}(\mathbf{C})}{\partial c_1}, \ldots, \frac{\partial \mathcal{U}(\mathbf{C})}{\partial c_m}\right\}$ of such general functions, and that conditions on these derivatives (and their ratios, etc.) give theorems about behavior.

One branch of non-expected utility theory—termed "generalized expected utility analysis"[7]—proceeds similarly, by working with derivatives of the preference function $\mathcal{V}(\cdot)$, and it is here that much of the robustness of expected utility analysis reveals itself. By way of motivation, recall some of the classical results of expected utility theory. For purposes of this exercise, assume that the set of potential outcome values $x_1 < \ldots < x_n$ is fixed, so that only the probabilities $\{p_1, \ldots, p_n\}$ are independent variables. Now, given an expected utility preference function $\mathcal{V}(\mathbf{P}) = \Sigma_{i=1}^n U(x_i) \cdot p_i$, don't think of $U(x_i)$ in its psychological role as the "utility of receiving outcome x_i," but rather in its purely mathematical role as the *coefficient* of $p_i = \text{prob}(x_i)$. If we plot these probability coefficients against x_i, as in Figure 6a, we can state the three most fundamental results of expected utility theory as follows:

First Order Stochastic Dominance Preference: $\mathcal{V}(\cdot)$ exhibits first order stochastic dominance preference if and only if its probability coefficients $\{U(x_i)\}$ form an increasing sequence, as in Figure 6a.

[7] E.g., Machina (1982, 1983).

Risk Aversion: $\mathcal{V}(\cdot)$ is risk averse if and only if its probability coefficients $\{U(x_i)\}$ form a concave sequence,[8] as in Figure 6a.

Comparative Risk Aversion: $\mathcal{V}_1(\cdot)$ is at least as risk averse as $\mathcal{V}_2(\cdot)$ if and only if the sequence of probability coefficients $\{U_1(x_i)\}$ is at least as concave[9] as the sequence of probability coefficients $\{U_2(x_i)\}$.

Now consider a general *non*-expected utility preference function $\mathcal{V}(\mathbf{P}) = \mathcal{V}(x_1, p_1; \ldots; x_n, p_n)$, and continue to treat the outcomes $x_1 < \ldots < x_n$ as fixed and the probabilities $\{p_1, \ldots, p_n\}$ as independent variables. Since $\mathcal{V}(\cdot)$ is not linear in the probabilities (not expected utility), it won't have probability coefficients. However, as long as $\mathcal{V}(\cdot)$ is differentiable, it will have a set of *probability derivatives* $\left\{\frac{\partial \mathcal{V}(\mathbf{P})}{\partial p_1}, \ldots, \frac{\partial \mathcal{V}(\mathbf{P})}{\partial p_n}\right\}$ at each distribution **P**, and calculus tells us that in many cases, theorems based on the *coefficients of a linear function* will also apply to the *derivatives of a nonlinear function.*

In fact, this is precisely the case with the above three results, and this extension from probability coefficients to probability derivatives is the essence of generalized expected utility analysis. In other words, for any non-expected utility preference function $\mathcal{V}(\cdot)$, pick a distribution **P**, and plot the corresponding sequence of probability derivatives $\left\{\frac{\partial \mathcal{V}(\mathbf{P})}{\partial p_1}, \ldots, \frac{\partial \mathcal{V}(\mathbf{P})}{\partial p_n}\right\}$ against x_i, as in Figure 6b. If these form an increasing sequence (as in the figure), then any *infinitesimal* stochastically dominating shift—say an infinitesimal drop in p_i and matching rise in p_{i+1}—will clearly be preferred. If the derivatives form a concave sequence (as in the figure), then any *infinitesimal* mean preserving increase in risk—such as an infinitesimal drop in p_i coupled with a mean preserving rise in p_{i-1} and p_{i+1}—will make the individual worse off.

Of course, these results are "local," since they link the derivatives $\left\{\frac{\partial \mathcal{V}(\mathbf{P})}{\partial p_1}, \ldots, \frac{\partial \mathcal{V}(\mathbf{P})}{\partial p_n}\right\}$ at a distribution **P** only to infinitesimal changes from **P**. However, we can take advantage of another feature of calculus, namely, that *global* conditions on derivatives are frequently equivalent to *global* properties of a function. This is the case with our three fundamental results. Thus, if the derivatives $\left\{\frac{\partial \mathcal{V}(\mathbf{P})}{\partial p_1}, \ldots, \frac{\partial \mathcal{V}(\mathbf{P})}{\partial p_n}\right\}$ are seen to form an increasing and concave sequence at *all* such distributions **P**, then *global* stochastically dominating shifts will always be preferred, and *global* increase in risk will always make the individual worse off. Formally, we can prove:

[8] Algebraically, $\{U(x_i)\}$ forms a concave sequence if and only if its point-to-point slopes $(U(x_2) - U(x_1))/(x_2 - x_1)$, $(U(x_3) - U(x_2))/(x_3 - x_2)$, etc. are successively nonincreasing.

[9] $\{U_1(x_i)\}$ is at least as concave than $\{U_2(x_i)\}$ if and only if each ratio of adjacent point-to-point slopes $[(U(x_{i+1}) - U(x_i))/(x_{i+1} - x_i)]/[(U(x_i) - U(x_{i-1}))/(x_i - x_{i-1})]$ is no greater for $\{U_1(x_i)\}$ than for $\{U_2(x_i)\}$.

First Order Stochastic Dominance Preference: A non-expected utility preference function $\mathcal{V}(\cdot)$ exhibits global first order stochastic dominance preference if and only if at each distribution **P**, its probability derivatives $\left\{\frac{\partial \mathcal{V}(\mathbf{P})}{\partial p_i}\right\}$ form an increasing sequence, as in Figure 6b.

Risk Aversion: $\mathcal{V}(\cdot)$ is globally averse to all (small and large) mean preserving increases in risk if and only if at each **P** its probability derivatives $\left\{\frac{\partial \mathcal{V}(\mathbf{P})}{\partial p_i}\right\}$ form a concave sequence, as in Figure 6b.

Comparative Risk Aversion: $\mathcal{V}_1(\cdot)$ is globally at least as risk averse as[10] $\mathcal{V}_2(\cdot)$ if and only if at each **P**, the sequence of probability derivatives $\left\{\frac{\partial \mathcal{V}_1(\mathbf{P})}{\partial x_i}\right\}$ is at least as concave as the sequence of probability derivatives $\left\{\frac{\partial \mathcal{V}_2(\mathbf{P})}{\partial x_i}\right\}$.

In light of this correspondence between expected utility's *probability coefficients* $\{U(x_i)\}$ and non-expected utility's *probability derivatives* $\left\{\frac{\partial \mathcal{V}(\mathbf{P})}{\partial x_i}\right\}$, we adopt the suggestive notation $U(x_i; \mathbf{P}) = \frac{\partial \mathcal{V}(\mathbf{P})}{\partial p_i}$, and call $\{U(x_i; \mathbf{P})\}$ the **local utility index** of $\mathcal{V}(\cdot)$ at **P**.

An important point: Do we really have to restrict ourselves just to changes in the probabilities of the *original outcomes* $\{x_1, \ldots, x_n\}$? No. At any distribution $\mathbf{P} = (x_1, p_1; \ldots; x_n, p_n)$, we can define the local utility index $U(x; \mathbf{P})$ for any *other* outcome level x, by observing that

$$\mathbf{P} = (x_1, p_1; \ldots; x_n, p_n) = (x_1, p_1; \ldots; x_n, p_n; x, 0) \tag{13}$$

so that we can define

$$U(x; \mathbf{P}) \equiv \frac{\partial \mathcal{V}(\mathbf{P})}{\partial \mathrm{prob}(x)} \equiv \left.\frac{\partial \mathcal{V}(x_1, p_1; \ldots; x_n, p_n; x, \wp)}{\partial \wp}\right|_{\wp = 0} \tag{14}$$

Thus, $U(\cdot; \mathbf{P})$ is really a local utility *function* over all outcome values x, and the isolated dots in Figure 6b—like the isolated utility values in Figure 6a—are really points on an entire *curve*. In this more complete setting, the non-expected utility conditions for first order stochastic dominance preference, risk aversion, and comparative risk aversion are that at every **P**, the function $U(x; \mathbf{P})$ must respectively be increasing in x, concave in x, and more concave in x—just like the conditions on $U(x)$ under expected utility theory. See Machina (1982, 1983, 1989), Allen (1987), Chew, Epstein

[10] For the appropriate definition of "at least as risk averse as" under non-expected utility, see Machina (1982, 1984).

and Zilcha (1988), Karni (1987, 1989) and Wang (1993) for additional extensions and applications of this kind of analysis.

Although the above suggests that the key to generalizing expected utility analysis is to think in terms of the *probability derivatives* of the preference function $\mathcal{V}(\mathbf{P}) = \mathcal{V}(x_1, p_1; \ldots; x_n, p_n)$, it is clear that the analysis of insurance and risk sharing problems will involve its *outcome derivatives* as well. Fortunately, we can show that, as long as we continue to think of $U(x; \mathbf{P}) = \dfrac{\partial \mathcal{V}(\mathbf{P})}{\partial \text{prob}(x)}$ as the "local utility function," the standard expected utility outcome derivative formula also generalizes to non-expected utility.[11] That is to say, if the local utility function $U(x; \mathbf{P}) = \dfrac{\partial \mathcal{V}(\mathbf{P})}{\partial \text{prob}(x)}$ is differentiable in x at every distribution $\mathbf{P}$, then

$$\frac{\partial \mathcal{V}(\mathbf{P})}{\partial x_i} \equiv \frac{\partial \mathcal{V}(x_1, p_1; \ldots; x_n, p_n)}{\partial x_i} \equiv \frac{\partial U(x_i; \mathbf{P})}{\partial x_i} \cdot p_i \equiv U'(x_i; \mathbf{P}) \cdot p_i \tag{15}$$

This gives us an immediate generalization of the expected utility *MRS* formula for non-expected utility indifference curves, namely

$$MRS_{\mathcal{V}}(x_1, x_2) \equiv -\frac{\partial \mathcal{V}(x_1, \bar{p}_1; x_2, \bar{p}_2)/\partial x_1}{\partial \mathcal{V}(x_1, \bar{p}_1; x_2, \bar{p}_2)/\partial x_2} \equiv -\frac{U'(x_1; \mathbf{P}_{x_1,x_2}) \cdot \bar{p}_1}{U'(x_2; \mathbf{P}_{x_1,x_2}) \cdot \bar{p}_2} \tag{16}$$

where $\mathbf{P}_{x_1,x_2} = (x_1, \bar{p}_1; x_2, \bar{p}_2)$ is the probability distribution corresponding to the point (x_1, x_2). It also gives us a generalization of the "marginal expected utility" formula, namely

$$\left.\frac{d\mathcal{V}(x_1 + k, p_1; \ldots; x_n + k, p_n)}{dk}\right|_{k=0} \equiv \sum_{i=1}^{n} U'(x_i; \mathbf{P}) \cdot p_i \tag{17}$$

It should come as no surprise that formulas like (15), (16) and (17) will come in handy in checking the robustness of standard expected utility-based insurance theory.

A settling of accounts: If a non-expected utility preference function $\mathcal{V}_1(\cdot)$ is at least as risk averse as another one $\mathcal{V}_2(\cdot)$, so that at each $\mathbf{P}$ its local utility function $U_1(\cdot; \mathbf{P})$ is at least as concave as $U_2(\cdot; \mathbf{P})$, then the Arrow-Pratt theorem and the *MRS* formula (16) directly imply the relative slope condition illustrated in Figure 5a. Similarly, the Arrow-Pratt theorem, *MRS* formula (8) and a little calculus imply the relative slope condition illustrated in Figure 5b. Just as required![12]

[11] This follows from applying Machina (1982, eq. 8) to the path $F(\cdot; \alpha) \equiv (x_1, p_1; \ldots; x_{i-1}, p_{i-1}; \alpha, p_i; x_{i+1}, p_{i+1}; \ldots; x_n, p_n)$.

[12] In some of our more formal analysis below (including the formal theorems), we use the natural extension of these ideas to the case of a preference function $\mathcal{V}(F)$ over cumulative distribution functions $F(\cdot)$ with local utility function $U(\cdot; F)$, including the smoothness notion of "Fréchet differentiability" (see Machina (1982)).

2.3 INDIVIDUAL DEMAND FOR INSURANCE

The previous section presented a set of tools—graphical and algebraic—for representing and analyzing non-expected utility risk preferences. It also showed that the analysis of non-expected utility preferences is much closer to classical expected utility theory than one might have thought. We now turn toward applying these tools to examining the robustness of standard insurance theory[13] in the absence of the expected utility hypothesis.

For most of this chapter, we shall assume that risk preferences—expected utility or otherwise—are differentiable both in the outcomes and in the probabilities.[14] In addition, since the results of insurance theory also almost all depend upon the property of risk aversion, even under the expected utility hypothesis, there is no point in dropping that assumption when undertaking our non-expected utility examination. But as noted above, since risk aversion under expected utility also means outcome convexity, we could never be sure whether the result in question was really driven by risk aversion alone, or by outcome convexity as well.[15] Thus, when examining insurance theory in the *absence* of the expected utility hypothesis, our "robustness check" could reveal each expected utility-based insurance result to be in one of the following categories:

- the result only requires the assumption of *risk aversion*, without either outcome convexity or expected utility
- the result requires *outcome convexity* (and hence also *risk aversion*), but not expected utility
- the result simply *doesn't hold at all* without the expected utility hypothesis

Naturally, when checking any given result, the higher up its category in this listing, the nicer it would be for non-expected utility theorists. And since robustness is a virtue, the nicer it would be for standard insurance theorists as well!

In the following, we assume that the individual possesses an initial wealth level w and faces the prospect of a random loss $\tilde{\ell}$, with probability distribution $(\ell_1, p_1; \ldots; \ell_n, p_n)$ (with each $\ell_i \geq 0$). An insurance policy consists of an **indemnity function** $I(\cdot)$ such that the individual receives payment $I(\ell)$ in the event of a loss of ℓ, as well as a **premium** of π, which must be paid no matter what. Thus, the individual's random wealth upon taking a policy (or "contract") $(I(\cdot), \pi)$ becomes[16]

[13] The reader wishing self-contained treatments of the vast body of insurance results can do no better than the excellent survey by Dionne and Harrington (1992, pp. 1–48) and volume by Eeckhoudt and Gollier (1995). For more extensive treatments of specific topics, see the rest of the papers in Dionne and Harrington (1992) as well as the papers in Dionne (1992) and the chapters in the present volume.

[14] We consider non-differentiabilities ("kinks") in the outcomes and probabilities in Sections 2.7 and 2.8.

[15] This point is nicely made by Karni (1992).

[16] Note that this framework abstracts from the problem of uninsurable "background risk," as studied for example by Doherty and Schlesinger (1983), Schlesinger and Doherty (1985), and Eeckhoudt and Kimball (1992).

$$w - \pi - \tilde{\ell} + I(\tilde{\ell}) \tag{18}$$

Of course, different forms of insurance involve different classes $\{(I_\alpha(\cdot), \pi_\alpha) \mid \alpha \in A\}$ of indemnity functions $I_\alpha(\cdot)$ and their corresponding premiums π_α, from which the individual may choose. In many cases, the premium for a given indemnity function $I(\cdot)$ takes the form $\pi = \lambda \cdot E[I(\tilde{\ell})]$, where $\lambda \geq 1$ is a **loading factor**. The results of standard insurance theory involve both characterization theorems and comparative statics theorems concerning individual maximization, bilateral efficiency, and group efficiency using the above framework.

For notational simplicity, we shall frequently work directly with random variables, such as $\tilde{\ell}$ or $w - \tilde{\ell}$, rather than with their probability distributions $(\ell_1, p_1; \ldots; \ell_n, p_n)$ or $(w - \ell_1, p_1; \ldots; w - \ell_n, p_n)$. In other words, given a random variable $\tilde{x}$ with probability distribution $(x_1, p_1; \ldots; x_n, p_n)$, we shall use the term $\mathcal{V}(\tilde{x})$ as shorthand for $\mathcal{V}(x_1, p_1; \ldots; x_n, p_n)$. Thus, for example, $\mathcal{V}(w - \pi - \tilde{\ell} + I(\tilde{\ell}))$ denotes $\mathcal{V}(w - \pi - \ell_1 + I(\ell_1), p_1; \ldots; w - \pi - \ell_n + I(\ell_n), p_n)$.

2.3.1 Demand for Coinsurance

The very simplest results in insurance theory involve individual demand for a level α of **coinsurance**, given a fixed loading factor $\lambda \geq 1$. Formally, this setting consists of the set of policies $\{(I_\alpha(\cdot), \pi_\alpha) \mid \alpha \in [0, 1]\}$, with

$$\begin{array}{rl} \text{Indemnity function:} & I_\alpha(\ell) \equiv \alpha \cdot \ell \\ \text{Premium:} & \pi_\alpha = \lambda \cdot \alpha E[\tilde{\ell}] \end{array} \quad \text{for } \alpha \in [0, 1] \tag{19}$$

In the expected utility framework, the individual's choice problem can therefore be written as

$$\begin{gathered} \max_{\alpha \in [0,1]} E[U(w - \alpha \cdot \lambda \cdot E[\tilde{\ell}] - \tilde{\ell} + \alpha \cdot \tilde{\ell})] \quad \text{or} \\ \max_{\alpha \in [0,1]} E[U(w - \lambda \cdot E[\tilde{\ell}] - (1-\alpha) \cdot (\tilde{\ell} - \lambda \cdot E[\tilde{\ell}]))] \end{gathered} \tag{20}$$

Denote the optimal choice in this problem by α^*. This setting was studied early on, in classic papers by Borch (1961), Mossin (1968) and Smith (1968). From the right side of (20) we see that marginal change in insurance coverage α adds/subtracts the random variable $(\tilde{\ell} - \lambda \cdot E[\tilde{\ell}])$ to/from the individual's random wealth. Accordingly, we can term the random variable $(\tilde{\ell} - \lambda \cdot E[\tilde{\ell}])$ the **marginal insurable risk variable**.

The most basic analytical results for coinsurance are:

CO.1 The first order condition for an interior optimum—i.e., a *necessary* condition for an interior global maximum—is that the expectation of the marginal insurable risk variable times the marginal utility of wealth is zero:

$$E[(\tilde{\ell}-\lambda\cdot E[\tilde{\ell}])\cdot U'(w-\alpha\cdot\lambda\cdot E[\tilde{\ell}]-\tilde{\ell}+\alpha\cdot\tilde{\ell})]=0 \tag{21}$$

and under risk aversion, this is a *sufficient* condition for a global optimum.

CO.2 If the individual is risk averse, then full insurance will be demanded if and only if it is *actuarially fair*. In other words, $\alpha^* = 1$ if and only if $\lambda = 1$.

CO.3 If two risk averse individuals face the same choice problem except that the first is *at least as risk averse* as the second, then the first will demand at least as much insurance as the second. In other words, if $U_1(\cdot)$ is a concave transformation of $U_2(\cdot)$, then $\alpha_1^* \geq \alpha_2^*$.[17]

Results CO.2 and CO.3 can both be illustrated in the Hirshleifer-Yaari diagram.[18] Consider Figure 7a, where the original uninsured position, point A, lies off the 45° line, its corresponding full insurance point would lie exactly on the 45° line, and the coinsurance "budget line" connects the two points. The value $\alpha \in [0, 1]$ corresponds to the position along the budget line from the uninsured point to the fully insured point. To see CO.2, note first that when insurance is actuarially fair, this budget corresponds to the (dashed) iso-expected value line emanating from A, and from risk aversion clearly implies that the optimal point on this line is its corresponding full insurance point B. Next, note that when insurance is actuarially unfair, the budget line from A is now *flatter* than the iso-expected value lines, so it is no longer tangent to the indifference curve through the (new) full insurance point C. This implies that the new optimal point, namely D, will involve less than full insurance. To see CO.3, consider Figure 7b and recall from Figure 4a (or equations (2) and (12)) that for expected utility maximizers, the (solid) indifference curves of the more risk averse person must be flatter than the (dotted) indifference curves of the less risk averse one in the region below the 45° line. This fact, coupled with the outcome-convexity property of risk averse expected utility indifference curves, guarantees that, when both start from the same uninsured point A', the more risk averse person will choose a greater level of coinsurance—point F rather than point E.

How about non-expected utility maximizers? In this case, the coinsurance problem becomes

$$\max_{\alpha\in[0,1]} \mathcal{V}(w-\alpha\cdot\lambda\cdot E[\tilde{\ell}]-\tilde{\ell}+\alpha\cdot\tilde{\ell}) \quad \text{or}$$

$$\max_{\alpha\in[0,1]} \mathcal{V}(w-\lambda\cdot E[\tilde{\ell}]-(1-\alpha)\cdot(\tilde{\ell}-\lambda\cdot E[\tilde{\ell}])) \tag{22}$$

[17] As demonstrated in Pratt (1964), further results which link increasing/decreasing absolute and/or relative risk aversion to changes in α as an individual's wealth changes can be derived as corollaries of result CO.3.

[18] So can result CO.1, if one calculates the slope of the budget lines in Figures 7a and 7b.

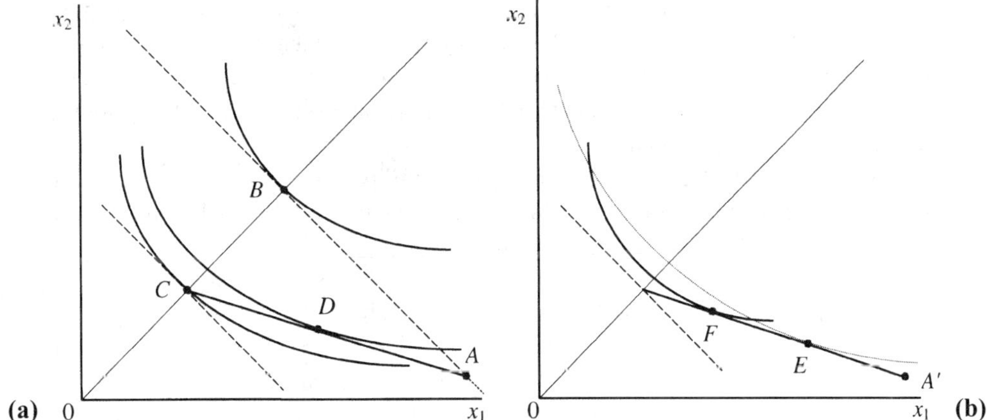

Figures 7a and 7b Optimal Coinsurance and Effect of Greater Risk Aversion on Coinsurance for Risk Averse Expected Utility Preferences

for some general non-expected utility preference function $\mathcal{V}(\cdot)$. Do any of the above expected utility-based results still hold? And if so, do they require just risk aversion, or do they also need outcome convexity?

To examine the robustness of CO.1, write (22) as

$$\max_{\alpha\in[0,1]} \mathcal{V}(w-\alpha\cdot\lambda\cdot E[\tilde{\ell}]-\ell_1+\alpha\cdot\ell_1, p_1;\ldots;w-\alpha\cdot\lambda\cdot E[\tilde{\ell}]-\ell_n+\alpha\cdot\ell_n, p_n) \quad (23)$$

Formula (15) allows us to differentiate with respect to α to get the non-expected utility first order condition

$$\frac{d\mathcal{V}(w-\alpha\cdot\lambda\cdot E[\tilde{\ell}]-\ell_1+\alpha\cdot\ell_1, p_1;\ldots;w-\alpha\cdot\lambda\cdot E[\tilde{\ell}]-\ell_n+\alpha\cdot\ell_n, p_n)}{d\alpha}$$
$$=\sum_{i=1}^{n}(\ell_i-\lambda\cdot E[\tilde{\ell}])\cdot U'(w-\alpha\cdot\lambda\cdot E[\tilde{\ell}]-\ell_i+\alpha\cdot\ell_i;\mathbf{P}_\alpha)\cdot p_i$$
$$=E[(\tilde{\ell}-\lambda\cdot E[\tilde{\ell}])\cdot U'(w-\alpha\cdot\lambda\cdot E[\tilde{\ell}]-\tilde{\ell}+\alpha\cdot\tilde{\ell};\mathbf{P}_\alpha)]=0 \quad (24)$$

where $\mathbf{P}_\alpha$ denotes the wealth distribution $w-\alpha\cdot\lambda\cdot E[\tilde{\ell}]-\tilde{\ell}+\alpha\cdot\tilde{\ell}$ arising from the purchase of α coinsurance. This is precisely the analogue of the expected utility first order condition (21) with the von Neumann-Morgenstern utility function $U(\cdot)$ replaced by the *local* utility function $U(\cdot;\mathbf{P}_\alpha)$ at the wealth distribution $\mathbf{P}_\alpha$,[19] where

$$\mathbf{P}_\alpha = w-\alpha\cdot\lambda\cdot E[\tilde{\ell}]-\tilde{\ell}+\alpha\cdot\tilde{\ell} \quad (25)$$

[19] This close correspondence of expected utility and non-expected utility first order conditions will come as no surprise to those who have read Chew, Epstein and Zilcha (1988). We'll come to this again below.

Note that the *necessity* of condition (24) does not even require risk aversion, just differentiability. However, it should be clear from the Hirshleifer-Yaari diagram that it will only be *sufficient* under full outcome convexity. Otherwise, an indifference curve could be tangent to the budget line from *below*, and the point of tangency would be a (local or global) minimum.

Extending result CO.2 to the non-expected utility case is straightforward, and doesn't require outcome convexity at all. When insurance is actuarially fair ($\lambda = 1$), we have that for any $\alpha < 1$, the random wealth

$$w - \alpha \cdot E[\tilde{\ell}] - \tilde{\ell} + \alpha \cdot \tilde{\ell} \equiv w - E[\tilde{\ell}] - (1-\alpha) \cdot (\tilde{\ell} - E[\tilde{\ell}]) \tag{26}$$

differs from the full insurance ($\alpha = 1$) wealth of $w - E[\tilde{\ell}]$ by the addition of a zero-mean random variable. Accordingly, risk aversion alone implies that when coinsurance is actuarially fair, full coverage is optimal. Similarly, when insurance is unfair ($\lambda > 1$), we have that

$$\left.\frac{d\mathcal{V}(w - \alpha \cdot \lambda \cdot E[\tilde{\ell}] - \tilde{\ell} + \alpha \cdot \tilde{\ell})}{d\alpha}\right|_{\alpha=1} = E[(\tilde{\ell} - \lambda \cdot E[\tilde{\ell}]) \cdot U'(w - \lambda \cdot E[\tilde{\ell}]; \mathbf{P}_1)]$$
$$= (1-\lambda) \cdot E[\tilde{\ell}] \cdot U'(w - \lambda \cdot E[\tilde{\ell}]; \mathbf{P}_1) < 0 \tag{27}$$

where $\mathbf{P}_1$ is the degenerate distribution of the full insurance wealth level $w - \lambda \cdot E[\tilde{\ell}]$. Thus, there will be values $\alpha < 1$ that are strictly preferred to the full insurance position $\alpha = 1$. This is all illustrated in Figure 8a, where indifference curves are risk averse but not outcome convex.[20]

It would seem that *if any* coinsurance result depended crucially on the assumption of outcome convexity, it would be result CO.3, which links greater risk aversion to greater coinsurance. This type of global comparative statics theorem is precisely the type of result we would expect to depend upon the proper curvature of indifference curves, and a glance at Figure 7b would seem to reinforce this view. However, one of the most important points of this chapter, which will appear a few times, is that even for a result like this, outcome-convexity is not needed.

The essence of this argument can be gleaned from Figure 8b. Recall that if preferences are risk averse but not outcome-convex, then there is the possibility of mul-

[20] *A Note on Beliefs*: Although CO.2 accordingly survives dropping the assumption of expected utility *risk preferences*, it *does not* survive dropping the assumption that the individual's subjective probabilities *exactly match* those of the "market," that is, the probabilities by which an insurance policy is judged to be actuarially fair or unfair. If—for reasons of moral hazard, adverse selection or simply personal history—the individual assigns a higher probability to state 2 than does the market, then the indifference curves in Figure 7a will be flatter than and *cut* the dashed lines at all certainty points, and an individual with a smooth (differentiable) $U(\cdot)$ may well select point *C* on an actuarially unfair budget line like *A*–*C*. How far must beliefs diverge for this to happen? Consider earthquake insurance priced on the basis of an actuarial probability of .0008 and a loading factor of 25%. Every smooth risk averter with a subjective probability greater than .001 will buy full insurance.

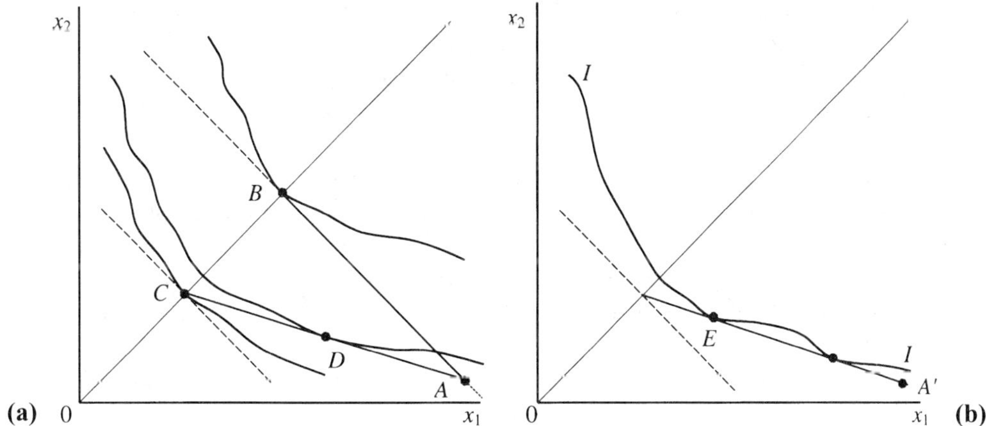

Figures 8a and 8b Optimal Coinsurance and Effect of Greater Risk Aversion on Coinsurance for Non-Expected Utility Preferences that are Risk Averse But Not Outcome-Convex

tiple global optima, as with the indifference curve in the figure. However, the essence of the comparative statics result CO.3 is *not* that each individual must have a unique solution, but that the less risk averse individual must *always* buy less insurance than the more risk averse individual.

To see that this still holds under non-expected utility, recall (from (12) and (16) or Fig. 5a) that the non-expected utility condition for comparative risk aversion is that at each point below the 45° line, the indifference curves of the more risk averse person are flatter than those of the less risk averse person. This means that any southeast movement along one of the *less* risk averse person's indifference curves must *lower* the preference function of the *more* risk averse person.

Now, to see that *every* optimum of the less risk averse person involves less insurance than *every* optimum of the more risk averse person, consider point E in Figure 8b, which is that optimum for the less risk averse person that involves the *most* insurance for them, and consider their indifference curve through E (call it I-I). Of course, I-I must lie everywhere on or above the insurance budget line. By the previous paragraph, any *more risk averse* person would prefer E to each point on I-I lying southeast of E, and hence (by the previous sentence) prefer E to every point on the *budget line* lying southeast of E. This then establishes that the *very least* amount of coinsurance this more risk averse person would buy is at E. If the more risk averse person is in fact *strictly* more risk averse, the two persons' indifference curves cannot *both* be tangent to the budget line at E. Rather, the indifference curve of the more risk averse person will be flatter at that point, which implies that the *least* insurance they would ever buy is strictly more than the *most* insurance that the less risk averse person would ever buy (namely, E). Risk aversion (and comparative risk aversion) alone ensure this result, and outcome convexity is not needed at all.[21]

A formal algebraic statement of this result, which includes general probability distributions and allows for a corner solution (at zero insurance), is:

Theorem 1. Let $w_0 > 0$ be base wealth, $\tilde{\ell} \geq 0$ a random loss, and $\lambda > 1$ a loading factor, such that $w_0 - \tilde{\ell}$ and $w_0 - \lambda \cdot E[\tilde{\ell}]$ are both nonnegative. Assume that the non-expected utility preference functions $\mathcal{V}_1(\cdot)$ and $\mathcal{V}_2(\cdot)$ are twice continuously Fréchet differentiable (see Note 12), strictly risk averse, and that $\mathcal{V}_1(\cdot)$ is strictly more risk averse than $\mathcal{V}_2(\cdot)$ in the sense that $-U_1''(x; F)/U_1'(x; F) > -U_2''(x; F)/U_2'(x; F)$ for all x and $F(\cdot)$. Consider the problem:

$$\max_{\alpha \in [0,1]} \mathcal{V}_i(w_0 - \alpha \cdot \lambda \cdot E[\tilde{\ell}] - \tilde{\ell} + \alpha \cdot \tilde{\ell}) \quad i = 1, 2 \tag{28}$$

If α_1^* is the smallest solution to this problem for $\mathcal{V}_1(\cdot)$, and α_2^* is the largest solution for $\mathcal{V}_2(\cdot)$, then $\alpha_1^* \geq \alpha_2^*$, with *strict inequality* unless $\alpha_1^* = 0$.

Proof in Appendix

In other words, regardless of the possible multiplicity of optima due to non-outcome convexity, we will never observe the more risk averse first individual purchasing a smaller amount of insurance than the second individual, and the only time they would ever purchase the same amount is if the terms are so unattractive that zero insurance is an optimum even for the first individual, in which case it is the *only* optimum for the second individual.

To sum up our robustness check on coinsurance: except for the additional status of the necessary condition (21) as a sufficient condition as well (which also requires outcome-convexity), *all three* of the coinsurance results CO.1, CO.2 and CO.3 generalize to non-expected utility preferences under the assumption of simple risk aversion alone. In other words, at least at this most basic level, the standard theory of demand for coinsurance is very robust.

2.3.2 Demand for Deductible Insurance

A second type of insurance contract, distinct from the coinsurance contract considered above, is **deductible** insurance. Given a fixed actuarial loading factor $\lambda \geq 1$, this setting consists of the set of contracts $\{(I_\alpha(\cdot), \pi_\alpha) \mid \alpha \in [0, M]\}$, where M is the largest possible value of the loss ℓ, and

[21] Readers will recognize this argument (and its formalization in the proofs of the theorems) as an application of the well-known "single-crossing property" argument from incentive theory, as in Mirrlees (1971), Spence (1974) and Guesnerie and Laffont (1984), and generalized and extended by Milgrom and Shannon (1994).

$$\begin{array}{rl} \text{Indemnity function:} & I_\alpha(\ell) \equiv \max\{\ell - \alpha, 0\} \\ \text{Premium:} & \pi_\alpha = \lambda \cdot E[I_\alpha(\tilde{\ell})] \end{array} \quad \text{for } \alpha \in [0, M] \tag{29}$$

In the expected utility framework, the individual's choice problem can therefore be written as

$$\max_{\alpha \in [0,M]} E[U(w - \lambda \cdot E[I_\alpha(\tilde{\ell})] - \tilde{\ell} + \max\{\tilde{\ell} - \alpha, 0\})] \quad \text{or}$$
$$\max_{\alpha \in [0,M]} E[U(w - \lambda \cdot E[\max\{\tilde{\ell} - \alpha, 0\}] - \min\{\tilde{\ell}, \alpha\})] \tag{30}$$

Denote the optimal choice by α^*. This problem has been studied by, among others, Mossin (1968), Gould (1969), Pashigian, Schkade and Menefee (1966), Moffet (1977), Schlesinger (1981), Drèze (1981), Karni (1983, 1985) and Eeckhoudt, Gollier and Schlesinger (1991).

The insurance budget line for this problem in the case of two states is illustrated in Figure 9. Given an initial (pre-loss) wealth point $W = (w, w)$, the uninsured point A reflects a small loss ℓ_1 in state 1 and a larger loss ℓ_2 in state 2. The thick line in the figure represents the kinked insurance budget line when insurance is actuarially unfair (otherwise, is it simply the dashed iso-expected value line through A). Starting at the deductible level $\alpha = \ell_2$ (i.e., no insurance) each unit drop in α lowers wealth in state 1 by the premium $\lambda \cdot \bar{p}_2$, and *raises* wealth in state 2 by $1 - \lambda \cdot \bar{p}_2$, while lowering the overall expected value of wealth. This generates a linear budget line from point A to

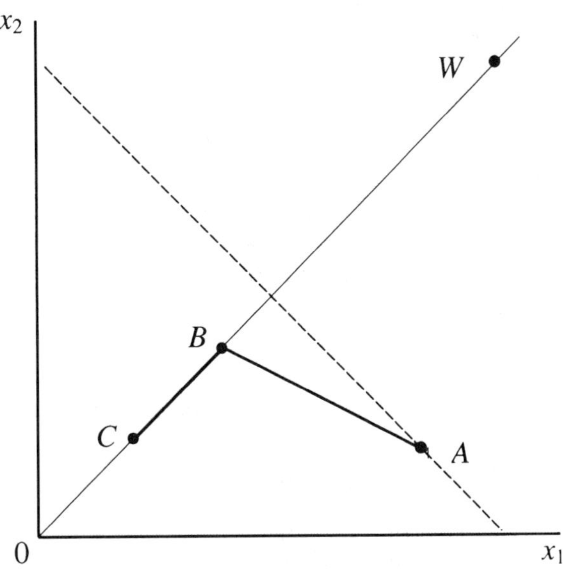

Figure 9 Insurance Budget Line for Deductible Insurance

the certainty line at point B, where α has dropped by $(\ell_2 - \ell_1)$ (so now $\alpha = \ell_1$), and the individual's wealth is equal to $w - \ell_1 - \lambda \cdot \bar{p}_2 \cdot (\ell_2 - \ell_1)$ in each state. Note that while a *still smaller* deductible $\alpha < \ell_1$ is possible, this is basically further insuring what is now a sure prospect, and doing so at actuarially unfair rates, so it would move the individual *down* the 45° line. In the limit, when $\alpha = 0$, wealth in each state would be $w - \lambda \cdot (\bar{p}_1 \cdot \ell_1 + \bar{p}_2 \cdot \ell_2)$ (i.e., point C).

The point of presenting Figure 9 is to show that, *for the two-state case*, the budget line for deductible insurance (at least the relevant part A–B) is so similar to the budget line for coinsurance that all of the graphical intuition obtained from Figures 7a,b and 8a,b concerning coinsurance will carry over to Figure 9 and to deductible insurance. But given the fact that most of the "action" of the deductible problem (30) occurs in the case of a *multitude* (or continuum) of states, we do not repeat the graphical analyses of Figures 7a,b and 8a,b here.

Rather, we proceed directly to our algebraic robustness check. To avoid the types of "kinks" that occur as α crosses the value of some discrete (i.e., positive probability) loss value ℓ_i, we assume that the random variable $\tilde{\ell}$ has a continuous cumulative distribution function $F(\cdot)$ with support $[0, M]$. We consider the corresponding basic results for deductible insurance:

DE.1 The first order condition for an interior optimum (i.e., the *necessary* condition for an interior global maximum) is:

$$E[[\lambda \cdot (1 - F(\alpha)) - \text{sgn}(\max\{\tilde{\ell} - \alpha, 0\})] \cdot U'(w - \lambda \cdot E[\max\{\tilde{\ell} - \alpha, 0\}] \\ - \min\{\tilde{\ell}, \alpha\})] = 0 \tag{31}$$

where $\text{sgn}(z) = +1/0/-1$ as $z >/=/< 0$.[22]

DE.2 If the individual is risk averse, then full insurance will be demanded if and only if it is *actuarially fair*. In other words, $\alpha^* = 0$ if and only if $\lambda = 1$.

DE.3 If two risk averse individuals face the same choice problem except that the first is *at least as risk averse* as the second, then the first will demand at least as much insurance as (i.e., have a lower deductible than) the second. In other words, if $U_1(\cdot)$ is a concave transformation of $U_2(\cdot)$, then $\alpha_1^* \leq \alpha_2^*$.[23]

The non-expected utility version of the deductible problem (30) is

$$\max_{\alpha \in [0, M]} \mathcal{V}(w - \lambda \cdot E[I_\alpha(\tilde{\ell})] - \tilde{\ell} + \max\{\tilde{\ell} - \alpha, 0\}) \quad \text{or}$$
$$\max_{\alpha \in [0, M]} \mathcal{V}(w - \lambda \cdot E[\max\{\tilde{\ell} - \alpha, 0\}] - \min\{\tilde{\ell}, \alpha\}) \tag{32}$$

[22] Thus, $\text{sgn}(\max\{\tilde{\ell} - \alpha, 0\})$ equals 1 when $\ell > \alpha$ and equals 0 when $\ell \leq \alpha$.
[23] This was shown by Schlesinger (1981) and Karni (1983).

Formula (15) allows us to differentiate these objective functions with respect to α, to get the non-expected utility first order condition:

$$\int_0^M [\lambda \cdot (1 - F(\alpha)) - \text{sgn}(\max\{\tilde{\ell} - \alpha, 0\})] \cdot U'(w - \lambda \cdot E[\max\{\tilde{\ell} - \alpha, 0\}] \\ - \min\{\ell, \alpha\}; F_\alpha) \cdot dF(\ell) = 0 \tag{33}$$

where $F_\alpha(\cdot)$ is the distribution of the random variable $w - \lambda \cdot E[\max\{\tilde{\ell} - \alpha, 0\}] - \min\{\tilde{\ell}, \alpha\}$. This is once again seen to be equivalent to the expected utility first order condition (30), with the von Neumann-Morgenstern utility function $U(\cdot)$ replaced by the *local* utility function $U(\cdot; F_\alpha)$ at the distribution $F_\alpha(\cdot)$ implied by the optimal choice. Thus, DE.1 generalizes to non-expected utility.

The "if" part of result DE.2, namely full insurance under actuarial fairness, follows immediately from risk aversion without outcome convexity, just as it did in the case of coinsurance. To see that the "only if" part does not require outcome convexity either, consider the case $\lambda > 1$ and evaluate the left hand side of (33) at the full insurance point $\alpha = 0$, to obtain

$$\left.\frac{d\mathcal{V}(w - \lambda \cdot E[\max\{\tilde{\ell} - \alpha, 0\}] - \min\{\tilde{\ell}, \alpha\})}{d\alpha}\right|_{\alpha=0} = [\lambda - 1] \cdot U'(w - \lambda \cdot E[\tilde{\ell}]; F_0) > 0 \tag{34}$$

where $F_0(\cdot)$ is the degenerate distribution of the full-insurance wealth level $w - \lambda \cdot E[\tilde{\ell}]$. Thus, in this case there will be values $\alpha > 1$ which are strictly preferred to the full insurance level $\alpha = 0$.

Finally, we turn to the comparative statics result DE.3: As it turns out, the argument behind Figure 8b and Theorem 1 applies to the case of deductible insurance as well:

Theorem 2. Let $w_0 > 0$ be base wealth, let $\tilde{\ell}$ be a random loss with support $[0, M]$ ($M < w_0$) and continuous cumulative distribution function $F_{\tilde{\ell}}(\cdot)$, and let $\lambda > 1$ be a loading factor. Assume that the non-expected utility preference functions $\mathcal{V}_1(\cdot)$ and $\mathcal{V}_2(\cdot)$ are twice continuously Fréchet differentiable, strictly risk averse, and that $\mathcal{V}_1(\cdot)$ is strictly more risk averse than $\mathcal{V}_2(\cdot)$ in the sense that $-U_1''(x; F)/U_1'(x; F) > -U_2''(x; F)/U_2'(x; F)$ for all x and $F(\cdot)$. Consider the problem:

$$\max_{\alpha \in [0, M]} \mathcal{V}_i(w_0 - \lambda \cdot E[\max\{\tilde{\ell} - \alpha, 0\}] - \tilde{\ell} + \max\{\tilde{\ell} - \alpha, 0\}) \quad i = 1, 2 \tag{35}$$

If α_1^* is the largest solution to this problem for $\mathcal{V}_1(\cdot)$, and α_2^* is the smallest solution for $\mathcal{V}_2(\cdot)$, then $\alpha_1^* \leq \alpha_2^*$, with *strict inequality* unless $\alpha_1^* = M$.

Proof in Appendix

That is, regardless of the possible multiplicity of optima due to non-outcome convexity, we will never observe the more risk averse first individual choosing a higher level of deductible (i.e., less insurance) than the second, and the only time they would choose the same level is if the terms are so unattractive that no insurance ($\alpha = M$) is an optimum even for the first individual, in which case it is the *only* optimum for the second. In a similar vein, Karni (1992) has shown that without expected utility, but with outcome convexity, one individual's optimal level of deductible for a conditional risk is greater than another's *if and only if* the former is more risk averse.

Perhaps surprisingly, or perhaps not, our robustness findings for at least the most basic aspects of deductible insurance parallel those of coinsurance: except for the additional status of condition (30) as a sufficient condition (which requires outcome-convexity), the deductible results DE.1, DE.2 and DE.3 generalize to the case of non-expected utility preferences.

2.4 PARETO-EFFICIENT BILATERAL INSURANCE CONTRACTS

The results of the previous section have examined the customer's optimal *amount* of insurance, taking the form of the insurance contract (either coinsurance or deductible) as given. However, an important set of results in insurance theory attempts to determine the optimal (i.e., Pareto efficient) *form* of insurance contract, given the nature of the insurer's costs and risk preferences. Will these results be robust to dropping the expected utility hypothesis?

The basic theorems on Pareto efficient bilateral insurance contracts concern the case where the insurer possesses an increasing cost function $C(I)$ for indemnity payments $I \geq 0$. These costs include the indemnity payment itself plus any additional processing or transactions costs. In the expected utility case, a Pareto efficient contract $(I(\cdot), \pi)$ can be represented as the solution to:

$$\max_{I(\cdot),\pi} E[U_1(w_1 - \pi - \tilde{\ell} + I(\tilde{\ell}))] \quad \text{s.t.:} \begin{cases} E[U_2(w_2 + \pi - C(I(\tilde{\ell})))] = U_2(w_2) \\ 0 \leq I(\ell) \leq \ell \end{cases} \tag{36}$$

where $U_1(\cdot)$ is the concave utility function of the *insured*, $U_2(\cdot)$ is the utility function of the *insurer*, and w_1 and w_2 are their respective initial wealth levels. The loss variable $\tilde{\ell}$ is assumed to have a continuous cumulative distribution function $F(\cdot)$ over some interval $[0, M]$.

Arrow (1963, Appendix)[24] considered the simplest case where the cost function takes the linear form $C(I) \equiv \lambda \cdot I$ (for $\lambda > 1$), and the insurer is risk neutral. Under these assumptions, the upper constraint in (36) directly implies the standard loading formula

[24] See also the related work in Arrow (1965c, 1974), the subsequent work by Raviv (1979) (discussed below), Blazenko (1985), Gollier (1987) and Marshall (1992), and the survey by Gollier (1992, Sect.2).

$$\pi = \lambda \cdot E[I(\tilde{\ell})] \tag{37}$$

and Arrow showed that the Pareto efficient indemnity function $I(\cdot)$ must take the deductible form

$$I(\ell) \equiv \min\{\ell - \alpha, 0\} \tag{38}$$

Needless to say, this forms an important justification for studying the individual's demand for insurance under the deductible structure, as we did in Section 2.3.2.

This result has been extended in a few directions by Raviv (1979), so that we can now consider the set of expected utility-based results:

PE.1 Given risk neutrality of the insurer and a linear cost function (with $\lambda > 1$), the Pareto efficient bilateral insurance contract must take the deductible form (38), for a positive deductible α.

PE.2 Given strict *risk aversion* of the insurer and a linear cost function (with $\lambda > 1$), the Pareto efficient bilateral insurance contract must take the form of coinsurance above a nonnegative deductible α, i.e.

$$\begin{aligned} I(\ell) &= 0 \quad \text{for } \ell \leq \alpha \\ 0 < I(\ell) &< \ell \quad \text{for } \ell > \alpha \\ 0 < I'(\ell) &< 1 \quad \text{for } \ell > \alpha \end{aligned} \tag{39}$$

PE.3 Given risk neutrality of the insurer and a strictly *convex* cost function $C(\cdot)$ (i.e., $C''(\cdot) > 0$), the Pareto efficient bilateral insurance contract must again take the form of coinsurance above a deductible, as in (39), where the deductible α is strictly positive.

Just as Arrow's original result (PE.1) gave a justification for the study of deductibles, the results PE.2 and PE.3 provide a justification for the study of the demand for coinsurance as we undertook in Section 2.3.1.[25]

Do these results extend to non-expected utility maximizers, and if so, is risk aversion sufficient to obtain them, or do we also need to assume outcome convexity? Under non-expected utility, the Pareto efficient contracts are characterized by the solutions to

$$\max_{I(\cdot),\pi} \mathcal{V}_1(w_1 - \pi - \tilde{\ell} + I(\tilde{\ell})) \quad \text{s.t.:} \begin{cases} \mathcal{V}_2(w_2 + \pi - C(I(\tilde{\ell}))) = \mathcal{V}_2(w_2) \\ 0 \leq I(\ell) \leq \ell \end{cases} \tag{40}$$

[25] Note, however, that derivative $I'(\ell)$ in PE.2 or PE.3 need not be constant, but as Raviv (1979, pp. 90, 91) has shown, depends upon each party's levels of risk aversion, as well as marginal indemnity cost $C'(I)$.

Concerning PE.1, note that under its assumptions, the standard loading formula (37) continues to follow from the constraint in (40). In such a case, Karni (1992) has proven that, given differentiability of $\mathcal{V}_1(\cdot)$, risk aversion alone ensures that any Pareto efficient insurance contract must continue to take the pure deductible form (38). Gollier and Schlesinger (1996) have also provided an ingenious proof of PE.1 based solely on first and second order stochastic dominance preference, and hence similarly independent of the expected utility hypothesis.

The robustness of PE.2 and PE.3 to non-expected utility can be demonstrated by using the same type of proof that Karni used to generalize PE.1. We present an informal sketch here. Let $(I^*(\cdot), \pi^*)$ be a Pareto efficient insurance contract between $\mathcal{V}_1(\cdot)$ (which is risk averse) and $\mathcal{V}_2(\cdot)$, under the assumptions of either PE.2 or PE.3.[26] In such a case, no joint differential change[27] $(\Delta I(\cdot), \Delta\pi)$ from $(I^*(\cdot), \pi^*)$ that continues to satisfy the conditions $\mathcal{V}_2(w_2 + \pi - C(I(\tilde{\ell}))) = \mathcal{V}_2(w_2)$ and $0 \leq I(\ell) \leq \ell$ should be able to raise the value of $\mathcal{V}_1(w_1 - \pi - \tilde{\ell} + I(\tilde{\ell}))$. However, from the cumulative distribution function version of (15), the effect of any such differential change $(\Delta I(\cdot), \Delta\pi)$ from $(I^*(\cdot), \pi^*)$ upon the value of $\mathcal{V}_1(w_1 - \pi - \tilde{\ell} + I(\tilde{\ell}))$ is given by the expression

$$\int_0^M U_1'(w_1 - \pi^* - \ell + I^*(\ell); F_{w_1-\pi^*-\tilde{\ell}+I^*(\tilde{\ell})}) \cdot [\Delta I(\ell) - \Delta\pi] \cdot dF_{\tilde{\ell}}(\ell) \tag{41}$$

and similarly, the effect of any differential change $(\Delta I(\cdot), \Delta\pi)$ from $(I^*(\cdot), \pi^*)$ upon the value of $\mathcal{V}_2(w_2 + \pi - C(I(\tilde{\ell})))$ is given by

$$\int_0^M U_2'(w_2 + \pi^* - C(I^*(\ell)); F_{w_2+\pi^*-C(I^*(\tilde{\ell}))}) \cdot [\Delta\pi - C'(I^*(\ell)) \cdot \Delta I(\ell)] \cdot dF_{\tilde{\ell}}(\ell) \tag{42}$$

Thus, any solution $(I^*(\cdot), \pi^*)$ to (40) must satisfy the following property:

> "No differential change $(\Delta I(\cdot), \Delta\pi)$ that makes (42) equal to zero can make (41) positive."

However, this is precisely the statement that the contract $(I^*(\cdot), \pi^*)$ satisfies the first order conditions for the *expected utility* problem (36), for the fixed von Neumann-Morgenstern utility functions $U_1(\cdot) = U_1(\cdot; F_{w_1-\pi^*-\tilde{\ell}+I^*(\tilde{\ell})})$ (which is concave) and $U_2(\cdot) = U_2(\cdot; F_{w_2+\pi^*-C(I^*(\tilde{\ell}))})$ (which under PE.2 is also concave), and we know from the expected utility versions of PE.2 and PE.3 that any pair $(I(\cdot), \pi)$ that satisfies these first order conditions, including therefore the pair $(I^*(\cdot), \pi^*)$, must satisfy the "coinsurance above a deductible" condition (39). Furthermore, under the assumptions of

[26] Thus, $(I^*(\cdot), \pi^*)$ is a solution to problem (40) for some given w_1 and w_2, though it needn't be a *unique* solution.

[27] By way of clarification, note that $\Delta\pi$ is a differential change in the scalar π, while $\Delta I(\cdot)$ is a differential change in the *entire function* $I(\cdot)$, in the sense being some differential change $\Delta I(\ell)$ in $I(\ell)$ for every value of ℓ.

PE.3, they must satisfy the additional property that the deductible is positive. Note that, like Karni, we needed to assume risk aversion of $\mathcal{V}_1(\cdot)$ (and also of $\mathcal{V}_2(\cdot)$ for PE.2), but not outcome convexity.[28]

Thus, another set of basic results in insurance theory seem to be quite robust to dropping the expected utility hypothesis.

2.5 PARETO-EFFICIENT MULTILATERAL RISK SHARING

An important part of the theory of insurance is the joint risk sharing behavior of a *group* of individuals. Research in this area was first initiated by Borch (1960, 1961, 1962) and Wilson (1968), and the modern theory of insurance markets can truly be said to stem from these papers.[29]

Under expected utility, this framework consists of a set $\{\theta\}$ of states of nature, and m individuals, each with von Neumann-Morgenstern utility function $U_i(\cdot)$ and random endowment $w_i(\theta)$. In this chapter, we consider the special case where there are a finite number of states $\{\theta_1, \ldots, \theta_T\}$, and where agents agree[30] on their probabilities $\{\text{prob}(\theta_1), \ldots, \text{prob}(\theta_T)\}$ (all positive). A **risk sharing rule** is then a set of functions $\{s_i(\cdot) \mid i = 1, \ldots, m\}$ that determines person i's allocation as a function of the state of nature θ_t. Under such a rule, person i's expected utility is given by

$$\sum_{i=1}^{T} U_i(s_i(\theta_t)) \cdot \text{prob}(\theta_t) \tag{43}$$

A sharing rule $\{s_i(\cdot) \mid i = 1, \ldots, m\}$ is **feasible** if it satisfies the constraint:

$$\sum_{i=1}^{m} s_i(\theta_t) \underset{\theta_t}{\equiv} \sum_{i=1}^{m} w_i(\theta_t) \tag{44}$$

and it is **Pareto-efficient** if there exists no other feasible rule which preserves or increases the expected utility of each member, with a strict increase for at least one member. Finally, define the **risk tolerance measure**[31] of a utility function $U_i(\cdot)$ by

$$\rho_i(x) \underset{x}{\equiv} -U_i'(x)/U_i''(x) \tag{45}$$

[28] Readers intrigued by this type of argument are referred to Chew, Epstein and Zilcha (1988) who, under slightly different assumptions (namely, uniqueness of maxima) demonstrate its surprising generality.

[29] See also Gerber (1978), Moffet (1979), Bühlman and Jewell (1979) and Eliashberg and Winkler (1981) for important subsequent contributions, and Lemaire (1990) and Gollier (1992, Sect.1) for insightful surveys.

[30] The case of differing beliefs, though clearly more realistic, is beyond the scope of this chapter.

[31] We say risk *tolerance* since $\rho_i(x)$ is the reciprocal of the standard Arrow-Pratt measure of absolute risk aversion.

In this framework, the three most basic analytical results for Pareto-efficient risk sharing are:

RS.1 A necessary condition for a risk sharing rule $\{s_i(\cdot) \mid i = 1, \ldots, m\}$ to be Pareto-efficient is that there exist nonnegative weights $\{\lambda_1, \ldots, \lambda_m\}$ such that

$$\lambda_i \cdot U_i'(s_i(\theta_t)) \underset{\theta_t}{\equiv} \lambda_j \cdot U_j'(s_j(\theta_t)) \quad i, j = 1, \ldots, m \tag{46}$$

and under risk aversion, this is a *sufficient* condition.

RS.2 Any Pareto-efficient risk sharing rule will satisfy the **mutuality principle** (e.g., Gollier (1992, p. 7)), namely, that the share $s_i(\theta_t)$ depends upon the state of nature θ_t *only* through the total group endowment $w(\theta_t) \equiv \Sigma_{k=1}^{m} w_k(\theta_t)$ in state θ_t. In other words, there exist functions $\{x_i(\cdot) \mid i = 1, \ldots, m\}$ such that

$$s_i(\theta_t) \underset{\theta_t}{\equiv} x_t(w(\theta_t)) \quad i = 1, \ldots; m \tag{47}$$

RS.3 In the case of a *continuum* of states of nature, members' **incremental shares** $\{x_i'(w)\}$ will be proportional to their respective risk tolerances, evaluated along the optimal sharing rule:

$$x_i'(w) \underset{w}{\equiv} \frac{\rho_i(x_i(w))}{\sum_{k=1}^{m} \rho_k(x_k(w))} \quad i = 1, \ldots, m \tag{48}$$

Do these results extend to non-expected utility? To check, take a set of m non-expected utility maximizers with preference functions $\{\mathcal{V}_1(\cdot), \ldots, \mathcal{V}_m(\cdot)\}$. The natural generalization of condition (46) would be that there exists a set of nonnegative weights $\{\lambda_1, \ldots, \lambda_m\}$ such that

$$\lambda_i \cdot U_i'(s_i(\theta_t); \mathbf{P}_i^*) \underset{\theta_t}{\equiv} \lambda_j \cdot U_j'(s_j(\theta_t); \mathbf{P}_j^*) \quad i, j = 1, \ldots, m \tag{49}$$

where $U_i(\cdot; \mathbf{P})$ and $U_j(\cdot; \mathbf{P})$ are the local utility functions of $\mathcal{V}_i(\cdot)$ and $\mathcal{V}_j(\cdot)$, and $\mathbf{P}_i^*$ and $\mathbf{P}_j^*$ are the probability distributions of the variables $s_i(\theta_t)$ and $s_j(\theta_t)$ respectively. To check the robustness of RS.1, assume (49) did not hold, so that there are some states θ_a, θ_b and individuals i, j such that

$$\frac{U_i'(s_i(\theta_a); \mathbf{P}_i^*)}{U_i'(s_i(\theta_b); \mathbf{P}_i^*)} \neq \frac{U_j'(s_j(\theta_a); \mathbf{P}_j^*)}{U_j'(s_j(\theta_b); \mathbf{P}_j^*)} \tag{50}$$

and hence

$$\frac{U_i'(s_i(\theta_a);\mathbf{P}_i^*)}{U_i'(s_i(\theta_b);\mathbf{P}_i^*)}\cdot\frac{\text{prob}(\theta_a)}{\text{prob}(\theta_b)}\neq\frac{U_j'(s_j(\theta_a);\mathbf{P}_j^*)}{U_j'(s_j(\theta_b);\mathbf{P}_j^*)}\cdot\frac{\text{prob}(\theta_a)}{\text{prob}(\theta_b)} \tag{51}$$

But from the n-state version of the *MRS* formula (16),[32] this would mean that the two individuals' marginal rates of substitution between consumption in states θ_a and θ_b are strictly unequal, so they would have an opportunity for mutually beneficial trade. Thus, the original sharing rule was not Pareto-efficient. This establishes that (49) is indeed a *necessary* condition for Pareto-efficiency. A standard Edgeworth box argument will establish that is also a *sufficient* condition provided outcome convexity holds, though not otherwise.

To check result RS.2, observe that if it did not hold, there would be two states θ_a, θ_b and an individual i such that $\Sigma_{k=1}^m w_k(\theta_a) = \Sigma_{k=1}^m w_k(\theta_b)$, but $s_i(\theta_a) > s_i(\theta_b)$. But by the feasibility condition (44), this means that there must exist some *other* individual j such that $s_j(\theta_a) < s_j(\theta_b)$. By risk aversion (concavity of local utility functions), this would imply

$$\frac{U_i'(s_i(\theta_a);\mathbf{P}_i^*)}{U_i'(s_i(\theta_b);\mathbf{P}_i^*)}\cdot\frac{\text{prob}(\theta_a)}{\text{prob}(\theta_b)}<\frac{\text{prob}(\theta_a)}{\text{prob}(\theta_b)}<\frac{U_j'(s_j(\theta_a);\mathbf{P}_j^*)}{U_j'(s_j(\theta_b);\mathbf{P}_j^*)}\cdot\frac{\text{prob}(\theta_a)}{\text{prob}(\theta_b)} \tag{52}$$

so that, as before, the two individuals have different marginal rates of substitution between consumption in states θ_a and θ_b, so the original sharing rule could not have been Pareto-efficient. Thus, the mutuality principle (RS.2) and the formula (47) also hold for non-expected utility risk sharers in this same setting. Observe that only risk aversion, and not outcome convexity, is needed for this result.

Finally, to show that the continuum-state-space result RS.3 also generalizes, combine (47) and (49) (which both continue to hold with a continuum of states) to write

$$\lambda_i\cdot U_i'(x_i(w);F_i^*)\underset{w}{\equiv}\lambda_j\cdot U_j'(x_j(w);F_j^*)\quad i,j=1,\dots,m \tag{53}$$

where $F_i^*(\cdot)$ and $F_j^*(\cdot)$ are the cumulative distribution functions of the (continuous) random variables $s_i(\theta)$ and $s_j(\theta)$ (see note 12). Differentiating (53) with respect to w and then dividing by (53) yields

$$\frac{U_i''(x_i(w);F_i^*)}{U_i'(x_i(w);F_i^*)}\cdot x_i'(w)\underset{w}{\equiv}\frac{U_j''(x_j(w);F_j^*)}{U_j'(x_j(w);F_j^*)}\cdot x_j'(w)\quad i,j=1,\dots,m \tag{54}$$

[32] Like the 2-state formula (16), its n-state equivalent follows immediately from equation (15).

and hence

$$\frac{\rho_j(x_j(w); F_j^*)}{\rho_i(x_i(w); F_i^*)} \cdot x_i'(w) \underset{w}{\equiv} x_j'(w) \quad i, j = 1, \ldots, m \tag{55}$$

where $\rho_i(x; F) \equiv -U_i'(x; F)/U_i''(x; F)$ is the risk tolerance measure of the local utility function $U_i(\cdot; F)$. Summing over $j = 1, \ldots, m$, noting that feasibility implies $\Sigma_{j=1}^{n} x_j'(w) \underset{w}{\equiv} 1$, and solving gives

$$x_i'(w) \underset{w}{\equiv} \frac{\rho_i(x_i(w); F_i^*)}{\sum_{k=1}^{m} \rho_k(x_k(w); F_k^*)} \quad i = 1, \ldots, m \tag{56}$$

In other words, each member's incremental share is proportional to their local risk tolerance, evaluated along the optimal sharing rule. (Recall that since $F_1^*(\cdot), \ldots, F_m^*(\cdot)$ are the distributions of $s_1(\theta), \ldots, s_m(\theta)$, they are determined directly by the optimal sharing rule.)

What does this all imply? It is true that we need outcome-convexity to guarantee the *sufficiency* of the Pareto-efficiency condition (49). However, it remains a *necessary* property of any Pareto-efficient allocation even without outcome-convexity. Otherwise, risk aversion alone (and sometimes not even that) suffices to generalize the basic risk sharing results RS.1, RS.2 and RS.3 to the case of non-expected utility maximizers.

2.6 SELF-INSURANCE VERSUS SELF-PROTECTION

This topic stems from the seminal article of Ehrlich and Becker (1972), who examined two important *non-market* risk reduction activities, namely **self-insurance**, where resources are expended to reduce the magnitude of a possible loss, and **self-protection**, where resources are expended to reduce the probability of that loss. In a two-state framework (the one they considered), the individual's initial position can be represented as the probability distribution $(w - \ell, p; w, 1 - p)$, that is to say, base wealth w with a p chance of a loss of ℓ.

The technology of self-insurance can be represented by function $\ell(\cdot)$ of an expenditure variable $\alpha \in [0, M]$, such that the first state loss becomes $\ell(\alpha)$, where $\ell'(\alpha) < 0$. In that case, an expected utility maximizer's decision problem is:

$$\max_{\alpha \in [0,M]} [p \cdot U(w - \ell(\alpha) - \alpha) + (1 - p) \cdot U(w - \alpha)] \tag{57}$$

The technology of self-protection can be represented by function $p(\cdot)$ of an expenditure variable $\beta \in [0, M]$, such that the probability of the loss becomes $p(\beta)$, where $p'(\beta) < 0$. In that case, an expected utility maximizer's decision problem is:

$$\max_{\beta \in [0,M]} [p(\beta) \cdot U(w - \ell - \beta) + (1 - p(\beta)) \cdot U(w - \beta)] \tag{58}$$

Needless to say, these activities could be studies in conjunction with each other, as well as in conjunction with *market* insurance, and Ehrlich and Becker do precisely that. Since then, the self-insurance/self-protection framework (with or without market insurance) has been extensively studied—see, for example, Boyer and Dionne (1983, 1989), Dionne and Eeckhoudt (1985), Chang and Ehrlich (1985), Hibert (1989), Briys and Schlesinger (1990), Briys, Schlesinger and Schulenburg (1991) and Sweeney and Beard (1992).

Konrad and Skaperdas (1993) examine self-insurance and self-protection in the case of a specific *non-expected utility* model, namely the "rank-dependent" form examined in Section 2.8 below. They find that most (though not all) of the expected utility-based results on self-insurance generalize to this non-expected utility model, whereas the generally ambiguous results on self-protection[33] must, of necessity, remain ambiguous in this more general setting.

A treatment anywhere near as extensive as Konrad and Skaperdas' analysis is beyond the scope of this chapter. However, we do examine what is probably the most "basic" theorem of self-insurance, namely that greater risk aversion leads to greater self-insurance, which was proven by Dionne and Eeckhoudt (1985) for expected utility and Konrad and Skaperdas (Proposition 1) for the non-expected utility rank-dependent form. Here we formally show that this comparative statics result extends to all smooth risk averse non-expected utility maximizers, whether or not they are outcome-convex:

Theorem 3. Assume that there are two states of nature with fixed positive probabilities $\bar{p}$ and $(1 - \bar{p})$. Let $w_0 > 0$ be base wealth, $\alpha \in [0, M]$ expenditure on self-insurance, and $\ell(\alpha) > 0$ be the loss in the first state, where $\ell'(\alpha) < 0$ and $M < w_0$. Assume that the non-expected utility preference functions $\mathcal{V}_1(\cdot)$ and $\mathcal{V}_2(\cdot)$ are twice continuously Fréchet differentiable, strictly risk averse, and that $\mathcal{V}_1(\cdot)$ is strictly more risk averse than $\mathcal{V}_2(\cdot)$ in the sense that $-U_1''(x; F)/U_1'(x; F) > -U_2''(x; F)/U_2'(x; F)$ for all x and $F(\cdot)$. Consider the problem:

$$\max_{\alpha \in [0,M]} \mathcal{V}_i(w_0 - \ell(\alpha) - \alpha, \bar{p}; w_0 - \alpha, 1 - \bar{p}) \quad i = 1, 2 \tag{59}$$

If α_1^* is the smallest solution to this problem for $\mathcal{V}_1(\cdot)$, and α_2^* is the largest solution for $\mathcal{V}_2(\cdot)$, then $\alpha_1^* \geq \alpha_2^*$, with *strict inequality* unless $\alpha_1^* = 0$ or $\alpha_2^* = M$.

Proof in Appendix

In other words, regardless of the possible multiplicity of optima due to non-outcome convexity, we will never observe the more risk averse first individual choos-

[33] Dionne and Eeckhoudt (1985), for example, show that greater risk aversion can lead to either more or less self-protection.

ing less self-insurance than the second individual, and the only time they would ever choose the same level is if the productivity of self-insurance is so weak that zero is an optimum even for the first individual (in which case it is the *only* optimum for the second) or else the productivity is so strong that full self-insurance ($\alpha = M$) is an optimum even for the second individual (in which case it is the *only* optimum for the first).

2.7 OUTCOME KINKS AND FIRST ORDER RISK AVERSION

Although the expected utility axioms neither require nor imply that preferences be differentiable in the *outcome levels*, the classical theory of insurance has followed the standard theory of risk aversion in usually assuming that $U(\cdot)$ is once (or twice) differentiable in wealth. But this needn't always be the case, and in this section we present some of the classical insurance model's results concerning kinked utility functions, and explore their robustness.

There are several situations where an expected utility maximizer's utility function—that is, the utility function they apply to their insurance decisions—might exhibit outcome kinks, even though their *underlying* risk preferences may be smooth in the payoffs. The simplest and probably most pervasive are piecewise linear income tax schedules, which imply that the utility of *before-tax* income will have kinks at the boundaries of each tax bracket. However, other cases where the marginal utility of money may discontinuously change include bankruptcy, and cases where a certain minimum level of wealth is needed for the acquisition of some indivisible good.

Figures 10a and 10b illustrate a risk averse von Neumann-Morgenstern utility function $U(\cdot)$ with a kink at $x = 100$, and its indifference curves in the Hirshleifer-Yaari diagram for fixed state probabilities $\bar{p}_1, \bar{p}_2$. Since $MRS_{EU}(x_1, x_2) = -(U'(x_1)\cdot \bar{p}_1)/(U'(x_2)\cdot \bar{p}_2)$ (eq.(2)), these indifference curves will be smooth and tangent to the iso-expected value lines[34] at all certainty points (x, x) *except* the point (100, 100), where there will be a convex (bowed toward the origin) kink. The curves will also be smooth at all *uncertainty points* (x_1, x_2) except where x_1 or x_2 equals 100 (i.e., along the vertical and horizontal dotted lines), where they will again have convex kinks. But even at these kinks we have a version of the *MRS* formula (2), this time between the left/right derivatives of $U(\cdot)$ and what may be called the **left/right marginal rates of substitution**:

$$MRS_{EU,L}(x_1, x_2) = -\frac{U_L'(x_1)\cdot \bar{p}_1}{U_R'(x_2)\cdot \bar{p}_2} \quad MRS_{EU,R}(x_1, x_2) = -\frac{U_R'(x_1)\cdot \bar{p}_1}{U_L'(x_2)\cdot \bar{p}_2} \tag{60}$$

[34] For clarity, the iso-expected values lines are not shown in Figure 10b, but do appear in Figure 11a.

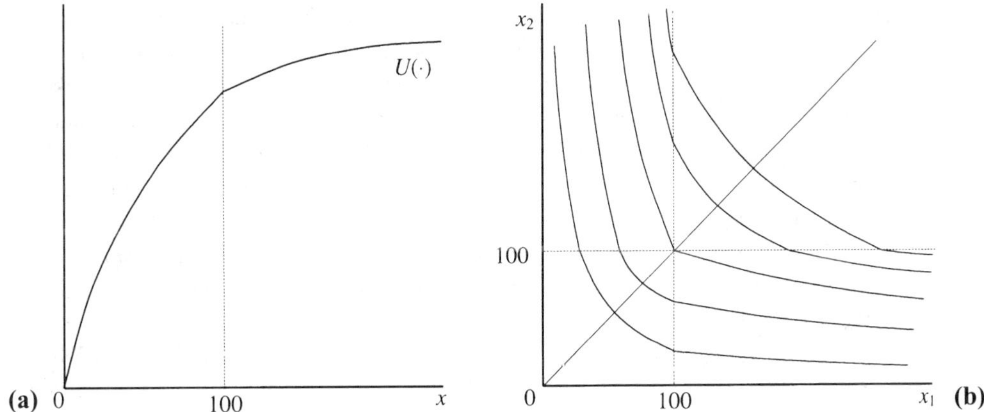

Figures 10a and 10b A Kinked von Neumann-Morgenstern Utility Function and Its Indifference Curves

Besides (60), the directional outcome derivatives also satisfy more general properties. For example, even at its kink points $(x_1, 100)$, $(100, x_2)$ or $(100, 100)$, we obtain the standard formulas linking the directional *total* derivatives and directional *partial* derivatives, for example

$$\left.\frac{d\mathcal{V}_{EU}(x_1+\alpha\cdot t,\,\bar{p}_1;\,x_2+\beta\cdot t,\,\bar{p}_2)}{dt^R}\right|_{t=0}$$
$$=\alpha\cdot\frac{\partial\mathcal{V}_{EU}(x_1,\,\bar{p}_1;\,x_2,\,\bar{p}_2)}{\partial x_1^R}+\beta\cdot\frac{\partial\mathcal{V}_{EU}(x_1,\,\bar{p}_1;\,x_2,\,\bar{p}_2)}{\partial x_2^R}\qquad \alpha,\beta>0 \tag{61}$$

Similarly, even when integrating along a line of kink points, say from (50, 100) to (150, 100), the fundamental theorem of calculus continues to link the global change in the preference function with its directional partial derivatives along the path, e.g.

$$\mathcal{V}_{EU}(150,\,\bar{p}_1;\,100,\,\bar{p}_2)-\mathcal{V}_{EU}(50,\,\bar{p}_1;\,100,\,\bar{p}_2)=\int_{50}^{150}\frac{\partial\mathcal{V}_{EU}(x_1,\,\bar{p}_1;\,100,\,\bar{p}_2)}{\partial x_1^R}\cdot dx_1 \tag{62}$$

That is, even if $U(\cdot)$ has a kink (or several kinks), the outcome kinks of the expected utility preference function $\mathcal{V}_{EU}(x_1, \bar{p}_1; x_2, \bar{p}_2) = U(x_1)\cdot\bar{p}_1 + U(x_2)\cdot\bar{p}_2$ (and its general form $\mathcal{V}_{EU}(x_1, p_1; \ldots; x_n, p_n) = \Sigma_{i=1}^{n} U(x_i)\cdot p_i$) are seen to be "well-behaved," in that they satisfy the above local and global properties of what is sometimes called the **calculus of directional derivatives**.

On the other hand, such expected utility maximizers do not satisfy result CO.2 of Section 2.3.1—that is, they may purchase full insurance even when it is actuarially unfair. This is illustrated in Figure 11a, where an individual with an uninsured position at point C, and facing an actuarially unfair budget line, maximizes expected utility by choosing the fully insured point (100, 100). However, if $U(\cdot)$ only has a single kink (or isolated kinks), this will be a knife-edge phenomenon: It is true that it can occur for any uninsured point $\hat{C}$ lying above the iso-expected value line through (100, 100) and below the subtangents of the indifference curve at that point. However, from any such $\hat{C}$ there is *exactly one* loading factor that will lead the individual to choose full insurance. Any greater or lesser loading factor from $\hat{C}$ leads to a *partial insurance* optimum on a higher or lower indifference curve than the one through (100, 100), and off of the certainty line.

Figure 11b illustrates another implication of kinked utility which is *not* a knife edge phenomenon. The uninsured positions A, B, C, D, E lie along a line of slope one, that is, they differ from each other only in the addition/subtraction of some sure amount of wealth. As such wealth increases raise the initial position from A to E, the optimal point first moves straight *upward* to (100, 100), then straight *rightward*. In other words, as wealth grows, the amount of loss insured rises to completeness and then starts to drop, so the Engle curve for insurance is first rising, then falling. To see that this is not a knife-edge implication, observe that since the optimal points are all convex kinks, this can occur for a range of loading factor values.

Segal and Spivak (1990) have defined and characterized the general behavior property corresponding to outcome kinks at certainty, and the sense in which risk preferences about such kinks are qualitatively different from smooth preferences about certainty points. Given an initial wealth x^* and a nondegenerate zero-mean risk $\tilde{\varepsilon}$, let $\pi(t)$ denote the individual's risk premium for the additive risk $t \cdot \tilde{\varepsilon}$, so the individual is

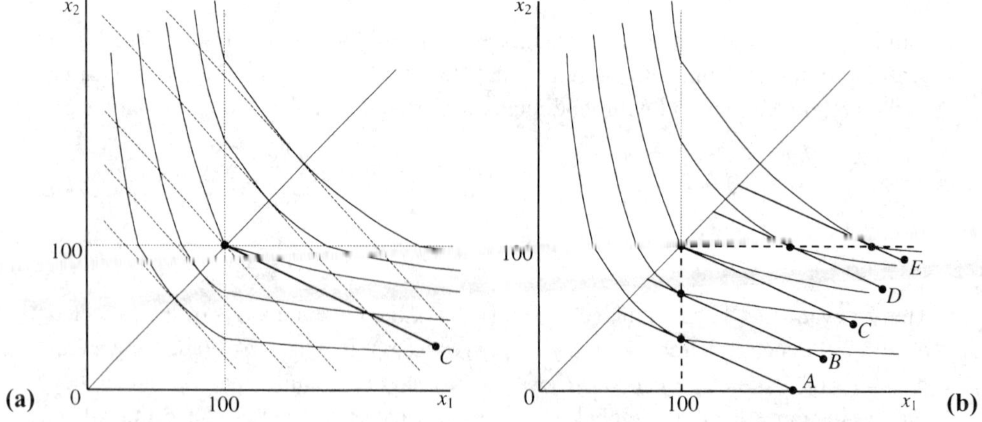

Figures 11a and 11b Full Purchase of Actuarially Unfair Insurance; Wealth Effects on the Demand for Coinsurance

indifferent between the sure wealth $x^* - \pi(t)$ and the risky wealth $x^* + t\cdot\tilde{\varepsilon}$. Note that $\pi(0) = 0$. Segal and Spivak define a risk averter as exhibiting

$$\textbf{first order risk aversion} \text{ at } x^* \quad \text{if} \quad \pi'(0) \neq 0$$
$$\textbf{second order risk aversion} \text{ at } x^* \quad \text{if} \quad \pi'(0) = 0 \quad \text{but } \pi''(0) \neq 0$$

Segal and Spivak show that if an individual (expected utility or otherwise) exhibits first order risk aversion at wealth level x^*, then for small enough positive k, they will strictly prefer x^* over the random variable $x^* + t\cdot(k + \tilde{\varepsilon})$ for all sufficiently small $t > 0$. This can be seen in Figure 11a, with $x^* = 100$, $x^* + 1\cdot(k + \tilde{\varepsilon})$ being the pre-insurance point C (with greater risk and greater expected value than x^*), and where the property "$x^* \succ x^* + t\cdot(k + \tilde{\varepsilon})$ for small enough t" is seen by the fact that the sure point (100, 100) is strictly preferred to nearby points on the insurance budget line. Segal and Spivak (1990) provide the following expected utility results linking properties of a utility function to its order of risk aversion about wealth x^*:

SS.1 If a risk averse von Neumann-Morgenstern utility function $U(\cdot)$ is not differentiable at x^* but has well-defined and distinct left and right derivatives at x^*, then the individual exhibits first order risk aversion at x^*

SS.2 If a risk averse von Neumann-Morgenstern utility function $U(\cdot)$ is twice differentiable at x^* with $U''(x) \neq 0$, then the individual exhibits second order risk aversion at x^*

Segal and Spivak's ideas, and their relevance to insurance, are not limited to preferences about complete certainty. An individual with the utility function as in Figure 10a, with a kink at x^*, will also exhibit **conditional first order risk aversion** about wealth level x^*: Consider any risk of the form [p chance of $x^* + t\cdot\tilde{\varepsilon}$: $(1 - p)$ chance of $\tilde{x}$]. Such distributions can arise in cases of **uninsured states**, such as war or certain "acts of God," in which no insurance indemnity is paid. Many (most?) insurance contracts explicitly specify such states, and usually retain the premium payment if they occur. The risk premium $\pi(t)$ in such cases solves

$$p\cdot E[U(x^*+t\cdot\tilde{\varepsilon})]+(1-p)\cdot E[U(\tilde{x})]=p\cdot U(x^*-\pi(t))+(1-p)\cdot E[U(\tilde{x}-\pi(t))] \quad (63)$$

For contracts that *refund* the premium if an uninsured state occurs, the final term in this equation becomes $(1 - p)\cdot E[U(\tilde{x})]$. In either case, we will again get $\pi(0) = 0$ and $\pi'(0) \neq 0$.[35]

[35] Can Figures 11a and 11b also be used to illustrate the demand for conditional insurance in states 1 and 2 when states 3, . . . , n are uninsured? Only when the insurance contract refunds the premium in every uninsured state. If the premium is retained in every state, then moving along the coinsurance budget line in the figure also changes the outcomes in states 3, . . . , n, so the x_1, x_2 indifference curves in the figure will shift.

Are these expected utility results robust when *linearity* in the probabilities is relaxed to *smoothness* in the probabilities? Segal and Spivak (1990, 1997) have already generalized SS.1 and SS.2 from von Neumann-Morgenstern utility to local utility functions: Given a risk averse non-expected utility $\mathcal{V}(\cdot)$, if its local utility function $U(x; \mathbf{P}^*_x)$ at the degenerate distribution $\mathbf{P}^*_x = (x^*, 1)$ has a kink at $x = x^*$, then $\mathcal{V}(\cdot)$ will exhibit *first order risk aversion* at x^*. Similarly, if $\mathcal{V}(\cdot)$'s local utility functions are all twice differentiable (and $U(x; \mathbf{P})$, $U'(x; \mathbf{P})$, $U''(x; \mathbf{P})$ are all continuous in $\mathbf{P}$), then $\mathcal{V}(\cdot)$ will exhibit *second order risk aversion* at all wealth levels. Their robustness proofs can also be extended to cover *conditional* first and second order risk aversion.

The above diagrammatic and comparative statics analysis is also robust to the case of smoothness in the probabilities. For example, let $\phi(x)$ denote the after-tax income corresponding to a pre-tax income of x, and let $\phi(\cdot)$ have a kink (with left/right derivatives) at $x = 100$. Given any underlying preference function $\hat{\mathcal{V}}(\cdot)$ over probability distributions of *after tax* income that is outcome-smooth (i.e., satisfies (15)), the individual's preferences over probability distributions of *pre-tax* income are given by the preference function $\mathcal{V}(\mathbf{P}) \equiv \mathcal{V}(x_1, p_1; \ldots; x_n, p_n) \equiv \hat{\mathcal{V}}(\phi(x_1), p_1; \ldots; \phi(x_n), p_n) \equiv \hat{\mathcal{V}}(\phi(\mathbf{P}))$, where $\phi(\mathbf{P})$ denotes the probability distribution $(\phi(x_1), p_1; \ldots; \phi(x_n), p_n)$. $\mathcal{V}(\cdot)$'s outcome kinks can be shown to be "well-behaved" in the sense described above, and $\mathcal{V}(\cdot)$ has local utility function and regular/directional outcome derivatives

$$\begin{aligned} U(x; \mathbf{P}) &\equiv \frac{\partial \mathcal{V}(x_1, p_1; \ldots; x_n, p_n)}{\partial \operatorname{prob}(x)} \equiv \frac{\partial \hat{\mathcal{V}}(\phi(x_1), p_1; \ldots; \phi(x_n), p_n)}{\partial \operatorname{prob}(\phi(x))} \\ &\equiv \hat{U}(\phi(x); \phi(\mathbf{P})) \end{aligned} \tag{64}$$

$$\frac{\partial \mathcal{V}(\mathbf{P})}{\partial x_i^{B/L/R}} = \frac{\partial \hat{\mathcal{V}}(\phi(x_1), p_1; \ldots; \phi(x_n), p_n)}{\partial \phi(x_i)} \cdot \phi'_{B/L/R}(x_i) \tag{65}$$

where "*B*/*L*/*R*" denotes either the regular ("Bi-directional") derivative if it exists, or otherwise the appropriate left/right derivative. Together, (64), (65) and outcome-smoothness of $\hat{\mathcal{V}}(\cdot)$ imply the regular/directional derivative version of the key generalized expected utility formula (15):

$$\frac{\partial \mathcal{V}(\mathbf{P})}{\partial x_i^{B/L/R}} = \hat{U}'_{B/L/R}(\phi(x_i); \phi(\mathbf{P})) \cdot p_i \cdot \phi'_{B/L/R}(x_i) = U'_{B/L/R}(x_i; \mathbf{P}) \cdot p_i \tag{66}$$

This again yields the *MRS* formula $MRS_{\mathcal{V}}(x_1, x_2) = -(U'(x_1; \mathbf{P}_{x1,x2}) \cdot \bar{p}_1)/(U'(x_2; \mathbf{P}_{x1,x2}) \cdot \bar{p}_2)$ at all smoothness points (where $x_1 \neq 100 \neq x_2$), and the left/right *MRS* formulas

$$MRS_{\mathcal{V},L}(x_1, x_2) = -\frac{U'_L(x_1; \mathbf{P}_{x1,x2}) \cdot \bar{p}_1}{U'_R(x_2; \mathbf{P}_{x1,x2}) \cdot \bar{p}_2} \quad MRS_{\mathcal{V},R}(x_1, x_2) = -\frac{U'_R(x_1; \mathbf{P}_{x1,x2}) \cdot \bar{p}_1}{U'_L(x_2; \mathbf{P}_{x1,x2}) \cdot \bar{p}_2} \tag{67}$$

when x_1 and/or x_2 equals 100. Thus, $\mathcal{V}(\cdot)$'s indifference curves are again smooth except for kinks at (100, 100) and on the vertical/horizontal lines $x_1 = 100$ and $x_2 = 100$. Finally, if preferences are also outcome-convex, then $\mathcal{V}(\cdot)$'s indifference curves will look almost exactly like those in Figure 10b, except that they will generally not satisfy the rectangle property of Section 2.2.1. This implies that both the full insurance phenomenon and "increasing then decreasing absolute risk aversion" phenomenon of payoff-kinked expected utility preferences will continue to hold.[36] In other words, these expected utility implications of non-differentiabilities in the *outcomes* ("outcome-kinks") are robust to dropping linearity in the *probabilities*.

A few specific non-expected utility functional forms for $\mathcal{V}(x_1, p_1; \ldots; x_n, p_n)$, and researchers who have studied them, are:

moments of utility $g\left(\sum_{i=1}^{n}\upsilon(x_i)\cdot p_i, \sum_{i=1}^{n}\upsilon(x_i)^2\cdot p_i, \sum_{i=1}^{n}\upsilon(x_i)^3\cdot p_i\right)$ Hagen (1989)

quadratic in probabilities[37] $\sum_{i=1}^{n}\upsilon(x_i)\cdot p_i + [\sum_{i=1}^{n}\kappa(x_i)\cdot p_i]^2$ Machina (1982)

weighted utility $[\sum_{i=1}^{n}\upsilon(x_i)\cdot p_i]/[\sum_{i=1}^{n}\tau(x_i)\cdot p_i]$ Chew (1983)

These forms all share the flexibility of expected utility, in that they can be used to represent outcome-smooth preferences, by choosing smooth constituent functions $g(\cdot)$, $\upsilon(\cdot)$, $\kappa(\cdot)$ and/or $\tau(\cdot)$, or used to represent preferences with fixed-location outcome-kinks as in Figure 10b, by choosing continuous constituent functions with kinks at those outcome values (or by the method of the previous paragraph). In the latter case, these forms will still: have local utility functions; satisfy the standard generalized expected utility properties concerning risk aversion, etc.; have what we have called well-behaved outcome kinks; satisfy the directional outcome derivative formula (66); and exhibit the first order and conditional first order risk aversion properties described above.

2.8 EXTENSIONS AND LIMITS OF ROBUSTNESS[38]

No theory can be robust to dropping *all* of its structure. We have seen that much of the classical theory of insurance, derived under the assumption that preferences are *linear* in the probabilities, extends to preferences that are smoothly *nonlinear* in the probabilities. At this point, it is natural to ask if this robustness extends any further, and if so, how far.

[36] Since the kinks generated here are convex kinks, this may occur even without full outcome convexity.

[37] This form is a special case of the more general quadratic form $\sum_{i=1}^{n}\sum_{j=1}^{m}K(x_i, x_j)\cdot p_i\cdot p_j$ studied by Chew, Epstein and Segal (1991). Those researchers have shown that when the function $K(x_i, x_j)$ is not smooth but rather takes the Leontief form $K(x_i, x_j) = \min\{x_i, x_j\}$, then preferences will *not* satisfy all the generalized expected utility robustness results. This type of issue is addressed in the following section.

[38] The material in this section, adapted from Machina (2000), owes much to the insightful comments in Karni (1995) and to subsequent discussions with Edi Karni, who is not responsible for its content.

By way of further Extensions, we have seen in the previous section how calculus can also be used for the exact analysis of *non-differentiable* functions, as long as they are not *too* non-differentiable. Consider the most basic result linking a function and its derivatives, namely the Fundamental Theorem of Calculus, which states that any globally smooth $f(\cdot)$: $R^1 \to R^1$ can be completely and exactly characterized in terms of its derivatives, via the formula $f(x) \equiv f(0) + \int_0^x f'(\omega) \cdot d\omega$. Global differentiability is *not* required for this formula to be exact: A continuous $f(\cdot)$ can have a finite or even countably infinite number of isolated kinks and the formula will still hold—we simply "integrate over the kinks." We have seen how this feature also holds in multivariate calculus: Provided the kinks in a multivariate function are "well-behaved," the Fundamental Theorem still links global changes in the function to line integrals and path integrals involving its partial derivatives. To get the total derivative of a function when its variables change, we simply paid attention to the directions in which they change, and used the appropriate left/right partial derivatives.

The application of these ideas in Section 2.7 involved kinks and directional derivatives in the *outcomes*. However, the mathematics applies equally well to changes in the *probabilities*, which we have seen to be the key independent variables of generalized expected utility analysis. Since a good proportion of generalized expected utility robustness results are obtained by use of line or path integrals over probability distributions, they will similarly extend to preferences with sufficiently well-behaved kinks in the probabilities, by the appropriate use of directional probability derivatives ("directional local utility functions").

But by way of Limits, we know that there also exist functions whose kinks are *too* nondifferentiable, even for the calculus of directional derivatives. The standard example of this in economics is the Leontief function $L(z_1, z_2) = \min\{z_1, z_2\}$, which fails to satisfy the standard relationship between total and partial derivatives at any of its kink points, even when directions are taken into account, for example

$$\left.\frac{dL(z+\alpha\cdot t, z+\beta\cdot t)}{dt^R}\right|_{t=0} \neq \alpha\cdot\frac{\partial L(z,z)}{\partial z_1^R}+\beta\cdot\frac{\partial L(z,z)}{\partial z_2^R} \quad \alpha,\beta>0 \tag{68}$$

and hence (for $\alpha = \beta = 1$)

$$\frac{dL(z,z)}{dz^R} \neq \frac{\partial L(z,z)}{\partial z_1^R}+\frac{\partial L(z,z)}{\partial z_2^R} \tag{69}$$

It turns out that one of the most important non-expected utility functional forms has Leontief-like outcome kinks that make it only partially amenable to generalized expected utility analysis. This form, first proposed by Quiggin (1982),[39] is now known as the "expected utility with rank-dependent probabilities" or simply **rank dependent**

[39] See also Weymark (1981) and Yaari (1987), who each independently proposed a special case of this functional form (the former in the context of inequality measurement), and Allais (1988).

form. In our setting of arbitrary finite-outcome distributions $\mathbf{P} = (x_1, p_1; \ldots; x_n, p_n)$, it takes the form

$$\begin{aligned} \mathcal{V}(x_1, p_1; \ldots; x_n, p_n) &= \upsilon(\hat{x}_1) \cdot G(\hat{p}_1) \\ &\quad + \upsilon(\hat{x}_2) \cdot [G(\hat{p}_1 + \hat{p}_2) - G(\hat{p}_1)] \\ &\quad + \upsilon(\hat{x}_3) \cdot [G(\hat{p}_1 + \hat{p}_2 + \hat{p}_3) - G(\hat{p}_1 + \hat{p}_2)] \\ &\quad \vdots \qquad\qquad\qquad\qquad\qquad\qquad\qquad \hat{x}_1 \le \ldots \le \hat{x}_n \\ &\quad + \upsilon(\hat{x}_{n-1}) \cdot [G(\hat{p}_1 + \ldots + \hat{p}_{n-1}) - G(\hat{p}_1 + \ldots + \hat{p}_{n-2})] \\ &\quad + \upsilon(\hat{x}_n) \cdot [G(1) - G(\hat{p}_1 + \ldots + \hat{p}_{n-1})] \\ &= \textstyle\sum_{i=1}^{n} \upsilon(\hat{x}_i) \cdot [G(\sum_{j=1}^{i} \hat{p}_j) - G(\sum_{j=1}^{i-1} \hat{p}_j)] \end{aligned} \tag{70}$$

where $\hat{x}_1, \hat{p}_1$ denotes the *lowest outcome* in the set $\{x_1, \ldots, x_n\}$ and its associated probability, $\hat{x}_2, \hat{p}_2$ denotes the *second lowest* outcome in $\{x_1, \ldots, x_n\}$ and its probability, etc. When two or more x_i values are equal, ties in defining the variables $(\hat{x}_1, \hat{p}_1), \ldots, (\hat{x}_n, \hat{p}_n)$ can be broken in any manner.

Provided $G(\cdot)$ is differentiable, the rank-dependent form *is* differentiable in the probabilities at any $\mathbf{P} = (x_1, p_1; \ldots; x_n, p_n)$, and as shown by Chew, Karni and Safra (1987) (or by equation (14)), has local utility function[40]

$$\begin{aligned} U(x; \mathbf{P}) &= \upsilon(x) \cdot G'(\textstyle\sum_{j=1}^{k} \hat{p}_j) + \sum_{k+1}^{n} \upsilon(\hat{x}_i) \cdot [G'(\sum_{j=1}^{i} \hat{p}_j) - G'(\sum_{j=1}^{i-1} \hat{p}_j)] \\ & x \in [\hat{x}_k, \hat{x}_{k+1}] \end{aligned} \tag{71}$$

$U(\cdot; \mathbf{P})$ is seen to consist of "piecewise affine transformations" of the function $\upsilon(\cdot)$, over the successive intervals $[\hat{x}_1, \hat{x}_2), \ldots, [\hat{x}_k, \hat{x}_{k+1}), \ldots$[41] The rank dependent form exhibits first order stochastic dominance preference if and only if $\upsilon(\cdot)$ is an increasing function, which from (71) is equivalent to the condition that $U(\cdot; \mathbf{P})$ is increasing in x at all $\mathbf{P}$. Chew, Karni and Safra (1987) showed that the form is globally averse to mean preserving spreads if and only if $\upsilon(\cdot)$ and $G(\cdot)$ are concave, which is equivalent to $U(\cdot; \mathbf{P})$ being concave in x at all $\mathbf{P}$.[42] They also showed that one rank dependent preference function $\mathcal{V}^*(\cdot)$ is more risk averse than another one $\mathcal{V}(\cdot)$ if and only $\upsilon^*(\cdot)$ and $G^*(\cdot)$ are concave transformations of $\upsilon(\cdot)$ and $G(\cdot)$, which is equivalent to the condition that at each $\mathbf{P}$, is $U^*(\cdot; \mathbf{P})$ is some concave transformation of $U(\cdot; \mathbf{P})$.[43]

[40] For the following equation, define $\hat{x}_0$ (resp. $\hat{x}_{n+1}$) as any value lower (resp. higher) than all of the outcomes in **P**.

[41] I.e., $U(\cdot; \mathbf{P}) \equiv a_k \cdot \upsilon(\cdot) + b_k$ over $[\hat{x}_k, \hat{x}_{k+1})$, where $a_k = G'(\Sigma_{i=1}^{k} \hat{p}_j)$ and $b_k = \Sigma_{i=k+1}^{n} \upsilon(\hat{x}_i) \cdot [G'(\Sigma_{j=1}^{i} \hat{p}_j) - G'(\Sigma_{j=1}^{i-1} \hat{p}_j)]$ are constant over each interval $[\hat{x}_k, \hat{x}_{k+1})$.

[42] From Note 41, $\upsilon(\cdot)$ concave is necessary and sufficient for $U(\cdot; \mathbf{P})$ to be concave *within* each interval $[\hat{x}_k, \hat{x}_{k+1})$, in which case $G(\cdot)$ concave (hence $G'(\cdot)$ decreasing) is necessary and sufficient for $U(\cdot; \mathbf{P})$ to be concave *across* these intervals.

[43] Again from Note 41, comparative concavity of $\upsilon^*(\cdot)$ and $\upsilon(\cdot)$ is necessary and sufficient for comparative concavity of $U^*(\cdot; \mathbf{P})$ and $U(\cdot; \mathbf{P})$ *within* each interval $[x_i, x_{i+1})$, in which case comparative concavity of $G^*(\cdot)$ and $G(\cdot)$ ($G^{*\prime}(\cdot)$ decreasing proportionately faster than $G'(\cdot)$) is necessary and sufficient for comparative concavity of $U^*(\cdot; \mathbf{P})$ and $U(\cdot; \mathbf{P})$ *across* these intervals.

Thus, many of the basic results of generalized expected utility analysis from Section 2.2.2 do apply to the rank dependent form.

However, neither the important relationship $\partial \mathcal{V}(\mathbf{P})/\partial x_i = U'(x_i; \mathbf{P})\cdot p_i$ (eq. (15)) linking the local utility function to the outcome derivatives, nor its directional generalization (66), hold for the rank dependent form, even when $\upsilon(\cdot)$ and $G(\cdot)$ are fully (even infinitely) differentiable. The failure of (15)/(66) can be verified by deriving $\partial \mathcal{V}(\mathbf{P})/\partial x_i$ from (70), deriving $U'(x_i; \mathbf{P})$ (which has distinct left and right derivatives) from (71), and observing they do not satisfy either (15) or (66). At this point—that is, in the analyses of rank dependent outcome changes—the calculus of generalized expected utility analysis finally breaks down.[44]

It is worth noting that the breakdown of (15)/(66) is not so much due to difficulties with the *probability derivatives* of the rank dependent form (recall the discussion following (71)), but rather to difficulties with its *outcome derivatives*, which exhibit the kind of Leontief-style kinks that exhibit the failures (68) and (69). For example, at any distribution $\mathbf{P} = (\ldots; x_i, p_i; \ldots; x_j, p_j; \ldots) = (\ldots; x, p_i; \ldots; x, p_j; \ldots)$ whose outcomes x_i and x_j have a common value, the rank dependent formula (70) will imply

$$\frac{d\mathcal{V}(\ldots; x, p_i; \ldots; x, p_j; \ldots)}{dx^R} \neq \frac{\partial \mathcal{V}(\ldots; x, p_i; \ldots; x, p_j; \ldots)}{\partial x_i^R} + \frac{\partial \mathcal{V}(\ldots; x, p_i; \ldots; x, p_j; \ldots)}{\partial x_j^R} \tag{72}$$

that is, the marginal benefit of increasing the common wealth level on the two-state event $\{i, j\}$ is *not* the sum of the marginal benefits in the individual states. For nonlinear $G(\cdot)$, this breakdown of the total derivative formula is generic, and can be shown to extend to constant-wealth events involving any number of states.[45] In other words, the calculus of directional outcome changes—and with it the generalized expected utility formulas (15)/(66)—breaks down for the rank dependent form.[46]

Should this be interpreted as a fundamental incompatibility between generalized expected utility analysis and the rank dependent functional form, so that insurance researchers must abandon either one or the other? No. Recall from the discussion following equation (71) that the two are in large part compatible. In addition, the rank

[44] For a discussion of this breakdown in the case of general probability distributions $F(\cdot)$, see Chew, Karni and Safra (1987) and Chew, Epstein and Segal (1991).

[45] This breakdown occurs in even the simplest of cases: the rank dependent formula (70) implies $d\mathcal{V}(x, \tfrac{1}{2}; x, \tfrac{1}{2})/dx^R = \upsilon'(x) \neq \upsilon'(x)\cdot[1 - G(\tfrac{1}{2})] + \upsilon'(x)\cdot[1 - G(\tfrac{1}{2})] = \partial \mathcal{V}(x, \tfrac{1}{2}; x, \tfrac{1}{2})/\partial x_1^R + \partial \mathcal{V}(x, \tfrac{1}{2}; x, \tfrac{1}{2})/\partial x_2^R$.

[46] One might argue that inequality (72) cannot be a reason for difficulty with the term $\partial \mathcal{V}(\mathbf{P})/\partial x_i$ in (15), since for given $\mathbf{P}$ there will typically not be any other outcome with the same value as x_i, so $\partial \mathcal{V}(\mathbf{P})/\partial x_i$ will typically not represent any *partial* derivative on the right side of (72). But since $\mathcal{V}(\cdot)$ treats the distributions $(\ldots; x_i, p_i; \ldots)$ and $(\ldots; x_i, p_i/2; x_i, p_i/2; \ldots)$ as identical, every term $\partial \mathcal{V}(\mathbf{P})/\partial x_i = \partial \mathcal{V}(\ldots; x_i, p_i; \ldots)/\partial x_i = d\mathcal{V}(\ldots; x_i, p_i/2; x_i, p_i/2; \ldots)/dx_i$ always corresponds to the *total* derivative on the *left* side of (72). Although the expression $U'(x_i; \mathbf{P})\cdot p_i$ from (15) and its directional analog in (66) are both seen to be additive with respect to such a division and partial shifting of the mass at x_i, (72) shows that $\partial \mathcal{V}(\mathbf{P})/\partial x_i$ cannot be.

dependent form has proven to be very analytically useful,[47] and for many questions, the presence/absence of outcome kinks will have no bearing on the results. When it does have bearing,[48] the choice between using an outcome-smooth preference function or the rank dependent form is no different than similar choices in other branches of economics, which treats both calculus *and* Leontief-type functional forms as indispensable tools.

2.9 INSURANCE AS A SOURCE OF NON-EXPECTED UTILITY PREFERENCES

Throughout this chapter, we have explored how the extension from expected utility to more general non-expected utility preferences does, or does not, affect the classical theory of insurance. As final topic, we consider the opposite direction of influence—namely, how an individual's opportunity to insure against *some* risks will generally induce non-expected utility preferences over the *other* risks they face.[49]

The theory of insurance in the presence of uninsurable risks has been well-studied in the literature.[50] Consider an individual whose final wealth $\tilde{w} = \tilde{x} + \tilde{y}$ consists of a **foreground risk** variable $\tilde{x}$ and an independent **background risk** variable $\tilde{y}$, with respective distributions $\mathbf{P} = (x_1, p_1; \ldots; x_n, p_n)$ and $\mathbf{Q} = (y_1, q_1; \ldots; y_m, q_m)$. The distribution of $\tilde{w}$ is thus given by the **additive convolution P ⊕ Q** of these two distributions, that is, by the distribution

$$\mathbf{P} \oplus \mathbf{Q} = \underbrace{(x_1 + y_1, p_1 \cdot q_1; \ldots; x_i + y_j, p_i \cdot q_j; \ldots; x_n + y_m, p_n \cdot q_m)}_{\substack{i=1,\ldots,n \\ j=1,\ldots,m}} \tag{73}$$

We assume that the individual's underlying preference function $\mathcal{V}(\cdot)$ takes the expected utility form, with von Neumann-Morgenstern utility function $U(\cdot)$. The expected utility of wealth $\tilde{w} = \tilde{x} + \tilde{y}$ can then be written as

[47] See, for example, Röell (1987), Quiggin (1982,1993), Ritzenberger (1996) and Bleichrodt and Quiggin (1997).

[48] The rank dependent form is sometimes justified on the grounds that its outcome kinks at certainty are needed to explain the fact that many individuals purchase complete insurance even though it is actuarially unfair. But from Note 20, we have seen that full insurance is *also* purchased by all risk averters with *smooth* preferences whose personal subjective probabilities are sufficiently more pessimistic than those of the insurer.

[49] The following is an example of the general observation of Markowitz (1959, Ch.11), Mossin (1969), Spence and Zeckhauser (1972) and others that induced risk preferences are generally not expected utility maximizing.

[50] E.g., Alarie, Dionne and Eeckhoudt (1992), Gollier and Pratt (1996), Mayers and Smith (1983), Nachman (1982), Pratt (1988), Pratt and Zeckhauser (1987), and the chapter by Gollier and Eeckhoudt (2000) in this volume.

$$\mathcal{V}(\mathbf{P} \oplus \mathbf{Q}) \equiv \sum_{i=1}^{n} \sum_{j=1}^{m} U(x_i + y_j) \cdot p_i \cdot q_j \equiv \sum_{i=1}^{n} \left[\sum_{j=1}^{m} U(x_i + y_j) \cdot q_j \right] \cdot p_i$$
$$\equiv \sum_{i=1}^{n} U_Q(x_i) \cdot p_i \tag{74}$$

where for any distribution $\mathbf{Q} = (y_1, q_1; \ldots; y_m, q_m)$, the utility function $U_{\mathbf{Q}}(\cdot)$ is defined by

$$U_Q(x) \overset{\text{def}}{\equiv} \sum_{j=1}^{m} U(x + y_j) \cdot q_j \tag{75}$$

Note that for any background risk variable $\tilde{y}_0$ with *fixed* distribution $\mathbf{Q}_0$, the individual's preferences over alternative foreground risks $\tilde{x}$—that is, their preferences over $\mathbf{P}$ distributions—are given by the *expected utility* preference function

$$\mathcal{V}_{Q_0}(\mathbf{P}) \overset{\text{def}}{\equiv} \mathcal{V}(\mathbf{P} \oplus \mathbf{Q_0}) \equiv \sum_{i=1}^{n} U_{Q_0}(x_i) \cdot p_i \tag{76}$$

Equation (76) is a very important result in the standard expected utility theory of insurance. It states that as long as the background risk $\tilde{y}_0$ is independent and has a fixed distribution $\mathbf{Q}_0$, the individual's preferences over alternative foreground risks $\tilde{x}$ will inherit the expected utility form, with $\mathbf{Q}_0$ influencing the shape, but not the existence, of the induced von Neumann-Morgenstern $U_{\mathbf{Q}_0}(\cdot)$. In other words, fixed-distribution background risk does *not* lead to departures from expected utility preferences over foreground risk variables. Since virtually all real-world insurance policies leave at least some background risk, equation (76) a provides a crucial justification for the assumption of expected utility preferences in the analysis of real-world insurance problems.[51]

However, say the background variable $\tilde{y}$ constitutes some *insurable* form of risk. That is, say the individual has the option of purchasing some form and/or level of insurance on $\tilde{y}$, such as full or partial coinsurance, or full or partial deductible. In the most general terms, we can represent this by saying that the individual can select a particular variable $\tilde{y}_\omega$, with distribution

$$\mathbf{Q}_\omega = (y_{1,\omega}, q_{1,\omega}; \ldots; y_{m_\omega,\omega}, q_{m_\omega,\omega}) \tag{77}$$

out of some set $\{\tilde{y}_\omega \mid \omega \in \Omega\}$, where the index $\omega \in \Omega$ represents the forms and/or levels of insurance available to the individual. (Note that not only do the payoffs $y_{j,\omega}$ and probabilities $q_{j,\omega}$ depend upon ω, but so can the *number* of different outcomes m_ω.

[51] See Pratt (1964, Thm.5), Kreps and Porteus (1979), and Nachman (1982) for analyses of how various properties of the underlying utility function $U(\cdot)$ do/do not carry over to the derived utility function $U_{\mathbf{Q}}(\cdot)$.

This reflects the fact that insurance can sometimes affect the number of different possible outcomes faced.)

Given this, the individual's preferences over foreground risks $\tilde{x}$ (i.e., **P** distributions) are represented by the **induced preference function**

$$\mathcal{V}^*(\mathbf{P}) \overset{\text{def}}{\equiv} \max_{\omega\in\Omega} \mathcal{V}(\mathbf{P}\oplus\mathbf{Q}_\omega) \equiv \mathcal{V}(\mathbf{P}\oplus\mathbf{Q}_{\omega(\mathbf{P})}) \equiv \sum_{i=1}^{n} U_{\mathbf{Q}_{\omega(\mathbf{P})}}(x_i)\cdot p_i \tag{78}$$

where

$$\omega(\mathbf{P}) \overset{\text{def}}{\equiv} \arg\max_{\omega\in\Omega} \mathcal{V}(\mathbf{P}\oplus\mathbf{Q}_\omega) \tag{79}$$

Observe how the "insurable background risk" preference function $\mathcal{V}^*(\cdot)$ from (78) differs from the "fixed background risk" function $V_{\mathbf{Q}_0}(\cdot)$ from (76). Since the choice of **P** can now affect the background risk distribution $\mathbf{Q}_{\omega(\mathbf{P})}$ and hence the function $U_{\mathbf{Q}_{\omega(\mathbf{P})}}(\cdot)$, the preference function $\mathcal{V}^*(\cdot)$ over foreground risk distributions **P** *no longer* takes the expected utility form, even though the individual's *underlying* preferences over wealth distributions *are* expected utility.

Such preferences depart from linearity in the probabilities in a very specific direction. Any induced preference function $\mathcal{V}^*(\cdot)$ from (78) must be **quasiconvex in the probabilities:** that is, if the distributions $\mathbf{P} = (x_1, p_1; \ldots; x_n, p_n)$ and $\mathbf{P}^* = (x_1^*, p_1^*; \ldots; x_{n^*}^*, p_{n^*}^*)$ satisfy $\mathcal{V}^*(\mathbf{P}) = \mathcal{V}^*(\mathbf{P}^*)$, then

$$\mathcal{V}^*(\lambda\cdot\mathbf{P}+(1-\lambda)\cdot\mathbf{P}^*) \le \mathcal{V}^*(\mathbf{P}) = \mathcal{V}^*(\mathbf{P}^*) \quad \text{for all } \lambda\in[0,1] \tag{80}$$

where the $\lambda{:}(1-\lambda)$ **probability mixture** of **P** and **P*** is defined by[52]

$$\lambda\cdot\mathbf{P}+(1-\lambda)\cdot\mathbf{P}^* \overset{\text{def}}{\equiv} (x_1, \lambda\cdot p_1; \ldots; x_n, \lambda\cdot p_n; x_1^*, (1-\lambda)\cdot p_1^*; \ldots; x_{n^*}^*, (1-\lambda)\cdot p_{n^*}^*) \tag{81}$$

To see that $\mathcal{V}^*(\cdot)$ will be quasiconvex in the probabilities, note that since $\mathcal{V}(\cdot)$ is linear in the probabilities, we have $\mathcal{V}(\lambda\cdot\mathbf{P}+(1-\lambda)\cdot\mathbf{P}^*) \equiv \lambda\cdot\mathcal{V}(\mathbf{P})+(1-\lambda)\cdot\mathcal{V}(\mathbf{P}^*))$, so that

$$\begin{aligned}
\mathcal{V}^*(\lambda\cdot\mathbf{P}+(1-\lambda)\cdot\mathbf{P}^*) &= \mathcal{V}((\lambda\cdot\mathbf{P}+(1-\lambda)\cdot\mathbf{P}^*)\oplus\mathbf{Q}_{\omega(\lambda\cdot\mathbf{P}+(1-\lambda)\cdot\mathbf{P}^*)}) \\
&= \lambda\cdot\mathcal{V}(\mathbf{P}\oplus\mathbf{Q}_{\omega(\lambda\cdot\mathbf{P}+(1-\lambda)\mathbf{P}^*)}) + (1-\lambda)\cdot\mathcal{V}(\mathbf{P}^*\oplus\mathbf{Q}_{\omega(\lambda\cdot\mathbf{P}+(1-\lambda)\mathbf{P}^*)}) \\
&\le \lambda\cdot\max_{\omega\in\Omega}\mathcal{V}(\mathbf{P}\oplus\mathbf{Q}_\omega) + (1-\lambda)\cdot\max_{\omega\in\Omega}\mathcal{V}(\mathbf{P}^*\oplus\mathbf{Q}_\omega) \\
&= \lambda\cdot\mathcal{V}^*(\mathbf{P}) + (1-\lambda)\cdot\mathcal{V}^*(\mathbf{P}^*) \\
&= \mathcal{V}^*(\mathbf{P}) = \mathcal{V}^*(\mathbf{P}^*)
\end{aligned} \tag{82}$$

[52] Thus, $\lambda\cdot\mathbf{P}+(1-\lambda)\cdot\mathbf{P}^*$ is the single-stage equivalent of a coin flip that yields probability λ of winning the distribution **P** and probability $(1-\lambda)$ of winning **P***.

In other words, the insurability (even partial insurability) of *background* risk induces preferences over *foreground* risks that depart from expected utility by exhibiting a weak (and what could well be strict) preference against probability mixtures of indifferent lotteries.

In those situations where the distribution $\mathbf{Q}_\omega$ is smoothly indexed by ω (e.g., coinsurance), and when the optimal choice $\omega(\mathbf{P})$ varies smoothly in $\mathbf{P}$, induced preferences will turn out to be smooth in the probabilities. In such cases, the special structure of (78) allows us to apply the envelope theorem to obtain a class of very powerful results. Since the first order condition for the maximization problem (79) is

$$\begin{aligned} 0 &= \mathcal{V}(\mathbf{P} \oplus \mathbf{Q}_{\omega(\mathbf{P})+d\omega}) - \mathcal{V}(\mathbf{P} \oplus \mathbf{Q}_{\omega(\mathbf{P})}) \\ &= \sum_{i=1}^{n} U_{\mathbf{Q}_{\omega(\mathbf{P})+d\omega}}(x_i) \cdot p_i - \sum_{i=1}^{n} U_{\mathbf{Q}_{\omega(\mathbf{P})}}(x_i) \cdot p_i \end{aligned} \qquad \text{for all } d\omega \text{ such that } \omega(\mathbf{P}) + d\omega \in \Omega \tag{83}$$

it follows from (78) that the local utility function $U^*(\cdot;\mathbf{P})$ of $\mathcal{V}^*(\cdot)$ is given by

$$\begin{aligned} U^*(x;\mathbf{P}) &\equiv_x \frac{\partial \mathcal{V}^*(\mathbf{P})}{\partial \operatorname{prob}(x)} \equiv \frac{d\sum_{i=1}^{n} U_{\mathbf{Q}_{\omega(\mathbf{P})}}(x_i) \cdot p_i}{d \operatorname{prob}(x)} \\ &\equiv U_{\mathbf{Q}_{\omega(\mathbf{P})}}(x) + \left.\frac{d\sum_{i=1}^{n} U_{\mathbf{Q}_\omega}(x_i) \cdot p_i}{d\omega}\right|_{\omega=\omega(\mathbf{P})} \cdot \frac{\partial \omega(\mathbf{P})}{\partial \operatorname{prob}(x)} \\ &\equiv U_{\mathbf{Q}_{\omega(\mathbf{P})}}(x) \equiv \sum_{j=1}^{m_\omega} U(x + y_j(\omega)) \cdot q_j(\omega) \end{aligned} \tag{84}$$

This implies, for example, that concavity of $U(\cdot)$ will be inherited by the local utility function $U^*(\cdot;\mathbf{P})$ at every $\mathbf{P}$, so that risk averse underlying preferences will imply a risk averse preference function $\mathcal{V}^*(\cdot)$ over foreground risks. Similarly, the property of third order stochastic dominance preference (positive third derivative of $U(\cdot)$)[53] is inherited by the local utility functions $U^*(\cdot;\mathbf{P})$, and hence by $\mathcal{V}^*(\cdot)$. Thus, although the property of *expected utility maximization* is not robust to the existence of insurable background risk, properties such as *risk aversion* and *third order stochastic dominance preference* can be robust. Further analyses of such induced preferences can be found in Kreps and Porteus (1979), Machina (1984) and Kelsey and Milne (1999).

2.10 CONCLUSION

Although the reader was warned that this robustness check would be more "broad" than "deep," even so, it is of incomplete breadth. There are several other important

[53] E.g., Whitmore (1970).

topics in the theory of insurance that remain unexamined. One is the effect of changes in *risk* (as opposed to *risk aversion*) upon the demand for insurance. This has been studied in the expected utility framework by Alarie, Dionne and Eeckhoudt (1992). The results of Machina (1989) on the robustness of the classic Rothschild-Stiglitz (1971) comparative statics analysis suggests that this might be another area in which standard expected utility-based results would generally extend.

Another potentially huge area is that of insurance under asymmetric information. This has already played an important role in the motivation of much of insurance theory, as for example, in the theory of adverse selection (e.g., Akerlof (1970), Pauly (1974), Rothschild and Stiglitz (1976)), and the theory of moral hazard (e.g., Arrow (1963,1968), Pauly (1968), Drèze (1986), Shavell (1979)).[54] Although this work has been primarily built on the basis of individual expected utility maximization, many of its classic results do not depend upon the expected utility property and hence can be expected to be robust. For example, the classic "lemons problem" of Akerlof (1970) derives from the effect of adverse selection on *beliefs* (i.e., actuarial or subjective probabilities) and hence is presumably quite robust to whether *risk preferences* are or are not expected utility. Similarly, the well-known Rothschild and Stiglitz (1976) analysis of pooling versus separating equilibria in insurance markets is conducted in the Hirschleifer-Yaari diagram, and although they do assume expected utility maximization, their results can be seen to follow from risk aversion and outcome-convexity of indifference curves.[55]

A final area is that of insurance under *ambiguity*, i.e., the absence of well-defined subjective probabilities. Although formal research on ambiguity and insurance has already begun (e.g., Hogarth and Kunreuther (1989,1992a,1992b)), the nature of many non-expected utility models of choice under ambiguity[56] departs sufficiently from classic expected utility theory that the robustness of standard insurance results to ambiguity is still very much an open question.

Important papers on non-expected utility and insurance, from various perspectives, include Cohen (1995), Doherty and Eeckhoudt (1995), Gollier (2000), Karni (1992, 1995), Konrad and Skaperdas (1993), Schlesinger (1997), Schmidt (1996), Schlee (1995) and Viscusi (1995). Non-expected utility researchers have been, and will continue to be, beholden to the fundamental contributions of expected utility theorists in the study of insurance. For the most part, the increased analytical and empirical power that non-expected utility models and analysis can contribute to insurance theory will not require that we abandon or the many fundamental and foundational insights we have received from the expected utility model.

[54] See also the chapters by Winter (2000) and Dionne, Doherty and Fombaron (2000) in this volume.

[55] The expected utility property only enters the Rothschild-Stiglitz analysis in their eq. (4) (p. 645), which gives conditions for an optimal insurance contract. As in the above analyses, these first order conditions will continue to hold for general (risk averse, outcome-convex) non-expected utility preferences, with individuals' von Neumann-Morgenstern utility functions replaced by their local utility functions.

[56] See, for example, the survey of Camerer and Weber (1992).

APPENDIX: PROOFS OF THEOREMS

Proof of Theorem 1. For notational simplicity, we can equivalently rewrite (28) as

$$\max_{\rho\in[0,1]} \mathcal{V}_i(c_0+\rho\cdot\tilde{z}) \quad i=1,2 \tag{A.1}$$

where $c_0 = w_0 - \lambda\cdot E[\tilde{\ell}]$, $\rho \equiv (1-\alpha)$, and $\tilde{z} \equiv \lambda\cdot E[\tilde{\ell}] - \tilde{\ell}$ with cumulative distribution function $F_{\tilde{z}}(\cdot)$. Proving the theorem is then equivalent to proving that if ρ_1^* is the largest solution to (A.1) for $\mathcal{V}_1(\cdot)$, and ρ_2^* is the smallest solution for $\mathcal{V}_2(\cdot)$, then $\rho_1^* \leq \rho_2^*$, with strict inequality unless $\rho_1^* = 1$.

For all $\rho \in [0, 1]$ and $c \geq c_0$, define the preference functions

$$\phi_i(\rho, c) \equiv \mathcal{V}_i(F_{c+\rho\cdot\tilde{z}}) \quad i=1,2 \tag{A.2}$$

where $F_{c+\rho\cdot\tilde{z}}(\cdot)$ is the cumulative distribution function of the random variable $c+\rho\cdot\tilde{z}$. By construction, each function $\phi_i(\rho, c)$ is continuously differentiable and possesses indifference curves over the set $\{(\rho, c)\mid \rho\in[0,1], c\geq c_0\}$ which are "inherited" from $\mathcal{V}_i(\cdot)$, as in Figure A.1. Since first order stochastic dominance preference ensures that $\partial\phi_i(\rho, c)/\partial c > 0$, these indifference curves cannot be either "backward bending" or "forward bending," although they can be either upward and/or downward sloping. Note that the horizontal line $c = c_0$ in the figure corresponds to the one-dimensional feasible set in the maximization problem (A.1). In other words, $\phi_i(\rho, c_0)$ equals the objective function in (A.1), so ρ_1^* and ρ_2^* are the largest and the smallest global maxima of $\phi_1(\rho, c_0)$ and $\phi_2(\rho, c_0)$, respectively.

We first show that, at any point in the set $\{(\rho, c)\mid \rho\in(0,1), c\geq c_0\}$, the marginal rates of substitution for the preference functions $\phi_1(\rho, c)$ and $\phi_2(\rho, c)$ must satisfy:

$$MRS_1(\rho, c) \equiv -\frac{\partial\phi_1(\rho, c)/\partial\rho}{\partial\phi_1(\rho, c)/\partial c} > -\frac{\partial\phi_2(\rho, c)/\partial\rho}{\partial\phi_2(\rho, c)/\partial c} \equiv MRS_2(\rho, c) \tag{A.3}$$

To demonstrate this inequality, assume it is false, so that at some such point (ρ, c) we had[57]

$$-\frac{\partial\phi_1(\rho, c)/\partial\rho}{\partial\phi_1(\rho, c)/\partial c} \leq k \leq -\frac{\partial\phi_2(\rho, c)/\partial\rho}{\partial\phi_2(\rho, c)/\partial c} \tag{A.4}$$

for some value k. Since k could have any sign, $c - \rho\cdot k$ could be either negative or nonnegative.

If $c-\rho\cdot k < 0$: In this case, $c+\rho\cdot\tilde{z} \geq 0$[58] implies $\rho\cdot\tilde{z}+\rho\cdot k > 0$ and hence $\tilde{z}+k>0$, which implies

[57] From here until the end of the paragraph following (A.8), all equations and discussion refer to this point (ρ, c).

[58] Since $c+\rho\cdot\tilde{z} \geq c_0+\rho\cdot\tilde{z} = w_0 - \lambda\cdot E[\tilde{\ell}] + \rho\cdot(\lambda\cdot E[\tilde{\ell}] - \tilde{\ell}) = \rho\cdot(w_0-\tilde{\ell}) + (1-\rho)\cdot(w_0 - \lambda\cdot E[\tilde{\ell}])$, non-

$$0 < \int (z+k) \cdot U_2'(c+\rho \cdot z;\, F_{c+\rho \cdot \tilde{z}}) \cdot dF_{\tilde{z}}(z) \tag{A.5}$$

(A.5), (15) and (A.2) then imply

$$k > -\frac{\int z \cdot U_2'(c+\rho \cdot z;\, F_{c+\rho \cdot \tilde{z}}) \cdot dF_{\tilde{z}}(z)}{\int U_2'(c+\rho \cdot z;\, F_{c+\rho \cdot \tilde{z}}) \cdot dF_{\tilde{z}}(z)} = -\frac{\partial \mathcal{V}_2(c+\rho \cdot \tilde{z})/\partial \rho}{\partial \mathcal{V}_2(c+\rho \cdot \tilde{z})/\partial c} = -\frac{\partial \phi_2(\rho, c)/\partial \rho}{\partial \phi_2(\rho, c)/\partial c} \tag{A.6}$$

which is a contradiction, since it violates (A.4).

If $c - \rho \cdot k \geq 0$: In this case, (A.4), (A.2) and (15) imply

$$k \geq -\frac{\partial \mathcal{V}_1(F_{c+\rho \cdot \tilde{z}})/\partial \rho}{\partial \mathcal{V}_1(F_{c+\rho \cdot \tilde{z}})/\partial c} = -\frac{\int z \cdot U_1'(c+\rho \cdot z;\, F_{c+\rho \cdot \tilde{z}}) \cdot dF_{\tilde{z}}(z)}{\int U_1'(c+\rho \cdot z;\, F_{c+\rho \cdot \tilde{z}}) \cdot dF_{\tilde{z}}(z)} \tag{A.7}$$

so that we have

$$\begin{aligned}
0 &\leq \int (z+k) \cdot \frac{U_1'(c+\rho \cdot z;\, F_{c+\rho \cdot \tilde{z}})}{U_1'(c-\rho \cdot k;\, F_{c+\rho \cdot \tilde{z}})} \cdot dF_{\tilde{z}}(z) \\
&= \int_{z+k>0} (z+k) \cdot \frac{U_1'(c+\rho \cdot z;\, F_{c+\rho \cdot \tilde{z}})}{U_1'(c-\rho \cdot k;\, F_{c+\rho \cdot \tilde{z}})} \cdot dF_{\tilde{z}}(z) \\
&\quad + \int_{z+k<0} (z+k) \cdot \frac{U_1'(c+\rho \cdot z;\, F_{c+\rho \cdot \tilde{z}})}{U_1'(c-\rho \cdot k;\, F_{c+\rho \cdot \tilde{z}})} \cdot dF_{\tilde{z}}(z) \\
&< \int_{z+k>0} (z+k) \cdot \frac{U_2'(c+\rho \cdot z;\, F_{c+\rho \cdot \tilde{z}})}{U_2'(c-\rho \cdot k;\, F_{c+\rho \cdot \tilde{z}})} \cdot dF_{\tilde{z}}(z) \\
&\quad + \int_{z+k<0} (z+k) \cdot \frac{U_2'(c+\rho \cdot z;\, F_{c+\rho \cdot \tilde{z}})}{U_2'(c-\rho \cdot k;\, F_{c+\rho \cdot \tilde{z}})} \cdot dF_{\tilde{z}}(z) \\
&= \int (z+k) \cdot \frac{U_2'(c+\rho \cdot z;\, F_{c+\rho \cdot \tilde{z}})}{U_2'(c-\rho \cdot k;\, F_{c+\rho \cdot \tilde{z}})} \cdot dF_{\tilde{z}}(z)
\end{aligned} \tag{A.8}$$

where the strict inequality for the "$z + k > 0$" integrals follows since in this case we have $c + \rho \cdot z > c - \rho \cdot k$, so comparative risk aversion implies $0 < U_1'(c + \rho \cdot z;\, F_{c+\rho \cdot \tilde{z}})/U_1'(c - \rho \cdot k;\, F_{c+\rho \cdot \tilde{z}}) < U_2'(c + \rho \cdot z;\, F_{c+\rho \cdot \tilde{z}})/U_2'(c - \rho \cdot k;\, F_{c+\rho \cdot \tilde{z}})$. Strict inequality for the "$z + k < 0$" integrals follows since in this case we have $c + \rho \cdot z < c - \rho \cdot k$, so the comparative risk aversion condition implies $U_1'(c + \rho \cdot z;\, F_{c+\rho \cdot \tilde{z}})/U_1'(c - \rho \cdot k;\, F_{c+\rho \cdot \tilde{z}}) > U_2'(c + \rho \cdot z;\, F_{c+\rho \cdot \tilde{z}})/U_2'(c - \rho \cdot k;\, F_{c+\rho \cdot \tilde{z}}) > 0$, but these ratios are each multiplied by the negative quantity $(z + k)$. This once again implies (A.5) and hence (A.6) and a contradiction. This then establishes inequality (A.3).

negativity of $c + \rho \cdot \tilde{z}$ on the set $\{(\rho, c) \mid \rho \in [0, 1], c \geq c_0\}$ follows from nonnegativity of $w_0 - \tilde{\ell}$ and $w_0 - \lambda \cdot E[\tilde{\ell}]$. Note that since $c \geq c_0 > 0$, the condition $c - \rho \cdot k < 0$ also implies that ρ must be nonzero, and hence positive.

Inequality (A.3) implies that, throughout the entire region $\{(\rho, c) \mid \rho \in (0, 1), c \geq c_0\}$, leftward movements along any $\phi_1(\rho, c)$ indifference curve must strictly lower $\phi_2(\rho, c)$, and rightward movements along any $\phi_2(\rho, c)$ indifference curve must strictly lower $\phi_1(\rho, c)$.

Assume $\rho_2^* < \rho_1^*$, as illustrated in Figure A.1. In this case, consider the point (ρ_2^*, c_0). As we move rightward along the $\phi_2(\rho, c)$ indifference curve that passes through this point, the value of $\phi_1(\rho, c)$ must strictly drop, so that $\phi_1(\rho, c)$ strictly prefers the point (ρ_2^*, c_0) to every point on the curve that lies to the right of (ρ_2^*, c_0). But since (ρ_2^*, c_0) is a global optimum for $\phi_2(\rho, c_0)$, this indifference curve must lie everywhere on or above the horizontal line $c = c_0$. Since $\partial\phi_1(\rho, c)/\partial c > 0$, this implies that $\phi_1(\rho, c)$ strictly prefers the point (ρ_2^*, c_0) to every point on the *line* $c = c_0$ that lies to the right of (ρ_2^*, c_0), which contradicts the assumption that there is a global maximum ρ_1^* which exceeds (i.e., lies to the right of) ρ_2^*. This, then, establishes that $\rho_1^* \leq \rho_2^*$.

To complete the proof, we must rule out $\rho_1^* = \rho_2^*$ unless $\rho_1^* = 1$. In the case $\rho_1^* < 1$, CO.2 and $\lambda > 1$ imply $\rho_2^* < 1$ so we would have $0 < \rho_2^* = \rho_1^* < 1$. However this case of identical *interior* optima would imply that both individuals' indifference curves had zero slope at the interior point $(\rho_1^*, c_0) = (\rho_2^*, c_0)$, which violates (A.3). *Q.E.D.*

Proof of Theorem 2. For notational simplicity, define

$$\eta(\ell, \alpha) \equiv \lambda \cdot E[\max\{\tilde{\ell} - \alpha, 0\}] + \ell - \max\{\ell - \alpha, 0\}$$
$$= \begin{cases} \lambda \cdot \int_\alpha^M (\varepsilon - \alpha) \cdot dF_{\tilde{\ell}}(\varepsilon) + \alpha & \text{if } \ell \geq \alpha \\ \lambda \cdot \int_\alpha^M (\varepsilon - \alpha) \cdot dF_{\tilde{\ell}}(\varepsilon) + \ell & \text{if } \ell < \alpha \end{cases} \quad \text{(A.9)}$$

This implies $\eta(\ell, \alpha) = \eta(\alpha, \alpha)$ if $\ell \geq \alpha$, and $\eta(\ell, \alpha) < \eta(\alpha, \alpha)$ if $\ell < \alpha$. We also have

$$\frac{\partial\eta(\ell, \alpha)}{\partial\alpha} = \begin{cases} -\lambda \cdot \int_\alpha^M 1 \cdot dF_{\tilde{\ell}}(\varepsilon) + 1 = -\lambda \cdot [1 - F_{\tilde{\ell}}(\alpha)] + 1 & \text{if } \ell > \alpha \\ -\lambda \cdot \int_\alpha^M 1 \cdot dF_{\tilde{\ell}}(\varepsilon) = -\lambda \cdot [1 - F_{\tilde{\ell}}(\alpha)] & \text{if } \ell < \alpha \end{cases} \quad \text{(A.10)}$$

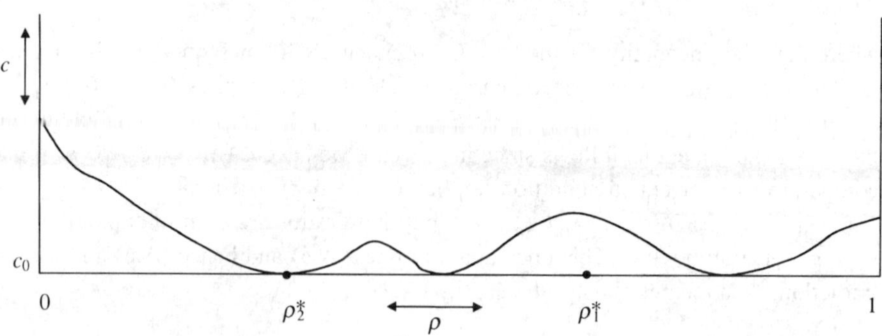

Figure A.1 Indifference Curve for the Preference Function $\phi_2(\rho, c)$

For all $\alpha \in [0, M]$ and $w \geq w_0$, let $F_{\alpha,w}(\cdot)$ denote the cumulative distribution function of the random variable

$$w - \lambda \cdot E[\max\{\tilde{\ell} - \alpha, 0\}] - \tilde{\ell} + \max\{\tilde{\ell} - \alpha, 0\} \equiv w - \eta(\tilde{\ell}, \alpha) \tag{A.11}$$

and define the preference functions

$$\phi_i(\alpha, w) \equiv \mathcal{V}_i(F_{\alpha,w}) \quad i = 1, 2 \tag{A.12}$$

By construction, each function $\phi_i(\alpha, w)$ is continuously differentiable and possesses indifference curves over the set $\{(\alpha, w) \mid \alpha \in [0, M], w \geq w_0\}$ which are "inherited" from $\mathcal{V}_i(\cdot)$, as in Figure A.2. Since first order stochastic dominance preference ensures that $\partial\phi_i(\alpha, w)/\partial w > 0$, these indifference curves cannot be either "backward bending" or "forward bending," although they can be either upward and/or downward sloping. Note that the horizontal line $w = w_0$ in the figure corresponds to the one-dimensional feasible set in the problem (35). In other words, $\phi_i(\alpha, w_0)$ equals the objective function in (35), so α_1^* and α_2^* are the largest and the smallest global maxima of $\phi_1(\alpha, w_0)$ and $\phi_2(\alpha, w_0)$, respectively.

We first show that, at any point in the set $\{(\alpha, w) \mid \in (0, M), w \geq w_0\}$, the marginal rates of substitution for the preference functions $\phi_1(\alpha, w)$ and $\phi_2(\alpha, w)$ must satisfy:

$$MRS_1(\alpha, w) \equiv -\frac{\partial\phi_1(\alpha, w)/\partial\alpha}{\partial\phi_1(\alpha, w)/\partial w} > -\frac{\partial\phi_2(\alpha, w)/\partial\alpha}{\partial\phi_2(\alpha, w)/\partial w} \equiv MRS_2(\alpha, w) \tag{A.13}$$

To demonstrate this inequality, assume it is false, so that at some such point (α, w) we had[59]

$$-\frac{\partial\phi_1(\alpha, w)/\partial\alpha}{\partial\phi_1(\alpha, w)/\partial w} \leq k \leq -\frac{\partial\phi_2(\alpha, w)/\partial\alpha}{\partial\phi_2(\alpha, w)/\partial w} \tag{A.14}$$

for some k. Since k could have any sign, $k + \lambda \cdot [1 - F_{\tilde{\ell}}(\alpha)]$ could be either nonpositive or positive.

If $k + \lambda \cdot [1 - F_{\tilde{\ell}}(\alpha)] \leq 0$: In this case, note from (A.10) that at the point (α, w), a differential increase in α of $d\alpha$ combined with a differential change in w of $dw = -\lambda \cdot [1 - F_{\tilde{\ell}}(\alpha)] \cdot d\alpha$ has zero differential effect on $w - \eta(\ell, \alpha)$ for each $\ell < \alpha$, and a strictly negative differential effect on $w - \eta(\ell, \alpha)$ for each $\ell > \alpha$. Since $\alpha \in (0, M)$ so that $\text{prob}(\tilde{\ell} > \alpha) > 0$, this implies a strictly negative differential effect on $\mathcal{V}_1(F_{\alpha,w})$. Hence, the value of dw necessary to have zero differential effect on $\mathcal{V}_1(F_{\alpha,w})$, must be greater

[59] From here until (A.18), all equations and discussion refer to this point (α, w).

than $-\lambda \cdot [1 - F_{\tilde{\ell}}(\alpha)] \cdot d\alpha$, and hence greater than $k \cdot d\alpha$. This implies that $MRS_1(\alpha, w) > k$, which is a contradiction since it violates (A.14).

If $k + \lambda \cdot [1 - F_{\tilde{\ell}}(\alpha)] > 0$: From (A.10), this implies that $k - \partial\eta(\ell, \alpha)/\partial\alpha > 0$ for $\ell < \alpha$. (A.14), (A.12) and (15) imply

$$k \geq -\frac{\partial \mathcal{V}_1(F_{\alpha,w})/\partial\alpha}{\partial \mathcal{V}_1(F_{\alpha,w})/\partial w} = -\frac{\int \left(-\frac{\partial\eta(\ell,\alpha)}{\partial\alpha}\right) \cdot U_1'(w - \eta(\ell,\alpha); F_{\alpha,w}) \cdot dF_{\tilde{\ell}}(\ell)}{\int U_1'(w - \eta(\ell,\alpha); F_{\alpha,w}) \cdot dF_{\tilde{\ell}}(\ell)} \tag{A.15}$$

so that

$$\begin{aligned}
0 &\leq \int \left(k - \frac{\partial\eta(\ell,\alpha)}{\partial\alpha}\right) \cdot \frac{U_1'(w - \eta(\ell,\alpha); F_{\alpha,w})}{U_1'(w - \eta(\alpha,\alpha); F_{\alpha,w})} \cdot dF_{\tilde{\ell}}(\ell) \\
&= \int_{\ell \geq \alpha} \left(k - \frac{\partial\eta(\ell,\alpha)}{\partial\alpha}\right) \cdot \frac{U_1'(w - \eta(\ell,\alpha); F_{\alpha,w})}{U_1'(w - \eta(\alpha,\alpha); F_{\alpha,w})} \cdot dF_{\tilde{\ell}}(\ell) \\
&\quad + \int_{\ell < \alpha} \left(k - \frac{\partial\eta(\ell,\alpha)}{\partial\alpha}\right) \cdot \frac{U_1'(w - \eta(\ell,\alpha); F_{\alpha,w})}{U_1'(w - \eta(\alpha,\alpha); F_{\alpha,w})} \cdot dF_{\tilde{\ell}}(\ell) \\
&= \int_{\ell \geq \alpha} \left(k - \frac{\partial\eta(\ell,\alpha)}{\partial\alpha}\right) \cdot \frac{U_1'(w - \eta(\alpha,\alpha); F_{\alpha,w})}{U_1'(w - \eta(\alpha,\alpha); F_{\alpha,w})} \cdot dF_{\tilde{\ell}}(\ell) \\
&\quad + \int_{\ell < \alpha} \left(k - \frac{\partial\eta(\ell,\alpha)}{\partial\alpha}\right) \cdot \frac{U_1'(w - \eta(\ell,\alpha); F_{\alpha,w})}{U_1'(w - \eta(\alpha,\alpha); F_{\alpha,w})} \cdot dF_{\tilde{\ell}}(\ell) \\
&< \int_{\ell \geq \alpha} \left(k - \frac{\partial\eta(\ell,\alpha)}{\partial\alpha}\right) \cdot \frac{U_2'(w - \eta(\alpha,\alpha); F_{\alpha,w})}{U_2'(w - \eta(\alpha,\alpha); F_{\alpha,w})} \cdot dF_{\tilde{\ell}}(\ell) \\
&\quad + \int_{\ell < \alpha} \left(k - \frac{\partial\eta(\ell,\alpha)}{\partial\alpha}\right) \cdot \frac{U_2'(w - \eta(\ell,\alpha); F_{\alpha,w})}{U_2'(w - \eta(\alpha,\alpha); F_{\alpha,w})} \cdot dF_{\tilde{\ell}}(\ell) \\
&= \int_{\ell \geq \alpha} \left(k - \frac{\partial\eta(\ell,\alpha)}{\partial\alpha}\right) \cdot \frac{U_2'(w - \eta(\ell,\alpha); F_{\alpha,w})}{U_2'(w - \eta(\alpha,\alpha); F_{\alpha,w})} \cdot dF_{\tilde{\ell}}(\ell) \\
&\quad + \int_{\ell < \alpha} \left(k - \frac{\partial\eta(\ell,\alpha)}{\partial\alpha}\right) \cdot \frac{U_2'(w - \eta(\ell,\alpha); F_{\alpha,w})}{U_2'(w - \eta(\alpha,\alpha); F_{\alpha,w})} \cdot dF_{\tilde{\ell}}(\ell) \\
&= \int \left(k - \frac{\partial\eta(\ell,\alpha)}{\partial\alpha}\right) \cdot \frac{U_2'(w - \eta(\ell,\alpha); F_{\alpha,w})}{U_2'(w - \eta(\alpha,\alpha); F_{\alpha,w})} \cdot dF_{\tilde{\ell}}(\ell)
\end{aligned} \tag{A.16}$$

Note that the "$\ell \geq \alpha$" integrals in the fourth and sixth lines of (A.16) are exactly equal. The strict inequality in (A.16) derives from the "$\ell < \alpha$" integrals in these two lines, since for these integrals we have: (i) $w - \eta(\ell, \alpha) > w - \eta(\alpha, \alpha)$, so the comparative risk aversion condition implies $U_2'(w - \eta(\ell, \alpha))/U_2'(w - \eta(\alpha, \alpha)) > U_1'(w - \eta(\ell, \alpha))/U_1'(w - \eta(\alpha, \alpha)) > 0$; (ii) the term $(k - \partial\eta(\ell, \alpha)/\partial\alpha)$ is positive; and (iii) since $\alpha \in (0, M)$, the distribution $F_{\tilde{\ell}}(\cdot)$ assigns positive probability to the range $\ell \in [0, \alpha)$.

From (A.16) we have

$$0 < \int\left(k - \frac{\partial\eta(\ell,\alpha)}{\partial\alpha}\right)\cdot U_2'(w-\eta(\ell,\alpha);F_{\alpha,w})\cdot dF_{\tilde{\ell}}(\ell) \tag{A.17}$$

and hence

$$k > \frac{\int\frac{\partial\eta(\ell,\alpha)}{\partial\alpha}\cdot U_2'(w-\eta(\ell,\alpha);F_{\alpha,w})\cdot dF_{\tilde{\ell}}(\ell)}{\int U_2'(w-\eta(\ell,\alpha);F_{\alpha,w})\cdot dF_{\tilde{\ell}}(\ell)} = -\frac{\partial\mathcal{V}_2(F_{\alpha,w})/\partial\alpha}{\partial\mathcal{V}_2(F_{\alpha,w})/\partial w} = -\frac{\partial\phi_2(\alpha,w)/\partial\alpha}{\partial\phi_2(\alpha,w)/\partial w} \tag{A.18}$$

which is a contradiction since it violates (A.14). This then establishes inequality (A.13).

Inequality (A.13) implies that, throughout the entire region $\{(\alpha, w) \mid \alpha \in (0, M), w \geq w_0\}$, leftward movements along any $\phi_1(\alpha, w)$ indifference curve must strictly lower $\phi_2(\alpha, w)$, and rightward movements along any $\phi_2(\alpha, w)$ indifference curve must strictly lower $\phi_1(\alpha, w)$.

Assume $\alpha_2^* < \alpha_1^*$, as illustrated in Figure A.2. In this case, consider the point (α_2^*, w_0). As we move rightward along the $\phi_2(\alpha, w)$ indifference curve that passes through this point, the value of $\phi_1(\alpha, w)$ must strictly drop, so that $\phi_1(\alpha, w)$ strictly prefers the point (α_2^*, w_0) to every point on the curve that lies to the right of (α_2^*, w_0). But since (α_2^*, w_0) is a global optimum for $\phi_2(\alpha, w_0)$, this indifference curve must lie everywhere on or above the horizontal line $w = w_0$. Since $\partial\phi_1(\alpha, w)/\partial w > 0$, this implies that $\phi_1(\alpha, w)$ strictly prefers the point (α_2^*, w_0) to every point on the *line* $w = w_0$ that lies to the right of (α_2^*, w_0), which contradicts the assumption that there is a global maximum α_1^* which exceeds (i.e., lies to the right of) α_2^*. This, then, establishes that $\alpha_1^* \leq \alpha_2^*$.

To complete the proof, we must rule out $\alpha_1^* = \alpha_2^*$ unless $\alpha_1^* = M$. In the case $\alpha_1^* < M$, DE.2 and $\lambda > 1$ imply $\alpha_2^* > 0$, so that equality of α_1^* and α_2^* would imply 0 <

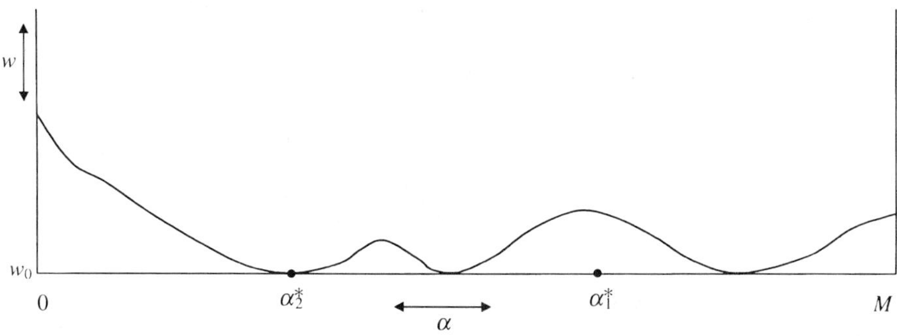

Figure A.2 Indifference Curve for the Preference Function $\phi_2(\alpha, w)$

$\alpha_2^* = \alpha_1^* < M$. However, this case of identical *interior* optima would imply that both individuals' indifference curves had zero slope at the interior point $(\alpha_1^*, w_0) = (\alpha_2^*, w_0)$, which violates (A.13). *Q.E.D.*

Proof of Theorem 3. For all $\alpha \in [0, M]$ and $w \geq w_0$, define the probability distribution

$$\mathbf{P}_{\alpha,w} \equiv (w_0 - \ell(\alpha) - \alpha, \bar{p}; w_0 - \alpha, 1 - \bar{p}) \tag{A.19}$$

and define the preference functions

$$\phi_i(\alpha, w) \equiv \mathcal{V}_i(\mathbf{P}_{\alpha,w}) \quad i = 1, 2 \tag{A.20}$$

By construction, each function $\phi_i(\alpha, w)$ is continuously differentiable and possesses indifference curves over the set $\{(\alpha, w) \mid \alpha \in [0, M], w \geq w_0\}$ which are "inherited" from $\mathcal{V}_i(\cdot)$, as in Figure A.3. Since first order stochastic dominance preference ensures that $\partial\phi_i(\alpha, w)/\partial w > 0$, these indifference curves cannot be either "backward bending" or "forward bending," although they can be either upward and/or downward sloping. Note that the horizontal line $w = w_0$ in the figure corresponds to the one-dimensional feasible set in the problem (59). In other words, $\phi_i(\alpha, w_0)$ equals the objective function in (59), so α_1^* and α_2^* are the smallest and largest global maxima of $\phi_1(\alpha, w_0)$ and $\phi_2(\alpha, w_0)$, respectively.

We first show that, at any point in the set $\{(\alpha, w) \mid \alpha \in (0, M), w \geq w_0\}$, the marginal rates of substitution for the preference functions $\phi_1(\alpha, w)$ and $\phi_2(\alpha, w)$ must satisfy:

$$MRS_1(\alpha, w) \equiv -\frac{\partial\phi_1(\alpha, w)/\partial\alpha}{\partial\phi_1(\alpha, w)/\partial w} < -\frac{\partial\phi_2(\alpha, w)/\partial\alpha}{\partial\phi_2(\alpha, w)/\partial w} \equiv MRS_2(\alpha, w) \tag{A.21}$$

From (A.20) and (15), we have

$$\begin{aligned}
-\frac{\partial\phi_1(\alpha, w)/\partial\alpha}{\partial\phi_1(\alpha, w)/\partial w} &= \frac{(1+\ell'(\alpha))\cdot U_1'(w-\ell(\alpha)-\alpha; \mathbf{P}_{\alpha,w})\cdot\bar{p} + U_1'(w-\alpha; \mathbf{P}_{\alpha,w})\cdot(1-\bar{p})}{U_1'(w-\ell(\alpha)-\alpha; \mathbf{P}_{\alpha,w})\cdot\bar{p} + U_1'(w-\alpha; \mathbf{P}_{\alpha,w})\cdot(1-\bar{p})} \\
&= 1 + \frac{\ell'(\alpha)}{1+\left(\dfrac{U_1'(w-\alpha; \mathbf{P}_{\alpha,w})}{U_1'(w-\ell(\alpha)-\alpha; \mathbf{P}_{\alpha,w})}\right)\cdot\left(\dfrac{1-\bar{p}}{\bar{p}}\right)} \\
&< 1 + \frac{\ell'(\alpha)}{1+\left(\dfrac{U_2'(w-\alpha; \mathbf{P}_{\alpha,w})}{U_2'(w-\ell(\alpha)-\alpha; \mathbf{P}_{\alpha,w})}\right)\cdot\left(\dfrac{1-\bar{p}}{\bar{p}}\right)} \\
&= -\frac{\partial\phi_2(\alpha, w)/\partial\alpha}{\partial\phi_2(\alpha, w)/\partial w}
\end{aligned} \tag{A.22}$$

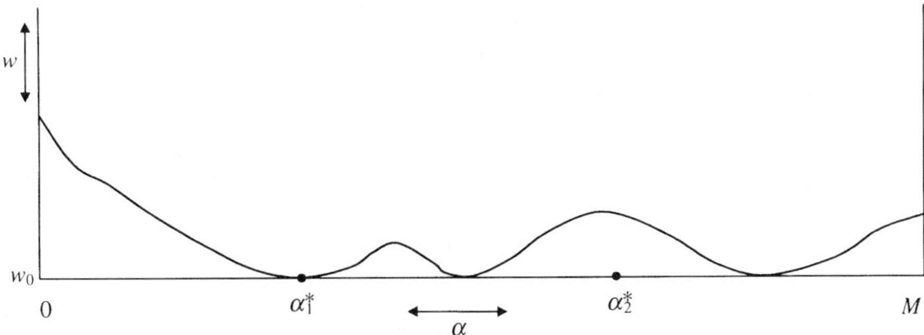

Figure A.3 Indifference Curve for the Preference Function $\phi_1(\alpha, w)$

where the strict inequality follows since (i) $w - \alpha > w - \ell(\alpha) - \alpha$ so the comparative risk aversion condition implies $U_2'(w - \alpha; \mathbf{P}_{\alpha,w})/U_2'(w - \ell(\alpha) - \alpha; \mathbf{P}_{\alpha,w}) > U_1'(w - \alpha; \mathbf{P}_{\alpha,w})/U_1'(w - \ell(\alpha) - \alpha; \mathbf{P}_{\alpha,w}) > 0$; (ii) these ratios occurs in *denominators*; and (iii) $\ell'(\alpha) < 0$.

Inequality (A.21) implies that, throughout the entire region $\{(\alpha, w) \mid \alpha \in (0, M), w \geq w_0\}$, rightward movements along any $\phi_1(\alpha, w)$ indifference curve must strictly lower $\phi_2(\alpha, w)$, and leftward movements along any $\phi_2(\alpha, w)$ indifference curve must strictly lower $\phi_1(\alpha, w)$.

Assume $\alpha_1^* < \alpha_2^*$, as illustrated in Figure A.3. In this case, consider the point (α_1^*, w_0). As we move rightward along the $\phi_1(\alpha, w)$ indifference curve that passes through this point, the value of $\phi_2(\alpha, w)$ must strictly drop, so that $\phi_2(\alpha, w)$ strictly prefers the point (α_1^*, w_0) to every point on the curve that lies to the right of (α_1^*, w_0). But since (α_1^*, w_0) is a global optimum for $\phi_1(\alpha, w_0)$, this indifference curve must lie everywhere on or above the horizontal line $w = w_0$. Since $\partial\phi_2(\alpha, w)/\partial w > 0$, this implies that $\phi_2(\alpha, w)$ strictly prefers the point (α_1^*, w_0) to every point on the *line* $w = w_0$ that lies to the right of (α_1^*, w_0), which contradicts the assumption that there is a global maximum α_2^* which exceeds (i.e., lies to the right of) α_1^*. This, then, establishes that $\alpha_2^* \leq \alpha_1^*$.

To complete the proof, we must rule out $\alpha_1^* = \alpha_2^*$ unless either $\alpha_1^* = 0$ or $\alpha_2^* = M$. If neither of these cases hold, we have $\alpha_1^* > 0$ and $\alpha_2^* < M$, so that equality of α_1^* and α_2^* would imply $0 < \alpha_1^* = \alpha_2^* < M$. However, this case of identical *interior* optima would imply that both individuals' indifference curves had zero slope at the interior point $(\alpha_1^*, w_0) = (\alpha_2^*, w_0)$, which violates (A.21). *Q.E.D.*

2.11 REFERENCES

Akerlof, G. (1970). "The Market for 'Lemons': Quality Uncertainty and the Market Mechanism," *Quarterly Journal of Economics* 84, 488–500. Reprinted in Akerlof (1984) and in Diamond and Rothschild (1989).

Akerlof, G. (1984). *An Economic Theorist's Book of Tales.* Cambridge: Cambridge University Press.

Alarie, Y., G. Dionne and L. Eeckhoudt (1992). "Increases in Risk and the Demand for Insurance," in Dionne (1992).

Allais, M. and O. Hagen (eds.) (1979). *Expected Utility Hypotheses and the Allais Paradox* (Dordrecht, Holland: D. Reidel Publishing Co.).

Allais, M. (1988). "The General Theory of Random Choices in Relation to the Invariant Cardinal Utility Function and the Specific Probability Function," in Munier (1988).

Allen, B. (1987). "Smooth Preferences and the Local Expected Utility Hypothesis," *Journal of Economic Theory* 41, 340–355.

Arrow, K. (1963). "Uncertainty and the Welfare Economics of Medical Care," *American Economic Review* 53, 941–969. Reprinted in Arrow (1971) and in part in Diamond and Rothschild (1989).

Arrow, K. (1965a). *Aspects of the Theory of Risk Bearing.* Helsinki: Yrjö Jahnsson Säätiö.

Arrow, K. (1965b). "Theory of Risk Aversion," in Arrow (1965a). Reprinted in Arrow (1971).

Arrow, K. (1965c). "Insurance, Risk, and Resource Allocation," in Arrow (1965a). Reprinted in Arrow (1971) and in Dionne and Harrington (1992).

Arrow, K. (1968). "The Economics of Moral Hazard: Further Comment," *American Economic Review* 58, 537–539. Reprinted in Arrow (1971).

Arrow, K. (1971). *Essays in the Theory of Risk-Bearing.* Amsterdam: North-Holland Publishing Company.

Arrow, K. (1974). "Optimal Insurance and Generalized Deductibles," *Scandinavian Actuarial Journal* 1, 1–42.

Blazenko, G. (1985). "The Design of an Optimal Insurance Policy: Note," *American Economic Review* 75, 253–255.

Bleichrodt, H. and J. Quiggin (1997). "Characterizing QALYs under a General Rank Dependent Utility Model," *Journal of Risk and Uncertainty* 15, 151–165.

Borch, K. (1960). "The Safety Loading of Reinsurance Premiums," *Skandinavisk Aktuarietidskrift* 163–184 Reprinted in Borch (1990).

Borch, K. (1961). "The Utility Concept Applied to the Theory of Insurance," *Astin Bulletin* 1, 245–255. Reprinted in Borch (1990).

Borch, K. (1962). "Equilibrium in a Reinsurance Market," *Econometrica* 30, 424–444. Reprinted in Borch (1990) and in Dionne and Harrington (1992).

Borch, K. (1990). *Economics of Insurance.* Amsterdam: North Holland Publishing Co. (Completed by K. Aase and A. Sandmo).

Boyer, M. and G. Dionne (1983). "Variations in the Probability and Magnitude of Loss: Their Impact on Risk," *Canadian Journal of Economics* 16, 411–419.

Boyer, M. and G. Dionne (1989). "More on Insurance, Protection and Risk," *Canadian Journal of Economics* 22, 202–205.

Briys, E. and H. Schlesinger (1990). "Risk Aversion and Propensities for Self-Insurance and Self-Protection," *Southern Economic Journal* 57, 458–467.

Briys, E., H. Schlesinger and J.-M. Schulenberg (1991). "Reliability of Risk Management: Market Insurance, Self-Insurance, and Self-Protection Reconsidered," *Geneva Papers on Risk and Insurance Theory* 16, 45–58.

Bühlman, E. and H. Jewell (1979). "Optimal Risk Exchanges," *Astin Bulletin* 10, 243–262.

Camerer, C. and M. Weber (1992). "Recent Developments in Modeling Preferences: Uncertainty and Ambiguity," *Journal of Risk and Uncertainty* 5, 325–370.

Chang, Y.M. and I. Ehrlich (1985). "Insurance, Protection from Risk and Risk Bearing," *Canadian Journal of Economics* 18, 574–587.

Chew, S. (1983). "A Generalization of the Quasilinear Mean With Applications to the Measurement of Income Inequality and Decision Theory Resolving The Allais Paradox," *Econometrica*, 51.

Chew, S., L. Epstein and U. Segal (1991). "Mixture Symmetry and Quadratic Utility," *Econometrica* 59, 139–163.

Chew, S., L. Epstein and I. Zilcha (1988). "A Correspondence Theorem Between Expected Utility and Smooth Utility," *Journal of Economic Theory* 46, 186–193.

Chew, S., E. Karni and Z. Safra (1987). "Risk Aversion in the Theory of Expected Utility with Rank Dependent Probabilities," *Journal of Economic Theory* 42, 370–381.

Cohen, M. (1995). "Risk Aversion Concepts in Expected- and Non-Expected Utility Models," *Geneva Papers on Risk and Insurance Theory* 20, 73–91. Reprinted in Gollier and Machina (1995).

Cook, P. and D. Graham (1977). "The Demand for Insurance and Protection: The Case of Irreplaceable Commodities," *Quarterly Journal of Economics* 91, 143–156. Reprinted in Dionne and Harrington (1992).

Debreu, G. (1959). *Theory of Value: An Axiomatic Analysis of General Equilibrium.* New Haven: Yale University Press.

Dekel, E. (1989). "Asset Demands without the Independence Axiom," *Econometrica* 57, 163–169.

Diamond, P. and M. Rothschild (eds.) (1989). *Uncertainty in Economics: Readings and Exercises, 2nd Ed.* New York: Academic Press.

Dionne, G. (ed.) (1992). *Contributions to Insurance Economics.* Boston: Kluwer Academic Publishers.

Dionne, G. (ed.) (2000). *Handbook of Insurance.* Boston: Kluwer Academic Publishers (this volume).

Dionne, G., N. Doherty and N. Fombaron (2000). "Adverse Selection in Insurance Markets," in Dionne G. (2000).

Dionne, G. and L. Eeckhoudt (1985). "Self Insurance, Self Protection and Increased Risk Aversion," *Economics Letters* 17, 39–42.

Dionne, G. and S. Harrington (eds.) (1992). *Foundations of Insurance Economics: Readings in Economics and Finance.* Boston: Kluwer Academic Publishers.

Doherty, N. and L. Eeckhoudt (1995). "Optimal Insurance without Expected Utility: The Dual Theory and the Linearity of Insurance Contracts," *Journal of Risk and Uncertainty* 10, 157–179.

Doherty, N. and H. Schlesinger (1983). "Optimal Insurance in Incomplete Markets," *Journal of Political Economy* 91, 1045–1054.

Drèze J. (1981). "Inferring Risk Tolerance from Deductibles in Insurance Contracts," *Geneva Papers on Risk and Insurance* 20, 48–52.

Drèze, J. (1986). "Moral Expectation with Moral Hazard," in Hildenbrand and Mas-Colell (1986).

Eeckhoudt, L. and C. Gollier (1995). *Risk: Evaluation, Management and Sharing*. New York: Harvester Wheatleaf.

Eeckhoudt, L., C. Gollier and H. Schlesinger (1991). "Increases in Risk and Deductible Insurance," *Journal of Economic Theory* 55, 435–440.

Eeckhoudt, L. and M. Kimball (1992). "Background Risk, Prudence, and the Demand for Insurance," in Dionne (1992).

Ehrlich, I. and G. Becker (1972). "Market Insurance, Self-Insurance, and Self-Protection," *Journal of Political Economy* 80, 623–648. Reprinted in Dionne and Harrington (1992).

Eliashberg, J., and R. Winkler (1981). "Risk Sharing and Group Decision Making," *Management Science* 27, 1221–1235.

Gärdenfors, P. and N. Sahlin (eds.) (1988). *Decision, Probability, and Utility: Selected Readings.* Cambridge: Cambridge University Press.

Gerber, H. (1978). "Pareto-Optimal Risk Exchanges and Related Decision Problems," *Astin Bulletin* 10, 25–33.

Gollier, C. (1987). "Pareto-Optimal Risk Sharing with Fixed Costs Per Claim," *Scandinavian Actuarial Journal* 13, 62–73.

Gollier, C. (1992). "Economic Theory of Risk Exchanges: A Review," in Dionne (1992).

Gollier, C. (2000). "Optimal Insurance Design: What Can We Do Without Expected Utility," in Dionne G. (2000).

Gollier, C. and L. Eeckhoudt (2000). "The Effects of Changes in Risk on Risk Taking: A Survey," in Dionne G. (2000).

Gollier, C. and M. Machina (1995). *Non-Expected Utility and Risk Management.* Dordrecht: Kluwer Academic Publishers.

Gollier, C. and J. Pratt (1996). "Risk, Vulnerability and the Tempering Effect of Background Risk," *Econometrica* 64, 1109–1124.

Gollier, C. and H. Schlesinger (1996). "Arrow's Theorem on the Optimality of Deductibles: A Stochastic Dominance Approach," *Economic Theory* 7, 359–363.

Gould, J. (1969). "The Expected Utility Hypothesis and the Selection of Optimal Deductibles for a Given Insurance Policy," *Journal of Business* 42, 143–151.

Guesnerie, R. and J.-J. Laffont (1984). "A Complete Solution to a Class of Principal-Agent Problems with an Application to the Control of a Self-Managed Firm," *Journal of Public Economics* 25, 329–369.

Hagen, O. (1979). "Towards a Positive Theory of Preferences Under Risk," in Allais and Hagen (1979).

Helpman, E., A. Razin, and E. Sadka (eds.) (1983). *Social Policy Evaluation: An Economic Perspective.* New York, Academic Press.

Hibert, L. (1989). "Optimal Loss Reduction and Risk Aversion," *Journal of Risk and Insurance* 56, 300–306.

Hildenbrand, W. and A. Mas-Colell (eds.) (1986). *Contributions to Mathematical Economics.* Amsterdam: North-Holland.

Hirshleifer, J. (1965). "Investment Decision Under Uncertainty: Choice-Theoretic Approaches," *Quarterly Journal of Economics* 79, 509–536. Reprinted in Hirshleifer (1989).

Hirshleifer, J. (1966). "Investment Decision Under Uncertainty: Applications of the State-Preference Approach," *Quarterly Journal of Economics* 80, 252–277. Reprinted in Hirshleifer (1989).

Hirshleifer, J. (1989). *Time, Uncertainty, and Information.* Oxford: Basil Blackwell.

Hirshleifer, J. and J. Riley (1979). "The Analytics of Uncertainty and Information—An Expository Survey," *Journal of Economic Literature* 17, 1375–1421. Reprinted in Hirshleifer (1989).

Hirshleifer, J. and J. Riley (1992). *The Analytics of Uncertainty and Information.* Cambridge: Cambridge University Press.

Hogarth, R. and H. Kunreuther (1989). "Risk, Ambiguity and Insurance," *Journal of Risk and Uncertainty* 2, 5–35.

Hogarth, R. and H. Kunreuther (1992a). "How Does Ambiguity Affect Insurance Decisions?" in Dionne (1992).

Hogarth, R. and H. Kunreuther (1992b). "Pricing Insurance and Warranties: Ambiguities and Correlated Risks," *Geneva Papers on Risk and Insurance Theory* 17, 35–60.

Karni, E. (1983). "Risk Aversion in the Theory of Health Insurance," in Helpman, Razin and Sadka (1983).

Karni, E. (1985). *Decision Making Under Uncertainty: The Case of State Dependent Preferences.* Cambridge, Mass.: Harvard University Press.

Karni, E. (1987). "Generalized Expected Utility Analysis of Risk Aversion with State-Dependent Preferences," *International Economic Review* 28, 229–240.

Karni, E. (1989). "Generalized Expected Utility Analysis of Multivariate Risk Aversion," *International Economic Review* 30, 297–305.

Karni, E. (1992). "Optimal Insurance: A Nonexpected Utility Analysis," in Dionne (1992).

Karni, E. (1995). "Non-Expected Utility and the Robustness of the Classical Insurance Paradigm: Discussion" *Geneva Papers on Risk and Insurance Theory* 20, 51–56. Reprinted in Gollier and Machina (1995).

Kelsey, D. and F. Milne (1999). "Induced Preferences, Non Additive Probabilities and Multiple Priors," *International Economic Review*, forthcoming.

Konrad, K. and S. Skaperdas (1993). "Self-Insurance and Self-Protection: A Nonexpected Utility Analysis," *Geneva Papers on Risk and Insurance Theory* 18, 131–146.

Kreps, D. and E. Porteus (1979). "Temporal von Neumann-Morgenstern and Induced Preferences," *Journal of Economic Theory* 20, 81–109.

Lemaire, J. (1990). "Borch's Theorem: A Historical Survey of Applications," in Loubergé (1990).

Loubergé, H. (ed.) (1990). *Risk, Information and Insurance.* Boston: Kluwer Academic Publishers.

Machina, M. (1982). "'Expected Utility' Analysis Without the Independence Axiom," *Econometrica* 50, 277–323.

Machina, M. (1983). "Generalized Expected Utility Analysis and the Nature of Observed Violations of the Independence Axiom," in Stigum and Wenstøp (1983). Reprinted in Gärdenfors and Sahlin (1988) and in Dionne and Harrington (1992).

Machina, M. (1984). "Temporal Risk and the Nature of Induced Preferences," *Journal of Economic Theory* 33, 199–231.

Machina, M. (1989). "Comparative Statics and Non-Expected Utility Preferences," *Journal of Economic Theory* 47, 393–405.

Machina, M. (1995). "Non-Expected Utility and the Robustness of the Classical Insurance Paradigm," *Geneva Papers on Risk and Insurance Theory* 20, 9–50. Reprinted in Gollier and Machina (1995).

Machina, M. (2000). "Payoff Kinks in Preferences over Lotteries," manuscript, Dept. of Economics, University of California, San Diego.

Markowitz, H. (1959). *Portfolio Selection: Efficient Diversification of Investments.* New Haven: Yale University Press.

Marshall, J. (1992). "Optimum Insurance with Deviant Beliefs," in Dionne (1992).

Mayers, D. and C. Smith (1983). "The Interdependence of Individual Portfolio Decisions and the Demand For Insurance," *Journal of Political Economy* 91, 304–311. Reprinted in Dionne and Harrington (1992).

Milgrom, P. and C. Shannon (1994). "Monotone Comparative Statics," *Econometrica* 62, 157–180.

Mirrlees, J. (1971). "An Exploration in the Theory of Optimal Income Taxation," *Review of Economic Studies* 38, 175–208.

Moffet, D. (1977). "Optimal Deductible and Consumption Theory," *Journal of Risk and Insurance* 44, 669–682.

Moffet, D. (1979). "The Risk Sharing Problem," *Geneva Papers on Risk and Insurance Theory* 11, 5–13.

Mossin, J. (1968). "Aspects of Rational Insurance Purchasing," *Journal of Political Economy* 79, 553–568. Reprinted in Dionne and Harrington (1992).

Mossin, J. (1969). "A Note on Uncertainty and Preferences in a Temporal Context," *American Economic Review* 59, 172–174.

Munier, B. (ed.) (1988). *Risk, Decision and Rationality.* Dordrecht: D. Reidel Publishing Co.

Nachman, D. (1982). "Preservation of 'More Risk Averse' Under Expectations," *Journal of Economic Theory* 28, 361–368.

Pashigian, B., L. Schkade and G. Menefee (1966). "The Selection of an Optimal Deductible for a Given Insurance Policy," *Journal of Business* 39, 35–44.

Pauly, M. (1968). "The Economics of Moral Hazard," *American Economic Review* 58, 531–537.

Pauly, M. (1974). "Overinsurance and Public Provision of Insurance: The Role of Moral Hazard and Adverse Selection," *Quarterly Journal of Economics* 88, 44–62. Reprinted in part in Diamond and Rothschild (1989).

Pratt, J. (1964). "Risk Aversion in the Small and in the Large," *Econometrica* 32, 122–136. Reprinted in Diamond and Rothschild (1989) and in Dionne and Harrington (1992).

Pratt, J. (1988). "Aversion to One Risk In the Presence of Others," *Journal of Risk and Uncertainty* 1, 395–413.

Pratt, J. and R. Zeckhauser (1987). "Proper Risk Aversion," *Econometrica* 55, 143–154.

Quiggin, J. (1982). "A Theory of Anticipated Utility," *Journal of Economic Behavior and Organization* 3, 323–343.

Quiggin, J. (1993). *Generalized Expected Utility Theory: The Rank-Dependent Model.* Boston, Mass.: Kluwer Academic Publishers.

Raviv, A. (1979). "The Design of an Optimal Insurance Policy," *American Economic Review* 69, 84–96. Reprinted in Dionne and Harrington (1992).

Ritzenberger, K. (1996). "On Games under Expected Utility with Rank Dependent Probabilities," *Theory and Decision* 40, 1–27.

Röell, A. (1987). "Risk Aversion in Quiggin's and Yaari's Rank-Order Model of Choice Under Uncertainty," *Economic Journal* 97 (Supplement), 143–159.

Rothschild, M. and J. Stiglitz (1970). "Increasing Risk: I. A Definition," *Journal of Economic Theory* 2, 225–243. Reprinted in Diamond and Rothschild (1989) and in Dionne and Harrington (1992).

Rothschild, M. and J. Stiglitz (1971). "Increasing Risk: II. Its Economic Consequences," *Journal of Economic Theory* 3, 66–84.

Rothschild, M. and J. Stiglitz (1976). "Equilibrium in Competitive Insurance Markets: The Economics of Markets with Imperfect Information," *Quarterly Journal of Economics* 90, 629–650. Reprinted in Diamond and Rothschild (1989) and in Dionne and Harrington (1992).

Samuelson, P. (1960). "The St. Petersburg Paradox as a Divergent Double Limit," *International Economic Review* 1, 31–37.

Schlee, E. (1995). "The Comparative Statics of Deductible Insurance in Expected- and Non-Expected Utility Theories," *Geneva Papers on Risk and Insurance Theory* 20, 57–72. Reprinted in Gollier and Machina (1995).

Schlesinger, H. (1981). "The Optimal Level of Deductibility in Insurance Contracts," *Journal of Risk and Insurance* 48, 465–481.

Schlesinger, H. (1997). "Insurance Demand Without the Expected Utility Paradigm," *Journal of Risk and Insurance* 64, 19–39.

Schlesinger, H. and N. Doherty (1985). "Incomplete Markets for Insurance: An Overview," *Journal of Risk and Insurance* 52, 402–423. Reprinted in Dionne and Harrington (1992).

Schmidt, U. (1996). "Demand for Coinsurance and Bilateral Risk-Sharing with Rank-Dependent Utility," *Risk, Decision and Policy* 1, 217–228.

Segal, U. and A. Spivak (1990). "First Order versus Second Order Risk Aversion," *Journal of Economic Theory* 51, 111–125.

Segal, U. and A. Spivak (1997). "First Order Risk Aversion and Non-Differentiability," *Economic Theory* 9, 179–183.

Shavell, S. (1979). "On Moral Hazard and Insurance," *Quarterly Journal of Economics* 93, 541–562. Reprinted in Dionne and Harrington (1992).

Smith, V. (1968). "Optimal Insurance Coverage," *Journal of Political Economy* 76, 68–77.

Spence, M. (1974). "Competitive and Optimal Responses to Signals: An Analysis of Efficiency and Distribution," *Journal of Economic Theory* 7, 296–332.

Spence, M. and R. Zeckhauser (1972). "The Effect of the Timing of Consumption Decisions and the Resolution of Lotteries on the Choice of Lotteries," *Econometrica* 40, 401–403.

Stigum, B. and F. Wenstøp (eds.) (1983). *Foundations of Utility and Risk Theory with Applications.* Dordrecht, Holland: D. Reidel Publishing Co.

Sweeney, G. and T. Beard (1992). "The Comparative Statics of Self-Protection," *Journal of Risk and Insurance* 59, 301–309.

Tobin, J. (1958). "Liquidity Preference as Behavior Toward Risk," *Review of Economic Studies* 25, 65–86.

Viscusi, K. (1995). "Government Action, Biases in Risk Perception, and Insurance Decisions," *Geneva Papers on Risk and Insurance Theory* 20, 93–110. Reprinted in Gollier and Machina (1995).

Wang, T. (1993). "L_p-Fréchet Differentiable Preference and 'Local Utility' Analysis", *Journal of Economic Theory* 61, 139–159.

Weymark, J. (1981). "Generalized Gini Inequality Indices," *Mathematical Social Sciences* 1, 409–430.

Whitmore, G. (1970). "Third Degree Stochastic Dominance," *American Economic Review* 60, 457–459.

Wilson, R. (1968). "The Theory of Syndicates," *Econometrica* 36, 119–132.

Winter, R. (2000). "Optimal Insurance under Moral Hazard" in Dionne G. (2000).

Yaari, M. (1965). "Convexity in the Theory of Choice Under Risk," *Quarterly Journal of Economics* 79, 278–290.

Yaari, M. (1969). "Some Remarks on Measures of Risk Aversion and On Their Uses," *Journal of Economic Theory* 1, 315–329. Reprinted in Diamond and Rothschild (1989).

Yaari, M. (1987). "The Dual Theory of Choice Under Risk," *Econometrica* 55, 95–115.

3 Optimal Insurance Design: What Can We Do With and Without Expected Utility?*

Christian Gollier

University of Toulouse

Abstract
This paper provides a survey on optimal insurance when insurers and policyholders have symmetric information about the distribution of potential damages. When transaction costs are proportional to transfers, it is shown that 1) there is at least one state of the world where no indemnity is paid, 2) the indemnity schedule is deterministic, implying in particular that umbrella policies are optimal, and 3) the optimal contract contains a straight deductible. This is proven without assuming expected utility. The use of expected utility generates additional results, e.g., in the case of nonlinear transaction costs.

Keywords: Optional insurance, symmetric information, transaction costs, expected utility, non expected utility.
JEL Classification Numbers: D80, G22.

3.1 INTRODUCTION

A well-known result is that it is socially efficient for a risk neutral agent to fully insure other risk-averse agents in the economy. This optimal risk-sharing arrangement allows for the elimination of costly risk premia that would have been borne by some risk-averse agents otherwise. In competitive markets for risks, that would be an equilibrium allocation if all parties would have the same information about the distribution of existing risks and if there would not be any transaction costs. This last hypothesis is clearly unrealistic, as insurance companies usually bear costs that amount up to 30% of their cash flows on lines as standard as automobile insurance or homeowner

* I am grateful to Louis Eeckhoudt and Harris Schlesinger not only for their useful comments on this chapter, but also for their continuing efforts to push me in this field.

insurance. Marketing costs, management costs and costs to audit claims are the three main sources of expenses for insurers.

Because these costs depend upon the type of contracts linking the insurer to its customers, it is not clear anymore that the optimal arrangement is full insurance. A reduction in indemnity paid in some states of the world has now the additional benefit to reduce transaction costs, which in turn generates a reduction in the insurance premium. The main problem that is addressed in the literature on optimal insurance is to determine the states of nature under which it is best to reduce indemnities. Symmetrically, starting from no insurance, one can address the question of which would be the states of the world that agents would like to insure first? Insurance indemnities are the most desirable, at the margin, where the wealth level is the smallest, if marginal utility is decreasing. Thus, when the marginal cost of insurance is constant, agents who are seeking for costly insurance should select a policy in which large losses are better indemnified than smaller losses, in absolute terms. This is the intuition behind the optimality of a straight deductible, a result first proven by Arrow (1963, 1971, 1974). A straight deductible is the insurance clause that maximizes the minimum final wealth level with a given insurance budget. It organizes a best compromise between the benefits of insurance coverage for risk-averse policyholders, and the willingness to limit (proportional) transaction costs.

Under expected utility (EU), the inverse relationship between marginal utility and wealth explains why it is better to cover the largest loss first.[1] But Zilcha and Chew (1990), Karni (1992), Schlesinger (1997) and Gollier and Schlesinger (1996) have shown that the Arrow's result is robust to any non-expected utility decision model that satisfies the second-degree stochastic dominance property. The objective of this paper is to show how several results that exist in this literature can be obtained under conditions that are much weaker than EU. As an example, when an agent faces several sources of risk, we know from Gollier and Schlesinger (1995) that it is optimal under EU to cover them through an "umbrella policy", i.e., a policy in which the indemnity is a function of the aggregate loss alone. We show in this paper that this remains true when EU is replaced by second-order stochastic dominance.

The results described above just rely on the concept of risk aversion, not on its measurement or intensity. However, a specific decision model is required when one turns to the question of the size of the optimal deductible. Clearly, it depends upon the degree of risk aversion of the policyholder. Depending upon how we model risk aversion, we will obtain different answers to this question. Other limits of a model-free analysis are when the insurer is risk-averse, or when one examines the optimal insurance contract with transaction costs that depend upon the size of the indemnity in a nonlinear way. In any of these cases, a more precise description of preferences must be made. Because of its long anteriority, most of the existing researches in this

[1] Eeckhoudt and Gollier (1995) provide a complete analysis of the insurance problem under EU.

field have been performed by using the expected utility model. We will cover this literature in this survey. More recently, new progresses have been made by extending the analysis to non-expected utility models.[2] These progresses are too recent to be surveyed.

3.2 THE BASIC FRAMEWORK

3.2.1 The Model

There is a set $\{\theta_1, \ldots, \theta_T\}$ of potential states of the world in the economy.[3] The uncertainty is represented by a vector of probabilities $(\pi_1, \ldots, \pi_T)$ where $\pi_t = Prob[\tilde{\theta} = \theta_t] > 0$, and $\Sigma_t \pi_t = 1$. All agents in the economy agree on these probabilities. Finally, the realization of $\tilde{\theta}$ is perfectly observable.

A risk-averse agent faces a risk of aggregate loss $x(\tilde{\theta})$ to his initial wealth w_0. The market provides insurance contracts for this risk. A contract is characterized by a premium P and indemnity schedule $I(\tilde{\theta})$. By selling this contract, the insurer gets P ex ante, and he promises to pay $I(\theta_t)$ if state θ_t occurs ex post, $t = 1, \ldots, T$.

Insurers are all identical and risk-neutral. They face a deadweight loss $c(I)$ whenever an indemnity I is paid. Function c is nondecreasing and is not a constant. We assume perfect competition on the insurance market. Therefore, the insurance tariff is given by the following equation:

$$P = E\left[I(\tilde{\theta}) + c(I(\tilde{\theta}))\right]. \tag{1}$$

The final wealth w_f of the policyholder purchasing policy (P, I) is

$$w_f(\theta) = w_0 - x(\theta) + I(\theta) - P, \tag{2}$$

in state θ.

Finally, one generally assumes that insurance markets are constrained to provide policies with nonnegative indemnity schedules: $I(\theta) \geq 0$ for all θ. In other words, ex-post increases in premium are prohibited, since a negative indemnity can be seen as an ex-post premium. There is a technical justification for imposing this constraint. Indeed, the condition $c' > 0$ is not realistic when the indemnity is negative. In this case, an increase in the transfer would *reduces* transaction costs![4]

[2] See for example Eeckhoudt and Doherty (1995) and Chateauneuf, Dana and Tallon (1997).

[3] For simplicity, we assume a finite number of states. All results remain true under continuous or mixed distribution functions.

[4] Gollier (1987a) allows for negative indemnities by assuming that transaction costs depend upon the absolute value of the indemnity. Surprisingly enough, in most cases, removing the constraint on the non-negativity of claims has no effect on the optimal contract.

3.2.2 The Concepts of Risk Aversion

The attitude towards risk of the policyholder is characterized by a real-valued preference functional $V(w_f(\tilde{\theta}))$. This means that risk $w_{f1}(\tilde{\theta})$ is preferred to risk $w_{f2}(\tilde{\theta})$ if and only if $V(w_{f1}(\tilde{\theta}))$ is larger than $V(w_{f2}(\tilde{\theta}))$. If V is linear in probabilities—a condition that can be derived from the independence axiom—, the model simplifies to EU.

In most of this paper, two basic assumptions will be made on the attitude towards risk of the policyholder. First, we assume that it satisfies first-degree stochastic dominance (FSD). That is, if $\hat{w}(\tilde{\theta})$ dominates $w(\tilde{\theta})$ in the sense of FSD, then the policyholder prefers $\hat{w}(\tilde{\theta})$ to $w(\tilde{\theta})$: $V(\hat{w}(\tilde{\theta})) \geq V(w(\tilde{\theta}))$. A FSD deterioration in risk is obtained by transferring probability masses from higher wealth states to lower wealth states. It can also be obtained by reducing wealth in any state of the world. Under EU, the FSD property holds if and only if utility is increasing in wealth.

The second assumption on the preference functional V is that if one risk $\hat{w}(\tilde{\theta})$ is a mean-preserving contraction (MPC) of another risk $w(\tilde{\theta})$ then the agent prefers the first to the second: $V(\hat{w}(\tilde{\theta})) \geq V(w(\tilde{\theta}))$. Risk $\hat{w}(\tilde{\theta})$ dominates risk $w(\tilde{\theta})$ in the sense of a MPC if w is obtained from $\hat{w}$ by adding a white noise to it:

$$w(\tilde{\theta}) =_d \hat{w}(\tilde{\theta}) + \varepsilon(\tilde{\theta}),$$

where $E[\varepsilon(\tilde{\theta}) \mid \hat{w}(\tilde{\theta}) = z] = 0$, for all z. Thus, the MPC property means that the agent dislikes any zero-mean lottery that would be added to his final wealth. This is a strong notion of risk aversion. It is a generalization of weak risk aversion, which is meant as the preference of the expectation $E\tilde{x}$ over the random variable $\tilde{x}$. The strong and the weak notion of risk aversion are equivalent in the EU model. They are both equivalent to the concavity of the utility function. But they are in general two separate concepts for more general preferences functionals. In order to derive results on optimal insurance policies, we will need to rely on the strong concept of risk aversion.[5]

3.2.3 On the Optimality of Partial Insurance

Before going to the specific analysis of the optimal insurance policy design, it is noteworthy that it is never optimal to get a positive indemnity in all states, because of the presence of transaction costs. More precisely, combining FSD with $c' \geq 0$ yields the following result:

Proposition 1. Suppose that c' is positive. If the preference functional V satisfies the first-degree stochastic dominance property, then there exists at least one state of nature in which no indemnity is paid to the policyholder.

[5] Cohen (1995) provides an excellent analysis of the various definitions of risk aversion and their connexions to each others.

Proof. Suppose by contradiction that $I(\theta) > 0$ for all θ. Consider an alternative contract with $\hat{I}(\theta, k) = I(\theta) - k$ for all θ. The premium to pay for this new contract is

$$\hat{P}(k) = E[\hat{I}(\tilde{\theta}, k) + c(\hat{I}(\tilde{\theta}, k))].$$

Observe that

$$\hat{P}'(0) = -1 - E[c'(I(\tilde{\theta}))].$$

The final wealth with the new contract is $\hat{w}_f(\theta, k) = w_0 - x(\theta) + \hat{I}(\theta, k) - \hat{P}(k)$ in state θ. Differentiating with respect to k yields

$$\frac{\partial \hat{w}}{\partial k}\Big|_{k=0} = -1 - \hat{P}'(0) = E[c'(I(\tilde{\theta}))],$$

which is positive by assumption. Since this is true for every θ, we proved that raising k from zero improves the distribution of final wealth in the sense of FSD. This concludes the proof. ■

Because indemnities generate deadweight losses, a uniform reduction in them across states has no other effect than to reduce these costs. The reduction in the indemnity in each state is entirely offset by the parallel reduction in premium. This uniform reduction will thus be done as long as it does not violate the constraint on the non-negativity of indemnities. In conclusion, this constraint will be binding in a subset of states of positive measure.

3.3 THE CASE OF LINEAR TRANSACTION COSTS

In this section, we assume that costs are linear with respect to the level of the indemnity: $c(I) = c_0 + \lambda I$. It implies that the insurance tariff is linear in the actuarial value of the policy:

$$P = c_0 + (1+\lambda)E[I(\tilde{\theta})].$$

Parameter c_0 can be seen as an entry fee for the policyholder. It has no other effect on the optimal insurance contract than the one generated by the induced reduction in wealth, which in turn affects the attitude towards risk. Notice also that if c_0 is too large, the agent may prefer not to buy coverage at all. Two main results are obtained in this framework: the inefficiency of random indemnity schedules, and the efficiency of deductible policies among deterministic schedules.

3.3.1 Deterministic Indemnity Schedule

Insurance is a device to reduce risk. Therefore, it is not a surprise that insurers will always pay a non-random indemnity in each state of nature. This is the substance of the following result:

Proposition 2. Consider the case of linear costs. Suppose that the policyholder is risk-averse in the sense that V satisfies the MPC property. Then the optimal indemnity depends upon the state of nature only through the aggregate loss suffered by the policyholder in that state: $[x(\theta_1) = x(\theta_2) \Rightarrow I(\theta_1) = I(\theta_2)]$.

Proof. Suppose by contradiction that $x(\theta_1) = x(\theta_2)$, but $I(\theta_1) < I(\theta_2)$. Consider another policy $(\hat{P}, \hat{I})$ where $\hat{I}(\theta) = I(\theta)$ for all $\theta \neq \theta_1, \theta_2$, and

$$\hat{I}(\theta_1) = \hat{I}(\theta_2) = \frac{\pi_1 I(\theta_1) + \pi_2 I(\theta_2)}{\pi_1 + \pi_2}.$$

It implies that the actuarial value of the policy is unchanged. Therefore, $\hat{P}$ equals P. Let $\hat{w}_f(\theta)$ be the final wealth with the new contract. Let also $\hat{W}$ denote $\hat{w}_f(\theta_1) = \hat{w}_f(\theta_2)$. We now prove that the risk $\hat{w}_f(\tilde{\theta})$ is a MPC of risk $w_f(\tilde{\theta})$. To do this, let us show that $w_f(\tilde{\theta})$ is obtained from $\hat{w}_f(\tilde{\theta})$ by adding a white noise $\varepsilon(\tilde{\theta})$ to it. Using this condition as a definition for ε, we obtain that

- $\varepsilon(\tilde{\theta}) \mid \hat{w}_f(\tilde{\theta}) \neq \hat{W}$ is degenerated at zero; and
- $\varepsilon(\tilde{\theta}) \mid \hat{w}_f(\tilde{\theta}) = \hat{W}$ takes value e_1 with probability $\frac{\pi_1}{\pi_1 + \pi_2}$, and value e_2 with probability $\frac{\pi_2}{\pi_1 + \pi_2}$, with

$$e_1 = -\frac{\pi_2}{\pi_1 + \pi_2}(I(\theta_2) - I(\theta_1)),$$

and

$$e_2 = \frac{\pi_1}{\pi_1 + \pi_2}(I(\theta_2) - I(\theta_1)).$$

Observe that the expectation of $\varepsilon(\tilde{\theta})$ conditional to any realization of $\hat{w}_f(\tilde{\theta})$ is zero. Therefore $\hat{w}_f(\tilde{\theta})$ dominates $w_f(\tilde{\theta})$ in the sense of MPC. Thus, all risk-averse policyholders dislike the old contract, which may not be efficient. ■

This Proposition means that the indemnity is a deterministic function of the aggregate loss.[6] Addıng noise to it would be detrimental to risk-averse policyholders, without increasing profits for insurers. If there are two states in which the aggregate losses are the same, but the indemnities differ, then there exists another contract that dominates the first in the sense of MPC. Consequently, only the aggregate loss suffered by the policyholder matters to determine the indemnity to be paid. This principle is usually violated in the real world. Indeed, it implies that the agent should not separately insure each risk that he faces. Rather, an "umbrella" policy is optimal, as shown by Gollier and Schlesinger (1995) in the specific case of expected utility. This result is obvious when the different risks faced by the agent are correlated. In particular, negative correlation allows for an homemade insurance that saves on external insurance costs.

To illustrate the benefit of an umbrella policy in the case of independent risks, let us consider the following numerical example. The agent faces two risks of loss, $\tilde{x}_1$ and $\tilde{x}_2$. These random variables are independent and identically distributed. They take value 0, 50 and 100 with equal probabilities. Observe that there are 9 states of nature in this economy. Let us also assume that $c_0 = 0$ and $\lambda = 0.5$. Consider first the strategy to purchase two separate contracts, one for each risk. Consider in particular separate contracts with a straight deductible of 50. This means that an indemnity of 50 is paid on a contract only if the worst loss occurs for the corresponding risk. The actuarial value of the contract is 50/3, the premium is 25, and the total insurance expense is 50. The distribution of final wealth is represented in Figure 1a. With probability 1/9, the agent incurs no loss, and he finishes with wealth $w_0 - 50$, the initial wealth minus the insurance expense. With probability 4/9, he suffers two losses of at least 50, ending up with wealth $w_0 - 150$, taking into account of the premiums paid, and the retained loss (50) on each risk. Finally, with probability 4/9, he suffers a loss on one risk, and no loss on the other risk, yielding final wealth $w_0 - 100$. By Proposition 1, this insurance strategy may not be optimal. Indeed, there are four states in which the aggregate losses are the same, but the aggregate indemnities differ. In particular, an aggregate loss of 100 may result from two partial losses of 50, or from a single loss of 100. In the former case, no indemnity at all is paid, whereas an indemnity of 50 is paid in the latter case.

Consider alternatively an umbrella policy with a deductible on the aggregate loss amounting to $D = 500/6$. One can verify that the premium for such a contract is 50, and that the distribution of final wealth is as in Figure 1b. With probability 2/9, the aggregate loss is 50, yielding final wealth equaling w_0 minus the premium (50), and minus the retained loss (50). With probability 6/9, the aggregate loss exceeds Dı100, generating a final wealth w_0 minus the premium and the deductible D.

[6] It has been proven by Eeckhoudt, Bauwens, Briys and Scarmure (1991) for the specific case of a binomila distribution.

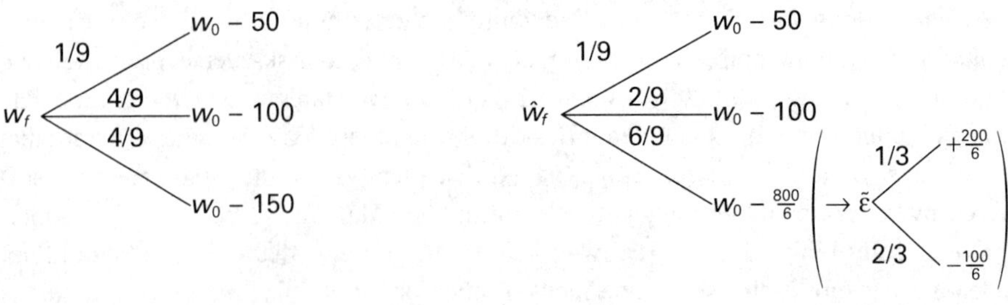

Figure 1a Separate Contracts with Deductibles Equal to 50

Figure 1b Umbrella Policy with a Deductible D = 500/6

Observe that the distribution in Figure 1a can be obtained from the one in Figure 1b by adding a zero-mean noise $\tilde{\varepsilon} = \left(\frac{200}{6}, 1/3; -\frac{100}{6}, 2/3\right)$ to its worst realization. This explains why no risk-averse agent, EU-maximizer or not, will purchase separate contracts, even when risks are independent. Explaining why separate contracts exists in reality is an important challenge for further research in this field.

We hereafter assume without loss of generality that $x(\theta) = \theta$ for all θ.

3.3.2 Optimality of a Deductible Policy

In this section, we prove the Arrow's result on the optimality of a straight deductible, without using expected utility. Arrow (1971) used basic tools of variational calculus to get the result. Raviv (1979) used dynamic optimization techniques. More recently, Spaeter and Roger (1997) introduced a topological concept named the angular norm to prove the optimality of a straight deductible. But Zilcha and Chew (1990), Karni (1992) and Gollier and Schlesinger (1996)[7] showed that this result is not dependent upon a decision model as specific as EU. Our proof is in the vein of Gollier and Schlesinger (1996) and Schlesinger (1997), who used the integral condition of Rothschild and Stiglitz (1970) to define a MPC. We do it here with the notion of transferring probability masses from the center of the distribution to its tails. From our point of view, this makes the proof shorter and more intuitive.

Proposition 3. Consider the case of linear costs. Suppose that the policyholder is risk-averse in the sense that V satisfies the MPC property. Then the optimal contract contains a straight deductible D: $I(x) = \max(0, x - D)$.

Proof. A deductible policy is characterized by the property that once a positive indemnity is paid in a state x_1, any marginal increase in the loss is fully indemnified.

[7] Zilcha and Chew (1990) and Karni (1992) used the restriction of Frechet differentiability, whereas Gollier and Schlesinger (1996) did not make any restriction on the model.

Suppose by contradiction that there exist two levels of loss, x_1 and x_2, with $x_1 < x_2$, such that $I(x_1) > 0$ and $I(x_2) < I(x_1) + x_2 - x_1$. The latter inequality is equivalent to

$$w_0 - x_2 + I(x_2) - P < w_0 - x_1 + I(x_1) - P,$$

or $w_f(x_2) < w_f(x_1)$. Now, consider an alternative indemnity schedule $\hat{I}$, which is unchanged with respect to I, except in case of loss x_1 or x_2. Take

$$\hat{I}(x_1) = I(x_1) - \varepsilon,$$

and

$$\hat{I}(x_2) = I(x_2) + \frac{\pi_1}{\pi_2}\varepsilon.$$

Observe that, by construction, this change has no effect on the premium, as the actuarial value of the policy is not affected. If ε is positive but small, the constraint on the nonnegativity of claims is not violated. This change affects the distribution of final wealth in the following way:

$$\hat{w}_f(x_1) < w_f(x_1) \quad \text{and} \quad \hat{w}_f(x_2) > w_f(x_2).$$

The expected final wealth is unchanged, but the larger final wealth level is reduced, whereas the smaller one is increased. This is a MPC.[8] No risk-averse agent would thus select the initial contract, which is inefficient. A symmetric proof can be done when $I(x_1) > 0$ and $I(x_2) > I(x_1) + x_2 - x_1$. ■

To illustrate, let us consider again the case of risk $\tilde{x}_1$ which takes value 0, 50 or 100 with equal probabilities. Assuming $c_0 = 0$ and $\lambda = 0.5$, a contract with a pure coinsurance rate of 50%, i.e., with $I(x) = x/2$, can be purchased for a premium $P = 37.5$. The distribution of final wealth in this case is represented in Figure 2a. Consider alternatively a contract with a straight deductible $D = 37.5$. The premium for this contract is also equal to 37.5. The final wealth is distributed as in Figure 2b if such a contract is purchased.

Observe that the distribution in Figure 2a can be obtained by adding a noise $\tilde{\varepsilon} = (+12.5, 1/2; -12.5, 1/2)$ to the worse realization of the random variable in Figure 2b. Since this noise has a zero mean, the distribution in Figure 2b is less risky in the sense of a MPC. We conclude that a contract with a 50% coinsurance rate will never be purchased, as it is dominated by a contract with a straight deductible. Proposition

[8] The equivalence between this characterization of an MPC and the definition using white noises is in Rothschild and Siglitz (1970).

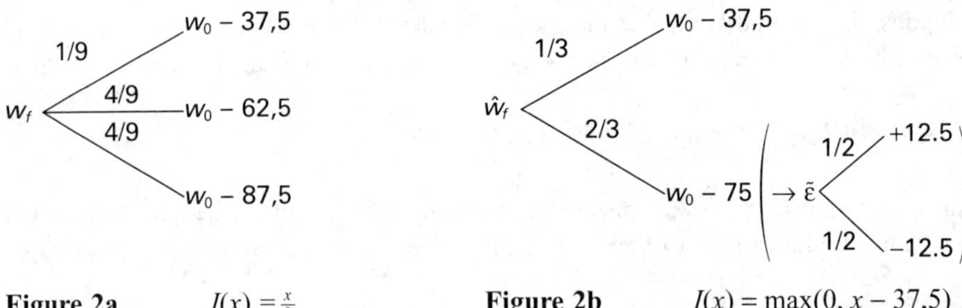

Figure 2a $I(x) = \frac{x}{2}$ **Figure 2b** $I(x) = \max(0, x - 37{,}5)$

3 shows that this technique can be extended to any contract that is not a straight deductible.

The intuition of this result has been presented in the introduction. In short, as it is apparent in Figure 2, a straight deductible efficiently concentrates the effort of indemnification on large losses. On the contrary, a contract with a constant coinsurance rate for example provides an inefficiently large amount of money when losses are small, and an inefficiently small amount when losses are large. The optimality of a straight deductible is the expression of the relevance of insurance for large risks. Small risks, i.e., risks whose largest potential loss is less than the optimal deductible should not be insured. I am willing to purchase insurance against the important risk for my kids and unemployed wife in case of my premature death. I am willing to purchase insurance for my house, which is my largest asset at this time. Given the cost of insurance, I am not willing to purchase insurance against the risk of broken glasses, or even against damages to my old car. I would be ready to bear the risk of paying for standard medical care, but I would like to get a large indemnity from my insurer in case of a costly surgical procedure. This is exactly what a policy with straight deductible provides!

3.3.3 Optimal Deductible

To sum up, under linear transaction costs, efficient indemnity schedules are deterministic functions of the loss, and they take the form of policies with a straight deductible. This has been obtained by assuming risk aversion alone, with no reference to any specific decision model. We now turn to the problem of the selection of the optimal deductible D.

Notice that adding the assumption of FSD for the preference functional implies that D is nonnegative. Otherwise, the indemnity would always be positive. This may not be optimal, as proven in Proposition 1. When the loading factor λ is zero, the optimal deductible vanishes. This corresponds to the optimality of full insurance. This is a trivial result, as a marginal increase in coverage would not change final wealth in expectation, whereas it would reduce its variability in the sense of a MPC.

The analysis is more complex when the loading factor λ is positive, as shown by Schlesinger (1981). In that case, a marginal increase in coverage, that is obtained by a reduction of D, reduces the expected final wealth. The agent must weight the benefit of insurance—which is to reduce the variability of wealth—with the cost of insurance. Let us consider the strategy of moving D from some small positive value to zero. Let $\tilde{x}$ be 0 with probability π_0 and $\tilde{y}$ with probability $1 - \pi_0$. Parameter $1 - \pi_0$ is the probability of an accident, and $\tilde{y}$ is the severity of the loss, that can be a random variable. The increase in the actuarial value of the full insurance policy D can be approximated as $(1 - \pi_0)D$. It implies that the reduction in expected wealth by selecting full insurance rather than contract D is $\lambda(1 - \pi_0)D$. This is the marginal net cost of insurance. The marginal cost of the last dollar of coverage or deductible is thus $\lambda(1 - \pi_0)$, which is strictly positive.

The benefit of reducing D to zero is the risk premium associated to the retained risk under policy D. The retained risk is $D\tilde{z}$, where $\tilde{z}$ takes value 0 with probability π_0, and value 1 otherwise. D is thus the size of the retained risk. Now remember that, in the EU model with a smooth utility function, the risk premium is approximately proportional to the variance of the retained risk, which is itself proportional to D^2. Thus, the *marginal* benefit of reducing D to zero is zero. Since we have shown that the marginal cost of the last dollar of deductible is positive, it may not be optimal to purchase it. This result is in Mossin (1968).

Proposition 4. Consider the case of linear costs in the expected utility framework. Suppose that the policyholder is risk-averse in the sense that V satisfies the MPC property. If $\lambda = 0$, then the optimal deductible is zero. If $\lambda > 0$, then the optimal deductible is positive.

Schlesinger (1997) provides a detailed analysis of this Proposition. This result has been generalized by Karni (1992) and Machina (1995) for non-expected utility models satisfying Frechet differentiability. Observe that the proof of this Proposition relies on the assumption that the risk premium is proportional to the variance of the retained risk, at least when the risk is small. This assumption holds for other models than the EU one. It is called second order risk aversion.[9] When risk aversion is of order 1, that is, when the risk aversion is approximately proportional to the standard deviation of the random variable, as in the EURDP model, the policyholder could optimally select full insurance even if λ is positive. This is because he has a positive benefit to the last dollar of coverage. Doherty and Eeckhoudt (1995) describes the case of the Yaari's dual model, where risk aversion is of the first order.

Some authors tried to quantify the optimal level of the deductible when λ is positive, using the EU model. The decision problem is to maximize $H(D) = Eu(w_0 - \min(\tilde{x}, D) - P(D))$ where $P(D) = (1 + \lambda)E \max(0, \tilde{x} - D)$. The first-order condition is written as

[9] For the definition of the order of risk aversion, see Segal and Spivak (1990).

$$H'(D) = (1 - F(D))[(1+\lambda)Eu'(w_0 - \min(\tilde{x}, D) - P(D)) - u'(w_0 - D - P(D))] = 0, \tag{3}$$

where F is the cumulative distribution of the random loss $\tilde{x}$. Drèze (1981) and Gollier (1992), using a Taylor approximation for this fist-order condition of the deductible selection problem, obtained the following conditions:

$$\frac{\lambda t}{1+\lambda} \leq \frac{D}{w_0 - D - P} \leq \frac{\lambda t}{\pi_0(1+\lambda)}, \tag{4}$$

where π_0 is the probability of no loss, and t is the index of relative tolerance, $t = -\frac{u'(w_0 - D - P)}{(w_0 - D - P)u''(w_0 - D - P)}$. When $\pi_0 \cong 1$, as for many insurance lines, we see that the optimal deductible of the umbrella policy, expressed as a fraction of total wealth, can be approximated by the product of the loading factor and the relative risk tolerance. A realistic value of λ is 0.3. The debate on realistic values for t is still open, but an acceptable interval would be $t \in [0.2, 0.5]$. This gives us an optimal deductible around 5 to 15% of total wealth.

We now turn to the comparative statics analysis of the optimal deductible in the EU model:

- We know from Mossin (1968) that an increase in risk aversion reduces the optimal D.[10] This is simple to understand from the observation that an increase in risk aversion raises the marginal benefit of reducing the deductible. This can be easily shown by using the first-order condition (3).
- This result directly implies that an increase in w_0 increases D under decreasing absolute risk aversion. Indeed, an increase in wealth is equivalent to a reduction in risk aversion when absolute risk aversion is decreasing.
- As usual, a change in λ has an ambiguous effect because of the presence of a wealth effect: an increase in λ makes self-insurance more desirable, but it also makes policyholders poorer. Under decreasing absolute risk aversion, this has a positive impact on insurance demand, which implies that the global effect is ambiguous.
- The analysis of the effect of a change in the distribution of the loss is more complex. The best result has been obtained by Jang and Hadar (1995), who have shown that an increase in the probability of an accident of a deterministic severity has a positive effect on D.[11] Finally, Eeckhoudt, Gollier and Schlesinger (1991) obtain results for the effect of an increase in risk of the distribution of damage

[10] Machina (1995) extends this result to non-expected utility models with Frechet differentiability.

[11] Eeckhoudt and Gollier (1999) extend this result to non-expected utility models with second-order risk aversion.

severity. Observe that when the change in distribution is a MPC that is concentrated in loss states x above the optimal deductible, the effect is obviously null. Indeed, the risk-neutral insurer absorbs 100% of the increase in risk without changing the premium. The policyholder is not affected by the change.

3.4 NONLINEAR TRANSACTION COSTS

To our knowledge, no econometric analysis has been performed to test for the linearity of transaction costs on insurance markets. In this section, we examine the case of nonlinear transaction costs.

3.4.1 Stochastic Indemnity Schedule

In the previous section, we have shown that the indemnity must be a deterministic function of the loss in the case of linear costs. When the transaction cost is a concave function of the indemnity, this may not be true. Indeed, randomizing indemnities generates a reduction in the expected transaction cost. If risk aversion is not too large, a random indemnity schedule may be optimal.

An interesting particular case of concave cost functions is due to the presence of a fixed cost per claim: when there is no claim at all the cost is zero, but even a small claim generates fixed costs for the insurer, as an audit cost, or processing the payment of the indemnity. There is an upward jump in cost at zero, which introduces a concavity to the cost function. Gollier (1987b) characterizes the best deterministic contract in that case. It exhibits a straight deductible, but with a clause that no indemnity would be paid if the loss is just slightly over the deductible. That clause eliminates "nuisance claims", i.e., claims that are too small with respect to the fixed auditing costs. More recent works in the literature on optimal audits show that stochastic audits and indemnities are optimal.[12]

3.4.2 No Overinsurance

In most models on optimal insurance, constraint $I(x) \leq x$ is imposed: no overinsurance is allowed. We know from Propositions 1 and 3 that this constraint is never binding in the case of linear costs. Huberman, Mayers and Smith (1983) claim that this constraint may be binding in the case of nonlinear costs. This is not true, as long as the policyholder is risk-averse.

[12] See Mookherjee and Png (1989) for a first result on this topic. The literature on optimal auditing is not covered in this survey. This is because our basic assumption is symmetric information, ex ante and *ex post*.

Proposition 5. Suppose that V satisfies the FSD property and the MPC property. Then, constraint $I(x) \leq x$ is never binding.

Proof. Suppose by contradiction that $0 < \max_x I(x) - x$. Let y be the argument of the maximum, and $\pi = Prob[\tilde{x} = y]$. It implies that this is in loss state y that the final wealth is the largest. Let also define $\hat{I}(x) = I(x)$ if $x \neq y$ and $\hat{I}(y) = I(y) - \varepsilon$, $\varepsilon > 0$. Suppose first that the new premium is $\hat{P}_1 = P - \pi\varepsilon$. Purchasing this new contract generates a MPC to the distribution of final wealth. Indeed, we reduce the largest potential wealth level, whereas we translate the distribution to the right to preserve the mean.

But in fact, the premium to pay for the new contract is not $\hat{P}_1$, but $\hat{P} = \hat{P}_1 - \pi(c(I(y)) - c(I(y) - \varepsilon))$. This is smaller than $\hat{P}_1$. Taking into account this additional reduction in premium yields an additional increase in V if it satisfies FSD. Thus, the initial contract is not efficient. ∎

The intuition is that overinsurance generates two effects that are detrimental to the welfare of the policyholder. First, a marginal increase of indemnity over the size of the loss yields an additional cost of insurance, which is detrimental to any V satisfying FSD. Second, this marginal change in indemnity generates a MPC to final wealth. Indeed, we know from Proposition 1, that there exists a $x \leq 0$ for which $I(x) = 0$. In consequence, the marginal change increases the wealth level at the right of the distribution of w_f. The net effect is thus a MPC.

Notice that the combination of Proposition 1 and Proposition 5 implies that $I(0) = 0$.

3.4.3 Optimal Design of the Indemnity Schedule

An interesting problem is to characterize the optimal policy when transaction costs are not linear. Under the EU model, Raviv (1979) showed that if $c(.)$ is increasing and convex, then

$$I'(x) = \left[1 + \frac{c''(I(x))}{1 + c'(I(x))} T(w_0 - x + I(x) - P)\right]^{-1} \tag{5}$$

when $I(x) > 0$. $T(z)$ is the absolute risk tolerance measured at z, i.e., $T(z) = -u'(z)/u''(z)$. When $c'' > 0$, the marginal indemnity is less than unity. The intuition is that large indemnities are relatively more costly. One can use the above formula when c is concave, provided the second-order condition of the decision problem is satisfied. In this case, the marginal indemnity is larger than 1. The extreme case is the presence of a fixed cost per claim, which generates an upward discontinuity to the indemnity function.

Spaeter (1997) examines whether the indemnity function is concave or convex with respect to the loss. She shows that if c is quadratic, then I'' is positive if and only if the policyholder is prudent. Prudence means that the third derivative of the utility function is positive.

3.5 OTHER REASONS FOR PARTIAL INSURANCE

This paper focussed on the existence of transaction costs to explain why partial insurance may be an equilibrium. Several other reasons can justify different forms of risk retention by the policyholder. The presence of asymmetric information between the two parties is a well-known argument which is examined at length in the literature. In the case of an adverse selection problem, accepting a positive risk retention ($I' < 1$ or $D > 0$) is a way for the policyholder to signal a low risk. When there is a moral hazard problem, imposing a retention of risk gives an incentive to policyholder to invest in prevention. Holmstrom (1978) characterizes the optimal insurance design under a moral hazard problem. We now discuss two other arguments: the existence of a random error in observing losses, and the risk aversion of the insurer.

3.5.1 Errors in Observation

Insurers often face the difficulty to estimate the size of damages. Gollier (1996) assumes that the insurer can indemnify the policyholder only on the basis of a proxy $\tilde{y} \mid x$ of the actual loss x. If the actual loss x equals the estimated loss y plus an independent white noise, then the optimal contract contains a straight deductible. The optimal deductible is negatively affected by the error if u is "risk vulnerable", a condition introduced by Gollier and Pratt (1996).[13] The existence of an error in estimating the loss reduces the quality of an insurance contract to cover the basic risk. Indeed, the insurance adds an additional indemnity risk to the wealth of the policyholder. Under risk vulnerability, this reduction in the quality of insurance *reduces* the demand for it. Only when u is not risk vulnerable, errors in estimating the loss generate an increase in risk retention at equilibrium. Indeed, in this case, the deterioration in the quality of the insurance product will be compensated for by an increase in its purchase.

A more realistic assumption is that the risk of error is increasing with the estimated loss. Gollier (1996) shows that under prudence ($u''' > 0$), the optimal insurance contains a disappearing deductible in that case: $I(y) = \max(0, J(y))$, with $J'(y) > 1$. The increase in expected wealth as the loss increases is used to forearm against the increased risk of error in the indemnity paid by the insurer.

[13] Risk vulnerability is linked to the third and the fourth derivative of the utility function. All familiar utility (exponential, power, logarithmic) functions satisfy this property.

3.5.2 Risk Aversion of the Insurer

We assumed in this paper that insurers are risk-neutral. This means that the minimum premium that is acceptable to them equals the expected indemnity plus the expected cost of insurance. This is a realistic assumption when individual risks are not correlated with the "market risk". It implies that individual risks are fully diversifiable by shareholders of insurance companies. Therefore, at equilibrium, they will not get any extra risk premium to bear individual risks. On the contrary, when risks are correlated with the market risk, the equilibrium insurance tariff must contain a risk premium for shareholders to accept to bear these risks. This is a relevant problem for catastrophic risks and some risks that are economic in nature (e.g., unemployment).

The general problem is to determine efficient risk-sharing arrangements in an economy of risk-averse agents. In fact, this problem is not different from the problem of the characterization of an equilibrium on financial markets. The link with the literature of finance is here very strong. The main difference between the theory of finance and the economics of insurance is the existence of much larger transaction costs ($\cong$ 30%) in insurance than in finance ($\cong$ 2%).[14]

Arrow (1953) provides the general framework for the analysis of the allocation of risks in an economy with no transaction costs. Borch (1960, 1962) examines optimal risk-sharing rules in a general EU framework. Wilson (1968), Buhlman and Jewell (1979), Raviv (1979), Eliashberg and Winkler (1981) and Blazenko (1985) considered the specific problem of a risk-averse insurer with utility function v who can insure a risk initially borne by a policyholder with utility function u. They obtain that

$$I'(x) = \frac{T_v(R - I(x) + P)}{T_v(R - I(x) + P) + T_u(w_0 - x + i(x) - P)}, \tag{6}$$

where R is the wealth of the insurer. The marginal indemnity equals absolute risk tolerance of the insurer expressed as a percentage of the group's absolute risk tolerance. The smaller the insurer's risk tolerance, the larger the risk transfer, and the larger the risk retention by the policyholder. It is interesting to observe that there is a simple way to obtain this rule in the case of a small risk with variance σ^2. If the risk is small, the use of the Arrow-Pratt approximation yields that the sum of the risk premiums supported by the policyholder and the insurer is written as

$$\Pi = \frac{1}{2}\frac{(1-I')^2\sigma^2}{T_u} + \frac{1}{2}\frac{I'^2\sigma^2}{T_v},$$

[14] The analogies are numerous. For example, the fact that $\lambda = 0$ implies that $D = 0$ is equivalent in finance to the fact that risk-averse investors will not invest in the risky asset if its expected return does not exceed the riskfree rate.

where $I' = I'(0)$ and $T_u = T_u(w_0)$ and $T_v = T_v(R)$. We look for the risk sharing arrangement which minimizes the sum of risk premiums in the economy: $\min_{I'} \Pi$. Solving the first-order condition of this problem directly yields $I' = T_v/(T_v + T_u)$.

Leland (1980) examined the sign of I''. In our context, the convexity of I would mean a contract similar to a deductible policy, whereas the concavity of I would correspond to a contract with a cap on indemnities. Leland shows that the sign of I'' depends upon which of the two functions u and v decreases at the fastest rate.

3.6 CONCLUSION

Most breakthroughs in the theory of optimal insurance have been made before the development of decision models alternative to expected utility. We are now realizing that many of these results can be extended at no cost to non-expected utility models. Arrow's result is the most striking example of this phenomenon. Arrow (1971) proved that a deductible insurance is optimal for a risk-averse expected-utility maximizer if transaction costs are linear. The complexity of the proofs of this result by Arrow and others has obscured our understanding of the optimality of deductibles in insurance for a long time. In fact, the literature has only recently recognized that this result is a direct consequence of the very general notions of strong risk aversion and of an increase in risk. Thus Arrow's result is robust to any decision model that satisfies this property. This conclusion is useful not only because it extends the initial proposition, but also because it provides a simple intuition for the optimality of a deductible policy.

However, various other results in insurance economics require a more precise modeling of risk preferences. And there, the expected utility model is still unbeatable to produce simple useful and testable properties of the optimal behavior under risk. The insurance market is likely to be a good candidate for testing those models.[15]

3.7 REFERENCES

Arrow, K.J. (1953). "Le Rôle des Valeurs Boursières pour la Répartition la Meilleure des Risques", Econometrie, 41–47. Paris: CNRS. Translated (1964) as "The Role of Securities in the Optimal Allocation of Risk-Bearing", *Review of Economics Studies* 31, 31–36.

Arrow, K.J. (1963). "Uncertainty and the Welfare Economics of Medical Care" American Economic Review, 53, 941–969.

Arrow, K.J. (1971). *Essays in the Theory of Risk Bearing*. Chicago: Markham Publishing Co.

Arrow, K.J. (1974). "Optimal Insurance and Generalized Deductibles", *Scandinavian Actuarial Journal* 1, 1–42.

Blazenko, G. (1985). "The Design of an Optimal Insurance Policy: Note", *American Economic Review* 75, 253–255.

[15] See Schlee (1995) for some insights about how to test EU and NEU models with insurance demand data.

Borch, K. (1960). "The Safety Loading of Reinsurance Premiums", *Skandinavisk Aktuarietskrift* 153–184.

Borch, K. (1962). "Equilibrium in a Reinsurance Market", *Econometrica* 30, 424–444.

Buhlmann, H. and W.S. Jewell (1979). "Optimal Risk Exchange", *Astin Bulletin* 10, 243–262.

Chateauneuf, A., R.-A. Dana and J.-M. Tallon (1997). "Optimal risk-sharing rules and equilibria with non-additive expected utility", *mimeo*, Paris 1.

Cohen, M. (1995). "Risk-aversion concepts in expected- and non-expected-utility models", *The Geneva Papers on Risk and Insurance Theory* 20, 73–91.

Doherty, N.A. and L. Eeckhoudt (1995). "Optimal insurance without expected utility: The dual theory and the linearity of insurance contracts", *Journal of Risk and Uncertainty* 10, 157–179.

Drèze, J.H. (1981). "Inferring Risk Tolerance from Deductibles in Insurance Contracts", *The Geneva Papers on Risk and Insurance* 6, 48–52.

Eeckhoudt, L., L. Bauwens, E. Briys and P. Scarmure (1991). "The Law of Large (Small?) Numbers and the Demand for Insurance", *Journal of Risk and Insurance* 58, 438–451.

Eeckhoudt, L. and C. Gollier (1995). *Risk: Evaluation, Management and Sharing*, New York: Harvester Wheatsheaf.

Eeckhoudt, L. and C. Gollier (1999). "The Insurance of Low Probability Events", *Journal of Risk and Insurance* 66, 17–28.

Eeckhoudt, L., C. Gollier and H. Schlesinger (1991). "Increase in Risk and Deductible Insurance", *Journal of Economic Theory* 55.

Eliashberg, J. and R. Winkler (1981). "Risk Sharing and Group Decision Making", *Management Science* 27, 1221–1235.

Gerber, H.U. (1978). "Pareto-Optimal Risk Exchanges and Related Decision Problems", *Astin Bulletin* 10, 155–179.

Gollier, C. (1987a). "The Design of Optimal Insurance without the Nonnegativity Constraint on Claims", *Journal of Risk and Insurance* 54, 312–324.

Gollier, C. (1987b). "Pareto-Optimal Risk Sharing with Fixed Costs per Claim", *Scandinavian Actuarial Journal* 13, 62–73.

Gollier, C. (1992). "Economic Theory of Risk Exchanges: A Review", in Dionne, G. (ed.), *Contributions to Insurance Economics*, Boston: Kluwer Academic Press.

Gollier, C. (1996). "The Design of Optimal Insurance When the Indemnity Can Depend Only Upon a Proxy of the Actual Loss", *Journal of Risk and Insurance* 63, 369–380.

Gollier, C. and J.W. Pratt (1996). "Risk Vulnerability and the Tempering Effect of Background Risk", *Econometrica* 64, 1109–1124.

Gollier, C. and H. Schlesinger (1995). "Second-Best Insurance Contract Design in an Incomplete Market", *Scandinavian Journal of Economics* 97, 123–135.

Gollier, C. and H. Schlesinger (1996). "Arrow's Theorem on the Optimality of Deductibles: A Stochastic Dominance Approach", *Economic Theory* 7, 359–363.

Holmstrom, B. (1978). "Moral Hazard and Observability", *The Bell Journal of Economics* 9, 74–91.

Huberman, G., D. Mayers and C.W. Smith (1983). "Optimal Insurance Policy Indemnity Schedules", *The Bell Journal of Economics* 14, 415–426.

Jang, Y.-S. and J. Hadar (1995). "A Note on Increased Probability of Loss and the Demand for Insurance", *The Geneva Papers on Risk and Insurance Theory* 20, 213–216.

Karni, E. (1992). "Optimal Insurance: A Nonexpected Utility Analysis", in Dionne, G. (ed.), *Contributions to Insurance Economics*, Boston: Kluwer Academic Press.

Leland, H.E. (1980). "Who Should Buy Portfolio Insurance?", *The Journal of Finance* 35, 581–596.

Machina, M. (1995). "Non-Expected Utility and the Robustness of the Classical Insurance Paradigm", in Gollier, C. and M. Machina (ed.), *Non-expected Utility and Risk Management*, Boston: Kluwer Academic Press, reprinted from *The Geneva Papers on Risk and Insurance Theory* 20, 9–50.

Mookherjee, D. and I. Png (1989). "Optimal Auditing, Insurance and Redistribution", *Quarterly Journal of Economics* 103, 399–415.

Mossin, J. (1968). "Aspects of Rational Insurance Purchasing", *Journal of Political Economy* 76, 533–568.

Pratt, J.W. (1964). "Risk Aversion in the Small and in the Large", *Econometrica* 32, 122 136.

Raviv, A. (1979). "The Design of an Optimal Insurance Policy", *American Economic Review* 69, 84–96.

Rothschild, M. and J. Stiglitz (1970). Increasing Risk: I. A Definition, *Journal of Economic Theory* 2, 225–243.

Schlesinger, H. (1981). "The Optimal Level of Deductibility in Insurance Contracts", *Journal of Risk and Insurance* 48, 465–481.

Schlesinger, H. (1997). "Insurance demand Without the Expected-Utility Paradigm", *Journal of Risk and Insurance* 64, 19–39.

Segal, U. and A. Spivak (1990). "First Order Versus Second Order Risk Aversion", *Journal of Economic Theory* 51, 11–125.

Schlee, E.E. (1995). "The Comparative Statics of Deductible Insurance in Expected- and Non-expected-utility Models", *The Geneva Papers on Risk and Insurance Theory* 20, 57–72.

Spaeter, S. (1997). "Optimal Insurance Policies When Prudence and Non-Linear Costs Are Jointly Considered", *mimeo*, CREST/ENSAE, Paris.

Spaeter, S. and P. Roger (1997). "The Design of Optimal Insurance Contracts: A Topological Approach", *The Geneva Papers on Risk and Insurance* 22, 5–20.

Wilson, R. (1968). "The Theory of Syndicates", *Econometrica* 36, 113–132.

Zilcha, I. and S.H. Chew (1990). "Invariance of the Efficient Sets When the Expected Utility Hypothesis is Relaxed", *Journal of Economic Behaviour and Organizations* 13, 125–131.

4 The Effects of Changes in Risk on Risk Taking: A Survey*

Louis Eeckhoudt

Catholic Faculties of Mons

Christian Gollier

University of Toulouse

Abstract

We examine an important class of decision problems under uncertainty that entails the standard portfolio problem and the demand for coinsurance. The agent faces a controllable risk—his demand for a risky asset for example—and a background risk. We determine how a change in the distribution in one of these two risks affects the optimal exposure to the controllable risk. Restrictions on first order and second order stochastic dominance orders are in general necessary to yield an unambiguous comparative statics property. We also review another line of research in which restrictions are made on preferences rather than on stochastic dominance orders.

Keywords: Comparative statics under uncertainty, increase in risk, background risk, portfolio decision, insurance demand.

JEL Classification Numbers: D80, G22.

4.1 INTRODUCTION

To start this survey, we present two problems that look very different at first glance. Consider an investor who has to allocate a given amount of money (w_0) between a safe asset paying a return (i) and a risky one paying a random return ($\tilde{x}$). If the mathematical expectation of $\tilde{x}$ exceeds i, it is optimal for an investor who obeys the axioms of expected utility to invest a strictly positive amount in the risky asset. Assume now that because of some good news, the prospects of the risky asset become "better" in the sense of improving the welfare of its holder. Intuition suggests that a rational investor should invest more in the risky asset because it has become relatively more attractive.

* We thank two referees for their useful comments on a preliminary version of the chapter.

We now turn to the second problem. We consider the case of an insured whose wealth w_0 may be reduced by a random damage $\tilde{y}$. To protect himself against this damage he can buy insurance that is sold with a positive and proportional loading by an insurance company. The company and the insured have identical information about the initial risk $\tilde{y}$. It is well-known that in this case, expected-utility maximizers should buy less than full insurance. Now assume that the insured receives a private information indicating that his risk deteriorates. Intuition suggests again that the insured should now demand more coverage to compensate for the deterioration in risk.

The examples of portfolio and insurance decisions illustrate a more general problem that is the topics of this survey: how do changes in risk affect risk taking (e.g., portfolio) or risk avoidance (e.g., insurance) by a decision-maker? We basically show that unless specific restrictions are made on the change in risk and/or on the shape of the utility function, a risk-averse decision-maker may very well decide to increase his exposure to a risk whose distribution deteriorates.

While they have the same formal structure, the two examples just described share another important feature: the decision-maker faces only one risk and by his single decision about this risk, he optimally controls the total risk he will assume. An important part of this survey will be devoted to a more realistic case recently developed in the literature under the general heading of "background risk". In this problem two risks are involved: one is exogenous and is not subject to transformations by the decision maker while the other one is endogenous and can be controlled in the way described in each of the two examples. The exogenous risk can be for example a risk related to labour income that is traditionally not insurable through standard insurance markets. The question raised in this new framework can be described as follows: how does the background risk affect the optimal decisions about the endogenous one? Is it true that e.g., a deterioration in the background risk will always reduce risk taking vis a vis the other risk?

Before turning to this question, we present our basic model in section 4.2 and we state some basic results about it. Section 4.3 is devoted to a presentation of the standard stochastic orders. In section 4.4, we survey results about the impact of a change in the distribution of the endogenous/controllable risk. As indicated earlier, the role and impact of background risk are examined in section 4.5. Some extensions and a concluding remark are provided respectively in sections 4.6 and 4.7.

4.2 A SIMPLE MODEL

The two problems presented in the introduction can be written in the following compact manner:[1]

[1] For more details, see Dionne-Eeckhoudt-Gollier (1993) and more especially pages 315–317. See also Eeckhoudt-Gollier (1995) and more specifically page 183, exercise 10.1. The reader who is interested in an insurance interpretation of some results in this survey may also refer to Alarie, Dionne and Eeckhoudt (1992).

$$\max_{\alpha} \; Eu(w_0 + \alpha\tilde{x} + \tilde{\varepsilon}) \tag{1}$$

where α is the decision variable, the value of which measures the extent of risk taking. The random variable $\tilde{\varepsilon}$ stands for the background risk. The utility function u is assumed to be increasing and concave. By assumption $\tilde{\varepsilon}$ is independent of $\tilde{x}$, the endogenous/controllable risk.[2]

Notice finally that for the problem to make sense the random variable $\tilde{x}$ must take negative and positive values otherwise the optimal α would be either $-\infty$ or $+\infty$. The absolute value of α expresses the exposure to risk $\tilde{x}$. Its optimal level—denoted α^*—has two properties that can be stated as follows:

- if the mathematical expectation of $\tilde{x}$ is strictly positive, so will be α^*. This property which was shown to be true in the absence of background risk remains valid in its presence (for a proof in an insurance context, see Doherty-Schlesinger (1983)).
- in the absence of background risk an increase in risk aversion decreases α^* (see Pratt (1964)). However as shown by Kihlstrom, Romer, Williams (1981), this relationship does not extend when an independent background risk is added to initial wealth. This result illustrates the importance of background risk the presence of which may invalidate results that hold true in its absence.

4.3 DETRIMENTAL CHANGES IN RISK

Suppose that random variable $\tilde{x}$ undergoes an exogenous change in distribution. The initial cumulative distribution function is denoted F, whereas the final one is denoted G. Economists usually consider two specific subsets of changes in risk: first order or second order stochastic dominance (respectively FSD and SSD). In order to define these stochastic dominance orders, one looks at the effect of a change in risk on a specific class of agents.

4.3.1 First Order Stochastic Dominance (FSD)

F dominates G in the sense of FSD if the expected utility under F is larger than under G for any increasing utility function:

$$\int u(x)dF(x) \geq \int u(x)dG(x) \quad \forall u \text{ increasing}. \tag{2}$$

Observe that among the set of increasing functions, we have the standard "step" (or indicator) function, which takes value 0 if x is less than a given y, otherwise it takes

[2] Gollier and Schlee (1997) examine the more general problem with a correlated background risk. Notice also that many results reviewed in this paper also hold when final wealth is a concave function of α and $\tilde{x}$.

value 1. Thus, applying the above definition to this function yields the necessary condition $1 - F(y) \geq 1 - G(y)$, or $F(y) \leq G(y)$. Notice also that any increasing function can be obtained by a convex combination of step functions, i.e., the set of step functions is a basis of the set of increasing functions. Observe finally that the expectation operator is linear, i.e., if u_1 and u_2 satisfy condition (2), then $\lambda u_1 + (1 - \lambda)u_2$ also satisfies (2). All this implies that requiring $F(y) \leq G(y)$ for all y is not only necessary, but also sufficient to guarantee that (2) holds. In conclusion, F dominates G in the sense of FSD if and only if

$$F(x) \geq G(x) \quad \forall x. \tag{3}$$

Among other properties,[3] it is worth remembering that after an FSD deterioration the mathematical expectation of a random variable necessarily decreases while the converse is not necessarily true.

4.3.2 Second Order Stochastic Dominance (SSD)

Whereas this notion was already known in the statistical literature for a long time,[4] it became popular in the economics and finance literature after the publication of Hadar and Russell's paper (1969). Distribution F dominates distribution G in the sense of SSD if all risk-averse agents prefer F to G. This is less demanding than FSD, since SSD requires F to be preferred to G just for increasing and concave utility functions, not for all increasing functions.

Observe that the set of "min" functions—$u(x) = \min(x, y)$—are increasing and concave. Thus a necessary condition for SSD is obtained by requiring condition (2) to hold for such functions. It yields

$$\int^y xdF(x) + y(1 - F(y)) \geq \int^y xdG(x) + y(1 - G(y)),$$

or, integrating by parts,

$$\int^y F(x)dx \leq \int^y G(x)dx. \tag{4}$$

Notice that any increasing and concave function can be obtained by a convex combination of "min" functions. Thus, using the same argument as before, it is true that condition (4) is not only necessary, but is also sufficient for F to dominate G in the sense of SSD.

If F dominates G in the sense of SSD and if F and G have the same mean, then G is said to be an increase in risk (IR). Rothschild and Stiglitz (1970) showed that

[3] For an excellent survey on stochastic dominance, see H. Levy (1992).
[4] See Hardy, Littlewood and Polya (1929).

any increase in risk can be obtained either by adding noise to the initial random variable, or by a sequence of mean-preserving spreads (MPS) of probabilities. A noise is obtained by adding a zero-mean lottery to any outcome of the initial random variable. A MPS is obtained by taking some probability mass from the initial density and by transfering it to the tails in a way that preserves the mean.

Finally, notice that any SSD deterioration in risk can be obtained by the combination of a FSD deterioration combined with an increase in risk.

4.4 THE COMPARATIVE STATICS OF CHANGES IN THE CONTROLLABLE RISK

In this section, we assume that some information is obtained that allows agents to revise the distribution of $\tilde{x}$, but $\tilde{\varepsilon}$ remains unaffected. The literature devoted to this topic was mostly developed under the assumption that there is no background risk. Most often, this is without loss of generality. Indeed, for every increasing and concave u, define the indirect utility function v as follows:

$$v(z) = Eu(z + \tilde{\varepsilon}). \tag{5}$$

This allows us to rewrite the initial problem (1) as

$$\max_{\alpha} \; Ev(w_0 + \alpha\tilde{x}). \tag{6}$$

Observe now that $u^{[n]}$, i.e., the nth derivative of u, and $v^{[n]}$ have the same sign, for any integer n. In particular v is increasing and concave. As long as no restriction on the utility function other than those on the sign of some of its derivatives is imposed, (1)and (6) are qualitatively the same problems.

As mentioned above, stochastic orders have been defined on the basis of how changes in distribution affect the welfare of some well-defined set of agents in the economy. In this section, we examine the effect of a disliked change in the distribution of $\tilde{x}$ on the optimal exposure α^* to this risk. For a while many researchers naturally extended the results about the agent's welfare to his optimal degree of risk taking. It turns out however that such an extension may not be correct.

The first-order condition on α^* under distribution F is written as:

$$\int xu'(w_0 + \alpha^* x)dF(x) = 0. \tag{7}$$

Given the concavity of the objective function with respect to the decision variable, the change in risk from F to G reduces the optimal exposure to risk if

$$\int xu'(w_0 + \alpha^* x)dG(x) \leq 0. \tag{8}$$

It happens that F dominating G in the sense of FSD or SSD is neither necessary nor sufficient for α^* to be reduced, i.e., for condition (8) to be satisfied whenever (7) is satisfied. It is stricking that a FSD deterioration in risk $\tilde{x}$ or an increase in risk $\tilde{x}$ can induce some risk-averse agents to increase the size α^* of their exposure to it! As counter-examples, let us examine the standard utility function $u(z) = z^{1-\gamma}/(1-\gamma)$. Consider in particular the case of a constant relative risk aversion $\gamma = 3$, which is within the range of degrees of risk aversion observed in the real world. Finally, take $w_0 = 2$ and an initial distribution of $\tilde{x} = (-1, 0.1; +4, 0.9)$. In this case, one can compute $\alpha^* = 0.6305$.

Suppose now that $\tilde{x}$ undergoes a FSD-deterioration with a new distribution $(-1, 0.1; +2, 0.9)$. Contrary to the intuition, the agent reacts by increasing his exposure to $\alpha^* = 0.7015$! Alternatively, suppose that $\tilde{x}$ undergoes an increase in risk to the new distribution $(-1, 0.1; +3, 0.45, +5, 0.45)$. Again, it is a puzzle that the agent reacts to this increase in risk by increasing his exposure to $\alpha^* = 0.6328$.

From examples such as these, researchers tried to restrict the model in order to exclude the possibility of such puzzles. Two directions of research have been followed. One can either restrict preference functionals, or one can restrict the set of changes in risk. We hereafter examine these two lines of research separately.

4.4.1 Restrictions on the Utility Function

This line of research has been explored by Rothschild and Stiglitz (1971), Fishburn and Porter (1976), Cheng, Magill and Shafer (1987) and Hadar and Seo (1990). All their findings rely on the following observation. Define the function $\phi(x; w_0) = xu'(w_0 + \alpha^* x)$, where α^* is the optimal exposure under F. We hereafter normalize it to unity. Combining conditions (7) and (8), the change in risk reduces the optimal exposure α^* if

$$\int \phi(x; w_0)dF(x) \geq \int \phi(x; w_0)dG(x). \tag{9}$$

4.4.1.1 Conditions for FSD Shifts

Suppose first that F dominates G in the sense of FSD. Which condition is required on ϕ to guarantee that (9) holds? Comparing this condition to condition (2) directly provides the answer to this question: ϕ must be an increasing function. Because

$$\frac{\partial \phi}{\partial x}(x; w_0) = u'(w_0 + x) + xu''(w_0 + x),$$

ϕ is increasing if

$$A^r(w_0 + x) - w_0 A(w_0 + x) \leq 1 \quad \forall x, \tag{10}$$

where $A(z) = -u''(z)/u'(z)$ and $A^r(z) = zA(z)$ are respectively the absolute and the relative degree of risk aversion measured at z. In conclusion, an FSD deterioration in $\tilde{x}$ always reduces the optimal exposure to it if relative risk aversion is uniformly less than unity. If condition (10) is not satisfied for some x, it is always possible to build a counter-example, as we have done above.

4.4.1.2 *Conditions for Increases in Risk*

The same argument can be used for increases in risk, which require ϕ to be concave in x. After some computations, we get that the second derivative of ϕ with respect to x is negative if and only if

$$P^r(w_0 + x) - w_0 P(w_0 + x) \leq 2 \quad \forall x, \tag{11}$$

where $P(z) = -u'''(z)/u''(z)$ and $P^r(z) = zP(z)$ are respectively the absolute and the relative degree of prudence measured at z. In conclusion, an increase in risk $\tilde{x}$ always reduces the optimal exposure to it if relative prudence is positive and less than 2. Notice that we built the counter-example above on the basis of $P^r(z) = \gamma + 1 = 4$.

4.4.2 Restrictions on the Change in Risk

4.4.2.1 *First-order Stochastically Dominated Shifts*

In this section, we present some restrictions on FSD in order to guarantee that all risk-averse agents reduce their exposure after the shift in distribution.

A first step in this direction was made in a slightly different context by Milgrom (1981) and later on by Landsberger and Meilijson (1990) and Ormiston and Schlee (1993). We say that F dominates G in the sense of the Monotone Likelihood Ratio order (MLR) if, crudely said, $\psi(x) = G'(x)/F'(x)$ is decreasing.[5] It is easy to verify that MLR is a particular case of FSD. If F dominates G in the sense of MLR, we obtain that

$$\int xu'(w_0 + x)dG(x) = \int xu'(w_0 + x)\psi(x)dF(x) \leq \psi(0)\int xu'(w_0 + x)dF(x) = 0. \tag{12}$$

The inequality is due to the fact that $x\psi(x)$ is always less than $x\psi(0)$. The last equality is the first-order condition on $\alpha^* = 1$ under F. In consequence, a MLR-deterioration in risk reduces the optimal exposure to it for all risk-averse agents.

Since the FSD condition is already rather restrictive, the MLR property is even more so. Hence it is worth trying to extend the result we have just stated. First, observe that one can replace the monotonicity of ψ by a weaker single-crossing condition:

[5] See Athey (1997) and Gollier and Schlee (1997) for a more formal definition. MLR plays a crucial role in information theory, or in modern industrial economics. When there is no information whether a random variable is distributed as F or G, the MLR condition means that the larger the outcome x, the more likely the distribution F.

$\psi(x)$ must single-cross the horizontal line at $\psi(0)$ from above. This is indeed the only thing that has been used in the proof (12). This single-crossing condition is much weaker than MLR.

Second, Eeckhoudt and Gollier (1995a) considered the ratio of the cumulative distributions, that is $\frac{G(x)}{F(x)}$ and coined the term "monotone probability ratio" (MPR) when this expression is non decreasing in x. As one can guess:

$$MLR \Rightarrow MPR \Rightarrow FSD$$

MPR is weaker than MLR, but is still a subset of FSD. It can be shown that the same comparative statics property holds under MPR. Hence the MPR condition is clearly an improvement on the MLR one.

4.4.2.2 Increases in Risk

Eeckhoudt and Hansen (1980) obtained a restriction on an increase in risk that yields the desired comparative statics property. They defined the notion of a "squeeze" of a density. This notion has been extended by Meyer and Ormiston (1985) who defined a strong increase in risk (SIR). A SIR is obtained when some probability weight is taken from the initial density of $\tilde{x}$ and sent either at its boundaries or outside the initial support. Meyer and Ormiston showed that all risk-averse agents reduce their exposure to a risk that undergoes a SIR.

In two subsequent papers, Black and Bulkley (1989) and Dionne, Eeckhoudt and Gollier (1993) weakened the notion of a SIR. Contrary to a SIR, these restrictions allow for transfering probability masses inside the initial support of the distribution of $\tilde{x}$. However, to maintain the desired comparative statics result, they had to make assumptions about the behavior of the likelihood ratio between the initial and the final densities.

Another sufficient condition for an increase in risk to have an unambiguous effect on α^* is the notion of a simple increase in risk, introduced by Dionne and Gollier (1992). A simple increase in risk is an IR such that F single-crosses G at $x = 0$.

To conclude this quick review, let us mention that much of this research resulted from A. Sandmo's discussion (1971) of the impact of the "stretching" of a random variable. A stretching of $\tilde{x}$ is obtained from its linear transformation into $\tilde{y}$ with $\tilde{y} = t\tilde{x} + (1 - t)E(\tilde{x})$ and $t > 1$. This transformation is mean-preserving since $E(\tilde{y}) = E(\tilde{x})$. This intuitive notion was later on generalized by Meyer and Ormiston (1989) under the terminology of the "deterministic transformation" of a random variable. However to obtain intuitive comparative statics results with such transformation the assumption of decreasing absolute risk aversion is required.

All the papers dealing with special cases of either FSD or IR that we have surveyed so far share a common trend: one starts with rather restrictive sufficient conditions to yield the desired comparative statics result and then one progressively relaxes them. The endpoint of these successive improvements is given by a set of necessary and sufficient conditions that we now present.

4.4.2.3 *The Necessary and Sufficient Condition*

Gollier (1995)and Gollier (1997) proposed a reversal in the agenda of research. Rather than trying to restrict the existing stochastic orders in order to obtain an unambiguous comparative statics property, one should solve the following problem: what is the stochastic order such that all risk-averse agents reduce their exposure to the risk that undergoes such a change in distribution? He coined the term "Central Dominance" (CR) for it.

Rothschild and Stiglitz (1971) already tried to solve this question, but their solution was wrong. Their argument went as follows: under which condition can we guarantee that

$$\int xu'(w_0+x)dG(x) \leq \int xu'(w_0+x)dF(x) \tag{13}$$

for all increasing and concave utility functions? Using the basis approach developed earlier in this paper, the condition is that (replace u by any "min" function):

$$\int^{y} xdG(x) \leq \int^{y} xdF(x)$$

for all y. Contrary to the claim of Rothschild and Stiglitz (1971), this condition is sufficient, but not necessary for CR. Indeed, condition (13) is sufficient but not necessary for the comparative statics property. The correct necessary and sufficient condition is that the LHS of (13) be negative whenever the RHS is zero. Basing the analysis on this observation, Gollier (1995) obtained a correct characterization of CR, which is

$$\exists m \in R: \quad \forall y: \quad \int^{y} xdG(x) \leq m\int^{y} xdF(x) \tag{14}$$

All sufficient conditions mentioned above are particular cases of CR. Interestingly enough, strong and simple increases in risk satisfy condition (14) with $m = 1$, which was the condition proposed by Rothschild and Stiglitz (1971). But conditions like MLR, MPR and the weakenings of SIR by Black and Bukley (1987) and others satisfy the condition with $m \neq 1$. Besides, whereas we already know that SSD is not sufficient for CR (see the numerical counter-examples), it also appears that SSD is not necessary. That is, it can be the case that all risk-averse agents reduce their α^* after a change which is *not* a SSD.

4.5 THE COMPARATIVE STATICS OF BACKGROUND RISK

In the previous section, we explained why the presence of a background risk is unimportant to determine the *sign* of the impact of a change in the distribution of the controllable risk. However, the background risk has an impact on the optimal *value* of the exposure to $\tilde{x}$.

In this section, we do the comparative statics analysis that is symmetric to the one performed in the previous section. We take the distribution of $\tilde{x}$ as given and we perturbate the distribution of background risk $\tilde{\varepsilon}$. Up to now, the literature focused mostly on the effect of *introducing* a background risk in the analysis. One compares the solution to program (6) to the solution of

$$\max_{\alpha} Eu(w_0 + \alpha\tilde{x}).$$

Remember that, as shown by Pratt (1964), the necessary and sufficient condition for an unambiguous comparison, independent of w_0 and the distribution of $\tilde{x}$, is that v be more risk-averse than u. In this case, the introduction of a background risk reduces the optimal exposure to $\tilde{x}$. Thus, the problem simplifies to determining whether

$$-\frac{Eu''(z+\tilde{\varepsilon})}{Eu'(z+\tilde{\varepsilon})} \geq -\frac{u''(z)}{u'(z)} \tag{15}$$

for all z. If $\tilde{\varepsilon}$ is degenerated at a negative value, this condition is just decreasing absolute risk aversion (DARA). But it is logical to concentrate the analysis on the introduction of a *pure* background risk, viz. $E\tilde{\varepsilon} = 0$.

The intuition that the introduction of a pure background risk should reduce the optimal exposure to other independent risks corresponds to the common wisdom that independent risks are substitutes. This intuition requires additional restrictions to the model, as shown by the following counter-example. Take $u(z) = \min(z, 50 + 0.5z)$, $w_0 = 101$ and $\tilde{x} = (-1, 0.5; +1.9, 0.5)$. Without background risk, one can compute $\alpha^* = 1$. But if pure background risk $\tilde{\varepsilon} = (-20, 0.5; +20, 0.5)$ is added to wealth w_0, the agent increases his optimal exposure to $\alpha^* = 10.53$!

Several authors tried to find conditions on u that implies that a pure background risk reduces α^*. If $\tilde{\varepsilon}$ is small, one can use second-order Taylor expansions of the numerator and denominator of the LHS of (15) to check that

$$-\frac{Eu''(z+\tilde{\varepsilon})}{Eu'(z+\tilde{\varepsilon})} \cong A(z) + 0.5\sigma_{\tilde{\varepsilon}}^2[A''(z) - 2A'(z)A(z)]. \tag{16}$$

Thus, a necessary and sufficient condition for any pure small background risk to reduce the optimal exposure to other risks is:

$$A''(z) \geq 2A'(z)A(z) \quad \forall z. \tag{17}$$

Absolute risk aversion may not be too concave. But what is necessary and sufficient for small risk is just necessary if one wants the comparative statics property to hold for any risk. Gollier and Scarmure (1994) proved that a sufficient condition is that absolute risk aversion be decreasing and convex. The proof of this result is immediate. Indeed, let us define $h(t) = u'(z + t)/Eu'(z + \tilde{\varepsilon})$. It yields

$$
\begin{aligned}
-\frac{Eu''(z+\tilde{\varepsilon})}{Eu'(z+\tilde{\varepsilon})} &= Eh(\tilde{\varepsilon})A(z+\tilde{\varepsilon}) \\
&= EA(z+\tilde{\varepsilon}) + E(h(\tilde{\varepsilon})-1)A(z+\tilde{\varepsilon}) \\
&\geq A(z+E\tilde{\varepsilon}) + cov(h(\tilde{\varepsilon}), A(z+\tilde{\varepsilon})) \\
&\geq A(z).
\end{aligned} \tag{18}
$$

The first inequality is a direct application of Jensen's inequality, and $A'' > 0$. The second inequality comes from the fact that h and A are two decreasing functions of ε. This concludes the proof.

The convexity of absolute risk aversion is compatible with its positivity and its decrease. It is also an intuitive assumption as it means that the risk premium to any (small) risk decreases with wealth in a decreasing way. Observe that the familiar utility functions with constant relative risk aversion γ are such that $A(z) = \gamma/z$, so $A' < 0$ and $A'' > 0$. Thus, there is no ambiguity of the effect of background risk for this set of utility functions.

Eeckhoudt and Kimball (1992) and Kimball (1993) obtained an alternative sufficient condition that they called "standard risk aversion". Risk aversion is standard if absolute risk aversion A and absolute prudence P are both decreasing in wealth. Decreasing prudence means that the effect on savings of a risk on future incomes is decreasing with wealth.

Gollier and Pratt (1996) obtained the necessary and sufficient condition for a background risk with a non-positive mean to increase the aversion to other independent risks. They coined the term (background) "Risk Vulnerability". They used a technique of proof that has been systematized in Gollier and Kimball (1997) to solve other problems dealing with multiple risks.

Up to now, we examined the effect of introducing a background risk. Eeckhoudt, Gollier and Schlesinger (1996) considered the more general problem of the effect of increasing the background risk, in the sense of a FSD or IR shift in distribution. In the case of an increase in background risk, they showed that the restrictions to impose on u to obtain an unambiguous effect on α^* are much more demanding than risk vulnerability. Meyer and Meyer (1997) relaxed these conditions on u at the cost of restricting the changes in risk. For example, standard risk aversion is sufficient when limiting the analysis to the effect of a strong increase in background risk.

4.6 EXTENSIONS

Let us go back to the problem analyzed in section 4.4. Indeed, the effect of a change in the distribution of $\tilde{x}$ and the effect of introducing a pure background risk are not without any link. Suppose that there is no background risk, but rather that the increase in risk of $\tilde{x}$ takes the form of adding an *independent* pure white noise $\tilde{\varepsilon}$ to it. The derivative of the objective function with the new risk $\tilde{x} + \tilde{\varepsilon}$ evaluated at the initial optimal exposure (normalized to 1) is written as

$$\begin{aligned} E(\tilde{x}+\tilde{\varepsilon})u'(w_0+\tilde{x}+\tilde{\varepsilon}) &= E\tilde{x}u'(w_0+\tilde{x}+\tilde{\varepsilon})+E\tilde{\varepsilon}u'(w_0+\tilde{x}+\tilde{\varepsilon}) \\ &= E\tilde{x}v'(w_0+\tilde{x})+E\tilde{\varepsilon}u'(w_0+\tilde{x}+\tilde{\varepsilon}) \\ &\leq E\tilde{\varepsilon}u'(w_0+\tilde{x}+\tilde{\varepsilon}) \\ &\leq 0. \end{aligned} \tag{19}$$

The first inequality is obtained by using the fact that $\alpha^* = 1$ under the initial risk $\tilde{x}$, together with the fact that v is more concave than u under risk vulnerability. The second inequality is a direct consequence of the fact that $E(\tilde{\varepsilon})= 0$. We conclude that risk-vulnerable agents reduce their exposure to a risk that has been increased in the sense of adding a zero-mean independent white noise to it. This result is in Gollier and Schlesinger (1996).

Recent developments of this field of research have been made to extend the basic model (1) to more than one source of endogenous risk. Landsberger and Meilijson (1990), Meyer and Ormiston (1994) and Dionne and Gollier (1996) considered the two-risky-asset problem, which is written as:

$$\max_{\alpha} Eu(w_0+\alpha\tilde{x}_1+(1-\alpha)\tilde{x}_2).$$

These authors determined whether imposing MLR, SIR or other restrictions on the change in the conditional distribution of $\tilde{x}_1$ generates the same conclusion in this more general context. Notice that rewritting final wealth as $w_0 + \alpha(\tilde{x}_1 - \tilde{x}_2) + \tilde{x}_2$ suggests that this problem is similar to the initial one, with a controllable risk $(\tilde{x}_1 - \tilde{x}_2)$, and a "background" risk $\tilde{x}_2$. But the two risks are here correlated.

Another line of research is related to the management of multiple endogenous risks, a problem which can be formulated as follows:

$$\max_{\alpha_1,\ldots,\alpha_n} Eu\left(w_0+\sum_{i=1}^{n}\alpha_i\tilde{x}_i\right).$$

Dionne and Gagnon (1996) focused on the case $n = 2$, which corresponds to the management of a portfolio with two risky assets and one riskfree asset. Eeckhoudt, Gollier and Levasseur (1994) examined the case where the $\tilde{x}_i$ are i.i.d., in which case all α_i^* are the same. They addressed the question of how α^* is affected by an increase in n. As an application, we have the optimal strategy of an agent who has to insure a fleet of vehicule. Gollier, Lindsey and Zeckhauser (1997) showed that an increase in n reduces α^* if relative risk aversion is constant and less than unity.

4.7 CONCLUSION

Stochastic dominance orders have been defined to determine the effect of a change in risk on the welfare of some category of economic agents. It is now apparent that these concepts are not well suited to perform comparative statics analyses. As an example, an increase in risk à la Rothschild-Stiglitz on the return of a risky asset may induce some risk-averse agents to increase their demand for it. Also, an increase in background risk à la Rothschild-Stiglitz may induce some risk-averse agents to raise their demand for another independent risk. In this paper, we summarize the main findings that allow to solve these paradoxes. We tried to convince the reader that most restrictions to preferences or to stochastic orders make sense even if some are rather technical.

We examined a simple model with a single source of endogenous risk, plus a background risk. We separately considered the case of a change in the distribution of the endogenous risk, and the case of a change in background risk. The current trends in this field is for the analysis of multiple risk taking situations, in which these two analyses are often combined to produce new results. Much progress must be still done on our understanding of the interaction between risks, but we now have the relevant tools and concepts to perform this work efficiently.

4.8 REFERENCES

Alarie, Y., G. Dionne and L. Eeckhoudt (1992). "Increases in Risk and the Demand for Insurance," in *Contributions to Insurance Economics*, Dionne Georges, ed., Kluwer Academic Press, Boston.

Athey, S. (1997). "Comparative Statics Under Uncertainty: Single Crossing Properties and Log-supermodularity," *mimeo*, MIT.

Black, J. and G. Bulkley (1989). "A Ratio Criterion for Signing the Effects of an Increase in Uncertainty," *International Economic Review*, 30, 119–130.

Cheng, H.C., M. Magill and W. Shafer (1987). "Some Results on Comparative Statics under Uncertainty," *International Economic Review*, 28, 493–507.

Dionne, G., L. Eeckhoudt and C. Gollier (1993). "Increases in Risk and Linear Payoffs," *International Economic Review*, 34, 309–319.

Dionne, G. and F. Gagnon (1996). "Increases in Risk and Optimal Portfolio," *mimeo*, Université de Montréal.

Dionne, G. and C. Gollier (1992). "Comparative Statics under Multiple Sources of Risk with Applications to Insurance Demand," *The Geneva Papers on Risk and Insurance Theory*, 17, 21–33.

Dionne, G. and C. Gollier (1996). "A Model of Comparative Statics for Changes in Stochastic Returns with Dependent Risky Assets," *Journal of Risk and Uncertainty*, 13, 147–162.

Doherty, N. and H. Schlesinger (1983). "Optimal Insurance in Incomplete Markets," *Journal of Political Economy*, 91, 1045–1054.

Eecckhoudt, L. and M.S. Kimball (1992). "Background Risk, Prudence, and the Demand for Insurance," in *Contributions to Insurance Economics*, Dionne Georges, ed., Kluwer Academic Press, Boston.

Eeckhoudt, L., C. Gollier and M. Levasseur (1994). "The Economics of Adding and Subdividing Independent Risks: Some Comparative Statics Results," *Journal of Risk and Uncertainty*, 8, 325–337.

Eeckhoudt, L. and C. Gollier (1995). *Risk: Evaluation, Management and Sharing*, Hearvester Wheatsheaf, 347 pages.

Fishburn, P. and B. Porter (1976). "Optimal Portfolios with One Safe and One Risky Asset: Effects of Changes in Rate of Return and Risk," *Mangement Science*, 22, 1064–1073.

Gollier, C. (1995). "The Comparative Statics of Changes in Risk Revisited," *Journal of Economic Theory*, 66, 522–536.

Gollier, C. (1997). "A Note on Portfolio Dominance," *Review of Economic Studies*, 64, 147–150.

Gollier, C. and M.S. Kimball (1997). "Toward a systematic approach to the economic effects of uncertainty: Characterizing untility functions," *Discussion paper*, U. of Michigan.

Gollier, C., J. Lindsey and R.J. Zeckhauser (1997). "Investment Flexibility and the Acceptance of Risk," *Journal of Economic Theory*, forthcoming.

Gollier, C. and J.W. Pratt (1996). "Risk Vulnerability and the Tempering Effect of Background Risk," *Econometrica*, 64, 1109–1123.

Gollier, C. and P. Scarmure (1994). "The Spillover Effect of Compulsory Insurance, The Geneva Papers on Risk and Insurance Theory," 19, 23–34.

Gollier, C. and E.E. Schlee (1997). "Increased Risk Taking with Multiple Risks," *mimeo*, University of Toulouse.

Gollier, C. and H. Schlesinger (1996). "Portfolio Choice Under Noisy Asset Returns," *Economics Letters*, 53, 47–51.

Hadar, J. and W. Russell (1969). "Rules for Ordering Uncertain Prospects," *American Economic Review*, 59, 25–34.

Hadar, J. and T.K. Seo (1990). "The Effects of Shifts in a Return Distribution on Optimal Portfolios," *International Economic Review*, 31, 721–736.

Hardy, G.H., J.E. Littlewood and G. Polya (1929). "Some Simple Inequalities Satisfied by Convex Functions," *Messenger of Mathematics*, 58, 145–152.

Kihlstrom, R., D. Romer and S. Williams (1981). "Risk Aversion with Random Initial Wealth," *Econometrica*, 49, 911–920.

Landsberger, M. and I. Meilijson (1990). "Demand for Risky Financial Assets: A Portfolio Analysis," *Journal of Economic Theory*, 12, 380–391.

Levy, H. (1992). "Stochastic Dominance and Expected Utility: Survey and Analysis," *Management Sciences*, 38, 555–593.

Meyer, D.J. and J. Meyer (1998). "Changes in Background Risk and the Demand for Insurance," *The Geneva Papers on Risk and Insurance Theory*, 23, 29–40.

Meyer, J. and M. Ormiston (1985). "Strong Increases in Risk and their Comparative Statics," *International Economic Review*, 26, 425–437.

Meyer, J. and M. Ormiston (1989). "Deterministic Tranformation of Random Variables and the Comparative Statics of Risk," *Journal of Risk and Uncertainty*, 2, 179–188.

Milgrom, P. (1981). "Good News and Bad News: Representation Theorems and Application," *Bell Journal of Economics*, 12, 380–391.

Ormistion, M.B. and E.E. Schlee (1993). "Comparative Statics under Uncertainty for a Class of Economic Agents," *Journal of Economic Theory*, 61, 412–422.

Pratt, J. (1964). "Risk Aversion in the Small and in the Large," *Econometrica*, 32, 122–136.

Rothschild, M. and J. Stiglitz (1970). "Increasing Risk: I. A Definition," *Journal of Economic Theory*, 2, 225–243.

Rothschild, M. and J. Stiglitz (1971). "Increasing Risk: II Its Economic Consequences," *Journal of Economic Theory*, 3, 66–84.

Sandmo, A. (1971). "On the Theory of the Competitive Firm Under Price Uncertainty," *American Economic Review*, 61, 65–73.

5 The Theory of Insurance Demand

Harris Schlesinger

University of Alabama

Abstract
This chapter presents the basic theoretical models of insurance demand in a one-period expected-utility setting. Models of coinsurance and of deductible insurance are examined along with their comparative statics with respect to changes in wealth, prices and attitudes towards risk. The similarities and difference between market insurance, self-insurance and self-protection are also presented. The basic models are then extended to account for default risk and for background risk.

Keywords: Insurance, risk aversion, deductibles, self-insurance, self-protection, default risk, background risk.
JEL Classification Numbers: D81, G22.

5.1 INTRODUCTION

The theory of insurance demand is often regarded as the purest example of economic behavior under uncertainty. Interestingly, whereas a decade ago most upper-level textbooks on microeconomics barely touched on the topic of uncertainty, much less insurance demand, textbooks today often devote substantial space to the topic. The purpose of this chapter is to present the basic model of insurance demand, that imbeds itself not only into the other papers in this volume and in the insurance literature, but also in many other settings within the finance and economics literatures. Since models that deal with nonexpected utility analysis are dealt with elsewhere in this volume, I focus only on the expected-utility framework.

If we were to view insurance as simply a case of optimal risk sharing, we would be led to a simple sharing rule due to Karl Borch (1962). However, for many reasons, not the least of which is the sheer size of the economy, such ideal risk sharing rarely seems to take place. Indeed, even Borch himself had to move from the level of the

* The author thanks Henri Loubergé, Ray Rees, his Insurance Economics class at the University of Konstanz, and an anonymous referee for helpful comments on a draft of this chapter. Remaining errors are an example of a market for which there is no insurance.

individual, past the level of the insurance company, and to the level of reinsurance in expositing his classic result. In this sense, we can view insurance as an intermediary. Although contingent contracts that allow for mutual risk sharing would be first best, such contracts are not feasible. We thus see insurers in the economy, who approximate the process by gathering and pooling the risks of a large number of individuals.

The device offered by the insurer is one in which, for a fixed premium, the insurer offers an indemnity for incurred losses. Of course, there are many variations on this theme, as one can see from gleaning the pages of this volume. From a purely theoretical viewpoint, the model presented in section 5.2 of this chapter should be viewed as a base model, from which all other models deviate.

In some ways, insurance is simply a financial asset. However, whereas most financial assets are readily tradable and have a risk that relates to the marketplace, insurance is a contract contingent on an individual's own personal wealth changes. This personal nature of insurance is what distinguishes it from other financial assets. It also exacerbates problems of informational asymmetry, such as moral hazard and adverse selection, which also are dealt with elsewhere in this volume.

The preponderance of insurance models isolate the insurance-purchasing decision. The consumer decides how much insurance to buy for a well-defined risk. And indeed, this chapter starts out the same way in section 5.2. However, when multiple risks face the consumer, it is not likely to be optimal to decide how to handle each risk separately. Rather, some type of overall risk-management strategy is called for. Even if we make an insurance decision in isolation, the presence of these other risks is most likely going to affect our choice. The second part of this chapter (Section 5.3) shows how the presence of other risks—so-called "background risk"—impacts the consumer's insurance-purchasing decision.

5.2 THE SINGLE RISK MODEL

Insurance contracts themselves can be quite complicated, but the basic idea is fairly simple. For a fixed premium P the insurer will pay the insured a contingent amount of money, that depends upon the value of a well-defined loss. This insurance payment is referred to as the *indemnity*.

To make the model concrete, consider an individual with initial wealth $W > 0$. Let the random variable $\tilde{x}$ denote the amount of the loss, where $0 \leq x \leq W$. The insurance indemnity is contingent only on x and will be written as $I(x)$. We often assume that $I(x)$ is nondecreasing in x and that $0 \leq I(x) \leq x$, though neither of these assumptions is necessary to develop a theory of insurance demand. We do, however, assume that the realization of $\tilde{x}$ is costlessly observable by all parties and that both parties agree on the distribution of the random variable $\tilde{x}$. Models that do not make these last two assumptions are dealt with elsewhere in this volume.

The insurer, for our purpose, can be considered as a risk-neutral firm that charges a market-determined price for its product. The individual is considered to be risk averse with von Neumann-Morgenstern utility of final wealth given by the function $u(\cdot)$, where u is assumed to be everywhere twice differentiable with $u' > 0$ and $u'' < 0$. The assumption of differentiability is not innocuous. It is tantamount in our model to assuming that risk aversion is everywhere of order 2.[1]

5.2.1 Proportional Coinsurance

The simplest type of indemnity payment is one in which the insurer pays a fixed proportion, say α, of the loss. Thus, $I(x) = \alpha x$. This type of insurance indemnity is often referred to as *coinsurance*, since the individual retains (or "coinsures") a fraction $1 - \alpha$ of the loss. If $\alpha = 1$, the insurer pays an indemnity equal to the full value of the loss and the individual is said to have *full insurance.*

An assumption that $0 \leq I(x) \leq x$ here is equivalent to assuming that $0 \leq \alpha \leq 1$. The case where $\alpha > 1$ is often referred to as *over insurance*. The case where $\alpha < 0$ is referred to by some as "selling insurance," but this description is incorrect. If $\alpha < 0$, the individual is taking a short position in his or her *own* loss; whereas selling insurance is taking a short position in someone else's loss.

To consider the insurance-purchasing decision, we need to specify the insurance premium as a function of the indemnity. The most general form of the premium is

$$P[I(\cdot)] = E[I(\tilde{x}) + c[I(\tilde{x})]]. \qquad (1)$$

Here E denotes the expectation operator and $c(\cdot)$ is a cost function, where $c[I(x)]$ denotes the cost of paying indemnity $I(x)$, including any market-based charges for assuming the risk $I(\tilde{x})$. Note that P itself is a *functional*, since it depends upon the function $I(\cdot)$.

As a base case, we often consider $c[I(x)] = 0\ \forall x$. This case is usually referred to as the case of *perfect competition* in the insurance market, since it implies that insurers receive an expected profit of zero, and the premium is referred to as a *fair premium.*[2]

The premium, as defined in (1), is a bit too general to suit our purpose here. See Gollier (2000) for more discussion of this general premium form. We consider here

[1] See Segal and Spivak (1990). Although extensions to the case where u is not everywhere differentiable are not difficult, they are not examined here. See Schlesinger (1997) for some basic results.

[2] Obviously real-world costs include more than just the indemnity itself, plus even competitive insurers earn a "normal return" on their risk. Thus, we do not really expect $c[I(x)] = 0$. However, real-world markets also allow for the insurer to invest premium income, which is omitted here, so that zero-costs might not be a bad approximation for our purpose of developing a simple model. The terminology "fair premium" is taken from the uncertainty literature, since such a premium in return for the random payoff $I(\tilde{x})$ represents a "fair bet" for the insurer.

the simplest case of (1) in which the expected cost is proportional to the expected indemnity; in particular

$$P(\alpha) = E(\alpha\tilde{x} + \lambda\alpha\tilde{x}) = \alpha(1+\lambda)E\tilde{x}, \tag{2}$$

where λ is called the *loading factor*, $\lambda \geq 0$. The individual's final wealth can then be expressed as a random variable, dependent upon the choice of α,

$$\tilde{Y}(\alpha) \equiv W - \alpha(1+\lambda)E\tilde{x} - \tilde{x} + \alpha\tilde{x}. \tag{3}$$

The individual's objective is choose α so as to maximize his or her expected utility

$$\max_{\alpha}\text{imize}\, E[u(\tilde{Y}(\alpha))], \tag{4}$$

where we might or might not wish to impose the constraint that $0 \leq \alpha \leq 1$.

Solving (4) is relatively straightforward, yielding a first-order condition for the unconstrained objective

$$\frac{dEu}{d\alpha} = E[u'(\tilde{Y}(\alpha)) \cdot (\tilde{x} - (1+\lambda)E\tilde{x})] = 0. \tag{5}$$

The second-order condition for a maximum holds trivially from our assumption that $u'' < 0$. Indeed, $d^2Eu/d\alpha^2$ is negative everywhere, indicating that any α^* satisfying (5) will be a global maximum. The fact that $E[u(\tilde{Y}(\alpha))]$ is globally concave in α also turns out to be key in later examining various comparative statics.

Evaluating $dEu/d\alpha$ at $\alpha = 1$ shows that

$$\left.\frac{dEu}{da}\right|_{\alpha=1} = -\lambda Eu'(\tilde{Y}(1)) \cdot E\tilde{x} + Cov(u'(\tilde{Y}(1)), \tilde{x}) = -\lambda Eu'(\tilde{Y}(1)) \cdot E\tilde{x} + 0, \tag{6}$$

where $Cov(\cdot,\cdot)$ denotes the covariance operator. Consequently, the sign of (6) will be zero if $\lambda = 0$ and will be negative if $\lambda > 0$. Together with the concavity of $Eu(\tilde{Y}(\alpha))$ in α, this implies the following result, usually referred to as *Mossin's Theorem*:[3]

Theorem. If proportional insurance is available at a fair price ($\lambda = 0$), then full coverage ($\alpha^* = 1$) is optimal. If the price of insurance includes a positive premium loading ($\lambda > 0$), then partial insurance ($\alpha^* < 1$) is optimal.

[3] The result is often attributed to Mossin (1968), with a similar analysis also appearing in Smith (1968).

Note that Mossin's Theorem does not preclude a possibility that $\alpha^* \leq 0$ in the unconstrained case. Indeed, evaluating $dEu/d\alpha$ at $\alpha = 0$ when $\lambda > 0$, yields

$$\left.\frac{dEu}{d\alpha}\right|_{\alpha=0} = -\lambda Eu'(\tilde{Y}(0)) \cdot E\tilde{x} + Cov(u'(\tilde{Y}(0)), \tilde{x}). \tag{7}$$

Since the covariance term in (7) is positive and does not depend on λ, we note that there will exist a unique value of λ such that the derivative in (7) equals zero. At this value of λ, zero coverage is optimal, $\alpha^* = 0$. For higher values of λ, $\alpha^* < 0$. Since $Eu(\tilde{Y}(\alpha))$ is concave in α, $\alpha = 0$ will be a constrained optimum whenever the unconstrained optimum is negative. In other words, if the price of insurance is too high, the individual will not purchase any insurance.

As long as the premium loading is nonnegative, $\lambda \geq 0$, the optimal level of insurance will be no more than full coverage, $\alpha^* \leq 1$. If, however, we allow for a negative premium loading, $\lambda < 0$, such as might be the case when the government subsidizes a particular insurance market, then over insurance, $\alpha^* > 1$, will indeed be optimal in the case where α is unconstrained. Strict concavity of $Eu(\tilde{Y}(\alpha))$ in α once again implies that full insurance, $\alpha = 1$, will be a constrained optimum for this case, when over insurance is not allowed.

It may be instructive for some readers to compare the above results with the so-called *portfolio problem* in financial economics. The standard portfolio problem has an investor allocate her wealth between a risky and a riskless asset. If we let A denote final wealth when all funds are invested in a riskless asset, and let $\tilde{z}$ denote the random excess payoff above the payoff on the riskless asset, the individual must choose a weight β, such that final wealth is

$$Y(\beta) = (1-\beta)A + \beta(A+\tilde{z}) = A + \beta\tilde{z}. \tag{8}$$

A basic result in the portfolio problem is that sgn β^* = sgn $E\tilde{z}$. If we set $A \equiv W - (1 + \lambda)E\tilde{x}$, $\tilde{z} \equiv (1 + \lambda)E\tilde{x} - \tilde{x}$, and $\beta = (1 - \alpha)$, then (8) is equivalent to (3). Noting that sgn $E\tilde{z}$ = sgn λ in this setting, our basic portfolio result is exactly equivalent to Mossin's Theorem. Using equation (8), we can think of the individual starting from a position of full insurance ($\beta = 0$) and then deciding upon the optimal level to coinsure, β^*. If $\lambda > 0$, then coinsurance has a positive expected return, so that any risk averter would choose $\beta^* > 0$ (i.e., $\alpha^* < 1$).

5.2.2 Effects of Changes in Wealth and Price

In the general case, it is often difficult to define what is meant by the *price* and the *quantity* of insurance. Since the indemnity is a function of a random variable and since the premium is a functional of this indemnity function, both price and quantity—the two fundamental building blocks of economic theory—have no direct counterparts for insurance. However, for the case of coinsurance, we have the level of coinsurance α and the premium loading factor λ, which fill in nicely as proxy measures of quantity and price respectively.

If the individual's initial wealth changes, but the loss exposure remains the same, will more or less insurance be purchased? In other words, is insurance a "normal" or an "inferior" good? Clearly, if $\lambda = 0$, then Mossin's Theorem implies that full insurance remains optimal. So let us consider the case where $\lambda > 0$, but assume that λ is not too large, so that $0 < \alpha^* < 1$. Since $Eu(\tilde{Y}(\alpha))$ is concave in α, we can determine the effect of a higher W by differentiating the first-order condition (5) with respect to W. Before doing this however, let us recall a few items from the theory of risk aversion.

If the Arrow-Pratt measure of local risk aversion, $r(y) = -u''(y)/u'(y)$, is decreasing in wealth level y, then preferences are said to exhibit decreasing absolute risk aversion (DARA). Similarly, we can define constant absolute risk aversion (CARA) and increasing absolute risk aversion (IARA). We are now ready to state the following result.

Proposition 1. Let the insurance loading λ be positive. Then for an increase in the initial wealth level W,

(i) the optimal insurance level α^* will decrease under DARA,
(ii) the optimal insurance level α^* will be invariant under CARA,
(iii) the optimal insurance level α^* will increase under IARA.

Proof. Let F denote the distribution of $\tilde{x}$. By assumption, the support of F lies in the interval $[0, W]$. Define $x_0 \equiv (1 + \lambda)E\tilde{x}$. Assume DARA. Then we note that $r(y_1) < r(y_0) < r(y_2)$ for any $y_1 > y_0 > y_2$, and, in particular for $y_0 = W - \alpha^*(1 + \lambda)E\tilde{x} - x_0 + \alpha x_0$. Now

$$
\begin{aligned}
\left.\frac{\partial^2 Eu}{\partial\alpha\partial W}\right|_{\alpha^*} &= \int_0^W u''(Y(\alpha^*))(x-(1+\lambda)E\tilde{x})dF \\
&= -\int_0^{x_0} r(Y(\alpha^*))u'(Y(\alpha^*))(x-(1+\lambda)E\tilde{x})dF - \\
&\quad \int_{x_0}^W r(Y(\alpha^*))u'(Y(\alpha^*))(x-(1+\lambda)E\tilde{x})dF \\
&< -r(y_0)\left[\int_0^W u'(Y(\alpha^*))(x-(1+\lambda)E\tilde{x})dF = 0\right].
\end{aligned} \tag{9}
$$

Thus increasing wealth causes α^* to fall.

The cases where preferences exhibit CARA or IARA can be proved in a similar manner. ■

We should caution the reader that DARA, CARA and IARA do not partition the set of risk-averse preferences. Indeed each of these conditions is shown to be sufficient for the comparative-static effects in Proposition, though none is necessary.

The case of CARA is often used as a base case, since such preferences eliminate any income effect. However, a more common and, by most standards, realistic assumption is DARA, which implies that insurance is an inferior good. One must use caution in using this interpretation however. It is valid only for the case of a fixed loss exposure $\tilde{x}$. Since real-world loss exposures typically increase as wealth increases, we do not necessarily expect to see richer individuals spending less on their insurance purchases, *ceteris paribus*.[4] We do, however, expect that they would spend less on the same loss exposure.

In a similar manner, we can examine the effect of an increase in the loading factor λ on the optimal level of insurance coverage. Differentiating the first-order condition with respect to λ obtains

$$\left.\frac{\partial^2 Eu}{\partial\alpha\partial\lambda}\right|_{\alpha^*} = -[E\tilde{x}Eu'(\tilde{Y}(\alpha^*))] - \alpha E\tilde{x}\frac{\partial^2 Eu}{\partial\alpha\partial W}. \tag{10}$$

The first term on the right-hand side of equation (10) captures the substitution effect of an increase in λ. This effect is negative due to the higher price of insurance. The second term on the right-hand side of (10) captures an income effect, since a higher premium would lower overall wealth, *ceteris paribus*. For a positive level of α, which we are assuming, this effect will be the opposite sign of $\partial^2 Eu/\partial\alpha\partial W$. For example, under DARA, this income effect is positive: the price increase lowers the average wealth of the individual, rendering him or her more risk averse. This higher level of risk aversion, as we shall soon see, implies that the individual will purchase more insurance. If this second (positive) effect outweighs the negative substitution effect, insurance can be considered a Giffen good.[5] More comprehensively, the following result is a direct consequence of equation (10) and Proposition 1.

Proposition 2. Let the insurance loading be positive, with $0 < \alpha^* < 1$. Then, insurance cannot be a Giffen good if preferences exhibit CARA or IARA, but may be Giffen if preferences exhibit DARA.

5.2.3 Changes in Risk and in Risk Aversion

If the loss distribution F changes, it is sometimes possible to predict the change in optimal insurance coverage α^*. Conditions on changes to F that are both necessary

[4] If the support of $\tilde{x}$ is $[0, L]$, it may be useful to define $W \equiv W_0 + L$. If the loss exposure is unchanged, an increase in W can be viewed as an increase in W_0. More realistically, an increase in W will consist of increases in both W_0 and L.

[5] A necessary and sufficient condition for insurance not to be Giffen is given by Briys, Dionne and Eeckhoudt (1989).

and sufficient for α^* to increase are not trivial, but can be found by applying a Theorem of Gollier (1995) to the portfolio problem, and then using the equivalence of the portfolio problem and the insurance problem. Although this condition is very complex, there are several sufficient conditions for α^* to rise due to a change in risk that are relatively straightforward. Since this topic is dealt with elsewhere in this volume (Eeckhoudt and Gollier, 2000), I do not detour to discuss it any further here.

A change in risk aversion, on the other hand, has a well-defined effect upon the choice of insurance coverage. First of all, we note that for an insurance premium that is fair, $\lambda = 0$, any risk-averse individual will choose an insurance policy with full coverage, $\alpha^* = 1$. If, however, insurance premia include a positive premium loading, $\lambda > 0$, then an increase in risk aversion will always increase the level of insurance. More formally,

Proposition 3. Let the insurance loading be positive, with $0 < \alpha^* < 1$. An increase in the individual's degree of risk aversion at all levels of wealth will lead to an increase in the optimal level of coverage, ceteris paribus.

Proof. Let α_u^* denote the optimal level of coverage under the original utility function u. Let v denote a uniformly more risk-averse utility function. We know from Pratt (1964), that there exists a function g:[Image u] $\rightarrow \Re$ such that $v(y) = g[u(y)]$, where $g' > 0$ and $g'' < 0$.

Since v is a risk-averse utility function, we note that $Ev(\tilde{Y}(\alpha))$ is concave in α. Thus, consider the following:

$$\left.\frac{dEv}{d\alpha}\right|_{\alpha_u^*} = \left.\frac{dEg[u]}{d\alpha}\right|_{\alpha_u^*} = \int_0^W g'[u(Y(\alpha_u^*))]u'(Y(\alpha_u^*))(x-(1+\lambda)E\tilde{x})dF$$
$$> g'[u(y_0)]\left\{\int_0^{x0} u'(Y(\alpha_u^*))(x-(1+\lambda)E\tilde{x})dF + \int_{x0}^W u'(Y(\alpha_u^*))(x-(1+\lambda)E\tilde{x})dF\right\} = 0 \tag{11}$$

where x_0 and y_0 are as defined in the proof of Proposition 1, and where the inequality follows from the concavity of g. This last expression equals zero by the first-order condition for α_u^*.

Since $Ev(Y(\alpha))$ is concave in α, the inequality in (11) implies that $\alpha_v^* > \alpha_u^*$.

5.2.4 Self-Insurance and Self-Protection

It is useful, at this point, to distinguish insurance from two other types of protection against loss. These alternatives were first examined in a classic article by Ehrlich and Becker (1972) and represent engineering-types of alternatives. That is, while insurance, which Ehrlich and Becker distinguish under the label "market insurance," offers third-party indemnification for losses that occur, these alternatives actually change the frequency and/or severity of the loss distribution. In particular, self-insurance lowers the financial severity of any loss that occurs, whereas self-protection reduces the likelihood that a loss occurs.[6] An example of self-insurance might be the installation a sprinkler system to protect against fire damages. An example of self-protection might be the installation of dead-bolt locks at home to keep potential thieves from entering.

In reality, the distinction between self-insurance and self-protection is often blurred. Indeed even in the above examples, the sprinkler might extinguish a fire in a waste basket, essentially lowering the chance of any loss occurring. Likewise, the dead-bolt lock might only take away from some of the thief's time spent in your house, thus lowering the level of damages. The point is that most investment to control losses simultaneously contains some degree of both self-insurance and self-protection. Moreover, changes in a loss distribution are not typically decomposable into self-insurance and self-protection types of changes.[7]

One way to view self-insurance in the general case is to redefine the "indemnity function" $I(x)$ as the deterministic reduction of the loss, which would have been of size x without self-insurance.[8] Thus, a loss that would have been x is now reduced to the amount $x - I(x)$. Instead of a "premium" $P[I(\cdot)]$, we can view P as the cost for achieving the loss-reduction schedule $I(\cdot)$. In this setting, it is not surprising that self-insurance and market insurance are substitutes, which was proven formally by Ehrlich and Becker for the simple case where there are only two states of nature: loss and no-loss, where the loss size without self-insurance is fixed.

Similarly, one way to view self-protection is to define the random variable $\tilde{L}$ as the size of a loss, conditional on the occurrence of a loss. We then let p denote the probability of a loss occurring. The loss amount $\tilde{x}$ thus has a distribution that contains an atom at zero. In particular, no loss occurs with probability $(l - p)$, and with probability p the consumer experiences a loss of random size L. To introduce self-protection, let c denote the level of investment in this type of activity. We assume that the loss probability is affected with $p \equiv p(c)$, where $p(\cdot)$ is a decreasing function. Final wealth can thus be viewed as a compound lottery. With probability $l - p(c)$ the level of wealth is $W - c$, and with probability $p(c)$ final wealth is $W - c - \tilde{L}$, where the distribution of loss severity L is assumed to be unaffected by c.

Whereas an investment in market insurance or in self-insurance will increase wealth in the "bad" states of nature at a cost of reduced wealth in the good states, the same cannot be said of self-protection. By increasing the expenditure on

[6] This terminology is still standard in the economics literature. These two activities are typically referred to as "loss reduction" and "loss prevention" respectively in the insurance literature.

[7] Ehrlich and Becker (1972) perform only a sketchy analysis of continuous loss distributions, and they provide no clear definitions of self-insurance and self-protection except for the simple two-state framework.

[8] If the reduction in loss size is stochastic, rather than deterministic, the analysis becomes much more complex.

self-protection c, final wealth is lower in every state of nature. However, self-protection alters the probabilities so that the best state of nature (no loss) is more likely. Given their very different structures, it is not surprising that self-protection is not generally a substitute for market insurance or self-insurance, and may indeed be a complement.[9]

If we turn our attention to the effects of risk aversion on the purchase of self-insurance, it is not surprising that self-insurance behaves much like market insurance. Under reasonable cost conditions, investment in self-insurance increases with higher levels of risk aversion. The same is not true for self-protection. Indeed, since self-protection lowers wealth in *all* states of nature, including the state with the highest loss, a more risk averse individual might optimally invest *less* in self-protection, in order to improve the worst possible wealth level.[10]

5.2.5 Deductible Insurance

Although proportional coinsurance is the simplest case of insurance demand to model, real-world insurance contracts often include fixed co-payments per loss or deductibles. Indeed, optimal contracts include deductibles under fairly broad assumptions, and under fairly simple but realistic pricing assumptions, straight deductible policies can be shown to be optimal.[11] In this section, we examine a few aspects of insurance demand when insurance is of the deductible type.

For deductible insurance, the indemnity is set equal to the excess of the loss over some predetermined level. Let L denote the supremum of the support of the loss distribution, so that L denotes the maximum possible loss. By assumption, we have $L \leq W$. Define the deductible level $D \in [0, L]$ such that $I(x) \equiv \max(0, x - D)$. If $D = 0$, the individual once again has full coverage, whereas $D = L$ now represents zero coverage. One complication that arises, is that the general premium, as given by equation (1), can no longer be written as a function of only the mean of the loss distribution, as in (2). Also, it is difficult to find a standard proxy for the *quantity* of insurance in the case of deductibles.[12]

In order to keep the model from becoming overly complex, we assume here that the distribution F is continuous, with density function f, so that $dF(x) = f(x)dx$. We will once again assume that the insurance costs are proportional to the expected indemnity, so that the premium for deductible level D is given by

[9] Ehrlich and Becker (1972) derive complementarily in a model with two states of nature, under certain cost conditions.

[10] Dionne and Eeckhoudt (1985) show these risk-aversion effects for the two-state model. Briys and Schlesinger (1990) extend this analysis by analyzing the effects of self-insurance and self-protection on the riskiness of final wealth. Sweeney and Beard (1992), show that there do not exist any conditions in an expected-utility framework that would lead to an individual always investing weak more in self-protection. See also the recent contributions of Jullien et al. (1999) and Dachraoui et al. (1999).

[11] See the essay by Gollier (2000) in this volume for a detailed analysis of the optimality of deductibles.

[12] Meyer and Ormiston (1998) make a strong case for using $E[I(\tilde{x})]$, although it is often much simpler to use D as an inverse proxy for insurance demand.

$$P(D) = (1+\lambda)E[I(\tilde{x})] = (1+\lambda)\int_D^L (x - D)dF(x) - (1+\lambda)\int_D^L [1 - F(x)]dx, \tag{12}$$

where the last equality is obtained via integration by parts.

Using Leibniz Rule, one can calculate the marginal premium reduction for increasing the deductible level,[13]

$$P'(D) = -(1+\lambda)(1 - F(D)). \tag{13}$$

By increasing the deductible level, say by an amount ΔD, the individual receives a lower payout in all states of the world for which the loss exceeds the deductible. The likelihood of these states is $1 - F(D)$. While it is true that the likelihood will also change as D changes, this effect is of secondary importance and, due to our assumption of a continuous loss distribution, disappears in the limit.

Following the choice of a deductible level D and using the premium as specified in (12), final wealth can be written as

$$\tilde{Y}(D) = W - P(D) - \min(\tilde{x}, D). \tag{14}$$

The individual's objective is now to choose the best deductible,

$$\underset{D}{\text{maximize}}\, E[u(\tilde{Y}(D))], \quad \text{where } 0 \le D \le L. \tag{15}$$

Assume that the premium loading is nonnegative, $\lambda \ge 0$, but not so large that we obtain zero coverage as a corner solution, $D^* = L$. The first-order condition for the maximization in (15), again using Leibniz rule, is

$$\begin{aligned} \frac{dEu}{dD} &= -P'\int_0^D u'(W - P - x)dF + (-P' - 1)\int_D^L u'(W - P - D)dF \\ &= -P'\int_0^D u'(W - P - x)dF + (-P' - 1)(1 - F(D))u'(W - P - D) = 0. \end{aligned} \tag{16}$$

The first term in either of the center expressions in (16) represents the marginal net utility benefit of premium savings from increasing D, conditional on the loss not exceeding the deductible level. The second term is minus the net marginal utility cost of a higher deductible, given that the loss exceeds the deductible. Thus, (16) has a standard economic interpretation of choosing D^* such that marginal benefit equals marginal cost.

[13] Leibniz rule states that $\dfrac{d}{dt}\displaystyle\int_{a(t)}^{b(t)} H(x,t)dx = H(b,t)b'(t) - H(a,t)a'(t) + \int_{a(t)}^{b(t)} \frac{\partial H}{\partial t}dx.$

The second-order condition for the maximization in (16) can be shown to hold as follows.

$$\frac{d^2Eu}{dD^2} = (1+\lambda)(-f(D))\int_0^D u'(W-P-x)dF + (-P')u'(W-P-D)f(D)$$
$$+(-P')^2\int_0^D u''(W-P-x)dF + (1+\lambda)(-f(D))(1-F(D))u'(W-P-D)$$
$$+(-P'-1)(-f(D))u'(W-P-D) + (-P'-1)^2(1-F(D))''(W-P-D). \qquad (17)$$

Multiplying all terms containing $f(D)$ in (17) above by $(1 - F(D))/(1 - F(D))$ and simplifying, yields

$$\frac{d^2Eu}{dD^2} = \frac{-f(D)}{1-F(D)}\left[-P'\int_0^D u'(W-P-x)dF + (-P'-1)(1-F(D))u'(W-P-D)\right]$$
$$+\left[(-P')^2\int_0^D u''(W-P-x)dF + (-P'-1)^2(1-F(D))u''(W-P-D)\right] < 0 \qquad (18)$$

The first term in (18) is zero by the first-order condition, while the second term is negative from the concavity of u, thus yielding the inequality as stated in (18).

To see that Mossin's Theorem can be extended to the case of deductibles, rewrite the derivative in (16) as

$$\frac{dEu}{dD} = (1-F(D))\left[(1+\lambda)\int_0^L u'(W-P-\min(x,D))dF - u'(W-P-D)\right]. \qquad (19)$$

If $\lambda = 0$, then (19) will be negative for any $D > 0$, and is easily seen to equal zero when $D = 0$. For $\lambda > 0$, (19) will be positive at $D = 0$, so that the deductible should be increased. Therefore, Mossin's Theorem also holds for a choice of deductible.

It also is straightforward to extend the comparative-static results of Propositions 1–3 to the case of deductibles as well, although we do not provide the details here.

5.3 THE MODEL WITH MULTIPLE RISKS

Although much is to be learned from the basic single risk model, rarely is the insurance decision made with no other uncertainty in the background. This so-called background risk might be exogenous or endogenous. In the latter case decisions on how to best handle risk cannot usually be decided in isolation on a risk-by-risk basis. Rather, some type of comprehensive risk management policy must be applied.[14]

[14] This question was first addressed by Mayers and Smith (1983) and Doherty and Schlesinger (1983). The special case of default risk was developed by Doherty and Schlesinger (1990), and Schlesinger and Schulenburg (1987).

However, even in the case where the background risk is exogenous and independent of the insurable risk, we will see that the mere presence of background risk affects the individual's insurance choice.

The existence of uninsurable background risk is often considered a consequence of incomplete markets for risk sharing. For example, some types of catastrophic risk might contain too substantial an element of nondiversifiable risk, including a risk of incorrectly estimating the parameters of the loss distribution, to be insurable. Likewise, nonmarketable assets, such as one's own human capital, might not find ready markets for sharing the risk. Similarly, problems with asymmetry of information between the insurer and the insured, such as moral hazard and/or adverse selection, might preclude the existence of insurance markets for certain risks.

We begin the next section by examining a type of secondary risk that is always present for an insurable risk, but almost universally ignored in insurance theory; namely the risk that the insurer does not pay the promised indemnity following a covered loss. The most obvious reason for nonpayment is that the insurer may be insolvent and not financially capable of paying its claims in full. However, other scenarios are possible. For instance, there might be some events that void insurance coverage, such as a probationary period for certain perils to be included, or exclusion of coverage in situations of civil unrest or war.[15] Even if the insurer pays the loss in full, it may decide to randomly investigate a claim thereby substantially delaying payment. In such an instance, the delay reduces the present value of the indemnity, which has the same effect as paying something less than the promised indemnity.

5.3.1 The Model with Default Risk

We consider here an insurance model in which the insurer might not pay its claims in full. To keep the model simple, we consider only the case of a full default on an insured's claim in which a loss of a fixed size either occurs or does not occur. Let the support of the loss distribution be $\{0, L\}$, where a loss of size L occurs with probability p, $0 < p < 1$. Let α once again denote the share of the loss paid as an indemnity by the insurer, but we now assume that there is only a probability q, $0 < q < 1$, that insurer can pay its claim, and that with probability $1 - q$ the claim goes unpaid.[16] As a base case, we consider a fair premium, which we calculate taking the default risk into account as $P(\alpha) = \alpha pqL$.

Obviously such a premium is not realistic, since for $q < 1$ it implies that the insurer will default almost surely. More realistically the insurance will contain a premium loading of $\lambda > 0$. Thus $P(\alpha) = \alpha p[(1 + \lambda)q]L$. Since P, α, p and L are known or observable, the consumer observes only $q(1 + \lambda)$, rather than q and λ separately. It is the

[15] Although not modeled in this manner, the possibility of a probationary period is examined by Eeckhoudt, et al. (1988), who endogenize the length of probation.

[16] In a two-state (loss vs. no loss) model, there is no distinction between coinsurance and deductibles. A coinsurance rate α is identical to a deductible level of $D = (1 - \alpha)L$.

consumer's *perception* of q and λ that will cause a deviation in insurance purchasing from the no-default-risk case. Since we only concern ourselves with how default risk affects insurance demand, the base case of a "fair premium" with $\lambda = 0$ seems like a good place to start.

Given our model, states of the world can be partitioned into three disjoint sets: states in which no loss occurs, states in which a loss occurs and the insurer pays its promised indemnity, and states in which a loss occurs but the insurer pays no indemnity. We assume that the individual's loss distribution is independent of the insurer's insolvency. Thus, the individual's objective can be written as

$$\underset{\alpha}{\text{maximize}}\ Eu = (1-p)u(Y_1) + pqu(Y_2) + p(1-q)u(Y_3) \tag{20}$$

where

$$Y_1 \equiv W - \alpha pqL$$

$$Y_2 \equiv W - \alpha pqL - L + \alpha L$$

$$Y_3 \equiv W - \alpha pqL - L$$

The first-order condition for maximizing (20) is

$$\frac{dEu}{d\alpha} = -(1-p)pqLu'(Y_1) + pq(1-pq)Lu'(Y_2) - p(1-q)pqLu'(Y_3) = 0. \tag{21}$$

Dividing through by L and rearranging, we can rewrite (21) as

$$u'(Y_2) = \beta u'(Y_1) + (1-\beta)u'(Y_3), \tag{22}$$

where $\beta = (1-p)/(1-pq)$, $0 < \beta < 1$. Thus we see that $u'(Y_2)$ is a weighted average of $u'(Y_1)$ and $u'(Y_3)$.[17] Given the concavity of $u(\cdot)$, equation (22) implies that

$$Y_1 > Y_2 > Y_3, \tag{23}$$

so that $\alpha^* < 1$. Clearly then, Mossin's Theorem does not hold in the presence of default risk.

In the presence of default risk, although we can purchase "nominally full insurance" with $\alpha^* = 1$, this does not fully insure the individual, since the insurer might

[17] Note that if there is no default risk with $q = 1$, then $u'(Y_1) = u'(Y_2)$ implying that $\alpha^* = 1$, as we already know from Mossin'sTheorem.

not be able to pay a valid claim. Indeed, in the case where the insurer does not pay a filed claim, the individual is actually worse off than with no insurance, since the individual also loses his or her premium. The higher the level of insurance, the higher the potential loss of premium. Thus it is not surprising that $\alpha^* = 1$ is not optimal.

It also is not difficult to show that, in contrast to the case with no default risk, an increase in risk aversion will not necessarily lead to an increase in the level of insurance coverage. Although a more risk-averse individual would value the additional insurance coverage absent any default risk, higher risk aversion also makes the individual fear the worst-case outcome (a loss and an insolvent insurer) even more. More formally, let $v(\cdot)$ be a more risk-averse utility function than $u(\cdot)$. As in section 1.3, we know there exists an increasing concave function g, such that $v(y) = g[u(y)]$ for all y.

Without losing generality, we can assume that $g'[u(Y_2)] = 1$, so that $g'[u(Y_1)] < 1 < g'[u(Y_3)]$. Now, calculating

$$\left.\frac{dEv}{d\alpha}\right|_{\alpha_u^*} = -g'[u(Y_1)](1-p)pqLu'(Y_1) + pq(1-pq)Lu'(Y_2) - g'[u(Y_3)]p(1-q)pqLu'(Y_3). \tag{24}$$

Comparing (24) with (21), we see that one of the negative terms on the right-hand side in (24) is increased in absolute magnitude while the other is reduced. However, it is not possible to predetermine which of these two changes will dominate, *a priori*. Thus, we cannot predict whether α^* will increase or decrease.

Using similar arguments, it is easy to show that insurance is not necessarily an inferior good under DARA, as was the case without default risk. A somewhat more surprising result is that, under actuarially fair pricing, an increase in the probability of solvency does not necessarily lead to a higher level of coverage. To see this, use the concavity of $Eu(Y(\alpha))$ in α, which is easy to check, and calculate

$$\left.\frac{\partial^2 Eu}{\partial\alpha\partial q}\right|_{\alpha^*} = p\alpha L[H(\alpha^*)] + p^2 qL[u'(Y_3) - u'(Y_2)], \tag{25}$$

where $H(\alpha)$ is defined as the derivative in the first-order condition (21), with $u(Y)$ replaced by the utility function $-u'(Y)$. The level of insurance coverage will increase, due to an increase in q, if and only if (25) is positive. Although the second term on the right-hand side of (25) is positive, the first term can be either positive or negative. For example, if u exhibits DARA, it is straightforward to show that $-u'$ is a more risk averse utility than u. Therefore, by our results on increases in risk aversion, $H(\alpha^*)$ might be either positive or negative.

There are two, and only two, circumstances in which the form of the utility function u will yield $d\alpha^*/dq > 0$, regardless of the other parameters of the model (assuming fair prices). The first is where u is quadratic, so that $H(\alpha) = 0$ for all α.

The second is where u satisfies CARA, and which case $-u'$ and u represent the same risk-averse preferences.[18] Hence, $H(\alpha^*) = 0$. We also know for any risk-averse utility u, that $d\alpha^*/dq > 0$ for q sufficiently close to $q = 1$. This follows since $\alpha^* = 1$ for $q = 1$, but $\alpha^* < 1$ for $q < 1$.

5.3.2 An Independent Background Risk

As opposed to a default risk, we now suppose that the insurer pays all of its claims, but that the individual's uninsured wealth prospect is $W + \tilde{\varepsilon} - \tilde{x}$, where $\tilde{x}$ once again represents the insurable loss and where $\tilde{\varepsilon}$ represents a zero-mean background risk that is independent of $\tilde{x}$. We assume that the support of the distribution of $\tilde{\varepsilon}$ is not the singleton $\{0\}$ and that $W + \tilde{\varepsilon} - \tilde{x} > 0$ almost surely. It is assumed that $\tilde{\varepsilon}$ cannot be insured directly. We wish to examine the effect of $\tilde{\varepsilon}$ on the choice of insurance level α^*.

The case of an independent background risk is easily handled by introducing the so-called *derived utility function* which we define as follows:

$$v(y) = Eu(y+\tilde{\varepsilon}) = \int_{-\infty}^{\infty} u(y+\varepsilon)dG(\varepsilon), \tag{26}$$

where $G(\cdot)$ is the distribution function for $\tilde{\varepsilon}$. Note that we can now write

$$\max_{\alpha} Eu(\tilde{Y}(\alpha)+\tilde{\varepsilon}) = \int_0^L \int_{-\infty}^{\infty} u(Y(\alpha)+\varepsilon)dG(\varepsilon)dF(x) = \int_0^L v(Y(\alpha))dF(x) = Ev(\tilde{Y}(\alpha)). \tag{27}$$

In other words, $v(Y(\alpha))$ is simply the "inner part" of an iterated integral. Finding the optimal insurance level for utility u in the presence of background risk $\tilde{\varepsilon}$, is identical to finding the optimal insurance level for utility v, absent any background risk.

For example, suppose u exhibits CARA or that u is quadratic. Then it is easy to show in each case that v is an affine transformation of u, so that background risk has no effect on the optimal choice of insurance.[19]

More generally, we know that more insurance will be purchased whenever the derived utility function $v(\cdot)$ is more risk averse than $u(\cdot)$. A sufficient condition for this to hold is *standard risk aversion* as defined by Kimball (1993). A utility function exhibits standard risk aversion "if every risk that has a negative interaction with a small reduction in wealth also has a negative interaction with any undesirable, independent risk." [Kimball (1993) p. 589] Here "negative interaction" means that risk magnifies the reduction in expected utility. Kimball shows that standard risk aversion

[18] This is easiest to see by noting that $-u'$ is an affine transformation of u.

[19] For CARA, $v(y) = ku(y)$ and for quadratic utility $v(y) = u(y) + c$, where $k = E[\exp(r\tilde{\varepsilon})] > 0$ and $c = -t\ \mathrm{var}(\tilde{\varepsilon})$ for some $t > 0$. Gollier and Schlesinger (1998) show that these are the only two forms of u for which v represents preferences identical to u.

is characterized by decreasing absolute risk aversion and decreasing absolute prudence, where absolute risk aversion is $r(y) = -u''(y)/u'(y)$ and absolute prudence is $\eta(y) = -u'''(y)/u''(y)$.

It is easy to show that DARA is equivalent to $\eta(y) > r(y)\ \forall y$. Since DARA implies prudence (i.e., $u'''(y) > 0$), then under DARA the function $-u'(y)$ represents a risk-averse utility of its own. The condition $\eta(y) > r(y)$ thus implies that $-u'(\cdot)$ is a more risk-averse utility than $u(\cdot)$. Similarly, we find that decreasing absolute prudence or "DAP" implies that $u''''(y) < 0$ and that $u''(\cdot)$ is a more risk-averse utility function than $-u'(\cdot)$.

Let $\pi(y)$ denote the risk premium, as defined by Pratt (1964), for utility $u(\cdot)$, given base wealth y and fixed risk $\tilde{\varepsilon}$. Similarly, let $\pi_1(y)$ and $\pi_2(y)$ denote the corresponding risk premia for utilities $-u'(\cdot)$ and $u''(\cdot)$ respectively. That is,

$$\begin{aligned} &Eu(y+\tilde{\varepsilon}) = u(y-\pi(y)) \\ &-Eu'(y+\tilde{\varepsilon}) = -u'(y-\pi_1(y)) \\ &Eu''(y+\tilde{\varepsilon}) = u''(y-\pi_2(y)). \end{aligned} \tag{28}$$

Standard risk aversion thus implies that $\pi_2(y) > \pi_1(y) > \pi(y) > 0\ \forall y$. Thus, we have the following set of inequalities

$$-\frac{v''(y)}{v'(y)} = \frac{-Eu''(y+\tilde{\varepsilon})}{Eu'(y+\tilde{\varepsilon})} = \frac{-u''(y-\pi_2)}{u'(y-\pi_1)} > \frac{-u''(y-\pi_1)}{u'(y-\pi_1)} > \frac{-u''(y)}{u'(y)}, \tag{29}$$

where the last inequality follows from DARA. Consequently $v(\cdot)$ is more risk-averse than $u(\cdot)$.[20]

Considering the maximization program (27), the above result taken together with our previous results on increases in risk aversion, implies the following:

Proposition 4. (a) If insurance has a zero premium loading, $\lambda = 0$, then full coverage is optimal in the presence of an independent background risk. (b) If insurance premia include a positive loading, $\lambda > 0$, then partial coverage is optimal in the presence of an independent background risk. (c) If insurance premia include a positive loading, $\lambda > 0$ and utility exhibits standard risk aversion, then more coverage is purchased in the presence of an independent zero mean background risk.

Remark. Parts (a) and (b) above do not require $E\tilde{\varepsilon} = 0$. They are direct applications of Mossin's Theorem to utility $v(\cdot)$. Although the discussion above is for proportional

[20] Another simple proof that standard risk aversion is sufficient for the derived utility function to be more risk averse appears in Eeckhoudt and Kimball (1992). Standard risk aversion is stronger than necessary, however. See Gollier and Pratt (1996).

coinsurance, part (c) of Proposition 4 also applies to deductibles, since it only relies upon $v(\cdot)$ being more risk-averse than $u(\cdot)$.

5.3.3 Nonindependent Background Risk

Obviously the background risk need not always be statistically independent of the loss distribution. For example, if $\tilde{\varepsilon} = \tilde{x}$ then final wealth is risk free without insurance, $Y = W$. Buying insurance on $\tilde{x}$ would only introduce risk into the individual's final wealth prospect. Consequently, zero coverage is optimal, even at a fair price, $\lambda = 0$. For example, suppose the individual's employer provides full insurance coverage against loss $\tilde{x}$. We can represent this protection by $\tilde{\varepsilon}$ as described here; and thus no further insurance coverage would be purchased.

Similarly, if $\tilde{\varepsilon} = -\tilde{x}$ then final wealth can be written as $\tilde{Y} = W - 2\tilde{x}$ with no insurance. Treating $2\tilde{x}$ as the loss variable, Mossin's Theorem implies that full insurance on $2\tilde{x}$ will be optimal at a fair price. This can be achieved by purchasing insurance with a coinsurance level of $\alpha^* = 2$. Although this is nominally "200% coverage," it is defacto merely full coverage of $2\tilde{x}$. If insurance is constrained to exclude over-insurance, then $\alpha = 1$ will be the constrained optimum. For insurance markets with a premium loading $\lambda > 0$, Mossin's Theorem implies that $\alpha^* < 2$. In this case, a constraint of no overinsurance might or might not be binding.

For more general cases of nonindependent background risk, it becomes difficult to predict the effects on insurance purchasing. Part of the problem is that there is no general measure of dependency that will lead to unambiguous effects on insurance demand. Correlation is not sufficient since other aspects of the distributions of $\tilde{x}$ and $\tilde{\varepsilon}$, such as higher moments, also are important in consumer choice.[21] Alternatives measures of dependence, many based on stochastic dominance, do not lead to definitive qualitative effects on the level of insurance demand.

For example, suppose we define the random variable $\tilde{\varepsilon}'$ to have the same marginal distribution as $\tilde{\varepsilon}$, but with $\tilde{\varepsilon}'$ statistically independent of $\tilde{x}$. We can define a partial stochastic ordering for $W + \tilde{\varepsilon} - \tilde{x}$ versus $W + \tilde{\varepsilon}' - \tilde{x}$. If, for example, we use second-degree stochastic dominance, we will be able to say whether or not the risk-averse consumer is better off or worse off with $\tilde{\varepsilon}$ or $\tilde{\varepsilon}'$ as the source of background risk; but we will not be able to say whether the level of insurance demanded will be higher or lower in the presence of background risk $\tilde{\varepsilon}$ versus background risk $\tilde{\varepsilon}'$.

Some recent work has used more sophisticated partial orderings to examine the behavior of insurance demand in the presence of a background risk that is not statistically independent from the loss distribution. For the most part, this work has focussed on comparing insurance demands with and without the background risk.[22]

[21] Doherty and Schlesinger (1983b) use correlation, but restrict the joint distribution of $\tilde{x}$ and $\tilde{\varepsilon}$ to be bivariate normal. For other joint distributions, correlation is not sufficient.

[22] Aboudi and Thon (1995) do an excellent and thorough job of characterizing many of the potential partial orderings, albeit in a discrete probability space, but they only whet our appetite for applying these orderings to insurance demand.

Eeckhoudt and Kimball (1992), for example, use one particular partial ordering, assuming that the conditional distribution of $\tilde{\varepsilon}$ given x_1 dominates the conditional distribution of $\tilde{\varepsilon}$ given x_2 via third-degree stochastic dominance, for every $x_1 < x_2$. Eeckhoudt and Kimball go on to show that such a negative dependency between $\tilde{\varepsilon}$ and $\tilde{x}$ leads to an increase in insurance demand in the presence of background risk, whenever preferences exhibit standard risk aversion. Important to note here, is that even with the strong third-degree stochastic dominance assumption, risk aversion alone is not strong enough to yield deterministic comparative statics.

One paper that does compare insurance demands for a change in background risk from $\tilde{\varepsilon}'$ to $\tilde{\varepsilon}$, where $\tilde{\varepsilon}'$ is statistically independent from $\tilde{x}$ and has the same marginal distribution as $\tilde{\varepsilon}$, is Tibiletti (1995). She uses the concept of concordance as her partial ordering. In particular, if $H(\varepsilon, x)$ is the joint distribution of the random vector $(\tilde{\varepsilon}, \tilde{x})$ and $G(\varepsilon, x)$ the distribution of $(\tilde{\varepsilon}', \tilde{x})$, then H is *less concordant* then G if $H(\varepsilon, x) \geq G(\varepsilon, x)\ \forall \varepsilon, x$. In other words, G dominates H by joint first—degree stochastic dominance. However, even using concordance, we need to make fairly restrictive assumptions on preferences to yield deterministic comparisons between optimal levels of insurance purchases. In particular, suppose we restrict the degree of relative prudence, $y\eta(y) = -yu'''(y)/u''(y)$, to be no greater than one. Then for H less concordant than G, more insurance will be purchased under H; i.e., more insurance is purchased in the presence of background risk $\tilde{\varepsilon}$ than in the presence of the independent background risk $\tilde{\varepsilon}'$.

Note that concordance is yet another measure of positive dependency between $\tilde{\varepsilon}$ and $\tilde{x}$. Thus the above result implies that if $\tilde{\varepsilon}$ and $\tilde{x}$ are, in a certain sense, negatively associated with each other, so that higher losses are more readily exacerbated by the simultaneous realization of low background wealth, then more insurance is purchased. In other words, the individual can partly compensate for downward fluctuations in background risk $\tilde{\varepsilon}$ by increasing his protection on the insurable loss $\tilde{x}$. While this result seems intuitively appealing, note that Tibiletti's result above, just as the result of Eeckhoudt and Kimball (1992), does *not* automatically follow if we assume only risk aversion for consumer preferences. In particular, if we assume that we change from zero background risk to a background risk that is negatively associated with $\tilde{\varepsilon}$ (either as measured by concordance, or as by Eeckhoudt and Kimball, 1992), there exist examples of risk-averse utility functions that would lead to the counter-intuitive result that insurance demand is lower in the presence of the background risk.[23]

[23] Although results are sparse and restrictive, this seems to be an area of much recent research activity. Tibiletti (1995) introduces the use of *copulas*, which allow one to write the joint distribution of $(\tilde{\varepsilon}, \tilde{x})$ as another joint distribution function of the marginal distributions of $\tilde{\varepsilon}$ and $\tilde{x}$, to analyze this problem. The use of particular functional forms for the *copulas* allows one to parameterize the degree of statistical association between $\tilde{x}$ and $\tilde{\varepsilon}$. See Frees and Valdez (1998) for a survey of the current use of *copulas*. The fact that a detrimental change in the background risk $\tilde{\varepsilon}$ does not necessarily lead to higher insurance purchases is examined by Eeckhoudt, Gollier and Schlesinger (1996), for the case where the deterioration can be measured by first- or second-degree stochastic dominance.

5.4 CONCLUDING REMARKS

Mossin's Theorem is often considered to be the cornerstone result of modern insurance economics. Indeed this result depends only on risk aversion for smooth preferences, such as those found in the expected-utility model.[24]

Although many results depend on stronger assumptions than risk aversion alone, research has turned in this direction. Stronger measures of risk aversion, such as those of Ross (1981) and of Kimball (1993), have helped in our understanding more about the insurance-purchasing decision.

One common "complaint," that I hear quite often from other academics, is that these restrictions on preferences beyond risk aversion are too limiting. These critics might be correct, if our goal is to guess at reasonable preferences and then see what theory predicts. However, insurance demand is not just a theory. I doubt there is anyone reading this who does not possess several insurance policies. If our goal in setting up simple theoretical models is to capture behavior in a positive sense, then such restrictions on preferences might be necessary. Of course, one can always argue that more restrictions belong elsewhere in our models, not on preferences.

As mentioned previously, the single-risk model as presented here should be viewed as a base case. As new insights about preferences become known, this model should extend in many ways. Indeed, many extensions already are to be found in this volume. Certainly there are enough current variations in the model so that every reader should find something of interest. I look forward to seeing the directions in which the theory of insurance demand is expanded in the years to come.

5.5 REFERENCES

Borch, K. (1962). "Equilibrium in a Reinsurance Market," *Econometrica* 30, 424–444.

Briys, E. and Harris Schlesinger (1990). "Risk Aversion and the Propensities for Self-Insurance and Self-Protection," *Southern Economic Journal* 57, 458–467.

Briys, E., G. Dionne and L. Eeckhoudt (1989). "More on Insurance as a Giffen Good," *Journal of Risk and Uncertainty* 2, 415–420.

Dachraoui, K., G. Dionne, L. Eeckhoudt and Ph. Godfroid (1999). "Proper Risk Behavior" Working Paper 99-01, Risk Management Chair, HEC-Montreal. http://www.hec/ca/gestiondesriques/papers.

Dionne, G. and L. Eeckhoudt (1985). "Self-Insurance, Self-Protection and Increased Risk Aversion," *Economics Letters* 17, 39–42.

Doherty, N. and H. Schlesinger (1983a). "Optimal Insurance in Incomplete Markets," *Journal of Political Economy* 91, 1045–1054.

Doherty, N. and H. Schlesinger (1983b). "The Optimal Deductible for an Insurance Policy when Initial Wealth is Random," *Journal of Business* 56, 555–565.

[24] Actually, this result hangs on the differentiability of the vonNeuman-Morgenstern utility function. "Kinks" in the utility function can lead to violations of Mossin's result. See, for example, Eeckhoudt, Gollier and Schlesinger (1997).

Doherty, N. and H. Schlesinger (1990). "Rational Insurance Purchasing: Consideration of Contract Nonperformance," *Quarterly Journal of Economics* 105, 143–153.

Eeckhoudt, L. and C. Gollier (2000). "The Effects of Changes in Risk on Risk Taking: A Survey" (this volume).

Eeckhoudt, L. and M. Kimball (1992). "Background Risk, Prudence, and the Demand for Insurance," in: G. Dionne, ed., *Contributions to Insurance Economics* (Boston: Kluwer Academic Publishers).

Eeckhoudt, L., C. Gollier and H. Schlesinger (1996). "Changes in Background Risk and Risk Taking Behavior," *Econometrica* 64, 683–689.

Eeckhoudt, L., C. Gollier and H. Schlesinger (1997). "The No Loss Offset Provision and the Attitude Towards Risk of a Risk-Neutral Firm," *Journal of Public Economics* 65, 207–217.

Eeckhoudt, L., J.F. Outreville, M. Lauwers and F. Calcoen (1988). "The Impact of a Probationary Period on the Demand for Insurance," *Journal of Risk and Insurance* 55, 217–228.

Ehrlich I. and G. Becker (1972) "Market Insurance, Self-Insurance and Self-Protection" *Journal of Political Economy*, 623–648.

Frees, E.W. and E. Valdez (1998). "Understanding Relationships using Copulas," *North American Actuarial Journal*, 2, 1–25.

Gollier, C. (1995). "The Comparative Statics of Changes in Risk Revisited," *Journal of Economic Theory* 66, 522–536.

Gollier, C. (2000). "Optimal Insurance Design: What can We Do with and without Expected Utility" (this volume)

Gollier, C. and J.W. Pratt (1996). "Risk Vulnerability and the Tempering Effect of Background Risk," *Econometrica* 5, 1109–1123.

Gollier, C. and H. Schlesinger (1998). "Preserving Preference Orderings of Uncertain Prospects under Background Risk," University of Toulouse working paper.

Jullien, B., B. Salanie and F. Salanie (1999) "Should More Risk Aversion Individuals Exert More Effort" *Geneva Papers on Risk and Insurance Theory*, 24, 19–28.

Kimball, M. (1993). "Standard Risk Aversion," *Econometrica* 61, 589–611.

Mayers, D. and C.W. Smith, Jr. (1983). "The Interdependence of Individual Portfolio Decisions and the Demand for Insurance," *Journal of Political Economy* 91, 304–311.

Meyer, J. and M.B. Ormiston (1998). "The Demand of Insurance when the Deductible Form of Indemnification is Optimal," Michigan State University working paper.

Mossin, J. (1968). "Aspects of Rational Insurance Purchasing," *Journal of Political Economy* 79, 553–568.

Pratt, J. (1964). "Risk Aversion in the Small and in the Large," *Econometrica* 32, 122–136.

Ross, S. (1983). "Some Stronger Measures of Risk Aversion in the Small and in the Large with Applications," *Econometrica* 3, 621–638.

Schlesinger, H. (1997). "Insurance Demand without the Expected-Utility Paradigm," *Journal of Risk and Insurance* 64, 19–39.

Schlesinger, H. and J.M. Gf. v.d. Schulenburg (1987). "Risk Aversion and the Purchase of Risky Insurance," *Journal of Economics* 47, 309–314.

Segal, U. and A. Spivak (1990). "First Order versus Second Order Risk Aversion," *Journal of Economic Theory* 51, 111–125.

Smith, V. (1968). "Optimal Insurance Coverage," *Journal of Political Economic* 68, 68–77.

Sweeney, G. and T.R. Beard (1992). "Self-Protection in the Expected-Utility-of-Wealth Model: An Impossibility Theorem," *Geneva Papers on Risk and Insurance Theory* 17, 147–158.

Part III
Asymmetric Information: Theory

6 Optimal Insurance under Moral Hazard

Ralph A. Winter

University of Toronto

Abstract
This chapter surveys the theory of optimal insurance contracts under moral hazard, revisiting the topic in light of developments in contract theory over the past twenty-five years. Moral hazard leads to less than full insurance, so that the insured retains some incentive to reduce accident costs. What form does the partial insurance contract take: a deductible, co-insurance or a ceiling on coverage? Posed in the most general form, the problem is identical to the hidden-action principal-agent problem. The insurance context provides some structure that allows more specific predictions. Optimal insurance contracts vary, for example, depending on whether effort affects the probability of an accident or its severity. The chapter characterizes the optimal insurance contract and integrates developments in contract renegotiation, contract dynamics and other extensions.

Keywords: Insurance, contracts, moral hazard, principal-agent.
JEL Classification Numbers: D8, G22.

6.1 INTRODUCTION

In the context of insurance, moral hazard refers to the impact of insurance on incentives to reduce risks. An individual facing an accident risk such as of the loss of a home, car or the risk of medical expenses, can generally take actions to reduce the risk. Without insurance, the costs and benefits of accident avoidance, or precaution, are internal to the individual and the incentives for avoidance are optimal. With insurance, some of the accident costs are borne by the insurer. The insured individual, bearing all of the costs of accident avoidance but only some of the benefits will under-invest in accident avoidance. The precaution decision is distorted relative by the failure of the individual to incorporate the external cost imposed on the insurer.

An insurance contract may specify the levels of precaution (the number of fire extinguishers, the frequency of inspection of equipment and so on). If the contract were *complete* in the sense of specifying the individual's care in all dimensions and in all future contingencies prior to the accident, then moral hazard would not be an issue. If an insurance contract is *incomplete*, however, in the sense that it does not fully specify the precaution to be taken by the insured, then the precaution decision taken after the contract is signed will be distorted by the externality imposed on the insurer. The optimal insurance contract will be designed, within the constraints of asymmetric information and enforceability, in anticipation of the moral hazard problem.

This chapter offers a synthesis of the economic theory of moral hazard in insurance. It reviews the sources of moral hazard, i.e., the reasons why insurance contracts may be incomplete, and then develops the economic implications of moral hazard. The focus is on the implications of moral hazard for optimal contracts.[1]

The term moral hazard originated in the insurance context that we will study here, but it is important to note that the meaning of the term has evolved and expanded. The concept and terminology of moral hazard now extend beyond the traditional context of insurance contracts to all types of contractual relationships. Labour contracts, for example, are designed with the knowledge that the effort and diligence of the employee cannot be specified completely in the contract and instead must be induced through incentives provided in the contract. The relationships between a homeowner and a contractor, a lawyer or service provider and a customer, partners in a joint venture, the editor of this volume and the author of this chapter, are all subject to moral hazard. Even a marriage is subject to moral hazard insofar as costs are imposed on one marriage partner whenever the other one shirks.[2] Moral hazard is often defined broadly as the conflict between the interests of an individual in an organization and the collective interest of the organization that arises when the contracts that comprise the organization are incomplete.

Indeed, the concept of moral hazard can, in the limit, encompass *any* externality. Law and social norms can be interpreted together as a social contract specifying the rights and obligations of individuals in a society.[3] All individuals are in the social contract, and externalities are the consequence of incompleteness in the social contract. Moral hazard in the broadest sense encompasses the distortions in individual decisions that result from incompleteness in the social contract.

A large part of the microeconomics literature over the past twenty-five years has

[1] This chapter is an update and extension of a previous survey (Winter (1992)).

[2] In an ideal marriage, costs imposed on the spouse are internalized an individual's own utility function. Love solves the moral hazard problem.

[3] To take a concrete example, drivers' decisions during morning rush hour, such as the speed, driving care and which route to take, are all decisions that impose costs on others. If all drivers could costlessly get on the internet before commuting to work in the morning and design an enforceable contract that specified these parameters for each driver then the externalities could be eliminated. In reality, of course, private contracts among drivers are incomplete in the extreme: they are non-existent. Highway regulations and tort law, in establishing rules and transfers among drivers in the events of accidents, can be interpreted as a (very incomplete) social contract specifying the obligations and rights of drivers.

been devoted to the implications of incomplete contracts (and the related concept, incomplete markets). In returning to the original context in synthesizing the implications of moral hazard in insurance, we draw on the developments in this literature.

It is well known and intuitive that the contractual response to moral hazard is to leave some of the risk uninsured, i.e., borne by the risk averse insured individual rather than transferred entirely to the insurer. Leaving the individual with *some* share of the consequences of a marginal change in precaution improves his incentives. The optimal contract will balance the risk-sharing benefits of greater insurance with the incentive benefits of less insurance.

What is perhaps less well understood is what *form* the risk-sharing takes. Will it involve a contract in which the individual bears the entire marginal cost of small losses, up to some limit—i.e., a deductible ? Or will the optimal contract involve full insurance of marginal losses up to some coverage limit with the individual bearing the full marginal cost at high losses; or will it involve some continuous sharing of the marginal accident costs? The focus of this review of moral hazard is the design of the contractual response to moral hazard.[4]

We begin in section 6.2 with the simplest moral hazard setting: a risk averse individual faces a known loss, L, with a probability $p(x)$ that depends upon the individual's effort x. In this simple case, the optimal form of the contract is not an issue; the optimal amount of insurance (and premium) is the entire problem. We extend this framework in section 6.3 to consider an individual facing with the same probability $p(x)$, an *uncertain* loss, $\tilde{L}$. In this case an insurance policy takes the form of a functional relationship between the realized loss and the insurance payment. Section 6.4 considers the case where the individual's effort affects the magnitude of the random loss contingent on an accident, rather than the probability of the accident. The parameters in this case are the probability of an accident, p, and the distribution of accident costs conditional upon the accident, $G(L; x)$. Section 6.5 then reviews the model of the optimal contract under a general distribution of losses. This connects the optimal insurance problem in terms of the standard principal-agent model. Section 6.6 outlines various extensions to the theory of moral hazard, including the issues of renegotiation, multi-dimensional care, and the dynamics of insurance contracts under moral hazard.

6.2 THE SIMPLEST MODEL

The simplest model of moral hazard is built on the following assumptions: An individual with initial wealth W and utility function $U(W)$ faces the risk of losing an

[4] The analysis of optimal contracts is partial equilibrium analysis. For treatment of the general equilibrium consequences of moral hazard, see Helpman and Laffont (1975).

amount of wealth, L. The probability of the loss is a function, $p(x)$, of the care, x, undertaken by the individual on avoiding the loss. The cost of care is one dollar per unit. The function $p(x)$ is assumed to be decreasing and convex, with $p'(0) = -\infty$. In the absence of insurance, after investing in care x the individual's final wealth is $W - x$ if there is no accident and $W - L - x$ if there is an accident.

Insurance coverage in the amount of q dollars at a premium of π changes the final wealth in the events of no accident and accident, respectively, to $W - x - \pi$ and $W - x - \pi - L + q$. The insurer cannot observe x but (because the market for insurance is assumed to be competitive) the insurer is willing to offer any insurance contract $[\pi, q]$ that yields zero profits.[5]

Before analyzing the optimal insurance problem under these assumptions, it is important to note various features of insurance that are *not* captured by this simple model. First, we represent care as a pecuniary expense, i.e., an expenditure of money or time. Many examples of care in insurance—security systems, locks, product safety decisions, fire sprinklers—fit this assumption. Care could, however, include diligence, the mental concentration of an automobile driver, or intensity of effort rather than expenditure. In the case of medical insurance, loss-avoidance costs would include physical discomfort that would result from cutting back on medical care.[6] Any reduction in discomfort beyond that which would be specified in a complete contract is the consequence of moral hazard, but would require a slightly different model than the ones in this chapter.

Second, we are adopting a model of *hidden action* rather than a model of *hidden information*, to use the distinction introduced by Arrow (1985) and now standard in the agency literature. Suppose that the cost per unit of care varied, instead of being equal to 1 as in our model. If the cost of care were uncertain at the time of contracting, and were realized subsequently and observed only by the individual insured (prior to the individual's effort decision) then we would have a model of hidden information. Even if care is observed in such a setting, the first-best contract would be unattainable.[7] We do not deal with hidden information settings in this paper.

Third, if the information asymmetry were present at the time of contracting instead of subsequently, we would have a particular type of hidden information:

[5] Constraining profits to be an arbitrary value rather than zero has no qualitative impact on the results in this section or throughout the chapter. The characterization of optimal competitive insurance contracts therefore extends directly to any *Pareto optimal* contracts, including the case where there is market power on the sellers' side of the market.

[6] The simple model also excludes the possibility that utility is state-dependent, which is suggested by this example. Under the assumption of state dependent utility, very different results are generated. Consider, for example, an individual who has tastes for only two activities: helicopter skiing and reading library books. This individual would rationally want *negative* insurance against the event of a debilitating accident, since negative insurance would transfer income into states of the world where his or her marginal utility of wealth is highest. After the insurance contract, the moral hazard problem would then be that the individual takes excessive care (because of the *positive* externality extended to the insurer in the event of an accident).

[7] For an analysis of hidden information contracts, see Mas-Colell, Whinston and Green (1996).

adverse selection (Akerlof (1970), Rothschild and Stiglitz (1976)). The assumption of symmetric information at the time of contracting means that we are abstracting from the problem of adverse selection. Adverse selection in insurance markets refers to the implications of insurers' inability to identify the risk types of individuals. Some of the contractual implications of adverse selection and moral hazard are identical. Under both moral hazard and adverse selection partial coverage for at least some individuals is optimal. Other implications, for example the self-selection of lower risk individuals into contracts with less coverage, distinguish adverse selection from moral hazard situations. Of course, in reality both problems occur together, and the simultaneous treatment of the two is an important area.[8]

Fourth, our moral hazard characterization characterizes the individual's care or precaution decision in a single dimension. There may in reality be many dimensions of care, only some of which cannot be contracted. We consider this extension in section 6.5. The conflict of interest between an insurer and an insured individual could be manifest in ways other than reduced care, such as in the selection of ventures or projects that are excessively risky. This moral hazard problem is ubiquitous in financial economics and is discussed in the concluding section.

Returning to the simple model at hand, we can characterize the optimal contract following a standard methodology in principal-agent theory. The level of care, x, cannot be contracted for since it is unobservable by the insurer. Rather than omitting the care, x, from the contract, however, we allow it to enter as a contractual parameter and restrict the set of contracts by an *incentive compatibility* constraint: only those contracts are allowed in which the care promised is credible, in the sense that it is the level of care that will actually be forthcoming given the incentives provided by the rest of the contract.

The optimal contract maximizes expected utility subject to the zero profit constraint, or participation constraint on the part of the insurer, and the incentive compatibility constraint of the insured:

$$(P1) \quad \max_{\pi,q,x}(1-p(x))U(W-\pi-x)+p(x)U(W-\pi-x-L+q) \tag{1}$$

subject to

$$\pi \geq p(x)q \tag{2}$$

$$x = \arg\max_{z}(1-p(z))U(W-\pi-z)+p(z)U(W-\pi-z-L+q) \tag{3}$$

The participation constraint ensures that the insurer would willingly offer the contract, and the incentive compatibility constraint ensures that the care level in the con-

[8] Stewart (1994) shows that the effects of moral hazard and adverse selection can be partially offsetting.

tract is credible in the sense that it will actually be chosen by the agent under the incentives provided by the rest of the contract.

The "first-best optimal" insurance contract corresponding to the problem (P1) is characterized by the same maximization problem, with the incentive compatibility constraint deleted. The effect of the incomplete contracting or moral hazard problem is to constrain the set of available contracts to those for which promises on non-enforceable dimensions of the contracts are credible.

In characterizing the solution to the problem (P1), as with more general principal-agent problems, three technical issues arise. The first issue is whether the incentive compatibility constraint be replaced by the first order condition of the agent's maximization problem. As Mirrlees (1975) first noted, because expected utility is often non-concave in care or effort, the set of care levels satisfying a first-order condition is different from the set satisfying the incentive compatibility constraint. The first-order conditions are satisfied at saddle points, local minima and local-but-not-global maxima as well as interior global maxima; on the other hand, the first-order conditions are not satisfied at corner solutions. For the current problem, however, our assumptions that $p(x)$ is convex and that $p'(0) = -\infty$, however, are sufficient for the second-order conditions on the problem expressed by (3). This assumption is therefore enough to justify the first-order approach to the characterization of any interior solution to (P1), i.e., a solution involving positive care.

We can therefore replace the incentive compatibility constraint (3) with the insured's first-order condition (assuming an interior level of care):

$$\begin{aligned} & p'(x)[U(W-\pi-x-L+q)-U(W-\pi-x)] \\ & \quad =[1-p(x)]U'(W-\pi-x)+p(x)U'(W-\pi-x-L+q) \end{aligned} \tag{4}$$

The second technical issue presented by the problem (P1) is that, in general, a break-even contract with the highest expected utility may involve *random* coverage. This possibility was demonstrated by Gjesdal (1982). A sufficient condition for the solution to be non-random would be for utility to be separable in income and effort; for the context of insurance, however, this separability is unrealistic as most forms of care involve pecuniary cost as we assume. Following Shavell (1979b: 544, nt 5) and almost all of the literature on moral hazard in insurance, we simply ignore the possibility of random contracts.

Consider the expected utility of the insured individual and the expected profits of the insurer as functions of the insurance contract, (π, q). The insured's valuation of the contract $[\pi, q]$ can be expressed as $\mathbf{U}(\pi, q) \equiv (1-p(X(\pi, q)))U(W-\pi-X(\pi, q)) + p(X(\pi, q))U(W-\pi-X(\pi, q)-L+q)$ where $X(\pi, q)$ is the optimal level of care defined by the incentive compatibility condition (3). The insurer's valuation can be similarly expressed as $\mathbf{V}((\pi, q)) = \pi - p(X(\pi, q)) \cdot q$. A contract solving (P1) must be Pareto optimal between the two parties to the contract, and can therefore be represented on the space of contracts by a tangency of an indifference and the zero expected profits curve. The third technical issue presented by the problem (P1) is that the indifference curves and the expected profit curves on this space may be *non-convex*. The non-convexity is in contrast to the standard consumer theory, and to the theory of optimal insurance in the absence of moral hazard.

The implications of the moral hazard non-convexities are investigated by Helpman and Laffont (1975) and Arnott and Stiglitz (1983, a and b) and reviewed in Arnott (1992). Among these implications is that equilibrium may fail to exist in competitive insurance markets, analogous to the failure of existence in competitive product markets when consumer utility is non-concave and demand functions, as a result, discontinuous. The principal implications, however, are for the case in which insurers are constrained to offer *uniform price contracts*, i.e., unlimited amounts of insurance at any premium. This constraint would arise if insurers could not observe the amount of insurance that an individual purchased from other insurers. We retain the assumption that contracts limiting the amount of coverage purchased by the individual are enforceable, as is generally the case for insurance contracts.

The solution to (P1) is described by its first order conditions when the incentive compatibility constraint (equation 3) has an interior solution. We can substitute the break-even constraint into the objective, and define $x(q)$ as the solution in x to the incentive compatibility constraint. This yields expected utility as a function of q alone. Differentiating this function, and substituting in (4) yields the condition (5) below for the optimal coverage. Let W_L and W_N be short-hand for the realized wealth given an accident and no accident, respectively; that is, $W_L \equiv W - \pi - x - L + q$ and $W_N \equiv W - \pi - x$.

$$\begin{aligned} EU'(q) = {} & -x'p'q[(1-p)U'(W_N)+pU'(W_L)] \\ & - p[(1-p)U'(W_N)+pU'(W_L)]+pU'(W_L) \end{aligned} \tag{5}$$

The three terms in this expression, following Shavell (1979), represent the marginal expected utility, with an additional dollar of coverage, from

(a) a change in the premium due to a change in the premium *rate* per dollar of coverage;
(b) a change in the premium due to an increased *level* of coverage; and
(c) a change in the level of coverage.

The latter two terms would be present even without the second constraint, i.e., these terms reflect the marginal benefits and costs of increased insurance even without moral hazard. Moral hazard is reflected only in the first term of the expression. The failure of **U** and **V** to be concave means that the optimal care level will vary discontinuously with changes in exogenous variables in the problem. Shavell (1979b) illustrates the discontinuity of optimal care as a function of the cost of care.

6.3 SELF-PROTECTION AND UNCERTAIN LOSSES

In the basic moral hazard model of section 2 we assumed that the cost of an accident is non-random. This framework is restrictive in that it allows one to address essentially only one question: How much insurance coverage is optimal under moral hazard? There are only two outcomes in the model: accident or no accident.

This section introduces the simplest extension that allows one to inquire into the *form* that insurance contracts take under moral hazard. Clearly moral hazard should lead to less insurance coverage—but does this reduction in insurance take the form of deductibles, co-insurance or upper limits on coverage? All three of these contractual features are observed in practice.

Following Ehrlich and Becker (1972), I distinguish between expenditure undertaken to reduce the probability of an accident and expenditure to reduce the size of the contingent loss. In Ehrlich and Becker's terminology, the former is *self-protection*. The latter these authors call self-insurance, although I will use the term *loss reduction* because "self-insurance" has more than one meaning in the insurance literature.

Expenditures on fire sprinklers reduce the size of a loss, but not the probability of an accident. Expenditures on a burglar alarm reduce the probability of a theft whereas the decision not to leave expensive silverware in an unlocked container reduces the loss if there is a household theft. In the case of earthquake insurance, all precaution is loss-reducing; we cannot under current technology change the probability of an earthquake. Driving an automobile more slowly and carefully reduces both the probability of an accident and the likely costs of an accident should it occur.

While many other expenditures lead to reductions in both the chance of an accident and the cost of an accident, it is instructive to consider separately the consequences of moral hazard in each type of expenditure. Posing the moral hazard or agency problem in the most general way possible yields few specific predictions; insight is gained by dissecting the kinds of moral hazard and investigating separately their implications for insurance contracts.

As it turns out, the consequences of each type of moral hazard for insurance contracts are quite different. For example, moral hazard on self-protection leads to a deductible under reasonable assumptions. The entire marginal loss (or "residual claim") accrues to the individual at low loss levels. Moral hazard on loss-reduction on the other hand leads to optimal insurance with the opposite feature: the individual is fully covered up to some ceiling; the marginal loss accrues entirely to the insurer at low loss levels.

In some contexts it is reasonable to assume that insurance payments cannot exceed losses. With this constraint and the constraint against negative payouts, we find that the two types of moral hazard each give rise to a simple insurance contract: a deductible in one case, and full coverage up to a limit, with co-insurance thereafter, in the other case.

To analyze the moral hazard on expenditures for self-protection, we retain substantial notation of Section 6.2. The function $p(x)$ represents the probability of an accident, as before, with $p' < 0$ and $p'' > 0$. We assume that the cost of care is one dollar per unit, and also assume that $p'(0) = -\infty$, which guarantees an interior solution on the optimal care. The event of an accident in this section refers to a random loss, with distribution function $G(L)$ and density $g(L)$. That is, G is the conditional distribution of L given the event $L > 0$. Self-protection then refers to an increase in the probability of a zero loss, with no change in the conditional distribution G. Loss-reduction refers to a first-order stochastic reduction in the random loss with no change in the probability of a loss.

A general insurance contract in this case consists of a premium π and a payment function or sharing rule $q(L)$ specifying how much the insurer promises to pay with each loss, L. Thus the insurer is assumed to be able to verify the size of the loss. As before, the optimal insurance contract maximizes expected utility subject to a break-even constraint for the insurer and an incentive-compatibility constraint for the individual.

In addition, we impose the constraint that the specified insurance payment $q(L)$ can never be negative. That is, the contract cannot specify a transfer from the insured to the insurer that is contingent upon particular realizations of the random loss. This limited liability constraint reflects an assumption that the insurer is aware of losses only when the insured reports them.

The following problem, (P2), characterizes the optimal contract with moral hazard on self-protection:

$$(P2) \quad \max_{\pi,q(L),x} (1-p(x))U(W-\pi-x)+p(x)\int U(W-\pi-x-L+q(L))g(L)dL$$

subject to

$$\pi - p(x)\int q(L)g(L)dL \geq 0 \tag{6}$$

$$x = \arg\max_{z} p(z)U(W-\pi-z)+[(1-p(z))]\int [U(W-\pi-z-L+q(L))]g(L)dL \tag{7}$$

$$q(L) \geq 0 \tag{8}$$

In this maximization problem, the constraint (6) is the break-even constraint; (7) is the incentive compatibility constraint; and (8) is the "reporting constraint" that insurance payments not be negative. For any interior solution to this problem, the incentive compatibility constraint can be replaced by a first order condition in an interior solution, because of the convexity of $p(\cdot)$. That is, the constraint (7) can be replaced by

$$[1-p(x)]U'(W-\pi-x)-p(x)\int[U'(W-\pi-x-L+q(L))]g(L)dL$$
$$-p'(x)\big[U(W-\pi-x)-\int[U(W-\pi-x-L+q(L))]g(L)dL\big]=0 \tag{9}$$

With this replacement, the problem (P2) is a problem of Lagrange, and an interior solution to the problem must satisfy a set of first-order conditions corresponding to the choice of each $q(L)$, as well as a first order condition on x, the level of care. Let W_L be shorthand for the wealth level given a loss of L, and W_0 be the wealth level with no accident ($W_0 = W - \pi - e$ and $W_L = W - \pi - x - L + q(L)$). Let the shadow prices on the first two constraints be λ_1 and λ_2.

At each L, either:

$$q(L)=0$$

or

$$p(x)U'(W_L)G(L)-\lambda_1 p(x)G(L)-\lambda_2[-p(x)G(L)U''(W_L)+p'(x)G(L)U'(W_L)]=0 \tag{10}$$

which implies that for all positive W_L,

$$\lambda_2 U''(W_L)+\left[1-\lambda_2\frac{p'(x)}{p(x)}\right]U'(W_L)-\lambda_1=0 \tag{11}$$

If equation (11) is solved at a particular loss, $\hat{L}$, by a wealth level $\hat{W}$, then $\hat{W}$ also solves the equation at any other loss. That is, (11) implies that at the optimum, W_L is independent of L wherever it is positive. From $W_L \equiv W - \pi - x - L + q(L)$, this implies that $q(L) = \max(0, L - D)$ for some constant D. It is easy to verify that D must be positive. In sum, we have proved:

Proposition 1. The optimal contract $[\pi^*, q^*(\cdot)]$ solving (P2), optimal insurance under moral hazard on self-protection, satisfies, for some constant D,

$$q^*(L)=\max(0, L-D)$$

That is, the optimal contract is full insurance above a deductible.

The intuition for this result is clear. Suppose that negative payouts were feasible. Because there is no moral hazard on the magnitude of the loss, large losses should be fully insured relative to small losses; the equalization of final wealth in all states with a positive loss is efficient. On the other hand, the moral hazard with respect to the event of a loss dictates that individuals face some penalty (reduction in wealth) in the event of the loss. This reduction in wealth will exceed the loss for small-loss states;

i.e., the pay-out will be negative. Incorporating the constraint against negative payments then yields the proposition.

6.4 LOSS REDUCTION AND MORAL HAZARD

The moral hazard problem under self-protection, or the reduction of the chance of an accident, was analyzed above given uncertainty about the size of the loss. In the case of moral hazard on loss reduction, the motivation for considering *uncertain* losses is even stronger: this moral hazard problem does not even exist unless the losses are random. For suppose that the loss conditional upon an accident is a deterministic function of unobservable expenditure by the individual. An insurance contract that covered only the loss associated with the first-best level of expenditure would leave the marginal cost of additional loss entirely on the insured, and would therefore elicit the first-best expenditure. The moral hazard problem would disappear.

Accordingly, we consider the moral hazard problem under the assumption that an additional unit of expenditure yields a reduction in the random loss in the sense of first-order stochastic dominance. We assume that conditional upon an accident, there are a finite number of possible loss values, $l_1, l_2, \ldots, l_n$ with $l_{i+1} > l_i$ for each i. These losses occur with probability $p_i(x)$, $i = 1, \ldots, n$ conditional upon an accident, i.e., conditional upon $L > 0$, given expenditure x. Loss-reduction refers to a first order stochastic drop in the conditional distribution of losses, with no change in the probability of an accident.

We adopt the constraint that insurance coverage given any loss cannot exceed the loss. This is based on the assumption that the individual could effect (without being observed by the insurer) a loss of any particular size. For example, if an item such as a bicycle is insured for more than its worth, it would purposely be lost. To avoid this moral hazard problem, the wealth of the individual in any state cannot be higher than the wealth in the event of no accident.

The probability of a positive loss is $\mathbf{p}$, the insurance payouts in the n accident states are $(q_1, q_2, \ldots, q_n)$ and the remaining notation is as in the previous section. The optimal insurance contract $(\pi^*; q_1^*, q_2^*, \ldots, q_n^*)$ solves the following problem

$$(P3) \quad \max_{\pi, q_1, \ldots; e} (1-\mathbf{p})U(W-\pi-e)+\mathbf{p}\sum_{i=1,\ldots,n} p_i(e)U(W-\pi-e-l_i+q_i)$$

subject to

$$\mathbf{p}\sum_{i=1,\ldots,n} p_i(e)q_i - \pi \leq 0 \tag{12}$$

$$e = \arg\max_z (1-\mathbf{p})U(W-\pi-z)+\mathbf{p}\sum_{i=1,\ldots,n} p_i(z)U(W-\pi-z-l_i+q_i) \tag{13}$$

$$q_i - l_i \leq 0 \tag{14}$$

In this problem (12) is the break-even constraint and (13) the incentive compatibility constraint. The constraint (14) reflects the assumption that an insurance policy which promised to pay out more than the loss in any state i would lead an individual to cause an accident. A constraint that the insurance payment is positive would also be justified (as in Section 6.3), but is never binding in this problem.

The first assumption that we impose on the problem is that every loss have positive probability when the first-best care level, e^*, is taken. (This assumption is familiar from the general principal-agent problem, to be reviewed in Section 6.5.) If this assumption did not hold, then the insurance contract could impose a penalty of zero coverage in outcomes that signalled a sub-optimal level of effort.

We adopt the assumption here that the incentive compatibility condition can be represented by the first-order condition to the individual's maximization problem. (This assumption is discussed below.) With this assumption, the constraint becomes

$$-(1-\mathbf{p})U'(W-\pi-e)-\mathbf{p}\sum_{i=1,\ldots,n}\{p_i(e)U'(W-\pi-e-l_i+q_i)$$
$$-\,p_i'(e)U(W-\pi-e-l_i+q_i)\}=0$$

The following proposition characterizes the insurance market reaction to moral hazard on loss-reduction activities. The technical condition of a monotone likelihood ratio is standard in principal-agent problems, and is discussed in Section 6.5.

Proposition 2. Assume:

- $p_i(e^*) > 0$ for every i;
- The incentive compatibility condition (13) can be represented by its first order condition;
- U exhibits non-increasing absolute risk aversion; and
- the distribution of losses satisfies the condition of monotone likelihood ratio.

Then the solution to (P3) satisfies:

a) $(l_i - q_i)$ is non-decreasing in l. That is, the amount of the risk borne by the individual is a non-decreasing function of the size of the loss.
b) There is some m such that:
For $i \leq m$, $q_i = l_i$ and the constraint (14) is binding.
For $i > m$, $q_i < l_i$.

Proof. Appendix

Part a) of the proposition states that the amount of the loss borne by the individual is a non-decreasing function of the realized loss. Part b) states that sufficiently small losses are fully covered by the optimal policy with moral hazard in loss- reduction activities, and that the constraint against over- insurance is binding for these losses. In contrast to the case of self-protection, optimal insurance contracts with moral hazard on loss-reduction activities involve full coverage of small losses (more than full coverage if possible) and on average, less than full coverage of the marginal dollar of high losses.

The intuition for this result is as follows. Ignore for the moment the constraint (14). Because there is no moral hazard problem on the *event* of an accident, efficient risk-bearing dictates that the individual's marginal utility of wealth in the event of no accident be equated to the expected marginal utility of wealth conditional upon the event of an accident. Wealth will be transferred, through insurance, between these two events to achieve this condition. But within the event of an accident, wealth will be transferred from high-loss states to low-loss states relative to the full insurance solution, in order to enhance incentives for loss-reduction, because of moral hazard. This leaves wealth in the low-loss states greater than in the event of no accident—that is, the insurance payment for a low loss exceeds the loss. With the constraint (14) binding, low losses are fully insured.

6.5 GENERAL ASSUMPTIONS ON THE DISTRIBUTION OF LOSSES

Up to this point, we have adopted specific assumptions on the impact of greater care on the distribution of losses faced by the insured. When we generalize the models of sections 6.2, 6.3 and 6.4 to allow for an arbitrary distribution of losses, with care affecting both the probability of a loss and the size of the loss, the result is the *Principal-Agent* model. This model is at the core of the theory of contracts in economics in a wide variety of contexts. An excellent overview of the model is provided in chapter 14 of MasColell, Whinston and Green (1995).

The interpretation of this general model as the optimal insurance contract under moral hazard is only one interpretation. The economic modelling of virtually any organization involves incentives, the allocation of risk-bearing and incomplete contracting. The most popular application of the principal-agent model is to the contractual relationship between managers of corporations and the owners in corporations; the model or its extensions can be interpreted in terms of a share-cropper and a landlord, or an employer and an employee where the actions or effort of the employee are not perfectly monitored by the employer; a manufacturer and a franchisee, and so on. Almost every economic relationship is influenced by risk and a trade-off between the efficient allocation of risk-bearing and the minimization of incentive distortions is fundamental.

Moral hazard arises in any contractual setting whenever an individual is not assigned the full costs and benefits, at the margin, of a decision that affects other parties to the contract. Moral hazard therefore arises in a contractual setting where the full *residual claim* (the total output or profit from the enterprise, minus a lump sum) is not assigned to each party making a decision after the contract. The manager of a firm that purchases the firm from its shareholders for a lump sum of money or an issue of riskless debt has resolved the moral hazard or agency problem, but a manager who has only partial equity in the firm has not.

There are three main reasons why an individual would not be assigned the full consequences of his decisions and, correspondingly, three types of principal-agent problems. First, the agent (a manager of a firm, for example) may not have the wealth to purchase the enterprise for its value to the principal or principals. A wealth constraint gives rise to the *limited liability* class of principal-agent models (e.g., Sappington (1983)). Second, there may be "multiple moral hazard": more than one agent, or individual whose actions affect the return to the enterprise. With only one residual claim to divide among many agents, each agent cannot receive the full benefits of additional effort at the margin (Alchian and Demsetz (1972), Holmström (1982), Carmichael (1983)). In either of these first two classes of agency models, moral hazard exists even if all parties are risk-neutral. Finally, in the class of principal-agent models that are of interest here, it is possible but not *optimal* to allocate the full residual claim to the agent. The agent's risk aversion implies that the principal should bear at least some part of the uncertainty that is tied to ownership of the residual claim. The actual contract is second best in that it compromises between the goal of efficient risk allocation and the achievement of efficient incentives. This is the essence of optimal insurance contracts under moral hazard.[9]

The following is the basic set of assumptions defining the Principal-Agent problem. Consider a principal and an agent who have property rights to an uncertain income stream. The random income stream depends on an input such as care or effort on the part of the agent, to be taken in the future. The income stream may represent a firm or project which is initially owned by the principal, the management of which is delegated to the agent; it may represent a project owned by the agent who must raise capital by promising some share of the income stream to the principal; or, it may represent a possible loss from current wealth if the agent insures with the principal.

Let e represent the effort of the agent in avoiding an accident, and θ the random state of the world. The principal and agent establish a *sharing rule* or contract to share the random income stream. In the insurance example, this contract describes the insurance payment to the agent, $I(L)$, as a function of the loss incurred by the agent. The loss $L(e, \theta)$ depends on the effort input by the agent as well as the state of the world. The critical assumption is that neither e nor θ can enter the contract. For example, neither is observable to the principal; alternatively, neither is observable to a third party enforcer of the contract (the courts). In most cases, it is analytically convenient

[9] Holmstrom and Milgrom (1991) discuss a fourth reason why residual claimancy contracts may not be feasible: the output, or benefit to the principal of the agent's effort, may not be observable. Their multitask agency model accomodates this possibility.

to re-parameterize the problem by letting $F(L, e)$ refer to the distribution of losses, L, given the care, e, undertaken by the agent.

The utility of the agent is represented by $U(W, e)$ which is increasing and concave in the agent's wealth, W and decreasing in effort. It simplifies the analysis to assume that the agent's utility is quasi-linear: $U(W, e) = u(w) - e$, in contrast to our assumption earlier in this essay that care is a pecuniary expense. The set of possible effort levels is denoted by A. The objective of the principal and agent is to choose a Pareto optimal sharing rule. If the principal owns the project, this is represented as maximizing the principal's utility subject to achieving a reservation level for the agent.

In the case of an optimal insurance contract with a competitive insurance market, however, the most natural formulation is the dual problem: maximize U subject to a break-even constraint on the part of the insurer. Furthermore, in the insurance context, the usual assumption is that the principal (the insurer) is risk-neutral because a large number of independent risks are insured. Finally, in most formulations, the effort on the part of the agent is assumed to be decided before the state θ is realized. The optimal contract under these assumptions is characterized by the maximization of the agent's expected utility subject to two constraints: the break-even constraint, and the incentive compatibility constraint:

$$(P4) \quad \max_{I(L),e} \int u(W - L - \pi + I(L)) f(L, e) dL - e$$

subject to

$$\pi - \int I(L) f(L, e) dL \geq 0 \tag{15}$$

$$e \in \arg\max_{a \in A} \int U(W - L - \pi + I(L)) f(L, a) dL - a \tag{16}$$

A necessary condition for the incentive compatibility constraint is the first-order condition corresponding to the maximization problem in the constraint. Where this first-order condition is *sufficient* as well as necessary for the constraint, the constraint can be replaced by the first-order condition. This method is referred to as the "first-order approach" to agency problems. Unfortunately, the first-order condition can identify not just global maxima but minima and local-but-not-global maxima. Mirrlees (1975), Rogerson (1985) and Jewitt (1988) contain analyses of circumstances under which the first-order approach is valid.

Where the first-order approach is valid, the incentive compatibility constraint becomes:

$$\int U(W - L - \pi + I(L)) f_e(L, e) dL - 1 = 0 \tag{17}$$

The resulting principal-agent problem (P4) becomes a standard Lagrangian maximization problem. Letting the shadow prices for the constraints (15) and (16) be λ and μ respectively, and solving the first-order conditions for (P4) yields the following standard necessary condition for the optimal contract:

$$\frac{1}{u'(W-L-\pi+I(L))}=\lambda+\mu\frac{f_e(L,e)}{f(L,e)} \tag{18}$$

This first-order condition reveals the trade-off between the insurance benefits of the contract, in transferring risk from the agent to the principal, and the incentives benefits of leaving the residual claim or effect of increased losses with the agent. If incentives were not an issue, so that μ and the last term of (18) disappeared, then this condition would imply that the agent's wealth be independent of the realization of L, and therefore that $L - I(L)$ were independent of L. In other words, the agent is fully insured. The extent to which a particular loss, L_1, is associated with a higher uninsured loss to the agent, $L_1 - I(L_1)$, relative to another loss, L_2, depends on the proportionate sensitivity of the likelihood of L_1 to effort relative to L_2—i.e., on the value of $f_e(L, e)/f(L, e)$ at L_1 and L_2. This measures the incentive benefit, in terms of mitigating the moral hazard problem, of deviating from the full insurance strategy of equalizing the agent's marginal utility of wealth at L_1 and L_2.

The principal-agent model is too general to reveal specific propositions on the form of the optimal insurance contract. Even the intuitive proposition that the agent's wealth is non-decreasing with output—in our context, that the agent's exposure to the loss is non-decreasing in the realized loss—is not automatic. To see this suppose that there are four possible values for the loss, 1, 2, 3 and 4 dollars, and that the effect of increasing the agent's effort is that the outcomes of 1 and 3 become more likely than 2 and 4. In this example, in the optimal contract the agent may bear less of the loss under the outcome of $L = 3$ than under the outcome $L = 2$. The latter outcome, even though it is more favourable to the insurer, signals a higher likelihood of low effort on the part of the agent. Attaching a penalty to this outcome encourages greater effort.

The example is ruled out by a condition referred to as the *monotonic likelihood ratio condition* (Milgrom (1981) and MasColell, Whinston and Green (1995)). For two effort levels, e_L and e_H, with $e_H > e_L$, the condition is that $f(L, e_L)/f(L, e_H)$ be increasing in L. That is, as L increases, the likelihood of generating a loss L from the low effort relative to the likelihood if effort is high, must increase. The monotone likelihood ratio is the essential condition that yields monotonicity of the sharing of accident losses between the agent and the principal.

Note that our framework in section 6.2, in which the accident probability but not the accident loss depended upon care, implied a constant likelihood ratio over all possible loss levels. The agent's exposure to the loss was, correspondingly, constant over sufficiently high loss levels.

A general result that is relevant for insurance contracts is proved by Shavell (1979): While moral hazard reduces the expected utility achieved with an insurance contract, under the assumptions of this section it never *eliminates* the gains to trade from insurance. There is always some gain from the first dollar of insurance coverage.

In sum, under general assumptions including the monotonic likelihood ratio property, moral hazard reduces but does not eliminate the gains from insurance, and is responded to optimally with a contract in which the agent bears an increasing, but not full, share of greater accident losses.

6.6 EXTENSIONS

The models of optimal insurance under moral hazard outlined in this essay are simplistic compared to the richness of real world markets. This concluding section reviews a number of ways in which the model of insurance contracts under moral hazard has been extended, or could be extended further.

6.6.1 Renegotiation

We have, to this point, ignored the possibility that the insurance company and the insured, or the principal and the agent, will renegotiate the insurance contract once it has been signed. The possibility of renegotiation must be addressed: an opportunity to achieve a Pareto superior outcome some time after the insurance contract has been signed will surely be exploited by the contractual parties. The standard model assumes that there is commitment against renegotiation. As Fudenberg and Tirole (1990, p. 1279) note, however, "While such commitment is likely to be credible in some situations, in others it may not be, especially if there are long lags between the agent's choice of action and the time when all of the (stochastic) consequences of that actions will have been revealed."

Suppose that the principal and the agent have signed an insurance contract in anticipation of moral hazard, according to the principles outlined in the previous section. Suppose further that there is a significant time interval between the time of the agent's action and the realization of uncertainty and that this timing is common knowledge. The principal and agent would, during this interval, face the opportunity for mutual gain from further contracting. Specifically, there would be no incentive cost to switching to a full insurance contract, since the agent's effort decision is history at this point.

What is the outcome of the moral hazard problem in this set of circumstances? Fudenberg and Tirole address this question in the following model (adapted to the insurance context). First, the parties sign an original or *ex ante* contract, c_1, which specifies the insurance coverage as a function of the realized accident loss. Then the agent chooses an effort level e. This effort generates the probability distribution $f(L, e)$ over the accident losses. The principal will observe the realized loss but not the effort. After the effort is undertaken, but before the realization of the loss, the parties have the opportunity to renegotiate, replacing c_1 with a new contract c_2. At the renegotiation stage, the principal is assumed to be able to implement the optimal mechanism, which generally involves the offer of a menu of insurance coverage functions, one for each level of effort that the agent may have undertaken.

As is standard in contractual games with renegotiation, the optimum can be achieved through the offer of a contract that is *renegotiation-proof*. If a contract c is offered and renegotiated to a contract c^*, then the principal and agent do as well by signing the contract c^* at the outset.

Fudenberg and Tirole show that the optimal contract in this model typically elicits randomization by the agent over choices of effort. To see why, suppose that only two levels of effort, e_L and e_H are possible. If the agent chose a pure strategy in the contract game, it would have to be e_L. It could not be e_H since the agent's choice of effort would be followed by renegotiation to full insurance (rather, this renegotiation incentive would be reflected in the original contract); the agent anticipating this would have no incentive to put out the higher effort. Therefore, a contract that induces the agent to choose a strategy with *some* probability on the high level of effort, cannot induce the *entire* probability on the high effort level, if it is to be renegotiation-proof.

Fudenberg and Tirole compare the outcome of this renegotiation contract game with the Principal Agent model under the standard commitment assumption. The renegotiation constraints in general lead the principal to elicit a different distribution over effort levels on the part of the agent than under the standard commitment model. In addition, depending on the class of the agent's utility function, any particular distribution of effort levels may be elicited with a different contract (including in particular a different level of rent or surplus to the agent) in the renegotiation game than when commitment is possible.

6.6.2 Multidimensional Care

Care or effort on the part of an insured agent does not in reality take on a single dimension, as we have assumed here. There are, for example, many activities that a homeowner can undertake to reduce the probability of fire or to lessen the damage if a fire does occur: "not dumping cigarette ashes in wastepaper baskets, not smoking in bed, not leaving the stove unattended while cooking, dousing the ashes in the fireplace before retiring, replacing frayed electrical cords immediately, keeping a functioning fire extinguisher in every room, spending extra on fire-resistant materials in home construction and household furnishings, ensuring easy exits from each room in the house, holding family fire drills, etc." (Arnott 1991: 327).

The problem of moral hazard is not manifest in all dimensions of care to the same degree. Some dimensions, such as the construction materials used in a home in the example above, are observable by the insurer; other aspects of care, such as refraining from smoking in bed, are not. The mental concentration of an automobile driver cannot be contractually specified, but the attendance in an advanced driving class or the choice by the driver of a car model, can be specified. How does the ability of the principal to observe some aspects of care affect the moral hazard problem?

The central tool for multi-dimensional principal-agent problems is the multi-task model of Holmström and Milgrom (1991). In this model, the agent makes a one-time choice of a vector of efforts $t = (t_1, \ldots, t_n)$ at personal cost $C(t)$. The efforts lead to expected gross benefits $B(t)$ which accrue directly to the principal. The function C is strictly convex and B is strictly concave. The agent's efforts generate as well a vector of informational signals

$$x = t + \varepsilon \tag{19}$$

where ε is normally distributed with mean vector zero and covariance matrix Σ.[10] (One limiting, special case is where some dimensions of effort are observable and others are not.)

The agent's utility over wealth is assumed to exhibit constant absolute risk aversion. Income effects in the demand for insurance are thus set aside. The agent's cost of effort is pecuniary. The agent's utility, from a contract specifying receipts by the agent of $w(x)$, interpreted in our context as the uninsured component of accident losses, is

$$E\{u[w(t+\varepsilon)-C(t)]\} \tag{20}$$

where $u(w) = -e^{-rw}$. The coefficient r measures the agent's degree of risk aversion. The agent's certainty-equivalent of the compensation package $w(\cdot)$ is CE defined by

$$u(CE) = E\{u[w(t+\varepsilon)-C(t)]\} \tag{21}$$

In the case of a linear compensation rule, $w(x) = \alpha' x + \beta$, the exponential form of the utility implies that the certainty equivalent is

$$CE = \alpha' t + \beta - C(t) - \frac{1}{2} r\alpha'\Sigma\alpha \tag{22}$$

where the term $\alpha'\Sigma\alpha$ is the variance of the agent's income under the scheme.

The principal's expected profit is $B(t) - E\{w[t+\varepsilon]\}$ which under the linear scheme equals $B(t) - \alpha' t - \beta$. Thus the combined certainty equivalent, or joint surplus, of the

[10] Holmstrom and Milgrom use the notation $x = \mu(t) + \varepsilon$ but note in their footnote 8 that this is no more general than $x = t + \varepsilon$.

principal and agent is $B(t) - C(t) - \frac{1}{2}r\alpha'\Sigma\alpha$. The principal-agent problem, with linear compensation rules and constant absolute risk aversion on the part of the agent, can thus be written very simply:

$$\max_{t,\alpha} B(t) - C(t) - \frac{1}{2}r\alpha'\Sigma\alpha \tag{23}$$

subject to

$$t = \arg\max_{\hat{t}} \alpha'\hat{t} - C(\hat{t}) \tag{24}$$

(The problem is expressed simply in terms of the slope α of the compensation rule; the intercept is determined subsequently.) For positive t, the incentive constraint (24) can be replaced by the first-order conditions $\alpha_i = C_i(t)$, $i = 1 \ldots n$. Solution of the resulting quadratic maximization problem yields as an optimum

$$\alpha^* = (I + r[C_{ij}]\Sigma)^{-1}\begin{pmatrix} B_1 \\ \vdots \\ B_n \end{pmatrix} \tag{25}$$

The above model contains an assumption that compensation rules are linear, or equivalently, that insurance payments are linear in realized losses. As Holmström and Milgrom point out, it contains as well a second assumption that is common in agency models and therefore likely to be overlooked: that the agent makes the effort decision once-and-for-all during the insurance relationship. Holmström and Milgrom demonstrate in an earlier article (Holmström and Milgrom (1987)), however, that these two assumptions are exactly offsetting: The solution to the linear/normal distribution agency problem is identical to the solution to a principal-agent problem in which (i) the agent chooses efforts continuously over the time interval [0, 1] to control the drift vector of a stationary Brownian motion process, and (ii) the agent can observe his accumulated performance before acting. In this model, the agent's compensation is a linear function of the final accumulated performance. As applied to the insurance context, the potential insight is that the simple linear form of some co-insurance contracts could be explained by the continuous effort decisions over time on the part of the insured individual (and the normality structure of the uncertainty).

Holmström and Milgrom apply the multi-task agency model to the explanation of a wide variety of contractual phenomena. With respect to the type of problem posed above—the optimal contract when some actions of the agent are observed and other actions are not—the authors show that the contract will reward the agent for actions that are complementary to those that are not observed. This encourages the agent to undertake more of the unobserved (hence, noncontractible) actions. In the insurance context, the purchase of new fire extinguishers is an investment that is complementary to the effort undertaken to monitor and replace existing fire extinguishers. Fire extinguishers are subsidized by insurers, or required in fire insurance contracts. Similarly, fire sprinkler systems may be required in commercial buildings as part of a building code, or as a requirement for lower insurance premiums.

An alternative, and natural, model of multi-dimensional care in insurance is the following. The agent can undertake two different kinds of care, 1 and 2, in amounts t_1 and t_2, and has a utility over wealth and care $U(W) - t_1 - t_2$. The probability of an accident is $p(t_1, t_2)$ and an accident leads to a loss L if it occurs. The Principal (insurer) can observe t_2 but not t_1 and is willing to provide insurance at a zero expected rate of profit. Unfortunately, in this model the impact of the non-observability of t_1, i.e., the moral hazard problem, on the observable care level t_2 cannot be determined unambiguously.

The impact on optimal insurance contracts of partial observability of insured's actions, both in terms of dimensionality as described here and in terms of "noisy" observability of actions, remains an important open issue.

6.6.3 Dynamics

Part of the conventional wisdom in insurance economics is that moral hazard problems are likely to be less severe under a repeated relationship between the insurer and the insured. Increased frequency of accidents because of failure on the part of an individual to take adequate care, the argument goes, will be met with increases in premiums. That is, the incentives to take adequate care are enhanced with "experience rating" of premiums. The central question in multiperiod moral hazard models has been the extent to which this conjecture is valid.

A basic starting point for this discussion is that with finite repetitions, this conventional wisdom is wrong. Suppose that the individual's utility exhibits constant absolute risk aversion, so that there are no income effects in the demand for insurance. Then when the relationship between the principal and agent is as modelled in Section 4, including the assumption of no informational signals being observed by the principal, with the repetition of the relationship a finite number of times, the contract and effort of the agent is *identical* to the single period case. Repetition has no impact on the moral hazard problem. Where the agent's degree of absolute risk aversion does vary with wealth, then contracts vary from period to period only because of the effect on the demand for insurance of changes in the individual's wealth.

The logic of this proposition is clear. Suppose that the principal and agent have access to the same interest rate for borrowing or lending in the capital market. Then a penalty for an accident in the current period, in the form of a higher premium in next period's contract, offers no additional degrees of freedom as compared with the static model. Such a penalty, contingent upon an accident the current period, is identical to a reduction in coverage for the current period equal to the present value of the increased future premium. The trade-off between optimal insurance and adequate incentives is unchanged by the repetition of the simplest moral hazard game.

The theory of repeated moral hazard proceeds by relaxing various of the assumptions in this "irrelevance proposition". The assumptions discarded in the various papers in the literature have been (i) finite number of periods; (ii) zero information on the part of the principal, and (iii) equal access to capital markets.

Rogerson (1985) relaxes the assumption that the principal and agent have equal access to capital markets. The long-term contract between the agent and the principal is governed by the goal of realizing the gains to trade arising from this difference in access (effectively, the gains from intermediation by the principal) and the usual goal of achieving the right mix of incentives and insurance. Rogerson shows that the expected wealth allocated to the agent by the contract may increase or decrease over time, depending on how quickly risk aversion decreases with wealth.

In another approach to long-term contracts under moral hazard, Becker and Stigler (1974) show that a strategy of increasing wages over time (relative to marginal product), together with a rule that shirking agents be fired if detected, can improve efficiency under moral hazard. The analysis of long-term contracts, however, is less relevant to the insurance context than to the context of long-term labour contracts. Life insurance contracts appear to be the only insurance contracts in which premiums are guaranteed for long periods, and for this type of insurance moral hazard is surely not a major issue.

A different branch of the literature on repeated moral hazard examines the extent to which the moral hazard problem can be resolved through "punishment strategies" by the principal when the principal infers that the agent has shirked, i.e., taken less than due care (Radner (1981), Rubinstein and Yaari (1983)). Expressed differently, this literature offers an explanation of experience rating, i.e. discounts on premiums offered to clients who possess a favourable record of part claims. It argues that experience rating provides a mechanism which enables the parties to the contract to mitigate or eliminate the moral hazard inefficiency.

The Rubinstein and Yaari (1983) analysis, in particular, is framed in the context of insurance markets. These authors show that if there are infinite periods, and no discounting (the insured and the insurer are interested in the average payoff in each period) then the insurer can eliminate the moral hazard problem by choosing an appropriate "no-claims-discount" (NCD) strategy. An NCD involves giving a discount for coverage in any period if the history of claims up to that period leads to an inference that the level of care is sufficiently high. Facing this announced strategy, it pays the insured to choose the first best care level in each period.

The insurer's problem is to determine exactly which claims histories should warrant a discount on the premium. If the definition of "excessive" claims is too strict, then the owner of the asset would end up paying a high premium too often, even when due care is exercised. If the definition is too lax, then the optimal care is not elicited.

Rubinstein and Yaari show that the two types of possible errors in inferring a deviation from optimal care are both minimized with a particular class of insurance premium strategies.

Radner (1981) has a similar model, although his equilibrium strategies do not satisfy the property of "perfection" as Rubinstein and Yaari (p. 95) point out. Both of these papers can be thought of as extensions of the "Folk Theorem" of repeated games to the class of games where a player makes a move in each period without full knowledge of the previous moves of the other player. Whatever the theoretical interest of these models, their implications for actual insurance contracts are limited by the assumptions of no discounting and infinite periods. A zero discount rate is simply counterfactual, and it is very difficult to determine the deviation from first best that arises when there is a discount rate.

The assumption of infinite periods is also unrealistic. In a finite period model, it is possible that individual's incentive to take adequate care is enhanced by a desire to achieve a reputation as one who is careful. This, however, becomes a model of adverse selection (hidden types) rather than a model of moral hazard alone. A conjecture is that the resolution of adverse selection, via revelation of information about types, can *reduce* welfare in a combined adverse selection-moral hazard model, because it eliminates the possibility of taking care to acquire a reputation with finite repetitions. In general, the literature on repeated moral hazard does not offer an implication for experience rating in actual contracts that is *testable* against the alternative hypothesis of adverse selection. Adverse selection clearly leads to experience rating (e.g., Hosios and Peters (1989)). There is no reason not to think that experience rating in actual insurance contracts is entirely explained by adverse selection.

An interesting case that has not been investigated in the repeated moral hazard literature is the case of long-lived, capital investments in care. In the case of product liability insurance, for example, "care" refers to the investment in safety in product design and the decision not to market excessively dangerous products. A decision to invest in care affects not just the immediate rate of accidents but the future rate as well. In a finitely repeated contract, when there is common knowledge at the beginning of the relationship (so that the problem is in this sense one of moral hazard), the incentive to take care is enhanced by the dependence of future premiums on past claims records: the future insurers "infer" the care decision from past claims. A conjecture is that even with a finite number of periods in the case of long-lived care decisions, repetition and the ability of premiums to respond to claims' histories does mitigate the moral hazard problem.

6.6.4 Other Extensions

A number of areas of the theory of moral hazard in insurance contracts remain fertile ground for further research. As I suggested above, a dynamic model of moral hazard in investment in safety capital, would yield important insights as well as a set of circumstances in which finite repetition of the insurance contracting does affect the nature of the contract.

The theory of moral hazard in insurance, indeed the theory of optimal insurance in general, has not been fully developed for the case of liability insurance purchased by a corporation with limited liability.[11] The presence of limited liability means that even without insurance, moral hazard is potentially a problem, as creditors bear some of the costs of lax effort on the part of equity holders. The specific moral hazard problem of deposit insurance, in the context of financial intermediary corporations, has received substantial attention (e.g., Grubel (1993)).

The basic assumption of moral hazard models is that some decisions about care on the part of the insured cannot be contracted for. But there are often both substitute or complementary inputs by the individual that are observable. As discussed in section 6.6, the theory of moral hazard in insurance contracts should be extended to analyze the contractual requirement of extra expenditure on contractible, loss-reducing activities as a response to moral hazard. A closely related topic is the investment by insurers themselves in loss-reduction and accident-avoidance (Schlesinger and Venezian (1986)). A conjecture is that these activities will be relied upon to a greater extent under moral hazard than in a complete insurance contract. The supply side of the insurance market is itself subject to moral hazard problems when there are guaranty laws, which limit the liability of insurance corporations in the event of insolvency (Brewer et al. 1997).

Finally, as Arnott (1991) discusses, the interaction of moral hazard and adverse selection in insurance markets deserves further exploration. A recent contribution on this topic is Stewart (1994), who argues that the effect of each type of problem is partially offset by the other. Moral hazard, as we have seen, elicits equilibrium insurance contracts with partial insurance. The addition of adverse selection induces low risk agents to choose contracts with even lower insurance coverage, so that these agents can be separated from high risk agents (who would refuse such contracts). This has the effect that the low risk agents bear more risk themselves, thus mitigating the low care levels associated with the moral hazard problem alone.

APPENDIX 6.1: PROOF OF PROPOSITION 2

Let w_i denote $W - \pi - x - l_i + q_i$, the individual's wealth in state i. The first-order conditions for this problem, corresponding to q_i, π and x are provided below. In these equations, λ_1, and λ_2 are the shadow prices for the break even constraint and the incentive compability constraint respectively.

$$(\forall i)\quad \mathbf{p}p_iU'(w_i) - \lambda_1\mathbf{p}p_i - \lambda_2\mathbf{p}p_iU''(w_i) + \lambda_2\mathbf{p}p_i'U'(w_i) - \lambda_{3i} = 0 \tag{26}$$

[11] An exception is Huberman, Mayers and Smith (1983).

$$-(1-\mathbf{p})U'(w_0)-\mathbf{p}\sum_i p_iU'(w_i)+\lambda_1$$
$$+\lambda_2\left((1-\mathbf{p})U''(w_0)+\mathbf{p}\sum_i [p_iU''(w_i)-p_i'U'(w_i)]\right)=0 \tag{27}$$

$$-(1-\mathbf{p})U'(w_0)-\mathbf{p}\sum_i p_iU'(w_i)+\mathbf{p}\sum_i p_i'U'(w_i)-\lambda_1\mathbf{p}\sum_i p_i'q_i$$
$$-\lambda_2\left[-(1-\mathbf{p})U''(w_0)-p\sum_i\{p_iU''(w_i)-p_i'U'(w_i)-p_i'U'(w_i)+p_i''U(w_i)\}\right]=0$$

To prove (a) of the proposition, we must show that $w_{j+1}\leq w_j$, for all $j=1,\ldots n-1$. If the constraint (14) is binding for both j and $j+1$, or only for j this is trivial. Consider the case where (14) is binding for neither j nor $j+1$. Equation (26) and $\lambda_i=0$, for $i=j, j+1$ imply that

$$1-\frac{\lambda_1}{U'(w_i)}+\lambda_2\cdot\frac{-U''(w_i)}{U'(w_i)}=-\lambda_2\frac{p_i'}{p_i} \tag{28}$$

As a function of w_i, the left hand side of (28) is strictly decreasing (the second term is strictly decreasing by the concavity of U and the third is nonincreasing by the assumption of non-increasing absolute risk aversion). It follows from Milgrom (1981: Proposition 5) that under the monotone likelihood ratio condition, the right hand side of (28) is nondecreasing in i. To maintain the equality (28) for all i, therefore, it must be that w_i is decreasing in i. The case where (14) is binding only for $j+1$ is similar. This proves part (a) of the proposition.

To prove part (b), suppose that $\lambda_{3i}=0$ for all i. Then equation (28) implies

$$U'(w_i)-\lambda_1-\lambda_2U''(w_i)+\lambda_2\frac{p_i'}{p_i}U'(w_i)=0 \tag{29}$$

Adding up all n first-order constraints represented by equation (26), subtracting (27) and simplifying yields

$$U'(w_0)-\lambda_1-\lambda_2U''(w_0)=0 \tag{30}$$

Next, note that $\Sigma_i p_i=1$ implies $\Sigma_i p_i'=0$. This and the fact that not all p_i' are zero implies p_i' are neither all negative nor all positive. The monotonicity in i of p_i'/p_i (see proof of (a) above) then implies that there exists $j, j\geq 1$ such that the last term of (29) is negative for all $i\leq j$, and positive for all $i>j$. Comparing with (30) and using the fact that the left hand side of (30) is decreasing in w_0 because $U'''>0$ for non-increasing absolute risk aversion utility functions, shows that $w_i>w_0$ for $i\leq j$. From the definitions of w_0 and w_i, this contradicts the constraint (14). Thus the supposition that $\lambda_{3i}=0$ for all i is contradicted, and the constraint (14) must therefore be binding for some i. Part (a) of the proposition implies that (14) is binding for small i. QED

APPENDIX 6.2: THE FIRST-ORDER APPROACH

Two assumptions are sufficient to justify the replacement of the incentive compatibility constraint with a first-order condition (Rogerson (1985)), in the case where the utility of the agent is separable in wealth and effort: the *monotone likelihood ratio condition* (MLRC) and the *concavity of the distribution function condition* (CDFC). Since the first-order approach is standard in modelling moral hazard and agency problems in general, it is a worthwhile digression in this survey to illustrate the basic problem with the first-order approach as well as the solution to the problem.

The first-order approach replaces the constraint that the agent choose an optimal level of care with a requirement that the agent choose a level of care at which his utility is at a stationary point. This is valid only when all stationary points are optima. In general, stationary points may also be saddle points, local minima or local maxima that are not global maxima. The first-order approach in general, therefore, expands the constraint set for the maximization problem and can lead to a different optimum, with a higher expected utility.

The MLRC is satisfied if, for $\hat{e} \leq \hat{\hat{e}}$, $p_i(\hat{e})/p_i(\hat{\hat{e}})$ is nonincreasing in i. Milgrom (1985) shows that the MLRC is equivalent to the following condition (expressed here in our context). Suppose that one starts with a prior on the agent's care level, observes only the outcome, i.e., the size of the loss, and then forms a posterior on the agent's care. Then the condition is that the observation of a higher loss allows the statistical inference that a lower care level was chosen in the sense of first-order stochastic dominance. This is, intuitively, a modest requirement on the distribution of output given care. Rogerson (1985) shows that MLRC implies the condition that increases in care cause the random loss to decrease in the sense of first-order stochastic dominance.

Define $F_j(e) = \Sigma_{i=1}^{j} p_i(e)$ as the distribution function associated with the probabilities $p_1(e), p_2(e), \ldots$. The concavity of the distribution function condition is satisfied if $F_j''(e)$ is nonpositive for every j and e. By the MLRC, $F_j(e)$ is increasing in e, i.e., the probability of realizing a loss lower than l_j is increasing in the care taken. The CDFC requires that the function increase at a decreasing rate, analogous to decreasing returns to scale.

Jewitt (1988) criticizes the Mirrlees-Rogerson conditions for the validity of the first-order approach, on the grounds that 1) the conditions do not work if the principal can observe more than one relevant statistic; and 2) the concavity of the distribution function is too restrictive a condition for even the basic principal-agent problem, being violated by some simple and reasonable examples. Jewitt (Theorem 1) replaces the conditions (the convexity condition in particular) with a set of four, easily tractable, convexity conditions on transformations of the distribution function and the utility function in the basic principal agent problem.

6.7 REFERENCES

Akerlof, G. (1970). "The Market for Lemons: Quality and the Market Mechanism," *Quarterly Journal of Economics*, 89, 488–500.

Alchian, A. and Demsetz, H. (1972). "Production, information costs, and economic organization", *American Economic Review*, LXII no. 5, 777–795.

Arnott, R. (1992). "Moral Hazard and Competitive Insurance Markets", in Dionne (1992).

Arnott, R. and Stiglitz, J. (1983a). "Equilibrium in Competitive Insurance Markets: The Welfare Economics of Moral Hazard", *Working Paper*, Queen's University, January 1983.

Arnott, R. and Stiglitz, J. (1983b). "The Basic Analytics of Moral Hazard: Ill-behaved Consumers with Well-behaved Utility Functions", *Working Paper*, Queen's University, November 1983.

Arnott, R. and Stiglitz, J. (1988a). "The Basic Analytics of Moral Hazard", *Scandinavian Journal of Economics* 90, 383–413.

Arnott, R. and Stiglitz, J. (1998b). "Randomization with Asymmetric Information", *Rand Journal of Economics*, 19, 344–362.

Arrow, K. (1970). "Uncertainty and the Welfare Economics of Medical Care", in K. Arrow, *Essays in the Theory of Risk-Bearing*, North-Holland.

Arrow, K. (1985). "The Economics of Agency," in *Principals and Agents: The Structure of Business*, ed. J. Pratt and R. Zeckhauser. Cambridge, MA: Harvard Business School Press.

Becker, G. (1968). "Crime and Punishment", *Journal of Political Economy*, March–April, 169–217.

Becker, G. and Stigler, G. (1974). "Law Enforcement, malfeasance, and compensation of enforcers", *Journal of Legal Studies*, 3, 1–18.

Boyer, M. and Dionne, G. (1983). "Variations in the Probability and Magnitude of Loss: Their impact on Risk", *Canadian Journal of Economics*, 16, 411–419.

Boyer, M. and Dionne, G. (1989). "More on Insurance, Protection and Risk", *Canadian Journal of Economics*, 22, 202–204.

Brewer, E., Mondschean, T. and Stahan, P. (1997). "The Role of Monitoring in Reducing the Moral Hazard Problem Associated with Government Guarantees: Evidence from the Life Insurance Industry," *Journal of Risk and Insurance*, vol. 64, no. 2 June, 301–322.

Carmichael, L. (1983). "The agent-agents problem: payment by relative output", *Journal of Labor Economics*, 1, 60–65.

Chang, Y.-M. and Ehrlich, I. (1985). "More on Insurance, Protection and Risk", *Canadian Journal of Economics*, 18, 574–587.

Dionne, G., ed. (1992). *Contributions to Insurance Economics*, Kluwer Academic Publishers.

Dionne, G. and Lasserre, P. (1987). "Dealing with Moral Hazard and Adverse Selection Simultaneously", *Working Paper*, Université de Montréal.

Ehrlich, I. and Becker, G. (1972). "Market Insurance, Self-Insurance and Self-Protection", *Journal of Political Economy*, 623–648.

Fudenberg, D. and Tirole, J. (1990). "Moral Hazard and Renegotiation in Agency Contracts," *Econometrica*, vol. 58, no. 6 November, 1279–1319.

Gjesdal, F. (1982). "Information and Incentives: The Agency Information Problem," *Review of Economic Studies* 49, 373–390.

Grossman, S. and Hart, O. (1983). "An Analysis of the Principal-Agent Problem", *Econometrica*, 51, no. 1 January, 7–45.

Grubel, H. (1993). "Government Deposit Insurance, Moral Hazard and the International Debt Crisis," in *Theory and measurement for economic policy*, Vol. 3, Elgar.

Harris, M. and Raviv, A. (1978). "Some Results on Incentive Contracts", *American Economic Review*, 68, no. 1 March, 20–31.

Helpman and Laffont, J.J. (1975). "On Moral Hazard in General Equilibrium", *Journal of Economic Theory*, 10, 8–23.

Holmström, B. (1979). "Moral Hazard and Observability", *The Bell Journal of Economics*, 10, no. 1 Spring, 74–92.

Holmström, B. (1982). "Moral Hazard in Teams", *The Rand Journal of Economics*, 13, 324–340.

Holmström, B. and Milgrom, P. (1987). "Aggregation and Linearity in the Provision of Intertemporal Incentives," *Econometrica*, 55, 303–329.

Holmström, B. and Milgrom, P. (1991). "Multitask Principal-Agent Analyses: Incentive Contracts, Asset Ownership and Job Design," *Journal of Law, Economics and Organization*, 7, 24–52.

Hosios, A. and Peters, M. (1989). "Repeated Insurance Contracts with Adverse Selection and Limited Commitment", *Quarterly Journal of Economics*, CIV, no. 2 May, 229–254.

Huberman, G., Mayers, D. and Smith, C. (1983). "Optimal Insurance Policy Indemnity Schedules", *Bell Journal of Economics*, August, 415–426.

Jewitt, I. (1988). "Justifying the First-Order Approach to Principal-Agent Problems", *Econometrica*, 56, no. 5 September, 1177–1190.

Kotowitz, Y. (1987). "Moral Hazard", in *The New Palgrave Dictionary of Economics*, 549–551.

Lambert, R. (1983). "Long-term Contracts and Moral Hazard", *Bell Journal of Economics*, August, 441–452.

MacDonald, G.M. (1984). "New Directions in the Economic Theory of Agency", *Canadian Journal of Economics*, XVII, no. 3 August, 415–440.

MasColell, A., Whinston, M. and Green, J. (1995). *Microeconomic Theory*, Oxford University Press.

Milgrom, P. (1981). "Good news and bad news: Representation Theorems and Applications," *Bell Journal of Economics*, 12, 380–391.

Mirrlees, J. (1975). "The Theory of Moral Hazard and Unobservable Behaviour. Part I", Mimeo, Nuffield College, Oxford.

Mookerjee, D. and Png, I. (1989). "Optimal Auditing, Insurance and Redistribution", *Quarterly Journal of Economics*, CIV, May, no. 2, 399–416.

Pauly, M. (1968). "The Economics of Moral Hazard: Comment", *American Economic Review*, 531–537.

Pauly, M. (1974). "Overinsurance and Public Provision of Insurance: The Roles of Moral Hazard and Adverse Selection", *Quarterly Journal of Economics*, 44–62.

Polinsky, A.M. (1983). *An Introduction to Law and Economics*, Little, Brown, Boston.

Polinsky, A.M. and Shavell, S. (1979). "The Optimal Tradeoff between the Probability and Magnitude of Fines", *American Economic Review*, 69, 880.

Radner, R. (1981). "Monitoring Cooperative Agreements in a Repeated Principal-Agent Relationship", *Econometrica*, 49, 1127–1148.

Radner, R. and Stiglitz, J. (1984). "A Non-concavity in the Value of Information", in *Bayesian Models in Economic Theory*, ed. by M. Boyer and R.E. Kihlstrom. North-Holland.

Rogerson, W.P. (1985). "Repeated Moral Hazard", *Econometrica*, 53, no. 1 January, 69–76.

Rogerson, W.P. (1985). "The First-Order Approach to Principal-Agent Problems", *Econometrica*, 53, no. 6 November, 1357–1367.

Rothschild, M. and Stiglitz, J.E. (1976). "Equilibrium in Competitive Insurance Markets: An Essay in the Economics of Imperfect Information," *Quarterly Journal of Economics*, 80, 629–649.

Rubinstein, A. and Yarri, M.E. (1983). "Repeated Insurance Contracts and Moral Hazard", *Journal of Economic Theory*, 30, 74–97.

Sappington, D. (1983). "Limited Liability Contracts between Principal and Agent", *Journal of Economic Theory* 29, 1–21.

Schlesinger, H. and Venezian, E. (1986). "Insurance Markets with Loss-Prevention Activity: Profits, Market Structure, and Consumer Welfare", *Rand Journal of Economics*, 17, no. 2 Summer, 227–238.

Shavell, S. (1979a). "Risk-Sharing and Incentives in the Principal and Agent Relationship", *The Bell Journal of Economics*, 10, no. 1 Spring, 55–73.

Shavell, S. (1979b). "On Moral Hazard and Insurance", *Quarterly Journal of Economics*, November, 541–562.

Singh, N. (1985). "Monitoring and Hierarchies: The Marginal Value of Information in a Principal-Agent Model", *Journal of Political Economy*, vol. 93, no. 3 June, 599–610.

Spence, M. and Zeckhauser, R. (1971). "Insurance, Information and Individual Action", *American Economic Review*, 380–387.

Stewart, J. (1994). "The Welfare Implications of Moral Hazard and Adverse Selection in Competitive Insurance Markets," *Economic Inquiry*, 32, no. 2 April, 193–208.

Stiglitz, J. (1983). "Risk, Incentives and Insurance: The Pure Theory of Moral Hazard", *The Geneva Papers on Risk and Insurance*, 8, no. 26 January, 4–33.

Winter, R. (1992). "Moral Hazard and Insurance Contracts", in Dionne (1992).

7 Adverse Selection in Insurance Markets*

Georges Dionne

HEC-Montreal

Neil Doherty

University of Pennsylvania

Nathalie Fombaron

Université Paris X-Nanterre

Abstract

In this survey we present some of the more significant results in the literature on adverse selection in insurance markets. Sections 7.1 and 7.2 introduce the subject and section 7.3 discusses the monopoly model developed by Stiglitz (1977) for the case of single-period contracts and extended by many authors to the multi-period case. The introduction of multi-period contracts raises many issues that are discussed in detail: time horizon, discounting, commitment of the parties, contract renegotiation and accidents underreporting. Section 7.4 covers the literature on competitive contracts. The analysis becomes more complicated since insurance companies must take into account competitive pressures when they set incentives contracts. As pointed out by Rothschild and Stiglitz (1976), there is not necessarily a Cournot-Nash equilibrium in presence of adverse selection. However, market equilibrium can be sustained when principals anticipate competitive reactions to their behaviour or when they adopt strategies that differ from the pure Nash strategy. Multi-period contracting is discussed. We show that different predictions on the evolution of insurer profits over time can be obtained from different assumptions concerning the sharing of information between insurers about individual's choice of contracts and accidents experience. The roles of commitment and renegotiation between the parties to the contract are important. Section 7.5 introduces models that consider moral hazard and adverse selection simultane-

* CRSH (Canada), FCAR (Québec) and FFSA (France) provided financial support to this study. Comments on an earlier version by K.J. Crocker, I. Cromb, B. Dahlby, C. Fluet, T. Nilssen, D.A. Malueg and P. Viala were very useful. We wish to thank Claire Boisvert for her valuable assistance in the preparation of the manuscript.

ously and section 7.6 treats adverse selection when people can choose their risk status. Section 7.7 discusses many extensions to the basic models such as risk categorization, different risk aversion, symmetric imperfect information, multiple risks, principals more informed than agents and uberrima fides.

Keywords: Adverse selection, insurance markets, monopoly, competitive contracts, self-selection mechanisms, single-period contracts, multi-period contracts, commitment, contract renegotiation, accidents underreporting, risk categorization.
JEL Classification Numbers: D80, D81, G22.

7.1 INTRODUCTION

In 1996, the European Group of Risk and Insurance Economists used its annual meeting to celebrate the twenty-year birthday of the Rothschild and Stiglitz (1976) article: "Equilibrium in Competitive Insurance Markets: An Essay in the Economics of Imperfect Information". At this meeting, many papers on adverse selection were presented and a subset of these presentations is now published in a 1997 issue of the Geneva Papers on Risk and Insurance Theory.

One of these articles was written by Rothschild and Stiglitz (1997) themselves. Their main topic was the role of competition in insurance markets, with an emphasis on underwriting in a world with imperfect information. They argue that insurance competition using underwriting on preexisting conditions (such as genetic conditions) can limit the welfare benefits of insurance. In this survey, we are mainly limited to a subset of situations involving imperfect information in the insured-insurer relationship since we analyse situations of standard adverse selection where the insured has more information about his risk than the insurer. However, we will consider extensions where insurers learning activities on individual characteristics that are not known by the insureds are introduced. We will also drop the assumption that risks are exogenous to individuals.

Adverse selection can be a significant resource allocation problem in many markets. In automobile insurance markets, risk classification is mainly explained by adverse selection. In health insurance, different insurance policies or contracts are offered to obtain some self-selection between different groups. In life insurance, the screening of new clients with medical exams is an accepted activity also justified by asymmetrical information between the insurer and the insured. These three resource allocation mechanisms can be complements or substitutes and adverse selection is not always a necessary condition for their presence. For example, in automobile insurance, we observe that insurers use risk classification and different deductible policies. Risk classification is usually justified by adverse selection, but the presence of different deductibles can also be explained by proportional transaction costs with different observable risks. A difficult empirical test is to verify whether the presence of different deductibles is justified by residual adverse selection or not! Another empirical test would be to verify whether bonus-malus schemes or multiperiod contracts with memory are explained in different markets by the presence of moral hazard, or by that of adverse selection or both. We shall not discuss these tests or these mechanisms in detail here, since other chapters of this book are concerned with these issues (Chiappori, 2000; Dionne, 2000). Instead, we will review the major allocation mechanisms that can be justified by the presence of adverse selection. An emphasis will be put on self-selection mechanisms in one-period contracting since a large part of the literature was devoted to this subject in the early literature (on risk classification, see Crocker and Snow, 2000). We will also discuss in detail some extensions of these basic models. Particularly, the role of multi-period contracting will be reviewed in detail. Finally, we will discuss the more recent contributions that focus on the effect of modifying the basic assumptions of the standard models. In particular, we will see how introducing moral hazard in the basic Rothschild and Stiglitz (1976) model affects the conclusions about both the nature and the existence of an equilibrium. The same exercise will be done for the monopoly model. Another subject will be insurance when individuals can choose their risk status. Other extensions concern the introduction of multiple risks, adverse selection and uberrima fides, the consideration of different risk averse individuals, the consideration of imprecise information about accident probabilities, and even, the case where the insurer is more informed than the insured about loss probabilities. This survey has to be considered as an update of Dionne and Doherty (1992).

7.2 BASIC ASSUMPTIONS AND SOME FUNDAMENTAL RESULTS

Without asymmetric information and under the standard assumptions of insurance models that we shall use in this article (same attitude toward risk and same risk aversion for all individuals in all classes of risk, one source of risk, risk neutrality on the supply side, no transaction cost in the supply of insurance, and no moral hazard), a Pareto optimal solution is characterized by full insurance coverage for all individuals in each class of risk. Each insured sets his optimal consumption level according to his certain wealth. No other financial institution is required to obtain this level of welfare. Both risk categorization and self-selection mechanisms are redundant. There is no need for multi-period insurance contracts since they are not superior to a sequence of one-period contracts. Finally, the two standard theorems of welfare economics hold and market prices of insurance are equal to the corresponding social opportunity costs.

In insurance markets, adverse selection results from asymmetric information between the insured (agent) and the insurer (principal). The insureds are heterogeneous with respect to their expected loss and have more information than the insurance company which is unable to differentiate between risk types. Naturally, the high risk individual has no incentive to reveal his true risk which is costly to observe by the insurer. As pointed out by Arrow, a pooling of risks is often observed in insurance markets. "In fact, however, there is a tendency to equalize rather than to differentiate premiums . . . This constitutes, in effect, a redistribution of income from those with a low propensity of illness to those with a high propensity . . ." (Arrow, 1963; p. 964).

Akerlof (1970) showed that if all insurers have imperfect information on individual risks, an insurance market may not exist, or if it exists, it may not be efficient. He proposed an explanation of why, for example, people over 65 have great difficulty in buying medical insurance: "the result is that the average medical condition of insurance applicants deteriorates as the price level rises—with the result that no insurance sales may take place at any price" (1970; p. 492). The seminal contributions of Akerlof and Arrow have generated a proliferation of models on adverse selection. In this survey we shall, however, confine attention to a limited subset. Many authors have proposed mechanisms to reduce the inefficiency associated with adverse selection: the "self-selection mechanism" in one period contracts which induces policyholders to reveal hidden information by selection from a menu of contracts, (Rothschild and Stiglitz, 1976; Stiglitz, 1977; Wilson, 1977; Miyazaki, 1977; Spence, 1978; Hellwig, 1986), the "categorization of risks" (Hoy, 1982; Crocker and Snow, 1985, 1986, 2000), and "multi-period contracting" (Dionne, 1983; Dionne and Lasserre, 1985, 1987; Kunreuther and Pauly, 1985; Cooper and Hayes, 1987; Hosios and Peters, 1989; Nilssen, 1990; Dionne and Doherty, 1994; Fombaron, 1997b, 2000). All of them address private market mechanisms. In the first case, insurers offer a menu of policies with different prices and quantity levels so that different risk types choose different insurance policies. Pareto improvements for resource allocation with respect to the single contract solution with an average premium to all clients can be obtained. In the second case, insurers use imperfect information to categorize risks and, under certain conditions, it is also possible to obtain Pareto improvements for resource allocation. In the third case, insurers use the information related to the past experience of the insured as a sorting device (i.e., to motivate high risk individuals to reveal their true risk ex ante).

Before proceeding let us comment briefly on some standard assumptions. We assume that all individuals maximize expected utility. The utility functions of the individuals in each risk group are identical, strictly concave and satisfy the von Neumann-Morgenstern axioms. Utility is time independent, time additive and state-independent. In many models there is no discounting. Individuals start each period with a given wealth, W, which is non random. To avoid problems of bankruptcy, the value of the risky asset is lower than W. All risks in the individual's portfolio are assumed to be insurable. Income received in a given period is consumed in that period; effectively there is no saving and no banking. Insurers are risk neutral and maximize the value of their cash flows or profits. Insurers write exclusive insurance contracts and there are no transaction costs in the supply of insurance. Finally, the insureds are assumed to be unable to influence either the probabilities of accident or the damages due to accidents; this rules out any problem of moral hazard.

To simplify the presentation we explicitly assume that insurers are risk neutral. An equivalent assumption is that insurers are well diversified in the sense that much of their total risk is diversified by their own equity holders in the management of their personal portfolios. The presence of transaction costs would not affect the qualitative conclusions concerning the effects of adverse selection on resource allocation in insurance markets (see Dionne, Gouriéroux and Vanasse, 1998, for more details). However, proportional transaction costs (or proportional loadings) are sufficient to explain partial insurance coverage and their explicit introduction in the analysis would modify some conclusions in the reference models. For example, each individual in each class of risk would buy less than full insurance in presence of full information and the introduction of adverse selection will decrease further the optimal coverage for the low risk individuals. Consequently the presence of adverse selection is not a necessary condition to obtain different deductibles in insurance markets.

The presence of many sources of non insurable risks or of many risky assets in individual portfolios is also an empirical fact that is not considered in the models. As long as these risks are independent, the conclusions should not be affected significantly. However, the optimal portfolio and insurance decisions in the presence of many correlated risks and asymmetrical information in one or in many markets is still an open question in the literature.

In reality, we observe that banks coexist with insurers who offer multi-period insurance contracts. The presence of saving and banking may change the conclusions obtained for multi-period contracts under asymmetrical information. Particularly, it may modify accidents reporting strategies and commitment to the contracts. However, with few exceptions (Allen, 1985, moral hazard; Dionne and Lasserre, 1987, adverse selection; Fudenberg, Holmstrom and Milgrom, 1986, moral hazard; Caillaud, Dionne and Jullien, 2000, insurance and debt with moral hazard. See Chiappori et al., 1994, for detailed discussion of different issues) research on principal-agent relationships has not envisaged the simultaneous presence of several alternative types of institutions.

The assumption of exclusive insurance contracting is discussed in Section 7.4 and some aspects of the discounting issues are discussed in Section 7.3. There remain the assumptions on the utility function. Although the theory of decision making under uncertainty has be challenged since its formal introduction by von Neumann and Morgenstern (Machina, 1987, 2000), it has produced very useful analytical tools for the study of optimal contracts such as, for example, optimal insurance coverage and the associated comparative statics, as well as the design of optimal contracts under moral hazard or the characterization of optimal insurance policies under adverse selection. In fact, very few contributions use non-linear models in insurance literature (see however Karni, 1992; Gollier, 2000; Doherty and Eeckhoudt, 1995) and none of these has addressed the adverse selection problem. In this survey we then limit the discussion to the linear expected utility model. We also assume that utility functions are not function of the states of the world and that all individuals in all classes of risks have the same level of risk aversion. As we will see, some of these assumptions are not necessary to get the desired results but permit the discussion to focus on differences in the risk types. They are discussed in more detail in 7.7.

7.3 MONOPOLY

7.3.1 Public Information

There are two possible states of the world ($x \in \{n, a\}$): state (n), "no accident" having the probability $(1 - p_i)$ and state (a), "accident" having the probability $0 < p_i < 1$. Consumers differ only by their probability of accident. For simplicity, there are two types of risk in the economy ($i \in \{H, L\}$ for high and low risk) with $p_H > p_L$. Each consumer owns a risky asset with monetary value $D(x)$; $D(a) = 0$ in state (a) and $D(n) = D$ in state (n). Therefore the expected damage for a consumer of type i ($E_i D(x)$) is $p_i D$.

Under public information and without transaction cost, a risk neutral private monopoly[1] would offer insurance coverage (net of premium) (β_i) for an insurance premium (α_i) such that a consumer will be indifferent between purchasing the policy and having no insurance (Stiglitz, 1977). In other words, the private monopolist maximizes his total profit over α_i, β_i and λ_i:

Problem 1

$$\underset{\alpha_i, \beta_i, \lambda_i}{Max} \sum q_i((1 - p_i)\alpha_i - p_i\beta_i) \tag{1}$$

under the individual rationality (or participating) constraints

$$V(C_i \mid p_i) - V(C^0 \mid p_i) \geq 0 \quad i = H, L \tag{2}$$

where $V(C_i \mid p_i)$ is the expected utility under the contract $C_i = \{\alpha_i, \beta_i\}$:

$$V(C_i \mid p_i) = p_i U(W - D + \beta_i) + (1 - p_i) U(W - \alpha_i);$$

$U(\cdot)$ is a twice differentiable, strictly increasing and strictly concave function of final wealth ($U'(\cdot) > 0$, $U''(\cdot) < 0$);

[1] For an analysis of several reasons why a monopoly behavior in insurance markets should be considered, see Dahlby (1987). For examples of markets with a monopoly insurer see D'Arcy and Doherty (1990) and Dionne and Vanasse (1992).

W is non random initial wealth;
C^0 denotes self-insurance; $C^0 = \{0, 0\}$ implies that
$V(C^0 \mid p_i) \equiv p_i U(W - D) + (1 - p_i)\, U(W)$; $V(C^0 \mid p_i)$ is the reservation utility. Below this level, individuals will self insure.
q_i is the number of policies sold to consumers of type i;
λ_i is a Lagrangian multiplier for constraint (2).

It is well known that full insurance, $\beta_i^* = D - \alpha_i^*$ (for $i = H, L$), is the solution to the above problem and that (2) is binding for both classes of risk, which means that

$$V\left(C_i^* \mid p_i\right) = V(C^0 | p_i) \quad i = H, L$$

or

$$\alpha_i^* = p_i D + z_i^*,$$

where z_i^* is the maximum unit-profit (or the Arrow-Pratt risk premium) on each policy. In other words z_i^* solves: $U(W - p_i D - z_i^*) = p_i U(W - D) + (1 - p_i) U(W)$.

The private monopoly extracts all the consumer surplus. However, there is no efficiency cost since each individual buys full insurance as under perfect competition.[2] This is the classical result that Pareto efficient risk sharing between a risk-averse agent and a risk-neutral principal shifts all the risk to the principal. To sum up we can write:

Proposition 1. In presence of public information about insureds' underlying risk, an optimal contract between a private monopolist and any individual of type i is characterized by:

a) full insurance coverage, $\beta_i^* = D - \alpha_i^*$;
b) no consumer surplus, $V(C_i^* \mid p_i) = V(C^0 \mid p_i)$.

Both solutions are shown at C_H^* and C_L^* in Figure 1 where C^0 is the "initial endowment" or self-insurance situation and where the vertical axis is wealth in the accident or loss state and the horizontal axis is wealth in the no-loss state.

Any point to the north-west of C^0 and below or on the 45° degree line represents the wealth of the insured with any contract where $\alpha_i \geq 0$ and $\beta_i \geq 0$. Since the monopoly solution implies no consumer surplus, it must lie on each risk type indifference

[2] As in the perfect discrimination case, the monopolist charges a price of insurance to each consumer equal to marginal cost. All potential consumer surplus is collected into monopoly profits so there is no dead weight loss. This result would not be obtained with a proportional loading or unit profit.

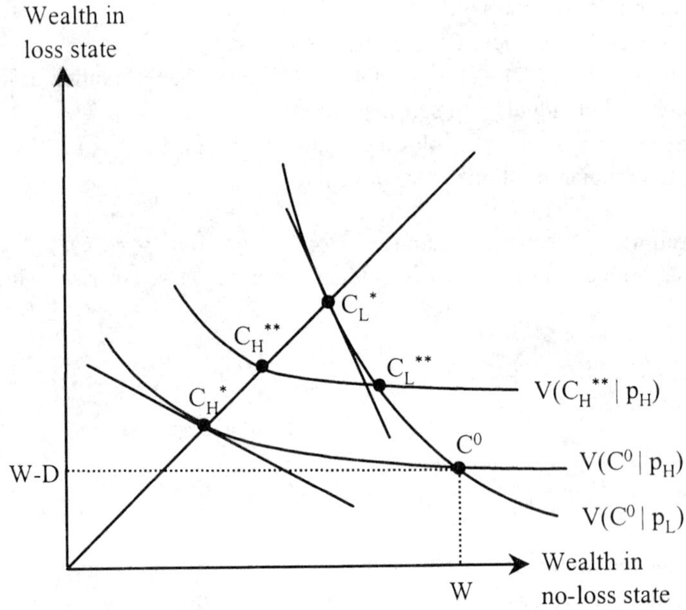

Figure 1 Monopoly model

curve passing through C^0. These indifference curves are strictly convex since $U(\cdot)$ is strictly concave by assumption.[3]

7.3.2 Private Information and Single-Period Contracts

Under private information the insurer does not observe the individual's risk types,[4] and must introduce mechanisms to ensure that agents will reveal this characteristic. Stiglitz (1977) extended the Rothschild-Stiglitz (1976) model to the monopoly case. In both contributions, price-quantity contracts[5] permit the separation of risks by introducing incentives for individuals to reveal their type. Low risk individuals reveal their identity by purchasing a policy which offers limited coverage at a low unit price. Thus they trade off insurance protection to signal their identity. Formally, risk revelation is obtained by adding two self-selection constraints to Problem 1:

[3] Since individuals of different types have the same degree of risk aversion, at each point in the figure, the absolute value of the slope of the high-risk indifference curve is lower than that of the low-risk individual. For example at point C^0, $U'(W)(1 - p_H)/U'(W - D)p_H < U'(W)(1 - p_L)/U'(W - D)p_L$. At equilibrium points C_H^* and C_L^*, the respective slopes (in absolute values) are $(1 - p_H)/p_H$ and $(1 - p_L)/p_L$. This is true since under full insurance, the insured of type i has $W - p_iD - z_i^*$ in each state.

[4] For models where neither the insurer nor the insured know the individuals' probabilities of accident, see Palfrey and Spatt (1985), Malueg (1988), Boyer, Dionne and Kihlstrom (1989), and De Garidel (1997).

[5] We limit our discussion to private market mechanisms. On public provision of insurance and adverse selection, see Pauly (1974) and Dahlby (1981).

$$V(C_i \mid p_i) - V(C_j \mid p_i) \geq 0 \quad i,j = H,L \quad i \neq j \tag{3}$$

Equation (3) guarantees that individual i prefers C_i to C_j. Let us use λ_{HL} and λ_{LH} for the corresponding Lagrangian multipliers where λ_{HL} is for the self-selection constraint of the H type risk and λ_{LH} is that for the L type. λ_{HL} and λ_{LH} cannot both be positive.[6] From Figure 1 it is easy to observe that, if the high risk individuals are indifferent between both contracts ($\lambda_{HL} > 0$), the low risk individuals will strictly prefer their own contracts ($\lambda_{LH} = 0$). Moreover, λ_{LH} cannot be positive when λ_{HL} is zero since this leads to a violation of (2). Therefore, a feasible solution can be obtained only when $\lambda_{HL} > 0$ and $\lambda_{LH} = 0$.

Figure 1 shows the solution to the maximization of (1) subject to (2) and (3) where low risk individuals choose a positive quantity of insurance[7] $\beta_L^{**} > 0$ and high risk individuals buy full insurance coverage ($\beta_H^{**} = \beta_H^*$). Separation of risks and profit maximization imply that $V(C_H^{**} \mid p_H) = V(C_L^{**} \mid p_H)$. As discussed above, it is clear that (2) and (3) cannot both be binding for the high risk individuals when it is possible for the low risks to buy insurance. In fact, Figure 1 indicates that C_H^{**} is strictly preferred to C_H^* which means that high risk individuals get some consumer surplus when the monopolist sells insurance to the low risk individuals. In other words, the rationality constraint (2) is not binding for the H individuals ($\lambda_H = 0$).

Another property of the solution is that good risk individuals do not receive any consumer surplus ($\lambda_L > 0$). However, as discussed above, they strictly prefer their contract to the contract offered to the bad risk individuals. In other words

$$V\left(C_L^{**} \mid p_L\right) = V(C^0 \mid p_L) \quad \text{and} \quad V\left(C_L^{**} \mid p_L\right) > V\left(C_H^{**} \mid p_L\right),$$

which means that the self-selection constraint is not binding for the low risk individuals while the rationality constraint is.

In conclusion, one-period contracts with a self-selection mechanism increase the monopoly profits under private information compared with a single contract without any revelation mechanism, but do not necessarily correspond to the best risk allocation arrangement under asymmetrical information. In particular, good risk individuals may not be able to buy any insurance coverage or, if they can, they are restricted to partial insurance. As we shall see in the next section, multi-period contracts can be

[6] Technically the preference structure of the model implies that indifference curves of individuals with different risks cross only once. This single crossing property has been used often in the sorting literature (Cooper, 1984).

[7] It is important to note that there is always a separating equilibrium in the monopoly case. However, the good risk individuals may not have any insurance coverage at the equilibrium. Property 4 in Stiglitz (1977) establishes that $C_L^{**} = \{0, 0\}$ when q_H/q_L exceeds a critical ratio of high to low risk individuals where q_i is the proportion of individuals i in the economy. The magnitude of the critical ratio is function of the difference in accident probabilities and of the size of the damage. Here, in order to have $C_L^{**} \neq \{0, 0\}$, we assume that q_H/q_L is below the critical ratio.

used to relax the binding constraints and to improve resource allocation under asymmetrical information. In summary

Proposition 2. In the presence of private information, an optimal one-period contract menu between a private monopoly and individuals of types H and L has the following characteristics:

a) $\beta_H^{**} = D - \alpha_H^{**}$; $\beta_L^{**} < D - \alpha_L^{**}$
b) $V(C_H^{**} \mid p_H) > V(C^0 \mid p_H)$; $V(C_L^{**} \mid p_L) = V(C^0 \mid p_L)$
c) $V(C_H^{**} \mid p_H) = V(C_L^{**} \mid p_H)$; $V(C_L^{**} \mid p_L) > V(C_H^{**} \mid p_L)$.

Proof. See Stiglitz (1977). ■

Stiglitz (1977) also considered a continuum of agent types and showed that some of the above results can be obtained under additional conditions. However, in general, the presence of a continuum of agent types affects the results.[8]

7.3.3 Multi-Period Insurance Contracts

Multi-period contracts are often observed in different markets. For example, in many countries, drivers buy automobile insurance with the same insurer for many years and insurers use bonus-malus systems (or experience rating) in order to relate insurance premiums to the individual's past experience (Lemaire, 1985; Henriet and Rochet, 1986; Hey, 1985; Dionne and Vanasse, 1992, 1997). Long term contracting also is observed in labour markets, workers' compensation insurance, service contracts, unemployment insurance and many other markets. The introduction of multi-period contracts in the analysis gives rise to many issues such as time horizon, discounting, commitment of the parties, myopic behaviour, accident underreporting, renegotiation. These issues are discussed in the following paragraphs.

Multi-period contracts are set, not only to adjust ex-post insurance premiums or insurance coverage to past experience, but also as a sorting device. They can be a complement or a substitute to standard self-selection mechanisms. However, in presence of full commitment, ex-ante risk announcement or risk revelation remains necessary to obtain optimal contracts under adverse selection.

In Cooper and Hayes (1987), multi-period contracts are presented as a complement to one period self-selection constraints. Since imperfect information reduces the monopolist's profits, the latter has an incentive to relax the remaining binding constraints by introducing contracts based on anticipated experience over time. By using price-quantity contracts and full commitment in long term contracts, Cooper

[8] In another context, Riley (1979a) showed that a competitive Nash equilibrium never exists in the continuum case (see also Riley, 1985).

and Hayes introduce a second instrument to induce self-selection and increase monopoly profits: experience rating increases the cost to high-risks from masquerading as low-risks by exposing them to second-period contingent coverages and premia.

Cooper and Hayes' model opens with a direct extension of the standard one-period contract presented above to a two-period world with full commitment on the terms of the contract. There is no discounting and all agents are able to anticipate the values of the relevant future variables. In order to increase profits, the monopolist offers contracts in which premiums and coverages in the second period are function of accident history in the first period. Accidents are public information in their model. The two period contract C_i^2 is defined by:

$$C_i^2 = \{\alpha_i, \beta_i, \alpha_{ia}, \beta_{ia}, \alpha_{in}, \beta_{in}\}$$

where a and n mean "accident" and "no accident" in the first period and where α_{il} and $\beta_{il}(l = a, n)$ are "contingent" choice variables. Conditional on accident experience, the formal problem consists of maximizing two-period expected profits by choosing C_L^2 and C_H^2 under the following constraints:

$$V(C_i^2 \mid p_i) \geq 2V(C^0 \mid p_i) \tag{4.1}$$

$$V(C_i^2 \mid p_i) \geq V(C_j^2 \mid p_i) \quad i, j = H, L \quad i \neq j \tag{4.2}$$

where

$$\begin{aligned} V(C_i^2|p_k) \equiv\ & p_k U(W - D + \beta_i) + (1 - p_k) U(W - \alpha_i) \\ & + p_k\, [p_k U(W - D + \beta_{ia}) + (1 - p_k)\, U(W - \alpha_{ia})] \\ & + (1 - p_k)[p_k U(W - D + \beta_{in}) + (1 - p_k)\, U(W - \alpha_{in})] \\ & k = i, j \quad i, j = H, L \quad i \neq j. \end{aligned}$$

The above constraints show that agents are committed to the contracts for the two periods. In other words, the model does not allow the parties to renegotiate the contract at the end of the first period. Moreover, the principal is committed to a loss related adjustment of the insurance contract in the second period negotiated at the beginning of the first period; the insured is committed, for the second period, to buy the coverage and to pay the premium chosen at the beginning of the first period. It is also interesting to observe from (4) that the decisions concerning insurance coverage in each period depend on the anticipated variations in the premiums over time. In other words, (4) establishes that variations in both premia and coverages in the second period are function of experience in the first period. Using the above model, Cooper and Hayes proved the following result:

Proposition 3. In the presence of private information and full commitment, the monopoly increases its profits by offering an optimal two-period contract having the following characteristics:

1) High risk individuals obtain full insurance coverage in each period and are not experience rated

   $\hat{\alpha}_H = \hat{\alpha}_{Hn} = \hat{\alpha}_{Ha}, \hat{\beta}_H = \hat{\beta}_{Ha} = \hat{\beta}_{Hn}$

   where $\hat{\beta}_H = D - \hat{\alpha}_H$
2) Low risk individuals obtain partial insurance with experience rating

   $\hat{\alpha}_{Ln} < \hat{\alpha}_L < \hat{\alpha}_{La}, \hat{\beta}_{La} < \hat{\beta}_L < \hat{\beta}_{Ln}$

3) Low risk individuals do not obtain any consumer surplus, and high-risk individuals are indifferent between the two contracts

   $$V(\hat{C}_L^2 \mid p_L) = 2V(C^0 \mid p_L),$$
   $$V(\hat{C}_L^2 \mid p_H) = V(\hat{C}_L^2 \mid p_H).$$

Proof. See Cooper and Hayes (1987). ■

The authors also discussed an extension of their two-period model to the case where the length of the contract may be extended to many periods. They showed that the same qualitative results as those in Proposition 3 hold with many periods.

Dionne (1983) and Dionne and Lasserre (1985, 1987) also investigated multi-period contracts in presence of both adverse selection[9] and full commitment on the part of the insurer. Their models differ from that of Cooper and Hayes in many respects. The main differences concern the revelation mechanism, the sorting device, commitment assumptions and the consideration of statistical information. Moreover, accidents are private information in their models. Unlike Cooper and Hayes, Dionne (1983) did not introduce self-selection constraints in order to obtain risk revelation. Instead risk revelation results from a Stackelberg game where the insurer offers a contract in which the individual has to select an initial premium by making a risk announcement in the first period. Any agent who claims to be a low risk pays a corresponding low premium as long as his average loss is less than the expected loss given his declaration (plus a statistical margin of error to which we shall return). If

[9] Townsend (1982) discussed multi-period borrowing-lending schemes. However, his mechanism implies a constant transfer in the last period that is not compatible with insurance in presence of private information.

that condition is not met, he is offered a penalty premium. Over time, the insurer records the agent's claims and offers to reinstate the policy at the low premium whenever the claims frequency become reasonable again.[10]

Following Dionne (1983) and Dionne and Lasserre (1985), the no-claims discount strategy consists of offering two full insurance premiums[11] ($F^1 = \{\alpha_H, \alpha_L\}$) in the first period and for $t = 1, 2, \ldots$

$$F^{t+1} \begin{cases} = \alpha_d \text{ if} \sum_{s=1}^{N(t)} \theta^s / N(t) < E_d D(x) + \delta_d^{N(t)} \\ = \alpha_k \text{ otherwise} \end{cases}$$

where

α_d is the full information premium corresponding to the declaration (d), $d \in \{H, L\}$

θ^s is the amount of loss in contract period s, $\theta^s \in \{0, D\}$

α_k is a penalty premium. α_k is such that $U(W - \alpha_k) < V(C_0 \mid p_H)$

$E_d D(x)$ is the expected loss corresponding to the announcement (d)

$\delta_d^{N(t)}$ is the statistical margin of error

$N(t)$ is the total number of periods with insurance; $N(t) \leq t$.

Therefore, from the construction of the model, $\sum_{s=1}^{N(t)} \theta^s / N(t)$ is the average loss claimed by the insured in the first $N(t)$ periods. If this number is strictly less then the declared expected loss plus some margin of error, the insurer offers α_d. Otherwise he offers α_k. The statistical margin of error is used in order not to penalize too often those who tell the truth. But it has to be small enough to detect those who try to increase their utility in announcing a risk class inferior to their true risk. From the Law of the Iterated Logarithm, one can show that

$$\delta_d^{N(t)} = \sqrt{2\gamma\sigma_d^2 \log\log N(t) / N(t)}, \quad \gamma > 1$$

[10] This type of "no-claims discount" strategy was first proposed by Radner (1981) and Rubinstein and Yaari (1983) for the problem of moral hazard (see also Malueg (1986) where the "good faith" strategy is employed). However, since the two problems of information differ significantly the models are not identical. First the information here does not concern the action of the agent (moral hazard) but the type of risk which he represents (adverse selection). Second, since the action of the insured does not affect the random events, the sequence of damage levels is not controlled by the insured. The damage function depends only on the risk type. Third, in the adverse selection model, the insured cannot change his declaration and therefore cannot depart from his initial risk announcement although he can always cancel his contract. Therefore, the stronger conditions used by Radner (1981) (robust epsilon equilibrium) and Rubinstein and Yaari (1983) ("long proof") are not needed to obtain the desired results in presence of adverse selection only. The Law of the Iterated logarithm is sufficient.

[11] In fact their formal analysis is with a continuum of risk types.

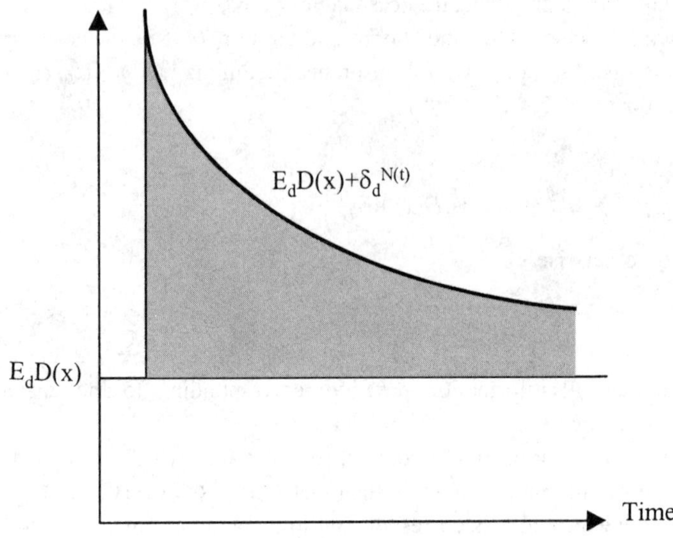

Figure 2 Graphical representation of $E_dD(x) + \delta_d^{N(t)}$

where σ_d^2 is the variance of the individual's loss corresponding to the declaration (d) and $\delta_d^{N(t)}$ converges to zero over time (with arbitrary large values for $N(t) = 1, 2$).

Graphically, we can represent $E_dD(x) + \delta_d^{N(t)}$ as in Figure 2:

As $N(t) \to \infty$, $E_dD(x) + \delta_d^{N(t)} \to E_dD(x)$.

Over time, only a finite number of points representing $(\Sigma\theta^s/N(t))$ will have a value outside the shaded area.

Proposition 4 below shows that the public information allocation of risks is obtainable using the no-claims discount strategy as $T \to \infty$ and as long as the agents do not discount the future.[12]

Proposition 4. Let i be such that:

$$\alpha_i - E_iD(x) \geq 0 \text{ and } U(W - \alpha_i) > V(C^0 \mid p_i).$$

Then, when $T \to \infty$, there exists a pair of optimal strategies for the individual of type i and the private monopoly having the following properties:

[12] In general, introducing discounting in repeated games reduces the incentives of telling the truth and introduces some inefficiency because players do not care for the future as they care for the current period. In other words, with discounting, players become less patient and cooperation becomes more difficult to obtain. See Sabourian (1989) and Abreu, Pearce and Stacchetti (1990) for detailed discussions on the discount factor issues in repeated contracts.

1) the strategy of the monopoly is a "no-claims discount strategy"; the strategy of insured i is to tell the truth about his type in period 1 and to buy insurance in each period;
2) the optimal corresponding payoffs are $\alpha_i^* - E_i D(x) = z_i^*$ and $U(W - \alpha_i^*) = V(C^0 \mid p_i)$, $i = H, L$;
3) both strategies are enforceable.

Proof. See Dionne and Lasserre (1985). ■

It is also possible to obtain a solution close to the public information allocation of risks in finite horizon insurance contracts. Dionne and Lasserre (1987) showed how a trigger strategy with revisions[13] may establish the existence of an ε equilibrium. This concept of ε equilibrium is due to Radner (1981) and was also developed in a moral hazard context. Extending the definition to the adverse selection problem, Dionne and Lasserre (1987) defined an ε equilibrium as a triplet of strategies (principal, low risk individual, high risk individual) such that, under these strategies, the expected utility of any one agent is at least equal to his expected utility under public information less epsilon. In fact, the expected utility of the high risk individual is that of the full information equilibrium.

As for the case of an infinite number of periods,[14] Dionne and Lasserre (1987) showed that it is in the interest of the monopolist (he obtains higher profits) to seek risk revelation on the part of the insured rather than simply use the statistical instrument to discriminate between low-risk and high-risk agents. In other words, their second main result shows that it is optimal to use statistical tools not only to adjust, ex-post, insurance premiums according to past experience, but also, to provide an incentive for the insured to announce, ex-ante, the true class of risk he represents. Finally, they obtained that a multi-period contract with announcement dominates a repetition of one-period self-selection mechanisms (Stiglitz, 1977) when the number of periods is sufficiently large and there is no discounting. This result contrasts with those in the economic literature where it is shown that the welfare under full commitment is equal to that corresponding to a repetition of one period contracts. In fact here, a multiperiod contract introduces a supplementary instrument (experience

[13] Radner's (1981) contribution does not allow for revisions after the initial trigger. However, revisions were always present in infinite horizon models [Rubinstein and Yaari (1983), Dionne (1983), Radner (1985), Dionne and Lasserre (1985)]. A trigger strategy without revision consists of offering a premium corresponding to a risk declaration as long as the average loss is less than the reasonable average loss corresponding to the declaration. If that condition is not met, a penalty premium is offered for the remaining number of periods. With revisions, the initial policy can be reinstate.

[14] See also Gal and Landsberger (1988) on small sample properties of experience rating insurance contracts in presence of adverse selection. In their model, all insureds buy the same contracts and resort to experience is made in the premium structure only. They show that the monopoly's expected profits are higher if based on contracts which take advantage of longer experience. Fluet (1998) shows how a result similar to Dionne and Lasserre (1985) can be obtained in a one period contract with fleet of vehicles.

rating) that increases efficiency (Dionne and Doherty, 1994; Dionne and Fluet, 1999; Fombaron, 1997b).

Another characteristic of Dionne and Lasserre (1987) model is that low risk agents do not have complete insurance coverage when the number of periods is finite; they chose not to insure if they are unlucky enough to be considered as high risk individuals. However, they always choose to be insured in the first period and most of them will obtain full insurance in each period. Finally, it must be pointed out that the introduction of a continuum of agent types does not create any difficulty in the sense that full separation of risks is obtained without any additional condition.

In Dionne (1983) and Dionne and Lasserre (1985) there is no incentive for accidents underreporting at equilibrium since there is no benefit associated with underreporting. When the true classes of risk are announced, insureds cannot obtain any premium reduction by underreporting accidents. When the number of periods is finite, matters are less simple since each period does matter. In some circumstances, the insured has to evaluate the trade-off between increased premiums in the future and no coverage in the present. This is true even when the contract involves full commitment as in Dionne and Lasserre (1987). For example, the unlucky good risk may prefer to receive no insurance coverage during a particular period in order to pass over a trigger date and have the opportunity to pay the full information premium as long as his average loss is less than the reasonable average loss corresponding to his class of risk.

We next address the incentive for policyholders to underreport accidents. The benefits of underreporting can be shown to be nil in a two-period model with full commitment and no statistical instrument and when the contract cannot be renegotiated over time (Dionne and Doherty, 1992). To see this, let us go back to the two-period model presented earlier (Cooper and Hayes, 1987) and assume that accidents are now private information. When there is ex ante full commitment by the two parties to the contract one can write a contract where the net benefit to any type of agent from underreporting is zero. High risk individuals have full insurance and no experience rating at equilibrium and low risk individuals have the same level of expected utility whatever the accident reporting at the end of the second period. However, private information about accidents reduces insurer's profits when we compare with the situation where accidents are public information.

In all the preceding discussions it was assumed that the insurer can precommit to the contract over time. It was shown that an optimal contract under full commitment can be interpreted as a single transaction where the incentive constraints are modified to improve insurance possibilities for the low risk individuals and to increase profits. Since there is full commitment and no renegotiation, accident histories are uninformative on the risk type. This form of commitment is optimal in Dionne (1983) and Dionne and Lasserre (1985) since, as in the Arrow-Debreu world, neither party to the contract can gain from renegotiation. However, in a finite horizon world, the role of renegotiation becomes important since self-selection in the first period implies that future contracts might be inefficient given the public information available after the initial period. When the good risks have completely revealed their type, it becomes advantageous to both parties, the insurer and the low risk individuals, to renegotiate a full insurance contract for the second period. Although the possibilities of renegotiation improve welfare in the second period, they violate the ex-ante self-selection constraints and reduce ex-ante welfare. In other words, renegotiation limits the commitment possibilities and reduces ex-ante parties welfare. For example, if the high risk individuals anticipe renegotiation in the second period, they will not necessarily reveal their type in the first period (Dionne and Doherty, 1994).

Formally, we can interpret the possibility of renegotiation as adding a new constraint to the set of feasible contracts: unless parties can precommit not to renegotiate then contracts must be incentive compatible and renegotiation-proof (Dewatripont, 1989; Bolton, 1990; Rey and Salanié, 1996). In order to reduce the possibilities for renegotiation in the second period, the insurer who is unable to commit not to renegotiate after new information is revealed, must set the contracts so that the insured type will not be perfectly known after the first period. This implies that the prospect of renegotiation reduces the speed of information revelation over time. In other words, the prospect of renegotiation can never improve the long term contract possibilities. In many circumstances, a sequence of one period contracts will give the same outcome as a renegotiated-proof long term contract; in other circumstances a renegotiation-proof long term contract dominates (when intertemporal and intertypes transfers and experience rating are allowed, for example) (Hart and Tirole, 1988; Laffont-Tirole, 1987, 1990, 1993; Dionne and Doherty 1994; Fombaron, 1997a; see the next section for more details).

Hosios and Peters (1989) presented a formal model that rules out any renegotiation by assuming that only one-period contracts are enforceable.[15] They also discussed the possibility of renegotiation in the second period when this renegotiation is beneficial to both parties. Although they cannot show formally the nature of the equilibrium under this alternative, they obtained interesting qualitative results. For example, when the equilibrium contract corresponds to incomplete risk revelation in the first period, the seller offers, in the second period, a choice of contract that depends on the experience of the first period. Therefore accident underreporting is possible without commitment and renegotiation. This result is similar to that obtained in their formal model where they ruled out any form of commitment for contracts that last for more than one period. Only one-period contracts are enforceable. They showed the following. results.[16]

[15] On limited commitment see also Freixas, Guesnerie and Tirole (1985), Laffont and Tirole (1987) and Dionne and Fluet (1999).

[16] However, separating equilibria are possible with discounting since future considerations are less relevant. In a model with commitment and renegotiation, Dionne and Doherty (1994) obtain a similar result: when the discount factor is very low a separating equilibrium is always optimal in a two-period framework. Intuitively, low discount factors reduce the efficiency of using intertemporal transfers or rents to increase the optimal insurance coverage of the low risk individuals by pooling in the first period. See Laffont and

Proposition 5. In absence of any form of commitment from both parties to the contract:

1) Without discounting, separating equilibria do not exist; only pooling and semi-separating equilibria are possible.
2) Accident underreporting can now affect the seller's posterior beliefs about risk types and insurance buyers may fail to report accidents in order to avoid premium increases.

Proof. See Hosios and Peters (1989). ■

This result implies that the insurer does not have full information on the risk types at the end of the first period; therefore, accidents reports become informative on the risk type contrary to the Cooper and Hayes model. However, the authors did not discuss the optimality of such two-period contract. It is not clear that a sequence of one period contracts with separating equilibrium does not dominate their sequence of contracts.

7.4 COMPETITIVE CONTRACTS

We now introduce a competitive context. Competition raises many new issues in both static and dynamic environments. The two main issues that will be discussed here are 1) the choice of an adequate equilibrium concept and the study of its existence and efficiency properties, and 2) the nature of information between competitive insurers (and consequently the role of government in facilitating the transmission of information between insurance market participants, particularly in long term relationships).

It will be shown that many well-known and standard results are function to the assumption on how the insurers share the information about both the individual's choice of contracts and accident experience.

In a first step, the situation where no asymmetric information affects the insurance market is presented as a benchmark. Then, issues raised by adverse selection problem and the remedies to circumvent it are discussed.

7.4.1 Public Information about an Individual's Characteristics

In a competitive market where insurance firms are able to discriminate among the consumers according their riskiness, we would expect that insureds are offered a menu

Tirole (1993) for a general discussion on the effect of discounting on optimal solutions in procurement when there is no uncertainty. See Dionne and Fluet (2000) for a demonstration that full pooling can be an optimal solution when the discount is sufficiently high and when there is no commitment. This result is due to the fact that, under no-commitment, the possibilities of rent transferts between the periods are limited.

of policies with a complete coverage among which they choose the one that corresponds with their intrinsical risk. Indeed, under competition, firms are now constrained to earn zero expected profits. When information on individual risk characteristics is public, each firm knows the risk type of each individual. The optimal individual contract is the solution to:

Problem 2

$$\underset{\alpha_i, \beta_i, \lambda_i}{Max}\ p_i U(W - D + \beta_i) + (1 - p_i)\, U(W - \alpha_i) + \lambda_i[(1 - p_i)\alpha_i - p_i\beta_i], \quad i = H, L$$

where $(1 - p_i)\alpha_i = p_i\beta_i$ is the zero-profit constraint.

As for the monopoly case under public information, the solution to Problem 2 yields full insurance coverage for each type of risk. However, on the contrary to monopoly, the optimal solutions C_H^* and C_L^* in Figure 3 correspond to levels of consumer welfare greater than in the no-insurance situation (C^0). As already pointed out, the monopoly solution under public information also yields full insurance coverage and does not introduce any distortion in risk allocation. The difference between the monopoly and competitive cases is that, in the former, consumer surplus is extracted by the insurer, while in the latter it is retained by both types of policyholder.

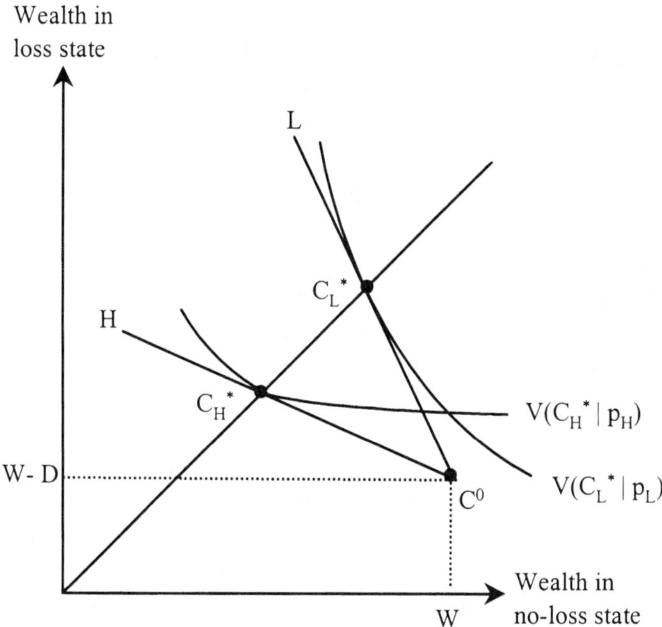

Figure 3 One-period competitive contracts with full information

Under competition, a zero-profit line passes through C^0 and represents the set of policies for which a type i consumer's expected costs are nil for insurers. The absolute value of its slope is equal to the (absolute) ratio $\frac{1-p_i}{p_i}$. Each point on the segment $[C^0C_i^*]$ has the same expected wealth for an individual of type i than that corresponding to C^0. The full information solutions are obtained when the ratio of slopes of indifference curves is just equal to the ratio of the probability of not having an accident to that of having an accident. To sum up,

Proposition 6. In an insurance world of public information about insureds' riskiness, a one-period optimal contract between any competitive firm on market and any individual of type i ($i = H, L$) is characterized by:

a) full insurance coverage, $\beta_i^* = D - \alpha_i^*$
b) no firm makes a surplus, $\pi(C_i^* \mid p_i) = 0$
c) consumers receive a surplus $V(C_i^* \mid p_i) > V(C^0 \mid p_i)$.

Characteristic b) expresses the fact that premiums are set to marginal costs and characteristic c) explains why individual rationality constraints (2) are automatically satisfied in a competitive context. Consequently, introducing competitive actuarial insurance eliminates the wealth variance at the same mean or corresponds to a *mean preserving contraction*.

In a usual way, under perfect information, competition allows to attain one-period solutions which are *first-best efficient*. This result does not hold when we introduce asymmetric information.

7.4.2 Private Information and Single-Period Contracts

In the presence of adverse selection, the introduction of competition may lead to fundamental problems with the existence and the efficiency of an equilibrium. When insurance firms cannot distinguish among different risk types, they lose money by offering the set of full information contracts (C_H^*, C_L^*) described above, since both types will select C_L^* (the latter contract requires a premium lower than C_H^* and in counterpart, covers also totally the incurring losses). Each insurer will make losses since the average cost is greater than the premium of C_L^*, which is the expected cost of group L. Under asymmetrical information, traditional full information competitive contracts are not adequate to allocate risk optimally. Consequently, many authors have investigated the role of sorting devices in a competitive environment to circumvent this problem of adverse selection. The first contributions on the subject in competitive markets are by Akerlof (1970), Spence (1974), Pauly (1974), Rothschild and Stiglitz (1976) and Wilson (1977). The literature on competitive markets is now very large and it is not our intention here to review all contributions. Our selection of models was made with criteria that will be identified and explained when it will become appropriate.[17]

A first division that we can make is between models of signaling (informed agents move first) and of screening (uninformed agents move first) (Stiglitz and Weiss, 1984). Spence (1974) and Cho and Kreps (1987) models are of the first type and are mainly applied to labor markets in which the workers (informed agents) move first by choosing an education level (signal). Then employers bid for the services of the workers and the latter select the more preferred bids. Cho and Kreps (1987) present conditions under which this three-stage game generates a Riley (1979a) single-period separating equilibrium.[18] Without restrictions (or criteria as those proposed by Cho and Kreps (1987)) on out-of-equilibrium beliefs, many equilibria arise simultaneously, which limit considerably the explanatory power of the traditional signaling models.[19]

Although it may be possible to find interpretations of the signaling models in insurance markets, it is generally accepted that the screening interpretation is more natural. Rothschild and Stiglitz (1976) and Wilson (1977) introduced to the literature insurance models with a screening behavior. In Rothschild and Stiglitz model only a two-stage game is considered. First, the uninformed insurer offers a menu of contracts to the informed customers who then choose among the contracts in the second stage.

Let us start with the Rothschild and Stiglitz (1976) model in which the insurers set premia with constant marginal costs. Each insurer knows the proportions of good risks and bad risks in the market but has no information on an individual's type. Moreover, each insurer cannot, by assumption, buy insurance from many insurers. Otherwise, the individual insurers would not be able to observe the individuals' total amount of insurance and would not be able to discriminate easily.[20] Each insurer observes all offers in the market. Finally, the insurer only needs to observe the claims he receives.[21]

Clearly, the properties of the equilibrium depend upon how firms react to rival offers. In a competitive environment, it seems reasonable to assume that each insurer

[17] See Cresta (1984) and Eisen (1989) for other analyses of problems of equilibria with asymmetric information.

[18] A Riley or reactive equilibrium leads the Rothschild-Stiglitz separating equilibrium regardless of the number of individuals in each class of risk.

[19] In fact, multiple equilibria are the rule in two-stage signaling models. However, when such equilibria are studied, the problem is to find at least one that is stable and dominates in terms of welfare. For a more detailed analysis of signaling models see the survey by Kreps (1989). On the notion of sequential equilibrium and on the importance of consistency in beliefs see Kreps and Wilson (1982).

[20] Jaynes (1978) and Hellwig (1988) analyzed the consequences of relaxing this assumption. More particularly, they showed under what conditions an equilibrium exists when the sharing of information about customers is treated endogenously as part of the game among firms. They showed that it is possible to overcome Rothschild-Stiglitz's existence problem of an equilibrium if insureds cannot buy more than one contract. Finally, Hellwig (1988) showed that the resulting equilibrium is more akin to the Wilson anticipatory equilibrium than to the competitive Nash equilibrium.

[21] In fact, this is a consequence of the exclusivity assumption. Moreover, since we consider static contracts, observing accident or claims does not matter. A conclusion, that will not be necessarily true in dynamic models.

takes the actions of its rivals as given. The basic model by Rothschild and Stiglitz described in the following lines considers that firms adopt a (pure) Nash strategy. Then, a menu of contracts in an insurance market is an equilibrium in the Rothschild and Stiglitz sense if a) no contract in the equilibrium set makes negative expected profits and b) there is no *other* contract added to the original set that earns positive expected profits.

Under this definition of the equilibrium, Rothschild and Stiglitz obtained three significant results:

Proposition 7. When insurers follow a pure Cournot-Nash strategy in a two-stage screening game:

a) A pooling equilibrium is not possible; the only possible equilibria are separating contracts.
b) A separating equilibrium may not exist.
c) The equilibrium, when it exists, is not necessarily a second-best optimum.

A pooling equilibrium is an equilibrium in which both types of risk buy the same contract. Recall that the publicly observable proportions of good-risk and bad-risk individuals are respectively q_L and q_H (with $q_H + q_L = 1$) and the average probability of having an accident is $\bar{p}$. This corresponds to the line C^0F in Figure 4a. To see why the Nash definition of equilibrium is not compatible with a pooling contract, assume that C_1 in the figure is a pooling equilibrium contract for a given insurer. By definition, it corresponds to zero aggregate expected profits; otherwise, another insurer in the market will offer another pooling contract. Because of the relative slopes of the risk type indifference curves, there always exists a contract C_2 that will be preferred to contract C_1 by the low-risk individuals. The existence of contract C_2 contradicts the above definition of a Nash equilibrium. Consequently, if there exists an equilibrium, it has to be a separating one in which different risk-type consumers receive different insurance contracts.

As for the monopoly case, the formal solution is obtained by adding one self-selection constraint (3) that guarantees individual i prefers C_i to C_j to Problem 2. By a similar argumentation to the one used in the determination of the optimal solution in the monopoly situation, it can be shown that only the self-selection constraint of the H risk type is binding at full insurance. Again the profit constraint is binding on each type so the problem is limited to find an optimal contract to the low-risk individual since that of the high risk individual corresponds to the public information case ($\alpha_H^{**} = \alpha_H^* = D - \beta_H^*$):

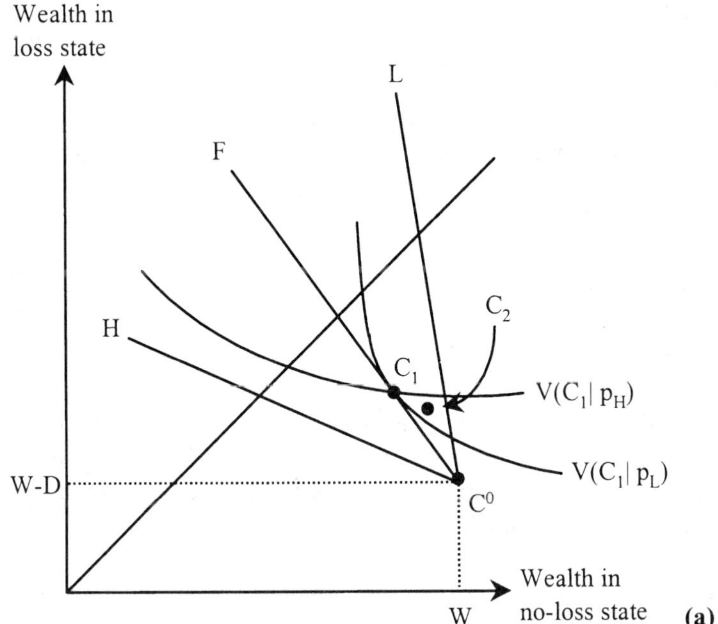

Figure 4a Inexistence of a Rothschild-Stiglitz pooling equilibrium

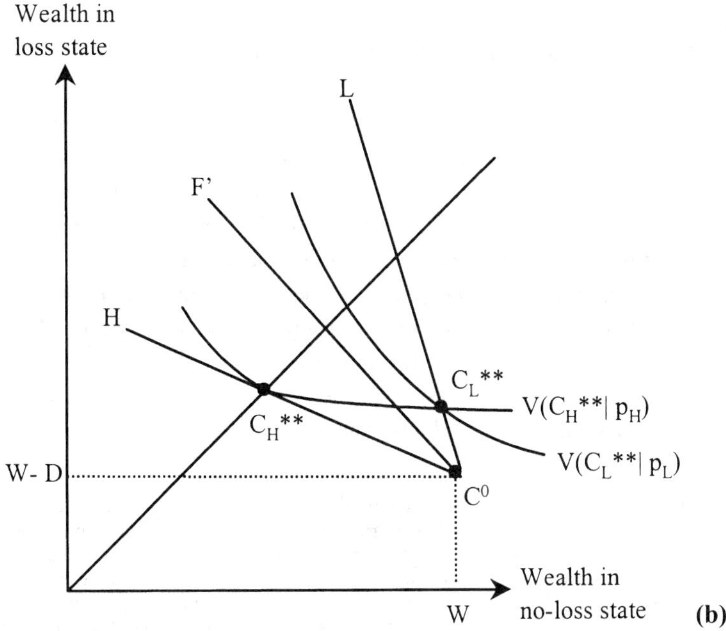

Figure 4b Existence of a Rothschild and Stiglitz separating equilibrium

Problem 3

$$\underset{\alpha_L, \beta_L, \lambda_L, \lambda_{HL}}{Max} \quad p_L U(W - D + \beta_L) + (1 - p_L) U(W - \alpha_L)$$

subject to the zero-profit constraint

$$(1 - p_L)\alpha_L = p_L \beta_L$$

and the self-selection constraint

$$U\left(W - \alpha_H^{**}\right) = p_H U(W - D + \beta_L) + (1 - p_H) U(W - \alpha_L).$$

At equilibrium, the high-risk individuals receive full insurance since the low-risk self-selection constraint is not binding. The solution of Problem 3 implies that the low-risk type receives less than full insurance.[22] We can summarize the description of the separating equilibrium with the following proposition:

Proposition 8. In the presence of private information, an optimal menu of separating one-period contracts between a competitive insurer and individuals of types H and L has the following characteristics:

a) $\beta_H^{**} = D - \alpha_H^{**}$; $\beta_L^{**} < D - \alpha_L^{**}$
b) $V(C_i^{**} \mid p_i) > V(C^0 \mid p_i)$, $i = H, L$
c) $V(C_H^{**} \mid p_H) = V(C_L^{**} \mid p_H)$; $\quad V(C_L^{**} \mid p_L) > V(C_H^{**} \mid p_L)$.

Graphically, C_H^{**} and C_L^{**} in Figure 4b correspond to a separating equilibrium. In equilibrium, high-risk individuals buy full insurance (C_H^{**}), while low-risk individuals get only partial insurance C_L^{**}.[23] Each firm earns zero expected profit on each contract. This equilibrium has the advantage for the low-risk agents that their equilibrium premium corresponds to their actuarial risk and does not contain any subsidy to the high-risk individuals. However, a cost is borne by low-risk insureds in that their equilibrium contract delivers only partial insurance compared with full insurance in the full information case. Only high-risk individuals receive the first-best allocation. Finally, the separating equilibrium is not necessarily second-best optimal when it is possible to improve the welfare of individuals in each class of risk. We will come back to this issue.

[22] Partial coverage is generally interpreted as a monetary deductible. However, in many insurance markets the insurance coverage is excluded during a probationary period that can be interpreted as a sorting device. Fluet (1992) analyzed the selection of an optimal time-deductible in presence of adverse selection.

[23] On the relationship between the coverage obtained by a low-risk individual under a monopoly compared to that under a pure Nash competitive equilibrium, see Dahlby (1987). It is shown, for example, that under constant absolute risk aversion, the coverage obtained by a low-risk individual under monopoly is greater than, equal to, or less than that obtained under competition as the monopolist's expected profit on a policy purchased by low-risk individuals is greater than, equal to, or less than its expected profit on the policy purchased by high-risk individuals.

The second important result from Rothschild and Stiglitz is that there are conditions under which a separating equilibrium does not exist. In general, there is no equilibrium if the costs of pooling are low to the low-risk individuals (few high-risk individuals or low q_H, which is not the case in Figure 4b since the line C^0F' corresponds to a value of q_H higher than the critical level q_H^{RS} permitting separating equilibria) or if the costs of separating are high (structure of preference). In the former case, given the separating contracts, the cost of sorting (partial insurance) exceeds the benefits (no subsidy) when profitable pooling opportunities exist. But, as already shown, a pooling contract cannot be an equilibrium. This negative result has prompted further theoretical investigations since many insurance markets do function even in the presence of adverse selection.

One extension for the existence of an equilibrium is to consider a mixed strategy in which an insurer's strategy is a probability distribution over a pair of contracts. Rosenthal and Weiss (1984) showed that a separating Nash equilibrium always exists when the insurers adopt this strategy. However, it is not clear that such strategy has any particular economic interpretation in insurance markets as in many other markets.[24] Another extension is to introduce a three-stage game in which the insurer may reject in the third stage the insured's contract choice made in the second stage. Hellwig (1986, 1987) showed that a pooling contract may correspond to a sequential equilibrium of the three-stage game or it can never be upset by a separating contract whenever pooling is Pareto preferred. Moreover, contrary to the Rothschild and Stiglitz two-stage model, the three-stage game always has a sequential equilibrium in pure strategies. The most plausible sequential equilibrium is pooling rather than sorting, while in a three-stage game in signaling models (Cho and Kreps, 1987) it is the pooling rather the separating equilibria that lack robustness. As pointed out by Hellwig (1987), the conclusions are very sensitive to the details of game specification.[25]

Another type of extension that permits the existence of equilibria is to allow firms to consider other firms' behavior or reactions in their strategies and then to abandon the Nash strategy in the two-stage game. For example, Wilson (1977) proposed an anticipatory equilibrium concept where firms drop policies so that those remaining (after other firms anticipated reactions) at least break even. By definition, a Wilson equilibrium exists if no insurer can offer a policy such that 1) this new policy yields nonnegative profits and 2) remains profitable after other insurers have withdrawn all unprofitable policies in reaction to the offer. The resulting equilibrium (pooling or separation) always exists. A Wilson equilibrium corresponds to the Nash equilibrium when a separating equilibrium exists; otherwise, it is a pooling equilibrium such as

[24] See also Dasgupta and Maskin (1986) and Rothschild and Stiglitz (1997). On randomization to improve market functioning in presence of adverse selection see Garella (1989) and Arnott and Stiglitz (1988).

[25] See also Fagart (1996a) for another specification of the game. Her paper is dealing with a game where two principals compete for an agent, when the agent has private information. By considering a certain type of uncertainty, competition in markets with asymmetric information does not always imply loss of efficiency.

C_1 in Figure 4a.[26] Finally, we may consider the Riley (1979) reactive equilibrium where competitive firms add new contracts as reaction to entrants. It is shown that an equilibrium always corresponds to separating contracts.

Wilson also considered subsidization between policies, but Miyazaki (1977) and Spence (1977) developed the idea more fully. They showed how to improve welfare of both classes of risk (or of all n classes of risk; Spence (1977)) with low-risk class subsidizing the high-risk class. In fact Spence showed that, in a model in which firms react (in the sense of Wilson) by dropping loss-making policies, an equilibrium always exists. In all the above models, each of the contracts in the menu available is defined to permit the low-risk policyholders to signal their true risk. The resulting equilibrium is a break-even portfolio of separating contracts, and exists regardless of the relative value of q_H. The separating solution has no subsidy between policies when $q_H \geq q_H^{WMS}$. More formally we have

Proposition 9. A Wilson-Miyazaki-Spence (WMS) equilibrium exists regardless of the value of q_H. When $q_H \geq q_H^{WMS}$, the WMS equilibrium corresponds to the Rothschild-Stiglitz equilibrium.

One such equilibrium (C_3, C_4) is presented in Figure 5 for the case of two risk classes with cross subsidization from the low to the high-risk group. The curve denoted by *frontier* in Figure 5 is the zero aggregate transfers locus defined such that the contracts pairs yield balanced transfers between the risk-types, and the subset (C_3, Z) in bold is the set of contracts for the low-risk individuals that are second-best efficient. The derivation of the optimal contracts with transfers is obtained by maximizing the following program:

Problem 4

$$\underset{\alpha_L, \beta_L, t, s}{Max} \; p_L U(W - D + \beta_L - t) + (1 - p_L) U(W - \alpha_L - t)$$

subject to the non-negative aggregate profits constraint

$$q_L t \geq q_H s$$

the zero-profit constraint before cross-subsidization

$$(1 - p_L)\alpha_L \geq p_L \beta_L$$

the self-selection constraint

$$U\left(W - \alpha_H^{**} + s\right) \geq p_H U(W - D + \beta_L - t) + (1 - p_H) U(W - \alpha_L - t)$$

[26] See Grossman (1979) for an analysis of the Wilson type equilibrium with reactions of insureds rather than reactions of sellers.

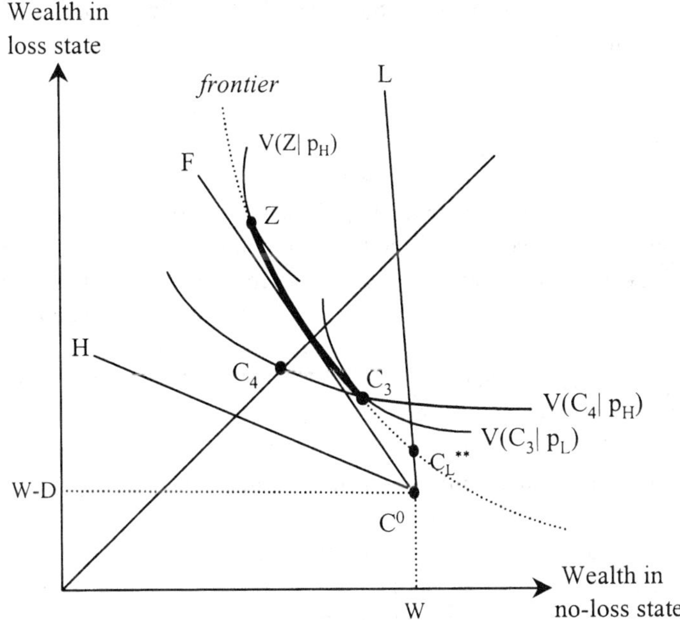

Figure 5 A Wilson-Miyazaki-Spence equilibrium

the positivity constraint

$$s \geq 0$$

where s and t are for subsidy and tax respectively.

When the positivity constraint is binding, (C_3, C_4) corresponds to the Rothschild Stiglitz contracts (C_H^{**}, C_L^{**}) without cross-subsidization. When the positivity constraint holds with a strict inequality, the equilibrium involves subsidization from low risks to high risks.[27]

The Wilson-Miyazaki-Spence (WMS) equilibrium (C_3, C_4) solves this program if (C_3, C_4) is second-best efficient in the sense of Harris and Townsend (1981). An allocation is second-best efficient if it is Pareto-optimal within the set of allocations that are feasible and the zero-profit constraint on the portfolio.[28] In competitive insurance markets, Crocker and Snow (1985) proved the following proposition, that can be seen as an analogue with the welfare first theorem (Henriet and Rochet, 1991):

[27] For a proof that the equilibrium can never imply subsidization from high-risks individuals to low-risks individuals, see Crocker and Snow (1985).

[28] See Crocker and Snow (1985, 1986) for more details. See Lacker and Weinberg (1999) for a proof that a Wilson allocation is coalition proof.

Proposition 10. A Wilson-Miyazaki-Spence (WMS) equilibrium is second-best efficient for all values of q_H.

Proof. See Crocker and Snow (1985).

Subsidization between different risk classes is of special interest for characterizing the notion of second-best optimality and simultaneously the shape of optimal redistribution in insurance markets. Indeed, the optimal allocation on these markets (given the incentive constraints imposed by adverse selection) involves cross-subsidization between risk types. Thus, the *second-best efficient* contracts resulting from this redistribution are described for low-risk individuals by the frontier in bold in Figure 5 (see Crocker and Snow, 1985). It can be shown that a Rothschild and Stiglitz equilibrium is second-best efficient if and only if q_H is higher than some critical value q_H^{WMS}, which is itself higher than the critical value q_H^{RS} permitting the existence of a Nash equilibrium. Then, as mentioned, a Nash equilibrium is not necessarily efficient. The same conclusion applies to the Riley equilibrium since it sustains the Rothschild and Stiglitz solution whatever q_H. In the income-states space, the shape of this curve can be convex as shown in Figure 5 (Dionne and Fombaron, 1996) under some unrestrictive assumptions about utility functions. More precisely, some conditions about risk aversion and prudence indexes guarantee the strict convexity of the efficiency frontier: the insurance coverage β_L offered to low-risks is a convex function in the subscribed premium α_L. Moreover, high risks are offered a coverage β_H which is a linear function in the premium α_H. It was shown by Dionne and Fombaron (1996) that this frontier can never be strictly concave under risk aversion. At least, a portion of the frontier must be convex.[29]

Despite the presence of non-convexities of this locus in the income-states space, the correspondence between optimality and market equilibrium is maintained (see Prescott and Townsend, 1984, for a general proof of this assertion and Henriet and Rochet, 1986, for an analysis in an insurance context). Consequently, the conventional question about the possibility of achieving a second-best efficient allocation by a decentralized market doesn't raise. So an analogue to the second optimality theorem holds for an informationally constrained insurance market (Henriet and Rochet, 1986): even though government cannot a priori impose risk-discriminating taxes on individuals, it can impose a tax on their contracts and so generate the same effect as if taxing directly individuals (Crocker and Snow, 1986).

Finally, as we will in section 7.7, another possibility to deal with equilibrium issues is to use risk categorization (see Crocker and Snow, 2000, for a more detailed analysis).

[29] For more general utility functions, the curvature can be both convex and concave but must necessarily be convex around the full insurance allocation under risk aversion. For more details, see Pannequin (1992) and Dionne and Fombaron (1996).

7.4.3 Multiperiod Contracts and Competition

The aspect of competition raises new technical and economic issues on multiperiod contracting. Indeed, the value of information affects considerably the process of decision-making in a competitive insurance market. Let us begin with Cooper and Hayes' (1987) analysis of two-period contracts with full commitment on the supply side.

7.4.3.1 Full Commitment

Cooper and Hayes used the Nash equilibrium concept in a two-period game where the equilibrium must be separating.[30] In fact, they considered two different behaviors about commitment on the demand side. First, both insurers and insureds commit themselves to the two-period contracts (without possibility of renegotiation) and second, the insurers commit to a two-period contract but the contract is not binding on insureds. We will refer these respective situations as contracts with *full commitment* and *with semi-commitment*, respectively. When competitive firms can bind agents to the two periods, it is easy to show that, in the separating solution, the contracts offered are qualitatively identical to that of the monopoly solution with commitment: high-risk agents receive full insurance at an actuarial price in each period while low-risk agents face price and quantity adjustments in the second period. Suppose that q_H is such that a Rothschild and Stiglitz equilibrium is second-best efficient. Then it can be shown that the two-period contract with full commitment dominates[31] a repetition of Rothschild and Stiglitz contracts without memory. As for the monopoly case, this result is due to the memory effect (see Chiappori et al., 1994 for a survey on the memory effect).

When the authors relax the strong commitment assumption in favor of semi-commitment, and consider that insureds can costlessly switch to other firms in the second period, they show that the presence of second-period competition limits but does not destroy the use of experience rating as a sorting device. The difference between the results with full commitment and semi-commitment is explained by the fact that the punishment possibilities for period-one accidents are reduced by the presence of other firms that offer single-period contracts in the second period.

The semi-commitment result was obtained by assuming that, in the second period, entrant firms offer single-period contracts without any knowledge of insureds' accident histories or their choice of contract in the first period. The new firms' optimal behavior is to offer Rothschild and Stiglitz separating contracts[32] to the market.[33] By

[30] In other words, they implicitly assumed that the conditions to obtain a Nash separating equilibrium in a single period contract are sufficient for an equilibrium to exist in their two-period model.

[31] For a proof of this assertion, see Fombaron 1997a.

[32] Actually, the Rothschild and Stiglitz contracts are not ever necessarily the best policy rival firms can offer. Assuming that outside options are fixed is restrictive. Such a issue is discussed in the next section.

[33] Recall here that the authors limited their focus on separating solutions.

taking this decision as given, the design of the optimal two-period contract by competitive firms with semi-commitment has to take into account at least one supplementary binding constraint (no-switching constraint) that reduces social welfare when we compare to full commitment. The formal problem consists of maximizing the low-risks' two-period expected utility by choosing C_H^2 and C_L^2 under the incentive compatibility constraints, the nonnegative intertemporal expected profits constraint and the *no-switching* constraints:

Problem 5

$$\max_{C_H^2, C_L^2} V(C_L^2 | p_L)$$

s.t.

$$V(C_i^2 | p_i) \geq V(C_j^2 | p_i) \quad i, j = H, L, \quad i \neq j$$

$$\pi (C_L | p_L) + [p_L \pi (C_{La} | p_L) + (1 - p_L) \pi (C_{Ln} | p_L)] \geq 0$$

$$V(C_{is} | p_i) \geq V\left(C_i^* | p_i\right) \quad i = H, L \quad s = a, n.$$

By the constraint of non-negative expected profits earned on the low risks' multiperiod contract, this model rules out the possibility for insurers to offer cross-subsidizations between the low and the high risks (and circumvent any problem of inexistence of Nash equilibrium). Since this constraint is obviously binding at the optimum, only intertemporal transfers are allowed by Cooper and Hayes.

Using the above model, Cooper and Hayes proved the following results, summarized by Proposition 11:

Proposition 11. Under the assumption that a Nash equilibrium exists, the optimal two-period contract with semi-commitment is characterized by the following properties:

1) High-risk individuals obtain full insurance coverage and are not experience rated: $V(C_{Ha}^* | p_H) = V(C_{Hn}^* | p_H) = V(C_H^* | p_H) = U(W - \alpha_H^1)$;
while low-risk individuals receive only partial insurance coverage and are experience rated: $V(C_{La}^* | p_L) < V(C_{Ln}^* | p_L)$;
2) High-risk agents are indifferent between their contract and that intended to low-risks, while low risks strictly prefer their contract:
$V(C_H^{2*} | p_H) = V(C_L^{2*} | p_H)$ and $V(C_L^{2*} | p_L) > V(C_H^{2*} > | p_L)$;
3) Both high and low risks obtain a consumer surplus:
$V(C_i^{2*} | p_i) > 2V(C^0 | p_i), \quad i = H, L;$

4) The pattern of temporal profits is highballing on low-risks' contracts and flat on high-risks' ones:
$\pi(C_L^* \mid p_L) \geq 0 \geq [p_L\pi(C_{La}^* \mid p_L) + (1 - p_L)\pi(C_{Ln}^* \mid p_L)]$
and $\pi(C_H^* \mid p_H) = \pi(C_{Ha}^* \mid p_H) = \pi(C_{Hn}^* \mid p_H) = 0$.

In other words, the presence of competition, combined with the agents' inability to enforce binding multiperiod contracts, reduces the usefulness of long term contracts as a sorting device and consequently, the potential gains of long term relationships. This conclusion is similar to that obtained in the monopoly case (in which the principal cannot commit on nonrenegotiation) since the no-switching constraints imposed by competition can be reinterpreted as rationality constraints in a monopolistic situation.

The fourth property in Proposition 11 means that, at equilibrium, firms make positive expected profits on old low-risk insureds (by earning positive profits on the low risks' first period contract) and expected losses on new low-risk insureds (by making losses on the second-period contract of low-risks who suffered a first-period loss, greater than positive profits on the low risks' contract corresponding to the no-loss state in the first period). In aggregate, expected two-period profits from low-risks are zero.

As in the monopoly situation, all the consumers self-select in the first period and only low-risk insureds are offered an experience-rated contract in the second period based on their accident history.[34] This arrangement provides an appropriate bonus for accident free experience and ensures that low risks who suffer an accident remain with the firm.[35] This temporal profit pattern, also labeled *highballing* by D'Arcy and Doherty (1990), was shown to stand in contrast with the *lowballing* predicted in dynamic models without commitment. In particular, D'Arcy and Doherty have compared the results obtained by Cooper and Hayes under the full commitment assumption with those of the *lowballing* predicted by Kunreuther and Pauly (1985) in a price competition. With about similar assumptions on commitment, Nilssen (1990) and Fombaron (1997b) also obtained a *lowballing* prediction in the classic situation of competition in price-quantity contracts.

Although Cooper and Hayes were the first to consider a repeated insurance problem with adverse selection and full commitment, some assumptions are critical. The first criticism refers to the ability for insurers to commit to long term relationships. Indeed, the assumption of precommitment by insurers straightforwardly converts a multiperiod program into a single-period problem where the incentive compatibility constraints are adequately modified to take into account the long-term nature of the relationship. Under this assumption, since the first-period contract

[34] But not on their contract choice.

[35] In fact, the corresponding expected utility of the low-risk individual who did not have an accident in the first period (and stays) is strictly greater at equilibrium to that corresponding to the entrant one-period contract.

choices do reveal the individual risks, the initial agreement on the second period contract could be renegotiated at the beginning of the second period (under full information) in a way that would improve the welfare of both parties. Consequently, the two-period contract with full commitment is Pareto-inefficient ex-post, i.e., relative to the information acquired by insurers at that time. Some recent articles in the literature have investigated other concepts of relationships between an insurer and his insureds, involving limited commitment: the *no-commitment* assumption represents the polar case of the full commitment situation (section 7.4.3.2) and the *commitment with renegotiation* appears to be an intermediate case between the full commitment and the no-commitment (section 7.4.3.3).

The second criticism refers to the *exogeneity of the outside options*. In Cooper and Hayes' model and in most dynamic models, firms are supposed to offer the same contract to a new customer, whatever his contractual path and his accident history. Behind this assumption on competitive behavior, it is implicitly assumed that the information revealed by the accident records and possibly by contractual choices does not become public.[36] However, this assumption is not very realistic with regard to the presence, in some countries, of a specific regulatory law that obliges the insurers to make public these data. This is the case in France and in most European countries for automobile insurance, where the free availability to accident records is a statutory situation. Consequently, models with endogenous outside options are more appropriate to describe the functioning of the competitive insurance market in these countries. This alternative approach will be discussed in the two next sections.

As a result to these above strong hypotheses, the literature obtains the same predictions than in the static model about the equilibrium existence issue[37] and about the self-selection principle. These predictions do not hold any longer when we assume limited commitment and/or endogenous outside options.

7.4.3.2 No-commitment

In this section, the attention is paid to competitive insurance models in which the contractual parties can only commit to one-period incentive schemes, i.e., where insurers can write short-term contracts, but not long-term contracts. The no-commitment is bilateral in the sense that each insured can switch to another company in period two if he decides to do so. Such situations are particularly relevant in liability insurance (automobile or health insurance for example) where long term contracts are rarely signed. Despite this inability to commit, both parties can sign a first-period contract that should be followed by second-period contracts which are conditionally optimal and experience-rated. This sequence of one-period contracts gives rise to a

[36] When an individual quits a company A and begins a new relationship with a company B, he is considered by the latter as a new customer on the insurance market.

[37] Cross-subsidizations between risk types remain inconsistent with equilibrium, so that problems for equilibrium existence also exist in a multiperiod context.

level of intertemporal welfare lower than that of full commitment but, in some cases, higher than in a repetition of static contracts without memory.

Kunreuther and Pauly (1985) were the first to study a multiperiod model without commitment in a competitive insurance context. However, their investigation is not really an extension of the Rothschild and Stiglitz' analysis since the authors consider competition in price and not in price-quantity.[38] They argue that insurers are unable to write exclusive contracts; instead they propose that insurers offer only pure price contracts (Pauly, 1974). Moreover, they assume that consumers are myopic: they choose the firm which makes the most attractive offer in the current period. At the other extreme, the classic dynamic literature supposes that individuals have perfect foresight in the sense that they maximize the discounted expected utility over the planning horizon.

Despite the major difference in the assumption about the way insurers compete, their model leads to the same lowballing prediction than other studies, like the ones developed by Nilssen (1990) and by Fombaron (1997b), both using the basic framework of the Rothschild and Stiglitz model where firms compete by offering price-quantity contracts. Insurers make expected losses in the first period (on the new customers) and earn expected profits on the policies they renew (on the old customers). The similarity in this pattern of intertemporal profits is mainly due to the fact these three contributions assume that insurers do not write long term contracts while, as we saw, Cooper and Hayes permitted long term contracting. In Nilssen's model, an important result is to show that pooling contracts could emerge in dynamic equilibrium (pooling on the new insureds) when the ability to commit lacks in the relationships, so making the cross-subsidizations compatible with equilibrium. Moreover, contrary to the Kunreuther and Pauly model, the absence of commitment does not rule out separation. His result has been extended in Fombaron (1997b) who shows that at equilibrium, semi pooling can emerge in the first period, followed by separation in the second period, and this is made possible by introducing mixed strategies played by insureds. This technical process, also labeled *randomization*, permits to defer the revelation of information and so, facilitates the respect of sequential optimality constraints required by models with limited commitment. It was used by Hosios and Peters (1989), as we saw, in a monopoly situation without commitment and by Dionne and Doherty (1994) in a competitive context with commitment and renegotiation. Moreover, in contrast with the mentioned-above literature, the model makes the outside options endogenous to the information revealed over time. The formal program presented below (Problem 6) is the most general. This program includes the Nilssen's model as a particular case (more precisely, for both $x_H = 1$, $x_L = 0$ and $C_i^{cc} = C_i^{RS}$ where $x_i \in [0; 1]$ measures the level of separation of type i). However, some results are contrasted in Table 1. This permits to compare the different results according to the assumptions in the models.

[38] They let insurers offer contracts specifying a per-unit premium for a given amount of coverage.

Table 1
Comparison of Multi-Period Competitive Models

Hypotheses	Full commitment	No-commitment			Commitment with renegotiation	
	Cooper & Hayes 1987	Kunreuther & Pauly 1985	Nilssen 1990	Fombaron 1997b	Dionne & Doherty 1994	Fombaron 2000
Price-quantity contracts	Yes	No	Yes	Yes	Yes	Yes
Insurers observe						
— total contract choice	Yes	No	Yes	Yes	Yes	Yes
— accidents	Yes	No (claims only)	Yes	Yes	Yes	Yes
Rivals observe						
— contract choices	No	No	Yes	Yes/No	Yes	Yes/No
— loss experience	No	No	No	Yes/No	No	Yes/No
Rivals' offers are endogenous	No	No	No	Yes	No	Yes

Results						
Type of equilibrium						
— first period	Separating	Pooling	Pooling or separating	Pooling, separating or semi-pooling	Pooling, separating or semi-pooling	Pooling, separating cr semi-pooling
— second period	Separating	Pooling	Separating	Separating	Separating	Separating
Cross-subsidization between						
— types	No	Yes in both periods	Yes in both periods	Yes in both periods	Yes in first period	Yes in both periods
— contracts	No	No	Yes in both periods	Yes in both periods	No	Yes in both periods
Temporal profit pattern	Highballing	Lowballing	Lowballing	Lowballing	Highballing	Highballing or lowballing
Consumer lock-in	No	Yes	Yes	Yes	No	Yes when lowballing
Equilibrium existence	$q_H \geq q_H^{RS}$ (sufficient condition for a Nash equilibrium)	No Nash equilibrium	$q_H \geq q_H^{RS}$ (sufficient condition for a NPB separating equilibrium)	For $q_H \geq q_H^{NC}$ ($>q_H^{RS}$) (sufficient condition for a NPBE)	For $q_H \geq q_H^{RS}$ (sufficient condition for a NPBE)	$\forall q_H$ for a NPBE

Concerning the interfirm communication, it is assumed in Fombaron (1997b), that companies learn about the risk characteristics of their insureds by observing claims records and contract choices, but will not share these private informations freely with rival firms. As a consequence, the rival firms do not have access to accident histories. However, they are assumed to observe in period 2 the contract any insured has chosen in period 1. There are many ways to obtain verified information about the terms of a contract. The most elementary consists for insurers of requiring that any insured shows his precedent contract[39] (generally, the contractual agreement mentions at least the amount of premium and the level of coverage). With regard to the assumption of asymmetric information about accident records between insurance market participants, the following model is not different from those developed by Cooper and Hayes (1987), Kunreuther and Pauly (1985), Nilssen (1990) or Dionne and Doherty (1994).

In Fombaron (1997b), a particular attention is paid to the value of informational asymmetry between competing insurers. When firms maximize, they take into account how their actions (i.e., their contract offers) affect over time the reactions of their rivals. So, each firm, in a monopolistic position in the second period, may act in a way to prevent the potential rivals to offer more appealing contracts than those offered to its clients.

Solving the two-period model without commitment requires to use the concept of Nash Perfect Bayesian Equilibrium[40] (NPBE). Given this notion of sequential equilibrium, we work backwards and begin by providing a description of the Nash equilibrium in the last period.

In period 2, $\widehat{C_{ia}}$ and $\widehat{C_{in}}$ solve the following subprograms imposed by the constraints of sequential optimality, for $s \in \{a, n\}$ respectively where a means accident in the first period and n means no-accident:

Problem 6

$$\widehat{C_{is}} \in \arg\max \sum_{i=H,L} q_{is}(x_i)\,\pi(C_{is} \mid p_i)$$
$$\text{s.t.}$$
$$V(C_{is} \mid p_i) \geq V(C_{js} \mid p_i) \quad i,j = H,L, \quad i \neq j$$
$$V(C_{is} \mid p_i) \geq V(C_i^{cc} \mid p_i) \quad i = H,L$$

where posterior beliefs[41] are defined by

[39] For a more detailed argumentation of information sharing, see Kunreuther and Pauly (1985) and D'Arcy and Doherty (1990).

[40] This concept implies that the set of strategies satisfies sequential rationality given the system of beliefs and that the system of beliefs is obtained from both strategies and observed actions using Bayes' rule whenever possible.

[41] Put differently, $q_{ia}(x_i)$ and $q_{in}(x_i)$ are the probabilities at the beginning of the second period that, among the insureds having chosen the pooling contract in the first period, an insured belongs to the i-risk class if he has suffered a loss or no loss in the first period respectively.

$$q_{ia}(x_i) = \frac{q_i p_i x_i}{\sum_{k=H,L} q_k p_k x_k}$$

$$\text{and } q_{in}(x_i) = \frac{q_i(1-p_i)x_i}{\sum_{k=H,L} q_k(1-p_k)x_k}, \quad i = H, L.$$

For given beliefs, the second-period optimization subprogram is similar, in some sense, to a single-period monopoly insurance model with adverse selection (Stiglitz, 1977, in section 7.3.2) for a subgroup of insureds and where no-switching constraints correspond to usual participation constraints. Indeed, in the absence of commitment and because of informational asymmetries between insurers, each informed firm can use his knowledge on his old insureds to earn positive profits in the second period. However, this profit is limited by the possibility that old insureds switch to another company at the beginning of the second period. Contrary to a rival company, a firm which proposes sets of contracts in the second period to his insureds can distinguish among accident-groups on the basis of past accident observations. Each company acquires over time an informational advantage relative to the rest of competing firms on the insurance market.

Formally, C_i^{cc} represents the best contract a rival uninformed company can offer to i-risk type. In other words, C_i^{cc} describes the switching opportunities of any insured i at the beginning of period 2. Clearly, since contract choices are observable by rival firms, C_i^{cc} depends on x_i. If no high risk self-selects in period 1, such that all high risks are pooled with low risks, the observation of contract choices does not reveal information on individual risk-types and, as a consequence, $C_i^{cc} = C_i^{RS}$. At the other extreme case, when the first-period contracts are fully separating, the contract choice reveals individual risk-types to any insurer on the insurance market and C_i^{cc} will be a first-best contract C_i^{FB}.

The PBE of the complete game is a sequence of one-period contracts (C_i^*, C_{ia}^*, C_{in}^*) for every $i = H$, L, such that:

Problem 7

$$\left(C_i^*, C_{ia}^*, C_{in}^*\right) \in \underset{(C_i, C_{ia}, C_{in})}{\arg\max}\, V(C_L \mid p_L) + \delta\left[p_L V(\widehat{C_{La}} \mid p_L) + (1-p_L)V(\widehat{C_{Ln}} \mid p_L)\right]$$

$$s.t.$$

$$x_i(1+\delta)V(C_i^{RS} \mid p_i) + (1-x_i)\left[V(C_i \mid p_i) + \delta\left(p_i V(\widehat{C_{ia}} \mid p_i) + (1-p_i)V(\widehat{C_{in}} \mid p_i)\right)\right]$$
$$\geq V(C_j \mid p_i) + \delta\left(p_i V(\widehat{C_{ja}} \mid p_i) + (1-p_i)V(C_{jn} \mid p_i)\right)$$

$$\sum_{i=H,L} q_i(x_i)\pi(C_i \mid p_i) + \delta\left[\sum_{i=H,L} q_{ia}(x_i)\pi(\widehat{C_{ia}} \mid p_i) + \sum_{i=H,L} q_{in}(x_i)\pi(\widehat{C_{in}} \mid p_i)\right] \geq 0$$

where $\widehat{C_{La}}$, $\widehat{C_{Ln}}$ solve Problem 6 for $s = a$, n respectively.

Problem 7 provides the predictions summarized in Proposition 12.

Proposition 12. In the presence of private information, each company may increase the individuals welfare by offering two contracts, a sequence of one-period contracts and a multiperiod contract without commitment having the following characteristics:

1) Both high and low-risk classes obtain partial insurance coverage in each period and are experience rated: $V(C_{ia}^* \mid p_i) \leq V(C_{in}^* \mid p_i)$, $i = H, L$;
2) High-risk are indifferent between a mix of a sequence of Rothschild Stiglitz contracts and the multiperiod contract, also subscribed by low-risk individuals: $x_H(1+\delta)V(C_H^{RS}|p_H)+(1-x_H)V\left(C_H^{2*}|p_H\right)=V\left(C_L^{2*}|p_H\right)$

   and the low-risks strictly prefer the multiperiod contract: $V\left(C_L^{2*} \mid p_L\right) > x_L(1+\delta)V(C_L^{RS} \mid p_L)+(1-x_L)V\left(C_L^{2*} \mid p_L\right)$, $x_L \in [0, 1]$;
3) High and low-risk individuals obtain a consumer surplus: $V\left(C_i^{2*} \mid p_i\right) > (1+\delta)V(C^0 \mid p_i)$, $i = H, L$;
4) Aggregate expected profits earned on the multiperiod contract increase over time: $\sum_{i=H,L} q_i(x_i)\pi\left(C_i^* \mid p_i\right) < \sum_{i=H,L}\sum_{s=a,n} q_{is}(x_i)\pi\left(C_{is}^* \mid p_i\right)$.

Concerning the existence property, it can be shown that a Nash Perfect Bayesian Equilibrium exists for some values of parameters (i.e., for every q_H such that $q_H \geq q_H^{NC}$ ($> q_H^{RS}$) where NC is for no commitment). As a consequence, the existence property of equilibrium is guaranteed for a set of parameters smaller than in the static model.

Similar assumptions on commitment and observations of individuals accident history explain that Nilssen (1990) and Fombaron (1997b) obtain similar predictions on lock-in (each firm earns a positive expected profit on its old customers since it controls information on past experience[42]). Moreover, different assumptions on allowed strategies (only pure strategies are played by insureds in Nilssen while in Fombaron, insureds are allowed to randomize between contracts), obviously lead to different properties of equilibrium in terms of existence (see Table 1).

Finally, in order to evaluate the effects of a regulatory law about interfirm communication, Fombaron (1997b) considered the extreme polar situation in which a regulatory law constrains insurers to make public records data such that rival firms do have access to all accident records. If competing firms have identical knowledge about insureds risks over time, no experience rating is sustainable in equilibrium and

[42] Cromb (1990) considered the effects of different precommitment assumptions between the parties to the contract on the value of accident history. Under fully binding contracts, the terms of the contract depend only on the number of accidents over a certain time horizon while under other assumptions (partially binding and no binding) the timing of accidents becomes important.

allocative inefficiency results from dynamic contractual relationships. The "too large" amount of revealed information is shown to destroy efficiency and existence of dynamic equilibria. In contrast, as we saw, when rival firms do not have access to accident records, equilibrium involves experience-rating and dynamic contracts achieve second-best optimality, since informational asymmetries between competing firms make cross-subsidization compatible with Nash equilibrium. As a consequence, insureds are always better off when accidents remain a private information.[43] The next section is devoted to an analysis of multiperiod contracts under an intermediary level of commitment from insurers.

7.4.4 Commitment and Renegotiation

Dionne and Doherty (1994) introduced the phenomenon of renegotiation in long term relationships in insurance markets. Two-period contracts are considered where insureds can leave the relation at the end of the first period and insurer is bound by a multiperiod agreement. The difference with Cooper and Hayes' model appears in the possibility of renegotiation. Indeed, insurers are allowed to make a proposition of recontraction with their insureds which can be accepted or rejected. In other words, parties cannot precommit not to make Pareto-improving changes based on information revealed at the end of the first period. As shown in Dionne and Doherty (1994), the Cooper and Hayes' solution is not renegotiation-proof. This means that sequential optimality fails since parties' objectives change over time. If renegotiation cannot be ruled out, the company and its insureds anticipate it, and this will change the nature of the contracts. Thus, in order to ensure the robustness against renegotiation procedure described above, we must impose either the constraint of pooling in the first period or the constraint of full insurance for both types in the second period in addition to standard constraints in Cooper and Hayes' optimization program. The new program can be written as Problem 7 except for the second-period constraints imposed by sequential optimality. Indeed, renegotiation-proofness means that the second-period contracts are robust to Pareto-improving changes and not only for increasing the insurers' welfare. Consequently, second period contracts cannot be solved as a subprogram which maximizes expected profits of insurers. In contrast, they must solve, in the last period, a standard competitive program which optimizes the low-risks welfare (in each group a and n). Moreover, no-switching constraints must appear in these subprograms in a similar way than in the model without commitment.

If we consider a general model in which all kinds of transfers are allowed (intertemporal and intertypes transfers), problem 6 can be rewritten in the context of semi-commitment with renegotiation as follows:

[43] In a context of symmetric incomplete information (see section 7.7.3), de Garidel (1997) finds also that accident claims should not be shared by insurers.

Problem 8

$$\widehat{C_{is}} \in \arg\max V(C_{Ls} \mid p_L) \quad \text{for } s = a,n$$

$$s.t.$$

$$V(C_{is} \mid p_i) \geq V(C_{js} \mid p_i) \quad i,j = H,L \quad i \neq j$$

$$\sum_{i=H,L} q_{is}(x_i)\pi(C_{is} \mid p_i) \geq \bar{\pi}_s$$

$$V(C_{is} \mid p_i) \geq V(C_i^{cc} \mid p_i) \quad i = H,L.$$

Dionne and Doherty (1994) first show that fully separating strategies, once made robust to renegotiation, degenerates to an outcome which amounts to that of a replication of single-period contracts in terms of welfare, when insureds are bound in relationships. If insureds are allowed to quit their company at the end of period 1, the program includes, in addition, no-switching constraints and as a result of this more constrained problem, the outcome will be worse in terms of welfare relative to a sequence of static contracts without memory. This negative result on separating contracts suggests efficiency will be attained by a partial revelation of information over time (as in no-commitment model). Dionne and Doherty then show that the solution may involve semi-pooling in the first period followed by separated contracts. They show that the equilibrium is fully separating when the discount factor is low and tends to a pooling for large discount factors. Moreover, they obtain a highballing configuration of intertemporal profits, contrary to the lowballing prediction resulting from models without commitment. Thus, commitment with renegotiation provides the same predictions than those in Proposition 12 except for the fourth result that becomes: $\sum_{i=H,L} q_i(x_i)\pi\left(C_i^* \mid p_i\right) > \sum_{i=H,L}\sum_{s=a,n} q_{is}(x_i)\pi\left(C_{is}^* \mid p_i\right)$.

However, if a more general model is considered (Fombaron, 2000), in which all kinds of transfers are allowed (intertemporal and interindividual transfers) and outside options are endogenous, results are different in some points of those obtained in Dionne and Doherty (see Table 1). More precisely, the configuration in equilibrium doesn't necessarily exhibit a decreasing profile of intertemporal profits for the company, so that the fourth result in Proposition 12 becomes here: $\sum_{i=H,L} q_i(x_i)\pi\left(C_i^* \mid p_i\right) \lesseqgtr \sum_{i=H,L}\sum_{s=a,n} q_{is}(x_i)\pi\left(C_{is}^* \mid p_i\right)$.

This means that the insureds' welfare optimization in period 2 (in models with commitment and renegotiation) instead the profits maximization (in models without commitment) doesn't necessarily rule out the possibility of lock-in.

More importantly, it is possible to establish that a competitive insurance market has always an equilibrium. This result is due to the compatibility of cross-subsidization with equilibrium, as opposed to the result in static models. The economic intuition can be the following: an additional instrument can serve to make rival offers less attractive. It consists for informed insurers of offering unprofitable contracts in the second period. This instrument is possibly used in a case of commitment with renegotiation but can not be enforced in no-commitment situations. Endly, as in models without commitment, insureds are always better off when the information about accident records remains private, i.e., in a statutory situation where no regulatory law enforces companies to make public records data.

Finally, the issue of consumer lock-in and the pattern of temporal profits should motivate researchers to undertake empirical investigations of the significance of adverse selection and of the testable predictions that permit discrimination between the competing models. To our knowledge, only two published studies have investigated these questions with multi-period data and their conclusions go in opposite directions. D'Arcy and Doherty (1990) found evidence of lowballing which supports the non-commitment assumption while Dionne and Doherty (1994) obtained that a significant group of insurers in California used highballing a result that is more in the line of some form of commitment. It is interesting to observe that this group of insurers attracts selective portfolios with disproportionate numbers of low risks. This result reinforces the idea that some form of commitment introduces more efficiency.

7.5 MORAL HAZARD AND ADVERSE SELECTION

Although in many situations principals face adverse selection and moral hazard problems simultaneously when they design contracts, these two types of asymmetrical information have been given separate treatments so far in the economic literature on risk-sharing agreements. Both information problems have been integrated into a single model where all the parties of the contract are risk neutral (Laffont and Tirole, 1986; Picard, 1987; Caillaud, Guesnerie, Rey and Tirole, 1988; Guesnerie, Picard and Rey, 1988). Although these models involve uncertainty, they are unable to explain arrangements where at least one party is risk averse. In particular they do not apply to insurance. More recently, some authors have attempted to integrate both information problems into a single model where the agent is risk averse.

As already discussed by Dionne and Lasserre (1988) such an integration of both information problems is warranted on empirical grounds. Applied studies are still few in this area, but they will find it difficult to avoid considering both kinds of information asymmetry.

7.5.1 Monopoly and Multi-Period Contracts

Dionne and Lasserre (1988) showed how it is possible to achieve a second-best allocation of risks when moral hazard and adverse selection problems are present simultaneously. While they draw heavily on the contributions of Rubinstein and Yaari (1983), Dionne (1983) and Dionne and Lasserre (1985), the integration of the two types of information problems is not a straightforward exercise. Since an agent who has made a false announcement may now choose an action that is statistically compatible with his announcement, false announcements may go undetected. They proposed a contract under which the agent cannot profit from this additional degree of freedom. Under a combination of moral hazard and adverse selection, several types of customers can adopt different care levels so that they have identical expected losses. When this happens, it is impossible to distinguish those who produce an efficient level of care from the others on the basis of average losses.

However, deviant behaviours can be detected by monitoring deviations from the mean. Thus the insurer's strategy can be written with more than one simple aggregate (as in Dionne and Lasserre, 1985, and Rubinstein and Yaari, 1983). In Dionne and Lasserre (1988) the principal has to monitor two aggregates, the average loss experienced by a given agent and its squared deviation from the mean. However, it was sufficient to get the desired result since in their model the information problem has only two dimensions. More generally, the insurer would have to monitor one moment of the distribution for each hidden dimension.

Combining moral hazard with adverse selection problems in models which use past experience, might involve some synergetic effects. In the model presented in Dionne and Lasserre (1988), the same information required to eliminate either the moral hazard problem alone (Rubinstein and Yaari), or adverse selection alone (Dionne and Lasserre), is used to remove both problems simultaneously. A related subject concerns the efficient use of past information, and the allocation of instruments, toward the solution of each particular information problem. For a long time, self-selection mechanisms have been proposed in response to adverse selection while nonlinear pricing was advocated against moral hazard. In one-period contracts both procedures used separately involve inefficiency (partial insurance) which can be reduced by the introduction of time in the contracts. Dionne and Lasserre showed that self selection may help solve moral hazard problems, as well as adverse selection problems. We will now discuss how the use of two instruments may improve resource allocation and welfare when both problems are present simultaneously in single-period competitive contracts.

In a static model which can be considered as a special case of the Dionne and Lasserre (1988) model, Chassagnon (1994) studies the optimality of a one-period model when both problems are present simultaneously. Three results are of interest in this paper: 1) the Spence-Mirlees propriety is not always verified. Indifference curves may have more than one intersection points; 2) contrarily to the Stiglitz (1977) model where the low risk individual may not have access to any insurance coverage, in Chassagnon model, there are configurations (in particular, the configuration du pas de danse) where all agents obtain insurance; finally, 3) both types of agents may receive a positive rent according to their relative number in the economy.

The model is specific in the sense that the accident probabilities keep the same order when the effort level is the same. Suppose that there are only two levels of efforts that characterize the accident probabilities of type i: $\underline{p}_i < \bar{p}_i$, $i = H, L$. In Chassagnon model, $\underline{p}_H > \underline{p}_L$ and $\bar{p}_H > \bar{p}_L$ while $\underline{p}_H$ can be lower than $\bar{p}_L$. In fact the effect of introducing moral hazard in the pure principal-agent one becomes interesting when the high risk individual is more efficient in care activities than the low risk individual. Otherwise, when $\underline{p}_H > \bar{p}_L$, the results are the same as in the pure adverse selection selection model where only the H type receives a positive rent.

7.5.2 Competitive Contracts

One of the arguments often used to justify the prohibition of risk categorization is that it is based on fixed or exogenous characteristics such as age, race and sex. However, as pointed out by Bond and Crocker (1990), insurers also use other characteristics that are chosen by individuals. They extended Crocker and Snow (1986) previous analysis of risk categorization in presence of adverse selection and examined the equilibrium and efficiency implications of risk categorization based on consumption goods that are statistically related to individual's risks, which they termed "correlative products".

Formally, their model introduces endogenous categorization in an environment characterized by both moral hazard and adverse selection. They show that, while there is a natural tension between the sorting of risk classes engendered by adverse selection and the correction of externalities induced by moral hazard, the use of risk classification improves efficiency in resource allocation. They also obtain that the sorting of risks based on correlative consumption may give a first-best allocation as Nash equilibria when adverse selection is not too severe and when the insurer can observe individual consumption of the hazardous good.

This is particularly interesting as an alternative view of how firms, in practice, may overcome the nonexistence of Nash equilibrium problems. They then considered the case where the insurer cannot observe both the individual's consumption and the individual's characteristics. However, the planner can observe aggregate production of the good. They showed that taxation of the consumption good has now two roles (reduces moral hazard and relaxes self-selection constraints) that permit Pareto improvements.

Cromb (1990) analyzed the simultaneous presence of moral hazard and adverse selection in competitive insurance markets and obtained that the addition of moral hazard to the standard Rothschild-Stiglitz (1976) model with adverse selection has qualitative effects on the nature and existence of equilibrium. Under certain circumstances the addition of moral hazard may eliminate the adverse selection problem but, more generally, it constitutes a new source of non-existence of a Nash equilibrium.

Chassagnon and Chiappori (1995) also proposed an extension to the pure adverse selection model in order to consider incentives or moral hazard: the individual's probability of accidents is no more completely exogenous; it depends on the agent's level of effort. In general, different agents choose different effort levels even when facing the same insurance contract. In fact the equilibrium effort level does not depend on the level of accident probability but on its derivative. Consequently, the *H* type may have more incentive to produce safety in order to have access to a low insurance premium but he may not have access to the efficient technology.

As in Chassagnon (1994), indifference curves may intersect more than one time which rules out the Spence-Mirlees condition. As a result, when an equilibrium exists, it may corresponds to many Rothschild and Stiglitz equilibria, a situation that is ruled out in the pure adverse selection model. Consequently, the equilibria must be ranked, and the authors use the Hahn's concept of equilibrium to select the Pareto efficient equilibrium among the Rothschild-Stiglitz candidates. In the pure adverse selection world, both equilibrium concepts are equivalent.

Another important conclusion is about the condition to obtain an equilibrium. It was shown in a previous section that a Rothschild-Stiglitz equilibrium exists if and only if there are enough high risk agents in the economy. When both problems are present simultaneously, this condition is no longer true. Depending on the parameters of the model, an equilibrium may exist whatever the proportions of agents of different types; or may even fail to exist whatever the respective proportions.

Finally, it is important to emphasize that the individual with the higher accident probability, at equilibrium, has always access to the more comprehensive insurance coverage, a conclusion that is shared by the standard model. However, here, this individual is not necessarily of type *H*. This result is important for empirical research on the presence of asymmetrical information problems.

7.6 ADVERSE SELECTION WHEN PEOPLE CAN CHOOSE THEIR RISK STATUS

An interesting twist on the adverse selection problem is to allow the information status of individuals to vary as well as the risk status. A traditional adverse selection problem arises when individuals know their risk status but the insurer does not. What will happen in a market where some insureds know their risk status and others do not? The answer to this one depends on whether the information status is observed by the insurer. And a further variation arises when the uninformed insureds can take a test to ascertain their risk status. Whether they choose to take the test depends on the menu they will be offered when they become informed and how the utility of this menu compares with the utility of remaining uninformed. Thus, the adverse selection problem becomes entwined with the value of information.

These questions are especially important in the health care debate. Progress in mapping the human genome is leading to more diagnostic tests and treatment for genetic disorders. It is important to know whether the equilibrium contract menus offered to informed insureds or employees are sufficiently attractive to encourage testing. Morever, the policy debate is extended by considering laws that govern access of outsiders (such as employers and insurers) to medical records. For example, many laws require that medical records cannot be released to outsiders without the consent of the patient.

7.6.1 A Full Information Equilibrium with Uninformed Agents

The basic analysis will follow Doherty and Thistle, 1996a. This model uses fairly standard adverse selection technology and is illustrated with health insurance. However, further work by Hoy and Polborn, 1999, has shown that similar results can be derived in a life insurance market where there is no natural choice of coverage and where individuals can buy from many insurers.

To start consider the simplest case in which there are initially three groups, uninformed, informed high risks and informed low risks which are labeled "U", "H" and "L" respectively. The contracts offered to each group will be labeled C_U, C_H and C_L. We assume that type U has a probability q_H of being high risk; so we can rank the *a priori* loss probabilities as $p_H > p_U > p_L$. Now if insurers know the information and risk status of any individual (i.e., they know whether she is U, H or L) the equilibrium competitive contracts are the first best contracts C_U^*, C_H^* and C_L^* depicted in Figure 6. Now this conclusion seems pretty obvious but there is a potential problem to be cleared before we can be comfortable with this equilibrium contract set. If all the uninformed chose to become informed, then the equilibrium contract set would contain only C_H^* and C_L^*. Thus, we must check when uninformed would choose to become informed and face a lottery over C_H^* and C_L^* (the former if the test showed them to be high risk and the latter if low risk). In fact, the decision to become informed and, with probability q_H, receive policy C_H^* and with probability q_L, receive policy C_L^*, is a fair lottery (with the same expected value as staying with C_U^*) and would not be chosen by a risk averse person. This confirms that the full information equilibrium is C_U^*, C_H^* and C_L^*.

7.6.2 Sequential Equilibrium with Insurer Observing Information Status But Not Risk Type

It is a short step from this to consider what happens when the information status is known to the insurer but not the risk status of those who are informed.[44] For this, and remaining cases in this section, we will look for sequential Nash equilibria. In this case, the insurer can offer a full information zero profit contract C_U^* to the uninformed

[44] This case may stretch plausibility a little since it is difficult to imagine an insurer being able to verify that someone claiming to be uninformed is not really an informed high risk. However, we will present the case for completeness.

and the normal Rothschild Stiglitz contracts, C_H^* and C_L^{**} as shown again in Figure 6. The intuition for this pair is clear when one consider that the uninformed can be identified and, by assumption, the informed high risks cannot masquerade as uninformed. But to confirm this is the equilibrium contract set, we must be sure that the uninformed choose to remain so. Recall from the previous paragraph, that the uninformed would prefer to remain with C_U^* than take the fair lottery of C_H^* and C_L^*. Now C_L^* would be strictly preferred by an informed low risk than the Rothschild Stiglitz policy C_L^{**} (which has to satisfy the high risk self selection constraint). Thus, by transitivity, the uninformed would prefer to remain with C_U^* than face the lottery of C_H^* and C_L^{**}.

7.6.3 Sequential Equilibrium When Insurer Cannot Observe Information Status or Risk Type

We now come to the more interesting case in which the information status of individuals cannot be observed. This raises the interesting possibility that people can take a test to become informed and, if the news is bad, pretend they are uninformed. Since the insurer cannot observe information status, he has now way of separating these wolves in sheeps' clothing from the uninformed sheep. This presents a problem for the uninformed. In order to signal that they are really uninformed, and thus avoid subsidizing the high risks, they must accept a contract that would satisfy a high risk self selection constraint. This contract, C_U'' is shown in Figure 6. Suppose for the time being they accept this contract. Now what zero profit contract can be offered to the informed low risks. To prevent the uninformed buying a low risk contract, the latter must satisfy an uninformed risk self selection constraint and such a contract set is C_L''. Now can this triplet, C_H^*, C_U'', C_L'' be a equilibrium? The answer depends on the costs of information.

If the uninformed could choose to stay at C_U'' or become informed and take a lottery over C_H^* and C_L'', what would they do. It turns out the value of the test is positive. Even though the test introduces more risk, there is a compensating factor which tips the balance in favor of the lottery. Remaining uninformed entails a real cost; policy C_U'' must bear risk to satisfy the high risk self selection constraint. Thus, the uninformed will remain so only if the cost of the test is sufficiently high. Accordingly the triplet C_H^*, C_U'', C_L'' can only be a Nash equilibrium if there are high costs of testing. If the test costs are low, we must consider another possible equilibrium. Suppose insurers expected all the uninformed to take the test, but they could not observe risk status after the test. In that case the only pair satisfying the high risk self selection constraint is the Rothschild Stiglitz pair, C_H^* and C_L^{**}. It is fairly straightforward to show that, if the uninformed remained so, she would choose C_L^{**} over C_H^*. Thus the choice for the uninformed is to keep C_L^{**} valued without knowledge of risk type, or face a lottery between C_H^* (valued with full information of high risk type) and C_L^{**} (valued with knowledge of low risk status). It turns out that the value of this lottery is zero. Thus,

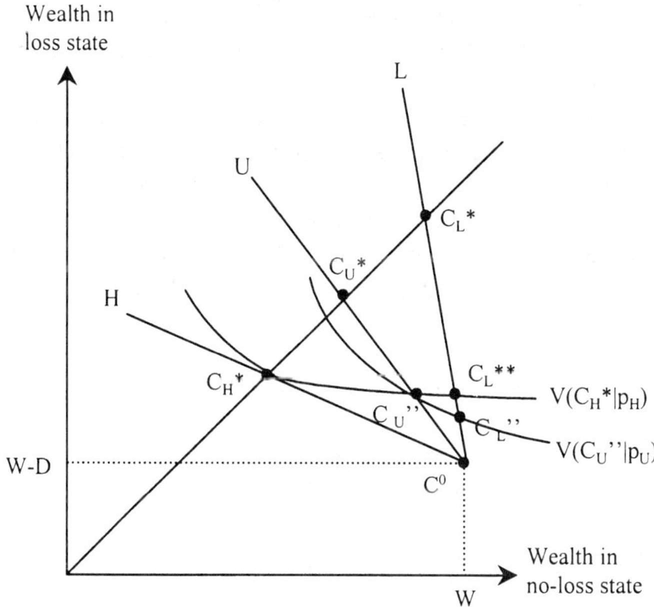

Figure 6 Endogenous information

if the cost of information was zero, and using a tie breaker rule, the uninformed would take the test and the pair, C_H^*, C_L^{**} is a sequential Nash equilibrium. But with any positive cost for the test, then this cannot be an equilibrium.

We can now summarize. If the costs of information are sufficiently high, there is a sequential equilibrium set C_H^*, C_U'', C_L''. If the information costs are positive but below this threshold, then no sequential Nash equilibrium exists. Finally, there is a knife edge case with an equilibrium of C_H^*, C_L^{**} which exists only with zero cost of information.

7.6.4 The Case of Consent Laws

One of the interesting policy applications of this analysis is consent laws. Many states have enacted laws governing the disposition of information from genetic (and other medical) tests. The typical law allows the patient to choose whether to divulge information revealed by the test to an employer or insurer. This issue was considered by Tabarrock (1994) who suggested that consent laws would encourage people to take the test. This was examined further by Doherty and Thistle, 1996b, who derive alternative Nash equilibria under consent laws. The principal feature of their analysis is that informed low risks can verify their low risk status by presenting the results of the test. Contrary, informed high risks will conceal their identity, i.e., withhold consent. This leads to a potential equilibrium containing policies of the set $A \equiv \{C_H^*, C_U'', C_L^*\}$

or set $B \equiv \{C_H^*, C_L^*\}$. For B to be an equilibrium, the uninformed must choose to take a diagnostic test when faced with this contract menu. The value of information, $I(B)$, turns out to be positive and this can only be an equilibrium if the information value exceeds it the cost of the diagnostic test, c. The other possible equilibrium, A, can only hold if the uninformed remain so. Since the value of information, also is positive, the equilibrium can only hold if the cost of the test is sufficiently high to discourage testing, $I(A) < c$. Thus, the possible equilibria are A if the cost of the test is sufficiently high and B if the cost of the test is sufficiently low. There are possible situations where no Nash equilibrium exists or where there are multiple equilibria. Summarizing:

$I(A) < c < I(B)$	multiple equilibria, A and B
$c < I(A), I(B)$	equilibrium set is B
$I(A), I(B) < c$	equilibrium set is A
$I(A) < c < I(B)$	no Nash equilibrium exists.

7.6.5 Moral Hazard, Public Health and AIDS Testing

If account is taken of the costs and benefits to patients of potential use of information in insurance markets when consent laws are in place, the value of information is positive and insurance markets can be concluded to encourage testing. Whether people actually take medical tests also depends on the costs of those tests and these costs are critical in determining which, if any, Nash equilibrium exists. One can generalize hear and talk not simply of the costs of the test but also of other benefits. Quite obviously, testing yields a medical diagnosis which can be useful in treating any revealed condition. In general we would expect this option for treatment to have a positive private and social value (see Doherty and Posey, 1998). Accounting for the private value of this option has the same effect as lowering the cost of the test and tends to favor the equilibrium contract set B in which all people take the test. But this opens up the wider issue of other costs and benefits to acquiring information of risk status.

The result that insurance markets tend to raise the private benefit from testing may be reassuring to those interested in public health who normally consider testing for diseases such as AIDS and inherited disorders to be socially beneficial. An interesting twist on this literature concerns the case of AIDS testing. Several studies have analyzed behavioral choices in sexual activities and their effect on the transmission of AIDS and the effectiveness of public health measures (Castillo-Chavez and Hadeler, 1994 and Kremer, 1996). But of particular interest here is the work of Philipson and Posner, 1993. They examine the effect of taking AIDS test on opportunities to engage in high risk sexual activity. Without going into detail, the point can be made by recognizing that people might take the test to verify their uninfected status so they can persuade partners to engage in high risk sexual activity. Without such certification, they may have been unable to secure partners for high risk sex. While this is only one part of their analysis, it is sufficient to illustrate their point that AIDS testing can conceivably *increase* the spread of the disease. But, in spite of the possible social costs to testing, it also shows there are private benefits to diagnostic tests since they expand opportunities for sexual trade.

This works tends to tilt the previous analysis of insurance equilibrium at least for the case of AIDS testing. The insurance equilibrium required a comparison of the costs of testing with the value of (insurance) information revealed by the test. The work of Philipson and Posner, 1993, gives an exogenous private benefit to testing. Such a private benefit is the same as a lowering of the cost of testing. Accordingly, it creates a bias in favor of those equilibria in which all individuals are fully informed of their risk status; i.e., contract set *B*.

7.7 CONCLUDING REMARKS: EXTENSIONS TO THE BASIC MODELS

7.7.1 Risk Categorization and Residual Adverse Selection

Adverse selection can explain the use of risk categorization in insurance markets based on variables that procure information at a low cost (Hoy, 1982). For example, in automobile insurance, age and sex variables are significant in explaining probabilities of accidents and insurance premia (Dionne and Vanasse, 1992, Puelz and Snow, 1994). Particularly, young male drivers (less than 25) are much more risky to insure than the average driver. Since it is almost costless to observe age and sex, an insurer may find it profitable to offer policies with higher premiums to young males. However, such categorization is now prohibited in some states and countries. For a survey on adverse selection and risk classification, see Crocker and Snow (2000).

Dahlby (1983, 1992) provided some empirical evidence that adverse selection is present in the Canadian automobile insurance market. He also suggested that his empirical results are in accordance with the Wilson-Miyazaki-Spence model that allows for cross-subsidization between individuals in each segment defined by a categorization variable such as sex or age: low-coverage policies (low risks) subsidizing high-coverage policies (high risks) in each segment.[45] This important statistical result raises the following question. Does statistical categorization enhance efficiency in the presence of adverse selection? In other words, can welfare be improved by using the public information on agents' characteristics (such that age and sex) in offering insurance contracts in presence of adverse selection? Crocker and Snow (1985, 1986) showed that, if the observable variables are correlated with hidden knowledge, costless imperfect categorization always enhances efficiency where efficiency is

[45] However, Riley (1983) argued that the statistical results of Dahlby (1983) are also consistent with both the Wilson anticipatory equilibrium (1977) and the Riley reactive equilibrium (1979). Both models reject cross-subsidization.

defined as in Harris and Townsend (1981). Another important contribution in Crocker and Snow (1986) concerns the existence of a balanced-budget tax-subsidy system that provides private incentives to use costless categorization. It is important to notice that the corresponding tax is imposed to contracts and not to individuals. If a redistribution is operated from gains earned on the group in which low risks are predominant (old male drivers for example) to the group in which high risks are predominant (young male drivers), the classification always permits to elarge the set of feasible contracts. The reason is that the use of categorization relaxes the incentive compatibility constraints. As a result, with appropriate taxes, no agent loses as a result of categorization. The results are shown for the Wilson-Miyazaki-Spence equilibrium concept but can also sustain an efficient allocation in a Nash equilibrium with a tax system (Crocker and Snow, 1986). Finally, these conclusions can be applied to the Wilson anticipatory equilibrium or to the Riley reactive equilibrium, for some values of parameters, both with a tax system. It then becomes clear that prohibiting discrimination on equity considerations imposes efficiency costs in insurance markets (such as automobile insurance where categorization based on age and sex variables is costless).

In a recent empirical study, Dionne, Gouriéroux and Vanasse (1997, 1998) (see also Gouriéroux, 1999) showed that risk classification is efficient to eliminate adverse selection from the portfolio of an insurer, in the sense that there was no residual adverse selection in the portfolio studied. They concluded that the insurer was able to control for adverse selection by using an appropriate risk classification procedure. Consequently, no other self-selection mechanism inside the risk classes (such as the choice of deductible) is necessary to reduce the impact of adverse selection. See Chiappori (2000) and Dionne (2000) for more detailed analyses of methodologies to isolate information problems in insurance data and Richaudeau (1999) for an application with a different data set.

7.7.2 Different Risk Aversion

Up to now, it was assumed that risk categories are determined up to the loss probability. However, residual asymmetric information between the insured and the insurers could consist of attitude toward risk. Villeneuve (1998) explores the implication of assuming that differences in risk aversion combined with differences in accident probabilities create a multi-dimensional adverse selection problem where the equilibrium allocation differs qualitatively from the classical results of Rothschild and Stiglitz (1976). Not only may positive profits be sustainable under several equilibrium concepts (Nash, Rothschild and Stiglitz, Wilson, Riley), but equilibria with random contracts are also possible. The former situation is more likely when low risk agents are more risk averse, wheras the latter is more likely when the low risk is less risk averse. Villeneuve explores precisely the origin of these phenomena. He gives necessary and sufficient conditions on the comparison of risk aversions that either guarantee or exclude atypical equilibria.

In a companion paper, Smart (1998) obtains similar results. In his model, indifference curves of customers may cross twice: thus the single crossing property does not hold. When differences in risk aversion are sufficiently large, firms cannot use policy deductibles to screen high risk customers. Types may be pooled in equilibrium or separated by raising premiums above actuarially fair levels. This leads to excessive entry of firms in equilibrium.

7.7.3 Symmetric Incomplete Information

According to recent empirical studies which test the presence of adverse selection in automobile insurance markets (Chiappori and Salanié, 1997, and Dionne, Gouriéroux and Vanasse, 1998), it seems that we can reject the presence of residual adverse selection. More precisely, even though there is some potential adverse selection on these markets, insurers are able to extract all information on risk type of individuals by the way of a very fine risk categorization.

By focusing on these recent empirical results, de Garidel (1997) rejects the presence of initial asymmetries of information and on the contrary, assumes that information between insurers and insureds is incomplete, but initially symmetric (at the beginning of a two-period contract). He provides a dynamic competitive model in which, each agent, together with his initial insurer, learns about his type through accidents. However, other insurers may not, depending on informational structures.

In the absence of ex-ante adverse selection, he shows that "(i) keeping information about accident claims private is welfare-improving, (ii) such a policy does not jeopardize the existence of an equilibrium, and (iii) this equilibrium exhibits both bonus and malus". Thus, in a two-period model, adverse selection arises endogenously through differentiated learning about type and leads to reconsider the widespread idea according to which competition in markets with adverse selection may be undesirable. Indeed, de Garidel shows that it is welfare-enhancing to produce adverse selection of this kind.

7.7.4 Principals more Informed than Agents

In the literature on decentralized markets under asymmetric information it is commonly assumed that the uninformed party possesses all the bargaining power. This is also the usual assumption of insurance models, whereas it is often argued that companies may be more able to assess the risk of an individual than this individual himself can. The paper by Bourgeon (1998) reverses this usual assumption, giving the relevant information to the insurers, in addition of the bargaining power. Under this hypothesis, the insurers' activity is not only to sell a particular good or service but also to produce a diagnosis of the buyers' needs. This is the case in some insurance markets, including health, where the sellers appear as the experts in the relationship.

Assuming risk-averse buyers and risk-neutral sellers, the focus of Bourgeon model is on symmetric steady state equilibria of the market game. The only candidates for equilibria are semi-separating ones, i.e., equilibria where the buyers carrying the good state of nature are partially pooled with the low state ones. The reason that invalidates separating equilibria is simply that they violate the sellers' incentive constraints: Assuming a separating equilibrium, the equilibrium contracts involve a full coverage of the damages, which are the same in both states accident and no-accident. The only difference between these contracts is thus the premium, which is higher for tne high-risk individuals. A seller would thus increase his profit by offering the high-risk contract to a low-risk buyer. A pooling equilibrium cannot occur because of a trickier reason related to the (limited) monopoly power of sellers: Knowing that her competitors propose a pooling contract, a seller offers a contract corresponding to the buyer's reservation value. But since the contract is pooling, the buyer cannot revise his beliefs and his reservation value is unchanged since his entrance in the market. Consequently, he has no reason to begin a time-consuming search and therefore, the market shuts down. If an equilibrium exists, it thus entails a search, which is long-lasting for all buyers carrying a bad state: Sellers always propose high-risk contract, but since there is a chance that the buyer's risk is low, he visits several sellers before accepting this contract. Moreover, he is never convinced, and consequently sellers charge a lower price than they would charge if the buyer knew the true information. The informational asymmetry is thus advantageous to the high-risk individuals, because they are not charged the entire risk premium corresponding to this state. When choosing a contract for a low-risk, a seller balances between offering the contract for low-risks, which is certain to be accepted by the buyer but gives small profits, and offering a high-risk contract, which is accepted only by some of the buyers but is more profitable.

In a static approach, Fagart (1996b) explores a competitive market of insurance where two companies compete for one consumer. Information is asymmetric in the sense that companies know the value of a parameter ignored by the consumer. The model is a signalling one, so that insureds are able to interpret offered insurance contracts as informative signals and may accept one among these offers or reject them. The features of the equilibrium solution are the following: the information is systematically revealed and profits are zero.

Villeneuve (1999a) studied the consequences for a monopolistic insurance firm of evaluating risk better than customers under the adverse selection hypothesis reversed. In a more general model (Villeneuve, 1999b), he suggests that information retention and inefficiency have to be expected in many contexts. Particularly, in a competitive insurance market, he shows that neither revelation of information nor efficiency are warranted, and that the surplus may be captured by some insurers rather than the consumers. Thus, in his model, the classical predictions of Rothschild and Stiglitz are reversed: types may be pooled, the high risk consumers may remain without insurance or obtain partial coverage, and profits are not always zero. The key argument is that the way consumers interpret offers may refrain competitive behavior in the ordinary sense.

7.7.5 Uberrima Fides

An insurance contract is under uberrima fides when an insured makes a full disclosure of all facts pertaining to his risk that are known to him ex-ante. Under this type of arrangement, the insurer asks questions about the individual risk at the signature of the contract, but keep the right to investigate the truth only when the claim is made, in order to reduce the audit costs. If the answers are found to be false, the insurer can refuse to pay the claim. This scheme provides a new way to select low risks at a lower social cost than the Rothschild-Stiglitz one. Some life insurers used individuals declarations about their smoking behavior in order to set insurance prices. In fact, Dixit (2000) shows that uberrima fides is Pareto-improving when compared to Rothschild-Stiglitz equilibrium.

7.7.6 Adverse Selection with Multiple Risks

Fluet and Pannequin (1997) consider two situations: one where insurers offer comprehensive policies against all sources of risk (complete insurance) and where different risks are covered by separate policies (incomplete contracts). In the second case, they analyse the possibility that the insurer has perfect information about the coverage of other risks by any insurer in the market. They show that, when market conditions allow for bundling (getting information to protect insurers against undesirable risks), the low risk individual in a particular market (or for a particular source of risk) does not necessarily buy partial insurance in that market as in the Rothschild and Stiglitz model.

Their analysis emphasizes the trade off between bundling and spanning. Multiple-risk contracts allow for perfect spanning (take into account of correlations between different risks) and for perfect bundling (take into account of all informations available to the insurers) while single contracts with imperfect information on contract choice for other risks are dominated since they do not permit risk diversification and information sharing. They show that the former is the more efficient which confirms the practice by insurers in many countries.

7.8 REFERENCES

Abreu, D., D. Pearce and E. Stacchetti (1990). "Toward a Theory of Discounted Repeated Games with Imperfect Monitoring," *Econometrica* 58, 1041–1064.

Akerlof, G.A. (1970). "The Market for 'Lemons': Quality Uncertainty and the Market Mechanism," *Quarterly Journal of Economics* 84, 488–500.

Allard, M., J.P. Cresta and J.C. Rocket (1997). "Pooling and Separating Equilibria in Insurance Markets with Adverse Selection and Distribution Costs," *Geneva Papers on Risk and Insurance Theory* 22, 103–120.

Allen, F. (1985). "Repeated Principal-Agent Relationships with Lending and Borrowing," *Economics Letters* 17, 27–31.

Arnott, R. (1992). "Moral Hazard and Competitive Insurance Markets," in G. Dionne (ed.), *Contributions to Insurance Economics*, Kluwer Academic Publishers.

Arnott, R. and J.E. Stiglitz (1988). "Randomization with Asymmetric Information," *Rand Journal of Economics* 19(3), 344–362.

Arrow, K.J. (1963). "Uncertainty and the Welfare Economics of Medical Care," *American Economic Review* 53, 941–969.

Bolton, B. (1990). "Renegotiation and the Dynamics of Contract Design," *European Economic Review* 34, 303–310.

Bond, E.W. and K.J. Crocker (1991). "Smoking, Skydiving and Knitting: The Endogenous Categorization of Risks in Insurance Markets with Asymmetric Information," *Journal of Political Economy* 99, 177–200.

Bourgeon, J.-M. (1998). "Decentralized Markets with Informed Sellers," *Working Paper* Thema, Université de Paris X-Nanterre.

Boyer, M., G. Dionne and R. Kihlstrom (1989). "Insurance and the Value of Publicly Available Information" in Studies in the Economics of Uncertainty in Honour of J. Hadar, T.B. Fomby and T.K. Seo. (eds.), Springer Verlag, 137–155.

Caillaud, B., G. Dionne and B. Jullien (2000). "Corporate Insurance with Optimal Financial Contracting," *Economic Theory*, 16, 1, 77–105.

Caillaud, B., R. Guesnerie, P. Rey and J. Tirole (1988). "Government Intervention in Production and Incentives Theory: A Review of Recent Contributions," *Rand Journal of Economics* 19, 1–26.

Castillo-Chavez, C. and K.P. Hadeler (1994). "A Core Group Model of Disease Transmission," *Working Paper*, Cornell University.

Chassagnon, A. (1994). "Antisélection et aléa moral dans un modèle principal-agent d'assurance," *Mimeo*, Chaire d'économie et d'économétrie de l'assurance, EHESS—ENSAE, DELTA.

Chassagnon, A. and P.A. Chiappori (1995). "Insurance Under Moral Hazard and Adverse Selection: the Case of Pure Competition," *Working Paper*, DELTA.

Chiappori, P.A. (1994). "Théorie des contrats et économétrie de l'assurance: quelques pistes de recherche," *Mimeo*, Chaire d'économie et d'économétrie de l'assurance, EHESS—ENSAE, DELTA.

Chiappori, P.A. (2000). "Econometric Models of Insurance under Asymmetric Information," Chapter 11 of this book.

Chiappori, P.A. and B. Salanié (1997). "Empirical Contract Theory: the Case of Insurance Data," *European Economic Review* 41, 943–950.

Chiappori, P.A., I. Macho, P. Rey and B. Salanié (1994). "Repeated Moral Hazard: The Role of Memory, Commitment, and the Access to Credit Markets," *European Economic Review* 38, 1527–1553.

Cho, I. and D. Kreps (1987). "Signalling Games and Stable Equilibria," *Quarterly Journal of Economics* CII, 179–222.

Cooper, R. (1984). "On Allocative Distortions in Problems of Self-Selection," *Rand Journal of Economics* 15, no. 4, 568–577.

Cooper, R. and B. Hayes (1987). "Multi-period Insurance Contracts," *International Journal of Industrial Organization* 5, 211–231, Reprinted in G. Dionne and S. Harrington (eds.), Foundations of Insurance Economics—Readings in Economics and Finance, Kluwer Academic Publishers, 1992.

Cresta, J.P (1984). "Théories des marchés d'assurance," Collection "Approfondissement de la connaissance économique", *Economica*, Paris.

Crocker, K.J. and A. Snow (1985). "The Efficiency of Competitive Equilibria in Insurance Markets with Adverse Selection," *Journal of Public Economics* 26, 207–219.

Crocker, K.J. and A. Snow (1986). "The Efficiency Effects of Categorical Discrimination in the Insurance Industry," *Journal of Political Economy* 94, 321–344, Reprinted in G. Dionne and S. Harrington (eds.), Foundations of Insurance Economics—Readings in Economics and Finance, Kluwer Academic Publishers, 1992.

Crocker, K.J. and A. Snow (1990). "The Social Value of Private Information in Environments with Adverse Selection," *Working Paper*, Penn State University.

Crocker, K.J. and A. Snow (1992). "The Social Value of Hidden Information in Adverse Selection Economics," *Journal of Public Economics* 48, 317–347.

Crocker, K.J. and A. Snow (2000). "The Theory of Risk Classification," Chapter 8 of this book.

Cromb, I.J. (1990). "Competitive Insurance Markets Characterized by Asymmetric Information," Ph.D. thesis, Queen's University.

Dahlby, B.G. (1981). "Adverse Selection and Pareto Improvements through Compulsory Insurance," *Public Choice*, 37, 547–558.

Dahlby, B.G. (1983). "Adverse Selection and Statistical Discrimination. An Analysis of Canadian Automobile Insurance," *Journal of Public Economics* 20, 121–130, Reprinted in G. Dionne and S. Harrington (eds.), Foundations of Insurance Economics—Readings in Economics and Finance, Kluwer Academic Publishers, 1992.

Dahlby, B.G. (1987). "Monopoly Versus Competition in an Insurance Market with Adverse Selection," *Journal of Risk and Insurance* LIV, 325–331.

Dahlby, B.G. (1992). "Testing for Assymmetric Information in Canadian Automobile Insurance," in *Contributions to Insurance Economics*, G. Dionne (ed.), Kluwer Academic Publishers.

D'Arcy, S.P. and N. Doherty (1990). "Adverse Selection, Private Information and Lowballing in Insurance Markets," *Journal of Business*, 63, 145–164.

Dasgupta, P. and E. Maskin (1986). "The Existence of Equilibrium in Discontinuous Economic Games, II: Applications," *Review of Economic Studies* 53(1), 27–41.

De Garidel, T. (1997). "Welfare-Improving Asymmetric Information in a Dynamic Insurance Market," *Working Paper* Delta.

Dewatripont, M. (1989). "Renegotiation and Information Revelation over Time: The Case of Optimal Labour Contracts," *Quarterly Journal of Economics* 104(3), 589–619.

Dionne, G. (1983). "Adverse Selection and Repeated Insurance Contracts," *Geneva Papers on Risk and Insurance* 8, 316–333. Reprinted in Dionne and S. Harrington (eds.), Foundations of Insurance Economics—Readings in Economics and Finance, Kluwer Academic Publishers, 1992.

Dionne, G. (2000). "The Empirical Measure of Information Problems with an Emphasis on Insurance Fraud," Chapter 12 of this book.

Dionne, G. and N. Doherty (1992). "Adverse Selection in Insurance Markets: A Selective Survey" in *Contributions to Insurance Economics*, G. Dionne (ed.), Kluwer Academic Publishers.

Dionne, G. and N. Doherty (1994). "Adverse Selection, Commitment and Renegotiation with Application to Insurance Markets," *Journal of Political Economy*, 209–235.

Dionne, G. and C. Fluet (2000). "Full Pooling in Multi-Period Contracting with Adverse Selection and Noncommitment," *Review of Economic Design*, 5, 1, 1–21.

Dionne, G. and N. Fombaron (1996). "Non-Convexities and the Efficiency of Equilibria in Insurance Markets with Asymmetric Information," *Economics Letters* 52, 31–40.

Dionne, G. and P. Lasserre (1985). "Adverse Selection, Repeated Insurance Contracts and Announcement Strategy," *Review of Economic Studies* 52, 719–723.

Dionne, G. and P. Lasserre (1987). "Adverse Selection and Finite-Horizon Insurance Contracts," *European Economic Review* 31, no 4, 843–862.

Dionne, G. and P. Lasserre, 1988 (revised 1989), "Dealing with Moral Hazard and Adverse Selection Simultaneously," *Working Paper*, Economics Department, University of Montreal.

Dionne, G. and C. Vanasse (1992). "Automobile Insurance Ratemaking in the Presence of Asymmetrical Information," *Journal of Applied Econometrics* 7, 149–165.

Dionne, G. and C. Vanasse (1997). "The Role of Memory and Saving in Long-Term Contracting with Moral Hazard: An Empirical Evidence in Automobile Insurance," *Mimeo*, Risk Management Chair, HEC.

Dionne, G., C. Gouriéroux and C. Vanasse (1997). "The Informational Content of Household Decisions with Application to Insurance Under Adverse Selection," CREST *Working Paper*.

Dionne, G., C. Gouriéroux and C. Vanasse (1998). "Evidence of Adverse Selection in Automobile Insurance Markets," in *Automobile Insurance: Road Safety, New Drivers, Risks, Insurance Fraud and Regulation*, G. Dionne and C. Laberge-Nadeau (eds.), Kluwer Academic Publishers.

Dixit, A. (2000). "Adverse Selection and Insurance with Uberrima Fides," *Mimeo*, Princeton University.

Doherty, N.A. (1990). "Adverse Selection, Screening and the Value of Information in Insurance Markets," *Mimeo*, University of Pennsylvania.

Doherty, N. and L. Eeckhoudt (1995). "Optimal Insurance without Expected Utility: The Dual Theory and the Linearity of Insurance Contracts," *Journal of Risk and Uncertainty* 10, 157–179.

Doherty, N. and H.J. Jung (1993). "Adverse Selection when Loss Severities Differ: First-Best and Costly Equilibria," *Geneva Papers on Risk and Insurance Theory* 18, 173–182.

Doherty, N. and L. Lipowski Posey (1998). "On the Value of a Checkup: Adverse Selection, Moral Hazard and the Value of Information," *Journal of Risk and Insurance* 65, 189–212.

Doherty, N. and H. Schlesinger (1983). "Optimal Insurance in Incomplete Markets," *Journal of Political Economy* 91, 1045–1054.

Doherty, N. and H. Schlesinger (1995). "Severity Risk and the Adverse Selection of Frequency Risk," *Journal of Risk and Insurance* 62, 649–665.

Doherty, N. and P. Thistle (1996a). "Adverse Selection with Endogenous Information in Insurance Markets," *Journal of Public Economics* 63, 83–102.

Doherty, N. and P. Thistle (1996b). "Advice and Consent: HIV Tests, Genetic Tests and the Efficiency of Consent Laws," *Working Paper*, Wharton School, University of Pennsylvania.

Eeckhoudt, L. and M. Kimball (1992). "Background Risk, Prudence, and the Demand for Insurance," in *Contributions to Insurance Economics*, G. Dionne (ed.), Kluwer Academic Publishers, 239–254.

Eisen, R. (1989). "Problems of Equilibria in Insurance Markets with Asymmetric Information," in *Risk, Information and Insurance*, H. Loubergé (ed.), Kluwer Academic Publishers.

Fagart, M.-C. (1996a). "Concurrence en contrats, anti-sélection et structure d'information," *Annales d'Economie et Statistiques* 43, 1–28.

Fagart, M.-C. (1996b). "Compagnies d'assurance informées et équilibre sur le marché de l'assurance," *Working Paper* Thema, 9626.

Fluet, C. (1992). "Probationary Periods and Time-Dependent Deductibles in Insurance Markets with Adverse Selection" in *Contributions to Insurance Economics*, G. Dionne (ed.), Kluwer Academic Publishers.

Fluet, C. (1998). "Commercial Vehicle Insurance: Should Fleet Policies Differ from Single Vehicle Plans?" in *Automobile Insurance: Road Safety, New Drivers, Risks, Insurance Fraud and Regulation*, G. Dionne and C. Laberge-Nadeau (eds.), Kluwer Academic Publishers.

Fluet, C. and F. Pannequin (1997). "Complete Versus Incomplete Insurance Contracts Under Adverse Selection with Multiple Risks," *Geneva Papers on Risk and Insurance Theory* 22, 81–101.

Fluet, C. and F. Pannequin (1995). "Insurance Contracts Under Adverse Selection with Random Loss Severity," *Working Paper*, Economic Department, Université du Québec à Montréal.

Fombaron, N. (1997a). "Contrats d'assurance dynamiques en présence d'anti-sélection: les effets d'engagement sur les marchés concurrentiels," thèse de doctorat, Université de Paris X-Nanterre, 306 pages.

Fombaron, N. (1997b). "No-Commitment and Dynamic Contracts in Competitive Insurance Markets with Adverse Selection," *Working Paper* Thema.

Fombaron, N. (2000). "Renegotiation-proof Contracts in Insurance Markets with Asymmetric Information," *Working Paper*, Thema.

Freixas, X., R. Guesnerie and J. Tirole (1985). "Planning Under Incomplete Information and the Ratchet Effect," *Review of Economic Studies* 52, 173–191.

Fudenberg, D., B. Holmstrom and P. Milgrom (1986). "Short-term Contracts and Long-term Agency Relationships," *Mimeo*, University of California, Berkeley.

Gal, S. and M. Landsberger (1988). "On 'Small Sample' Properties of Experience Rating Insurance Contracts," *Quarterly Journal of Economics*, 233–243.

Garella, P. (1989). "Adverse Selection and the Middleman," *Economica* 56, 395–399.

Gollier, C. (2000). "Optimal Insurance Design: What Can We Do With and Without Expected Utility?," Chapter 3 of this book.

Gouriéroux, C. (1999). "The Econometrics of Risk Classification in Insurance," *Geneva Papers on Risk and Insurance Theory* 24, 119–138.

Grossman, H.I. (1979). "Adverse Selection, Dissembling, and Competitive Equilibrium," *Bell Journal of Economics* 10, 336–343.

Guesnerie, R., P. Picard and P. Rey (1988). "Adverse Selection and Moral Hazard with Risk Neutral Agents," *European Economic Review* 33, 807–823.

Harris, M. and R. Townsend (1981). "Resource Allocation under Asymmetric Information," *Econometrica* 49, 33–64.

Hart, O.D. and J. Tirole (1988). "Contract Renegotiation and Coasian Dynamics," *Review of Economic Studies* 55, 509–540.

Hellwig, M.F. (1986). "A Sequential Approach to Modelling Competition in Markets with Adverse Selection," *Mimeo*, University of Bonn.

Hellwig, M.F. (1987). "Some Recent Developments in the Theory of Competition in Markets with Adverse Selection," *European Economic Review* 31, 319–325.

Hellwig, M.F. (1988). "A Note on the Specification of Interfirm Communication in Insurance Markets with Adverse Selection," *Journal of Economic Theory* 46, 154–163.

Henriet, D. and J.C. Rochet (1986). "La logique des systèmes bonus-malus en assurance automobile: une approche théorique," *Annales d'Économie et de Statistique*, 133–152.

Hey, J. (1985). "No Claim Bonus?," *Geneva Papers on Risk and Insurance* 10, 209–228.

Hosios, A.J. and M. Peters (1989). "Repeated Insurance Contracts with Adverse Selection and Limited Commitment," *Quarterly Journal of Economics* CIV, no 2, 229–253.

Hoy, M. (1982). "Categorizing Risks in the Insurance Industry," *Quarterly Journal of Economics* 97, 321–336.

Hoy, M. (1989). "The Value of Screening Mechanisms Under Alternative Insurance Possibilities," *Journal of Public Economics* 39, 177–206.

Hoy, M. and M. Polborn (1999). "The Value of Genetic Information in the Life Insurance Market," *Working Paper*, University of Guelph. Forthcoming in *Journal of Public Economics*.

Jaynes, G.D. (1978). "Equilibria in Monopolistically Competitive Insurance Markets," *Journal of Economic Theory* 19, 394–422.

Karni, E. (1992). "Optimal Insurance: A Nonexpected Utility Analysis," in G. Dionne (ed.), *Contributions to Insurance Economics*, Kluwer Academic Publishers.

Kremer, M. (1996). "Integrating Behavioral Choice into Epidemiological Models of AIDS," *Quarterly Journal of Economics* 111, 549–573.

Kreps, D. (1989). "Out-of-Equilibrium Beliefs and Out-of-Equilibrium Behaviour," in *The Economics of Information, Missing Markets and Games* (F. Hahn, ed.), Oxford: Clarendon Press, 7–45.

Kreps, D. and R. Wilson (1982). "Sequential Equilibria," *Econometrica* 50, 863–894.

Kunreuther, H. and M. Pauly (1985). "Market Equilibrium with Private Knowledge: An Insurance Example," *Journal of Public Economics* 26, 269–288, Reprinted in G. Dionne and S. Harrington (eds.), Foundations of Insurance Economics—Readings in Economics and Finance, Kluwer Academic Publishers, 1992.

Lacker, J.M. and J.A. Weinberg (1999). "Coalition-Proof Allocations in Adverse-Selection Economies," *Geneva Papers on Risk and Insurance Theory* 24(1), 5–18.

Laffont, J.J. and J. Tirole (1986). "Using Cost Observation to Regulate Firms," *Journal of Political Economy* 94, 614–641.

Laffont, J.-J. and J. Tirole (1987). "Comparative Statics of the Optimal Dynamic Incentive Contracts," *European Economic Review* 31, 901–926.

Laffont, J.-J. and J. Tirole (1990). "Adverse Selection and Renegotiation in Procurement," *Review of Economic Studies*, 597–625.

Laffont, J.-J. and J. Tirole (1993). "A Theory of Incentives in Procurement and Regulation," Boston, MIT Press.

Landsberger, M. and I. Meilijson (1996). "Extraction of Surplus Under Adverse Selection: The Case of Insurance Markets," *Journal of Economic Theory* 69, 234–239.

Lemaire, J. (1985). "Automobile Insurance: Actuarial Models," Kluwer-Nighoff Publishing, Boston, 247 pages.

Ligon, J. and P.D. Thistle (1996). "Information Asymmetries and Informational Incentives in Monopolistic Insurance Markets," *Journal of Risk and Insurance* 63(3), 434–459.

Machina, M.J. (1987). "Choice Under Uncertainty: Problems Solved and Unsolved," *Journal of Economics Perspectives* 1, 121–154. Reprinted in G. Dionne and S. Harrington (eds.), Foundations of Insurance Economics—Readings in Economics and Finance, Kluwer Academic Publishers, 1992.

Machina, M.J. (2000). "Non-Expected Utility and the Robustness of the Classical Insurance Paradigm," Chapter 2 of this book.

Malueg, D.A. (1986). "Efficient Outcomes in a Repeated Agency Model Without Discounting," *Journal of Mathematical Economics* 15, 217–230.

Malueg, D.A. (1988). "Repeated Insurance Contracts with Differential Learning," *Review of Economic Studies*, LV, 177–181.

Miyazaki, H. (1977). "The Rate Race and Internal Labour Markets," *Bell Journal of Economics* 8, 394–418.

Nilssen, T (1990). "Consumer Lock-in with Asymmetric Information," *Working Paper*, Norvegian School of Economics and Business. Forthcoming in *International Journal of Industrial Organization*.

Palfrey, T.R. and C.S. Spatt (1985). "Repeated Insurance Contracts and Learning," *Rand Journal of Economics* 16(3), 356–367.

Pannequin, F. (1992). "Théorie de l'assurance et de la sécurité sociale," thèse de doctorat, Université de Paris I.

Pauly, M.V. (1974). "Overinsurance and the Public Provision of Insurance: The Roles of Moral Hazard and Adverse Selection," *Quarterly Journal of Economics* 88, 44–62.

Philipson T. and R. Posner (1993). "Private Choice and Public Health: The AIDS Epidemic in an Economic Perspective" Harvard University Press, Cambridge MA.

Picard, P. (1987). "On the Design of Incentives Schemes Under Moral Hazard and Adverse Selection," *Journal of Public Economics* 33, 305–331.

Prescott, E. and R. Townsend (1984). "Pareto Optima and Competitive Equilibria with Adverse Selection and Moral Hazard," *Econometrica* 52, 21–45.

Puelz, R. and A. Snow (1994). "Evidence of Adverse Selection: Equilibrium Signaling and Cross-Subsidization in the Insurance Market," *Journal of Political Economy* 102, 236–257.

Radner, R. (1981). "Monitoring Cooperative Agreements in a Repeated Principal-Agent Relationship," *Econometrica* 49, 1127–1148.

Radner, R. (1985). "Repeated Principal-Agent Games with Discounting," *Econometrica* 53, 1173–1198.

Rea, S.A. (1987). "The Market Response to the Elimination of Sex Based Annuities," *Southern Economic Journal* 54, 55–63.

Rea, S.A. (1992). "Insurance Classifications and Social Welfare," in *Contributions to Insurance Economics*, G. Dionne (ed.), Kluwer Academic Publishers.

Rey, P. and B. Salanié (1996). "On the Value of Commitment with Asymmetric Information," *Econometrica* 64, 1395–1414.

Richaudeau, D. (1999). "Automobile Insurance Contracts and Risk of Accident: An Empirical Test Using French Individual Data," *Geneva Papers on Risk and Insurance Theory* 24(1), 97–114.

Riley, J.G. (1979a). "Informational Equilibrium," *Econometrica* 47, 331–359.

Riley, J.G. (1979b). "Non-Cooperative Equilibrium and Markets Signalling," *American Economic Review*, May, 303–307.

Riley, J.G. (1983). "Adverse Selection and Statistical Discrimination: Further Comments," *Journal of Public Economics* 20, 131–137.

Riley, J.G. (1985). "Competition with Hidden Knowledge," *Journal of Political Economy* 93, 958–976.

Rothschild, M. and J. Stiglitz (1976). "Equilibrium in Competitive Insurance Markets: An Essay on the Economics of Imperfect Information," *Quarterly Journal of Economics* 90, 629–650, Reprinted in G. Dionne and S. Harrington (eds.), Foundations of Insurance Economics—Readings in Economics and Finance, Kluwer Academic Publishers, 1992.

Rothschild, M. and J. Stiglitz (1997). "Competition and Insurance Twenty Years Later," *Geneva Papers on Risk and Insurance Theory* 22, 73–79.

Rubinstein, A. and M. Yaari (1983). "Repeated Insurance Contracts and Moral Hazard," *Journal of Economic Theory* 30, 74–97.

Sabourian, H. (1989). "Repeated Games: A Survey," in *The Economics of Information*, Missing Markets and Games (F. Hahn, ed.), Oxford: Clarendon Press, 62–105.

Smart, M. (1998). "Competitive Insurance Markets with Two Unobservables," *Mimeo*, Economics Department, University of Toronto. Forthcoming in *International Economic Review*.

Spence, M. (1973). "Job Market Signalling," *Quarterly Journal of Economics* 87, 355–374.

Spence, M. (1978). "Product Differentiation and Performance in Insurance Markets," *Journal of Public Economics* 10, 427–447.

Stiglitz, J. (1977). "Monopoly, Nonlinear Pricing, and Imperfect Information: The Insurance Market," *Review of Economic Studies* 44, 407–430.

Stiglitz, J. and A. Weiss (1984). "Sorting Out the Differences Between Screening and Signalling Models," *Working Paper*, Princeton University.

Tabarrok, A. (1994). "Genetic Testing: An Economic and Contractarian Analysis," *Journal of Health Economics* 13, 75–91.

Townsend, R. (1982). "Optimal Multiperiod Contracts and the Gain from Enduring Relationships under Private Information," *Journal of Political Economy* 90, 1166–1185.

Villeneuve, B. (1998). "Concurrence et antisélection multidimensionnelle", *Mimeo IDEI*, Toulouse.

Villeneuve, B. (1999a). "The Consequences for a Monopolistic Insurance Firm of Evaluating Risk Better than Customers: The Adverse Selection Hypothesis Reversed," forthcoming in *The Geneva Papers on Risk and Insurance Theory*.

Villeneuve, B. (1999b). "Information Retention and Inefficiency in Competitive Markets for Services", *Mimeo*, IDEI, Toulouse.

Watt, R. and F.J. Vazquez (1997). "Full Insurance Bayesian Updated Premiums, and Adverse Selection," *Geneva Papers on Risk and Insurance Theory* 22, 135–150.

Whinston, M. (1983). "Moral Hazard, Adverse Selection and the Optimal Provision of Social Insurance," *Journal of Public Economics* 22, 49–71.

Wilson, C. (1977). "A Model of Insurance Markets with Incomplete Information," *Journal of Economic Theory* 16, 167–207.

Young, V.R. and M.J. Browne (1997). "Explaining Insurance Policy Provisions Via Adverse Selection," *Geneva Papers on Risk and Insurance Theory* 22, 121–134.

8 The Theory of Risk Classification

Keith J. Crocker

University of Michigan Business School

Arthur Snow

University of Georgia

Abstract

Risk Classification is the avenue through which insurance companies compete in order to reduce the cost of providing insurance contracts. While the underwriting incentives leading insurers to categorize customers according to risk status are straightforward, the social value of such activities is less clear. This chapter reviews the literature on risk classification, and demonstrates that the efficiency of permitting categorical discrimination in insurance contracting depends on the informational structure of the environment, and on whether insurance applicants become informed by the classification signal.

Keywords: Risk categorization, classification, informational asymmetry, information, insurance.

JEL Classification Numbers: D82, G22.

8.1 INTRODUCTION

The efficiency and equity effects of risk classification in insurance markets have been a source of substantial debate, both amongst economists and in the public policy arena.[1] The primary concerns have been the adverse equity consequences for individuals who are categorized unfavorably, and the extent to which risk classification enhances efficiency in insurance contracting. While adverse equity effects are endemic to any classification scheme that results in heterogeneous consumers being charged actuarially fair premiums, whether such classification

[1] See Crocker and Snow (1986) for references to U.S. Supreme Court rulings disallowing gender-based categorization in pensions, and to discussions of the laws and public policies related to categorization practices. Tabarrok (1994) provides further references to the policy and popular debate on categorical discrimination.

enhances market efficiency depends on specific characteristics of the informational environment.

In this contribution we set out the theory of risk classification in insurance markets and explore its implications for efficiency and equity in insurance contracting. Our primary concern is with economic efficiency and the role of risk classification in mitigating the adverse selection that arises when insurance applicants are better informed about their riskiness than insurers. We are also interested in the role of classification risk, that is, uncertainty about the outcome of a classification procedure. This uncertainty imposes a cost on risk averse consumers and is thus a potential cause of divergence between the private and social value of information gathering. In addition, the adverse equity consequences of risk classification bear directly on economic efficiency as they contribute to the social cost of classification risk.

8.2 RISK CLASSIFICATION IN THE ABSENCE OF HIDDEN KNOWLEDGE

We begin by considering as a benchmark the case in which both insurers and insurance applicants are symmetrically uninformed about the applicants' propensities for suffering an insurable loss.

8.2.1 Homogeneous Agents

Formally, the insurance environment consists of a continuum of risk averse consumers, each of whom possesses an initial wealth $\overline{W}$ and may suffer a (publicly-observed) loss D with known probability $\overline{p}$. Each consumer's preferences are represented by the von Neumann-Morgenstern utility function $U(W)$, which is assumed to be strictly increasing and strictly concave, reflecting risk aversion.

A consumer may purchase insurance against the loss by entering into a contract $C \equiv (m, I)$, which specifies the premium m paid to the insurer and the indemnification I received by the insured when the loss occurs. A consumer's expected utility under the insurance contract C is given by

$$V(\overline{p}, C) \equiv \overline{p}U(W_D) + (1 - \overline{p})U(W_N), \tag{1}$$

where $W_D \equiv \overline{W} - m - D + I$ and $W_N \equiv \overline{W} - m$ denote the consumer's state-contingent wealth levels. The expected profit of providing the insurance contract C is given by

$$\pi(\overline{p}, C) \equiv m - \overline{p}I. \tag{2}$$

In order to be feasible, a contract must satisfy the resource constraint

$$\pi(\bar{p}, C) \geq 0, \tag{3}$$

which requires that the premium be sufficient to cover the expected insurance indemnity.

In this setting, an optimal insurance contract is a solution to the problem of maximizing (1) subject to the feasibility constraint (3), which results in full coverage for losses ($I = D$) at the actuarially fair premium ($m = \bar{p}D$). This contract, which is depicted as F in Figure 1, is also the competitive equilibrium for an insurance market with free entry and exit when all consumers have the same (publicly observed) probability $\bar{p}$ of suffering loss.

8.2.2 Classification with Heterogeneous Agents

We now turn to the case in which both insurers and insurance applicants have access to a costless and public signal that dichotomizes applicants into two groups. After the signal has been observed, a proportion λ of the agents are known to be *high risk* with probability p^H of suffering the loss, while $1 - \lambda$ are *low risk* with loss propensity p^L, where $p^H > p^L$ and $\bar{p} = \lambda p^H + (1 - \lambda)p^L$. When each individual's type (p^H or p^L) is publicly observable, insurers in a competitive market equilibrium offer full coverage ($I = D$) to all consumers, and charge the actuarially fair premium $m^\tau = p^\tau D$ appropriate for the p^τ-types. These contracts are depicted as H^* (L^*) for p^H-types (p^L-types) in Figure 1.

Notice that competitive pressures force firms to implement risk classification based upon the insureds' publicly observed characteristic, p^τ. Any insurer attempting to offer a contract that would pool both high and low risks (such as F) recognizes that a competitor could offer a profitable contractual alternative that would attract only the low risks. The exodus of low risks caused by such cream-skimming would render the pooling contract unprofitable.

The introduction of symmetric information about risk type accompanied by categorization based on this information increases the utility of some of the insured agents (low risks, who receive L^*), but reduces the utility of others (high risks, who receive H^*) relative to the pre-classification alternative (when both types receive F). From an efficiency perspective, however, the relevant question is whether the insureds *expect* to be better off when moving from a status-quo without information and risk-based categorization to a regime with information and risk classification. If an individual who is classified as a p^τ-type receives the contract C^τ, then the expected utility of the insured in the classification regime is

$$E\{V\} \equiv \lambda V^H + (1-\lambda)V^L \tag{4}$$

where $V^i \equiv V(p^i, C^i)$ for $i \in \{H, L\}$. The corresponding resource constraint is

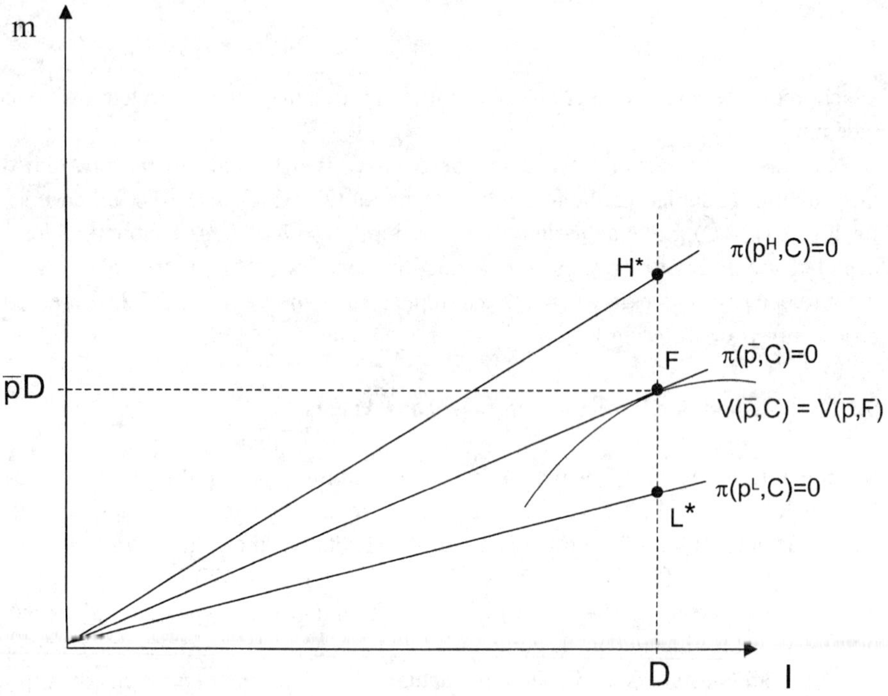

Figure 1

$$\lambda\pi(p^H, C^H) + (1-\lambda)\pi(p^L, C^L) \geq 0, \tag{5}$$

requiring that premiums collected cover expected indemnity payments per capita.

An *efficient classification contract* is a solution to the problem of maximizing (4) subject to (5), which turns out to be the pooling contract, depicted as F in Figure 1, and which provides full coverage at the pooled actuarially fair premium $\bar{p}$ D. The intuition behind this result is revealed in Figure 2, which illustrates the utilities possibilities frontier for the classification regime as locus XFY. The concavity of XFY is dictated by the risk aversion of consumers, and movement along the frontier from X towards Y makes L-types (H-types) better (worse) off. From equation (4), we infer that the slope of an indifference curve for the expected utility of an insured confronting classification risk, dV^H/dV^L, is $-(1-\lambda)/\lambda$. By the concavity of U and Jensen's inequality, the pool F is the unique optimum for the consumer anticipating risk classification.

We conclude that the efficient contract in the classification regime ignores the publicly observed signal, and treats all insureds the same independently of their types. Put differently, when information is symmetric between insurers and insureds, uni-

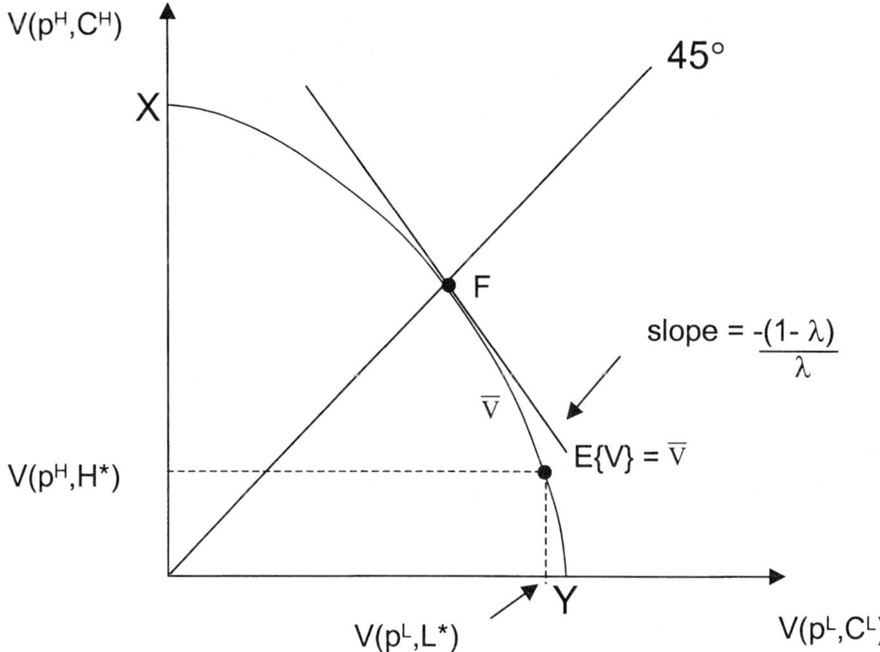

Figure 2

formed insureds prefer to remain uninformed if they anticipate that the information revealed will be used to classify the risks. The reason is that the pooling contract *F* provides full coverage against two types of risk, the *financial risk* associated with the occurrence of the loss state, and the *classification risk* faced by insurance applicants, who may find out that they are high risk. The competitive equilibrium contracts H^* and L^* satisfy the resource constraint (5) and, therefore, are candidate solutions for optimal classification contracts. However, while they provide complete protection from financial risk, they leave consumers wholly exposed to classification risk. Thus, insurers would use public information to classify insurance applicants, even though risk classification based on new information actually reduces efficiency in this setting, and is therefore undesirable.

8.3 RISK CLASSIFICATION IN THE PRESENCE OF HIDDEN KNOWLEDGE

We now turn to an environment in which the individuals to be insured all initially possess private information about their propensities for suffering loss, as in the model introduced by Rothschild and Stiglitz (1976). Each consumer has prior hidden knowledge of risk type, p^H or p^L, but insurers know only that they face a population of consumers in which a proportion λ $(1-\lambda)$ have the loss probability p^H (p^L). Given the nature of the informational asymmetry, in order to be attainable a pair of insurance contracts (C^H, C^L) must satisfy the incentive compatibility (self-selection) constraints

$$V(p^\tau, C^\tau) \geq V(p^\tau, C^{\tau'}) \quad \text{for every } \tau, \tau' \in \{H, L\} \tag{6}$$

as a consequence of the Revelation Principle exposited by Myerson (1979) and Harris and Townsend (1981).

In this informationally constrained setting, an efficient insurance contract can be characterized as a solution to the problem of maximizing the expected utility of low-risk consumers $V(p^L, C^L)$ subject to the resource constraint (5), the incentive constraints (6), and a utility constraint on the welfare of high-risk types

$$V(p^H, C^H) \geq \bar{V}^H. \tag{7}$$

As discussed by Crocker and Snow (1985a), a solution to this problem yields full (partial) coverage for H-types (L-types); both the resource constraint (5) and the utility constraint (7) hold with equality; and the incentive constraint (6) binds (is slack) for high (low) risks.

One element of the class of efficient contracts is depicted in Figure 3 as $\{\hat{C}^H, \hat{C}^L\}$. By construction, the locus FA depicts the set of contracts awarded to low risks that, when coupled with a full-insurance contract to which high risks are indifferent, satisfies the resource constraint with equality.[2] Also depicted is the Rothschild-Stiglitz separating allocation (H^*, A), which is the Pareto dominant member of the family of contracts that satisfy the incentive constraints (6) and the requirement that each type of contract break even individually. The Rothchild-Stiglitz allocation is not an element of the (second-best) efficient set unless the proportion of H-types (λ) is sufficiently large.

At this juncture, it is useful to elaborate on the differences between the efficiency approach that we have adopted in this chapter, and the equilibrium analyses that have characterized much of the insurance literature. The potential for the non-existence of a Nash equilibrium in pure strategies that was first observed by Rothschild and Stiglitz

[2] Even though the shape of the locus AF is ambiguous, concavity is guaranteed around F. Indeed, the slope of this locus (see Crocker and Snow (1986) page 448) is the right-hand side of condition (c) evaluated at $\delta = 0$: $\dfrac{\lambda(1-p^H)U'(W_1^L)+(1-\lambda)(1-p^L)U'(W_2^H)}{\lambda p^H U'(W_2^L)+(1-\lambda)p^L U'(W_2^H)}$. Since we have $W_1^H = W_2^H = W_1^L = W_2^L$ at F, the slope can be rewritten as follows: $\dfrac{\lambda(1-p^H)+(1-\lambda)(1-p^L)}{\lambda p^H+(1-\lambda)p^L}$. This reduces to $\dfrac{1-\bar{p}}{\bar{p}}$, which is the slope of the aggregate zero-profit line. So the AF locus is tangent to the aggregate zero-profit line (see Dionne and Fombaron (1996)).

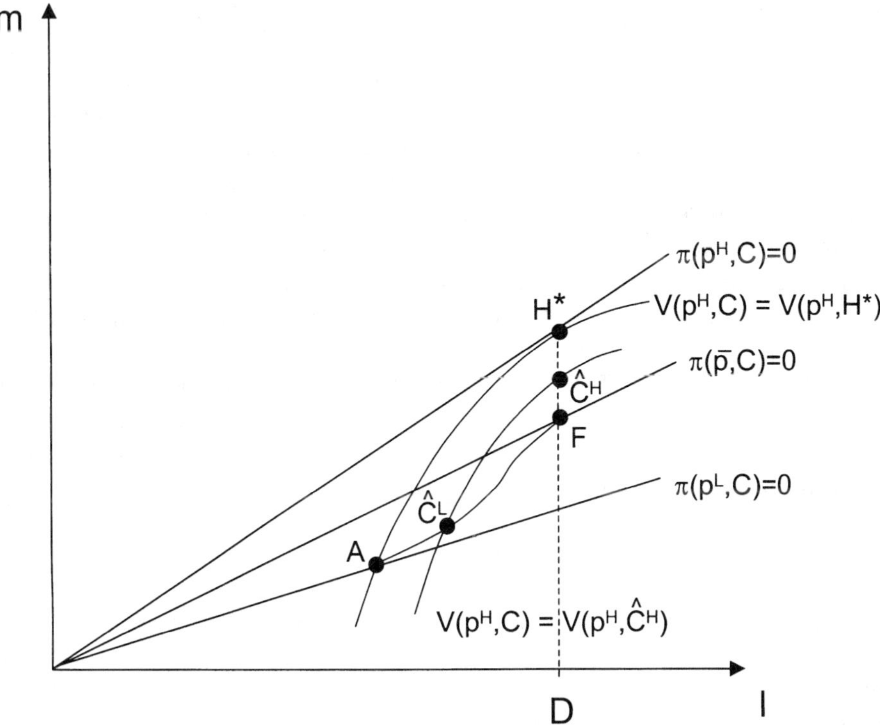

Figure 3

is an artifact of the incentives faced by uninformed insurers who compete in the offering of screening contracts to attract customers. This result has spawned a substantial body of work attempting to resolve the nonexistence issue, either through the application of non-Nash equilibrium concepts (Wilson (1977); Riley (1979); Miyazaki (1977)) or by considering alternative extensive form models of the insurance process with Nash refinements (Hellwig (1987); Cho and Kreps (1987)). Unfortunately, the insurance contracts supported as equilibrium allocations generally differ, and depend on the particular concept or extensive form being considered.

In contrast, the characterization of second-best efficient allocations that respect the informational asymmetries of the market participants is straightforward. The model is that of a social planner guided by the Pareto criterion, and who has the power to assign insurance allocations to the market participants.[3] While the planner is omnipotent, in the sense of having the ability to assign any allocation that does not violate the economy's resource constraints, it is not omniscient, and so is constrained

[3] Both Harris and Townsend (1981) and Myerson (1979) have demonstrated that no alternative organization of the economy's allocation process can dominate the allocations attainable by a social planner.

to have no better information than the market participants.[4] Hence, the issue of how firms compete in the offering of insurance contracts does not arise, since the social planner assigns allocations by dictatorial fiat subject to the (immutable) informational and resource constraints of the economy. This exercise permits an identification of the best outcomes that could, in principle, be attained in an economy. Whether any particular set of equilibrium mechanics can do as well is, of course, a different issue, and one that we consider in more detail in Section 8.5 below.

Finally, as we close this section, notice that risk classification, accomplished through self-selection based on hidden knowledge of riskiness, is required for efficient contracting in this environment. Specifically, with the exception of the first-best pooling allocation F, all efficient allocations are second best, as they entail costly signaling by low-risk types. These consumers retain some risk by choosing a contract that incorporates a positive deductible, but in so doing they are best able to exploit opportunities for risk pooling given the potential adverse selection of low-risk contracts by high-risk consumers.

8.3.1 Categorization Based on Immutable Characteristics

We suppose for the purposes of this section that consumers differ by an observable trait that is immutable, costless to observe, and correlated with (and, hence informative about) the unobservable risk of loss. Examples of such categorizing tools are provided by, but not restricted to, an insured's gender, age or race, which may be imperfectly correlated with the individual's underlying probability of suffering a loss. The interesting question is whether the information available through categorical discrimination, which can be used by insurers to tailor the contracts that are assigned to insureds based upon their observable characteristics, enhances the possibilities for efficiency.

In the first attempt to examine the implications of permitting insurers to classify risks in this environment, Hoy (1982) considered the effects of categorization on market equilibria. Since there was, and still is, little consensus on the identity of the allocations supported by equilibrium behavior, Hoy considered the pure strategy Nash equilibrium of Rothschild and Stiglitz, the "anticipatory" equilibrium of Wilson (1977), and the equilibrium suggested by Miyazaki (1977) which assumes anticipatory behavior but permits cross-subsidization within an insurer's portfolio of contractual offerings. Hoy found that the efficiency consequences of permitting risk classification were ambiguous, depending on the particular equilibrium configuration posited. The primary reason for this ambiguity is that, with the exception of the

[4] So, for example, in the efficiency problem just considered, the goal of the social planner is to maximize the expected utility of one arbitrarily selected agent (V^L) subject to the constraints of (i) not making the other agent worse off than a specified level of expected utility $\bar{V}^H$ ($V^H \geq \bar{V}^H$); (ii) the economy's resource constraint (5); and (iii) the informational constraints of the market participants (6). By varying $\bar{V}^H$, the entire set of (second-best) efficient allocations may be determined.

Miyazaki equilibrium, none of the allocations supported by the equilibrium behaviors considered is guaranteed to be on the efficiency frontier.[5] Thus, a comparison of the equilibrium allocations pre- and post-categorization provides no insights regarding whether permitting categorization enhances the efficiency possibilities for insurance contracting.

A more fruitful approach is explored by Crocker and Snow (1986), who compare the utilities possibilities frontier for the regime where categorization is permitted to the one in which it is not. Throughout the remainder of this section, we assume that each insurance applicant belongs either to group A or to group B, and that the proportion of low-risk applicants is higher in group A than in group B. Letting λ_k denote the proportion of H-types in group k, we have $0 < \lambda_A < \lambda_B < 1$, so that group membership is (imperfectly) informative. Assuming that a proportion ω of the population belongs to group A, it follows that $\omega\lambda_A + (1 - \omega)\lambda_B = \lambda$.

Let $C_k \equiv (C_k^H, C_k^L)$ denote the insurance contracts offered to the members of group k. Since insurers can observe group membership but not risk type, the contractual offerings must satisfy separate incentive constraints for each group, that is,

$$V(p^\tau, C_k^\tau) \geq V(p^\tau, C_k^{\tau'}) \quad \text{for all } \tau,\ \tau' \in \{H, L\} \tag{8}$$

for each group $k \in \{A, B\}$. In addition, contracts must satisfy the resource constraint

$$\begin{aligned} &\omega[\lambda_A \pi(p^H, C_A^H) + (1-\lambda_A)\pi(p^L, C_A^L)] + (1-\omega)[\lambda_B \pi(p^H, C_B^H) \\ &\quad + (1-\lambda_B)\pi(p^L, C_B^L)] \geq 0, \end{aligned} \tag{9}$$

which requires that the contracts make zero profit on average over the two groups combined.

To demonstrate that risk categorization may permit Pareto improvements[6] over the no-categorization regime, it proves useful to consider the efficiency problem of maximizing $V(p^L, C_B^L)$ subject to the incentive constraints (8), the resource constraint (9), and the utility constraints

[5] Since Hoy was concerned with comparing equilibrium allocations in the pre- and post-categorization regimes, the pertinent efficiency issue—can be the winners from categorization compensate, in principle, the losers—was not considered. As Crocker and Snow (1986) demonstrate, the answer to this question, at least in the case of the Miyazaki equilibrium, is that they can.

[6] An actual Pareto improvement requires that at least one type of agent be made better off while no agents are made worse off. A potential Pareto improvement requires only that the winners from the regime change be able, in principle, to compensate the losers, so that the latter would be made no worse off from the move. As Crocker and Snow (1985b) have demonstrated, there exists a balanced-budget system of taxes and subsidies that can be applied by a government constrained by the same informational asymmetries as the market participants, and which can transform any potential Pareto improvement into an actual improvement. In the discussion that follows, we will use the term "Pareto improvement" to mean "potential Pareto improvement", recognizing throughout that any potential improvements can be implemented as actual improvements.

$$V(p^\tau, C_A^\tau) \geq V(p^\tau, \hat{C}^\tau) \quad \text{for } \tau \in \{H, L\}; \text{ and} \tag{10}$$

$$V(p^H, C_B^H) \geq V(p^H, \hat{C}^H), \tag{11}$$

where $\hat{C} \equiv (\hat{C}^H, \hat{C}^L)$ is an efficient allocation in the no-categorization regime. By construction, we know that this problem has at least one feasible alternative, namely the no-categorization contract $\hat{C}$ which treats the insureds the same independently of the group (A or B) to which they belong. If $\hat{C}$ is the solution, then the utilities possibilities frontier for the categorization and the no-categorization regimes coincide at $\hat{C}$. However, if $\hat{C}$ does not solve the problem, then categorization admits contractual opportunities Pareto superior to $\hat{C}$ and the utilities possibilities frontier for the categorization regime lies outside the frontier associated with the no-categorization regime.

Let δ denote the Lagrange multiplier associated with the utility constraint (7) for the efficiency problem in the no-categorization regime, and let μ_H be the multiplier associated with the incentive constraint (6) for $\tau = H$. The following result is from Crocker and Snow (1986, p. 329).

Result. Categorization permits a Pareto improvement to be realized over efficient contracts without categorization if and only if

$$\frac{\delta}{\mu_H} < \frac{\lambda - \lambda_A}{\lambda_A(1-\lambda)}. \tag{12}$$

For the inequality to hold, it is sufficient that $\delta = 0$, which necessarily obtains whenever the utility constraint, $\bar{V}^H$, in (7) is set sufficiently low. When $\delta > 0$, the location of the utilities possibilities frontiers depends on the informativeness of the categorization. When categorization is more informative, λ_A is smaller and the right hand side of (12) is larger. If categorization were uninformative ($\lambda = \lambda_A$), then (12) could never hold, and if categorization were perfectly informative ($\lambda_A = 0$), then (12) would always be satisfied. Finally, the inequality can never hold when $\mu_H = 0$, which occurs when the incentive constraint (6) for the efficiency problem in the no-categorization regime is slack. Contract F is the only efficient contract for which the incentive constraint is slack, so that the utilities possibilities frontiers always coincide at F regardless of the degree of informativeness of the categorization. The relative positions of the utilities possibilities frontiers for the categorization and the no-categorization regimes for those in group A are depicted in Figure 4, while a similar diagram applies to those in group B.

To evaluate the efficiency of categorization, we employ the Samuelson (1950) criterion for potential Pareto improvement. Risk classification through *a priori* categorization by insurers is defined to be efficient (inefficient) if there exists (does not exist) a utility distribution in the frontier for the no-categorization regime Pareto dominated

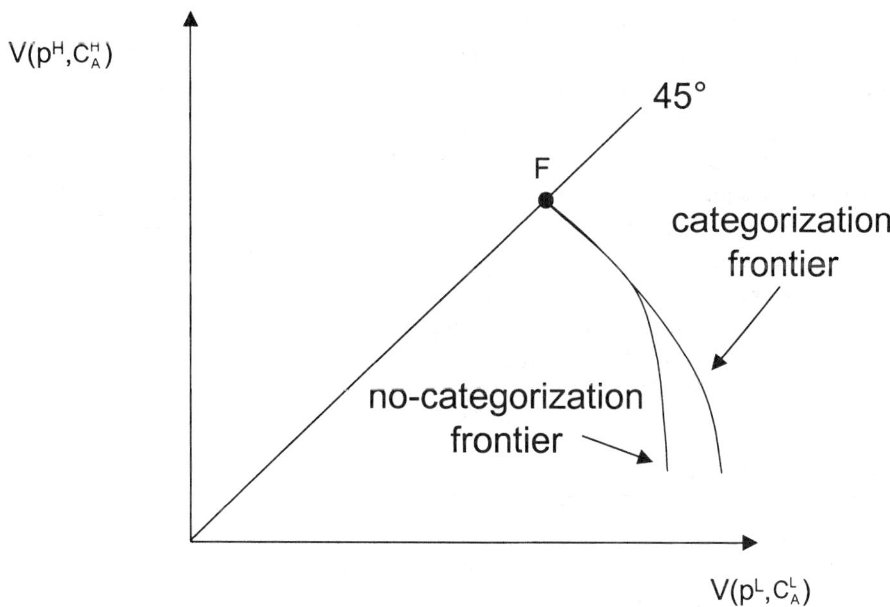

Figure 4

by a distribution in the frontier for the categorization regime, and there does not exist (exists) a distribution in the categorization frontier Pareto dominated by one in the no-categorization frontier. Since costless categorization shifts outward the utilities possibilities frontier over some regions and never causes the frontier to shift inward, we conclude that categorization is efficient.

Crocker and Snow (1985b) show that omniscience is not required to implement the hypothetical lump-sum transfers needed to effect movement along a utilities possibilities frontier. Although the appropriate lump-sum transfers cannot be assigned directly to individual consumers, since their risk types are hidden knowledge, these transfers can be built into the premium-indemnity schedule so that insurance applicants self-select the taxes or transfers intended for their individual risk types. In this manner, a government constrained by the same informational asymmetry confronting insurers can levy taxes and subsidies on insurance contracts to implement redistribution, while obeying incentive compatibility constraints and maintaining a balanced public budget. Our application of the Samuelson criterion is thus consistent with the informational environment.

8.3.2 Categorization Based on Consumption Choices

In contrast to categorical discrimination based on observable but immutable characteristics, in many situations consumers use products, such as cigarettes or stodgy automobiles, with the anticipation that such consumption will affect their opportunities for insuring. The actuarial relationship between the consumption of such a *correlative product* and underlying risk may be the consequence of a direct causal link (smoking and heart disease) or merely a statistical relationship (people who drive stodgy automobiles are more likely to be careful drivers). In both cases, however, the observed consumption of a correlative product permits insurers to design contracts that mitigate the problems of moral hazard and adverse selection inherent in insurance markets with private information.

To analyze the efficiency effects of permitting insurers to classify applicants on the basis of their consumption choices, Bond and Crocker (1991) assume that consumers' utility functions have the additively separable form

$$U(W)+\theta G(x) \tag{13}$$

where W and x are the consumer's wealth and consumption of the correlative product, respectively, and θ is a taste parameter. There are two types of consumers distinguished by their taste for the correlative product $\theta \in \{\theta^H, \theta^L\}$ where $\theta^H > \theta^L$. The proportion of θ^H-types in the population is λ.

Each consumer faces two possible wealth states, so W_D (W_N) represents consumption of other goods (that is, wealth net of expenditures on the correlative productive) in the loss (no-loss) state. The probability of the loss state for a θ^τ-type consumer is $p^\tau(x)$, with $\partial p^\tau(x)/\partial x \geq 0$ and $1 \geq p^H(x) \geq p^L(x) \geq 0$ for every x. Thus, the consumption of the correlative product either affects directly, or may be positively correlated with, the potential for loss. While we restrict our attention to the case of hazardous goods whose level of consumption increases the probability of a loss ($\partial p^\tau/\partial x > 0$) or where the consumer's taste for the product is positively correlated with loss propensity ($p^H(x) > p^L(x)$), consideration of other correlative relationships is straightforward.

Under the assumption that consumers purchase the hazardous good x before the wealth state is revealed, the expected utility of a type θ^τ individual is

$$V^\tau(W_D, W_N, x) \equiv p^\tau(x)U(W_D)+(1-p^\tau(x))U(W_N)+\theta^\tau G(x). \tag{14}$$

When the hazardous good is supplied by a competitive market at marginal cost c, the state-contingent wealth of an insured is now $W_N \equiv \overline{W} - m - cx$ and $W_D \equiv \overline{W} - m - cx + I - D$. The expected profit of providing the insurance policy $\{m, I\}$ to a θ^τ-type agent who consumes x is

$$\pi^\tau(m, I, x) \equiv m - p^\tau(x)I. \tag{15}$$

A *contract* $C \equiv \{m, I, x\}$ determines the consumption bundle for the insured, and an *allocation* (C^H, C^L) is a pair of contracts assigned to insureds based upon their types. Feasible contracts must satisfy the resource constraint

$$\lambda\pi^H(C^H)+(1-\lambda)\pi^L(C^L)\geq 0, \tag{16}$$

which ensures that premiums are sufficient to cover expected indemnity payments per capita.

When the insureds' taste parameters and the consumption of the hazardous good can be observed publicly, first-best allocations are attainable. In that event, an efficient allocation, denoted ($C^{L}*$, $C^{H}*$), is a solution to the problem of maximizing $V^L(C^L)$ subject to (16) and a utility constraint on H-types, $V^H(C^H) \geq \bar{V}^H$. An efficient allocation results in full insurance for ($W_D^\tau = W_N^\tau = W^\tau$) for both types of agents, and consumption levels for the hazardous good, x^τ, that equate each type of consumer's marginal valuation of consumption with its marginal cost, that is,

$$\frac{\theta^\tau G'(x^\tau)}{U'(W^\tau)}=c+D\partial p^\tau(x^\tau)/\partial x, \tag{17}$$

Notice that the marginal cost of the hazardous good includes its production cost c as well as its marginal effect on the expected loss.

The interesting case from the perspective of risk classification arises when consumption of the hazardous good, x, is observable but the consumer's taste parameter, θ, is private information. In this setting with asymmetric information, allocations must satisfy the incentive constraints

$$V^\tau(C^\tau)\geq V^\tau(C^{\tau'}) \quad \text{for all } \tau,\ \tau'\in\{H, L\}. \tag{18}$$

This case is referred to as *endogenous risk classification* since the consumers' insurance opportunities may depend on their choices regarding consumption of the hazardous good.

An efficient allocation is a solution to the problem of maximizing $V^L(C^L)$ subject to $V^H(C^H) \geq \bar{V}^H$, the incentive constraints (18), and the resource constraint (16). There are two classes of solutions, which differ based on whether any of the incentive constraints (18) are binding.

8.3.3 First-Best Allocations: A Pure Strategy Nash Equilibrium

When the incentive constraints (18) do not bind at a solution to the efficiency problem, the efficient allocation provides full coverage to all individuals and charges actuarially fair premiums $p^\tau(x^\tau)D$ that depend on the amount of the hazardous good consumed (as determined by (17)). The insurance premium offered is bundled with a consumer's observed consumption of the hazardous good, so that individuals are classified based upon their consumption choices for x. An efficient allocation in this case is depicted as ($C^{H}*$, $C^{L}*$) in Figure 5.

The moral hazard aspect of hazardous goods consumption is reflected by the cur-

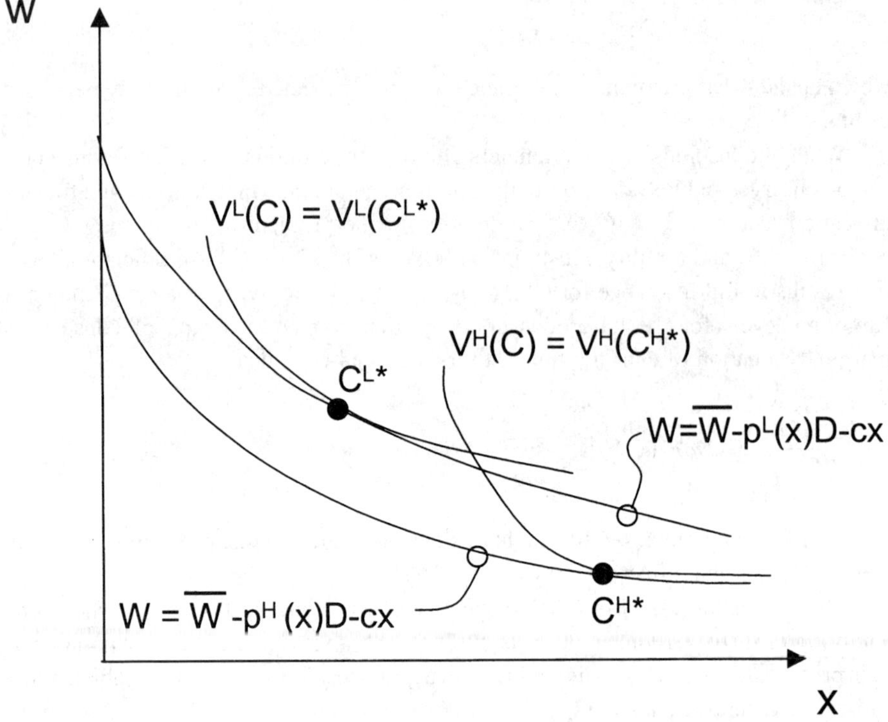

Figure 5

vature of a consumer's budget constraint $W = \overline{W} - p^\tau(x)D - cx$, which reflects the fact that the risk of loss depends on consumption of the hazardous good, given $\partial p^\tau(x)/\partial x \neq 0$. The potential for adverse selection arises because the budget constraint for θ^H-types lies below that for θ^L-types, since $p^H(x) > p^L(x)$. In the special case where there is no adverse selection ($p^H(x) = p^L(x)$), the budget constraints of the two types of consumers coincide, and a first-best allocation solves the efficiency problem. Effectively, the insurer levies a Pigovian tax based upon the observed consumption levels of the hazardous good, thereby forcing the insured to internalize the moral hazard externality. Introducing a small amount of private information still permits the attainment of first-best allocations, as long as the difference in loss probabilities ($p^H(x) - p^L(x)$) is not to great.

It is easy to see that the first-best allocation (C^{H*}, C^{L*}) is necessarily a Nash equilibrium in pure strategies whenever the incentive constraints (18) are not binding. This result provides an important insight concerning the desirability of permitting insurers to classify applicants on the basis of their consumption of goods that directly affect loss propensities. In the polar case, where the level of hazardous good consumption completely determines an individual's loss probability (so $p^H(x) = p^L(x) \equiv p(x)$), endogenous risk classification allows first-best allocations to be attained as Nash equilibria. Indeed, to disallow such categorization would cause a reversion to the typical adverse selection economy where the Nash equilibrium, if it exists, lies strictly inside the first-best frontier.

Even in cases where endogenous risk classification is imperfect, so that some residual uncertainty about the probability of loss remains after accounting for consumption of the hazardous good ($p^H(x) \neq p^L(x)$), the pure strategy Nash equilibrium exists and is first-best efficient as long as the risk component unexplained by x is sufficiently small. Consequently, insurers may alleviate the problems of adverse selection in practice by extensively categorizing their customers on the basis of factors causing losses, which may partly offset the insureds' informational advantage and permit the attainment of first-best allocations as equilibria.

8.3.4 Second-Best Allocations

When incentive constraints are binding at a solution to the efficiency problem, an optimal allocation generally results in distortions in both the insurance dimension and in the consumption of the hazardous good. While the nature of a second-best allocation depends on the specifics of the model's parameters, there are several generic results.

Result. When the incentive constraint (18) binds for the θ^H-type consumers, an efficient allocation is second best. Also,

(i) if $p^H(x) > p^L(x)$, then θ^H-types (θ^L-types) receive full coverage (are under-insured); and

(ii) if $\left\{ \begin{array}{l} \text{either } p^H(x) = p^L(x) \text{ (no adverse selection case)} \\ \text{or } \dfrac{\partial p^\tau(x)}{\partial x} = 0 \text{ (pure adverse selection case) and } \dfrac{\theta^H}{\theta^L} = \dfrac{p^H}{p^L} \end{array} \right\}$

then θ^L-types (θ^H-types) under-consume (over-consume) the hazardous good relative to the socially optimal level (17).

These results indicate the extent to which there is a tension between discouraging consumption of the hazardous good to mitigate moral hazard, on the one hand, and using such consumption as a signal to mitigate adverse selection, on the other. An optimal contract reflects a balance between the signaling value of hazardous goods consumption and the direct social costs imposed by the consumption of products that increase the probability of loss.

As an example, consider those who ride motorcycles without wearing safety helmets, which is a form of hazardous good consumption. On the one hand, those who choose to have the wind blowing through their hair are directly increasing their probabilities of injury (the *moral hazard* effect), which increases the cost of riding motorcycles. On the other hand, the taste for not wearing helmets may be correlated with a propensity of the rider to engage in other types of risk-taking activities (the *adverse selection* effect), so that the choice to ride bear-headed may be interpreted by insurers as an imperfect signal of the motorcyclist's underlying risk. Interestingly, to require the use of safety helmets eliminates the ability of insurers to utilize this signal, with deleterious effects on efficiency.

8.4 RISK CLASSIFICATION AND INCENTIVES FOR INFORMATION GATHERING

As discussed originally by Dreze (1960) and subsequently by Hirshleifer (1971), because information resolves uncertainty about which of alternative possible outcomes will occur, information destroys valuable opportunities for risk averse individuals to insure against unfortuitous outcomes. This phenomenon lies behind the observation, made earlier in section A, that new information used by insurers to classify insurance applicants has an adverse effect on economic efficiency. As emphasized in the "no-trade" theorem of Milgrom and Stokey (1982), if applicants were able to insure against the possibility of adverse risk classification, then new information would have no social value, either positive or negative, as long as consumers initially possess no hidden knowledge.

By contrast, the results of Crocker and Snow (1986) and Bond and Crocker (1991) show that new information can also create valuable insurance opportunities when consumers are privately informed. Information about each consumer's hidden knowledge, revealed by statistically correlated traits or behaviors, allows insurers to sort consumers more finely, and thereby to reduce the inefficiency caused by adverse selection. In this section, we investigate the effects of risk classification on incentives for gathering information about underlying loss probabilities.

8.4.1 Symmetric Information

Returning to the benchmark case of symmetric information, we now suppose that some consumers initially possess knowledge of being either high-risk or low-risk, while other consumers are initially uninformed. Being symmetrically informed, insurers can classify each insurance applicant by informational state and can offer customers in each class a contract that provides full coverage at an actuarially fair premium. Thus, with reference to Figure 1, informed consumers receive either H^* or L^*, while uninformed consumers receive the first-best pooling contract F.

Observe that uninformed consumers in this setting have no incentive to become informed, since they would then bear a classification risk. In Figure 2, the line tangent to the utilities possibilities frontier at point F corresponds to an indifference curve for an uninformed consumer.[7] Clearly, the pooling contract F is preferred to the possibility of receiving H^* with probability λ or L^* with probability $1 - \lambda$, that is,

$$V(\bar{p}, F) > \lambda V(p^H, H^*) + (1-\lambda)V(p^L, L^*),$$

where $\bar{p} = \lambda p^H + (1 - \lambda)p^L$. Since all three of the contracts (F, L^*, H^*) fully insure consumers against the financial risk associated with the loss D, becoming informed in this environment serves only to expose a consumer to classification risk, with no countervailing gain in efficiency. The incentive for uninformed consumers to remain uninformed is consistent with socially optimal information gathering, since the classification risk optimally discourages individuals from seeking information.

8.4.2 Initial Acquisition of Hidden Knowledge

Hidden knowledge can be acquired either purposefully or serendipitously as a by-product of consumption or production activities. In this section we consider environments in which some consumers initially possess *hidden knowledge* of their riskiness, while others do not. Moreover, we assume that insurers cannot ascertain *a priori* any consumer's informational state. Figure 6 illustrates the Pareto dominant separating allocation in which each contract breaks even individually, which is the analogue to the Rothschild and Stiglitz equilibrium with three types (p^H, $\bar{p}$ and p^L) of consumers.[8] Consumers with hidden knowledge of risk type (either p^H or p^L) select contract H^* or contract L, while those who are uninformed (perceiving their type to be $\bar{p}$) select contract B on the pooled fair-odds line. Notice that the presence of uninformed consumers adversely affects low-risk types, who could otherwise have received the (preferred) contract A. Thus, the presence of uninformed consumers may exacerbate the adverse selection inefficiency caused by the hidden knowledge of informed consumers.

In this setting, and in contrast to the case of symmetric information in 8.4.1 above, uninformed consumers *do* have an incentive to become informed despite the classification risk they must bear as a result. Ignoring any cost of acquiring information, and assuming for the moment that contracts H^* and L continue to be offered, the expected gain to becoming informed is given by

[7] Since the expected utility of an uninformed agent is $\lambda V^H + (1 - \lambda)V^L$ where V^i represents the agent's utility in the informational state i, the slope of the associated indifference curve is $dV^H/dV^L = -(1 - \lambda)/\lambda$.

[8] The Rothschild and Stiglitz allocation is the Pareto dominant member of the class of *informationally consistent* allocations, which is defined as the set of contracts that satisfy self-selection, and that each make zero profit given the class of customers electing to purchase them. While the analysis of the previous sections indicate that these allocations are not always elements of the efficient set (for some parameter configurations), we will, in the interests of expositional ease, assume that they are in the arguments that follow. This is without loss of generality, for in cases where cross-subsidization between risk types is required for efficiency, the same arguments will apply, except with the zero-profit loci relabeled to effect the desired level of subsidy.

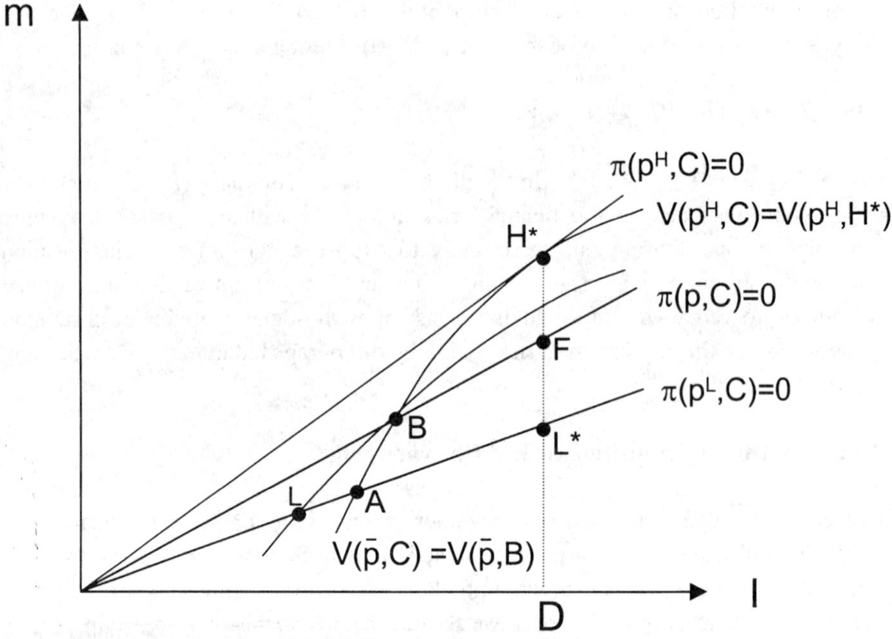

Figure 6

$$\lambda V(p^H, H^*) + (1-\lambda)V(p^L, L) - V(\bar{p}, B) = (1-\lambda)[V(p^L, L) - V(p^L, B)],$$

where the equality follows from the fact that

$$V(\bar{p}, B) \equiv \lambda V(p^H, B) + (1-\lambda)V(p^L, B),$$

and from the binding self-selection constraint requiring that $V(p^H, H^*) = V(p^H, B)$. The incentive constraints also require that $V(p^L, L)$ exceeds $V(p^L, B)$. Hence, for an uninformed consumer, the expected gain in utility to becoming informed of risk type (p^H or p^L) is unambiguously positive. Finally, when all consumers possess hidden knowledge, contract A replaces contract L, which enhances the expected value of becoming informed, while also raising the utility of low-risk insureds. We conclude that, in the presence of adverse selection, risk classification through self-selection provides an incentive for uninformed consumers to acquire hidden knowledge, and that this action enhances the efficiency of insurance contracting by reducing, in the aggregate, the amount of signaling required to effect the separation of types.

This result strengthens the finding reported by Doherty and Posey (1998), who adopt the additional assumption that high-risk consumers, whose test results have indicated a risk in excess of p^H, can undergo a treatment that reduces the probability of loss to p^H. They emphasize the value of the treatment option in showing that initially

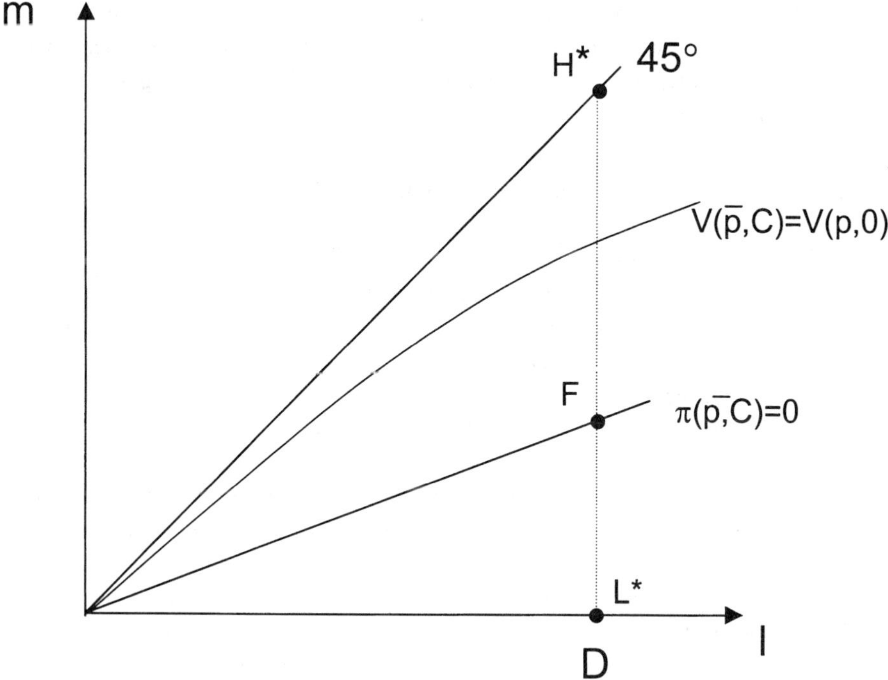

Figure 7

uninformed consumers choose to acquire hidden knowledge. Our demonstration of this result abstracts from the possibility of treatment, and reveals that risk classification is valuable to uninformed consumers in markets where some consumers possess hidden knowledge, despite uncertainty about the class to which one will be associated. Thus, private incentives for information gathering accurately reflect the social value of initially acquiring hidden knowledge.

A case of special concern arises when information reveals whether a loss has occurred, as when an incurable disease is diagnosed. Figure 7 illustrates this situation with $p^H = 1$ and $p^L = 0$. The equilibrium indifference curve for H-type consumers coincides with the forty-five degree line, while that for L-types coincides with the horizontal axis. Although informed consumers possess no insurable risk, uninformed consumers do possess an insurable risk. However, when insurers are unable to distinguish between insurance applicants who are informed and those who are not, the market fails to provide any insurance whatsoever.[9] This result, obtained by Doherty

[9] The problem arises because the H-types have no insurable risks when $p^H = 1$. Whenever $p^H \neq 1$, the allocations B and L depicted in Figure 6 are non-degenerate (in the sense that they do not correspond with the origin). This holds even when $p^L = 0$, although in this particular case the allocation L would reside on the horizontal axis. In contrast, when $p^H = 1$, B and L necessarily correspond with the origin, so there are no insurance opportunities for the uninformed agent (since B is degenerate). This argument holds for any $p^L \geq 0$.

and Thistle (1996), represents the extreme case in which uninformed consumers have no incentive to acquire hidden knowledge. Notice that the acquisition of such knowledge has no social value as well, so that private incentives are once again in accord with economic efficiency.

8.4.3 Acquisition of Additional Hidden Knowledge

Henceforth, we assume that all consumers possess hidden knowledge. In this section, we investigate the private and social value of acquiring additional hidden knowledge. Since hidden knowledge introduces inefficiency by causing adverse selection, it is not surprising to find that additional hidden knowledge can exacerbate adverse selection inefficiency. However, we also find that additional hidden knowledge can expand opportunities for insuring, and thereby mitigate adverse selection inefficiency.

We assume that all insurance applicants have privately observed the outcome of an experiment (the α-experiment) that provides information about the underlying probability of loss, and we are concerned with whether the acquisition of additional hidden knowledge (the β-experiment) has social value. Prior to observing the outcome of the α-experiment, all consumers have the same prior beliefs, namely that the loss probability is either p^1 or p^2 ($>p^1$) with associated probabilities denoted by $P(p^1)$ and $P(p^2)$ such that

$$\bar{p} = p^1 P(p^1) + p^2 P(p^2).$$

After the α-experiment, consumers who have observed $\alpha^\tau \in \{\alpha^L, \alpha^H\}$ have formed posterior beliefs such that

$$p^\tau = p^1 P(p^1|\alpha^\tau) + p^2 P(p^2|\alpha^\tau).$$

A proportion $\lambda = P(\alpha^H)$ have observed α^H.

At no cost, consumers are permitted to observe a second experiment (the β-experiment) whose outcome $\beta^t \in \{\beta^1, \beta^2\}$ reveals the consumer's actual loss probability $p^t \in \{p^1, p^2\}$. In what follows, the notation $P(\beta^i, \alpha^j)$ denotes the joint probability of observing the outcome (β^i, α^j) of the two experiments, where $i \in \{1, 2\}$ and $j \in \{H, L\}$.

For this environment, Crocker and Snow (1992) establish the following propositions concerning the efficiency implications of the additional hidden knowledge represented by the second experiment β. The experiment has a positive (negative) social value if the utilities possibilities frontier applicable when consumers anticipate observing β prior to contracting lies (weakly) outside (inside) the frontier applicable when observing β is not an option.

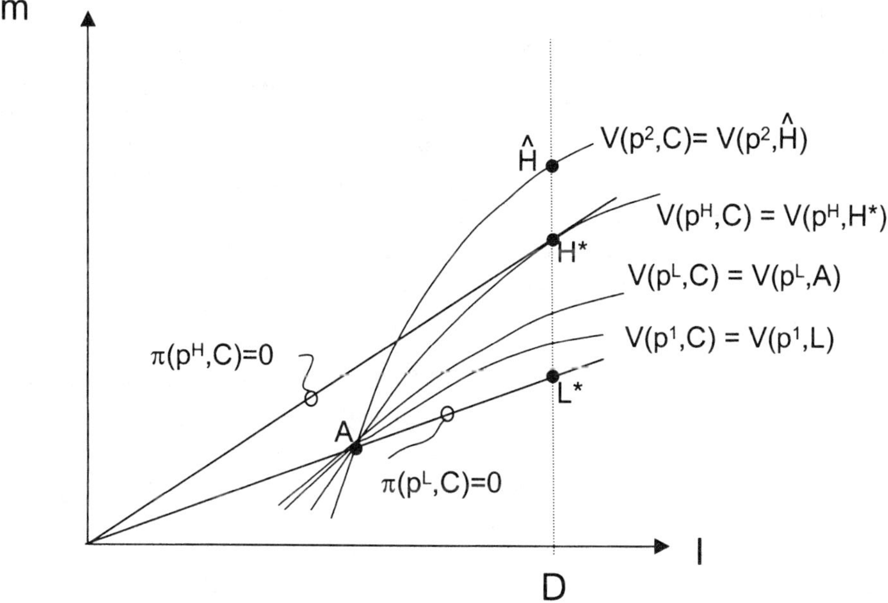

Figure 8

Result. The additional hidden knowledge represented by experiment β has a positive social value if

$$p^2P(\beta^2,\alpha^L)-p^1P(\beta^1,\alpha^H)\leq \min\{P(\beta^2,\alpha^L)-P(\beta^1,\alpha^H),\ P(\beta^2)(p^2-p^1)/(1-p^H)\},$$

but has a negative social value if

$$p^2P(\beta^2,\alpha^L)-p^1P(\beta^1,\alpha^H)\geq \max\{0,[p^2P(\beta^2)-p^HP(\alpha^H)]/p^H\}.$$

So, for example, if the probability difference $P(\beta^2, \alpha^L) - P(\beta^1, \alpha^H)$ is positive, then the weighted difference $p^2\ P(\beta^2, \alpha^L) - p^1\ P(\beta^2, \alpha^H)$ cannot be too large, for then the acquisition of the hidden knowledge β would have negative social value. Similarly, if the probability difference is negative, then the weighted difference must also be negative in order for β to have positive social value. Although these conditions are not necessary for additional hidden knowledge to have a positive or negative social value, they depend only on exogenous parameters of the informational environment without regard to consumers' risk preferences.

Figure 8 illustrates the sources of social gains and losses from additional hidden knowledge. In the absence of experiment β, a typical efficient separating allocation is depicted by the pair (H^*, A). Once consumers have privately observed β, the pair

(H^*, A) is no longer incentive compatible. The α^L-type consumers who discover their type to be p^2 now prefer H^* to their previous allocation A, while the α^H-types who find out that their loss propensity is p^1 now prefer A. The effect of consumers' acquiring additional hidden knowledge through the β-experiment is to alter irreversibly the set of incentive compatible allocations, and to render previously feasible contracts unattainable. From a social welfare perspective, for the β-experiment to have positive social value, there must exist allocations that (i) are incentive compatible under the new (post β-experiment) informational regime, (ii) allow consumers to be expectationally at least as well off as they were at (H^*, A) prior to the experiment; and (iii) earn nonnegative profit.

It is easy to verify that the incentive compatible pair $(\hat{H}, A)$, when evaluated by consumers ex ante, prior to observing β, affords α^L-types (α^H-types) the same expected utility they enjoy at A (H^*).[10] Notice that α^L-types who observe β^2 no longer bear signaling costs since they no longer choose the deductible contract A, while α^H-types who observe β^1 now absorb signaling costs. Since, by construction, consumers are indifferent between not observing the β-experiment and receiving (H^*, A), or observing the β-experiment and being offered $(\hat{H}, A)$, the acquisition of the additional hidden information has positive social value if the contracts $(\hat{H}, A)$ yield positive profit to the insurer.[11] Whether this occurs depends on the proportion of consumers signaling less when newly informed, $p^2P(\beta^2, \alpha^L)$, relative to the proportion signaling more, $p^1P(\beta^1, \alpha^H)$, as indicated by conditions stated in the *Result* above.

Private incentives for information gathering may not accord with its social value in the present environment. We will illustrate this result in a setting where insurance markets attain separating equilibria in which contracts break even individually. First, notice that, if α^L-types acquire access to the β-experiment, then α^H-types prefer also to become informed, even though they may be worse off than if neither type has access to the β-experiment. To see this, refer to Figure 9, which illustrates the equilibrium when only α^L-types will observe β and receive either H^2 or L, and α^H-types will not observe β and bear adverse selection costs by receiving H instead of H^*. The α^H-types would be indifferent between remaining uninformed and receiving H, or observing β and afterwards selecting either H^2 or H, since

$$P(\beta^2|\alpha^H)V(p^2, H^2) + P(\beta^1|\alpha^H)V(p^1, H) = V(p^H, H)$$

given the equality $V(p^2, H^2) = V(p^2, H)$ implied by incentive compatibility. Moreover, it follows that α^H-types would strictly prefer to observe β and afterwards select H^2

[10] For example, the expected utility of α^L-types is given by $P(\beta^2 | \alpha^L)V(p^2, H^2) + P(\beta^1 | \alpha^L)V(p^1, A)$, where the allocation H^2 is depicted in Figure 9 below. Using the self-selection condition $V(p^2, H^2) = V(p^2, A)$, we can rewrite this expression as $P(\beta^2 | \alpha^L)V(p^2, A) + P(\beta^1 | \alpha^L)V(p^1, A)$, which is equal to $V(p^L, A)$. Thus, the pair (H^2, A) provides α^L-types the same expected utility they enjoy at A.

[11] These profits could then be rebated to the consumers through lower premiums, so that they would be made strictly better off in the post β-experiment regime.

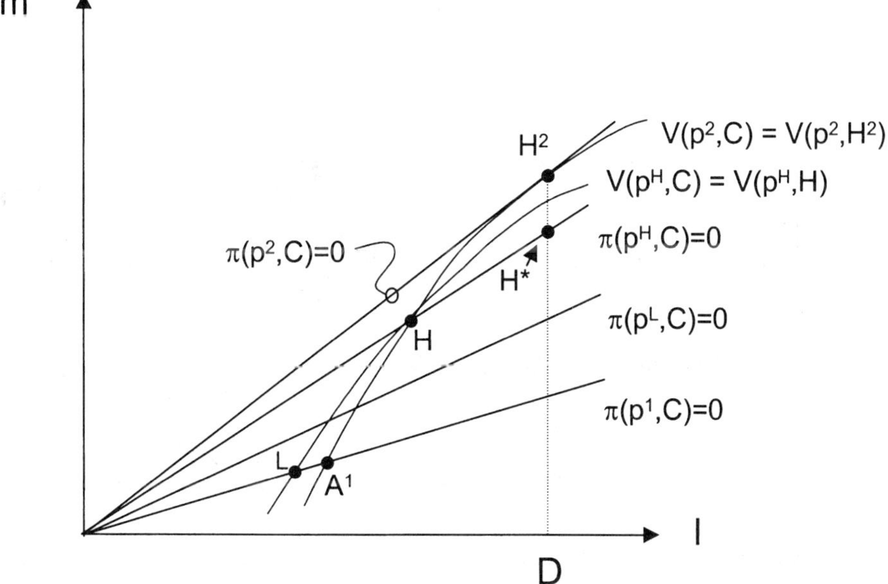

Figure 9

or A^1, even though they may be worse off than they would have been receiving H^*, which is rendered unattainable once α^L-types have private access to experiment β. Thus, once the α^L-types become informed, it is in the best interests of α^H-types to do so as well.

Second, note that α^L-types will demand the β-experiment even if their gains are negligible and are more than offset by the harm imposed on α^H-types, so that the social value of the β-experiment is negative. To demonstrate this result, refer to Figure 10 which illustrates a "knife-edge" case where α^L-types are just indifferent to acquiring additional hidden knowledge.[12] The α^H-types, however, are necessarily worse off, since

$$V(p^H, H^*) > V(p^H, A^1) = P(\beta^2|\alpha^H)V(p^2, H^2) + P(\beta^1|\alpha^H)V(p^1, A^1),$$

where the equality follows from the self-selection condition $V(p^2, H^2) = V(p^2, A^1)$. If α^L-types were to experience a small expected gain from acquiring additional hidden knowledge, they would demand access to the β-experiment even though this information would be detrimental to efficiency in insurance contracting. In such an

[12] By construction in Figure 10, the α^L-types are indifferent between A, and observing the β-experiment followed by a selection of H^2 or A^1.

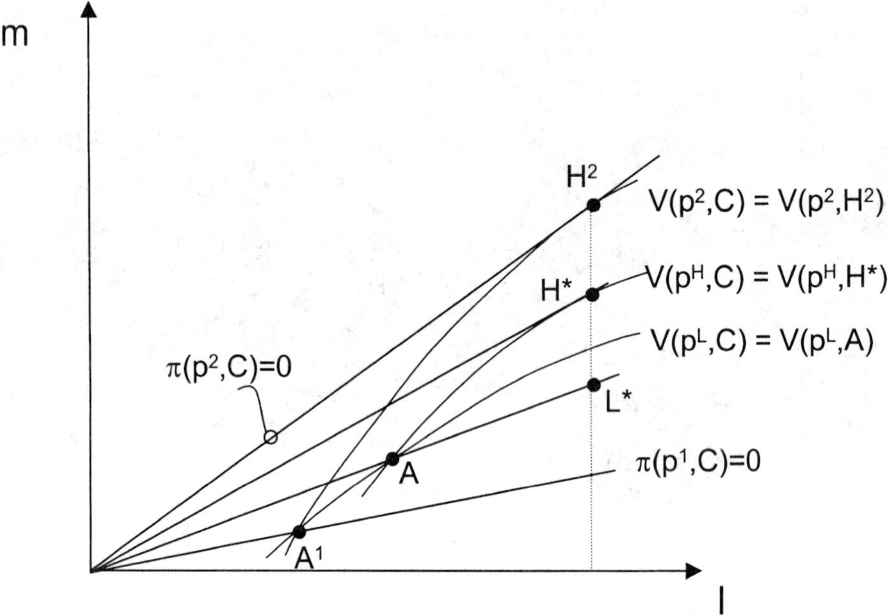

Figure 10

environment, private incentives for information gathering do not reflect its social value. The problem is that the acquisition of private information by some consumers generates an uncompensated externality for others through its effect on the incentive constraints.

8.4.4 Acquisition of Public Information

In this section we examine incentives for gathering public information. We continue to assume that all consumers initially possess hidden knowledge, having privately observed the outcome of experiment α. Outcomes of the second experiment β, however, are now observed publicly.

Let us first consider the case in which the β-experiment reveals to insurers, but not to consumers, information about the latter's underlying loss probability. A special case of this environment is considered by Crocker and Snow (1986), where the consumer has already observed the outcome of the α-experiment (α^H or α^L) which is fully informative of the individual's underlying probability of loss, and in which the β-experiment consists of observing consumer traits, such as gender, that are imperfectly correlated with the private information held by insurance applicants. The β-experiment provides no information to consumers, who already know their types, but

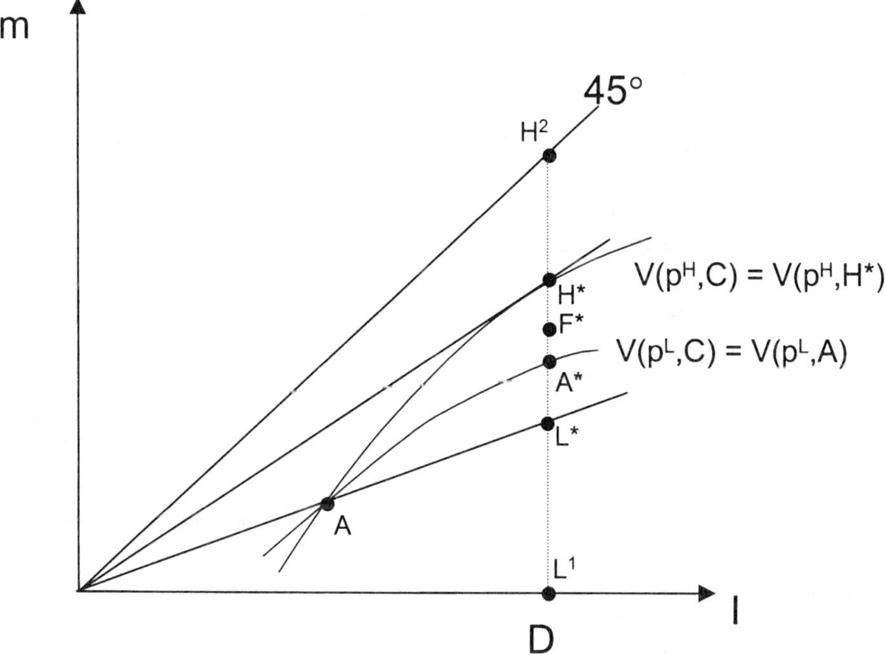

Figure 11

is informative to the informationally constrained insurers. As discussed earlier in section 8.3, this type of categorization, in which the outcome of the β-experiment is publicly observable, enhances efficiency when consumers know *a priori* the outcomes that they will observe for the β-experiment (i.e., their gender). Specifically, a consumer of either β type is at least as well off with categorization based upon β as without it.

Since the β-experiment is not informative for consumers concerning their loss propensities, and does not in any other way influence their preferences, the set of feasible contracts does not depend on whether consumers have prior knowledge of β. Moreover, because each consumer, regardless of β type, is at least as well off with categorization, each consumer must expect to be at least as well off when the outcome of the β-experiment is not privately known ex ante. Thus, it is efficient for insurers to categorize applicants on the basis of a publicly observed experiment that is informative for insurers but not for insurance applicants.

The analysis is somewhat different when the β-experiment reveals to consumers information about their underlying loss propensities. In this instance, public information could have a negative social value. As an example, Figure 11 illustrates the extreme situation in which the underlying probability $p^1 = 0$ or $p^2 = 1$ is perfectly revealed by the outcome of the experiment β. Pooling contracts based on β that provide

H^* to those revealed to have incurred the loss and A^* to everyone else would allow consumers to attain the same expected utility levels they would realize in the absence of experiment β, when they self-select either H^* or A. Whenever the pair (H^*, A^*) at least breaks even collectively, experiment β has positive social value. It follows that β is socially valuable if and only if the first-best pooling contract lies below the point $F^* \equiv \lambda H^* + (1 - \lambda)A^*$ in Figure 11. In that event, those consumers revealed to have incurred the loss can be fully compensated by redistributing some of the gains realized by those who have not incurred the loss, permitting attainment of an allocation Pareto superior to (H^*, A).

When the first-best pooling contract lies above F^*, no redistribution of the gains can fully compensate those revealed to have incurred the loss. In these instances, public information has a negative social value. No insurable risk remains after the public information is revealed, hence its social value is determined by the stronger of two opposing effects, the efficiency gains realized by eliminating adverse selection and the costs of classification risk.[13]

As in the case of hidden information, private incentives for gathering public information may not accord with its social value when consumers initially possess hidden knowledge. In the example depicted in Figure 11, the market outcome (H^2, L^1) that occurs when public information is available prior to contracting provides an expected utility equal to the expected utility of the endowment, which is always below the expected utility realized by α^L-types at A and α^H-types at H^*. It follows that, in the present context, the costs of risk classification always discourage the gathering of public information whether or not that information would enhance efficiency.

In contrast with the symmetric information environment, in which public information used to classify consumers has negative social value, when consumers initially possess hidden knowledge, public information can have a positive social value. In the symmetric information environment, the use of public information imposes classification risk on consumers with no countervailing gains in contractual efficiency. However, in markets with asymmetric information, risk classification reduces adverse selection inefficiencies, and these gains may outweigh the costs of classification risk.

8.5 COMPETITIVE MARKET EQUILIBRIUM AND EXTENSIONS OF THE BASIC MODEL

Although we have emphasized efficiency possibilities in a stylized model of risk classification by insurers, our discussion has practical implications insofar as no crit-

[13] The result of Crocker and Snow (1992) showing that public information always has positive social value applies in a linear signaling environment with risk neutral consumers, so the classification risk has no social cost.

ical aspect of insurance contracting is omitted from the model that would have a qualitative effect on efficiency possibilities, and unregulated markets for insurance exploit potential efficiency gains. In this section, we address the issue of market equilibrium and the implications of several innovations of the model to account for additional features relevant to insurance contracting.

8.5.1 Competitive Market Equilibrium

As shown by Hoy's (1982) original analysis of risk categorization based on immutable characteristics, predictions concerning the performance of an unregulated, competitive insurance market depend on the equilibrium concept employed to account for the presence of asymmetric information. Although the appropriate equilibrium concept remains an unsettled issue, empirical evidence reported by Puelz and Snow (1994) is consistent with theories that predict the separating Rothschild and Stiglitz allocation (i.e., the pure Nash strategy equilibrium suggested by Rothschild and Stiglitz (1976), the non-Nash reactive equilibrium proposed by Riley (1979) in which insurers anticipate profitable competing entrants, or the take-it-or-leave-it three-stage game analyzed by Cho and Kreps (1987) in which the informed insurance applicants move first), rather than those predicting either a pooling allocation (which can occur in the non-Nash anticipatory equilibrium suggested by Wilson (1977) in which the exit of unprofitable contracts is anticipated, the dissembling equilibrium advanced by Grossman (1979), or the three-stage game analyzed by Hellwig (1987) in which the uninformed insurers move first) or separation with all risk types paying the same constant price per dollar of coverage (as in the linear-pricing equilibrium suggested by Arrow (1970) and analyzed by Pauly (1974) and Schmalensee (1984)).

The evidence reported by Puelz and Snow, however, is also inconsistent with the presence of cross-subsidization between types, first analyzed by Miyazaki (1979) in labor market context, and cross-subsidization is necessary for second-best efficiency in the stylized model unless high-risk types are sufficiently prevalent, as shown by Crocker and Snow (1985a). Moreover, if competition always leads to the Rothschild and Stiglitz allocation, then the model predicts that the market fails to exploit efficiency gains available through risk categorization based on immutable traits, since all categories have the same risk types represented, so that customers in every category would choose from the same menu consisting of the Rothschild and Stiglitz contracts.

Bond and Crocker (1991) have shown that categorization based on the observed consumption of a product that is correlated with underlying risk alleviates and, in some instances, can eliminate the problem of adverse selection. If endogenous risk classification is imperfect, then further categorization based on immutable traits may be exploited by an unregulated market even in the absence of cross-subsidization when different categories have different risk types represented as a result of the insurer's simultaneous risk classification based on behavior by the insured that influences the risk of loss. This possibility has yet to be explored, but may explain the statistical significance found by Puelz and Snow for both correlative products (e.g., type of vehicle and coverage of other risks) and immutable traits (e.g., age and gender) in the pricing of insurance contracts.

Our discussion of incentives for information gathering reveals that, when categorization is informative for insurance applicants, incentive compatibility constraints are irreversibly altered, and the social value of this type of information could therefore be positive or negative depending on parameters of the environment. As our analysis shows, private incentives for information gathering may not be consistent with efficiency. In unregulated markets, public information or additional hidden knowledge may be acquired when it has negative social value, but go unexploited when it has positive social value.

8.5.2 Extensions of the Model

We have abstracted from a number of considerations that may be of practical relevance to insurance contracting. Here we shall take note of three which appear to be particularly relevant to risk classification.

8.5.2.1 Multiple Periods

Categorization of risks through experience rating is a common practice in insurance contracting, which we have ignored in this review by analyzing an atemporal model. The analysis of Cooper and Hayes (1987) reveals the critical factors that influence contracting with asymmetric information in temporal contexts. For an environment with adverse selection, (costless) experience rating has positive social value if and only if experience is serially correlated with hidden knowledge, as when risk of loss is hidden knowledge and unchanging over time.

The overriding factor determining whether unregulated, competitive markets exploit the efficiency gains of experience rating is the ability of insurers and insurance customers to commit credibly to long-term contracts. If they can, and the market attains the pure strategy Nash equilibrium, then high-risk types receive full and fair insurance, while the coverage and premium for low-risks types is adjusted in the second period based on experience in the first. However, if insurance customers cannot credibly commit to a two-period contract, then experience rating is less valuable as a sorting device, and when renegotiation is introduced, the separating equilibrium degenerates to replications of the single-period equilibrium, as shown by Dionne and Doherty (1994). Hosios and Peters (1989) showed that accident underreporting is possible with no commitment, further limiting the market's ability to exploit efficiency gains available through experience rating.

8.5.2.2 Moral Hazard

We have abstracted from moral hazard as a source of informational asymmetry, focusing exclusively on adverse selection. In many insurance markets, however, both informational asymmetries influence contracting possibilities and, as shown by Cromb (1990), the pure strategy Nash equilibrium can be strongly affected by the presence of an unobservable action taken by the insured that influences the risk of loss. In some instances, moral hazard eliminates the adverse selection problem, and thereby eliminates any social value to risk categorization. In other instances, moral hazard constitutes a new source of nonexistence of a pure strategy Nash equilibrium, and the social value of risk categorization may be enhanced if risk types can be grouped in categories for which the Nash equilibrium exists.

8.5.2.3 Risk Preferences

In the stylized model, all insurance applicants have the same preferences for risk bearing, giving rise to a single crossing of indifference curves for applicants of different risk type. In practice, the willingness to bear risk differs among consumers and is also not directly observable by insurers. Smart (1996), analyzing a partial equilibrium model of insurance contracting, shows that incentive compatibility constraints and the market equilibrium can be fundamentally altered when risk preferences as well as risk type are hidden knowledge, since indifference curves of different risk types may cross twice because of differences in the willingness to bear risk.

In some instances, the qualitative properties of the incentive constraints and the pure strategy Nash equilibrium are not affected, but when differences in risk aversion are sufficiently great, a pure strategy Nash equilibrium does not exist, although a non-Nash, reactive equilibrium does exist and entails pooling of different risk types at a contract offering partial coverage that earns a strictly positive profit. For environments in which insurers cannot by regulation or market conditions earn economic rents, the nature of equilibrium remains an open question. In these instances, categorization based on observable traits, either immutable or endogenous, that are correlated with willingness to bear risk may provide insurers with information that reduces the variation in risk aversion within categories sufficiently to create marketable insurance contracts.

8.6 SUMMARY AND CONCLUSIONS

In insurance markets with symmetric information, opportunities for risk pooling can be fully exploited so that perfectly competitive market outcomes are first-best efficient, and consumers are charged actuarially fair premia for insurance coverage. In such markets, information and attendant risk classification have negative social value, even when the information is public, because of the classification risk that must be borne by consumers.

For insurance markets with asymmetric information, risk classification enhances efficiency possibilities. Whether effected through self-selection by insurance applicants possessing hidden knowledge of riskiness (signaling by choice of deductible) or through *a priori* categorization by insurers based on observable traits or behaviors correlated with riskiness (gender, age, race, smoking, or driving sporty cars), risk classification provides insurers with information that relaxes the incentive compatibility constraints and mitigates adverse selection inefficiency.

The unambiguous social benefit of permitting insurers to categorize applicants based upon observable characteristics (such as gender, age or race) that are imperfectly correlated with underlying loss probabilities depends crucially on the assumption that such classification is informative to insurers, but not to their customers. When applicants are fully informed of their underlying loss probabilities, the use of risk classification by insurers expands, and in no way diminishes, the set of feasible (incentive compatible) insurance contracts. Put differently, the pre-categorization insurance contracts are always feasible in the post-categorization regime. It is the nesting of the regimes that guarantees the efficiency of categorical discrimination.

In contrast, when consumers obtain information about their underlying loss probabilities from the classification procedure (such as in the case of a genetic test), the act of categorization immutably and irreversibly alters the feasible set of insurance contracts. The insurance possibilities that were feasible prior to the classification procedure are precluded by the consumers' changed information sets, which alters the incentive constraints faced by the social planner when designing optimal insurance contracts. Since the pre- and post-categorization regimes are not nested when consumers are informed by the classification procedure, such classification has ambiguous social value.

The adverse equity consequences of risk classification are of special concern to policy analysts when information reveals that some consumers are, in fact, uninsurable. As emphasized by Hoy (1989), these concerns are compounded when action could be taken to diminish the severity of loss, but consumers are discouraged from gathering information and taking such action. We have shown that in markets with either symmetric or asymmetric information, private incentives for initially acquiring hidden knowledge accurately reflect its social value. However, in markets with asymmetric information, private incentives for gathering either public information or additional hidden knowledge are not necessarily consistent with the goal of efficiency in insurance contracting.

The adverse equity consequences of risk classification are precisely the effects that underlie the costs of classification risk. Although we have emphasized these costs as the factor responsible for discouraging consumers from gathering information that has positive social value, we may also observe that these costs appropriately discourage the gathering of information that has negative social value.

8.7 REFERENCES

Arrow, Kenneth J. (1970). "Political and Economic Evaluation of Social Effects and Externalities," in *The Analysis of Public Output*, Julius Margolis, ed. New York: Columbia University Press (for NBER).

Bond, Eric W. and Keith J. Crocker. (1991). "Smoking, Skydiving and Knitting: The Endogenous Categorization of Risks in Insurance Markets with Asymmetric Information," *Journal of Political Economy* 99, 177–200.

Cho, In-Koo. and David M. Kreps. (1987). "Signaling Games and Stable Equilibria," *Quarterly Journal of Economics* 102, 179–221.

Cooper, Russell and Beth Hayes. (1987). "Multi-period Insurance Contracts," *International Journal of Industrial Organization* 5, 211–231.

Crocker, Keith J. and Arthur Snow. (1985a). "The Efficiency of Competitive Equilibria in Insurance Markets with Asymmetric Information," *Journal of Public Economics* 26, 201–219.

Crocker, Keith J. and Arthur Snow. (1985b). "A Simple Tax Structure for Competitive Equilibrium and Redistribution in Insurance Markets with Asymmetric Information," *Southern Economic Journal* 51, 1142–1150.

Crocker, Keith J. and Arthur Snow. (1986). "The Efficiency Effects of Categorical Discrimination in the Insurance Industry," *Journal of Political Economy* 94, 321–344.

Crocker, Keith J. and Arthur Snow. (1992). "The Social Value of Hidden Information in Adverse Selection Economies," *Journal of Public Economics* 48, 317–347.

Cromb, I.J. (1990). "Competitive Insurance Markets Characterized by Asymmetric Information," Ph.D. thesis, Queens University.

Dionne, Georges and Neil A. Doherty. (1994). "Adverse Selection, Commitment and Renegotiation with Application to Insurance Markets," *Journal of Political Economy*, 102, 209–235.

Dionne, Georges and Nathalie Fombaron, (1996). "Non-convexities and The Efficiency of Equilibria in Insurance Markets with Asymmetric Information," *Economics Letters* 52, 31–40.

Doherty, Neil A. and Lisa Posey. (1998). "On the Value of a Checkup: Adverse Selection, Moral Hazard and the Value of Information," *Journal of Risk and Insurance* 65, 189–212.

Doherty, Neil A. and Paul D. Thistle. (1996). "Adverse Selection with Endogenous Information in Insurance Markets," *Journal of Public Economics* 63, 83–102.

Dreze, Jacques H. (1960). "Le paradoxe de l'information," *Economie Appliquee* 13, 71–80; reprinted in *Essays on Economic Decisions Under Uncertainty*, Cambridge University Press: New York (1987).

Grossman, Herschel I. (1979). "Adverse Selection, Dissembling, and Competitive Equilibrium". *Bell Journal of Economics* 10, 336–343.

Harris, Milton and Robert M. Townsend. (1981). "Resource Allocation under Asymmetric Information," *Econometrica* 49, 33–64.

Hellwig, Martin (1987). "Some Recent Developments in the Theory of Competition in Markets with Adverse Selection," *European Economic Review* 31, 391–325.

Hirshleifer, Jack. (1971). "The Private and Social Value of Information and the Reward to Inventive Activity," *American Economic Review* 61, 561–574.

Hosios, Arthur J. and Michael Peters. (1989). "Repeated Insurance Contracts with Adverse Selection and Limited Commitment," *Quarterly Journal of Economics* 104, 229–253.

Hoy, Michael. (1982). "Categorizing Risks in the Insurance Industry," *Quarterly Journal of Economics* 97, 321–336.

Hoy, Michael. (1989). "The Value of Screening Mechanisms under Alternative Insurance Possibilities," *Journal of Public Economics* 39, 177–206.

Milgrom, Paul and Nancy Stokey. (1982). "Information, Trade and Common Knowledge," *Journal of Economic Theory* 26, 17–27.

Miyazaki, Hajime. (1977). "The Rat Race and Internal Labor Markets," *The Bell Journal of Economics* 8, 394–418.

Myerson, Roger B. (1979). "Incentive Compatibility and the Bargaining Problem," *Econometrica* 47, 61–73.

Pauly, Mark V. (1974). "Overinsurance and Public Provision of Insurance: The Roles of Moral Hazard and Adverse Selection". *Quarterly Journal of Economics* 88, 44–62.

Puelz, Robert and Arthur Snow. (1994). "Evidence on Adverse Selection: Equilibrium Signaling and Cross-Subsidization in the Insurance Market," *Journal of Political Economy* 102, 236–257.

Riley, John G. (1979). "Informational Equilibrium," *Econometrica* 47, 331–359.

Rothschild, Michael and Joseph E. Stiglitz. (1976). "Equilibrium in Competitive Insurance Markets: An Essay on the Economics of Imperfect Information," *Quarterly Journal of Economics* 90, 630–649.

Samuelson, Paul A. (1950). "Evaluation of Real National Income," *Oxford Economic Papers* N.S. 2, 1–29.

Schmalensee, Richard. (1984). "Imperfect Information and the Equitability of Competitive Prices". *Quarterly Journal of Economics* 99, 441–460.

Smart, Michael. (1996). "Competitive Insurance Markets with Two Unobservables," *Working Paper UT-ECIPA-msmart-96-01*, Department of Economics, University of Toronto.

Tabarrok, Alexander. (1994). "Genetic Testing: An Economic and Contractarian Analysis," *Journal of Health Economics* 13, 75–91.

Wilson, Charles A. (1977). "A Model of Insurance Markets with Incomplete Information," *Journal of Economic Theory* 16, 167–207.

9 The Economics of Liability Insurance

Scott E. Harrington
University of South Carolina

Patricia M. Danzon
University of Pennsylvania

Abstract
Emphasizing general liability insurance, we describe basic relationships between legal liability law, liability insurance, and loss control, including the practical limitations of liability rules and insurance markets as mechanisms for promoting efficient deterrence and risk-spreading. After a brief introduction to the role of liability rules in providing incentives for loss control, we consider the implications of limited wealth and limited liability for the demand for liability insurance and accident deterrence. We then discuss the effects of correlated risk on liability insurance markets, the nature and causes of liability insurance contract disputes, causes of the U.S. tort liability / liability insurance crisis in the mid 1980s, and efficiency of the U.S. tort liability / liability insurance system.

Keywords: liability insurance, tort liability, deterrence, limited liability.
JEL Classification Numbers: G22, K13.

9.1 INTRODUCTION

The demand for and supply of liability insurance arise from the legal liability of individuals and businesses for bodily injury, property damage, and financial losses caused to third parties, as distinct from first-party insurance which covers losses suffered directly by the policyholder. Private passenger auto liability insurance is by far the largest liability-related line of business in terms of premium volume in the United States (see Figure 1). However, the lines that have grown most rapidly and often attracted the most attention in recent years are workers' compensation insurance and commercial general liability (GL) insurance, which includes product liability,

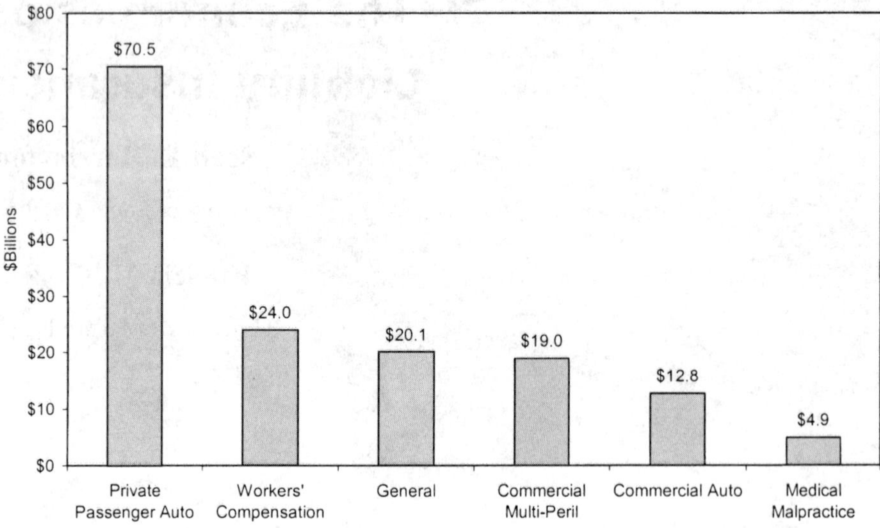

Figure 1 U.S. Liability Insurance Net Premiums Written in 1997

directors and officers liability, environmental liability, professional liability, municipal liability and related coverages.[1] In particular, the mid-1980s commercial liability insurance "crisis" received widespread attention, influenced tort liability reforms in many states, and motivated substantial academic work on liability insurance price dynamics.

This chapter provides an overview of the economics of liability insurance. Particular attention is given to basic relationships between legal liability law, liability insurance, and loss control, and general liability insurance is emphasized.[2] There is a large law and economics literature on tort liability that is at least indirectly related to liability insurance. Our approach is necessarily selective (and no doubt influenced by our perspective and prior work). The objective is to introduce key elements of the literature that deal directly with liability insurance and/or are most relevant to liability insurance. We include discussion of the inherent tension between the theory of efficient liability rules and the practical limitations of liability rules and liability insurance markets as mechanisms for promoting efficient deterrence and risk-spreading.

Section 9.2 sets the context by introducing basic theory on the role of liability

[1] Much of the exposure to liability losses in these areas is self-insured and thus is not reflected in premium volume. Commercial multi-peril coverage (Figure 1) also includes coverage for many general liability hazards. General liability insurance often is called "other liability" insurance; this term is used in insurance company annual statements filed with regulators. We use the term general liability throughout.

[2] Other chapters in this volume consider auto liability and workers' compensation. See Danzon and Harrington (1992) for our earlier introduction to the liability insurance literature.

rules in providing incentives for loss control. Section 9.3 considers the implications of limited wealth and limited liability for the demand for liability insurance and deterrence of harm through the tort liability system. Sections 9.4 and 9.5 discuss the problems of correlated risk in liability insurance markets and liability insurance contract disputes. Section 9.6 discusses the causes of the U.S. tort liability / liability insurance crisis in the mid 1980s. Some of the main issues in the debate over the efficiency of the U.S. tort liability / liability insurance system are briefly reviewed in Section 9.7. Section 9.8 contains concluding observations.

9.2 LEGAL LIABILITY, DETERRENCE, AND INSURANCE

9.2.1 Efficient Deterrence

Overview

Since the pioneering work by Coase (1960), Calabresi (1970) and Posner (1972, 1973), the burgeoning field of law and economics has applied standard tools of positive and normative economics to analyze to the structure of common law, including the law of tort liability. This analysis has shown that, given certain restrictive assumptions, liability rules can be designed to achieve a Pareto optimal allocation of resources to risk reduction in contexts where market forces alone would fail because of imperfect information or transactions costs. This extensive literature on optimal liability rules is only briefly introduced here to provide a framework for understanding key issues related to liability insurance.[3] This sub-section focuses on the role of liability rules in providing incentives to control risky activities and prevent losses in the absence of limited wealth and limited liability.

Accidents involving third parties can arise in many circumstances, including the use of automobiles and other consumer products, the use of professional services such as medical care, and exposure to workplace and environmental hazards. The production of safety (risk reduction or loss control) can be modeled either in a standard production framework (Brown, 1973) or as a joint product or spillover associated with other beneficial activities (Williamson et al., 1967; Shavell, 1980; Polinsky, 1980). Formally, the activity of one party, the "injurer," can result in risk of injury to another party, the "victim." The probability or size of loss may depend on the both the level of the activity and the amount of care per unit of activity exercised by the injurer (unilateral accidents), and possibly also on activity level and care per unit taken by the victim (bilateral accidents).

For bilateral accidents where both injurers and victims choose levels of care and activity levels, the social optimum is defined as the solution to the problem of maxi-

[3] For reviews of this literature, see Polinsky (1983), Posner (1998), Shavell (1987), Landes and Posner (1987), Cooter and Ulen (1999) and references cited therein. Also see Miceli (1997).

mizing the sum of injurers' and victims' utilities from engaging in their activities, net of their costs of care and expected accident losses (using the notation in Shavell, 1987, pp. 43–44):

$$\text{Max}[u(s) - sx] + [v(t) - ty - stl(x, y)]$$

where

s = injurer's activity level,
$u(s)$ = injurer's gross dollar benefits from the activity,
t = victim's activity level,
$v(t)$ = victim's gross dollar benefits from the activity,
x = injurer's level of care, measured in unit costs,
y = victim's level of care, measured in unit costs, and
stl(x, y) = expected accident losses.[4]

The optimal values x^*, y^*, s^*, and t^* are defined by the first order conditions

$tl_x(x, y) = -1$
$sl_y(x, y) = -1$
$u'(s) = x + tl(x, y)$
$v'(t) = y + sl(x, y)$

These conditions imply that the marginal cost of care must equal the marginal benefit in terms of reduction in expected accident costs, and that the marginal utility of increasing activity must equal the sum of the marginal cost of taking optimal care and the increase in expected accident costs.

The standard results of the Coase theorem apply. Optimal investment in all dimensions of risk reduction will be achieved, regardless of the liability rule, if both parties are informed about the risks and if negotiation is costless. An important corollary is that if risks are obvious and if the parties are in an ongoing contractual relation, as employer/employee or producer/consumer, then market prices will reflect the potential victim's demand for safety and induce optimal levels of safety. Market contracts will also generate an optimal allocation of risk between the parties and optimal levels of compensation in the event of injury.[5]

In the case of accidents involving strangers, transaction costs may prevent the achievement of a first best solution by voluntary contract. And even in buyer-seller

[4] Since the product of st and $l(x, y)$ is defined as expected losses, the model implicitly allows for losses to be of differing severity.

[5] For formal models and empirical estimates of the wage premium for risk-bearing in risky employments, and use of such estimates to infer a willingness-to-pay for safety or "value of life", see, e.g., Viscusi (1983) and Viscusi and Moore (1987).

situations where contracting costs are low, Spence (1977) shows that if consumers misperceive risk, producers have non-optimal incentives for care and consumers will be non-optimally insured. Liability rules are one among several possible policy tools for achieving efficient levels of loss control and risk allocation where voluntary contracting in private markets fails. Regulatory standard setting, taxes and subsidies, fines and injunctions are other possible corrective policies. Among other dimensions, liability rules differ from regulatory standard setting in that they do not proscribe a specific course of action ex ante. Rather, liability rules define general conditions for allocating the cost of accidents and determining the amount of damages payable.[6]

Negligence and Strict Liability

The two benchmark liability rules are negligence and strict liability. Under a negligence rule, the injurer is liable only if he or she failed to take "due care" and this failure was the "cause" of injury to the victim. Under a simple strict liability rule, the injurer is liable if his activities caused an injury to the victim, regardless of the injurer's level of care. In the United States, negligence is the prevailing rule for personal and professional liability (including medical malpractice) and for automobile injuries, except in states that have explicitly adopted automobile insurance no-fault statutes that limit tort liability for minor injuries. Strict liability is exemplified by workers' compensation statutes whereby employers are absolutely liable for statutory benefits for work-related injuries, regardless of their own or employee negligence. For product-related injuries, manufacturers can be sued under theories of negligence and strict liability, but liability is strict only for injuries caused by *defective* products.[7] Important variants of these benchmark rules are the application of a contributory negligence defense (which shifts liability to the victim if he or she failed to take due care, regardless of the defendant's care), and comparative negligence, whereby damages are apportioned between the parties in proportion to their degree of negligence.

Brown (1973) first formally modeled the effects of these alternative liability rules on levels of care. He assumed noncooperative (Nash) behavior in a context of bilateral accidents with level of care the only determinant of risk; risk neutrality of both parties; costless administration; and perfect information, in the sense that courts know the level of care actually taken and the parties know safety production functions and the due standard of care. Under these assumptions, three liability rules are potentially efficient: negligence, with or without a contributory negligence defense, and strict liability with a contributory negligence defense. Strict (no) liability is potentially efficient only in the context of unilateral accidents where victim (defendant) care is

[6] See Shavell (1984) for comparison of tort liability and safety regulation as methods to promote loss control.

[7] This notion of product defect reintroduces an issue of reasonable care, defined by some weighing of risks and benefits of additional care, analogous to a due care standard under a negligence rule. Thus strict liability for products is not absolute liability in the sense of the simple theoretical models.

irrelevant. Haddock and Curran (1985), Cooter and Ulen (1987) and Rubinfeld (1987) show that it is possible to define an efficient comparative negligence rule.[8]

Shavell (1980) generalized Brown's model to allow both levels of activity and levels of care as determinants of risk. The conclusions now depend critically on the potential victim's information about accident risk. If average risk is misperceived, no liability rule is fully efficient. If victims know at least the average risk, a negligence rule is potentially efficient provided that the formulation of the due care standard includes both the level of care and the level of risky activities (see also Polinsky, 1980). More generally, the due care standard must include all relevant dimensions of precautions in order to achieve optimal investment in all dimensions of safety.

Damages

Tort awards simultaneously provide deterrence to injurers and compensation to victims. Viewing tort liability as a system of (conditional) compulsory insurance (Oi, 1973; Danzon, 1984b), it is unique among systems of social and private insurance in that the amount of compensation is determined after the injury. Compensation is usually by settlement but with ultimate recourse to a jury trial without contractual or statutory limits, and is intended to provide full compensation of pecuniary and non-pecuniary loss. This reflects the dual function of tort awards, as compensation to victims and penalties to defendants.

A single award is optimal for both deterrence and compensation only in a restricted set of circumstances. If the victim suffers only a monetary loss (utility is not state-dependent) and if the injurer is either risk neutral or can fully insure at actuarial rates, an award equal to the loss simultaneously provides optimal insurance to the victim and optimal deterrence to the injurer. When the victim suffers a non-pecuniary loss (utility is state dependent), optimal compensation still requires the equalization of the marginal utility of wealth in the two states of the world. However, the size of award necessary to achieve this result depends on whether the injury raises or lowers the marginal utility of wealth (Cook and Graham, 1977). Thus, the optimal compensatory award generally is no longer identical to the optimal deterrence penalty on the injurer. Spence (1977) shows that a first best result requires supplementing compensatory awards with a system of fines, paid initially to the state and refunded as subsidies to the risky activity. Danzon (1985a) shows that the optimal compensatory award to the victim is inversely related to the load on the defendant's liability insurance.[9] Rea (1981) demonstrates that lump sum awards are

[8] Cooter and Ulen (1987) argue that a comparative negligence rule is superior to a negligence rule when injurers and victims bear risk and there is evidentiary uncertainty. Rubinfeld (1987) reinforces this conclusion when injurers and victims are heterogeneous.

[9] These conclusions follow from the standard assumption that the optimal damage award is chosen to maximize the utility of the victim, subject to a reservation level of utility for the defendant. Thus by assumption the incidence of costs of liability is on victims. This is reasonable assuming a perfectly elastic long-run supply of the products or services that are subject to strict liability. But with imperfectly elastic supply in the short run, the incidence of unanticipated changes in liability costs is partly on defendants (Danzon, 1990).

more efficient than periodic payments contingent on losses actually incurred. Contingent periodic payment overinsures the victim and encourages ex post moral hazard.[10]

9.2.2 Liability Insurance, Moral Hazard, and Experience Rating

Risk Neutrality / Actuarially Fair Premiums and No Judgement Proof Problem

Early models of the effects of liability on levels of activity and care ignore the role of liability in allocating risk by assuming that losses are purely financial and either risk neutrality or actuarially fair insurance. They also ignore the judgement proof problem that arises when the potential injurer's liability for harm is bounded by the party's wealth and the doctrine of limited liability. Shavell (1982) formally examined the demand for liability insurance, introducing risk aversion of victims and injurers and the availability of first-party and liability insurance into a model of unilateral accidents with pecuniary losses only.[11] A first best solution now requires (a) a level of care that minimizes expected accident losses plus the cost of care, and (b) an optimal allocation of risk for both parties.[12] The demand for liability insurance and its effect on social welfare depend critically on the information available to courts and to insurers.

With perfect information and a negligence rule with the standard of care optimally defined and perfectly implemented, there is no demand for liability insurance. It is cheaper for defendants to be non-negligent than to be negligent and insure against the resulting liability. Since defendants are not liable, they bear no risk.[13] Under strict liability, if injurers are risk averse and liability insurance is not available, a first best outcome is not attainable as long as optimal risk-spreading requires setting damage awards at less than full compensation. Both victims and injurers bear risk. Injurers may take excessive care or engage suboptimally in risky activities. When liability insurance is available and insurers can observe defendant care (perfect experience rating), injurers can be fully protected against risk while preserving optimal incentives for care, and optimal damage awards provide full compensation to victims. Thus

[10] Noncontingent periodic payment of awards, where the amount is determined at time of trial or settlement (also called "structured settlements") are potentially more efficient than lump sum awards if the defendant is permitted to provide for the payment of these future damages by the purchase of an annuity or other financial instrument. This transfers from the jury to financial markets the issue of determining expected rates of inflation and interest (Danzon, 1984). Perhaps more important, structured settlements may reduce income tax costs.

[11] Corporate demand for liability insurance may be explained by risk aversion of customers, suppliers, managers, or employees, or by other factors, such as indirect losses, that cause firm value to be a concave function of firm cash flows (Mayers and Smith, 1982; Froot et al., 1993).

[12] Formally, the problem is to maximize expected utility of the victim, subject to constraints of (a) a reservation utility level for the defendant, (b) an overall resource constraint, (c) victims and injurers choose first-party and liability insurance to maximize their respective utilities, and (d) insurers break even. If insurance is not available, then the choice between liability rules depends on which party is better able to bear risk. In particular, strict liability is preferable to negligence if injurers are risk neutral or better able to bear risk.

[13] A first best outcome is achieved only if victims can eliminate risk by buying actuarially fair first-party insurance.

liability insurance unambiguously improves social welfare and permits a first best solution for level of care and allocation of risk.

With imperfect information, demand for liability insurance under a negligence rule is affected by information available to claimants, courts, and insurers. If victims or courts systematically commit Type 1 errors, failing to seek and award damages, respectively, in all instances of negligence, then with actuarial insurance it is cheaper for defendants to be negligent and to insure against the resulting liability than to always be non-negligent. Conversely, if claimants or courts commit Type 2 errors, making erroneous claims or findings of negligence, then defendants are exposed to a risk akin to strict liability and will demand liability insurance (Shavell, 1982, 1987; Danzon, 1985a). Even if the level of care is correctly defined on average, random errors can generate a demand for liability insurance.[14] If the insured's level of care is observable to the insurer, the optimal contract would exclude coverage if the defendant acted negligently. But obviously if insurers had the information necessary to implement such a policy, the courts could use the information and eliminate the errors that generated the demand for insurance in the first place.

Under strict liability, if insurers cannot observe defendants' care, defendants will choose less than full coverage and the outcome for both level of care and allocation of risk is not first best. Thus, in the single period context moral hazard induced by asymmetric information results in a trade-off between loss prevention and risk-spreading in the context of liability insurance, as for first-party insurance (Shavell, 1979; also see Winter, 1992). But Shavell concludes that even with imperfect experience rating, government intervention in liability insurance markets is not warranted. This assumes that government has no information advantage, damage awards are optimally set, and defendants are not judgement proof (see below).

Efficient Co-Payments

If the probability and size of injury depend only on the defendant's level of care and there is a proportional loading, theorems of optimal first-party insurance imply that optimal co-payment would include a deductible, a co-insurance rate, or both in the single period case. In the multi-period case, the optimal policy is experience rated. When care is not observable, policyholders may prefer a policy that requires insurers to invest in information, rather than levy co-payments automatically for all claims or all paid claims. Paid claims do not convey perfect information about whether negligence occurred even if courts are unbiased because over 90 percent of paid claims are settled out of court. The decision to settle and amount of settlement may be influenced by many factors other than the defendant's level of care and plaintiff's true damages, including the parties' misperceptions of the expected verdict, costs of

[14] Calfee and Craswell (1984) analyze effects of uncertain legal standards on compliance under a negligence regime in the absence of liability insurance.

litigation, risk aversion, concerns over precedent, and other factors.[15] The private and socially optimal policy would attempt to protect the insured from these exogenous risks and relate co-payment only to losses caused by suboptimal care.

When the courts lack perfect information about the defendant's care, the victim's damages, or the injury production function, both parties have incentives to invest in legal effort to influence the outcome.[16] But when both the insurer and the policyholder can affect the magnitude of the settlement, no simple loss sharing contract can simultaneously provide both with optimal marginal incentives. In general, if it is costly for policyholders to monitor the insurer's legal defense effort, the privately optimal co-payment is lower than on first-party coverage with comparable policyholder moral hazard and even lower if defense effort reduces plaintiffs' incentives to file claims (Danzon, 1985a).[17] When claim outcomes depend on legal defense effort, defendants may choose policies with too little co-payment: from a social standpoint, too many resources may be devoted to fighting claims and too few to preventing injuries. Private and social optima diverge unless potential victims are in a contractual relationship with defendants and accurately perceive the nature of the defendant's insurance coverage and its likely effects on claim outcomes—but in that case the liability rule is irrelevant.

Deductibles are common for product liability and professional liability policies for attorneys, accountants, corporate directors and officers, but not for medical malpractice, where rating based on the physician's individual claim record is relatively limited.[18] If more experience rating is statistically feasible than occurs for some forms of liability insurance, such as medical malpractice, this suggests a lack of demand. The apparent lack of co-payment for malpractice, for example, may be deceptive if physicians face significant co-payment in the form of uninsurable time and disutility of being sued, or higher premium costs if they are denied coverage by more selective, lower cost insurers (Danzon, 1985a). To the extent co-payment and experience rating exist, it is usually based on additional information to distinguish Type 2 errors from valid claims, rather than automatic co-payment for all paid claims, consistent with the hypothesis that the risk of judicial "error" contributes to the lack of demand for experience rated policies.[19] Ellis et al. (1988) show that automatic experience rating based

[15] A large literature and often technical literature addresses selection of disputes for litigation and settlement strategy (e.g., Priest and Klein, 1984; Spier, 1994; Siegelman and Waldfogel, 1999). Cooter and Rubenfeld (1989) review early work.

[16] For product liability and medical malpractice, plaintiff and defense legal expenditures each average about one half of the net compensation received by plaintiffs (Danzon, 1985b; Kakalik and Pace, 1987). For the effects of costly litigation on the efficiency of liability rules see, for example, Polinsky and Rubinfeld (1988) and Cooter and Rubinfeld (1989). Also see Sarath (1991).

[17] For example, a deductible undermines the insurer's incentives to fight claims that can be settled for less than the deductible. Incurring legal expense in excess of damages may be a privately optimal strategy if it deters other potential claims.

[18] Several studies have shown that the actual distribution of claims and awards is inconsistent with a purely random distribution, after controlling for specialty (Rolph, 1981; Ellis et al., 1988; Sloan et al., 1989a and b).

[19] Professional liability policies explicitly exclude coverage of intentional acts. The existence of a

on Bayesian conditional means would impose significant risk on physicians and create inequities in premiums across physicians with identical true risks. Thus the lack of experience rating for some types of professional liability insurance may reflect a rational demand for protection against the risk of judicial error and being erroneously rated.

Bundling Defense and Indemnity

The optimal insurance contract under conditions of moral hazard has been extensively studied in the context of first-party insurance (see, e.g., Winter, 1992). For liability insurance against loss caused by the policyholder to a third party, control of moral hazard is more complex. As discussed above, the liability insurance loss depends not only on the policyholder's activity and care, but also on the insurer's defense and the policyholder's cooperation in this defense. Thus, there are both ex ante and ex post moral hazard problems. A distinguishing feature of liability insurance is the nearly universal bundling of indemnity and defense coverage in a single contract: most liability insurance contracts specify the right and duty of the insurer to defend the policyholder and the right of the insurer to control the defense.

The bundling of defense and indemnity in liability insurance contracts reflects three main influences. First, with imperfect information about care and the application of liability rules, potential injurers often face substantial risk associated with legal defense costs. Their total loss exposure reflects the sum of judgements and defense costs. It is hardly surprising that parties that seek coverage for indemnity to third parties also seek coverage for defense. Second, insurers have specialized expertise in defending claims, which favors the purchase of defense services from insurers (e.g., Mayers and Smith, 1982). Third, and as suggested in our earlier discussion of co-payments, bundling indemnity and defense helps provide efficient incentives for minimizing the sum of indemnity and defense costs (see Danzon, 1984b; Cooter and Rubenfeld, 1989; Syverud, 1990). For claims that exceed the deductible and are materially below the policy limit, a liability insurer has a clear incentive to minimize this sum, which generally is consistent with policyholder preferences ex ante.[20] In contrast, separation of the financial responsibility for defense and indemnity would dilute incentives for cost minimization and/or lead to higher monitoring costs.

demand for and supply of coverage for punitive damages in states where this is permitted suggests a significant risk of Type 2 errors, despite the higher standard of proof (gross negligence or willful misconduct) for punitive awards.

[20] Buyers with preferences that are inconsistent with cost minimization may make arrangements with accommodating insurers. Also see MacInnes (1997). Possible incentive conflicts when the likely court award would be near or above the policy limit are discussed briefly below.

9.3 LIMITED LIABILITY, INSURANCE, AND DETERRENCE

9.3.1 Limited Wealth and Limited Coverage

A fundamental factor that distinguishes liability coverage from property insurance is that the harm suffered by the injured party may exceed the assets of the injurer that are available to pay damages in view of limited liability and bankruptcy law.[21] As a result, potential injurers generally will not seek full insurance coverage for liability (see Sinn, 1982; Huberman et al., 1983; Keeton and Kwerel, 1984; Shavell, 1986). As we explain in detail below, limited coverage for potential legal liability can affect levels of risky activity and care. It is first useful, however, to consider the demand for upper limits on liability insurance coverage when activity and care are exogenous.[22]

In an article that often has been overlooked by subsequent work, Sinn (1982) analyzes the demand for liability (and human wealth) insurance when the gross loss can exceed the socially guaranteed minimum level of wealth. Using a simple two-state framework (loss and no loss), he shows that the incentive to buy full coverage for loss increases with the degree of risk aversion and with the amount of wealth in the no-loss state, and decreases with the (exogenous) probability of loss, the severity of loss, and the lower bound on net wealth in the loss state. His analysis of the demand for partial insurance has qualitatively similar implications. Upper limits on coverage are shown to be optimal because beyond some point the expected benefit of additional coverage is smaller than its cost, given that the price of coverage must reflect the cost of paying losses that otherwise would fall on other parties.

Sinn's key result is illustrated in Figure 2. $U(Y)$ is a state-independent von Neumann-Morgenstern utility of wealth function with $U'(Y) > 0$ and $U''(Y) < 0$. The party's wealth in the no-loss state is W. The minimum guaranteed wealth is M. This amount represents the minimum value of real assets, financial assets, and human capital permitted under bankruptcy law. L denotes the harm in the loss state, which arises with probability α.

If M were less than W-L, the amount of harm would be less than the party's net wealth at risk, and the party's net wealth without insurance would either be W-L or W. In this case, the party's expected utility of wealth, $E(U(Y))$, is a linear function of expected wealth, $E(Y)$, and is represented by the chord between the origin and the point (W, $U(W)$). As is well known and following directly from Jensen's inequality, expected utility without insurance is lower than the utility of expected wealth given that U is concave. The party will therefore demand full coverage for the loss if the premium is actuarially fair (i.e., if $P = \alpha L$).

[21] The same general issue arises in the case of medical expense insurance, where the cost of care provided could exceed the assets of the patient or patient's family. Easterbrook and Fischel (1985) provide comprehensive discussion of the rationale for the limited liability doctrine.

[22] Raviv (1979) provides an early treatment of upper limits of coverage that does not consider bounds on wealth net of indemnity for losses.

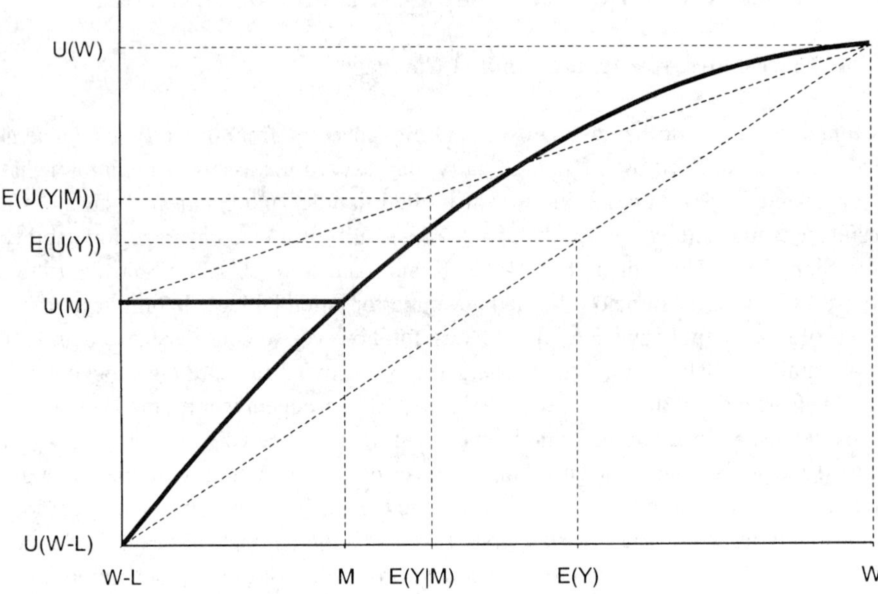

Figure 2 Demand for Liability Insurance with Limited Wealth and Liability

In contrast, when $M > W\text{-}L$, as is shown, the party does not have to pay the full loss if uninsured. Utility of wealth becomes "kinked" due to the lower bound on wealth. Expected wealth without insurance, which we denote $E(Y|M) = \alpha M + (1 - \alpha)W$, obviously increases because of the constraint on minimum wealth. Expected utility without insurance, $E(U(Y|M))$, now falls on the chord between the points (W-L, U(M)) and (W, U(W)). The utility of expected wealth need not exceed expected utility without insurance because utility is no longer uniformly concave. Thus, the utility of wealth with full coverage at actuarially fair rates, $U(E(Y|M))$, need not exceed expected utility without insurance, $E(U(Y|M))$, as is illustrated in Figure 2. This result is more likely, ceteris paribus, when M is large, L is large, and W is small. For sufficiently large (small) α, $U(E(Y|M))$ is less (greater) than $E(U(Y|M))$. Intuitively, the willingness of parties to insure declines when part of the premium is required to finance loss that they would not have to bear if uninsured.[23]

Huberman, Mayers, and Smith (1983) consider the demand for liability insurance with bankruptcy protection, assuming a continuous loss distribution. Like Sinn (1982), they show that bankruptcy protection can lead parties to demand upper limits

[23] To illustrate with a simple example (also see Shavell, 1986), consider a party with \$10,000 of assets at risk who faces a 0.01 probability of causing \$100,000 of harm to others. The party's expected loss without insurance is \$100 (=0.01 × \$10,000); the actuarially fair premium for full liability insurance protection is \$1,000. An unwillingness to insure fully in this case is hardly surprising.

on liability coverage. They illustrate the demand for upper limits assuming exponential utility. Because expected utility is not differentiable with a lower bound on net wealth, they note that the general solution to the assumed maximization problem is "complicated and there is no obvious economic interpretation of the derived restrictions" (p. 418).

The key conclusion that a lower bound on net wealth reduces the demand for liability insurance arises from the resulting convex portion of the constrained utility function. Similar results are implied in the case where corporations are assumed to maximize firm value provided that firm value is a convex function of realized payoffs for sufficiently low realizations. More generally, this result is closely related to the literature on why firm's hedge or insure (e.g., Mayers and Smith, 1982; Stulz, 1985; Froot et al., 1993; also see MacMinn and Han, 1990, and chapter 16 in this volume). Limited assets and lower bounds on wealth due to limited liability / bankruptcy law reduce incentives for firms to hedge risk and buy liability insurance.[24]

9.3.2 The Judgement Proof Problem and Compulsory Liability

If injurers lack sufficient assets to fully satisfy a judgement, incentives to purchase liability insurance are diminished. Incentives to take precautions also may be diluted (Calabresi, 1970; Keeton and Kwerel, 1984; Shavell, 1986; also see Sykes, 1984, 1994; Beard, 1990, and Posey, 1993). Under a negligence rule, if the injurer's wealth is below a critical level that is less than the potential loss, incentives for care are suboptimal. Under strict liability, if insurance is perfectly experience rated, full coverage is purchased and the level of care is efficient if injurers' wealth exceeds some critical level; at lower levels of wealth, injurers do not insure, and the level of care is suboptimal. If insurers cannot observe care, above some (higher) critical level of wealth, injurers buy partial coverage but care is suboptimal.

Many authors have considered whether making the purchase of liability insurance compulsory can restore efficient incentives for safety (e.g., Shavell, 1986; also see Keeton and Kwerel, 1984).[25] Shavell (1986) shows that compulsory insurance can restore efficient incentives for care under both negligence and strict liability, provided that enforcement is complete and that insurers can observe defendants' care and rate premiums appropriately.[26] However, if injurers' care is unobservable, compulsory coverage that fully protects injurers' assets will lead to an inefficiently

[24] A large amount of anecdotal evidence on the demand for liability and workers' compensation insurance is consistent with the prediction that parties with low wealth will demand little or no coverage.

[25] A related literature considers whether compulsory first-party insurance against catastrophic property losses can improve incentives for efficient investment and precautions (e.g., Kaplow, 1991). Similar issues arise with respect to uninsured medical care.

[26] Other possible remedies are vicarious liability (see Sykes, 1984, 1994) and imposing asset requirements for participating in the activity. Shavell (1986) shows that imposing asset requirements equal to the maximum possible loss may overdeter, because it is socially efficient for parties to participate in an activity if their assets equal the expected loss, which is less than the maximum possible loss.

low level of care, even though it reduces incentives to engage in an excessive level of risky activity. Although compulsory coverage is analogous to a tax on risky activity, moral hazard associated with liability insurance may reduce care compared to the case where the potential injurer is exposed to a material loss absent insurance.

In the United States, insurance (or ex ante proof of financial responsibility) is compulsory for workers' compensation and certain forms of environmental liability in all states, and in most states for automobile liability. Two arguments can be made for compulsory coverage even in the absence of individual experience rating. First, and as suggested above, with experience rating at the level of the group but not the individual, compulsory coverage still internalizes accident costs to the responsible activity or class of individuals. The cost of insurance operates like a tax on the activity and achieves general but not specific deterrence (optimal level of the activity, conditional on non-optimal care per unit of activity). Second, compulsory insurance helps assure the compensation function of tort liability.

On the other hand, concern with the resulting distributive effects between classes of injurers and victims may influence the political demand for compulsory insurance, associated enforcement, and price regulation of compulsory coverage in ways that undermine its deterrent function.[27] Moreover, the efficiency case for compulsory coverage rests implicitly on the assumption that the tort liability / liability system is efficient. As we elaborate in Section VII, many observers challenge this assumption, arguing that the tort liability system leads to excessive deterrence, as well as suboptimal compensation. Also, the redistributive effects of compulsory coverage are to some extent regressive. The case for compulsory coverage therefore often is an uneasy one, at least for some types of risk, such as the risk of auto accidents. As a practical matter, the judgement proof problem may lead to inefficiently high levels of risky activity and inefficiently low levels of care. Limited liability and tort liability law may induce strategies that attempt to shield assets from judgements and, in extreme cases, may induce planned bankruptcy (see Ringleb and Wiggins, 1990; Ackerlof and Romer, 1993; Swanson and Mason, 1998; also see LoPucki, 1996). The judgement proof problem has received substantial attention in recent years and has kindled debate over the efficiency of the traditional doctrine of limited liability, at least for corporations that own corporations or that have many diversified shareholders (see, e.g., Hansmann and Kraakman, 1991).

[27] Keeton and Kwerel (1984) raise the theoretical possibility that subsidized liability insurance could be efficient. On the other hand, if compulsory coverage leads to a political demand for rate regulation that guarantees availability of coverage for high risks at subsidized rates, incentives for care will likely be undermined. The political economy of compulsory automobile insurance is analyzed in Harrington (1994b); for workers' compensation, see Danzon and Harrington (1998).

9.4 LIABILITY INSURANCE WITH CORRELATED RISK

9.4.1 Sources of Correlated Risk

The dependence of liability losses on social norms and legal standards creates a positive correlation of losses among policyholders that affects the demand for liability insurance and optimal form of contract. Positive correlation of liability risks derives in part from the dependence of number of claims and size of awards on unanticipated changes in law and social norms.[28] By the operation of legal precedent, a ruling by one court can influence the outcome of related cases.

The correlated risk associated with common factors that affect liability losses generally increases with the duration of insurer liability, which is typically longer for liability insurance than for first-party insurance. Delay between the writing of the policy and the ultimate disposition of all claims is caused partly by delay in the legal process of settling claims. More significant time lapse derives from discovery-based statutes of limitations which do not begin to run until the injury and its cause have been or with reasonable diligence should have been discovered, which could be many years for some medical and environmental losses. The longer the duration of liability, the greater the risk than unanticipated information about hazards or new legal standards will shift the distribution of expected loss for all outstanding policies. Socio-legal risk has become more significant with the expansion of liability for defects in product design and warnings and the adoption of statutory liability for environmental damage and clean-up (see below). A single ruling can influence hundreds or even thousands of claims.[29]

9.4.2 Effects on Premiums and Contract Design

The basic theory of insurance prices implies that "fair" premiums equal the discounted value of all expected costs associated with writing coverage including the expected

[28] The effect of correlated risk on "crises" and cycles in the supply of liability insurance is discussed below. There are two aspects of correlated risk: (a) unfavorable realizations in underlying loss distributions that are correlated across policyholders, and (b) errors in forecasting the mean of the underlying distributions. The actuarial literature refers to the former aspect as process risk and the latter as parameter uncertainty. The economics / behavioralist literature sometimes calls the latter type of risk "ambiguity" (see Kunreuther et al., 1993).

[29] Many of the thousands of asbestos claims arise out of exposure to asbestos in the 1940s and 1950s and are based on allegations of failure to warn of the hazards of asbestos exposure. Epstein (1982) argues that even if the medical risks were knowable at the time of exposure, the tort liability of asbestos manufacturers could not have been anticipated because at that time a worker's sole recourse would have been through a workers' compensation claim against his employer. Similarly, environmental liability under Superfund could not have been anticipated. Even if courts admit a state of the art defense for product injuries in principle, some degree of retroactivity is implicit in basic common law rules of procedure and damages, and some courts have explicitly disallowed a state of the art defense. Retroactivity in tort is discussed in Henderson (1981), Schwartz (1983), Danzon (1984b), and Abraham (1988b).

cost of claim payments, underwriting expenses, income taxes, and capital (see Myers and Cohn, 1986, and Cummins and Phillips, 2000). The amount of capital that is committed to support underwriting has a major impact on the fair premium level because of the tax and agency costs of capital, as well as any systematic risk for which investors demand compensation. Higher levels of capital lead to higher premiums and lower default risk (e.g., Myers and Cohn, 1986; Cummins and Lamm-Tennant, 1994).

Increases in risk associated with changes in tort liability rules, proclivities to bring suit, and other factors require insurers to hold more capital to be equally safe. Total capital costs increase as more capital is held, thus providing a positive link between increased risk of claim cost forecast error and prices.[30] Increased risk of forecast error for liability insurance claims need not imply that liability insurance necessarily requires more capital than certain other types of coverage. For example, the long-tail associated with liability claims may allow insurers time to respond gradually to unexpected increases in costs, an option not available for catastrophe property losses. A key point, however, is that intertemporal increases in risk for a line of business will increase the amount of capital and price needed to offer coverage in that line.[31]

Severely correlated risk also may affect the optimal form of contract and, perhaps, the optimal organizational form of insurers. Doherty and Dionne (1993; also see Marshall, 1974) show that correlated risk may cause claims-made policies to dominate occurrence policies and suggest that mutual forms of organization may have a comparative advantage over stock forms. Danzon (1984b, 1985) makes similar arguments in explaining the switch from occurrence to claims-made coverage and the growth of physician-owned mutuals following the medical malpractice "crisis" of the 1970s (also see Doherty, 1991, and Winter, 1994). An alternative mechanism for sharing risk with respect to the distribution of aggregate losses is use of a contract that provides for retroactive adjustment in the premium, through dividends or assessments on policyholders. Such contracts are costly to enforce when there is asymmetric information between insurer and policyholder in observing the true loss or when the realized loss depends in part on the insurer's incentive for legal defense (Danzon, 1985a). The mutual form, which eliminates the policyholder-shareholder conflict, may thus have an advantage in assuring optimal investment in legal defense and offering contracts with retroactive adjustment or multiperiod policies. Conversely, mutual insurers are less able then stock insurers to raise external capital following large losses, which could increase the capital that mutuals need to hold ex ante.

[30] Sommer (1996) and Phillips et al. (1998) provide evidence using insurer level data that insurance prices are positively related to measures of underwriting risk and capital. Also see Cummins and Lamm-Tennant (1994). Viscusi (1993) obtains inconclusive evidence of a relationship between premium rates and measures of ambiguity using ISO ratemaking files for 1980–84.

[31] A developing alternative to insurers/reinsurers holding more equity capital on their balance sheets is to use capital market instruments, such as Act of God bonds, or insurance derivative contracts. However, the use of these types of instruments to manage long-tailed liability risk appears problematic given the long claims tail and lack of a suitable index that is highly correlated with changes in the value of claim liabilities (Harrington et al., 1995).

The effect of correlated risk on the optimal structure of damage awards and duration of liability (statutes of limitations) is discussed informally in Danzon (1984b) and Rubinfeld (1984) but has not been analyzed rigorously in formal models. More generally, the effect of the current structure of liability rules on the risk faced by liability insurers has played a major role in the debate over tort reform and liability insurance "crises" (see Sections 9.6 and 9.7).

9.5 CONTRACT INTERPRETATION AND LITIGATION

The demand for and supply of liability insurance also are influenced both directly and indirectly by the existence and likelihood of extensive litigation over contractual terms in the event of large claims against policyholders. Hundreds of millions of dollars have been spent on liability insurance coverage litigation during the past two decades. Much of this litigation has dealt with the interpretation of general liability insurance policies for environmental claims and clean-up orders stemming from the Comprehensive Environmental Response, Compensation, and Liability Act (CERCLA) of 1980. This Act imposed strict, retroactive, and joint and several liability on firms involved in the creation, transport, and disposal of environmental toxins. Abraham (1988b, 1991a) discusses the numerous aspects of environmental coverage litigation. Doherty and Smith (1993) argue that litigation over coverage terms is much more likely in the event of large claims involving multiple policyholders, suggesting that the large stakes dwarf reputation and other market forces that otherwise discourage litigation. Much general liability coverage litigation involves contracts sold during the 1950s through 1970s. In most cases the litigants have long since terminated their contractual relationships.

Specific issues that have been extensively litigated for occurrence liability insurance coverage include: (a) the meaning and timing of the occurrence of loss, (b) whether government ordered or negotiated clean-up costs are covered damages, (c) the meaning of the policy exclusion of pollution damage and damage that is "expected or intended" by the insured, and (d) allocation of responsibility for indemnity and defense among insurers when an occurrence is deemed to have spanned multiple policies (e.g., Abraham, 1888b, 1991a, in the context of environmental litigation).[32] Court resolution of these issues often has been influenced by the doctrine of *contra proferentem* (ambiguous terms should be construed against the drafter) and by the doctrine of reasonable expectations (see, e.g., Rappaport, 1995). A large legal literature deals with these issues. Economic analyses have focused more on the effects of correlated risk on the price of coverage, the optimality of occurrence versus claims made coverage, and optimal policy for dealing with environmental clean-up (see Danzon, 1984; Menell, 1991; also see Doherty and Dionne, 1993). While this literature may shed

[32] Cummins and Doherty (1997) analyze the allocation issue; also see Doherty (1997) and Fischer (1997).

light on possible intentions of the contracting parties, it generally is not dispositive with respect to coverage issues.

A large legal literature also deals with insurer and policyholder obligations with respect to defense and settlement (see Abraham, 1991a, and Syverud, 1990). Key issues have included the interpretation of contractual provisions that require the policyholder to (a) promptly notify the insurer of the claim, (b) cooperate in the insurer's defense, and (c) forego voluntary payments to the claimant without the insurer's consent. An important aspect of this litigation is whether and/or the extent to which the policyholder's actions or omissions must materially prejudice the insurer's rights in order to void coverage for indemnity and the insurer's duty to defend.

Syverud (1990) provides detailed discussion of the duty to defend, and he examines insurer incentives and efficient legal rules when the settlement or judgement is highly likely to equal or exceed the policy limits. In such cases the insurer's incentive to minimize the sum of indemnity and defense costs may be dulled, with the result that the policyholder may face greater risk of a judgement above policy limits. He discusses the potential efficiency of a legal standard that imposes the duty on the insurer to settle the claim as if there were no policy limit. He also suggests that traditional contractual remedies, as opposed to bad faith actions, are sufficient to provide insurers with incentives to comply with this type of standard.

9.6 THE LIABILITY INSURANCE CRISIS

The so-called liability insurance crisis of the mid-1980s received enormous attention by policymakers, businesses, insurers, attorneys, and the general public. This episode influenced the enactment of a variety of tort reforms by the states, and it stimulated extensive research and debate on the causes of the crisis, the dynamics of liability insurance prices, and the efficiency of the U.S. tort liability / liability insurance system. Figures 3 and 4 illustrate some of the main stylized facts of the crisis using industry aggregate data for general liability insurance. Premiums increased sharply in 1985–86 following several years of progressively larger operating losses to insurers, caused in part by declining premium rates in the early 1980s (Figure 3). The premium increases were coupled with widespread reports of availability problems, such as lower available policy limits.

Reported claim costs for general liability for accidents in 1985 and 1986 increased sharply compared to the early 1980s (Figure 4). Revised estimates of claim costs for these years ("developed" losses) a decade later were materially lower than the initial estimates, consistent with unexpectedly favorable loss development, over-reaction to deteriorating experience in the early 1980s, and/or ex ante overstatement of losses by insurers during these years.[33] However, the developed loss data also indicate

[33] The "developed" losses shown in Figure 4 are those reported 9 years after the accident year for accident years 1980–1988. The losses for later accident-years are those reported as of year-end 1997.

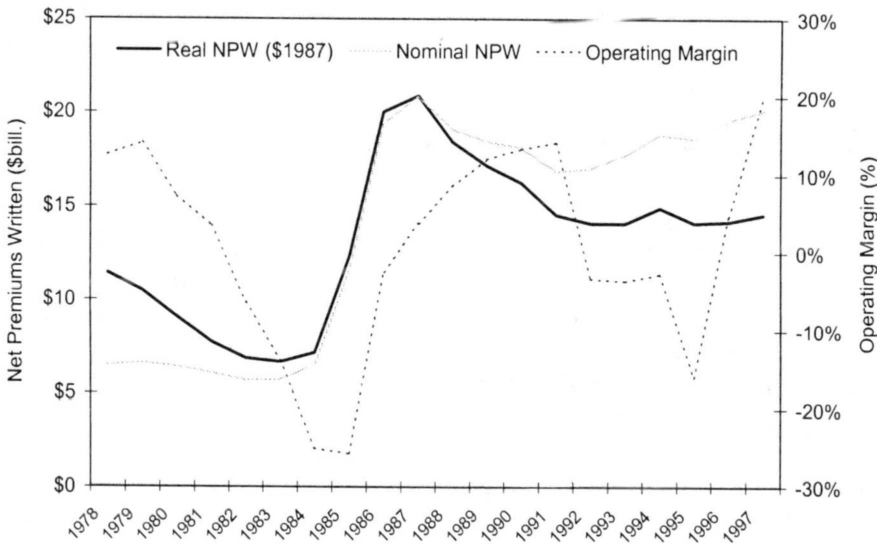

Figure 3 U.S. General Liability Insurance Net Premiums Written and Operating Margins: 1978–1997

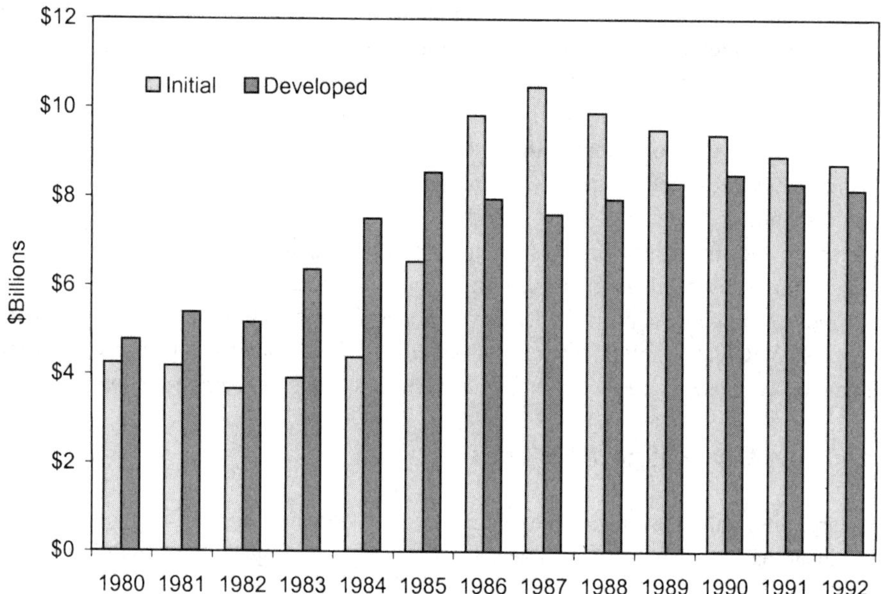

Figure 4 Initially Reported and Developed Incurred Losses for U.S. General Liability Insurance: Accident Years 1980–1992

substantial loss growth during the mid 1980s. This section first provides brief background on commercial liability insurance markets. We then summarize theoretical and empirical work on the causes of crisis.

9.6.1 Competition, Price Volatility, and the Underwriting Cycle

The structure of the market for most property-liability insurance lines, including general liability insurance, generally has been regarded as highly competitive (e.g., MacAvoy, 1977, Danzon, 1984b, Clarke et al., 1988, Harrington, 1988; Winter, 1988; also see Joskow, 1973). Market concentration generally is low whether measured at the state or national level, especially for commercial lines, such as general liability. Most studies concur that there exist no substantial barriers to entry in liability insurance. Absent cooperative arrangements for the pooling of data on claim costs, large insurers might have a significant advantage over small insurers in forecasting future claims. Current institutional arrangements for cooperative activity are likely to reduce the fixed costs of ratemaking for individual firms and mitigate this potential entry barrier (see, for example, Danzon, 1983, 1992). While subject to the usual measurement problems, studies of accounting returns on insurer capital indicate that property-liability insurer returns have been average or below average compared to other industries.

The "underwriting cycle" is an interesting feature of the industry. Property-liability insurance markets have been characterized historically by "soft" markets, in which prices are stable or falling and coverage is readily available, followed by "hard" markets, in which prices rise rapidly and availability declines. Several studies provide evidence that reported underwriting profit margins follow a second-order autoregressive process that is consistent with a cycle (see Harrington and Niehaus, 2000). These patterns have not been adequately explained by changes in the main factors that affect the discounted expected costs of providing coverage.[34] The traditional view of underwriting cycles by industry analysts emphasizes fluctuations in capacity to write coverage caused by changes in surplus and insurer expectations of profitability on new business. Competition purportedly drives prices down to the point where underwriting losses deplete capital; insurers ultimately constrain supply in order to prevent financial collapse. Price increases then replenish surplus until price-cutting resumes.

9.6.2 Causes of the 1980s Crisis

A large literature has sought to explain the mid-1980s hard market in general liability insurance, arguably the most severe hard market for any property-liability insur-

[34] Cummins and Outreville (1987) examine the question of whether cycles in reported underwriting results are simply caused by financial reporting procedures and lags in price changes due to regulation. They note that these phenomena are unlikely to explain large price fluctuations in the commercial liability insurance market in the mid-1980s. In a related vein, Doherty and Kang (1988) essentially argue that

ance coverage during the 20th century.[35] Possible explanations that have been proffered and analyzed include changes in the discounted expected cost of providing coverage, adverse selection, negative shocks to insurer capital from unexpected growth in claim costs, excessive price cutting by some insurers in the early 1980s, and alleged insurer collusion during the hard market. These explanations are not mutually exclusive. With the exception of the collusion hypothesis, which is prima facie inconsistent with market structure and price dynamics, each of these explanations has some force.

Growth in Expected Costs

Growing Expected Claim Costs and Declining Interest Rates. Several studies have attempted to explain rapid growth in premiums and availability problems in the commercial liability insurance market during the mid-1980s by changes in the cost of providing coverage. Harrington (1988) and Harrington and Litan (1988) provide evidence that rapid premium growth in general liability insurance was associated with upward revisions in loss reserves for prior years' business and rapid growth in reported losses for new accidents (see Figure 4). The results suggest that growth in reported losses for new accidents and decreases in interest rates (which increased the present value of expected claim costs) can explain much of the premium growth. However, premiums grew more slowly than implied by changes in the estimated discounted value of reported losses on new business during the early 1980s and more rapidly than implied by such changes during 1985–86. As is clear from Figure 4, incorporating subsequent revisions in loss forecasts for accidents in the mid 1980s would materially increase the unexplained portion of price changes.

Higher Taxes. The Tax Reform Act of 1986 substantially increased income taxes on property-liability insurers, in part by requiring discounting of loss reserves for tax purposes. Logue (1996) argues that this increase in effective tax rates, which was anticipated in 1985, may have had a material effect on the price increases in long-tailed liability lines during 1985–86. Bradford and Logue (1996), however, conclude that while changes in tax law likely had a material effect on prices for long-tailed liability lines, the effect was small relative to changes in loss experience.

Increased Risk. Clarke et al. (1988) attributed price increases and availability problems to growth in the expected value and uncertainty of future liability claim costs (also see Abraham, 1988a,b). Several studies argue that greater uncertainty increased prices needed to cover expected future costs including the cost of capital (e.g., Danzon, 1984, Clarke et al., 1988, and Winter, 1988). That liability insurance claim

cycles reflect slow adjustment of premiums to the present value of future costs, but they do not identify causes of lags in adjustment. See chapter 20 in this volume for further discussion.

[35] See Harrington (1990), Abraham (1988a, 1991b), Cummins, Harrington, and Klein (1991), and Winter (1991a) for further background and discussion of possible causes. Also see Trebilcock (1988).

costs became less predictable during the 1980s seems plausible given growth in jury awards, punitive damages, and expansive interpretations of liability insurance contract terms by the courts.[36] However, distinguishing a change in the ex ante distribution of costs from unfavorable realizations with stable distributions is problematic with available data. Clarke et al. (1988) show that the standard deviation of loss ratios for general liability insurance increased during the 1980s compared to the 1970s. This result could largely reflect unfavorable realizations of claim costs during the latter period, as opposed to an ex ante increase in uncertainty. Cummins and MacDonald (1991) analyze liability insurance claim data during the late 1970s and early 1980s. They provide empirical evidence suggesting an ex ante increase in the variability of claim cost distributions.[37]

Adverse Selection. Priest (1987) argues that expansion in tort law and associated increases in uncertainty aggravated adverse selection to the point where coverage sometimes became unavailable at any price during the 1980s hard market. He also suggests that an unraveling of insurance pools, which increased prices as relatively low risk buyers ceased to buy coverage, can explain much of the general liability insurance price increases. The anecdotal evidence about widespread availability problems strongly suggests that adverse selection aggravated the hard market.[38] Other observers and evidence, however, generally suggest that increased adverse selection was not a primary cause of the crisis (see, e.g., Abraham, 1991, and Winter, 1991a).

Summary. The overall evidence suggests that growth in conditional expectations of claim costs, lower interest rates, higher taxes, increased risk, and increased adverse selection combined to have a material effect on general liability insurance prices during the mid 1980s. Nonetheless, these cost-based explanations have a difficult time explaining the suddenness of the premium increases. This is especially true given evidence that the frequency of lawsuits and the size of awards, while subject to substantial secular growth, did not increase sharply during 1984–86 (see, for example, Hensler et al., 1988; U.S. GAO, 1988) Indeed, the suddenness and severity of the mid 1980s hard market provided a major impetus to look for other explanations.

Shocks to Capital

The events in the U.S. commercial liability insurance market in the 1980s helped spawn a large literature on the effects of shocks to capital, such as a large, unexpected

[36] Abraham (1988b) argues that expansive court decisions concerning contract language contributed to availability problems in the market for environmental impairment liability coverage in the mid 1980s.

[37] Increased variability in liability insurance claim costs need not be caused by an increase in idiosyncratic variation in individual awards and, of course, does not imply that court awards are largely unpredictable. Osborne (1999), for example, provides evidence of substantial predictability of awards given pre-trial information.

[38] Berger and Cummins (1992) formally model adverse selection in liability insurance where buyer loss distributions are characterized by mean-preserving spreads.

increase in claim costs, on the supply of insurance.[39] Theoretical contributions include studies by Winter (1988, 1991b, 1994), Gron (1994a), Cagle and Harrington (1995), Doherty and Garven (1995), and Cummins and Danzon (1997). While the details differ, the main implication is that shocks to capital can cause otherwise inexplicable price increases and quantity reductions consistent with a hard market. The intuition is simple. The supply of capital to the industry is inelastic in the short run due to market imperfections. A sudden reduction in capital therefore causes insurers to reduce supply to prevent a large increase in insolvency risk, which would jeopardize insurer-specific assets and reduce the price that default-risk sensitive buyers would be willing to pay for coverage.[40] The higher prices and lower quantities associated with the backward shift in supply then help to replenish insurer capital, gradually shifting the supply curve out, thus lowering price and increasing quantity.

The most important prediction of the capital shock models is that insurance prices and insurer profits will be negatively related to insurer capital, and loss ratios (ratios of losses to premiums) should be positively related to capital. Winter (1994) regresses an "economic loss ratio" for general liability insurance on lagged values of insurer capital relative to its previous five-year average and interest rates. The coefficients on the lagged capital variables are positive and statistically significant in most of his specifications. During the 1980s, however, the correlation between insurer capital and the economic loss ratio is negative. Thus, his empirical model is unable to explain the liability insurance crisis.[41] Gron (1994b) analyzes industry aggregate underwriting profit margins for four lines of business including general (other) liability. The results suggest a negative relationship between underwriting profits and the ratio of capital to GDP, which is consistent with the notion that prices increase when capital (capacity) falls.[42]

Cummins and Danzon (1997) estimate a two-equation system for price (economic loss ratio) and capital using insurer level panel data for general liability insurance during 1979–87. Their results suggest a negative relation between prices and capital and that insurers are more likely to raise capital following a price increase. However, they conclude that shocks to surplus cannot explain the sharp price increases of

[39] A detailed review of this literature is contained in chapter 20 of this volume.

[40] Some authors suggest that regulatory constraints, such as restrictions on the allowable ratio of premiums to capital, exacerbate the supply shift (see Winter, 1991b, for detailed analysis of this case). In practice, however, constraints on premiums relative to capital are informal. As is true for risk-based capital requirements adopted in the 1990s, these constraints are unlikely to be binding for most insurers at once, even at the time of a hard market.

[41] Winter suggests that ex post unfavorable realizations of losses or omission of reinsurance capacity from the capital variables may explain the 1980s results. Berger et al. (1992) analyze shocks to reinsurance supply during the 1980s crisis and provide evidence that shocks disrupted the price and availability of reinsurance.

[42] Gron (1994a) regresses both the difference between premiums and underwriting expenses and the difference in the ratio of all lines premiums to underwriting expenses on lagged capital and a variety of control variables. The results indicate that changes in the margin between premiums and underwriting expenses are negatively related to lagged values of capital, providing some support for the capital shock model.

1985–86. Doherty and Garven (1995) use insurer panel data first to estimate the sensitivity of insurer underwriting returns to interest rate changes and then explain cross-firm differences in interest rate sensitivity. Their results suggest that capital shocks due to interest rate changes influence prices.

Like the expected-cost growth explanations, the lack of sharp evidence of a sudden and large reduction in capital during 1984–85 represents a weakness of the capital shock explanation of the mid 1980s hard market. The theory and empirical evidence nonetheless suggest that upward revisions in loss reserves, which depleted capital, and increases in the discounted expected cost of providing coverage can explain much of what occurred. In addition, the capital shock literature has materially increased understanding of price and capital dynamics in the insurance industry.

Excessive Price Cutting in the Early 1980s

Did "excessive" price cutting in the early 1980s aggravate losses and contribute to the mid-1980s hard market? Winter's model (1988, 1994) implies that positive shocks to capital may explain the soft phase of the underwriting cycle and short-run prices below long-run equilibrium prices. In effect, costs associated with paying out "excess" capital in the form of dividends or share repurchases might make selling policies for less than the long-run equilibrium price less costly than either paying out the capital or having it insufficiently utilized to support additional output.[43]

McGee (1986) suggests that heterogeneous expectations of future claim costs among insurers could affect pricing behavior during soft markets. Harrington (1988a) suggests that aggressive behavior by firms with little to lose in the event of default and risk insensitive policyholders could influence price reductions during soft markets. Harrington and Danzon (1994) consider whether some firms may price below cost because of moral hazard that results from limited liability and risk-insensitive guaranty programs. They also consider whether other insurers may price below cost due to heterogeneous information concerning future claim costs and resulting winner's curse effects. A key aspect of these hypotheses is that aberrant behavior by a relatively small number of firms may induce market wide responses. When faced with underpricing, other firms may cut prices to preserve market share and thus avoid loss of quasi-rents from investments in tangible and intangible capital. Harrington and Danzon use cross-section data from the early 1980s to test whether moral hazard and/or heterogeneous information contributed to differences in general liability insurance prices and premium growth rates among firms. They provide some evidence that is consistent with moral hazard but not winner's curse effects.

Collusion

The McCarran-Ferguson Act, which was enacted by the U.S. Congress in 1945, establishes the primacy of state insurance regulation and provides the insurance industry

[43] Yuengert (1991) also considers the issue of whether excess capacity leads to soft markets.

with a limited exemption from federal antitrust law. This exemption protects certain cooperative activities to the extent that the activities are regulated by the states or unless boycott, coercion, or intimidation is involved.[44] The development of advisory rates and policy forms by the Insurance Services Office (ISO) became the subject of considerable controversy during and following the 1980s hard market. The attorneys general of nearly twenty states filed a federal antitrust suit against the ISO and numerous insurers, and the Congress proposed repeal or narrowing of the industry's antitrust exemption.[45] An NAIC committee proposed prohibiting expense and profit loadings in advisory rates, and the ISO voluntarily complied, instead disseminating only developed and trended loss costs. Several observers argued that the ISO advisory rate system aggravated rate increases during the crisis. A few (e.g., Angoff, 1988) suggested that advisory rates served as a "focal point" for collusive price increases.

After the enactment of the McCarran-Ferguson Act, it is likely that prior approval regulation encouraged insurers to use rates developed by rate service organizations (see Joskow, 1973, MacAvoy, 1977). However, the institutional environment gradually evolved away from ratemaking in concert for most lines of business. Most authors argue that market structure and pricing behavior are prima facie inconsistent with collusive price increases and that rate service organizations enhance efficiency (see Danzon, 1983, 1992; Clarke et al., 1988; Winter, 1988; and Joskow and McLaughlin, 1991).

9.7 EFFICIENCY OF THE TORT LIABILITY / LIABILITY INSURANCE SYSTEM

The United States tort liability / liability insurance system has been the subject of enormous debate during the past two decades. One polar view is that the tort liability system is reasonably efficient and, if anything, requires further expansion to achieve efficient deterrence. The alternative polar view is that the tort liability system has devolved into a system of expensive and unpredictable rent seeking by plaintiffs' and their attorneys, which in turn creates an excessive and highly unpredictable tax on the U.S. economy.[46] This section identifies some of the main points in this debate.

[44] Many states provide insurers with similar exemptions from state antitrust statutes.

[45] The attorneys general antitrust suits alleged that the ISO, the Reinsurance Association of America, and a number of insurers and brokers engaged in collusion and boycott when making changes in the standard form of general liability coverage during 1984–85. The major charges dealt with the inclusion of an optional claims-made form, the inclusion of the retroactive date in the claims-made form, the absolute pollution exclusion, and a proposal (not adopted) to include insurer defense costs within policy limits. After the U.S. Supreme Court allowed the case to go forward, holding in part that the McCarran exemption did not protect some of the alleged conduct, the suits were settled. The ISO agreed to modest restructuring and the inclusion of outside board members as part of the settlement. Ayers and Siegelman (1989) suggest an exclusionary explanation for the suits; Priest (1989) provides a rebuttal.

[46] Huber (1990) and Olson (1992) provide provocative renditions of this latter view.

9.7.1 Efficient Compensation versus Efficient Deterrence

Ignoring deterrence, it generally is recognized that the tort liability system is an inefficient mechanism of compensation for harm and risk-spreading. The policy dilemma is that deterrence cannot be ignored. Most characteristics of the tort liability system that seem clearly inefficient from a compensation perspective provide at least some deterrent to harm. Because it is exceedingly difficult to provide concrete evidence of whether a particular tort liability rule is efficient, it is likewise difficult to reach intellectual consensus, let alone political consensus, on whether material changes in the tort liability system would enhance efficiency.

Transaction Costs of Third-Party versus First-Party Insurance

It is popular to compare liability insurance to first-party insurance and to note that, from the standpoint of delivering compensation to the victim, the loading in liability insurance premiums appears to be much greater. For example, roughly 40 cents of the product liability or medical malpractice insurance dollar reaches the victim as compensation; roughly 40 cents is litigation expense, divided evenly between plaintiff and defense, and the remainder is insurance overhead (Munch, 1977; Kakalik and Pace, 1986). By contrast, the loading for large group first-party medical insurance may be less than 10 cents of the insurance dollar, although higher for small groups and individual policies. Of course, a simple comparison of loading charges is an inappropriate measure of overall efficiency since part of the purpose of the litigation expense component of liability insurance is enforcement of liability rules which in principle serve a deterrent as well as a compensation function. Thus, from a social perspective, liability and first-party insurance perform different functions and are used in contexts that make them non-comparable. About all that can be said is that the administrative costs of tort liability are not justified if the impact of legal rules on deterrence is less than some critical level (see Shavell, 1987, ch. 11).

Epstein (1986) and Priest (1987) examine product liability as an insurance market and argue that it is much less efficient than first-party insurance for purposes of controlling moral hazard and adverse selection on the part of consumers. But in the context of two party accidents such as consumer product injuries, first-party insurance is relatively inefficient at controlling moral hazard on the part of producers, just as liability insurance does little to control moral hazard on the part of consumers. There is an exact parallel here between liability insurance and liability rules: just as one-sided liability rules such as caveat emptor and strict liability without a contributory negligence defense are inefficient for controlling bilateral accidents, the associated insurance arrangements similarly fail to provide efficient incentives for care to the party that is immune from liability. It is not obvious a priori that first-party insurance is more efficient than liability insurance for bilateral accidents.

Non-Pecuniary Losses, Collateral Sources, and Punitive Damages

Two common examples of alleged inefficiency in tort damages from the perspective of optimal compensation and risk-spreading are damages for pain and suffering and punitive damage awards. Requiring injurers to compensate the injured for non-pecuniary losses, such as pain and suffering, and not allowing offset for the injured party's collateral sources of compensation can be justified on efficiency grounds. The basic argument is that failure to hold injurers liable for the "full" loss leads to inefficient incentives to control losses. However, damages for non-pecuniary losses are inefficient from a compensation and risk-spreading incentive, as has been emphasized in the literature on automobile insurance no-fault laws and more recently in the products liability literature. Whether rational consumers would choose to insure non-pecuniary losses is theoretically ambiguous, given that higher marginal utility of wealth following such losses cannot be ruled out from first principles. Many authors presume that higher marginal utility following non-pecuniary losses is unlikely, citing the relative dearth of first-party insurance for non-pecuniary losses as support (e.g., Rubin, 1993, for detailed discussion). Viscusi and Evans (1990) use survey data on wage premia that chemical workers would demand to be exposed to various chemicals. Their analysis provides some support for the hypothesis that marginal utility declines following non-pecuniary loss. These arguments and evidence, however, are not dispositive. The theory is ambiguous, insurance markets for non-pecuniary loss might fail due to transaction costs and moral hazard, and the empirical evidence on pre- and post-loss marginal utility is slender. Thiel (1998; also see Croley and Hansen, 1995) provides detailed discussion of these issues.[47]

Similarly, requiring defendants to pay punitive damages in some circumstances can be justified as necessary to promote efficient deterrence, for example, if incentives for injured parties to bring suit are inadequate for certain types of harm (e.g., Shavell, 1987). Although some highly publicized punitive damage awards may appear to be ludicrous on the face, it often can be argued, at least by plaintiffs' and plaintiffs' counsel, that these damages are necessary to discourage injurious activity that might not be efficiently deterred through compensatory damages alone.

Distributive Effects

A popular view among some segments of society is that litigation, including in many cases punitive damages, is necessary to promote social justice (i.e., to "bring large corporations to heel," to "send a message," and so on). While addressing issues of justice/fairness is beyond the scope of this chapter, implicit in this view is that an expansive tort liability system achieves a progressive redistribution of income.

[47] Thiel (1998) also argues that incorporating concern for post-accident utility into pre-accident preferences can motivate rational consumers to demand compensation for pain and suffering even if marginal utility does not increase following non-pecuniary loss. The argument may border on tautology: consumers demand compensation for pain and suffering because knowing that it will be paid ex post makes them happier ex ante.

However, the distributional effects of the tort liability system are complex, with some if not most of the costs borne by consumers of products and services and individuals involved in mundane albeit risky activities. A number of studies have analyzed ways in which the tort liability / liability insurance system could have regressive distributional effects. If consumers with different levels of wealth purchase the same risky products, for example, the increment in price necessary to cover the expected cost of product injury will be invariant to income, but the expected indemnity from tort liability action increases with wages. Moreover, compulsory auto liability laws generally can be expected to transfer some wealth from low-wealth persons who otherwise would drive uninsured to higher-wealth persons who would buy coverage voluntarily (e.g., Harrington, 1994b).

9.7.2 Endogeneity of Insurance, Liability Rules, and Litigation

Much of the law and economics literature on tort liability focuses on efficient deterrence, often either explicitly or implicitly assuming that injurers are either risk neutral or can purchase actuarially fair insurance. A smaller but important literature adopts a positive approach to explain why certain liability rules have been adopted in particular circumstances, arguing that strong incentives exist for efficiency in common law (e.g., Landes and Posner, 1981, 1987). The implication—that common law tort liability rules efficiently deter harm—provides a strong intellectual foundation for the current U.S. tort liability system, thereby undercutting the case that material changes in tort liability law would produce significant efficiencies. Nonetheless, it can be argued that the tort liability system is biased in several respects towards excessive awards. Intuition and analysis suggest that the incentives of injured parties to maximize damages ex post are inefficient ex ante (see Kaplow and Shavell, 1996). A sizable literature considers the efficiency of contingency fee systems in this regard. There is also evidence that jury decisions, in particular the size of awards, are influenced by knowledge of the defendant's liability insurance coverage, although in principle this usually is not admissible evidence.[48]

More generally, many persons argue that the shift to strict product liability in recent years and other expansions in tort liability reflect in large part the perception of courts that corporate defendants can obtain and pass on the costs of liability insurance more readily than individuals can obtain first-party insurance. Indeed, the risk-spreading rationale clearly played a central role in the adoption of strict liability. The earlier discussion in this chapter makes it clear, however, that risk-spreading through product markets and liability insurance is far from costless. Syverud (1994) argues further that feedback effects between liability insurance coverage and litigation have

[48] For example, Chin and Peterson (1985) find that jury verdicts are significantly higher for the same type of injury if the defendant is a corporation or physician, rather than an individual. Danzon (1980) provides evidence of a positive relation between award and limits of the defendants' insurance coverage.

produced socially excessive levels of litigation and costs (also see D'Arcy, 1994). The basic argument is that expanding tort liability increases the demand for liability insurance, which in turn leads to additional and expansive litigation because of the greater prevalence of liability coverage. Bias on the part of sympathetic jurors, costly risk-spreading through product and liability insurance markets, and the cost-increasing effects of widespread liability insurance coverage on incentives to litigate undermine the efficient deterrence justification for the current U.S. tort liability system.

9.7.3 Evidence on Deterrence

Despite the policy interest in the effect of liability rules on resource allocation to loss control and the possible dulling effect of liability insurance, empirical evidence is limited and inconclusive. One fundamental problem is the unobservability of relevant rules of common law and of injury rates as opposed to claim rates. Moreover, the rate of injuries, claim frequency and severity, legal expenditures, and legal rules are simultaneously determined. Data necessary to identify the structural equations of this system are generally not available. Several studies have estimated the effects of liability on resource allocation in medical care, but without a measure of injury rates have been unable to distinguish cost-justified improvements in injury prevention that liability is intended to induce from wasteful "defensive medicine" (e.g., Danzon, 1989). Other studies have estimated the impact of a limited set of legal rules on the frequency and severity of claims (for medical malpractice, see Danzon, 1984, 1986; Danzon and Lillard, 1984; Sloan et al., 1989a,b; for product liability, see Viscusi, 1989, and the literature on tort reform discussed below). None of these studies have measured whether liability insurance with imperfect experience rating undermines the incentive effects of liability rules.[49]

Measurement of the relevant law and insurance parameters is generally easier where liability is governed by statute rather than common law, as in workers' compensation and no-fault automobile regimes. Data on accident rates as opposed to claim rates are also available, although subject to reporting error. Most of the evidence is for work-related injuries and automobile accidents (see chapters 12 and 13 in this volume). Empirical studies, for example, provide evidence of a positive relation between workers' compensation benefit levels and claim rates, in part due to increased reporting of injuries by workers, and that experience rating influences claim rates. A number of studies of automobile injuries (e.g., Zador and Lund, 1986; McEwin, 1989; Devlin, 1992; and Cummins and Weiss, 1999; also see Landes, 1982) provide evidence of a relationship between auto no-fault laws and motor vehicle fatality rates or claims, especially outside of the United States.

[49] Consistent with a possible disciplining effect on the level of risky activity, Core (1999) presents evidence that insurers charge higher premiums for directors and officers liability insurance to firms with weaker measures of corporate governance.

Nonetheless, the relative dearth of direct and reliable evidence of the deterrent effects of tort liability impedes conclusions about the efficiency of various tort liability rules and procedures. While some advances on this dimension are likely in the future, the general problem will likely remain. If more hard evidence on deterrent effects were available, reliable estimates of the costs of deterrence and whether other means of achieving deterrence would involve lower or higher costs would still often be unavailable.

9.7.4 Effects of Tort Reform

Many states adopted modest "reforms" in their tort liability systems following the mid-1980s hard market in commercial liability insurance, such as partial limits on pain and suffering awards and partial modification of the collateral source rule. These changes to some extent paralleled earlier changes in laws governing medical malpractice liability. The policy debate over tort reform often hinges, at least in part, on how much a reform might be expected to reduce premium rates (e.g., Harrington, 1994a). A number of studies analyze the effects of tort reforms on liability insurance claims and claim costs (see Danzon, 1984a; Viscusi et al., 1993; Born and Viscusi, 1994; Lee et al., 1994). The evidence generally suggests that some of the reforms helped reduce claim costs. However, reliable analysis of the effects of changes in tort law on injuries, claim costs, and premiums must confront several challenging econometric issues. These include the large variety of statutory changes clustered in calendar time for a relatively small number of cross-sectional units (states), as well as potential endogeneity / self-selection issues.

9.8 CONCLUSIONS

The theory of efficient deterrence of harm through tort liability is one of the main pillars of modern law and economics. The basic notion that tort liability rules can help minimize the total cost of risk in society is fundamentally sound. Unfortunately, numerous complications arise from imperfect information, limited wealth / limited liability, and a variety of factors that impede and increase the cost of risk-spreading through liability insurance. Liability insurance is often a blunt and costly instrument for transmitting tort liability incentives to potential injurers. There is an unavoidable trade-off between efficient deterrence and efficient compensation / risk-spreading. Although the key policy issues often are theoretically ambiguous and resistant to reliable empirical analysis, increased understanding of the limits of liability rules and liability insurance markets as mechanisms for promoting efficient deterrence and risk-spreading represents major intellectual progress.

Our own reading of the theory and evidence, only a portion of which is introduced in this chapter, is that efficiency could be enhanced by restricting tort liability in a number of ways (e.g., by allowing greater freedom to restrict damages by contract, see Rubin, 1993, by requiring losers in litigation to pay winners' legal costs under more circumstances, and/or by statutory limits on pain and suffering awards, punitive damages, and perhaps the doctrine of joint and several liability). Given enough concern about reduced deterrence, such restrictions might be combined with greater reliance on other tools for deterring harmful activity and inadequate precautions. We won't opine on how much living standards would improve given suitable changes in the U.S. tort liability system, apart from suggesting that the increase would be non-trivial. It appears likely, however, that efficiency-increasing changes to the tort liability system will be slow and incremental unless or until there is compelling evidence that the system produces widespread and sizable reductions in living standards. The costs of the present system's excesses and the potential benefits of reform are sufficiently opaque to encourage a bias toward the status quo. The system's excesses are not unlike a physical ailment that reduces the quality of life, but which does not appear life-threatening. The victim adapts and applies minor remedies; more invasive treatment is eschewed unless symptoms deteriorate.

9.9 REFERENCES

Abraham, Kenneth S. (1988a). "The Causes of the Insurance Crisis." Walter Olson, ed. *New Directions in Liability Law*. New York: The Academy of Political Science.

Abraham, Kenneth S. (1988b). "Environmental Liability and the Limits of Insurance." *Columbia Law Review*. 88, 942–988.

Abraham, Kenneth S. (1991a). "Environmental Liability Insurance Law." *Englewood Cliffs*, N.J.: Prentice-Hall Law & Economics.

Abraham, Kenneth S. (1991b). "The Once and Future Crisis." *Journal of Risk and Uncertainty*. 4, 353–371.

Akerlof, G.A. and Paul M. Romer (1993). "Looting: The Economic Underworld of Bankruptcy for Profit." *Brookings Paper on Economic Activity*. 2, 1–60.

Angoff A. (1988). "Insurance Against Competition: How the McCarran-Ferguson Act Raises Prices and Profits in the Property-Casualty Insurance Industry. *Yale Journal on Regulation*. 5, 397–415.

Ayres, Ian and Peter Siegelman (1989). "The Economics of the Insurance Antitrust Suits: Toward an Exclusionary Theory." *Tulane Law Review*. 63, 971–997.

Beard, T.R. (1990). "Bankruptcy and Care Choice." *Rand Journal of Economics*. 21, 624–634.

Berger, Lawrence A. (1988). "A Model of Underwriting Cycles in the Property-Liability Insurance Industry." *Journal Risk and Insurance*. 55, 298–306.

Berger, Lawrence A. and J. David Cummins (1992). "Adverse Selection and Equilibrium in Liability Insurance Markets." *Journal of Risk and Uncertainty*. 5, 273–288.

Berger, Lawrence A., J. David Cummins and Sharon Tennyson (1992). "Reinsurance and the Liability Insurance Crisis." *Journal of Risk and Insurance*. 5, 253–272.

Born, Patricia and W. Kip Viscusi. "Insurance Market Responses to the 1980s Liability Reforms: An Analysis of Firm Level Data." *Journal of Risk and Insurance*. 61, 194–218.

Bradford, David F. and Kyle D. Logue (1996). "The Effects of Tax Law Changes on Prices in the Property-Casualty Insurance Industry." *NBER Working Paper 5652*.

Brown, John (1973). "Toward an Economic Theory of Liability." *Journal Legal Studies*. 2, 323–350.

Butler Richard J. and Jack D. Worrall (1983). "Workers' Compensation: Benefit and Injury Claim Rates in the Seventies." *Review of Economics and Statistics*. 65, 580–589.

Cagle, Julie and Scott E. Harrington (1995). "Insurance Supply with Capacity Constraints and Endogenous Insolvency Risk." *Journal of Risk and Uncertainty*. 11, 219–232.

Calabresi, Guido (1970). "The Costs of Accidents." Yale University Press, New Haven.

Calfee, John and Richard Craswell (1984). "Some Effects of Uncertainty on Compliance with Legal Standards." *Virginia Law Review*. 70, 965–1003.

Chin, Audrey and Mark A. Peterson (1985). "Deep Pockets, Empty Pockets: Who Wins in Cook County Jury Trials." R-3249-ICJ. The RAND Corporation. Santa Monica CA.

Clarke, Richard N., Frederick Warren-Boulton, David K. Smith and Marilyn J. Simon (1988). "Sources of the Crisis in Liability Insurance: An Empirical Analysis." *Yale Journal on Regulation*. 5, 367–395.

Coase, Ronald (1960). "The Problem of Social Cost." *Journal of Law and Economics*. 3, 1–44.

Cook, Philip and Donald Graham (1977). "The Demand for Insurance and Protection: The Case of Irreplaceable Commodities." *Quarterly Journal of Economics*. 91, 143–156.

Cooter, Robert and Ulen, Thomas (1987). "The Economic Case for Comparative Negligence." *New York Law Review*.

Cooter, Robert and Ulen, Thomas (1999). "Law and Economics." Addison-Wesley.

Cooter, Robert and Rubinfeld, Daniel L. (1989). "Economic Analysis of Legal Disputes and Their Resolution." *Journal Economic Literature*. 27, 1067–1097.

Core, John E. (1999). "The Directors and Officers Insurance Premium: An Outside Assessment of the Cost of Weak Corporate Governance." *Mimeo*. The Wharton School.

Craswell, Richard and John Calfee (1986). "Deterrence and Uncertain Legal Standards." *Journal of Law, Economics, and Organization*. 2, 279–303.

Crowley, Steven and Jon Hanson (1995). "The Nonpecuniary Costs of Accidents: Pain and Suffering Damages in Tort Law." *Harvard Law Review*. 108, 1785–1834.

Cummins, J. David and Neil A. Doherty (1996). "Allocating Continuous Occurrence Liability Losses Across Multiple Insurance Policies." *Environmental Claims J*. 8, 5–42.

Cummins, J. David and Joan Lamm-Tennant (1994). "Capital Structure and the Cost of Equity Capital in the Property-Liability Insurance Industry." *Insurance: Mathematics and Economics*. 15, 187–201.

Cummins, J. David and James MacDonald (1991). "Risky Probability Distributions and Liability Insurance Pricing." In *Journal David Cummins, Scott Harrington, and Robert Klein, eds. Cycles and Crises in Property/Casualty Insurance: Causes and Implications for Public Policy*. Kansas City, Mo.: National Association of Insurance Commissioners.

Cummins, J. David and Francois Outreville (1987). "An International Analysis of Underwriting Cycles in Property-Liability Insurance." *Journal Risk and Insurance*. 54, 246–262.

Cummins, J. David and Mary Weiss (1999). "The Incentive Effects of No-Fault Automobile Insurance." In Georges Dionne and Claire Laberge-Nadeau, eds. Automobile Insurance: Road Safety, New Drivers, Risks, Insurance Fraud, and Regulation. Centre for Research on Transportion 25th Anniversary Series. Montreal: Kluwer Academic Publishers.

Cummins, J. David and Richard A. Phillips (2000). "Applications of Financial Pricing Models in Liability Insurance," in this book.

Danzon, Patricia (1980). "The Disposition of Medical Malpractice Claims." R-2622-HCFA. The RAND Corporation. Santa Monica CA.

Danzon, Patricia (1983). "Rating Bureaus in U.S. Property Liability Insurance Markets; Anti or Pro-Competitive?" *Geneva Papers on Risk and Insurance*. 8, 371–402.

Danzon, Patricia (1984a). "The Frequency and Severity of Medical Malpractice Claims." *Journal Law and Economics*. 27, 115

Danzon, Patricia (1984b). "Tort Reform and the Role of Government in Private Insurance Markets." *Journal of Legal Studies*. 13, 517–549.

Danzon, Patricia (1985a). "Liability and Liability Insurance for Medical Malpractice." *Journal Health Economics*. 4, 309–331.

Danzon, Patricia (1985b). "Medical Malpractice: Theory, Evidence and Public Policy." Cambridge, Mass: Harvard University Press.

Danzon, Patricia (1986). "New Evidence on the Frequency and Severity of Medical Malpractice Claims." *Law and Contemporary Problems*. 49, 57–84.

Danzon, Patricia (1990). "Alternative Liability Regimes for Medical Injuries." *Geneva Papers on Risk and Insurance*. 54, 3–21.

Danzon, Patricia (1990). "Liability for Medical Malpractice: Incidence and Incentive Effects." *Paper presented at the Rand Conference on Health Economics*, March 1990.

Danzon, Patricia (1992). "The McCarran-Ferguson Act. Anticompetitive or Procompetitive." *Regulation: Cato Review of Business and Government*. 15, 38–47.

Danzon, Patricia and Scott E. Harrington (1992). "The Demand for and Supply of Liability Insurance." In Georges Dionne, ed. *Contributions to Insurance Economics*. Boston, Mass.: Kluwer Academic Publishers.

Danzon, Patricia and Scott E. Harrington (1998). "Rate Regulation of Workers' Compensation Insurance: How Price Controls Increase Costs." Washington, D.C.: American Enterprise Institute.

Danzon, Patricia and Lee Lillard (1983). "Settlement out of Court: The Disposition of Medical Malpractice Claims." *Journal Legal Studies*. 12, 2.

D'Arcy, Stephen (1994). "The Dark Side of Insurance." In Sandra Gustavson and Scott Harrington, eds. *Insurance, Risk Management, and Public Policy*. Boston, Mass.: Kluwer Academic.

Devlin, Rose Anne (1992). "Liability Versus No-Fault Automobile Insurance Regimes: An Analysis of the Experience in Quebec." In Georges Dionne, ed. *Contributions to Insurance Economics*. Boston, Mass.: Kluwer Academic Publishers.

Doherty, Michael G. (1997). "Allocating Progressive Injury Liability Among Successive Insurance Policies." *University of Chicago Law Review*. 64, 257–285.

Doherty, Neil (1991). "The Design of Insurance Contracts when Liability Insurance Rules are Uncertain." *Journal of Risk and Insurance*. 58, 227–246.

Doherty, Neil and Han Bin Kang (1988). "Price Instability for a Financial Intermediary: Interest Rates and Insurance Price Cycles." *Journal of Banking and Finance*.

Doherty, Neil and Georges Dionne (1993). "Insurance with Undiversifiable Risk: Contract Structure and Organizational Form of Insurance Firms." *Journal of Risk and Uncertainty*. 6, 187–203.

Doherty, Neil and Clifford Smith, Jr. (1993). "Corporate Insurance Strategy: The Case of British Petroleum." *Continental Bank—Journal of Applied Corporate Finance*. 6, 4–15.

Easterbrook, Frank and Daniel Fischel (1985). "Limited Liability and the Corporation." *University of Chicago Law Review*. 52, 89–117.

Ellis, Randall P., Cynthia L. Gallup and Thomas G. McGuire (1990). "Should Medical Professional Liability Insurance be Experience Rated?" *Journal Risk and Insurance*. 57, 66–78.

Epstein, Richard A. (1982). "Manville: The Bankruptcy of Product Liability." *Regulation*. September–October.

Epstein, Richard A. (1986). "Product Liability as an Insurance Market." *Journal Legal Studies*.

Fischer, James M. (1997). "Insurance Coverage for Mass Exposure Tort Claims: the Debate over the Appropriate Trigger Rule." *Drake Law Review*. 45, 625–696.

Froot, Kenneth, David Scharfstein and Jeremy Stein (1993). "Risk Management: Coordinating Corporate Investment and Financing Policies." *Journal of Finance*. 48, 1629–1658.

Gould, John (1973). "The Economics of Legal Conflicts." *Journal Legal Studies*. 2, 279–300.

Gron, Anne (1994a). "Capacity Constraints and Cycles in Property-Casualty Insurance Markets." *Rand Journal of Economics*. 25, 110–127.

Gron, Anne (1994b). "Insurance Evidence of Capacity Constraints in Insurance Markets." *Journal of Law and Economics*. 37, 349–377.

Haddock, David and Christopher Curran (1985). "An Economic Theory of Comparative Negligence." *Journal of Legal Studies*. 14, 49–72.

Hannsman, Henry and R. Kraakman (1991). "Toward Unlimited Shareholder Liability for Corporate Torts." *Yale Law J.* 100, 1897–1934.

Harrington, Scott E. (1988a). "Prices and Profits in the Liability Insurance Market." In Robert Litan and

Clifford Winston, eds. *Liability: Perspectives and Policy*. Washington, D.C.: The Brookings Institution.

Harrington, Scott E. (1990). "Liability Insurance: Volatility in Prices and in the Availability of Coverage." In *Tort Law and the Public Interest*. Peter Schuck, ed. New York, N.Y.: W.W. Norton.

Harrington, Scott E. (1994a). "State Decisions to Limit Tort Liability: An Empirical Analysis of No-Fault Automobile Insurance Laws." *Journal of Risk and Insurance*. 61.

Harrington, Scott E. (1994b). "Taxing Low Income Households in Pursuit of the Public Interest: The Case of Compulsory Automobile Insurance." In *Insurance, Risk Management, and Public Policy*. Sandra Gustavson and Scott Harrington, eds. Boston, Mass.: Kluwer Academic.

Harrington, Scott E. and Patricia Danzon (1994). "Price Cutting in Liability Insurance Markets." *Journal of Business*. 67, 511–538.

Harrington, Scott E. and Robert E. Litan (1988). "Causes of the Liability Insurance Crisis." *Science* 239, 737–741.

Harrington, Scott E., Steven Mann and Greg Niehaus (1995). "Insurer Capital Structure Decisions, Correlated Risk, and the Viability of Insurance Futures and Options Contracts." *Journal of Risk and Insurance*. 62, 482–508.

Harrington, Scott E. and Grey Niehaus (2000). "Volatility and Underwriting Cycles," in this book.

Henderson, James A. (1981). "Coping with the Time Dimension in Products Liability." *California Law Review*. 69, 919

Hensler, Deborah, et al. (1988). "Trends in Tort Litigation: The Story Behind the Statistics." *Santa Monica*, Cal.: The Rand Corporation.

Huber, Peter (1990). "Liability: The Legal Revolution and its Consequences". New York: Basic Books.

Huberman, Gur, David Mayers and Clifford Smith (1983). "Optimal Insurance Policy Indemnity Schedules." *Bell Journal of Economics*. 14, 415–426.

Joskow, Paul (1973). "Cartels, Competition, and Regulation in the Property-Liability Insurance Industry." *Bell Journal of Economics and Management Science*. 4, 375–427.

Joskow, Paul and Linda McLaughlin (1991). "McCarran-Ferguson Act Reform: More Competition or More Regulation." *Journal of Risk and Uncertainty*. 4, 373–401.

Kakalik James S. and Nicholas M. Pace (1986). "Costs and Compensation Paid in Tort Litigation." *Santa Monica*. CA. The RAND Corporation. R-3391-ICJ.

Kaplow, Louis (1991). "Incentives and Government Relief for Risk." *Journal of Risk and Uncertainty*. 4, 167–175.

Kaplow, Louis and Steven Shavell (1996). "Accuracy in the Assessment of Damages." *Journal of Law and Economics*. 39, 191–210.

Keeton, William R. and Evan Kwerel (1984). "Externalities in Automobile Insurance and the Uninsured Driver Problem." *Journal of Law and Economics*. 27, 149–180.

Kunreuther, Howard, Robin Hogarth and Jacqueline Meszaros (1993). "Insurer Ambiguity and Market Failure." *Journal of Risk and Uncertainty*. 7, 53–70.

Landes, Elizabeth M. (1982). "Insurance, Liability, and Accidents: A Theoretical and Empirical Investigation of the Effects of No-Fault Accidents." *Journal of Law and Economics*. 25, 49–65.

Landes, William M. (1971). "An Economic Analysis of the Courts." *Journal Law and Economics*. 14, 61–107.

Landes, William M. and Richard Posner (1981). "The Positive Economic Theory of Tort Law." *Georgia Law Review*. 15, 851–924.

Landes, William M. (1987). "The Economic Structure of Tort Law." Harvard University Press. Cambridge, MA.

Lee, Han-Duck, Mark Browne and Joan Schmit (1994). "How Does Joint and Several Liability Tort Reform affect the Rate of Tort Filing? Evidence from State Courts." *Journal of Risk and Insurance*. 61, 295–316.

Logue, Kyle D. (1996). "Toward a Tax-Based Explanation of the Liability Insurance Crisis." *Virginia Law Review*. 82, 895–959.

LoPucki, Lynn M. (1996). "The Death of Liability." *Yale Law J.* 106, 1–92.

MacAvoy, Paul, ed. (1977). "Federal-State Regulation of the Pricing and Marketing of Insurance." Washington, D.C.: American Enterprise Institute.

McEwin (1989). "No-fault and Road Accidents: Some Australian Evidence." *International Review of Law and Economics*. 9, 13–24.

McGee, Robert T. (1986). "The Cycle in Property/Casualty Insurance." *Federal Reserve Bank of New York Quarterly Review*. 22–30.

McInnes, Melayne (1997). "Liability, Litigation, Insurance, and Incentives. Mimeo." Yale University.

MacMinn, Richard and Li-Ming Han (1990). "Limited Liability, Corporate Value, and the Demand for Liability Insurance." *Journal of Risk and Insurance*. 57, 581–607.

Marshall, John M. (1974). "Insurance Theory: Reserves versus Mutuality." *Economic Inquiry*. 12, 476–492.

Mayers, David and Clifford W. Smith, Jr. (1981). "Contractual Provisions, Organizational Structure, and Conflict Control in Insurance Markets." *Journal of Business*. 54, 407–434.

Mayers, David (1982). "On the Corporate Demand for Insurance." *Journal of Business* 55, 281–296.

Menell, P.S. (1991). "The Limitations of Legal Institutions for Addressing of Envirnmental Risks." *Journal of Economic Perspectives*. 5, 93–113.

Miceli, Thomas J. (1997). "Economics of the Law: Torts, Contracts, Property, and Litigation." Oxford University Press.

Munch, Patricia (1977). (See also Danzon). "The Costs and Benefits of the Tort System if Viewed as a Compensation System." P-5921 The RAND Corporation. Santa Monica CA.

Myers, Stewart C. and Richard A. Cohn (1986). "A Discounted Cash Flow Approach to Property-Liability Insurance Rate Regulation.' In Journal David Cummins and Scott E. Harrington, eds. *Fair Rate of Return in Property-Liability Insurance*. Boston: Kluwer.

Oi, Walter (1973). "The Economics of Product Safety." *Bell Journal of Economics and Management Science*. 4, 3–28.

Olson, Walter K. (1992). "The Litigation Explosion: What Happened When America Unleashed the Lawsuit." Truman Talley Books.

Osborne, Evan (1999). "Courts as Casinos? An Empirical Investigation of Randomness and Efficiency in Civil Litigation." *Journal of Legal Studies*. 28, 187–204.

Phillips, Richard, J. David Cummins and Franklin Allen (1998). "Financial Pricing of Insurance in the Multiple-Line Insurance Company." *Journal of Risk and Insurance*. 65, 597–636.

Polinsky, A. Mitchell (1980). "Strict Liability vs. Negligence in a Market Setting." *American Economic Review*. 70, 363–370.

Polinsky, A. Mitchell (1983). "An Introduction to Law and Economics." Boston: Little-Brown.

Polinsky, A. Mitchell and Rubinfeld, Daniel L. (1988). "The Welfare Implications of Costly Litigation," *Journal Legal Studies*. 17, 151–164.

Posey, Lisa L. (1993). "Limited Liability and Incentives when Firms can Inflict Damages Greater than Net Worth." *International Review of Law and Economics*. 13, 325–330.

Posner, Richard (1972). "A Theory of Negligence." *Journal of Legal Studies*. 2, 205–221.

Posner, Richard (1973). "Economic Analysis of Law." Boston: Little-Brown.

Posner, Richard (1998). "Economic Analysis of Law." 5th ed. Aspen Publishing.

Priest, George (1987). "The Current Insurance Crisis and Modern Tort Law." *Yale Law J.* 96, 1521–1590.

Priest, George (1989). "Antitrust Suits and the Public Understanding of Insurance." *Tulane Law Review*. 63, 999–1044.

Priest, George and Benjamin Klein (1984). "The Selection of Disputes for Litigation." *Journal of Legal Studies*. 13, 1.

Rappaport, Michael B. (1995). "The Ambiguity Rule and Insurance Law: Why Insurance Contracts Should not be Construed Against the Drafter." *Georgia Law Review*. 30, 173–257.

Raviv, Artur (1979). "The Design of an Optimal Insurance Policy." *American Economic Review*. 69, 84–96.

Rea, Samuel (1981). "Lump Sum versus Periodic Damage Awards." *Journal of Legal Studies*. 10, 131–154.

Rea, Samuel (1982). "Non-Pecuniary Loss and Breach of Contract." *Journal of Legal Studies*. 11, 35–54.

Ringleb, A.H. and S.N. Wiggins (1990). "Liability and Large-Scale, Long-term Hazards." *Journal of Political Economy*. 98, 574–595.

Rolph, John E. (1981). "Some Statistical Evidence on Merit Rating in Medical Malpractice Insurance." *Journal Risk and Insurance*. 48, 247.

Rubin, Paul H. (1993). "Tort Reform by Contract." Washington, D.C.: American Enterprise Institute.

Rubinfeld, Daniel L. (1984). "On the Optimal Magnitude and Length of Liability in Torts." *Journal Legal Studies*. 15, 551–563.

Rubinfeld, Daniel L. (1987). "The Efficiency of Comparative Negligence." *Journal of Legal Studies*. 16, 375–394.

Ruser, John H. (1986). "Workers' Compensation Insurance, Experience Rating and Occupational Injuries." *The Rand Journal of Economics*. 16, 487–503.

Sarath, Bharat (1991). "Uncertain Litigation and Liability Insurance." *Rand Journal of Economics*. 22, 218–231.

Schwartz, Gary (1983). "Retroactivity in Tort Law." *New York University Law Review*. 58, 796.

Shavell, Steven (1979). "On Moral Hazard and Insurance." *Quarterly Journal of Economics*. 93, 541–562.

Shavell, Steven (1980). "Strict Liability versus Negligence." *Journal of Legal Studies*. 9, 1–25.

Shavell, Steven (1982). "On Liability and Insurance." *Bell Journal of Economics*. 13, 120–132.

Shavell, Steven (1984). "Liability for Harm versus Regulation of Safety." *Journal of Legal Studies*. 13, 357–374.

Shavell, Steven (1986). "The Judgement Proof Problem." *International Review of Law and Economics*. 6, 45–58.

Shavell, Steven (1987). "Economic Analysis of Accident Law." Cambridge, Mass.: Harvard University Press.

Siegelman, Peter and Joel Waldfolgel (1999). "Toward a Taxonomy of Disputes: New Evidence through the Prism of the Priest/Klein Model." *Journal of Legal Studies*. 28, 101–130.

Sloan, Frank A., Paula M. Mergenhagen and Randall R. Bovbjerg (1989a). "Effects of Tort Reform on the Value of Closed Medical Malpractice Claims: A Microanalysis." *Journal of Health Economics, Policy, and Law* 14, 663–689.

Sloan, Frank A. (1989b). "Medical Malpractice Experience of Physicians." *Journal of American Medical Association*. 262, 3291–3297.

Sommer, David W. (1996). "The Impact of Firm-Risk and Property-Liability Insurance Prices." *Journal of Risk and Insurance*. 63, 501–514.

Spence, Michael (1977). "Consumer Misperceptions, Product Failure and Product Liability." *Review of Economic Studies*. 64, 561–572.

Spier, Kathryn (1994). "Settlement Bargaining and the Design of Damages." *Journal of Law, Economics, and Organization*. 10, 84–95.

Summers, John (1983). "The Case of the Disappearing Defendant: An Economic Analysis." *University of Pennsylvania Law Review*. 132, 145–185.

Swanson, Timothy and Robin Mason (1998). "Long-Tailed Risks and Endogenous Liabilities." *Geneva Papers on Risk and Insurance: Issues and Practice*. 87, 182–195.

Sykes, Alan O. (1984). "The Economics of Vicarious Liability." *Yale Law Journal*. 93, 1231–1280.

Sykes, Alan O. (1994). "'Bad Faith' Refusal to Settle by Liability Insurers: Some Implications for the Judgment Proof Problem." *Journal of Legal Studies*. 23, 77–110.

Syverud, Kent (1990). "The Duty to Settle." *Virginia Law Review*. 76, 1113–1209.

Syverud, Kent (1994). "On the Demand for Liability Insurance." *Texas Law Review*. 72, 1629–1654.

Thiel, Stuart E. (1998). "Is There a Demand for Pain and Suffering Coverage?" *Mimeo*. University of Michigan Law School.

Trebilcock, Michael (1988). "The Role of Insurance Considerations in the Choice of Efficient Civil Liability Rules." *Journal of Law, Economics, and Organization*. 4, 243–264.

U.S. General Accounting Office (1988). "Product Liability: Extent of 'Litigation in federal Courts Questioned." GAO/HRD-88-35BR.

Viscusi, W. Kip (1983). "Risk by Choice: Regulating Health and Safety in the Workplace." Harvard University Press. Cambridge, MA.

Viscusi, W. Kip (1989). "The Interaction between Product Liability and Workers' Compensation as Ex Post Remedies for Workplace Injuries." *Journal of Law, Economics, and Organization*. 5, 185–209.

Viscusi, W. Kip (1993). "The Risky Business of Insurance Pricing." *Journal of Risk and Uncertainty*. 7, 117–139.

Viscusi, W. Kip and Michael J. Moore (1987). "Workers' Compensation: Wage Effects, Benefit Inadequacies and the Value of Health Losses." *Review of Economics and Statistics*. 69, 249–261

Viscusi, W. Kip, Richard Zeckhauser, Patricia Born and Glenn Blackmon (1993). "The Effects of 1980s Tort Reform Legislation on General Liability and Medical Malpractice Insurance." *Journal of Risk and Uncertainty*. 6, 165–186.

Wiggins, S.N. and A.H. Ringleb (1992). "Adverse Selection and Long-term Hazards: The Choice between Contract and Mandatory Liability Rules." *Journal of Legal Studies*. 21, 189–215.

Williamson, Oliver, Douglas Olson and August Ralston (1967). "Externatilites, Insurance, and Disability Analysis." *Economica*. 34, 235–253.

Winter, Ralph A. (1988). "The Liability Crisis and the Dynamics of Competitive Insurance Markets." *Yale Journal on Regulation*. 5, 455–499.

Winter, Ralph A. (1991a). "The Liability Insurance Market." *Journal of Economic Perspectives*. 5, 115–136.

Winter, Ralph A. (1991b). "Solvency Regulation and the Property-Liability 'Insurance Cycle.'" *Economic Inquiry*. 29, 458–471.

Winter, Ralph A. (1992). "Moral Hazard and Insurance Contracts." In Georges Dionne, ed. *Contributions to Insurance Economics*. Boston, Mass.: Kluwer Academic Publishers.

Winter, Ralph A. (1994). "The Dynamics of Competitive Insurance Markets." *Journal of Financial Intermediation*. 3, 379–415.

Worrall, John and David Appel (1982). "The Wage Replacement Rate and Benefit Utilization in Workers' Compensation Insurance." *Journal of Risk and Insurance*. 49, 361–371.

Yuengert, Andrew (1991). "Excess Capacity in the Property/Casualty Insurance Industry." Federal Reserve Bank of New York Research Foundation.

Zador, Paul and Adrian Lund (1986). "Re-Analysis of the Effects of No-Fault Auto Insurance on Fatal Crashes." *Journal of Risk and Insurance*. 50, 631–669.

10 Economic Analysis of Insurance Fraud*

Pierre Picard

Université Paris X-Nanterre

Abstract

We survey recent developments in the economic analysis of insurance fraud. The paper first sets out the two main approaches to insurance fraud that have been developed in the literature, namely the costly state verification and the costly state falsification. Under costly state verification, the insurer can verify claims at some cost. Claims' verification may be deterministic or random. Under costly state falsification, the policyholder expends resources for the building-up of his or her claim not to be detected. We also consider the effects of adverse selection, in a context where insurers cannot distinguish honest policyholders from potential defrauders, as well as the consequences of credibility constraints on anti-fraud policies. Finally, we focus attention on the risk of collusion between policyholders and agents in charge of marketing insurance contracts.

Keywords: Fraud, audit, verification, falsification, collusion, build-up.
JEL Classification Numbers: D80, G22.

10.1 INTRODUCTION

Insurance fraud is a many-sided phenomenon.[1] Firstly, there are many different degrees of severity in insurance fraud, going from build-up to the planned criminal fraud, through opportunistic fraud. Furthermore, insurance fraud refers primarily to the fact that policyholders may misreport the magnitude of their losses[2] or report an

* I am particularly grateful to two referees for their detailed comments on a previous version of this chapter.

[1] See the chapter by Georges Dionne in this book on empirical evidence about insurance fraud.

[2] Note that a claimant is not fraudulent if he relies in good faith on an erroneous valuation of an apparently competent third party—see Clarke (1997)—. However, insurance may affect fraud in markets for credence goods, i.e., markets where producers may provide unnecessary services to consumers who are never sure about the extent of the services they actually need. See Darby and Karni (1973) on the definition of credence goods and Dionne (1984) on the effects of insurance on the possibilities of fraud in markets for credence goods.

accident that never occured, but there is also fraud when a policyholder does not disclose relevant information when he takes out his policy or when he deliberatly creates further damages to inflate the size of claim. Lastly, insurance fraud may result from autonomous decision-making of opportunist individuals, but often it goes through collusion with a third party.

Since Becker (1968) and Stigler (1970), the analysis of fraudulent behaviors is part and parcel of economic analysis and there is a growing theoretical literature dealing with insurance fraud. Making progress in this field is all the more important that combating insurance fraud is nowadays a major concern of most insurance companies.

This survey of recent developments in the economic theory of insurance fraud is organized as follows. Sections 10.2–10.4 set out the two main approaches to insurance fraud that have been developed in the literature: the costly state verification and the costly state falsification. Both approaches should be considered as complementary. Under the costly state verification hypothesis, the insurer can verify damages but he then incurs a verification (or audit) cost. Under costly state falsification, the policyholder expends some resources for the building-up of his or her claim not to be detected by the insurer. In Section 10.2, we first describe the general framework used in most parts of our study, namely a model in which a policyholder has private information about the magnitude of his losses and who may file fraudulent claims. We then turn to the analysis of costly state verification procedures under deterministic auditing. In practice, claim handlers are, to some extent, entrusted with claims verification but, more often than not, state verification involves some degree of delegation. Indeed, there are specific agents, such as experts, consulting physicians, investigators or attorneys who are in charge of monitoring claims. Under deterministic auditing, claims are either verified with certainty or not verified at all, according to the size of the claim. Recent developments in the economic theory of insurance fraud surveyed in sections 10.3 and 10.4 emphasize the fact that policyholders may engage in costly claims falsification activities, possibly by colluding with a third party such as an auto mechanic, a physician or an attorney. Section 10.3 remains within the costly state verification approach. It is devoted to the analysis of audit cost manipulation: policyholders may expend resources to make the verification of damages more difficult. Section 10.4 addresses the (*stricto sensu*) costly state falsification approach: at some cost, policyholders are supposed to be able to falsify the actual magnitude of their losses. In other words, they can take acts that misrepresent the actual losses and then the claims' build up cannot be detected. Sections 10.5 to 10.7 set out extensions of the costly state verification model in various directions. Section 10.5 focuses on random auditing. Section 10.6 characterizes the equilibrium of a competitive insurance market where trades are affected by adverse selection because insurers cannot distinguish honest policyholders from potential defrauders. Section 10.7 focuses on credibility constraints that affect antifraud policies. Section 10.8 focuses on collusion between policyholders and agents in charge of marketing insurance contract. Section 10.9 concludes. Proofs and references for proofs are gathered in an appendix.

10.2 COSTLY STATE VERIFICATION: THE CASE OF DETERMINISTIC AUDITING

Identical insurance buyers own an initial wealth W and they face an uncertain monetary loss x, where x is a random variable with a support $[0, \bar{x}]$ and a cumulative distribution $F(x)$. The no-loss outcome—i.e., the "no-accident" event—may be reached with positive probability. Hence x is distributed according to a mixture of discrete and continuous distributions: x has a mass of probability $f(0)$ at $x = 0$ and there is a continuous probability density function $f(x) = F'(x)$ over $(0, \bar{x}]$. In other words $f(x)/[1 - f(0)]$ is the density of damages conditional on a loss occurring.

The insurance policy specifies the (non negative) payment $t(x)$ from the insurer to the policyholder if the loss is x and the premium P paid by the policyholder. The realization of x is known only to the policyholder unless there is verification, which costs c to the insurer.

For the time being, we assume that the insurer has no information at all about the loss suffered by the policyholder unless he verifies the claim through an audit, in which case he observes the loss perfectly.[3] We will later on consider alternative assumptions, namely the case where the insurer has partial information about the loss suffered (he can costlessly observe whether an accident has occurred but not the magnitude of the loss) and the case where the claim is a falsified image of true damages.

The policyholder's final wealth is $W_f = W - P - x + t(x)$. Policyholders are risk-averse. They maximize the expected utility of final wealth $EU(W_f)$, where $U(\cdot)$ is a twice differentiable von Neumann-Morgenstern utility function, with $U' > 0$, $U'' < 0$.

A *deterministic auditing policy* specifies whether a claim is verified or not depending on the magnitude of damages. More precisely, following Townsend (1979), we define a deterministic audit policy as a verification set $M \subset [0, \bar{x}]$, with complement M^c, that specifies when there is to be verification. A policyholder who experiences a loss x may choose to file a claim $\hat{x}$. If $\hat{x} \in M$, the claim is audited, the loss x is observed and the payment is $t(x)$. If $\hat{x} \in M^c$, the claim is not audited and the payment to the policyholder is $t(\hat{x})$.

A contract $\delta = \{t(\cdot), M, P\}$ is said to be *incentive compatible* if the policyholder thruthfully reveals the actual loss, i.e., if $\hat{x} = x$ is an optimal strategy for the policy-

[3] On insurance fraud with imperfect auditing, see Abadie (1999). On imperfect auditing, in contexts which are different from insurance fraud, see Baron and Besanko (1984) and Puelz and Snow (1995).

holder. Lemma 1 establishes that any contract is weakly dominated[4] by an incentive compatible contract, in which the payment is constant in the no-verification set M^c and always larger in the verification set than in the no-verification set.

Lemma 1. Any contract $\delta = \{t(\cdot), M, P\}$ is weakly dominated by an incentive compatible contract $\tilde{\delta} = \{\tilde{t}(\cdot), M, P\}$ such that:

$$\tilde{t}(x) = t_0 \quad \text{for} \quad x \in \tilde{M}^c$$

$$\tilde{t}(x) > t_0 \quad \text{for} \quad x \in \tilde{M}$$

where t_0 is some constant.

The characterization of the incentive compatible contracts described in Lemma 1 is quite intuitive. In the first place, truthful revelation of the actual loss is obtained by paying a constant indemnity in the no-verification set, for otherwise the policyholder would always report the loss corresponding to the highest payment in this region. Secondly, if the payment were lower for some level of loss located in the verification set than in the no-verification set, then, for this level of loss, the policyholder would announce falsely that his loss is in the no-verification set.[5]

Lemma 1 implies that we may restrict our characterization of optimal contracts to such incentive compatible contracts. This is proved by defining $\tilde{t}(x)$ as the highest indemnity payment that the policyholder can obtain when his loss is x, by choosing $\tilde{M}$ as the subset of $[0, \bar{x}]$ where the indemnity is larger than the minimum and by letting $\tilde{P} = P$. This is illustrated in Figure 1, with $M = (x^*, \bar{x}]$, $\tilde{M} = (x^{**}, \bar{x}]$, $\tilde{t}(x) = t_0$ if $x \le x^{**}$ and $\tilde{t}(x) = t(x)$ if $x > x^{**}$. Under δ, for any optimal reporting strategy the policyholder receives t_0 when $x \le x^{**}$ and he receives $t(x)$ when $x > x^{**}$, which corresponds to the same payment as under $\tilde{\delta}$. Furthermore, under δ, any optimal strategy $\hat{x}(x)$ is such that $\hat{x}(x) \in M$ if $x > x^{**}$, which implies that verification is at least as frequent under δ (for any optimal reporting strategy) as when the policyholder tells the truth under $\tilde{\delta}$. Thus, δ and $\tilde{\delta}$ lead to identical indemnity payments whatever the true level of the loss and expected audit costs are lower when there is truthtelling under $\tilde{\delta}$ than under δ.

From now on, we restrict ourselves to such incentive compatible contracts. The optimal contract maximizes the policyholder's expected utility

$$EU = \int_M U(W - P - x + t(x))dF(x) + \int_{M^c} U(W - P - x + t_0)dF(x) \tag{1}$$

[4] Dominance is in a Pareto-sense with respect to the expected utility of the policyholder and to the expected profit of the insurer.

[5] If both payments were equal, then it would be welfare improving not to audit the corresponding level of loss in the verification region and simultaneously to decrease the premium. Note that Lemma 1 could be presented as a consequence of the Revelation Principle (see footnote 21).

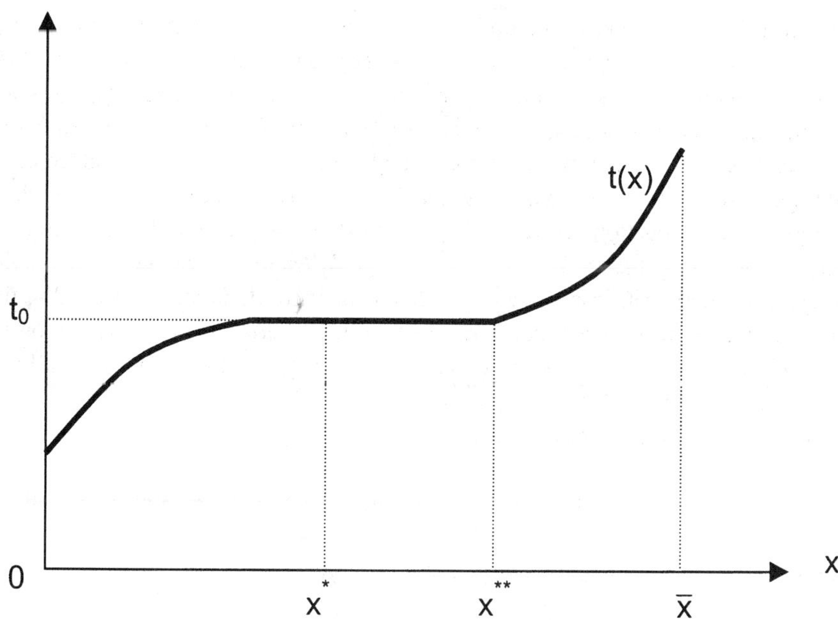

Figure 1

with respect to P, t_0, $t(\cdot)$: $M \rightarrow R_+$ and $M \subset [0, \bar{x}]$, subject to a constraint that requires the expected profit of the insurer $E\Pi$ to meet some minimum preassigned level normalized at zero

$$E\Pi = P - \int_M [t(x) + c]dF(x) + \int_{M^c} t_0\, dF(x) \geq 0 \tag{2}$$

and to the incentive compatibility constraint

$$t(x) > t_0 \text{ for all } x \text{ in } M \tag{3}$$

Lemma 2. For any optimal contract, we have

$$t(x) = x - k > t_0 \text{ for all } x \text{ in } M$$

and

$$M = (m, \bar{x}] \text{ with } m \in [0, \bar{x}]$$

Lemma 2 shows that it is optimal to verify the claims that exceed a threshold m and also to provide full insurance of marginal losses when $x > m$. The intuition of these results are as follows. The optimal policy shares the risk between the insured and the insurer without inducing the policyholder to misrepresent his loss level. As shown in Lemma 1, this incentive compatibility constraint implies that optimally the indemnity schedule should be minimal and flat outside the verification set, which means that no insurance of marginal losses is provided in this region. On the contrary, nothing prevents the insurer to provide a larger variable coverage when the loss level belongs to the verification set. Given the concavity of the policyholder's utility function, it is optimal to offer the flat minimal coverage when losses are low and to provide a larger coverage when losses are high. This leads us to define the threshold m that separates the verification set and its complement. Furthermore, conditionally on the claim being verified, i.e., when $x > m$, sharing the risk optimally implies that full coverage of marginal losses should be provided.

Hence, the optimal contract maximizes

$$EU = \int_0^m U(W - x - P + t_0)\,dF(x) + [1 - F(m)]U(W - P - k)$$

with respect to P, $m \geq 0$, $t_0 \geq 0$ and $k \geq t_0 - m$ subject to

$$E\Pi = P - t_0 F(m) - \int_{m+}^{\bar{x}} (c + x - k)\,dF(x) \geq 0$$

At this stage it is useful to observe that EU and $E\Pi$ are unchanged if there is a variation in the coverage, constant among states, compensated by an equivalent variation in the premium, i.e., $dEU = dE\Pi = 0$ if $dt_0 = dk = dP$, with m unchanged. Hence, the optimal coverage schedule is defined up to an additive constant. Without loss of generality, we may assume that no insurance payment is made outside the verification set, i.e., $t_0 = 0$. We should then have $t(x) = x - k > 0$ if $x > m$, or equivalently $m - k \geq 0$. In such a case, the policyholder files a claim only if the loss level exceeds the threshold m. This threshold may be viewed as a deductible.

Note that the optimal coverage is no more indeterminate if we assume, more realistically, that the cost c is the sum of the audit cost and of an administrative cost which is incurred whenever a claim is filed, be it verified or not. In such a case, choosing $t_0 = 0$ in the no-verification set is the only optimal solution since it saves the administration cost—see Picard (1999).

The optimal contract is derived by maximizing

$$EU = \int_0^m U(W - x - P)\,dF(x) + [1 - F(m)]U(W - P - k) \tag{4}$$

with respect to $m \geq 0$, k and P, subject to

$$E\Pi = P - \int_{m+}^{\bar{x}} (c + x + k)\,dF(x) \geq 0 \tag{5}$$

$$m - k \geq 0 \tag{6}$$

Proposition 1. Under deterministic auditing, an optimal insurance contract $\delta = \{t(\cdot), M, P\}$ satisfies the following conditions:

$$M = (m, \bar{x}] \quad \text{with} \quad m > 0$$
$$t(x) = 0 \quad \text{if} \quad x \leq m$$
$$t(x) = x - k \quad \text{if} \quad x > m$$

with $0 < k < m$.

The optimal contract characterized in proposition 1—(established by Gollier (1987)—is depicted in Figure 2. First, it states that it is optimal to choose a positive threshold m. The intuition is as follows. When $m = 0$, all positive claims are verified and it is optimal to offer full coverage, i.e., $t(x) = x$ for all $x > 0$. Starting from such a full insurance contract an increase $dm > 0$ entails no first-order risk-sharing effect. However, this increase in the threshold cuts down the expected audit cost, which is beneficial to the policyholder. In other words, in the neighbourhood of $m = 0$ the trade-off between cost minimization and risk-sharing always tips in favor of the first objective.

Secondly, we have $0 < k < m$ which means that partial coverage is provided when $x > m$. Intuitively, the coverage schedule is chosen so as to equalize the marginal utility

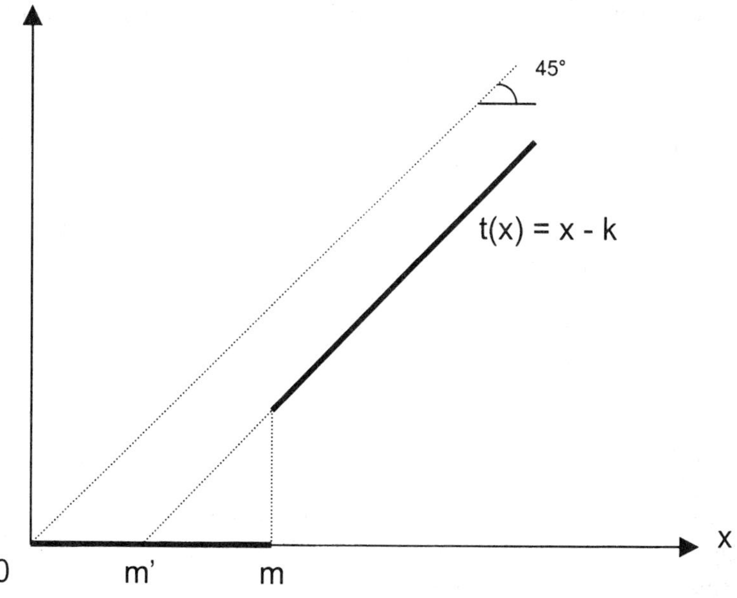

Figure 2 Optimal insurance coverage under deterministic auditing

of final wealth in each state of the verification set with the expected marginal utility of final wealth, because any increase in the insurance payment has to be compensated by an increase in the premium paid whatever the level of the loss. We know that no claim is filed when $x < m$, which implies that the expected marginal utility of final wealth is larger than the marginal utility in the no-loss state. Concavity of the policyholder's utility function then implies that a partial coverage is optimal when the threshold is crossed.

Thus far we have assumed that the insurer has no information at all about the loss incurred by the policyholder. In particular, the insurer could not observe whether a loss occured ($x > 0$) or not ($x = 0$). Following Bond and Crocker (1997), we may alternately assume that the fact that the policyholder has suffered some loss is publicly observable. The size of the loss remains private information to the policyholder: verifying the magnitude of the loss costs c to the insurer.

This apparently innocuous change in the information structure strongly modifies the shape of the optimal coverage schedule. The insurer now pays a specific transfer $t = t_1$ when $x = 0$, which occurs with probability $f(0)$. Lemmas 1 and 2 are unchanged and we now have

$$EU = f(0)U(W - P + t_1) + \int_{0_+}^{m} U(W - x - P + t_0)\,dF(x) + [1 - F(m)]U(W - P - k)$$

$$E\Pi = P - t_1 f(0) - t_0[F(m) - f(0)] - \int_{m_+}^{\bar{x}} (c + x - k)\,dF(x)$$

The optimal contract maximizes EU with respect to P, $m \geq 0$, $t_0 \geq 0$, $t_1 \geq 0$ and $k \geq t_0 - m$ subject to $E\Pi \geq 0$. We may choose $t_1 = 0$, since P, t_0, t_1 and k are determined up to an additive constant: no insurance payment is made if no loss occurs.

Proposition 2. Under deterministic auditing, when the fact that the policyholder has suffered some loss is publicly observable, an optimal insurance contract $\delta = \{t(\cdot), M, P\}$ satisfies the following conditions:

$$\begin{aligned}
&M = (m, \bar{x}] \quad \text{with} \quad m > 0 \\
&t(0) = 0 \\
&t(x) = t_0 \quad \text{if} \quad 0 < x \leq m \\
&t(x) = x \quad \text{if} \quad x > m
\end{aligned}$$

with $0 < t_0 < m$.

Proposition 2 is established by Bond and Crocker (1997). It is depicted in Figure 3. When an accident occurs but the claim is not verified (i.e., $0 < x \leq m$), the incentive compatibility requires the insurance payment to be constant: we then have $t(x) = t_0$. The payment should be larger than t_0 when the claim is verified (i.e., when $x > m$).

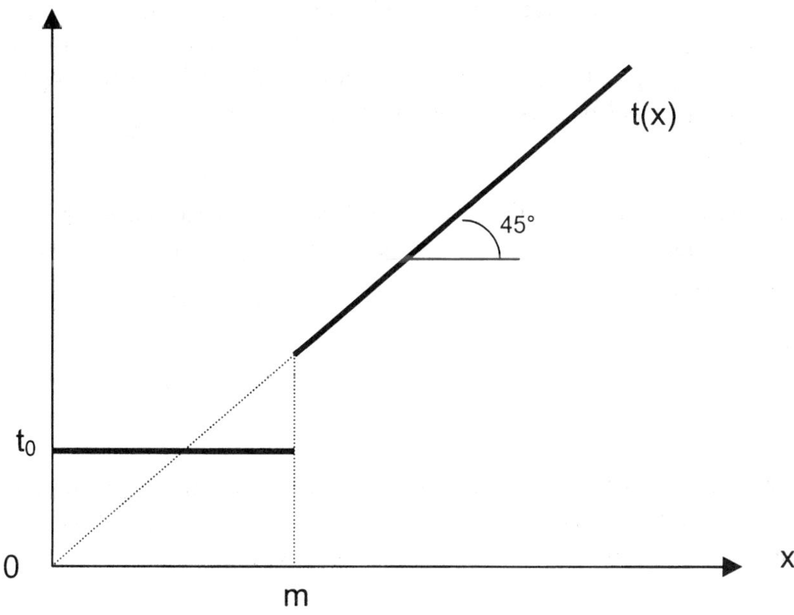

Figure 3 Optimal insurance coverage under deterministic auditing when the insurer can observe whether an accident has occurred but not the magnitude of the actual loss

Optimal risk sharing implies that the policyholder's expected marginal utility (conditional on the information of the insurer) should be equal to the marginal utility in the no-accident state. This implies first that, in the no-verification region, an optimal insurance contract entails overpayment of small claims (when $0 < x < t_0$) and underpayment of large claims (when $t_0 < x \leq m$). Secondly, there is full insurance in the verification region (i.e., when $x > m$).

Neither Figure 2 nor Figure 3 looks like the coverage schedule that are most frequently offered by insurers for two reasons: first because of the upward discontinuity at $x = m$ and secondly because of overpayment of smaller claims in the case of Figure 3. In fact, such contracts would incite the policyholder to inflate the size of his claim by intentionally increasing the damage. Consider for example the contract described in Proposition 1 and illustrated by Figure 2. A policyholder who suffers a loss x less than m but greater than m' would profit by increasing the damage up to $x = m$, insofar as the insurer is not able to distinguish the initial damage and the extra damage.[6] In

[6] In fact, the policyholder would never increase the damage if and only if $t(x) - x$ were non-increasing over $[0, \bar{x}]$. Given that $t(x)$ is non-decreasing (see Lemma 2), this no-manipulability condition implies that $t(x)$ should be continuous. Note that extra damages may either deliberately by the policyholder (arson is a good example) or made thanks to a middleman, such as as car repairer or a health case provider. In such cases, gathering verifiable information about intentional overpayment may be be too time consuming to the insurer. See Bourgeon and Picard (1999) on corporate fire insurance when these is a risk of arson.

such a case, the contract defined in proposition 1 is dominated by a contract with a straight deductible, i.e., $t(x) = Sup\{0, x - m'\}$ with $M = (m', \bar{x}]$. As shown by Huberman, Mayers and Smith (1983) and Picard (1999), in different settings, a straight deductible is indeed optimal under such circumstances.

We thus have:

Proposition 3. Under deterministic auditing, when the policyholders can inflate their claims by intentionally increasing the damage, the optimal insurance contract $\delta = \{t(\cdot), M, P\}$ is a straight deductible

$$t(x) = Sup\,\{0, x - m\}$$

with $m > 0$ and $M = (m, \bar{x}]$.

Proposition 3 explains why insurance policies with straight deductibles are so frequently offered by insurers, in addition to the wellknown interpretations in terms of transaction costs (Arrow, 1971) or moral hazard (Holmström, 1979).

10.3 COSTLY STATE VERIFICATION: DETERMINISTIC AUDITING WITH MANIPULATION OF AUDIT COSTS

In the previous section, the policyholder was described as a purely passive agent. His only choices were whether he files a claim or not and, should the occasion arise, what is the size of the claim? As a matter of fact, in many cases, the policyholder involved in an insurance fraud case plays a much more active part. In particular, he may try to falsify the damages in the hope of receiving a larger insurance payment. Usually, falsification goes through collusion with agents, such as healthcare providers, car repairers or attorneys, who are in position to make it more difficult or even impossible to prove that the claim has been built up or deliberately created.[7] Even if fraudulent claiming may be detered at equilibrium, the very possibility for policyholders to falsify claims should be taken into account in the analysis of optimal insurance contracts.

Two main approaches to claims falsification have been developed in the literature. Firstly, Bond and Crocker (1997) and Picard (1999) assume that the policyholder may manipulate audit costs, which means that they expend resources to make the

[7] On collusion between physicians and workers, see the analysis of workers' compensations by Dionne and St-Michel (1991) and Dionne, St-Michel and Vanasse (1995). See Derrig, Weisberg and Chen (1994) on empirical evidence about the effect of the presence of an attorney on the probability of reaching the monetary threshold that restrict the eligibility to file a tort claim in the Massachusetts no-fault automobile insurance system. In the Tort system, Cummins and Tennyson (1992) describe the costs to motorists experiencing minor accidents of colluding with lawyers and physicians as the price of a lottery ticket. The lottery winnings are the motorist's share of a general damage award.

verification of claims more costly or more time consuming to the auditor. In this approach, detering the policyholder from manipulating audit cost is feasible and, sometimes, optimal. What is most important is the fact that the coverage schedule affects the incentives of policyholders to manipulate audit costs, which gives a specific moral hazard dimension to the problem of designing an optimal insurance contract. In another approach, developed by Crocker and Morgan (1997), it is assumed that policyholders may expend resources to falsify the actual magnitude of their losses in an environment where verification of claims is not possible. Here also the coverage schedule affects the incentives to claims falsification, but the cost of generating insurance claims through falsification differs among policyholders according to their true level of loss. These differential costs make it possible to implement loss-contingent insurance payments with some degree of claims falsification at equilibrium.

In this section and the following, we review both approaches in turn. For the sake of expositional clarity, we refer to them as costly state verification with manipulation of audit cost and costly state falsification, although in both cases the policyholder falsifies his claim, i.e., he prevents the insurer observing the true level of damages. In the first approach, the policyholder deters the auditor from performing an informative audit while in the second one he provides a distorted image of his damages.

The audit cost manipulation hypothesis has been put forward by Bond and Crocker (1997) in the framework of a model with deterministic auditing. They assume that policyholders may take actions (refered to as *evasion costs*) that affect the audit cost. Specifically, Bond and Crocker assume that, after observing their loss x, a policyholder may incur expenditures $e \in \{e_0, e_1\}$, with $e_1 > e_0$, which randomly affects the audit cost. If $e = e_i$, then the audit cost is $c = c^H$ with probability p_i and $c = c^L$ with probability $1 - p_i$, with $i \in \{0, 1\}$, $c^H > c^L$ and $p_1 > p_0$. In other words, a large level of manipulation expenditures makes it more likely that the audit cost will be large. Without loss of generality, assume $e_0 = 0$. Let us also simplify by assuming $c^L = 0$. These expenditures are in terms of utility so that the policyholder's utility function is now $U(W_f) - e$.

Bond and Crocker assume that the actual audit cost is verifiable, so that the insurance contract may be conditioned on c. Under deterministic auditing, an insurance contract δ is then defined by a premium P, a state-contingent coverage schedule $t^i(x)$ and a state-contingent verification set $M^i = (m^i, \bar{x}]$, where $i = H$ if $c = c^H$ and $i = L$ if $c = c^L$. Bond and Crocker also assume that the insurer can observe whether an accident has occurred, but not the size of the actual damages and (without loss of generality), they assume that no insurance payment is made if $x = 0$.

An optimal *no-manipulation* insurance contract maximizes the expected utility of the policyholder subject to:

- The insurer's participation constraint
- Incentive compatibility constraints that may be written as

$$t^i(x) = \begin{cases} t_0^i & \text{if} \quad x \in (0, m^i] \\ > t_0^i & \text{if} \quad x \in (m^i, \bar{x}] \end{cases}$$

for $i = H$ or L.

- The constraint that the policyholder does not engage in audit cost manipulation whatever his loss, i.e.,

$$\begin{aligned} &p_1 U(W - x - P + t^H(x)) + (1 - p_1)U(W - x - P + t^L(x)) - e_1 \\ &\quad \leq p_0 U(W - x - P + t^H(x)) + (1 - p_0)U(W - x - P + t^L(x)) \end{aligned}$$

for all x in $(0, \bar{x}]$.

Bond and Crocker (1997) show the following proposition.

Proposition 4. The optimal no-manipulation insurance contract $\delta = \{t^H(\cdot), t^L(\cdot), m^H, m^L, P\}$ has the following properties:

(i) $m^H < \bar{x}$ and $m^L = 0$
(ii) $t^H(x) = x$ for $x > m^H$ and $t^H(x) = t_0^H$ for $0 < x \leq m^H$
(iii) $t^L(x) = x$ for $\tilde{x} \leq x \leq \bar{x}$ and $t^L(x) = S(x)$ for $0 < x < \tilde{x}$ where $S(x)$ is given by

$$(p_1 - p_0)[U(W - x - P + t_0^H) - U(W - x - P + S(x)] - e_1 = 0.$$

The optimal no-manipulation contract is depicted in Figure 4. If there were no possibility of audit cost manipulation, then the optimal insurance contract would involve $m^L = 0$ and $t^L(x) = x$ for all x (since $c_L = 0$) and $m^H > 0$, $t^H(x) = x$ if $x > m$ and $0 < t_0^H < m_H$ (see Proposition 2). This suggests that manipulating audit cost (i.e., choosing $e = e_1$) may be a profitable strategy for low values of x. Proposition 4 shows that overcompensating easily verified losses is an appropriate strategy to mitigate the policyholder's incentive to engage in audit cost manipulation. This overcompensation is defined by the $S(x)$ function. $S(x)$ denotes the minimum payoff in the c^L state that makes the policyholder indifferent between manipulating or not and $\tilde{x}$ is the threshold under which the policyholder chooses to evade if he is offered the full insurance contract in the c^L state.

Since overcompensating is costly to the insurer, it may be optimal to allow for some degree of manipulation at equilibrium. Bond and Crocker provide a characterization of this optimal contract with audit cost manipulation at equilibrium. In particular, they show that there is still a subintervall $[s_2, s_1]$ in $(0, m^H)$ where the insurer overcompensates the loss in the c^L state, with $t^L(x) = S(x) > x$ when $s_2 \leq x < s_1$. Finally they show that, when U exhibits constant absolute risk aversion, then the optimal contract in the presence of audit cost manipulation results in lower payoffs and less mon-

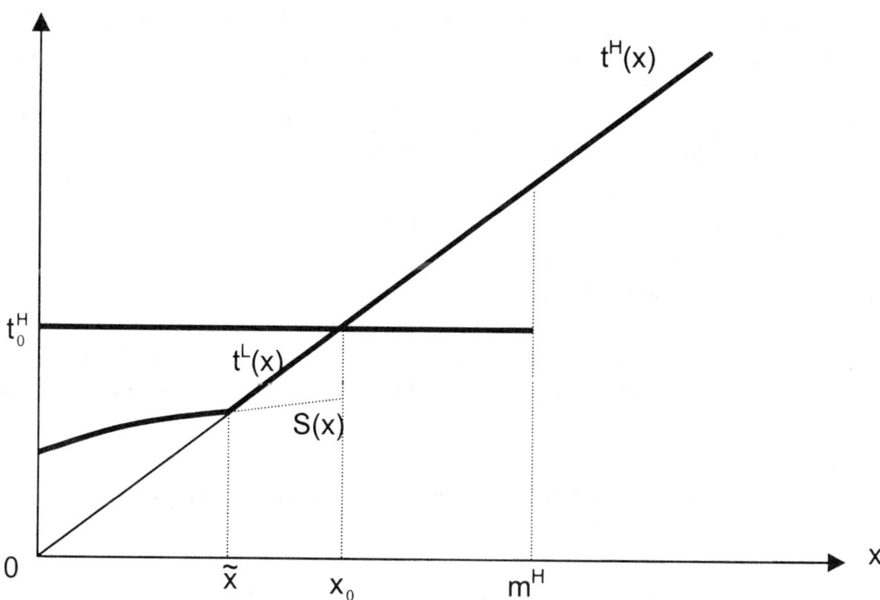

Figure 4 Optimal no-manipulation contract in the Bond-Crocker (1997) model

itoring in the c^H state than would an optimal contract in an environment where claims manipulation was not possible.[8]

The analysis of Bond and Crocker (1997) is interesting firstly because it is a first step toward a better understanding of the active part that policyholders may take in insurance fraud. Furthermore, it provides a rationale for the fact that insurers may be willing to settle small claims generously and without question when the loss is easily monitored to forestall a claim that may be larger and more difficult to verify. From a normative point of view, the Bond-Crocker analysis suggests that the appropriate way to mitigate build-up is not to increase the amount of monitoring but to design coverage schedules in such a way that policyholders have less incentive to engage in fraudulent claiming.

Two other aspects of the Bond-Crocker model have to be emphasized. First, the optimal coverage schedule is such that small claims are overcompensated whatever the audit cost, which may incite the policyholder to intentionally bring about damages. This issue has already been addressed in section 3 and we will not hark back to it any further. Secondly, Bond and Crocker assume that the actual audit cost is verifiable so

[8] The CARA assumption eliminates wealth effects from incentives constraints.

that the insurance coverage may be conditioned on it. This is a very strong assumption. In most cases, claims verification is performed by an agent (an expert, a consulting physician, an attorney, an investigator . . .) who may have private information about the cost entailed by a specific claim. Picard (1999) focuses attention on the agency relationship that links the insurer and the auditor when policyholders may manipulate audit costs and the insurer does not observe the cost incurred by the auditor. His analysis may be summarized as follows.

The auditor sends a report $\tilde{x} \in [0, \bar{x}]$ which is an evaluation of the magnitude of the loss. Let $\tilde{x} = \varnothing$ when no audit is performed. Observing the magnitude of the loss costs c_a to the auditor. The policyholder may incur a manipulation cost e and, in such a case, the cost of elicitating *verifiable* information about the size of the damages becomes $c_a + b\,e$, where the parameter $b > 0$ characterizes the manipulation technology. Furthermore, verifiable information is necessary to prove that the claim has been built up (i.e., to prove that $x < \hat{x}$). The insurer does not observe the audit cost. He offers an incentive contract to his auditor to motivate him to gather verifiable information about fraudulent claims. Let t and r be respectively the insurance payment and the auditor's fees. Contracts $T(\cdot)$ and $R(\cdot)$ specify t and r as functions of the auditor's report.[9] We have $t = T(\tilde{x})$ and $r = R(\tilde{x})$ where T: $[0, \bar{x}] \cup \varnothing \to R_+$ and T: $[0, \bar{x}] \cup \varnothing \to R$.

The auditor-policyholder relationship is described as a three stage audit game. At stage 0, a loss x, randomly drawn in $[0, \bar{x}]$, is privately observed by the policyholder.[10] At stage 1, the policyholder reports a claim $\hat{x} \in [0, \bar{x}]$ and he incurs the manipulation cost $e \geq 0$. At stage 2, the claim is audited whenever $\hat{x} \in M = (m, \bar{x}]$. When $\hat{x} \in M$, the auditor observes x and he reports $\tilde{x} \in \{x, \hat{x}\}$ to the insurer. If $\tilde{x} = x \neq \hat{x}$, the auditor incurs the cost $c_a + be$ so that his report incorporates verifiable information. If $\tilde{x} = \hat{x}$, the auditor's cost is only c_a. The payments to the policyholder and to the auditor are respectively $T(\tilde{x})$ and $R(\tilde{x})$.

In this setting, an allocation is described by $\delta = \{t(\cdot), M, P\}$, with $M = (m, \bar{x}]$ and by $\omega(\cdot)$: $[0, \bar{x}] \to R$, where $\omega(x)$ is the auditor's equilibrium payoff (net of the audit cost) when the loss is equal to x.

Contracts $\{T(\cdot), R(\cdot)\}$ are said to implement the allocation $\{\delta, \omega(\cdot)\}$ if at a perfect equilibrium of the audit game, there is no audit cost manipulation (i.e., $e = 0$ for all x), the claim is verified if and only if $x \in M$ and the net payoffs—defined by $T(\cdot)$ and $R(\cdot)$—are equal to $t(x)$, $\omega(x)$ when the loss is equal to x.[11]

In such a setting, the equilibrium audit cost is $\omega(x) + c_a$ if $x \in M$ and $\omega(x)$ if $x \in M^c$. Furthermore, the auditor's participation constraint may be written as

[9] The payment $R(\cdot)$ is net of the standard audit cost c_a.

[10] Contrary to the Bond-Crocker (1997) model, it is assumed that the insurer cannot observe whether an accident has occurred, i.e., he cannot distinguish the event $\{x = 0\}$ from $\{x > 0\}$. Furthermore, the manipulation cost e is in monetary terms and not in utility terms as in Bond-Crocker (1997).

[11] Picard (1999) shows that allowing for audit cost manipulation (i.e., $e > 0$) at equilibrium is a weakly dominated strategy for the insurer.

$$\int_0^{\bar{x}} V(\omega(x))\,dF(x) \geq \bar{\upsilon} \tag{7}$$

where $V(\cdot)$ is the auditor's von Neumann-Morgenster utility function, with $V' > 0$, $V'' \leq 0$ and $\bar{\upsilon}$ is an exogenous reservation utility level.

The optimal allocation $\{\delta, \omega(\cdot)\}$ maximizes the policyholder's expected utility, subject to the insurer's and the auditor's participation constraints and to the constraint that there exist contracts $\{T(\cdot), R(\cdot)\}$ that implement $\{\delta, \omega(\cdot)\}$.

Picard (1999) characterizes the optimal allocation in a setting where the policyholder can inflate their claim by intentionally increasing the damages, which implies that $t(x) - x$ should be nonincreasing (see section 2). His main result is the following:

Proposition 5. When the auditor is risk averse ($V'' < 0$), the optimal insurance contract is a deductible with coinsurance for high levels of damages:

$$\begin{aligned} &t(x) = 0 && \text{if} \quad 0 \leq x \leq m \\ &t(x) = x - m && \text{if} \quad m \leq x \leq x_0 \\ &t'(x) \in (0,1) && \text{if} \quad x_0 \leq x \leq \bar{x} \end{aligned}$$

with $0 \leq m < x_0 \leq \bar{x}$ and $M = (m, \bar{x}]$.

Furthermore, the auditor's fees (expressed as function of the size of the claim) are

$$\begin{aligned} &r = r_1 - bt(x) && \text{if} \quad x > m \\ &r = r_0 && \text{if} \quad x \leq m \end{aligned}$$

where r_0 and r_1 are constant.

Picard (1999) also gives sufficient conditions for $m > 0$ and $x_0 < \bar{x}$. The contracts characterized in Proposition 5 are depicted in Figure 5. We have $t(x) = 0$ when x is in the no-verification set $[0, m]$. Hence, the threshold m may be interpreted as a deductible under which no claim is filed. In the verification set, there is coinsurance of large losses (i.e., the slope of the coverage schedule is less than one when $x > x_0$). Furthermore, the insurer should pay contingent fees to his auditor: the auditor's fees are (linearly) decreasing in the insurance indemnity payment.

The intuition for these results is as follows Let $x \in M$. A deviation from truthful revelation of loss without audit cost manipulation (i.e., $\hat{x} = x$, $e = 0$) to $\hat{x} = x' > x$, $e > 0$ is profitable to the policyholder if $T(x') - e > T(x)$ provided the claim is accepted by the auditor, which implies $R(x') \geq R(x) - be$. Both conditions are incompatible (for all e) if

$$R(x') + bT(x') \leq R(x) + bT(x)$$

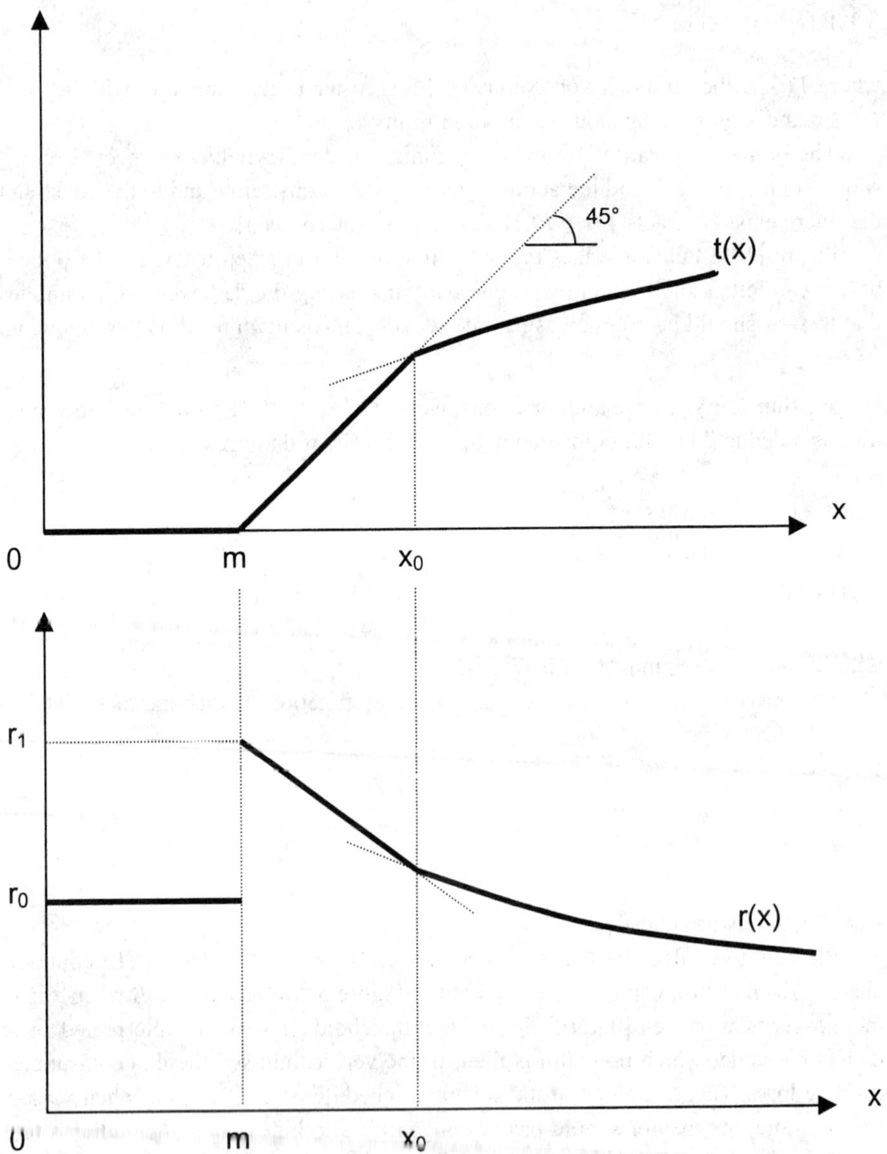

Figure 5 Optimal insurance contract and auditor's contingent fees

For all $x \in M$, we have $t(x) = T(x)$, $\omega(x) = R(x)$. This means that $\omega(x) + bt(x)$ should be nonincreasing for manipulation of audit cost to be detered. In other words, a 1 \$ increase in the indemnity payment should lead at least to a b \$ decrease in the auditor's fees. Because the auditor is risk averse, it would be suboptimal to have $\omega'(x) < -bt'(x)$, which gives the result on contingent fees. Because of condition $\omega'(x) = -bt'(x)$, a greater scope of variation in insurance payments entails a greater variability in the auditor's fees and thus a larger risk premium paid to the auditor for his participation constraint to be satisfied. Some degree of coinsurance for large losses then allows the insurer to decrease the auditor's expected fees which is ultimately beneficial to the policyholder. This argument does not hold if the auditor is risk-neutral and, in that case, a straight deductible is optimal. Inversely, a ceiling on coverage is optimal when the auditor is infinitely risk-averse or when he is affected by a limited liability constraint.

10.4 COSTLY STATE FALSIFICATION

Let us come now to the analysis of state falsification first examined by Lacker and Weinberg (1989)[12] and applied to an insurance setting by Crocker and Morgan (1997):[13] the policyholders are in position to misrepresent their actual losses by engaging in costly falsification activities. The outcome of these activities is a claim denoted by $y \in R_+$. The insurer only observes y: contrary to the costly state verification, setting verifying the actual magnitude of damages is supposed to be prohibively costly. Hence, an insurance contract only specifies a coverage schedule $t = T(y)$. Claims falsification is costly to the policyholder, particularly because it may require colluding with an agent: an automechanics, a physician, an attorney . . . Let $C(x, y)$ be the falsification cost. The policyholder's final wealth becomes

$$W_f = W - x - P + T(y) - C(y,x).$$

Let $y(x)$ be the (potentially falsified) claim of a policyholder who suffers an actual loss x. Given a falsification strategy $y(\cdot)$: $[0, \bar{x}] \to R_+$, the policyholder's final wealth may be written as a function of his loss:

$$W_f(x) \equiv W - x - P + T(y(x)) - C(y(x), x) \tag{8}$$

An optimal insurance contract maximizes $EU(W_f(x))$ with respect to $T(\cdot)$ and P subject to

$$P \geq \int_0^{\bar{x}} T(y(x))\, dF(x) \tag{9}$$

$$y(x) \in \text{Arg}_{y'} \text{ Max } T(y') - C(y', x) \quad \text{for all } x \in [0, \bar{x}] \tag{10}$$

[12] See also Maggi and Rodriguez-Clare (1995).

[13] See also Crocker and Tennyson (1999) and Dionne and Gagné (1997) on econometric testing of theoretical predictions of models involving costly state falsification.

(9) is the insurer's participation constraint and (10) specifies that $y(x)$ is an optimal falsification strategy of a type-x policyholder.

Since the payments $\{P, T(\cdot)\}$ are defined up to an additive constant, we may assume $T(0) = 0$ without loss of generality. For the time being, let us restrict attention to linear coverage schedule, i.e., $T(y) = \alpha y + \beta$. Our normalization rule gives $\beta = 0$. Assume also that the falsification costs borne by the policyholder depend upon the absolute amount of misrepresentation $(y - x)$ and, for the sake of simplicity, assume $C = \gamma(y - x)^2/2$, where γ is an exogenous cost parameter. (10) then gives

$$y(x) \equiv x + \frac{\alpha}{\gamma} \tag{11}$$

Hence the amount of falsification $y(x) - x$ is increasing in the slope of the coverage schedule and decreasing in the falsification cost parameter. The optimal coverage schedule will tradeoff two conflicting objectives: providing more insurance to the policyholder, which requires increasing α, and mitigating the incentives to claim falsification by lowering α.

The insurer's participation constraint (9) is binding at the optimum, which gives

$$P = \int_0^{\bar{x}} \left(\alpha x + \frac{\alpha^2}{\gamma} \right) dF(x) = \alpha Ex + \frac{\alpha^2}{\gamma}$$

(8) then gives

$$W_f(x) = W - (1 - \alpha)x - \alpha Ex - \frac{\alpha^2}{2\gamma}$$

Maximizing $EU(W_f(x))$ with respect to α leads to the following first-order condition

$$\frac{\partial EU}{\partial \alpha} = E\left\{ \left(x - Ex - \frac{\alpha}{\gamma} \right) U'(W_f(x)) \right\} = 0 \tag{12}$$

and thus

$$\frac{\partial EU}{\partial \alpha}\Big|_{\alpha=1} = -\frac{1}{\gamma} U'\left(W - Ex - \frac{1}{2\gamma} \right) < 0 \tag{13}$$

$$\frac{\partial EU}{\partial \alpha}\Big|_{\alpha=0} = E\{(x - Ex)U'(W - x)\} > 0 \tag{14}$$

We also have

$$\frac{\partial^2 EU}{\partial \alpha^2} = -\frac{1}{\gamma} EU'(W_f(x)) + E\left\{ \left(x - Ex - \frac{\alpha}{\gamma} \right)^2 U''(W_f(x)) \right\} < 0 \tag{15}$$

which implies that $0 < \alpha < 1$ at the optimum. Hence, under costly state falsification, the optimal linear coverage schedule entails some degree of coinsurance and (11) shows that there exists a certain amount of claims falsifications at equilibrium. This characterization results from the trade-off between the above mentioned conflicting objectives: providing insurance to the policyholder and detering him from engaging in costly claim falsification activities.

This trade-off is particularly obvious when $U(\cdot)$ is quadratic. In that case, we may write

$$EU(W_f) = EW_f - \eta Var(W_f) \quad \eta > 0 \tag{16}$$

and straightforward calculations give

$$\alpha = \frac{2\eta\gamma\sigma^2}{1+2\eta\gamma\sigma^2} \tag{17}$$

at the optimum, where $\sigma^2 \equiv Var\ x$.

Hence, the coinsurance coefficient α is an increasing function of the cost parameter γ, of the risk aversion index η and of the variance of the loss. We have

$$T(y(x)) = \alpha x + \frac{\alpha^2}{\gamma}$$

which give $T(y(x)) > x$ if $x < x_0$ and $T(y(x)) < x$ if $x > x_0$ with $x_0 = \alpha^2/\gamma(1-\alpha)$. Hence in that case, the optimal indemnification rule overcompensates small lossess and it overpays larger ones. This is depicted in Figure 6.

Assume now that the insurer observes whether a loss occured or not, as in the paper by Crocker and Morgan (1997). Then an insurance contract is defined by a premium P, an insurance payment t_0 if $x = 0$ and an insurance coverage schedule $T(y)$ to be enforced if $x > 0$. In that case, a natural normalization rule is $t_0 = 0$. We still assume that $T(y)$ is linear: $T(y) = \alpha y + \beta$. For the sake of simplicity, we also assume that $U(\cdot)$ is quadratic.

The insurer's participation constraint and (11) give

$$P = \alpha Ex + [1 - f(0)]\left(\frac{\alpha^2}{\gamma} + \beta\right) \tag{18}$$

which implies

$$W_f = W - \alpha Ex - [1 - f(0)]\left(\frac{\alpha^2}{\gamma} + \beta\right) \quad \text{if } x = 0$$

$$W_f = W - \alpha Ex - [1 - f(0)]\left(\frac{\alpha^2}{\gamma} + \beta\right) - (1-\alpha)x + \beta + \frac{\alpha^2}{2\gamma} \quad \text{if } x > 0$$

and we obtain

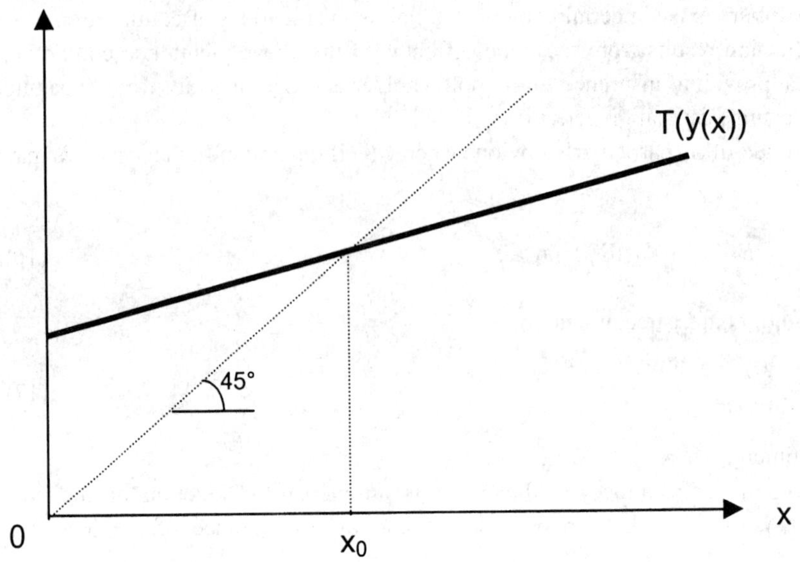

Figure 6 Equilibrium indemnification under costly state falsification

$$EW_f = W - Ex - \frac{\alpha^2}{2\gamma}[1 - f(0)] \tag{19}$$

and

$$Var(W_f) = f(0)[1 - f(0)]\left(\beta + \frac{\alpha^2}{2\gamma}\right)^2 + (1-\alpha)^2\sigma^2 - 2f(0)(1-\alpha)\left(\beta + \frac{\alpha^2}{2\gamma}\right)Ex \tag{20}$$

Maximizing $EU(W_f)$ defined by (16) with respect to α and β gives the following result

$$\alpha = \frac{2\eta\gamma\tilde{\sigma}^2}{1+2\eta\gamma\tilde{\sigma}^2} \tag{21}$$

$$\beta = (1-\alpha)\bar{x} - \frac{\alpha^2}{2\gamma} \tag{22}$$

where $\tilde{\sigma}^2 = Var(x \mid x > 0)$ and $\bar{x} = E(x \mid x > 0)$ i.e., $\tilde{\sigma}^2$ and $\bar{x}$ are respectively the variance and the expected value of the magnitude of damages conditional on a loss occurring.

(21) is similar to (17) and it may be interpreted in the same way. The fact that α is strictly positive (and less than one) means that some degree of insurance is provided but also that there is claims falsification at equilibrium. β may be positive or

negative, but the insurance payment $T(y(x))$ is always positive.[14] As in the previous case, small losses are overcompensated and there is undercompensation for more severe losses.

Crocker and Morgan (1997) obtain a similar characterization without restricting themselves to a linear-quadratic model. They characterize the allocations, $\{t(\cdot), y(\cdot), P\}$, with $t(\cdot)$: $[0, \bar{x}] \to R_+$ and $y(\cdot)$: $(0, \bar{x}] \to R_{++}$, that may be implemented by a coverage schedule $T(y)$.[15] For such an allocation, there exists $T(\cdot)$: $R_+ \to R_+$ such that

$$y(x) \in \text{Arg}\ \max_{y'}\{T(y') - C(y',x)\}$$

and

$$t(x) = T(y(x)) \quad \text{for all } x$$

The Revelation Principle (Myerson, 1979) applies in such a context, which means that implementable allocations may be obtained as the outcome of a revelation game in which

1. The insurance payment t and the action y are defined as functions of a message $\tilde{x} \in [0, \bar{x}]$ of the policyholder, i.e., $t = t(\tilde{x})$, $y = y(\tilde{x})$.
2. Truthtelling is an optimal strategy for the policyholder, i.e.,

$$x \in \text{Arg}\ \max_{\tilde{x}}\{t(\tilde{x}) - C(y(\tilde{x}), x)\} \tag{23}$$

for all x in $(0, \bar{x}]$.

Such an allocation $\{t(\cdot), y(\cdot)\}$ is said to be incentive compatible. The optimal allocation maximizes the polilcyholder's expected utility $EU(W_f(x))$ with respect to $t(\cdot)$, $y(\cdot)$ and P subject to the insurer's participation constraint and to incentive compatibility constraints. Using a standard technique of incentives theory, Crocker and Morgan characterize the optimal solution of a less-constrained problem in which a first-order truthtelling condition is substituted to (24). They obtain the following result.[16,17]

[14] When β is negative, the optimal coverage schedule is equivalent to a deductible $m = -\beta/\alpha$ with a coinsurance provision for larger losses, i.e., $T(y) = Sup\{0, \alpha(y - m)\}$.

[15] Crocker and Morgan assume that the insurer can observe whether a loss occurred or not. Hence, there may be falsification only if $x > 0$.

[16] There are some minor differences between the Crocker-Morgan's setting and ours. They are not mentioned for the sake of brevity.

[17] The second-order condition for incentive compatibility requires $y(x)$ to be monotonically increasing. If the solution to the less constrained problem satisfies this monotonicity condition, then the optimal allocation is characterized as in proposition 6. See Crocker and Morgan (1997) for a numerical example. If this is not the case, then the optimal allocation entails bunching on (at least) an interval $(x', x'') \subset [0, \bar{x}]$, i.e., $y(x) = \hat{y}$, $t(x) = \hat{t}$ for all x in (x', x''). In such a case, the coverage schedule $T(y)$ that sustains the optimal allocation is not differentiable at $y = \hat{y}$.

Proposition 6. The optimal solution to the insurance problem under claims falsification satisfies

(i) $y(0_+) = 0$, $y(\bar{x}) = \bar{x}$ and $y(x) > x$ if $0 < x < \bar{x}$
(ii) $t'(0_+) = t'(\bar{x}) = 0$ and $t'(x) > 0$ if $0 < x < \bar{x}$
(iii) $t(0_+) > 0$ and $t(\bar{x}) < \bar{x}$.

Proposition 6 extends the results already obtained in this section to a more general setting, with a non linear coverage schedule. The optimal solution always entails some degree of falsification except at the top (when $x = \bar{x}$) and at the bottom (when $x \to 0_+$). The insurance payment is increasing in the magnitude of the actual damages and it provides overinsurance (respect. underinsurance) for small (respect. large) losses.

10.5 COSTLY STATE VERIFICATION: THE CASE OF RANDOM AUDITING

We now come back to the costly state verification setting. Under *random auditing*, the insurer verifies the claims with a probability that depends upon the magnitude of damages. The insurance payment may differ depending on whether the claim has been verified or not. A policyholder who suffers a loss x files a claim $\hat{x}$ that will be audited with probability $p(\hat{x})$. If there is an audit, the true damages are observed by the insurer and the policyholder receives an insurance payment $t_A(x, \hat{x})$. If there is no audit, the insurance payment is denoted $t_N(\hat{x})$.

When a policyholder with damages x files a claim $\hat{x}$, his expected utility is

$$[1 - p(\hat{x})]U(W - P - x + t_N(\hat{x})) + p(\hat{x})U(W - P - x + t_A(x, \hat{x}))$$

The *Revelation Principle* applies to this setting and we can restrict attention to incentive compatible insurance contracts, that is to contracts where the policyholder is given incentives to report his loss truthfully. Such incentive compatible contracts are such that

$$\begin{aligned}&[1 - p(x)]U(W - P - x + t_N(x)) + p(x)U(W - P - x + t_A(x, x)) \\ &\geq [1 - p(\hat{x})]U(W - P - x + t_N(\hat{x})) + p(\hat{x})U(W - P - x + t_A(x, \hat{x}))\end{aligned} \tag{24}$$

for all x, $\hat{x} \neq x$.

Let us assume that the net payment from the policyholder to the insurer $P - t_A(x, \hat{x})$ is bounded by a maximal penalty that can be imposed in case of misrepresentation of damages (i.e., when $x \neq \hat{x}$). This maximal penalty[18] may depend on the true level of damages x and will be denoted $B(x)$. Hence, we have

$$P - t_A(x, \hat{x}) \leq B(x) \quad \text{if} \quad x \neq \hat{x} \tag{25}$$

For instance, Mookherjee and Png (1989) assume that the wealth of the policyholder is perfectly liquid and that his final wealth can be at most set equal to zero in case of false claim detected by audit. We have $B(x) \equiv W - x$ in that case. Fagart and Picard (1999), assume that the policyholder is affected by a liquidity constraint and that the liquid assets of the policyholder have a given value B. The maximal penalty is then $B(x) = B$ for all x. Another interpretation of (25) is that $B(x) \equiv B$ is an exogenously given parameter that represents the cost (in monetary terms) incurred by a policyholder who is prosecuted after he filed a fraudulent claim detected by audit.[19]

This upper bound on the penalty plays a crucial role in the analysis of optimal insurance contracts under random auditing. Indeed, by increasing the penalty, the insurer could induce truthtelling by the policyholder with a lower probability of auditing, which, since auditing is costly, reduces the cost of the private information. Consequently, if there were no bound on the penalty, first-best optimality could be approximated with very large fines and a very low probability of auditing. Asymetry of information would not be a problem in such a case.

In equilibrium, the policyholder always reports his loss truthfully. Hence, it is optimal to make the penalty as large as possible since this provides maximum incentive to tell the truth without affecting the equilibrium pay-offs.[20] We thus have

$$t_A(x, \hat{x}) = P - B(x) \quad \text{if} \quad x \neq \hat{x}$$

Finally, we assume that the policyholder's final wealth W_f should be larger than a lower bound denoted $A(x)$. This bound on the policyholder's final wealth may simply

[18] The Revelation Principle does not apply any more if the maximal penalty also depend on the claim $\hat{x}$. In such a case, there may be false report at equilibrium.

[19] Under this interpretation, it may be more natural to assume that the policyholder should pay the penalty B in addition to the premium P, since the latter is usually paid at the beginning of the time period during which the insurance policy is enforced. In fact, both assumptions are equivalent when the policyholder is affected by a liquidity constraint. Indeed, in such a case, it would be optimal to fix the insurance premium P at the largest possible level (say $P = \bar{P}$) and to compensate adequately the policyholder by providing large insurance payments t_N and t_A unless a fraudulent claim is detected by audit. This strategy provides the highest penalty in case of fraud, without affecting equilibrium net payments $t_N - P$ and $t_A - P$. If the law of insurance contracts specifies a penalty $\hat{B}$ to be paid in case of fraudulent claim, we have $P - t_A(x, \hat{x}) \leq \bar{P} + \hat{B}$ which corresponds to (25) with $B(x) \equiv \bar{P} + \hat{B}$.

[20] In a more realistic setting, there would be several reasons for which imposing maximal penalties on defrauders may not be optimal. In particular, audit may be imperfect so that innocent individuals may be falsely accused. Furthermore, a policyholder may overestimate his damages in good faith. Lastly, very large fines may create incentives for policyholders caught cheating to bribe the auditor to overlook their violation.

result from a feasibility condition on consumption. In particular, we may have $W_f \geq 0$ which gives $A(x) = 0$ for all x. The lower bound on final wealth may also be logically linked to the upper bound on the penalty: when $B(x)$ corresponds to the value of liquid assets of the policyholder, we have $P - t_N(x) \leq B(x)$ and $P - t_A(x, x) \leq B(x)$ for all x which implies $W_f \geq W - x - B(x) \equiv A(x)$. Mookherjee and Png (1989) assume $B(x) = W - x$, which gives $A(x) = 0$. Fagart and Picard (1999) assume $B(x) = B$, which gives $A(x) = W - x - B$.

Let $t_A(x) \equiv t_A(x, x)$. Under random auditing, a contract will be denoted $\delta = \{t_A(\cdot), t_N(\cdot), p(\cdot), P\}$. An optimal contract maximizes

$$EU = \int_0^{\bar{x}} \{[1 - p(x)]U(W - P - x + t_N(x)) + p(x)U(W - P - x + t_A(x))\}\, dF(x) \tag{26}$$

with respect to P, $t_A(\cdot)$, $t_N(\cdot)$ and $p(\cdot)$ subject to the followwing constraints:

$$E\Pi = P - \int_0^{\bar{x}} \{[1 - p(x)]t_N(x) + p(x)[t_A(x) + c]\}\, dF(x) \geq 0 \tag{27}$$

$$\begin{aligned}&[1 - p(x)]U(W - P - x + t_N(x)) + p(x)U(W - P - x + t_A(x)) \\ &\quad \geq [1 - p(\hat{x})]U(W - P - x + t_N(\hat{x})) + p(\hat{x})U(W - x - B(x)) \quad \text{for all } x, \hat{x} \neq x\end{aligned} \tag{28}$$

$$W - P - x + t_N(x) \geq A(x) \quad \text{for all } x \tag{29}$$

$$W - P - x + t_A(x) \geq A(x) \quad \text{for all } x \tag{30}$$

$$0 \leq p(x) \leq 1 \quad \text{for all } x \tag{31}$$

(27) is the insurer's participation constraint. Inequalities (28) are the incentive compatibility constraints that require the policyholder to be willing to report his level of loss truthfully. (29), (30) and (31) are feasibility constraints.[21]

Mookherjee and Png (1989) have established a number of properties of an optimal contract. They are synthetized in proposition 7 hereafter. In this proposition $v(x)$ denotes the expected utility of the policyholder when his loss is x, i.e.,

$$v(x) = [1 - p(x)]U(W - P - x + t_N(x) + p(x)U(W - P - x + t_A(x)).$$

Proposition 7. Under random auditing, an optimal insurance contract $\delta = \{t_A(\cdot), t_N(\cdot), p(\cdot), P\}$, has the following properties:

[21] Deterministic auditing may be considered as a particular case of random auditing where $p(x) = 1$ if $x \in M$ and $p(x) = 0$ if $x \in M^c$, and Lemma 1 may be obtained as a consequence of the incentive compatibility conditions (28). If x, $\hat{x} \in M^c$, (28) gives $t_N(x) \geq t_N(\hat{x})$. Interverting x and $\hat{x}$ gives $t_N(\hat{x}) \geq t_N(x)$. We thus have $t_N(x) = t_0$ for all x in M^c. If $x \in M$ and $\hat{x} \in M^c$, (28) gives $t_A(x) \geq t_N(\hat{x}) = t_0$. If $t_A(x) = t_0$ for $x \in [a, b] \subset M$, then it is possible to choose $p(x) = 0$ if $x \in [a, b]$, and to decrease P, the other elements of the optimal contract being unchanged. The policyholder's expected utility would increase, which is a contradiction. Hence $t_A(x) > t_0$ if $x \in M$.

(i) $p(x) < 1$ for all x if $v(x) > U(W - x - B(x))$ for all x

(ii) $t_A(x) > t_N(x)$ for all x such that $p(x) > 0$

(iii) If $p(\hat{x}) > 0$ for some $\hat{x}$ then there exists x such that $v(x) = [1 - p(\hat{x})]U(W - x - P + t_N(\hat{x})) + p(\hat{x})U(W - x - B(x))$

(iv) If $v(x) > u(W - x - B(x))$ for all x and $t_N(\hat{x}) = Min\{t_N(x), x \in [0, \bar{x}]\}$, then $p(\hat{x}) = 0$ and $p(x'') > p(x')$ if $t_N(x'') > t_N(x')$.

In Proposition 7, the condition "$v(x) > U(W - x - B(x))$ for all x" means that non-trivial penalties can be imposed on those detected to have filed a fraudulent claim. Let us call it "condition **C**". Mookherjee and Png (1989) assume $B(x) = W - x$, which means that the final wealth can be set equal to zero if the policyholder is detected to have lied. In such a case, **C** means that the final wealth is always positive at the optimum and a sufficient condition for **C** to hold is $U'(0_+) = +\infty$. If we assume $B(x) \equiv B$, i.e., the penalty is upward bounded either because of a liquidity constraint or because of statutory provisions, then **C** holds if B is large enough.[22] If **C** does not hold at equilibrium, then the optimal audit policy is deterministic and we are back to the characterization of Section 2. In particular, the $B = 0$ case reverts to deterministic auditing.

From (i) in proposition 4, all audits must be random if **C** holds. The intuition for this result is that under **C**, the policyholder would always strictly prefer not to lie if his claim were audited with probability one. In such a case, decreasing slightly the audit probability reduces the insurer's expected cost. This permits a decrease in the premium P, and thus an increase in the expected utility of the policyholder, without inducing the latter to lie. (ii) shows that the policyholder who has been verified to have reported his damages truthfully should be rewarded. The intuition is as follows. Assume $t_A(x) < t_N(x)$ for some x. Let $t_A(x)$– respect. $t_N(x)$– be increased (respect. decreased) slightly so that the expected cost $p(x)t_A(x) + [1 - p(x)]t_N(x)$ is unchanged. This change does not disturb the incentive compatibility constraints and it increases the expected utility which contradicts the optimality of the initial contract. If $t_A(x) = t_N(x)$, the same variation exerts no first-order effect on the expected utility (since we start from a full insurance position) and it allows the insurer to reduce $p(x)$ without disturbing any incentive compatibility constraint. The expected cost decreases, which enables a decreases in the premium P and thus generates an increase in the expected utility. This also contradicts the optimality of the initial contract. (iii) shows that for any level of loss $\hat{x}$ audited with positive probability, there exists a level of loss x such that the policyholder who suffers the loss x is indifferent between filing a truthful claim and reporting $\hat{x}$. In other words, when a claim $\hat{x}$ is audited with positive probability, a decrease in the probability of audit $p(\hat{x})$ would induce misreporting by the policyholder for (at least) one level of loss x. Indeed if this were not the case, then one could lower $p(\hat{x})$ without disturbing any incentive compatibility constraint. This

[22] See Fagart and Picard (1999).

variation allows the insurer to save on audit cost and it enables a decrease in the premium. The policyholder's expected utility increases which contradicts the optimality of the initial contract. Finally, (iv) shows that, under **C**, the claim corresponding to the lowest indemnity payment in the absence of audit should not be audited. All other claims should be audited and the larger the indemnity payment in the absence of audit, the larger the probability of audit. Once again, the intuition is rather straightforward. A policyholder who files a fraudulent claim $\hat{x}$ may be seen as a gambler who wins the prize $t_N(\hat{x})$ if he has the luck not to be audited and who will pay $B(x)$ if he gets caught. The larger the prize, the larger the audit probability should be for fraudulent claiming to be detered. Furthermore it is useless to verify the claims corresponding to the lowest prize since it always provides a lower expected utility than truthtelling.

The main difficulty if one wants to further characterize the optimal contract under random auditing is to identify the incentive compatibility constraints that are binding at the optimum and those that are not binding. In particular, it may be that, for some levels of damages, many (and even all) incentive constraints are binding and, for other levels of damages none of them are binding.[23] Fagart and Picard (1999) provide a full characterization of the optimal coverage schedule and of the audit policy when the policyholder has constant absolute risk aversion and the penalty is constant (i.e., $B(x) \equiv B$).

Proposition 8. Assume $U(\cdot)$ exhibits constant absolute risk aversion and **C** holds at the optimum. Then there exist $m > 0$ and $k \in (0, m)$ such that

$$t_A(x) = x - k \text{ and } t_N(x) = x - k - \eta(x) \quad \text{if} \quad x > m$$

$$t_A(x) = t_N(x) = 0 \quad \text{if} \quad x \leq m$$

with $\eta'(x)$, $\eta(m) = m - k$, $\eta(x) \to 0$ when $x \to \infty$.

Furthermore, we have

$$0 < p(x) < 1, \; p'(x) > 0, \; p''(x) < 0 \quad \text{when} \quad x > m$$

$$p(m) = 0$$

$$p(x) \to \bar{p} \in (0, 1) \quad \text{when} \quad x \to \infty$$

The optimal contract characterized in proposition 8 is depicted in Figure 7. No claim is filed, when the magnitude of damages is less than m. When the damages

[23] Technically, this rules out the possibility of taking up the differential approach initially developed by Guesnerie and Laffont (1984) and widely used in the literature on incentives contracts under adverse selection.

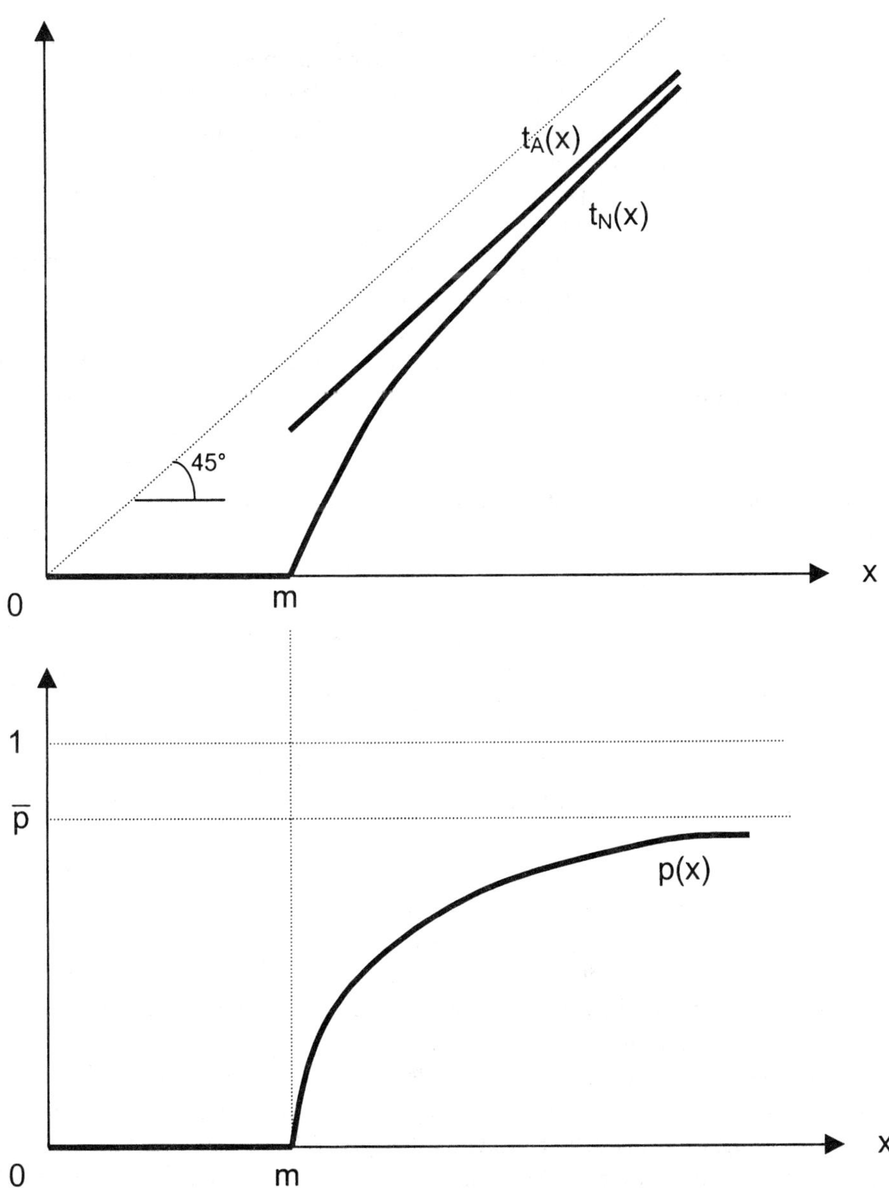

Figure 7 Optimal insurance contract under random auditing when $U(\cdot)$ is CARA

exceed the threshold, then the insurance payment is positive and it is larger when the claim is audited than when it is not—which confirms proposition 7-(ii)—. However the difference is decreasing when the magnitude of damages is increasing and this difference goes to zero when the damages go to infinity (when $\bar{x} = +\infty$). Marginal damages are fully covered in case of audit, i.e., $t_A'(x) = 1$ if $x > m$. In other words, the insurance coverage includes a constant deductible k if the claim is verified. If the claim is not verified, then there is also an additional deductible that disappears when the damages become infinitely large. Furthermore the probability of audit is a concave increasing function of the damages and this probability goes to a limit $\bar{p} < 1$ when x goes to infinity.

To understand the logic of these results, observe that any variation in insurance payment (with a compensating change in the premium) entails two effects. Firstly, if affects the risk sharing between the insurer and the policyholder and, of course, this is the *raison d'être* of any insurance contract. Secondly, it may also modify the audit policy for incentive compatibility constraints not to be disturbed. This second effect is more difficult to analyze because the effects of variations in insurance payment on the incentive to tell the truth are intricate. As above, we may describe the decision making of the policyholder as if he were a gambler. When the true level of damages is x, filing a fraudulent claim $\hat{x} \neq x$ amounts to choose the lottery "earning $t_N(\hat{x})$ with probability $1 - p(\hat{x})$ or losing B with probability $p(\hat{x})$" in preference to the lottery "earning $t_N(x)$ with probability $1 - p(x)$ or earning $t_A(x)$ with probability $p(x)$". If the incentive compatibility constraint corresponding to x and $\hat{x}$ is tight, then any increase in $t_N(\hat{x})$ should be accompanied by an increase in $p(\hat{x})$ for fraudulent claiming to be detered. However, simultaneously, the increase in $t_N(\hat{x})$ may also affect the optimal strategy of a policyholder who has actually experienced a loss $\hat{x}$ and who (for instance) intended to file another fraudulent claim, say $\hat{x}' \neq \hat{x}$. This policyholder may come back to truthfulling after the increase in $t_N(\hat{x})$, even if $t_N(\hat{x}')$ is slightly increased. This sequence is possible if the preferences of our gambler over lotteries depend upon his wealth, i.e., upon the magnitude of his loss. This suggests that, without simplifying assumptions, analyzing the consequences of a variation in the coverage schedule on the policyholder's strategy may be quite intricate.

The problem is much more simple under constant absolute risk aversion since weath effects disappear from the incentive constraints when utility is exponential. Fagart and Picard (1999) have considered this case. They show that, when $U(\cdot)$ is CARA, the only incentive constraints that may be binding at the optimum correspond to loss levels $x \in I \subset [0, \bar{x}]$ for which the policyholder receives the smallest indemnity payment. This results from the fact that, when $U(\cdot)$ is CARA, the loss x disappears from (28). We know from Proposition 5-(ii) and (iv) that the claim is not audited in that case, which allows us to assume $t_N(x) = t_A(x) = 0$ if $x \in I$ since, as before, the optimal insurance coverage schedule $\{t_N(\cdot), t_A(\cdot), P\}$ is defined up to an additive constant. The best risk-sharing is reached when $I = [0, m]$, with $m > 0$. Under constant absolute risk aversion, the fact that small claims should not be audited can thus be extended to the case of random auditing.

When the loss exceeds m, it is optimal to provide a positive insurance payment. Any increase in $t_N(x)$ should be accompanied by an increase in $p(x)$ for fraudulent claiming to be detered. Let $\phi(t_N)$ be the probability of audit for which the lottery "earning $t_N(x)$ with probability $1 - p(x)$ or losing B with probability $p(x)$" and the status quo (i.e., a zero certain gain) are equivalent for the policyholder when his true loss level $\tilde{x}$ is in I. The probability $\phi(t_N)$ does not depend on $\tilde{x}$ when $U(\cdot)$ is CARA and we have $\phi' > 0$, $\phi'' < 0$. The optimal audit probability is such that $p(x) = \phi(t_N(x))$ for all $x > m$.

Let $c\ \phi'(t_N(x))dt_N(x)$ be the additional expected audit cost induced by a marginal increase in the insurance payment $dt_N(x)$. Adding this additional expected audit cost to the variation in the insurance payment itself gives the additional expected total cost $[1 + c\ \phi'(t_N(x))]dt_N(x)$. When a claim is audited, the additional cost induced by an increase in the insurance payment is just $dt_A(x)$. The difference in additional cost per \$ paid as coverage explains why a larger payment should be promised in case of audit—i.e., $t_A(x) > t_N(x)$—. More precisely, $\phi'' < 0$ implies that $1 + c\ \phi'(t_N(x))$ is decreasing when $t_N(x)$ is increasing. Hence, the difference in the addditional expected cost per \$ paid as coverage decreases when $t_N(x)$ increases. This explains why the additional deductible $t_A(x) - t_N(x) \equiv \eta(x)$ is decreasing and disappears when x is large.[24]

10.6 MORALE COSTS AND ADVERSE SELECTION

Thus far we have assumed that the policyholders are guided only by self-interest and that they didn't feel any morale cost after filing a fraudulent claim. In other words, there was no intrinsic value of honesty to policyholders. In the real world, thank God, dishonesty creates morale problems and a lot of people are detered to file fraudulent claim even if the probability of being caught is small and the fine is moderate.[25] However, more often than not, the insurers are unable to observe the morale cost incurred by their customers which lead to an adverse selection problem.[26] In such a situation, the optimal audit policy as well as the competitive equilibrium in the insurance market (in terms of coverage and premium) may be strongly affected by the distribution of morale costs in the population of policyholders. In particular,

[24] Let $\overline{U}(x) = [1 - p(x)]U(W - P - x + t_N(x)) + p(x)U(W - P - x + t_A(x))$ be the expected utility of a policyholder who has incurred a loss x. Using $p(m) = 0$ shows that $\overline{U}(x)$ is continuous at $x = m$.

[25] See Tennyson (1994) on consumer attitudes toward insurance fraud. She shows that tolerant attitudes toward fraud are more often expressed by individuals who have negative perceptions of the fairness of insurance institutions and of insurance market outcomes, particularly by those who face poorly functioning or noncompetitive insurance markets.

[26] This asymetric information problem may be mitigated in a repeated relationship framework.

the consequences of insurance fraud will be all the more severe that the proportion of purely opportunistic policyholders (i.e., individuals without any morale cost) is large.

We will approach this issue in the following setting, drawn from Picard (1996).[27] Assume that the insurance buyers face the possibility of a loss L with probability $\delta \in (0, 1)$. Hence, for the sake of simplicity, the size of the loss is now given. The insurance contract involves a premium P and a level of coverage t. The insurer audits claims with a probability $p \in [0, 1]$ at cost c. To simplify further the analysis, we assume that the insurance payment t is the same, whether the claim is audited or not. The reservation utility is $\overline{U} = \delta U(W - L) + (1 - \delta)U(W)$. The policyholders may be either opportunist, with probability θ or honest with probability $1 - \theta$, with $0 < \theta < 1$. Honest policyholders truthfully report losses to their insurer: they would suffer very large morale cost when cheating. Opportunists may choose to fraudulently report a loss. Let α be the (endogenously determined) probability for an opportunist to file a fraudulent claim when no loss has been incurred. The insurers cannot distinguish honest policyholders from opportunists.

Law exogenously defines the fine, denoted B, that has to be paid by a policyholder who is detected to have lied. Let $\tilde{p}$ denote the audit probability that makes an opportunist (who has not experienced any loss) indifferent between honesty and fraud. Honesty gives $W_f = W - P$ where W (respect. W_f) still denotes the initial (respect. final) wealth of the policyholder. Fraud gives $W_f = W - P - B$ if the claim is audited and $W_f = W - P + t$ otherwise. Hence $\tilde{p}$ is given by

$$U(W - P) = \tilde{p}U(W - P - B) + (1 - \tilde{p})U(W - P + t)$$

which implies

$$\tilde{p} = \frac{U(W - P + t) - U(W - P)}{U(W - P + t) - U(W - P - B)} \equiv \tilde{p}(t, P) \in (0, 1)$$

Consider a contract (t, P) chosen by a population of individuals that includes a proportion $\sigma \in [0, 1]$ of opportunists. Note that σ may conceivably differ from θ if various contracts are offered on the market. Given (q, P, σ), the relationship between a policyholder and his insurer is described by the following three stage game:

- At stage 1, *nature* determines whether the policyholder is honest or opportunist, with probabilities $1 - \sigma$ and σ respectively. Nature also determines whether the policyholder experiences a loss with probability δ.
- At stage 2, the *policyholder* decides to file a claim or not. Honest customers always tell the truth. When no loss has been incurred, opportunists defraud with probability α.

[27] See also Boyer (1999) for a similar model.

- At stage 3, when a loss has been reported at stage 2, the insurer audits with probability p.

Opportunists who do not experience any loss choose α to maximize

$$EU = \alpha[pU(W - P - B) + (1 - p)U(W - P + t)] + (1 - \alpha)U(W - P)$$

which gives

$$\left.\begin{array}{ll} \alpha = 0 & \text{if } p > \tilde{p}(t, P) \\ \alpha \in [0, 1] & \text{if } p = \tilde{p}(t, P) \\ \alpha = 1 & \text{if } p < \tilde{p}(t, P) \end{array}\right\} \tag{32}$$

The insurer chooses p to maximize its expected profit $E\Pi$ or equivalently to minimize the expected cost C defined by

$$C = IC + AC$$

with

$$E\Pi = P - C$$

where IC and AC are respectively the expected insurance coverage and the expected audit cost.[28]

Insurance coverage is paid to the policyholders who actually experience a loss and to the opportunists who fraudulently report a loss and are not audited. We have

$$IC = t[\delta + \alpha\sigma(1 - \sigma)(1 - p)] \tag{33}$$

$$AC = pc[\delta + \alpha\sigma(1 - \delta)] \tag{34}$$

As in the previous sections, we assume that the insurer can commit to his audit policy which means that he has a Stackelberg advantage in the audit game: the audit probability p is chosen to minimize C given the reaction function of opportunists. Since in the next section we want to contrast such an equilibrium with a situation where the insurer cannot commit to its audit policy, we refer to this commitment equilibrium with the upper index c. Let $\alpha^c(t, P, \sigma)$, $p^c(t, P, \sigma)$ and $C^c(t, P, \sigma)$ be respectively the equilibrium strategies of opportunists and insurers and the equilibrium

[28] For the sake of simplicity, we assume that no award is paid to the insurer when an opportunist is caught cheating. The fine B is entirely paid to the government.

expected cost in an audit game (q, P, σ) under commitment to audit policy. Proposition 9 characterize these functions.

Proposition 9. Under commitment to audit policy, the equilibrium of an audit game (t, P, σ) is characterized by

$$p^c(t, P, \sigma) = 0 \text{ and } \alpha^c(t, P, \sigma) = 1 \quad \text{if} \quad c > c_0(t, P, \sigma)$$

$$p^c(t, P, \sigma) = \tilde{p}(q, P) \text{ and } \alpha^c(t, P, \sigma) = 0 \quad \text{if} \quad c \leq c_0(t, P, \sigma)$$

$$C^c(t, P, \sigma) = \min\{t[\delta + \sigma(1-\delta)], \delta[t + \tilde{p}(t, P)c]\}$$

where

$$c_0(t, P, \sigma) = \frac{(1-\delta)\sigma t}{\delta \tilde{p}(t, P)}$$

The proof of proposition 9 is straightforward. Only two strategies may be optimal for the insurer: either fully preventing fraud by auditing claims with probability $p = \tilde{p}(t, P)$ which gives $\alpha = 0$[29] or abstaining from any audit ($p = 0$) which gives $\alpha = 1$. The optimal audit strategy is chosen so as to minimize C. Using (33) and (34) gives the result. Proposition 9 shows in particular that, given the contract (t, P), preventing fraud through an audit policy is optimal if the audit cost c is low enough and the proportion of opportunists σ is large enough.

We now consider a competitive insurance market with free entry, where insurers compete by offering policies. An adverse selection feature is brought in the model because the insurers cannot distinguish opportunists from honest policyholders. Following the approach of Wilson (1977), a market equilibrium is defined as a set of profitable contracts such that no insurer can offer another contract which remains profitable after other insurers have withdrawn all non-profitable contracts in reaction to the offer. Picard (1996) characterizes the market equilibrium by assuming that honest individuals are uniformly distributed among the best contracts, likewise for opportunists. This assumption will be called **A**. Let[30]

$$(t^c, P^c) = \arg\max_{t,P} \{\delta U(W - L + t - P) + (1-\delta)U(W - P) \quad \text{s.t.} \quad P \geq C^c(t, P, \theta)\}$$

Proposition 10. Under **A**, (t^c, P^c) is the unique market equilibrium when the insurers can commit to their audit policy.

[29] $\alpha = 0$ is an optimal strategy for opportunists when $p = \tilde{p}(t, P)$ and it is the *only* optimal strategy if $p = \tilde{p}(t, P) + \varepsilon$, $\varepsilon > 0$.

[30] We assume that (t^c, P^c) is a singleton.

According to Proposition 10, a market equilibrium is defined by a unique contract (t^c, P^c) that maximizes the expected utility of honest policyholders under the constraint that opportunists cannot be set aside.[31] The arguments at work in the proof of proposition 10 can be summarized as follows. Let us first note that all contracts offered at equilibrium are necessarily equivalent for honest customers, otherwise some equilibrium contracts would only attract opportunists. Given **A**, this would imply that $\alpha = 1$ is the equilibrium strategy of opportunists for such contract and these contracts could not be profitable. Equilibrium contracts are also equivalent for opportunists. Assume *a contrario* that opportunists concentrate on a subset of equilibrium contracts. For these contracts, the proportion of opportunists is larger that θ and honest individuals prefer (t^c, P^c) to these contracts. A contract $(t^c - \varepsilon, P^c)$, $\varepsilon > 0$ would attract all honest individuals for ε small and would remain profitable even if opportunists finally also opt for this new contract. This contradicts the definition of a market equilibrium. Hence, for any contract (t, P) offered at equilibrium, the insurers' participation constraint is $P \geq C^c(t, P, \theta)$. If (t^c, P^c) is not offered, then another contract could be proposed that would be strictly preferred by honest individuals and that would remain profitable whatever the reaction of opportunists. Hence (t^c, P^c) is the only possible market equilibrium. Another contract $(\tilde{t}, \tilde{P})$, offered in addition to (t^c, P^c) will be profitable if it attracts honest individuals only[32] and if $\tilde{P} > \delta\tilde{t}$. If $(\tilde{t}, \tilde{P})$ were offered, the insurers that go on offering (t^c, P^c) loss money. Indeed in such a case we necessarily have $\alpha^c(t^c, P^c, \tilde{\sigma}) = 1$ where $\tilde{\sigma}$ is the proportion of opportunists in the population of insureds who still choose (t^c, P^c) after $(\tilde{t}, \tilde{P})$ has be offered with $\tilde{\sigma} > \theta$.[33]

We then have

$$\begin{aligned} C^c(t^c, P^c, \sigma^c) &= t^c[\delta + \tilde{\sigma}(1-\delta)] \\ &> t^c[\delta + \theta(1-\delta)] \geq C^c(t^c, P^c, \theta) = P^c \end{aligned}$$

which proves that (t^c, P^c) becomes non-profitable. Hence (t^c, P^c) will be withdrawn and all individuals will turn toward the new contract $(\tilde{t}, \tilde{P})$. This new contract will show a deficit and it will not be offered, which establishes that (t^c, P^c) is the market equilibrium.

The market equilibrium is depicted in Figures 8 and 9. The perfect information market equilibrium is A with full insurance offered at fair premium.

Maximizing $EU = \delta U(W - L - P + t) + (1 - \delta)\, U(W - P)$ with respect to $t \geq 0$, $P \geq 0$ subject to $P = \delta[t + c\tilde{p}(t, P)]$ gives $t = \hat{t}$ and $P = \hat{P}$ at point B. We denote η_B the expected utility at B and we assume $\eta_B > \overline{U}$, i.e., the origin of the axis is over the

[31] Proposition 10 shows that a pooling contract is offered at equilibrium: there does not exist any separating equilibrium where honest and opportunist individuals would choose different contract. This result is also obtained by Boyer (1999) in a similar framework.

[32] Opportunists cannot benefit from separating and (t^c, P^c) is the best pooling contract for honest individuals.

[33] We have $\tilde{\sigma} = 1$ if all honest policyholders choose $(\tilde{t}, \tilde{P})$ and $\tilde{\sigma} = \dfrac{2\theta}{\theta+1}$ if $(\tilde{t}, \tilde{P})$ and (t^c, P^c) are equivalent for honest policyholders.

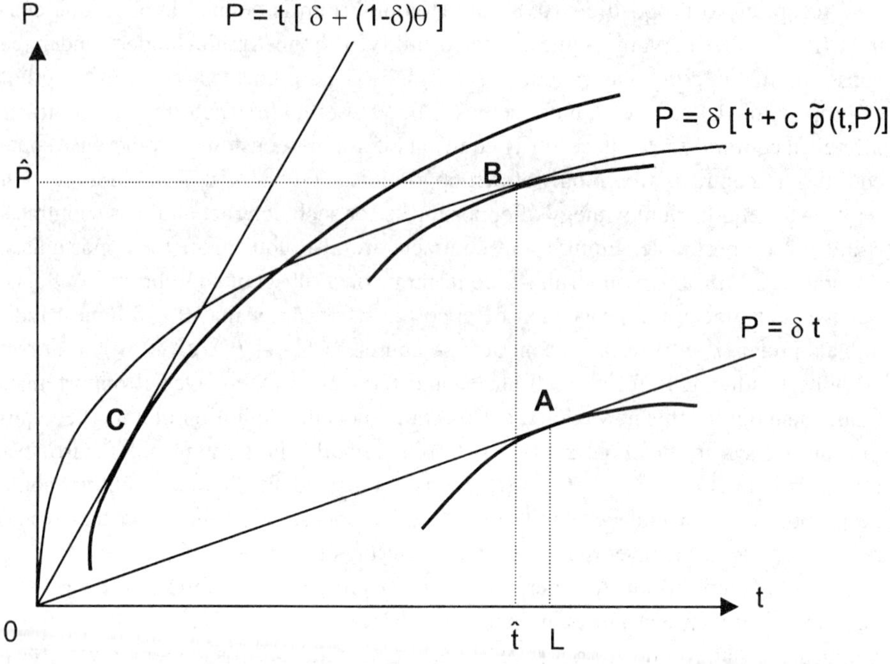

Figure 8 The market equilibrium is at point B when $\theta > \hat{\theta}$

indifference curve that goes through B. This assumption is satisfied if the audit cost c is not too large. Maximizing EU with respect to $t \geq 0$, $P \geq 0$ subject to $P = t[\delta + (1 - \delta)\theta]$ gives $t = \bar{t}$ and $P = \bar{P}$ at point C. We denote $\eta_C(\theta)$ the expected utility at C, with $\eta'_C(\theta) < 0$. Let $\hat{\theta} \in (0, 1)$ such that $\eta_B = \eta_C(\hat{\theta})$. When $\theta > \hat{\theta}$, the market equilibrium is at B: the insurers audit claims with probability $\tilde{p}(\hat{t}, \hat{P})$ and the opportunists are detered from defrauding. When $\theta < \hat{\theta}$, the market equilibrium is at C: the insurers do not audit claims because the proportion of opportunists is too small for verifying claims to be profitable and the opportunists systematically defraud. Hence, when $\theta < \hat{\theta}$, there is fraud at equilibrium.

10.7 THE CREDIBILITY ISSUE

In a situation where there are many opportunist policyholders, it is essential for insurers to credibly announce that a tough monitoring policy will be enforced, with a high probability of claim verification and a high level of scrutiny for suspected fraud. In the model introduced in the previous section, this was reached by announcing that claims are audited with probability $\tilde{p}(t, P)$. However, since auditing is costly to the insurer, a commitment to such a tough audit policy may not be credible.

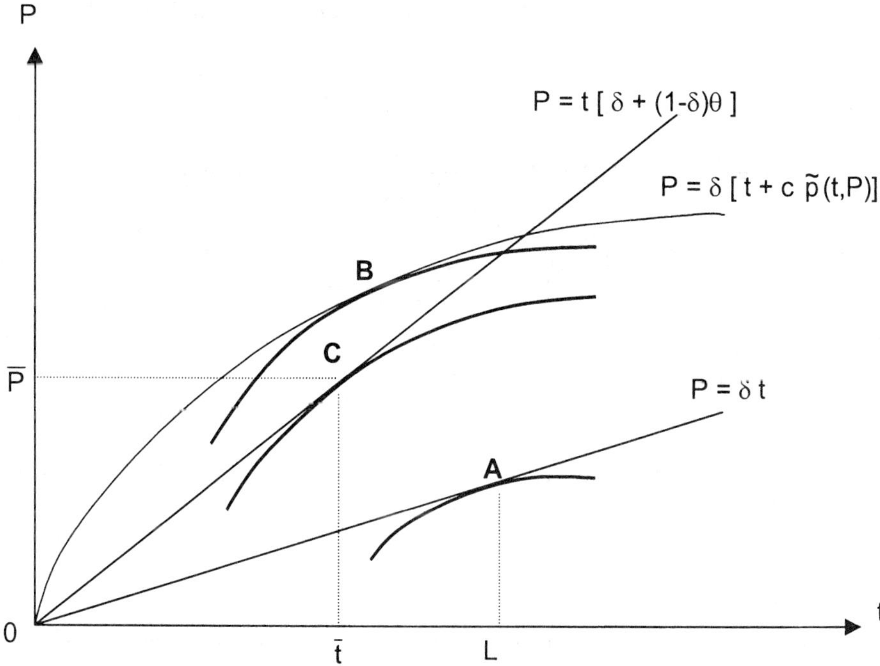

Figure 9 The market equilibrium is at point C when $\theta < \hat{\theta}$

In the absence of commitment, i.e., when the insurer has no Stackelberg advantage in the audit game, the auditing strategy of the insurer is constrained to be a best response to opportunists' fraud strategy, in a way similar to tax compliance games[34] studied by Graetz, Reinganum and Wilde (1986) and Melumad and Mookherjee (1989).[35] In the framework of the model of the previous section under no commitment to audit policy, the outcome of an audit game (t, P, σ) corresponds to a perfect Bayesian equilibrium, where: (a) the fraud strategy is optimal for an opportunist given the audit policy (b) the audit policy is optimal for the insurer given beliefs about the probability of a claim to be fraudulent (c) the insurer's beliefs are obtained from the probability of loss and opportunists strategy using Bayes' rule.

Let $\alpha^n(t, P, \sigma)$ and $p^n(t, P, \sigma)$ be the equilibrium strategy of opportunists and of insurers, respectively, in an audit game in the absence of commitment to an audit policy and let $C^n(t, P, \sigma)$ be the corresponding expected cost.

[34] See Andreoni, Erard and Feinstein (1998) for a survey on tax compliance.

[35] Cummins and Tennyson (1994) analyze liability claims fraud within a model without Stackelberg advantage for insurers: each insurer chooses his fraud control level to minimize the costs induced by fraudulent claims.

Proposition 11. Without commitment to an audit policy, the equilibrium of an audit game (t, P, σ) is characterized by[36]

$$p^n(t, P, \sigma) = 0 \text{ and } \alpha^n(t, P, \sigma) = 1 \quad \text{if} \quad c > c_1(t, \sigma)$$

$$p^n(t, P, \sigma) = \tilde{p}(t, P) \text{ and } \alpha^n(t, P, \sigma) = \frac{\delta c}{\sigma(1-\delta)(t-c)} \quad \text{if} \quad c < c_1(t, \sigma)$$

$$C^n(t, \sigma) = \min\left\{t[\delta + \sigma(1-\delta)], \frac{\delta t^2}{t-c}\right\}$$

where

$$c_1(t, \sigma) = \frac{\sigma(1-\sigma)t}{\sigma(1-\sigma)+\delta}.$$

The proof of proposition 11 may be sketched as follows. Let π be the probability for a claim to be fraudulent. Bayes' rule gives

$$\pi = \frac{\alpha\sigma(1-\delta)}{\alpha\sigma(1-\delta)+\delta} \tag{35}$$

Once a policyholder puts in a claim, the (conditional) insurer's expected cost is

$$\overline{C} = p[c + (1-\pi)t] + (1-p)t \tag{36}$$

The equilibrium audit policy minimizes $\overline{C}$ with respect to p which gives

$$\left.\begin{array}{ll} p = 0 & \text{if } \pi t < c \\ p \in [0, 1] & \text{if } \pi t = c \\ p = 1 & \text{if } \pi t > c \end{array}\right\} \tag{37}$$

The equilibrium of the no-commitment audit game is a solution (α, p, π) to (32), (35) and (37). Let us compare Proposition 11 to Proposition 9. At a no-commitment equilibrium, there is always some degree of fraud: $\alpha = 0$ cannot be an equilibrium strategy since any audit policy that totally prevents fraud is not credible. Furthermore, we have $c_1(t, \sigma) < c_0(t, P, \sigma)$ for all t, P, σ which means that the optimal audit strategy $p = \tilde{p}(t, P, \sigma)$ that discourages fraud is optimal for a larger set of contracts in the commitment game than in the no-commitment game. Lastly, we have $C^n(t, \sigma) \geq C^c(t, P, \sigma)$ with a strict inequality when the no-commitment game involves $p > 0$ at equilibrium. Indeed, at a no-commitment equilibrium, there must be some degree of fraud for an audit policy to be credible which increases insurance expected cost.[37]

[36] We assume $t > c$ and we neglect the case $c = c_1(t, \sigma)$. See Picard (1996) for details.

[37] As shown by Boyer (1999), when the probability of auditing is strictly positive at equilibrium (which occurs when θ is large enough), then the amount of fraud $(1 - \delta)\theta\alpha^n(t^n, P^n, \theta) = \delta c/(t^n - c)$ does not depend on θ. *Note* that t^n does not (locally) depend on θ when $c < c_1(t^n, \theta)$.

The analysis of market equilibrium follows the same logic as in the commitment case. Let

$$(t^n, P^n) = \arg\ \max_{t,P}\{\delta U(W - L + t - P) + (1-\delta)U(W - P)$$
$$s.t.\quad P \geq C^n(t, P, \theta)$$

be the pooling contract that maximizes the expected utility of honest policyholders.[38]

Proposition 12. Under **A**, (t^n, P^n) is the unique market equilibrium when the insurers cannot commit to their audit policy.

The expected utility of honest policyholders is higher at the commitment equilibrium than at the no-commitment equilibrium. To highlight the welfare costs of the no-commitment constraint, let us focus attention on the case where θ is sufficiently large so that, in the absence of claims' verification, honest customers would prefer not to take out an insurance policy than to pay high premiums that cover the cost of systematic fraud by opportunists. This means that point C is at the origin of the axis in Figures 8 and 9, which occurs if $\theta \geq \theta^*$, with

$$\theta^* = \frac{\delta[U'(W - L) - U'(W)]}{\delta U'(W - L) + (1-\delta)U'(W)} \in (0,1)$$

In Figure 10, the commitment equilibrium is at point B (i.e., $\theta < \hat{\theta}$) and the no-commitment equilibrium is at the origin of the axis: the, the market shuts down completely at $t = t^n = 0$.

Hence, besides the inevitable market inefficiency induced by the cost of auditing (i.e., going from A to B in Figure 10), the inability of insurers to commit to an audit policy induces an additional welfare loss (from B to 0). How can this particular inefficiency be overcome? Two solutions have been put forward in the literature. A first solution, developed by Melumad and Mookherjee (1989) in the case of income tax audits, is to delegate authority over an audit policy to an independent agent in charge of investigating claims. An incentive contract offered by the insurer to the investigator could induce a tough monitoring strategy, and precommitment effects would be obtained by publicly announcing that such incentives have be given to the investigator. Secondly, Picard (1996) shows that transferring audit costs to a budget balanced common agency may help to solve the commitment problem. The common agency takes charge of part of the audit expenditures decided by insurers and is financed by lump-sum participation fees. This mechanism mitigates the commitment problem and may even settle it completely if there is no asymmetric information between the agency and the insurers about audit costs.

[38] We assume that (t^n, P^n) is a singleton.

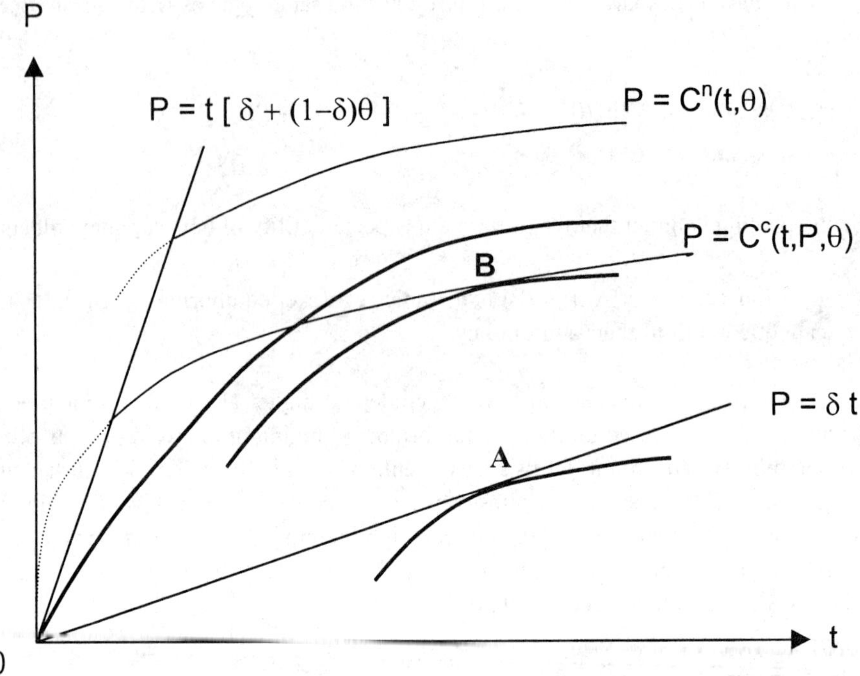

Figure 10 Case where the market shuts down at a no-commitment equilibrium

10.8 COLLUSION WITH AGENTS

In many cases, insurance fraud goes through collusion between policyholders and a third party. For instance, collusion with auto mechanics, physicians or attorneys is a channel through which an opportunist policyholder may manage to falsify his claims. Falsification costs—taken as exogenous in the sections 3 and 4—then are the outcome of hidden agreement between policyholders and such agents.

In this section, we focus on collusion between policyholders and agents in charge of marketing insurance contracts. We also consider another type of fraud, namely the fact that policyholders may lie or not disclose relevant information when they take out their policy.[39] We will assume that the agent observes a number of characteristics of the customer that allow him to estimate correctly the risks and to price the policy. These characteristics cannot be verified by the insurer. Agents also provide promotional services that affect the demand for the policies offered by the insurer but promotional effort cannot either be verified by the insurer.[40] The insurer only observes

[39] On this kind of fraud when insurers can (at some cost) verify the policyholders' types, see Dixit (2000).

[40] The choice of distribution system affects the cost to the insurers of elicitating additional promotional effort of their sales force. For instance, exclusive representation prevents the agents from diverting potential customers to other insurers who pay larger commissions. Likewise giving independent agents ownership of policy expirations provides incentives for agents to expend effort to attract and retain customers—see Kim, Mayers and Smith (1996).

two signals of his agent's activity, namely net premiums written and indemnity payments.

The key element we want to focus on is the fact that agents may be willing to offer unduly advantageous contracts to some policyholders in order to compensate low promotional efforts. This possibility should lead the insurer to condition his agents' commissions at the same time on cashed premiums and on indemnity payments. Of course, the issue of how an insurer should provide incentives to his selling agents—be they exclusive or independent—is important independently of insurance fraud. However, in a situation where the insurer does not perfectly monitor his agents, there is some scope for collusion between agents and policyholders which facilitates insurance fraud. The agent may be aware of the fact that the customer tells lies or that he conceals relevant information but he overlooks this violation in order not to miss an opportunity to sell one more insurance policy. Hence, in such a case, the defrauder is in fact the policyholder-agent coalition itself. In what follows we sketch a model that captures some consequences of insurance fraud through collusion between policyholders and agents.

Consider an insurance market with n risk-neutral firms of equal size. Each firm employs l exclusive agents to sell insurance contracts.[41] Let e be the promotional effort expended by an agent. Let k be the loading factor used to price the policies written by the agent. For any customer, the agent is supposed to be able to correctly estimate the expected indemnity payments Et. Let $\hat{k}$ be the loading factor decided upon by the insurer. Hence, if expected indemnity payments are truthfully reported by the selling agent to the insurer, the pricing rule should lead the agent to charge a premium $(1 + \hat{k})Et$. However, by misreporting expected indemnity payments, the agent is able to write policies with an actual loading factor lower than $\hat{k}$. In what follows, e and k are the decision variables of the agent.

Let P and Q be respectively the aggregate premiums collected by a given agent and the aggregate indemnity payments made to his customers during a period of time. We assume

$$P = \frac{1}{n\ell}[g(e,k)+\varepsilon_1] \text{ with } g'_e > 0 \text{ and } g'_k < 0 \tag{38}$$

where ε_1 is an idiosyncratic random parameter that varies among agents, with $E\varepsilon_1 = 0$. ε_1 is unknown when the selling agent chooses e and k and cannot be observed by the insurer. Larger promotional efforts increase demand for insurance contracts sold by the agent which increases the amount of collected premiums. Furthermore, we assume that the elasticity of demand for coverage (in terms of expected insurance demand) with respect to loading $1 + k$ is larger than one. Hence a higher loading factor—or, equivalently, less downward misreporting of expected insurance payments

[41] Modelling promotional effort in an independent agency system would be more complex since, in such a system, the agent's decisions are simultaneously affected by incentives provided by several insurers.

by the agent to the insurer—decreases the premiums cashed. Note that the coefficient $1/n\ell$ in (38) reflects the market share of each agent. We also have

$$Q = \frac{1}{n\ell}\left[h(e,k) + \frac{\varepsilon_1}{1+k} + \varepsilon_2\right] \tag{39}$$

where $h(e, k) \equiv g(e, k)/1 + k$, with $h'_e > 0$, $g'_k < 0$ and where ε_2 is another idiosyncratic random parameter, uncorrelated with ε_1, such that $E\varepsilon_2 = 0$.

Let $\psi(e)$ be the cost to the agent of providing promotional effort at level e, with $\psi' > 0$, $\psi'' > 0$. The agents are supposed to be risk-averse.

If insurers were able to monitor the promotional effort and to verify the expected indemnity payments of the policies written by their agents, they would be in position to choose e and k so as to maximize their expected profit written as

$$E\Pi = \ell[EP - EQ - EC]$$

where C denotes the commission paid to each agent. Under perfect information about the agent's behaviour it is optimal to pay fixed commissions so that net earnings $C - \psi(e)$ are equal to a given reservation payment normalized at zero. We thus have $C = \psi(e)$, which gives

$$E\Pi = \frac{1}{n}[g(e,k) - h(e,k)] - \ell\psi(e) \tag{40}$$

Maximizing $E\Pi$ with respect to e and k gives the first best solution $e = e^*$ and $k = k^*$. A free entry perfect information equilibrium is defined by $E\Pi = 0$ which gives an endogenously determined number of firms $n = n^*$.

Assume now that the insurers do not observe the promotional effort expended by the agents. They can neither verify the expected indemnity payments associated with the policies written by their agent. Opportunist policyholders would like to purchase insurance priced at a loading factor lower than $\hat{k}$ by not disclosing relevant information about the risks incurred to the insurer. It is assumed that this hidden information cannot be revealed to the insurer if an accident occurs. The agent observes the risks of the customers but he may choose not to report this information truthfully to the insurer in order to get larger sales commissions. The insurer may control the agent opportunism by conditioning his commissions both on cashed premiums and on indemnity payments. However, because of the uncertainty that affects premiums and losses, risk premiums will have to be paid to selling agents which will ultimately affect the firm's profitability.

Assume that the commission paid to an agent depends linearly on P on Q, i.e.

$$C = \alpha P - \beta Q + \gamma$$

Assume also that the agents' utility function V is quadratic, which allows us to write

$$EV = EC - \rho Var(C) - \psi(e) \quad \rho > 0$$

The agent's participation constraint $EV \geq 0$ is binding at the optimum, which gives

$$\begin{aligned} EC &= \rho Var(C) + \psi(e) \\ &= \frac{\rho}{(n\ell)^2}\left[\alpha^2\sigma_1^2 + \beta^2\frac{\sigma_1^2}{(1+k)^2} + \beta^2\sigma_2^2\right] \end{aligned}$$

where $\sigma_1^2 = Var(\varepsilon_1)$ and $\sigma_2^2 = Var(\varepsilon_2)$. We obtain

$$E\Pi = \frac{1}{n}[g(e,k) - h(e,k)] - \ell\psi(e) - \frac{\rho}{n^2\ell}\left[\alpha^2\sigma_1^2 + \beta^2\frac{\sigma_1^2}{(1+k)^2} + \beta^2\sigma_2^2\right]$$

The insurer maximizes $E\Pi$ with respect to $e \geq 0$, $k \geq 0$, α and β subject to the agent's incentive compatibility constraint

$$\begin{aligned} (e,k) \in \underset{e',k'}{\text{ArgMax}}\, EV = &\frac{\alpha}{n\ell}g(e',k') - \frac{\beta}{n\ell}h(e',k') + \gamma - \psi(e') \\ &- \frac{\rho}{(n\ell)^2}\left[\alpha^2\sigma_1^2 + \beta^2\frac{\sigma_1^2}{(1+k')^2} + \beta^2\sigma_2^2\right] \end{aligned}$$

If there is some positive level of promotional effort at the optimum, the incentive compatibility constraint implies $\alpha > 0$ and $\beta > 0$. In words, the insurers should condition the sales commissions at the same time on collected premiums and on indemnity payments. Because of the risk premium paid to the agent, the expected profit of the insurer is lower than when he observes e and k. The equilibrium levels of e and k also differ from their perfect information levels e^* and k^*. Lastly, at a free entry equilibrium, the number of firms in the market is lower than when the insurer has perfect information about his agent's activity.

Insurance fraud through collusion between policyholders and agents may also occur in the claims settlement phase, particularly in an independent agency system. As emphasized by Mayers and Smith (1981), independent agents usually are given more discretion in claims administration than exclusive agents and they may intercede on the policyholder's behalf with the company's claims adjuster. Influencing claims settlement in the interest of their customers is all the more likely that independent agents may credibly threat to switch their business to another insurer.

10.9 CONCLUSION

Although the theory of insurance fraud is far from being complete, this survey allows us to draw some tentative conclusions. Firstly, insurance fraud affects the design of optimal insurance policies in several ways. On the one hand, because of claims' monitoring costs, an optimal contract exhibits non-verification with constant net payouts to insureds in the lower loss states and (possibly random) verification for some severe losses. In some cases, a straight deductible contract is optimal. On the other hand, the possibility for policyholders either to manipulate audit costs or to falsify claims should lead insurers to offer contracts that exhibit some degree of coinsurance at the margin. The precise form of coinsurance depends on the specification of the model. For instance, it may go through a ceiling on coverage or through overcompensation for small losses and undercompensation for large losses. However, the fact that insurers should not be offered policies with full insurance at the margin seems a fairly robust result as soon as they may engage in costly activities that affect the insurer's information about damages. Secondly, insurance fraud calls for some cooperation among insurance companies. This may go through the development of common agencies that build data bases about past suspicious claims, that develop quantitative method for better detecting fraudulent claims[42] and that spread information among insurers. In particular data bases may help to mitigate the inefficiency associated with adverse selection, that is with the fact that insurers are unable to distinguish potential defrauders from honest policyholders. Cooperation among insurers may also reduce the intensity of the credibility constraints that affect antifraud policies. Freeriding in antifraud policies could be analyzed along the same lines and it also calls for more cooperation among insurers. Thirdly, insurance fraud frequently goes through collusion with a third party, be it the agent of the policyholder or of the insurer. Contractual relationships between insurers and these third parties strongly affects the propensity of policyholders to engage in insurance fraud activities. In particular, conditioning sales commissions paid to agents on a loss-premium ratio results from a compromise between two objectives: providing incentives to make promotional effort and detering collusion with customers. Risk premiums borne by agents are then an additional cost of the distribution system, which ultimately affects the efficiency of insurance industry. Preventing collusion between a policyholder and his own agent is a still more difficult challenge. Vertical integration of these agents by insurance companies (for instance through affiliated automechanics networks) is likely to mitigate the intensity of collusion in such cases.[43]

[42] See Derrig and Ostaszewski (1995) and Weisberg and Derrig (1992).

[43] See Brundin and Salanié (1997).

APPENDIX

Proof of Lemma 1

Let

$$\begin{aligned}\tilde{t}(x) &= Sup\{t(x),\ t(y), y \in M^c\}\\ t_0 &= Inf\{\tilde{t}(x), x \in [0, \bar{x}]\}\\ \tilde{M} &= \{x \mid \tilde{t}(x) > t_0\}\\ \tilde{P} &= P\end{aligned}$$

Obviously, the contract $\tilde{\delta} = \{\tilde{t}(.), \tilde{M}, \tilde{P}\}$ is incentive compatible. Hence $\tilde{\delta}$ and δ yield the same insurance payment.

Let $\hat{x}(x)$ be an optimal claim of the policyholder under δ when he suffers a loss x. Let $x_0 \in \tilde{M}$. We then have $\tilde{t}(x_0) > \tilde{t}(x_1)$ for some x_1 in $[0, \bar{x}]$. This gives $\hat{x}(x_0) \in M$, otherwise $\hat{x}(x_0)$ would be a better claim than $\hat{x}(x_1)$ under δ when $x = x_1$. Audit costs are thus lower under $\tilde{\delta}$ than under δ. ■

Proof of Lemma 2[44]

Let

$$\mathcal{L} = U(W - P - x + t(x))f(x) + \lambda[t(x) + c] \quad \text{if} \quad x \in M$$

be the Lagrangean, with λ a multiplier associated with the non-negative expected profit constraint. When P, t_0 and M are fixed optimally, the schedule $t(.)$: $M \to R_+$ is such that

$$\frac{\partial \mathcal{L}}{\partial t} = U'(W - P - x + t(x))f(x) - \lambda f(x) = 0$$

This allows us to write

$$t(x) = x - k \text{ for all } x \text{ in } M$$

where k is a constant.

Assume there exist $0 \leq a_1 < a_2 < a_3 \leq a_4 \leq \bar{x}$ such that

$$[a_1, a_2) \cup (a_3, a_4] \subset M$$

[44] This proof follows Bond and Crocker (1997).

$(a_2, a_3) \subset M^c$

Let

$$M* = M - \{[a_1, a_2) \cup (a_3, a_4]\}$$

$$M_*^c = M^c - [a_2, a_3]$$

We have

$$\begin{aligned} EU = &\int_{M*} U(W - P - k)dF(x) + \int_{M*} U(W - P - x + t_0)dF(x) \\ &+ \int_{a_1}^{a_2} U(W - P - k)dF(x) + \int_{a_2}^{a_3} U(W - P - x + t_0)dF(x) \\ &+ \int_{a_3}^{a_4} U(W - P - k)dF(x) \end{aligned} \tag{41}$$

and

$$\begin{aligned} E\Pi = P &- \int_{M*} (x - k + c)\, dF(x) - \int_{M_*^c} t_0\, dF(x) \\ &- \int_{a_1}^{a_2} (x - k + c)\, dF(x) - \int_{a_2}^{a_3} t_0\, dF(x) \\ &- \int_{a_2}^{a_4} (x - k + c)\, dF(x) = 0 \end{aligned} \tag{42}$$

Differentiating (42) with respect to a_2 and a_4 gives

$$da_3 = \frac{(a_2 - k + c - t_0) f(a_2)\, da_2}{a_3 - k + c - t_0}$$

which implies

$$dEU = f(a_2)\, \Delta\, (t_0 - a_2 + k - c)\, da_2$$

with

$$\Lambda = \frac{U(W - k - P) - U(W - P - a_3 + t_0)}{a_3 - k - t_0 + c} - \frac{U(W - k - P) - U(W - P - a_2 + t_0)}{a_2 - k - t_0 - c}$$

The concavity of U guarantees that $\Delta > 0$. Furthermore $a_2 - k \geq t_0$ since $[a_1, a_2) \subset M$. We thus have $dEU > 0$ if $da_2 < 0$. ■

Proof of Proposition 1

Let us delete the constraint (6). We may check that it is satisfied by the optimal solution of this less constrained problem. Assigning a multiplier $\lambda \geq 0$ to the nonnegative profit constraint, the first-order optimality conditions on k, P and m are respectively

$$[1 - F(m)][U'(W - P - k) - \lambda] = 0 \tag{43}$$

$$\int_0^m U'(W - x - P)\,dF(x) + [1 - F(m)]U'(W - P - k) = \lambda \tag{44}$$

$$\begin{aligned} &U(W - m - P)f(m_+) - U(W - P - k)f(m_+) + \lambda(c + m - k)f(m_+) \leq 0 \\ &\quad = 0 \quad \text{if} \quad m > 0 \end{aligned} \tag{45}$$

(43), (44) and $F(m) \geq f(0) > 0$ for all $m \geq 0$ give

$$U'(W - P - k) = \frac{1}{F(m)} \int_0^m U'(W - x - P)\,dF(x)$$

which implies $0 < k < m$ if $m > 0$ and $k = 0$ if $m = 0$.

Assume $m = 0$. Substituting $k = m = 0$ in (45) then gives $\lambda c f(0_+) \leq 0$, hence a contradiction. ■

Proof of Proposition 2

The first order optimality conditions on k, P and t_0 are respectively

$$[1 - F(m)]\,[U'(W - P - k) - \lambda] \tag{46}$$

$$f(0)U'(W - P) + \int_{0_+}^m U'(W - x - P + t_0)\,dF(x) + [1 - F(m)]U'(W - P - k) = \lambda \tag{47}$$

$$\int_{0_+}^m U'(W - x - P + t_0)\,dF(x) = \lambda[F(m) - f(0)] \tag{48}$$

(46), (47), (48) and $F(m) \geq f(0) > 0$ for all $m \geq 0$ give $k = 0$ and $\lambda = U'(W - P)$. Using (48) then yields

$$[F(m) - f(0)]U'(W - P) = \int_{0_+}^m U(W - x - P + t_0)\,dF(x)$$

which implies $0 < t_0 < m$ if $m > 0$.

Consider m as a fixed parameter. Let $\Phi(m)$ be the optimal expected utility as a function of m. The envelope theorem gives

$$\begin{aligned} \Phi'(m) = {} & U'(W - m - P + t_0)f(m) - U(W - P - k)f(m) \\ & + \lambda(t_0 + c + m - k)f(m) \quad \text{if} \quad m > 0 \end{aligned}$$

when $m \to 0$, then $t_0 \to 0$. Using $k = 0$ then gives

$$\lim_{m\to 0} \Phi'(m) = \lambda c f(0_+) > 0$$

which implies $m > 0$ at the optimum. ■

Proof of Proposition 3. See Picard (1999).

Proof of Proposition 4. See Bond and Crocker (1997).

Proof of Proposition 5. See Picard (1999).

Proof of Proposition 6. See Crocker and Morgan (1997).

Proof of Proposition 7. See Mookherjee and Png (1989) and Fagart and Picard (1999).

Proof of Proposition 8. See Fagart and Picard (1999).

Proof of Proposition 9. See Picard (1996).

Proof of Proposition 10. See Picard (1996).

Proof of Proposition 11. See Picard (1996).

Proof of Proposition 12. See Picard (1996).

10.1 REFERENCES

Abadie, L. (1999). "An economic analysis of insurance fraud with imperfect auditing", *mimeo*, Université de Toulouse.

Andreoni J., B. Erard and J. Feinstein (1998). "Tax compliance", *Journal of Economic Literature*, vol. XXXVI, 818–860.

Arrow, K. (1971). *Essays in the Theory of Risk Bearing*, North-Holland, Amsterdam.

Baron, D.P. and D. Besanko (1984). "Regulation, asymmetric information and auditing", *Rand Journal of Economics*, 15, N° 4, 447–470.

Becker, G. (1968). "Crime and punishment: an economic approach", *Journal of Political Economy*, 76, 169–217.

Bond, E.W. and K.J. Crocker (1997). "Hardball and the soft touch: the economics of optimal insurance contracts with costly state verification and endogenous monitoring costs", *Journal of Public Economics*, 63, 239–264.

Bourgeon, J-M. and P. Picard (1999). "Reinstatement or insurance payment in corporate fire insurance", forthcoming in the *Journal of Risk and Insurance.*

Boyer, M.M. (1999). "When is the proportion of criminal elements irrelevant? A study of insurance fraud when insurers cannot commit" in *Automobile Insurance: Road Safety, New Drivers, Risks, Insurance Fraud and Regulation*, edited by G. Dionne and C. Laberge-Nadeau, Kluwer Acdemic Publishers.

Brundin, I. and F. Salanié (1997). "Fraud in the insurance industry: an organizational approach", *mimeo*, Université de Toulouse.

Clarke, M.A. (1997). *The Law of Insurance Contracts*, Lloyd's of London Press Ltd.

Crocker, K.J. and J. Morgan (1997). "Is honesty the best policy? Curtailing insurance fraud through optimal incentive contracts", *Journal of Political Economy*, 106, N° 2, 355–375.

Crocker, K.J. and S. Tennyson (1999). "Costly state falsification or verification? Theory and evidence from bodily injury liability claims", in *Automobile Insurance: Road Safety, New Drivers, Risks, Insurance Fraud and Regulation*, edited by G. Dionne and C. Laberge-Nadeau, Kluwer Academic Publishers.

Cummins, J.D. and S. Tennyson (1992). "Controlling automobile insurance costs", *Journal of Economic Perspectives*, 6, N° 2, 95–115.

Cummins, J.D. and S. Tennyson (1994). "The tort system 'lottery' and insurance fraud: theory and evidence from automobile insurance", *mimeo*, The Wharton School, University of Pennsylvania.

Darby, M.R. and E. Karni (1973). "Free competition and the optimal amount of fraud", *Journal of Law and Economics*, 16, 67–88.

Derrig, R.A. and K.M. Ostaszewski (1995). "Fuzzy Techniques of Pattern Recognition in Risk and Claim Classification", *Journal of Risk and Insurance*, 62, 447–482.

Derrig, R.A., H.I. Weisberg and X. Chen (1994). "Behavioral factors and lotteries under no-fault with a monetary threshold: a study of Massachusetts Automobile Claims", *The Journal of Risk and Insurance*, 61, N° 2, 245–275.

Dionne, G. (1984). "The effects of insurance on the possibilities of fraud", *The Geneva Papers on Risk and Insurance*, 9, N° 32, 304–321.

Dionne, G. and R. Gagné (1997). "The non-optimality of deductible contracts against fraudulent claims: an empirical evidence in automobile insurance", *Working Paper* 97-05, HEC-Montréal, Chaire de Gestion des Risques. Forthcoming in *Review of Economics and Statistics*.

Dionne, G. and P. St-Michel (1991). "Workers' compensation and moral hazard", *Review of Economics and Statistics*, Vol. 83, 2, 236–244.

Dionne, G., P. St-Michel and C. Vanasse (1995). "Moral hazard, optimal auditing and workers' compensation", in *Research in Canadian Workers' Compensation*, T. Thomason and R.P. Chaykowski eds. IRC Press, Queen's University at Kingston, 85–105.

Dixit, A. (2000). "Adverse selection and insurance with *Uberrima Fides*", Mimeo Princeton University.

Fagart, M.C. and P. Picard (1999). "Optimal insurance under random auditing", *Geneva Papers on Risk and Insurance Theory*, 29, N° 1, 29–54.

Gollier, C. (1987). "Pareto-optimal risk sharing with fixed costs per claim", *Scandinavian Actuarial Journal*, 62–73.

Graetz, M.J., J.F. Reinganum and L.L. Wilde (1986). "The tax compliance game: Toward an interactive theory of law enforcement", *Journal of Law, Economics and Organization*, 2, N° 1, 1–32.

Guesnerie, R. and J.J. Laffont (1984). "A complete solution to a class of principal-agent problems, with an application to the control of a self-managed firm", *Journal of Public Economics*, 25, 329–369.

Holmström, B. (1979). "Moral hazard and observability", *Bell Journal of Economics*, Vol. 10 (1), 74–91.

Huberman, G., D. Mayers and C.W. Smith Jr. (1983). "Optimum insurance policy indemnity schedules", *Bell Journal of Economics*, 14, Autumn, 415–426.

Kim, W.-J., D. Mayers and C.W. Smith, Jr. (1996). "On the choice of insurance distribution systems", *Journal of Risk and Insurance*, 63, N° 2, 207–227.

Lacker, J.M. and J.A. Weinberg (1989). "Optimal contracts under costly state falsification", *Journal of Political Economy*, 97, 1347–1363.

Maggi, G. and A. Rodriguez-Clare (1995). "Costly distortion of information in agency problems", *The Rand Journal of Economics*, 26, 675–689.

Mayers, D. and C.S. Smith, Jr. (1981). "Contractual provisions, organizational structure, and conflict control in insurance markets", *Journal of Business*, 54, 407–434.

Melumad, N.D. and D. Mookherjee (1989). "Delegation as commitment: The case of income tax audits", *Rand Journal of Economics*, 20, N° 2, 139–163.

Mookherjee D. and I. Png (1989). "Optimal auditing insurance and redistribution", *Quarterly Journal of Economics*, CIV. 205–228.

Myerson, R. (1979). "Incentive compatibility and the bargaining problem", *Econometrica*, 47, 61–74.

Picard, P. (1996). "Auditing claims in insurance market with fraud: the credibility issue", *Journal of Public Economics*, 63, 27–56.

Picard, P. (1999). "On the design of optimal insurance contracts under manipulation of audit cost", forthcoming in the *International Economic Review*.

Puelz, R. and A. Snow (1995). "Optimal incentive contracting with *ex-ante* and *ex-post* moral hazards: theory and evidence", *mimeo*, Southern Methodist University, University of Georgia.

Stigler, G.L. (1970). "The optimal enforcement of laws", *Journal of Political Economy*, 78, 526–536.

Tennyson, S. (1994). "Economic institutions and individual ethics: a study of consumer attitudes toward insurance fraud", *mimeo*, Department of Insurance and Risk Management, University of Pennsylvania.

Townsend, R. (1979). "Optimal contracts and competitive markets with costly state verification", *Journal of Economics Theory*, XXI, 265–293.

Weisberg, H.I. and R. Derrig (1993). "Quantitative methods for detecting fraudulent automobile bodily injury claims", *Automobile Insurers Bureau of Massachusetts Filing on Fraudulent Claims Payment*, DOI Docket G93-24, Boston.

Wilson, C. (1977). "A model of insurance markets with incomplete information", *Journal of Economic Theory*, 16, 167–207.

Part IV
Asymmetric Information: Empirical Analysis

11 Econometric Models of Insurance under Asymmetric Information*

Pierre-André Chiappori

University of Chicago

Abstract

The paper surveys recent empirical studies that test for or evaluate the importance of asymmetric information in insurance relationships. I first discus the main conclusions reached by insurance theory in both a static and a dynamic framework. A particular emphasis is put on the testable consequences that can be derived from existing models. I review several studies exploiting these theoretical insights in a static context. Then I briefly consider the dynamic aspects.

Keywords: Insurance, adverse selection, moral hazard, contract theory, tests.
JEL Classification Numbers: D80, G22, C25, G11.

11.1 INTRODUCTION

Modern insurance economics have been deeply influenced by the developments of contract theory. Our understanding of several crucial aspects, such as the design of optimal insurance contracts, the form of competition on insurance markets or the role of public regulation, just to name a few, systematically refers to the basic concepts of contract theory—moral hazard, adverse selection, commitment, renegotiation and others. Conversely, it is fair to say that insurance has been, and to a large extent still remains, one of the most important and promising fields of empirical application for contract theory.

It can even be argued that, by their very nature, insurance data provide nearly ideal material for testing the predictions of contract theory. Chiappori (1994) and

* The author is endebted to G. Dionne, I. Hendel, B. Salanié and two referees for useful suggestions and comments. Financial support from the Chaire d'Economie de l'Assurance (Paris) is gratefully aknowledged. Errors are mine.

Chiappori and Salanié (1996) remark that most predictions of contract theory are expressed in terms of a relationship between the form of the contract, a "performance" that characterizes the outcome of the relationship under consideration, and the resulting transfers between the parties. Under moral hazard, for instance, transfers will be positively correlated to but less volatile than outcomes, in order to conjugate incentives and risk sharing; under adverse selection, the informed party will typically be asked to choose a particular relationship between transfer and performance within a menu. The exact translation of the notions of "performance" and "transfer" varies with the particular field at stake. Depending on the context, the "performance" may be a production or profit level, the performance of a given task or the occurrence of an accident; whereas the transfer can take the form of a wage, a dividend, an insurance premium and others.

In all cases, empirical estimation of the underlying theoretical model would ideally require a precise recording of (i) the contract, (ii) the information available to both parties, (iii) the performance, and (iv) the transfers. In addition, the contracts should be to a large extent standardized, and large samples should be considered, so that the usual tools of econometric analysis can apply. As it turns out, data of this kind are quite scarce. In some contexts, the contract is essentially implicit, and its detailed features are not observed by the econometrician. More frequently, contracts do not present a standardized form because of the complexity of the information needed either to characterize the various (and possibly numerous) states of the world that should be considered, or to precisely describe available information.[1] In many cases, part of the information at the parties' disposal is simply not observed by the econometrician, so that it is de facto impossible to condition on it as required by the theory. Last but not least, the "performance" is often not recorded, and even not precisely defined. In the case of labor contracts, for instance, the employee's "performance" is often the product of a supervisor's subjective estimation, that is typically not recorded in the firm's files (and, in any case, will typically not be available to the econometrician).

In contrast, most insurance contracts fulfill all of the previous requirements. Individual insurance contracts (automobile, housing, health, life, etc.) are largely standardized. The insurer's information is accessible, and can generally be summarized through a reasonably small number of quantitative or qualitative indicators. The "performance"—whether it represents the occurrence of an accident, its cost, or some level of expenditure—is very precisely recorded in the firms' files. Finally, insurance companies frequently use data bases containing several millions of contracts, which is as close to asymptotic properties as one can probably be. It should thus be no surprise that empirical tests of adverse selection, moral hazard or repeated contract theory on insurance data have recently attracted renewed attention.

In what follows, I shall concentrate on empirical models that explicitly aim at testing for or evaluating the importance of asymmetric information in insurance rela-

[1] This problem, for instance, is frequently encountered with data related to firms' behavior.

tionships. This obviously excludes huge parts of the empirical literature on insurance, that are covered by other chapters of this volume. Also, I will leave aside the important literature on fraud—a topic that is explicitly addressed by the contributions of P. Picard and G. Dionne. Similarly, I shall only allude to a few studies relating to information asymmetries in health insurance.

The structure of this contribution is as follows. Section 11.2 discusses the main conclusion reached by insurance theory in a both a static and a dynamic framework. A particular emphasis is put on the testable consequences that can be derived from existing models. Section 11.3 reviews several studies exploiting these theoretical insights in a static context. Section 11.4 briefly considers the dynamic aspects of the issue. Finally, concluding comments are in the last section.

11.2 EMPIRICAL TESTS OF INFORMATION ASYMMETRIES: THE THEORETICAL BACKGROUND

It is by now customary to outline two polar cases of asymmetric information, namely adverse selection and moral hazard. Each case exhibits specific features that must be understood before any attempt at quantifying their empirical importance.[2]

11.2.1 Adverse Selection[3]

11.2.1.1 Definition

Adverse selection arises when one party—generally, the subscriber—has a better information than the other party—the insurer—about some parameters that are relevant for the relationship. In most theoretical models, the asymmetry is relative to the level of risk: the client is assumed to know better either her accident probability, or the (conditional) distribution of losses incurred in case of accident, or both. A key feature is that, in such cases, the agent's informational advantage is directly related to the insurer's (expected) cost of providing the contract.

While theoretical models concentrate upon one particular source of adverse selection—the agent's better knowledge of her risk—the empirical relevance of this exclusive emphasis is not always guaranteed. In many real-life applications, risk is not the only possible source of informational asymmetry, and arguably not the most important one. For instance, individuals also have a better knowledge of their own preferences, and particularly their level of risk aversion—an aspect that is often disregarded in theoretical models.

A possible justification for this lack of interest is that, in principle, adverse selection on preferences, per se, has negligible consequences upon the form and the

[2] For a clear and comprehensive presentation of the various theoretical models, the reader is referred to Salanié (1997).

[3] See also the contribution by Dionne, Doherty and Fombaron in this volume.

outcome of the relationship, at least in a competitive context. Pure competition typically imposes that companies charge a fair premium, at least whenever the latter can be directly computed (which is precisely the problem when the agent's risk is not known). Hence, the equilibrium contract should not depend on the subscriber's preferences, whether the latter are public or private information. To be a little more specific: in a model of perfectly competitive insurance markets with symmetric information, the introduction of hidden information on preferences only will not alter the equilibrium outcome.

This conclusion should however be qualified, for at least two reasons. For one thing, perfect competition is a natural assumption within a simplified theoretical model, but much less so in reality. Fixed costs, product differentiation, price stickiness, switching costs and cross-subsidization are part of the real world; oligopoly is probably the rule rather than the exception. In such a context, firms are able to make positive profit, and the latter is related to the agents' demand elasticity—which directly reflects risk aversion. To take an extreme case, it is well known that in a principal-agent framework—equivalent to some monopoly position of the insurance company—adverse selection on risk aversion does matter for the form of the optimal contract.

A second caveat is that even when adverse selection on preferences *alone* does not matter, it may still, when added to asymmetric information of a more standard form, considerably modify the properties of equilibria. In a standard Rothschild-Stiglitz context, for instance, heterogeneity in risk aversion may result in violations of the classical single-crossing property of indifference curves "a la Spence-Mirrlees", which in turn generates new types of competitive equilibria.[4] More generally, situations of bi- or multi-dimensional adverse selection are much more complex than the standard ones, and may require more sophisticated policies.[5]

11.2.1.2 What Does the Theory Predict?

The previous remarks only illustrate a basic conclusion: when it comes to empirical testing, one should carefully check the robustness of the conclusions under consideration to various natural extensions of the theoretical background. Now, what are the main robust predictions emerging from the theoretical models?

A first distinction, at this stage, must be made between exclusive and non exclusive contracts. The issue, here, is whether individuals are free to buy an arbitrary number of contracts from different insurance companies, or whether the insurer can impose an exclusive relationship. In the field of insurance, both situations coexist; for

[4] See Villeneuve (1996), Chassagnon (1996) and Araujo and Moreira (2000). The same remark applies to models with adverse selection and moral hazard, whether adverse selection is relative to risk, as in Chassagnon and Chiappori (1997), or to risk aversion, as in Julien, Salanié and Salanié (1996).

[5] Typically, they may require more instrument than in the standard models. In addition, one may have to introduce randomized contracts, and bunching may take specific forms. See Rochet and Choné (1998).

instance, automobile insurance contracts are almost always exclusive, whereas annuities or life insurance are typically sold without exclusivity.

Non Exclusive Contracts and Price Competition. Non exclusivity strongly restricts the set of possible contracts. For instance, no convex price schedule can be implemented: if unit prices rise with quantities (which is typically what adverse selection requires), agents can always "linearize" the schedule by buying a large number of small contracts from different insurers.[6] The same holds true for quantity constraints, which can be considered as a particular form of price convexity. To a large extend, the market will in that case entail standard (linear) price competition.

In this context, adverse selection has well-known consequences. Since all agents face the same (unit) price, high risk individuals are de facto subsidized (with respect to fair pricing), whereas low risk agents are taxed. The latter are likely to buy less insurance, or even to leave the market. A first prediction of the theory is precisely that, in the presence of adverse selection, the market typically shrinks, and the high risk agents are over-represented among buyers. In addition, purchased quantities should be positively correlated with risk; i.e., high risk agents should, everything equal, buy more insurance. Both predictions are testable using insurers' data.

Finally, the presence of adverse selection will have an impact on prices. Because of the over-representation (in number and in quantities) of high risk agents in the insurers' portfolios, unit prices will, at equilibrium, exceed the level that would obtain in the absence of adverse selection. Although the latter is not observable, it may in some cases be computed from the average characteristics of the general population. A typical example is provided by annuities, since the distribution of life expectancy conditional on age is well documented. It is in principle possible to compute the fair price of a given annuity, and to compare it to actual market price. A difference that exceeds the "normal" loading can be considered as indirect evidence of adverse selection (provided, of course, that the "normal" level of loading can be precisely defined).

Exclusive Contracts. In the alternative situation of exclusivity, theoretical predictions depend, among other things, on the particular definition of an equilibrium that is adopted—an issue on which it is fair to say that no general agreement has been reached. Using Rothschild and Stiglitz's concept, equilibrium may fail to exist, and cannot be pooling. However, an equilibrium a la Riley always exists. The same property holds for equilibria a la Wilson; in addition, the latter can be pooling or separating, depending on the parameters. Referring to more complex settings—for instance, game-theoretic frameworks with several stages—does not simplify the problem, because the properties of equilibria are extremely sensitive to the detailed structure

[6] The benefits of linearization can be mitigated by the presence of fixed contracting costs. For large levels of coverage, however, this limitation is likely to be negligible.

of the game (for instance, the exact timing of the moves, the exact strategy spaces, ...), as emphasized by Hellwig (1987).

These remarks again suggest that empirically testing the predictions coming from the theory is a delicate exercise; it is important to select properties that can be expected to hold in very general settings. Following Chiappori and Salanié (2000), one can argue that three conclusions seem fairly robust, namely:

1. under adverse selection, agents are likely to be faced with menus of contracts, among which they are free to choose.
2. contracts with more comprehensive coverage are sold at a higher (unit) premium; or, more precisely, the marginal premium rate (i.e., the increase in premium required for each additional dollar of coverage) should increase with coverage (*convex pricing*).
3. contracts with more comprehensive coverage are chosen by agents with higher expected accident costs.

The first prediction is essentially qualitative. It is also quite general, and holds true for different types of adverse selection (i.e., agents may differ by their risk, but also by their wealth, preferences, risk aversion, etc.), at least within an imperfect competition context. The second prediction, in most circumstances, is a direct consequence of individual rationality in general: even in the absence of adverse selection, an agent will not choose a contract with higher deductible (or more coinsurance) unless its unitary price is lower, at least if pricing is approximately fair.[7] Testing for this property is an interesting perspective; however, it requires an explicit and adequate estimation of the firm's pricing policy. Such a task may, in practice, reveal quite difficult. While abstract models generally assume proportional costs, in real life fixed costs and (dis)economies of scale and scope play an important role, and are responsible for many non linearities in the pricing policy. The latter may be very difficult to disentangle from those due to asymmetric information. If, because of adverse selection, the price schedule is less concave than it would otherwise be, there is little hope that such a subtle impact can be empirically identified at all.

On the contrary, testing the third property does not require an estimation of the firm's pricing policy. If agents, facing an identical menu of contracts (sold at identical fares), self select on the basis of some private information they have about their riskiness, then a positive correlation between coverage and expected costs should be observed, whatever the prices. It should be noted that this prediction seems quite robust. For instance, it does not require single crossing, and it holds when moral hazard or multidimensional adverse selection are introduced.

[7] This needs not be true when loading is high, because agents with lower risk will typically prefer less coverage, even at a (slightly) higher unit price. However, insurance companies are unlikely to charge a higher unit price to less risky customers in any case.

This claim must however be qualified, or at least clarified. What must be stressed, at this point, is that this prediction is valid within a group of *observationally identical* agents. In practice, insurance companies use observable characteristics to categorize individual risks. As far as pricing *across* classes thus constructed is concerned, the previous conclusions are totally irrelevant. Some agents may be offered contracts entailing both higher unitary premium and larger deductible;[8] the point being that they cannot choose the class they will be categorized into. The self-selection issue applies only *within* such classes. The empirical translation is that one must systematically consider probability distributions that are *conditional on all observables*. Although this requirement is in principle straightforward, how this conditioning is actually performed on "real" data is one of the key problems of this line of empirical investigation.

Finally, although most models predict a positive correlation between equilibrium coverage and risk, the literature has identified a few cases in which this correlation can be reversed. One is when the informational advantage is on the insurer's side, as studied by Villeneuve (1996). The problem, here, is that the insurer's claim that a client's risk is high can only be credible if it does not result in increased profit for the insurer. This revelation constraint, in general, requires partial coverage of risky agents and full coverage of safer ones. Another case is the "cherry-picking" model of de Meza and Webb (1999). In this context, risk averse agents are both more willing to buy insurance and more likely to adopt a cautious behavior that results in smaller accident probability. The authors show that this combination of adverse selection on risk aversion and moral hazard may, in the presence of loading, generate a negative correlation between risk and coverage at equilibrium.

11.2.2 Moral Hazard

Moral hazard occurs when the accident probability is not exogenous, but depends on some decision made by the subscriber (e.g., effort of prevention). When the latter is observable and contractible, then the optimal decision will be an explicit part of the contractual agreement. For instance, an insurance contract covering a fire peril may impose some minimal level of firefighting capability, or at least adjust the rate according to the existing devices. When, on the contrary, the decision is not observable, or not verifiable, then one has to examine the incentives the subscriber is facing. The curse of insurance contracts is that their mere existence tends to decrease incentives to reduce risk. In the extreme case of complete insurance (when the insured's welfare does not depend at all on the occurrence of an accident), incentives are killed, resulting in maximum accident probabilities. In general, different contracts provide different incentives, hence result in different observed accident rates. This is the bottom line of most empirical tests of moral hazard.

[8] This is typically the case of automobile insurance for young drivers, for instance.

An additional distinction that is specific to insurance economics is between an *accident* and a *claim*. Moral hazard is ex ante when the consequence of the agent's effort is a decrease in *accident* probability or severity (this is typical of prevention). But insurance companies are interested in claims, not in accidents. Whether an accident results in a claim is the agent's decision, and is as such influenced by the form of the insurance contract. Of course, the previous argument holds for both case: more comprehensive coverage discourages accident prevention *and* increases incentives to file a claim for small accidents. However, the econometrician will in general be eager to distinguish between "true" moral hazard (resulting in changes in the accident rates) and incentives to file a claim, if only because the welfare implications are typically very different. For instance, a deductible is more likely to be welfare increasing when it reduces accident probability than when its only effect is to discourage victims from filing a claim (unless, of course, the technology of the insurance industry—say, the presence of fixed costs—makes the processing of small claims very inefficient).[9]

Quite interestingly, the basic moral hazard story is very close to the adverse selection one, except for an inverted causality. Under adverse selection, people are characterized by different levels of risk (that will ex post be translated into different accident rates); because of these discrepancies, they choose different contracts. In a context of moral hazard, agents first choose different contracts; then they are faced with different incentive schemes, hence adopt more or less cautious behavior, which ultimately results in heterogeneous accident probabilities. In both cases, however, the conclusion is that, controlling for observables, the choice of a contract will be correlated with the accident probability—again, more comprehensive coverage being associated to higher risk.

This suggests that it may be difficult to distinguish between adverse selection and moral hazard in the static framework (i.e., using cross-sectional data). An econometrician may find out that, conditionally on observables, agents covered by a comprehensive automobile insurance contract are more likely to have an accident. Deciding whether they chose full coverage because they knew their risk was higher, or they became more risky because the comprehensive contract they chose (for some exogenous and independent reason) killed most incentives to drive safely, is a much harder task.

Distinguishing Adverse Selection from Moral Hazard. The adverse selection versus moral hazard puzzle can be solved in different ways. One is to use natural experiments. Assume that the incentive structure that a given population faces is modified for exogenous reasons (typically, a reform of the regulatory framework). Resulting changes in people's behavior (if any) cannot be attributed to adverse selection (since the population remains unchanged); then moral hazard is a natural inter-

[9] A related problem is fraud, defined as any situation where a subscriber files a claim for a false accident or overstates its severity in order to obtain a more generous compensation. The optimal contract, in that case, typically require selective auditing procedures (see the Chapters by G. Dionne and P. Picard in this volume).

pretation. Ideally, the population would be randomly split into various subgroups, one of which (at least) keeps the old scheme. Such a "reference" group allows to sort out the changes that are specifically driven by the new regulation. The celebrated Rand study on medical expenditures (see Manning et al. 1987) provides a perfect illustration of such a context.

This basic idea may in some occasions apply even in the absence of an actual "experiment" of this kind. Any context where similar individuals are facing different incentive schemes can do, provided one can be sure that the selection into the various schemes is not related to risk-relevant characteristics. A few examples of such "pseudo natural experiments" will be provided later on.

Finally, and perhaps more fruitfully, the distinction between adverse selection and moral hazard may exploit the different dynamic properties of the various cases. Two approaches can be chosen here. One is to assume that existing contracts are optimal. The recent developments of dynamic contract theory can then be used to characterize the main qualitative patterns these optimal contracts should exhibit in each case. Testable predictions obtain, that can be compared to existing contracts. The second approaches does not rely on optimality assumptions. Rather, it takes existing contracts as given, and characterizes the agent's optimal response in the various contexts. For instance, one may test for moral hazard by deriving the dynamic properties of the optimal experience rating schemes, and check whether existing schemes correspond to this model. Alternatively, one may take the existing experience rating mechanisms as given, and study the induced dynamics of effort and accidents. Then these can be compared to observed behavior. Note that first approach only requires data on contracts, whereas the second, while more general (since it does not assume optimal contracts), is more demanding and requires individual data on contracts and accidents.

11.2.3 The Dynamics of Optimal Contracts

In repeated interactions, the transfers at any period (and in particular the premium paid by the agent) will typically be contingent on the past history of the relationship. While this notion of "experience rating" is general, the particular form it takes in optimal contracts will in general depend on the type of asymmetry and on the parties' ability to commit.

Repeated Adverse Selection. As a first polar case, consider the case where the basic adverse selection model is repeated. Cooper and Hayes (1987) provide a full characterization of the optimal contract under the assumption that both the insurer and the insured can fully commit on their future behavior. While high risk agents are fully covered by a time-invariant contract, the contract for low-risk individuals entails both partial coverage at each period and experience rating.[10] The empirical relevance of this result is however debatable since the corresponding contract is not immune to

[10] This property apparently contradicts a standard result of the repeated adverse selection literature,

renegotiation. The agents' type is indeed fully revealed at the first period through her choice of a contract. At any subsequent period, both parties can then increase their (ex post) well-being by agreeing on a different continuation that provides full insurance to low-risk agents as well. If a renegotiation of this type cannot be prevented, however, it will be anticipated by low risk agents at the first period, which aggravates the first-period revelation problem. Hart and Tirole (1988) and Laffont and Tirole (1993) characterize the optimal long term contract under full commitment when renegotiation cannot be ruled out. They show that it entails partial pooling. At any period, two contracts are available, one of which only entails full coverage at a high unit price. Low-risk agents always prefer the partial coverage contract, whereas high-risk agents are indifferent and are randomly distributed across the two contracts. In particular, while the choice of full coverage signals a high risk type with probability one, the partial coverage contract always attracts agents of both types (except for the last period), which avoids the renegotiation problem. This intuition is extended to a competitive insurance framework by Dionne and Doherty (1994). Their model entails one-sided commitment: the insurer can commit to keep its clients, whereas a client is always free to leave the relationship. They show that, in a two-period framework, the optimal renegotiation-proof contract entails semi-pooling in the first period and separation in the second. More importantly, the contract will exhibit "highballing" features; i.e., the insurance company will typically make positive profits in the first period, compensated by low, below-cost second period prices. An important remark is that this property is empirically testable. Moreover, it does not necessarily require individual data, since the highballing prediction can be tested at the firm level.[11]

Repeated Moral Hazard. Repeated moral hazard constitutes a second natural polar case. A first intuition is that the law of large number should, in this case, be of considerable help. Assuming that the agent's effort strategy is stationary, a "long enough" observation of accident rates should allow the principal to very precisely infer the action chosen. Then an adequate punishment scheme should lead to outcomes close to the first-best. Rubinstein and Yaari (1983) show indeed that when neither the principal nor the agent has a preference for the present, the first-best can be implemented, at least when the interaction is infinitely repeated.

From an empirical perspective, however, the Rubinstein and Yaari model suffers from several limitations. It requires very patient agents and an infinitely repeated interaction, two assumptions that may seem at least debatable. Another major problem that

stating that the optimal long term contract under full commitment is the repetition of the one-period optimal contract. The difference is due to a particular feature of insurance models: the occurence of an accident during the relationship provides information about the agent's type *independently of the agent's strategy*. It is then possible to increase efficiency by signing contracts that are contingent on this information, which is the exact definition of experience rating.

[11] Finally, the no commitment case is particularly complex in the competitive context, in particular because it generates difficult existence problems. See Fombaron (1997) for a recent characterization.

any repeated contract model should face, at least when empirical applications are at stake, is how to model the agent's access to financial markets. Most theoretical models assume that the payments at each period directly determine the agent's consumption, i.e., that the agent can neither save nor borrow to improve the allocation of her consumption over time.[12] Such an assumption has to be considered with suspicion. One can probably accept that some agents may face credit constraints (although the actual importance of these effects seems actually small for a majority of people). In the repeated moral hazard context, however, Rogerson (1985) has shown that the optimal contract with no access to financial markets is such that the agent would actually like to *save more* than what is implied by the contract. Hence ignoring financial markets amounts to assuming that agents cannot freely save, a very strange assumption indeed.

Allowing for the agent's access to financial markets, however, raises other problems. In general, the agent's transactions on financial markets are not observable by the insurer. As a consequence, whenever the risk aversion of the agent depends on her wealth (i.e., her preferences are not CARA), the second-period relationship entails an additional element of adverse selection on preferences, that is moreover endogenous to the first period strategies. Chiappori et al. (1994) show that this fact dramatically reduces the set of available contracts. They prove, in particular, that only contracts entailing the minimum effort level for all periods but the very first are renegotiation-proof, at least among the set of non randomized contracts. The particular case of CARA preferences and monetary cost of effort, on the other hand, had been previously studied by Fudenberg, Holmstrom and Milgrom (1990). The absence of income effect due to the constant absolute risk aversion assumption turns out to greatly simplify the problem. Fudenberg, Holmstrom and Milgrom show that the (second-best) optimal contract can then be implemented without memory, i.e., through deductible only (and without experience rating). The empirical scope of this result is however limited by the restrictiveness of the two key assumptions.

Symmetric Learning. A third, and possibly more promising case is when information is symmetric, in the sense that both the customer and the insurance company initially ignore the customer's risk. At each period of the relationship, they learn from the outcome (say, the number of accidents during the period), and symmetrically revise their prior. Assuming that the firm is able to commit whereas the client is not, Harris and Holmstrom (1982) show that in the optimal contract the premium is upwards rigid.[13] Unlucky agents are not penalized for the occurrence of an accident, in the sense that their premium does not increase. On the contrary, lucky agents are rewarded for the absence of accident during the period (this is a direct consequence

[12] In other word, the insurance contract is used to smooth the agent's consumption not only across states of the world, but also across periods.

[13] The initial Harris and Holmstrom model consider wage dynamics. The transposition to insurance is straightforward.

of the absence of commitment on the agent's side). Note that the existence of this "bonus" is costly ex ante, because it restricts the agent's insurance coverage. Under bilateral commitment, the optimal contract would not depend on the occurrence of an accident, thus providing insurance against the classification risk as well (i.e., the risk of being believed to be a high risk).[14]

These features can be contrasted with the contracts that obtain without commitment from the insurer. Then the occurrence of an accident at period t always worsens the insurer's posterior about the agent's type and results in higher premia in period $t+1$. Since both types of contract coexist in practice, these qualitative properties can be empirically distinguished, a fact that has been used in the empirical literature.[15] Finally, the Harris and Holmstrom model has been recently extended by de Garidel (1997), who analyzes the issue of information transmission between the incumbent insurer and its potential competitors.

Dynamic Behavior Under (Possibly) Suboptimal Contracts. Even when contracts are suboptimal, the dynamics of outcomes (say, accident occurrence) will typically differ under moral hazard and adverse selection. Adverse selection (and more generally any heterogeneity that is residual to the insurance company's classification model) typically results in "positive contagion" phenomena: more accidents in the past signal a high risk agent, who is more likely to have other accidents in the future. On the contrary, under moral hazard, the experience rating schemes are typically such that the marginal cost of a new accident increases with the number of past accidents. This point is formally established by Chiappori and Heckman (2000), who consider an experience rating scheme for automobile insurance where the premium is multiplied by some constant larger (resp. smaller) than one for each year with (resp. without) accident (the so-called "bonus/malus" scheme). They show that, under general assumptions, effort at each period is an increasing function of the premium level at the beginning of the period.[16] In other words, more accidents in the past result in stronger incentives, more prevention effort and lower accident rates in the future. This "negative contagion" property can be tested, provided individual, dynamic data are available.

[14] In principle, the upward rigidity prediction only holds without agent's access to financial markets. Indeed, the first best could otherwise be implemented. The idea is to charge a very high first period premium, then choose at any subsequent period a uniform premium that leaves the agents with the best history just indifferent between staying or leaving (all other agents strictly prefer to stay). Such a contract, however, requires that the agent borrows a large amount at the beginning of the relationship; it cannot be implemented in the presence of credit constraints.

[15] Interestingly enough, this model also generates strong testable predictions on the dynamics of transfers between the principal and the agent, even when the agent's "performance" (here, the occurence and the severity of an accident) is not observable. This property is not utterly appealing in the insurance context, where accidents are typically observed. But it may become quite attractive in different contexts, such as labor contracts. See Chiappori, Salanié and Valentin (1999) for a detailed investigation of the so-called "late beginner" effect.

[16] In practice, the "bonus/malus" coefficient is often capped. Then the effort monotonicity property obtains only for values of the bonus coefficient that are "far enough" from the cap.

11.2.4 Claims Versus Accidents

As mentioned above, a key feature of insurance data is that the insurer can only observe claims, not accidents. In most cases, the decision to file a claim is made by the subscriber, and must be understood as a response to specific incentives. Should the costs of filing a claim exceed the expected benefits—say, because the expected cost is below the deductible, or experience rating implies that the claim will result in higher future premia—then the insured is always free not to report the accident.

This simple remark has two consequences. One is that the incentives to file a claim should be monitored by the insurance company, particularly when the processing of a small claim involves important fixed costs for the company. A deductible, for instance, is often seen by insurance companies as a simple and efficient way of avoiding small claims. More related to the present topic is the fact that the empirical distribution of claims will in general be a truncation of that of accidents—since "small" accidents are typically not declared. Moreover, the truncation is endogenous; it depends on the contract (typically, on the size of the deductible or the presence of experience rating), and also on the individual characteristics of the insured (if only because the cost of higher future premia is related to the expected frequency of future accidents). This can potentially generate severe biases. If a high deductible discourages small claims, a (spurious) correlation will appear between the choice of the contract and the the number of filed claims, even in the absence of adverse selection or ex ante moral hazard. The obvious conclusion is that any empirical estimation must very carefully control for potential biases due to the distinction between accidents and claims.

11.3 EMPIRICAL ESTIMATIONS OF ASYMMETRIC INFORMATION IN THE STATIC FRAMEWORK

While the theoretical analysis of contracts under asymmetric information began in the 70s, the empirical estimation of insurance models entailing either adverse selection or moral hazard is more recent. Among early contributions, one may mention Boyer and Dionne (1987) and Dahlby (1983), who does not reject the presence of some asymmetric information. However, Dahlby uses aggregate data only, so that it is not clear whether his results would be robust to the inclusion of more detailed individual data.

11.3.1 Non Exclusivity and Price Competition

11.3.1.1 Annuities

In a non exclusivity context, several studies have been devoted to the market for annuities. The latter provide a typical example of non exclusive contracts. Also, the information available to the insurance company is generally rather sparse. Despite the similarities between annuities and life insurances (in both cases, the underlying risk is related to mortality), it is striking to remark that while life insurance contracts (at least above some minimum amount) are contingent to detailed information upon the subscriber's health state, the price of an annuity only depends on the buyer's age. This suggests that adverse selection may play an important role in this context.

A first line of research has concentrated upon prices. In an important contribution, Friedman and Warshawski (1990) compute the difference between the implicit contingent yield on annuities and the available yield on alternative forms of wealth holding (in that case, US government bonds). Even when using longevity data compiled from company files, they find the yield of annuities to be about 3% lower than US bonds of comparable maturity, which they interpret as evidence of adverse selection in the company's portfolio. Similar calculations on UK data by Brugiavini (1990) find a 3% difference, but only when longevity is estimated on the general population.

A related but more direct approach studies the distribution of mortality rates in the subpopulation of subscribers, and compares it to available data on the total population in the country under consideration. Brugiavini (1990) documents the differences in life expectancy between the general population and the subpopulation actually purchasing annuities. For instance, the probability, at age 55, to survive till age 80 is 25% in the general population but close to 40% among subscribers. In a similar way, the yield difference computed by Friedman and Warshawski (1990) is 2% larger when computed from data relative to the general population.

A final prediction of the theory is that the amount purchased should be positively correlated with (realized) longevity. However, neither paper does test for this property.

11.3.1.2 Life Insurance

Life insurance contracts provide another typical example of non exclusive contracts, although adverse selection might in this case be less prevailing. In a recent paper, Cawley and Philipson (1997) use direct evidence on the (self-perceived and actual) mortality risk of individuals, as well as the price and quantity of their life insurance. They first find that unit prices fall with quantities, indicative of the presence of bulk discounts. More surprising is the result that quantities purchased appear to be *negatively* correlated with risk, even when controlling for wealth. This strongly suggests that the market for life insurance may not be affected by adverse selection, probably because of the large amount of information available to the insurer in that case.[17]

[17] As argued above, the negative correlation finding can be explained in two different ways. The "cherry-picking" effect requires moral hazard to play an important role; it may be the case, for instance, that "timid" agents buy more insurance and invest more in medical prevention. The "informed principal" argument, on the other hand, is less convincing in this case, since in principle it requires exclusive contracts.

11.3.2 Exclusive Contracts

11.3.2.1 The Hedonic Approach (Puelz and Snow 1994)

The alternative approach—i.e., the analysis of competition in exclusive contracts—has attracted renewed attention during the last decade. An important contribution, due to Puelz and Snow (1994), relies upon a hedonic model of insurance pricing. Using individual data from an automobile insurer in Georgia, they build a two-equation model of insurance contracts. The first equation represents the pricing policy adopted by the insurance firm. It takes the form:

$$P_i = g(D_i, X_i, \varepsilon_i)$$

where P_i and D_i are the premium and the deductible in the contract chosen by individual i, the X_i are individual-specific exogenous variables and ε_i is an econometric error term. This allows to directly test the second prediction in subsection 11.2.1.2—namely, that higher premia should be associated to lower deductible. This property is indeed confirmed by the data. However, as argued above, this result, per se, cannot provide a strong support to the existence of adverse selection. Whatever the reason for offering a menu of contracts, one hardly expects rational agents to choose contracts with a higher unitary premium *and* a larger deductible. More interesting is the test they propose for the third prediction—i.e., that the choice of a contract offering a more comprehensive coverage should be correlated with a higher accident probability. For this purpose, they estimate a second equation that describes the agent's choice of deductible. The decision depends on the agent's "price of deductible" $\hat{g}_D$, as estimated from a third regression using instrumental variables, and on his (unobserved) accident probability. Since the latter is unobservable, it is proxied by a dummy variable RT_i that equals one if the individual had an accident and zero otherwise. This leads to an equation of the form:

$$D_i = h(\hat{g}_{Di}, RT_i, X_i, \eta_i)$$

where η_i is another error term. The Rothschild-Stiglitz model predicts that higher risks buy better coverage, i.e., a lower deductible, so that h should decrease in RT. Puelz and Snow specify their pricing equation as a linear model and estimate it by ordinary least squares. Since there are only three levels of deductible in their data set, they estimate the contract choice equation (again linear) by ordered logit; they find a negative coefficient for RT_i (although the choice of deductible does not vary much with the risk type).

11.3.2.2 Problems with the Hedonic Approach

There are several problems in the Puelz-Snow approach, that provide an interesting illustration of the difficulties encountered by any attempt at testing the predictions of contract theory. A first (and somewhat technical) one is related to the approximation of the (unknown) accident probability by the dummy variable *RT*. This procedure introduces a measurement error in the second equation. In linear models, the estimates would be biased towards zero, which would reinforce the conclusion of Puelz-Snow. In an ordered logit, it is not clear which way the bias goes.

A second concern is that the data set under consideration comprises individuals of various ages and driving records. This important heterogeneity may be troublesome for two reasons. One is heteroskedasticity. Presumably, the distribution of the random shocks, and especially of η_i, will depend on the driver's seniority. Within a nonlinear model such as the ordered logit, this will bias the estimation. The second and more disturbing problem relates to experience rating. Insurers typically observe past driving records; these are highly informative on probabilities of accident, and, as such, are used for pricing Omitting these variables will typically generate a bias, that tends precisely to overestimate the level of adverse selection: the corresponding information is treated by the econometrician as being private, whereas it is in fact common to both parties. However, the introduction of past experience is a quite delicate task, because it is (obviously) endogenous. Not only are panel data required, but endogeneity then raises specific econometric problems that will be discussed in the next section. Thirdly, nothing is done in the paper to distinguish between ex ante and ex post moral hazard. Higher deductible tend, everything equal, to discourage accident reporting, which has little to do with accident prevention but can generate spurious correlation.

A final (and quite general) problem relates to the use of a highly constrained functional form. In the second equation, in particular, the relationship of the latent variable to the accident probability π and the price $\hat{g}_D$ is taken to be linear. This needs not be the case. To illustrate this point, Chiappori and Salanié (2000) consider the case of constant absolute risk aversion. Then the individual's choice of deductible is of the form:

$$D_i = \frac{1}{\sigma_i}\log\frac{1-\pi_i}{\pi_i}\frac{-\hat{g}_{Di}}{1+\hat{g}_{Di}}$$

which is highly nonlinear. They argue that, in fact, applying the Puelz-Snow procedure to data generated by a *symmetric* information model, according to this formula, may well result in the kind of negative estimates they get, simply because the accident term captures in fact some of the omitted nonlinearities.

A particularly elegant illustration of this fact is provided by Dionne, Gouriéroux and Vanasse (1998). Their idea is to first run a probit on the "accident" variable, then to introduce the resulting *predictors* $\hat{\pi}_i$ of this probit in the right-hand side of the second equation (for the choice of deductible), together with the dummy RT_i. They find that the $\hat{\pi}$ variable has a large and highly significant negative coefficient, whereas the *RT* variable is no longer significant. This, obviously, has nothing to do with adverse selection, as $\hat{\pi}_i$ is by construction a function of *observed* variables only; it suggests, a contrario, that the negative influence of *RT* in the initial model can be spurious and due to misspecification.

11.3.2.3 Avoiding Possible Misspecifications

Several studies have attempted to correct for these biases. Chiappori (1994) and Chiappori and Salanié (2000) propose a very general approach, that may potentially apply to most problems entailing adverse selection. The idea is to simultaneously estimate two (non linear) equations. One relates to the choice of the deductible. In the (simplest) case of a binomial decision, it takes the form

$$y_i = \mathbb{I}[f(X_i, \beta) + \varepsilon_i > 0] \tag{3.1}$$

where, as above, the X_i are individual-specific exogenous variables, the β are parameters to be estimated, and ε_i is an econometric error term. Note that, contrarily to Puelz and Snow, the accident variable *RT* is *not* included in the right hand side. Nor is the premium; the idea, here, is that the latter is computed as a function of observables only, so that any information it conveys is already included in $f(X_i, \beta)$—provided, of course, that the corresponding functional form is flexible enough.

The second equation takes the occurrence (and/or severity) of an accident as the dependent variable. In the simplest case, the latter is the dummy for the occurrence of an accident (our previous *RT* variable), and the equation takes the form:

$$RT_i = \mathbb{I}[g(X_i, \gamma) + \eta_i > 0] \tag{3.2}$$

Note that this setting can easily be generalized. For instance, a recent contribution by Richaudeau (1999) takes into account the number of accident, modelled as following a negative binomial distribution.[18] Equation (3.2) is estimated using a count data model; the η_i are approximated by their "generalized residual" counterpart. In the same way, the distribution of accident costs (conditional on occurrence) can be introduced at that stage.

The key idea, then, is to simultaneously estimate the two equations, allowing for general correlation across the error terms. According to standard theory, asymmetric information should result in a positive correlation, under the convention that $y_i = 1$ (resp. $RT_i = 1$) corresponds to more comprehensive coverage (resp. the occurrence of an accident). One obvious advantage of this setting is that is does not require the estimation of the pricing policy followed by the firm, which is probably an extremely difficult task—and a potential source of important bias.

To circumvent the non linearity problems discussed above, as well as the issues raised by experience rating, Chiappori and Salanié consider a subsample of inexperi-

[18] In practice, Richaudeau includes among the regressors of the second equation the generalized residual obtained in the contract choice probit. Under the null of no correlation, the coefficient should be zero. Using a very complete French data base, he cannot reject the null.

enced drivers, and introduce a large number of exogenous variables, allowing for cross-effects. They use both a parametric and a non parametric approach. The latter relies upon the construction of a large number of "cells", each cell being defined by a particular profile of exogenous variables. Under the null (in the absence of adverse selection), within each cell the choice of contract and the occurrence of an accident should be independent, which can easily be checked using a χ^2 test.

This method can be given a general form. Following the presentation proposed by Dionne, Gouriéroux and Vanasse (1997) and Gouriéroux (1999), a general strategy can be summarized as follows. Let Y, X and Z respectively denote the endogenous variable under consideration (say, the occurrence of an accident), the initial exogenous variables and the decision variables at the agent's disposal (say, the choice of a particular contract within a given menu). Let $l(Y \mid X, Z)$ denote the probability distribution of Y conditional on X and Z. In the absence of adverse selection, the agent's choice conveys no information upon the endogenous variable. The translation is that:

$$l(Y \mid X,Z) = l(Y \mid X)$$

Obviously, this relationship can be given different but equivalent forms, such as:

$$l(Z \mid X,Y) = l(Z \mid X)$$

or

$$l(Y,Z \mid X) = l(Y \mid X) l(Z \mid X)$$

(the latter version expressing the fact that, conditionally on X, Y and Z should be independent).

Interestingly enough, in all the empirical applications to automobile insurance just listed (with the exception of the initial paper by Puelz and Snow), independence is not rejected; in other words, these studies find no evidence of adverse selection. The conclusion is that, at least in the context of automobile insurance, adverse selection may not be a crucial issue. One remark must be stressed at this point. According to the previous arguments, the existence of a positive correlation across the residuals cannot be interpreted as establishing the presence of asymmetric information without some precautions: as argued above, any misspecification can indeed lead to a spurious correlation. Parametric approaches, in particular, are highly vulnerable to this type of flaws, especially when they rely upon some simple, linear form. But the argument is not symmetric. Suppose, indeed, that some empirical study does *not* reject the null (i.e., the absence of correlation). Although, in principle, this result might as well be due to a misspecification bias, this explanation is much less credible in that case; for it must be the case that, while (fully conditional) residuals are actually positively correlated, the bias goes in the opposite direction with the *same* (absolute) magnitude—so that it exactly offsets the correlation. In other words, misspecifications are much more likely to bias the results *in favor* of the presence of adverse selection.

Accidents Versus Claims. A related issue is the distinction between accidents and claims discussed in the theory section. A regression using claims as the dependent variable is likely to generate misleading results, because a larger deductible automatically discourages small accidents reporting, hence reduces the number of claims even when the accident rate remains constant. This is a serious problem, that can be addressed in two different ways. The solution proposed by Chiappori and Salanié (2000) is to discard all accidents where one vehicle only is involved. Whenever two automobiles are involved, a claim is much more likely to be filed in any case.[19] A more restrictive version is to exclusively consider accidents involving bodily injuries, since reporting is mandatory in that case; the cost being a drastic reduction in the number of accidents.

Alternatively, one can explicitly model the filing decision as part of the accident process. For any accident, the agent computes the net benefit of filing a claim, and reports the accident only when this benefit is positive (or above some threshold). Although accidents involving no claims are generally not observed,[20] adequate econometric techniques can be used. Note, however, that these require the estimation of a complete structural model, as in Dionne, Gouriéroux and Vanasse (1998).

11.3.3 Adverse Selection Versus Moral Hazard

Natural Experiments. As argued above, the previous tests are not specific of adverse selection. Moral hazard would typically lead to the same kind of correlation, although with a different causality. In order to distinguish between adverse selection and moral hazard, one need some additional structure. Of particular interest are the situations where a "natural experiment" takes place. Assume that, for some exogenous reason (say, a change in regulation), a given, exogenously selected set of agents experiences a sudden and exogenous modification in the incentive structure they are facing. Then the resulting changes in behavior can be directly studied; and adverse selection is no longer a problem, since it is possible to concentrate upon agents that remained insured throughout the process.[21] A typical example is provided by the changes in automobile

[19] In principle, the two drivers may agree on some bilateral transfer and thus avoid the penalties arising from experience rating. Such a "street-settled" deal is however quite difficult to implement between agents who meet randomly, will probably never meet again, and cannot commit in any legally enforceable way (since declaration is in general compulsory according to insurance contracts). We follow the general opinion in the profession that such bilateral agreements can be neglected.

[20] Some data sets do, however, record accidents that did not result in claims. Usually, such data sets have been collected independently of insurance companies. See Richaudeau (1999).

[21] In addition, analyzing the resulting attrition (if any) may in some cases convey interesting information on selection issues.

insurance regulation in Québec, where a "no fault" system was introduced in 1978, then deeply modified in 1992. Dionne and Vanasse (1996) recently provided a careful investigation of the effects of these changes. They show that the new system provided strong incentives to increase prevention, and that, as a result, the average accident frequency dropped significantly during the years that followed its introduction. They conclude that changes in agents' behavior, as triggered by new incentives, did have a significant effect on accident probabilities.[22]

A limitation of any work of this kind is that, strictly speaking, it establishes a simultaneity rather than a causality. What the Dionne and Vanasse study shows is that, on a given period, accident probabilities have changed significantly, and that this evolution immediately followed a structural change in regulation. But, of course, the two phenomena might stem from simultaneous and independent causes. Such a "coincidence" may be more or less plausible. In the particular case of the Quebec reform, for instance, the incentive explanation remains by far the more convincing one, given both the magnitude of the drop in sinistrality and the absence of other major changes that could account for it during the period under consideration.

Still, an ideal experiment would involve a "reference" sample that is not affected by the change, so that the effects can be estimated in differences (or more precisely differences of differences), allowing for very convincing tests. A paper by Dionne and St-Michel (1991) provides a good illustration of this idea. They study the impact of a regulatory variation of coinsurance level in the Quebec public insurance plan on the demand for days of compensation. The main methodological contribution of the paper is to introduce a distinction between injuries, based on the type of diagnosis (easy or difficult). This distinction is based on information obtained from the medical literature; it reflects the fact that it is much easier for a physician to detect a fracture than, say, lower back pain. If moral hazard is more prevalent when the information asymmetry is larger, theory predict that the regulatory change will have more significant effects on the number of days of compensation for those cases where the diagnose is more problematic. This prediction is clearly confirmed by empirical evidence. A more generous insurance coverage, resulting from an exogenous regulatory change, is found to increase the number of days of compensations, but only for the cases of difficult diagnoses. Note that the effect thus identified is ex post moral hazard. The reform is unlikely to have triggered significant changes in prevention; and, in any case, such changes would have affected all types of accidents.

Additional evidence is provided by Fortin et al. (1994), who examine how the Canadian Worker's Compensation (WC) and the Unemployment Insurance (UI) programs interact to influence the duration of workplace accidents. Here, the duration is estimated from a mixed proportional hazard model, where the baseline hazard is estimated non parametrically, and unobserved heterogeneity is taken into account using

[22] See Browne and Puelz (1998) for a similar study on US data.

a gamma distribution. They show that an increase in the generosity of Worker's Compensation in Quebec leads to an increase in the duration of accidents. In addition, a reduction in the generosity of Unemployment Insurance is, as in Dionne and St-Michel, associated with an increase in the duration of accidents that are difficult to diagnose. The underlying intuition is that worker's compensation can be used as a substitute to unemployment insurance. When a worker goes back to the labor market, he may be unemployed and entitled to UI payments for a certain period. Whenever worker's compensation is more generous than unemployment insurance, there will be strong incentives to delay the return to the market. In particular, the authors show that the hazard of leaving WC is 27% lower when an accident occurs at the end of the construction season, when unemployment is seasonally maximum.[23]

In two recent papers, Chiappori, Durand and Geoffard (1998) and Chiappori, Geoffard and Kyriadizou (1998) use data on health insurance that display similar features. Following a change in regulation in 1993, French health insurance companies modified the coverage offered by their contracts in a non uniform way. Some of them increased the level of deductible, while other did not. The tests use a panel of clients belonging to different companies, who were faced with different changes in coverage, and whose demand for health services are observed before and after the change in regulation. In order to concentrate upon those decisions that are essentially made by consumers themselves (as opposed to those partially induced by the physician), the authors study the occurrence of a physician visit, distinguishing between general practitioner (GP) office visits, GP home visits and specialist visits. They find that the number of home visits significantly decreased for the "test group" (i.e., agents who experience a change of coverage), but not for the reference group (for which the coverage remained constant). They argue that this difference is unlikely to result from selection, since the two populations are employed by similar firms, display similar characteristics, and that participation to the health insurance scheme was mandatory.

"Quasi Natural Experiments". Natural experiments are valuable but scarce. In some cases, however, a static context exhibits specific features that keep the flavor of a natural experiment, although no exogenous *change* of the incentive structure can be observed. The key remark is that any situation were identical agents are, for *exogenous* reasons, faced with different incentive schemes can be used for testing for moral hazard. The problem, of course, is to check that the differences in schemes are purely exogenous, and do not reflect some hidden characteristics of the agents. For instance, Chiappori and Salanié (1997) consider the case of French automobile insurance, where young drivers whose parents have low past accident rates can benefit from a reduction in premium. Given the particular properties of the French experience

[23] See also Fortin and Lanoie (1992), Bolduc et al. (1997), and the survey by Fortin and Lanoie in this volume.

rating system, it turns out that the marginal cost of accident is reduced for these drivers. In a moral hazard context, this should result in less cautious behavior and higher accident probabilities. If, on the contrary, the parents' and children's driving abilities are (positively) correlated, a lower premium should signal a better driver, hence translate into less accidents. The specific features of the French situation thus allow to distinguish between the two types of effects. Chiappori and Salanié find evidence in favor of the second explanation: the accident rates of the "favored" young drivers are, other things equal, smaller than average by a small but significant percentage.

A contribution by Cardon and Hendel (1998) extends these ideas in a very stimulating way. They consider a set of individuals who face different menus of employer-based health insurance policies, under the assuption that there is no selection bias in the allocation of individuals across employers. Two types of behavior can then be observed. First, agents choose one particular policy within the menu at their disposal; second, they decide on the level of health expenditures. The authors identify a fully structural model, which allows them to simultaneously estimate a selection equation that describe the policy choice, and estimate the price elasticity of demand controlling for selection bias. The key ingredient for identifying the specific effects of moral hazard is that while people are free to choose any contract in the menu they face, they cannot choose the menu itself; and different menus involve different coinsurance levels. The "quasi-experimental" features stem precisely from this random assignment of people to different choice sets. Even if less risky people always choose the contract with minimum coinsurance, the corresponding coinsurance rates will differ across firms. In other words, it is still the case that identical people in different firms face different contracts (i.e., different coinsurance rates) for exogenous reasons (i.e., because of the choice made by their employer).[24] Interestingly enough, the authors find no evidence of adverse selection, while price elasticities are negative and very close to those obtained in the Rand survey alluded to above. This suggest that moral hazard, rather than adverse selection, may be the main source of asymmetric information in that case.

11.4 DYNAMIC MODELS OF INFORMATION ASYMMETRIES

As indicated above, tests based on the dynamics of the contractual relationship can either study the qualitative features of existing contracts assuming they are optimal in the relevant context, or take existing contracts as given and investigate the testable properties of the induced individual behavior.

[24] As Cardon and Hendel put it: ". . . the coinsurance is an endogenous variable . . . but since different individuals face different choice sets, the premium at which insurance was offered becomes a useful instrument for the coinsurance" (1998, p. 21).

Tests Assuming Optimal Contracts. Only a few empirical studies consider the dynamics of insurance relationships. An important contribution is due to Dionne and Doherty (1994), who use a model of repeated adverse selection with one-sided commitment. Their main purpose is to test the "highballing" prediction, according to which the insurance company should make positive profits in the first period, compensated by low, below-cost second period prices. They test this property on Californian automobile insurance data. According to the theory, when various types of contracts are available, low risk agents are more likely to choose the experience rated policies. Since these are characterized by highballing, the loss to premium ratio should rise with the cohort age. If insurance companies are classified according to their average loss per vehicle (which reflects the "quality" of their portfolio), one expects the premium growth to be negative for the best quality portfolios; in addition, the corresponding slope should be larger for firms with higher average loss ratios. This prediction is confirmed by the data. Insurance companies are classified into three subgroups. The slope coefficient is negative and significant for the first group (with lowest average loss), positive and significant for the third group, non significant for the intermediate group. They conclude that the "highballing" prediction is not rejected.

Recently, Hendel and Lizzeri (1999) have provided very convincing tests of the symmetric learning model a la Harris and Holmstrom (1982) on life insurance data. They use a rich contract data base that includes information on the entire profile of future premiums. Some contracts involve commitment from the insurer, in the sense that the dynamics of future premium is fixed in advance and cannot depend on the evolution of the insuree's health. For other contracts, however, future premia are contingent on health. Specifically, the premium increases sharply unless the insured is still in good health (as certified, for instance, by a medical examination). In this context, the symmetric learning model generates very precise predictions on the comparison between contracts with and without commitment. Contracts with non contingent future premia should entail front loading, representing the cost of the insurance against the classification risk. They should also lock-in a larger fraction of the consumers, hence exhibit a lower lapsation rate; in addition, only better risk types are likely to lapse, so that the average quality of the insurer's client portfolio should be worse, which implies a higher present value of premiums for a fixed period of coverage. Hendel and Lizzeri show that all of these predictions are satisfied by existing contracts.[25] Finally, the authors study accidental death contracts, i.e., life insurance

[25] The main puzzle raised by these findings is that a significant fraction of the population does not choose commitment contracts, i.e., does not insure against the classification risk. The natural explanation suggested by theory (credit rationing) is not very convincing in that case, since differences in premiums between commitment and no commitment contracts are small (less than $300 per year), especially for a client pool that includes executives, doctors, businessmen and other high income individuals. Heterogeneous risk perception across individuals is a better story, but formal tests still have to be developped. Obviously, more research is needed on this issue.

contracts that only pay if death is accidental. Strikingly enough, these contracts, where learning is probably much less prevalent, exhibit none of the above features.

Another characteristic feature of the symmetric learning model is that any friction reducing the clients' mobility, although ex post inefficient, is often ex ante beneficial, because it increases the agents' ability to (implicitly) commit and allows for a larger coverage of the classification risk. Using this result, Crocker and Moran (1998) study employment-based health insurance contracts. They derive and test two main predictions. One is that when employers offer the same contract to all of their workers, the coverage limitation should be inversely proportional to the degree of worker commitment, as measured by his level of firm-specific human capital. Secondly, some contracts offer "cafeteria plans", whereby the employee can choose among a menu of options. This self-selection device allows the contract to change in response to interim heterogeneity of insurees. In this case, the authors show that the optimal (separating) contract should exhibit more complete coverage, but that the premiums should partially reflect the health status. Both predictions turn out to be confirmed by the data. Together with the results obtained by Hendel and Lizzeri, this fact that strongly suggests the symmetric learning model is particularly adequate in this context.

Behavioral Dynamics Under Existing Contracts. Natural as it seems, the assumption that contracts are always optimal may for some applications be problematic. For one thing, theory is often inconclusive. Little is known, for instance, on the form of optimal contracts in a repeated moral hazard framework, at least in the (realistic) case where the agent can freely save. And the few results we have either require utterly restrictive assumptions (CARA utilities, monetary cost of effort) or exhibit features (randomized contracts, for instance) that sharply contrast with real life observations. Even skeptics of bounded rationality theories may accept that such very sophisticated constructs, that can hardly be understood by the average insurance salesman (let alone the average consumer), are unlikely to be implemented on a large scale.[26]

Another potential deviation from optimality comes from the existence of regulations, if only because regulations often impose very simple rules that fail to reproduce the complexity of optimal contracts. An interesting example is provided by the regulation on experience rating by automobile insurance companies, as implemented in some countries. A very popular rule is the "bonus/malus" scheme, whereby the premium is multiplied by some constant larger (resp. smaller) than one for each year

[26] A more technical problem with the optimality assumption is that it tends to generate complex endogeneity problems. Typically, one would like to compare the features of the various existing contracts. The optimality approach requires that each contract is understood as the optimal response to a specific context, so that differences in contracts simply reflect differences between the "environments" of the various firms. In econometric terms, contracts are thus, by assumption, endogenous to some (probably unobserved) heterogeneity across firms, a fact that may, if not corrected, deeply bias the estimations.

with (resp. without) accident. Theory strongly suggests that this scheme is too simple in a number of ways. In principle, the malus coefficient should not be uniform, but should vary with the current premium and the driver's characteristics; the deductible should vary as well; etc.[27]

Still, one can take this (probably suboptimal) scheme as given, and use theory to derive the main testable features of individual behavior for the various models at stake. In a recent contribution, Chiappori and Heckman (2000) test in this context the "negative contagion" prediction that can be derived in a moral hazard framework. The idea is that, for experience rating schemes of this kind, the occurrence of an accident typically increases the marginal cost of a future accidents. This should strengthen incentives to drive safely, hence reduce the probability of future accidents. The problem, however, is that any unobserved heterogeneity among individuals will generate an opposite, "positive contagion" phenomenon, since bad drivers had more accidents in the past and will probably have more accidents in the future. Technically, the "negative contagion" effect obtains only *conditionally* on agents' characteristics, including unobserved ones. The challenging econometric puzzle, at this point, is to disentangle the two aspects. In principle, this is feasible whenever panel data are available. Chiappori and Heckman use French data, for which regulation imposes that insurers increase the premium by 25% in case an accident occurs; conversely, in the absence of any accident during one year, the premium drops by 5%.[28] The technique they suggest relies upon existing result on the distinction between pure heterogeneity and state dependence (see Heckman (1978)). To get the intuition in a simple way, assume the system is malus only (i.e., the premium increases after each accident, but does not decrease subsequently), and consider two sequences of 4 years records, $A = (1, 0, 0, 0)$ and $B = (0, 0, 0, 1)$, where 1 (resp. 0) corresponds to the occurrence of an accident (resp. no accident) during the year. In the absence of moral hazard, and assuming away learning phenomena, the probability of the two sequences should be exactly identical; in both cases, the observed accident frequency is 25%. Under moral hazard, however, the first sequence is more probable than the second: in A, the sequence of three years without accident happens after an accident, hence when the premium, and consequently the marginal cost of future accidents and the incentives to take care are maximum.[29] In other words, for a given average frequency of accidents, the precise timing of the occurrences can provide valuable information upon the importance of incentives or disincentives effects. More surprisingly, Chiappori and Heckman show that a precise record of the sequence is not even needed when the distribution of new

[27] Of course, the precise form of the optimal scheme depends on the type of model. It is however basically impossible to find a model for which the existing scheme is optimal.

[28] In addition, several non linearities have been introduced; e.g., there exist both a floor and a ceiling on the resulting "bonus/malus" coefficient.

[29] Interestingly enough, if, as argued by many insurers, there is learning, in the sense that experienced drivers are better drivers, then A is more likely than B.

contracts is stationary (conditionally on observable). The knowledge of each individual's number of years of driving and number of accidents is then sufficient to test for moral hazard.

11.5 CONCLUSION

As argued in the introduction, empirical applications of contract theory is likely to become a burgeoning field; and it is a safe bet that insurance data will play an important role in these developments. Several studies have already contributed to a better knowledge of the impact of adverse selection and moral hazard in various markets. In several cases, the importance of information asymmetries has been found to be limited. This by no means implies, however, that such phenomena are of no importance in insurance. For one thing, the existence and the consequences of informational asymmetries vary considerably across markets. For instance, various (alas unpublished) studies have found strong adverse selection effects in private unemployment insurance markets.[30]

In addition, there exist a number of crucial normative issues where our theoretical and empirical knowledge of asymmetric information are likely to play a crucial role. The economics of discrimination in insurance provide an important example. The availability of an always larger range of medical tests allows insurance companies to classify people according to their health risk in a more precise way. A classic remark by Hirshleifer (1971) is that this progress comes with a cost—namely, the classification risk becomes uninsurable. The induced changes can have a major impact on individuals' lives; think, for instance, of the consequences of the introduction of the HIV test, or the forthcoming developments of genetic testing. A possible solution consists in regulating the use of such data by insurance companies. For instance, many countries restrict (and sometimes prohibit) the use of HIV tests for health insurance pricing. For an economist, however, the potential perverse effect of this regulation is to replace explicit discrimination by adverse selection, which may sometimes result either in similar discrimination plus signalling inefficiencies, or even in market collapse. Policy recommendations on this issue must rely on both a theoretical understanding of the issue and an empirical evaluation of the magnitude of the effects. Obviously, these problems are crying out for more work.

Finally, a better understanding of actual behavior is likely to require new theoretical tools. The perception of accident probabilities by the insurees, for instance, is a very difficult problem on which little is known presently. Existing results, however, strongly suggest that standard theoretical models relying on expected utility maximization using the "true" probability distribution may fail to capture some key aspects

[30] This is particularily true for unemployment insurance contracts linked to mortgages. See Chiappori and Pinquet (1998) for an overview in the French case.

of many real-life situations. Here again, the application of existing theory to insurance data is likely to reveal an extremely promising research direction.

11.6 REFERENCES

Araujo, A. and H. Moreira (2000). "Adverse Selection Problems without the Spence-Mirrlees Condition", *Mimeo*, IMPA.

Bolduc, D., B. Fortin, F. Labrecque and P. Lanoie (1997). "Incentive Effects of Public Insurance Programs on the Occurence and the Composition of Workplace Injuries", *CIRANO Scientific Series*, Montreal, 97s-24.

Boyer, M. et G. Dionne (1989). "An Empirical Analysis of Moral Hazard and Experience Rating", *Review of Economics and Statistics*, 71, 128–34.

Browne, M. and R. Puelz (1998). "The Effect of Legal Rules on the Value of Economic and Non-Economic Damages and the Decision to File", *mimeo*, University of Wisconsin-Madison.

Brugiavini, A. (1990). "Longevity Risk and the Life Cycle", *PhD Dissertation*, LSE, London.

Cardon, J. and I. Hendel (1998). "Asymmetric Information in Health Insurance: Evidence From the National Health Expenditure Survey", *Mimeo*, Princeton University.

Cawley. J. and T. Philipson (1997). "An Empirical Examination of Information Barriers to Trade in Insurance", *Mimeo*, University of Chicago.

Chassagnon, A. (1996). "Anti-selection: modèle générique et applications", thèse de doctorat, DELTA-EHESS.

Chassagnon, A. and P.A. Chiappori (1997). "Insurance Under Moral Hazard and Adverse Selection: the Competitive Case", *mimeo*, DELTA.

Chiappori, P.A. (1994). "Assurance et économétrie des contrats: quelques directions de recherche", *mimeo*, DELTA.

Chiappori, P.A., F. Durand and P.Y. Geoffard (1998). "Moral Hazard and the Demand for Physician Services: First Lessons from a French Natural Experiment", *European Economic Review*, 42, 499–511.

Chiappori, P.A., P.Y. Geoffard and E. Kyriadizou (1998). "Cost of Time, Moral Hazard, and the Demand for Physician Services", *Mimeo*, University of Chicago.

Chiappori, P.A. and J. Heckman (2000). "Testing for Adverse Selection versus Moral Hazard from Dynamic Data", *Mimeo*, University of Chicago.

Chiappori, P.A., I. Macho, P. Rey and B. Salanié (1994). "Repeated Moral Hazard: Memory, Commitment, and the Access to Credit Markets", *European Economic Review*, 1527–53.

Chiappori, P.A. and J. Pinquet (1998). "Assurance chômage des emprunteurs", *Rapport pour la Direction de la prévision du Ministère de l'économie et des finances*; forthcoming in *Revue Francaise d'Economie*.

Chiappori, P.A. and B. Salanié (1996). "Empirical Contract Theory: The Case of Insurance Data", *European Economic Review*, 41, 943–51.

Chiappori, P.A. and B. Salanié (2000). "Testing for Asymmetric Information in Insurance Markets", *Journal of Political Economy*, 108, 56–78.

Chiappori, P.A., B. Salanié and J. Valentin (1999). "Early Starters vs Late Beginners", *Journal of Political Economy*, 107, 731–60.

Cooper, R. and B. Hayes (1987). "Multi-period Insurance Contracts", *International Journal of Industrial Organization*, 5, 211–31.

Crocker, K. and J. Moran (1998). "Contracting with Limited Commitment: Evidence from Employment-Based Life Insurance Contracts", *Working Paper*, University of Michigan, Ann Arbor.

Dahlby, B. (1983). "Adverse Selection and Statistical Discrimination: An Analysis of Canadian Automobile Insurance", *Journal of Public Economics*, 20, 121–30.

Dahlby, B. (1992). "Testing for Asymmetric Information in Canadian Automobile Insurance", in *Contributions to Insurance Economics*, G. Dionne ed, Kluwer.

de Garidel, T. (1997). "Pareto Improving Asymmetric Information in a Dynamic Insurance Market", D.P. 266, LSE, London.

de Meza, D. and D. Webb (1999). "The Timid and the Reckless: Risk Preference, Precaution and Over-insurance", WP, LSE, London.

Dionne, G. Ed. (1992). *Contributions to Insurance Economics*, Kluwer, Boston.

Dionne, G. and N. Doherty (1994). "Adverse Selection, Commitment and Renegotiation: Extension to and Evidence from Insurance Markets", *Journal of Political Economy*, 102–2, 210–35.

Dionne, G., C. Gouriéroux and C. Vanasse (1997). "The Informational Content of Household Decisions, With an Application to Insurance under Adverse Selection", W.P., HEC, Montreal.

Dionne, G., C. Gouriéroux and C. Vanasse (1998). "Evidence of Adverse Selection in Automobile Insurance Markets", in Dionne G. and C. Laberge-Nadeau (eds): *Automobile Insurance*, Kluwer Academic Publishers.

Dionne, G. and P. St-Michel (1991). "Worker's Compensation and Moral Hazard", *Review of Economics and Statistics*, LXXIII, 236–44.

Dionne, G. and C. Vanasse (1992). "Automobile Insurance Ratemaking in the Presence of Asymmetrical Information", *Journal of Applied Econometrics*, 7, 149–65.

Dionne, G. and C. Vanasse (1996). "Une evaluation empirique de la nouvelle tarification de l'assurance automobile au Quebec", *Mimeo*, Universite de Montreal.

Fombaron, N. (1997). "Contracts d'assurance dynamiques en présence d'antiselection: the effects d'engagement sen lis marches' concunentreds" Ph.D. thesis, Universite de Pari X-Nanture, 305 pages.

Fortin, B. and P. Lanoie (1992). "Substitution Between Unemployment Insurance and Workers' Compensation", *Journal of Public Economics*, 49, 287–312.

Fortin, B., P. Lanoie and C. Laporte (1995). "Is Workers' Compensation Disguised Unemployment Insurance", *CIRANO Scientific Series*, Montreal, 95s-48.

Fortin, B. and P. Lanoie (1998). "Incentries Effects of Workers' Compensation: a Survey". In this book.

Friedman, B.M. and M.J. Warshawski (1990). "The Cost of Annuities: Implications for Savings Behavior and Bequests", *Quarterly Journal of Economics*, 420, 135–54.

Fudenberg, D., B. Holmstrom and P. Milgrom (1990). "Short-Term Contracts and Long-Term Agency Relationship", *Journal of Economic Theory*, 51, 1–31.

Gouriéroux, C. (1999). "The Econometrics of Risk Classification in Insurance", *Geneva Papers on Risk and Insurance Theory*, 24, 119–39.

Harris, M. and B. Holmstrom (1982). "A Theory of Wage Dynamics", *Review of Economic Studies*, 49, 315–33.

Hart, O. and J. Tirole (1988). "Contract Renegotiation and Coasian Dynamics", *Review of Economics Studies*, 55, 509–40.

Heckman, J.J. (1978). "Simple Statistical Models for Discrete Panel Data Developed and Applied to Test the Hypothesis of True State Dependence Against the Hypothesis of Spurious State Dependence, *Annales de l'INSEE*, 30–1, 227–69.

Hellwig, M. (1987). "Some Recent Developments in the Theory of Competition in Markets with Adverse Selection", *European Economic Review*, 31, 154–63.

Hendel, I. and A. Lizzeri (1999). "The Role of Commitment in Dynamic Contracts: Evidence from Life Insurance", *Working Paper*, Princeton University.

Hirshleifer, J. (1971). "The Private and Social Value of Information and the Reward to Inventive Activity", *American Economic Review*, 61, 561–74.

Jullien, B., B. Salanié and F. Salanié (1999). "Should More Risk-Averse Agents Exert More Effort?", *Geneva Papers on Risk and Insurance Theory*, 24, 19–28.

Laffont, J.-J. and J. Tirole (1993). *A Theory of Incentives in Procurement and Regulation*, Cambridge, MIT Press.

Manning, W. et al. (1987). "Health Insurance and The Demand for Medical Care: Evidence from A Randomized Experiment", *American Economic Review*, 77(3), 251–77.

Puelz, R. and A. Snow (1994). "Evidence on Adverse Selection: Equilibrium Signalling and Cross-Subsidization in the Insurance Market", *Journal of Political Economy*, 102, 236–57.

Richaudeau, D. (1999). "Automobile Insurance Contracts and Risk of Accident: An Empirical Test Using French Individual Data", *The Geneva Papers on Risk and Insurance Theory*, 24, 97–114.

Rochet, J.C. and P. Choné (1998). "Ironing, Sweeping, and Multidimensional Screening", *Econometrica*, 66, 783–827.

Rogerson, W. (1985). "Repeated Moral Hazard", *Econometrica*, 53, 69–76.

Rothschild, M. and J. Stiglitz (1976). "Equilibrium in Competitive Insurance Markets", *Quarterly Journal of Economics*, 90, 629–49.

Rubinstein, A. and M. Yaari (1983). "Repeated Insurance Contracts and Moral Hazard", *Journal of Economic Theory*, 30, 74–97.

Salanié, B. (1997). *The Economics of Contracts: A Primer*, MIT Press.

Villeneuve, B. (1996). "Essais en économie de l'assurance", thèse de doctorat, DELTA-EHESS.

12 The Empirical Measure of Information Problems with Emphasis on Insurance Fraud*

Georges Dionne

HEC-Montreal

Abstract

We discuss the difficult question of measuring the effects of asymmetric information problems on resource allocation. Two of them are retained: moral hazard and adverse selection. One theoretical conclusion, shared by many authors, is that information problems may introduce significant distortions into the economy. However, we can verify, in different markets, that efficient mechanisms have been introduced in order to reduce these distortions and even eliminate, at the margin, some residual information problems. This conclusion is stronger for adverse selection. One explanation is that adverse selection is related to exogenous characteristics while moral hazard is due to endogenous actions that may change at any point in time.

Keywords: Empirical measure, information problem, moral hazard, adverse selection, insurance fraud.

JEL Classification Numbers: D80, G22, C25, G11.

12.1 INTRODUCTION

The study of information problems in economics began in the early 1960s. The two best known problems, moral hazard and adverse selection, were introduced into the literature in 1963 by Kenneth Arrow in a classic article published in the American Economic Review. In 1970, Akerlof came up with the first analysis of a market equilibrium in the presence on adverse selection. Optimal contracts were first character-

* I would like to thank Marie-Gloriose Ingabire for her help with bibliographical research, FCAR-Quebec and CRSH-Canada for their financial support. I would also like to mention the researchers who helped me develop several of the ideas on the subject over the years: P.A. Chiappori, K. Dachraoui, N. Doherty, C. Fluet, N. Fombaron, R. Gagné, C. Gouriéroux, P. Lasserre, P. Picard, B. Salanié, P. St-Michel, C. Vanasse, P. Viala. I thank P. Lanoie, C. Fluet, and B. Villeneuve who proposed interesting improvements to the first version of this chapter.

ized for adverse selection in articles by Pauly (1974), Rothschild and Stiglitz (1976), and Wilson (1977), and for ex-ante moral hazard by Holmstorm (1979) and Shavell (1979). Even if the problem of ex-post moral hazard was defined early on by Pauly (1968), it was later formalized by Townsend (1979) and Gale and Hellwig (1985).

In the early 1980s, several theoretical developments were advanced to account for different facts observed in several markets. Specifically, dealing only with models of two-party contracts, multi-period contractual relations were introduced; the renegotiation of contracts was formalized; the problem of contractual commitments was analyzed; and simultaneous treatment of several problems became a consideration. Other noteworthy proposals were developed to explain hierarchical relations in firms and in organizations (see the references).

The contracts most often studied are insurance contracts, banking contracts, work and sharecropping contracts, and types of auctions, etc. Several forms of contracts observed in these different markets were catalogued in various theoretical contributions. The best known are partial insurance coverage (co-insurance and deductibles), compensation based on hours worked and performance, compensation of executives with stock purchase options, debt, bonus-malus, temporal deductibles, venture capital contracts with warrants, etc. There was also rationalization of several corporate organizational practices such as the use of foremen, internal and external controls, decentralization of certain decisions, and the centralization of more difficult-to-control decisions.

The empirical study of information problems began much later. The main motivation was to distinguish the stylized (qualitative) facts used to construct certain models from real or more quantitative facts. For example, in classroom and theoretical journals, different automobile insurance deductibles can very well be used to justify adverse selection, but there is no evidence that insurers established this partial coverage for that reason. It can also be argued that labor contracts with performance compensation are used to reduce moral hazard in firms, but it has not necessarily been empirically demonstrated that there is less moral hazard in firms using this form of compensation than in other firms that use fixed compensation but set up other incentives or other control mechanisms to deal with the information problem.

Another strong motivation for empirically verifying the effects of information problems is the search for ways to reduce their negative impact on resource allocation. For example, we know that partial insurance is effective in reducing ex-ante moral hazard, as it exposes the insured person to risk. On the other hand, this mechanism is not effective against ex-post moral hazard, as the accident has already occurred. Partial insurance may even have pernicious effects and encourage the padding of costs (Dionne and Gagné, 1997). The audit is the most effective instrument against ex-post moral hazard. This shows the importance of identifying the real problem when attempting to correct imperfections.

When it comes to empirically measuring information problems and assessing the effectiveness of mechanisms set up to correct them (relationship between the nature of contracts and their performance), a number of complications soon arise. For one thing, several information problems may be present, simultaneously, in the data base studied; the theoretical predictions must then be carefully defined so as to distinguish the effects of different information problems on the parameters of the contracts to be estimated. Moreover, firms have a whole range of mechanisms (substitutes or complementary) at their disposal and they may be selected for reasons other than information problems or for information problems other than the ones to be taken up in a particular study. In other words, the information problems under consideration are often neither a necessary nor a sufficient condition to justify the existence of certain mechanisms.

Treating several information problems simultaneously is difficult, as the literature does not offer many theoretical predictions, even when available range of contributions is reviewed. But if we simply limit ourselves to verify whether a market contains any residual information asymmetry, regardless of its origin, it is easier to demonstrate its absence, since there is no need to distinguish between the different forms of information asymmetry. Otherwise, we have to ascertain which form is still present and document its cause in order to analyze the instruments which could mitigate or eliminate it.

As a rule, the distinction between moral hazard and adverse selection can be brought down to a problem of causality (Chiappori, 1994, 2000). With moral hazard, the non-observable actions of individuals that affect the way contracts work are consequences of the forms of contracts. For example, a contract may increase the risk of the activity, because it reduces the incentives to act with prudence. With pure adverse selection, the nature of different risks already exists before the contract is written. The contracts selected will flow from the risks present. There is thus a form of reverse causality between the two information problems. When an exogenous change occurs in an insurance contract, we can limit our test to the way it affects existing policy holders and isolate a moral hazard effect. Or, we could make comparisons to see whether the chance of catastrophe differs between new and old policy holders and check for any bias caused by adverse selection.

Another difficulty in the empirical measurement of information problems is the fact that researchers are not privy to any more information than decision makers. Two solutions have been adopted to make up for that difficulty: (1) use of confidential polls and (2) development of econometric strategies capable of isolating the desired effect. The experimental approach is a third avenue that I shall not deal with in detail (see, however, Section 12.4 for an example).

The polling method has the advantage of providing direct access to private information not available to the other parties to the contracts. Such information makes it possible to measure directly motivations for choosing specific contractual clauses as well as the behaviour of agents. The drawback of this method is that it is very costly. It can also be biased, because it is very difficult to explain all the complexity of the problem studied to respondents and because several alternative explanations might have been overlooked in the questionnaires.

The development of econometric strategies requires a good knowledge of the theoretical problem under study and of the econometric methods suitable to the project. This is why the most productive research teams are composed of theoreticians and econometricians. The objective is to isolate effects that are not directly observable by both parties to the contract but which are taken into account by certain variables or combination of variables. As discussed by Chiappori (1994), econometric work consists in distinguishing between two types of information. The first type is composed of variables observable by the two parties to the contract. These variables can be used to make estimates conditional on the characteristics observed. The second type is linked to that which is not observable by econometricians (and by at least one contractual party), but which may explain choices of contracts or behaviours. In the case of adverse selection, choices of contract can be interpreted by econometricians as being a bias of endogenous selection. One way of taking this into account is to estimate simultaneously the decisions of agents by introducing hidden connections (or informational asymmetries) between the decisions. One known form is the non-null correlation between the random terms of the different equations (Chiappori and Salanié, 2000).

Quality of data is a determining factor in the measurement of desired effects. The data must correspond directly to the contractual relations studied and to the duration of the contractual periods. There must also be access to data broken down contract by contract. The work of formulating raw data for the purposes of research should not be underestimated. Raw data are used in the day-to-day operations of firms which are not concerned with research problems and do not always contain the direct information on variables needed for the problem studied.

Econometric specifications must correspond to the theoretical models under consideration, if erroneous conclusions are to be avoided. Often, we choose (or are forced) to use only part of the information available to decision-makers, and thus bias the effects of certain variables so that they capture the effects of other forgotten or inaccessible variables.

Finally, the agents party to different contracts are often risk averse and display different levels of such aversion. This last characteristic is also difficult to observe and can itself be a source of asymmetric information. Some authors have recently proposed models taking into account the varying degrees of aversion to risk, but there are very few predictions capable of isolating the effects of information problems as they relate to varying degrees of risk aversion among agents (see Dionne, Doherty and Fombaron, 2000, for a longer discussion in relation to adverse selection).

The rest of my exposé will take up examples of the empirical verification of the presence or absence of a residual information problem in a market. These examples highlight the various difficulties which are not always well understood by those who tackle the empirical measurement of information problems. The first is a test for the presence of adverse selection in the portfolio of a private insurer. The question to ask is the following: Are the choices of deductibles explained by this information problem or not?

The second example deals with labor contracts and methods of compensation. Methods of compensation are often observable by econometricians, whereas individual effort is not. Furthermore, individual output can hardly be used to deduce effort, because it depends on several other factors, such as the outcome of a random variable or other non-observable staffing practices.

We next treat ex-post moral hazard in markets covering work accidents and medical services. The main difficulty is assigning variations in demand to price effects, moral hazard, and adverse selection. Many studies show that a change in coverage will affect consumption, but few are capable of determining whether the cause is a problem of moral hazard, for example. A section on insurance fraud will also be presented. We will see how parameters of standard insurance contracts may affect incentives to defraud.

Finally, we shall discuss market equilibrium in reference to adverse selection in markets for used cars. Can the price differences observed for the same quality be explained by adverse selection?

12.2 MEASUREMENT OF RESIDUAL ADVERSE SELECTION IN THE PORTFOLIO OF AN INSURER

Adverse selection has been dealt with in several theoretical essays (for example, see Dionne, Doherty and Fombaron, 2000). In this section, we limit ourselves to insurance contracts. Two mechanisms have been proposed in the literature to account for this resource allocation problem: deductibles and classification of risks. The two are complementary and the empirical questions with which we are concerned are the following:

Does the effective use of risk classification suffice to account for this information problem?

Or:

Do we need additional self-selection mechanisms? In other words, is there any residual adverse selection in classes of risk that justify the use of deductibles?

Before answering these questions, we should summarize the relevant theoretical contributions associated with them. Crocker and Snow (1985, 1986, 2000) proposed models showing that the classification of risks does improve the welfare of all individuals if two conditions are respected. The variables used to evaluate the individual risks must be easily observable (or observable at low cost). They must also be correlated with the individual risks.

We can easily certify that most of the variables involved in the classification of risks for automobile insurance contracts are easily observed by insurers. To check the second condition, we need to estimate individual frequencies of accidents in terms of these same variables of ratemaking. This is why it is so important to have high quality data on an insurer's portfolio.

The next step is to check whether deductibles in different classes of risk, are chosen in terms of individual risks. The model constructed by Rothschild and Stiglitz (1976) and Wilson (1977) predicts that high risks will choose lower deductible than low risks. Puelz and Snow (1994) used accidents at the end of the contractual period to approximate individual risks. They found that those who were the most accident prone chose the lowest deductible.

This finding is not convincing, for it is subject to an econometric specification error. The authors estimated two equations: one equation dealing with insurance pricing and the other equation dealing with choice of deductible. They used the second equation to test for the presence of adverse selection. As their choice-of-deductible equation contained only a few explanatory variables, the coefficient of the "accidents" variable may capture information other than that related to residual adverse selection.

The standard method for correcting this specification problem is to introduce the mathematical expectation of the number of accidents (or its predicted value obtained from the estimates of the accidents distribution) in the choice-of-deductible equation (Dionne, Gouriéroux, and Vanasse, 1998, or Chiappori and Salanié, 2000, for an equivalent approach; see also Section 12.5 of this chapter for more details). In doing this second regression, we check to see if the accident variable is still significant. If not, this means that there is no residual information in the risk classes. If the predicted variable is significant and bears the same sign as the accident variable in the first step, we cannot conclude that it measures adverse selection, since its prediction was obtained with variables observable by the insurer. The fact that it is significant is usually due to non-linearities not modeled in the equation. These non-linearities can be eliminated by increasing the interactions between variables in the choice-of-deductible equation, as do insurers when setting their premia.

Finally, we may conclude that there is a residual information problem in the portfolio when there is still a statistical link between the deductible variable and the accident variable in a model well specified. For example, the presence of residual adverse selection might have prevented the standard econometric specification method from completely correcting the problem. But the true residual information problem may be other than adverse selection. Other tests are necessary to isolate the true information problem.

There are numerous lessons to be drawn from this example. On this point, the theoretical environment has been well documented. The theoretical predictions of Rothschild and Stiglitz have had currency for more than twenty years and have been taught in microeconomics courses for a good many years. Some authors before Puelz and Snow had proposed tests for the theory, but the data used were not always adequate and often too aggregate.

Puelz and Snow had access to a good quality data base. They rather successfully isolated the relevant empirical questions, but they did not consider all of the instruments an insurer could use to take adverse selections into account effectively. Moreover, they failed to correctly interpret their econometric results and, most unfortunately, they never suspected that their conclusion on the residual adverse selection measured in the portfolio might be the result of an econometric specification.

This does not mean that there is no adverse selection in the automobile insurance markets. The fact that insurers classify risks is in large part explained by adverse selection. But, the absence of residual information asymmetry in the classes of risk shows that, when this classification is correctly done, the choice of deductible is not needed to treat adverse selection. In other words, the Rothschild and Stiglitz (1976) model is not useful in this portfolio.

Others will want to point out that moral hazard may also be present in this portfolio and that we probably did not screen for all the factors capable of explaining how deductibles relate to the differing degrees of policy holders' risk aversion. The second criticism is easier to handle. Let's start with that one.

Though rare, works treating differences in aversion to risk conclude that, in cases of adverse selection, good risks, who have a stronger risk aversion, may ask for coverage other than the one imposed by the self-selection constraint of the low risk (more expensive than actuarial, better than that of the good-to-weak aversion category, but still partial) (Villeneuve, 1996 and Smart, 1998).

Risk aversion cannot be directly observed. To screen for it, as in Puelz and Snow, we (Dionne, Gouriéroux, Vanasse, 1998) used the amounts of insurance coverage chosen by individuals as protection against potential civil liability losses. Some of these variables are significant and of the right sign when we calculate the choice-of-deductible equation for damages to the car combined with the predicted accident variable. But we also show that it is possible to make these variables non-significant by increasing the number of variables and the number of interactions between the variables insurers use in setting their rates. This finding implies that the methods for classifying policy holders can take into account not only the differences between individual risks but also the differences in risk aversion.

To adequately account for moral hazard in insurance contracts along with adverse selection, we must have access to a model capable of making theoretical predictions in an environment where the two information problems are simultaneously present. This exercise was dealt with by Chassagnon and Chiappori (1995) in a competitive market context. They found that agents who are less worried about protection choose contracts with the broadest coverage and the lowest deductibles (see also Dionne and Lasserre, 1987).

If we are limited to static contracts with data covering just one period, it is difficult to ascertain where the causality of moral hazard and adverse selection is heading. Panel data and experiments can help define the two information problems. The data of Dionne, Gouriéroux and Vanasse (1998, 2000) contained information on the bonus-malus of the company's clients. This information can here be considered as another good instrument for taking moral hazard into account. The preliminary results show that use of these variables have no impact on conclusions concerning the presence of residual adverse selection (see also Dionne and Gagné, 2000, for discrimination between information problems. We shall come back on this contribution in Section 12.5).

Another test concerns the type of commitment we may observe in dynamics insurance contracts. Dionne and Doherty (1994) proposed such a test by analyzing the variation of insurers loss premium ratio as a function of the premium rate. They verified that some automobile insurers use commitment to attract selective portfolios with disproportionate numbers of low risks. These results are consistent with the commitment and renegotiation model and reject both the no-commitment and the full commitment models. However, we must emphasize that these preliminary results represent an indirect test of the theory since the authors did not have access to the more accurate data. As mentioned by the authors, a direct test would require that data on different risk groups or cohorts be available as well data on the insurance prices faced by the different cohorts over time.

12.3 EX-ANTE MORAL HAZARD AND CHOICES OF WORK CONTRACTS

There is, by definition, ex-ante moral hazard if one of the parties to a contract can affect the results of the contractual relation by non-observable actions before realization of the random variables (Holmstrom, 1979; Shavell, 1979) (see Arnott, 1992, and Winter, 2000, for reviews of the insurance literature with moral hazard). In the simple model that we shall now treat, the realized output is observable but we do not know whether its value is due to the agent's effort or to the outcome of a random variable. We thus have a problem of identification to solve, if we want to check for the presence of residual moral hazard. (For other applications, see Dionne, Gagné, Gagnon and Vanasse, 1997, and Dionne and Vanasse, 1997.)

One useful prediction that models with moral hazard have made for the labour market is that forms of compensation can have an impact on work incentive: a worker paid based on performance should work harder than a worker paid an hourly wage. In other words, there should be less moral hazard when workers are paid based on performance, since their compensation is exposed to risks whose impact they can vary by their efforts.

Empirically, the hardest factor to measure in the model is the worker's effort, as this means gaining access to a variable the employer cannot observe and which can still be used to see whether methods of compensation have any impact on effort. Foster and Rosenzweig (1994) used calories consumed by workers as an approximation of the effort they expend.

They propose a simple theoretical model of workers' health in which body mass (kg/square meter) is affected by food intake, illness, and work effort. They show that it is possible, for the types of jobs studied, to make a direct connection between forms of compensation and the calories consumed. More specifically, in periods where workers have access to methods of compensation that reward more high powered performance, they work harder and consume more calories, thus justifying the direct theoretical link between method of compensation and consumption of calories.

To test their model, they used panel data containing information on 448 farming families in the Philippines; the members of these families may work either for themselves or for outsiders, under different forms of compensation. These individuals were interviewed four times concerning their wages, their modes of compensation, the type of work done, and the quantity of calories consumed over the previous 24 hours. A period of four months separated the interviews.

The results from estimation of the health function indicate that self-employment and piece work significantly reduce the body mass index as compared with unemployment, whereas work compensated on an hourly basis shows no significant effect. This seems to indicate either less effort or a measurable presence of moral hazard on the part of those who are paid with an hourly rate.

Now, what about the link between methods of payment and the performance rate per calorie consumed? They found that the calories consumed are associated with higher pay and performance in self-employment and piece work. Consequently, workers receiving these modes of payment consume more calories and, thus, can be said to work harder.

The next important question we must ask is the following one: Is this a test for moral hazard or for adverse selection? In other words, do workers themselves choose their type of work and mode of compensation?

The authors tried to answer this question by checking to see whether their data contained any sample selection effect. They used two methods to do this: Heckman's two-step Probit selection (1979) and Lee's multinomial Logit selection (1983). Both models render identical results.

It should be pointed out that 47.1% of the subjects worked under different regimes during the same period. But this statistic does not suffice to qualify the choices as random, since only 28% worked for hourly wages in all four periods.

Taking explicitly into account workers' choices of types of compensation tends to strengthen rather than weaken the results. Modes of compensation actually have a bigger impact on the use of calories with the selection model. This implies that those who choose incentive pay at the margin do so because they truly want to work harder. But, unlike what the authors suggest, the model tested is not a pure moral-hazard model. It is rather a mixed model containing aspects of adverse selection and moral hazard. The best physically endowed and most highly motivated will choose the highest paying but most demanding work.

In fact, to isolate a pure moral-hazard effect, it practically takes an exogenous change in a compensation regime or in some other parameter impinging on all the agents. We are now going to study changes of this nature as we turn to ex-post moral hazard.

12.4 EX-POST MORAL HAZARD, DEMAND FOR MEDICAL SERVICES, AND DURATION OF WORK LEAVES

In our applications, ex-post moral hazard deals with non-observable actions on the part of agents, actions which occur during or after the outcome of the random variable or accident (Townsend, 1979, and Gale and Hellwig, 1985). For example, an accident can be falsified to obtain better insurance compensation. This form of moral hazard is often associated with fraud or falsification (Crocker and Morgan, 1998; Crocker and Tennyson, 1998; Bujold, Dionne, and Gagné, 1997; Picard, 2000). Partial insurance of agents is not optimal in reducing this form of moral hazard, for the agent knows the state of the world when he makes his decision. Claims auditing is more appropriate, but it is costly, resulting in the potential presence of this moral hazard in different markets.

The main difficulty in isolating the ex-post moral hazard effect in different levels of insurance coverage is separating the effects of price and income variations from the effects of asymmetric information. Contrary to what is often read in the literature, not every variation in consumption following upon a variation in insurance coverage can be tied to ex-post moral hazard. When compared with full-coverage regimes, it is perfectly conceivable that a health insurance regime with partial coverage might be explained by transaction costs and patients' decision to curtail consumption of certain services because they must share in the cost. If for some reason, the transaction costs drop and the insurance coverage expands, the consumption of medical services will increase, since their price will be cheaper. But this increase will not be due to moral hazard. It will simply be a classic effect of demand. There are still too many articles in the literature which confuse variations in demand with moral hazard.

Another big difficulty in isolating moral hazard is linked to the possibility that potential policy holders, better informed than the insurer about the state of their health over the next period of the contract, will make an endogenous choice of insurance regime. As a rule, those expecting health problems choose more generous insurance regimes, even if the per unit cost is higher. This is a well-known adverse selection effect.

In the famous Rand corporation study (Manning et al., 1987 and Newhouse, 1987) dealing with the effects of changes in insurance coverage on the demand for medical services, the experimental method used was capable of isolating the elasticity of the demand from the effects of adverse selection by random selection of families who might be subject to exogenous changes in insurance coverage but who were not free to choose their insurance coverage ex-ante. They thus successfully calculated elasticities of demand much lower than those obtained in other studies that did not screen for the effect of endogenous choices of insurance regimes (adverse selection).

Their measurement of the elasticity of demand for medical services is not a measurement of ex-post moral hazard. It is, in fact, very unlikely that there is any moral hazard in their data, considering all the screening done.

Let us now consider work accidents. As we indicated above, using an exogenous change in an insurance regime can isolate moral hazard. An exogenous change in an insurance regime can be interpreted as a laboratory experiment, if certain conditions are met. As for laboratory animals, it is possible to restrict the choices of insurance available to the subjects.

It is also important to have a control group which undergoes the same insurance changes, but which does not have the same information problems as those expected. For example, if we suspect that some workers with specific medical diagnoses (hard to diagnose and verify) have greater information asymmetry with the insurer, there have to be other workers having undergone the same insurance changes at the same time but whose information asymmetry is weaker (easy to diagnose and verify). The reason for this is that it is hard to isolate an absolute effect with real economic data, because other factors not screened for may lead to changes in behaviour. The control group allows us to isolate a relative effect arising from the information problem, all things being equal. To simplify the analysis, it is preferable that the period under study should be short enough to get around having to screen for several changes at once.

Dionne and St-Michel (1991) managed to bring together all these conditions in a study of change in coverage for salary losses associated with work accidents (see B. Fortin and P. Lanoie, 1992, 1995, 2000, for similar studies and for a survey of different issues associated to workers compensation). The change in insurance coverage studied was exogenous for all the workers. Other forms of insurance were not really available, even if, in theory, it is always possible to buy extra insurance in the private sector if one is not satisfied with the public regime. But very few individuals do so in Quebec for this type of compensation. The fact that there are state monopolies over several types of insurance coverage in Quebec, makes it easier for us to meet this condition.

Dionne and St-Michel (1991) showed, first of all, that the increase in insurance coverage had a significant positive effect on the duration of absence from work. But this effect cannot be interpreted as being moral hazard, for it may simply be associated with an increase in the demand for days off due to their lower cost. Next, the authors checked to see whether this effect was only significant for diagnoses with greater asymmetry of information (hard to diagnose) between the worker and the insurer as represented by a doctor. This second finding confirms that the only effect observed on the duration of absences was that of moral hazard, since the workers of the control group (those without information asymmetry, easy to diagnose) did not modify their behaviour. Moreover, the change-of-regime variable without interaction with diagnostics, was no longer significant when the diagnostic-change-of-insurance variables were adjusted. This implies that there is no demand effect. However, the change of regime achieved the desired redistribution effects sought after by allowing poorer workers to have access to more insurance.

We may conclude that an ex-post moral hazard effect has been isolated (see Cummins and Tennyson, 1996, Butler et al., 1996a, Ruser, 1998, and Dionne, St-Michel and Vanasse, 1995, for similar results). It is, in fact, highly unlikely that the change in regime studied had any impact on ex-ante prevention activities which might affect the seriousness of work accidents. There is no reason to think that the average worker can practice such selective prevention as to influence diagnostics ex-ante. But, ex-post, when he knows his diagnosis, he can take undue advantage of the situation of asymmetric information. Some workers might be more tempted to provoke accidents or to say falsely that they had an accident in order to have access to more compensation, when the rates are more generous. These activities were not distinguished from other forms of moral hazard by Dionne and St-Michel, since they can be interpreted as ex-post moral hazard.

It is also difficult to find the link between this result and adverse selection. On the one hand, workers could not choose their insurance coverage in this market and, on the other hand, it is highly unlikely that the change in insurance regime had any short-term effect on workers' choice of more or less risky jobs.

Bernard Fortin and Paul Lanoie (2000) present a review of the literature on the incentive effects of work accident compensation. They use the classification of different forms of moral hazard proposed by Viscusi (1992). The form of ex-post moral hazard we just described can be classified moral hazard as duration of claims, which they distinguish from moral hazard as substitution hazard. This distinction can be explained, for example, by the fact that compensation for work accidents are more generous than those for unemployment insurance. Activities resulting in accidents are called causality moral hazard, which is ex-post moral hazard (bordering on ex-ante moral hazard), since the action takes place at the time of the accident. The result obtained by Dionne and St-Michel captures these three forms of ex-post moral hazard. It is even possible that workers may have substituted workers' compensations for unemployment insurance.

Can we now perform closer analysis and distinguish between the three forms of ex-post moral hazard: incentives provoking hard-to-verify accidents; decisions to prolong length of absence in hard-to-check diagnoses; or decisions to substitute accident compensations for unemployment insurance, or even falsification? This distinction would be important as it is not obvious that the mechanisms for correcting the situation would be the same for each of these forms of asymmetric information.

The last three forms are difficult to distinguish, since they belong to the same market. However, it is possible to separate new accidents from older ones using indicative variables. We know, for example, that the accidents provoked occur early on Monday mornings (see also Fortin and Lanoie, 1998, and Derrig, 1997) and that, among seasonal workers, requests to extend work absences pick up with the approach of unemployment insurance periods. Further research must be done on this subject.

12.5 INSURANCE FRAUD

Insurance fraud has become an important economic problem. In the Québec automobile insurance market, the cost of fraud was estimated at $100 million in 1994, just under 10% of total claims (Caron and Dionne, 1997). The Insurance Bureau of Canada has estimated that the total annual cost of liability insurance fraud was about $2 billion in Canada (Medza, 1998), while it is estimated to be nearly $70 billion per year in the United States for all types of claims (Foppert, 1994).

The causes of the rapid growth of insurance fraud are numerous: changes in morality, increased poverty, modifications in the behaviour of the intermediaries (medical doctors or mechanics for instance), attitude of insurers, etc. (Dionne, Gibbens and St-Michel, 1993). In two papers, Dionne and Gagné (1997, 2000) highlight the nature of insurance contracts. In both cases, they use the theoretical model proposed by Picard (1996) to obtain an equilibrium without commitment of the parties. In the second one (2000), they test whether the presence of a replacement cost endorsement can be a cause of fraudulent claims for automobile theft. This endorsement was introduced in the automobile insurance market to increase the protection of the insureds against depreciation.

Traditional insurance markets do not offer protection against the replacement value of an automobile. Rather, they cover current market value, and when a theft occurs, the insurance coverage is largely partial with respect to the market value of a new automobile. A replacement cost endorsement gives the opportunity to get a new vehicle in the case of theft or in the case of total destruction of the car in a collision, usually if the theft or the collision occurs in the first two years of ownership of a new automobile. In case of total theft, there is no deductible. Ex-ante and without asymmetric information, this type of contract can be optimal. The only major difference is the expected coverage cost which can easily be reflected in the insurance premium.

Intuitively, a replacement cost endorsement may decrease the incentives toward self-protection since it can be interpreted as more than full insurance when the market value of the insured car is lower than the market value of a new car. The presence of a replacement cost endorsement in the insurance contract may also increase the incentives to defraud for the same reason. For example, the insured may have an incentive to set up a fraudulent theft because of the additional protection given by the replacement cost endorsement. This particular type of fraud is known as opportunistic fraud since it occurs when an opportunity occurs and usually not when an insurance contract for a new vehicle is signed. Alternatively, under adverse selection, an individual may choose to include in his coverage a replacement cost endorsement because he knows he will be more at risk.

A first objective of the study by Dionne and Gagné (2000) was to test how the introduction of a replacement cost endorsement affects the distribution of thefts in the automobile insurance market. Another significant objective was to propose an empirical procedure allowing the distinction between the two forms of moral hazard. In other words, they seek to determine whether an increase in the probability of theft may be explained by a decrease in self-protection activities or by an increase in opportunistic fraud. They also took into account the adverse selection possibility since the insured ex-ante decision to add a replacement cost endorsement to the insurance policy might be explained by unobservable characteristics that also explain higher risks.

As discussed in Section 12.2, Dionne, Gouriéroux and Vanasse (1998) proposed a method that was applied to adverse selection. In their article, Dionne and Gagné (2000) extend this method in order to take into account both forms of moral hazard simultaneously. Furthermore, their approach makes it possible to isolate adverse selection.

Let us first consider y, an endogeneous binary variable indicating the occurrence of a theft. The decision or contract choice variable z (in this case the presence of a replacement cost endorsement; in Section 12.2, the choice of a particular deductible) will provide no additional information on the distribution of y if the prediction of y based on z and other initial exogenous variables $\boldsymbol{x}$ coincides with that based on $\boldsymbol{x}$ alone. Under this condition, we can write the conditional distribution of y as

$$\phi_y(y \mid \boldsymbol{x}, z) = \phi_y(y \mid \boldsymbol{x}) \tag{1}$$

where $\phi(\bullet \mid \bullet)$ denotes a conditional probability density function. A more appropriate but equivalent form for different applications is

$$\phi_z(z \mid \boldsymbol{x}, y) = \phi_z(z \mid \boldsymbol{x}) \tag{2}$$

In that case, the distribution of z is estimated and when condition (2) holds, this distribution is independent of y which means that the distribution of theft is independent of the decision variable z, here the replacement cost endorsement, since (1) and (2) are equivalent. The empirical investigation of Dionne and Gagne relies on the indirect characterization as defined by (2). It can be interpreted as the description of how the individual's decision affects his future risks (moral hazard) or of what his decision would be if he knew his future risks (adverse selection).

This type of conditional dependence analysis is usually performed in a parametric framework where the model is a priori constrained by a linear function of $\boldsymbol{x}$ and y, that is

$$\phi_z(z \mid \boldsymbol{x}, y) = \phi_z(z \mid \boldsymbol{x}'a + by).$$

This practice may induce spurious conclusions, since it is difficult to distinguish between the informational content of a decision variable and an omitted nonlinear effect of the initial exogenous variables. A simple and pragmatic way of taking into account these potential nonlinear effects of $\boldsymbol{x}$ is to consider a more general form

$$\phi_z(z \mid \boldsymbol{x}, y) = \phi_z(z \mid \boldsymbol{x}'a + by + cE(y \mid \boldsymbol{x})) \tag{3}$$

where $E(y \mid \boldsymbol{x})$ is an approximated regressor of the expected value of y computed from the initial exogenous information. Assuming normality, $E(y \mid \boldsymbol{x})$ is computed with the parameters obtained from the estimation of y using the *Probit* method.

The above framework can be applied to test for different types of information asymmetries. The failure of condition (2) to hold may allow a distinction between different types of information problems depending on how y is defined. Dionne and Gagné (2000) defined y using 5 different contexts or sub-samples (s):

- $s = 0$ when no theft occurred;
- $s = 1$ if a partial theft occurred at the beginning of the cost endorsement contract;
- $s = 2$ if a partial theft occurred near the end of the cost endorsement contract;
- $s = 3$ if a total theft occurred at the beginning of the cost endorsement contract;
- $s = 4$ if a total theft occurred near the end of the cost endorsement contract.

Using such a categorization, they identified the different types of information problems: adverse selection, ex-ante moral hazard and ex-post moral hazard or opportunistic fraud.

If we are in presence of a pure adverse selection effect, the time dimension (that is, the proximity of the expiration of the replacement cost endorsement in the contract, since it is valid for only two years after buying a new car) would not have any importance. In other words, the effect of pure adverse selection would be significant and of approximately the same size whether it is a new contract or an old one. However, the effects may not be of the same magnitude. Therefore, with a pure adverse selection effect, condition (2) should not hold in all sub-samples considered (i.e., $s = 1$, 2, 3 and 4).

Assuming that the same self-protection activities are involved in the reduction of the probabilities of both types of theft (partial and total), condition (2) should not hold under ex-ante moral hazard for both types of theft. In that case, the presence of a replacement cost endorsement in the insurance contract reduces self-protection activities leading to an increase in the probabilities of partial and total theft. In addition, since the benefits of prevention are decreasing over time, ex-ante moral hazard increases over time. Thus, as for adverse selection, ex-ante moral hazard implies that condition (2) does not hold in all sub-samples considered, but with a stronger effect near the end of the contract (i.e., sub-samples 2 and 4) than at the beginning (i.e., sub-samples 1 and 3).

In the case of opportunistic fraud, the pattern of effects is different. Because the incentives to defraud are very small or even nil in the case of a partial theft, condition (2) should hold in both sub-samples 1 and 2. Also, because the benefits of fraud for total theft are small at the beginning of the contract but increasing over time with a replacement cost endorsement, condition (2) should also hold in the case of a total theft at the beginning of the contract ($s = 3$). However, near the end the contract, the incentives to defraud reach a maximum only in the case of a total theft when the insurance contract includes a replacement cost endorsement. It follows that with a fraud effect, condition (2) would not be verified in sub-sample 4.

Their empirical results show that the total theft occurrence is a significant factor in the explanation of the presence of a replacement cost endorsement in an automobile insurance contract only when this endorsement is about to expire. The total theft occurrence is not a significant factor neither at the beginning of the contract, nor at a middle stage.

As suggested by Chiappori (1998), one possibility to obtain separation from claim data is to use a dynamic model. The data of Dionne and Gagné (2000) did not allow them to go in that direction. The originality of their methodology, although in the spirit of Chiappori (1998), was to use different contracting dates for the replacement cost endorsement but claims over one period. Consequently, Dionne and Gagné (2000) were first able to separate moral hazard from adverse selection since the latter should have the same effect at each period according to the theory. Finally, they were able to separate between the two forms of moral hazard by using partial and total thefts and by assuming that the same preventive actions affect both distributions. Their results do not reject the presence of opportunistic fraud in the data which means that the studied endorsement has a direct significant effect on the total number of car thefts in the analyzed market.

In their 1997 article, Dionne and Gagné discuss the effect of higher deductible on the costs of claims explained by falsification. Since the significant contribution of Townsend (1979), an insurance contract with a deductible is described as an optimal contract in the presence of costly state verification problems. In order to minimize auditing costs and guarantee insurance protection against large losses to risk averse policy-holders, this optimal contract reimburses the total reported loss less the deductible when the reported loss is above the deductible and pays nothing otherwise. The contract specifies that the insurer commits itself to audit all claims with probability one and this deductible contract is optimal only for the class of deterministic mechanisms. Consequently, we should not observe any fraud, notably in the form of build-up, in markets with deductible contracts, since the benefits of such activity are nil. However, fraud is now a significant problem in automobile insurance markets for property damages where deductible contracts are often observed.

The recent literature on security design has proposed different extensions to take into account different issues regarding the optimal insurance contracts. Three main issues related to the empirical model of Dionne and Gagné (1997) are discussed in this literature. First, the deductible model implies that the principal fully commits to the contract in the sense that he will always audit all claims even if the perceived probability of lying is nil. It is clear that this contract is not renegotiation proof: at least for small losses above the deductible, the insurer has an incentive not to audit the claim and save the auditing cost. However, if the client anticipates such a behaviour from the insurer, he or she will not necessarily tell the truth when filing the claim!

One extension to the basic model was to suggest that random audits are more appropriate to reduce auditing costs. However, the optimal insurance contract is no longer a deductible contract and the above commitment issue remains relevant. Another extension is to suggest that costly state falsification is more pertinent than costly state verification for insurance contracting with ex-post moral hazard. The optimal contract under costly state falsification leads to insurance overpayments for small losses and under-compensation for severe accidents. We do not yet observe such contracts for property damages in automobile insurance markets, although they seem to be present for bodily injuries in some states or provinces (Crocker and Tennyson, 1996).

The empirical hypothesis of Dionne and Gagné (1997) is as follows: when there is a sufficient high probability the fraud will succeed, the observed loss following an accident is higher when the deductible of the insurance contract is higher. Because they only have access to reported losses, a higher deductible also implies a lower probability of reporting small losses to the insurer. In order to isolate the fraud effect related to the presence of a deductible in the contract, they introduce some corrections in the data to eliminate the potential bias explained by incomplete information.

Their results are quite significant. They imply that when there are no witnesses (other than the driver and his or her passengers) on the site of the accident, the losses reported to the insurance companies are somewhere between 24.6% and 31.8% higher for those insured with a $500 deductible relatively to those with a $250 deductible. Furthermore, they are confident that this increase corresponds to build-up, because their result is closely related to the presence of witnesses. Since the mean loss reported in their sample is $2552.65, these increases correspond to increases of the reported losses from $628 to $812, which is far more than the difference between the two deductibles ($250). Thus, it seems than when an insured decides to defraud, not only does he or she try to recover the deductible, but also to increase his or her net wealth (for instance, by increasing the net value of the automobile).

It may be argued that the choice of the deductible is the consequence of an extension of the traditional adverse selection problem because the insured anticipates higher expected losses. However, if this ex-ante argument were right, we should observe a significant effect of the deductible on reported losses even when the presence of witnesses is more likely, which was not the case. It would be surprising to obtain such an ex-ante effect only in the case of accidents without witnesses, because it is difficult to anticipate the type of accident and its severity when choosing the deductible ex-ante.

It may also be the case that insurers can affect the probability of successful falsification by increasing the frequency of audits in the case of claims for which no witnesses are involved and for which the policy bears a high deductible. In other words, insurers may use the presence of witnesses as a fraud indicator. If it is the case, the results show that insurers are not fully efficient in their investigations since there is still a significant effect associated with the deductible in the reported loss equation. This interpretation is supported by the fact that insurers only detect 33% of fraud when they audit (Caron and Dionne, 1997).

Recent contributions (Crocker and Morgan, 1998; Crocker and Tennyson, 1996) tend to show that other types of contracts are more effective than deductible contracts in reducing this type of ex-post moral hazard when falsification activities are potentially present. However, they limit the behaviour of the insurer to full commitment. The full characterization of an optimal contract in presence of ex-post moral hazard is then an open question in the literature.

12.6 ADVERSE SELECTION AND THE QUALITY OF THE PRODUCT IN A MARKET

Akerlof (1970) was the first to propose a model with asymmetric information on the quality of products. This pathbreaking article has motivated many researchers to study the second-hand markets for durable goods. In general, owners of used goods know better the quality of their good than a potential buyer. Kim (1985) proposed a model suggesting that traded used cars should be of higher quality. Bond (1982) did test a similar proposition but did not find any evidence of adverse selection on the market for used pick up trucks. However Lacko (1986) did report some evidence for older cars only, a result also obtained by Genesove (1993). We now consider in detail this paper.

The main hypotheses to be considered for testing the presence of adverse selection are the following:

(a) During the transaction, one party is better informed than the other about the product's quality: usually the seller.
(b) Both of the parties involved in the transaction value quality.
(c) The price is not determined by either party but by the market.
(d) There is no market mechanism such as guarantees or reputation to eliminate adverse selection.

To test for residual adverse selection, Genesove (1993) analyzed the market for used cars sold by auction in the United States, where buyers have only a few moments to look at the cars and cannot take them for a test drive before purchase. The auction is simple: a series of ascending bids where the seller has the option of accepting or refusing the second highest bid. Sixty per cent of the sellers accept to relinquish their cars. The auction lasts one minute and a half, including the time to put the car up for auction and the time to remove it once the last bid is made! As a rule, the second price should correspond to the average quality of the cars offered, and buyers are supposed to be aware of this level of quality.

Genesove wanted to test whether any observable characteristic of the seller could be used to predict the average quality of the cars sold. In the presence of perfect information on the quality of the product, the characteristics of the seller would be of no importance. Only the quality of the product would count in explaining price equilibrium.

He thus considered two types of sellers participating in these auctions: those who sold only used cars (UC) and those who sold used cars and new cars (NC). Each seller participates in two markets: the auction market where the buyer makes no distinction in quality and a more traditional market where the real quality is more likely to be observed by the buyer.

It can be shown that the equilibrium price will be equal to the price matching the average quality each type of seller will offer. Thus, a seller whose cars are of superior quality to the average quality offered by this type will not put them up for auction unless there is a surplus in stock. In this case, he may offer some for auction, starting with those of lower quality. Moreover, the average quality of the two types may vary, as sellers may have different stock management systems. The author, in fact, shows that those who offer the two types of cars (used and new) have cars whose average quality is higher.

The motive behind stock management is important in finding an equilibrium. If the only motive for putting used cars up for auction is to take advantage of information asymmetry as shown in Akerlof's model, it is hard to obtain an equilibrium in a market where buyers are ready to pay for average quality and sellers are motivated to offer cars of only inferior or average quality. However, during a period of surplus stock, some sellers may have cars worth less than market value that they may be motivated to sell at the average-quality price, in order to gain a bonus. In other words, buyers in this type of market would have to value cars more highly than sellers to obtain an equilibrium. Gibbons and Katz (1991) have used this type of argument to obtain an equilibrium in the work market with specific human capital.

Empirically, a positive bonus in an auction market is only possible in a situation of asymmetric information where the buyer pays the average-quality price associated with the type of seller. Thus a seller who is more likely to sell in this market because he often has surpluses will usually sell better quality cars and obtain, at the equilibrium, a higher average price for the same quality of car.

The author verified that, though the data covered cars from 1988 to 1984 and earlier, there is a significant bonus only for 1984 cars. This allows him to conclude that residual adverse selection is weak in this kind of market. This implies that enough information circulates by other mechanisms to reduce the informational bonus to zero. These mechanisms are reputation and guarantees. Sellers are not truly anonymous in the auction market. The seller must be present to accept or refuse the second price. Furthermore, there are limited guarantees protecting buyers during the first hour following the auction. So, as for the automobile insurance example, in Section 12.2, private markets use effective mechanisms for reducing residual adverse selection.

Two extensions are now discussed in the literature. The first one proposes to use price and quantity profiles overtime across brands of cars in order to isolate evidence of adverse selection (Hendel and Lizzeri, 1999). There will be evidence of adverse selection if the car that has a steeper price decline overtime also has the lower trade volume. This contrasts with the depreciation story where the faster price decline should correspond to a larger volume of trade. The second extension is to show that leasing can solve the lemons problem (Guha and Waldman, 1996; Hendel and Lizzeri, 1998).

12.7 CONCLUSION

We have taken up the difficult question of the empirical measurement of the effects of information problems on the allocation of resources. Two problems drew our attention: moral hazard and adverse selection.

One conclusion which seems to be accepted by a number of authors is that information problems may create considerable distortions in the economy in contrast with a situation of full and perfect information. But we have also found that effective mechanisms have been established to reduce these distortions and to eliminate residual problems at the margin.

This conclusion seems stronger for adverse selection than for moral hazard, at least in the markets studied. One possible explanation, which should be investigated in detail, is that adverse selection concerns exogenous factors, whereas moral hazard hinges on endogenous actions which are always open to modification.

Finally, given the specific nature of the problems studied—lack of information—we must be always prudent in our conclusions, since the effect measured cannot be 100% verified. There will always be a lingering **doubt**!

12.8 REFERENCES

Abraham, A.F. and S.J. Carroll (1998). "The Frequency of Excess Claims for Automobile Personal Injuries", in Dionne, G. and Laberge-Nadeau, C. (eds.), *Automobile Insurance: Road Safety, New Drivers, Risks, Insurance Fraud and Regulation*, Kluwer Academic Press, Norwell, 131–150.

Akerlof, G.A. (1970). "The Market for 'Lemons': Quality Uncertainty and the Market Mechanism," *Quarterly Journal of Economics*, 84, 488–500.

Arnott, R.J. (1992). "Moral Hazard and Competitive Insurance Markets," in G. Dionne (ed.), *Contributions to Insurance Economics*, Boston: Kluwer Academic Publishers.
Arrow, K. (1963). "Uncertainty and the Welfare Economics of Medical Care," *American Economic Review*, 53, 941–969.
Bell, C. (1977). "Alternative Theories of Sharecropping: Some Tests Using Evidence from Northeast India," *Journal of Development Studies*, 13, 317–346.
Bond, E.W. (1982). "A Direct Test of the 'Lemons' Model: The Market for Used Pickup Trucks," *American Economic Review*, 72, 836–840.
Bond, E.W. and K.J. Crocker (1997). "Hardball and the Soft Touch: The Economics of Optimal Insurance Contracts with Costly State Verification and Endogenous Monitoring Costs," *Journal of Public Economics*, 63, 239–264.
Boyer, M.M. (1998). "Over-Compensation as a Partial Solution to Commitment and Renegotiation Problems: the Case of Ex-Post Moral Hazard," *Working Paper* 98-04. Risk Management Chair, HEC-Montreal.
Boyer, M. and G. Dionne (1989). "An Empirical Analysis of Moral Hazard and Experience Rating," *The Review of Economics and Statistics*, 71, 128–134.
Bujold, L., G. Dionne and R. Gagné (1997). "Assurance valeur à neuf et vols d'automobiles: une étude statistique," *Assurances*, 65, 49–62.
Butler, R.J., D.L. Durbin and N.M. Helvacian (1996a). "Increasing Claims for Soft Tissue Injuries in Workers' Compensation: Cost Shifting and Moral Hazard" *Journal of Risk and Uncertainty*, 13(1), 73–87.
Butler, R.J., H.H. Gardner and B.D. Gardner (1996b). "More than Cost Shifting: Moral Hazard Lowers Productivity," *Mimeo*, University of Minnesota.
Butler, R.J. and J. Worall (1963). "Workers' Compensation: Benefit and Injury Claims Rates in the Seventies," *Review of Economics and Statistics*, 65, 580–589.
Butler, R.J. and J.D. Worall (1991). "Claims Reporting and Risk Bearing Moral Hazard in Workers' Compensation," *Journal of Risk and Insurance*, 58, 191–204.
Caillaud, B., G. Dionne and B. Jullien (2000). "Corporate Insurance with Optimal Financial Contracting," *Economic Theory*, 16, 1, 77–105.
Caron, L. and G. Dionne (1997). "Insurance Fraud Estimation: More Evidence from the Quebec Automobile Insurance Industry," *Assurances*, 64(4), 567–578.
Chassagnon, A. and P.A. Chiappori (1995). "Insurance under Moral Hazard and Adverse Selection: the Case of Pure Competition," *Cahier de recherche*, DELTA.
Chiappori, P.A. (1994). "Théorie des contrats et économétrie de l'assurance: quelques pistes de recherche," *Cahier de recherche*, DELTA.
Chiappori, P.A. (1998). "Asymmetric Information in Automobile Insurance: an Overview," in: G. Dionne and C. Laberge-Nadeau (eds.), *Automobile Insurance: Road Safety, New Drivers, Risks, Insurance Fraud, and Regulation*, Boston: Kluwer Academic Publishers, 1–12.
Chiappori, P.A. (2000). "Econometric Models of Insurance under Asymmetric Information," in this book.
Chiappori, P.A. and B. Salanié (2000). "Testing for Asymmetric Information in Insurance Markets," *Journal of Political Economy*, 108, 1, 56–78.
Crocker, K.J. and J. Morgan (1998). "Is Honesty the Best Policy? Curtailing Insurance Fraud through Optimal Incentive Contracts," *Journal of Political Economy*, 26, 355–375.
Crocker, K.J. and A. Snow (1985). "The Efficiency Effects of Competitive Equilibrium in Insurance Markets with Adverse Selection," *Journal of Public Economics*, 26, 207–219.
Crocker, K.J. and A. Snow (1986). "The Efficiency Effects of Categorical Discrimination in the Insurance Industry," *Journal of Political Economy*, 94, 321–344.
Crocker, K.J. and A. Snow (2000). " The Theory of Risk Classification," in this book.
Crocker, K.J. and S. Tennyson (1997). "Contracting with Costly State Falsification: Theory and Empirical Results from Automobile Insurance," *Manuscript*. Ann Arbor: University of Michigan, Business School.

Crocker, K.J. and S. Tennyson (1998). "Costly State Falsification or Verification? Theory and Evidence from Bodily Injury Liability Claims," in G. Dionne and C. Laberge-Nadeau (eds.), *Automobile Insurance: Road Safety, New Drivers, Risks, Insurance Fraud and Regulation*, Boston: Kluwer Academic Publishers, 119–130.

Cummins, J.D. and Tennyson, S. (1996). "Moral Hazard in Insurance Claiming: Evidence from Automobile Insurance," *Journal of Risk and Uncertainty* 12(1), 29–50.

Dachraoui, K. and G. Dionne (1999). "Capital Structure and Compensation Policies," *Working paper* 99-03, Risk Management Chair, HEC-Montreal.

Dahlby, B.A. (1983). "Adverse Selection and Statistical Discrimination: An Analysis of Canadian Automobile Insurance," *Journal of Public Economics*, 20, 121–130.

Dahlby, B.A. (1992). "Testing for Asymmetric Information in Canadian Automobile Insurance," in G. Dionne (ed.), *Contributions to Insurance Economics*, Boston: Kluwer Academic Publishers, 423–444.

D'Arcy, S. and N. Doherty (1990). "Adverse Selection, Private Information and Low Balling in Insurance Markets," *Journal of Business*, 63, 145–164.

Derrig, R.A. (1997). "Insurance Fraud and the Monday Effect in Workers' Compensation Insurance," *Mimeo*, Boston.

Diamond, P.A. (1977). "Insurance Theoretic Aspects of Workers' Compensation," in A. Blinder and P. Friedman (eds.) *Natural Resources: Uncertainty and General Equilibrium Systems*. New York: Academic Press.

Dionne, G., N. Doherty and N. Fombaron (2000). "Adverse Selection in Insurance Markets," in this book.

Dionne, G. and N. Doherty (1994). "Adverse Selection, Commitment, and Renegotiation: Extension to and Evidence from Insurance Markets," *Journal of Political Economy*, 102, 209–235.

Dionne, G. and C. Fluet (2000). "Full Pooling in Multi-Period Contracting with Adverse Selection and Noncommitment," *Review of Economic Design*, 5, 1, 1–21.

Dionne, G. and R. Gagné (1997). "The Non-Optimality of Deductible Contracts Against Fraudulent Claims: Empirical Evidence in Automobile Insurance," *Working paper* 97-05, Risk Management Chair, HEC-Montreal. Forthcoming in *Review of Economics and Statistics*.

Dionne, G. and R. Gagné (2000). "Replacement Cost Endorsement and Opportunistic Fraud in Automobile Insurance," *Working paper*. 00–01, Risk Management Chair, HEC-Montreal.

Dionne, G., R. Gagné, F. Gagnon and C. Vanasse (1997). "Debt, Moral Hazard, and Airline Safety: Empirical Evidence," *Journal of Econometrics*, 79, 379–402.

Dionne, G., A. Gibbens and P. St-Michel (1993). "An Economic Analysis of Insurance Fraud", Les Presses de l'Université de Montréal.

Dionne, G., C. Gouriéroux and C. Vanasse (1998). "The Informational Content of Household Decisions with Applications to Insurance under Adverse Selection," *Working paper* 98-02, Risk Management Chair, HEC-Montreal.

Dionne, G., C. Gouriéroux and C. Vanasse (1998). "Evidence of Adverse Selection in Automobile Insurance Markets" in G. Dionne and C. Laberge-Nadeau (eds.), *Automobile Insurance: Road Safety, New Drivers, Risks, Insurance Fraud and Regulation*, Boston: Kluwer Academic Publishers, 13–46.

Dionne, G., C. Gouriéroux and C. Vanasse (2000) "Testing for Evidence of Adverse Selection in the Automobile Insurance Market" Forthcoming in *Journal of Political Economy*.

Dionne, G. and P. Lasserre (1987). " Adverse Selection, Repeated Insurance contracts, and Announcement Strategy," *Review of Economic Studies*, 70, 719–723.

Dionne, G. and P. Lasserre (1987). "Dealing with Moral Hazard and Adverse Selection Simultaneously," *Working paper*, Centre for the Study of Risk and Insurance, University of Pennsylvania.

Dionne, G. and P. St-Michel (1991). "Workers' Compensation and Moral Hazard," *Review of Economics and Statistics*, 73, 236–244.

Dionne, G., P. St-Michel and C. Vanasse (1995). "Moral Hazard, Optimal Auditing, and Workers' Compensation," in T. Thomason and R.P. Chaykowski (eds.) *Research in Canadian Workers' Compensation*, Queen's: IRC Press, 85–105.

Dionne, G. and C. Vanasse (1992). "Automobile Insurance Ratemaking in the Presence of Asymmetrical Information," *Journal of Applied Econometrics*, 7, 149–165.

Dionne, G. and C. Vanasse (1997). "The Role of Memory and Saving in Long-Term Contracting with Moral Hazard: An Empirical Evidence in Automobile Insurance," *Mimeo*, Risk Management Chair, HEC-Montreal.

Fluet, C. (1992). "Probationary Periods and Time-Dependent Deductible in Insurance Markets with Adverse Selection," in G. Dionne (ed.), *Contributions to Insurance Economics*, Boston: Kluwer Academic Publishers, 359–376.

Fombaron, N. (1997). "No-Commitment and Dynamic Contracts in Competitive Insurance Markets with Adverse Selection," *Mimeo*, THEMA, Université de Paris X-Nanterre.

Foppert, D. (1994). "Waging War Against Fraud," *Best's Review: Property-Casualty Ed.*, 94.

Fortin, B. and P. Lanoie (1992). "Substitution Between Unemployment Insurance and Workers' Compensation," *Journal of Public Economics*, 49, 287–312.

Fortin, B. and P. Lanoie (2000). "Incentives Effects of Workers' Compensation: A Survey," in this book.

Fortin, B., P. Lanoie and C. Laporte (1995). "Is Workers' Compensation Disguised Unemployment Insurance?" *Cirano Scientific Series*, Montreal, 95s–48.

Foster, A.D. and M.R. Rosenzweig (1993). "Information, Learning, and Wage Rates in Low-Income Rural Areas," *Journal or Human Resources*, 28, 759–790.

Foster, A.D. and M.R. Rosenzweig (1994). "A Test for Moral Hazard in the Labor Market: Contractual Arrangements, Effort, and Health," *The Review of Economics and Statistics*, 76, 213–227.

Gale, D. and M. Hellwig (1985). "Incentive-Compatible Debt Contracts: the One-Period Problem," *Review of Economic Studies*, 52, 647–663.

Genesove, D. (1993). "Adverse Selection in the Wholesale Used Car Market," *Journal of Political Economy*, 101, 644–665.

Gibbons, R. and I. Katz (1991). "Layoffs and Lemons," *Journal of Labor Economics*, 9, 351–380.

Gouriéroux, C., A. Monfort and A. Trognon (1984a). "Pseudo Maximum Likelihood Methods: Theory," *Econometrica*, 52, 681–700.

Gouriéroux, C., A. Monfort and A. Trognon (1984b). "Pseudo- Maximum Likelihood Methods: Application to Poisson Models," *Econometrica*, 52, 701–720.

Greenwald, B.C. (1986). "Adverse Selection in the Labor Market," *Review of Economic Studies*, 53, 325–347.

Guha, R. and M. Waldman (1996). "Leasing Solves the Lemons Problems," *Working Paper*, Cornell University.

Hausman, J.A., B.H. Hall and Z. Criliches (1984). "Econometric Models for Count Data with an Application to the Patents-R&D Relationship," *Econometrica*, 52, 910–938.

Heckman, J. (1979). "Sample Bias As a Specification Error," *Econometrica*, 47, 153–162.

Hellwig, M. (1987). "Some Recent Developments in the Theory of Competition in Markets with Adverse Selection," *European Economic Review*, 31, 319–325.

Hendel, I. and A. Lizzeri (1999). "Adverse Selection in Durable Goods Markets," *American Economic Review*, 89, 1097–1115.

Hendel, I. and A. Lizzeri (1998). "The Role of Leasing Under Adverse Selection," NBER *Working Paper* 6577.

Holmstrom, B. (1979). "Moral Hazard and Observability," *Bell Journal of Economics*, 10, 74–91.

Kaplow, L. (1994). "Optimal Insurance Contracts when Establishing the Amount of Losses is Costly," *Geneva Papers on Risk and Insurance Theory*, 19, 139–152.

Kiefer, N. (1988). "Economic Duration Data and Hazard Functions," *Journal of Economic Literature*, 26, 646–679.

Kim, J. (1985). "The Market for Lemons Reconsidered: A Model of the Used Car Market with Asymmetric Information," *American Economic Review*, 75, 836–843.

Krueger, A.B. (1990). "Incentives Effects of Workers' Compensation Insurance," *Journal of Public Economics*, 41, 73–99.

Laffont, J.J. (1997). "Collusion et information asymétrique," *Actualité économique*, 73, 595–610.

Lanoie, P. (1991). "Occupational Safety and Health: A Problem of Double or Single Moral Hazard," *Journal of Risk and Insurance*, 58, 80–100.

Lee, L. (1983). "Generalized Econometric Models with Selectivity," *Econometrica*, 51, 507–512.

Leigh, J.P. (1985). "Analysis of Workers' Compensation Using Data on Individuals," *Industrial Relations*, 24, 247–256.

Manning, W.G. et al. (1987). "Health Insurance and the Demand for Medical Care: Evidence from a Randomized Experiment," *American Economic Review*, 77, 251–277.

Medza, R. (1998). "They Cheat, You Pay," in G. Dionne and C. Laberge-Nadeau (eds.), *Automobile Insurance: Road Safety, New Drivers, Risks, Insurance Fraud, and Regulation*, Boston: Kluwer Academic Publications, 191–193.

Meyer, B.D. (1990). "On Unemployment Insurance and Unemployment Spells," *Econometrica*, 58, 757–782.

Meyer, B.D., W.K. Viscusi and D.L. Durbin (1995). "Workers' Compensation and Injury Duration: Evidence from a Natural Experiment," *American Economic Review*, 85, 322–340.

Mookherjee, D. and I. Png (1989). "Optimal Auditing, Insurance and Redistribution," *Quarterly Journal of Economics*, 104, 205–228.

Newhouse, J.P. (1987). "Health Economics and Econometrics," *American Economic Review*, 77, 269–274.

Pauly, M. (1968). "The Economics of Moral Hazard: Comment," *American Economic Review*, 58, 531–537.

Pauly, M. (1974). "Overprovision and Public Provision of Insurance," *Quarterly Journal of Economics*, 88, 44–62.

Picard, P. (1996). "Auditing Claims in Insurance Markets with Fraud: The Credibility Issue," *Journal of Public Economics*, 63(1), 27–56.

Picard, P. (1997). "On the Design of Optimal Insurance Policies Under Manipulation of Audit Costs," *Working Paper*, THEMA. *International Economic Review* (forthcoming).

Picard, P. (2000). "Economic Analysis of Insurance Fraud," in this book.

Pinquet, J. (1998). "Allowance for Hidden Information by Heterogeneous Models and Applications to Insurance Rating," in G. Dionne and C. Laberge-Nadeau (eds.) *Automobile Insurance: Road Safety, New Drivers, Risks, Insurance Fraud, and Regulation*, Boston: Kluwer Academic Publications, 47–78.

Puelz, R. and A. Snow (1994). "Evidence on Adverse Selection: Equilibrium Signaling and Cross-Subsidization in the Insurance Market," *Journal of Political Economy*, 102, 236–257.

Rothschild, M. and J. Stiglitz (1976). "Equilibrium in Competitive Insurance Markets," *Quarterly Journal of Economics*, 90, 629–649.

Ruser, J.W. (1991). "Workers' Compensation and Occupational Injuries and Illnesses," *Journal of Labor Economics*, 9, 325–350.

Ruser, J.W. (1998). "Does Workers' Compensation Encourage Hard to Diagnose Injuries," *Journal of Risk and Insurance* 65, 101–124.

Shavell, S. (1979). "Risk Sharing and Incentives in the Principal and Agent Relationship," *Bell Journal of Economics*, 10, 55–73.

Smart, M. (1998). "Competitive Insurance Markets with Two Unobservables," *Mimeo*, Economics Department, University of Toronto. Forthcoming in *International Economic Review*.

Stiglitz, J.E. (1982). "Alternative Theories of Wage Determination and Unemployment: The Efficiency Wage Model," in M. Gersovitz, C. Diaz-Alejandor, G. Ranis and M.R. Rosenzweig (eds.), *The Theory and Experience of Economic Development*, London: George Allen and Unwin.

Thomason, T. (1993). "Permanent Partial Disability in Workers' Compensation: Probability and Costs," *Journal of Risk and Insurance*, 60, 570–590.

Townsend, R.M. (1979). "Optimal Contracts and Competitive Markets with Costly State Verification," *Journal of Economic Theory*, 21, 265–293.

Villeneuve, B. (1996). "Essais en économie de l'assurance," *doctoral thesis*, DELTA-CREST.

Viscusi, W.K. (1992). "Fatal Injuries," New York: Oxford University Press.

Weisberg, H.I. and R.A. Derrig (1991). "Fraud and Automobile Insurance: A Report on Bodily Injury Liability Claims in Massachusetts," *Journal of Insurance Regulation*, 9, 497–541.

Weisberg, H.I. and R.A. Derrig (1993). "Quantitative Methods for Detecting Fraudulent Automobile Bodily Injury Claims," *Automobile Insurance Fraud Bureau of Massachusetts*, Boston, 32 pages.

Wilson, C. (1977). "A Model of Insurance Market with Incomplete Information," *Journal of Economic Theory*, 16, 167–207.

Wilson, C. (1980). "The Nature of Equilibrium in Markets with Adverse Selection," *Bell Journal of Economics*, 11, 108–130.

Winter, R. (2000). "Moral Hazard in Insurance Markets," in this book.

13 Incentive Effects of Workers' Compensation: A Survey*

Bernard Fortin

Université Laval

Paul Lanoie

HEC-Montréal

Abstract

This survey covers extensively the theoretical and the empirical work that was done on the incentive effects related to the existence of workers' compensation (WC) in the North American context. It first analyzes the economic rationale for compulsory WC. Then it studies the impact of WC on behavior. Three types of effects can be distinguished: 1) WC may influence frequency, duration and nature of claims through a variety of incentive effects. Under asymmetrical information about accident prevention activities, WC may affect safety behavior of both employers and employees and the risk level in the market place. Under asymmetrical information about the true nature of workplace injuries, insured workers may attempt to report false or off-the-job accidents and to undertake activities in order to obtain higher WC benefits, especially in the case of hard-to-diagnose injuries. Moreover, substitution between WC and other insurance programs may be observed. The decision of reporting a workplace accident may also be affected by the generosity of WC benefits. 2) WC may induce changes in occupational wages rates and 3) WC may affect firms' productivity. So far, the literature has focused mainly on the first type of effects. The main results show that increases in WC insurance are associated with an increase in the frequency of injuries (elasticities ranging from 0.4 to 1), and with an increase in the average duration of claims (elasticities ranging from 0.2 to 0.5). Furthermore, increases in WC are associated with more reporting of injuries that are hard-to-diagnose and, in the same line, there are some evidence (at least in Canada) of substitution between unemployment insurance and WC insurance. Lastly, there are empirical results showing that the presence of WC insurance induces important reductions in wage rates, while an emerging literature suggests that changes in WC insurance may also have negative productivity effects.

* The authors thank Michel Sylvain for able research assistance. They are also grateful to Georges Dionne and two anonymous referees for helpful comments.

Keywords: Workplace accidents, workers' compensation, incentive, moral hazard.
JEL Classification Numbers: J3, K2, G22.

13.1 INTRODUCTION

The social cost of workplace accidents is important. In a typical year in the United States, more than 50 times as many working days are lost to work injuries than to labor strikes, and from one-half to one-third as many working days are lost to work injuries than to unemployment (Krueger, 1988). Not surprisingly, policy makers have been concerned by this phenomenon and workers' compensation (WC) insurance has been made compulsory in most North American jurisdictions, covering more than 90 percent of the workforce.

WC insurance is a form of no-fault insurance in case of a workplace accident, where workers give up the right to sue their employer in exchange for a right to compensation. Firms are considered liable for workplace accidents. In the U.S., the majority of firms meet their obligation to provide insurance from contracts with private insurance carriers. In Canada, firms pay insurance premiums as a percentage of their total payroll to a Workers' Compensation Board (WCB), which compensates accident victims and pays for their medical expenses related to workplace injuries. Insurance premiums are usually adjusted to reflect the past claim records of firms (experience-rating). WC claims result from work injuries that produce an impairment that can be classified by duration (temporary or permanent) and severity (total or partial). Most indemnity claims are for temporary total impairment, where the injured worker returns to work with no residual impairment. Claimants then receive a percentage of their pre-injury wage throughout the duration of the claim (typically 66% of gross wage in the U.S. and 90% of net wage in Canada).[1]

It is important to consider the implications of the WC system since it operates in a market context. The system may have a variety of effects on employees and employers. Three types of effects can be distinguished.[2] First, WC may influence frequency, duration and nature of claims through a variety of incentive effects. In particular, WC insurance may lead to moral hazard problems, which arise when informational asymmetries are used for personal gains.[3] The first is that of *ex ante* injury hazard. Since insurance covers the financial and medical losses associated with the injury, workers' incentive to exercise care will diminish with increases in coverage. Moreover, because employers fund WC benefits through premiums linked at least in part to their firm's safety record, there is an incentive to increase the investment in health and safety capital when there is an increase in WC insurance coverage. These pressures may result in changes in risk or, more precisely, in the frequency or the duration of injuries.

[1] In both countries, benefits are not taxable.
[2] This classification is similar to that adopted by Moore and Viscusi (1991).
[3] The description that follows uses Viscusi's (1992) classification.

A second form of moral hazard, termed *ex ante* causality hazard, arises because it is sometimes difficult to identify which accidents are caused by the job. Therefore, workers may file claims for accidents that have not occurred, or for off-the-job accidents. A third form might be termed *ex post* duration hazard. With an increase in the insurance coverage, injured workers may be tempted to take action in order to prolong the duration of the period over which benefits are paid out.

A particular case of the previous forms of moral hazard, termed *insurance substitution* hazard, may arise, given that WC is in general more generous than unemployment insurance (UI). Workers may be tempted to undertake activities in order to benefit from WC instead of UI, when they are confronted with a lay-off. For instance, they may report false or off-the-job accidents or, given that they have been injured on the job, they may try to increase the duration of their period of recovery compensated by WC.

The decision to file an accident report may also be affected by the level of WC benefits (reporting incentives) since, in some circumstances, an injured worker may have some discretion over whether to ignore an injury and to continue working or to report the injury and to receive WC benefits.

A second potentially important effect of the WC system is on wages. The change in risk described above may affect workers' wage through changes in compensating differentials, or simply because social insurance for job injuries will increase the attractiveness of risky employment to workers, thus reducing the required compensating differential. Third, WC benefits may lead to more absenteeism and the loss of firm specific human capital, which in turn may induce productivity effects.

To our knowledge, the present survey is the first to cover all these aspects related to the existence of workers' compensation. As will be shown, the literature has focused on the first type of effects described above and is mainly North American. Section 13.2 discusses the theoretical rationale for government regulation of WC insurance and presents the theoretical arguments, which relate changes in WC insurance coverage to changes in certain outcomes (frequency, duration and nature of claims, wage and productivity). Section 13.3 provides a survey of the empirical work that was done on these issues. Section 13.4 presents some concluding remarks and discusses the lessons to be learned by policy makers from this literature.

13.2 THEORETICAL WORK

13.2.1 Economic Rationale for WC Insurance

A Model with no Market Imperfection

Some authors, such as Thaler and Rosen (1976), allege that the presence of both wage differentials for risky jobs and private insurance markets implies that WC is unnecessary. In their hedonic model based on Rosen (1974), the labor market is perfectly competitive, workers are risk averse and have perfect information about risks of accidents. They are also perfectly mobile between jobs. Firms differ in terms of certain intrinsic risks of accidents but can influence the probability of accidents through undertaking safety expenditures. Moreover, the marginal cost of reducing risks varies across firms.

The model also assumes a perfect insurance market: the cost of insurance against injuries equals its actuarial value and insurers know the true probability of accident in each firm. Conditional upon facing a given accident probability, each worker will purchase an optimal amount of insurance coverage. This level of insurance will equate his (ex post) marginal utility in all states of the world (that is, with and without injury). Workers will move to firms whose wage rate-risk of injuries combination maximizes their well-being. If all workers are identical, firms with higher risk of accident will have to pay a higher wage rate to attract workers. This is the case even if workers are perfectly insured against accidents, since the insurance premium is increasing with the level of risk prevailing in a firm.

In such a world, wage differentials across firms compensate workers for the welfare reduction associated with a risk of accident. In equilibrium, each firm's marginal cost for risk reduction equals its workers' marginal benefit from risk reduction. Moreover, wage differentials induce a social optimal allocation of workers across firms and a social optimal effort within each firm to reduce hazard. This analysis formalizes the basic insights of Adam Smith's theory of equalizing wage differentials as applied to the risk of occupational accidents.

In the case where preferences against risk of accidents vary across workers, workers with low risk aversion will choose to work in high-risk firms.[4] Therefore, the wage premium provided by high-risk firms will understate the one required by individuals working in low-risk firms. Again, under the assumptions of the model, this sorting equilibrium will be socially optimal.

This model can also be generalized to the case where workers can influence their risk of injury through costly accident-preventing effort. As long as firms have full information about the level of effort chosen by workers, competitive equilibrium will also lead to a social optimum. In equilibrium, safety input provided by each party will be such that its marginal cost for one party will equal to its marginal benefit to both parties. This rule is analogous to the efficiency condition in public goods theory (Lanoie, 1991).

In this model, workers insure themselves in a competitive market. However, as long as firms are risk-neutral, one could argue that they are a natural source of insurance to their risk-averse workers (see Rea, 1981). Of course, under the assumptions

[4] This will be the case if insurance is imperfect (nonzero loading or administrative charges and hence incomplete coverage), if preferences are state dependent or if there are interpersonal differences in physical capacities to cope with job risk. In all these cases, risk-averse workers will not fully insure against accidents. Therefore their risk choice will depend on their degree of risk aversion (see Thaler and Rosen, op.cit., p. 272).

of the model, one should not expect this possibility to affect the injury rate at any firm and therefore the safety level and the allocation of workers across firms will still be Pareto-optimal. However, one should observe smaller compensating wage differentials in higher risk firms since a part of their workers' total compensation will include WC insurance. In such a world, the introduction of a public WC system that is perfectly experience rated and that involves no administrative costs, will lead to a safety level and an allocation of labor similar to the one observed in a competitive market. Moreover, if WC benefits are not perfectly experience rated, higher risk firms will be implicitly subsidized by the public system. Therefore they will have less incentive to undertake safety expenditures. In that case, WC insurance will lead to a sub-optimal allocation of resources (Ehrenberg, 1988).

This model shows that, in a world of complete information and perfect markets, either public WC insurance is unnecessary or is harmful. However, this result breaks down with incomplete information or imperfect markets, and the literature on accident prevention discusses such situations.

Problems of Imperfect Information

Problems of imperfect information in the "market for workplace accidents" have attracted much attention recently. There are at least six possible types of imperfect information that may affect this market: 1) Employers and insurers may not be able to identify workers who are accident-prone; 2) Insurers may not be able to identify employers who offer risky jobs; 3) employees and employers may be incorrect in their estimates of occupational risk and of their influence on the level of risk; 4) the employer may not be able to monitor the precautions taken by employees; 5) the insurer may not be able to monitor employers' and employees' precautions; 6) the insurer may not be able to monitor the nature of injury. The two first types of misinformation leads to what is commonly called adverse selection. The fourth and fifth types reflect *ex ante* injury hazard and the sixth type involves *ex ante* causality hazard or *ex post* duration hazard.

Let us first consider the case of adverse selection. This phenomenon is a manifestation in insurance markets of the more general concept of "lemons" (Akerlof, 1970). A worker may have a much better idea than the insurer of whether he is a high- or low-risk (first type of misinformation) or a firm may have more information than the insurer on its risk (second type of misinformation). In the face of this asymmetric information problem, the insurance market is either inefficient or fails entirely, the ultimate outcome depending on the precise behavior of insured and insurer (e.g., see Hellwig, 1987). One solution (or a partial solution) is to restrict the range of choice the insured is allowed. A particular relevant possibility is to impose compulsory insurance to prevent lower risks opting out. It should be stressed that this policy does not necessary require the public provision of WC insurance. The government could make WC compulsory, while not supplying insurance itself. In fact, in a number of American States, WC insurance is mandatory but is privately provided

(Butler, 1994). In a dynamic context, experience rating could also mitigate the adverse selection problem. Thus low risk firms are more likely to be attracted by experience rated contracts, which will reduce the "shrinking" effect of adverse selection on the insurance market.

The third type of imperfect information concerns workers' knowledge about the safety level prevailing at different firms in the market. This problem has been analyzed by Oi (1974), Diamond (1977) and Rea (1981). Following an assumption first adopted by Adam Smith, these authors suppose that workers underestimate risk. Akerlof and Dickens (1982) have argued that the psychic costs of fear of accidents may induce a cognitive dissonance phenomenon that makes workers underestimate their perceived probability of accidents and choose a sub-optimal level of accident-preventing effort.

Under the assumption that workers underestimate risk, Diamond and Oi argue that mandatory insurance (privately or publicly provided) and safety regulation are justified because they raise the expected utility of risk averse workers. However, their analysis assumes that employees' safety precautions are not affected by the regulation of insurance. In contrast, Rea (1981) alleges that mandatory insurance and safety regulation may lead workers to undertake more risk and therefore to substitute wages for safer jobs. As a result, safety could fall even in the absence of moral hazard. Moreover, if this effect is strong enough, WC could lower workers' expected utility, evaluated with true probabilities. This analysis has some similarities with the well-known Peltzman (1975) effect, according to which automobile safety regulations such as compulsory seat belt may induce automobilists to drive less carefully. This may lead to an increase in the number and the severity of car accidents and, if this effect is strong enough, to a reduction in total welfare.

Carmichael (1986) disagrees with the assumption that workers underestimate risk. He integrates imperfect information by exploring the role of a firm's reputation in repeated games. His model suggests that it takes time for workers to learn about changes in safety in a firm which leads, generally, to an underprovision of safety. In contrast with Rea, Carmichael is able to make unambiguous statements about the welfare-improving nature of government intervention related to occupational safety and health. In particular, he shows that a marginal increase in the level of compensation benefits leads to unambiguous improvement in welfare.

The fourth and fifth types of misinformation involve a particular type of moral hazard: *ex ante* injury hazard. It defines the effect of insurance on the choice of self-protection activities by the insured when the insurer cannot observe or enforce these activities (asymmetric information). Let us consider the case of individual expenditure on a preventive activity, x, which can reduce the probability of an insured event. The socially efficient level of x is that at which its marginal cost is equal to its social benefit in terms of its effect on the reduction of insured losses. But if losses are fully insured and the insurer cannot monitor individual preventive activities, the private incentive is to spend little on it. As a result, this *ex ante* moral hazard typically leads to an underprovision of self-protection activities by the insured, as far as the substitution effect is concerned (see Pauly, 1974; Holmstrom, 1979; Arnott and Stiglitz, 1988, and Arnott, 1992, for careful analyses of the effects of moral hazard).

Private insurers have adopted a number of devices to reduce this problem. In particular, incentive mechanisms may seek to share the cost between the insured and the insurer: frequent claimants may pay higher premiums; deductibles make the insured person pay the first $X of any claim; with coinsurance, the insured person pays a fraction of any claim. However, none provides a complete solution to the ex ante moral hazard, since the root of the problem is the imperfect information of insurers about the behavior of the insured.

In the "market place for accidents", this problem is compounded with the possibility of *ex ante* "double moral hazard" (Lanoie, 1991). Indeed, a workplace accident not only depends on precaution levels of the worker but also on those of the firm. Therefore, the level of WC insurance may affect the (nonenforceable) precaution levels of the two parties. In fact, a rise of the level of insurance benefits gives opposite incentives to both parties, at least when the firm is experience-rated by the insurer or is the insurance provider. It decreases the cost of an accident to the worker (inducing less precaution), while it increases the cost of accident to the firm (inducing more precaution). As a result, *ex ante* double moral hazard does not necessarily lead to an underprovision of precaution by both parties. Whether or not it does depends not only on the substitutability or the complementary of the precaution levels of the two parties, but also on the chosen level of insurance (Lanoie, 1991).

In such a context, can a government intervene to induce a Pareto improvement in the level of precaution? As in all cases involving misinformation problems, the answer to this question partly depends on the information the government has at its disposal. Technological constraints make the case of a government better informed that the private insurance sector unlikely. Therefore a more relevant question is whether the government, with no more information than the private sector, can improve welfare with publicly provided WC insurance. Lanoie shows, in contrast with Carmichael (1986), that the impact of a legislated increase in WC benefits does not necessarily lead to a welfare improvement. An explanation for the ambiguity is that, in Carmichael's approach, the probability of accidents depends only on the firm's safety expenditure while Lanoie's approach allows it to vary according to both workers' and firm's safety expenditure.

The last type of misinformation concerns *ex ante causality hazard* and *ex post* duration hazard. When the insurer is not perfectly informed about the state of the world, an insured worker may take action in order to increase the level of his WC benefits. For instance, he may be encouraged to simulate injuries (e.g., Staten and Umbeck, 1982; Butler et al., 1996; Bolduc et al., 1997) or to file a claim that occurs off the job (e.g., Smith, 1989), especially in the case of hard-to-diagnose injuries such as sprains, strains and low back problems. He may also attempt to obtain a longer period of recovery compensated by WC by exaggerating the severity of his injury or by investing resources in order to find and convince a physician to write an appropriate medical report (Dionne and St-Michel, 1991; Fortin and Lanoie, 1992).

Theoretical models that take into account not only the standard *ex ante* injury hazard but also the *ex post* duration hazard and the *ex ante* causality hazard, show that usual WC insurance contracts are suboptimal when the last two types of moral hazard are present (e.g., Mookherjee and Png, 1989; Dionne and St-Michel, 1991). In particular, partial coverage insurance alone is not optimal. The standard approach suggests to identify claims exhibiting predisposing characteristics toward falsification and then to subject these claims to auditing procedures. This approach is based on the application of the costly state verification framework (Townsend, 1979) to the context of insurance contracts (Kaplow, 1994; Bond and Crocker, 1997). It suggests that reports should be audited more extensively in the case of injuries that are hard-to-diagnose, since *ex post* duration and *ex ante* causality hazards are likely to be more severe in that case. A basic problem with this solution is the intrinsical incapacity for the insurer to verify the nature of the injury. For example, in the case of WC claims involving sprains or soft-tissue injuries, it is almost impossible for the insurer to obtain an accurate measure of the costs imposed to the claimant. Another approach that deals with this problem has been suggested by Crocker and Morgan (1998). They propose an *ex ante* insurance contract that mitigates the incentives for the falsification of claims. The basic idea is to reduce the sensitivity of the compensation to the observed (and, possibly, falsified) losses. The result is an efficient contract that provides overinsurance for small losses and underinsurance for severe injuries. Their approach provides simple but testable restrictions, that could in principle be tested with WC data.

The above discussion suggests that, due to partial information concerning the risk of accidents and to the presence of a variety of informational asymmetries, the private labor and insurance markets are likely to fail to provide the optimal level of safety and the optimal allocation of workers across occupations. Moreover, our analysis of adverse selection suggests that compulsory WC insurance could improve welfare.[5] However, this does not imply that publicly provided WC is necessarily Pareto-improving. While the goal of this social insurance may be to improve the potential market failures, our analysis suggests that it is not clear that it is necessarily the case. In publicly provided WC, there is also a potential for moral hazard problems and other adverse incentives. It is thus important to analyze both theoretical and empirical impact of WC on variables such as 1) the frequency, duration and nature of claims; 2) the level of occupational wage rates and 3) the level of labor productivity.

[5] There is not much empirical evidence supporting the idea that adverse selection is of major concern in the "market of workplace accidents". Therefore, it is not clear that compulsory insurance will necessarily increase welfare, since it may also impose costs on agents who are constrained in their choices by this policy. Also, as we mentioned, compulsory insurance is not the only way to deal with adverse selection. Besides, a merit good argument could partly justify this measure (especially if workers underestimate their true accident probability).

13.2.2 Theoretical Effects of WC Insurance

Effect on the Frequency, Duration and Nature of Claims

This section analyses the theoretical impact of WC insurance on both the occurrence (frequency and duration) of claimed accidents and their nature. These effects are certainly those that have been most studied in the economic literature on WC. Moreover, we pay a particular attention to the impact of other social insurance programs such as unemployment insurance (UI) on these variables. Indeed, recent literature has shown that one is likely to observe a substitution between UI benefits and WC compensation.

Effect on the Frequency of Claims

A change in parameters of a WC program, such as the level of benefit coverage, will affect the frequency of WC claims through a number of incentive effects. Thus, for a given wage rate and a given level of safety expenditures by the firm, an increase in the level of WC benefits will induce workers to reduce their accident-preventing efforts and it may lead them to report false accidents or accidents that occurred off the job. These factors will tend to raise the number of reported accidents. Moreover, not all workers who are injured on the job report their accident to the WC Board, since there are various costs associated with filing for WC benefits. These costs include the value of time and resources needed to see a doctor and to fill up requested forms, the costs associated with the probability of being controlled and to have to undertake other medical examinations. An injured worker will do so only as long as the expected marginal benefits of filing a claim exceeds its marginal cost. Therefore, one should expect incentives to report workplace accidents to be positively related with the WC benefit level, especially in the case of minor injuries (Krueger, 1990a).

On the other hand, as long as WC benefits are at least partially experience rated at the firm level, an increase in benefit coverage will raise a firm's costs associated with its own accident experience. Therefore, employers will have more incentive to spend resources on safety prevention, for a given level of accident-preventing effort from its employees. Moreover, higher benefits will increase employers' incentive to challenge claims. These effects will reduce the number of (accepted) claims.

From this analysis, it is clear that the impact of a change in WC benefits on the frequency of claims is ambiguous since, *ceteris paribus*, it creates safety and reporting incentives working in opposite directions for employers and employees. Moreover, the net result depends on the degree of complementary or substitutability between safety efforts of each party as well as on the nature of the labor contract (Ehrenberg, 1988; Krueger 1990a; Lanoie, 1992a). Empirical analyses are required to resolve this ambiguity.

Effect on the Duration of Claims

Behavior of employers and employees not only influence the rate of reported injuries but also their duration. As discussed earlier, following an increase in the level of WC benefits, workers may have incentives to take action in order to obtain a longer period of recovery compensated by WC (ex post duration hazard). Indeed, a higher benefit level generates both substitution and income effects that induce an injured worker to increase his leisure (assumed to be a normal good) by prolonging his period on WC. Of course, this possibility is limited by the level of resources required to obtain the needed medical report. These costs reflect the probability of contestation and rejection of the physician's report. This may involve a costly and stressful process of examinations by other physicians, of testimony in arbitrage, and possible delays in WC benefits payments (Fortin and Lanoie, 1992). Moreover, through their negative effect on the level of workers' safety efforts, higher benefits will also raise the duration of claims, as long as lower safety efforts increase not only the probability but also the expected severity of injuries.

On the employers' side however, higher partially experience rated WC benefits will play in the opposite direction, by encouraging them to increase their safety expenditures and by increasing their incentives to challenge claims. Again the net impact of higher benefits on the duration of claims is ambiguous and empirical studies are needed to shed light on this issue.

Effect on the Nature of the Claims

As discussed above, higher benefits may induce a worker to simulate injuries, to file a claim for injuries that occur off the job (as long as benefit coverage is more generous under WC than under disability insurance) or, given that he had a workplace accident, to obtain a longer period compensated by WC. However, the costs of these actions for the worker will depend on the nature of accidents. Thus one should expect these costs to be smaller for accidents that are harder to diagnose. Therefore, higher benefits should not only influence the frequency and the duration of claims but also the nature of injuries compensated by WC. In particular, they should increase the relative importance of reported hard-to-diagnose injuries.

This suggests one way to isolate ex post duration hazard and ex ante causality hazard on the one hand, from ex ante injury hazard (effects on safety behavior) and from effects on reporting injuries occurring on the job, on the other. The idea is to verify whether higher benefit coverage induces more important effects, in terms of frequency and duration, on injuries that are hard-to-diagnose, such as back-related problems, in comparison with injuries such as contusions, friction burn or fractures, than are much easier to diagnose (Dionne and St-Michel, 1991; Bolduc et al., 1997; Fortin et al. 1999).

Effect of Unemployment Insurance on Occurrence and Nature of Claims (Insurance Substitution Hazard)

Many reasons may suggest the existence of a potentially strong interdependency in the effects of UI and WC programs. The basic reason is that, as emphasized by

Ehrenberg (1988), the structure of both programs are quite similar. In particular, both provide insurance against an adverse consequence (workplace injury or unemployment) that leads to time away from work. Therefore, as long as the risk of these events is partially determined by employer and employee behavior, one could expect behavior in the labor market to be affected interactively by the characteristics of both systems. Thus as long as the worker's net wage replacement ratio provided by UI is smaller than the corresponding WC benefit ratio, some workers suffering from a workplace injury may, *ceteris paribus*, have incentives to take action in order to prolong their period of recovery, especially in industries where the level of unemployment is relatively high. Indeed, in these industries, many injured workers may expect to be unemployed and to receive UI benefits after their period of recovery. Moreover, workers who expect a period of unemployment (e.g., in seasonal industries) may have incentive to use fewer resources in attempting to prevent workplace accidents. In addition, some workers may be encouraged to shirk in order to increase their chances of receiving WC rather than UI benefits.

Fortin and Lanoie (1992) and Bolduc et al. (1997) have provided theoretical models that show, under plausible assumptions, that lower UI benefits will raise both frequency and duration of WC claims, especially in the case of hard-to-diagnose injuries.

Effect on Wage Rates

A number of studies have theoretically analyzed the impact of WC on the wage rates (Ehrenberg, 1988; Lanoie, 1990). As shown above, in a world of perfect competition with perfect information and public WC, higher benefits that are perfectly experience rated would reduce wage rates so as to offset the increase in WC costs. Total workers' remuneration (including the value, for workers, of more generous WC insurance) would thus not be affected by the policy. In other words, the downward shift in the labor demand curve in a given industry would be offset by the downward shift in the corresponding labor supply curve.

As long as the WC system is not perfectly experience rated, the reduction of wage rates in high-risk industries or occupations would be larger than the increase in firms' WC liability, while the contrary would be observed in low-risk industries. This will be the case if one takes into account the required increase in the portion of costs that are not dependent on firms' own accident experience to fund higher benefits (cross-subsidizing effect). Therefore, the level of compensating wage differential would be reduced in favor of high-risk industries.

Moreover, under asymmetrical information, workers in high-risk industries will have incentives to reduce precaution levels and to prolong the duration of their compensated accidents. On the firms' side, incentives will play in the opposite direction. Therefore, the impact of moral hazard and reporting behavior is ambiguous on reported injuries and therefore on the wage rates.

Effect on Labor Productivity
A theoretical and empirical literature is recently emerging on the effects of WC insurance on labor productivity. Butler et al. (1997c), and Butler and Gardner (1994) present a model of management in which managers tend to use the disability system as a mean of getting rid of the less productive employees. They show that workers receiving disciplinary notices (i.e., those with "management" problems) are more likely to enter in disability status. Furthermore, Butler et al. (1999) argue that, as WC benefits increase, work absenteeism increases and firm specific human capital will be lost (holding labor and physical capital constant) and output will fall.

13.3 EMPIRICAL WORK

13.3.1 Studies on Frequency, Duration and Nature of Claims

This section will present the empirical work that was done to investigate the different effects of workers' compensation insurance. We will follow the same outline as in the preceding section. A first group of studies has examined the impact of changes in WC benefits on the frequency, duration and nature of claims, and the potential interaction between social insurance programs.

Claim Frequency Studies
Recall that, theoretically, the effect of WC benefits changes on injury rates is ambiguous; it depends on the relative magnitude of employee and employer responses to such changes. This question has been studied extensively in the North American context. Typically, the authors estimate an equation which relates the injury rate to a variable capturing the generosity of WC benefits and a set of control variable for aspects such as demographic characteristics of manpower, industrial sector, or unionization. All reported studies in Table 1 are either American or Canadian; many of them were actually performed by a team of researchers surrounding Richard J. Butler and John D. Worrall. Table 1 reports the authors, the data used, the definition of the dependent variable, the definition of the benefit variable and representative benefits elasticities obtained for each study.

A variety of **data sources** has been used in these studies: aggregate data at the state level (Chelius, 1977, 1982, 1983; Worrall and Appel, 1982; Butler and Worrall, 1983; Ruser, 1985; Butler, 1994), data at the industry level (Butler, 1983; Bartel and Thomas, 1985; Curington, 1986; Worrall and Butler, 1988, 1990; Lanoie, 1992a, 1992b; Lanoie and Streliski, 1996), data at the firm level (Chelius and Kavanaugh, 1988; Ruser, 1991) and micro data at the individual level (Leigh, 1985; Krueger, 1990a; Moore and Viscusi, 1990; Thomason, 1993; Thomason and Pozzebon, 1995; Butler et al., 1997).

Table 1
Representative Estimates of the Effect of Workers' Compensation Benefits on Injury Rates

Study	Unit of observation and sample	Benefit variable	Dependent variable	Benefit elasticity
Bartel and Thomas (1982)	Various industries in 22 states during the period 1972 through 1978	Expected benefit for a temporary total disability	Lost work days (for job injuries) per full-time employee	0.626
Bartel and Thomas (1985)	Three digit SIC manufacturing industries per year; industries from 1972 to 1978; data are averaged over 22 states	Expected benefit for a representative wage earner who files a claim for a temporary total disability	Lost workdays per 100 full-time worker (occupational illnesses are excluded)	0.346
Butler (1983)	Manufacturing industries per year; 15 industries over 32 years in South Carolina	Constructed by taking the average observed wages and then computing the expected benefits (accounting for minimum and maximum insurable income)	Injury rate index constructed with the principal components analysis. Includes four categories: death, dismemberment and disfiguration, permanent partial injury and temporary total injury	From 0.29* to 1.13*
Butler (1994)	Cross-section time-series data base covering 39 states during the period 1954 through 1984	Wage replacement ratio expected on the basis of the wage distribution in each state	Number of claims in non agricultural sectors per employee	0.4***
Butler and Worrall (1983)	State per year; 35 states from 1972 to 1978	See Butler (1983)	The number of claims filed by nonself-insuring firms per thousand employees Three types of injury: ☐ temporary total ☐ minor permanent partial ☐ major permanent partial	 0.352* 0.4* 1.1*
Butler et al. (1997)	Microdata on WC Claims within one firm in 3 states: California (1990–1991), New-York (1990–1992), Connecticut (1993)	Maximum replacement dollar amount by state	Change in the claim frequency between the year before the change in maximum benefit and the year after	Between 0.39 and 1.07, significant

Table 1
(Continued)

Study	Unit of observation and sample	Benefit variable	Dependent variable	Benefit elasticity
Chelius (1977)	Cross-section of industries in 18 states	Ratio of weekly WC benefits to weekly wages in a given industry, year and state compared to the same ratio for all other states	Injury rate	Positive and significant impact
Chelius (1982)	Manufacturing industries in 36 states from 1972 to 1978	Ratio of weekly WC benefits to weekly wages in a given industry, year and state compared to the same ratio for all other states	Ratio of the number of injuries per 100 full-time workers in a given industry, time period and state to the number of injuries in all other states Occupational illnesses are excluded	Positive and significant impact
Chelius (1983)	Manufacturing industries in 28 states from 1972 to 1978	Ratio of weekly WC benefits to weekly wages in a given industry, year and state compared to the same ratio for all other states	Ratio of the number of injuries per 100 full-time workers in a given industry, time period and state to the number of injuries nationwide	Positive and significant impact
Chelius and Kavanaugh (1988)	The maintenance staff at 2 New Jersey community colleges; quarterly observations from 1979:1 to 1984:3	A dummy variable equaling 1 when WC benefits were lowered	WC claims rate for claims lasting more than 7 days	0.346***
Curington (1986)	18 manufacturing industries in New-York from 1964 to 1976	Ratio of the New-York maximum weekly benefit for temporary total disability relative to the average weekly wage for each industry	Number of compensated WC claims per 1,000 full-time equivalent employees (Occupational illness cases are excluded and the injured worker must have been unable to work for seven days)	Not reported (significant positive effect)

Kaestner and Carroll (1997)	State specific one SIC industry for 1983–1988 amounting to 1,516 observations	Measure of total benefit (medical and income replacement)	Number of lost workday cases per 100 employees	Positive and significant impact
Kniesner and Leeth (1989)	Simulation exercise calibrated to reproduce the American labor market in the early 1970s	The median after-tax income replacement rate for a married man in USA	They considered three types of injuries: non impairing injury, permanent partial disability and permanent total disability	0.21**
Krueger (1990a)	Micro-level data from current population survey; information is available on 27,000 individuals for two consecutive years 1983–84 or 1984–85	Potential temporary total WC benefit	A 0–1 variable marking the transition into the WC program All types of industrial accidents and illness are considered	0.741**
Lanoie (1992a)	Quebec data at the industry level; 28 industries for the period 1974–1987	The rate of wage replacement in case of a temporary total disability	Two variables: FREQUENCY: log $[RATE_{it}/(1 - RATE_{it})$ where RATE is the total number of accidents (including diseases) with at least one workday lost divided by the number of full-time employees.	Non-significant
			PERMRATE: Same definition as FREQUENCY with the numerator of RATE being the number of permanent disability cases	Non-significant
Lanoie (1992b)	Quebec data at the industry level covering 28 industries for the period 1983–87	The variable is based on the net wage replacement ratio obtained by a disabled worker in case of temporary total disability	Log $[RATE_{it}/(1 - RATE_{it})$ where RATE is the total number of accidents (including diseases) with at least one workday lost divided by the number of full-time employees.	0.523*
Lanoie and Streliski (1996)	Quebec data at the industry level covering 28 industries for the period 1983–90	The variable is based on the net wage replacement ratio obtained by a disabled worker in case of temporary total disability	See Lanoie (1992a)	2.38**

Table 1
(Continued)

Study	Unit of observation and sample	Benefit variable	Dependent variable	Benefit elasticity
Leigh (1985)	11,88[illegible] American workers; period 1977 to 1979	A proxy measure of the potential benefit a worker on WC would receive	A dummy variable which takes the value 1 if respondent receives any WC benefit	0.3*
Moore and Viscusi (1990)	1,173 individual workers; for 1982	The potential weekly benefits based on the temporary total disability	Number of fatal accidents per 100,000 workers	0.02**
Oshsfeldt and Morrisey (1997)	State level data, for two-digit SIC code industry over the 1975–1985 period	Lost workdays due to non-fatal injury per 100 workers	☐ Maximum weekly payment divided by the average wage ☐ Minimum weekly payment divided by average wage ☐ Waiting period	☐ Positive impact of the maximum payment ☐ Negative impact of the minimum payment and the waiting period
Ruser (1985)	25 manufacturing industries across a maximum of 41 states for the years 1972 to 1979	The average weekly real income benefit paid to a worker during the period of recovery from a total temporary disability	☐ Injuries per 100 full-time workers (All types of injuries) ☐ Injuries with lost workdays per 100 full-time workers (excluding fatality cases)	0.062* 0.116***
Ruser (1991)	Longitudinal microdata set of 2,788 manufacturing establishments for the years 1979 to 1984	The average real weekly WC benefit for production worker's divided by 100	Frequency of lost-workdays injury and illness cases per 100 workers years (excluding fatalities)	From 0.2 to 0.82 (mostly significant)
Thomason (1993)	Claimants of the state WC; 5 states for the period 1979 to 19[illegible]1 (about 16,000 observations)	The weekly permanent partial benefit payment	A dummy variable that takes the value 1 if the claim was classified as a permanent partial disability and 0 if it was not	0.4***

Thomason and Pozzebon (1995)	A national sample of individual Canadian workers; 1986–87 and 1988–89 longitudinal panels (about 52,000 observations)	A measure of worker's expected temporary total disability benefits	A 0–1 variable constructed with this question: Did you receive income from WC in past year?	From 0.363*** to 0.410***
Worrall and Appel (1982)	The claims data, from the NCCI, include all indemnity and non-comp. medical (medical only) claims for the period 1958–1977 in the State of Texas	The average weekly indemnity benefit for temporary total disability	□ Temporary total disability claims divided by the medical-only claims	0.614***
			□ All indemnity claims divided by the medical-only claims	0.465***
Worrall and Butler (1988)	15 industries from South-Carolina pooled over the period 1940–1971	The expected WC benefit for the average worker	Annual injuries per employee resulting in permanent partial injuries	2.46
			Annual injuries per employee resulting in temporary total injuries	0.16**
Worrall and Butler (1990)	15 industries from South-Carolina for the period 1940–1971	The expected WC benefit for the average worker	□ Temporary total injuries per employee	1.09***
			□ Permanent partial injuries per employee	2.79***
			□ Permanent dismemberment or disfigurement	1.74***

* Significantly different from 0 at the 0.10 level. ** Significantly different from 0 at the 0.05 level. *** Significantly different from 0 at the 0.01 level.

Most authors take the total number of claims to construct the injury rate used as the **dependent variable**, while some of them are interested in certain categories of injuries: most of the studies by Butler and associates distinguish between temporary total, permanent partial and permanent total disabilities; Moore and Viscusi (1990) distinguish between fatal and nonfatal injuries; Lanoie, (1992a), and Lanoie and Streliski (1996) distinguish between temporary and permanent disabilities, and Thomason (1993) only considers the permanent partial disability cases. These distinctions are often advocated to control for "reporting effects". Indeed, permanent disabilities or death cases are likely to have always been reported in the same fashion to WCBs through time, so that any detected effect of WC benefits would not be attributable to changes in the reporting behavior.

The **measure of benefits** also varies across studies. American studies performed with data at the state level often use the wage replacement ratio prevailing for temporary total disability cases. Butler, Worrall and associates use a measure of the wage replacement ratio expected on the basis of the wage distribution in each state (which accounts for the minimum and maximum insurable income).[6] Studies with data at the industry level use the industry wage and the maximum insurable income to define a wage replacement ratio per industry (Curington, 1986; Lanoie, 1992a, 1992b; Lanoie and Streliski, 1996). Since they include data on people who had an accident and on people who had not, studies with micro-level data involve the calculation of potential workers' compensation benefits for each individual (instead of a representative or "averaged" individual, as the aggregated analyses do).

Virtually all these empirical analyses, which use conventional regression techniques, find that claims frequency increases as workers' compensation increases. This implies, in line with our theoretical discussion, that employee responses are stronger than employer responses. The **results** suggest that a 10 percent increase in benefits is associated with a 4 to 10 percent increase in claims frequency (with an average elasticity of about 0.6 across the various studies). These results do not seem to be influenced by the type of data used, and findings in Canadian studies, especially in Thomason and Pozzebon (1995) and in Lanoie (1992b), are in the same order of magnitude. Interestingly, Butler (1983), Butler and Worrall (1983) and Worrall and Butler (1990), who consider three types of disability cases (temporary total, permanent partial and permanent total), all show that the estimated elasticity increases with the injury duration.

The only study to report a negative and significant relationship between benefits and frequency is Moore and Viscusi (1990).[7] They find that benefits increases do tend to decrease the number of fatal injuries. This result is not necessarily surprising since, for this category of claims, it is plausible that the employee response to benefits changes, as described above, may be dominated by employer responses.

[6] This measure is fully described in Butler (1983).

[7] Such a result is also present in a simulation exercise of Kniesner and Leeth (1989).

Among the limitations of these studies, one should first note that the use of aggregate data at the state level in many American studies is debatable since it is probably difficult to account for all unobservable or difficult-to-quantify differences in state laws and program administration. This estimation strategy was probably appropriate in early studies when no other data source was available, but recently, most authors have turned themselves to more disaggregated data. Second, most of these studies fail to consider in their specification other institutional aspects that could influence workplace safety like experience rating and safety regulation. There are some exceptions: Ruser (1985) controls for experience rating, Bartel and Thomas (1985), and Curington (1986) account for OSHA[8] activities, while Lanoie (1992a, 1992b) and Lanoie and Streliski (1996) control for both experience rating and "OSHA-type" safety regulations. Interestingly, Ruser (1985), Bartel and Thomas (1985), and Lanoie (1992a) find lower elasticities than in the rest of the literature: 0.35 for Ruser and non-significant results for Bartel and Thomas (1985) and Lanoie (1992a).[9] Omitted variables problem exists also with other employee benefit programs in effect (provision of sick days, existence of employer provided short-term and long-term insurance- in addition to WC), and the relative generosity of these programs. Third, as discussed in the theoretical section, from a policy point of view, it is important to distinguish between legitimate changes in injury rates following increases in WC coverage (the reporting effect), and changes that could reflect an abusive use of the system. Therefore, the question of moral hazard is crucial in this debate.

Duration Studies

Generally, the severity of injuries is proxied by the duration of claims (average duration at the state or at the industry level, and actual duration at the individual level).[10] Theoretically, the impact of benefits changes on severity rates is ambiguous for the same reasons given at the beginning of the preceding section and because, at the aggregate level, changes in benefits may result in a change of the mix of injuries, leading to a different average duration. For instance, if higher benefits lead to an increase in the reporting of small injuries that would otherwise have gone unreported, the average severity in a state, or in an industry, may decline without any real improvement in workplace safety.

As one can see from Table 2, again, the research on this question has been mainly done in North America. Fewer studies are available than for claim frequency, and they tend to be more recent. This could partly explain why most of them have been performed with individual data. Certain studies examine the duration of all claims as their **dependent variable (**Krueger, 1990b; Lanoie, 1992a, 1992b; and Lanoie and Streliski, 1996; Meyer et al., 1996), but a number of them are based on specific

[8] OSHA: Occupational Safety and Health Agency.

[9] Lanoie (1992b)'s results are in the range of the rest of the literature, while Curington does not report his elasticity estimates.

[10] Butler et al. (1997) use the cost per claim as a measure of severity.

Table 2
Representative Estimates of the Effect of Workers' Compensation Benefits on Injury Duration

Study	Unit of observation and sample	Benefit variable	Dependent variable	Benefit elasticity
Butler and Worrall (1985)	Claim for low-back injuries beginning in 1979 in Illinois	Weekly benefits under WC	Expected duration of workplace	A 10% increase in benefits increases the average claim duration by 0.23 weeks
Butler and Worrall (1991a)	Sample of low-back claims that started in 1985 from 12 states	See Butler and Worrall (1985)	Expected duration of claims	0.04*
Butler et al. (1997)	Microdata on WC Claims within one firm in 3 states: California (1990–1991), New-York (1990–1992) and Connecticut (1993)	Maximum replacement dollar amount by state	Change in the cost of claims between the year before the change in maximum benefit and the year after	Between 0.06 and 2.90
Curington (1986)	18 manufacturing industries in New-York from 1964 to 1976	Ratio of the New-York maximum weekly benefit for temporary total disability relative to the average weekly wage for each industry	A severity index that integrates the actual days lost from work for temporary impairments with a measure of permanent impairment (Occupational illness cases are excluded and the injured worker must have been unable to work for seven days)	Not reported (non significant negative effect)
Curington (1994)	Permanent partial disability cases closed by the New-York WCB from 1964 through 1983	The weekly benefit received	Number of weeks of work absence for:	
			☐ minor permanent partial impairments	0.13 to 0.24
			☐ severe permanent partial imp.	0.75 to 1.34 (mostly significant)

Johnson and Ondrich (1990)	WC clients with diverse permanent partial disabilities from Florida, New-York and Wisconsin injured in 1970	The WC benefit received	Expected duration of work absence	0.96*** to 1.16***
Johnson, Butler and Baldwin (1995)	Survey of 8,690 Ontario workers with a permanent partial disability claim between June 1989 and June 1990	Benefit-wage ratio	Duration of first absences	Non-significant effect
Krueger (1990b)	Temporary total claims in Minnesota filed in 1986 and closed by July 1989 (25,446 observations)	The observed weekly benefit	Log of duration in weeks	1.67**
Lanoie (1992b)	Quebec data at the industry level covering 28 industries for the period 1983–87	The variable is based on the net wage replacement ratio obtained by a disabled worker in case of temporary total disability	Log (AWL) where AWL is the average number of workdays lost per accident. (includes all type of accidents)	Non-significant effect
Lanoie and Streliski (1996)	Quebec data at the industry level covering 28 industries for the period 1983–90	The variable is based on the net wage replacement ratio obtained by a disabled worker in case of temporary total disability	Log (AWL) where AWL is the average number of workdays lost per accident (includes all type of accidents)	0.67*
Meyer, Viscusi and Durbin (1995)	Indemnity claims beginning in 1979 in Michigan (M) and Kentucky (K) (about 3,000 observations)	The fraction of previous earning replaced by WC	The measure of duration is the number of weeks of temporary total benefits paid plus anticipated future weeks if the claims is still open	0.29*** to 0.4*** (M) 0.33 to 0.55** (K)
Worrall and Butler (1985)	Male workers who experiment a nonwork state due to low back temporary total injury in Illinois beginning in 1979	Replacement ratio (the wages that are replaced by WC benefits)	Expected duration of work absence	0.463***

* Significantly different from 0 at the 0.10 level. ** Significantly different from 0 at the 0.05 level.

categories of claims: Butler and Worrall (1985); Worrall and Butler (1985); and Butler and Worrall (1991a) consider low-back injury claims, while Johnson and Ondrich (1990), Curington (1994) and Johnson et al. (1995) are using permanent partial disability claims. The rationale for focusing on different types of injuries is not always clear. For instance, Butler and Worrall (1991a) choose the low-back claims "in order to minimize the impact of unobservable heterogeneity due to differences in the type of claim, or in the administration of a claim" (p. 164). Curington (1994) chooses permanent partial disabilities to complete the picture since most studies are based on temporary total claims. The **measures of WC benefits** used in these studies are very similar to those in the claim frequency studies.

Concerning the **estimation technique**, most authors use simple regression models to estimate the impact of WC parameters. However the basic problem is that these parameters may be correlated with other unobservable explaining variables. As well known, OLS estimators will be inconsistent in this case. For instance, introducing a simple dummy variable to assess the impact of a reform in the WC system will produce a biased estimator as long as the reform is correlated with unobserved variables that vary over time. To deal with this problem, certain authors have based their analysis on "natural experiments" (Curington, 1994; Meyer et al., 1996; Butler et al., 1997a). This approach can be used when the data allow to distinguish between a treatment group (who has been affected by a reform) and a control group (who has not). The natural experiment approach typically uses difference (treatment group vs control group) in means differences (post-reform vs pre-reform) estimates. Under standard assumptions (including the basic one that the reform does not influence the sorting of individuals between the two groups), this "difference-in-differences" estimator will be consistent.

Recently, many researches focusing on the duration of claims have used hazard models. As explained in Kiefer (1988), these models are based on conditional probability (e.g., the probability of an individual leaving WC in the tenth week, given that he has been absent nine weeks). Without entering in all the technical details, it is commonly accepted (e.g., see the discussion in Meyer, 1990) that hazard models are superior to regression analysis to investigate spells duration, especially when time-dependent covariates are relevant (changing benefits over the duration of a claim) and when spells are left- or right-censored.

The principal **finding** of these studies is that the duration of disabilities varies directly with WC benefits. The benefit elasticity in these studies is about 0.2 to 0.5, with certain outliers (Johnson and Ondrich find an elasticity around 1, while Krueger's (1990b) results are in the 1.5–2 range).

Among the methodological issues and possible limitations related to this work, one should note again that most of these studies fail to consider in their specification other institutional aspects that could influence safety. Another more technical issue is the assumed parametric form of the baseline hazard in studies using hazard models. Most previous work in this area has relied on parametric methods, which assume, despite a lack of theoretical support, a specific form for the baseline hazard (e.g., Weibull). Only Fortin et al. (1999) (to be discussed in details in the next section) use the mixed proportional hazard model devised by Meyer (1990) that does not impose a parametric form on the baseline hazard. Another important issue is related to unobserved heterogeneity. As is well known, ignoring unobserved heterogeneity may lead to a dynamic selection bias in the parameter estimates and in the estimate of the baseline hazard. For example, as time goes by, it is possible that workers who do not return to the labor market after an accident are those with an intrinsic bad health condition. If one does not account for this unobserved heterogeneity, one may end up with the false impression that the hazard declines through time. A convenient and commonly used distribution for the random variable reflecting unobserved heterogeneity is the gamma, but there is no consensus on the best distribution to adopt.

Studies Related to the Nature of Claims

As discussed above, problems of moral hazard, which arise when informational asymmetries are used for personal gain, are of different types. First, Butler and Worrall (1991b) develop an approach that allows one to distinguish between certain of these types (the studies presented in this section are summarized in Table 3). Their approach can be summarized in the following way: Assume that all workers receiving WC are being paid the maximum weekly benefit for wage replacement. If the WCB raises this maximum by 10 percent, the total value of benefits will increase, *ceteris paribus*, by 10 percent (the actuarial effect). If, instead of a 10% increase, we observe a 15% increase in total benefits paid, the extra 5% might be expected to have arisen from two effects: workers and firms may have changed their level of prevention (the "risk bearing effect" which is equivalent to the ex ante injury hazard we defined earlier), and/or workers may have made more claims, for longer periods etc. (the "claims reporting effect", which is a combination of the ex post duration hazard, the ex ante causality hazard and the claims reporting effect we defined earlier).

Butler and Worrall argue that evidence concerning the relative impacts of these two effects can be obtained by investigating the responsiveness of WC payments to changes in the wage-replacement benefit rate. If it is assumed that there is no claims reporting effect on medical expenses—workers have no reason to claim medical expenses, so an increase in wage-replacement should not produce additional medical claims—any change in medical claims which follows an increase in wage-replacement must have arisen from the risk-bearing effect.

They tested this hypothesis using data from 33 states during the period 1954–1981 and found that a 10 percent increase in benefits led to a 13.2 percent increase in total benefits paid for wage replacement and to a 3.6 percent decrease in medical expenses. They conclude from this that the risk bearing effect was –3.6% and that the claim reporting effect was +6.8% (if total claims increased by 3.2% more than the acturial effect, when the risk bearing effect suggested that they should have decreased by 3.6%, then the claim reporting effect must have been 3.2 + 3.6 = 6.8). Aiuppa and

Table 3

Studies Focusing on Moral Hazard Issues Estimates of the Effect of Workers' Compensation Benefits on Injury Rate or Injury Duration[1]

Study	Unit of observation and sample	Benefit variable	Dependent variable	Benefit elasticity
Bolduc, Fortin, Labrecque, Lanoie (1997)	Micro data 10,000 workers in the Quebec construction industry over each month of the period 1977–1986	The level of benefits divided by the net marginal wage	A three alternative dependent variable: 1) a difficult-to-diagnose accident 2) a easy-to-diagnose accident 3) no accident	**Injury rate:** From 0.83** to 1.45** (1) From 0.72** to 1.03** (2)
Butler, Durbin and Helvacian (1996)	Individual claim data from 15 states for the period 1980 to 1989	Expected level of temporary total benefits in each state-year divided by wages	A multiple choice variable with four injury types: Sprains/straims Laceration/contusion Fracture/crushing All others	**Injury rate:** 0.164** 0.383*** 0.25*** 0.298***
Dionne and St-Michel (1991)	5,000 closed cases of work-related injuries which are associated to total temporary disability	Dichotomous variable representing a greater insurance coverage	In (number of days of compensation)	**Injury duration:** Not reported (significant positive effect)
Fortin and Lanoie (1992)	Quebec data at the industry level: 30 industries for the period 1974–1987	Net wage replacement ratio for a worker with a temporary total disability	Average number of workdays lost per accident (including diseases)	**Injury duration:** From 0.9** to 1.4** **Injury rate:** From 1.6 to 1.9
Fortin, Lanoie and Laporte (1999)	Longitudinal WC administrative micro-data on more than 30,000 workers in the Québec construction industry for the period 1976–1986	The WC replacement ratio (benefits divided by pre-WC net marginal wage) calculated individually for each year	Expected duration of absence	**Injury duration:** 0.71 before 1979 1.09 after 1979
Johnson et al., 1998	9,599 WC claimants in Ontario from June 1989 to June 1990.	Ratio of temporary total disability benefits to pre-injury wage	Probability of returning to work	−2.61 back cases −1.64 non-back cases[2]
Ruser, 1998	Survey of 38,402 cases conducted by the BLS in 1992	1) Average not wage replacement rate 2) Waiting period 3) Dummy variable indicating that the worker can choose his worker	Back sprains Cuts Fractures Carpal tunnel syndrome	Stronger effect of benefits and waiting period on hard-to-diagnose injuries relative to those that are easy-to-diagnose

* Significantly different from 0 at the 0.10 level. ** Significantly different from 0 at the 0.05 level. *** Significantly different from 0 at the 0.01 level.

[1] Because they do not calculate benefit elasticities the studies of Butler and Worral (1991b), Staten and Umbeck (1982), Smith (1989), Card and McCall (1996) and Derrig (1997) are not reported in this Table.

[2] These are significant estimated coefficients in a logit regression.

Trieshmann (1998) used the same approach in the French context with aggregate data from 16 regional offices of the Caisse Nationale for 1973–1991. Their results are close to Butler and Worrall's, showing a risk bearing effect of –0.90 and a claim reporting effect of 0.78, for an overall effect of –0.12 (which is said to be underestimated since the benefit variable used is a maximum instead of an expected value).

This is an interesting approach. However, it depends crucially on the assumption that the claims reporting effect (as they define it) has no impact on medical claims, which could be debatable, especially if this effect leads to a change in the mix of injuries that are reported (this point will be discussed in more details below).

Other authors have used more directly the nature of claims to detect the presence of moral hazard problems. A group of researchers has investigated how difficult-to-diagnose injuries evolve with changes in benefits (ex ante causality hazard and ex post duration hazard). Given that each study has adopted a different approach, we have to discuss them in turn.

Staten and Umbeck (1982) are the first to present evidence of moral hazard from the behavior of air traffic controllers. In the 1970s, these workers were covered by a disability program which, in case of a work-related claim, was providing them with a compensation equal to a fixed percentage of their pay (around 75% non-taxable) for the duration of the claim. Given the type of job of these people, an injury did not need to be physical; stress-related disorders that prevented the employees from working would qualify. Certain changes in the 1970s in the rules governing disability claims made claiming disabilities more attractive for controllers. The 1974 rule changes made monitoring false claims generally more complicated and made catching a fake stress-related claim especially difficult.

A controller who wanted to fake a claim for stress-related disability needed to show the disability was job-related to collect, and the examiners were directed to look for specific events that could have contributed to the stress. This created the incentive to manufacture on-the-job incidents that could have caused the stress. The natural candidate here was a "separation violation", in which planes for which the controller was responsible came too close to one another. Two sorts of separation violations are recorded: System Errors and Near Mid-Air Collisions. The former represents any violations of the standard separation requirements; the later are much more serious and directly life threatening. Because either sort of violation would do equally well for the purposes of filing a claim, a controller who did not want to cause unnecessary danger would be more willing to generate a minor violation than a near collision. And, in fact, the authors show that the number of System Errors jumped significantly after the 1974 change, but there was only a small, statistically insignificant change in the number of Near Mid-Air Collisions.

Smith (1989) raised the possibility that workers' compensation may be paying for some off-the-job injuries. He argues that these injuries reported as work-related would probably be difficult to diagnose, relatively easy to conceal, and tend to be reported early in the shift, especially on Mondays. From a sample of about 57,000 injury cases that occurred in 1978 and 1979 in seven states,[11] Smith finds that of the three largest categories of claims, strains and sprains are reported earlier in the day. Moreover, the propensity to report strains and sprains earlier in the day is significantly increased on Mondays and on days following a three-day weekend. Smith estimates that 4% of strains and sprains are misrepresented as having occurred on the job.

Card et McCall (1996) reexamine this question with a 10 percent random sample of "first reports" of injury filed with the Minnesota Department of Labor and Industry between 1985 and 1989. Combining these administrative data on workplace injury claims with CPS data on medical insurance coverage, and using different estimation techniques, they are not able to show that workers with low medical coverage rates are more likely to report a Monday injury than other workers. They conjecture that the "Monday effect" may be a consequence of the return to work after a "week end hiatus".

Derrig (1997) proposes a more direct test of the "Monday effect" in light of recently available data from the Insurance Fraud Bureau (IFB) of Massachusetts. Summarizing WC claims and taking accepted IFB fraud referrals as proxies for fraud claims, he finds no significant difference in the distributions of each day of the week, even adjusting for days after holidays. Similar empirical distributions are consistent with the hypothesis of elevated true claim injuries on Mondays, and their accompanying fraud level. Similar distributions are not consistent with the off-the-job injury explanation of the Monday effect.

In a recent paper, Ruser (1998) reactivates the debate. Using a survey of 38,402 cases conducted by the BLS, finds that more generous wage replacement and the workers' choice of doctor do raise the probability that any of injury is reported on Monday (or the day after a long weekend) relative to other week days.

Dionne and St-Michel (1991) investigate the presence of moral hazard by looking at the variation in days on WC for injuries with difficult-to-diagnose conditions relative to those with less difficult-to-diagnose conditions. They split injuries into two dimensions based on injury severity (minor versus major injuries) and whether the condition was easy or more difficult to diagnose. Like Smith, they reason that moral hazard responses will be greatest for the difficult-to-diagnose injuries: lower back pain (minor injury) and spinal disorder (major injury). Their analysis is based on a change in Quebec coinsurance parameters occurring in 1979. They consider a sample of about 5,000 injury cases (half before the change and half after). Their OLS estimates show that, as insurance coverage increased in 1979, days spent on difficult-to-diagnose claims rose significantly more than did claims with easy diagnosis. They also find that, once the interaction with diagnosis difficulty was controlled, the 1979 shift had no independent effect on the average duration of claims. This means that most of the impact of the increasing generosity of the regime on durations came through an increase in days by those with difficult-to-diagnose injuries.

[11] These states are: Colorado, Delaware, Montana, New York, North Carolina, Virginia and Wisconsin.

In the same vein, Johnson et al. (1998) explore how the probability to return to work after an injury is affected by the nature of the injury. They find that the disincentive effect of disability benefits on the probability of return to work is substantially larger for back cases versus non-back cases (–2.61 for back cases versus –1.64 for non-back cases).[12] Ruser (1998) also reports evidence that a higher wage replacement rate and a shorter waiting period increase the fraction of hard-to-diagnose injuries relative to those that are easy-to-diagnose.

Interestingly, Dionne and St-Michel's approach can be interpreted as a way to isolate the effect of moral hazard using a "natural experiment" methodology. The treatment group (workers with difficult-to-diagnose claims) incurs the same change of regime as the control group (those with easy-to-diagnose claims) but has not the same information problem. Basically, they introduce a dummy variable for whether the observation is after the reform, a dummy variable for whether the claimant belongs to the treatment group and an interaction variable of these two latter variables. The coefficient associated with the interaction variable is a measure of the *ex post* moral hazard effect of the reform and corresponds to a difference-in-differences estimator.[13] A similar approach has recently been used by other researchers in the field (e.g., Bolduc et al., 1997; Fortin et al., 1999).

Workers are not the only parties in the disability process that are sensitive to financial incentives. In this perspective, Butler et al. (1996) analyze the existence of behaviors associated with moral hazard from health care providers in U.S. HMOs (Health Maintenance Organization). HMOs are per capita payment programs in which physicians contract to meet all the health care needs of an individual (or a family) for an annual fee. However, they get paid on a fee-for-service basis for workers' compensation injuries, on top of their per capita fees, and so are financially better off when they classify as many of their treatments as work related as possible. Physicians outside HMOs face different payment systems: fee-for-service doctors get paid the same for treating a broken bone arising from an accident at home as they do for the same type of break occurring on the job.

This leads to the hypothesis that, as HMO coverage expands, relatively more sprains and strains are expected because these are difficult-to-diagnose injuries. To test this hypothesis, they use a database on the types of WC claims across states and over time (15 states for the time period 1980–1989). Estimations are done with a multinomial logit model in which they assume that the typical worker may experience one of five states: 1) no injury; 2) sprains and strains (including low back); 3) lacerations and contusions; 4) fractures and crushing injuries; and 5) all other types of injuries. The elasticities for the replacement ratio indicate that a 10% increase in benefits leads to a 1.25% increase in sprains and strains. A 10% increase in the

[12] These are estimated coefficients in a logit.

[13] Dionne (1998) and Chiappori (1999) provide a useful discussion which emphazises the interest of exploiting natural experiments of this kind to obtain consistent estimates of moral hazard effects. See also the two chapters by the same authors in this book.

proportion of the population covered by HMOs leads to about a 0.8% increase in the proportion of strains and sprains.[14]

Interaction Between Social Insurance Programs

Fortin and Lanoie (1992) examine indirectly the presence of moral hazard behaviors (insurance substitution hazard) through the interaction between WC and unemployment insurance (UI). In particular, they argue that, since WC is in general more generous than UI (which is the case in most industrialized countries, see Lanoie, 1994), workers about to be laid-off may have incentives to reduce their prevention efforts so as to benefit from WC instead of UI. Workers suffering from a workplace accident may also be tempted to take action in order to obtain a longer period of recovery compensated by WC, especially if they know that they would be laid-off when returning on the labor market. These arguments lead to the following theoretical predictions: 1) an increase in the wage replacement rate under WC should lead to a higher frequency and/or longer duration of claims; 2) an increase in the wage replacement rate under UI should have the converse effect.

They tested this hypothesis with a pooled time-series and cross-section database at the industry level (30 Quebec industries covering the period 1974–1987). They find that a raise of 1% in WC benefits leads to an increase of the average duration of accidents in the 0.9–1.4% range, while an increase in UI payments reduces the average duration of accidents with an elasticity in the 0.5–0.7 range. The results with respect to injury frequency are not conclusive.

The moral hazard problem described above is more likely to be important when injuries are difficult-to-diagnose (e.g., low-back injuries) and in industries where the level of unemployment is such that many workers may expect to be unemployed and to receive UI benefits after their recovery. This is the case in seasonal industries such as the Canadian construction industry, which is less active during winter because of weather constraints.

Fortin et al. (1999) estimate the effect of WC and UI benefits on the expected duration of claims using a unique panel data set allowing them to investigate more fully the issues that we just raised. The database is composed of longitudinal WC administrative micro-data on more than 30,000 workers in the Quebec construction industry for the period 1976–1986. For the empirical work, they use a mixed proportional hazard model, devised by Meyer (1990), that does not impose a parametric form on the baseline hazard and that takes unobserved heterogeneity into account using a gamma distribution. They find that, for hard-to-diagnose injuries, an increase of 1% in the generosity of WC is associated with an increase of 0.71–1.09% in the expected spell duration, while the elasticity with respect to UI benefits is –0.54 (a result similar to that found in Fortin and Lanoie, 1992). Furthermore, the fact that an accident occurs

[14] Note also that Butler et al. (1997b) investigate the impact of the rapid expansion of HMOs in the 80's on the claim cost per employee. Their results are inconclusive and depend on the inclusion or not of state dummy variables.

in December rather than in July (December corresponds to the end of the construction season for most workers) induces an increase of 21.2% in the expected duration. This is another piece of evidence that there is substitution between WC and UI in the construction industry.

Bolduc et al. (1997) extend this work to show that WC insurance may affect the composition of reported occupational injuries. Based on an expected utility framework, their theoretical model predicts that, under reasonable assumptions, an increase in the WC wage replacement ratio (or a decrease in the UI wage replacement ratio) leads to a larger increase in the probability of reporting a difficult-to-diagnose injury than in the probability of reporting an easy-to-diagnose injury. The initial database used in this study is the same as the one used in Fortin et al. (1999). The parameters of the model are estimated using a three alternative multinomial probit framework with random effects.[15] Their results confirm their predictions. In particular, the impact of an increase in the WC replacement ratio on the probability of accidents ranges (in terms of elasticity) from 0.83 to 1.45 for difficult-to-diagnose injuries and from 0.72 to 1.03 for easy-to-diagnose injuries (for the period 1979–1986). Furthermore, the impact of an increase in the UI ratio ranges (in terms of elasticity) from −1.93 to −2.32 for the difficult-to-diagnose injuries, and from −1.20 and −1.47 for the easy-to-diagnose injuries. In line with these results, they also show that the probability to report a difficult-to-diagnose injury is significantly greater in winter (the dead season in the construction industry) than in other seasons.

13.3.2 Wage Effects

Another current of empirical literature is investigating the question: who actually pays for workers' compensation?[16] In particular, is it possible that the cost of workers' compensation be shifted, completely or partly, to workers through lower wages? As discussed above, this question can be analyzed through conventional labor demand and supply curves. WC is a form of payroll tax that shifts down labor demand, resulting in a lower wage at the new equilibrium. The magnitude of the wage change depends on the relative elasticities of labor demand and supply. Another approach is to consider that the existence of workers' compensation has some value for workers that could lead them to accept lower wages. Specifically, the existence of WC may mean lower risk premia (or compensating wage differentials) for risky jobs, which would also entail a wage reduction. As discussed earlier, given the level of experience rating, this impact could vary across low and high-risk industries.

We have identified six empirical studies that have investigated the relationship between WC costs and wage levels. They are summarized in Table 4. In general, they use, as their **dependent variable**, a conventional measure of the wage (like the after-

[15] The empirical approach is actually an extension to panel data of the approach developed in Bolduc et al. (1996) and Bolduc and Ben-Akiva (1991).

[16] For an excellent survey, see Chelius and Burton (1995).

Table 4
The Impact of Workers' Compensation Programs on the Wage

Study	Data	Measure of Benefits or WC costs	Results
Arnould and Nichols (1983)	Sample of the 1970 population census (USA), 1/10,000 sample (⊃ 1,800)	Percentage of wages recouped under state WC laws	Negative impact of WC on the wage
Butler (1983)	Fifteen industries in South Carolina, 1940–1972	Benefit index capturing the average real annual payments for injuries resulting in death, permanent disabilities and temporary total disabilities	A1$ increase in expected benefits leads to a wage decrease between 11.5 and 14.0 ¢
Dorsey and Walzer (1983)	National sample of 5,843 blue collar (May 1978)	The rate for workers compensation liability insurance expressed in dollars per $100 of payroll	1% increase in WC costs leads to a 1.4% wage decline
Gruber and Krueger (1991)	National sample of 15,244 individuals in five high-risk jobs: carpenters, truck drivers, hospital employees, gasoline station employees and plumbers (1979, 80, 81, 87, 88)	Corresponding workers' compensation rate per $100 of payroll	86.5 percent of WC costs are shifted on workers through lower wages
Kaestner and Carroll (1997)	National sample of 7,638 individuals from the 1988 current population survey (CPS)	Measure of WC benefits that includes a portion for medical benefits	A 1 percent increase in benefits leads to a 0.78 percent decline in wage
Moore and Viscusi (1990)	See Table 1	See Table 1	An increase of $1,000 in annual WC cost leads to an annual wage reduction of $890

tax weekly male wage of production employees; Butler, 1983). The workers' compensation variable is either a traditional measure of workers' compensation benefits, as those described above, or a measure of workers' compensation costs (e.g., Dorsey and Walzer use the rate paid for WC liability expressed in dollars per $100 of payroll, Kaestner and Carroll (1997) use a measure of WC benefits that include medical benefits). Most authors (except Butler, 1983) have used micro data at the individual level, and some of them have focused on workers in risky jobs (e.g., Gruber and Krueger, 1991, use data from a national sample of individuals in five high-risk jobs: carpenters, truck drivers, nonprofessional hospital employees, gasoline station employees, and plumbers.)

In general, the **results** show **substantial impacts** of workers' compensation on the wage (except for Butler, 1983). Dorsey and Walzer (1983) find that, for every 1 percent increase in workers' compensation costs, wages decline by 1.4 percent. Moore and Viscusi (1990) conclude that higher compensation benefits, from the employer's perspective, more than pay for themselves. Gruber and Krueger (1991) show that 86% of workers' compensation costs are shifted onto workers in the form of lower wages.[17] Kaestner and Carroll (1997) find that a 1% increase in benefits leads a 0.78% decrease in wage.[18]

As one limitation of this literature, one should note that the authors have little to say on why the impact would be so strong. As put by Chelius and Burton (1995, p. 157) "the conclusion that higher workers' compensation costs could be more than compensated by lower wage is a radical one that, undoubtedly, will be sharply contested by many members of the workers' compensation community".

13.3.3 Labor Productivity Effects

As mentioned earlier, a recent literature has focused on the effect of WC on labor productivity. In particular, Butler et al. (1997c), and Butler and Gardner (1994) have tested the hypothesis that managers partly get rid of their low productivity workers through the WC program. Butler et al. (1997c) show that workers receiving disciplinary notices (i.e., those with "management" problems) are much more likely to enter in disability status. A notice increases the probability of filing a claim from about 12 to 15 percent.

Moreover, Butler et al. (1999) test the hypothesis that higher WC benefits reduce labor productivity through its impact on absenteeism and firm specific human capital. For this matter, they use a database covering 14 U.S. manufacturing sectors from 1980 to 1991. These data include information on value added, employment, capital, WC

[17] In the same vein, Gunderson and Hyatt (1996) present evidence on the extent to which injured workers in Ontario (1979–1988) paid, through lower wages, for "reasonable accommodation" requirements designed to facilitate their return to work after their injury.

[18] These authors also explore the impact of WC insurance market regulation on wages. They find that wages are higher in states with deregulated WC insurance.

benefits and specific human capital. These two last aspects are crucial in their analysis. Benefits are measured by the total amount of WC benefits paid in the industry divided by the total payroll, a measure that displays little variability in the sample.[19] As a proxy of firm specific capital, they use the "average job industry specific job tenure of employees" from the CPS. Assuming that output follows a Cobb-Douglas process, estimations are made in which value added is regressed on employment, capital, tenure, benefits and an interaction term between tenure and benefits. The estimated implied elasticities are ranging from 0.05 to 0.3. These results (especially those in the upper range) are a bit surprising since the benefits measure displays little variability. This suggests that the database used is probably not the most appropriate one to study this phenomenon.[20]

13.4 CONCLUDING REMARKS AND POLICY DISCUSSION

To our knowledge, this survey is the first one to cover extensively the theoretical and the empirical work that was done on the incentive effects related to the existence of workers' compensation in the North American context. Three types of effects have been distinguished: 1) Through various incentive effects (ex ante and ex post moral hazard, substitution between WC and unemployment insurance, reporting incentives) WC may affect the frequency, duration and nature of claims; 2) WC may induce changes in the wage level and 3) WC may affect firms' productivity. So far, the literature has focused on the first type of effects. The main results have shown that increases in WC insurance are associated with an increase in the frequency of injuries (elasticities ranging from 0.4 to 1), and with an increase in the average duration of claims (elasticities ranging from 0.2 to 0.5). Furthermore, increases in WC are associated with more reporting of injuries that are difficult-to-diagnose and, in the same line, there are some evidence (at least in Canada) of substitution between unemployment insurance and WC insurance. Lastly, there are empirical results showing that the presence of WC insurance induces important reductions in wage rates, while an emerging literature suggests that changes in WC insurance may also have negative productivity effects.

For **policy makers**, our results raise the question of the appropriate rate of wage replacement provided by WC in case of workplace accident. Are the rates actually in place too high or too low? Pressure groups have their opinion which are probably irreconcilable. Unions want higher replacement rates, while business associations often criticize the great cost of workers' compensation insurance (although the results showing that WC cost is transferred to workers through lower

[19] Mean: 0.03 and standard deviation: 0.0098.

[20] They also tackle the question with state longitudinal data (1954–1991), but they no longer have information on the capital stock (by state) and job tenure.

wages put this criticism in a different perspective). Of course, it is difficult to determine theoretically or empirically what is the **optimal rate of replacement**.[21] The literature on moral hazard (e.g., Arnott, 1991) only tells us that the replacement rate should be less than 100%!

Should policy makers be worried by the empirical results showing that increases in WC are associated with increases in the level of workplace risk (duration and frequency of injuries)? Not necessarily, as discussed earlier, these results indicate that employees response to changes in WC are stronger than employer responses. This is a likely outcome if experience rating is not pervasive, which seems to be the case in most jurisdictions, especially for small firms. This could suggest that further increases in WC replacement rate should be accompanied by more intense experience rating if one wants to control total WC costs. One should recognize, however, that movements in that direction are not likely; for instance, five Canadian provinces have reduced their WC replacement rates within the last five years.

More worrying are the results of the studies related to moral hazard. In relation with these results, one should note that U.S. WC costs, as a percent of payroll, rose from 1.96 in 1980 to 2.36 in 1990, a 19% increase in the real costs of U.S. workplace accident insurance. At the same time, real benefits increases were modest, and workplace fatalities—presumably a good proxy for job safety—fell steadily from 13 per 100,000 to 9 per 100,000 by 1990,[22] which means that it is unlikely that the increased costs are attributable to more dangerous workplaces. One relatively unexplored explanation of this cost trend is the change in the mix of claims reimbursed. This explanation is somewhat supported by the results indicating that increases in WC insurance are associated with more difficult-to-diagnose injuries (soft-tissue injuries and low-back pain) and longer duration of such claims.

In fact, the results presented above could suggest that more resources should be devoted to the screening of the difficult-to-diagnose claims, especially those arising on Mondays, those that are treated by an HMO physician, and those occurring in a period surrounding a lay-off. One should keep in mind, however, that if the efficiency cost of detection (medical exams, litigation etc.) is larger than the efficiency cost of moral hazard, then it might not be optimal to put more resources in detection. In fact, as long as there is no major improvement in the way physicians can detect these types of injury (especially low-back pain), it is clear that behaviors associated with moral hazard will persist.

The issue of substitution between UI and WC investigated by three Canadian studies raise the question of the optimal gap between the wage replacement rate under

[21] There is some work on the optimal replacement rate provided by unemployment insurance (for instance, see Hansen and Imrohoroglu, 1992). Viscusi and Evans (1990). through an estimation of state-dependent utility functions, present a calculation showing that, in the U.S., the optimal rate of income replacement under WC is 0.68 of the gross wage. However, their analytical framework does not account for moral hazard.

[22] These figures are taken from Butler et al. (1996).

UI and that under WC. From the moral hazard literature, one can make the argument that, because abusing from WC (finding an accommodating physician etc.) is probably more difficult than abusing from UI, the insurance coverage should be lower for UI than for WC. However, there is no study on the optimal gap between the generosity of the two regimes. Lanoie (1994) provides a comparative analysis of the WC and UI systems in 14 OECD countries. It turns out that Canada is one of the countries (with Australia) where the gap between the generosity of the two regimes is the largest. This suggests that actions reducing this gap (reducing WC insurance coverage or increasing the generosity of UI) may be warranted.

Lastly, another worrying finding is that of Butler et al. (1999) showing that increases in WC benefits are associated with lower productivity. However, as discussed above, more research on this issue is certainly required before we have a clear picture of the links between WC benefits and productivity.

13.5 REFERENCES

Aiuppa, T. and J. Trieshmann (1998). "Moral Hazard in the French Workers' Compensation System", *Journal of Risk and Insurance* 65, 125–133.

Akerlof, G.A. (1970). "The Market for "Lemons": Qualitative Uncertainty and the Market Mechanism", *Quarterly Journal of Economics* 84, 488–500.

Akerlof, G.A. and W.T. Dickens (1982). "The Economic Consequences of Cognitive Dissonance", *American Economic Review* 72, 307–319.

Arnott, R.J. (1992). "Moral Hazard and Competitive Insurance Markets", in G. Dionne (ed.), *Contributions to Insurance Economics*, Kluwer Academic Publisher, Boston.

Arnott, R.J. and J.E. Stiglitz (1988). "The Basic Analytics of Moral Hazard", *Scandinavian Journal of Economics* 90, 383–413.

Arnould, R.J. and L.M. Nichols (1983). "Wage-Risk Premiums and Workers' Compensation: A Refinement of Estimates of Compensating Wage Differentials", *Journal of Political Economy* 91, 332–340.

Bartel, A. and L.G. Thomas (1982). "Enforcement, Industrial Compliance and Workplace Injuries", Research paper 477a, Columbia University Graduate School of Business, New York.

Bartel, A. and L.G. Thomas (1985). "Direct and Indirect Effects of Regulation: A New Look at OSHA's Impact", *Journal of Law and Economics* 28, 1–25.

Bolduc, D., B. Fortin and M.-A. Fournier (1996). "The Impact of Incentive Policies on the Practice Location of Doctors: A Multinomial Probit Analysis", *Journal of Labor Economics* 14, 703–732.

Bolduc, D. and M. Ben-Akiva (1991). "A Multinomial Probit Formulation for Large Choice Sets", Proceedings of the 6th International Conference on Travel Behavior.

Bolduc, D., B. Fortin, F. Labrecque and P. Lanoie (1997). "Incentive Effects of Public Insurance Programs on the Occurrence and the Composition of Workplace Injuries", Cahier de recherche IEA-97-07, Institut d'économie appliquée, École des Hautes Études Comerciales, Montréal.

Bond, E.W. and K.J. Crocker (1997). "Contracting with Costly State Falsification: Theory and Empirical Results from Automobile Insurance", *Journal of Public Economics* 63, 239–264.

Butler, R.J. (1983). "Wage and Injury Rate Response to Shifting Levels of Workers' Compensation", in J. Worrall (ed.), *Safety and the Workforce: Incentives and Disincentives in Worker's Compensation*, Cornell University Press, Ithaca, NY, 61–86.

Butler, R.J. (1994). "The Economic Determinants of Workers' Compensation Trends", *Journal of Risk and Insurance* 61, 383–401.

Butler, R.J., D.L. Durbin and N.M. Helvacian (1996). "Increasing Claims for Soft Tissue Injuries in Workers' Compensation: Cost Shifting and Moral Hazard", *Journal of Risk and Uncertainty* 13, 73–87.

Butler, R.J. and H.H. Gardner (1994). "Worker Productivity Failure and Disability", mimeo, University of Minnesota.

Butler, R.J., H.H. Gardner and B.D. Gardner (1999). "More than Cost Shifting: Moral Hazard Lowers Productivity", forthcoming in the *Journal of Risk and Insurance*.

Butler, R.J., B.D. Gardner and H.H. Gardner (1997c). "Claimant Learning in Workers' Compensation: Do Past Claims Cause Future Claims?", mimeo, University of Minnesota.

Butler, R.J., B.D. Gardner and H.H. Gardner (1997a). "Workers' Compensation Costs when Maximum Benefits Change", *Journal Risk and Uncertainty* 15, 259–269.

Butler, R.J., R.P. Hartwig and H. Gardner (1997b). "HMOs, Moral Hazard and Cost Shifting in Workers' Compensation", *Journal of Health Economics* 16, 191–206.

Butler, R.J. and J. Worrall (1983). "Workers' Compensation: Benefit and Injury Claims Rates in the Seventies", *Review of Economics and Statistics* 65, 580–589.

Butler, R.J. and J.D. Worrall (1985). "Worker Injury Compensation and the Duration of Nonwork Spells", *Economic Journal* 95, 714–724.

Butler, R.J. and J.D. Worrall (1991a). "Gamma Duration Models with Heterogeneity", *Review of Economics and Statistics*, 161–166.

Butler, R.J. and J.D. Worrall (1991b). "Claims Reporting and Risk Bearing Moral Hazard in Workers 'Compensation", *Journal of Risk and Insurance*, 191–204.

Card, D. and B.P. McCall (1996). "The Monday Effect", *Industrial and Labor Relations Review* 49, 690–706.

Carmichael, L. (1986). "Reputation for Safety: Market Performance and Policy Remedies", *Journal of Labor Economics* 4, 458–472.

Chelius, J. (1977). "Workplace Safety and Health", American Enterprise Institute, Washington.

Chelius, J. (1982). "The Influence of Workers' Compensation on Safety Incentives", *Industrial and Labor Relations Review* 35, 235–242.

Chelius, J. (1983). "Worker's Compensation and the Incentive to Prevent Injuries", in J.D. Worrall (ed.), *Safety and the Work Force: Incentives and Disincentives in Worker's Compensation*, Cornell University Press, Ithaca, NY.

Chelius, J. and K. Kavanaugh (1988). "Workers' Compensation and the Level of Occupational Injuries", *Journal of Risk and Insurance* 55, 315–323.

Chelius, J. and J.F. Burton (1995). "Who Actually Pays for Workers' Compensation?: The Empirical Evidence", *Workers' Compensation Year Book*.

Chiappori, P.A. (1999). "Asymmetric Information in Automobile Insurance: an Overview", *Assurances* 4, 629–644.

Crocker, K.T. and J. Morgan (1998). "Is Honesty the Best Policy? Curtailing Insurance Fraud through Optimal Incentive Contracts", *Journal of Political Economy* 106, 355–375.

Curington, W.P. (1986). "Safety Regulation and Workplace Injuries", *Southern Economic Journal* 53, 51–71.

Curington, W.P. (1994). "Compensation for Permanent Impairment and the Duration of Work Absence: Evidence from Four Natural Experiments", *The Journal of Human Resources* 29, 888–910.

Derrig, R.A. (1997). "Insurance Fraud and The Monday Effect in Workers' Compensation Insurance", mimeo, Boston.

Diamond, P.A. (1977). "Insurance Theoretic Aspects of Workers' Compensation", in A. Blinder and P. Friedman (eds.), *Natural Resources, Uncertainty and General Equilibrium Systems*, Academic Press, New York.

Dionne, G. (1998). "La mesure empirique des problèmes d'information", *L'Actualité Economique* 74, 585–606.

Dionne, G. and P. St-Michel (1991). "Workers' Compensation and Moral Hazard", *Review of Economics and Statistics* 73, 236–244.

Dorsey, S. and N. Walzer (1983). "Workers' Compensation, Job Hazards, and Wages", *Industrial and Labor Relations Review* 36, 642–654.

Ehrenberg, R.G. (1988). "Workers' Compensation, Wages, and the Risk of Injury", in J. Burton Jr. (ed.), *New Perspectives in Workers' Compensation*, ILR Press.

Fortin, B. and P. Lanoie (1992). "Substitution between Unemployment Insurance and Workers' Compensation", *Journal of Publics Economics* 49, 287–312.

Fortin, B., P. Lanoie and C. Laporte (1999). "Is Worker's Compensation a Substitute for Unemployment Insurance?", *Journal of Risk and Uncertainty*, 18, 165–188.

Gruber, J. and A.B. Krueger (1991). "The Incidence of Mandated Employer—Provided Insurance: Lessons from Workers' Compensation Insurance", in D. Bradford (ed.) *Tax Policy and the Economy*, MIT Press, Cambridge MA, 111–143.

Gunderson, M. and D. Hyatt (1996). "Do Injured Workers Pay for Reasonable Accomodation?", *Industrial and Labor Relations Review* 50, 92–104.

Hansen, G.D. and A. Imrahoroglu (1992). "The Role of Unemployment Insurance in an Economy with Liquidity Constraints and Moral Hazard", *Journal of Political Economy* 100, 118–142.

Hellwig, M. (1987). "Some Recent Developments in the Theory of Competition in Markets with Adverse Selection", *European Economic Review* 31, 319–325.

Holmstrom, B. (1979). "Moral Hazard and Observability", *Bell Journal of Economics* 10, 74–91.

Johnson, W.G. and J.I. Ondrich (1990). "The Duration of Post-Injury Absences from Work", *Review of Economics and Statistics* 72, 578–586.

Johnson, W.G., R.J. Butler and M. Baldwin (1995). "First Spells of Work Among Ontario Workers", in T. Thomason and R. Chaykowski (eds.), *Research in Canadian Workers' Compensation*, Industrial Relations Centre Press, Kingston, 72–84.

Johnson, W.G., M.L. Baldwin and R.J. Butler (1998). "Back Pain and Work Disability: the Need for a New Paradigm", *Industrial Relations* 37, 9–34.

Kaplow, L. (1994). "Optimal Insurance Contracts When Establishing the Amount of Losses is Costly", *Geneva Papers Risk and Insurance Theory* 19, 139–152.

Kaestner, R. and A. Carroll (1997). "New estimates of the Labor Market Effects of Workers' Compensation Insurance", *Southern Journal of Economics* 63, 635–651.

Kiefer, N. (1988). "Economic Duration Data and Hazard Functions", *Journal of Economic Literature* XXVI, 646–679.

Kniesner, T.J. and J.D. Leeth (1989). "Separating the Reporting Effects from the Injury Rate Effects of Worker's Compensation Insurance: a Hedonic Simulation", *Industrial and Labor Relations Review* 42, 280–293.

Krueger, A.B. (1988). "Moral Hazard in Workers' Compensation Insurance", mimeo, Princeton University.

Kruger, A.B. (1990a). "Incentive Effects of Workers' Compensation Insurance", *Journal of Public Economics* 41, 73–99.

Krueger, A.B (1990b). "Workers' Compensation Insurance and the Duration of Workplace Injuries, *NBER Working Paper* 3253.

Lanoie, P. (1990). "The Case of Risk Premia for Risky Jobs Revisited", *Economics Letters* 32, 181–185.

Lanoie, P. (1991). "Occupational Safety and Health: a Problem of Double or Single Moral Hazard", *Journal of Risk and Insurance* 58, 80–100.

Lanoie, P. (1992a). "Safety Regulation and the Risk of Workplace Accidents in Québec", *Southern Economic Journal* 58, 950–965.

Lanoie, P. (1992b). "The Impact of Occupational Safety and Health Regulation on the Risk of Workplace Accidents: Quebec, 1983–87", *Journal of Human Resources* 27, 643–660.

Lanoie, P. (1994). "Aspects économiques de la santé et sécurité au travail", *Relations Industrielles/Industrial Relations* 49, 62–84.

Lanoie, P. and D. Streliski (1996). "L'impact de la réglementation en matière de santé et sécurité du travail sur le risque d'accident au Québec: de nouveaux résultats", *Relations Industrielles/Industrial Relation* 51, 778–801.

Leigh, J.P. (1985). "Analysis of Workers' Compensation using Data on Individual", *Industrial Relations* 24, 247–256.

Meyer, B. (1990). "On Unemployment Insurance and Unemployment Spells", *Econometrica* 58, 757–782.

Meyer, B.D., W.K. Viscusi and D.L. Durbin (1995). "Workers' Compensation and Injury Duration: Evidence from a Natural Experiment", *American Economic Review* 85, 322–340.

Mookherjee, D. and I. Png (1989). "Optimal Auditing, Insurance and Redistribution", *Quarterly Journal of Economics* 104, 205–228.

Moore, M.J. and W.K. Viscusi (1990). *Compensation Mechanisms for Job Risks: Wages, Workers' Compensation and Product Liability*, Princeton University Press.

Moore, M.J. and W.K. Viscusi (1992). "Social Insurance in Market Contexts: Implications of the Structure of Workers' Compensation for Job Safety and Wages", in G. Dionne (ed.) *Contributions to Insurance Economics*, Boston: Kluwer Academic Publisher, 399–422.

Oi, W. (1974). "An Essay on Workmen's Compensation and Industrial Safety", in *Supplemental Studies for the National Commission on State Workmen's Compensation Laws*, Vol. I, 41–106.

Ohsfeldt, R.L. and M.A. Morrisey (1997). "Beer Taxes. Workers' Compensation and Industrial Injury", *Review of Economics and Statistics*, 155–159.

Pauly, M. (1974). "Overprovision and Public Provision of Insurance", *Quarterly Journal of Economics* 88, 44–62.

Peltzman, S. (1975). "The Effects of Automobile Safety Regulation", *Journal of Political Economy* 83, 669–699.

Rea S. Jr. (1981). "Workmen's Compensation and Occupational Safety under Imperfect Information", *American Economic Review* 70, 80–93.

Rosen, S. (1974). "Hedonic Prices and Implicit Markets: Product Differentiation in Pure Competition", *Journal of Political Economy* 82, 34–55.

Ruser, John (1985). "Workers' Compensation Insurance, Experience Rating and Occupational Injuries", *Rand Journal of Economics* 16, 487–503.

Ruser, John W. (1991). "Workers' Compensation and Occupational Injuries and Illnesses, *Journal of Labor Economics* 9, 325–350.

Ruser, J.W. (1998). "Does Workers' Compensation Encourage Hard to Diagnose Injuries?", *Journal of Risk and Insurance* 65, 101–124.

Smith, R.S. (1989). "Mostly on Mondays: Is Workers' Compensation Covering Off-The-Job Injuries?", in P.S. Borba and D. Appel (eds.) *Benefits, Costs, and Cycles in Workers'Compensation*, Boston, Kluwer Academic Press, 115–127.

Staten, M.E. and J. Umbeck (1982). "Information Costs and Incentive to Shirk: Disability Compensation of Air Traffic Controllers", *American Economic Review* 72, 1023–1037.

Thaler, R. and S. Rosen (1976). "The Value of Life Saving", in N.E. Terleckyj (ed.), *Household Production and Consumption*, NBER Press, New York.

Thomason, T. (1993). "Permanent Partial Disability in Workers' Compensation: Probability and Costs", *Journal of Risk and Insurance* 60, 570–590.

Thomason, T. and S. Pozzebon (1995). "The Effect of Workers' Compensation Benefits on Claim Incidence in Canada: an Analysis of Micro-Level Data", in T. Thomason and R.P. Chaykowski (eds.), *Research in Canadian Workers' Compensation*, IRC Press, Queen's University, Kingston, 53–70.

Townsend, R.M. (1979). "Optimal Contract and Competitive Markets with Costly State Verification", *Journal of economic Theory* 21, 265–293.

Viscusi, W.K. (1992). *Fatal Injuries*, Oxford University Press, New York.

Viscusi, W.K. and W.N. Evans (1990). "Utility Functions that Depends on Health Status: Estimates and Economic Implications", *American Economic Review* 80, 353–374.

Worrall, J.D. and D. Appel (1982). "The Wage Replacement Rate and Benefit Utilization in Workers' Compensation Insurance", *Journal of Risk and Insurance* 49, 361–371.

Worrall, J. and R.J. Butler (1985). "Benefit and Claim Duration", in J.D. Worrall and D. Appell (eds.), *Workers' Compensation Benefits: Adequacy, Equity and Efficiency*, Ithaca, N.Y., ILR Press, 57–70.

Worrall, J.D. and R.J. Butler (1988). "Experience Rating Matters", in D. Appel and P.S. Borda (eds.), *Workers' Compensation Insurance Pricing*, Boston, Kluwer Academic Press.

Worrall, J.D. and R.J. Butler (1990). "Heterogeneity Bias in Estimating of the Determinants of Workers' Compensation Loss Distribution", in P.S. Borda and D. Appel (eds.), *Benefits, Costs and Cycles in Worker's Compensation*, Boston, Kluwer Academic Publisher.

14 Experience Rating through Heterogeneous Models*

Jean Pinquet

University Paris X-Nanterre

Abstract

This paper presents statistical models which lead to experience rating in insurance. Serial correlation for risk variables can receive endogeneous or exogeneous explanations. The paper recalls that the main interpretation for automobile insurance is exogeneous, since positive contagion is always observed for the number of claims reported and since true contagion should be negative. This positive contagion can be explained by the revelation throughout time of a hidden features in the risk distributions. These features are represented by heterogeneity components in a heterogeneous model. Prediction on longitudinal data can be performed through the heterogeneous model, and the paper provides consistent estimators for models related to number and cost of claims. Examples are given for count data models with a constant or time-varying heterogeneity components, one or several equations, and for a cost-number model on events. Empirical results are presented, which are drawn from the analysis of a French data base of automobile insurance contracts.

Keywords: Observed and real contagion, overdispersion, fixed and random effects models, Poisson and linear models with heterogeneity, experience rating.
JEL Classification Numbers: C13, C14, C23, C25, C30, G22.

14.1 INTRODUCTION

The assessment of individual risks in non life insurance raises problems which occur in any statistical analysis of longitudinal data. An insurance rating model computes risk premiums, which are estimations of risk levels, themselves expectations of risk variables. These variables are either numbers of claims or are related to their severity

* Thanks to Georges Dionne, Bernard Salanié, two anonymous referees and the participants in the ASTIN conference at Lausanne for their comments. This paper benefited from a discussion with Daniel Mac Fadden, and from comments of Jerry Hausman and Jean Lemaire on related papers. Financial support from the Fédération Française des Sociétés d'Assurance is acknowledged.

(the cost of the claim, or the duration of a compensation). The risk levels assessed in this paper are the frequency of claims, the expected cost per claim and the pure premium, which refers to the expected loss or to its estimation.

Owing to the difficulty to maintain cross subsidies between different risk levels in a competitive setting, the design of a fair rating structure is a major concern for actuaries. A risk premium may depend on the rating factors of the current period (think of the type of car, the occupation of the policyholder, the geographical area for automobile insurance), but also on the past. An a priori rating model uses only the present rating factors for risk assessment. The allowance for the history of the policyholder in a rating model derives from interpretations of serial correlation for longitudinal data which can be summarized in the following way.

- Within an endogeneous framework, the history of individuals modify their risk levels. Statistical literature uses the terms "true contagion" (referring to epidemiology), or "state dependence". A car accident may modify your perception of danger behind the wheel, and lower your risk level as a policyholder. Actual insurance rating schemes often provide incentives to careful driving (see Section 14.1) and should induce negative contagion.
- If an exogeneous approach is retained, serial correlation for risk variables is seen as only apparent, and results from the revelation of hidden features in the risk distributions. Think for instance of annual mileage, and of features of the behaviour which do not depend on the history. This unobserved heterogeneity can be represented by a heterogeneity component in the distributions of a statistical model.

For a heterogeneous model, the heterogeneity component is the realization of a random variable. This model with random effects provides distributions for generic individuals (see Section 14.3), whereas the distributions for real individuals belong to a model with fixed effects. The distributions of the heterogeneous model are mixtures of distributions in the a priori rating model.

Once estimated, the heterogeneous model can be used to perform prediction on longitudinal data. It allows experience rating in insurance (see Lemaire (1985, 1995), Dionne and Vanasse (1989, 1992), Pinquet (1997a)). In a Bayesian setting, the prediction is derived from the expectation of a random effect with respect to a posterior distribution. This distribution takes into account the history of the individual, and so does the prediction, although serial independence is assumed for the actual distributions. The history of the individual is viewed here as revealing the unobserved heterogeneity.

A "bonus-malus" coefficient derived from such a model estimates the ratio of expectations of a random effect with respect to prior[1] and posterior distributions. This

[1] The distribution is prior to the individual, but not to the data. We follow a frequentist approach, and we estimate the mixing distribution on the whole sample.

coefficient grants a credibility to the history of the policyholder in the assessment of its risk level. Linear credibility predictors can also be obtained from a linear regression derived in the model with random effects (Bühlmann (1967, 1970)). In that case, predictors can often be derived from estimated moments of the random effects, regardless of a parametric specification for the mixing distribution. The links between heterogeneous models and prediction on longitudinal data are presented in Section 14.4, and examples are given for models related to number and cost of claims.

Prediction of risk levels can also be obtained from the "credibility models" used by actuaries. For a long time, they performed experience rating from a weighted average between the global and the individual claim history (see Mowbray (1914), Whitney (1918)). The weight granted to the individual was named a "credibility coefficient", referring to the credibility that could be given to the history of the policyholder. Bailey (1945) and Bühlmann (1967) related experience rating in insurance with Bayesian models.

The story which is told here to obtain predictors is purely exogeneous. However, endogeneous effects do exist in insurance. In Section 14.5, we develop two points connected with indentifiability and predictability. On one hand, it is very difficult to disentangle exogeneous and endogeneous explanations of serial correlation for longitudinal data. Observed contagion on risk variables results from apparent contagion (which reveals unobserved heterogeneity), and from real contagion. If an information allowing to differentiate real contagion effects among individuals is not available, you cannot hope to estimate the two components of observed contagion. On the other hand, predictors depend on observed contagion, but not on its nature.

A major difficulty for statistical inference on heterogeneous models is that their likelihood does not have a closed form in most cases. Nevertheless, Poisson and linear models with heterogeneity can be consistently estimated from residuals computed in the a priori rating model. The method is presented in Section 14.7, and examples are given in Section 14.8 for count data models with constant or time-varying heterogeneity components, one or several equations, and for a cost-number model on events. The key result is the following. A risk premium of a policyholder, computed in the a priori rating model, converges towards the risk level of the related generic individual if the data generating process belongs to the model with random effects. This result holds whatever are the values of the rating factors and of the mixing distribution.

The models estimated in Section 14.8 address the following issues.

- The allowance for the date of claims in the prediction of their frequency.
- The prediction of risks for stratified portfolios (e.g., each stratum is the set of contracts subscribed by a company).
- Suppose that individuals are observed at different levels. Think for instance about the number and cost of claims, numbers of claims of different types, and events which are not claims like offences against the highway safety code. A multi equa-

tion model with a joint distribution for the random effects performs prediction from the history observed on all the equations.

- As an example, a cost-number model on claims leads to a bonus-malus system for the pure premium (the expected loss). The bonus-malus coefficients will depend on the number of claims reported, the frequency premium, and on the relative severity of the claims.

Lastly, empirical results are presented in Section 14.9, which are drawn from the analysis of a French data base of automobile insurance contracts.

14.2 TARIFF STRUCTURES AND EXPERIENCE RATING SCHEMES IN THE INSURANCE INDUSTRY

There is a trend towards deregulation in the insurance industry, but compulsory bonus-malus systems are still in force in Europe (except in Spain, Portugal and United Kingdom). Within this framework, an insurance premium is the product of a basic premium and of a bonus-malus coefficient. The bonus-malus coefficient usually depends on the history of claims at fault. For a given period, this coefficient is derived from a transition table between the preceding coefficient and the number of claims reported during the last period (see Lemaire (1995) for numerous examples).

Let us consider for instance the rules of computation for bonus-malus coefficients in France. A new driver begins with a bonus-malus coefficient equal to one, and this coefficient is equal to 0.95 after one year if no claim at fault is reported. The coefficient is equal to $(1.25)^n$ if n claims at fault are reported during the first year, and is bounded by 3.5. The same rules are applied later to the new coefficient. Besides, there is a lower bound of 0.5 for the coefficient. If the bonus-malus coefficient is equal to 0.95, you have a five percent bonus, whereas a claim at fault entails a twenty five percent malus. In this example, the bonus-malus coefficient is roughly an exponential function of the number of claims at fault, if you forget the other features of the system. In other countries, the average coefficient after a given number of years is usually a convex function of the number of claims.

In situations of complete deregulation, actuaries often compute premiums from models which use rating factors and features of the history as regression components. The French bonus-malus system could more or less be obtained in this way, if you retain the lagged number of claims as a regression component.

The optimal bonus-malus systems described in this paper compute coefficients which are equal to one on average whatever are the rating factors. This fairness property is not fulfilled by bonus-malus systems such as the French one. If the boni and mali do not depend on the frequency of claims, the average bonus-malus coefficient increases with the frequency.

Fairness in the rating structure is made necessary because of the difficulty to maintain cross subsidies between different risk levels in a competitive setting. Hence, risk premiums are usually seen as estimations of expectations of risk variables conditional on an information available to the insurance company. A question is raised about the private or public nature of this information. Insurance companies are not forced by competition to use private information on their policyholders in their rating structure. A compulsory bonus-malus system makes this information partly public, since it provides a summary of the policyholder's behaviour which can be shown to every competitor of the insurance company. An information rent for insurance companies is then more likely to be created in a deregulation setting (see Kunreuther and Pauly (1985)).

Actual bonus-malus systems always have a "crime and punishment" flavour. The events which trigger a malus are usually claims at fault. If a no-fault system is in force as in several states of the United States and in Quebec, claims at fault are often replaced in the experience rating scheme by offences against the highway safety code. You can also think of mixing the history of claims and offences in the rating structure. In the USA, insurers have direct access to records of the Motor Vehicles Division. In states with a tort compensation system (i.e., fault is determined if the accident involves a third party), insurance companies use both types of events in their experience rating schemes. A speeding ticket related to more than fifteen m.p.h. above the speed limit entails the same penalty as an accident at fault, and so does failure to stop at a traffic light, or failure to respect a stop sign. The worst offence consists in overtaking a school bus while its red lights are blinking. It is worth nine points, instead of five for the aforementioned events.

14.3 MODELS WITH HETEROGENEITY: DEFINITIONS AND EXAMPLES OF INTEREST FOR INSURANCE RATING

14.3.1 Definitions

The starting point is a model (subsequently called "basic model") on the observable information. Its likelihood with respect to a dominating measure is parameterized by θ_1, and denoted as $l^0(y_i|\theta_1, x_i)$ for the individual i. Since data are longitudinal, x_i and y_i are sequences of variables. For an insurance rating problem, $y_i = (y_{i1}, \ldots, y_{iT_i})$, where y_{it} $(t = 1, \ldots, T_i)$ is a vector of risk variables. In the same way, x_i is a sequence of vectors of regression components derived from the rating factors. The basic model provides the a priori rating structure. Besides x_i, the vector of observable exogeneous variables, we suppose that there exist hidden variables, relevant for the explanation of y_i. These variables are represented by u_i, a heterogeneity component for i. The likelihood conditional on u_i is denoted as $l^*(y_i|\theta_1, x_i, u_i)$. These distributions, supposed to be the actual ones in the prediction, will be said to belong to a "fixed effects" model, where the individual heterogeneity component is the fixed effect. We suppose that the past is by no means correlated with the future in the basic and in the fixed effects model. The number variables have independent increments, they are independent between different equations, and the costs of claims are independent.

We suppose that there exists u^0 such that

$$l^*(y_i|\theta_1, x_i, u^0) = l^0(y_i|\theta_1, x_i) \forall y_i, \theta_1, x_i. \tag{1}$$

In the heterogeneous model, u_i is the realization of a random variable U_i, the "random effect". Its distribution is defined from a vector θ_2 in a parametric setting. The likelihood is

$$l(y_i|\theta, x_i) = E_{\theta_2}[l^*(y_i|\theta_1, x_i, U_i)]; \quad (\theta = (\theta_1, \theta_2)), \tag{2}$$

where the expectation is taken with respect to U_i. The parameter θ is written as a list for convenience. The U_i are i.i.d., and we write

$$\theta_1 \in \Theta_1 \subset \mathbb{R}^{k_1}; \quad \theta_2 \in \Theta_2 \subset \mathbb{R}^{k_2}; \quad \theta \in \Theta = \Theta_1 \times \Theta_2 \subset \mathbb{R}^k.$$

For all the models considered later, the random effect has a Dirac distribution in u^0 under the assumption $\theta_2 = 0$, or: $\theta_2 = 0 \Leftrightarrow U_i \equiv u^0 \forall i$. From (1) and (2), the last equivalence entails

$$l(y_i|\widetilde{\theta_1}, x_i) = l^0(y_i|\theta_1, x_i) \forall\, y_i, \theta_1, x_i, \quad \text{with } \widetilde{\theta_1} = (\theta_1, 0). \tag{3}$$

Thus, the basic model appears to be embedded in the heterogeneous model that is derived from it.

In the examples considered later, the distributions conditional on the fixed effect belong to the basic model, and we can write:

$$l^*(y_i|\theta_1, x_i, u_i) = l^0(y_i|\theta_1 + g(u_i), x_i); \, l(y_i|\theta, x_i) = E_{\theta_2}[l^0(y_i|\theta_1 + g(U_i), x_i)].$$

Hence, the distributions in the heterogeneous model are mixtures of distributions of the basic model. If a semiparametric approach is retained, the vector θ_2 gives moments constraints on the mixing distribution.

Mixing distributions are usually parameterized by variances and covariances between the random effects. The parameter space Θ_2 is usually a cone, and $\theta_2 = 0$ belongs to its boundary. An important geometrical feature of a heterogeneous model is that the basic model belongs to the boundary of its parameter space.

Hidden exogeneous variables are correlated with the observable ones: for instance, the age of a vehicle is a good proxy for annual mileage. The price of secondhand cars depends more on their age than on their mileage. Thus the less you drive, the more you are financially incited to buy a car secondhand, and to keep it as long as possible. This explains the significant influence of the age of the vehicle on the frequency risk. Now the random effect is given independently of the observable exogeneous variables in equation (2). This apparent contradiction is solved if this random effect is seen as allowing for a residual heterogeneity.

To see this, write a causality relationship as follows:

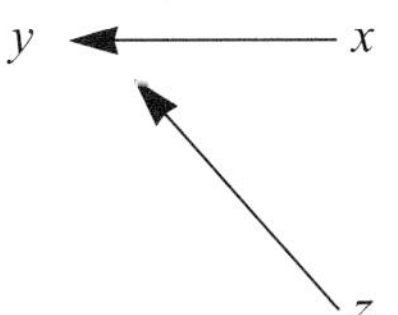

y: risk variables (endogeneous)

x: rating factors (exogeneous, observable)

z: hidden variables (exogeneous)

$$l(y|x) = E[\tilde{l}(y|X, Z)|\, X = x].$$

The likelihood for the heterogeneous model is defined here from a distribution given conditionally on all the exogeneous variables, and from a joint distribution for these variables.

Consider for instance cross section count data, and write

$$\tilde{l}(y|x, z) = P_\lambda(y) = \exp(-\lambda)\frac{\lambda^y}{y!}, \quad \lambda = \exp(x\alpha + z\beta)$$

(x and z are written as line-vectors, α and β are column-vectors). Derive the linear regression of Z with respect to X, i.e.

$$Z = X\alpha + V, E(X'V) = 0; \quad \left(a = [E(X'X)]^{-1} E(X'Z)\right).$$

If the intercept is one of the exogeneous variables, we have $E(V) = 0$, and $Cov(X, V) = E(X'V) - E'(X)E(V) = 0$. Suppose now that X and V are independent. Then the distribution conditional on x of $Z - xa$ is that of V for all x, and we can write

$$l(y|x) = E[\tilde{l}(y|x, xa + V)] = E[l^*(y|\theta_1, x, U)],$$

with

$$l^*(y|\theta_1, x, u) = P_\lambda(y); \quad \lambda = \exp(x\theta_1 + u), \theta_1 = \alpha + a\beta;$$

$$u = v\beta = (z - E(Z|X = x))\beta; \quad V(U) = V(Z\beta) - V(E(Z|X)\beta).$$

As $U = V\beta$ is independent of X, the random effect receives the interpretation given before (see Mundlak (1978) for developments on linear models for panel data). A distribution in the heterogeneous—or random effects—model is that of a generic individual. It is defined conditionally on the observable exogeneous variables, and its likelihood is derived as an average with respect to hidden variables.

14.3.2 Examples of Heterogeneous Models

We give examples for heterogeneous models which can be used to perform experience rating. They are derived from a priori rating models for which we recall some basic features.

14.3.2.1 Single Equation Models for Number of Events

We distinguish two cases.

Time-independent Heterogeneity Component. Start from a Poisson model

$$N_{it} \sim P(\lambda_{it})_{i=1,\ldots,p;t=1,\ldots,T_i}, \quad (\lambda_{it} = \exp(x_{it}\theta_1)),$$

where n_{it} is the number of events observed for the individual i in period t (add a duration d_{it} if the durations are not equal). The regression components are usually indicators of levels. Each level can be either related to a rating factor (e.g., a given value for the occupation of the policyholder, a given interval for his age, etc.), or to a class of a partition of the portfolio. In this case, partitions are obtained from successive dichotomies induced by the rating factors (i.e., a given value for the occupation vs. the other values, younger than a given threshold vs. older than this threshold, etc.). This is a segmentation approach, very popular in the marketing world, and also used in the insurance industry. Of course, these two methods ("scores" and segmentations) can be mixed.

The frequency premium (an estimation of the expectation of N_{it}) is equal to $\hat{\lambda}_{it} = d_{it}\exp(x_{it}\widehat{\theta}_1)$. The maximum likelihood estimator of θ_1 in the Poisson model is the solution to the equation

$$\sum_{i,t}(n_{it} - \hat{\lambda}_{it})x_{it} = 0,$$

which is an orthogonality relationship between the regression components and number-residuals. The preceding equation means that the sum of the frequency premiums is equal to the total number of claims for every subsample associated to a given level. This is a fairness property of the rating structure.

As for references on Poisson models, let us quote

- Boyer, Dionne and Vanasse (1992) for empirical examples, and comparisons with competing models (linear, logit, probit, multinomial logit, and negative binomial).
- Cameron and Trivedi (1998) for a thorough survey of the literature.

Let us define now fixed and random effects models. Denote the distributions in the fixed effects model as

$$N_{it} \sim P(\lambda_{it} w_i)_{i=1,\ldots,p;t=1,\ldots,T_i}.$$

The heterogeneity component u_i is equal either to w_i, or to $\log(w_i)$. It depends on the type of distribution retained for u_i. For the heterogeneous model, the distribution of the random effect is parameterized by the variance. The greater is the variance, the greater will be the weight given to the history of the policyholder in the prediction. Let us quote for instance

- Gamma distributions for the W_i, with an expectation equal to one. Here, we write $U_i = W_i$ (hence $u^0 = 1$ in equation (1)). The distributions of the N_{it} in the heterogeneous model are negative binomial. This model is the most popular in actuarial literature since the likelihood is analytically tractable, and since the bonus-malus coefficients are explicit and easily interpretable with respect to the credibility granted to the history of the policyholder.
- Log-normal distributions for the W_i. With $U_i = \log(W_i)$, we can write $\lambda_{it} W_i = \exp(x_{it}\theta_1 + U_i))$, hence $u^0 = 0$ in equation (1). The likelihood of the heterogeneous model is not analytically tractable, and bonus-malus coefficients are not explicit. But the advantage is that elaborate formulations of time-dependence for the heterogeneity component can be considered as generalizations. Besides, the Gaussian distribution is naturally extended to the multivariate case, leading to heterogeneous models with several equations.

Time-dependent Heterogeneity Component. It is natural to retain this kind of specification since hidden and relevant exogeneous variables may vary with time, as do the observable ones. If you think of the behaviour of the policyholder, you might consider either shocks induced by events like a divorce, a lay-off, or continuous modifications due to alcohol addiction, for instance. The two following specifications would suit respectively these two situations.[2]

Using the preceding fixed effects model (w_i is replaced by w_{it}), we can retain for instance

[2] Notice that the exogeneous specification retained here could be used to predict data governed also by endogeneous causes, like incentive effects due to the experience rating scheme. We come back to this point in Section 14.5.

- $U_{it} = W_{it} = R_i S_{it}$. The two families of random effects R_i and S_{it} are i.i.d. and independent from one another. In this model, the autocorrelation function between the random effects is constant, and the individual white noise process $(S_{it})_{t=1,\ldots,T_i}$ is related to shocks in the distributions of generic individuals. The specification retained here for the random effects is semiparametric, and moments of these random effects will be estimated in Section 14.8.1 regardless of a parametric specification.
- $U_{it} = \log(W_{it})$. The distribution of U_{it} is that of U_t, where $(U_t)_{t\geq 1}$ follows a stationary Gaussian process. A time-dependent autocorrelation function for the random effects entails an allowance for the age of events in the prediction of their frequency. In this setting, actuarial literature provides prediction formulas through credibility models with geometric weights (see Gerber and Jones (1975), Sundt (1981)). Estimators will be given in Section 14.8.2.

The first model quoted here follows the same approach as the negative binomial model with random effects (Hausman et al. (1984)). The latter is obtained from distributions with fixed effects, defined as follows. Write

$$N_{it} \sim P(\widetilde{\lambda}_{it}), \text{ with: } \widetilde{\lambda}_{it} \sim \gamma(\mu_{it}, \delta_i); \quad \mu_{it} = \exp(x_{it}\beta).$$

Here, the regression components are included in the shape parameter of the gamma distribution (and not in the scale parameter, as in the usual formulation of a Poisson model with gamma random effects). One can write

$$\widetilde{\lambda}_{it} = \frac{G_{it}}{\delta_i}, G_{it} \sim \gamma(\mu_{it}); \quad E(N_{it}) = E(\widetilde{\lambda}_{it}) = \frac{\mu_{it}}{\delta_i}.$$

In the negative binomial model with random effects, δ_i is the realization of Δ_i, with

$$\Delta_i = \frac{A_i}{B_i}, A_i \sim \gamma(a); \quad B_i \sim \gamma(b).$$

The $(A_i, B_i, G_{it})_{\substack{i=1,\ldots,p \\ t=1,\ldots,T_i}}$ are supposed to be independent. This model can be seen as a Poisson model with dynamic random effects, because the random effect λ^*_{it} can be written in the following way:

$$\lambda^*_{it} = \frac{G_{it}}{\Delta_i}; \quad \frac{\Delta_i}{1+\Delta_i} \sim \beta_1(a,b); \quad E(\lambda^*_{it}) = E(N_{it}) = \frac{b\mu_{it}}{a-1};$$

$$\lambda^*_{it} = E(\lambda^*_{it}) R_i S_{it}; \quad R_i = \frac{1/\Delta_i}{E(1/\Delta_i)}; \quad S_{it} = \frac{G_{it}}{E(G_{it})};$$

$$E(R_i) = E(S_{it}) = 1 \forall i, t; \quad V(R_i) = \frac{a+b-1}{b(a-2)}; \quad V(S_{it}) = \frac{1}{\mu_{it}} = \frac{b}{(a-1)E(N_{it})}.$$

The time-independent random effect R_i has a finite variance if $a > 2$. The likelihood is analytically tractable (see Hausman et al. (1984)).

Let us investigate the consequences of distribution mixing by the heterogeneous model. Starting from the fixed effects model $N_{it} \sim P(\lambda_{it}u_{it})$, the equidispersion equation is $V(N_{it}) = E(N_{it})$.

Usual formulas for total variance and covariance are

$$\begin{aligned} &V(N) = E_U[V(N|u)] + V_U[E(N|u)]; \\ &Cov(N_1, N_2) = E_U[Cov(N_1, N_2|u)] + Cov_U(E(N_1|u), E(N_2|u)). \end{aligned} \tag{4}$$

Here, the conditional and the unconditional expectations are taken respectively in the fixed and random effects models. Besides, E_U, V_U and Cov_U refer to expectations taken with respect to U, which replaces u in the conditional moments. For the Poisson model with random effects, we have

$$V(N_{it}) = E[\lambda_{it}U_{it}] + V[\lambda_{it}U_{it}] \Rightarrow V(N_{it}) - E(N_{it}) = \lambda_{it}^2 V(U_{it}).$$

Mixing Poisson distributions entails overdispersion. Consider the case where the heterogeneity component is constant, and where the mixing distribution is parameterized by the variance. Local overdispersion can be proved for every random effects model of this sort from the local expansion

$$E_{\theta+d\theta}(S_\theta) = I(\theta)d\theta + o(d\theta),$$

which expresses the Fisher information matrix as the Jacobian of the expectation of the score (Pinquet (1996)).

Besides, $Cov(N_{it}, N_{it'}) = \lambda_{it}\lambda_{it'}Cov(U_{it}, U_{it'})$ in the heterogeneous model. Mixing distributions entails serial correlation.

The Information Matrix statistic (White (1982)) allows to question whether the individual random effects are identically distributed. Denote the score and Hessian in the basic model as $S^0_{\theta_1,x_i}$ and $H^0_{\theta_1,x_i}$ for the individual i. The Information Matrix statistic for cross section count data is equal to

$$IM = \sum_i \left[S^0_{\theta_1,x_i}(S^0_{\theta_1,x_i})' + H^0_{\theta_1,x_i} \right]_{\theta_1=\hat{\theta}^0_1} = \sum_i \left[(n_i - \widehat{\lambda}_i)^2 - \widehat{\lambda}_i \right] x_i' x_i.$$

It gives information on the links between overdispersion of residuals and the distribution of the exogeneous variables.

14.3.2.2 Multi Equation Models for Number of Events

A multi equation model deals with several types of claims, or other events like offences against the highway safety code. Suppose that we have q equations. There is a scalar and time-independent heterogeneity component for each equation. The distributions in the fixed effects model are $N_{it}^j \sim P(\lambda_{it}^j w_{ij})$; $\lambda_{it}^j w_{ij} = \exp(x_{it}^j \theta_{1j} + u_{ij})$; $i = 1, \ldots, p$; $j = 1, \ldots, q$; $t = 1, \ldots, T_i$. Besides $(\theta_{1j})_{j=1,\ldots,q}$, the $V_{jl} (1 \leq l \leq j \leq q)$, variances and covariances of the random effects are the parameters for the heterogeneous model.

The number variables are supposed to be independent in the model with fixed effects. This implies that the different types of events do not overlap, an assumption which may lead to redefine them. As an example, let us describe the model given by Johnson and Kotz (1969). Write N_E the number of events of type E, and consider two events A and B which can occur at the same time. We have

$$N_A = N_{A \cap B} + N_{A-B}; \quad N_B = N_{A \cap B} + N_{B-A},$$

and the variables $N_{A \cap B}$, N_{A-B} and N_{B-A} can be supposed independent since the three events do not overlap. Suppose that A and B represent claims involving two different guarantees. The prediction of the three fixed effects would make it possible to design a bonus-malus system on both guarantees.

Multi equation models can be used to allow for the severity of claims involving third party liability, from the dichotomy between claims with or without bodily injury (see Picard (1976)).

14.3.2.3 Models for Cost of Events

The distributions families investigated here (gamma, and log-normal) are indexed by two parameters: a shape parameter, and a scale parameter, which is a function of the rating factors. The fixed and random effects are also included in the scale for property damages parameter. Usually, the log-normal distributions provide a better fit to costs of claims for property damages than gamma distributions (see Cummins et al. (1990) for a survey of distribution families on costs).

Let c_{itj} be the cost of the jth claim reported by the policyholder i in period t ($1 \leq j \leq n_{it}$, if $n_{it} \geq 1$). We suppose here that the costs are positive.

Gamma Distributions. The cost distributions in the a priori rating model are written in the following way

$$C_{itj} \sim \gamma(d, b_{it}), b_{it} = \exp(z_{it}\beta),$$

or $b_{it}C_{itj} \sim \gamma(d)$. The coefficient b_{it} is the scale parameter, a multiplicative function of the regression components, that are represented by the line-vector z_{it}. Let $\hat{c}_{it} = \hat{d}/\hat{b}_{it} = \hat{d}/\exp(z_{it}\hat{\beta})$ be the estimation of the expected cost for each claim reported by the policyholder i in period t. If we suppose that the costs are independent, the maximum likelihood estimator of β is the solution of the following equation:

$$\sum_{i,t}\left(\sum_{j=1}^{n_{it}} 1-(c_{itj}/\hat{c}_{it})\right) z_{it} = \sum_{i,t} cres_{it} z_{it} = 0.$$

The cost-residual $cres_{it}$ estimates the relative severity of the claims reported by the policyholder i in period t. The likelihood equation for β can be interpreted as an orthogonality relationship between the regression components and cost-residuals.

The distributions conditional on the fixed effect u_{ci} are

$$C_{itj} \sim \gamma(d, b_{it} u_{ci}),$$

with $U_{ci} \sim \gamma(\delta, \delta)$ in the heterogeneous model. Hence, $C_{itj} = D_{itj}/(b_{it} U_{ci})$, where the two variables D_{itj} and U_{ci} follow gamma distributions and are independent. The variable C_{itj} follows a GB2 distribution (see Cummins et al. (1990)).

Log-normal Distributions. The other distribution family investigated in this paper is the normal distribution family for the logarithms of costs

$$\log C_{itj} \sim N(z_{it}\beta, \sigma^2) \Leftrightarrow \log C_{itj} = z_{it}\beta + \varepsilon_{itj}, \varepsilon_{itj} \sim N(0, \sigma^2).$$

The heterogeneous model derived from the log-normal distributions on the basic model is

$$\log C_{itj} = z_{it}\beta + \varepsilon_{itj} + U_i; \quad U_i \sim N(0, \sigma_U^2),$$

where ε_{itj} and the random effect U_i are independent.

14.3.2.4 Model for Number and Cost of Events

Here, a joint distribution must be specified for the random effects included in the number and cost equations. If the random effects are independent, the bonus-malus coefficient for the pure premium is equal to the product of the coefficients related to frequency and expected cost per claim. But one may think that the behaviour of the policyholder influences the two random effects in a similar way and that the correlation is positive.

We will estimate the following model.

- The distributions conditional on u_{ni} and u_{ci}, the heterogeneity components for number and cost distributions of the policyholder i, are respectively derived from Poisson and linear models. Write

$$N_{it} \sim P(\lambda_{it} \exp(u_{ni})); \quad \log C_{itj} = z_{it}\beta + \varepsilon_{itj} + u_{ci}, \quad \text{with}$$

$$\lambda_{it} = \exp(w_{it}\alpha), \varepsilon_{itj} \sim N(0, \sigma^2), t = 1, \ldots, T_i; \quad j = 1, \ldots, n_{it}.$$

- In the heterogeneous model, U_{ni} and U_{ci} follow a bivariate normal distribution with a null expectation and a variance matrix equal to

$$V = \begin{pmatrix} V_{nn} & V_{nc} \\ V_{cn} & V_{cc} \end{pmatrix}.$$

The parameters are

$$\theta_1 = \begin{pmatrix} \alpha \\ \beta \\ \sigma^2 \end{pmatrix}; \quad \theta_2 = \begin{pmatrix} V_{nn} \\ V_{cn} \\ V_{cc} \end{pmatrix}.$$

Here, Θ_2 is the cone of positive semidefinite matrices, embedded in the space of symmetric matrices with a dimension 2, which is identified to $\mathbb{R}^3$. Specifications with dynamic random effects are given by Gouriéroux (1999).

14.4 HETEROGENEOUS MODELS AND PREDICTION ON LONGITUDINAL DATA THROUGH A REVELATION PRINCIPLE

14.4.1 Prediction through Expectation with Respect to a Posterior Distribution

Let us suppose an individual observed on T periods: $\mathcal{Y}_T = (y_1, \ldots, y_T)$ is the sequence of risk variables, and $\mathcal{X}_T = (x_1, \ldots, x_T)$ that of the regression components. The sequences $\mathcal{X}_T$ and $\mathcal{Y}_T$ replace x_i and y_i in the preceding sections. The date of forecast T must be given here, and the individual index can be suppressed, since the policyholder can be considered separately in the prediction. Besides, belonging to the working sample is not mandatory for this policyholder.

We want to predict a risk for the period $T + 1$, by means of a heterogeneous model. For the period t, this risk R_t is the expectation of a function of Y_t (y_t is the realization of Y_t).

We now include a heterogeneity component u_t. The distribution of Y_t in the model with fixed effects depends on θ_1, x_t and u_t. This applies to R_t, and we can write $R_t = h_{\theta_1}(x_t)\, g(u_t)$, for the three types of risk dealt with later (frequency of claims, expected cost per claim, pure premium), with g a real-valued function.

A predictor for the risk in period $T + 1$ can be written as $h_{\theta_1}(x_{T+1})\hat{g}^T(u_{T+1})$, with $\hat{g}^T(u_{T+1})$ a predictor of $g(u_{T+1})$ defined from

$$\hat{g}^T(u_{T+1}) = E_\theta[g(U_{T+1})|\mathcal{X}_T, \mathcal{Y}_T] = \frac{E_{\theta_2}\left[g(U_{T+1})\prod_{t=1}^{T} l^*(y_t|\theta_1, x_t, U_t)\right]}{E_{\theta_2}\left[\prod_{t=1}^{T} l^*(y_t|\theta_1, x_t, U_t)\right]}$$

$$= \arg\min_a E_{\theta_2}\left[(g(U_{T+1}) - a)^2 \prod_{t=1}^{T} l^*(y_t|\theta_1, x_t, U_t)\right].$$

Here, we assumed serial independence for the Y_t in the fixed effects model (observed contagion is supposed to be only apparent). For convenience, we denoted the likelihood for each period as for the whole sequence of periods. The expectations are taken with respect to the random effect. If we replace θ_1 and θ_2 by their estimations in the heterogeneous model, we obtain the a posteriori premium

$$\hat{R}^T_{T+1} = h_{\hat{\theta}_1}(x_{T+1})\hat{g}^T(u_{T+1}) = h_{\hat{\theta}_1}(x_{T+1})E_{\hat{\theta}}[g(U_{T+1})|\mathcal{X}_T, \mathcal{Y}_T],$$

computed for the period $T + 1$. It can be written as

$$(h_{\hat{\theta}_1}(x_{T+1})E_{\hat{\theta}_2}[g(U_{T+1})]) \times \frac{E_{\hat{\theta}}[g(U_{T+1})|\, x_1, \ldots, x_T; y_1, \ldots, y_T]}{E_{\hat{\theta}_2}[g(U_{T+1})]}. \tag{5}$$

The first term is an a priori premium, based on the rating factors of the current period. The second one is a bonus-malus coefficient: it estimates the ratio of two expectations of the same variable, computed for prior and posterior distributions. Owing to the equality: $E_\theta[E_\theta(g(U_{T+1})|\mathcal{X}_T, \mathcal{Y}_T)] = E_\theta[g(U_{T+1})] = E_{\theta_2}[g(U_{T+1})]$, the premiums obey to a fairness principle.

This method of prediction is usually referred to as "Bayesian", since it rests on distribution mixing. However, two interpretations can be given for mixtures.

- Distribution mixing can be derived from a prior knowledge of data. You could think of a statement like "young boys are more risky drivers than young girls" for automobile insurance. This knowledge is represented by a prior distribution on the parameters of a statistical model. Once data are observed, a posterior likelihood on the parameters can be computed. This "likelihoodist" approach (Jeffreys (1939)) is not very relevant for automobile rating. The numerous regression components make it difficult to translate a prior knowledge in terms of distributions for parameters.
- Here, distribution mixing expresses an unobserved heterogeneity, and means a lack of knowledge on the data. The mixing distribution is not given *ex ante*, but is estimated from the data.

14.4.2 Linear Credibility Predictors

A popular approach to experience rating in actuarial literature is the computation of predictors as linear functions of risk variables, usually number of claims (Bühlmann (1967, 1970)). The predictor of the fixed effect is obtained from a linear regression in the model with random effects, whereas it could be any function of $x_1, \ldots, x_T$, $y_1, \ldots, y_T$ in the preceding section. Whereas the expected value principle forces the mixing distribution to belong to a given parametric family, the linear credibility approach constrains the shape of the predictor.

In many situations, linear credibility predictors are obtained from moments of the mixing distribution, regardless of a parametric specification for this distribution (see Section 14.9.1 for empirical results).

14.4.3 Examples of Prediction Through Heterogeneous Models

We give here examples of predictors which are derived from the models presented in Section 14.3.2.

14.4.3.1 The Negative Binomial Model for Number of Claims

We drop the individual index, and write $N_t \sim P(\lambda_t w)$, with $W \sim \gamma(a, a)$ and $U = W$ in the heterogeneous model. With the notations of the preceding section, we have $R_t = E(N_t) = \lambda_t u$; $\lambda_t = \exp(x_t\theta_1)$; $V(U) = \sigma^2 = \theta_2 = 1/a$. Since $E_{\theta_2}(U) = 1$ for every θ_2, the bonus-malus coefficient derived from (5) is equal to

$$E_{\hat{\theta}}[U|\mathcal{X}_T, \mathcal{Y}_T] = \frac{\hat{a} + \sum_{t=1}^{T} n_t}{\hat{a} + \sum_{t=1}^{T} \widehat{\lambda_t}} = \frac{1 + \left(\widehat{\sigma^2} \sum_{t=1}^{T} n_t\right)}{1 + \left(\widehat{\sigma^2} \sum_{t=1}^{T} \widehat{\lambda_t}\right)} \tag{6}$$

(see Dionne and Vanasse (1989, 1992)).

14.4.3.2 Linear Credibility Prediction in a Single Equation Model

The last expression is also obtained with a linear credibility approach. The bonus-malus coefficient is equal to $1 + \hat{c}\sum_{t=1}^{T}(n_t - \widehat{\lambda_t})$, where $\hat{c}$ is obtained from the linear regression

$$\hat{c} = \arg\min_c \hat{V}\left[\frac{U}{E(U)} - c\left(\sum_{t=1}^{T} N_t\right)\right] = \frac{\widehat{\sigma^2}}{1 + \left(\widehat{\sigma^2} \sum_{t=1}^{T} \widehat{\lambda_t}\right)}.$$

The estimated variance is computed in the model with random effects. The results proved in Section 14.7 show that the predictor is obtained without any specification of the mixing distribution (only the first and second moments of the random effects are supposed to exist). The bonus-malus coefficient is the one obtained in equation (6). The frequency premiums $\widehat{\lambda_t}$ are computed in the Poisson model without fixed or random effects, and $\widehat{\sigma^2}$ (given in equation (12)) is a consistent estimator of $CV^2(U) = V(U)/E^2(U)$.

14.4.3.3 *The GB2 Model for Cost of Claims*

We derive here bonus-malus coefficients for expected cost per claim, with the expected value principle. Performing this only through the heterogeneous model on cost distributions supposes that the random effects in the equations for number and cost of claims are independent.

The bonus-malus coefficients depend on the relative severity of the claims, which is assessed by cost-residuals. A cost-residual relates the cost of a claim to an estimation of its expectation.

We use the first heterogeneous model defined in Section 14.3.2.3. Here, $R_t = E(C_{tj}) = d/(b_t u)$; $g(u) = 1/u$. Given the history of the policyholder, the posterior distribution of U is a $\gamma(\delta + d(\Sigma_t n_t), \delta + \Sigma_{t,j} b_t c_{tj})$, and:

$$\widehat{1/u}^{T+1} = E_\theta\left[\frac{1}{U}|X_T, \mathcal{Y}_T\right] = \frac{\delta + \sum_{t,j} b_t c_{tj}}{\delta - 1 + d\left(\sum_t n_t\right)}.$$

We have $E_{\theta_2}(1/U) = \delta/(\delta - 1)$ (we suppose $\delta > 1$, a necessary condition for $1/U$ to have a finite expectation). Omit the period index, denote the number of claims reported by the policyholder during the first T periods as tn_T, and write $\eta = (\delta - 1)/d$. Then the bonus-malus coefficient is:

$$\frac{E_{\hat\theta}\left[\frac{1}{U}|X_T, \mathcal{Y}_T\right]}{E_{\hat\theta_2}\left[\frac{1}{U}\right]} = \frac{\hat\eta + \sum_{j=1}^{tn_T}(c_j / E_{\hat\theta}(C_j))}{\hat\eta + tn_T}. \tag{7}$$

14.4.3.4 *The Log-normal Model for Cost of Claims*

From the second model described in Section 14.3.2.3, we have $R_t = E(C_{tj}) = \exp(z_t\beta + (\sigma^2/2))$; $g(u) = \exp(u)$. We write $tn_T = \Sigma_{t=1}^{T} n_t$, $lcres_T = \Sigma_{j=1}^{tn_T}(\log c_j - E_{\hat\theta_1}(\log C_j))$ (we omit the period index). Then (see Pinquet (1997a)), the bonus-malus coefficient is

$$\frac{E_{\hat\theta}[\exp(U)|X_T, \mathcal{Y}_T]}{E_{\hat\theta_2}[\exp(U)]} = \exp\left[\frac{lcres_T - (tn_T\,\widehat{\sigma_U^2}/2)}{(\widehat{\sigma^2}/\widehat{\sigma_U^2}) + tn_T}\right],$$

where $lcres_T$ represents the relative severity of the claims reported by the policyholder.

14.4.3.5 *Random Effects vs. Fixed Effects Models*

In this section, we compare predictors to estimators, i.e.,

- Bonus-malus coefficients, which are connected with the prediction of a heterogeneity component.
- Estimators of the heterogeneity component, this one being viewed as a parameter in a fixed effects model.

The comparison is performed on the examples presented in Sections 14.4.3.1 and 14.4.3.3. Let us investigate first a Poisson model with fixed effects, i.e., $N_{it} \sim P(\lambda_{it}u_i)$, $\lambda_{it} = \exp(x_{it}\theta_1)$, where u_i is a parameter. The likelihood equations are

$$\widehat{u_i}^{FE} = \frac{n_i}{\widehat{\lambda}_i^{FE}}; \quad \sum_{i,t}\left(n_{it} - \left(\widehat{u_i}^{FE}\widehat{\lambda_{it}}^{FE}\right)\right)x_{it} = 0,$$

where $\widehat{\lambda_{it}}^{FE} = \exp(x_{it}\widehat{\theta}_1^{FE})$, $\widehat{\lambda}_i^{FE} = \Sigma_t\widehat{\lambda_{it}}^{FE}$. A constraint must be added on the parameters to identify the model. We retain $\bar{u} = 1/p\Sigma_{i=1}^{p}u_i = 1$, since the mean of the random effect is equal to one in the negative binomial model. Notice that $\widehat{u_i}^{FE}$ can be seen as an individual "loss to premium" ratio, if losses are measured by the number of claims. Denote the bonus-malus coefficient as $\widehat{u_i}^{RE}$ (FE and RE stand respectively for Fixed Effects and Random Effects). From equation (6), we write

$$\widehat{u_i}^{RE} = \frac{\hat{a}+n_i}{\hat{a}+\widehat{\lambda}_i^{RE}} \simeq (1-\alpha_i)\underbrace{E(U_i)}_{=1} + \alpha_i\widehat{u_i}^{FE}; \quad \alpha_i = \frac{\widehat{\lambda}_i^{RE}}{\hat{a}+\widehat{\lambda}_i^{RE}} = \frac{\widehat{\lambda}_i^{RE}\widehat{\sigma^2}}{1+\widehat{\lambda}_i^{RE}\widehat{\sigma^2}},$$

if we suppose that $\widehat{\lambda}_i^{RE} \simeq \widehat{\lambda}_i^{FE}$. They have indeed the same limit (see Hausman (1978, 1984) for a test of random effects vs. fixed effects in linear and Poisson models).

In the weighted average which defines the bonus-malus coefficient, α_i can be seen as the credibility granted to the history of the policyholder, since it is applied to "the loss to premium" ratio which summarizes this history. In empirical studies, a is close to 1.5. If $\widehat{\lambda_{it}}$ is equal to 0.1, α_i increases by 6% per annum at the beginning.

Let us interpret the French bonus-malus coefficients as credibility predictors. Suppose that the frequency premium of the new driver is equal to 0.1. If we express the bonus-malus coefficients as weighted averages of the preceding type, we obtain

$$0.95 = (1-\alpha_1) + (\alpha_1 \times 0); \quad \alpha_1 = 5\%;$$
$$1.25 = (1-\alpha_2) + (\alpha_2 \times (1/0.1)); \quad \alpha_2 \simeq 2.8\%$$

for a beginner who reported, either no claim, or one claim at fault during the first year. The bonus-malus coefficients are weighted averages between one, the coefficient applied to beginners, and $n/\hat{E}(N)$, which summarizes the history of the policyholder. In the prediction, the credibility granted to the history is measured by α_1 and α_2.

The GB2 model defined in Section 14.3.2.3 for cost of claims can be interpreted in the same way. The model with fixed effects is $C_{itj} \sim \gamma(d, b_{it}u_i)$, and the estimator of u_i is such that (we drop the time index)

$$\frac{1}{\widehat{u}_i^{FE}} = \frac{\sum_{j=1}^{ni} c_{ij} / \widehat{c_{ij}}^{FE}}{n_i}.$$

If we suppose that $\bar{u} = 1$, and that $\hat{d}^{FE}/\widehat{b_{ij}}^{FE} = \widehat{c_{ij}}^{FE} \simeq \widehat{c_{ij}}^{RE}$, we obtain from equation (7):

$$\widehat{1/u_i}^{RE} = \frac{\hat{\eta} + \sum_{j=1}^{ni} \left(c_{ij} / \widehat{c_{ij}}^{RE}\right)}{\hat{\eta} + n_i} \simeq (1-\alpha_i) + \alpha_i \frac{1}{\widehat{u}_i^{FE}},$$

where $\alpha_i = n_i/(\hat{\eta} + n_i)$ is the credibility granted to the history of the policyholder.

14.4.4 James-Stein Predictors

Credibility predictors are also found in classical statistical literature, and referred to as “James-Stein estimators”. Stein (1956) proves that a random vector following a multivariate normal distribution is not admissible, if seen as an estimator of its mean.[3] Shrinking this vector allows to obtain an other estimator which beats the preceding one everywhere in the parameter space, in terms of mean squared error.

Efron and Morris (1977) provide James-Stein predictors for the batting averages of 18 major-league baseball players as they were recorded after their first 45 times at bat in the 1970 season. This batting average is denoted as y, and is defined as the number of hits divided by the number of times at bat. If $\bar{y}$ is the grand batting average ($\bar{y} = 0.265$), the James-Stein predictor of the batting average of the player number i for the whole season is equal to

$$z_i = \bar{y} + 0.212(y_i - \bar{y}) = (1 - 0.212)\bar{y} + 0.212 y_i.$$

This predictor outperforms y and $\bar{y}$ as predictors of the batting average for the whole season. The coefficient 0.212 can be seen as a shrinkage coefficient or as a credibility granted to the history of the player. As the first 45 times at bat are observed after

[3] This result holds under the assumption that the variances-covariances matrix is known (say, equal to identity) and if the dimension of the vector is greater than two.

one month of competition, the ability of a baseball player is revealed much faster than the risk level of an automobile policyholder.

In this example, the starting point in the prediction is the individual mean. Then an other prediction is obtained from a shrinkage of the individual means around the grand mean. At the opposite, the starting point in actuarial literature is a grand mean, possibly estimated conditionally on rating factors. If distribution mixing is possible from the data, then more heterogeneity is added to the premiums as described in this section.

14.5 HETEROGENEITY, STATE DEPENDENCE AND PREDICTION ON LONGITUDINAL DATA

14.5.1 Real and Observed Contagion for Automobile Insurance Data

Actual bonus-malus systems throughout the world are described in Lemaire (1995). For most of them, a claim reported increases the cost of the malus applied to the next claims. Thus, these systems induce a "hunger for bonus", and have a real incentive effect on policyholders (see Lemaire (1977) for a model of optimal claiming behaviour). If true contagion should be negative, positive contagion is observed for every guarantee in automobile insurance. Policyholders who reported claims in the past will report more in the future than those who did not.

Let us give numerical results on positive observed contagion. Consider a portfolio of policyholders observed during two periods (a period is equal or less than a year). We split the population between those who did not report claims of a given type during the first period, and those who did. We discard the policyholders who reported two or more claims during the first period (the following results are easier to interpret). Since the frequency per period is very inferior to one, these policyholders are much less numerous that those who reported one claim. For the population which reported i claim (i = 0, 1), denote as f_i (resp. $\hat{f}_i$) the average frequency (resp. estimated frequency) of claims during the second period. The estimated frequency is derived from the estimation of a Poisson model on the whole population. What is always observed is that f_1/f_0 and $(f_1/\hat{f}_1)/(f_0/\hat{f}_0)$ are greater than one. For claims involving third party liabilityor property damage, f_1/f_0 is usually close to 1.5 or 1.6, whereas $\hat{f}_1/\hat{f}_0$ is close to 1.1. But the ratio f_1/f_0 can be superior to 1.8 for a guarantee such as car theft.

The two results quoted here (the suspected negative contagion, and the observed positive contagion) raise identifiability issues. We discuss them in the following section.

14.5.2 Identifiability of the Nature of Observed Contagion

This indentifiability issue is also referred to as an opposition "heterogeneity vs. true state dependence" (Heckman and Borjas (1980)). It has been addressed for a long time by statistical literature for count data models. While commenting a paper written by Neyman (1939), Feller (1943) quotes the opposite interpretations of the negative binomial distributions in terms of heterogeneity (Greenwood and Yule (1920)), and in terms of state dependence (Pólya and Eggenberger (1923)). Feller concludes to the impossibility of identifying the nature of the distributions.

Let us go back to the example of the preceding section. Suppose for instance that you have $f_1/f_0 = 1.54$; $\hat{f}_1/\hat{f}_0 = 1.1$. Thus a claim reported in the first period entails a forty percent malus for the frequency, which is obtained beyond the a priori rating structure. If real contagion is negative, this means that the ratio of the fixed effects between the two classes (the policyholders who reported one or no claim during the first period) is greater than 1.4. Observed contagion results from real and apparent contagion. You cannot hope to estimate the two components of observed contagion from the data if you do not have an information allowing to differentiate the endogeneous effects on the sample.

A sudden modification of the experience rating scheme is an example of such an information. In Quebec for instance, the public monopoly which provides automobile insurance coverage for bodily injury liability decided to introduce experience rating in 1992. Before this date, the rating structure was without memory, and the history of recent offences against the highway safety code was then introduced. The frequency of claims decreased by twenty percent since (Dionne and Vanasse (1997)). You could explain this result by an incentive effect of the experience rating scheme. Now the frequencies are not observed at the same time, so you might also relate this modification to a structural change of the frequency. In the same way, a reduction of observed contagion after 1992 could be explained by the negative contagion due to the experience rating scheme, if you supposed that apparent contagion did not vary throughout time.

Such situations where a test group is compared to a control group are usually referred to as experiments. If the comparison between the two groups cannot be blurred by any cause (such as the generation effect in the preceding example, or a selection bias), you obtain a controlled experiment. Otherwise, you have a natural experiment. These frameworks are necessary to obtain results in terms of identification. Endogeneous effects which could not be differentiated on the individuals (like the modifications of risk perception due to the history of accidents) cannot be estimated from the data.

As a conclusion, the identification of the nature of observed contagion can be obtained at best partially, and under conditions which are not often fulfilled in practice.

14.5.3 Identifiability and Predictability: The Pólya Process Applied to Generic or Real Individuals

We show on an example that prediction on longitudinal data does not depend on the nature of observed contagion. We compare in this section the predictors derived from exogeneous and endogeneous interpretations of the same process.

Let $(N_t)_{t\geq 0}$ be a Markov process with integer values. We restrict to "pure birth" processes, which means that the only transition intensities different from 0 are those from n to $n + 1$ ($n \in \mathbb{N}$). Denote this transition intensity at the time t as $\lambda_n(t)$. The process shows true contagion if the transition intensities depend on n. If number of claims are dealt with, the transition intensity can be seen as an instantaneous frequency risk. It is natural then to start from

$$\lambda_n(t) = \lambda(t)\frac{a+n}{a+\Lambda(t)}, \quad \Lambda(t) = \int_0^t \lambda(u)du, \tag{8}$$

a formulation similar to the prediction derived from the negative binomial model (Section 14.4.3.1).

Now, the Markov process $(N_t)_{t\geq 0}$ derived from $N_0 \equiv 0$ and from the preceding values of $\lambda_n(t)$ is a Pólya process (see Lundberg (1940), Feller (1957)). If we write the negative binomial distributions as mixtures of Poisson distributions, i.e., $NB(\lambda, a) = \int_0^{+\infty} P_{\lambda u} dR(u)$, $R = \gamma(a, a)$, we obtain $N_t \sim NB(\Lambda(t), a)$.

On the other hand, a Pólya process can be seen as a mixture of Poisson processes. Let $\mathbb{P}_\lambda$ be a Poisson process, i.e., a pure birth Markov process on $\mathbb{N}^{\mathbb{R}^+}$ starting from 0 at $t = 0$, with $\lambda_n(t) = \lambda(t)\ \forall n \in \mathbb{N}, \forall t \geq 0$. Write $\mathbb{P}ol_{\lambda,a} = \int_0^{+\infty} \mathbb{P}_{\lambda u} dR(u)$, $R = \gamma(a, a)$ a mixture of Poisson processes, with a gamma mixing distribution. Straightforward computations (see Bühlmann (1970) for instance) prove that this mixture is the aforementioned Pólya process.

In this example, the prediction does not depend on the nature of observed contagion. If the Pólya process is applied to generic individuals, the premium derived from Section 14.4.3.1 is equal to the estimated transition intensity given in equation (8) for real individuals. More general formulations easily show that the prediction only depends on observed contagion, and not on the way this observed contagion splits into real and apparent contagion.

The negative binomial distributions provide a good fit to automobile insurance data (see Boyer, Dionne and Vanasse (1992) for empirical results, and Winkelmann (1994) for a survey of goodness-of-fit tests for count data). They are the marginal distributions of the Pólya process, and a pessimistic conclusion is that it is difficult to identify the nature of the contagion.

"Pessimism for identifiability, optimism for predictability" is the opinion of the author, concerning the opposition between heterogeneity and state-dependence for dynamic data. Risk distributions can be related to generic or real individuals, according to the fact that the observed contagion is apparent or real. The example shows the difficulty of answering to a question such as: "does the history of an individual reveal hidden features of its distributions, or does it modify these distributions?".

Actuarial models certainly do not tell the truth on the data, when they consider observed contagion as only apparent. But the truth is out of reach and does not need to be known for prediction.

14.6 ESTIMATION AND TESTS FOR HETEROGENEOUS MODELS: A SURVEY OF THE LITERATURE

Statistical methods which can be used for the estimation of heterogeneous models are recalled in this section. The following section presents a method designed by the author for these models.

Maximum likelihood estimation (m.l.e.) of parametric models is the basic way to describe a data generating process. We recall its convergence properties in a misspecification context.

Let $(P_{\theta_1})_{\theta_1 \in \Theta_1}$ be a parametric family of equivalent probability measures (they have the same negligible Borelians). If μ is a measure equivalent to the $(P_{\theta_1})_{\theta_1 \in \Theta_1}$, and if $l_{\theta_1} = dP_{\theta_1}/d\mu$ is a density, write $\widehat{\theta_1}^0 = \arg\max \Sigma_{i=1}^{p} \log l_{\theta_1}(Y_i)$, where $(Y_i)_{i=1,\ldots,p}$ is an i.i.d. sample of variables, with a distribution equal to Q. The parameter is denoted as θ_1 because later m.l.e. will be performed in the a priori rating model. This model is related to the null hypothesis, hence the superscript 0 for the estimator of θ_1. If Q (the data generating process) does not belong to $(P_{\theta_1})_{\theta_1 \in \Theta_1}$, the model is misspecified. We write $l_Q = dQ/d\mu$ (Q is supposed to be equivalent to the $(P_{\theta_1})_{\theta_1 \in \Theta_1}$), and $EQ(f) = \int f(y)dQ(y) = E[f(Y)]$, if the distribution of Y is Q. In the same way, we write $E_\theta(f) = \int f(y)dP_\theta(y)$. A usual result (Akaike (1973)) is

$$\lim_{p \to +\infty} \widehat{\theta_1}^0 = \arg\max_{\theta_1} E_Q(\log l_{\theta_1}) = \arg\min_{\theta_1} KL(Q/P_{\theta_1}),$$

where $KL(Q/P_{\theta_1}) = E_Q(\log l_Q - \log l_{\theta_1})$ is the Kullback-Leibler criterion, a dissimilarity index between equivalent probability measures. The limit of $\widehat{\theta_1}^0$ is called the pseudo-true value, and is denoted as $\theta_1^*(Q)$.

The probability measure under the arrow refers to the data generating process. The pseudo-true value is the least unfavourable solution with respect to the Kullback-Leibler dissimilarity index.

As an example of pseudo-true value, let $(P_m)_{m \in M}$ be a family of equivalent distributions, parameterized by the expectation. If m is this expectation, suppose that the densities with respect to an equivalent measure μ have a linear exponential structure, i.e.

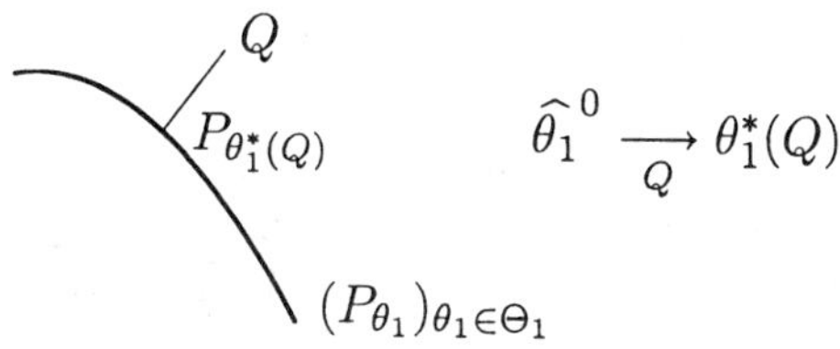

Figure 1 Pseudo-true Value

$$l_m(y) = (dP_m/d\mu)(y) = \exp[A(m) + B(y) + C(m)y].$$

Then (see Gouriéroux, Monfort and Trognon (1984a)), we have

$$m^*(Q) = E_Q(Id) = \int y dQ(y) \tag{9}$$

for any data generating process equivalent to the $(P_m)_{m \in M}$. Setting the expectations equal yields the least unfavourable solution.

Let us take an example with regression components in the distributions. We retain cross section count data, and the data generating process is a mixture of Poisson distributions. The regression components are connected with θ_1, and the variance of the mixing distribution is σ^2. If N is the endogeneous variable, suppose that $E(N|\theta_1, \sigma^2, x) = \exp(x\theta_1)$. The expectation of N does not depend on the variance of the mixing distribution, and the heterogeneous model is said well specified with respect to expectation. This is the case for the negative binomial model. Suppose that a Poisson model with the same regression components is estimated on the data. Poisson distributions have a linear exponential structure. Hence the Poisson distribution with a parameter equal to $m = exp(x\theta_1)$ minimizes the Kullback-Leibler dissimilarity index with the true distribution of N. As this result holds for every value of x, we obtain the limit of $\widehat{\theta_1}^0$, the m.l.e. for the Poisson model

$$\widehat{\theta_1}^0 \xrightarrow[\theta_1, \sigma^2]{} \theta_1^*(\theta_1, \sigma^2) = \theta_1.$$

Hence the m.l.e. on a Poisson model provides consistent estimation for the related parameters of the same model with heterogeneity, if the latter is well specified with respect to expectation. Consistent estimators for other Poisson models with heterogeneity and well specified with respect to expectation can be found in Gouriéroux, Monfort and Trognon (1984b).

Moment-based methods provide estimators in a semiparametric setting. Let $(f_\theta)_{\theta \in \Theta}$ be a parametric family of maps from $\mathbb{R}^m$ to $\mathbb{R}^k$, with $\Theta \subset \mathbb{R}^k$. These maps can also be defined conditionally on regression components and instruments. Let $\mathcal{P}$ be a set of probability measures defined on $\mathbb{R}^m$ (for instance, those which are equivalent to a given measure on $\mathbb{R}^m$). We write

$$\forall \theta \in \Theta: P_\theta = \left\{P \in \mathcal{P} / E_P(f_\theta) = \int f_\theta(y) dP(y) = 0\right\}.$$

Here, P_θ is a family of probability measures defined implicitly. Such a formulation can be retained for mixing distributions specified only by some moments, as it is assumed in the linear credibility approach (see Section 14.2). Suppose that $(Y_i)_{i \in \mathbb{N}^*}$ is a sequence of i.i.d. variables ranging in $\mathbb{R}^m$. The estimator $\hat{\theta}^{GMM}$ derived from the generalized method of moments is defined from

$$\overline{f_{\hat{\theta}^{GMM}}} = \frac{1}{p}\sum_{i=1}^{p} f_{\hat{\theta}^{GMM}}(Y_i) = 0.$$

Under usual identifiability, smoothness and boundedness conditions, the estimator is consistent (Hansen (1982)). This means here that, if the distribution of the $(Y_i)_{i\in\mathbb{N}^*}$ belongs to P_θ (and not equals P_θ as in the parametric setting), then $\hat{\theta}^{GMM}$ converges towards θ if the size of the sample goes to infinity.

Let us apply this result to a Poisson model with heterogeneity, which is well specified with respect to expectation. We have $V(N|\theta_1,\sigma^2, x) = E(N|\theta_1,\sigma^2, x) + \sigma^2E^2(N|\theta_1,\sigma^2, x)$, with $E(N|\theta_1,\sigma^2, x) = \exp(x\theta_1)$. Hence

$$E[f_{\theta,x}(N)] = 0; \quad \theta = \begin{pmatrix}\theta_1\\ \sigma^2\end{pmatrix}; \quad f_{\theta,x}(n) = \begin{pmatrix}(n-\exp(x\theta_1))x'\\ (n-\exp(x\theta_1))^2 - n - \sigma^2[\exp(x\theta)]^2\end{pmatrix}.$$

Let $n_1, \ldots, n_p, x_1, \ldots, x_p$ be a sample of count variables and regression components. The m.l.e. on the Poisson model, $\widehat{\theta_1}^0$, is defined from the orthogonality relation $\Sigma_i(n_i - \widehat{\lambda}_i)x_i' = 0$, $\widehat{\lambda}_i = \exp(x_i\widehat{\theta_1}^0)$. Hence, the GMM estimators for the Poisson model with heterogeneity are

$$\widehat{\theta_1} = \widehat{\theta_1}^0; \quad \widehat{\sigma^2} = \frac{\sum_i\left[(n_i - \widehat{\lambda}_i)^2 - n_i\right]}{\sum_i \widehat{\lambda}_i^2}.$$

Notice that the estimator of σ^2 is not bound to be positive. A positive sign means an overdispersion of residuals.

The methods recalled up to now pertain to exact inference. They use a criterion (likelihood or moment conditions) which has a closed form. Such is not always the case, and we will quote briefly approximate inference methods.

The likelihood of a heterogeneous model is an expectation, which can be approximated if it does not have a closed form. Two types of computation can be investigated.

- Numerical integration of the likelihood. If it is viewed as a parameter, the approximation is a biased and deterministic estimator. See Davis and Rabinowitz (1984) for methods of numerical integration using Gaussian quadrature rules, and Lillard (1993) for empirical results.
- Monte-Carlo methods interpret the likelihood as the expectation of a function of a distribution-free variable. An average derived from independent draws of this variable for each individual leads to a simulation-based estimator. The likelihood is then approximated by a random and unbiased variable. Owing to the concavity of the logarithm, the estimator of the log-likelihood has a negative bias. The asymptotic properties of these estimators are given by Gouriéroux and Monfort

(1991). Consistency is obtained if the number of simulations converges towards infinity with the size of the sample.

We come back to the method of moments. If the expectation of the statistic does not have a closed form, it can be estimated by simulations. If the simulation errors are independent across observations and sufficiently regular with respect to the parameters, the simulation-based estimators can be consistent even if the number of draws are fixed for each individual. Consistency is obtained if a linearity property allows the simulation errors to be averaged out over the sample. A proof of these properties and applications to discrete response models are found in Mac Fadden (1989).

Before estimating the heterogeneous model, the opportunity of mixing the distributions of the basic model, which gives the a priori rating structure, should be tested for. Here, the heterogeneous model contains the basic model at the boundary of the parameter space (see equation (3)). Thus, the heterogeneous model does not necessarily outperform the basic model on a likelihood criterion. Let us denote the m.l.e. for the basic model as $\widehat{\theta_1}^0$. The Lagrangian with respect to θ_2 of the log-likelihood, computed for $\theta_1 = \widehat{\theta_1}^0$; $\theta_2 = 0$, is denoted as $\mathcal{L}$. Since Θ_2 spans $\mathbb{R}^{k_2}$, the space in which it is embedded, the Lagrangian can be defined from the unique extension of a linear form from Θ_2 to $\mathbb{R}^{k_2}$.

The heterogeneous model will outperform the basic model on a likelihood criterion if $\mathcal{L}$ does not belong to Θ_2^-, the negative dual of Θ_2. Under this condition, the data allow distribution mixing from the a priori rating model. Thus, a natural test for the nullity of θ_2 is the score test, or the Lagrange multiplier test (Rao (1948), Aitchison and Silvey (1958, 1959)). As compared with usual competitors such as the likelihood ratio test or the Wald test, its advantages are the following.

- The estimation related to the alternative hypothesis is avoided, a useful property here since the heterogeneous models often do not have a closed form for the likelihood.
- The asymptotic normality of $\mathcal{L}$ is maintained if the null lies at the boundary of the parameter space, which is the case here.
- Due to the local approach used in the score test, one given test can be relevant for a whole class of alternative hypotheses, a result with a semiparametric flavour. Once again, this is the case here, and the test does not depend on the parameterized family retained for the mixing distribution.

The seminal paper on tests for heterogeneity based on the score with respect to the parameters of the mixing distribution was written by Neyman (1959). This paper, published in a Festschrift for Harald Cramér, provided a test which was later referred to as the "$C(\alpha)$ test" (Neyman and Scott (1966)), where C stood for Cramér. More details on this contribution can be found in the biography of Jerzy Neyman written by Constance Reid (1998).

The Lagrangian can be expressed from the first and second derivatives, with respect to the heterogeneity component, of the log-likelihood for the fixed effects model. For instance, if $\theta_2 = \sigma^2$ (the heterogeneity component is scalar and time-independent), we have

$$\mathcal{L} = \frac{1}{2}\sum_i (res_i^2 - s_i);$$

$$res_i = \left(\frac{\partial}{\partial u}\log l^*\left(y_i|\widehat{\theta_1}^0, x_i, u\right)\right)_{u=u^0}; \quad s_i = -\left(\frac{\partial^2}{\partial u^2}\log l^*\left(y_i|\widehat{\theta_1}^0, x_i, u\right)\right)_{u=u^0},$$

with the notations of Section 14.3. The heterogeneous model outperforms the basic model on a likelihood criterion if the Lagrangian is positive, which means an overdispersion of residuals.

Consider the Poisson model with heterogeneity investigated in this section. The score test for nullity of σ^2 at the level α is obtained from the one-sided critical region

$$\frac{\sum_i\left[\left(n_i - \widehat{\lambda}_i\right)^2 - n_i\right]}{\sqrt{2\sum_i \widehat{\lambda}_i^2}} \geq u_{1-\alpha},$$

where u is the quantile of a $N(0, 1)$ distribution (see Cameron and Trivedi (1986), Dean and Lawless (1989)).

14.7 SCORE-BASED INFERENCE FOR LINEAR AND POISSON MODELS WITH HETEROGENEITY

14.7.1 An Informal Presentation

A heterogeneous model, with its—in most cases—analytically intractable likelihood, appears to be very "dark" for inference. On the other hand, the basic model is "enlightened" (its likelihood has a closed form). A digression may explain the method retained by the author.

A short story

A man walks in a dark night. At some moment, he notices an other man, bent to the ground, near a street lamp. He asks him:
"What are you looking for?"
The man near the street lamp (he is insane):
"I am looking for my keys."

The passer-by: "Did you lose them here?"
The insane: "No, I lost them there, in the dark."
The passer-by: "So, why are you looking for them here?"
The insane: "Don't be stupid! Because there is light here, of course!"

The bunch of keys searched by the statistician analysing data through a probabilistic paradigm is the distribution which generated the data. The situation of the insane is actually worse than that of the statistician, because there is little chance that the position of the keys modifies the way in which light is shed by the street lamp. Now, besides the estimation of a parametric model, the statistician can analyse residuals. Residuals are obtained by replacing the parameters by an estimation in any parameterized statistic (Cox and Snell (1968)). They are widely used in misspecification tests, and the most important example is the score test. Now residuals can also be used to perform consistent estimation of some heterogeneous models. Staying where there is light (the basic model), it is possible to locate the keys without venturing in the dark (the heterogeneous model).[4] The statistic used to perform consistent estimation is precisely the score used in the score test.

14.7.2 A More Formal Presentation

Consistent estimators for linear and Poisson models with heterogeneity can be obtained from

- the computation of a pseudo-true value, obtained here as the limit of the m.l.e. on the basic model, whereas the data generating process includes heterogeneity with respect to this model.
- The estimation of some moments of the mixing distribution, from residuals computed in the basic model. The statistic used here is the score with respect to the parameters of the mixing distribution, hence the name of the method. A still more formal presentation is given in Pinquet (1999).

We will present the method from an example. Consider the Poisson model with heterogeneity estimated in Section 14.6. Here, the expectation may depend on the variance of the mixing distribution. If we write $N \sim P(\exp(x\theta_1)u)$ in the fixed effects model, we have

$$E(N) = \exp(x\theta_1)E(U) = \exp(x(\theta_1 + \log[E(U)]e_1)).$$

The intercept is supposed to be the first of k regression components, and e_1 is the first vector of the canonical base of $\mathbb{R}^k$. From Section 14.6, we know that the Poisson dis-

[4] Unfortunately, it is less than probable that the keys of the statistician are in this darkness, since reality is only partially captured by the heterogeneous model.

tribution with a parameter equal to $m = \exp(x(\theta_1 + \log[E(U)]e_1))$ minimizes the Kullback-Leibler dissimilarity index with the mixture of Poisson distributions. As this result holds for every x, it is easily seen that the pseudo-true value is equal to $\theta_1^* = \theta_1 + \log[E(U)]e_1$. It is the limit of $\widehat{\theta}_1^{\,0}$, the m.l.e. on the Poisson model, whereas the data generating process is a mixture of these distributions. We obtain

$$\hat{E}^0(N) = \exp\left(x\widehat{\theta}_1^{\,0}\right) \to \exp(x\theta_1^*) = \exp(x\theta_1)E(U) = E(N). \tag{10}$$

Due to the interpretation given in Section 14.3.1 for a model with random effects, this result can be expressed as follows. The frequency premium of an individual, computed in the a priori rating model, converges towards the frequency risk of the related generic individual if the data generating process belongs to the model with random effects. This property holds whatever is the value of the rating factors and of the mixing distribution.

The variance of N in the model with random effects is

$$V(N) = E(N) + [\exp(x\theta_1)]^2 V(U). \tag{11}$$

From $E(N) = \exp(x\theta_1)E(U)$, we obtain

$$E\left[\frac{(N - E(N))^2 - N}{E^2(N)}\right] = \frac{V(U)}{E^2(U)} = CV^2(U).$$

With the notations of Section 14.6, and with the limit given in equation (10), we will obtain on a sample

$$\widehat{CV^2(U)} = \frac{\sum_i \left(n_i - \widehat{\lambda}_i\right)^2 - n_i}{\sum_i \widehat{\lambda}_i^2} \to CV^2(U). \tag{12}$$

A moment of the mixing distribution is consistently estimated from the m.l.e. on the Poisson model. From equations (10), (11) and (12), we have

$$\widehat{\lambda}_i + \left(\widehat{\lambda}_i^2 \widehat{CV^2(U)}\right) \to V(N_i) \forall i.$$

Thus we obtain a consistent estimation of the variance (computed in the random effects model) of the count variable, an estimation obtained from the m.l.e. on the Poisson model. Such results are useful for the computation of linear credibility predictors (see Section 14.9.1 for an example).

From equation (12), consistent estimators can be obtained for parametric specifications of the mixing distribution. Suppose that the distribution of U is log-normal, i.e. $U = \exp(\sigma T)$, $T \sim N(0, 1)$. Then $CV^2(U) = \exp(\sigma^2) - 1$, and $\widehat{\sigma^2} = \log(1 + \widehat{CV^2(U)})$ is a consistent estimator of σ^2. Predictors of the frequency with the expected value principle and log-normal mixing distributions are convex functions of the number of claims, for a given value of the frequency premium.

For linear and Poisson models with heterogeneity, the preceding example can be generalized as follows. Let $m_0(\theta_1, x)$ be the expectation of risk variables in the a priori rating model, defined conditionally on rating factors and parameters. We denote the expectation of the related generic individual in the model with random effects as $m(\theta, x)$. We write $(\theta = (\theta_1, \theta_2))$, where θ_2 is the vector of parameters for the mixing distribution. We have the following property

$$\exists \theta_1^* : \Theta \rightarrow \Theta_1 / m(\theta, x) = m_0(\theta_1^*(\theta), x) \forall x, \forall \theta.$$

In the preceding example, we had $\theta_1^*(\theta_1, \sigma^2) = \theta_1 + \log[E_{\sigma^2}(U)]e_1$. This property holds for linear and Poisson models with heterogeneity, but not for other linear exponential models with random effects like logit and probit equations.

The pseudo-true value $\theta_1^*(\theta)$ is then the limit of $\widehat{\theta_1}^0$, the m.l.e. on the a priori rating model, if the data generating process belongs to the model with random effects. If Y is the vector of risk variables for which the expectation is estimated, we have

$$\hat{E}^0(Y) = m_0\left(\widehat{\theta_1}^0, x\right) \xrightarrow[\theta]{} m_0(\theta_1^*(\theta), x) = m(\theta, x) = E(Y) \forall x, \forall \theta. \tag{13}$$

As $m_0(\widehat{\theta_1}^0, x)$ is a risk premium computed in the a priori rating model, this limit can be interpreted as we did after equation (10) for the frequency risk.

This property leads to consistent estimation of some moments of the mixing distribution from residuals computed in the a priori rating model. For Poisson models with random effects, linear credibility predictors can be computed from these estimated moments.

Owing to the unconstrained approach with respect to the parameters of the mixing distribution, the estimator $\widehat{\theta_2}$ is not bound to belong to the parameter space Θ_2. This property allows it to be asymptotically normal (and efficient) under the null, although it converges in that case towards 0, which belongs to the boundary of Θ_2. The author thinks that this property is not a drawback. Extremal estimators, obtained from the maximization of an objective function (e.g., an explicit likelihood, or a likelihood approximated numerically or by simulation) will be obtained at the boundary of the parameter space, if the heterogeneous model does not fit the data. In that case, prediction through the whole heterogeneous model is as impossible as with estimators obtained outside the parameter space.[5] With the preceding method, predictors can be

[5] More precisely, an estimation of θ_2 obtained at the boundary of Θ_2 but different from 0 (the vertex of Θ_2) would lead you to a submodel with random effects. The unconstrained approach retained here also indicates clearly which submodel to choose.

computed iff $\widehat{\theta_2}$ belongs to θ_2. This condition is easy to interpret, because it can be expressed in terms of overdispersion, relative overdispersion, positive contagion for residuals, etc. (see the following section). Besides, the probability that $\widehat{\theta_2}$ belongs to Θ_2 can be consistently estimated under the null (see Pinquet (1997b)).

14.8 EXAMPLES OF CONSISTENT ESTIMATORS FOR HETEROGENEOUS MODELS

We give examples for the heterogeneous models quoted in Section 14.3.2. The estimators given here are explicit, consistent, asymptotically normal and asymptotically efficient at the null. Remember that the null hypothesis is connected with the basic model (no unobserved heterogeneity).

14.8.1 Single Equation Model for Number of Events, with a Constant Autocorrelation Function for the Random Effect

The fixed effects model is

$$N_{it} \sim P(\lambda_{it} u_{it}); \quad \lambda_{it} = \exp(x_{it}\theta_1); \quad u_{it} = r_i s_{it}.$$

Besides θ_1, the parameters of the heterogeneous model are $\sigma_r^2 = V(R_i)$ and $\sigma_s^2 = V(S_{it})$. If the expectations of the R_i and S_{it} are equal to one (the model with random effects is well specified with respect to expectation), consistent estimators for σ_r^2 and σ_s^2 are

$$\widehat{\sigma_r^2} = \widehat{\sigma_r^2}^1; \quad \widehat{\sigma_s^2} = \frac{\widehat{\sigma_s^2}^1}{1+\widehat{\sigma_r^2}^1},$$

with

$$\widehat{\sigma_r^2}^1 = \frac{\sum_i \sum_{t \neq t'} (n_{it} - \hat{\lambda}_{it})(n_{it'} - \hat{\lambda}_{it'})}{\sum_i \sum_{t \neq t'} \hat{\lambda}_{it} \hat{\lambda}_{it'}}; \quad \widehat{\sigma_r^2}^1 + \widehat{\sigma_s^2}^1 = \frac{\sum_{i,t} \left[\left(n_{it} - \widehat{\lambda_{it}}^2 \right) - n_{it} \right]}{\sum_{i,t} \widehat{\lambda_{it}}^2}.$$

The estimators $\widehat{\sigma_r^2}^1$ and $\widehat{\sigma_s^2}^1$ are obtained after the score test from a linearization of the score computed for $\theta_1 = \widehat{\theta_1}^0$; $\theta_2 = 0$. They are given here in a semiparametric setting, since they are obtained regardless of a parametric specification for the mixing distribution. Notice that

$$\widehat{\sigma}_r^{\,1}, \widehat{\sigma_r^2} > 0 \Leftrightarrow \sum_i \sum_{t \neq t'} (n_{it} - \hat{\lambda}_{it})(n_{it'} - \hat{\lambda}_{it'}) > 0;$$

$$\widehat{\sigma_s^2}^{1}, \widehat{\sigma_s^2} > 0 \Leftrightarrow \frac{\sum_{i,t}\left[(n_{it} - \hat{\lambda}_{it})^2 - n_{it}\right]}{\sum_{i,t} \hat{\lambda}_{it}^2} > \frac{\sum_i \sum_{t \neq t'} (n_{it} - \hat{\lambda}_{it})(n_{it'} - \hat{\lambda}_{it'})}{\sum_i \sum_{t \neq t'} \hat{\lambda}_{it} \hat{\lambda}_{it'}}$$

$$\Leftrightarrow \frac{\sum_{i,t}\left[(n_{it} - \hat{\lambda}_{it})^2 - n_{it}\right]}{\sum_{i,t} \hat{\lambda}_{it}^2} > \frac{\sum_i \left[(n_i - \hat{\lambda}_i)^2 - n_i\right]}{\sum_i \hat{\lambda}_i^2}. \tag{14}$$

The estimators $\widehat{\sigma_r^2}$ and $\widehat{\sigma_r^2}^{1}$ are positive if there is positive contagion for the data. In other words, the residuals of an individual which are computed at different periods must have rather the same sign. The sign of $\widehat{\sigma_s^2}$ and $\widehat{\sigma_s^2}^{1}$ depends on the comparison of two measures of relative overdispersion. Here, a link is made between results on overdispersion for count data (Cox (1983), Cameron and Trivedi (1986)), Dean and Lawless (1989), and results on linear models for panel data (Balestra and Nerlove (1966)).

Individuals which belong to a stratified sample are identified with a double index. The model estimated here can be applied to stratified samples, if we view a stratum as an individual and individuals in a stratum as periods. The design of experience rating schemes for fleets of vehicles is a current research topic for the editor of this book and for the author (Desjardins, Dionne, Pinquet, 2000, Dionne, Desjardins, Pinquet, 1999).

14.8.2 Single Equation Model for Number of Events, with a Varying Autocorrelation Function for the Random Effect

We start from the fixed effects model

$$N_{it} \sim P(\lambda_{it} w_{it}); \quad w_{it} = \exp(u_{it}).$$

Suppose that there exists a stationary Gaussian process $(U_t)_{t \geq 1}$, where the distribution of U_{it} is that of U_t for individuals observed on more than t periods. We write

$$\sigma^2 = V(U_t); \quad Cov(U_{t+h}, U_t) = \sigma^2 \rho(h).$$

We do not specify the distribution family for the $(U_t)_{t \geq 1}$, but a correlogram for the process can be consistently estimated. The statistics

$$\widehat{\sigma^2} = \log\left(1 + \frac{\sum_{i,t}\left[(n_{it} - \widehat{\lambda_{it}})^2 - n_{it}\right]}{\sum_{i,t} \widehat{\lambda_{it}}^2}\right)$$

and

$$\widehat{\sigma^2}\widehat{\rho(h)} = \log\left(1 + \frac{\sum_{i/T_i>h}\sum_{T_i\geq t>h}(n_{it}-\widehat{\lambda_{it}})(n_{i,t-h}-\hat{\lambda}_{i,t-h})}{\sum_{i/Ti>h}\sum_{Ti\geq t>h}\widehat{\lambda_{it}}\hat{\lambda}_{i,t-h}}\right)$$

converge respectively to σ^2 and $\sigma^2\,\rho(h)$, with $0 < h < T_{\max}$, ($T_{\max}$ is the maximal number of periods). Owing to the unconstrained estimation of the moments of the mixing distribution, the $\widehat{\rho(h)}$ are not bound to belong to $[-1, 1]$.

14.8.3 Multi Equation Model for Number of Events

With the notations of 14.3.2.2, the statistics

$$\hat{V}^1_{jj} = \frac{\sum_i\left[\left(n_i^j - \widehat{\lambda_i^j}\right)^2 - \widehat{\lambda_i^j}\right]}{\sum_i \widehat{\lambda_i^j}^2}; \quad \hat{V}^1_{jl} = \frac{\sum_i\left(n_i^j - \widehat{\lambda_i^j}\right)\left(n_i^l - \widehat{\lambda_i^l}\right)}{\sum_i \widehat{\lambda_i^j}\widehat{\lambda_i^l}} \quad (j \neq l),$$

are the estimators of V_{jj} and V_{jl} derived after the score test from a linearization of the score. Numbers and frequency-premiums are summed on all the periods. If $W_j = \exp(U_j)$, where U_j has the distribution of the U_{ij}, it can be shown that

$$\hat{V}^1_{jl} \to \frac{E[W_j W_l]}{E[W_j]E[W_l]} \forall j, l.$$

This property leads to linear credibility predictors obtained with a semi-parametric approach.

In a parametric setting, suppose that $U \sim N_q(0, V)$. From: $E[W_jW_l]/(E[W_j]\, E[W_l])$ $= \exp(V_{jl}) - 1$, we infer that

$$\hat{V}_{jl} = \log\left(1 + \hat{V}^1_{jl}\right)\forall j, l$$

give a consistent estimator of V. The prediction for longitudinal data with the expected value principle can be performed through a Choleski decomposition of $\hat{V}$, if $\hat{V}$ is positive definite.

Empirical results connected with this model are given in Pinquet (1998) for optimal bonus-malus systems derived from different types of claims. With a linear credibility approach, the bonus-malus coefficient for each type of claim can be seen as a linear combination of "loss to premium" ratios, with a first increasing, then time-vanishing credibility for the other types.

If compared to the case where only one type of claim is allowed for, the other main results for the prediction of a given type of claim are the following.

- Not surprisingly, each claim of this type becomes less meaningful in the prediction, since more types of events are taken into account.
- The revelation throughout time of hidden features in the number distributions is enhanced. The improvement increases with the frequency of the other types, and with the squared covariances between the random effects.

14.8.4 Cost-number Model on Events

With the notations of 14.3.2.4, consistent estimators are

$$\hat{V}_{nn} = \log(1+\hat{V}^1_{nn}), \hat{V}^1_{nn} = \frac{\sum_i (n_i - \hat{\lambda}_i)^2 - n_i}{\sum_i \hat{\lambda}_i^2}; \quad \hat{V}_{cn} = \frac{\sum_i (n_i - \hat{\lambda}_i)(tlc_i - \hat{E}^0(TLC_i))}{\left(\sum_i \hat{\lambda}_i^2\right)(1+\hat{V}^1_{nn})},$$

$$\hat{V}_{cc} = \frac{\sum_i \left[(tlc_i - \hat{E}^0(TLC_i))^2 - n_i\widehat{\sigma^2}^0\right]}{\left(\sum_i \hat{\lambda}_i^2\right)(1+\hat{V}^1_{nn})} - \hat{V}^2_{cn}$$

$$= \frac{\sum_{i|n_i\geq 2} \sum_{1\leq j,k\leq n_i, j\neq k} lcres_{ij} lcres_{ik}}{\left(\sum_{i|n_i\geq 2} n_i(n_i-1)\right) + 2\sum_i \hat{\lambda}_i(n_i - \hat{\lambda}_i)} - \hat{V}^2_{cn}. \tag{15}$$

Besides,

i) $lcres_{ij}$ is equal to $\log(c_{ij}) - z_{ij}\hat{\beta}^0$, a cost-residual (we dropped the time index) obtained from ordinary least squares, and $\widehat{\sigma^2}^0$ is the m.l.e. for the variance of the regression.
ii) $tlc_i = \Sigma_{j=1}^{n_i} \log(c_{ij})$; $\hat{E}^0(TLC_i) = \Sigma_{j=1}^{n_i} z_{ij}\hat{\beta}^0$.

The pseudo-true values (used to obtain the preceding results) lead to consistent estimators for the parameters of the basic model. We obtain

$$\hat{\alpha} = \hat{\alpha}^0 - \frac{\hat{V}_{nn}}{2} e_{n,1}; \quad \hat{\beta} = \hat{\beta}^0 - \hat{V}_{cn} e_{c,1}; \quad \widehat{\sigma^2} = \widehat{\sigma^2_0} - \hat{V}_{cc}, \tag{16}$$

where $e_{n,1}$ and $e_{c,1}$ are the first vectors of the canonical base of $\mathbb{R}^{k_n}$ and $\mathbb{R}^{k_c}$. Both intercepts are supposed to be the first of k_n and k_c regression components for number and cost distributions. These values are derived from the limit

$$\hat{E}^0(Y_i) \to E(Y_i)\forall i; \quad Y_i = \left(N_i, \sum_{j=1}^{n_i} \log(C_{ij}), \sum_{j=1}^{n_i} C_{ij}\right)$$

(see equation (13)).

A consistent estimator of V_{cc} under the assumption $V_{cn} = 0$ can be recognized in the ratio of the last expression. It is equal to

$$\hat{V}_{cc}^{0} = \frac{\sum_{i/n_i \geq 2} \sum_{1 \leq j,k \leq n_i, j \neq k} lcres_{ij} lcres_{ik}}{\sum_{i/n_i \geq 2} n_i(n_i - 1)} = \frac{\sum_i \left[\left(\sum_{j=1}^{n_i} lcres_{ij} \right)^2 - \sum_{j=1}^{n_i} lcres_{ij}^2 \right]}{\sum_{i/n_i \geq 2} n_i(n_i - 1)}$$

This estimator is the average of products of paired off residuals, that are related to the same policyholder and to different claims. It measures the observed contagion for the relative severities of the claims. If the past is of some use in the prediction of the future through a revelation principle, this must have been observed in the past, and this is the meaning of a positive sign for $\hat{V}_{cc}^{0}$.

A bonus-malus coefficient for the pure premium of the insurance contract i can be derived from a predictor of $\exp(u_{ni} + u_{ci})$ obtained with the expected value principle. This predictor is obtained from simulations. A Choleski decomposition of $\hat{V}$ (supposed to be positive definite) must be performed first.

A linear credibility prediction can be performed with this model. The bonus-malus coefficient for the policyholder i is equal to $1 + a_{ni}(n_i - \hat{\lambda}_i) + a_{ci}(tlc_i - \hat{E}^0(TLC_i))$, where a_{ni} and a_{ci} are the solutions of the linear system

$$m_{nn}^{i} a_{ni} + m_{nc}^{i} a_{ci} = b_n; \quad m_{cn}^{i} a_{ni} + m_{cc}^{i} a_{ci} = b_c,$$

with

$$m_{nn}^{i} = 1 + \hat{\lambda}_i \hat{V}_{nn}^{1}; \quad m_{nc}^{i} = \hat{\lambda}_i \widehat{V_{cn}}(1 + \hat{V}_{nn}^{1}); \quad b_n = \exp(\widehat{V_{nn}} + \widehat{V_{cn}}) - 1;$$

$$m_{cn}^{i} = m_{nc}^{i}; \quad m_{cc}^{i} = \widehat{\sigma^2}^{0} + \left[\hat{\lambda}_i(1 + \hat{V}_{nn}^{1})\left(\widehat{V_{cn}}^{2} + \widehat{V_{cc}}\right)\right]; \quad b_c = (\widehat{V_{cn}} + \widehat{V_{cc}})\exp(\widehat{V_{nn}} + \widehat{V_{cn}}).$$

14.9 EMPIRICAL RESULTS

The samples from which empirical results are drawn are part of the automobile policyholders portfolio of a French insurance company.

14.9.1 Allowance for a Time-Dependent Heterogeneity Component in a Poisson Model

The main results obtained in this section are the following:

- Starting from a model with a constant heterogeneity component, the time-dependence is found significant for our sample.

- The allowance for a time-dependent heterogeneity component (under a condition given in (14)) leads us to give in the prediction less credibility to the history of the individual.

In this section, we explain the number of claims at fault. The rating factors are

- The characteristics of the vehicle: group, class, age.
- The characteristics of the insurance contract: type of use, geographical area.

Other rating factors are the policyholder's occupation, as well as the year when the period began (in order to allow for a generation effect). The regression components (more than thirty) are indicators related to the different levels of the rating factors. The periods have not the same duration, and the parameters of the Poisson distributions are proportional to the duration.

The policyholders in the working sample are observed on one, two or three periods. More precisely, we have

	Number of policyholders observed on:
at least one period	85,909
at least two periods	68,344
three periods	44,428

The working sample is here a non balanced panel data set. From the estimation a Poisson model, we obtain

$$\sum_{i,t}(n_{it}-\hat{\lambda}_{it})^2=10{,}104.3;\quad \sum_{i,t}\hat{\lambda}_{it}^2=633.1;\quad \sum_i n_i=9{,}552;$$

$$\sum_i(n_i-\hat{\lambda}_i)^2=10{,}537.1;\quad \sum_i\hat{\lambda}_i^2=1{,}346.1;$$

The semiparametric estimators derived from Section 14.8.1 are

$$\widehat{\sigma_r^2}=\widehat{\sigma_r^2}^1=\frac{\sum_i\sum_{t\neq t'}(n_{it}-\hat{\lambda}_{it})(n_{it'}-\hat{\lambda}_{it'})}{\sum_i\sum_{t\neq t'}\hat{\lambda}_{it}\hat{\lambda}_{it'}}=\frac{10{,}537.1-10{,}104.3}{1{,}346.1-633.1}=0.607.$$

$$\widehat{\sigma_r^2}^1+\widehat{\sigma_s^2}^1=\frac{\sum_{i,t}\left[(n_{it}-\hat{\lambda}_{it})^2-n_{it}\right]}{\sum_{i,t}\hat{\lambda}_{it}^2}=0.872\Rightarrow\widehat{\sigma_s^2}^1=0.265;\quad \widehat{\sigma_s^2}=\frac{\widehat{\sigma_s^2}^1}{1+\widehat{\sigma_r^2}^1}=0.165.$$

The variance of the white noise process (the S_{it}) is thus less important than that of the time independent component.

Consider an insurance contract observed during one period. We compute bonus-malus coefficients for the second period from linear credibility predictors. If U_1, U_2

are the random effects related to the two periods, we distinguish two cases for the prediction.

i) The heterogeneity component does not depend on time. Then $U_1 = U_2$, and we will restrict to heterogeneous models which are well specified with respect to expectation. This assumption could be relaxed in the computations that follow. Hence $E(U_1) = E(U_2) = 1 \ \forall \sigma_u^2 = V(U_1) = V(U_2)$.

ii) The heterogeneity component is time-dependent, and the heterogeneous model is the one estimated in Section 14.8.1. Here, $U_1 = RS_1$; $U_2 = RS_2$.

The bonus-malus coefficient for the second period is obtained as $\hat{a} + \hat{b}n_1$, where n_1 is the number of claims reported during the first period, and

$$(\hat{a}, \hat{b}) = \arg\min_{a,b} \hat{E}\left[(U_2 - a - bN_1)^2\right]$$

(see Section 14.4.2). Here, the expectation is taken in the model with random effects. As $E(U_2) = 1$, we obtain

$$\hat{a} + \hat{b}n_1 = 1 + \hat{b}(n_1 - \hat{E}(N_1)) = (1-\alpha) + \alpha \frac{n_1}{\hat{E}(N_1)}; \quad \hat{b} = \frac{\widehat{Cov}(N_1, U_2)}{\hat{V}(N_1)}; \quad \alpha = \hat{b}\hat{E}(N_1).$$

From the identities recalled in equation (4), we have

$$\hat{V}(N_1) = \hat{E}(\lambda_1 N_1) + \hat{V}(\lambda_1 N_1); \quad \widehat{Cov}(N_1, U_2) = 0 + \widehat{Cov}(\lambda_1 U_1, U_2).$$

Let $\widehat{\lambda_1}$ be the frequency premium for the first period, and derived from a Poisson model without fixed or random effects. From the comments given after equation (10), we retain $\hat{E}(N_1) = \widehat{\lambda_1}$. Then we obtain $\hat{V}(N_1) = \widehat{\lambda_1} + \widehat{\lambda_1}^2\widehat{\sigma_u^2}$; $\widehat{Cov}(\lambda_1 U_1, U_2) = \widehat{\lambda_1}\widehat{\sigma_u^2}$ if the heterogeneity component does not depend on time, whereas $\widehat{Cov}(\lambda_1 U_1, U_2) = \widehat{\lambda_1}\widehat{Cov}(RS_1, RS_2) = \widehat{\lambda_1}\widehat{\sigma_r^2}$ in the other case. In the first case, a consistent estimator of σ_u^2 is for instance

$$\widehat{\sigma_u^2} = \frac{\sum_{i,t}\left[(n_{it} - \hat{\lambda}_{it})^2 - n_{it}\right]}{\sum_{i,t}\hat{\lambda}_{it}^2} = \widehat{\sigma_r^2}^1 + \widehat{\sigma_s^2}^1,$$

where $\widehat{\sigma_r^2}^1$ is a consistent estimator of σ_r^2 in the second model. As

$$\alpha_1 = \frac{\widehat{\lambda_1}\widehat{\sigma_u^2}}{1 + \widehat{\lambda_1}\widehat{\sigma_u^2}}; \quad \alpha_2 = \frac{\widehat{\lambda_1}\widehat{\sigma_r^2}}{1 + \widehat{\lambda_1}\widehat{\sigma_u^2}}$$

are the two credibility coefficients obtained in the two models, the conclusion drawn from the two last equations is the following. If $\widehat{\sigma_s^2}$, the estimated variance of the white noise recalled in this section is positive (conditions are given in equation (14)), the allowance for a time-dependent heterogeneity component leads us to grant less credibility to the history of the policyholder in the prediction. With the preceding estimations, we obtain

$$\frac{\alpha_2}{\alpha_1}=\frac{\widehat{\sigma_r^2}}{\widehat{\sigma_u^2}}=\frac{\widehat{\sigma_r^2}^1}{\widehat{\sigma_r^2}^1+\widehat{\sigma_s^2}^1}\simeq 0.7.$$

14.9.2 Allowance for Cost of Claims in Bonus-Malus Systems

We give here some results developed in full length in Pinquet (1997a).

The working sample includes 38772 policyholders and 71126 policyholders-periods. These policyholders reported 3493 claims. The average duration of the periods is nine months, and the annual frequency of claims is 6.7%. Here, we retained claims involving the property damage guarantee. The rating factors are those of the preceding section, plus the level of the deductible.

A well known result in actuarial literature is that log-normal distributions provide a better fit to the data than the gamma distributions. This result is verified on our data. Not surprisingly, there is more residual heterogeneity for gamma than for log-normal distributions, since heterogeneity expresses misspecification.

Let us estimate a joint distribution for the random effects related to number and cost of claims, through an estimation of the heterogeneous model described in Sections 14.3.2.4 and 14.8.4.

The statistics required for consistent estimation are:

$$\sum_i n_i = 3,493;\quad \sum_i n_i(n_i-1)=590;\quad \sum_i\left(n_i-\hat{\lambda}_i\right)^2-n_i=216.24;$$

$$\sum_i \hat{\lambda}_i^2=389.48;\quad \sum_i\left(n_i-\hat{\lambda}_i\right)\left(tlc_i-\widehat{tlc}_i\right)=7.96;$$

$$\sum_i\left[\left(tlc_i-\widehat{tlc}_i\right)^2-n_i\widehat{\sigma}^{2^0}\right]=\sum_{i/n_i\geq 2}\ \sum_{1\leq j,k\leq n_i,\,j\neq k} lcres_{ij}lcres_{ik}=100.80.$$

Let us estimate the covariance between the two random effects:

$$\hat{V}_{nn}^1=\frac{\sum_i\left(n_i-\hat{\lambda}_i\right)^2-n_i}{\sum_i\hat{\lambda}_i^2}=0.555\Rightarrow \hat{V}_{cn}=\frac{\sum_i\left(n_i-\hat{\lambda}_i\right)\left(tlc_i-\widehat{tlc}_i\right)}{\left(\sum_i\hat{\lambda}_i^2\right)\left(1+\hat{V}_{nn}^1\right)}=0.013.$$

From equation (15), we have

$$\hat{V}_{cc} = \frac{\sum_i \left[\left(tlc_i - \widehat{tlc}_i\right)^2 - n_i \widehat{\sigma^2}^0 \right]}{\left(\sum_i \hat{\lambda}_i^2\right)\left(1 + \hat{V}_{nn}^1\right)} - \hat{V}_{cn}^2 = 0.166;$$

$$\hat{V}_{nn} = \log(1 + \hat{V}_{nn}^1) = 0.442 \Rightarrow \hat{r}_{cn} = \frac{\hat{V}_{cn}}{\sqrt{\hat{V}_{cc}\hat{V}_{nn}}} = 0.048.$$

The correlation between the random effects is positive, but close to zero.

We compute the bonus for expected cost per claim and pure premium for a contract without claim reported. It is a function of the cumulated frequency premium. We obtain the results in Table 1.

Because of the positive correlation between the two random effects, a cost-bonus does appear, but it is very low.

The bonus-malus coefficients for frequency, expected cost per claim and pure premium are functions of three items. *i*) The number of claims. *ii*) The frequency premium computed for all the periods in the Poisson model without fixed or random effects. *iii*) The relative severity of the claims, as measured by the sum of cost-residuals computed in the log-normal model.

We now compute bonus-malus coefficients for policyholders who reported one claim. They are a function of the cost-residual $\log(c_1) - z_1\hat{\beta}$ (c_1 is the cost of the claim, and z_1 represents the policyholder's characteristics when the claim occurred), and of the frequency premium. If the frequency premium is equal to 0.1, we obtain the coefficients in Table 2.

Table 1

Boni for Expected Cost Per Claim and Pure Premium (Contracts without Claims Reported)

frequency premium	0.05	0.1	0.2	0.5	1	2
expected cost per claim bonus (%)	0.1	0.1	0.2	0.5	0.9	1.5
pure premium bonus (%)	2.7	5.3	9.7	19.9	31.2	44.7

Table 2

Bonus-Malus Coefficients (One Claim Reported)

residual for the logarithm of cost	frequency of claims coefficient	expected cost per claim coefficient	pure premium coefficient
−1	1.421	0.847	1.200
0	1.437	0.996	1.427
1	1.456	1.17	1.700

Bonus-malus coefficients for the frequency of claims, the expected cost per claim and the pure premium are given here for three levels of the relative severity of the claim. Consider for instance two claims explained by the same rating factors. A difference of two between the residuals is equivalent to a ratio of e^2 (i.e., more than seven) for the two costs. In the preceding table, significant differences between severities of claims have little influence on the frequency-malus. The increase of the coefficient with the severity is due to the positive correlation between the two random effects. The relative severity does have an influence on the coefficient for expected cost per claim. This influence depends mostly on the variance of the random effect in the cost distributions. Because of the correlation between the two random effects, the coefficients related to pure premium are not exactly equal to the product of the coefficients for frequency and expected cost per claim, but differences are very low.

14.10 REFERENCES

Akaike, H. (1973). "Information Theory and an Extension of the Likelihood Principle," *Proceedings of the Second International Symposium on Information Theory.*

Aitchison, J. and S.D. Silvey (1958). "Maximum Likelihood Estimation of Parameters Subject to Restraints," *The Annals of Mathematical Statistics* 29, 813–828.

Bailey, A.L. (1945). "A Generalized Theory of Credibility," *Proceedings of the Casualty Actuarial Society* 32, 13–20.

Balestra, P. and M. Nerlove (1966). "Pooling Cross-Section and Time Series Data in the Estimation of a Dynamic Model: the Demand for Natural Gas," *Econometrica* 34, 585–612.

Boyer, M., G. Dionne and C. Vanasse (1992). "Econometric Models of Accident Distributions," in *Contributions to Insurance Economics*, Kluwer Academic Publishers (Editor: G. Dionne).

Bühlmann, H. (1967). "Experience Rating and Credibility," *ASTIN Bulletin* 4, 199–207.

Bühlmann, H. (1970). *Mathematical Methods in Risk Theory*. Die Grundlehren der Mathematischen Wissenschaften in Einzeldarstellungen, Springer Verlag.

Cameron, A.C. and P.K. Trivedi (1986). "Econometric Models Based on Count Data: Comparisons and Applications of some Estimators and Tests," *Journal of Applied Econometrics* 29–54.

Cameron, A.C. and P.K. Trivedi (1998). *Regression Analysis of Count Data*. Econometric Society Monographs, Cambridge University Press.

Cox, D.R. and E.J. Snell (1968). "A General Definition of Residuals," *Journal of the Royal Statistical Society* B 30, 248–275.

Cox, D.R. (1983). "Some Remarks on Over-Dispersion," *Biometrika* 70, 269–274.

Cummins, J.D., G. Dionne, J.B. Mac Donald and B.M. Pritchett (1990). "Application of the GB2 Distribution in Modelling Insurance Loss Processes," *Insurance: Mathematics and Economics* 9, 257–272.

Davis, P. and P. Rabinowitz (1984). *Methods of Numerical Integration*. New York: Academic Press.

Dean, C. and J.F. Lawless (1989). "Tests for Detecting Overdispersion in Poisson Regression Models," *Journal of the American Statistical Association* 84, 467–472.

Dionne G., Desjardins, D. and J. Pinquet (1999). "L'évaluation des Risques d'Accident des Transporteurs Rontiers: Des Résultats Preliminaires *Assurances*, 67, 449–479.

Desjardins, D., G. Dionne and J. Pinquet (2000). "Experience Rating Schemes for Fleets of Vehicles," Mimeo, Risk Management Chair, HEC-Montreal.

Dionne, G. and C. Vanasse (1989). "A Generalization of Automobile Insurance Rating Models: the Negative Binomial Distribution with a Regression Component," *ASTIN Bulletin* 19, 199–212.

Dionne, G. and C. Vanasse (1992). "Automobile Insurance Ratemaking in the Presence of Asymmetrical Information," *Journal of Applied Econometrics* 7, 149–165.

Dionne, G. and C. Vanasse (1997). "The Role of Memory and Saving in Long-Term Contracting with Moral Hazard: An Empirical Evidence in Automobile Insurance," Mimeo, Risk Management Chair, HEC-Montreal.

Efron, B. and C. Morris (1977). "Stein's Paradox in Statistics," *Scientific American* 236, 119–127.

Eggenberger, F. and G. Pólya (1923). "Über die Statistik Verketteter Vorgänge," *Zeitschrift für Angewandte Mathematik und Mekanik* 1, 279–289.

Feller, W. (1943), "On a General Class of 'Contagious' Distributions," *The Annals of Mathematical Statistics* 14, 389–400.

Feller, W. (1957). *An Introduction to Probability Theory and its Applications*. Vol I, Wiley.

Gerber, H. and D. Jones (1975). "Credibility Formulas of the Updating Type," *Transactions of the Society of Actuaries vol. XXVII*, 31–52.

Gouriéroux, C., A. Monfort and A. Trognon (1984a). "Pseudo Likelihood Methods: Theory," *Econometrica* 52, 681–700.

Gouriéroux, C., A. Monfort and A. Trognon (1984b). "Pseudo Likelihood Methods: Applications to Poisson Models," *Econometrica* 52, 701–720.

Gouriéroux, C. and A. Monfort (1991). "Simulation Based Inference in Models with Heterogeneity," *Annales d'Economie et de Statistiques* 20–21, 69–107.

Gouriéroux, C. (1999). *Statistique de l'assurance*. Economica.

Greenwood, M. and G.U. Yule (1920). "An Inquiry into the Nature of Frequency Distribution Representative of Multiple Happenings with Particular Reference to the Occurrence of Multiple Attacks of Disease or of Repeated Accidents," *Journal of the Royal Statistical Society* 83, 255–279.

Hansen, L.P. (1982). "Large Sample Properties of Generalized Method of Moments Estimators," *Econometrica* 50, 1029–1054.

Hausman, J.A. (1978). "Specification Tests in Econometrics," *Econometrica* 46, 1251–1271.

Hausman, J.A., B.H. Hall and Z. Griliches (1984). "Econometric Models for Count Data with an Application to the Patents-R&D Relationship," *Econometrica* 52, 909–938.

Heckman, J.J. and G.J. Borjas (1980). "Does Unemployment Cause Future Unemployment? Definitions, Questions and Answers from a Continuous Time Model of Heterogeneity and State Dependence," *Economica* 47, 247–283.

Jeffreys, H. (1939). *Theory of probability*. Oxford University Press.

Johnson, N.L. and S. Kotz (1969). *Distribution in Statistics: Discrete Distributions*. Boston: Houghton Mifflin Co.

Kunreuther, H. and M.V. Pauly (1985). "Market Equilibrium with Private Knowledge: An Insurance Example," *Journal of Public Economics* 26, 269–288. Reprinted in *Foundations of Insurance Economics*, Kluwer Academic Publishers (editors: G. Dionne and S. Harrington).

Lemaire, J. (1977). "La Soif du Bonus," *ASTIN Bulletin* 9, 181–190.

Lemaire, J. (1985). *Automobile Insurance: Actuarial Models*. Huebner International Series on Risk, Insurance and Economic Security.

Lemaire, J. (1995). *Bonus-Malus Systems in Automobile Insurance*. Huebner International Series on Risk, Insurance and Economic Security.

Lillard, L. (1993). "Simultaneous Equations for Hazards (Marriage Duration and Fertility Timing)," *Journal of Econometrics* 56, 189–217.

Lundberg, O. (1940). *On Random Processes and their Applications to Sickness and Accident Statistics*. Thesis, University of Stockholm, Uppsala. Second Edition: Uppsala, Almquist & Wiksells 1964.

Mac Fadden, D. (1989). "A Method of Simulated Moments for Estimation of Discrete Response Models Without Numerical Integration," *Econometrica* 57, 995–1026.

Mowbray, A.H. (1914). "How Extensive a Payroll Exposure Is Necessary To Give a Dependable Pure Premium," *Proceedings of the Casualty Actuarial Society* 1, 24–30.

Mundlak, Y. (1978). "On the Pooling of Time Series and Cross-Section Data," *Econometrica* 46, 69–85.

Neyman, J. (1939). "On a New Class of 'Contagious' Distributions, Applicable in Entomology and Bacteriology," *The Annals of Mathematical Statistics* 10, 35–57.

Neyman, J. (1959). "Optimal Asymptotic Tests of Composite Statistical Hypotheses," *Probability and Statistics. The Harald Cramér Volume*, 213–234. Wiley, New-York.

Neyman, J. and E.L. Scott (1966). "On the Use of $C(\alpha)$ Optimal Tests of Composite Hypotheses," *Bulletin of the International Statistical Institute* 41 I, 477–497.

Picard, P. (1976). "Généralisation de l'Etude sur la Survenance des Sinistres en Assurance Automobile," *Bulletin Trimestriel de l'Institut des Actuaires Français*, 204–267.

Pinquet, J. (1996). "Hétérogénéité Inexpliquée," Document de Travail THEMA 9611.

Pinquet, J. (1997a). "Allowance for Cost of Claims in Bonus-Malus Systems," *ASTIN Bulletin* 27, No. 1, 33–57.

Pinquet, J. (1997b). "Testing for Heterogeneity through Consistent Estimators," Document de Travail THEMA 9714.

Pinquet, J. (1998). "Designing Optimal Bonus-Malus Systems from Different Types of Claims," *ASTIN Bulletin* 28, No. 2, 205–220.

Pinquet, J. (1999). "Allowance for Hidden Information by Heteregeneous Models, and Applications to Insurance Rating", *Automobile Insurance*, Kluwer Academic Publishers (Editors: Georges Dionne and Claire Laberge-Nadeau), 47–78.

Rao, C.R. (1948). "Large Sample Tests of Statistical Hypothesis Concerning Several Parameters with Applications to Problems of Estimation," *Proceedings of the Cambridge Philosophical Society* 44, 50–57.

Reid, C. (1998). *Neyman*. Springer Verlag. Second Edition of *Neyman-From Life*.

Silvey, S.D. (1959). "The Lagrangian Multiplier Test," *The Annals of Mathematical Statistics* 30, 389–407.

Stein, C. (1956). "Inadmissibility of the Usual Estimator for the Mean of a Multivariate Normal Distribution," *Proceedings of the 3rd Berkeley Symposium on Mathematical Statistics and Probability* (J. Neyman and L. Le Cam, eds.). University of California Press 1, 197–206.

Sundt, B. (1981). "Credibility Estimators with Geometric Weights," *Insurance: Mathematics and Economics* 7, 113–122.

White, H. (1982). "Maximum Likelihood Estimation of Misspecified Models," *Econometrica* 50, 1–25.

Whitney, A.W. (1918). "The Theory of Experience Rating," *Proceedings of the Casualty Actuarial Society* 4, 274–292.

Winkelmann, R. (1994). *Count Data Models (Econometric Theory and an Application to Labor Mobility)*. Springer Verlag. Second Edition: 1997.

Part V
Risk Management

15 Innovation in Corporate Risk Management: the Case of Catastrophe Risk

Neil A. Doherty

University of Pennsylvania

Abstract

Recent financial innovation in managing catastrophe risk, such as catastrophe bonds and catastrophe options, may be seen as a specific response to the problem of insurance and reinsurance capacity. This view is bolstered by a clear upward revision of estimates of loss potential. An equally compelling case can be made that such innovation is a natural expression of a conceptual revolution, in which the nature of risk and its impact on firms, has been reworked. This so called revolution is known in financial circles simply as "risk management".

The first prong of new risk management, why risk is costly to firms, arose from an apparent contradiction between the theory and practice of financial management. The second prong of risk management is that it is inclusive in nature. I will start with a summary of the results of recent literature on why risk is costly to firms and I will identify the generic pairs of strategies that are available to manage risk costs. The structure reveals how reinsurance, financial instruments, insurance policy design, leverage management and organizational form can be used jointly or selectively to manage insurer risk.

Keywords: Catastrophe bonds, catastrophe options, risk management, financial risk management, insurance policy design, leverage management, organizational form.
JEL Classification Numbers: D80, G22.

15.1 INTRODUCTION

Recent financial innovation in managing catastrophe risk, such as catastrophe bonds and catastrophe options, may be seen as a specific response to the problem of insurance and reinsurance capacity. This view is bolstered by a clear upward revision of estimates of loss potential. Recent earthquakes in Kobe and Northridge, as well as events such as hurricane Andrew, have shifted estimates of maximum potential loss by an order of magnitude. Furthermore, the emergence of modeling firms using large technical and financial data bases, has provided the insurance marketplace with credible estimates of single events that could overwhelm the insurance industry. For example, the U.S. industry faces the real possibility of a $50 to $100 billion loss through a major Midwest or Western earthquake or from a hurricane such as Andrew hitting Miami. Comparing this loss potential with an aggregate industry surplus of about $250 billion, illustrates the precarious financial position of the industry. In this view of the world, financial innovation may be seen as an attempt to diversify such potential catastrophe losses over the much larger (approximately $13 trillion) capital markets.

An equally compelling case can be made that such innovation is a natural expression of a conceptual revolution, in which the nature of risk and its impact on firms, has been reworked. This so called revolution is known in financial circles simply as "risk management" and its application spreads across all firms (insurance and non insurance firms) and all manner of risk (insurable and non insurable risk). The timing of this conceptual revolution is not accidental. The potential for managing risk requires the availability of suitable hedging instruments and the blossoming derivative markets have provided the supply. While the term "risk management" has been borrowed from insurance usage, the new risk management is a separate beast. The two defining characteristics of risk management (at least as applied to firms) are a very precise consideration of why risk is costly to firms and an embracing of all types of risk in a co-coordinated strategy. The new risk management is an "integrated risk management".

The first prong of new risk management, why risk is costly to firms, arose from an apparent contradiction between the theory and practice of financial management. The intellectual climate of the 1970's and 1980's was dominated by the capital asset pricing model and its derivatives. Under this view of the world, risk to a corporation passes to its stakeholders, notable its shareholders. But since shareholders can, and do diversify their portfolio holdings, there should be no gain in value to the firm that hedges risk. Why would investors reward hedging firms when investors could replicate any gain on their own account and at low cost? Despite the compelling logic, firms and investors did indeed seem to place value on corporate hedging. The contradiction is resolved in a more convincing explanation of why risk is costly to firms. The explanation has to do with transaction costs. Risk evokes a number of transaction costs for firms and these costs are borne by the firms owners. By lowering risk, one can lower the transaction costs and increase the expected value of gains to investors.

Merely to point out that there was a misunderstanding about why risk created costs to firms, seems a little pedantic. Why does it matter as long as we reduce risk and thereby enhance corporate value? It turns out that there are important practical reasons for wishing to know why risk was causing a problem. If we know the nature of the transaction cost, we can derive a whole new set of risk management strategies. The cost of risk can be addressed not only by reducing the risk, but also by reducing the transaction cost. This pairing of strategies will be called "duality". For example, one reason risk destroys value arises from non-linear tax schedules. One can create after tax value either by reducing risk or by engaging in transactions that effectively linearize taxes. Similarly, risk is costly to a firm with significant financial leverage since risk creates incentive conflicts between fixed income and residual stakeholders. The dual risk management strategies are to hedge the risk or change the leverage. These complimentary risk management strategies can be identified only if we know precisely why risk was a problem.

The second prong of risk management is that it is inclusive in nature. This is sometimes referred to as "global" risk management. The idea is simple. Risk to a firm can come from a number of sources. For example, a manufacturing firm may be exposed to risk from changes in demand, interest rates, commodity prices and insurable exposures. What ultimately matters is the combined impact of all risk exposures and risk management strategy is most effective if it addresses combined risk. This point should be obvious to insurance folk. Just as an insurer can combine insurable exposures and control relative portfolio risk, so a non insurable firm can diversify across its many types of risk (financial, economic, insurable etc). Thus, it would be strange if a firm that accepted enormous fluctuations in value from daily commodity price changes should decide that a $10 million deductible on a liability policy exposed the firm to too much risk.

To bring this discussion back towards the subject of catastrophe risk, first note a corollary of the two features of risk management. Given it is the transaction costs that arise from corporate structure that create risk costs for firms, and that the ownership shares of both insurance and non insurance firms are traded in the same market, the same general principles of risk management should apply to insurance and non insurance firms. I will start with a summary of the results of recent literature on why risk is costly to firms and I will identify the generic pairs of strategies that are available to manage risk costs. This approach can then be applied to the risk management choices for an insurance firm. The structure provides a much richer set of strategies than is usually identified (insurers typically contemplate only reinsurance and leverage management) and shows how the new financial instruments for hedging catastrophe risk have the potential to provide value to the insurance firm. The structure reveals how reinsurance, financial instruments, insurance policy design, leverage management and organizational form can be used jointly or selectively to manage insurer risk. Moreover, these various approaches vary in their ability to relieve the firm of the various transaction costs that seeded the interest in risk management in the first place.

15.2 WHY IS RISK COSTLY TO FIRMS?

15.2.1 Tax Non-Linearities

Risk is costly to firms because it aggravates a set of transaction costs and thereby decreases corporate value.[1] One simple cost of risk arises from non-linearities in tax schedules. The tax functions facing firms typically are convex i.e., higher levels of corporate earnings usually encounter higher rates of marginal taxation. To some degree, this convexity is built into the tax schedule; initial corporate earnings, like the first dollars of individual earnings, are untaxed at the Federal level. Above this threshold, earnings pass through several marginal rates, settling on a constant rate which currently is 34% in the U.S. But convexity also arises from other features of the tax code. Firms are allowed deductions for certain expenditures such as depreciation and loss carry backs. The effects of such deductions is to increase the range of income which attracts a zero marginal rate. When deductions are exhausted, the tax rate restores to the normal rate thus giving rise to convexity.

Given tax convexity, Jensen's inequality implies that expected taxes will be reduced if the riskiness of earnings is reduced. It follows that the after tax value of the firm will rise if the firm hedges earnings risk. If earnings are risky, upside variation causes a large increase in taxes but downside variation causes little reduction of taxes. Thus, earnings stabilization will avoid the large potential upside increase in taxes without sacrificing much of a tax decrease on the downside. In this manner, hedging can create value by reducing expected taxes.[2]

15.2.2 Managerial Compensation

A second cost of risk to firms arises from its effect on optimal contract design. The efficient management compensation contract involves a trade off between risk sharing and efficiency. Risk sharing considerations favor payment of flat salary to managers since shareholders have a comparative advantage in diversifying. The flat salary avoids payment of a risk premium to risk averse and undiversified managers. But efficiency favors compensation that aligns the interests of shareholders and managers, i.e., performance related compensation such as bonuses, options, etc, that are related to earnings or share value. The problem is that performance related compensation exposes managers to risk and requires the inclusion of a risk premium. In practice, the optimal compensation package usually is one that compromises between efficient incentives and risk sharing, e.g., a base salary plus some performance compensation.

Now, if earnings and share price are purged of risk that is outside managers control by appropriate hedging, the trade off between risk sharing and efficiency is

[1] For explanations of the cost of risk see Mayers and Smith 1982, Shapiro and Titman 1985, Froot, Scharfstein and Stein, 1993.

[2] See Smith and Stulz, 1985.

avoided. This means that the compensation packet can focus only on the efficiency goal and thus be loaded with incentive compensation, without the need to pay the manager a risk premium.

A variation on this idea is that firms often deal with creditors who are risk averse and hold an undiversified position in the firm. A specific example is the case of insurance firms. Insurance exists because policyholders are risk averse and relatively undiversified. The quality of the insurance product is degraded by the prospect of insurer default. Being risk averse, policyholders will be reluctant to bear this risk, even if it is priced into the insurance contract. The insurer that is able to reduce default risk by hedging, will be at a competitive advantage. Ceteris paribus, policyholders will be more likely to purchase its policies and/or pay a higher premium than for the policies of a more risky insurer. Thus, a demand for reinsurance, is induced from direct insurance demand (Doherty and Tinic, 1982).

15.2.3 Direct Costs of Financial Distress

If a firm becomes bankrupt then, according to the absolute priority rule, shares expire worthless and the firm resorts to the creditors. Any transaction costs, such as legal fees, court fees, accounting costs, will be borne *ex post*, by the creditors. In addition to direct costs of bankruptcy, there may be indirect costs, or opportunity costs, which also will fall on creditors. When a firm is administered by the court, the normal incentive structure which leads agents to perform efficiently may be disturbed. Contracts written with managers, agents, employees and others often have rewards and penalties associated with performance. During a bankruptcy, these contracts are sometimes challenged especially if they seem retroactively generous given the firm's current plight. Moreover, new contracts written during such a period are overseen by the court. Will these contracts written under court supervision, carry the same incentive provisions as contracts written during a normal period under which the firm is monitored continuously by the capital market? To the extent that incentive compatibility is sacrificed during bankruptcy, the performance of the firm will suffer. The foregone value will be lost to the creditors who now "own" the firm. Similarly, value may be lost if the selection of investment projects is affected by court supervision. For example, during solvent operations, and capital market accountability, the firm may be aggressive in its project selection and earn the appropriate premium associated with such entrepreneurial activity. If the bankrupt firm is less entrepreneurial in its project selection, any loss of value will fall on the creditors.

The various transaction costs of bankruptcy theoretically fall *ex post* upon the creditors since equity claims have expired worthless.[3] *Ex ante*, these costs will be

[3] In practice, distressed firms are not always re-organized according to the absolute priority rule. Many distressed firms are re-organized in out-of-court settlements or "workouts". These settlements usually, leave the shareholders with some value and the (usually lower) transaction costs associated with workouts will fall jointly (according to negotiation) on both classes of stakeholder.

anticipated in the value of the bonds. Absent any risk premia, the bonds will be reduced by the expected value of the bankruptcy costs. The discount in bond values will reflect investor expectations as to the prospective size of the bankruptcy costs, together with investor expectations about the probability of bankruptcy. Accordingly, any strategy which reduces the probability of bankruptcy (such as hedging) will enhance the value of the firm's bonds and thus reduce the cost of capital.

15.2.4 Agency Costs and the Under-Investment Problem

Apart from the transaction costs associated with actual financial distress, the prospect of future financial distress causes a number of other problems. The most documented of these is a form of agency which arises between shareholders and creditors, that is often called the "under investment problem". Shareholders have some control over the decision making processes within the firm through their ability to appoint and compensate the management team (and less directly through their ability to buy and sell shares). Creditors lend their money to the firm without such control over its decision making. Thus, the shareholders are in an agency relationship with respect to the bondholders. This relationship generates opportunities for shareholders to transfer wealth from bondholders by selecting projects with asymmetric payoffs to different classes of investors.

The agency conflict between shareholders and creditors arises from the non-linear nature of claims. Given limited liability, and the residual nature of the equity claim, shareholders will tend to over-value high risk investment projects since part of the downside risk is "put" to the bondholders. This implies that, either the firm will loose value as it fails to select value maximizing investment projects, or that resolution of the agency conflict requires costly controls that limit the discretionary power of managers.[4] Either way, the value of the firm will be reduced. Moreover, if bondholders anticipate such expropriation by high risk project choice, then the cost of debt financing will increase. In this way, the costs of inefficient project selection will fall *ex ante* on the shareholders. This loss of value can be avoided if the shareholders can credibly commit to hedge any high risk associated with new and existing projects. As risk is hedged, the value of the default put falls, and the incentive to select low NPV-high risk projects is removed.[5]

15.2.5 Costly Access to Capital and the "Crowding Out" of Investment Projects

After a firm suffers a loss of assets, such as fire damage to a plant, it is presented with an investment opportunity, i.e., to re-invest in the construction of a replacement plant. Reinvestment only will add value if the net present value is positive. Reinvestment

[4] See Jensen and Meckling, 1976 and Myers, 1977.
[5] See Mayers and Smith 1987.

can be financed in two ways. Under *post loss* financing, the funds are secured (from internal or external sources) after the loss has occurred. *Pre-loss* financing occurs if the funds to reinvest in future prospective losses, are secured and paid for before the loss occurs. Insurance is such a source. Premiums are paid in anticipation of possible losses, and the insurance proceeds can be used to finance re-investment without any future interest or dividend obligation. Thus, insurance may be seen as a source of financing for losses, in much the same way as debt and equity are sources of financing. Some financing source is necessary for the firm to capture the net present value of reinvestment. The decision to purchase insurance involves a comparison between the transaction costs associated with insurance (such as commissions, overheads, and moral hazard frictions) with the transaction costs of more conventional capital sources such as debt and equity. It can be seen that one of the benefits of hedging or insurance, is that it permits the firm to undertake value adding re-investment opportunities, which might be lost if post-loss financing is not forthcoming or is too costly.

The analysis of the previous paragraph was developed by Doherty (1985) to analyze insurance and reinvestment decisions. A more general rational for hedging has been developed by Froot, Scharfstein and Stein (FSS) which I will call the "crowding out" hypothesis. The first element is that capital sources have different costs. FSS evoke the work of Myers and Majluff to argue that external capital is more costly than internal capital. The costs associated with capital are then used by FSS to develop their rationale for hedging. First, firms derive their value from identifying and undertaking new investment projects. A healthy and growing firm may be investing in research and development, developing new products and rationalizing existing operations. Such firms face a continuing need for capital to fund their investment opportunities. Given the pecking order of the costs of financing, one would expect such firms to adopt a financial strategy (e.g., a dividend policy) to fund as much as feasible of the project budget from internal sources. Now suppose that such a firm takes a sudden loss in liquidity from an uninsured fire or liability suit, a sharp deterioration in exchange rates or an unanticipated rise in the price of a commodity that is used intensively in production. The loss in liquidity compromises the firm's ability to undertake its desired investment projects. Empirical evidence cited by FSS suggests that for each dollar of unhedged loss, project budgets will be cut by about 30 cents. More recent evidence from Minton and Schrand also supports this opportunity cost. They show that capital expenditure for firms with high cash flow volatility is about 19% below the mean and expenditures for those with low volatility is about 11% above the mean. Hedging avoids this loss and protects the ability of the firm to fund its investment program.

15.3 GLOBALITY, DUALITY AND FOUR PRINCIPLE STRATEGIES

The title of this section seems to suggest a conundrum; is it two, four or many? Actually I am addressing four separate issues all of which have an important bearing on the emergence of new risk management instruments and strategies. The issue of globality refers to the idea of assessing the joint impact of all risk from all sources on the value of the firm and forming a co-coordinate risk management strategy. Duality refers to the result that strategies for dealing with the effects of risk on corporate value, come in pairs. Whatever the reason that risk is costly, value can be created either by hedging the risk or by adapting the structure of the firm or its operations such that risk can be borne with lower cost. I will call the second type of strategy "risk accommodation". From these paired strategies, we will isolate four principle generic strategies that lie at the heart of recent financial innovation.

15.3.1 Globality

The various rationales of the cost of risk to a firm suggest that the point of impact is at a highly aggregate level. For example, the tax non-linearity explanation implies that it is the risk of the earnings of the taxable entity in a given jurisdiction, that bestows costs on the firm (i.e., for Federal U.S. taxes, the relevant financial number is the U.S. taxable income). For a U.S. firm, it does not matter whether the income comes from the Idaho plant or the Illinois distribution operation, these values are aggregated for tax purposes. Nor does it matter whether the source of the risk is an insurance exposure or an interest rate fluctuation which impacts earnings. All that matters is the joint impact of all sources of risk on taxable income. When considering financial distress rationales, or the crowding out hypothesis, the level of aggregation is higher. What matters is the joint impact of all sources of risk to the firm on its probability of insolvency, on its leverage and cost of capital, on its share price, etc. Again the riskiness of an insurance exposure (or an interest exposure, a foreign exchange exposure, etc.) does not matter in isolation. What matters is the joint effect of all risk from all sources on the firm's "bottom line". And just as the pooling of many insurance policies will result in a low level of relative risk (assuming low correlation) so too will the combination of various types of risk to the firms (insurable, financial, interest rate, marketing, etc) lead to similar benefits of diversification. This is no more than the law of large numbers (the very basis of insurance). The agency costs between fixed income stakeholders and residual claimants of the firm arise without reference to the source of risk. Moreover, the crowding out of new investments is likely to be equally severe if the depletion of internal funds was the result of an uninsured liability loss or a sudden shift in the price of the firm's major raw materials.

15.3.2 Duality

In Section II, I outlined five mechanisms by which risk can reduce corporate value. The idea of duality is simple. If risk destroys value, then value potentially can be restored either by reducing risk or by organizing the firm and its operations so that the risk is less costly. In Table 1, I lay out all five forms of risk cost and against each

Table 1

Type of risk cost	Hedge	Risk accommodation
Tax non-linearities	Hedge	Tax Arbitrage-Reinsurance
Financial Distress—agency conflict	Hedge	Reduce Leverage
Financial Distress—transaction costs	Hedge	Reduce Leverage
Cost of Capital—Crowding Out	Hedge	Alternative Financing
Incentive Compatible Compensation	Hedge	Re-write compensation contract

describe two strategies; hedging or accommodation. Consider each of the mechanisms starting with tax convexity. If taxes are convex, then expected taxes will fall as risk falls. Firms have a second option in tackling this problem; they can leave the risk alone but effectively "linearize" their tax obligations. There is a quasi market for firms to "trade" tax shields. The most well known aspect of this market is that for leasing which is driven largely by the lessor retaining ownership of an asset and exploiting its comparative tax advantage over the lessee in depreciating the asset. Similarly, there is some evidence to suggest that reinsurance trade is partly explained as an arbitrage between insurers with different marginal tax rates. (Keun ock Lew 1991, Garven and Louberge 1996).

The second mechanism by which risk reduces value was that it compromises the ability of firms to write managerial compensation schemes with efficient incentives. One risk management strategy is simply to hedge the risk so that directors can write incentive compatible compensation schemes (i.e., link compensation to stock price or earnings) without having to pay managers a risk premium. The second strategy is to link managerial compensation to alternative (accounting) performance measures that are purged of risk. This is known as a "phantom hedge" since the risk in earnings (etc) need not be actually hedged. Instead an accounting measure is derived as though there were a hedge in place, and then compensation is based on the accounting measure. Ideally such measures should carry a strong signal of management performance, but should have little extraneous noise; i.e., they should have a low noise to signal ratio.

A similar dual strategy set is available to address the remaining risk mechanisms. The expected value of bankruptcy costs and the agency costs between creditors and equityholders arise jointly from the effects of risk and leverage. Two risk management strategies immediately suggest themselves; reduce risk or reduce leverage. Similarly, with the crowding out hypothesis, reducing risk by hedging will mitigate the problem. But here too leverage management can be used as a complementary or competing strategy. For example, the problem of crowding out can be reduced by maintaining a lower leverage and by reducing dividends. In this way, the firm will be in a stronger position to finance new investment projects from preferred sources of capital even after an unhedged loss.

15.3.3 Four Principle Strategies

Of the various strategies identified in Table 1 I will isolate four generic types that are central to the discussion.

Asset Hedge

An "asset hedge" can be defined as an asset which provides a hedge against the risk in some other asset. A portfolio comprising the basic asset and the hedging asset has little or no risk. The asset hedge can be represented in a portfolio F in which an amount \$ is invested in two assets. The first basic asset has a payoff of A_B for each dollar invested. The second asset, the hedging asset, has a per dollar payoff of A_H. The capital \$ is allocated over the two assets in the ratio $\{1:h\}$ and the correlation coefficient ρ_{BH} is negative (in the limit approaching negative unity).

$$\text{ASSET HEDGE} \quad F = \$(A_B + hA_H) \quad \text{where} \quad 0 > \rho_{BH} \geq -1 \tag{1}$$

If $\rho_{BH} = -1$, then some hedge ratio h^* can be chosen such that the portfolio is riskless; i.e., $\mathrm{COV}\{\$(A_B + h^*A_H)\} = 0$. A reinsurance policy is a traditional form of asset hedge for the insurer. A newer instrument is the catastrophe option which is an option written on the value of an index of insurance company claims and yields a payoff when the index triggers a pre-set value (the striking price).

Liability Hedge

A hedge can be achieved on the opposite side of the balance sheet. Instead of the hedging asset, the portfolio includes a liability L_H as follows.

$$\text{LIABILITY HEDGE} \quad F = \$(A_B - hL_H) \quad \text{where} \quad 0 < \rho_{BH} \leq 1 \tag{2}$$

If $\rho_{BH} = 1$, then some hedge ratio h^* can be chosen such that the portfolio is riskless; i.e., $\mathrm{COV}\{\$(A_B - h^*L_H)\} = 0$. Many of the newer risk management strategies are indeed liability hedges.

Postloss Equity Re-Capitalisation

The reasons for managing corporate risk included the avoidance of bankruptcy costs and the protection of the firm's continuing ability to pay for sudden losses and to finance investment opportunities. One way to address these concerns is to re-capitalise the firm after a loss. The gain is that the firm receives an injection of funds when it is most needed without an increase in leverage. Moreover, an insurer may unable to pay for cat losses from current liquid assets, despite having substantial illiquid assets, especially the franchise value of future operations. Re-capitalisation is essentially a tool to release these illiquid assets and permits the firm to continue operating and preserve its franchise value. I will examine two strategies. The first is simple postloss equity financing.[6] A feature of this strategy is that the price at which new equity can be issued is reduced by the loss. A second strategy is for the insurer to purchase a put option on its own stock that can be exercised after a catastrophe of defined magnitude. These new instruments have recently been assembled under the trade name "Cateputs".

Leverage Management

Risk accommodation strategies are several, depending on the particular type of risk cost. Tax arbitrage can be appropriate to mitigate the effects of tax non-linearities, and re-writing of managerial compensation contracts can mitigate the adverse effects of risk on managerial decision-making. But I will venture that the most important risk accommodation strategy involves the control of leverage. This strategy can be used to address *ex post* costs of financial distress, the agency costs that arise from leverage and prospective insolvency and the crowding out of new investments. Leverage management may simply involve reduction of the level of leverage. This reduces the agency cost between creditors and residual claimants and reduces the expected value of bankruptcy costs. Moreover, if a sudden loss arises, the firm will find itself in a stronger position to approach capital markets for new funding (either to reconstruct destroyed assets or to fund new investment projects). Alternatively, dividend policy may be used to address directly the crowding out problem. Lower dividend payouts will enhance the ability of the firm to fund future projects from internal funds and reduce the probability that projects will be lost for lack of access to low cost capital.

In applying the above structure to the management of catastrophe loss, I will not discuss leverage management for insurers in any detail. This lack of attention does not reflect its lack of importance as a risk management strategy. Quite the reverse. The use of surplus management and reinsurance to reduce leverage and there by reduce the probability of ruin, is the subject of an extensive actuarial literature. The newer innovations in insurer risk management have concentrated on new types of hedges, such as cat bonds and futures and this is where I will focus. Indeed it is these new types of financial instruments that are providing competition for traditional reinsurance policies.

15.4 CATASTROPHE RISK: INSURANCE, REINSURANCE & FINANCIAL INNOVATION

15.4.1 Reinsurance: Credit Risk, Basis Risk and Moral Hazard

Simple diversification will not always remove risk from a primary insurer's liability portfolio. For example, liability insurance is subject to significant correlation, since

[6] See Doherty 1985 for a risk managment analysis of this strategy. This is compared with postloss debt financing and pre-loss (insurance) financing.

changes in liability rules can simultaneously affect all policies in an insurer's portfolio. Catastrophe insurance is subject to even more apparent correlation. Thus, the law of large numbers cannot be relied upon to remove relative risk. Reinsurance is the traditional hedging instrument available to primary insurers. However, its use does involve significant transaction cost which are now discussed.

Credit Risk[7]

Catastrophe hedging instruments face design choices that trade off various inefficiencies against each other. Reinsurance can be used to illustrate these trade offs. First, there is credit risk; the risk that the reinsurer will be unable to pay its obligation to the ceding firm. The recent $17 billion Andrew losses and the $12 billion Northridge losses revealed some chinks in the insurance industry's armor and estimates of a repeat of the 1906 San Francisco earthquake have forecast widespread insolvencies amongst primary firms (Doherty, Kleffner and Kunreuther 1991). Such insolvencies would be transmitted to reinsurers. Indeed, the defaults could be disproportionately large in the reinsurance industry. Typically, a catastrophe reinsurance contract only covers the right hand tail of the primary's loss distribution (a "stop loss" coverage). Normally the expected payout of the reinsurer is quite small but the variance is high. Thus, the coefficient of variation for cat reinsurace is usually very high. While the reinsurance premiums is usually based on the expected payout with a loading related to risk, the high risk-return ratio requires high risk capital or carries a high ruin probability. It has been estimated that large catastrophes would probably cause widespread insolvencies. Initial estimations of potential industry payouts for large catastrophes (Cummins and Doherty 1996) support this conclusion with the number of insolvencies rising disproportionately with the size of the catastrophic loss.

Basis Risk

While credit risk is present with reinsurance, basis risk is resolved. Reinsurance payoffs are geared to losses sustained by the primary insurer. Contracts usually cover the primary firm's portfolio losses on designated lines of business (treaty reinsurance), or specific primary policies (facultative reinsurance). Moreover, policies share risk between primary insurer and reinsurer according to linear or non-linear formulae. Thus, while the primary firm will retain some risk, there is no mismatch between the asset on which the reinsurance payoff is defined and the asset to be hedged. In other words, there is no basis risk. It is possible to imagine a "reinsurance" contract with

[7] An aspect of credit risk that is not developed in this paper is liability risk. Litigation does arise between primary insurers and reinsurers over contract wording or over the conduct of the parties. The prospect of non delivery on a reinsurance contract, and the costs of enforcing legal claims against reinsurers are significant costs. The new instruments that are discussed later can be expected to face similar liability risk. For example, one can expect cases in which investors maintain that the dimensions of risk were not properly represented or that the issuer did not act appropriately to control the level of risk.

basis risk. If an insurer purchased a reinsurance contract with a payoff structured on the industry losses, rather than on the primary firm's own losses, there would be basis risk. The extent of basis risk would depend on the correlation between industry and firm losses; the lower the correlation, the higher the basis risk. The discussion of basis risk is important since it forms an important design element in structuring new hedges and it can be used to mitigate another inefficiency, moral hazard.

Moral Hazard

Moral hazard is the flip side of basis risk. Moral hazard arises with all insurance policies. With reinsurance contracts, moral hazard can take two generic forms; *ex ante* or *ex post* moral hazard. *Ex ante* moral hazard arises when, due to reinsurance protection, the primary insurer fails to take actions to reduce future losses or takes actions that increase losses. This occurs because the reinsurer cannot monitor the primary continuously and condition the reinsurance contract on the primary's behavior. Thus, the primary firm may be lax in its underwriting procedures, pay inadequate attention to spread of risk and fail to provide adequate risk audits for potential new policies. Naturally, the reinsurer will anticipate this behavior and some level of monitoring will take place. But monitoring is costly and the combination of the costs of monitoring and the excess losses suffered due to inadequate underwriting provides a measure of the costs of moral hazard. These costs are substantial. Industry sources frequently put the transaction cost of reinsurance at 20% of premiums or higher. These direct costs take the form of commissions and premium loading. In addition, many reinsurance relationships are implicitly long term and implicitly experience rated, to compensate for costly monitoring. These temporal relationships constrain the parties and contribute to the costs of moral hazard. It may be noticed that moral hazard arises from the quality of the hedge; i.e., from the absence of basis risk. Consequently, the structuring of a catastrophe hedge, provides the opportunity for trading off these two features.

Ex post moral hazard arises when the loss settlement practices of the insurer are relaxed due to the presence of reinsurance. This is a particular problem for catastrophic losses. The loss settlement capacity of any insurer (and of the industry) is reasonably geared to the normal levels of loss frequency. When an event such as hurricane Andrew arises, primary firms simply do not have the capacity to inspect and negotiate claims settlements thoroughly. Thus, it becomes more difficult to prevent the "build up" of claims (policyholders including uninsured damage in the claim or exaggerating the size of the loss) or outright fraud on the part of policyholders. However, the incentive for the primary insurer to control its claims will be relaxed if it has reinsurance protection. The primary may be able to avoid the abnormal transaction costs of settling claims, and even buy some goodwill with its policyholders by making generous settlements with policyholders and passing the costs of excess settlements to its reinsurer. Also, insurers are often pressured by regulators to be prompt and generous in settling losses in a highly publicized catastrophe. When protected by reinsurance, the primary insurer can achieve regulatory goodwill and pass the cost to the reinsurers.

Of course, there are constraints on this type of behavior. For moderate losses, the primary firm may well consider its reputation in the reinsurance market before engaging in such opportunistic behavior. Primary insurers will seek future reinsurance protection and a history of moral hazard will hardly stand them in good stead. In the event of severe catastrophes, the normal constraints on such insurer moral hazard will be especially dulled. When insurers are facing financial stress, their reputation in returning to reinsurance markets in the future, is unlikely to be so constraining.

A More Formal Look at Moral Hazard and Reinsurance

Let us look at moral hazard a little more formally. The object is to see how moral hazard affects the design of reinsurance contracts and the structure of reinsurance markets. In particular, I wish to be able to show why reinsurance locks the parties together into long term relationships and why these relationships appear so costly relative to hedging instruments traded on financial exchanges. To start, consider a very simple single period valuation model of an insurer. At the beginning of the year the insurer contributes equity capital of E and receives premiums P (net of expenses). The initial funds $E + P$ are invested at a random rate of return r_i for one year and then losses L (also random) are paid. Thus, the terminal value of the insurer's equity is:

$$T = (E + P)(1 + r_i) - L \tag{3}$$

Now add reinsurance. At the beginning of the year, the insurer pays an amount R as a reinsurance premium. The policy assumed is a treaty stop loss policy which pays the insurer when losses on an underlying insurance portfolio I, exceed a deductible (striking price) S. The payoff to the reinsurance can be represented as a call option and we use the notation $C(I; S)$. The term "h" is the hedge ratio, which may be interpreted here as the proportion of the primary's losses above S that is reinsured. Naturally, the premium also depends on I and S (i.e., $R = R(I; S)$). In normal arrangements, the reinsurance coverage is based on the ceding insurer's portfolio, or some particular lines. There is no inherent basis risk other than that assumed by the ceding company by accepting a deductible. Thus, for reinsurance, we can consider I and L as identical. With other hedging instruments, basis risk can be present and we will keep the distinct notation. The final element is mitigation. The insurer is able to reduce the level of expected loss, by spending an amount "a" on mitigation (better underwriting, loss control, loss adjustment, etc). While mitigation is a direct cost to the insurer, losses will decline as more is spent on mitigation. The terminal value of equity can be shown as:

$$E(T) = \{E - P - R(I;S)\}(1 + E(r_i)) - E(L(a)) + hC(I;S) - a \tag{4}$$

Now consider that optimal choice of mitigation for the primary insurer.[8] Using normal optimization techniques, this can be represented by the first order condition:

$$\frac{\partial E(T)}{\partial a} = -\frac{\partial E(L(a))}{\partial a} - 1 + h\frac{\partial C}{\partial I}\frac{\partial I}{\partial L}\frac{\partial L}{\partial a} = 0 \tag{5}$$

The first term $(-\partial E(L(a))/\partial a)$ shows the effects of increasing mitigation spending by \$1 on the primary's expected losses; the second term (-1) shows the direct cost of increasing mitigation expense by \$1; and the third term $\{h(\partial C/\partial I)(\partial I/\partial L)(\partial L/\partial a)\}$ shows the effect of the additional mitigation (and therefore reduced expected claims for the primary) on the expected recovery under the reinsurance policy. If there were no reinsurance, the primary insurer would fully internalize the benefits of spending on safety and the third term would drop out leaving (6) in the form $-\partial E(L(a))/\partial a = 1$. This can be interpreted as follows. The primary will spend an amount on mitigation until the additional dollar of expenditure on mitigation brings a reduction of one dollar in expected losses. However, reinsurance disturbs this balance. With reinsurance, the third term becomes important and this will serve to reduce the primary's choice of mitigation. Any benefit to the primary in terms of reduced policyholder claims, simply reduces the reinsurance recovery. The higher the deductible the lower the choice of mitigation. Since reinsurers will rationally anticipate this reduction in mitigation in the reinsurance premium, the primary will end up paying in advance for additional incurred losses. If there were no contracting costs, the primary could commit to a given level of mitigation and the reinsurance contract would be priced accordingly. However, this commitment requires monitoring costs for commitment and these costs can be high.[9] This is the nature of the moral hazard problem. However, we can use a little more structure to evoke a well known solution.

Denote the primary insurer's profit (before any transaction costs of risk considered in section II) as $\Pi_P = \Pi_P(R, L, S, h) - a$. To account for the various costs of risk, I will assume that the insurer's value is a concave function of Π_P but I will also use the common device of assuming that value is separable in mitigation a.

[8] This analysis establishes the optimal mitigation given the basis risk. For some problems the basis risk can be determined exogenously and this will require joint solution of mitigation and basis risk. The appropriate methodology is to estimate optimal mitigation as a functional relationship of basis risk; then to choose the value maximizing level of basis risk subject to the *ex* post optimization of mitigation.

[9] For example, an important aspect of primary insurer mitigation is the level of resources it allocates to settling losses and its willingness to avoid making generous loss settlement to capture goodwill from customers and regulators.

The difficulty of pre-commitment is that the level of mitigation is not easy to measure. The primary has to settle claims after a cat loss. The level of mitigation relates partly to the expenditures undertaken by the primary in settling policyholder losses. This itself is fairly easy to measure this expenditure but to specify in advance what level of expenditure is appropriate for any given loss is more complicated.

$$V_P = \int U\{\Pi_P(R,L,S,h)\} f(L;a)dL - a \tag{6}$$

Where $f(L; a)$ is the conditional probability of observing losses L given mitigation level of a. Notice that $U\{\cdot\}$ resembles a utility function and concavity is analogous to risk aversion. However, here we mean that the various transaction costs of risk suggests that more risk yields lower value and thus a concave mapping of Π_P into V_P. The primary's optimal choice of "a" can now be represented by the following first order condition which is called the "incentive constraint".

$$\int U\{\Pi_P(R,L,S,h)\} f_a(L;a)dL = 1 \tag{7}$$

Now consider the optimal *ex ante* design of the reinsurance contract. To avoid unnecessary restriction of the problem, let the reinsurance premium R be a function of the revealed losses L (in other words, allow retrospective rating). Moreover, we can represent the comparative advantage of the reinsurer by assuming that it can diversify catastrophe risk and that it is effectively risk neutral. Designing an optimal policy now can be presented as a standard "principal-agent" problem. If the reinsurer (the principal) cannot directly monitor "a", it can choose to condition the premium, R, on the revealed value of L. With standard assumptions, the problem becomes one of minimizing V_P subject to the incentive constraint and a second (participation) constraint to ensure that the primary will actually purchase the contract offered. The solution is well known; *the optimal reinsurance premium R is a non decreasing function of the revealed loss L.*[10] The optimal design of the reinsurance contract is one with retrospective premiums.

The adaptation of the standard one period principal agent problem to the design of reinsurance yields retrospective premiums. The single period model has been extended to many periods[11] with the analogous result that the payment between the principal and the agent be related to prior losses (experience rating).[12] This prediction is testable, though casual observation of the reinsurance market suggests that it follows the model. While I am not aware of formal tests, long term relationships are normal in this market and it is common practice for poor claims experience against the reinsurer to be recovered in future premiums. This practice has been formalized over recent years with the introduction of finite reinsurance. By defining a fixed period, and limiting indemnity in relation to accumulated premiums, the reinsurance contract

[10] See Kreps chapter 16 for a presentation of this problem (not in a reinsurance setting) and for the necessary assumptions.

[11] See Lambert (1986) (again not in a reinsurance setting).

[12] The presence of long term contract and *ex post* rating can also be explained by other information problems. If information on which to base premiums is asymmetrically distributed, then prior rated contracts may not be closed. However, both parties may still gain from *ex post* rating, since this Bayesian update is observed equally by both parties.

begins to look more like a debt instrument. But whether formally, or informally, setting reinsurance premiums to actual loss experience increases the degree of risk retained by the primary insurer; this additional retention being part of the cost of addressing the moral hazard.

Of course, reinsurers also can address moral hazard by increasing the resources devoted to monitoring the behavior of the ceding firms and conditioning the reinsurance coverage on this behavior. If reinsurers can monitor at low cost, then it will be more efficient to do so than to impose risk on the primary through *ex post* rating. In practice one would expect to see some monitoring and some rating. In this case, the costs of moral hazard would be incurred partly in monitoring cost, partly in imposing risk on the primary through *ex post* rating and, to the extent that these did not completely eliminate expropriatory behavior, partly through increased claims.

15.4.2 Alternative Risk Management Strategies For the Primary Insurer

The four principle risk management strategies identified for the firm were asset hedges, liability hedges, *ex* post financing and leverage management. This structure helps us to organize the instruments that are beginning to appear, but also it is useful to think through new strategies. In Figure 1 the three vertical shafts identify three types of risk for the primary insurer; these are not exhaustive but illustrative. First, consider asset hedge strategies. The obvious one is reinsurance and we can target

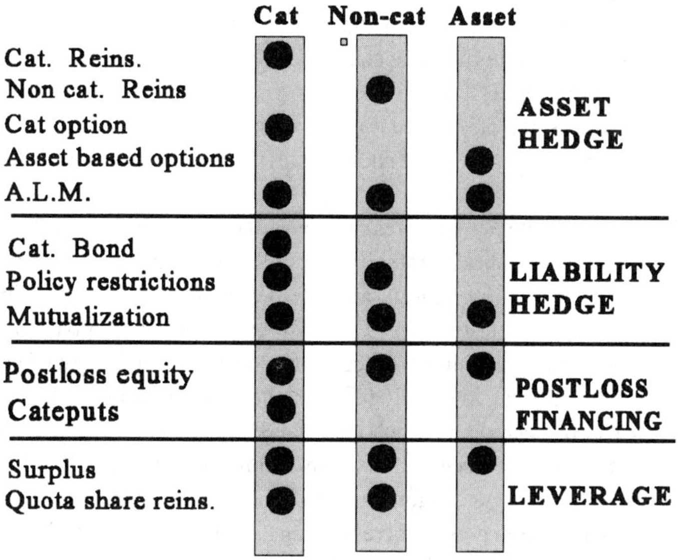

	Cat	Non-cat	Asset	
Cat. Reins.	●			ASSET HEDGE
Non cat. Reins		●		
Cat option	●			
Asset based options			●	
A.L.M.	●	●	●	
Cat. Bond	●			LIABILITY HEDGE
Policy restrictions	●	●		
Mutualization	●	●	●	
Postloss equity	●	●	●	POSTLOSS FINANCING
Cateputs	●			
Surplus	●	●	●	LEVERAGE
Quota share reins.	●	●		

Figure 1

this to catastrophe risk, other insurance risk, or possibly blanket coverage for all lines. Catastrophe risk also can be hedged by a catastrophe future of the type sold on the Chicago Board of Trade which will be discussed presently, but which is in effect a reinsurance policy sold by investors instead of reinsurers. The insurer can hedge its asset risk (i.e., risk on its stock and bond portfolios) by appropriate financial instruments such as stock options, interest rate futures, etc. Similarly, the insurer can cross hedge; i.e., choose to hold its reserves in financial assets that are positively correlated with insured losses. This is, of course, asset liability portfolio management.

Figure 1 also shows possible liability hedges. Liability hedges involve debt forgiveness should the loss experience be unusually large. Two such approaches can be distinguished according to who holds the debt. The insurer can issue debt to financial institutions or investors. When such debt contains a provision for forgiveness (principal, interest or both) on the basis of insured loss experience, then we shall call it a cat (catastrophe) bond or an "act of god" bond. But insurers, by their very nature, issue debt like instruments in the form of insurance policies. It is possible to include in this policy "debt" a forgiveness provision which reduces the amount payable to policyholders, depending on individual policyholder loss experience, the insurer's aggregate loss experience or the insurer's overall profits. One possible provision is to reduce the proportion of each individual's loss that is payable, as the insurer's aggregate loss rises. In a crude way, this is achieved by having different deductibles for cat loss and non cat loss. For example, it is usual practice to insure earthquake risk in California with a deductible that is a percentage of the property value; but to have no deductible for non catastrophe losses. We show this as "policy restrictions" in Figure 1 and focus the hedge on cat losses. A more direct hedging device it to require all policyholders to contribute higher premiums (or accept reduced policyholder dividends) if aggregate profitability falls. Indeed this is simply mutual insurance and mutual insurance is a liability hedge. Since pure mutualization gives the policyholder an equity stake in the whole insurance operation, we show "mutualization" as hedging risk in all three columns.

The third set of strategies involves postloss financing. These involve re-capitalising the insurer after loss. These strategies respond particularly to the Froot Scarfstein and Stein "crowding out" hypothesis and are designed to provide the insurer with a new source of capital after the loss. This will enable the firm to pay for cat losses, fund new investment opportunities and continue to operate to reap future profits. The two strategies identified in Figure 1 differ in the price at which postloss equity is issued. Equity can be issued at the postloss market value; i.e., reflecting the devaluation caused by the loss. The second is to pre-commit to a fixed purchase price; thus the instrument becomes a put option and partly hedges the loss.

The fourth set of strategies involve leverage management. We will not dwell on these strategies in this section, since there is an extensive literature on the determination of appropriate leverage for insurers. Of course this wheel is important; I simply do not wish to re-invent it here.

15.4.2a Asset Hedges

Catastrophe Options

New types of catastrophe instruments are often explained in terms of the need to provide direct access to capital markets to supplement the limited capacity of reinsurance markets. Noting that catastrophe risk is not highly correlated with capital market returns, then the required rate of return to attract capital is the risk free rate. Current rates on line for reinsurance are sufficiently high to be able to beat the risk free rate. But this explanation is incomplete. If attractive investment opportunities are available to investors from shorting catastrophe risk, why is there not an influx of capital into reinsurance firms? It seems that high rates on line support the high transaction costs associated with reinsurance rather than excess returns to reinsurance shareholders. Thus, if new instruments are to compete successfully with reinsurance and to be attractive to investors, they must be designed to lower transaction costs. Moreover, since the dominant transaction costs is that due to moral hazard (excess losses, the additional costs of monitoring, and locking parties into long term relationships), then successful securitization of catastrophe risk requires more effective ways of dealing with moral hazard. Also important is the ability of new instruments to address credit risk.

With reinsurance, the source of the moral hazard was the absence of basis risk. This can be seen by the term $\partial I/\partial L$ in equation 5. Since reinsurance is defined on the primary's loss L, then $I = L$ and $\partial I/\partial L = 1$. This means that there is no basis risk and the third term in (5) operates to reduce the optimal level of mitigation. As the term $\partial I/\partial L$ gets closer to zero, there will be more basis risk, leaving (5) in the form $-\partial E(L(a))/\partial a \approx 1$. In this case, there would be little moral hazard and the primary would mitigate close to the social optimum. As we shall see, one of the main defining features of cat options, and some other new instruments, is their introduction of basis risk as a method of addressing moral hazard.

Catastrophe options are traded on the Chicago Board of Trade. The basic structure of these contracts is similar to other options and, except for the difference in basis risk, resembles stop loss reinsurance. The CBOT contracts are defined on various industry (mostly quarterly) indices of property liability losses. The indices are defined by region within the U.S. There is a national index, regional indices (Western, Midwestern, Southeastern, Northeastern and Eastern) and state indices (California, Florida and Texas). When index losses exceed the striking price, the contract pays the difference between the index value and the striking price. The basic instrument can be used to derive many trading strategies (spreads, strips, etc.) in much the same fashion as stock options.

The effects of hedging with catastrophe options can be presented in the same formula used for reinsurance.[13] The trading strategy shown is a long position in a call. In equation 4, the term $R(I; S)$ can be re-interpreted as the price of the option. Here "h" is the number of contracts purchased and $C(I; S)$ is the payout on a standard contract on index "I" with strike price "S". However, since the insurer pays its own losses "L", but receives a payoff based on the chosen index "I", there is basis risk (L does not equal I). The size of the basis risk will vary. First, the insurer's own losses will contribute to the index, but for many insurers this will be modest. Second, to the extent that the primary has a portfolio similar to that of the other insurers comprising the index, the basis risk will be small. Indeed one would expect the hedging demand for CBOT options to be strongest for insurers with representative portfolios.

The major benefit of defining the option on the index, is that it controls moral hazard. The primary insurer that is able to practice *ex ante* or *ex post* mitigation, will receive much of the benefit of that activity in the form of reduced claims. However, this benefit will not be offset by a reduction in the payoff to the option, except to the limited extent that the primary's reduced losses affects the index. The idea can be illustrated by a simple example. Suppose that an insurer has a portfolio that represents 5% of the market covered by the index and correspondingly wishes to buy a call option that pays 0.05 times the payoff on the amount by which industry losses exceed "S". Since "I" is the sum of industry losses ($I \equiv \Sigma L_i$), then spending of "a_i" on safety by insurer "i" will reduce the index at the rate $\partial L/\partial a_i$. But since the primary is hedging only five percent of changes in the index, then the primary's payoff on its call position will be reduced only at the rate $(0.05)\partial L/\partial a_i$.[14] In contrast, spending on mitigation reduces the primary's own claims obligations to its policyholders at the full rate $\partial L/\partial a_i$. Thus, mitigation yields a large marginal net benefit to the primary (0.95 times $\partial L/\partial a_i$).

Catastrophe options face similar credit risk to reinsurance. Many financial instruments use "mark to market" to address credit risk. When the instrument is written on an underlying asset whose price evolves as a smooth process, "mark to market" offers considerable credit protection. This device prevents the build up of large liabilities. However, the temporal path of catastrophe insurance liabilities is anything but smooth. With storms, the lead time is, at most a few days. With earthquakes, the liability can

[13] Other hedging strategies can be derived. One that offers some continuity with traditional reinsurance strategies is to buy a spread. This involves holding a call option with one striking price and selling another call with a higher striking price. The effect is to obtain a layer of hedge protection between a range of index losses. Apart from the fact that the loss is defined on the index, this arrangement is similar to layered reinsurance arrangements.

[14] The same concepts can be described in the appropriate terminology. CBOT options are denominated in payment of $200 for every $100 million change in the index. Each $100 million in the index is referred to as a "point" Thus, the primary wishing to hedge for a 5% of the amount by which the index exceeded a chosen striking price, would purchase 25,000 units. Thus, if the strike price was 400 and the index was 450, the payoff on this position would be (450–400) times (200) times 25,000 = $250 million. Notice that $250 million is exactly 5% of the amount by which industry losses ($45 billion) exceed the strike price ($40 billion).

change from zero to billions of dollars in one second. "Mark to market" is of little use. Sellers of catastrophe bonds are required to maintain a margin account. However, this device offers only limited protection unless the account is maintained at a level equal to (or close to) the maximum possible loss. Thus, catastrophe options impose some credit risk. The CBOT options offer a second line of defense. The CBOT maintains a security fund. However, the scale of this fund is small compared with the multi billion dollar liabilities that are plausible with these instruments. This is not to say that the credit risk is severe, only that it is potentially severe. The degree of credit risk depends on the spread of liability amongst investors who take short positions in these instruments. The point is that the structural design of this, and other asset hedges, introduces credit risk. As we shall see below, the structural design of the liability hedges avoids this problem.

15.4.2b Liability Hedges

Catastrophe Bonds

Debt forgiveness instruments go by several names; insurance linked bonds, Act of God bonds, catastrophe bonds and (anciently) bottomry. The idea is very old, dating to the medieval origins of insurance in Italy. A primitive arrangement was for merchants to fund ventures by borrowing to pay for the ship and/or cargo. However, in the event of the loss of ship or cargo, the debt would be forgiven. Thus, the lenders were "insuring" the vessel and its cargo. The idea has recently re-appeared. Recently, bond issues have been announced by insurers, that have forgiveness provisions in the event of catastrophic losses; the consideration being a higher interest rate. The generic design can allow for interest and/or principal forgiveness which can be total, partial or scaled to the size of the loss. Moreover, the forgiveness can be triggered either by catastrophic losses to the issuing firm, or to catastrophic losses measured on some composite index of insurer losses.

The effects of hedging with cat. bonds can be analyzed with equation (8). The insurer issues debt with a face value D which must be repaid with interest at a rate r. However, the debt can be forgiven (here I illustrate with the principal being forgiven not the interest) according to a loss index I. The forgiveness is shown by the term $hC(I; S)$ which indicates that the cat bond is really a simple bond with an embedded call option written on the catastrophe loss.

$$T = \{E + P + D\}(1 + E(r_i)) - E(L(a)) - D\{1 - hC(I;S) + r\} - a \tag{8}$$

The analysis of moral hazard is similar to that for asset hedges. Condition (9) below shows the first order condition for mitigation for the primary insurer which is identical to condition (5). The first term shows the effect of mitigation on the primary insurer's losses; the second term shows the increased marginal cost of mitigation; and the third term is the effect of reduced mitigation (and therefore increased losses) on the cat bond forgiveness.

$$\frac{\partial E(T)}{\partial a} = -\frac{\partial E(L(a))}{\partial a} - 1 + h\frac{\partial C}{\partial I}\frac{\partial I}{\partial L}\frac{\partial L}{\partial a} = 0 \tag{9}$$

The interpretation of (9) depends on whether there is basis risk or not (i.e., whether I equals L). Consider that the cat bond is forgiven on the basis of the primary's own catastrophic losses, $I = L$. This moral hazard effect is similar to that under reinsurance. If the cat bond is forgiven dollar for dollar against the primary's own catastrophe losses, the primary has little, or no, incentive to control those losses. Controlling losses simply increases the amount of debt that must be repaid (the first and third terms would simply cancel out). With no cat bond, the primary would have reaped all the benefit of mitigation and would have chosen a level of mitigation at which marginal benefit equaled marginal cost.

Now if the cat bond is forgiven on the basis of some industry index of catastrophe losses, $I \neq L$, the moral hazard is similar to that for the catastrophe option. The primary spending on mitigation will only reduce the debt forgiveness to the extent of its share of the index. Thus, the primary contracting for forgiveness at the rate of 5% of the index (i.e., \$5 of debt is forgiven for every \$100 increase in industry losses) will reap a net benefit from mitigation equal to 95% of the reduction in its direct claims.

This analysis shows that cat bonds can be designed to achieve different balances between basis risk and moral hazard. Given freedom to select indices, the primary may well be able to identify some industry portfolio with similar exposure to its own. If it can, the basis risk from writing the cat bond on this index will be small, and the moral hazard problem will be largely mitigated. If the primary's portfolio is not represented well by a convenient industry loss index, then the hedging properties of an index based cat bond will be poor, even though moral hazard is addressed. In such circumstances, a cat bond based on the primary's own losses may be preferable with other controls (e.g., monitoring) used to address the moral hazard.

Cat bonds avoid the credit risk to the issuer, that is found with reinsurance or catastrophe options. Bondholders provide the hedge to the insurer by forgiving existing debt. Thus, the value of the hedge is independent of the bondholders' assets and the issuing primary insurer has no risk of non-delivery on the hedge. In essence, the cat bond is similar to a reinsurance contract in which the reinsurer opens a margin account equal to the maximum expected loss. Moreover, the primary insurer has access to the margin account. This avoids all possibility of default to the primary.[15]

[15] The risk to the bondholder is of interest. Had the primary issued a non forgiveness bond, it would have been subject to default risk. However, one of the most likely causes for default on such an issue would be that the primary insurer suffered catastrophic losses. What the cat bond does, is to turn the default risk (i.e., the implicit default put) into an explicit embedded option.

A variation on the theme of debt forgiveness is the conversion of the debt into another asset, notably equity. This idea it to embody a conversion option in the debt, but the option is exercised by the issuer, not the bondholder. This can be called "reverse convertible debt" (RCD). A pure form for RCD is simply to permit the issuer to choose conversion at a fixed ratio of shares for bonds. When the share price falls, for whatever reason, the option will be "in the money". This instrument provides a partial hedge against a fall in share price and it does not matter whether the cause was a catastrophic loss or a fall in the value of the primary's asset portfolio. Doherty (1995) has shown that this instrument can be potentially useful for non insurance firms since it can be used to resolve incentive conflicts between stakeholders and it avoids the transaction costs of bankruptcy. Indeed the resolution of these problems can be so effective that RCD has greater value than regular debt (i.e., the conversion option can have negative value). A more limited version of RCD for primary insurers could embody an event trigger; the conversion option can be exercised in the event of a defined catastrophe which could be based on firm losses or an index.

The value created for the primary on conversion is the difference between the outstanding debt obligation and the value of the equity used to redeem that obligation. Investors holding such bonds could well find them attractive despite their short position in the embedded option, since the conversion option carries more favorable incentives than the implicit default put in non-convertible debt. RCD may also be attractive to policyholders. I will note below the analogy between debt and the primary's policy liabilities. Drawing on this analogy, scaling the payout of policyholder claims to the size of a catastrophe, is equivalent to a mutual insurance in which scaling is achieved by policyholder dividends. There are strong theoretical and practical reasons why mutualization of catastrophe risk is an efficient form of risk sharing and there is a pressing case for considering contract design as part of a risk management program.

Policy Conditions and Mutualization

Perhaps the most direct way in which the insurer can hedge its catastrophe risk is to require that the policyholder bear some of this risk. To explore this further, it is useful to take a small detour into the economics of insurance. Much of intellectual and lay thinking about insurance, focusses on an ideal in which the policyholder is fully insured for all loss. At an intellectual level, this ideal can be derived by assuming that policyholders are risk averse, but that all risk can be diversified by the insurer by holding a large portfolio of independent policies. The law of large numbers implies that such a portfolio will leave the insurer with a highly predictable per policy average loss, and thus the competitive insurer will charge little, or no, risk premium. Being risk averse, individuals will fully insure since they can avoid risk without facing any significant loading of the premium above the expected value of loss.

With catastrophe risk, the law of large numbers is violated since losses are highly correlated. Thus, the insurer cannot rely simply on many policies to diversify its risk away. Moreover, if risk is costly to the insurer (why otherwise would we be discussing hedging strategies?), then the insurer would be forced to charge a risk premium and the optimal amount of insurance would be less than full coverage. It is important to understand that "optimal" reflects the interests of insurer and insured. The risk premium reflects the cost of risk bearing and this is a real social cost. The insured is better off having less insurance (and avoiding part of the risk premium) than being fully insured and facing the full risk premium. In short, the insured in trading off expected wealth against risk.

Now this reasoning can be refined in several ways following the seminal work of Karl Borch (1962), (which pre-dated and fully anticipated the capital asset pricing model). Where risk cannot be fully diversified, the optimal insurance arrangement from all policyholders' perspectives, is one in which all are full insured for idiosyncratic (read diversifiable) risk, but in which each shares in the social loss. This is tantamount to a mutual insurance arrangement; each policyholder is insured for catastrophe risk, but the proportion of insurance depends on the size of the catastrophe. In practice, this can be accomplished by a mutual which pays everyone's claim, but which reduces its dividend to all policyholders (or assesses them) by an amount related to total losses.[16]

The second way in which this reasoning can be refined is to address moral hazard between the policyholder and the primary insurer. This is closely related to the moral hazard occurring at the interface between the primary insurer and the reinsurer. For example, the *ex post* moral hazard that can arise between the primary insurer and reinsurer, stems from the lack of appropriate actions by the primary to prevent policyholders from "building up" claims or filing fraudulent claims. In short, the moral hazard that arises between primary and reinsurer is largely a "pass through" of the moral hazard between the policyholder and the primary. Policyholder moral hazard can be addressed by requiring that the policyholder share the loss, normally through the use of a deductible or policy limit (see Shavell 1979 and Stiglitz 1983). This idea has been extended by Smith and Stultzer (1994) who have shown that sharing risk through dividends also helps control moral hazard.

[16] To argue that mutualization of this sort is "optimal" is often misunderstood. Policyholders would certainly be better off if they could fully insure at no risk premium. But this is not an option in a competitive market since investors would require that the insurer cover any cost of bearing undiversified risk. Thus the real choice for policyholders is (a) to have a policy with a large risk loading which would induce policyholders to accept a large deductible or coinsurance or (b) to accept a policy which covers idiosyncratic risk but which requires the policyholder to contribute in proportion to total losses. The argument here is that option (b) is better for policyholders than option (a). Notice that this argument is identical to the reasoning of the capital asset pricing model. In that model it is shown that the optimal investment strategy is for risk averse investors to hold a diversified portfolio (i.e., the market portfolio) such that each shares in the total market risk but each diversifies away idiosyncratic risk.

15.4.2c Postloss Equity Financing

Post-loss Equity Issues

Another approach to insurer risk management is postloss financing. This may or may not, involve a hedging arrangement. Perhaps the most obvious motivation for this type of strategy relates to Froot, Sharfstein and Stein's "crowding out" rationale for managing corporate risk. When a insurer sustains abnormally large losses, its internal capital is depleted and its ability to fund new investment project is compromised. The most prominent "project" is for the firm to continue to operate into the future and to reap future profits. Refer to the present value of such earnings as the "franchise value" and consider a firm that suffers very large losses but still has a significant franchise value. The firm can still have a positive equity value, but the franchise component of that value is illiquid. Thus, if losses exhaust its available funds (the surplus), then it may be unable to continue to operate and lose the value of its franchise. The problem seems to be that the franchise value is not liquid, and therefore cannot be used to pay for current losses. We will show that postloss equity financing provides a method for releasing the franchise value or, more generally, for releasing illiquid assets. For the moment, we will assume that there is no hedge in this arrangment and that the postloss issue is common equity.

The value of insurer at the end of one period is:

$$T_1 = ((E+P)(1+r_0)-L)+\sum_t \frac{P_t - E(L_t)}{1+r_t} = S_1 + F_1 \tag{10}$$

where $S_1 \equiv (E_1 + P)(1 + r_0) - L$ is the end of first period surplus/deficit (the value of the first bracket) and $F_1 \equiv \Sigma_t(P_t - E(L_t))/(1 + r_t)$ is the franchise value of the firm at the end of the first period (i.e., the expected value of its future expected cash flows). If the realization of L is very large, the firm will be insolvent and T_1 is negative. Assuming F is positive, there will be some intermediate value of L for which T_1 is positive but where S_1 is negative. For such values, the firm is still solvent but faces a liquidity crunch. Thus, we refer to $T_1 > 0$ as solvent and $S_1 < 0$ as a liquidity crunch.

The effect of the liquidity crunch is illustrated in Figure 2. Assuming the franchise value can be captured despite shortage of first period surplus, the value of equity is shown as the solid line. Note that when losses exceed $S_1 + F_1$, the firm is insolvent and equity falls to zero. However, if the surplus is negative then the franchise can be lost if the firm cannot translate this into a liquid form to pay current losses. The dashed line shows that when losses exceed $(E_1 + P)(1 + r)$, the value of equity falls to zero, despite the positive franchise value.

The liquidity crunch can be overcome by an equity injection of E_2 at the beginning of the second period. Assume this is common equity.

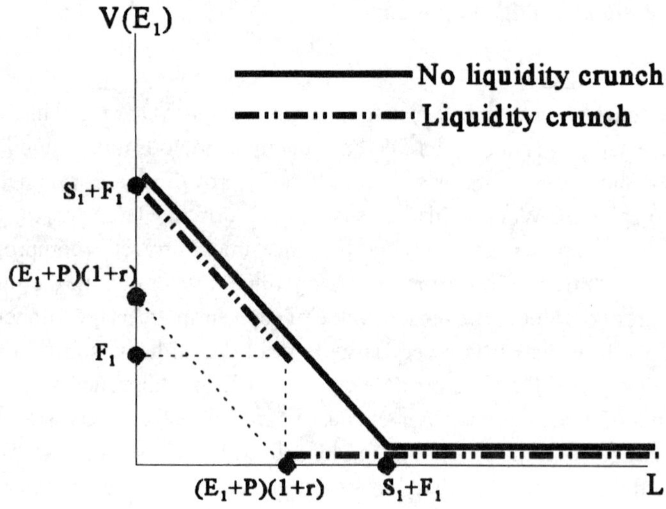

Figure 2

$$T_1^{+} = ((E_1 + P)(1 + r_0) - L) + E_2 + \sum_t \frac{P_t - E(L_t)}{1 + r_t} = S_1 + E_2 + F_1 \tag{11}$$

Now, if N_2 shares are issued after the realization of L, the market value of the new equity, E_2, will be:

$$E_2 = \frac{N_2}{N_1 + N_2}[S_1 + E_2 + F_1] = \frac{N_2}{N_1}[S_1 + F_1] \tag{12}$$

Thus, the issue of N_2 new shares will command a positive value only if the franchise value F_1 is sufficient to overcome any shortfall of current resources, S_1, from current losses L_1. If this condition is met, there is some number of shares that can be issued at market price *after loss*, such that the net after loss value of the firm ($NV \equiv S_1 + F_1$) can be captured by the original shareholders. To see this, note the after loss value of the original equity $V(E_1)$ will be the ratio $N_1/(N_1 + N_2)$ time the total equity value T_1^{+} shown in (11):

$$V(E_1) = \frac{N_1}{N_1 + N_2}[S_1 + E_2 + F_1] \tag{13}$$

Substituting from (12) for E_2 gives

$$V(E_1) = [S_1 + F_1] \tag{14}$$

Thus, as long as a firm is solvent, it can always overcome the liquidity crunch to capture net value for existing shareholders by a postloss share issue. If the loss exceeds the equity value, there is no price at which new shares can be sold without a formal re-organization.

In order to capture the franchise value, despite the negative surplus, a dilution of equity must occur. To raise enough shares to cover the deficit E_2 must equal (negative) S_1. Substituting, for E_2 from (12) gives:

$$\frac{N_2}{N_1}(S_1 + F_1) = -S_1 \tag{15}$$

Solving for N_2, the firm must issue

$$N_2 = N_1 \frac{-S_1}{S_1 + F_1} \tag{16}$$

Thus, if the deficit ($S_1 < 0$) was so large that it almost wiped out the franchise value, $S_1 \rightarrow F_1$, then the insurer would have to issue an almost infinite numbert of shares, i.e., ceding almost all control to new shareholders.

Postloss equity capitalization can be useful following less traumatic losses. A more modest liquidity crisis can arise without severe financial distress. With large losses and a asset portfolio predominantly illiquid, the insurer will be forced to a "fire sale" or to other forms of control such as delaying claims payments to policyholders. The former results in a direct asset loss, the latter may compromise reputation and future profitability. If the *ex ante* advantages of holding a relatively illiquid portfolio are substantial, then postloss equity financing provides a method of avoiding the potential liquidity crunch.

In summary, postloss financing can be used to by a distressed insurer to capture the "illiquid" franchise value, as long as the firm value, including franchise value, is positive. While the ideas has been developed to cope with the extreme case in which suplus S_1 is negative, the notion translates easily to less dramatic liquidity crunches. If S_1 is positive but part of the assets are illiquid, then postloss financing can be a useful method of providing liquidity. The appropriate test is how the transaction costs associated with liquidizing assets compare with those of a new postloss equity issue.

This analysis assumes that insurer equity value falls following a catastrophe loss. This assumption can be set against some recent evidence. Insurer stock prices showed a *positive* response to the 17th October 1989 Loma Prieta earthquake (Shelor, Anderson and Cross 1992; and Aiuppa, Carney and Krueger, 1993). This has been interpreted as a capturing the potential for price increases in a regulated market. However, Hurricane Andrew, a much larger loss for the industry, seems to have induced significant negative price effects (Lamb 1995). Insofar as positive price responses do occur, then post-loss equity re-capitalization can occur with relatively little stock dilution.

Catastrophe equity puts (CE Puts)

The discussion of postloss financing sets the stage for CE puts. One version of this type of instrument, known as a Cateput, was designed by Aon, have recently been used by Centre Re in a pair of transactions with insurers. The cateput is a postloss equity financing arrangement, but with price of the equity issue fixed before the loss (and not the postloss market price as considered above). Thus, there is a striking price or exercise price, x, which differs (except by coincidence) from the postloss share price, p_1. This is a put option contract which gives the option to the insurer to sell a given number N_2 of shares to the counterparty (e.g., a reinsurer) after a defined loss and at a fixed price. The second innovation, is that there is a another trigger; the insurer's losses must lie between pre-determined upper and lower bounds (this can be called the *exercise window*) before the capitalization option can be exercised. I will assume that the postloss equity issue is of common shares.

Since the insurer has the option to sell equity after the defined catastrophe at a specified exercise price, it will do so only if the value of the original shareholders' equity after exercise of this option, exceeds both (a) its value of with this option exercised and (b) its value if equity is issued at market price. First note that the value raised in a new equity issue is the number of shares covered by the option N_2 times the exercise price, x. The total value of equity after exercise is now $S_1 + N_2x + F_1$. Thus, exercise will increase the original owners' equity if:

$$\frac{N_1}{N_1+N_2}(S_1+N_2x+F_1) > S_1+F_1 \tag{17}$$

From which it is easily deduced that exercise will only be chosen if $x > (S_1 + F_1)/N_1 \equiv p_1$. The possibility for gain to the insurer on exercise makes this instrument a hedge. Strictly, the hedge is not against losses per se, but against a fall in the insurer's share price (this will be qualified when the exercise window is discussed). Thus, the value created for the insurer stems partly from the fact that postloss capitalization secures the franchise value and partly from the efficieny gains associated with reductions in corporate risk.

The market value of the postloss equity sold to the counterparty is $[N_2/(N_1 + N_2)][S_1 + N_2x + F_1]$ which will be less than its purchase price under the put option if $x > p_1$. Consequently, the put option will command a initial price which, following normal option technology, will depend upon the parameters of the underlying equity distribution (which depend on insurer leverage, loss distribution, investment distribution, etc) the exercise price, the current equity price, maturity and the risk free rate.

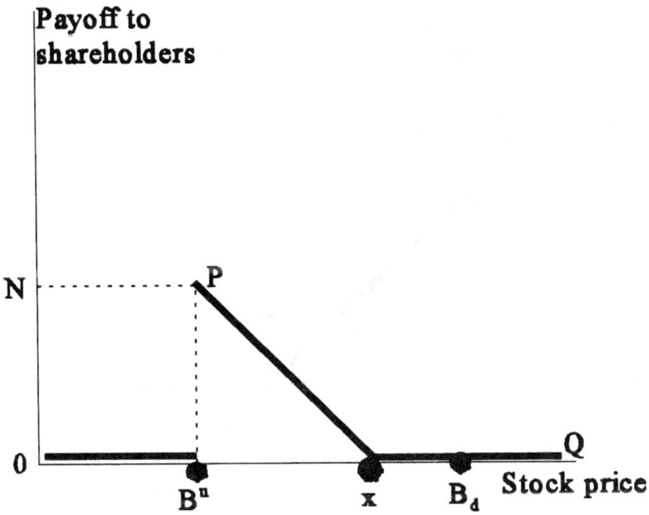

Figure 3

Since the option is written on the underlying stock, its pricing would appear to be fairly conventional. However, there is the unusual twist introduced by the second trigger. The option can only be excercised if the catastrophe losses to the insurer lies between a lower and upper bound; the *exercise window*. The exercise window is important, particularly the upper boundary. One would expect a close negative relationship between the insurer's cat losses and its post-loss share price. For small losses, there is little need for re-capitalisation and there is little likelihood that the share price would fall below a pre-arranged striking price. Thus, the lower trigger is not very interesting and the potential exercise could be controlled simply by choice of a sufficiently low exercise price. However, if cat losses are very high, the share price will fall sufficiently that the share value will fall well below the exercise price and the insurers payoff from exercise will be substantial. The upper loss boundary therefore becomes a method of limiting the risk to the counterparty and this will be reflected in a lower price for the option.

Figures 3 and 4 illustrate CE puts and the effects of the exercise window. Bearing in mind that the put option will assume positive value when either of two triggers kick in; either the loss is of sufficient size or the share price falls below the exercise price. Considering also that losses translate into lower share prices, the loss boundaries can be represented on the horizontal axis and are shown as B_d for the lower boundary and B^u as the upper boundary. In Figure 3, the lower boundary, B_d is set sufficiently low that it does not bind and is somewhat redundant. In Figure 4, the lower bound on losses is set sufficiently high that it kicks in only after share prices will have fallen to below the exercise price. Thus, when the exercise price is triggered, the option is not

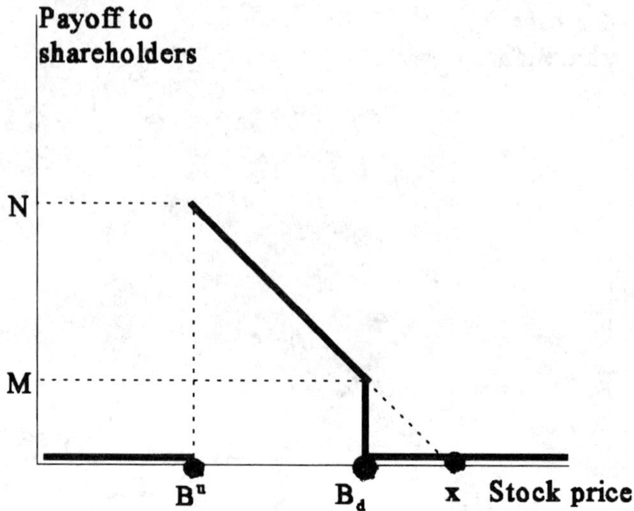

Figure 4

available because of thc loss trigger. Only when the loss trigger is activated, does the option become payable. The crucial issue in Figure 4 is the discontinuity of the payout, with a big jump when the lower loss bound is activated. This can have dysfunctional incentive as discussed below.

The moral hazard issues surrounding CE Puts are parallel to those for other instruments already discussed. Insofar as contracts offer the insurer indemnification for its own losses, there is a moral hazard cost. When contract payouts are indexed to industry losses, the moral hazard problem is mitigated. With CE Puts, the payout is not indexed and the insurer's behaviour in underwriting and settling losses has direct implications for the realized value of losses and therefore for stock price. The purchase of the put relaxes incentives for loss control and, unless the counter-party is able to monitor, losses are likely to increase. However, there is an interesting twist. Consider the lower boundary B_d illustrated in Figures 3 and 4. The first problem is that, if the lower loss bound is high relative to the exercise price, the loss boundary may activate when the put option is already "in the money" as shown in Figure 4. This gives the insurer a discrete incentive to relax control of loss payout for a given catastrophic event, in order to activate the trigger. The threshold dollar of loss payouts that hits B_d can bring an enormous payoff if, as shown in Figure 4, the option can then be exercised well below its exercise price. The payoff is OM in Figure 4. On the upper side the incentive is reversed. If losses on the insurer are just above the upper trigger, B^u then a small reduction in loss payouts will bring a sudden payoff on the option of ON. These boundaries resemble a concept known as a "knock out" option in which a normal option is annihilated if a specified stock price in penetrated before maturity.

While the indemnification feature of the CE Put carries adverse incentives, the "knock out" characteristics of the loss boundaries are downright perverse. The incentive problem arises from limiting the hedge to one of catastrophe risk, but paying according to stock price. Two alternative designs are, first, to design a non specific hedge; i.e., that covers any fall in share price regardless of cause and, second to keep the notion of a catastrophe hedge but remove the more perverse edges. The first approach is to treat the lower boundary as either redundant or carrying perverse incentives and thus to discard it. The upper bound is more problematic since the counterparty migh wish to limit its liability. A more friendly structure can be envisioned in which the option is not annihilated when losses penetrate the barrier, but rather the payout is capped at a level N in Figure 3. Allowing for the discard of both loss bounds, the payoff structure is shown in Figure 3 as NPxQ. This payout structure can be replicated by a portfolio comprising a long put with exercise price x; a short put with exercise price B^u; and a short position in a bond valued at N.[17]

The second approach is to retain the notion of a catastrophe trigger but to avoid the payout discontinuities. This can be achieved by having a "floating" exercise price equal to the share price immediately before the defined catastrophe that triggers payout. The upper discontinuity can be avoided by simply capping the payout rather than terminating it entirely when the upper threshold is exceeded.

15.5 INNOVATION: MARKET ENHANCEMENT AND TECHNICAL EFFICIENCY

Innovation serves two general functions. First, innovation is market enhancing. Figure 5 shows the relevant properties of hedging instruments. The defining characteristic is its ability to control basis risk. Incidentally, hedging instruments can encounter moral hazard and credit risk. Innovation extends the range of choice in this three dimensional space. The figure shows the characteristics of the main instruments considered, but the point is that product design provides for continuous trade offs to be made across this space. The value of market enhancement arises because insurers are not identical. The issue can be simplified by considering the trade off between moral hazard and basis risk. In Figure 5, the line AB shows the potential choices available to the purchaser of a hedge; positions closer to A involve less basis risk and more moral hazard. The shape and position of line AB depends on technical issues and this will be discussed presently. Now, an insurer with a geographically diversified portfolio, may prefer to resolve moral hazard, not by reinsurance, but by accepting some basis risk by trading CBOT options (close to A on line AB). For this insurer, the basis risk will be fairly modest since its portfolio corresponds closely in structure to the "market portfolio" of insurance exposures. Another insurer with a more concentrated

[17] This portfolio also suggests a pricing scheme since each component can be priced separately.

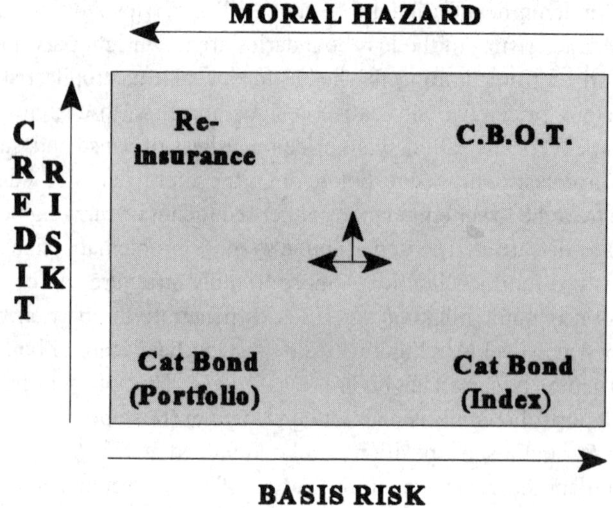

Figure 5

book of business, may find the basis risk in an available index to be unacceptable and will prefer reinsurance (close to B on line AB).

Market enhancement does increase efficiency, but the second function of innovation is to change technical efficiency. Consider the trade off between moral hazard and basis risk shown in Figure 5 as line AB. If this line can be shifted towards the origin, the efficiency loss from hedging will be reduced. To illustrate, note that reinsurance addresses this trade off in one of two ways. First a traditional reinsurance contract does not have basis risk, but bonds the parties in a long term relationship (and/or the primary is monitored) as a way of controlling moral hazard. By choosing the level of attachment for the reinsurance contract, the insurer can select a position on the AB line; higher retention involves more risk acceptance and less moral hazard. The second way is for the reinsurance contract to be restructured as a debt like instrument, as happens with finite reinsurance. This limits the hedging properties of the reinsurance contract (introduces basis risk) but does mitigate moral hazard. Now the primary has less incentive to let claims get out of control and less reinsurer monitoring is required. By changing the mix of debt and insurance in the finite risk plan, different points in moral hazard—basis risk space can be achieved. The question is now, which method involves the most efficient trade off; changing the reinsurance attachment point, or changing the insurance debt mix. Increasing efficiency means lowering the trade off line in Figure 6 from AB to CB.

Other options for increasing technical efficiency can be imagined. In a recent paper, John Major (1996) showed that, if insurers are allowed to hedge using a state-

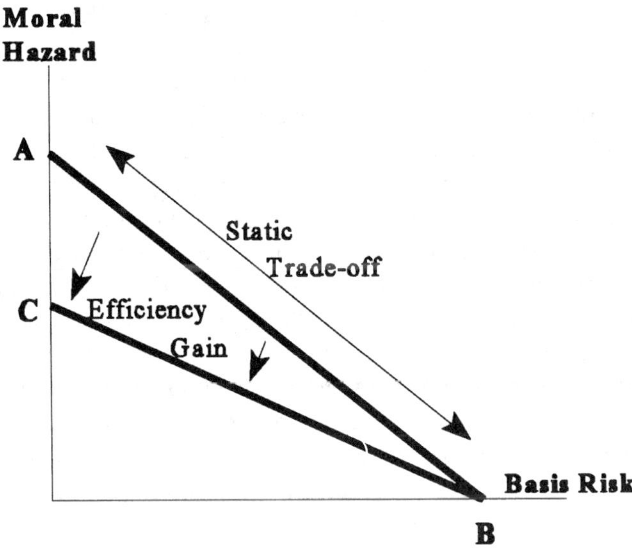

Figure 6

wide index of industry loss experience, they can achieve significant reductions in volatility. But, state-wide indices do involve some basis risk which will differ between firms according to their portfolio mixes. If indices were available for industry loss experience by zip code, then the basis risk could be reduced significantly. This reduction in basis risk arises partly because the insurer will be more concentrated, and have a larger market share, in some zip codes. Lowering the basis risk is achieved by increasing the hedge ratio in these high concentration zip codes. But this strategy will increase moral hazard, because the hedging insurer's losses comprise a significant portion of the industry losses in the zips. Now the technical question is this. Is it more efficient to use a state index and trade off moral hazard and basis risk with a fairly high hedge ratio; or should one use a zip code index and a lower hedge ratio? I.e., which strategy is depicted by line AB, and which by line CB?

Other possibilities for changing technical efficiency can be envisioned. For example, reinsurer monitoring is one method of controlling *ex post* moral hazard. Another is for the primary insurer to write direct contracts with appropriate incentives to policyholders for *ex post* loss mitigation (e.g., deductibles, coinsurance, retrospective premium adjustments). The rate at which moral hazard and basis risk can be traded off against each other with these two approaches may well differ for any insurer, and may well differ across insurers. The only safe conjecture is that there is no "one size fits all". It is this diversity that will permit value to be created through innovation, as insurers seek to find combinations of basis risk, credit risk and moral hazard that match their financial and organizational structure.

15.6 SOME ACTUAL AND POTENTIAL STRATEGIES

Hedging by Primary Insurers

A straightforward use of the catastrophe instruments is for a primary insurer to replace, or supplement, reinsurance with cat options and bonds. Several insurers have made limited use of the traded CBOT catastrophe options though the size of this market is still modest (the size of the private market is unknown). Use of cat bonds is rarer. The most visible example lies in a recent USAA announcement for a $500 million dollar issue that would be forgiven on the issuer's own loss experience. As discussed, this strategy does not avoid moral hazard since the issuer's gain from reducing its losses is offset by a reduction in the debt under the cat bond. Moreover, unlike reinsurance where contractual relationships are set up to resolve incentive conflicts, the cat bond issue has no natural mechanism to combat moral hazard. Thus, investors will be looking for mechanisms that lie outside the terms of the issue to deal with moral hazard. Is the issue linked with other hedging instruments that provide appropriate monitoring? For example, does the issuer still have adequate conventional reinsurance in place, so that bondholders can "free ride" off the monitoring provided by the reinsurer. Alternatively, is the direct portfolio written with appropriate incentives (e.g., deductibles, dividends) to provide appropriate controls over policyholder moral hazard? This sort of investigation by potential purchasers goes somewhat beyond the normal credit monitoring required by prudent bond investors. The additional monitoring would be less crucial had the issue been based on an industry loss index, but this would introduce basis risk.

Providing Reinsurance Capacity

An alternative use for cat instruments is to enable the issue to extend reinsurance capacity. Many catastrophe reinsurers will seek to control risk by international diversification. It would be common for a specialty Bermuda catastrophe reinsurer to have a portfolio with risk in North and South America, Europe, Japan and the Antipodes. Such an insurer could issue bonds based on worldwide catastrophe risk to hedge its existing portfolio while maintaining an acceptably low level of basis risk. Taking this approach further, the bond issue could also provide the basis for extending its capacity to offer reinsurance to primaries. This thinking seems to lie behind a recent cat bond issue announced in Geneva in August 1996 by the American International Group (A.I.G.). This issue provides for scaled forgiveness of debt, according to the number of catastrophes recorded in the publication Sigma (published by the Swiss Re.). The index is based on five regions across the world and a catastrophe is defined as industry losses above a set value that varies according to the region. The debt is progressively forgiven and will be completely forgiven with five events within the operational period. A.I.G. intention appears to be to use this issue to offer retrocessions to catatrophe reinsurers.

An expression that is now sometimes heard in connection with this type of activity is "intermediating basis risk". The idea is this. A reinsurer with a wide spread of business can write a hedge contract based on a very broad index without assuming a high level of basis risk. Were a primary with a much less diversified portfolio to write a hedge using the same index, the basis risk would be very high. Thus, the reinsurer "intermediates the basis risk" by hedging on the index and using this hedge to expand conventional reinsurance to primaries. This should be viewed with a little caution. By absorbing the basis risk and offering conventional reinsurance, all the moral hazard issues in the reinsurer-primary relationship remain. This type of activity can expand capacity, but does not address the moral hazard problem. Thus, the potential to add value, depends on which explanation for financial innovation is valid. If innovation simply addresses a diversification problem, the intermediating basis risk can potentially add capacity and add value. If innovation is needed to respond to moral hazard and similar frictions, then intermediating basis risk does nothing to address the root cause.

The California Earthquake Authority

In an attempt to increase the availability of earthquake insurance, the State of California has formed the California Earthquake Authority. The state initiative includes provisions that permit insurers to offer earthquake insurance with appropriate limitations of coverage, (such as deductibles and limited coverage on house contents), and a financial structure to "reinsure" the industry in the event of a very large loss. The structure includes potential assessments on policyholders and various layers of financing including reinsurance. Of particular interest is a bond layer of $1.5 billion with interest forgiveness. The principal is secured by using a portion of the proceeds of the issue to purchase U.S. Treasury strips. The interesting feature of this initiative is that it combines many of the features discussed in this paper. Policyholders are required to participate both in their individual losses and in the collective loss. Moreover, the issue of interest forgiveness cat bonds allows insurers to supplement conventional reinsurance hedges with cat bonds.

Facilitating Third World Investment

Other uses can be imagined. Insurance is rarely bought on private dwellings in the third world even though many regions are subject to severe catatrophe risk. However, development banks such as the World Bank who often lend to these countries for the construction of industrial and infra-structure projects, seem to be showing increasing concern about possible default following catastrophic events. A plausible hedging scenario could jointly address this default risk and the need for mitigation. Loss mitigation is usually most cost effective at the point of construction. Development bank loans could be used to fund projects with embodied mitigation. If this issue is made as a catastrophe bond, the development bank could use the additional interest to purchase a catastrophe option designed to repay interest and principal in the event of a defined disaster. Thus, unlike normal cat bonds in which the option is embedded, the option could be stripped out and sold separately. Such a scheme jointly addresses the hedging issue and loss prevention. Moreover, by linking with project finance, mitigation can be introduced at the point of construction of the asset when it is most cost effective. The trick in designing an operation scheme would be to define the trigger to minimize *ex post* moral hazard on the part of the borrowing government. For their part, those shorting the cat call could conceivably partly hedge their exposure in exchange rate futures which are likely to be highly sensitive to the triggering event.

15.7 REFERENCES

Aiuppa, Thomas A., Robert J. Carney and Thomas M. Krueger (1993). "An Examination of Insurance Stock Prices Following the 1989 Loma Prieta Earthquake", *Journal of Insurance Issues and Practices*, 16, 1–14.

Babbel, David, F., Anthony M. and Santomero (1996). "Risk Management by Insurers: An Analysis of the Process," Working Paper, Financial Institutions Center, Wharton School, University of Pennsylvania.

Borch, Karl (1962). "Equilibrium in a Reinsurance Market", *Econometrica*, 30, 424–444.

Cummins, J. David and N.A. Doherty (1996). "Can Insurers Pay for the "Big One": Measuring the Capacity of the Insurance Industry to Respond to Catastrophic Losses", working paper, Wharton School, University of Pennsylvania.

Doherty, Neil A. (1985). "Corporate Risk Management: A Financial Analysis" McGraw Hill.

Doherty, Neil A. (1996). "Corporate Insurance: Competition from Capital Markets" in *Universal Banking*, (eds. A. Saunders and I. Walter), Salomon Center, New York University, New York. Reprinted in *Assurances*, 65, 43–90.

Doherty, Neil A. and James R. Garven (1986). "Price Regulation in Property-Liability Insurance: A Contingent Claims Approach", *Journal of Finance*, 41, 1031–1050.

Doherty, Neil, Anne E. Kleffner and Howard Kunreuther (1992). "Should Society Deal with the Earthquake Problem?", (with H. Kunreuther and A. Kleffner), *Regulation*.

Doherty, Neil and Seha Tinic (1981). "A Note on Reinsurance under Conditions of Capital Market Equilibrium" *Journal of Finance*, 36, 949–953.

Froot, Kenneth, David Scharfstein, and Jeremy Stein (1993). "Risk Management: Co-ordinating Investment and Financing Problems", *Journal of Finance*, 48, 1629–1658.

Garven James R. and Henri Louberge (1996). "Reinsurance, Taxes and Efficiency: A Contingent Claims Model of Insurance Market Equilibrium", *Journal of Financial Intermediation*, 5, 74–93.

Garven, James. R. and Richard D. MacMinn (1993). "Underinvestment Problem, Bond Covenants and Insurance", *Journal of Risk and Insurance*, 60, 635–646.

Jensen, Michael C. and Meckling, William H. (1976). "Theory of the Firm: Managerial Behavior, Agency Cost and Ownership Structure", *Journal of Financial Economics*, 3, 305–360.

Kreps, David (1990). *A Course in Microeconomic Theory*" Princeton University Press, Princeton, N.J.

Lamb, Reinhold P. (1995). "An Exposure Based Analysis of Property Liability Insurer Stock Values Around Hurrican Andrew", *Journal of Risk and Insurance*, 62, 111–123.

Lambert, R. (1983). "Long Term Contracts and Moral Hazard", *Bell Journal of Economics*, 8, 441–452.

Lew, Keun ock (1990). "Reinsurance and The Firm Value", Ph.D. Dissertation, Wharton School, University of Pennsylvania.

Major, John, A. (1996). "Index Hedge Performance: Insurer Market Penetration and Basis Risk", paper presented at National Bureau of Economic Research conference, Palm Beach, Florida.

Mayers David and Clifford W. Smith Jnr (1983). "On the Corporate Dermand for Insurance" *Journal of Business*, 55, 281–296.

Minton, Bernadette A. and Catherine Schrand (1999). "The Impact of Cash Flow Volatility on Discretionary Investment and the Costs of Debt and Equity Financing", Working Paper, Wharton School, University of Pennsylvania.

Myers, Stewart C. (1977). "Determinants of Corporate Borrowing", *Journal of Financial Economics*, 5, 147–175.

Myers, Stewart C. and Nicholas S. Majluf (1984). "Corporate Financing and Investment Decisions When Firms Have Information That Investors Do Not Have". *Journal of Financial Economics*, 13, 187–221.

Nance, D.R., C.W. Smith and C.W. Smithson (1993). "On the Determinants of Corporate Hedging", *Journal of Finance*, 267–284.

Shapiro, Alan C. and Sheridan Titman (1985). "An Integrated Approach to Corporate Risk Management", *Midland Corporate Finance Journal*, 3, #2, 41–56.

Shavell, Stephen (1979). "On Moral Hazard and Insurance", *Quarterly Journal of Economics*, 93, 541–562.

Shavell, Stephen (1979). "Risk Sharing and Incentives in the Principal and Agent Relationship", *Bell Journal of Economics*, 10, 55–73.

Shelor, Roger M., Dwight C. Anderson and Mark L. Cross (1992). "Gaining from Loss: Property-Liability Insurer Stock Prices in the Aftermath of the 1989 California Earthquake", *Journal of Risk and Insurance*, 5, 476–488.

Smith, Clifford W. Jnr and Rene Stultz (1985). "The Determinants of Firm's Hedging Policies", *Journal of Financial and Quantitative Analysis*, 28, 391–405.

Smith, B.D. and M.J. Stultzer (1994). "A Theory of Mutual Formation and Moral Hazard", working paper, University of Minnesota.

Stiglitz, J. (1983). "Risk, Incentives and Insurance: The Pure Theory of Moral Hazard", *Geneva Papers on Risk and Insurance*, 8(26), 4–33.

16 On Corporate Insurance

Richard MacMinn

University of Texas at Austin

James Garven

Louisiana State University

Abstract

Although insurance contracts are regularly purchased by corporations and play an important role in the management of corporate risk, only recently has this role received much attention in the finance literature. This paper provides a formal analytic survey of recent theoretical developments in the corporate demand for insurance. Insurance contracts are characterized as simply another type of financial contract in the nexus of contracts that comprise the corporation. The model developed here focuses specifically on the efficiency gains that can be derived from using corporate insurance contracts to reduce bankruptcy costs, agency costs, and tax costs.

Keywords: Corporate risk management, Fisher model, costly bankruptcy, asymmetric taxes, asset substitution, underinvestment.
JEL Classification Numbers: D81, G22, G32, H25.

16.1 INTRODUCTION

Insurance contracts are regularly purchased by corporations and play an important role in the management of corporate risk.[1] In spite of this fact, only recently has this role received much attention in the finance literature, even though insurance contracts are simply another type of financial contract in the nexus of contracts that comprise the corporation.

[1] As a use of funds, corporate property-casualty insurance premium payments are economically significant, typically exceeding dividend payments by an order of magnitude of 30–40 percent (see Mayers and Smith (1982) and Davidson *et al.* (1992)). Survey evidence compiled by Tillinghast-Towers Perrin and Risk and Insurance Management Society (1995) finds that direct property-casualty insurance costs for most U.S. and Canadian business organizations typically average around 0.4% of revenues. Similar findings on the economic significance of corporate insurance purchases obtain for other industrialized countries; e.g., Yamori (1999) reports that in 1994, Japanese non-financial corporations paid 2.3 percent of their operating profits for property-casualty insurance premiums.

In the insurance literature, the incentive to buy insurance is often assumed to be risk aversion.[2] Risk aversion might be is a sufficient motivation for the closely held corporation but it is not sufficient for the publicly held corporation. According to Mayers and Smith (1982) "The corporate form provides an effective hedge since stockholders can eliminate insurable risk through diversification." Equivalently, the value of the insured corporation is the same as the value of the uninsured corporation. If these claims hold, then insurance is not a necessary tool in managing corporate risk. A characterization of the market conditions in which the claim does and does not hold should be important to corporate managers as well as insurance companies. The claim is intuitively appealing. If the corporation is viewed as a set of financial contracts, then it is a generalization of the 1958 Modigliani-Miller Theorem (see Modigliani and Miller (1958)). The generalized theorem says that the composition of the contract set is irrelevant. The irrelevance claim was established in MacMinn (1987); that analysis also provided a number of relevance results. This analysis provides a generalization and extension of the earlier results. The model presented here demonstrates some of the market conditions in which insurance is an important tool for managing corporate risk.

The first step is to formally establish the claim that corporations need not buy insurance since competitive risk markets already provide sufficient opportunity to diversify risk. To establish or refute this claim requires a model of the economy that includes stock, bond and insurance markets. Those markets are introduced in the next section of this paper. The basic model includes debt, equity and insurance. The model is used first to develop the corporate objective function and then to investigate the insurance decision. The analysis shows that as long as bankruptcy is costless, markets are competitive and efficient then the risk adjusted net present value of the insurance decision is zero and the claim that insurance is irrelevant is formally established.

In the section on Costly Bankruptcy, the model is altered to allow for the transaction costs of bankruptcy. Mayers and Smith (1982) note that bankruptcy costs provide the firm with an incentive to insure because, by shifting risk to the insurance company, the firm decreases the probability that the cost is actually incurred. The analysis here, as in MacMinn (1987), shows that the total market value of the insured firm is equal to that of the uninsured firm plus the present value of the savings on bankruptcy costs; equivalently, the analysis shows that the value of the insured firm exceeds the value of the uninsured firm. This provides the corporation with an incentive to insure.

In the section on Agency Problems, the basic model is generalized so that it incorporates conflict of interest problems between corporate management and bondholders. Conflict of interest problems arise when the corporate manager, acting in the

[2] For example, Borch (1960, 1962) and Blazenko (1986) motivate insurer demand for reinsurance on this basis.

interests of stockholders, has the incentive to select actions that are not fully consistent with the interests of other groups of claimholders. Two classic examples of the conflict of interest problems are developed. The analysis necessary to show how the insurance contract may be used to limit the divergence between the interests of claim holders and management is developed. The first agency conflict considered is usually referred to as the "under-investment" problem, e.g., see Myers (1977), MacMinn (1987), Mayers and Smith (1987), and Garven and MacMinn (1993). In this example, the manager of a levered firm has an incentive to limit the scale of investment because the additional returns from further investment accrue primarily to bondholders rather than shareholders. The analysis here shows that insurance can be used to eliminate this underinvestment problem. The investment decision approaches the socially optimal level as insurance is used to reduce the probability of insolvency.

The second agency conflict considered is usually referred to as the asset substitution problem, or equivalently, as the risk-shifting problem, e.g., see Jensen and Meckling (1976), Green (1984), Mayers and Smith (1982), MacMinn (1987) and MacMinn (1993). Once a corporation has obtained debt financing, it is well known that by switching from a relatively safe investment project to a riskier one, the corporation can increase the value of its equity at the expense of its bondholders. Mayers and Smith (1982) discuss this conflict and note that rational bondholders recognize this incentive to switch and incorporate it into the bond price. Consequently, an agency cost is represented in the bond price and a reduction in the total market value of the firm. Mayers and Smith also note that an important role played by insurance in this corporate environment is in bonding the corporation's investment decision. They suggest that the incentive to include insurance covenants in bond contracts increases with firm leverage. The analysis here shows that the asset substitution problem only exists for highly levered firms and that an indenture provision, requiring insurance, can be structured so that any incentive for risk-shifting is eliminated. Thus, the model shows how insurance may be used to eliminate this agency cost.

In the section on Tax Asymmetries, the basic model is altered to allow for the corporate income tax as well as agency costs. It is well known that under the U.S. corporate tax code, income and losses to the firm are taxed in an asymmetric fashion. A number of potential sources for tax asymmetries exist, including incomplete tax loss offsets and progressive marginal tax rates. Several articles have utilized asymmetric taxes to rationalize a number of different aspects of financial contracting, including optimal capital structure (see DeAngelo and Masulis (1980)), leasing (see Heaton (1987)), corporate risk management (see Green and Talmor (1985) and Campbell and Kracaw (1990)), corporate insurance demand (Mayers and Smith (1982)), corporate hedging (Smith and Stulz (1985)), and the demand for reinsurance (Garven and Louberge (1996)). The analysis presented here shows that the asymmetric nature of the corporate income tax constitutes a sufficient condition for the corporation to purchase insurance. Taxes reinforce further the basic result that optimally insured firms command higher market values than otherwise identical uninsured firms. Insurance is viewed here as a mechanism that enables the firm to 1) optimally trade off agency and tax-related costs, and 2) replace a risky tax shelter (represented by loss costs related to property risks) with a safe tax shelter (represented by debt service costs).

The final section of this paper presents some conclusions and comments on the role that insurance contracts play in managing corporate risk. It also provides a brief discussion of some empirical implications, as well as suggestions for future research.

Before continuing any further, a caveat is in order. Most insurance models, beyond those designed to simply consider the reallocation of risk, might be classified as hidden action or hidden knowledge models. The hidden action is an action, e.g., an investment or production decision, taken by an agent that cannot be observed by the principals or claim holders; models characterized by hidden action or equivalently moral hazard problems are considered here. The cases covered are not exhaustive. Mayers and Smith (1982) argue that insurance is a mechanism that can be used to reduce the impact of regulatory constraints and that is consistent with the current model structure. Froot, Scharfstein and Stein (1993) posit a "crowding out" hypothesis to rationalize corporate hedging decisions that may also provide a useful framework for addressing the demand for corporate insurance.[3] The hidden knowledge is a difference in information possessed by insiders versus outsiders or by different groups of claim holders in this setting; models characterized by hidden knowledge or equivalently, in some cases, by adverse selection, require more closure than the current model provides. The monitoring role of insurance noted by Mayers and Smith among others would fit this category. The work done on optimal contracting by Caillaud, Dionne and Jullien (2000) would also fit this category. These are important considerations and await a more general version of the model outlined here. The focus here will be on the efficiency gains that can be derived from using corporate insurance contracts to reduce bankruptcy costs, agency costs, and tax costs.

16.2 BASIC MODEL

Assume that there are many individual investors indexed by i in the set I, and that there are many firms indexed by f in the set F. There are two dates, $t = 0$ and $t = 1$, that will be subsequently referred to as *now* and *then*, respectively. All decisions are

[3] In the Froot, Scharfstein and Stein model, hedging adds value by enabling the firm to avoid external financing costs associated with capital market imperfections. Hedging helps to ensure that a corporation has sufficient and less costly internal funds available to take advantage of attractive investment opportunities. Corporate insurance contracts can play a similar role. Since insurance premiums are paid *ex ante* in anticipation of possible future losses, *ex post* claims payments enable firms to reinvest in valuable corporate assets without having to rely upon external capital markets. Furthermore, as Doherty (1997a) points out, insurance is a "leverage neutral" loss financing strategy because it enables the firm to fund losses without having to rely upon issuing new equity or debt or relying upon internal funds that would otherwise be used to invest in other capital projects.

made *now* and all payoffs from those decisions are received *then*. The payoffs depend on which state of nature ξ in the set Ξ occurs *then*. The model is developed with debt, equity and insurance. The Fisher model is used in this setting.[4]

There are many individual investors. Investor i is endowed with income *now* and *then* represented by the pair (y_{i0}, y_{i1}). Furthermore, investor i has a consumption pair (c_{i0}, c_{i1}) and an increasing concave utility function u_i: $D \rightarrow R$, where D is a subset of $R \times R^n$; u_i expresses the individual's preferences for consumption *now* versus *then*. In order to introduce uncertainty, let $(\Xi, \mathcal{F}, \Psi)$ denote the probability space for individual i, where Ξ is the set of states of nature, $\mathcal{F}$ is the event space, and X is the probability measure. If the number of states of nature is finite, i.e., $\Xi = \{\xi_1, \xi_2, \ldots, \xi_n\}$, then the event space $\mathcal{F}$ is the power set, i.e., the set of all subsets of Ξ. To make the uncertainty operational, suppose that the investor can only transfer dollars between dates by buying or selling stock, bond, or insurance contracts. In this complete markets setting, suppose that a basis stock of type ξ is a promise to pay one dollar if state ξ occurs and zero otherwise, and let its price be denoted as $p(\xi)$.[5] Then the investor's budget constraint may be expressed as

$$c_{i0} + \sum_{\Xi} p(\xi) c_{i1}(\xi) = y_{i0} + \sum_{\Xi} p(\xi) y_{i1}(\xi) \tag{1}$$

The left-hand side of equation (1) represents the risk-adjusted present value of the consumption plan, while the right hand side represents the risk-adjusted present value of income. Now the investor's constrained maximization problem can be stated as

$$\begin{aligned} &\max imize \int_{\Xi} u_i(c_{i0}, c_{i1}(\xi)) d\Psi(\xi) \\ &subject\ to\ c_{i0} + \sum_{\Xi} p(\xi) c_{i1}(\xi) = y_{i0} + \sum_{\Xi} p(\xi) y_{i1}(\xi) \end{aligned} \tag{2}$$

This is the classic statement of the investor's problem; it may also be expressed in terms of a portfolio of financial contracts and more financial contracts can be introduced. As long as any new contracts are spanned by the basis stock, the financial markets remain complete. Any spanned contract has a value equal to that of a portfolio of basis stock that provides the same payoff structure *then*.[6] Hence, letting $\Pi(a, \xi)$ denote a corporate payoff *then* that depends on the state of nature and an action taken by management. That action may be an investment decision or a production decision. Both decisions are examined in the subsequent analysis. The value of the unlevered corporate payoff is $S(a)$ where

$$S(a) = \int_{\Xi} \Pi(a, \xi) dP(\xi) \tag{3}$$

[4] See Fisher (1930). The Fisher model is developed under uncertainty in Hirshleifer (1965) and MacMinn and Martin (1988).

[5] These stock contracts form a basis for the payoff space.

[6] This may be demonstrated by direct calculation but it also clearly follows by a no-arbitrage argument.

and $P(\xi)$ represents the sum of basis stock prices up to state ξ. If the firm issues a zero coupon bond with a promised payment of b dollars *then*, the value of the bond issue is $B(a, b)$, where

$$\begin{aligned} B(a,b) &= \int_{\Xi} \min\{\Pi(a,\xi), b\}\, dP \\ &= \int_{B} \Pi(a,\xi)\, dP + \int_{\Xi \setminus B} b\, dP \end{aligned} \tag{4}$$

B represents the bankruptcy event, i.e., $B = \{\xi \mid \Pi(a, \xi) < b\}$ and $\Xi \setminus B$ represents the complement of the bankruptcy event relative to Ξ. The stock or equity value in this levered case is $S(a, b)$ where

$$S(a,b) = \int_{\Xi \setminus B} (\Pi(a,\xi) - b)\, dP. \tag{5}$$

In each case the value represents a risk-adjusted present value of a contract payoff.[7]

Next we introduce insurance. Suppose the corporation faces property risks. Let the corporate payoff be $\Pi = R - L + \max\{0, L - d\}$, where R represents the quasi-rent *then* on an investment of I dollars *now*, L represents the property losses and d represents the deductible on the insurance; the insurance contract payoff is $\max\{0, L - d\}$. Let i denote the premium *now* on the insurance contract. In this setting, the premium value is

$$i = \int_{\Xi} \max\{0, L - d\}\, dP. \tag{6}$$

Finally, the model provides enough structure to allow the derivation of the corporate objective function that incorporates the insurance decision along with the financing and investment decisions.

Theorem 1. Suppose the corporate manager receives a salary package (y_0, y_1) and m shares of stock in the corporation *then*. Suppose the manager pursues her own self-interest in making decisions on personal and corporate account. The decisions on personal account may be separated from those on corporate account and the decisions on corporate account are made to maximize the objective function $F = S + B - I - i$.

Proof. The pursuit of self-interest yields the following constrained maximization problem:

$$\begin{aligned} &\max imize \int_{\Xi} u(c_0, c_1(\xi))\, d\Psi(\xi) \\ &subject\ to\ c_0 + \sum_{\Xi} p(\xi) c_1(\xi) = y_0 + \sum_{\Xi} p(\xi) y_1(\xi) + S^m, \\ &and\ S^n + B = I + i, \end{aligned} \tag{7}$$

[7] See MacMinn (1990) for more on this interpretation.

where S^m is the manager's equity stake and S^n is the value of the issue of new shares of stock. Letting S^o denote the current shareholder value and N denote the number of existing shares, note that

$$S^m = \frac{m}{N+m+n} S, \; S^n = \frac{m+n}{N+m+n} S, \text{ and } S^o = \frac{N}{N+m+n} S. \tag{8}$$

The constrained maximization function includes the budget constraint and financing constraint, i.e., the personal account and corporate account constraints.

The Lagrange function for this constrained maximization problem is

$$\begin{aligned} L(a,b,n,\lambda,\delta) = {} & \int_{\Xi} u \, d\Psi + \lambda\left(m_{i0} + \sum_{\Xi} p m_1 + S^m - c_{i0} - \sum_{\Xi} p c_1\right) \\ & + \delta(S^n + B^n - I - i). \end{aligned} \tag{9}$$

Direct calculation shows that the manager makes decisions on corporate account to maximize $\lambda\, S^m + \delta\, (S^n + B - I - i)$. Direct calculation also shows that

$$\delta = \lambda \frac{m}{N}. \tag{10}$$

and it follows that

$$\begin{aligned} \lambda S^m + \delta(S^n + B - I - i) &= \lambda\left(S^m + \frac{m}{N}(S^n + B - I - i)\right) \\ &= \lambda \frac{m}{N}(S^o + S^n + B - I - i) \\ &= \lambda \frac{m}{N}(S + B - I - i). \end{aligned} \tag{11}$$

QED

Theorem 1 establishes a financial market version of Fisher's famous separation theorem. Like Fisher's result, this theorem shows that decisions made on corporate account are separable from decisions made on personal account. The manager will make the finance, insurance and other corporate decisions to maximize the current shareholder value S^m subject to a financing constraint. The manager's measure of risk aversion will affect the saving and portfolio decisions made on personal account, but not those decisions made on corporate account.

It is possible to see the irrelevance result in this setting. If the insurance decision is a matter of indifference to shareholders then the current shareholder value must be independent of the insurance decision. Let $U > L(\xi)$ for all ξ so that a deductible of U corresponds to no insurance. The following theorem shows that insurance is irrelevant in the absence of some of the problems addressed in subsequent sections.

Theorem 2. The current shareholder value of the uninsured firm equals that of the insured firm, in the absence of taxes, agency, and information problems.

Proof. The uninsured current shareholder value is

$$F^{u}(a,b,U) = -I + \int_{\Xi} (R-L)\,dP \tag{12}$$

The current shareholder value of the insured firm is

$$\begin{aligned} F(a,b,d) &= -i - I + S(a,b,d) + B(a,b,d) \\ &= -i - I + \int_{\Xi} \Pi\, dP \\ &= -\int_{\Xi} \max\{0, L-d\}dP - I + \int_{\Xi} (R - L + \max\{0, L-d\})\,dP \\ &= -I + \int_{\Xi} (R-L)\,dP \\ &= F(a,b,U) \end{aligned} \tag{13}$$

The second equality in (13) follows by (4) and (5) while the third equality follows by (6). QED

16.3 COSTLY BANKRUPTCY[8]

In this section, the impacts of bankruptcy costs are considered. Suppose that there is a cost $c > 0$ associated with the bankruptcy event. The uninsured firm's earning is $R(a, \xi) - L(\xi)$. The bankruptcy event for an uninsured firm is $B = [0, \delta)$, where δ is the boundary of the insolvency event and is implicitly defined by the condition $R(a, \delta) - L(\delta) - b = 0$. The stock value of the levered uninsured firm's stock is $S(a, b, U)$, where

$$S(a,b,U) = \int_{\delta}^{\omega} [R(a,\xi) - L(\xi) - b]\,dP, \tag{14}$$

Similarly, the value of the levered uninsured firm's debt, given costly bankruptcy, is $B(a, b, U)$, where

$$B(a,b,U) = \int_{0}^{\delta} (R(a,\xi) - L(\xi) - c)\,dP + \int_{\delta}^{\omega} b\,dP \tag{15}$$

It follows that the total value of the levered uninsured firm is

[8] This section is similar to MacMinn (1987).

$$
\begin{aligned}
V(a,b,U) &= B(a,b,U) + S(a,b,U) \\
&= \int_0^{\delta} (R(a,\xi) - L(\xi) - c)\,dP + \int_{\delta}^{\omega} b\,dP + \int_{\delta}^{\omega} [R(a,\xi) - L(\xi) - b]\,dP \\
&= \int_0^{\omega} (R(a,\xi) - L(\xi))\,dP + \int_0^{\delta} c\,dP
\end{aligned} \tag{16}
$$

The current shareholder value is

$$
F(a,b,U) = -I + V(a,b,U) \tag{17}
$$

The last term on the right-hand side of equation (16) is the risk adjusted present value of the bankruptcy costs. It may be noted that the 1958 Modigliani-Miller theorem holds here if either the bankruptcy cost is zero or the bankruptcy set is empty; otherwise, the firm's capital structure is relevant. Of course, this value does not incorporate insurance and it seems apparent that insurance allows the firm to avoid some bankruptcy costs.

Consider the value of the levered insured firm compared to the value of an otherwise identical levered uninsured firm. Suppose that the insurance is purchased before the firm levers or in conjunction with the bond issue. The insured firm purchases a policy with a deductible of d for the premium i, where i is given by equation (6). By purchasing such a policy, the net earnings for the insured firm in any state becomes $R(a, \xi) - L(\xi) + \max\{0, L(\xi) - d\} = R(a, \xi) - min\{L(\xi), d\}$. The bankruptcy event of the insured firm is $[0, \beta)$ where β is implicitly defined by the condition $R(a, \beta) - L(\beta) + \max\{0, L(\beta) - d\} - b = 0$. Note that $\beta < \delta$. Then the value of the levered insured firm is

$$
\begin{aligned}
V(a,b,d) &= B(a,b,d) + S(a,b,d) \\
&= \int_0^{\beta} (R(a,\xi) - L(\xi) + \max\{0, L(\xi) - d\} - c)\,dP + \int_{\beta}^{\omega} b\,dP \\
&\quad + \int_{\beta}^{\omega} [R(a,\xi) - L(\xi) + \max\{0, L(\xi) - d\} - b]\,dP \\
&= \int_0^{\omega} (R(a,\xi) - L(\xi) + \max\{0, L(\xi) - d\})\,dP - \int_0^{\beta} c\,dP
\end{aligned} \tag{18}
$$

Similarly, the current shareholder value is

$$
\begin{aligned}
F(a,b,d) &= -I - i + V(a,b,d) \\
&= -I - i + \int_0^{\omega} (R(a,\xi) - L(\xi) + \max\{0, L(\xi) - d\})\,dP - \int_0^{\beta} c\,dP \\
&= -I + \int_0^{\omega} (R(a,\xi) - L(\xi))\,dP - \int_0^{\beta} c\,dP
\end{aligned} \tag{19}
$$

and the difference in current shareholder values is

$$
\begin{aligned}
F(a,b,d)+F(a,b,U) &= -I-i(d)+V(a,b,d)+I+i(U)-V(a,b,U)\\
&= \int_0^{\delta} c\,dP - \int_0^{\beta} c\,dP\\
&= \int_{\beta}^{\delta} c\,dP\\
&> 0
\end{aligned} \tag{20}
$$

where $i(d)$ is the insurance premium for a deductible of d and $i(U) = 0$ is the insurance premium for a deductible of U. The increase in value, due to insurance, is simply the present value of the saving in bankruptcy costs. Hence, the firm has an incentive to insure as noted in the following theorem.

Theorem 3. A transaction cost $c > 0$ in the event of bankruptcy is sufficient to show that insuring increases current shareholder value.

16.4 AGENCY PROBLEMS

In this section, the use of insurance contracts in resolving conflict of interest problems between corporate manager and bondholders is analyzed. Since the corporate manager also represents the interests of stockholders, there is a potential for conflict between the manager and bondholders, or equivalently, between the manager and the bondholders' trustee. This will be the case if it is possible for the manager to take actions that benefit one group, which are detrimental to the other. If the bonds represent safe debt then there is no conflict. If not, then an agency problem may exist.

The agency relationship can be thought of as a contract between the principal, i.e., the bondholders' trustee,[9] and an agent, i.e., the corporate manager. The agent acts on behalf of the principal. The contract specifies the bounds on the actions that may be taken by the agent. If the contract covers all possible contingencies then there is no real delegation of authority and therefore no agency problem. If the contract is incomplete so that the agent has some discretion in the selection of actions then there is at least the potential for a conflict of interest. The conflict occurs because both the principal and the agent behave in accordance with their own self-interests. The prin-

[9] The legal trustee for the bondholders may be treated as the single principal. It should be added that the trustee acts on behalf of the bondholders. The trustee's problem is the selection of bond covenants that limit the divergence of interests between corporate management and the bondholders. In general, the trustee may have a problem in selecting covenants that provide a solution to the conflict because of the different risk aversion measures of the bondholders. In the two cases considered here, however, the bondholders will unanimously support a covenant that provides management with the incentive to maximize the risk adjusted net present value of the corporation. It should also be noted that in general there might be an agency problem between the trustee and bondholders (i.e., between the agent and the principals). In the cases considered here that problem does not arise because of the unanimity.

cipal can limit the divergence of interests by providing provisions in the contract that give the agent the appropriate incentives to act in the principal's interest; in addition, the principal can monitor the activity of the agent. However it is not usually possible to specify the contract in such a way as to completely eliminate the conflict of interest problem. Hence, it will usually be the case that there is a difference between the action taken by the agent and the action that is in the best interests of the principal. Jensen and Meckling (1976) define agency cost as the sum of the monitoring expenditures of the principal, the bonding expenditures of the agent, and the residual loss; this residual loss is the loss in the market value of the corporation.[10]

Underinvestment

The first agency problem considered here occurs when the manager makes investment decisions. Jensen and Smith (1985) note that one source of conflict is underinvestment. They observe that

> . . . when a substantial portion of the value of the firm is composed of future investment opportunities, a firm with outstanding risky bonds can have incentives to reject positive net present value projects if the benefit from accepting the project accrues to the bondholders (Jensen and Smith (1985), p. 111).

The incentive need not be so extreme that it causes the manager to reject a project; the manager may under-invest by limiting the size of the project. Suppose the firm's earnings are $\Pi(I, \xi) = R(I, \xi) - c - L(I, \xi)$, where R represents the quasi-rents from the investment projects, c represents a fixed obligation to creditors, and L represents property losses. The fixed obligation c may be a commitment on previously issued bonds, but it need not be limited to that. Suppose Π is increasing and concave in the investment level I. Let X denote the event that the firm cannot pay its claimants and creditors. Let B denote the firm's bankruptcy event. The event X is a subset of B. Then, with no corporate taxes, the market value of the firm's equity is $S(b, d, I)$, where

$$S(b,d,I) = \int_{\Xi \setminus B} (\Pi + (L-d) - b)\,dP, \tag{21}$$

where $\Xi \setminus B = \{\xi \in \Xi \mid \Pi(I, \omega) - (L - d) - b \geq 0\} = [\beta, \omega]$. Note that β is the boundary of the insolvency event here and will be positive even if no new debt is issued, i.e., $b = 0$. The market value of the corporation's creditor stake is $C(b, d, I)$ where

[10] Jensen and Meckling (1976) also define the residual loss as the dollar equivalent of the loss in expected utility experienced by the principal. Although this notion of residual loss is measurable for a particular principal, this definition poses problems when a trustee represents many principals because the residual loss of any bondholder will depend on the bondholder's measure of risk aversion and on the proportion of the contract owned.

$$C = \int_B \frac{c}{b+c}((R-L)+L-d)\,dP + \int_{\Xi \setminus B} c\,dP. \tag{22}$$

Suppose that the corporate payoff *then* is the sum of the payoffs from the corporate projects or operating divisions.[11] It is possible to motivate the underinvestment problem by noting how the creditor value is affected by changing the investment level on a project. Note that the value increases in the scale of the investment if there is a positive probability of insolvency, i.e., $P\{B\} > 0$, since

$$\begin{aligned}\frac{\partial C}{\partial I} &= \left(\frac{c}{b+c}(R(I,\beta)-d)-b\right)p(\beta)\frac{\partial \beta}{\partial I} + \frac{c}{b+c}\int_B \frac{\partial R}{\partial I}\,dP \\ &= \frac{c}{b+c}\int_{\Xi} \frac{\partial R}{\partial I}\,dP \\ &> 0.\end{aligned} \tag{23}$$

This inequality provides analytic content for Jensen and Smith earlier statement.

The underinvestment may be relative to either the investment that would maximize the value of an unlevered corporation, or the investment that is socially efficient.[12] The socially efficient investment maximizes the value of all the corporate stakeholders; equivalently, the socially efficient investment satisfies the following first order condition

$$\int_{\Xi} \frac{\partial \Pi}{\partial I}\,dP - 1 = 0. \tag{24}$$

This condition implicitly defines an investment level I^v that maximizes the value of all the stakeholders' claims on the firm. The extent of the underinvestment will be measured relative to the level of investment indicated here.

Theorem 1 shows that the corporate manager will make the investment decision for the corporation to maximize current shareholder value, or equivalently, the risk-adjusted net present value. The objective function is[13]

$$\begin{aligned}F &= B(b,d,I) + S(b,d,I) - I - i \\ &= \int_B \frac{b}{b+c}((R-L)+(L-d))\,dP + \int_{\Xi \setminus B} (\Pi + (L-d))\,dP - I - i\end{aligned} \tag{25}$$

[11] Here it suffices to think of the payoff as being the sum of old and new project payoffs, i.e., $\Pi(I, \xi) = \Pi_o(\xi) + \Pi_n(I, \xi)$.

[12] This is efficiency in the Pareto sense. An investment is socially efficient if it is not possible to make one investor better off without making another worse off.

[13] The objective function takes the form $B + S - I - i$, where B denotes the value of any new debt issue. Using corporate value here is inappropriate because there can be an old debt issue.

The following first order condition implicitly defines the optimal investment I^m that is selected by corporate management acting in the interests of current shareholders:

$$\begin{aligned}\frac{\partial F}{\partial I} &= \int_B \frac{b}{b+c}\frac{\partial R}{\partial I}dP + \int_{\Xi\setminus B}\frac{\partial R}{\partial I}dP - 1 - \frac{\partial i}{\partial I} \\ &= \int_\Xi \frac{\partial \Pi}{\partial I}dP - 1 - \int_B \frac{c}{b+c}\frac{\partial R}{\partial I}dP \\ &= 0. \end{aligned} \tag{26}$$

The first order condition in equation (26) shows that the manager under-invests, equivalently, $I^m < I^v$, where I^m and I^v represent the investment levels that maximize current shareholder value and total stakeholder value, respectively.

Insurance can play an important role in alleviating the underinvestment problem. The decision sequence is critical. To ensure that current shareholders receive the benefit of positive risk-adjusted net present value investment decisions, the insurance contract must precede the investment. If insurance can be used to eliminate insolvency risk then the first order condition in (26) shows that the underinvestment problem would be eliminated. The next theorem shows that even if insurance cannot eliminate the insolvency risk and the underinvestment problem, it can be effectively used to reduce the impact of this problem.

Theorem 4. If the probability of insolvency is positive, i.e., $P\{B\} > 0$, then the optimal investment increases with insurance coverage.

Proof. It suffices to show that

$$\frac{\partial I}{\partial d} = -\frac{\dfrac{\partial^2 F}{\partial d\,\partial I}}{\dfrac{\partial^2 F}{\partial I^2}} < 0. \tag{27}$$

The concavity of F makes the denominator negative and so the optimal investment is decreasing in the deductible if the numerator is negative. Note that the numerator is

$$\frac{\partial^2 F}{\partial d\,\partial I} = -\frac{c}{b+c}\frac{\partial R(I,\beta)}{\partial I}p(\xi)\frac{\partial \beta}{\partial d} < 0, \tag{28}$$

and the sign in (28) follows since the quasi-rent increases in the investment and the boundary of the insolvency event increases in the deductible. QED

This theorem shows that insuring mitigates the underinvestment problem. If the firm insures and increases its investment then it protects bond and general creditor values and so facilitates the movement of all additional value from investment to existing shareholders. The theorem also suggests that full insurance is optimal.

Asset Substitution

The second agency problem considered here is typically referred to as either the asset substitution or risk-shifting problem. It is encountered by the corporation in selecting the set of assets and liabilities that constitute the firm. The problem can occur when the firm selects among mutually exclusive investment projects (e.g., MacMinn (1990)), selects a portfolio of investment projects (e.g., Green (1984)), makes operating decisions, restructures, (e.g., MacMinn and Brockett (1995), etc. Jensen and Smith note that

> . . . the value of the stockholders' equity rises and the value of the bondholders' claim is reduced when the firm substitutes high risk for low risk projects (Jensen and Smith (1985), p. 111).[14]

Rational bondholders are aware of the incentive to shift risk and so it is reflected in a lower value for the corporation's debt issues, or equivalently, in a higher interest rate on the debt. An insurance mechanism is constructed here that can reduce or eliminate the risk-shifting incentive and so another source of the agency cost of debt.

In order to demonstrate the agency problem, suppose the corporation is considering an operating decision after its finance and insurance decisions have been made. Let q denote the operating decision *now* and let $\Pi(q, \xi)$ denote the random earnings. Suppose earnings are positive for all states.[15] Suppose also that the project satisfies the Principle of Increasing Uncertainty (PIU) (see Leland (1972); MacMinn and Holtmann (1983)); let the random payoff be defined by a function that maps the operating decision and state into earnings. Then the payoff is $\Pi(q, \xi)$ and by the PIU, $D_2\Pi > 0$ and $D_{12}\Pi > 0$.[16] These derivative properties say that the payoff increases in state as does the marginal payoff.[17] The PIU also implies that, after correcting for the changes in the expected payoff, an increase in scale increases risk in the Rothschild-Stiglitz sense.[18]

To establish the existence of the asset substitution problem consider the relationship between the scale and the level of debt. If the firm levers itself to finance the project then the stock value is $S(b, q)$ and

[14] See Green (1984) and Hirshleifer (1965) for similar statements.

[15] The assumption $\Pi > 0$ for all $\xi \in \Xi$ simply allows the result $V^i = V^u$, for any insurance scheme, to be used here.

[16] This notation denotes the partial derivative of Π with respect to its first argument and the cross partial of Π with respect to its first and second arguments, respectively.

[17] The state space is still assumed to be finite but it is easier to see the mean-preserving spread when Π_f is drawn as a continuous function of state.

[18] See Rothschild and Stiglitz (1970) for a definition of increasing risk. See MacMinn and Holtmann (1983) for a demonstration of this equivalence result.

$$S(b,q) - \int_B (\Pi(q,\xi) \quad b)\, dP(\xi)$$
$$= \int_\beta^\omega (\Pi(q,\xi) - b)\, dP(\xi), \tag{29}$$

where $B = \{\xi \mid \Pi(q, \xi) - b < 0\}$; β is the boundary of the insolvency event and is implicitly defined by the relation $\Pi(q, \beta) - b = 0$. Once the funds have been raised, the firm makes its operating decision to maximize shareholder value. The condition for an optimal operating decision is

$$\frac{\partial S}{\partial q} = \int_\beta^x \frac{\partial \Pi}{\partial q}\, dP = 0. \tag{30}$$

It follows by the PIU that the output scale increases with leverage if the probability of insolvency is positive, i.e., $P\{\Pi - b < 0\} > 0$. To see this, note that

$$\frac{\partial q}{\partial b} = -\frac{\dfrac{\partial^2 S}{\partial b \partial q}}{\dfrac{\partial^2 S}{\partial q \partial q}}$$
$$= -\frac{-\dfrac{\partial \Pi(q,\zeta)}{\partial q} p(\zeta) \dfrac{\partial \zeta}{\partial b}}{\dfrac{\partial^2 S}{\partial q^2}}$$
$$> 0. \tag{31}$$

The inequality in (31) follows because the marginal payoff is negative at the boundary of the financial distress event by the PIU, the denominator is negative by the concavity of the payoff function, and the boundary state β of the financial distress event is an increasing function of leverage.

Also observe that the increase in scale reduces the debt and corporate values. The value of the bond issue is $B(b, q)$, where

$$B(b,q) = \int_0^\beta \Pi\, dP + \int_\beta^\omega b\, dP. \tag{32}$$

The corporate value is

$$V(q) = B(b,q) + S(b,q) = \int_0^\omega \Pi\, dP. \tag{33}$$

The operating scale affects the probability of distress and the bond payoff in the distress event. Note that

$$\frac{\partial B}{\partial q} = \int_0^{\beta} \frac{\partial \Pi}{\partial q} dP < 0 \tag{34}$$

by the PIU. Hence, the increase in risk suffices to reduce the bond value. The same increase in risk, of course, increases the stock value. Although it may be less apparent, the increase in risk reduces the corporate value if the probability of financial distress is positive. To see this, observe that equation (21) implicitly defines operating scale that maximizes the stock value; let q^s denote that scale. The next equation implicitly defines that operating scale that maximizes the corporate value; let q^v denote that scale:

$$\frac{\partial V}{\partial q} = \int_0^{\omega} \frac{\partial \Pi}{\partial q} dP = 0. \tag{35}$$

By comparing equations (30) and (35), it is apparent that the PIU yields $q^s > q^v$ and so $V(q^s) < V(q^v)$. Therefore, in the absence of any mechanism to avoid the agency problem, the levered corporation has an incentive to increase the scale of its operation and so increase the risk of its debt issues. The agency cost of debt, in this case is $V(q^v) - V(q^s)$.

Now, consider whether a bond covenant requiring insurance can be written in a way that eliminates the risk-shifting problem. Let i denote the insurance premium. Without the insurance the corporate payoff is $\Pi(q, \xi) = R(q, \xi) - L(\xi)$, where R and L represent the quasi-rent and property loss, respectively. With insurance, the corporate payoff is $R - L + \max\{0, L - d\}$ where d is the deductible on the insurance. The insurance premium is the risk-adjusted presented value of the net loss, i.e.,

$$i = \int_0^{\omega} \max\{0, L - d\} dP. \tag{36}$$

The corporation makes the finance and insurance decisions *now*, knowing the impact that those decisions have on the subsequent production decisions. Green (1984) and MacMinn (1993) have shown that convertible bonds can be used to solve the risk-shifting problem. MacMinn (1987) showed that insurance contracts can also solve the risk-shifting problem. It is also possible to eliminate the problem by issuing equity rather than debt. Hence, there are capital structure choices that are not considered in the literature. The analysis here is a generalization of the literature.

Theorem 5. If the probability of insolvency is positive, i.e., $P\{B\} > 0$, then insuring the property risk is optimal.

Proof. Recall that the corporation makes an insurance decision and capital structure decision and subsequently makes the production. The production decision is a function of the leverage and insurance decisions. Hence, the condition for an optimal insurance decision is

$$\begin{aligned}\frac{\partial F}{\partial d} &= \frac{\partial V}{\partial q}\frac{\partial q}{\partial d} + \frac{\partial V}{\partial d} - \frac{\partial i}{\partial d} \\ &= \int_0^{\omega}\left(\frac{\partial R}{\partial q}\frac{\partial q}{\partial d} - 1\right)dP + \int_0^{\omega} dP \\ &= 0. \end{aligned} \tag{37}$$

Evaluating this derivative at q^s yields

$$\frac{\partial F}{\partial d} = \frac{\partial q}{\partial d}\int_0^{\beta}\frac{\partial R}{\partial q}dP < 0. \tag{38}$$

The sign follows because the operating scale increases in the deductible and the marginal payoff or quasi-rent is negative in the financial distress event. Therefore a positive probability of financial distress makes it optimal, *ceteris paribus*, to purchase insurance. QED

Theorem 5 represents one more example of the link between finance decisions and operating decisions. This particular application of the risk-shifting problem is very common and the result shows that insurance can be effective in mitigating the effects of risk-shifting and so credibly committing the firm to a particular operating decision. The theorem shows that the insurance allows the current shareholder value to be increased despite the fact that, viewed by itself, the insurance is a zero risk-adjusted net present value decision. It may also be observed that the theorem implies that it is optimal to increase the insurance coverage as long as there is any insolvency risk; this, in turn, implies that full insurance is optimal if it does not eliminate the insolvency risk.

16.5 TAX ASYMMETRIES

The tax model has traditionally been the most important in corporate finance. The corporate tax motivates the use of debt and helps explain the optimal use of that contract either in the small or in the large. In the insurance literature either the convex random tax liabilities or differences in capital gain versus income tax rates are used to show that insurance can add value. A different perspective is provided here by introducing a second source of risk. The risk that has been introduced in the previous sections is an economic index and can be thought of as a market risk. The property risk[19]

[19] Pure risk, accident risk, and property risk are used synonymously here.

may arise as a consequence of accident or weather conditions and so be modeled with another index. That is the approach taken here.

In the economy constructed here the state space is expanded so that $(\xi, \zeta) \in \Xi \times Z$; ξ, as before, is interpreted as an index of economic conditions and $\Xi = [0, \omega]$ is the set of these index numbers. The state ζ represents an accident state and $Z = \{0, 1\}$ is the set of these states. The pure or equivalently accident risk is a random variable $\Lambda: Z \to R$.[20] Let $\Lambda(0) = 0$ and $\Lambda(1) = L$. The corporate payoff is $\Gamma = \Pi - \Lambda$, where Π is the random corporate payoff without the accident risk. This generalization of the financial model introduces a new valuation problem. Even if investors purchasing stock in the corporation know that a particular economic state will occur *then*, the corporate payoff is still uncertain until the accident state has been resolved. The introduction of a pure risk causes incompleteness in an otherwise complete financial market system. If the corporation does not hedge or otherwise insure the property risk then risk averse investors will hedge it. The financial values expressed here are a consequence of that hedging behavior.[21]

Suppose the property loss L occurs with probability θ so that no loss occurs with probability $1 - \theta$. Suppose the loss L is large enough so that there is a positive probability of bankruptcy if the accident occurs but not so large that there is a positive probability of bankruptcy if the accident does not occur.[22] Let the tax liability of the corporation be denoted by $T = t\max\{0, \Pi - b - \Lambda\}$ where t is the tax rate; this assumes that the principle and interest are deductible.[23] The equity payoff is $\Pi - b - \Lambda - T$ and so the stock value is[24]

$$S = \int_0^{\delta} ((1-\theta)(1-t)(\Pi(q,\xi) - b))\,dP + \int_{\delta}^{\omega} ((1-\theta)(1-t)(\Pi(q,\xi) - b) + \theta(1-t)(\Pi(q,\xi) - b - d))\,dP \tag{39}$$

where δ is the boundary of the bankruptcy event and is implicitly defined by the condition $\Pi(q, \delta) - b - L - T(b, d, q, \delta) = 0$. The after-tax value of the firm is

$$V = \int_0^{\delta} ((1-\theta)(1-t)\Pi + (1-\theta)tb + \theta(\Pi - d))\,dP + \int_{\delta}^{\omega} ((1-t)\pi + tb - \theta(1-t)d)\,dP. \tag{40}$$

Let the corporate objective be the current shareholder value $F = V - I - i$, as

[20] Any random variable may be interpreted as a function mapping index numbers into the real line. A speculative risk maps Ξ into the real line while a pure risk maps Z into the real line.

[21] See (MacMinn 1999) for on the hedging behavior that provides these values.

[22] The probability of bankruptcy is endogenous and so to be complete one would have to allow for a positive probability of bankruptcy for any accident loss as long as the leverage is sufficient. That generality is not necessary to make the point that is demonstrated here.

[23] The assumption is only made to simplify the analysis and make the models here approximately the same.

[24] Note that the shareholders may receive a payoff in what has been called the bankruptcy event. Now, however, the bankruptcy event also depends on whether or not an accident occurs.

before, but where corporate value is now specified by equation (40). Here, as elsewhere, suppose the manager makes the financing decisions then the operating decisions.

The manager, acting in the interests of current shareholders, makes the finance and insurance decisions to maximize the objective function F. The first order condition for a bond issue is

$$\frac{\partial F}{\partial b}=(1-\theta)t\int_0^{\delta}dP+t\int_{\delta}^{\omega}dP+\frac{\partial q}{\partial b}\left\{\int_0^{\delta}\left((1-\theta)(1-t)\frac{\partial \Pi}{\partial q}+\theta\frac{\partial \Pi}{\partial q}\right)dP\right.$$
$$\left.+\int_{\delta}^{\omega}(1-t)\frac{\partial \Pi}{\partial q}dP\right\}=(1-\theta)t\int_0^{\delta}dP+t\int_{\delta}^{\omega}dP+\frac{\partial q}{\partial b}\left\{\int_0^{\delta}\theta\frac{\partial \Pi}{\partial q}dP\right\}. \tag{41}$$

The second equality in equation (41) follows due to the subsequent first order condition for an optimal output. The first two terms on the right hand side of equation (41) represent the marginal value of the debt tax shelter while the last term on the right hand side represents the marginal agency cost of the bond issue. Equation (41) implies the result that the firm issues bonds and pushes the bond issue to the point at which the marginal value of the tax shelter equals the marginal cost of the agency problem. Hence, *ceteris paribus*, equation (41) implies a risky debt issue.

The manager also makes an insurance decision to maximize current shareholder value. The first order condition is

$$\frac{\partial F}{\partial d}=-\theta\int_0^{\delta}dP-(1-t)\theta\int_{\delta}^{\omega}dP+\theta\int_0^{\omega}dP$$
$$+\frac{\partial q}{\partial d}\left\{\int_0^{\delta}\left((1-\theta)(1-t)\frac{\partial \Pi}{\partial q}+\theta\frac{\partial \Pi}{\partial q}\right)dP+\int_{\delta}^{\omega}(1-t)\frac{\partial \Pi}{\partial q}dP\right\}$$
$$=\theta t\int_{\delta}^{\omega}dP+\frac{\partial q}{\partial d}\left\{\int_0^{\delta}\theta\frac{\partial \Pi}{\partial q}dP\right\}. \tag{42}$$

The second equality follows due to the subsequent first order condition for an optimal output. The first term on the right hand side of equation (42) represents the marginal value of the tax shelter while the second term on the right hand side represents the marginal agency cost. Equation (42) implies the result that the firm increases its deductible, equivalently, reduces its insurance to the point at which the marginal value of the tax shelter equals the marginal agency cost. Equation (42) does not yield a conclusion like the bond issue equation because setting the deductible to zero does not eliminate the default risk; the contrary is more nearly true.

Despite the limitations in interpreting the first order condition in equation (42), it is possible to demonstrate a demand for insurance in this version of the model. It is possible for the firm to increase its leverage with a bond issue and counter the increase in the agency cost by simultaneously increasing its insurance coverage. A one to one trade-off in the size of the bond issue and the size of the deductible suffices to eliminate the agency cost at the margin and to increase the value of the tax shelter. Hence, there is a tax driven demand for insurance. The result is summarized in the following theorem.

Theorem 6. The corporate tax suffices to generate a demand for insurance.
Sketch of Proof. Suppose that for every dollar increase in leverage, the firm reduces the deductible by a dollar. Then the firm can generate an increase in value. Letting $v = (1, -1)$ and D_vF denote the derivative of the objective function in the direction v, observe that[25]

$$\begin{aligned} D_vF(b,d) &= \frac{\partial F}{\partial b} - \frac{\partial F}{\partial d} \\ &= (1-\theta)t\int_0^{\infty} dP \\ &> 0. \end{aligned} \tag{43}$$

follows by direct calculation. QED

Theorem 6 shows a rather strong motivation to insure. The property risk represents a risky tax shelter while the bond represents a certain tax shelter; the theorem shows that it is optimal to replace a risky with a safe tax shelter.[26] This is an intuitive result but it does require the introduction of the second index and so it is not a result that has been reported in the literature. It should be noted that the direction the financing takes, i.e., $v = (1, -1)$, does isolate the effect from the agency cost of debt because the probability of bankruptcy is held constant. Once the exchange of tax shelters is complete the firm still has the incentive specified in (41) to increase the size of the debt issue to the point at which the marginal benefit due to the tax shelter equals the marginal agency cost of the debt.

16.6 CONCLUDING REMARKS

The notion of risk management implies that the corporation plays an active role in reducing the risk of the corporate payoff in much the same way that an individual investor would reduce risk by diversifying his portfolio. The analysis here shows that

[25] The derivative of a function in a direction $v = (v_1, v_2)$ is $D_vF = v_1D_1F + v_2D_2F$.

[26] Of course, it should be recalled that the principal and interest are being deducted here. In a setting in which only interest on debt is deductible a similar result should hold if the interest rate, i.e., coupon interest on the issue, is sufficiently large relative to the probability of the loss.

it is not always necessary for the corporation to actively pursue any risk reduction policy (i.e., risk management is irrelevant). This is the case if the corporation's risk management operation does not affect the payoffs that investors can achieve by diversifying their own portfolios. The first and most naive version of the financial markets model demonstrates this case.

The corporation has an active role to play in managing risk if it can alter the payoff distribution in a way that investors cannot duplicate on personal account. In the sections on costly bankruptcy and agency problems, the analysis shows that minor modifications of the financial markets model provide the corporation with an incentive to purchase insurance. Two results emerge from the analysis. The first is that current shareholder value is greater for an insured than an uninsured firm in an economy with costly bankruptcy. This is the case because the firm can reduce the bankruptcy cost and this is something that individual investors cannot achieve on personal account. This result is not substantially altered by the introduction of a corporate tax and debt. The second result is that insurance may be used to reduce or eliminate some of the agency costs of debt. The corporate manager who selects the investment level can alleviate the underinvestment problem by insuring and so increase current shareholder value. This agency cost is like a deadweight loss; in the process of eliminating it the manager can make all the corporate claimholders better off. The asset substitution, or equivalently, risk-shifting problem can also be alleviated by insuring. The analysis here shows that the firm with bankruptcy risk will, *ceteris paribus*, over-produce. The firm can increase current shareholder value by providing a credible commitment that it will not over-produce and insurance represents one way of providing such a credible commitment.

Although this model is based upon conventional indemnity contracts, in recent years there has been a proliferation of new derivative securities such as catastrophe bonds, exchange-traded catastrophe options, credit derivatives and weather derivatives that can be expected to play increasingly important roles in the management of risk. The catastrophe (CAT) instruments have been used primarily by insurers and reinsurers to expand reinsurance capacity for catastrophes, but there is every reason to expect non-insurance companies that are already accustomed to hedging financial risks with derivatives to consider the CAT instruments, credit and other derivatives as viable alternatives to conventional indemnity contracts. Doherty (1997b) notes that by linking payoffs to indices that are correlated with the insured's loss but over which the insured has little control, such instruments help to resolve moral hazard problems. This benefit must be traded off against basis risk. While the current model does not incorporate alternative risk transfer mechanisms such as derivatives, the framework provided is robust enough to accommodate such instruments and would be a very fruitful avenue for future research.

While a fair amount of attention has been paid to developing theories concerning the corporate demand for insurance, the empirical implications of these theories have largely gone untested. This has primarily been due to the difficulty in obtaining data on corporate insurance purchases. Mayers and Smith (1990) and Garven and Lamm-Tennant (1999) attempt to overcome this problem by examining the demand for reinsurance by insurance companies.[27] While these authors report empirical results that are not inconsistent with the bankruptcy and agency cost theories, unfortunately it is not possible to unambiguously distinguish empirically between these theories.[28] Furthermore, Garven and Lamm-Tennant's results on tax convexity are inconclusive. Studies of the corporate demand for insurance by non-financial firms that have some bearing on the theories presented here have been conducted by Davidson, Cross, and Thornton (1992), Core (1997) and Yamori (1999). Davidson *et al.* find no evidence that the purchase of insurance affects the cost of equity capital, a result that is consistent with the notion that shareholder risk aversion does not motivate the corporate demand for insurance. Core finds, among other things, that firms with higher financial distress probabilities are more likely to purchase directors' and officers' liability insurance. Yamori reports that more highly levered firms insure more, but like Garven and Lamm-Tennant his results on tax convexity are inconclusive. Future empirical research in this area will need to focus upon building empirical models that make use of better databases that have less severe data limitations as well as accomplish a better job of empirically discriminating between the theories discussed in this survey.

16.7 REFERENCES

Borch, K. (1960). "The Safety Loading of Reinsurance Premiums." *Scandinavian Actuarial Journal* 163–184.

Borch, K. (1962). "Equilibrium in a Reinsurance Market." *Econometrica* 30, 424–444.

Blazenko, G. (1986). "The Economics of Reinsurance." *Journal of Risk and Insurance* 53, 258–277.

Caillaud, B., G. Dionne and B. Jullien. (2000). "Corporate Insurance with Optimal Financial Contracting." *Economic Theory* 16, 1, 77–105.

Core, J.E. (1997). "On the Corporate Demand for Directors' and Officers' Insurance." *Journal of Risk and Insurance* 64, 63–87.

Campbell, T.S. and W.A. Kracaw. (1990). "Corporate Risk Management and the Incentive Effects of Debt." *Journal of Finance* 45, 1673–1686.

Davidson, W.N., M.L. Cross and J.H. Thornton. (1992). "Corporate Demand for Insurance: Some Empirical and Theoretical Results." *Journal of Financial Services Research* 6, 61–72.

DeAngelo, H. and R.W. Masulis. (1980). "Optimal Capital Structure under Corporate and Personal Taxation." *Journal of Financial Economics* 8, 3–27.

Doherty, N.A. (1997a). "Corporate Insurance: Competition from Capital Markets and Financial Institutions." *Assurances* 65, 63–94.

Doherty, N.A. (1997b). "Innovations in Managing Catastrophe Risk." *Journal of Risk and Insurance* 64, 713–718.

[27] Data availability is a less severe problem in this industry because insurance companies are required by regulatory fiat to systematically report their reinsurance transactions.

[28] Mayers and Smith find, among other things, that firms with lower Best's ratings reinsure more, while Garven and Lamm-Tennant find that more reinsurance is demanded the higher the firm's leverage and the lower the correlation between the firm's investment-returns and claims-costs.

Fisher, I. (1930). *The Theory of Interest*. New York: MacMillan.

Garven, J.R. and R.D. MacMinn. (1993). "The Underinvestment Problem, Bond Covenants and Insurance." *Journal of Risk and Insurance* 60, 635–646.

Garven, J.R. and J. Lamm-Tennant. (1999). "The Demand for Reinsurance: Theory and Empirical Tests." Louisiana State University/Villanova University Working Paper.

Garven, J.R. and H. Loubergé. (1996). "Reinsurance, Taxes and Efficiency: A Contingent-claims Model of Insurance Market Equilibrium." *Journal of Financial Intermediation* 5, 74–93.

Green, R.C. (1984). "Investment Incentives, Debt and Warrants." *Journal of Financial Economics* 13, 115–136.

Green, R.C. and E. Talmor. (1985). "The Structure and Incentive Effects of Corporate Tax Liabilities." *Journal of Finance* 40, 1095–1114.

Heaton, H. (1986). "Corporate Taxation and Leasing." *Journal of Financial and Quantitative Analysis* 21, 351–359.

Hirshleifer, J. (1965). "Investment Decision under Uncertainty: Choice-Theoretic Approaches." *Quarterly Journal of Economics* 89, 509–536.

Jensen, M. and W. Meckling. (1976). "Theory of the Firm: Managerial Behavior, Agency Costs and Ownership Structure." *Journal of Financial Economics* 3, 305–360.

Jensen, M.C. and C.W. Smith. (1985). "Stockholder, Manager, and Creditor Interests: Applications of Agency Theory." In *Recent Advances in Corporate Finance*, ed. E. Altman and M. Subrahmanyam. Richard D. Irwin.

Leland, H. (1972). "Theory of the Firm Facing Uncertain Demand." *American Economic Review* 62, 278–291.

MacMinn, R.D. (1999). "On Corporate Risk Management and Insurance." University of Texas Working Paper.

MacMinn, R.D. and P.L. Brockett. (1995). "Corporate Spin-offs as a Value Enhancing Technique When Faced With Legal Liability." *Insurance, Mathematics and Economics* 16, 63–68.

MacMinn, R.D. (1987). "Insurance and Corporate Risk Management." *Journal of Risk and Insurance* 54, 658–677.

MacMinn, R.D. (1993). "The Risk-Shifting Problem and Convertible Bonds," *Advances in Quantitative Analysis of Finance and Accounting*, v2, Part B, 181–200.

MacMinn, R.D. (1990). "Uncertainty, Financial Markets, and the Fisher Model." University of Texas Working Paper.

MacMinn, R.D. and A. Holtmann. (1983). "Technological Uncertainty and the Theory of the Firm." *Southern Economic Journal* 50, 120–136.

MacMinn, R.D. and J.D. Martin. (1988). "Uncertainty, the Fisher Model, and Corporate Financial Theory." *Research in Finance* 7, 227–264.

Mayers, D. and C.W. Smith. (1982). "On the Corporate Demand for Insurance." *Journal of Business* 55, 281–296.

Mayers, D. and C.W. Smith. (1987). "Corporate Insurance and the Underinvestment Problem." *Journal of Risk and Insurance* 54, 45–54.

Modigliani, F. and M.H. Miller. (1958). "The Cost of Capital, Corporation Finance and the Theory of Investment." *American Economic Review* 48:3, 261–297.

Myers, S.C. (1977). "The Determinants of Corporate Borrowing." *Journal of Financial Economics* 5, 147–175.

Myers, Stewart C. and Nicholas S. Majluf. (1984). "Corporate Financing and Investment Decisions When Firms Have Information That Investors Do Not Have." *Journal of Financial Economics* 13, 187–221.

Rothschild, M. and J.E. Stiglitz. (1970). "Increasing Risk: I. A Definition." *Journal of Economic Theory* 2, 225–243.

Smith, C.W. and R.M. Stulz. (1985). "The Determinants of Firms' Hedging Policies." *Journal of Financial and Quantitative Analysis* 20, 391–405.

Tillinghast-Towers Perrin and Risk and Insurance Management Society. (1995). *1995 Cost of Risk Survey*, Tillinghast-Towers Perrin Risk Management Publications, Stamford, CT.

Yamori, N. (1999). "An Empirical Investigation of the Japanese Corporate Demand for Insurance: A Note." Forthcoming, *Journal of Risk and Insurance*.

17 Financial Risk Management in the Insurance Industry

J. David Cummins

University of Pennsylvania

Richard D. Phillips

Georgia State University

Stephen D. Smith

Georgia State University and Federal Reserve Bank of Atlanta

Abstract

This chapter has two objectives. The first objective is to survey the finance literature on corporate hedging and financial risk management with an emphasis on how the general literature applies in insurance. We begin by reviewing the theoretical rationales for widely-held, risk-neutral, profit-maximizing firms to practice risk management and then go on to discuss the empirical literature on corporate hedging. The second objective is to develop a theoretical model to provide a new explanation for why widely-held insurers manage risk. Insurers are hypothesized to invest in multiple period, private assets where the payoffs are not fully realized if the assets have to be liquidated prior to their expiration. Avoiding adverse shocks to capital that would trigger a liquidation provides the motivation for risk management in our model.

Keywords: Risk management, corporate hedging, private information, financial intermediaries, insurance.

JEL Classification Numbers: D80, G22, G13, G31.

17.1 INTRODUCTION

This chapter has two objectives. The first objective is to provide a survey of the literature on corporate hedging and financial risk management with an emphasis on how the general literature applies in insurance. We begin by reviewing the theoretical rationales for risk-neutral, profit-maximizing firms to practice risk management and then go on to discuss the empirical literature on corporate hedging. The second objective is to develop a new theoretical model to explain why the managers of risk-neutral insurance companies engage in risk management.[1] Insurers are hypothesized to invest in multiple period, private assets where the payoffs are not fully realized if the assets have to be liquidated prior to their expiration. Avoiding adverse shocks to capital that would trigger a liquidation provides the motivation for risk management in our model.

This paper draws upon three strands of modern financial theory. The first strand is perfect-markets asset pricing theory as applied to widely held firms whose shares are traded in frictionless and complete markets. This theory is based on the assumption that shares are owned by diversified investors, who eliminate non-systematic risk through their portfolio choices.[2] Investors are risk averse and choose portfolios that are optimal in terms of their taste for risk. In its simplest form, the theory envisions investors as balancing risk and return by choosing portfolios that are linear combinations of a riskless asset (e.g., Treasury bills) and the market portfolio of risky assets. Because investors can achieve an optimal risk-return position by varying the weights placed on the riskless asset and the market portfolio, such investors do not want the individual corporations that constitute the market portfolio to manage non-systematic risk. Rather, investors want firms to maximize the market value of their net worth. In perfect markets financial theory, this generally implies that firms should be risk neutral, i.e., they should take advantage of any projects available to them that have positive net present values, without regard to non-systematic project risk.[3] Because corporate risk management is costly (e.g., because it requires the use of costly managerial resources, the payment of premia for options and other derivatives used to manage risk, etc.) and because investors can engage in "home-made" risk management, expenditures on risk management at the corporate level constitute a deadweight loss to investors.

The second strand of financial theory discussed in this paper attempts to explain the existence of corporate risk management. This theory was developed because it has been observed that corporations do manage risk, in spite of the strong proscription against this type of activity in perfect-markets financial theory. In fact, the existence

[1] We follow the standard practice in the insurance economics literature in referring to insurance companies as "insurers" throughout our discussion. Insurers are assumed to be owned by shareholders who hire managers to operate the firm.

[2] Financial theory divides risk into two major types—*non-systematic risk*, which can be eliminated by investing in a diversified portfolio, and *systematic risk*, which cannot be eliminated through diversification. Non-systematic risk is considered to be firm or industry specific, whereas systematic risk affects the entire market and thus cannot be diversified away.

[3] Systematic project risk is recognized through the discount factor used to calculate the net present value of the project, i.e., it is recognized in the cost of capital. See Brealey and Myers (1996) for further discussion.

of corporate risk management can be explained by reference to *imperfections* in financial markets. Financial theorists have identified two broad categories of imperfections to explain the existence of corporate risk management. One class of imperfections consists of factors that impose costs on firms that do not manage risk. Managing risk in response to these imperfections is generally value maximizing, i.e., the market value of corporate net worth will be higher if this type of risk management is carried out than if it is not. The second class of imperfections that motivate risk management are typically associated with managerial behavior, i.e., instead of maximizing the value of the firm, managers may maximize their own utility. The extent to which this behavior is consistent with value maximization is unclear. If risk management is costless then allowing managers to hedge risk at the corporate level may be value enhancing to the extent risk averse managers demand less compensation due to the decreased likelihood that adverse outcomes will threaten their job security. However, if risk management is costly, then shareholders may have to undertake certain activities, such as the development of incentive-based compensation contracts or undertake costly monitoring, to ensure the resources of the firm are devoted to the maximization of the firm's net worth and not the manager's own utility. The value maximizing and managerial risk aversion motivations for risk management are discussed in detail in section 2 of this chapter.

The third strand of financial theory explored in this paper deals with information asymmetries and private information, both of which are assumed away in perfect markets financial theory. This theory views insurers as financial intermediaries that borrow funds from policyholders by issuing insurance policies and then "intermediate" these funds into portfolios of invested assets. Private information can be present in both the underwriting and the investment operations of an insurer. Information asymmetries are generally present between the company and its policyholders as the policyholders typically know more about their risk characteristics than does the insurer. This information asymmetry can lead to the problem adverse selection and, in the extreme case, lead the market to fail as explained in the important article by Rothschild and Stiglitz (1976) as well as much subsequent research. The company-policyholder asymmetry also presents an opportunity for the insurer to develop *private information*, i.e., information on its policyholders that is known by the insurer but not by its competitors. By insuring a policyholder over a period of time, the insurer acquires information on the policyholder's risk characteristics that is not available to competing insurers. The insurer may be able to exploit this private information to earn economic rents from policyholders that have been with the company for a period of time (see D'Arcy and Doherty 1990).

Financial intermediaries also can acquire private information in their investment operations. Generally, this involves acquiring more information about a borrower or a complex security than is possessed by the market as a whole. For example, there is considerable evidence that banks acquire information about certain types of borrowers that is difficult for other investors to replicate (Diamond 1991). This information gives banks a competitive advantage over other banks and the capital markets in dealing with these borrowers; and banks can exploit this information to earn economic rents (Rajan 1992). Likewise, insurers have an informational advantage in investing in certain types of assets. E.g., life insurers are the major source of privately placed bonds in the U.S. capital market. Privately placed bonds are analogous to bank loans in terms of providing opportunities for insurers to gain an informational advantage.[4] Insurers also invest in structured securities and other complex long-dated financial assets where the expected return on the assets may be higher due to the level of private information they contain.

In this chapter, we provide a new rationale for corporate risk management based on private information. We develop a model motivated by the observation that insurers engage in contracts covering multiple time periods for which the payoffs on those contracts may not be fully realized until they expire. For example, D'Arcy and Doherty (1990) provide empirical evidence that insurers may be willing to underprice (take a loss on) newly issued policies based on rents they expect to earn from the subset of new policyholders who stay with the company for a period of years. The motivation for underpricing new policies is that insurers cannot fully discriminate between good and bad risks who are applicants for insurance. However, by observing policyholders over a period of time, they are able to identify the bad risks and either charge them higher premiums or eliminate them from the policyholder pool. Insurers earn a profit on the good risks that remain that more than offsets the losses created by having some bad risks in the pool at the outset. The good risks are hypothesized to remain with the insurer even though their premiums are higher than would be experienced in an informationally efficient, competitive market because competitors do not observe the private information that has been accumulated and hence cannot distinguish the good risks from the bad risks that have been eliminated from the pool. Thus, the good risks do not have an incentive to leave the insurer and go back into the market.[5]

[4] Such private information would not arise for widely traded, standardized securities such as Treasury bonds and corporate equities. For private information to develop, the investor must have a unique opportunity to obtain information that is not available to others. The relationship between banks and their borrowers and between insurers and the issuers of privately placed bonds may give rise to such information.

[5] Implicit in this discussion is the assumption that the price charged to new policyholders is higher than the price the good risks have to pay if they remain with the insurer, which in turn is higher than the price the good risks would pay in an informationally efficient, competitive market. Recall that the price charged to new risks is a pooled price applying to both bad risks and good risks. Consequently, insurers could lose money on the pooled price when selling to both bad and good risks and still have sufficient slack in pricing to earn positive rents when insuring only the good risks. Another issue, discussed by D'Arcy and Doherty (1990), is that the insurer's competitors could adopt the strategy of offering insurance at favorable rates to policyholders who can present a valid renewal offer from another insurer; and, in fact, at least one major company has based a marketing campaign on this approach. In effect, by making the renewal offer, the insurer has revealed some of its private information, which can potentially be captured by competitors. D'Arcy and Doherty suggest various ways that the insurer could protect its private information by "scrambling" the renewal signal.

We refer to contractual relationships in which insurers earn economic rents from private information as *private assets*—a term encompassing both insurance policy relationships as well as investments such as privately placed bonds and other opaque assets. In our model, we assume that private assets must be held for a specified period of time in order for positive rents to be realized. We make the simplifying assumption that if insurers are forced to liquidate some or all of their positions in the private assets at some intervening time period due to a shock to the capital resources of the firm, they will only collect the par value of their investment and therefore be forced to pass up the opportunity to realize the benefits of private information. In the case of insurance policies, an adverse shock to capital may lead to a ratings downgrade or regulatory intervention that causes a "flight to quality" by the insurer's profitable long-term policyholders. In the case of investments, an adverse shock may create cash flow problems that require the insurer to liquidate long-dated private investments on unfavorable terms.

Insurers can reduce the probability of having to liquidate their positions in private assets in the intervening time periods in one of two ways. First, they can reduce the level of investment they make in the private assets and hold additional levels of cash (or some other highly liquid security). The cost of adopting such a strategy is the opportunity cost of not being able to more fully participate in a private asset with a higher expected return. This is a particularly serious problem if the private asset involves the firm's core business, as in the case of an insurer issuing insurance policies. Alternatively, insurers can engage in risk management to reduce the chance that a given shock to capital will require liquidation of the private asset. To the extent that practicing risk management is less costly than holding cash, insurers will have an incentive to transfer as much of the risk of the shock away from the firm as they can.

The theories we discuss in this chapter are quite general and also provide motivations for non-insurance firms to manage risk. However, there are two principal reasons why the discussion should be of particular interest to insurance economists: (1) Because of the nature of insurance enterprise, financial firms such as insurers are more susceptible to the agency costs associated with shareholder/manager and shareholder/customer informational asymmetries than are corporations in general. For example, insurers tend to invest in liquid asset classes which can be subject to rapid change. Financial firms thus can enter, exit, expand, and contract businesses rapidly, making them difficult to monitor effectively (Merton and Perold 1993; Perold 1999). In addition, financial firms are "opaque" in the sense that some of their activities are not publicly disclosed or disclosed only with significant time lags (Ross 1989). For example, insurers do not publicly report the adequacy of loss reserves and they disclose detailed data on their asset portfolios only in their annual regulatory statements. Information asymmetries are also endemic in the relationship between insurers and their customers. It is not a coincidence that Rothschild and Stiglitz (1976) and many subsequent papers on adverse selection have used insurance markets as the primary example of adverse selection. Thus, the deadweight costs of capital due to informational asymmetries are particularly severe in this industry, which should lead to a higher demand for risk management by insurers. (2) As financial intermediaries, the suppliers of an insurer's debt capital are also its customers; and the customers of an insurer are particularly averse to insolvency risk (credit quality) and will strictly prefer to conduct business with highly rated firms (Merton and Perold 1993; Phillips, Cummins, and Allen 1998).[6]

The chapter proceeds as follows: Section 17.2 provides a brief overview of the financial rationale for corporate hedging from the prior literature. Section 17.3 provides a summary of the empirical evidence investigating the economic factors associated with risk management and the use of derivative securities. In section 17.4, we present our theoretical analysis providing a new rationale for corporate hedging. Section 17.5 concludes the chapter.

17.2 THE RATIONALE FOR CORPORATE RISK MANAGEMENT: A SURVEY OF RECENT LITERATURE

As mentioned above, a perfect-markets approach to financial theory views corporate risk management as creating deadweight costs that reduce firm value. However, because widely held corporations do engage in risk management, researchers have developed a richer set of hypotheses to explain why corporations manage risk. One set of motivations for risk management are viewed as contributing to the maximization of firm value. These factors include various market imperfections, incentive conflicts, and information asymmetries that are hypothesized to create motivations for value-maximizing corporate managers to engage in hedging activities (see, for example, Smith and Stulz 1985; Froot, Scharfstein, and Stein 1993; Stulz 1996; and Tufano 1996). However, it is also recognized that corporations may engage in risk management activities based upon objective functions other than those that are purely value-maximizing. Such activities typically arise due to managerial risk aversion and imperfectly controlled incentive conflicts between managers and owners (Smith and Stulz 1985; Stulz 1996). This section reviews the literature that explains both the value maximizing and alternative motivations for corporate hedging.

[6] Investors are willing to supply capital to firms with various levels of insolvency risk as long as they are appropriately compensated. Customers of insurers have a greater concern about credit quality because they have purchased insurance in most cases to reduce their exposure to unfavorable contingencies that threaten their financial security. A bond investor can protect against bond defaults by specific issuers by investing in a diversified portfolio. An insurance policyholder, on the other hand, cannot diversify by purchasing numerous small insurance policies from a large number of insurers. Thus, credit risk acquires greater significance to buyers of insurance than to investors in corporate debt.

Value Maximizing Motivations for Hedging

One rationale for value-maximizing firms to engage in hedging activities is the avoidance of the costs of financial distress. Financial distress costs include the direct costs of bankruptcy such as legal fees and court costs. Financial distress costs also encompass indirect costs that arise even if the insurer does not enter bankruptcy, such as reputational losses and the disruption of relationships with employees, suppliers, and customers. For example, key managers may seek employment elsewhere if the firm encounters financial difficulties, suppliers may be reluctant to grant trade credit to a financially vulnerable firm, and customers may shift their business to competing firms in a "flight to quality."[7]

Financial distress costs also can arise if cash flows are adversely affected by unhedged risks that force managers to forego profitable investment projects. This is the classic under-investment problem, first identified by Myers (1977).[8] The under-investment problem arises because the presence of debt in the firm's capital structure may lead the firm to forego positive net present value projects if the gains primarily accrue to bond holders rather than shareholders. The problem is more likely to occur in highly leveraged firms, providing a motivation for firms to hedge to avoid shocks to equity that result in high leverage ratios. A related problem, identified by Froot, Scharfstein, and Stein (1993) arises if external funds are more costly than internal funds, due to, say, information asymmetries between managers and shareholders. For example, managers are likely to be better informed about the expected cash flows from a potential project than are shareholders. Firms may hedge to reduce the volatility of their cash flows and thus help to ensure the availability of internal funds to take advantage of attractive projects.

The hypothesis that firms engage in risk management to avoid financial distress costs seems particularly applicable to the insurance industry. In the insurance industry, managers are likely to have more information about the adequacy of loss reserves than do the insurer's owners, leading to higher costs for external than for internal capital. In addition, insurers are subject to stringent state solvency regulation, enforced through regulatory site audits, detailed reporting requirements, and computerized audit ratio tests (see Klein 1995). Recently adopted risk-based capital standards require insurance commissioners to institute corrective action and ultimately to seize control of financially troubled insurers when their equity capital falls below certain thresholds. This regulatory "option" on the equity of the firm reduces the value of the owners' interest in the firm (Cummins, Harrington, and Niehaus 1995). Both corporate and personal lines policyholders are very sensitive to an insurer's financial ratings and are likely to take their business elsewhere if the insurer's financial condition begins to deteriorate.

[7] See Andrade and Kaplan (1998) for one attempt to measure the costs of financial distress.
[8] See also Mayers and Smith (1987).

There are a number of risks faced by insurers that may motivate them to hedge using derivatives and other risk management strategies (Santomero and Babbel 1997). Both life and property-liability insurers issue insurance contracts that create liabilities with maturities of fifteen years or more, and both types of insurers tend to invest heavily in long-term financial assets such as bonds. These long-term assets and liabilities expose insurers to interest rate risk that can adversely affect the market values of assets, liabilities, and equity. The empirical evidence suggests that both property-liability and life insurers tend to have positive equity duration gaps, with the duration of assets exceeding the duration of liabilities (Cummins and Weiss 1991; Staking and Babbel 1995), and insurers seek to hedge the resulting duration and convexity risk (Santomero and Babbel 1997).[9]

In addition to high-grade, publicly-traded bonds, insurers also invest in assets with higher default risk, higher return volatilities, and/or lower liquidity, providing a potential motivation for hedging such risks. For example, investments in real estate may expose insurers to more price and liquidity risk than they would like to retain. Many life insurers also invest heavily in privately placed bonds and mortgages, which often contain embedded options and are also subject to liquidity risk. Both life and property-liability insurers invest in collateralized mortgage obligations (CMOs), which carry similar risks. With the increasing internationalization of financial markets, insurers have begun to invest more heavily in foreign securities, either as a hedge against foreign liabilities or simply to enhance portfolio diversification and take advantage of attractive yields. Insurers thus have the motivation to reduce their exposure to foreign currencies by hedging the exchange rate risk resulting from foreign assets and liabilities. Investment in corporate equities exposes insurers to systematic risk from market fluctuations, which cannot be eliminated through diversification but can be managed through trading in derivatives such as stock options.

Various categories of liabilities also potentially expose insurers to abnormal risks. For life insurers, these include group annuities and individual life insurance and annuities. Group annuities are held by sophisticated institutional investors such as corporate pension plans, who are sensitive to both yields and insurer financial ratings. Individual life insurance and annuities are relatively long maturity contracts that contain numerous embedded options, making them particularly sensitive to interest rate and/or equity volatility risk. For example, many asset accumulation policies include minimum yield guarantees, in effect incorporating put options that are automatically exercised against the insurer when investment yields decline or, in the case

[9] Duration and convexity risk refer to the risk of changes in the market values of assets and liabilities due to changes in interest rates. The market values of assets and liabilities equal the present value of their cash flows. If interest rates increase, the present value of the cash flows decline. If assets have longer durations than liabilities, for example, an interest rate increase will reduce the market value of assets by more than it reduces the market value of liabilities, leading to a decline in the market value of equity that can create financial distress costs.

of equity-linked annuities, during periods of downturns in the stock market. Life insurers also issue guaranteed investment contracts (GICs), similar to structured notes, that are purchased primarily by institutional investors. GICs are yield-sensitive and contain embedded options that are likely to be exercised in response to changes in interest rates and other economic fluctuations.

A related motivation for risk management by insurers and other financial intermediaries has been suggested by Allen and Santomero (1998). They point out that most investors do not actively participate directly in securities markets due to participation costs. Participation costs include the costs of learning about specific securities and continuously monitoring one's investment portfolio and trading to maintain the target level of risk. Because of these costs, a significant amount of investment takes place through intermediaries. Allen and Santomero (1998) argue that an important role played by intermediaries is to create products with relatively stable distributions of returns that require less monitoring by investors than an actively traded portfolio. Maintaining stable return distributions (e.g., on products such an equity-linked annuities) provides another motivation for insurers to manage risk.

Yet another motivation to undertake corporate hedging to maximize shareholder value is provided by the convexity of the corporate income tax schedule (Smith and Stulz 1985).[10] This convexity implies that expected tax payments can be reduced by lowering the volatility of the taxable income stream through the use of derivatives or other risk management techniques. The tax schedules affecting both life and property-liability insurers have convex segments, and property-liability insurers, in particular, are known to engage in active tax management (Cummins and Grace 1994).

Managerial Risk Aversion

As suggested earlier, managerial risk aversion and incentive conflicts between managers and owners provide alternative rationales for corporate hedging. behavior, i.e., instead of maximizing the value of the firm, managers may maximize their own utility. Managers may behave in a risk averse manner, taking less risk than would be optimal for the firm's owners, because their human capital and wealth are poorly diversified. Thus, they may be more concerned about losing their jobs which can lead to reductions in firm value to the extent hedging is not costless and/or it is costly for shareholders to monitor the actions of the managers. The extent to which this behavior is consistent with value maximization is unclear. If risk management is costless, then allowing managers to hedge risk at the corporate level may be value enhancing to the

[10] The tax schedule is strictly convex if its slope is increasing in income (i.e., if it has positive first and second derivatives). For convex tax schedules, the expected value of the tax payment is increasing in the risk of the income stream.

extent risk averse managers demand less compensation due to the decreased likelihood that adverse outcomes will threaten their job security. However, if risk management is costly then shareholders may have to undertake certain activities, such as the development of incentive-based compensation contracts or undertake costly monitoring, to ensure the resources of the firm are devoted to the maximization of the firm's net worth and not the manager's own utility.[11] Stock option plans are considered to be especially effective in this regard.

Many firms in the insurance industry are especially susceptible to friction costs created by managerial risk aversion. A substantial proportion of the firms in the industry are mutuals or closely-held stocks, where managers are likely to exhibit risk aversion because of suboptimal diversification of personal wealth, organization-specific capital, and/or the absence of effective mechanisms for owners to use as disciplining and incentive devices.

The mutual ownership form lacks effective mechanisms that owners can use to control, monitor, and discipline managers, such as the alienable claims, voting rights in elections for directors, and the proxy and takeover fights available to the owners of stock companies. The opportunities to align owner and shareholder interests through management compensation systems (such as stock option plans) also are more limited in the mutual ownership form. Thus, mutual managers are likely to behave in a risk-averse manner, placing a higher priority on avoiding or hedging risks that may threaten their jobs than on maximizing firm value. This reasoning suggests the hypothesis that managers of mutuals are more likely to engage in derivatives activity than comparable stock insurers.

An alternative prediction about mutuals is provided by the managerial discretion hypothesis, which suggests that mutuals will be relatively successful in less complex and less risky activities than stocks (Mayers and Smith 1988). To the extent that less complex and less risky activities give rise to less need for hedging, the managerial discretion hypothesis would predict that mutuals may be less active in the use of derivatives and other risk management techniques than stocks. Of course, these two hypotheses are not mutually exclusive, i.e., mutuals on average may be less risky and less complex than stocks, while at the same time mutual managers exhibit greater risk aversion than managers of similar stock insurers.

Another reason why mutual managers may fail to maximize value is provided by the *expense preference* hypothesis (e.g., Mester 1989). This hypothesis holds that mutual managers are more likely to generate expenses due to excessive consumption of perquisites and other activities that are not consistent with cost minimization.

[11] Another managerial motivation for hedging involves the use of risk management to signal managerial skill in the presence of asymmetric information (Breeden and Viswanathan 1996; DeMarzo and Duffie 1995).

Again, the rationale is that the owners of mutuals have less effective mechanisms to motivate and control managers than do the owners of stock insurers.

A final argument with regard to mutuals is that their lack of access to the capital markets may lead to rational risk averse behavior. Mutuals cannot issue new equity following an adverse shock due to higher than expected loss payments or investment losses but rather must wait for retained earnings to restore lost capital. Thus, they run the risk of having to forego attractive investment opportunities following a shock to capital and/or losing customers due to downgrades of their financial ratings. Mutuals thus may be more active in risk management than stocks in order to avoid these adverse consequences.

17.3 CORPORATE RISK MANAGEMENT: EMPIRICAL EVIDENCE

Corporations can manage risk using a wide variety of tools. The choice of investment projects, diversification across product lines, choices involving operating and financial leverage, and shareholder dividend strategies all can be viewed as techniques for managing risk. However, unlike some of these traditional methods for managing risk, derivative securities exist only for purposes of risk management. Consequently, empirical analyses of firms' use of derivatives provide somewhat "cleaner" results concerning why firms may choose to engage in risk management. It is also the case that the volume of activity in derivatives contracts has grown dramatically over the past two decades. Consequently, we focus the remainder of our discussion on empirical evidence on corporate risk management through the use of derivatives.

Most of the motivations for corporate hedging are generic, although they apply in varying degrees across industries. Consequently, it is informative to consider empirical evidence on risk management by both non-insurance and insurance firms. However, because we are primarily interested in the insurance industry, our discussion of non-insurance firms focuses on particularly noteworthy studies rather than trying to present a comprehensive survey.

Risk Management by Non-Insurance Firms

A major study investigating the question of the "motive" for risk management is by Tufano (1996), who looks at managerial compensation schemes and hedge ratios in the gold mining industry to determine whether risk management is motivated by value maximization or managerial risk aversion. Tufano argues that risk-averse managers whose compensation comes in large part through acquiring shares in the firm will want to hedge their risk. Such a policy would not necessarily benefit diversified shareholders. Tufano contrasts these managers with managers who earn a relatively large portion of their compensation through stock options. In this situation managers can walk away from the options should the firm do poorly, but if the firm does well their positions will provide high payoffs. With this form of incentive compensation, even risk-averse managers would be more willing to tolerate gold price, and therefore earnings, volatility and thus would find hedging to be less advantageous.[12] Tufano's empirical evidence suggests that managers with high option holdings manage risk less than those with high stock holdings consistent with the managerial risk-aversion hypothesis of risk management. Tufano finds almost no evidence in favor of the various rationales that would make risk management a value-maximizing decision.

Contrary to Tufano's results, some authors have provided evidence that is more consistent with the value-maximization theories of risk management. Numerous authors have investigated whether firms engage in risk management in an effort to reduce the probability of incurring financial distress costs. An early study by Wall and Pringle (1989) found support for the hypothesis as they report that firms with lower credit ratings are more likely than higher-rated firms to use interest rate swaps.[13] Other authors have considered the more general question of whether the firm's capital structure is related to the likelihood that the firm will engage in risk management via derivatives contracting. The evidence presented in these studies is mixed. For example, neither Mian (1996) nor Nance, Smith, and Smithson (1993) report any evidence to suggest that derivatives trading is related to the capital structure of the firm. A more recent study by Geczy, Minton, and Schrand (1997) investigates the relationship between the capital structure of the firm and the decision to manage foreign currency exposures using derivatives. This study differs from its predecessors by recognizing the simultaneity of a firm's capital structure and risk-management decisions. Even after controlling for simultaneity, however, the authors conclude that there does not appear to be a relationship between a firm's capital structure and the decision to use derivatives.

Two exceptions to these studies of nonfinancial firms are Dolde (1996) and Graham and Rogers (1999). Dolde finds a significant relationship between risk management and the leverage of the firm after controlling for the firm's underlying exposure to various financial risks. Graham and Rogers (1999), like Geczy, et al., investigate the hedging and debt policy decisions of the firm using a simultaneous equations approach. They find that the use of derivatives is positively related to firm leverage. Thus, these authors find evidence to suggest highly levered firms appear more likely to use derivatives to avoid the expected costs of financial distress; or as Graham and Rogers argue, firms that use derivatives can maintain higher leverage ratios and maximize firm value by increasing their interest-expense tax deductions.

[12] It is well-known that the value of a stock option is increasing in the risk of the underlying stock. Intuitively, this is because the holder of the option benefits from upside fluctuations in the stock price but loses nothing beyond the option premium in the event of downside fluctuations (see Hull 1993).

[13] For a discussion of the various types of derivative securities, see Hull (1993).

The evidence from studies investigating the decision by non-insurance financial firms to use derivatives as a way to avoid financial distress costs is also mixed. Carter and Sinkey (1998) provide weak evidence that the capital structure and risk-management decisions of U.S. commercial banks are related. Gunther and Siems (1995), who also analyze U.S. banks, report no significant relationship between the decision to use derivatives and the capital structure of the bank. Focusing only on banks that are active in derivatives markets, Gunther and Siems find that banks reporting a higher volume of derivatives activity also have higher capital ratios. This result is in fact inconsistent with the financial distress hypothesis, at least as it is usually defined in the literature.

Mixed evidence has also been presented on the use of derivatives to lower the firm's expected tax burden. In their study of non-financial companies, Nance, Smith, and Smithson (1993) find that firms with higher investment tax credits are more likely to engage in derivative transactions. In an analysis of firms reported on Compustat, Graham and Smith (1999) conclude that approximately 50 percent of the firms in their sample face convex tax schedules and therefore have an incentive to reduce the volatility of their income stream. However, in a subsequent study, Graham and Rogers (1999) use a similar methodology to estimate the convexity of the tax schedule for a large sample of firms across many industries and are unable to find any relationship between derivative holdings and tax convexity.

A number of authors have found strong evidence documenting that firms use derivatives to reduce the variability of their income stream and thus help to ensure that adequate internal funds are available to take advantage of attractive investments. Gay and Nam (1999), for example, provide results consistent with the hypothesis that non-financial firms with both low levels of liquidity and high growth opportunities tend to hedge more. This finding is consistent with managers trying to mitigate the need to seek costly external funds to finance positive net present value projects. Other authors have found similar results. For example, Geczy, Minton, and Schrand (1997) and Nance, Smith, and Smithson (1993) both found that companies with less liquidity or companies that use less preferred stock, as opposed to using straight debt, are more likely to use derivatives to avoid shocks to the internal capital resources. A recent study by Ahmed, Beatty, and Takeda (1997), investigating 152 U.S. commercial banks, also finds support for the costly external finance hypothesis.

Risk Management by Insurance Firms

Cummins, Phillips, and Smith (CPS) (1997; 2000) analyze the factors that motivate both life and property-liability insurance firms to participate in derivatives markets as well as the drivers of the volume of derivatives transactions for insurers that decide to participate (see also Colquitt and Hoyt 1997). Based on 1994 data, CPS find that about 10.9 percent of life insurers and 6.9 percent of property-liability insurers use derivatives. However, usage is much more widespread in the largest size quartile, where 34.4 percent of life and 21.1 percent of property-liability insurers are active in derivatives markets. The transactions volume for life insurers far exceeds that of property-liability insurers. The transactions volume for life insurers is concentrated in bond and interest rate derivatives, as expected if insurers are using derivatives to hedge interest rate (duration and convexity) risk. Life insurers also show significant activity in foreign currency derivatives, consistent with the argument that insurers use derivatives to manage exchange rate risk. The leading categories of derivatives transactions for property-liability insurers include equity call options, foreign currency contracts, and bond and interest rate derivatives, again consistent with the management of price volatility, foreign exchange rate risk, and interest rate risk.

Following Gunther and Siems (1995), CPS (2000) conduct a multivariate probit analysis of the decision by insurers to participate in derivatives markets and a log-normal regression analysis investigating the volume of derivatives transactions by insurers. The authors investigate both decisions as they argue hedging is not costless, either in terms of fixed or variable costs. Thus, if the participation decision is driven by fixed costs, only firms with high enough levels of risk exposure, for example, due to a high tolerance for risk per unit of expected return, would find it worthwhile to enter the derivatives market. However, conditional on being active in derivatives, firms/managers with high appetites for risk will generally hedge less at the margin to the extent that each additional unit imposes marginal costs in the form of risk premiums. As evidence in support of this hypothesis, the authors report that many of the risk measures employed in the study often display exactly the opposite signs in the participation and volume regressions. This suggests that among firms having a large enough exposure to warrant participation in derivatives markets, those with the largest exposures are less willing to incur the marginal cost associated with eliminating the exposure.

The participation investigation in the CPS analysis also provides a considerable amount of support for the hypothesis that insurers hedge to maximize value. They present evidence consistent with the use of derivatives to reduce the expected costs of financial distress. For example, the decision to use derivatives is inversely related to the capital-to-asset ratio for both life and property-liability insurers. CPS also provide evidence consistent with the use of derivatives by insurers to hedge asset volatility, liquidity, and exchange rate risks. They find significant regression coefficients on several variables related to asset risk exposure such as the proportions of assets in privately placed bonds and collateralized mortgage obligations. Life insurers appear to use derivatives to manage interest rate risk and the risk from embedded options present in their individual life insurance and GIC liabilities. There is also some evidence that tax considerations play a role in motivating derivatives market participation decisions by insurers.

On the other hand, the CPS analysis provides little or no support for the hypothesis that corporate hedging in the insurance industry is motivated by managerial risk aversion. However, their data source did not contain several important variables that would have provided a more complete test of this hypothesis, including the proportion of an insurer's stock owned by managers and the incentive features in managerial compensation plans. The use of such variables to analyze the risk aversion hypothesis is a promising area for future research.

17.4 CORPORATE HEDGING, MULTIPERIOD CONTACTS, AND PRIVATE INFORMATION

In this section, we provide a new rationale for corporate hedging using a simple model that provides conditions under which value-maximizing managers of insurers will find risk management desirable. Specifically, we assume that firms such as insurers invest in multi-period, private assets that have higher returns than publicly traded assets. However, the returns are not realized unless the assets are held to their maturity date. If the assets have to be liquidated prior to maturity, the firm receives only the par value of the investment and foregoes the assets' returns. The firm thus has a motivation to hedge risk in order to avoid an adverse shock to capital that may force the insurer to liquidate some or all of its holdings of the private asset. As discussed above, the private assets may be insurance policies, privately placed bonds, or some other type of complex, opaque investment. Although the model applies generally to any firm that can invest in private assets, we believe that it is especially applicable to insurers because of the information asymmetries arising from insurance underwriting and the prominent role played by insurers in the markets for privately placed bonds and other structured securities.

To develop the theory more formally, we consider a three date model where the returns from investing in the private asset are received at date two. Assume that there are $i = 1, \ldots, N$ firms, each endowed with capital, K, and having access to two types of securities. The first security is short-term and yields a riskless yield per period, per unit of investment, of R, where $R > 0$. The other security is a long-lived private asset yielding a random gross return per unit of investment, $\tilde{\theta}_i$, at date two, $0 \leq \tilde{\theta}_i \leq \infty$. The realization of $\tilde{\theta}_i$, θ_i, is assumed to be private information with $E_0(\tilde{\theta}_i) > (1 + R)^2$, where $E_0(\cdot)$ is the expectation taken at time zero. We assume that $\tilde{\theta}_i = 0$ with positive probability, so that, absent the expenditure of costs for monitoring, firms are unable to credibly issue securities to outside claim-holders.

We will let I_i denote the level of investment in the private security at date zero, $I_i \leq K$, $\forall\ i$ and we assume the firm cannot add to the long-lived security at date one. In addition, if any portion is sold before maturity (date two), the portion sold returns its par value, or initial investment.[14] Absent any frictions in the capital markets, the

[14] In this model we assume the firm will recoup its initial investment in the private technology asset. However, the finance literature modeling distressed asset sales predicts that firms forced to liquidate some

first best solution is clearly $I_i = K$ for any-value maximizing firm i, and the present value of the firm at date 0 will equal $V_i^0 = \frac{KE(\tilde{\theta}_i)}{(1+R)^2}$.

The first friction we introduce to the model involves a shock to the firm's value at time one, $\tilde{Z}_i$, with $E_0(\tilde{Z}_i) = 0 \ \forall \ i$. The shocks are used as a summary measure for economy-wide and idiosyncratic factors that may influence the value of the firm at the intermediate date. In particular, we assume that $\tilde{Z}_i = \beta_i \, (\tilde{\rho} - 1) + \tilde{\varepsilon}_i$ where $\tilde{\rho}$ is an observable economy-wide shock with $E(\tilde{\rho}) = 1$, $\tilde{\varepsilon}_i$ is an idiosyncratic shock with $E(\tilde{\varepsilon}_i) = 0$ and β_i is a sensitivity coefficient with respect to the economy-wide shock. We consider two cases regarding the support for the distribution of $\tilde{Z}_i$. In the first case, we assume the support to be bounded on the interval $[a_i, b_i]$ with $b_i = K$. Doing so ensures the firm will always be able to meet any shock equal to the firm's initial endowment, K. In the second case, shown in the appendix to this chapter, we relax this assumption and assume the upper bound of the support of $\tilde{Z}_i$ can be larger than the firm's initial endowment, i.e., $b_i > K$.

Recall that the gross return on the private asset, $\tilde{\theta}_i$, is realized at date two. Given a joint distribution of $\tilde{\theta}_i$ and $\tilde{Z}_i$ at time zero, say $g(\theta_i, Z_i)$, it is possible to write this in the form $g(\theta_i, Z_i) = h(\theta_i|Z_i)f(Z_i)$, where $h(\theta_i|Z_i)$ is the conditional density of θ_i given a realization of $\tilde{Z}_i$, and $f(Z_i)$ is the marginal density of $\tilde{Z}_i$.

The problem facing firm i at date zero is to choose I_i to maximize the current value of its date two payoff. We use recursive programming to solve this problem. First, define ϕ_i to be the value of the firm's liquid assets at time 1. I.e., ϕ_i is

$$\phi_i = (K - I_i)(1+R). \tag{1}$$

Then, for a given choice of I_i at date zero, if $Z_i < \phi_i$ the present value of firm i at date 1 will be

$$V_i^1 = \frac{E(\tilde{\theta}_i|\tilde{Z}_i = Z_i)I_i}{(1+R)} + \frac{(\phi_i - Z_i)(1+R)}{(1+R)} \tag{2}$$

That is, the firm is able to cover its shock using only its liquid asset position. Alternatively, if the shock is greater than the liquid assets of the firm, $Z_i \geq \phi_i$, the firm will be forced to sell some or all of its investment in the private security before maturity and realizes only the par value at time 1. The present value in this case at date 1 will be

or all of their investment in private technology assets will often be forced to accept price discounts. For a theoretical discussion, see Schleifer and Vishny (1992). Pulvino (1998) provides some recent empirical support for this prediction. The benefits of risk management would be even greater for insurers if they were forced to liquidate a portion of their investment in the private technology assets at a discount.

$$V_i^1 = \frac{E(\tilde{\theta}_i|\tilde{Z}_i - Z_i)(I_i + \phi_i - Z_i)}{(1+R)} \tag{3}$$

where $E(\tilde{\theta}_i|\tilde{Z}_i = Z_i) = \int \tilde{\theta}_i h(\theta_i|Z_i)d\theta_i$.

Working backwards, taking expectations at time zero and discounting, we have that the time zero value of firm i, V_i^0, is given by

$$V_i^0 = \frac{E_0(\tilde{\theta})I_i}{(1+R)^2} + \int_{a_i}^{\phi_i} \frac{(\phi_i - Z_i)f(Z_i)}{(1+R)} dZ_i + \int_{\phi_i}^{b_i} \frac{(\phi_i - Z_i)E(\tilde{\theta}_i|\tilde{Z}_i)f(Z_i)}{(1+R)^2} dZ_i. \tag{4}$$

We now consider the firm's investment decision under two alternative assumptions regarding the joint distribution of $\tilde{\theta}_i$ and $\tilde{Z}_i$.

Case 1. Firm level endowment shocks, $\tilde{Z}_i$, at date 1 reveal no information regarding the realization of the return on the private technology asset, $\tilde{\theta}_i$, at date 2.

In Case 1, we assume that $E(\tilde{\theta}_i|\tilde{Z}_i) = E_0(\tilde{\theta}_i)\ \forall\ Z_i$. This assumption is weaker than assuming independence but stronger than the assumption that $\tilde{\theta}_i$ and $\tilde{Z}_i$ are uncorrelated. In this case the first order condition is given by

$$\frac{\partial V_i^0}{\partial I_i} = \frac{E_0(\tilde{\theta}_i)}{(1+R)^2} - \frac{E_0(\tilde{\theta}_i)}{(1+R)}[1 - F(\phi_i)] - F(\phi_i) = 0 \tag{5}$$

where $F(\phi_i) = \int_{a_i}^{\phi_i} f(Z_i)dZ_i$. Notice that in this case the second order condition for a maximum is satisfied since

$$\frac{\partial^2 V_i^0}{\partial I_i^2} = -f(\phi_i)E_0(\tilde{\theta}_i) + f(\phi_i)(1+R) < 0 \tag{6}$$

and, by assumption, $E_0(\tilde{\theta}_i) > (1 + R)^2 > (1 + R) > 0$.

Let $I_i = I_i^*$ solve equation (5). Our focus on the demand for risk management revolves around examining the difference in the value of the firm in the absence of shocks, $V_i^0(K) = KE_0(\tilde{\theta}_i)/(1 + R)^2$, and the second best value of the firm, given by (4) and evaluated at $I_i = I_i^*$. Call this $V_i^0(I_i^*)$. Define D_i to be this difference

$$D_i = V_i^0(K) - V_i^0(I_i^*). \tag{7}$$

We argue that anything making D_i larger will encourage value maximizing firms to be more likely to engage in risk management activities to the extent that these contracts can be used to reduce D_i by mitigating the influence of the shocks. To the extent that the shocks contain some macroeconomic component, traded off-balance-sheet contracts can be effective in minimizing (7).

To investigate changes in the difference function, equation (7), first note that for any factor, call it x, we know that

$$\frac{\partial D_i}{\partial x} = \frac{\partial D_i}{\partial I_i^*}\frac{\partial I_i^*}{\partial x} + \frac{\partial D_i}{\partial x}. \tag{8}$$

However, we also note that at I^*

$$\frac{\partial D_i}{\partial I_i^*} = \frac{\partial V^{i^0}(K)}{\partial I_i^*} - \frac{\partial V^{i^0}(I_i^*)}{\partial I_i^*} = 0. \tag{9}$$

This last result follows from the fact that $\frac{\partial V^{i^0}(I_i^*)}{\partial I_i^*} = 0$ and $V_i^0(K)$ is not a function of I_i^*. Equations (8) and (9) demonstrate that we only need to consider the direct effect of changes in any of the underlying factors on the difference between the first best value of the firm, $V_i^0(K)$, and the second best value of the firm $V_i^0(I_i^*)$.

Given this result, consider changes in expected return on the private technology asset, $E_0(\tilde{\theta}_i)$. Using the definition of $V_i^0(K)$ and equation (4), we have

$$\frac{\partial D_i}{\partial E_0(\tilde{\theta}_i)} = \frac{K - I^*}{(1+R)^2} - \int_{\phi_i}^{b_i} \frac{(\phi_i - Z_i)f(Z_i)}{(1+R)^2} dZ_i > 0. \tag{10}$$

So, our first result is that the demand for risk management will be higher by firms with more valuable private, but illiquid securities.

Our next result concerns the demand for risk management as a function of the distribution of shocks. This can be easily analyzed by re-writing equation (4) (and recalling $E_0(\tilde{Z}_i) = 0$) as

$$V_i^0 = \frac{E_0(\tilde{\theta}_i|\tilde{Z}_i)I_i^*}{(1+R)^2} + \frac{(K - I_i^*)E_0(\tilde{\theta}_i)}{(1+R)} + \int_{a_i}^{\phi_i} \frac{F(Z_i)dZ_i}{(1+R)}\left(1 - \frac{E_0(\tilde{\theta}_i)}{(1+R)}\right) \tag{11}$$

where the last term is obtained by integrating by parts. Consider an alternative shock, call it $\tilde{Y}_i$, with distribution function G, and $E_0(\tilde{Y}_i) = 0$. If $\tilde{Y}_i$ is also confined to the closed interval $[a_i, b_i]$, then Rothschild and Stiglitz (1970) have shown that if "$\tilde{Y}_i$ has more weight in its tails than $\tilde{Z}_i$" and both have the same mean, then $\int_{a_i}^{Y_i} [G(Z_i) - F(Z_i)]dZ_i = T(Y_i) \geq 0$ and $T(a_i) = T(b_i) = 0$.

It follows immediately from the fact that $E_0(\tilde{\theta}_i) > (1 + R)$ and equation (11) that, for any value of I_i^*, equation (11) is lower if the firm faces the riskier shock $\tilde{Y}_i$ when compared to $\tilde{Z}_i$. Thus, our second result is that, ceteris paribus, firms who face a riskier distribution of shocks will have more incentive to engage in risk management. Stated differently, firm value will be higher for those firms who can reduce the riskiness of the distribution of shocks they face, all other things held equal.

To explore this result, note that since $\tilde{Z}_i = \beta_i(\tilde{\rho} - 1) + \tilde{\varepsilon}_i$, any risk management contract whose payoff is tied to $\tilde{\rho}$ can be used to reduce the weight in the tails of the distribution of $\tilde{Z}_i$. For example, consider a forward contract that pays off $\tilde{\rho}$ at date one. Define H_i to be the number of forward contracts held short at a forward price of p_f. With H_i forward contracts, the net shock the firm now faces, $\tilde{Z}_i^h$, is

$$\tilde{Z}_i^h = -H_i(\tilde{\rho} - \rho_f) + \tilde{Z}_i. \tag{12}$$

If we assume costless hedging, i.e., $\rho_f = 1$, then

$$\begin{aligned} \tilde{Z}_i^h &= (\beta_i - H_i)(\tilde{\rho} - 1) + \tilde{\varepsilon}_i \\ &= \tilde{x}_i^h + \tilde{\varepsilon}_i. \end{aligned} \tag{13}$$

Appealing to the Rothschild and Stiglitz once again, $\tilde{Z}_i^h$ is more risky than $\tilde{\varepsilon}_i$ if $\tilde{x}_i^h$ is a mean zero random variable and $E(\tilde{x}_i^h|\varepsilon_i) = 0 \ \forall \ \varepsilon_i$. Thus, choosing $H_i = \beta_i$ will eliminate the firm's exposure to the economy-wide risk (i.e., $\tilde{x}_i^h = 0$) and therefore reduce the riskiness of the firm's shock to include only its idiosyncratic component. It follows, therefore, given the Rothschild and Stiglitz result, that the value of the firm is maximized by eliminating the economy-wide portion of the firm's risk exposure and reducing the riskiness of the shocks that the firm faces. Moreover, when hedging is costless, no other terms in the firm valuation equation (equation 11), are affected since $E_0(H_i(\tilde{\rho} - 1)) = H_i(E_0(\tilde{\rho}) - 1) = 0, \ \forall \ H_i$. We also note the obvious point that if the amount of idiosyncratic risk and market risk are inversely related, firms with high levels of idiosyncratic risk will tend to have smaller positions in risk management contracts (e.g., H_i will be smaller).

Case 2. Firm level endowment shocks, $\tilde{Z}_i$, at date 1 reveal new information regarding the realization of the return on the private technology asset, $\tilde{\theta}_i$, at date 2.

The second case we consider involves relaxing the assumption that $E(\tilde{\theta}_i|Z_i) = E_0(\tilde{\theta}_i) \ \forall \ Z_i$. I.e., we allow for the possibility that the size of the shock to the firm's endowment may be correlated with the return the firm can expect on its private technology asset. For example, an unexpected strengthening in the foreign currency exchange rate between the U.S. and Korea may also signal that the underlying credit worthiness of a fixed income asset issued by a Korean corporation may also have changed. In this case, the value of the firm at date 0, using equation (4) and the fact that covariance is a linear operator, we have that

$$V_i^{0'} = V_i^0 - \frac{Cov_0[(E(\tilde{\theta}_i)|Z_i), Z_i|b_i \geq Z_i \geq \phi_i]}{(1+R)^2} \tag{14}$$

where V_i^0 is the value of the firm if $E(\tilde{\theta}_i|Z_i) = E_0(\tilde{\theta}_i)\ \forall\ Z_i$ and Cov(·) is the covariance operator. Notice that, for a given level of I_i, the value of the firm will be lower if the conditional (on Z_i) time one value of the private asset is increasing in Z_i. This result contrasts with the standard portfolio theory idea that one would want to minimize the variance of terminal wealth by seeking out assets whose value would be high when other, negative, shocks to endowment are high (i.e., Z_i is large).

The intuition for our result can be seen by recognizing that, for $\phi_i \leq Z_i \leq b_i$, some of the private security must be liquidated. Consider two private assets, with the same unconditional expectation. Suppose that for the first asset $E(\tilde{\theta}_i^1|Z_i)$ is increasing in Z_i, while, for the second, $E(\tilde{\theta}_i^2|Z_i)$ is decreasing in Z_i. Then value will, ceteris paribus, increase by choosing the second asset since the opportunity cost of liquidation $[E(\tilde{\theta}_i|Z_i) - (1 + R)]$ is low when the security must be liquidated. For example, if negative endowment shocks are being caused by a poor overall economy, value would be enhanced by holding private securities whose value, conditional on the economy, is also low. That is, the opportunity cost of having to liquidate the private asset at time 1 is lower when the size of the shock and the expected return are negatively related. Re-interpreting the shocks to be interest rate related changes in liability values, it is straightforward to show that firms may increase value by acquiring assets whose values are less, rather than more, sensitive to decreases in interest rates, e.g., mortgage backed securities.

Thus, we would argue that firms for which asset values and endowment shocks are positively dependent are more likely to utilize risk management tools, while those in the opposite position will tend to have built in insurance against the realizations of these opportunity cost.

We have not yet considered the case where the shocks to capital may result in bankruptcy. While we provide a brief set-up of this problem in the Appendix to this chapter, we note that many of the results obtained here remain. However, it is no longer the case that an increase in the riskiness of cash flows will always result in a higher demand for hedging since bankruptcy provides an option to the firm which increases in value with increases in the riskiness of cash flows. Therefore, a mean preserving spread in the distribution of shocks may increase value to the extent the increases in the value of the limited liability option may partially or totally offset the additional demand for risk management that arises from the desire to avoid liquidating the valuable private asset.

To summarize, the model yields three main predictions:

a. The demand for risk management will be higher for firms with more valuable private but illiquid investments.
b. Firms that face riskier random shock distributions will have a greater demand for risk management than firms facing less risky random shocks.
c. Firms for whom private asset returns and random endowment shocks are positively correlated are more likely to engage in risk management, whereas firms in the opposite position have a natural hedge against the costs of random shocks.

To test these propositions, one would need to have data on the composition of insurer investment portfolios in order to determine the volume of private investments, the relative rates of return on these investments, and the correlation between private investment returns and random shocks. Life insurers hold substantial amounts of privately placed bonds and mortgages, which are likely to reflect private information. Both life and property-liability insurers hold structured securities and collateralized mortgage obligations, which also can be considered to have some characteristics of private assets.

Considering insurance policies as an insurer's projects or "assets," evidence presented in D'Arcy and Doherty (1990) is consistent with the argument that insurers accumulate private information by insuring drivers over a period of time and that this private information allows them to charge relatively higher prices the longer the driver has been with the company. The amount of private information on corporate insurance buyers, on the other hand, is likely to be relatively less because the commercial insurance market is more price competitive, commercial buyers are more sophisticated than personal lines policyholders, and commercial buyers tend to have statistically credible loss data that can be easily be provided to competing insurers. Thus, we might expect personal lines insurers to have more valuable private information than that possessed by commercial lines insurers. This provides some indication of the types of hypotheses shown here might be testable based on our model.

Evidence presented in Cummins, Phillips, and Smith (1997; 2000) is also consistent with the main predictions of our model. For example, the probability that both life and property-liability insurers will engage in derivatives transactions is positively related to the ratio of stocks to total assets, consistent with firms with riskier random shock distributions having a greater demand for risk management. In addition, for life insurers, participation in derivatives markets is positively related to the percentage of reserves in individual life insurance and annuity products and in GICs. Both individual life and annuities and GICs are relatively illiquid, multiple period contracts in which insurers are likely to acquire private information. Property-liability insurers with higher ratios of products liability reserves to total liabilities are more likely to participate in derivatives markets, as expected if products liability is a line with relatively high volatility. These findings are intriguing, and it is hoped that they will motivate additional research in this area.

17.5 CONCLUSION

This chapter provides a review of the rationales that are often advanced to explain why corporations manage risk. Because the pure theory of finance views expenditures on corporate hedging as dead-weight costs that destroy firm value, the financial rationales for hedging usually involve the existence of market frictions and transactions costs that can be mitigated through corporate hedging. Firms may have a motive to hedge to reduce the expected costs of financial distress, including the disruption of relationships with key employees, suppliers, and customers. Another set of reasons for corporate hedging include the avoidance of shocks to internal capital that may force the firm to forego profitable investment opportunities and the reduction of expected taxes due to the convexity of the corporate income tax schedule. An alternative, and non-mutually exclusive, hypothesis is that hedging is motivated by managerial risk aversion, i.e., by the desire of managers to maximize their own utility rather than to maximize firm value.

The chapter also reviews the empirical literature on a specific type of hedging activity undertaken by firms—the trading of financial derivatives. For non-financial firms and banks, the evidence on the use of derivatives to maximize firm value is rather mixed. One prominent paper (Tufano, 1996) finds that risk management by gold mining firms seems to be driven primarily by executive compensation plans, i.e., by managerial utility maximization. The evidence from research on the relationship between the use of derivatives and firm capital structure and, more generally, the use of derivatives to reduce financial distress costs also has been mixed. Stronger evidence has been found that firms use derivatives to lower their expected tax payments and to reduce the variability of their cash flows to help ensure adequate internal funds. Cummins, Phillips, and Smith (1997; 2000) present convincing evidence that insurers use derivatives to reduce financial distress costs and to hedge risks resulting from investment return volatility, liquidity, and exchange rate risk. They also find evidence supporting the hypothesis that insures use derivatives to hedge risks affecting the value of liabilities. We expect corporate hedging through derivatives and other devices to become increasingly important in the years to come and to provide numerous research opportunities for economists.

The chapter also provides a theoretical analysis that leads to a new rationale for corporate hedging. We postulate a firm that has the opportunity to invest in a long-lived investment project which has an especially attractive return due to private information or other factors. However, the return is realized only if the project is held until maturity. The firm is subject to random shocks that may necessitate the liquidation of part or all of the project prior to maturity. If liquidation occurs, the firm receives only the par value of the investment and must forgo the attractive return that could have been realized at maturity. The potential loss of this return motivates the firm to engage in hedging. The theory leads to the predictions that the demand for hedging will be positively related to the expected return on the long-lived investment project and also positively related to the riskiness of the random shocks faced by the firm. A counter-intuitive prediction is that the demand for hedging will be greater if the random shock and the return on the long-lived project are positively correlated. The intuition behind this result is that the firm will be more averse to liquidating the project due to a shock in states of the world where the payoff is higher. We conclude the theoretical discussion with some suggestions for testing our hypotheses.

APPENDIX A

In this appendix we consider the case where the shocks to capital may result in bankruptcy—i.e., where $b_i > K$ under the assumption that the shock $\tilde{Z}_i$ conveys no information about the realization of the return on the private asset $\tilde{\theta}_i$. In this case the insurer will be insolvent for $Z_i > I_i + (K - I_i)(1 + R) = I_i + \phi_i$. Reworking the programming problem, we have that V_i^1 is still given by either equation (1) (if $Z_i \leq \phi_i$), equation (2) (if $\phi_i < Z_i < \phi_i + I_i$) or $V_i^1 = 0$ (if $Z_i \geq \phi_i + I_i$)). In this case, assuming that $\tilde{\theta}_i$ and $\tilde{Z}_i$ are independent and dropping the "i" subscript for notational convenience, the time zero value of firm i is given by

$$V^0 = \int_a^{\phi}\left[\frac{IE_0(\tilde{\theta}) + (\phi - Z)(1+R)^2}{(1+R)^2}\right]f(Z)dZ + \int_{\phi}^{\phi+I}\left[\frac{E_0(\tilde{\theta})(I+\phi-Z)}{(1+R)^2}\right]f(Z)dZ. \tag{A.1}$$

Equation (A.1) can also be written, after some manipulation, as

$$\begin{aligned} V^0 = &\int_a^{\phi}\left[\frac{(\phi - Z)((1+R) - E_0(\tilde{\theta}))}{(1+R)^2}\right]f(Z)dZ + \frac{E_0(\tilde{\theta})(I+\phi)}{(1+R)^2} \\ &- \int_{\phi+I}^{b}\left[\frac{E_0(\tilde{\theta})(I+\phi-Z)}{(1+R)^2}\right]f(Z)dZ. \end{aligned} \tag{A.2}$$

In this case the first order condition can be written as

$$\frac{\partial V^0}{\partial I} = 0 = \left[\frac{E_0(\tilde{\theta}_i) - (1+R)}{(1+R)}\right]F(\phi) - \left[\frac{E_o(\tilde{\theta}_i)R}{(1+R)^2}\right]F(\phi + I). \tag{A.3}$$

Checking the second order conditions, we have that

$$\frac{\partial^2 V_0}{\partial I^2} = -[E_0(\tilde{\theta}_i) - (1+R)]f(\phi) + \frac{R^2}{(1+R)^2} E_0(\tilde{\theta}_i) f(\phi + I). \tag{A.4}$$

Using equation (A.3), it is straightforward to show that the second-order condition will hold (i.e., equation (A.4) will be negative) if Z is drawn from a distribution that is log concave, i.e., if $\frac{\partial^2 \ln[F(Z)]}{dZ^2} \leq 0$. To see this, note that equation (A.4) will be negative if and only if

$$\frac{f(\phi)}{f(\phi + I)} > \frac{R^2 E_0(\tilde{\theta}_i)}{[E_0(\tilde{\theta}_i) - (1+R)](1+R)^2} = \frac{RF(\phi)}{(1+R)F(\phi + I)} \tag{A.5}$$

where the last equality follows from setting equation (A.3) equal to zero and solving for $E_0(\tilde{\theta}_i) - (1 + R)$. It follows that a sufficient condition for equation (A.5) to hold is that $\frac{f(\phi)}{F(\phi)} \geq \frac{f(\phi + I)}{F(\phi + I)}$ (since $R < 1 + R$). Log concavity of F guarantees that this inequality will hold.

Some of the earlier comparative statistics go through even in the case where bankruptcy is possible. The analog to equation (7) is given by

$$D = \frac{KE_0(\tilde{\theta})}{(1+R)^2} - \int_a^{\phi} \left[\frac{IE_0(\tilde{\theta}) + (\phi - Z)(1+R)^2}{(1+R)^2} \right] f(Z)dZ - \int_{\phi}^{\phi + I} \left[\frac{E_0(\tilde{\theta})(I + \psi - Z)}{(1+R)^2} \right] f(Z) \tag{A.6}$$

It is straightforward to show that, as before, $\frac{\partial D}{\partial E_0(\tilde{\theta}_i)} > 0$, so that firms with more valuable private assets will choose to engage in risk management. To see this, recall that

$$\frac{\partial D}{\partial E_0(\tilde{\theta})} = \frac{K}{(1+R)^2} - \frac{IF(\phi + I)}{(1+R)^2} - \int_{\phi}^{\phi + I} \frac{(\phi - Z)}{(1+R)^2} dF(Z). \tag{A.7}$$

It follows immediately that (A.7) is non-negative since $IF(\phi + I) < K$ and $Z > \phi$ over the range ϕ to $(\phi + I)$.

It is less straightforward to determine whether or not firms facing more risky distributions for their shocks will be more inclined to engage in risk management since limited liability provides shareholders with an option whose value is increasing in the volatility of the shocks. Therefore, a mean preserving spread in the distribution of shocks increases firm value and this may partially or totally offset the additional demand for risk management that arises from the desire to avoid liquidating the valuable private asset. Finally, while we omit details, the desire to hold assets whose conditional values are inversely related to shocks is still true.

17.6 REFERENCES

Ahmed, Anwer S., Anne Beatty and Carolyn Takeda (1997). "Evidence on Interest Rate Risk Management and Derivatives Usage by Commercial Banks," Working Paper, University of Rochester, Rochester, NY.

Allen, Franklin and Anthony M. Santomero (1998). "The Theory of Financial Intermediation," *Journal of Banking and Finance* 21, 1461–1485.

Andrade, Gregor and Steven N. Kaplan (1998). "How Costly is Financial (not Economic) Distress? Evidence from Highly Leveraged Transactions that Became Distressed," *Journal of Finance* 53, 1443–1493.

Breeden, Douglas and S. Viswanathan (1996). "Why Do Firms Hedge? An Asymmetric Information Model," Working paper, Duke University, Durham, N.C.

Brealey, Richard A. and Stewart C. Myers (1996). *Principles of Corporate Finance*, 5th edition (New York: Mc-Graw-Hill).

Carter, David, and Joseph F. Sinkey (1998). "The Use of Interest Rate Derivations by End-Users: The Case of Large Community Banks." *Journal of Financial Services Research* 14, 17–34.

Colquitt, L. Lee and Robert E. Hoyt (1997). "Determinants of Corporate Hedging Behavior: Evidence from the Life Insurance Industry," *Journal of Risk and Insurance* 64, 649–671.

Cummins, J. David and Elizabeth Grace (1994). "Tax Management and Investment Strategies of Property-Liability Insurers," *Journal of Banking and Finance* 18, 43–72.

Cummins, J. David, Scott E. Harrington and Gregory Niehaus (1995). "Risk-Based Capital Requirements for Property-Liability Insurers: A Financial Analysis," in Edward Altman and Irwin Vanderhoof, eds., *The Financial Dynamics of the Insurance Industry* (Homewood, IL: Irwin Professional Publishers).

Cummins, J. David, Richard D. Phillips and Stephen D. Smith (1997). "Corporate Hedging in the Insurance Industry: The Use of Financial Derivatives by US Insurers." *The North American Actuarial Journal* 1, 13–49.

Cummins, J. David, Richard D. Phillips and Stephen D. Smith (2000). "Derivatives and Corporate Risk Management: Participation and Volume Decisions in the Insurance Industry," forthcoming *Journal of Risk and Insurance*.

Cummins, J. David and Mary A. Weiss (1991). "The Structure, Conduct, and Regulation of the Property-Liability Insurance Industry," in R.W. Kopcke and R.E. Randall, eds., *The Financial Condition and Regulation of Insurance Companies* (Boston: Federal Reserve Bank of Boston).

DeMarzo, Peter and Darrell Duffie (1995). "Corporate Incentives for Hedging and Hedge Accounting," *Review of Financial Studies* 8, 743–772.

D'Arcy, Stephen P. and Neil A. Doherty (1990). "Adverse Selection, Private Information, and Lowballing in Insurance Markets," *Journal of Business* 63, 145–161.

Diamond, Douglas W. (1991). "Monitoring and Reputation: The Choice Between Bank Loans and Directly Placed Debt," *Journal of Political Economy* 99, 689–721.

Dolde, Walter (1996). "Hedging, Leverage, and Primitive Risk," *The Journal of Financial Engineering* 4, 187–216.

Froot, Kenneth A., David S. Scharfstein and Jeremy C. Stein (1993). "Risk Management: Coordinating Investment and Financing Policies," *Journal of Finance* 68, 1629–1658.

Gay, Gerald D. and Jouahn Nam (1999). "The Underinvestment Problem and Derivatives Usage by Corporations." *Financial Management* 27, 53–69.

Geczy, Christopher, Bernadette A. Minton and Catherine Schrand (1997). "Why Firms Use Currency Derivatives," *Journal of Finance* 52, 1323–1354.

Graham, John R. and Clifford W. Smith, Jr. (1999). "Tax Incentives to Hedge," *Journal of Finance* 54, 2241–2262.

Graham, John R. and Daniel A. Rogers (1999). "Is Corporate Hedging Consistent with Value Maximization? An Empirical Analysis," Duke University, working paper.

Gunther, Jeffery W. and Thomas F. Siems (1995). "The Likelihood and Extent of Bank Participation in Derivative Activities," Working Paper, Federal Reserve Bank of Dallas, Dallas TX.

Hull, John C. (1993). *Options, Futures, and Other Derivative Securities* (Englewood Cliffs, NJ: Prentice-Hall).

Klein, Robert W. (1995). "Insurance Regulation In Transition," *Journal of Risk and Insurance* 62, 363–404.

Mayers, David and Clifford W. Smith, Jr. (1987). "Corporate Insurance and the Underinvestment Problem," *Journal of Risk & Insurance* 54, 45–54.

Mayers, David and Clifford W. Smith, Jr. (1988). "Ownership Structure Across Lines of Property-Liability Insurance," *Journal of Law and Economics* 31, 351–378.

Merton, Robert C. and André Perold (1993). "Theory of Risk Capital in Financial Firms," *Journal of Applied Corporate Finance* 16–32.

Mester, L.J. (1989). "Testing for Expense Preference Behavior: Mutual Versus Stock Savings and Loans," *Rand Journal of Economics* 20, 483–498.

Mian, Shehzad L. (1996). "Evidence on Corporate Hedging Policy," *Journal of Financial and Quantitative Analysis* 31, 419–439.

Myers, Stewart C. (1977). "Determinants of Corporate Borrowing," *Journal of Financial Economics* 5, 147–175.

Nance, Deana R., Clifford W. Smith, Jr. and Charles W. Smithson (1993). "On the Determinants of Corporate Hedging, *Journal of Finance* 68, 267–284.

Perold, Andre (1999). "Capital Allocation in Financial Firms," Working Paper, Harvard University, Cambridge, MA.

Phillips, Richard D., J. David Cummins and Franklin Allen (1998). "Financial Pricing of Insurance in the Multiple-Line Insurance Company," *Journal of Risk and Insurance* 65, 597–636.

Pulvino, Todd C. (1998). "Do Asset Fire Sales Exist? An Empirical Investigation of Commercial Aircraft Transactions," *Journal of Finance* 53, 939–978.

Rajan, Raghuram G. (1992). "Insiders and Outsiders: The Choice Between Informed and Arm's-length Debt," *Journal of Finance* 67, 1367–1400.

Ross, Stephen (1989). "Institutional Markets, financial Marketing, and Financial Innovation," *Journal of Finance* 44, 541–556.

Rothschild, Michael and Joseph E. Stiglitz (1970). "Increasing Risk: I. A Definition," *Journal of Economic Theory* 2, 225–243.

Rothschild, Michael and Joseph E. Stiglitz (1976). "Equilibrium In Competitive Insurance Markets: An Essay on the Economics of Imperfect Information," *Quarterly Journal of Economics* 90, 629–649.

Santomero, Anthony and David Babbel (1997). "Financial Risk Management By Insurers: An Analysis of the Process," *Journal of Risk and Insurance* 64, 231–270.

Shleifer, Andrei and Robert W. Vishny (1992). "Liquidation Values and Debt Capacity: A Market Equilibrium Approach," *Journal of Finance* 47, 1343–1366.

Smith, Clifford W. Jr. and René M. Stulz (1985). "The Determinants of Firms' Hedging Policies," *Journal of Financial and Quantitative Analysis* 20, 391–405.

Staking, Kim B. and David F. Babbel (1995). "The Relation Between Capital Structure, Interest Rate Sensitivity, and Market Value in the Property-Liability Insurance Industry," *Journal of Risk and Insurance* 62, 690–718.

Stulz, René M. (1996). "Rethinking Risk Management," *Journal of Applied Corporate Finance* 9, 8–24.

Stulz, René M. (1990). "Managerial Discretion and Optimal Financing Policies," *Journal of Financial Economics* 26, 3–27.

Tufano, Peter (1996). "Who Manages Risk? An Empirical Examination of Risk Management Practices in the Gold Mining Industry," *Journal of Finance* 51, 1097–1137.

Wall, Larry D. and John Pringle. 1989. "Alternative Explanations of Interest Rate Swaps: An Empirical Analysis." *Financial Management* 18, 119–149.

18 Linking Insurance and Mitigation to Manage Natural Disaster Risk*

Howard Kunreuther

University of Pennsylvania

Abstract

The insurance industry has suffered very large losses in the past 10 years from natural disasters and has the potential for experiencing even greater losses in the future. This chapter examines the role that insurance coupled with cost-effective risk mitigation measures (RMMs) can play in managing the risks from natural disasters. Large insurers have incentives to provide premium reductions to encourage RMMs if the allowable premiums are sufficiently high that they can pass the savings in losses to the property owner or if they are required to continue providing their current policyholders with coverage. Small insurers also have incentives to encourage their policyholders to adopt mitigation measures through premium reductions so as to reduce their chances of insolvency from a large-scale disaster. They may also want to consider purchasing reinsurance to cover a portion of their excess losses. Well-enforced building codes can complement insurance by forcing the adoption of cost-effective RMMs. They may be needed because many property owners underestimate the risks from disasters. In addition, mitigation measures not only reduce losses to the property itself but may produce positive externalities by reducing other costs of a disaster. The chapter concludes by outlining the roles that financial institutions, real estate developers and municipalities can play in developing incentives for the adoption of cost-effective RMMs and suggesting directions for future research.

Keywords: Insurance, natural disaster, risk mitigation, risk management, reinsurance.

JEL Classification Numbers: S80, G22.

* Special thanks to two anonymous referees for their helpful comments on an earlier version of this paper. I have benefited greatly from discussions with my colleagues from the Wharton *Managing Catastrophic Risk Project* on topics covered in the paper: Vivek Bantwal, Peter Burns, David Croson, David Cummins, Neil Doherty, Patricia Grossi, Robert Klein, Paul Kleindorfer, Robert Meyer and Tony Santomero. Partial support from NSF Grant # 524603 and the Wharton Risk Management and

18.1 INTRODUCTION

The insurance industry is now fully aware that they are highly vulnerable to potential losses from natural disasters. Insured losses from Hurricane Andrew, which swept ashore along the Florida coastline in August 1992, topped $15 billion. If the storm had taken a more northerly track so it would have hit downtown Miami and Miami Beach, total insured damage could have approached $50 billion. (Insurance Research Council and Insurance Institute for Property Loss Reduction 1995). Insured damage from the Northridge earthquake in southern California exceeded $12 billion. Had a similar quake hit central Los Angeles the insured bill could have been over $50 billion. A large quake in central Tokyo could have cost over $800 billion. (Giles 1994).

Companies now recognize that they will have to turn to risk mitigation measures (RMMs) to reduce their chances of insolvency from future catastrophic events. For example, studies following Hurricane Andrew estimated that 25 percent of the $15 billion insured damage from the disaster could have been prevented had building codes been enforced (Insurance Research Council and Insurance Institute for Property Loss Reduction (1995). A group of insurers formed the Insurance Institute for Property Loss Reduction (IIPLR) in the early 1990s. This independent, nonprofit organization, now named the Insititute for Business and Home Safety (IBHS), has undertaken research and studies designed to encourage actions which reduce deaths, injuries, property damage and economic losses from natural disasters. The substantial interest today by insurers in loss prevention measures to reduce natural disaster damage has a parallel in the automobile arena, when insurers created the Institute for Highway Safety whose principal mission is to design safer cars.

This paper focuses on when insurers would want to encourage individuals to adopt cost-effective RMMs using premium reductions as an incentive to reduce their chances of insolvency and/or improve their future expected profits. A cost-effective risk mitigation measure (RMM) is defined to be one where the expected discounted benefits in the form of reduced losses exceeds the upfront cost of the measure. Section 18.2 addresses why insurers are concerned with potential insolvencies from future natural disasters. Section 18.3 then turns to the positive role that RMMs can play in improving the profitability of large insurers and addressing the insolvency concerns of small insurers. Section 18.4 focuses on the role of building codes in dealing with the misinformation problems of property owners and reducing externalities. In Section 18.5 I explore other incentives for encouraging mitigation using insurance as a vehicle. The concluding section discusses future research directions.

Decision Processes Center is gratefully acknowledged. Portions of the paper are based on an invited paper presented at the Fifth Alexander Howden (Australia) Conference on Disaster Insurance, Gold Coast, August, 1997.

18.2 INSURERS CONCERN WITH INSOLVENCY

A principal reason that mitigation is of central importance to insurers today is their fear of insolvency from future natural disasters. Mayers and Smith (1982) used modern finance theory to challenge the assumption that insurers are risk neutral with respect to losses. Employees of an insurance firm may be risk averse due to the costs of finding another job if their company becomes insolvent so that the insurer will want to charge higher premiums against risks with potentially catastrophic losses to reflect this concern. In fact, risk aversion is one reason that property/liability companies are willing to purchase reinsurance at premiums that exceed their actuarial risks (Mayers and Smith 1990).[1]

Insurers will also have incentives to limit their risk of insolvency to the extent that they have acquired franchise value that can only be recouped if they remain in business. Research suggests that the managers of mutual insurance companies should be able to exercise greater discretion in promoting the safety of their companies than stock insurers. In fact, the owners of stock insurance firms with low levels of capital and little franchise values may have an incentive to incur excessive risks (Cummins 1988).[2]

With respect to decision making in an insurance firm, Stone (1973a, b) suggested that an underwriter who wants to determine the premium to charge will first focus on keeping the probability of insolvency below some threshold level (q^*). One reason that an insurer would want to do this is to improve its ability to set higher premiums and hence improve its cash flow. More specifically, suppose that the insurer has a portfolio of N policies, each of which can lead to a loss L. Then the underwriter will recommend a premium P so that the probability of insolvency would be less than q^*.

Empirical studies of underwriters pricing decisions reveals that risks with more uncertain losses or greater ambiguity will cause them to want to charge higher premiums for a given portfolio of risks (Kunreuther and Roth Chapter 2 1998). The situation will be most pronounced for highly correlated losses, such as earthquake policies sold in one region of California.

A safety-first model of underwriter behavior is consistent with the Mayers and Smith (1990) rationale as to why insurance firms want to purchase reinsurance. In fact, a rule that focuses on keeping the chances of insolvency below q^* explicitly recognizes the role that risk plays in the decision process and the role that mitigation measures and reinsurance can play in alleviating these concerns. A more formal model for the underwriter's decision process based on a safety first model is specified in Appendix 1.

Interview data with several insurance companies in the United States concerned with the impact of recent natural disaster losses on their future activity provides evi-

[1] Doherty and Tinic (1982) have argued that demand for reinsurance is generated by insurers anticipating policyholders' aversion to bankruptcy.

[2] I am grateful to one of the referees of this paper for pointing this out.

dence that firms follow a safety first model.[3] In the aftermath of Hurricane Andrew and the Northridge earthquake, company executives indicated that they were concerned that they could not survive a future catastrophe given their current portfolio and the amounts of reinsurance coverage that they could obtain at reasonable prices. In other words they felt that their chances of insolvency based on their current portfolio exceeded their threshold level of concern (q^*).

When insurers are in this position they can pursue one or more of the following options to reduce their chances of insolvency. They can try and reduce the number of policies they write in catastrophic-prone areas. They can request from the relevant state insurance commissioners that they be allowed to raise their premium P to current and/or future policyholders. They can encourage their policyholders through economic incentives or require them to adopt mitigation measures as a way of reducing future claim payments. Insurers can also try and obtain more reinsurance coverage and/or raise more capital to hold as reserves.[4]

In practice state regulation often precludes insurers from canceling as many policies as they would like and raising premiums.[5] Since Hurricane Andrew the percentage of homeowners policies in Florida that an insurer can cancel or nonrenew in any one year is required to be less than 5 percent statewide and 10 percent in any one county. Permitted rate increases have also been less than what insurers would like to charge (Lecomte and Gahagan 1998).[6] These restrictions have led to new developments in the state. There have been cross-subsidies between policyholders with property owners on the coast being cross-subsidized by those who reside in less hazard-prone areas regions of the state (Klein 1997). In addition residual markets, state catastrophe funds and guarantee funds have been created and have lead to a form of risk-sharing between insurers.

18.3 LINKING MITIGATION WITH INSURANCE

There has been considerable research on the decision to invest in loss prevention or RMMs by consumers (Ehrlich and Becker (1972), Dionne and Eeckhoudt (1985) and

[3] These observations are based on a series of personal interviews with insurers and reinsurers conducted by Jacqueline Meszaros as part of a National Science Foundation study to the University of Pennsylvania on "The Role of Insurance and Regulation in Dealing with Catastrophic Risk".

[4] See Kleffner and Doherty (1996) for a more detailed analysis of the impact of the relative costs of these measures and the characteristics of the insurers who use them. Russell and Jaffee (1997) discuss the impact of catastrophes on the cash flow management problem and how current tax law prevents insurers from accumulating reserves to fund catastrophe losses.

[5] For more detail on the role that regulation plays in the rating setting process for risks of natural disasters see Klein 1998.

[6] During the 1996 Florida state legislative session companies were allowed to accelerate nonrenewals. An insurer, with approval of the commissioner could use its entire quota of nonrenewals allowed through June 1, 1999 in the first year. Several major insurers filed for permission to do that, and those filings were approved.

Kunreuther and Kleffner (1992). Those who have insurance coverage will want to invest in mitigation measures if the premium reduction is large enough to justify the extra costs of investing in the loss prevention measure. The question we are addressing in this chapter is what type of premium incentives will insurers want to provide to their policyholders to encourage them to adopt RMMs? The answer depends both on the surplus of the insurer, the rate structure as well as the concerns that both the insurer and policyholder have with insolvency.

To motivate the discussion I construct a simple example of an insurer who wants to determine how much coverage to provide against the earthquake risk. A concrete example has the virtue of showing the impact that loss prevention can have on insurers behavior and the resulting tradeoffs between profitability and insolvency. We first examine the case of a large insurer who has sufficient surplus that the probability of insolvency under its current portfolio of risks is less than q^*. Hence its only rationale for encouraging its policyholders to adopt mitigation measures is to improve its profitability. We then turn to a small insurer where the insolvency constraint is operative. Now the insurer faces a tradeoff between encouraging its policyholders to adopt mitigation or purchasing reinsurance to reduce its loss payments following a disaster.

An Illustrative Example

Consider an insurer who provides full earthquake coverage for a single type structure (e.g., a wood frame home). The insurer estimates the chances of an earthquake in the region to be $p = 1/100$. The insurer will incur a loss (L') if an RMM is adopted and a loss ($L'' > L'$) if it is not mitigated. For this example, $L' = \$200,000$ and $L'' = \$250,000$ so the RMM reduces damage by \$50,000 should a quake occur. Based on this information the insurer can calculate the expected loss for a structure with mitigation which is $[E(L') = 1/100\ (\$200,000) = \$2,000]$ or the expected loss without mitigation which is $[E(L'') = 1/100\ (\$250,000) = \$2,500]$. In other words the expected annual benefit from mitigation is \$500.

Suppose that an insurer has written N earthquake policies on this type structure in a given region of the country and has calculated the probability that n or more homes will be damaged by the quake given there is less than perfect correlation between losses. Table 1 provides a set of annual probabilities and respective values of L'' and L' for 0 to 8 losses for the case where an insurer has written $N = 100$ earthquake policies.

The question for the insurer is what premium to charge the property owner to encourage her to adopt mitigation with the objective of maximizing expected profits while keeping the probability of insolvency (q) below some threshold level (q^*). For purposes of this example, let $q^* = 1/120$.

In addition to internal organizational concerns with insolvency noted above, an insurer may be required to show the regulator that it is financially viable by having a

Table 1
Probabilities of Damage and Respective Losses for Insurers with and without Mitigation in Place

Number of Losses (n)	Probability (# of losses ≥ n)	Loss with No Mitigation (L″)	Loss with Mitigation (L′)
0	1	$ 0	$ 0
1	1/20	$ 250,000	$ 200,000
2	1/40	$ 500,000	$ 400,000
3	1/80	$ 750,000	$ 600,000
4	1/120	$ 1,000,000	$ 800,000
5	1/140	$ 1,250,000	$ 1,000,000
6	1/160	$ 1,500,000	$ 1,200,000
7	1/180	$ 1,750,000	$ 1,400,000
8	1/200	$ 2,000,000	$ 1,600,000

Note: The probabilities of losses of 1 or more homes in this table is based on the assumption that there is imperfect correlation between structures that are damaged from an earthquake. If there was perfect correlation than either all homes would be damaged with probability p = 1/100 or no homes would be damaged with p = 99/100.

probability of insolvency which is q^* or less. Furthermore policyholders may be willing to pay a higher premium if they know that the chances of the insurer becoming insolvent is reduced. In the analysis which follows, it will be assumed that a reduction in q will have **no** impact on the premium. To the extent that lower credit risks leads to higher premiums then this provides insurers with an additional economic rationale to encourage homeowners to adopt RMMs.

Behavior by a Large Insurer

Consider a large capitalized insurer, Alpha, who has enough initial capital and premium income so it is not concerned with the insolvency constraint and does **not** require reinsurance. Let S_L represent Alpha's financial resources which consists of its initial surplus and premium income based on charging the actuarially fair premium without mitigation. In the context of the data in Table 1 suppose that $S_L = \$1.2$ million. In this case Alpha will still have positive capital on hand unless it suffered more than four losses with no structures mitigated (i.e., $L = L''$). The probability of this occurring is $\frac{1}{140}$ so that the insurer has satisfied its insolvency constraint.

For this reason, Alpha's sole objective is to maximize expected profits and it has no desire to purchase reinsurance. Suppose Alpha has the freedom to charge whatever rate the market will bear. This implies that the insurer will charge a premium at least as high as its expected loss so that $P' \geq E(L') = \$2{,}000$ if mitigation is adopted and $P'' \geq E(L'') = \$2{,}500$ when mitigation is not utilized.

Suppose that a property owner has purchased coverage at the actuarial rate when no mitigation is in place. Let M be the minimum premium reduction from P'' that will lead the property owner to adopt mitigation. If $M < P'' - P'$, then Alpha will offer a policy with mitigation where the premium will range between P' and $P'' - M$. The actual premium depends on the competitive nature of the market and the extent of search by customers. Thus if $M = \$300$, insurers will offer policies for mitigated homes that range from \$2,000 to \$2,200.[7]

Turning to the impact that mitigation has on reducing q, suppose Alpha was able to encourage all its customers to adopt an RMM, and had $S_L = \$1.2$ million. From Table 1 its probability of insolvency with mitigation is reduced to $q = 1/180$ since it can now absorb six losses rather than the four losses it was able to cover when an RRM was not adopted. From an insurer's vantage point, mitigation truncates the worst case scenarios by reducing the losses on individual structures.

Suppose that the regulator set a maximum premium (P_R) below the actuarial cost but Alpha was **not forced** to provide coverage to those who wanted it. If $P_R < P'$ then it would not offer any coverage even if the homeowner adopted mitigation since it would be losing money on the insurance policy. If, on the other hand, $P_R > P'$, then Alpha will be willing to offer coverage to those who mitigate at a premium reduction as high as $P_R - P'$. For those who do not mitigate it would only offer them a policy if $P_R \geq P''$.

If Alpha was forced to provide coverage to its existing policyholders, then it would still want to offer a premium reduction as an incentive for them to adopt mitigation no matter what P_R the regulator set. In fact, to minimize its expected loss Alpha would be willing to reduce its premium by as much as $P'' - P' = \$500$.

Behavior by Small Insurers

In addition to encouraging mitigation through premium reductions, reinsurance can be utilized to reduce the chances of insolvency for smaller insurers impacted by the insolvency constraint.[8] Consider an excess of loss reinsurance contract for dealing with catastrophic risks. The primary insurer would be responsible for all losses up to a specified amount and the reinsurance company would reimburse the insurer for a layer of losses up to some pre-specified maximum dollar figure. For example, if the reinsurance contract specified \$5 million in excess of \$1 million and the total losses were \$10 million, then the primary insurer would pay the \$10 million in losses, and the reinsurer would reimburse the insurer for \$5 million of this amount. Had the insured loss been below \$1 million, then the insurer would be responsible for all of it.

[7] If $M > P'' - P$, then the homeowner will ***not*** have an incentive to mitigate. If the RMM is cost-ineffective, then there is good reason why the property owner should not want to adopt it. On the other hand, individuals may choose not to incur the upfront costs of an RMM because of budget constraints or insufficient appreciation of the long-term benefits of loss reduction due to short time horizons or hyperbolic discounting. Section 18.5 addresses ways to make cost-effective RMMs more attractive to the homeowner.

[8] An excellent summary of alternative reinsurance arrangments can be found in McIsaac and Babbel (1995).

Behavior with No Moral Hazard. We first discuss the case where the insurer behaves in the same way as if it did not have reinsurance so that there is no moral hazard. The same example used for evaluating Alpha's pricing strategy can illustrate the maximum amount that a small capitalized insurer would pay for reinsurance if it were forced to insure its current policyholders. We define a small capitalized insurer to be an entity where the insolvency constraint is binding, so that it is forced to sacrifice some expected profits to make sure that $q = q^*$. One way of viewing the concern with q^* of these insurers is that a regulatory authority requires them to show that they have enough surplus on hand to be solvent in case actual losses are greater than expected losses.

The necessity of meeting insolvency conditions provides a partial explanation as to why some insurers are willing to pay high prices for reinsurance. Let S_S represent the surplus of a small capitalized company called Beta. It has financial resources of S_S = \$700,000 consisting of its initial surplus (A_S = \$450,000) and premium income (\$250,000) based on selling 100 earthquake policies at premium P'' = \$2,500 with no mitigation in place. If Beta has to maintain its current portfolio, then it will **not** meet its insolvency constraint. As seen from Table 1, should it suffer 3 quake losses, it will have claims totalling \$750,000 which exceeds S_S by \$50,000. The probability of suffering 3 or more losses is $q = 1/80 > q^* = 1/120$. By turning to the reinsurance market for an excess loss treaty, Beta can lay off some of its claims and should be willing to pay a relatively high price to do so.

Suppose that Beta negotiated an excess of loss treaty with a reinsurer for \$250,000 excess of \$500,000 to cover the costs of the third loss should an earthquake occur. This type of treaty arrangement would reduce its probability of insolvency from $q = 1/80$ to $q = 1/120$, thus satisfying the regulator's concern with insolvency. Two questions naturally emerge: (1) How much *would* the reinsurer want to charge for such a policy based on actuarial costs? and (2) How much *could* the reinsurer charge Beta for such a policy based on Beta's need to meet an insolvency constraint?

The first question can be answered using the data from Table 1. The reinsurer is only concerned with the probability of Beta suffering three or more losses, in which case it will have to pay Beta \$250,000. The probability of such an event occurring is $p = 1/80$. Hence the actuarially fair reinsurance premium is R = 1/80 (\$250,000) = \$3,333. Beta, on the other hand, is willing to pay considerably more for such a policy to meet its insolvency constraint. With S_S = \$700,000 it will theoretically be willing to pay up to \$200,000 for such a policy if it still will make positive expected profits on other lines of coverage.[9] This is shown in Appendix 2 for an insurer who wants to determine the maximum it would have to pay to meet the insolvency constraint imposed by the regulator.

Of course, no insurer would ever pay anything close to \$200,000 for a policy

[9] The small insurer is not making any positive expected profits on earthquake coverage by assumption. The premiums without mitigation are simply the expected losses.

which only promises them $250,000 with a probability of $p - 1/80$. On the other hand, a small capitalized insurer is very likely to be willing to pay the reinsurer somewhat more than the actuarial fair premium of $3,333. How much the reinsurer will actually charge for this excess loss protection depends on the degree of competition in the market and the tradeoffs between making a quick profit tomorrow vs maintaining a long-term relationship with the insurer by charging a reasonable price for excess loss coverage.

One way of avoiding reinsurance charges is for insurers like Beta to provide premium reductions to their policyholders as a way of encouraging them to adopt mitigation measures. In the above example, if Beta were able to induce all of its policyholders to mitigate their home, then their losses from an earthquake is given in the last column of Table 1. In this situation, the $700,000 that Beta has in surplus will be able to pay for the claims associated with 3 losses ($600,000). Hence Beta will **not** need to purchase reinsurance to meet the regulator's concern with insolvency if its policyholders adopt RMMs.

As shown in Appendix 2 Beta is willing to provide a sufficiently large premium reduction to encourage mitigation by its policyholders to satisfy the insolvency constraint, knowing that it will lose money on its earthquake book of business. The only reason to agree to pay this premium is if it costs the insurer less than reinsurance and it enables Beta to make sufficient expected profits on other risks to more than offset the expected earthquake losses.

The maximum discount that Beta would be willing to give its policyholders to encourage them to adopt an RMM depends on Beta's current surplus relative to potential claims in the future. The detailed calculations are shown in Appendix 2. The informal argument can be summarized as follows. Beta wants to show the regulator that it has S_S = $600,000 on hand to cover at least three earthquake losses when mitigation is in place. Since S_S = $700,000 it will be able to reduce its total premium by as much as $100,000 and still meet this constraint assuming that its expected profits from this and other lines of coverage was still positive.

This means that Beta would be willing to reduce the premiums for each of its policyholders by up to $1,000 if that is what it took to convince their policyholders to adopt a mitigation measure and Beta would still be making a positive. Since the actuarially fair reduction in premiums based on Table 1 is only $500, Beta would be willing to reduce its profits to reduce its expected loss on its earthquake book of business in order to meet its insolvency constraint. Of course, when reinsurance is available, Beta will make tradeoffs between the reinsurance premium it will have to pay for coverage and the premium reduction it will offer property owners in exchange for mitigation.

Behavior with Moral Hazard. In setting their premiums, reinsurers are concerned with problems of ex ante and ex post moral hazard. Ex ante moral hazard occurs when the primary insurer fails to take actions to reduce future losses or takes actions that increase losses simply because the reinsurer cannot monitor the insurer's behavior [Pauly (1974), Marshall (1976), Shavell (1979) and Dionne and Harrington (1992).] Ex post moral hazard arises when the insurer relaxes its loss settlement process because it knows that the reinsurer will cover some of its claims. [Spence and Zeckhauser (1971) and Dionne and Harrington (1992)].

Below we focus only on ex post moral hazard. More specifically the insurer considers skimping on its claims processing because it can pass some of the loss payments to the reinsurer. To keep the analysis simple all policyholders are assumed to be identical and each one experiences the same loss from the disaster. The primary insurer incurs two types of expenditures: (1) an administrative cost for processing claims and adjusting the losses and (2) the claims payments from the losses themselves. Both these costs will increase as the number of losses increases. When the primary insurer bears all the losses itself, then it will diligently process the claims and adjust the losses at a cost of C_i if there are i losses from the disaster. It would then incur total insurance claims costs of iL.

If the reinsurer were to cover the entire set of losses, then the primary insurer would shirk in its claims-adjusting process and incur a cost of $C_i^* < C_i$ causing each loss to increase to $L^* > L$. To examine the financial implications of this type of ex post moral hazard, the primary insurer will be assumed **not** to shirk if it must absorb the entire difference in the loss costs itself. This implies that

$$i(L^* - L) > C_i - C_i^* \quad \text{for all } i \tag{1}$$

With an excess loss treaty, the reinsurer has the opportunity to reduce the ex post moral hazard by arranging the lower and upper attachment points so that the primary insurer will bear enough of the costs of shirking at both the front end and the back end to want to behave more responsibly. The lower attachment point means that the primary insurer is responsible for any losses below this amount (i.e., a deductible on a reinsurance policy). The upper attachment point refers to the upper limit of the reinsurers excess loss contract. If an insurer experiences losses above that amount, then it must bear the residual losses.

Suppose that the insurer has an excess loss treaty with the reinsurer whereby the insurer pays for the first D dollars of the loss, the reinsurer pays the next R dollars and then the primary insurer is responsible for any loss above $D + R$. The insurer faces the following tradeoff. If it is negligent in its claims adjustment process it can reduce its costs by $C_i - C_i^*$ but now faces higher loss costs, some of which may be shifted to the reinsurer. If total losses are below D, then the primary insurer bears the extra loss cost on its own; if total losses are between D and $D + R$ then both the insurer and reinsurer share the extra loss costs; any losses above $D + R$ are borne by the insurer. Hence the primary insurer will not want to shirk if the savings from the administrative costs are wiped out by higher expenditures at either the front and/or back ends.

If the reinsurer offers an excess loss contract, there are two conditions when the primary insurer will **not** want to shirk because the increase in loss costs exceed the savings in administration costs:

Condition 1: If the losses after shirking from the disaster are below D. (i.e., $iL^* < D$). In this case the insurer must bear the entire claims costs itself.

Condition 2: If the losses without shirking are above $D + R$ (i.e., $iL > D + R$). In this case the insurer bears all the ***extra costs*** of shirking itself.

On the other hand, the insurer will always want to shirk if it can pass on enough of the excess in loss costs to the reinsurer to justify the savings in administrative costs. Let $TC(S)$ = the total costs to the insurer of shirking and $TC(NS)$ = the total costs to the insurer of not shirking. Given Conditions 1 and 2, then the primary insurer will incur the following costs when it shirks and doesn't shirk:

$$TC(S) = \min\{iL^*, D\} + \mathrm{Max}\{0, iL^* - R\} + C_i^* \tag{3}$$

$$TC(NS) = \min\{iL, D\} + \mathrm{Max}\{0, iL - R\} + C_i \tag{4}$$

The primary insurer will always want to shirk whenever $TC(S) < TC(NS)$. This implies that shirking will always occur whenever the increase in loss costs is less than the savings in administrative costs from shirking as shown by the following inequality derived from (3) and (4):

$$[\min\{iL^*, D\} - \min\{iL, D\}] + \mathrm{Max}\{0, iL^* - R\} - \mathrm{Max}\{0, iL - R\} < C_i - C_i^* \tag{5}$$

A simple example illustrates when shirking becomes worthwhile. Suppose that $i = 10$ $L^* = 100$, $L = 80$ $D = 50$ and $R = 850$. The total cost of shirking is 200. The LHS of (5) is 150 reflecting the extra costs that the insurer has to pay above $D + R$ for shirking with the reinsurer incurring an extra cost of 50. Whenever $C_i - C_i^* > 150$ then the insurer will want to shirk.[10] In general, as D increases and R decreases the primary insurer will have less incentive to shirk because it will have to bear a larger proportion of the losses itself. In other words, larger deductibles and lower maximum coverage limits placed by the reinsurer reduce the possibility of ex post moral hazard by the primary insurer.[11]

When there are shortages of claims adjustors, then as the number of losses increases the settlements will expected to become more generous particularly if there is additional pressure on the insurers to settle more quickly to help the community back on its feet. Reinsurers will now have higher payments for reasons having nothing

[10] Note that if the reinsurer sets $D + R > 1000$ then it will cover the entire amount of the losses above the deductible whether the insurer shirks or doesn't shirk. In this case whenever $C_i > C_i^*$ the insurer will want to shirk.

[11] The relationship between the reinsurer and insurer is similar to that between the insurer and a policyholder.

to do with ex post moral hazard unless insurers are even more generous in making claims when they are reinsured than when they have to bear the costs themselves.

18.4 ROLE OF BUILDING CODES

The above analysis implicitly assumed that insurers would encourage property owners to undertake RMMs through premium reductions.[12] There would be no need for building codes if the following set of conditions were met in practice: Homeowners have perfect information on the risks associated with natural disasters and invest in cost-effective mitigation measures because they maximize their discounted expected utility. Insurers utilize the information on the risk from natural disasters to price their coverage and provide premium discounts to those who adopt these RMMs. Finally, all the costs from disasters are allocated to specific individuals and property. It is precisely because none of these conditions are fulfilled in practice that building codes serve a useful purpose as shown below.

Addressing Misinformation Problems

Property owners may fail to adopt cost-effective RMMs either because they have budget constraints, underestimate the benefits from adopting the RMM and/or the probability of a disaster occurring (Kunreuther 1996). To illustrate these points, suppose a family only feels it can only afford \$300 for investing in a measure which costs \$2,000. The homeowner may perceive the probability of an earthquake causing damage to his or her home next year to be 1/500, while experts estimate it to be 1/100. They may compute the expected discounted benefits from the mitigation measure only over the next several years while the relevant time horizon is the expected length of life of the structure. Furthermore the homeowner may have difficulty assessing a home's hazard resistance in the absence of code enforcement.

There is also limited interest by engineers and builders in designing safer structures if it means incurring costs that they feel will hurt them competitively. Interviews with structural engineers concerned with the performance of earthquake-resistant structures indicate that they have **no** incentive to build structures that exceed existing codes because they have to justify these expenses to their clients and would lose out to other engineers who did not include these features in the design (May and Stark 1992). Without building codes, they would even be less interested in undertaking measures that will enable the structure to withstand the forces of a disaster.

Well-enforced building codes correct misinformation that potential property owners have regarding the safety of the structure. Suppose the property owner believes that the losses from an earthquake to the structure is $L' = \$20{,}000$ and the developer

[12] Alternatively codes could have specified that structures meet certain requirements but there was poor enforcement of these regulations.

knows that it is $L'' = \$25{,}000$ because it is not well constructed. There is no incentive for the developer to relay the correct information to the property owner because the developer is not held liable should a quake cause damage to the building. If the insurer is unaware of how well the building is constructed, then this information cannot be conveyed to the potential property owner through a premium based on risk. Inspecting the building to see that it meets code provides accurate information to the property owner.

Reducing Externalities

Cohen and Noll (1981) provide an additional rationale for building codes. When a building collapses it may create externalities in the form of economic dislocations and other social costs that are beyond the economic loss suffered by the owners. These may not be taken into account when the owners evaluate the importance of adopting a specific mitigation measure. Consider the following examples of externalities:

Triggering Damage to Other Structures. Suppose that an unbraced concrete block structure had a 20 percent chance of toppling in an earthquake, bursting a pipeline and creating a fire which would severely damage 10 other homes, each of which would suffer \$40,000 in damage. Had the house been bolted to its foundation this series of events would not have occurred. The insurer who provided coverage against these fire-damaged homes under a standard homeowner's policy would then have had an additional expected loss of \$80,000 (i.e., $.2 \times 10 \times \$40{,}000$) due to the lack of building codes requiring concrete block structures to be braced in earthquake prone areas.

One option would be for homes adjacent to those that are unbraced to be charged a higher fire premium by their insurers to reflect the additional hazard from living next to the unprotected house. In fact, this additional premium should be charged to the unprotected structure that caused the damage, but this cannot legally be done. Hence, each of the 10 homes that are vulnerable to fire damage from the quake would have to be charged this extra premium.[13] Alternatively the house that caused the pipeline to burst could be liable for the damage to the other structures but this also does not have a legal basis today in the United States.

The relevant point for this analysis is that when there are additional annual expected benefits from mitigation that cannot be captured through premiums by private insurers, then well-enforced building codes may be necessary. All financial institutions and insurers who are responsible for the 10 other properties at risk would favor building codes to protect their investments and/or reduce the insurance premiums they would otherwise have to charge for coverage against fire following earthquake.

[13] If insurance was provided by the government rather than the private sector then this problem would not exist. The government would have an incentive to charge the unprotected home a premium reflecting the additional risk caused to other homes from not bracing its foundation.

Social Costs Arising from Property Damage. If a family is forced to vacate its home because of damage from a quake which would have been obviated if a building code had been in place, then this is an additional cost which needs to taken into account when determining the benefits of mitigation. Suppose that the family is expected to need food and shelter for t days (e.g., $t = 50$) at a daily cost of $D = \$100$. Then the additional expense after a disaster occurs from not having mitigated is $t \times D$ (i.e., $50 \times \$100 = \$5{,}000$). If the annual chances of the disaster occurring is $p = 1/100$, then the annual expected extra cost to the taxpayer of not mitigating is $p \times t \times D$ (i.e., $1/100 \times 50 \times \$100 = \$50$). Although this may not appear to be a very large figure, it amounts to an expected discounted cost of over \$560 for a 30 year period if an 8% discount rate is utilized. Should there be a large number of households that need to be provided with food and shelter, these costs could be substantial.

In addition to these temporary food and housing costs, the destruction of commercial property could cause business interruption losses and the eventual bankruptcy of many firms. In a study estimating the physical and human consequences of a major earthquake in the Shelby County/Memphis, Tennessee area, located near the New Madrid fault, Litan et al. (1992, pp. 65–66) found that the temporary losses in economic output stemming from damage to workplaces could be as much as \$7.6 billion based on the magnitude of unemployment and the accompanying losses in wages, profits and indirect "multiplier" effects. Their report suggests that selective building codes for certain structures could be beneficial, in the light of these additional economic benefits.

18.5 ENCOURAGING MITIGATION THROUGH OTHER INCENTIVES AND REGULATIONS

Private insurance coupled with building codes can be important components of a program for reducing losses from natural disasters while providing financial protection for those who suffer damage. This section discusses ways to supplement these two policy tools with other measures through the active involvement of other interested parties notably financial institutions, the real estate community and the community itself.

Premium Reductions Linked with Long-Term Loans

As shown in Section 18.3 insurance premium reductions for undertaking loss prevention measures can encourage property owners to adopt them. However, they may be reluctant to adopt these measures due to budget constraints. Building codes do not solve the affordability issue so that one may want to turn to banks and financial institutions for a creative solution to this problem.

One way to make this measure financially attractive to the property owner is for the bank to provide funds for mitigation through a home improvement loan with a payback period identical to the life of the mortgage. Consider the following example, where the cost of bracing the roof on property in a hurricane-prone coastal area is $1,500. If the meteorologists' best estimate of the annual probability of a hurricane is $p = 1/100$, and the reduction in loss from bracing the roof is $27,500, then the expected annual benefit is $275. A 20-year loan for $1,500 at an annual interest rate of 10 percent would result in payments of $170 per year. If the annual insurance premium reduction reflected the expected benefits of the mitigation measure (i.e., $275), then the insured homeowner will have lower *total* payments by investing in mitigation than not undertaking the measure.

Banks and financial institutions normally require homeowners insurance as a condition for a mortgage. In the above example the property owner would not have to think twice about taking out a home improvement loan since this would reduce the total annual payments by $105. On the other hand, if insurance were not required, as is the case today with earthquake coverage, then long-term loans may still not be effective in encouraging the adoption of mitigation measures and one might have to rely primarily on code enforcement. Even if insurance is required but the regulated rates are ***not*** based on risk, then the insurer may have no financial incentive to reduce the price of coverage to reflect the full gains from mitigation. For example, if the premium reduction were less than $170 per year, then the property will have no financial incentive to take out a loan unless she felt there were other benefits from mitigation aside from the property damage reduction from a future hurricane.

Many poorly constructed homes are owned by low-income families who cannot afford the costs of mitigation measures on their existing structure. Equity considerations argue for providing this group with low-interest loans and grants so that they can either adopt cost-effective mitigation measures or relocate to a safer area. Since low-income victims are likely to receive federal assistance to cover uninsured losses after a disaster, subsidizing these mitigation measures can also be justified on efficiency grounds.

Seals of Approval on Structures Meeting Code

Cost-effective risk-reduction measures should be incorporated in building codes and a seal of approval should given to each structure that meets or exceeds the code. A seal of approval provides accurate information to the property owner and forces the developer and real estate agent to let the potential buyer know why the structure has not been officially approved for safety. It may have the added benefit of increasing the property value of the home, since buyers should be willing to pay a premium for a safer structure.

Banks and financial institutions could require that structures be inspected and certified against natural hazards as a condition for obtaining a mortgage. This inspection, which would be a form of buyer protection, is similar in concept to termite and radon inspections normally required when property is financed. The success of such a program requires the support of the building industry, of realtors, and of a cadre of well-qualified inspectors providing accurate information on the condition of the structure.

Evidence from a July 1994 telephone survey of 1241 residents in six hurricane-prone areas along the Atlantic and Gulf Coasts supports this type of program. Over 90 percent of the respondents felt that local home builders should be required to follow building codes, and 85 percent considered it very important that local building departments conduct inspection of new residential construction (Insurance Institute for Property Loss Reduction 1995).

Community-based insurance incentives

One way to encourage communities to develop and enforce building codes is to provide insurance premium reductions to all policyholders in the area based on the stringency of the standard The more effective a community program is in reducing future disaster losses, the greater the insurance premium reduction.

Such a Community Rating System (CRS) was created by the Federal Insurance Administration in 1990 as a way to recognize and encourage community flood plain management activities that exceed the minimum National Flood Insurance Program (NFIP) standards (Pasterick 1998). Inspired by the CRS, the Institute for Business and Home Safety (IBHS) helped create the Building Code Effectiveness Grading Schedule (BCEGS) for use in adjusting private sector insurance premiums. This rating system administered by the Insurance Services Office, measures how well building codes are enforced in communities around the United States. Although it is not yet implemented, the goal of the program is that property located in communities that have well-enforced codes will benefit through lower insurance premiums.

Tax Incentives for Mitigation

One way for communities to encourage its residents to engage in mitigation measures is to provide them with tax incentives. For example, if a family lowered the chances of its home being damaged from a hurricane by installing a mitigation measure, it would get a rebate on its state taxes to reflect the lower costs of disaster relief. Alternatively ones property taxes could be lowered for the same reason.

In practice, communities often create a monetary disincentive to invest in mitigation. A property owner, who improves his home by making it safer, is likely to have the property reassessed at a higher value and hence have to pay higher taxes. California has been cognizant of this problem and voters passed Proposition 127 in 1990 which exempts seismic rehabilitation improvements to buildings from being reassessed to increase property taxes.

The City of Berkeley has taken an additional step to encourage home buyers to retrofit their newly purchased homes by instituting a transfer tax rebate. The city has a 1.5 percent tax levied on property transfer transactions; up to one-third of this amount can be applied to seismic upgrades during the sale of property. Qualifying upgrades include foundation repairs or replacement, wall bracing in basements, shear wall installation, water heater anchoring and securing of chimneys. Since 1993 these programs have been applied to 6,300 houses, representing approximately $4.4 million in foregone revenues to the city (Earthquake Engineering Research Institute 1998).

The principal reason for utilizing tax rebates to encourage mitigation is because of the externalities associated with these measures. As pointed out above, these added benefits cannot be captured through insurance premium reductions which normally cover damage only to the property. Taxes are associated with a broader unit of analysis such as the community, state or even federal level. To the extent that the savings in disaster costs relate to these units of government, tax rebates are most appropriate.

Role of Liability

The liability system has the potential of being a powerful tool for encouraging key interested parties to enforce relevant standards and regulations. Contractors who did not utilize a building code could be responsible for paying the damage to poorly designed homes battered by a hurricane. Banks who did not require homeowners in high hazard areas to purchase flood insurance, which is required as a condition for a federally insured mortgages, could be forced to pay the claims that the property owner would have collected from his flood policy.

In practice the liability system has not been utilized in this way. However, there are signs that this may be changing. A step in making banks more responsible for enforcing flood insurance requirements was taken by the Flood Disaster Protection Act of 1990 where fines were levied on any financial institution that let a policy lapse (Pasterick 1998). Florida anticipates developing a statewide building code where contractors who are found to not meet the standards would be fined and lose their license.

18.6 FUTURE RESEARCH DIRECTIONS

This chapter has suggested ways that mitigation can be linked with insurance and other policy tools for reducing future losses from natural disasters. Future research needs to focus on ways of improving estimates of the risk as well as determining what we mean by a cost-effective mitigation measures. These two areas are discussed in turn. The paper concludes by examining the role that micro-model simulations can play in analyzing alternative mitigation and insurance programs.

Improving Estimates of Risk

Insurers will benefit from improved estimates of the risk associated with catastrophes in two ways. First, by obtaining better data on the probabilities and consequences of disasters, insurers will be able to more accurately set their premiums and tailor their portfolios to reduce the chances of insolvency. The improved information should enable them to more accurately determine their needs for protection through reinsurance or capital market instruments. Second, more accurate data on risk also reduces the asymmetry of information between insurers and other providers of capital. Investors are more likely to supply additional capital as they become increasingly confident in the estimates of the risks of insured losses from natural disasters.

In setting rates for catastrophic risks, insurers have traditionally looked backwards, relying on historical data to estimate future risks.[14] This process is likely to work well if there is a large database of past experience from which to extrapolate into the future. Low-probability high-consequence events, such as natural disasters, by their nature make for small historical databases. Thus, there is a need to integrate scientific estimates of the probabilities and consequences of events of different magnitudes with the evidence from past experience.[15]

Advances in information technology have encouraged catastrophe modeling that can simulate a wide variety of different scenarios reflecting the uncertainties in different estimates of risk. For example, it is now feasible for insurers to evaluate the impact of different exposure levels on both expected losses and maximum possible losses by simulating a wide range of different estimates of seismic events using the data generated by scientific experts. Similar studies can be undertaken to evaluate the benefits and costs of different building codes and loss prevention techniques (Insurance Services Office 1996).

The growing number of catastrophe models has presented challenges to users who are interested in estimating the potential damage to their portfolio of risks. Each model uses different assumptions, different methodologies, different data, and different parameters in generating their projections. Their conflicting results make it difficult for the insurer to know what premiums to set to cover their risks; they also make it difficult for reinsurance and capital market communities to feel comfortable investing their money in providing protection against catastrophic risk. Hence the need for a better understanding as to why these models differ and the importance of reconciling these differences in a more scientific manner than has been done up until now. Bringing the leading modelers together with the insurers, reinsurers, and capital markets to discuss how their data are generated may reduce the mystery that currently surrounds these efforts.

[14] I am grateful to Terry van Gilder of Risk Management Solutions, formerly chief underwriter at Chubb, for characterizing the decision process of insurers in this way.

[15] For example, new advances in seismology and earthquake engineering are discussed in Federal Emergency Management Agency (1994) and Office of Technology Assessment (1995).

Encouraging Adoption of Cost-Effective Mitigation Measures

There is a need to specify the types of cost-effective mitigation measures that could be applied to new and existing structures and how they can be made part of a hazard management program. Only then can insurers, builders, and financial institutions work together to incorporate these measures as part of building codes and provide property owners with appropriate rewards for adopting them.

Several programs have been initiated in the past several years which recognize the importance of involving the key stakeholders concerned with disaster losses and developing a set of economic incentives which make the mitigation measures appealing to these concerned parties. The programs also are based on a much broader set of costs and benefits than has been traditionally considered in evaluating mitigation measures. It would be worthwhile to evaluate how well these programs have worked to determine the ingredients for successfully implementing mitigation measures.

Project Impact. This FEMA initiative challenges the country to undertake actions that protect families, businesses and communities by reducing the effects of natural disasters. There are three primary tenets of the Project Impact initiative: mitigation is a local issue; private sector participation is essential to mitigation efforts, and mitigation is a long-term effort requiring long-term commitment.

Project Impact seeks to achieve the goal of loss reduction through a community-based partnership consisting of key stakeholders from the private sector, non-profit organizations, and local, state and federal governments. The community must first examine its risk for natural disasters and identify its vulnerabilities to those risks. Next, it must identify and prioritize risk reduction actions and mitigation activities. Finally, the local leaders must build support for these actions and publicize their successes to ensure continued cooperation and support. There are currently 57 Project Impact communities in different stages of development (Heinz Center 1999).

The Showcase Community Program. The Institute for Business and Home Safety (IBHS) is an initiative of the insurance industry dedicated to reducing losses from natural disasters. Because much of the impetus for loss reduction must occur at the local level, IBHS has established the Showcase Community Program to operationalize the goals of its strategic plan. The program is designed to help a community reduce its vulnerability to natural disasters.

To support the Showcase Community Program, IBHS has developed Statements of Understanding with a number of groups, including the Central United States Earthquake Consortium (CUSEC), the American Red Cross, the Electric Power Research Institute (EPRI), Disaster Recovery Business Alliance (DRBA℠), the American Society of Civil Engineers, and the American Society of Home Inspectors. These organizations provide professional expertise, additional personnel, and energy that help to sustain locally driven efforts. In addition, IBHS member companies are engaged in the Showcase Communities program by supporting child daycare center retrofits, sponsoring DRBA^{SM} activities, providing speakers at community events, and through other activities.

Micro-Model Simulations

A broader strategy for undertaking research in this area involves the analysis of the impact of disasters or accidents of different magnitudes on different structures. In order to determine expected losses and the maximum probable losses arising from worst case scenarios, it may be necessary to undertake long-term micro-model simulations. For example, one could examine the impacts of earthquakes or hurricanes of different magnitudes on the losses to a community or region over a 10,000 year period. In the process one could determine expected losses based on the probabilistic scenario of these disasters as well as the maximum possible loss during this period based on a worst case scenario.

By constructing large, medium and small *representative* insurers with specific balance sheets, types of insurance portfolios, premium structures and a wide range of potential financial instruments, one could examine the impact of different disasters on the insurer's profitability, solvency and performance through a simulation. Such an analysis may also enable one to evaluate the performance of different mitigation measures and building codes on certain structures in the community on both expected losses as well as worst case scenarios. One could also consider the impact that reinsurance will have on both the insurer's expected profits and insolvency with and without RMMs in place. An example of the application of such an approach to a model city in California facing an earthquake risk can be found in Kleindorfer and Kunreuther (1999).

This type of simulation modeling must rely on solid theoretical foundations in order to delimit the boundaries of what is interesting and implementable in a market economy. Such foundations will apply to the decision processes of (re-)insurance companies, public officials and property owners in determining levels of mitigation, insurance coverage and other protective activities. In the area of catastrophic risks, the interaction of these decision processes, which are central to the outcome, seem to be considerably more complicated than in other economic sectors, perhaps because of the uncertainty and ambiguity of the causal mechanisms underlying natural hazards and their mitigation.

A current research program jointly being undertaken by the Financial Institutions Center and the Risk Management and Decision Processes Center at the Wharton School, University of Pennsylvania is addressing all the above issues. We are particularly interested in understanding the impact of different institutional arrangements in other countries on the role that insurance coupled with mitigation and other policy tools can play in reducing losses from future natural disasters.

APPENDIX 1 A SAFETY-FIRST MODEL OF UNDERWRITER BEHAVIOR[16]

Suppose an insurer has N policies associated with a risk and must decide what premium (P) it will charge. Let S be the insurer's financial resources to pay claims. It consists of its initial surplus (A) plus the premiums from its N policies (NP). The insurer has determined the probability p_i that it will have i losses each with claims payment L from different events.

A safety first model implies that the insurer's objective is to find a premium P which will

$$\text{Max}[A + NP - \sum p_i\, i\, L] \tag{1}$$

subject to the following insolvency constraint

$$\text{Probability}\left[\sum_{i=1}^{8}[A + NP) - i\,L] \leq 0\right] \leq q^* \tag{2}$$

where q^* = maximum probability of insolvency insurer will tolerate

APPENDIX 2 MODELING INSURERS BEHAVIOR WITH RESPECT TO MITIGATION

Consider the following scenario as it relates to insurers decision processes with respect to the premiums they are willing to charge for mitigation and how much they are willing to pay for reinsurance coverage:

Notation

p = annual probability of a loss for a single house (e.g., p = 1/100)
L'' = Loss without mitigation (e.g., L'' = \$250,000)
L' = Loss with mitigation (e.g., L' = \$200,000)
$E(L'') = p\, L''$ = Expected Annual Loss without Mitigation (e.g., \$2,500)
$E(L') = p\, L'$ = Expected Annual Loss with Mitigation (e.g., \$2,000)
$P'' = E(L'')$ = actuarially fair premium without Mitigation
$P' = E(L')$ = actuarially fair premium with Mitigation
M = Minimum premium reduction from P'' for homeowner to adopt mitigation

[16] More details on this model as well as an empirical test of its descriptive power appears in Berger and Kunreuther (1994).

Assumptions

The insurer provides coverage for a single type structure (e.g., concrete block house) in an earthquake prone area.

The insurer has written N earthquake policies on the single type structure. It may have other insurance policies in force but the concern here is **only** on its earthquake business.

The insurer has calculated the probability that n or more homes will be damaged by a severe quake (i.e., there is not a perfect correlation between losses) and has estimated the resulting losses with and without mitigation in place. Table 1 presents these data for an illustrative example.

Large and Small Capitalized Insurer Premium Setting Processes

Large—Capitalized Insurers (No Insolvency Constraint)

Alpha has N earthquake policies and must decide what premium (P_L) it will charge. Let S_L = Alpha's financial resources to pay claims which consists of its initial surplus (A_L) plus the premiums from its N policies (NP_L). It has determined the probability (p_i) that it will have i losses from an earthquake. The size of each loss L will be L'' if the property owner doesn't mitigate or L' if she does.

Alpha's objective is to choose a premium $P_L \geq P''$ so as to

$$\text{Max}\left[A_L + NP_L \quad \sum_i p_i\, i\, L\right] \tag{1}$$

subject to the following insolvency constraint

$$\text{Probability}\left[\sum_{i=1}^{8}[A_L + N(P_L) - i\,L] \leq 0\right] \leq q^* = \frac{1}{120} \tag{2}$$

where q^* = maximum probability of insolvency that insurer will tolerate

In the example given in the paper, Alpha is assumed to have S_L = \$1.2 million so that the insolvency constraint given by (2) will be met when mitigation is not in place and a premium $P_L = P''$ is charged. As seen from Table 1, (2) will also be satisfied if mitigation is adopted by property owners and $P_L = P'$.

Hence Alpha will set a premium which maximizes (1). It is interested in reducing the premium from P'' only if it will encourage the property owner to mitigate their home and increase the insurer's expected profit. The insurer knows that the range of premium reductions that satisfies both these conditions is between M and $P'' - P'$. Note that M is the minimum premium reduction from P'' that will lead the property owner to adopt mitigation. If $M > P'' - P'$ then mitigation will not be encouraged because the insurer will be forced to provide a reduction in premium that will cause them to reduce their expected profits on their earthquake business. If $M < P'' - P'$, in an imperfectly competitive market the insurer will charge $P \geq P'$ to encourage mitigation.

Small Capitalized Insurers (Insolvency Constraint is Exceeded without Mitigation)
Beta has N earthquake policies and must decide what premium (P_S) it will charge. Let S_S = the small insurer's financial resources to pay claims which consists of its initial surplus (A_S) plus the premiums from its N policies (NP_S). It has a probability p_i that it will have i losses (L) from an earthquake. The size of each loss L will be L'' if the property owner doesn't mitigate; L' if he does mitigate.

The small insurer's objective is to choose a premium $P_S \leq P''$ so as to

$$\text{Max}\left[A_S + NP_S - \sum_i p_i \, i \, L\right] \tag{3}$$

subject to the following insolvency constraint

$$\text{Probability}\left[\sum_{i=1}^{8}[A_S + N(P_S) - i\,L] \leq 0\right] \leq q^* \tag{4}$$

where q^* = maximum probability of insolvency

Beta is assumed to have ***insufficient*** financial resources (S_S) when mitigation is not in place, so that the insolvency constraint given by (4) for $L = L''$ will *not* be met. Beta must continue to provide earthquake coverage to its existing policyholders. Otherwise, it would have an incentive to cancel some policies to satisfy (4) without having to rely on mitigation or reinsurance.

In the example in the paper S_S = \$700,000 consisting of A_S = \$450,000 and actuarial premiums for 100 policies 100 (P'') = \$250,000. The small insurer can either purchase reinsurance and/or encourage mitigation through premium reduction to meet (4). We will briefly examine each of these decisions using the data from Table 1.

Purchasing Reinsurance

Suppose that a reinsurer is willing to provide coverage of \$250,000 to protect Beta against losses exceeding \$500,000 (i.e., \$250,000 in excess of \$500,000). The reinsurer will suffer a loss of \$250,000 in excess of \$500,000 if there 3 or more losses. This probability is given by 1/80 so that the actuarially fair premium is R = 1/80(\$250,000) = \$3,300.

For the example above we can determine the maximum reinsurance premium ($R_{\max}$) Beta would pay for this excess coverage to satisfy (4) assuming that it will still make positive expected profits by providing this coverage. Specifically with reinsurance of \$250 (thousand) in excess of \$500 (thousand), (4) becomes:

$$\text{Prob}\left[\left\{\sum_{i=1}^{2}[\$700 - R_{\max} - i\,L''] + [\$700 - R_{\max} - 750 + 250]\right.\right.$$
$$\left.\left. + \sum_{i=4}^{8}[\$700 - R_{\max} - i\,L'' + 250] \leq 0\right\}\right] \leq \frac{1}{120} \tag{5}$$

where the figures are in thousands of dollars.

$R_{\max}$ is determined by finding the value where the surplus of the insurer is exactly zero when there are 3 losses. To see this, note from Table 1 that Beta's surplus will be greater than zero if it suffers 0, 1 or 2 losses and that the probability of suffering four or more losses is less than 0.01. Hence if $q^* = \frac{1}{120}$, the value of R_{max} is determined by solving:

$$\$700 - R_{max} - 750 + 250 = 0. \qquad (6)$$

Based on (6) $R_{max} = \$200$. This means that, in theory, the insurer is willing to pay as much as \$200,000 for reinsurance. Of course, such a payment will yield an expected loss to Beta on its earthquake insurance business since premiums without mitigation reflected the actuarial loss. Beta may still choose to pay a large sum for earthquake reinsurance if it will make sufficient positive expected profits on other risks to want to stay in business. The actual reinsurance premium for this example will be somewhere between \$3,333 and this upper limit depending on the degree of competition in the reinsurance market and the expected profits that the insurer can earn on other policy lines.

Encouraging Mitigation Through Premium Reductions

As an alternative to reinsurance Beta may actually be willing to set a premium P_S that is below the actuarially fair rate to encourage its current policyholders to adopt mitigation measures. Claim payments following an earthquake will be reduced and Beta may then be able to meet the insolvency constraint given by (4).

From Table 1 one sees that if $q^* = \frac{1}{120}$ then Beta needs to set premiums so it has sufficient surplus to cover 3 losses. With mitigation its claims are reduced from \$750,000 to \$600,000 when 3 structures are damaged. Hence to determine P_S which satisfies (4) Beta computes.

$$\$450{,}000 - 100P_S - \$600{,}000 = 0 \qquad (6)$$

This means that $P_S = \$1{,}500$, a premium below the actuarially fair value of $P' = \$2{,}000$. Thus Beta is willing to lose money on its earthquake business to encourage mitigation and satisfy its insolvency constraint.

18.7 REFERENCES

Berger, Lawrence and Kunreuther, Howard (1994). "Safety First and Ambiguity" *Journal of Actuarial Practice* 2, 273–291.

Cohen, Linda and Noll, Roger (1981). "The Economics of Building Codes to Resist Seismic Structures" *Public Policy* Winter 1–29.

Cummins, David (1988). "Risk Based Premiums for Insurance Guaranty Funds" *Journal of Finance* 43, 823–839.

Dionne, Georges and Eeckhoudt, Louis (1985). "Self-Insurance, Self Protection and Increased Risk Aversion" *Economic Letters* 17, 39–42.

Dionne, Georges and Harrington, Scott, eds. (1992). *Foundations of Insurance Economics* (Kluwer: Boston).

Doherty, Neil and Tinic, S.M. (1982). "A Note on Reinsurance under Conditions of Capital Market Equilibrium" *Journal of Finance* 36, 949–953.

Earthquake Engineering Research Institute (1998). *Incentives and Impediments to Improving the Seismic Performance of Buildings*. Oakland, CA: Earthquake Engineering Research Institute.

Ehrlich, Isaac and Becker, Gary (1972). "Market Insurance, Self-Insurance and Self Protection" *Journal of Political Economy* 80, 623–648.

Federal Emergency Management Agency (1994). *Assessment of the State-of—the Art Earthquake Loss Estimation* Washington, D.C.: National Instiution of Building Sciences.

Giles, Martin (1994). "A Survey of Insurance" *The Economist* 3–22, Dec. 3.

Heinz Center (1999). *The Hidden Costs of Coastal Hazards* Washington, D.C: Island Press.

Insurance Institute for Property Loss Reduction (IBHS) (1995). *Homes and Hurricanes: Public Opinion Concerning Various Issues Relating to Home Builders, Building Codes and Damage Mitigation* Boston, MA: IBHS.

Insurance Research Council and Insurance Institute for Property Loss Reduction (1995). *Coastal Exposure and Community Protection: Hurrican Andrew's Legacy* [Wheaton, Ill (IRC) and Boston (IBHS)].

Insurance Services Office (1996). *Managing Catastrophic Risk* (New York, N.Y.: Insurance Services Office).

Kleffner, Anne and Doherty, Neil (1996). "Costly Risk Bearing and the Supply of Catastrophic Insurance" *Journal of Risk and Insurance* 63, 567–571.

Klein, Robert (1998). "Regulation and Catastrophe Insurance." *In* H. Kunreuther and R. Roth, Sr., eds., *Paying the Price: The Status and Role of Insurance Against Natural Disasters in the United States.* Washington, D.C: Joseph Henry Press.

Klein, Robert (1997). "The Regulation of Catastrophe Insurance: An Initial Overview" (mimeo) June.

Kleindorfer, Paul and Kunreuther, Howard (1999). "Challenges Facing the Insurance Industry in Managing Catastrophic Risks" Solutions" in Kenneth Froot (ed) *The Financing of Property/Casualty Risks* (Chicago: University of Chicago Press).

Kunreuther, Howard (1996). "Mitigating Disaster Losses Through Insurance". *Journal of Risk and Uncertainty.* 12, 171–187.

Kunreuther, Howard and Roth, Richard, Sr. (ed.) (1998). *Paying the Price: The Status and Role of Insurance Against Natural Disasters in the United States* (Washington, D.C: The Joseph Henry Press).

Kunreuther, Howard and Kleffner, Anne E. (1992). "Should Earthquake Mitigation Measures Be Voluntary or Required?" *Journal of Regulatory Economics* 4, 321–335.

Lecomte, Eugene and Gahagan, Karen (1998). "Hurricane Insurance Protection in Florida" *In* H. Kunreuther and R. Roth, Sr., eds., *Paying the Price: The Status and Role of Insurance Against Natural Disasters in the United States.* Washington, D.C: Joseph Henry Press.

Litan, Robert, Krimgold, Frederick, Clark, Karen and Khadilkar, Jayant (1992). *Physical Damage and Human Loss: The Economic Impact of Earthquake Mitigation Measures* (New York: Insurance Information Institute Press).

Marshall, John (1976). "Moral Hazard" *The American Economic Review* 66, 880–890.

May, Peter and Stark, Nancy (1992). "Design Professions and Earthquake Policy" *Earthquake Spectra* 8, 115–132.

Mayers, David and Smith, Clifford (1982). "On Corporate Demand for Insurance" *Journal of Business* 55, 281–296.

Mayers, David and Smith, Clifford (1990). "On Corporate Demand for Insurance: Evidence from the Reinsurance Market" *Journal of Business* 63, 19–40.

McIsaac, Donald and Babbel, David (1995). *The World Bank Primer on Reinsurance* Washington, D.C.: USGPO).

Office of Technology Assessment (1995). *Reducing Earthquake Losses* (Washington, D.C.: USGPO).

Pasterick and Edward (1998). "The National Flood Insurance Program" *In* H. Kunreuther and R. Roth, Sr., eds., *Paying the Price: The Status and Role of Insurance Against Natural Disasters in the United States.* Washington, D.C: Joseph Henry Press.

Pauly, Mark (1974). "Overinsurance and Public Provision of Insurance: The Role of Moral Hazard and Adverse Selection" *Quarterly Journal of Economics* 88, 44–62.

Russell, Thomas and Jaffee, Dwight (1997). "Catastrophe Insurance, Capital Markets, and Insurable Risk" *Journal of Risk and Insurance* 64, 205–230.

Shavell, Steven (1979). "On Moral Hazard and Insurance" *Quarterly Journal of Economics* 93, 541–562.

Spence, Michael and Zeckhauser, Richard (1971). "Insurance, Information and Individual Action" *American Economic Review* 61, 380–387.

Stone, John (1973). "A Theory of Capacity and the Insurance of Catastrophic Risks: Part I," and "Part II," *Journal of Risk and Insurance*, 40, 231–243 (Part I) and 40, 339–355 (Part II).

Part VI
Insurance Pricing

19 Applications of Financial Pricing Models in Property-liability Insurance

J. David Cummins

University of Pennsylvania

Richard D. Phillips

Georgia State University

Abstract

This chapter provides a comprehensive survey of the literature on the financial pricing of property-liability insurance and provides some extensions of the existing literature. Financial prices for insurance reflect equilibrium relationships between risk and return or, minimally, avoid the creation of arbitrage opportunities. We discuss insurance pricing models based on the capital asset pricing model, the intertemporal capital asset pricing model, arbitrage pricing theory, and option pricing theory. Discrete time discounted cash flow models based on the net present value and internal rate of return approaches are also discussed as well as pricing models insurance derivatives such as catastrophic risk call spreads and bonds. We provide a number of suggestions for future research.

Keywords: Insurance pricing, financial pricing, securitization.
JEL Classification Numbers: G22, G13, G31.

19.1 INTRODUCTION

This chapter surveys the literature on the financial pricing of insurance and provides some extensions of the existing literature. Financial pricing differs from traditional actuarial pricing by taking into account the role played by markets in determining the price of insurance. Thus, policy prices should reflect equilibrium relationships between risk and return or, minimally, avoid the creation of arbitrage opportunities. By contrast, traditional actuarial models, such as the actuarial premium principle models (Goovaerts, de Vylder, and Haezendonck 1984), take a supply-side perspective, incorporating the assumption that prices are primarily determined by the insurer. The traditional supply-side approach is gradually being replaced by the financial pricing approach, reflecting models developed by both actuaries and financial economists.[1]

Financial theory views the insurance firm as a levered corporation with debt and equity capital. The insurer raises debt capital by issuing insurance contracts, which are roughly analogous to the bonds issued by non-financial corporations. However, insurance liabilities are not like conventional bonds but more like structured securities, where payoffs are triggered by various contingencies. The payment times and amounts for property-liability insurance policies are stochastic, determined by contingent events such as fires, earthquakes, and liability judgments. The types of risks incorporated in insurance liabilities drive both the pricing and capital structure decisions of insurers. Insurance policies also differ from bonds issued by non-financial corporations because the holders of the insurer's debt instruments are also its customers (Merton and Perold 1993). Consequently, the insurer's debt instruments should be priced to earn a fair economic profit reflecting the risks borne by the insurer. The derivation of the fair profit is one of the principal themes of this chapter.

Insurance financial pricing models have been developed to price this special class of liabilities using various strands of financial theory. The earliest models were based on the capital asset pricing model (CAPM). These models provide important insights but are too simple to be used in realistic situations, especially in light of financial research showing that factors other than the CAPM beta determine security returns (e.g., Fama and French 1993, 1996, Cochrane 1999). More promising are discrete and continuous time discounted cash flow (DCF) models, analogous to the net present value (NPV) and internal rate of return (IRR) models used in corporate capital budgeting. Option models also provide important insights into insurance pricing. The most recent research focuses on the pricing of financial instruments based on losses from property catastrophes such as hurricanes and earthquakes.

Although the primary focus in this chapter is on the theory of insurance pricing, we also briefly discuss some significant empirical contributions on the topic. We first provide a conceptual overview of the capital structure of insurance firms, with insurance policies viewed as risky debt capital. We then turn to a discussion of financial pricing models, beginning with the most basic model, the insurance capital asset pricing model (CAPM). More complex and realistic models are then discussed, including the newly-developed catastrophic risk (CAT) bonds and options.

[1] Recent actuarial papers reflecting the financial approach include Gerber and Landry (1997) and Gerber and Shiu (1998).

19.2 INSURANCE AS RISKY DEBT

Insurance companies are levered corporations that raise debt capital by issuing a specific type of financial instrument—the insurance policy. This section outlines the insurance pricing problem, describes the characteristics of insurance debt that should be reflected in financial pricing models, and discusses insurer capital structure.

In order to operate an insurance enterprise, the firm's owners commit equity capital to the firm (the reasons for doing so are discussed below) and then issue insurance policies, which are characterized by an initial premium payment, i.e., a cash inflow to the insurer, followed by a stream of cash outflows representing loss payments. During the period between the premium payment and the final satisfaction of all claims against the policy, the insurer invests the unexpended premium balance as well as the equity capital committed to the firm, receiving investment income. The equity capital is assumed to flow back to the owners as the loss obligations are satisfied. The firm's underwriting profit (the difference between premium inflows and loss outflows) and investment income expose the insurer to income tax liabilities which generate additional cash flows. Thus, the principal cash flows that must be taken into account in insurance pricing consist of premiums, losses, investment income, equity capital, and taxes.

Timing differences between the funds that flow into the company as the result of the commitment of capital and issuance of insurance policies generate the firm's assets as well as two liability accounts—the unearned premium reserve and the loss reserve. The unearned premium reserve reflects premiums that have been paid to the company for coverage not yet provided and is similar to a short-term loan (most policy coverage periods are a year or less) with no unusual risk characteristics. The loss reserve, which arises because claim payments lag premium payments and loss occurrences, represents the company's estimate of the losses it will eventually have to pay less the payments that have already been made.[2] The loss reserve is similar to an exotic option or structured security. Neither the magnitude nor the timing of loss payments are known in advance but rather depend upon contingent events such as the occurrence of accidents and the outcomes of liability lawsuits. In addition, loss cash flows can be generated by events that were unknown and/or impossible to predict when the policies were issued such as liabilities arising from exposure to environmental and asbestos exposures.[3] Because the realizations of the loss cash flows may be correlated

[2] In economic terms, the true value of the reserve is its market value which reflects the timing of expected loss payments on claims known to the insurer, an expectation of payments on accidents incurred which have not been reported to the insurer as of the statement date, a risk premium, and its value as a tax shield. However, in most industrialized countries, regulators require that insurers state their policy obligations at nominal (non-discounted) values.

[3] Actuaries often refer to the uncertainty regarding the ultimate amount of loss as *process risk*. The risks associated with the inability to accurately model the frequency and severity of all future loss events is known as *parameter risk*.

with movements in the overall financial market, insurance prices should incorporate risk premia to compensate insurers for bearing market risk.

Equity capital is the other major component of the capital structure of an insurance company. Although holding equity capital is costly due to regulation, the double taxation of dividends, and the various agency costs associated with operating an insurance company, insurers maintain capital in excess of regulatory requirements for a variety of reasons. Avoiding financial distress costs provides one important motivation for insurers to hold capital. Financial distress costs include direct costs resulting from bankruptcy as well as indirect costs which may affect the firm's ability to retain its relationships with key employees, customers, or suppliers. Merton and Perold (1993) argue that insurers also hold capital because the customers of insurers, who purchase insurance to reduce their exposure to unfavorable contingencies, are particularly concerned about the ability of the insurer to satisfy its financial obligations. Insurers also may hold equity because they issue illiquid contracts containing private information (D'Arcy and Doherty 1990, Cummins, Phillips, and Smith 1998, 2000). The benefits of this private information are only realized over time and the contracts cannot be liquidated for their full value should the firm suffer a shock to its capital resources. Finally, various agency costs, borne by the shareholders of the firm, also can be mitigated by holding additional levels of capital (e.g., Myers and Majluf 1984). Evidence that P/L insurers have strong motivations for holding equity capital is provided by the capital-to-asset ratio in the U.S. P/L industry, which equaled 33 percent in 1995. By comparison, the capital-to-asset ratio for life insurers and commercial banks are much lower, approximately 6.5 and 3.5 percent in 1995.[4]

Insurers invest primarily in financial assets, with a heavy emphasis on stocks and bonds. Insurers select assets with the objective of maximizing return while maintaining acceptable levels of credit risk exposure in their bond portfolios, exposure to price volatility from their stock portfolios, and exposure to price and exchange rate volatility from assets denominated in foreign currencies. In addition, insurers manage the duration and convexity of their asset and liability portfolios to reduce their exposure to interest rate risk (Staking and Babbel 1995). Many insurers also use off-balance-sheet contracts such as financial derivatives to manage their exposure to these same risks (Cummins, Phillips, and Smith 1997, 1998, Santomero and Babbel 1997).

The risks that should be taken into account in pricing insurance contracts are summarized in Table 1. Insurance pricing models differ in the degree to which these risks are recognized. The existing insurance financial pricing models tend to focus on systematic risk, inflation risk, and interest rate risk. More research is needed on unified models that incorporate all types of risk.

[4] The capital-to-asset ratios are from the Federal Reserve Flow of Funds Accounts (Washington, D.C.: Board of Governors of the Federal Reserve System).

Table 1
Pricing Characteristics and Risks in Property-Liability Insurance

Uncertainty Regarding Frequency and Severity (Process Risk)
Uncertainty Regarding Models to Estimate Losses (Parameter Risk)
Interest Rate (Duration and convexity) Risk
Inflation Risk
Payout Pattern Risk
Systematic (Market) Risk
Default Risk

19.3 A SIMPLE CAPM FOR INSURANCE PRICING

The first financial models of the insurance firm were based on a very simple algebraic approach. The first model of this type was developed by Ferrari (1969). His paper presents the basic algebraic model of the insurer but does not link the model to the concept of market equilibrium. An important advance in insurance financial pricing was the linkage of the algebraic model of the insurance firm with the capital asset pricing model (CAPM). The resulting model is often called the *insurance CAPM.*

The insurance CAPM was developed in Cooper (1974), Biger and Kahane (1978), Fairley (1979), and Hill (1979). The derivation begins with the following simple model of the insurance firm:

$$\tilde{Y} = \tilde{I} + \tilde{\Pi}_u = \tilde{r}_a A + \tilde{r}_u P \tag{1}$$

where $\tilde{Y}, \tilde{I}$ = net income and investment income, respectively,
$\tilde{\Pi}_u$ = underwriting profit (loss) = premium income less expenses and losses,
A = invested assets of the firm
P = premiums collected from policyholders to compensate insurers for the risks they underwrite,
$\tilde{r}_a$ = rate of investment return on assets, and
$\tilde{r}_u$ = rate of return on underwriting (as a proportion of premiums).

Tildes indicate stochastic variables. Writing (1) as return on equity and using the balance sheet identity $A = R + G$, where R = (undiscounted) reserves and G = equity, one obtains:

$$\tilde{r}_e = \tilde{r}_a\left(\frac{R}{G}+1\right) + \tilde{r}_u\frac{P}{G} = \tilde{r}_a(ks+1) + \tilde{r}_u s \tag{2}$$

where s = P/G = the premiums-to-equity (or premiums-to-surplus) ratio, and
k = R/P = the liabilities-to-premiums ratio (*funds generating factor*).

Equation (2) indicates that the rate of return on equity for an insurer is generated by both *financial leverage* ($R/G + 1$) and *insurance leverage* (P/G). The leverage factor for investment income is a function of the premium-to-surplus ratio and the funds generating factor. The latter approximates the average time between the policy issue and claims payment dates. The underwriting return is leveraged by the premium-to-surplus ratio. Taking expectations in (2), one obtains the insurer's expected return on equity.

Equation (2) is essentially an accounting model. The model is given economic content by assuming that the equilibrium expected return on the insurer's equity is determined by the CAPM. The CAPM formula for the expected return on the insurer's stock is

$$E(\tilde{r}_e) = r_f + \beta_e[E(\tilde{r}_m) - r_f] \tag{3}$$

where $E(\tilde{r}_e)$ = expected return on the insurer's equity capital,
β_e = the insurer's equity beta coefficient = $\text{Cov}(\tilde{r}_e, \tilde{r}_m)/\text{Var}(\tilde{r}_m)$,
$E(\tilde{r}_m)$ = expected return on the market portfolio, and
r_f = the risk-free rate of interest.

The insurance CAPM is obtained by equating the CAPM rate of return on the insurer's equity with the expected return given by equation (2) and solving for the expected underwriting profit.[5] The result is:

$$E(\tilde{r}_u) = -k\, r_f + \beta_u[E(\tilde{r}_m) - r_f] \tag{4}$$

where $\beta_u = \text{Cov}(\tilde{r}_u, \tilde{r}_m)/\text{Var}(\tilde{r}_m)$ = the beta of underwriting profits.

The insurer must earn (in expectation) the return $E(\tilde{r}_u)$ on underwriting in order to avoid penalizing equity (if the return is too low) or charging policyholders too much (if the return is too high). The first term in equation (4), $-k\, r_f$, represents an interest credit for the use of policyholder funds. The second component of $E(\tilde{r}_u)$ is the insurer's reward for risk-bearing: the underwriting beta multiplied by the market risk premium. The risk premium reflects only systematic risk, i.e., policies are treated as free of default risk.

Several limitations of the insurance CAPM have motivated researchers to seek more realistic models. One problem is the use of the funds generating factor (k) to represent the payout tail. Myers and Cohn (1987) argue that k is only an approximation of the discounted cash flow (DCF) approach. A second limitation is that the model ignores default risk. As a practical matter, errors in estimating underwriting betas

[5] The derivation also uses the CAPM pricing relationship for the insurer's expected asset return, $E(\tilde{r}_a)$, i.e., $E(\tilde{r}_a) = r_f + \beta_a[E(\tilde{r}_m) - r_f]$ as well as the relationship $\beta_e = \beta_a(ks + 1) + \beta_u s$.

can be significant (Cummins and Harrington 1985). A final serious limitation is that most recent studies have shown that security returns are related to other factors in addition to the CAPM beta coefficient. A more modern version of the insurance CAPM could easily be developed that incorporate multi-factor asset pricing models. Most of the models discussed below deal with one or more of the limitations of the CAPM.

19.4 DISCRETE TIME DISCOUNTED CASH FLOW (DCF) MODELS

Paralleling corporate finance, DCF models for insurance pricing have been developed based on the net present value (NPV) and the internal rate of return (IRR) approaches. The NPV approach was applied originally by Myers and Cohn (1987) and extended by Cummins (1990) and Taylor (1994). The NPV model is an application of *adjusted present value* (APV) method, which requires each cash flow to be discounted at its own risk-adjusted discount rate (RADR) (see Brealey and Myers 1996). The IRR approach was originally developed by the National Council on Compensation Insurance (NCCI) and is further discussed in Taylor (1994).[6] In this section we provide a general discussion of the DCF approach to insurance pricing using notation taken from Taylor (1994).[7] Taylor's model is more rigorously developed than earlier models, and he explicitly derives the conditions under which the NPV and IRR models give the same results.

We begin by defining some additional notation. Specifically, let

P = the premium paid by policyholders for insurance coverage,
a_t = the proportion of the premium paid at time t,
$\tilde{L}$ = the total amount of losses under the policy,
c_t = the proportion of losses paid at time t,
$\tilde{L}_t = c_t\tilde{L}$ = the amount of the loss payment at time t,
$E(\tilde{r}_l) = r_f + \beta_l[E(\tilde{r}_m) - r_f]$ = the expected value of the loss discount rate $\tilde{r}_l$,
$E(\tilde{r}_a) = r_f + \beta_a[E(\tilde{r}_m) - r_f]$ = the expected return on the insurer's invested assets,
$\beta_x = \text{Cov}(\tilde{r}_x, \tilde{r}_m)/\text{Var}(\tilde{r}_m)$ = the beta coefficient for cash flow x ($x = l, a$),
G_t = the insurer's equity capital at time t, and
τ = tax rate for investment and underwriting income.[8]

[6] Of course, the internal rate of return model in insurance is subject to the same well-known pitfalls that have been identified in corporate finance more generally. See, for example, Brealy and Myers (1996). However, as Brealy and Myers point out, "used properly, it gives the same answer" as the net present value (NPV) method (Brealy and Myers, p. 85).

[7] Taylor (1994) provides the set of conditions under which the net present value model and the internal rate of return models will yield identical premia. Our discussion is a simplified version of his model. The reader is referred to the original paper for more details.

[8] Although we believe that our modeling of income taxes is reasonably generic, the models would have to be modified for use in jurisdictions that have other types of tax formulas.

As above, tildes indicate random variables. The insurer is assumed to issue policies at time 0. In general, premiums are received at times $\{0, 1, \ldots, T-1\}$ and losses are paid at times $\{1, 2, \ldots, T\}$, where T is the last loss payment date. We assume that $c_t > 0$ at all times $\{1, 2, \ldots, T\}$, but premium payments may be zero at some possible premium payment dates. An important special case is where all premiums are paid at time zero, i.e., $a_t = 0$, $t \neq 0$. Expenses (other than loss payments) are assumed to be zero. The asset and liability discount rates, the risk-free rate, the expected return on the market portfolio, and the beta coefficients are all assumed to be constant over the payout period. Insurer underwriting profits and investment income are taxed at the constant rate τ.

An important feature of the discounted cash flow approach to insurance pricing is the concept of the *surplus flow*. The insurer is assumed to commit equity capital (surplus) to the enterprise at time 0, and the capital is assumed to flow back to the insurer over the loss payment period. A specific pattern of surplus flow is required in order for the net present value and IRR methods to yield identical premiums. Myers and Cohn assumed that surplus is released as losses are paid. However, Taylor (1994) shows that their assumption will not lead to equivalency of the NPV and IRR premiums. Taylor shows instead that the surplus must be released in proportion to reductions in reserves. We return to this point below.

The insurer's market value balance sheet consists of the market value of its assets on one side and the market value of its debt and equity on the other. Debt capital consists of loss reserves, i.e., no bonds or other types of non-insurance debt capital are used. The market value of liabilities can be defined as:

$$R_t^m = \sum_{t=1}^{T}\left[\frac{L_t(1+v_t)}{[1+E(r_l)]^t} - \frac{P_{t-1}}{[1+r_f]^{t-1}}\right] = R_t^{ml} - R_t^{mp} \tag{5}$$

where R_t^m = the market value of reserves at time t,

v_t = loading factor applied to expected costs of period t in their contribution to loss reserves, and

R_t^{ml}, R_t^{mp} = the loss and premium components, respectively, of equation (5).

The factor v_t reflects loadings that are held in reserves until realization at time t. The loadings are needed to pay the taxes on underwriting and investment income (see below). The premium component R_t^{mp} represents a receivables account and could be equivalently treated as an asset item. The *leverage factor* can be defined as $\theta_t^{-1} = R_t^{ml}/G_t$, $t = 0, 1, \ldots, T$.

Taylor (1994) derives the following formula for the cash flows to/from the insurer's owners:

$$\tilde{F}_t = (G_{t-1} - G_t) + (1-\tau)\tilde{\Pi}_t \tag{6}$$

where $\tilde{F}_t$ = net cash flow to (from) owners in period t. $\tilde{\Pi}_t$ = the insurer's profit at time t, defined as follows:[9]

$$\tilde{\Pi}_t = G_{t-1}(1-\tau)\left[E(\tilde{r}_a)+[E(\tilde{r}_a)-E(\tilde{r}_l)]\frac{R_{t-1}^{ml}}{G_{t-1}}+v_t\frac{L_t}{G_{t-1}}-[E(\tilde{r}_a)-r_f]\frac{(R_{t-1}^{mp}-P_{t-1})}{G_{t-1}}+\tilde{z}_{t-1}\right] \tag{7}$$

The profit is after-tax and has five components, corresponding to the five terms inside the brackets in equation (7). The first, $E(\tilde{r}_a)$, corresponds to the investment income earned on the insurer's equity. The second, equal to $[E(\tilde{r}_a) - E(\tilde{r}_l)]$ leveraged by $(\theta_{t-1})^{-1}$, reflects investment income on reserves less the rate of return credit needed to write up discounted reserves for an additional period as they approach maturity, the latter being a deduction in determining taxable income (Cummins 1990). The third, involving v_t, represents the release to profits of the loading margin in the loss reserve. The fourth term represents the reduction in income attributable to premiums not yet received by the insurer; and the fifth term, $\tilde{z}_{t-l}$, is a mean-zero random variable to capture deviations of losses and investment income from their expected values.

The insurer's return on equity (ROE) in period t can be obtained by dividing through equation (6) by G_{t-1}. Because we have assumed no changes in the underlying variables such as expected investment returns and taxes, the expected return on equity should be constant over the entire runoff period. Thus, it is of interest to inquire about the conditions that will lead to a constant ROE. Using equations (6) and (7), the CAPM formulas for $E(\tilde{r}_a)$ and $E(\tilde{r}_l)$, and the definition of θ_t, ROE can be written as

$$\tilde{r}_e = (1-\tau)\left[E(\tilde{r}_a)+[E(\tilde{r}_a)-E(\tilde{r}_l)]\theta_{t-1}^{-1}\left(1-\frac{\beta_a}{\beta_a-\beta_l}\frac{R_{t-1}^{mp}-P_{t-1}}{R_{t-1}^{ml}}\right)+v_t\frac{L_t}{G_{t-1}}+\tilde{z}_t\right] \tag{8}$$

Considering the second term inside of the brackets, involving $(\theta_{t-1})^{-1}$, it is clear that this term will be constant if $\theta_{t-1} = \theta$, $\forall\ t$, where θ is a constant, and the term involving R_t^{mp} and R_t^{ml} is constant. An important special case where this will occur is when all premiums are received at time zero. Otherwise, the condition imposes a constraint on the ratio of the reserve for deferred premiums to the reserve for unpaid losses.

In the no-tax case where $v_t = 0\ \forall\ t$, the v_t term in equation (8) vanishes, so we do not need to worry about this term creating non-constant ROE. When $v_t \neq 0$, the condition that the v_t term in (8) must satisfy in order for ROE to be constant is the following:

$$v_t\frac{L_t}{R_{t-1}^{ml}} = \frac{\theta\tau}{1-\tau}ROE \tag{9}$$

[9] The profit is the amount that must be earned in order for the insurer to earn its cost of capital on the policy. We are not suggesting that monopoly rents play a role in this model.

where ROE = the constant value for ROE being sought in the analysis. Because the right hand side of equation (9) is a constant, this condition implies that the emergence of profits should vary inversely with the ratio L_t/R^{ml}_{t-1}, i.e., profit emerges proportionately to the ratio of paid losses to the (present valued) loss reserve. This differs significantly from the approach in Myers and Cohn (1987), who assume that "underwriting profits are accrued as losses are *paid*" (p. 68, emphasis added). Taylor's result in equation (9) shows that the MC assumption about the emergence of profit will not lead to ROE being constant over time, even when the underlying parameters are constant.

We are now ready to compare the IRR and NPV models. Consider first the IRR model. This model specifies that the premium P is the solution of the following equation:

$$\sum_{t=0}^{T} \frac{E(\tilde{F}_t)}{[1+E(\tilde{r}_e)]^t} = 0 \tag{10}$$

where $\tilde{F}_t$ is given by equation (6). It is convenient in discussing the method to assume that all premiums are paid at time zero. Then equations (8) and (9) imply that

$$E(\tilde{r}_e) - E(\tilde{r}_a) + [E(\tilde{r}_a) - E(\tilde{r}_l)]\theta^{-1} - \tau[E(\tilde{r}_a) + [E(\tilde{r}_a) - E(\tilde{r}_l)]\theta^{-1}] + (1-\tau)v_t \frac{L_t}{G_{t-1}} \tag{11}$$

But by equation (10) the last two terms in (11) sum to zero, so $E(\tilde{r}_e) = E(\tilde{r}_a) + [E(\tilde{r}_a) - E(\tilde{r}_l)]\theta^{-1}$, where θ^{-1} is the constant ratio of the present value of unpaid losses to capital. Therefore, under these conditions we have a constant ROE.

This result has several important implications. First, the constant ROE generated by the model is the required rate of return implied by the CAPM, which can be rewritten as $E(\tilde{r}_e) = E(\tilde{r}_a)(1 + R^{ml}/G) - E(\tilde{r}_l)\,(R^{ml}/G)$, where $R^{ml}/G = \theta^{-1}$ = the ratio of the present value of reserves to equity capital, which is constant for all t. Thus, the insurer earns a leveraged return on assets at rate $E(\tilde{r}_a)$ and pays for the use of policyholder funds at the rate $E(\tilde{r}_l)$, where both $E(\tilde{r}_a)$ and $E(\tilde{r}_l)$ are determined by the CAPM. Second, the profit loadings (v_t) emerge at exactly the time and amount needed to offset the income tax on the ROE, so that the insurer earns the pre-tax ROE. The policyholder pays the firm's income tax in accordance with the argument that the owners will not commit capital to the insurer if it is subjected to another layer of taxation because the owners have the option of investing directly in the capital markets. And, third, like the insurance CAPM, the model does not recognize insolvency risk. Thus, θ is indeterminate, and there is nothing explicitly in the model to prevent the insurer from infinitely leveraging the firm. Thus, the model incorporates the implicit assumption that market discipline or regulation prevent infinite leveraging.

The fourth implication provides a link between the IRR and the MC net present value models. This argument is a bit more subtle and the reader is referred to Taylor (1994) for a rigorous proof. However, the intuition is that the equation defining the IRR (equation (10)) implies that no profit emerges at time zero. This in turn implies that $R_0^m = 0$ in equation (5) and thus that the premium satisfies the following equation.

$$\sum_{t=1}^{T} \frac{P_{t-1}}{(1+r_f)^{t-1}} = \sum_{t=1}^{T} \frac{L_t(1+v_t)}{(1+E(\tilde{r}_l))^t} \tag{12}$$

If v_t is zero for all t, equation (12) is exactly the Myers-Cohn model for the case of no taxes.

To produce a constant CAPM return on equity, one could calculate premiums using the IRR model in equation (12). Alternatively, we can restate the MC model using the surplus release pattern postulated by Taylor. To do this, we first note that the APV approach requires that the insurer's tax liability be broken down into its components, with each component discounted at the appropriate rate. The insurer's expected tax liability can be disaggregated as follows:

$$Tax_t = \tau\{E(\tilde{r}_a)[G_{t-1} + R_{t-1}^{ml} - (R_{t-1}^{mp} - P_{t-1})] - E(\tilde{r}_l)R_{t-1}^{ml} + r_f(R_{t-1}^{mp} - P_{t-1})\} \tag{13}$$

The first expression in equation (13), equal to the expected investment return times the bracketed expression, is the investment return on the insurer's assets at the start of the period, where assets (A_{t-1}) equal equity (G_{t-1}) plus reserves ($R^{ml} - R^{mp}$) plus premiums received (P_{t-1}). The second term ($-E(\tilde{r}_l)\ R_{t-1}^{ml}$) is a deduction for losses paid and for the write-up of the remaining loss reserve to reflect the reduced time to maturity. The third component is the interest write up to accrue the premium account towards maturity, i.e., a financing charge for unpaid premiums.

The present value of the tax components is added to the present value of losses to obtain the NPV premium. To obtain the premium, it is necessary to specify a RADR for each component of the tax. For the last term, the answer is obvious: $r_f(R_{t-1}^{mp} - P_{t-1})$ is a riskless flow and therefore is discounted at the risk free rate, r_f. For the first term, which is a risky investment flow, determined by the risky rate of return $\tilde{r}_a$, the answer is not so obvious. However, it turns out that this flow as well is discounted at the risk free rate. This result is known as the *Myers' theorem*, developed by Myers (1984) and proved more rigorously in Derrig (1994) and Taylor (1994).

The Myers' theorem can be demonstrated easily. Assume an investment of 1 at time 0 in the risky asset. The return on the asset, which is unknown at time 0, will be $\tilde{\boldsymbol{r}}_a$. The investor will receive this risky return at time 1 and will pay a tax of $\tau\,\tilde{\boldsymbol{r}}_a$. The question is: what is the present value at time 0 of this tax flow? The result is obtained by observing that the investor is able to deduct the amount of the initial investment (i.e., 1) before paying the tax. Although the investment return is risky, the deduction is not.

We are seeking the following present value:

$$\text{PV(Tax)} = \text{PV}(\tau\tilde{\boldsymbol{r}}_a) = \tau\text{PV}(\tilde{\boldsymbol{r}}_a)$$

However, we also recognize that the investor will have both the principal and interest at time 1, i.e., $(1 + \tilde{r}_a)$, and can deduct 1 before paying the tax. Therefore, we can write

$$PV(Tax) = \tau PV[(1+\tilde{r}_a)-1]$$

But we have assumed that capital markets are efficient, so the present value of the risky amount $(1 + \tilde{r}_a)$ is 1, i.e., the appropriate discount factor for this term is $(1 + \tilde{r}_a)$. The deduction of 1 is riskless and thus is discounted at the risk free rate. Therefore, we have

$$PV(Tax) = \tau PV[(1+\tilde{r}_a)-1] = \tau[1-1/(1+r_f)] = \tau r_f/(1+r_f)$$

that is, the present value of the tax on a risky investment of \$1 is the risk-free rate times the tax rate, discounted at the risk-free rate.

The only component for which we still need a discount rate is the loss deduction. The loss deduction depends on risky losses so that the appropriate discount rate is $E(\tilde{r}_l)$. Consequently, the revised form of the Myers-Cohn model, which we term the *Myers Cohn-Taylor (MCT) net present value model*, is given by:

$$\sum_{t=0}^{T-1} Pa_t = \sum_{t=1}^{T} L\frac{c_t}{[1+E(\tilde{r}_L)]^t} + \tau\left[\sum_{t=1}^{T}\frac{r_f(A_{t-1}+R_{t-1}^{ml})}{(1+r_f)^t} - \sum_{t=1}^{T}\frac{E(\tilde{r}_l)R_{t-1}^{ml}}{[1+E(\tilde{r}_L)]^t}\right] \tag{14}$$

Premiums based on this model will generate a constant (expected) cost of capital throughout the runoff period for the policies being priced, and it will give the same premium as the IRR model.

Although the discrete time models we have discussed here are useful and practical financial pricing models, they are not without limitations. E.g., multi-factor models that price various sources of risk should be used instead of the CAPM in discounting risky cash flows (see Cochrane 1999). Research identifying the sources of priced risk in insurance markets would be an important advance in this field.

Recent work in the theory of risk management also suggest that the models presented here may be in need of further development. Because of various capital market imperfections, the cost of raising capital external to the firm will be more costly than capital generated from internal sources (Froot, Scharfstein, and Stein 1993). Thus, firms have an incentive to manage risk at the individual firm level to decrease the likelihood of having to raise costly external capital. Froot and Stein (1998) have developed a capital budgeting model that allows for the possibility that external capital is more costly than internal capital. They argue that the discount rate on lines of business which co-vary positively with overall firm capital levels should have higher discount rates than lines of business which co-vary negatively. Their work suggests that in the presence of financing imperfections, the optimal discount rate will depend not only upon the economy-wide systematic risks, but will also include a firm and line specific adjustment determined by how the losses underwritten on a particular line of business are expected to correlate with the internal capital levels of the firm. Future research validating (or rejecting) this hypothesis would greatly increase our understanding about how intermediaries price their products and also about the sources of friction in insurance markets.

19.5 OPTION PRICING MODELS

Like options, insurance policies can be thought of as derivative financial assets (contingent claims) with payments that depend upon changes in the value of other assets. Payments under primary insurance policies are triggered by changes in the value of insured assets, while reinsurance payments depend upon the experience of the primary insurer. Thus, it is natural to consider option models for pricing insurance.

The basic paradigm for pricing derivatives is the no-arbitrage principle. No arbitrage exists in perfect and frictionless markets if the payoffs on the derivative security can be replicated using existing securities with known prices. The price of the derivative is found by forming a portfolio of primitive securities whose payoffs exactly replicate the payoffs on the derivative. Since the prices of the primitive securities are assumed to be known, the price of the derivative must be exactly equal to the value of the replicating portfolio.

Financial economics theory has shown that when markets are complete and arbitrage free there exists a pseudo-probability measure, known as the *risk-neutral measure*, under which *all* uncertain cash flow streams can be priced using the risk-free rate of interest (Duffie 1996). The equal return feature is just a fiction, of course—returns on most assets, including options, are not actually equal to the risk-free rate. Rather, the risk neutral valuation technique prices securities *as if* returns were risk-free. Thus, the price of any uncertain cash flow stream can be determined by taking expectations of the future cash flows using the risk neutralized probability distribution and then discounting at the risk-free.

The discussion of option pricing models of insurance we present in this chapter parallels the evolution of the literature in which the principles of no arbitrage and risk-neutral valuation are standard assumptions. However, it should be noted that the assumptions of no-arbitrage and completeness in insurance markets are non-trivial as they imply there exists a sufficient number of linearly independent financial instruments to hedge all risks and replicate the payoffs on any insurance contract. This assumption is more realistic for some insurance products than for others. For example, the valuation of crop insurance using no-arbitrage arguments is relatively straightforward since the underlying risk (the commodity price) can be replicated using the spot markets and existing traded securities such as futures and options. Identifying the set of securities which completes the market for other insurance products is more difficult and suggests a possible limitation of this literature as well as offering opportunities for future research. For example, the literature on incomplete markets has received little attention in the context of insurance financial pricing.

19.5.1 Basic Option Models In Insurance

Single period option models provide some important insights into insurance pricing.[10] A simple example is the pricing of excess of loss reinsurance on a portfolio of primary insurance policies which is sufficiently large and has loss severity sufficiently small so that the evolution of claim costs can be approximated by a Brownian motion process. Consider such an excess of loss reinsurance agreement in which the reinsurer agrees to pay the losses of the primary insurer in the event these losses exceed a fixed retention amount M up to a maximum limit of U. In this case, the insurance policy is a call option spread, paying {Max[0, $Y - M$] – Max[0, $Y - U$]} at maturity, where Y = losses. Under the appropriate conditions, the Black-Scholes approach leads to the following formula for the reinsurance premium:

$$P_R = e^{-r_f\tau}\int_M^U (X-M)\frac{1}{X\sigma\sqrt{2\pi}}e^{-\frac{1}{2}\left(\frac{\ln X-\mu}{\sigma}\right)^2}dX + [M-U]\left[1-N\left(\frac{\ln U-\mu}{\sigma}\right)\right] \tag{15}$$

where $\mu = r_f - \sigma^2/2$ and N(·) is the standard normal distribution function.

Another application of option modeling in insurance is to analyze insolvency risk. This application utilizes the put-call parity formula:

$$A = C(A,L,\tau) + [Le^{-r_f\tau} - P(A,L,\tau)] \tag{16}$$

where A = the value of firm assets,
L = the value of firm liabilities,
$C(A, L, \tau)$ = a call option on asset A, with striking price L, and time to maturity τ, and
$P(A, L, \tau)$ = a put option on asset A, with striking price L and time to maturity τ.

The options are assumed to be European options, implying that they can only be exercised at the maturity date. The option model of the firm expresses the ownership interest as the value of the call option because the owners have the right to receive the residual value of the firm at the expiration date. If $A > L$ at that date, the owners pay off the liabilities and receive the amount $A - L$. If $A < L$, the owners default,

[10] Relatively early articles using single period option models to study insurance problems include Merton (1978), Doherty and Garven (1986) and Cummins (1988).

turning the firms assets over to the debt holders. The value of the policyholders' interest in the firm (i.e., the fair value of the insurance at any time prior to the option exercise data) is given by the bracketed expression in (16), the riskless present value of liabilities minus the put value. The put represents a discount in the price of insurance to reflect the expected value of the owners' option to default if $A < L$ and is called the *insolvency put.*[11] Thus, the fair price of insurance is the riskless present value of losses less the insolvency put.

Basic option models have some limitations that restrict their applicability to many real world insurance problems.[12] Three examples are: (1) The models are restricted to a single payoff, even though most real-world property-liability policies have multiple cash flows. (2) There is only one class of liabilities, whereas most insurers write multiple lines of insurance. And (3) they require that the optioned variable be continuous. Thus, discrete jumps in loss values are ruled out. To relax the multiple period assumption, it would be possible to adapt other types of financial models such as the *compound options model* discussed in Geske (1977, 1979) or perhaps a coupon bond model. In the following sections, we discuss some attempts to generalize the models to incorporate multiple classes of liabilities and jump processes.

19.5.2 A Multi-Class Option Model

Because most insurers are multiple-line operations, it is of interest to extend the basic insurance option model to the case of multiple liabilities (Cummins and Danzon 1997, Phillips, Cummins, and Allen 1998). To conserve notation, the model is derived with two liability classes. Assume that insurer assets and liabilities follow diffusion processes:

$$dA = \mu_A A dt + \sigma_A A dz_A$$

$$dL_1 = \mu_{L_1} L_1 dt + \sigma_{L_1} L_1 dz_{L_1} \tag{17}$$

$$dL_2 = \mu_{L_2} L_2 dt + \sigma_{L_2} L_2 dz_{L_2}$$

where A, L_1, L_2 = market values of assets and liabilities (classes 1 and 2),
μ_A, σ_A = drift and diffusion parameters for assets,

[11] Cummins (1988) uses the put-call parity relationship to obtain the premium for guaranty insurance as the value of the put, $P(A, L, \tau)$.

[12] Nevertheless, the simple option models may perform better than might be expected. D'Arcy and Garven (1990) tested the performance of several financial pricing models in explaining actual underwriting profit margins over a sixty year period ending in 1985. They found that the most accurate models were basic option pricing models (Doherty and Garven 1986, Cummins 1988) and an industry rule of thumb model, the total return model. The insurance CAPM and the NPV models did not perform as well as the option and total return models.

μ_{Li}, σ_{Li} = drift and diffusion parameters for liability class i, $i = 1, 2$, and
dz_A, dz_{L1}, dz_{L2} = increments of the Brownian motion processes for the asset and liability classes 1 and 2.

The Brownian processes are related as follows: $dz_A\, dz_{L1} = \rho_{A1}\, dt$, $dz_A\, dz_{L2} = \rho_{A2}\, dt$, $dz_{L1}\, dz_{L2} = \rho_{12}\, dt$, where ρ_{Ai}, $i = 1,2$, = instantaneous correlation coefficients between the Brownian processes for assets and liability classes 1 and 2, respectively, and ρ_{12} = the instantaneous correlation coefficient for liability classes 1 and 2.

Both assets and liabilities are assumed to be priced according to an asset pricing model, such as the inter-temporal capital asset pricing model (ICAPM), implying the following return relationships:

$\mu_A = r_f + \pi_A$, for assets, and
$\mu_{Li} = r_{Li} + \pi_{Li}$, for liability classes $i = 1, 2$.

where r_{Li} = the inflation rate in liability class i, and
π_j = the market risk premium for asset $j = A, L_1, L_2$.

The Fisher relationship is assumed to hold so that $r_f = r + r_I$, where r = the real rate of interest and r_I = economy-wide rate of anticipated inflation. The economy-wide rate of inflation will not in general equal the inflation rates on the two classes of insurance liabilities. If assets (and liabilities) are priced according to the ICAPM, the risk premium would be:[13]

$$\pi_j = \rho_{jm}(\sigma_j / \sigma_m)[\mu_m - r_f]$$

where μ_m, σ_m = the drift and diffusion parameters of the Brownian motion process for the market portfolio, and
ρ_{jm} = the correlation coefficient between the Brownian motion process for asset j and that for the market portfolio.

The value of an option on the two-liability insurance company can be written as $P(A, L_1, L_2, \tau)$, where τ = time to expiration of the option. Differentiating P using Ito's lemma and invoking the ICAPM pricing relationships for assets and liabilities yields the following differential equation:

$$Pr_f = r_f P_A A + r_{L_1} P_{L_1} L_1 + r_{L_2} P_{L_2} L_2 - P_\tau + \frac{1}{2}\sigma_A^2 P_{AA} A^2 + \frac{1}{2}\sigma_{L_1}^2 L_1^2 P_{L_1 L_1} + \frac{1}{2}\sigma_{L_2}^2 P_{L_2 L_2} L_2^2 + P_{AL_1} A L_1 \sigma_{A1} + P_{AL_2} A L_2 \sigma_{A2} + P_{L_1 L_2} \sigma_{12} L_1 L_2 \qquad (18)$$

[13] Alternatively, the risk premium could be defined using the consumption CAPM (Breedon 1979). The consumption CAPM assumes risk premia are related to the rate of return on aggregate real consumption instead of assuming that asset risk premia are related to movements in securities markets. Empirical tests of the consumption CAPM, however, suggest the model does no better explaining security returns than

Risk and the drift parameters (μ_j) have been eliminated by using the ICAPM and taking expectations. This also could be done by using a hedging argument, provided that appropriate hedging assets are available.

The next step is to use the homogeneity property of the option model to express the model in terms of the asset-to-liability ratio x, the option value-to-liability ratio $p = P/L$, and the liability proportions $w_1 = L_1/L$ and $w_2 = L_2/L$, where $x = A/L$ and $L = L_1 + L_2$. The result is the following differential equation:

$$pr_n = xp_x r_n - p_\tau + \frac{1}{2}x^2 p_{xx}\sigma_n^2 \tag{19}$$

where $r_n = r_f - w_1 r_{L1} - w_2 r_{L2}$,

$\sigma_n^2 = \sigma_A^2 + w_1^2\sigma_{L1}^2 + w_2^2\sigma_{L2}^2 - 2w_1\sigma_{A1} - 2w_2\sigma_{A2} + 2w_1w_2\sigma_{12}$,

σ_j^2 = the diffusion parameter for process j ($j = A$ = assets, $j = L1, L2$ = liability classes 1 and 2), and

σ_{jk} = the covariance parameter for processes j and k, A = assets, 1,2 = classes 1 and 2.

Equation (19) is the standard Black-Scholes differential equation, where the optioned asset is the asset-to-liability ratio (x).

This model can be used to price various contingent claims on the insurer by solving the equation subject to the appropriate boundary conditions. For example, the call option $c(x, 1, \tau)$ = the value of owners' equity, is the solution to equation (19) with boundary condition $c(x, 1, 0) = \text{Max}(x - 1, 0)$. The put option $g(x, 1, \tau)$ = the guaranty fund premium is the solution of (19) with boundary condition $g(x, 1, 0) = \text{Max}(1 - x, 0)$. The value of policy liabilities is obtained from the parity relationship as $b(x, 1, \tau) = \exp(-r\tau) - g(x, 1, \tau)$. The striking price in each case is equal to 1 because of the normalization of asset and option values by L. The option values are given by the usual Black-Scholes call and put option formulas (see Ingersoll (1987)).[14]

19.5.3 Implications of the Multi-Class Model

A number of interesting implications about insurance markets can be gleaned from equation (19). For example, the equation reveals that a portfolio effect exists for insurers that write multiple policies or multiple lines. To be specific, assume the existence of two insurers, with assets A_i, liabilities L_i, and risk parameters σ_i, $i = 1, 2$. The put values for the two insurers separately are $g_i(A_i, L_i, \tau)$, $i = 1, 2$. Now suppose that the two companies are merged, with no change in the asset or liability parameters. Assuming there is no correlation between the asset and liability processes and the correla-

does the traditional CAPM (Breeden, Gibbons, and Litzenberger 1989). Thus, the value of using the consumption CAPM in insurance pricing is an open question.

[14] Using the homogeneity property, the options on x can be rescaled in dollars by multiplying by L.

tion coefficient between the liability processes ρ_{12} is not equal to one, it is easy to show the put value for the merged insurer, $g(A_1 + A_2, L_1 + L_2, \tau)$ must be less than or equal to the put values of the two insurers separately owing to the convexity of European puts (Merton 1973). Intuitively, the portfolio of puts from the separate insurers is worth at least as much as the put on the portfolio because situations exist where one of the individual puts finishes in the money but the portfolio does not. Thus, equation (19) implies that value is created by pooling different classes of risks in a portfolio and multiple line insurers have an advantage over mono-line insurers in that they can offer equally safe insurance with less capital as long as the liability processes are not perfectly correlated

The multi-class option model has also been used by Cummins and Danzon (1997) to gain some insights into the supply of insurance. They consider a company which has an existing portfolio of policies L_1 with one year until maturity. Its assets are A_1, and its existing portfolio will pay no additional premiums. The company has the opportunity to write a new block of policies, L_2. To write the new policies, it may have to issue new equity. The company is seeking a strategy for issuing new equity and pricing the new policies.

Assuming that markets are efficient and that the policyholders know the characteristics of insurers, pricing will depend upon the *liquidation rule*, i.e., the rule governing the disposition of the company's assets in the event of insolvency. Assume that the liquidation rule compensates policyholders in proportion to the nominal value of their claims against the company, so that policy class i obtains proportion $w_i = L_i/(L_1 + L_2)$ of assets.[15] Then, the fair premium for the new policyholders is: $L_2\,[\exp(-r\tau) - w_2 g_S(x, \tau)]$, where $g_S(x, \tau)$ = the put option on the company after the new policies and new equity are issued and $x = (A_1 + A_2)/(L_1 + L_2)$.

Because the pricing rule of the new policyholders is satisfied for a wide range of x values, the amount of the equity issue is indeterminate unless additional structure is imposed on the problem. For example, equity owners could gain by issuing the new policies and obtaining little or no new equity. This would expropriate value from the existing (class 1) policyholders without affecting the new policyholders, who pay the fair value for their coverage. In a competitive, efficient market, it is unlikely that the equity owners would be able to gain by expropriation. Expropriating value from the old policyholders would adversely affect the firm's reputation and its future cash flows. For example, the new policyholders might not be willing to pay the "fair value" if it appears that the owners have a history of expropriating wealth from policyholders by changing the capital structure or risk characteristics of the firm.

Assume that the firm's objective is for the value of equity after the equity/policy issue to be at least as large as the sum of its equity before the equity/policy issue and the amount of new capital raised (E), i.e.,

[15] This is consistent with the way insurance insolvencies are handled in practice (National Association of Insurance Commissioners 1993).

$$C_s(A_1 + A_2, L_1 + L_2, \tau) \geq C_1(A_1, L_1, \tau) + E \tag{20a}$$

Substituting for the value of the call options on the both sides of the inequality yields:

$$\begin{aligned} &A_1 + A_2 - (L_1 + L_2)e^{-r\tau} + (L_1 + L_2)p(x,\tau) \geq A_1 - L_1 e^{-r\tau} + L_1 p_1(x_1,\tau) + E \\ &A_2 - L_2[e^{-r\tau} - p(x,\tau)] + L_1[p(x,\tau) - p_1(x_1,\tau)] \geq E \end{aligned} \tag{20b}$$

Focusing on the second line in (20b), it should be clear that the premium of the new policyholders is (−1 times) the first bracketed expression on the left hand side of the inequality sign. The difference between A_2 and the premium must equal the new equity (E) since there is no other source of funds. Thus, the condition for writing the policies reduces to the following:

$$p(x,\tau;\sigma^2) - p(x_1,\tau;\sigma_1^2) \geq 0 \tag{21}$$

where σ_1^2, σ^2 = the risk parameters of the firm before and after the policy issue.

In general, if the firm is safer after the new policies are issued, i.e., if $p(x, \tau, \sigma^2) < p(x_1, \tau, \sigma_1^2)$, the stockholders will lose money on the transaction.[16] They will gain if the firm is more risky following the policy issue, so that $p(x, \tau, \sigma^2) > p(x_1, \tau, \sigma_1^2)$. Expression (20a) is satisfied as an equality only if the value of the put (per dollar of liabilities) is the same before and after the policy issue.

Unless the new policies are unusually risky or highly correlated with the old policies, the risk parameter of the firm after the policies are issued will be less than it was before due to the diversification effect. Since $\partial p(x, \tau)/\partial\sigma > 0$ and $\partial p(x, \tau)/\partial x < 0$, this implies that the firm can operate at a lower leverage ratio without expropriating value from the old policyholders.

This model may help to explain market behavior observed during insurance price and availability crises. For example, assume that the risk of policy class 2 is sufficiently high that $\sigma^2 > \sigma_1^2$. Then, in order to avoid expropriation, the leverage ratio must increase, leading to higher costs for the new policies. If there is an optimal leverage ratio (or range) and unexpected losses reduce the ratio to a suboptimal level, it may be difficult to restore the optimal ratio immediately. Expressions (20a), (20b), and (21) imply that the firm cannot raise the ratio without incurring a capital loss unless it charges more than the optimal premium to the new policyholders. Writing more business at a suboptimal leverage ratio may affect the reputation of the firm and therefore dampen future cash flows. Thus, the firm would prefer to write business at higher-than-market prices even if this means reducing its volume.[17]

[16] The put value is directly related to risk, i.e., $\partial p/\partial\sigma > 0$. The comparative statics of the Black-Scholes model are discussed in Ingersoll (1987).

[17] Some restriction on entry is necessary in order for firms to restore optimal leverage ratios by writing at higher-than-fair prices. New entry may be difficult in lines such as liability insurance due to information asymmetries, regulation, and other market imperfections.

The multi-class options model also has implications for the price of insurance. Consistent with the basic options model, the multi-class model also suggests that the price will be inversely related to the value of the insolvency put, i.e., safer firms should command higher prices. Empirical evidence that insurance prices are inversely related to the expected policyholder costs of insolvency is provided by Sommer (1996), Cummins and Danzon (1997), and Phillips, Cummins, and Allen (PCA) (1998).

19.5.4 Option Models and the Allocation of Equity Capital

A recent topic that has been addressed by several papers in the actuarial and financial literature is the allocation of equity capital (surplus) by line of business (e.g., Kneuer 1987, Butsic 1999, Merton and Perold 1993, Cummins, Phillips, and Allen 1998, Perold 1999, Myers and Read 1999, Cummins 2000). The usual objective in capital allocation is to assess a cost of capital charge to each line based upon the amount of capital assigned to the line and the riskiness of the line. The allocation of capital is motivated by the observation that holding capital in a financial institution is costly due to regulation, taxation, and agency costs. The general argument is that lines which consume more capital should bear a higher proportion of the firm's overall cost of capital than lines which consume less capital. Capital consumption is determined by the impact of the line of business on the insurer's insolvency put option.

In capital allocation, a typical objective is to attain a specified target level of the expected policyholder deficit (EPD) or insolvency put option. E.g., a firm may want to have an insolvency put value of no more than 5 percent of liabilities. The allocation of capital among lines in the multiple line firm is problematical because writing multiple lines leads to diversification effects whereby the amount of capital needed to attain the EPD target in the multiple line firm will be less than the sum of the capital needed to attain the target if each line were operated as a separate or "stand-alone" firm. The impact of diversification is non-linear in the option modeling context, and it is not obvious how to allocate the diversification effect.

Merton and Perold (1999) and Perold (1999) propose a marginal approach to allocating capital. To facilitate the discussion of their methodology, we consider a firm with three lines of business—labeled lines 1, 2, and 3. We assume that the multi-class option model presented in the preceding section is used in conducting the capital allocation. In this context, the M-P method of capital allocation is conducted in two steps: (1) Calculate the equity capital required to obtain the EPD target by firms that combine two of the businesses. There are three possible combinations: businesses 1&2, businesses 1&3, and businesses 2&3. (2) Calculate the marginal capital required to attain the target when the excluded business is added to the two-business firms, i.e., the marginal capital required if a firm consisting of two businesses were to add the third business. The capital allocated to a given business is equal to the marginal capital required when it is added to the appropriate two-business firm. Because the calculation is made for each two firm combination, the method provides a unique capital allocation for each of the business lines comprising the firm.[18]

Merton and Perold (1993) argue that capital allocations based on stand-alone capital are likely to lead to incorrect decisions about the projects undertaken by the firm and the performance evaluation of lines of business. They also argue that allocating all capital among lines may lead to the rejection of positive net present value projects. Their view is that the unallocated capital should be held at the "corporate" level rather than being charged to any specific division.

An alternative to the Merton and Perold approach which does allocate 100 percent of capital has been proposed by Myers and Read (M-R) (1999). They also use an option pricing model to allocate capital but reach different conclusions from Merton and Perold. Whereas Merton and Perold allocate capital at the margin by adding entire lines or division to the firm (a *macro* marginal allocation), Myers and Read allocate capital by determining the effect of very small changes in loss liabilities for each line of business (a *micro* marginal allocation). Myers and Read allocate capital by differentiating the insolvency put with respect to the amount of liabilities resulting from each line of business, essentially deriving the effect on the put of infinitesimal changes in the liabilities from each line. They argue that their approach leads to a unique allocation of the firm's entire capital across its lines of business.

Examples presented in Cummins (2000) indicate that the amounts of capital allocated to each line of business can differ *substantially* between the Merton-Perold and Myers-Read methods. Thus, the two methods will not yield the same pricing and project decisions. The Myers-Read method has considerable appeal because it avoids the problem of how to deal with the unallocated capital under the Merton-Perold approach. In addition, most decision making regarding pricing and underwriting *is* marginal in the sense of Myers and Read, i.e., typically involving very small changes to an existing portfolio. However, more research is needed to determine which model is more consistent with value maximization.

A different perspective on the multiple line firm problem is provided by Phillips, Cummins, and Allen (PCA) (1998). Unlike Merton-Perold and Myers-Read, they assume that no friction costs are present in the market for insurance. They derive the following formula for the market value of line i's claim on the insurer:

$$P_i = L_i e^{-(r_f - r_{L_i})\tau} - w_{L_i} B(A, L, \tau) \tag{22}$$

where P_i = the market value of line i's claim on the firm,
L_i = the nominal losses owed to line i,
r_f, r_{Li} = the risk-free rate and the liability inflation rate of line i,

[18] The order in which the businesses are combined into firms does not matter because all three two-business combinations are used, i.e., the allocated capital of each business is obtained on the assumption that two of the businesses have already been combined.

$w_{li} \;= L_i/L,$
A, L = total assets and total liabilities of the insurer, and
$B(A, L, \tau)$ = the insurer's overall insolvency put.

Or, in other words, the market value of line i's claim on the firm at time τ before the policy expiration date is equal to the nominal expected value of its loss liabilities at the expiration date $L_i e^{r_{L_i}\tau}$, discounted at the risk-free rate, minus the line's share of the firm's overall insolvency put option. Thus, the discount for insolvency risk in line i's claim on the firm depends upon the overall insolvency risk of the firm and not just on the line-specific levels of risk. Intuitively, this is because each line of business has access to the firm's entire capital in the event that losses are larger than expected.

One of the implications of the surplus allocation result in the PCA analysis is that the market value of the line-specific claims on the insurer should be equal after controlling for differences in line-specific growth rates and the overall risk level of the firm, regardless of differences in the risk characteristics of the individual lines of business. PCA test their theoretical prediction by comparing a measure of price for short-tail lines to the same measure for long-tail lines and show that prices are consistent with the predictions, i.e., after controlling for the overall insolvency risk of the firm and line-specific growth rates, there is no significant difference between the price measures for the short and long-tail lines.

A linkage can be developed between the PCA and the Myers-Read models of capital allocation in the presence of friction costs. That is, the price to be charged to line i would be equal to the market value of line i's claim on the firm from equation (22) plus the costs of the marginal capital that must be added to the firm to maintain a target insolvency put, where marginal capital is obtained using the formulas in Myers and Reed (1999). Further theoretical and empirical exploration of this approach could provide a new class of insurance option pricing models.

19.5.5 The Insurer as a Down-and-Out Option

One of the implications of the simple option model of the firm is that the equity owners can gain at the expense of the debt holders by increasing the risk of the firm (the derivative of a call option with respect to the risk parameter is positive). Nevertheless, in actual securities and insurance markets, stockholders usually do not exploit this feature of the call option. One way to explain this is through reputational arguments, as suggested above. Another approach is to examine penalties and restrictions that might be imposed on firms adopting expropriative strategies.

One type of restriction that is often used in bond markets is the safety covenant. For example, the bond agreement may specify that the firm will be reorganized if its value ever drops to a specified level. Although insurance contracts usually do not include safety covenants, regulation has a similar effect. Specifically, under the U.S. risk-based capital system, regulators are required to seize an insurer if its equity capital falls below a specified level $K > 0$ (see Cummins, Harrington, and Niehaus 1994). This regulatory "option" terminates the equity holders' claim in the firm if the difference between assets and liabilities ever reaches the boundary. Because the chance of reaching the boundary is an increasing function of risk, the risk-based capital system changes equity owner incentives with regard to risk-taking.

Risk-based capital can be modeled using a type of option known as the *down-and-out option* (see Merton 1973, Cox and Rubenstein 1985). Let $W(A, L, \tau)$ equal the value of a down-and-out call option on an insurer with assets A and face value of liabilities L. The time-to-expiration of the option is τ. Prior to τ if the value of the assets ever reaches the *knock-out boundary* $K = b\,L\exp(-\eta\tau)$, the stockholders' interest in the firm is terminated and the assets revert to the debt holders, where b and η are constants.

To analyze the insurance case, assume that $\eta = 0$. Then the knock-out boundary is constant, and the value of the firm reverts to the debt holders if assets fall to $b\,L$. Also assume that the call option has an infinite life, i.e., $\tau = \infty$.[19] The formula for the infinite down-and-out call is:

$$W(A,L) = A - bL\left(\frac{A}{bL}\right)^{-2r_f/\sigma^2} \tag{23}$$

where σ^2 = the dispersion parameter of the insurer. Because the value of an infinite-lived conventional call option equals the value of the assets (the value of an infinite-lived conventional put is zero), equation (23) implies that the value of the firm's debt is $D(A, L) = bL(A/bL)^{-\gamma}$, where $\gamma = 2r_f/\sigma^2$.

The effects of changes in risk on the equity and debt of the down-and-out firm are as follows:

$$\frac{\partial W}{\partial \sigma^2} = -\frac{\partial D}{\partial \sigma^2} = -bL\ln\left(\frac{bL}{A}\right)\left(-\frac{2r_f}{\sigma^4}\right) \tag{24}$$

Expression (24) is < 0 if $bL < A$. Thus, increases in risk reduce the equity holders' share of the value of the firm and increase the debt holders' share. Equity holders have an incentive not to increase risk because this increases the chance that their share in the firm will be forfeited to the debt holders due to the knock-out feature. This provides a useful model of the value of the firm under solvency regulation.

Like the standard Black-Scholes model, the down-and-out option can be generalized to multiple asset and liability classes. For one asset class and two types of liabilities, the value of the down-and-out option is given by equation (23), with dispersion parameter σ_n^2 (defined following equation (19)).

[19] These assumptions are used to simplify the discussion. A closed form solution exists for finite-lived down-and-out options with $\eta > 0$. See Cox and Rubenstein (1985, p. 410).

If the liquidation rule allocates assets in proportion to nominal liabilities, the analysis of the firm's decision to accept new business is similar to the multi-variate Black-Scholes analysis discussed above. The firm will issue new business provided that the equity value of the firm after the policy (and stock) issue is greater than the value of the firm before the issue plus the amount of new capital raised. The condition is expressed as follows:

$$W(A_1 + A_2, L_1 + L_2) - W(A_1, L_1) \geq E$$

$$A_2 - bL_2\left(\frac{x}{b}\right)^{-2r_f/\sigma^2} - bL_1\left[x^{-2r_f/\sigma^2} - x_1^{-2r_f/\sigma_1^2}\right] \geq E \tag{25}$$

where $x = (A_1 + A_2)/(L_1 + L_2)$,
$x_1 = A_1/L_1$,
σ^2 = dispersion parameter after the policy issue, and
σ_1^2 = dispersion parameter before the policy issue.

Since new debt holders will pay the fair value of their coverage, there is neither a gain nor a loss in equity if the term in brackets in (25) is equal to zero. The dispersion of the firm typically will be lower following the policy issue. Thus, the firm should be able to operate at a lower leverage ratio after issuing new policies. The down-and-out model provides an alternative options interpretation of the insurance firm which may provide a better description of observed insurer behavior than the Black-Scholes model.

19.6 PRICING CAT CALL SPREADS AND BONDS

A number of new financial instruments have been introduced recently to accomplish the securitization of insurance risk. The securitization process involves the development of financial instruments whose payoffs are triggered by losses from hurricanes, earthquakes, oil spills and other contingent events traditionally financed through insurance. The most prominent insurance derivatives are catastrophic risk (CAT) call spreads and bonds, where the payoffs are triggered by losses from property catastrophes. CAT call spreads are option contracts that pay off on the basis of an industry loss index, while the payoff on most CAT bonds is triggered by the losses of the specific insurer issuing the bonds.

CAT futures were first introduced by the Chicago Board of Trade (CBOT) in 1992, call spreads were introduced in 1993, and a major design change was implemented in 1995. We abstract from most of the institutional details of the CBOT contracts and focus instead on the key mathematical features that enter into the pricing of this type of contract. Define an industry loss index, *I*, which is based on the value of losses from catastrophic events over a clearly defined period of time. For the CBOT contracts, the loss index is compiled by Property Claims Services (PCS), a statistical agent sponsored by the insurance industry, based on surveys of insurers following property catastrophes. The index is equal to the insured catastrophic property loss divided by $100 million, e.g., a $2 billion event would have an index value of 20. The CBOT securities are call spreads on the index, so that the payoff is defined as: $P = \text{Max}[0, I\text{-}M] - \text{Max}[0, I\text{-}U]$, where M = the lower strike price and U = the upper strike price of the option. E.g., a 20/40 spread would be triggered by an industry-wide loss of > $2 billion and pay a maximum of 20 points for losses ≥$4 billion, with each point worth $200. The pricing of CBOT-type contracts has been investigated by Cummins and Geman (1995). They model the stochastic process representing CAT losses as having a continuous component, modeled as a geometric Brownian motion process, and a discrete component based on a Poisson jump model. They do not find a closed form expression for the option price but are able to price the contracts using Monte Carlo simulations.

To develop a more general model of CAT options, it would be necessary to address the problem of incomplete markets. Naik and Lee (1990) show that when jump risk is systematic (i.e., correlated with the market portfolio), the market is incomplete. Consequently, risk-neutral valuation techniques cannot be applied without imposing additional restrictions such as constant jump magnitudes (as in Cummins and Geman 1995) and non-systematic jump risk (as in Merton 1978). If such restrictions are unrealistic, it is necessary to resort to equilibrium pricing, resulting in utility dependent option values. Insurance pricing with jumps in the incomplete markets setting is an important area for future research.[20]

To price CAT bonds, we adopt Merton's (1978) approach to the incomplete markets problem, i.e., the assumption that catastrophic risk is non-systematic.[21] We again abstract from the institutional details and focus primarily on the mathematical structure. CAT bonds are debt instruments issued by an insurer and sold to investors. The investors contribute capital in exchange for the bonds. The capital is placed in a single purpose reinsurer (SPR) that exists solely to handle the CAT bond issue. The SPR is set up in the form of a trust that holds the proceeds of the bond issue. The bonds are invested in safe securities such as Treasury bonds. Because of the formation of the trust and the investment of proceeds in low risk securities, the SPR is virtually free of credit risk. The insurer agrees to pay interest on the bonds. However, repayment of principal is contingent on the insured event.[22] If the contingent event occurs, the bond covenant permits the insurer to withdraw funds from the trust

[20] Chang (1995) has developed an option pricing model incorporating jumps in both complete and incomplete markets settings.

[21] Evidence that property catastrophe losses are not correlated with returns on the stock market is provided in Litzenberger, Beaglehole, and Reynolds (1996) and Canter, Cole, and Sandor (1997).

[22] For example, the bond may call for full repayment of principal unless a hurricane occurs in a specified geographical region such as Florida that satisfies certain severity criteria such as the amount of insured property loss and/or physical severity criteria such as the Saffir-Simpson rating of the storm.

to pay losses arising from the event; and the bond holders forfeit some or all of their principal.

Because of the assumption that CAT risk is uncorrelated with the stock market, CAT bonds can be considered *zero-beta securities*. The zero-beta feature also suggests a simple pricing model for these securities. Specifically, in asset pricing theory, zero-beta securities should earn the risk-free rate. However, because there is some probability that the principal will not be repaid, the bond coupon rate on these securities should be sufficient to deliver the risk-free rate to investors after taking into account the potential loss of principal. Assuming a one-period bond, this suggests the following pricing model:

$$P(1+r_f) = P(1+r_c - \lambda) \tag{26}$$

where P = the bond principal,
r_c = the coupon rate on the bond, and
λ = the expected loss of principal due to an insured event expressed as a proportion of principal.

It is easy to see that the coupon rate should be: $r_c = r_f + \lambda$. Thus, to price the bond, one needs to estimate the expected loss from the contingent event.

Cummins, Lewis, and Phillips (CLP) (1999) provide an estimate of λ based upon the frequency and severity of hurricanes and earthquakes using both historical loss data provided by PCS and simulated losses from Risk Management Solutions (RMS), a modeling firm specializing in the simulation of catastrophic events. They estimate the expected loss for a contract covering the layer from \$25 to \$50 billion dollars in total industry losses to range from less than 1 percent to 2.4 percent, depending on the probability distributions selected to model the frequency and severity distributions and the data source (PCS or RMS). Thus, a CAT bond covering losses in this layer might be issued at the Treasury rate plus a maximum of 240 basis points. Actual CAT bond issues have generally been sold at higher margins above the Treasury rate, although the risk premia have declined over time as investors have become more familiar with these bonds.

19.7 CONTINUOUS TIME DISCOUNTED CASH FLOW MODELS

19.7.1 Certainty Model

Continuous time models for insurance pricing have been developed by Kraus and Ross (KR) (1982) and Cummins (1988). As an introduction, consider the Kraus-Ross continuous time model under conditions of certainty.

To simplify the discussion, assume that the current value of losses is determined by a draw from a random process at time 0. Loss payments occur at instantaneous rate θ, while loss inflation is at exponential rate ρ, and discounting is at rate r_f. The differential equation for the rate of change in outstanding losses at time t, in the absence of inflation, is: $dC_t/dt = -\theta C_t$. Solving this equation for C_t yields the amount of unpaid claims at any given time (the reserve): $C_t = C_0\, e^{-\theta t}$. Thus, the assumption is that the claims runoff follows an exponential decay process with average time to payout = $1/\theta$.

Considering inflation (π), the rate of claim outflow at any given time is: $L_t = \theta C_t e^{\pi t}$. The premium is the present value of losses, obtained as follows:

$$P = \int_0^\infty L_t e^{-r_f t} dt = \int_0^\infty \theta C_0 e^{(\pi-\theta-r_f)t} dt = \frac{\theta C_0}{r_f + \theta - \pi} \tag{27}$$

In (27), π could be >, =, or < economy-wide inflation. The model also can be used to estimate the market value of reserves, R_τ:

$$R_\tau = \int_\tau^\infty \theta L_0 e^{-(\theta+r_f-\pi)t} dt = \frac{\theta L_0}{\theta + r_f - \pi} e^{-(\theta+r_f-\pi)\tau} \tag{28}$$

19.7.2 Uncertainty Models

Kraus and Ross also introduce a continuous time model under uncertainty. This model is based on arbitrage pricing theory (APT). The KR model allows for market-related uncertainty in both frequency and severity.

The following differential equation governs the claims process: $dC/dt = \alpha_t - \theta C_t$, where α_t = accident frequency. The frequency process affects the evolution of outstanding claims for a period of length T (the policy period). After that point, no new claims can be filed. During the entire period (0 to ∞) claims inflation takes place according to the price index q_t. The parameters α_t and q_t are governed by the k economic factors of arbitrage pricing theory. These factors are modeled as diffusion processes:

$$dx_i = m_i x_i dt + \sigma_i x_i dz_i, \quad i = 1, 2, \ldots, k. \tag{29}$$

The parameters are log-linear functions of the factors, e.g.:

$$\log(q) = \sum_{i=1}^{k} q_i \log(x_i) + \log(q_0) \tag{30}$$

where q_0 = the price level of the average claim at policy inception.

Arbitrage pricing theory implies that the value of outstanding claims at any time t, $V(x, C, t)$, where x is the vector consisting of the x_i, is governed by the following differential equation:

$$E\left[\frac{dV}{V}\right]+\left[\frac{\theta qC}{V}-r_f\right]dt=\sum_{i=1}^{k}\lambda_i\sigma_i\left[Cov\left(\frac{dV}{V},\frac{dx_i}{x_i}\right)\Big/Var\left(\frac{dx_i}{x_i}\right)\right]dt \tag{31}$$

where λ_i = the market price of risk for factor $i = (r_{mi} - r_f)/\sigma_i$, and
r_{mi} = the market return on a portfolio that is perfectly correlated with the ith risk factor.

The premium formula is obtained by applying the multivariate version of Ito's lemma (see Ingersoll 1987) and then solving the resulting differential equation. The formula is:

$$P=\left(\frac{\theta\alpha_0 q_0 L_0}{\rho+\theta}\right)\left[\frac{1-e^{-\rho_\alpha\tau}}{\rho}\right] \tag{32}$$

where $\rho = r_f - \pi - \Sigma_i\, \lambda_i\sigma_i q_i$,
$\rho_\alpha = r_f - \pi_\alpha - \Sigma_i\, \lambda_i\sigma_i(q_i + \alpha_i)$,
$\pi = \Sigma_i\, [.5\sigma^2 q_i(q_i - 1) + q_i m_i]$,
$\pi_\alpha = \Sigma_i\, [.5\sigma^2(\alpha_i + q_i(\alpha_i + q_i - 1) + (\alpha_i + q_i)m_i]$.

The premium given by (32) is similar to the premium for the certainty case except for the presence of the market risk loadings (λ_i terms) in the denominator. These loadings are the company's reward for bearing systematic risk. The α_i and q_i are the "beta coefficients" of the model.

For the company to receive a positive reward for risk bearing, the risk loading term must be negative, i.e., losses must be negatively correlated with some of the market factors such that the net loading is < 0. The model requires estimates of the market prices of risk for the k risk factors as well as the beta coefficients for insurance. This would be difficult given the available data. Like most other financial pricing models for insurance, this model gives the price for an insurance policy that is free of default risk.

A continuous time model that prices default risk has been developed by Cummins (1988). Assets and liabilities follow geometric Brownian motion:

$$\begin{aligned} dA &= (\alpha_A A - \theta L)dt + A\sigma_A dz_A \\ dL &= (\alpha_L L - \theta L)dt + L\sigma_L dz_L \end{aligned} \tag{33}$$

where α_A, α_L = asset and liability drift parameters,
σ_A, σ_L = asset and liability risk (diffusion) parameters,
A, L = stock of assets and liabilities,
θ = the claims runoff parameter, and
$dz_A(t)$, $dz_L(t)$ = possibly correlated standard Brownian motion processes.

The asset and liability processes are related as follows: $\rho_{AL} = Cov(dz_A, dz_L)$.

The model is more realistic than the standard options model since it does not have a fixed expiration date but rather allows the liabilities to run off over an infinite time horizon, i.e., it models liabilities as a perpetuity subject to exponential decay.[23] Cummins uses the model to obtain the market value of default risk, $D(A, L)$. Using Ito's lemma to differentiate D and then using either a hedging argument or the ICAPM to eliminate the risk terms, one obtains the confluent hypergeometric differential equation. The solution is:

$$D(x) = \frac{\Gamma(2)}{\Gamma(2+a)} b^a x^{-a} e^{-b/x} M(2, 2+a, b/x) \tag{34}$$

where $a = 2(r_r + \theta)/Q$, $b = 2\theta/Q$, $Q = \sigma_A^2 + \sigma_L^2 - 2\,\sigma_A\,\sigma_L\,\rho_{AL}$, and M = Kummer's function (see Abramowitz and Stegun 1972).

This perpetuity model has significant potential for pricing blocks of policies subject to default risk. It poses easier estimation problems than the Kraus-Ross model since one need only estimate the variance and covariance parameters of assets and liabilities rather than betas and factor risk premia.

19.7.3 Pricing Multiple Claim Insurance Contracts

Shimko (1992) develops an equilibrium valuation model for insurance policies which extends the prior literature in three important ways. First, his model explicitly recognizes the non-linear payoff structures resulting from the deductibles and maximum policy limits found in many insurance policies. Second, both the frequency and severity of losses are allowed to vary systematically. By contrast, many of the option pricing models of insurance assume the liabilities of the insurer evolve as smooth geometric Brownian motion, which essentially combines these two features into one process. Third, Shimko's model allows for multiple claims over the lifetime of the policy.

Shimko assumes the claim amount C, conditional upon a claim being filed, for an individual will follow a geometric Brownian motion process:

$$dC_t = \alpha_c C_t dt + \sigma_c C_t dZ_{ct}. \tag{35}$$

To incorporate the deductible and policy limit provisions, the payoff to the policy-holder conditional upon a claim being filed at time t will equal

$$S_t = \min[\max(C_t - D, 0), M] \tag{36}$$

[23] A perpetual put option model incorporating jumps that also might be applicable to insurance pricing has been developed by Gerber and Shiu (1998).

where S_t is the payoff, D is the deductible, and M is the policy limit. The arrival of claims is modeled as a non-stationary Poisson process where the expected intensity of claims arrival is a geometric diffusion process equal to

$$d\lambda_t = \alpha_\lambda \lambda_t dt + \sigma_\lambda \lambda_t dZ_{\lambda t} \tag{37}$$

where the constant term α_λ measures the non-stochastic expected growth in claim frequency over the time period while σ_λ is the instantaneous volatility. The model allows for correlation between the claim arrival and amount processes where $dZ_{ct}dZ_{\lambda t} = \rho_{c\lambda}dt$ is the instantaneous correlation between C and λ.

To solve for the value of the insurance policy, V, Shimko considers two cases. In the first case he simplifies the problem and assumes the policy has a maximum indemnity payment M equal to positive infinity and a positive deductible D. Invoking the ICAPM equilibrium pricing relationships discussed earlier, he finds a closed form solution for the policy value V. The formula is quite complicated and therefore is not presented here. However, there is an intuitive interpretation which is useful to discuss.

The value of the policy is given by

$$V(C, \lambda, \tau; D) = \lambda W(C, \tau; D) \tag{38}$$

where W represents the expected payout by the insurance company conditional on a claim being filed by the policyholder and λ is the expected number of claims. Shimko shows that W is equal to the fair value of the cash flows needed to replicate the cash flows of the insurance contract. The replicating cash flows are as follows: (1) At the beginning of the policy period, if the claim amount is greater than the deductible, the insurer must purchase a risky perpetuity that pays Cdt and must sell a risk-free perpetuity that pays Ddt. If $C < D$ at time zero, do nothing. (2) Over the policy period the insurer must continuously revise the position. Whenever $C > D$, the insurer must go long in the risky perpetuity and short the risk-free perpetuity; otherwise hold nothing. (3) At the end of the policy period, the insurer must liquidate its positions.

To solve for the more general case when the policy includes a per-claim maximum indemnity limit, M, the revised valuation formula is[24]

$$V(C, \lambda, \tau; D, M) = \lambda W(C, \tau; D) - \lambda W(C, \tau; M + D). \tag{39}$$

The intuition behind this result is readily apparent after we rewrite equation (36) as

$$S_t = \min[\max(C_t - D, 0), M] = \max(C_t - D, 0) - \max[C_t - (D + M), 0] \tag{40}$$

[24] Readers familiar with Shimko's paper will note this formula differs from his equation for the value of the insurance policy with a maximum indemnity limit shown on page 235. The difference arises as we define the maximum indemnity payment M to be the largest payment the insurance company will make to its policyholder. This interpretation of a policy limit is standard in the insurance literature.

Thus, the payout to the policyholder is truncated from above as the policyholder takes a short position in a second insurance policy with a deducible equal to $(D + M)$, relieving the insurer from paying large losses.

The model which Shimko develops has a number of interesting implications. First, consider the case when there is no deductible, i.e., $D = 0$. In this is case, the cash flows needed to replicate the payoffs on the insurance contract are quite simple. Whenever $C > 0$ at time zero, the insurer must purchase a risky perpetuity that continuously pays λCdt over the term of the contract and will be liquidated at policy termination. The fair value of this cash flow is

$$V(C, \lambda, \tau; D = 0) = \frac{\lambda C}{\delta} - e^{-\delta\tau} \frac{\lambda C}{\delta} \tag{41}$$

where τ is the term of the insurance policy and δ is the risky discount rate. If there is no correlation between the claims arrival and/or the conditional claim amount processes and the market portfolio, the discount rate δ will only be a function of the risk-free rate of interest and the expected growth rates of the claims arrival and amount processes, α_λ and α_c. Thus, when there is no deductible and no market risk, there is no reward for underwriting risky liability payments. In addition, increases or decreases in the riskiness of the claims arrival and/or amount processes will have no effect on the fair value of the insurance policy. Only positive correlation between the loss processes and the market portfolio will be priced in the contract. Thus, In the absence of market risk, a risk premium based upon the volatility of the liability processes cannot be justified.

When a positive deductible is introduced into the model, greater levels of volatility will increase the value of the insurance contract. When both a positive deductible and a policy limit are introduced, the effect of increasing volatility on the value of the insurance contract is ambiguous. On one hand, increasing levels of volatility will increase the value of the policyholder's long position in the first risky perpetuity in (41). However, the increased volatility also makes it more likely the policy limit will be reached, increasing the value of the short perpetuity in (41). Either effect can dominate.

19.8 CONCLUSIONS

This paper discusses the principal financial pricing models that have been developed for property-liability insurance and proposes some extensions. Insurance pricing models have been developed based on the capital asset pricing model, the intertemporal capital asset pricing model, arbitrage pricing theory, and options pricing theory. The models assume either that insurance policies are priced in accordance with principles of market equilibrium or minimally that arbitrage opportunities are avoided.

Additional research is needed to develop more realistic insurance pricing models. For example, most of the models assume that interest rates are non-stochastic even though insurers face significant interest rate risk. Modeling multiple-line firms with multi-period claim runoffs also poses challenging problems. With few exceptions, existing financial models do not price the risk of insolvency. Estimation problems, especially for betas and market risk premia, are a major problem given the existing insurance data. Option models and perpetuity models may offer solutions to some of these problems, since they rely on relatively few parameters and can be modified to incorporate stochastic interest rates. However, the options models often rely upon market completeness and no-arbitrage arguments which are difficult to justify for some insurance contracts. Additional research is needed on the pricing of insurance in incomplete markets.

In addition to models now in existence, models based on multi-factor asset pricing theory (Fama and French 1993, 1996), martingale pricing (Duffie 1988), and lattice modeling (Boyle 1988) may provide promising avenues for future research. Modifications of the perfect information, perfect markets results for information asymmetries also will become increasingly important as the field continues to advance. Also, future work which incorporates frictions in capital markets (Froot and Stein 1998) may add additional insights into the behavior of prices in insurance markets. We also expect to see further advances in pricing models and concepts for CAT bonds and options as the market for these innovative products continues to develop. Finally, researchers have applied fuzzy set theory (FST) to financial pricing (e.g., Cummins and Derrig 1997, Young 1996). We did not explore this topic in the present paper because providing an explanation of fuzzy mathematics sufficient for readers to understand the application would require too much space. However, FST may be a promising approach to explore in future research because it provides a rigorous set of rules for incorporating vague or imprecise information (e.g., expert judgment, etc.) into insurance ratemaking. Thus, FST has the potential to add another dimension to the standard financial pricing techniques, which implicitly assume a degree of precision in the information used in pricing that is rarely realized in practice.

19.9 REFERENCES

Abramowitz, Milton and Irene A. Stegun (1972). *Handbook of Mathematical Functions* (New York: Dover Publications).

Biger, Nihum and Yehuda Kahane (1978). "Risk Considerations In Insurance Ratemaking," *Journal of Risk and Insurance* 45, 121–132.

Boyle, Phelim (1988). "A Lattice Framework for Option Pricing With Two State Variables," *Journal of Financial and Quantitative Analysis* 23, 1–12.

Brealey, Richard A. and Stewart C. Myers (1996). *Principles of Corporate Finance*, 5th ed. (New York: McGraw-Hill).

Breedon, D.T. (1979). "An Intertemporal Asset Pricing Model with Stochastic Investment and Consumption Opportunities," *Journal of Financial Economics* 6, 273–296.

Breedon, D.T., M.R. Gibbons and R.H. Litzenberger (1989). "Empirical Test of the Consumption-Oriented CAPM," *Journal of Finance* 44, 231–262.

Brennan, M.J. (1979). "The Pricing of Contingent Claims In Discrete Time Models," *Journal of Finance* 24, 53–68.

Butsic, Robert (1999). "Capital Allocation for Property-Liability Insurers: A Catastrophe Reinsurance Application," Casualty Actuarial Society 1999 Spring Forum, Reinsurance Call Papers, Casualty Actuarial Society, New York.

Canter, Michael S., Joseph B. Cole and Richard Sandor (1997). "Insurance Derivatives: A New Asset Class for the Capital Markets and a New Hedging Tool for the Insurance Industry," *Journal of Applied Corporate Finance* 10 (Fall), 69–83.

Chang, Carolyn W. (1995). "A No-Arbitrage Martingale Analysis for Jump-Diffusion Valuation," *Journal of Financial Research* 18, 351–381.

Cochrane, John H. (1999). "New Facts in Finance," National Bureau of Economic Research Working Paper No. W7169, Cambridge, MA.

Cooper, Robert W. (1974). *Investment Return and Property-Liability Insurance Ratemaking* (Philadelphia: S.S. Huebner Foundation, University of Pennsylvania).

Cox, John D. and Mark Rubinstein (1985). *Options Markets* (Englewood Cliffs, N.J.: Prentice-Hall).

Cummins, J. David (1988). "Risk-Based Premiums for Insurance Guaranty Funds," *Journal of Finance* 43, 823–839.

Cummins, J. David (1990). "Multi-Period Discounted Cash Flow Ratemaking Models in Property-Liability Insurance," *Journal of Risk and Insurance* 57, 79–109.

Cummins, J. David (2000). "Allocation of Capital in the Insurance Industry," *Risk Management and Insurance Review*, in press.

Cummins, J. David and Patricia M. Danzon (1997). "Price Shocks and Capital Flows in Liability Insurance." *Journal of Financial Intermediation* 6, 3–38.

Cummins, J. David and Richard A. Derrig (1988). *Classical Models of Insurance Solvency* (Norwell, MA: Kluwer Academic Publishers).

Cummins, J. David and Richard A. Derrig (1989). *Financial Models of Insurance Solvency* (Norwell, MA: Kluwer Academic Publishers).

Cummins, J. David and Richard A. Derrig (1997). "Fuzzy Financial Pricing of Property-Liability Insurance," *North American Actuarial Journal* 1, 21–40.

Cummins, J. David and Helyette Geman (1995). "Pricing Catastrophe Insurance Futures and Call Spreads: An Arbitrage Approach," *Journal of Fixed Income* 4, 46–57.

Cummins, J. David and Scott E. Harrington (1985). "Property-Liability Insurance Rate Regulation: Estimation of Underwriting Betas Using Quarterly Profit Data," *Journal of Risk and Insurance* 52, 16–43.

Cummins, J. David and Scott E. Harrington (1987). *Fair Rate of Return In Property-Liability Insurance* (Norwell, MA: Kluwer Academic Publishers).

Cummins, J. David, Scott E. Harrington and Gregory Niehaus (1994). "Risk-Based Capital Requirements for Property-Liability Insurers: A Financial Analysis." In Edward Altman and Irwin Vanderhoof, eds., *The Financial Dynamics of the Insurance Industry* (Homewood, IL: Irwin Professional Publishers, 1994).

Cummins, J. David, Christopher M. Lewis and Richard D. Phillips (1999). "Pricing Excess-of-Loss Reinsurance Contracts against Catastrophic Loss," in Kenneth Froot, ed., *The Financing of Catastrophe Risk* (Chicago: University of Chicago Press).

Cummins, J. David, Richard D. Phillips and Stephen D. Smith (1997). "Corporate Hedging in the Insurance Industry: The Use of Financial Derivatives by US Insurers." *The North American Actuarial Journal* 1, 13–49.

Cummins, J. David, Richard D. Phillips and Stephen D. Smith (2000). "Derivatives and Corporate Risk Management: Participation and Volume Decisions in the Insurance Industry," forthcoming in *Journal of Risk and Insurance*.

Cummins, J. David, Richard D. Phillips and Stephen D. Smith (2000). "Financial Risk Management in the Insurance Industry," in Georges Dionne, ed., *Handbook of Insurance* (Norwell, MA: Kluwer Academic Publishers).

D'Arcy, Stephen P. and Neil A. Doherty (1990). "Adverse Selection, Private Information, and Lowballing in Insurance Markets," *Journal of Business* 63, 145–161.

D'Arcy, Stephen P. and James R. Garven (1990). "Property-Liability Insurance Pricing Models: An Empirical Evaluation," *Journal of Risk and Insurance* 57, 391–430.

Derrig, Richard A. (1994). "Theoretical Considerations of the Effect of Federal Income Taxes on Investment Income in Property-Liability Ratemaking," *Journal of Risk and Insurance* 61, 691–709.

Doherty, Neil and James Garven (1986). "Price Regulation in Property/Liability Insurance: A Contingent Claims Approach," *Journal of Finance* 41, 1031–1050.

Duffie, Darrell (1996). *Dynamic Asset Pricing Theory* (Princeton, NJ: Princeton University Press).

Fairley, William (1979). "Investment Income and Profit Margins In Property-Liability Insurance: Theory and Empirical Tests," *Bell Journal* 10, 192–210.

Fama, Eugene F. and Kenneth R. French (1993). "Common Risk Factors in the Returns on Stock and Bonds," *Journal of Financial Economics* 33, 3–56.

Fama, Eugene F. and Kenneth R. French (1996). "The CAPM Is Wanted, Dead or Alive," *Journal of Finance.* 51, 1947–1958.

Ferrari, J. Robert (1969). "A Note on the Basic Relationship of Underwriting, Investments, Leverage and Exposure to Total Return on Owners' Equity," *Proceedings of the Casualty Actuarial Society* 55, 295–302.

Froot, Kenneth A., David S. Scharfstein and Jeremy C. Stein (1993). "Risk Management: Coordinating Corporate Investment and Financing Policies," *Journal of Finance* 48, 1629–1658.

Froot, Kenneth A. and Jeremy C. Stein (1998). "Risk Management, Capital Budgeting, and Capital Structure Policy for Financial Institutions: An Integrated Approach," *Journal of Financial Economics* 47, 55–82.

Gerber, Hans U. (1982). "On the Numerical Evaluation of the Distribution of Aggregate Claims and Its Stop-Loss Premiums," *Insurance: Mathematics and Economics* 1, 13–18.

Gerber, Hans U. and Bruno Landry (1997). "Skewness and Stock Option Prices," *North American Actuarial Journal* 1, 50–62.

Gerber, Hans U. and Elias S.W. Shiu (1998). "Pricing Perpetual Options for Jump Processes," *North American Actuarial Journal* 2, 101–107.

Geske, Robert (1977). "The Valuation of Corporate Liabilities As Compound Options," *Journal of Financial and Quantitative Analysis* 541–552.

Geske, Robert (1979). "The Valuation of Compound Options," *Journal of Financial Economics* 7, 63–81.

Goovaerts, M.J., F. de Vylder and J. Haezendonck (1984). *Insurance Premiums: Theory and Applications* (New York: North-Holland).

Hill, Raymond (1979). "Profit Regulation in Property-Liability Insurance," *Bell Journal* 10, 172–191.

Ingersoll, Jonathan E. Jr. (1987). *Theory of Financial Decision Making* (Totowa, NJ: Rowman & Littlefield).

Johnson, Norman L. and Samuel Kotz (1972). *Distributions in Statistics: Continuous Multivariate Distributions* (New York: John Wiley & Sons).

Kneuer, Paul J. (1987). "Allocation of Surplus in a Multiline Insurer," *Discussion Paper Proceedings, Casualty Actuarial Society*, 191–228.

Kraus, Alan and Stephen Ross (1982). "The Determination of Fair Profits for the Property-Liability Insurance Firm," *Journal of Finance* 33, 1015–1028.

Litzenberger, Robert H., David R. Beaglehole and Craig E. Reynolds (1996). "Assessing Catastrophe Reinsurance-linked Securities as a New Asset Class," *Journal of Portfolio Management,* 76–86.

Merton, Robert C. (1973). "Theory of Rational Option Pricing," *Bell Journal of Economics and Management Science* 4, 141–183.

Merton, Robert C. (1978). "On the Cost of Deposit Insurance When There Are Surveillance Costs," *Journal of Business* 51, 439–452.

Merton, Robert and Andre Perold (1993). "Theory of Risk Capital In Financial Firms," *Journal of Applied Corporate Finance*.

Myers, Stewart (1984). "Testimony Prepared for the Massachusetts Automobile Insurance Rate Hearings," Massachusetts Rating Bureau Filing for 1985 Automobile Rate Hearings, Boston.

Myers, Stewart and Richard Cohn (1987). "Insurance Rate Regulation and the Capital Asset Pricing Model," in J.D. Cummins and S.E. Harrington, eds., *Fair Rate of Return In Property-Liability Insurance* (Norwell, MA: Kluwer Academic Publishers).

Myers, Stewart C. and Nicholas S. Majluf (1984). "Corporate Financing and Investment Decisions When Firms Have Information That Investors Do Not Have," *Journal of Financial Economics* 13, 187–221.

Myers, Stewart C. and James A. Read, Jr. (1999). "Surplus Allocation for Insurance Companies," working paper, Massachusetts Institute of Technology, Cambridge, MA.

Naik, V. and M. Lee (1990). "General Equilibrium Pricing of Options on the Market Portfolio With Discontinuous Returns," *Review of Financial Studies* 3, 493–521.

National Association of Insurance Commissioners (1993). "Insurers Rehabilitation and Liquidation Model Act," in *Model Laws, Regulations, and Guidelines* (Kansas City, MO).

Perold, Andre F. (1999). "Capital Allocation in Financial Firms," Working Paper, Harvard University.

Phillips, Richard D., J. David Cummins and Franklin Allen (1998). "Financial Pricing of Insurance in the Multiple Line Insurance Company," *Journal of Risk and Insurance* 65, 597–636.

Santomero, Anthony M. and David F. Babbel (1997). "Financial Risk Management by Insurers: an Analysis of the Process," *Journal of Risk and Insurance* 64, 231–270.

Shimko, David C. (1992). "The Valuation of Multiple Claim Insurance Contracts," *Journal of Financial and Quantitative Analysis* 27, 229–246.

Sommer, David W. (1996). "The Impact of Firm Risk on Property-Liability Insurance Prices," *Journal of Risk and Insurance* 63, 501–514.

Staking, Kim B. and David F. Babbel (1995). "The Relation Between Capital Structure, Interest Rate Sensitivity, and Market Value in the Property-liability Insurance Industry, *Journal of Risk & Insurance* 62, 690–718.

Taylor, Greg (1994). "Fair Premium Rating Methods and the Relations Between Them," *Journal of Risk and Insurance* 61, 592–615.

Young, Virginia R. (1996). "Insurance Rate Changing: A Fuzzy Logic Approach," *Journal of Risk and Insurance* 63, 461–484.

20 Volatility and Underwriting Cycles

Scott E. Harrington and Greg Niehaus

University of South Carolina

Abstract

This paper describes and illustrates the main ideas and findings of research on the volatility and cyclical behavior of insurance prices relative to those predicted by a perfectly competitive market in long-run equilibrium. After presenting evidence that insurance market prices indeed follow a second order autoregressive process, we examine several lines of research that have tried to explain the cyclical behavior of insurance prices. Particular emphasis is given to the theoretical developments of and empirical results supporting capital shock models, which primarily explain periods of high insurance prices. We then summarize the idea that moral hazard and/or winners curse effects can explain periods of low insurance prices. Finally, the potential effects of regulation on insurance price volatility are summarized.

Keywords: Capital shocks, insurance pricing, regulation, capital market imperfections, autoregressive processes.

JEL Classification Numbers: G22, G13, G31.

20.1 INTRODUCTION

Markets for many types of property-liability insurance have exhibited soft market periods, where prices and profitability are stable or falling and coverage is readily available to consumers, and subsequent hard market periods, where prices and profits increase abruptly and less coverage is available. The mid 1980s liability insurance crisis was the most recent severe hard market. The dramatic increases in business liability insurance premiums and reductions in the supply of coverage for some sectors received enormous attention in the media and by policymakers. The mid-1980s experience also spawned extensive research on this hard market episode and the general causes of fluctuations of price and availability of coverage in insurance markets. Subsequent large catastrophe losses in the late 1980s and early 1990s has fueled

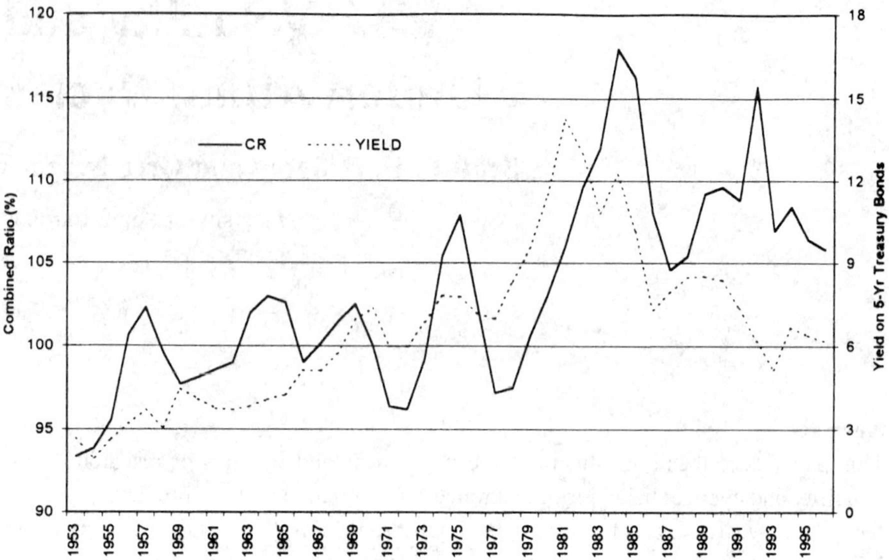

Figure 1 US Combined Ratios and 5-Year Treasury Yields: 1953–96

additional interest and research on short run dynamics of reinsurance and primary market pricing following large losses.

Conventional wisdom among many practitioners and other observers is that soft and hard markets occur in a regular cycle, commonly known as the underwriting cycle. Casual examination of aggregate US underwriting profitability over time, as measured by the combined ratio (see Figure 1), and of aggregate US premiums in relation to gross domestic product (a proxy for aggregate demand for insurance, see Figure 2) suggests material volatility with a cyclical pattern.

This paper introduces the literature on underwriting cycles and volatility in insurance prices and profits.[1] Our purpose is to describe and illustrate the main ideas and findings of research concerning the extent and causes of volatility and cycles. While most empirical research in this area focuses on the behavior of insurance prices, the underwriting cycle lore also relates to the quantity of coverage that is offered by insurers. For example, in hard market periods, coverage may even be rationed for some types of insurance. Due to data availability problems, however, predictions about quantity adjustments generally are not tested. Consistent with the literature, our review focuses on pricing issues with appropriate mention of the predictions of certain models with respect to the quantity of coverage.

[1] See Harrington and Danzon (2000) in this volume for additional discussion of the liability insurance crisis.

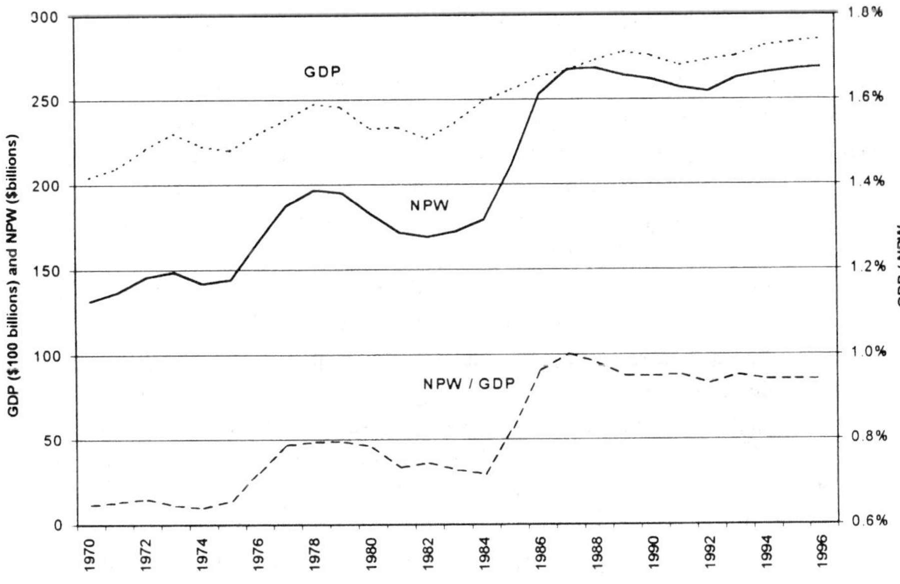

Figure 2 US Net Premiums Written and Gross Domestic Product: 1970–96

Section 20.2 provides an overview of the major determinants of insurance prices in a perfectly competitive insurance market in long-run equilibrium. Section 20.3 defines unexplained and possibly cyclical variation in prices and underwriting results compared to this benchmark. We then provide a synopsis of the evidence from simple time series models that indicates that underwriting results follow a second-order autoregressive process. We illustrate these findings using data on aggregate underwriting profits for US property-liability insurance market during the period 1955–96. We also briefly discuss several comparatively recent studies that have investigated whether underwriting results have unit roots and are cointegrated with a number of macroeconomic factors.

The growing body of theoretical and empirical work on the effects of shocks to capital on the supply of insurance is introduced in Section 20.4. Section 20.5 provides an overview of research that focuses on the extent and causes of price reductions during soft markets. Section 20.6 considers regulatory influences on volatility and cycles. Section 20.7 concludes.

20.2 THE PERFECT MARKETS MODEL

Standard financial theory predicts that in long-run equilibrium competitively determined insurance premiums, commonly known as *fair premiums*, will equal risk-adjusted discounted values of expected cash outflows for claims, sales expenses, income taxes, and any other costs, including the tax and agency costs of capital (e.g., Myers and Cohn, 1986; or, for some bells and whistles, see Doherty and Garven, 1986). We use the term *perfect markets model* to refer to this model, with the additional assumptions (see Cummins and Outreville, 1987, and Harrington and Danzon, 1994) that (1) expectations are rational (optimal) forecasts conditional on information available when policies are sold, and that (2) insurer capital is sufficient to produce a negligible level of insolvency risk.

Given this framework, volatility in insurance premiums, prices, and profit rates can be viewed as having two components: (1) volatility that can be explained by the perfect markets model, i.e., by changes in fair premiums, and (2) volatility that cannot be explained by changes in fair premiums. The perfect markets model also implies that the quantity of coverage sold will vary inversely with changes in fair premiums and directly with the demand for coverage, and that quantity will not be rationed.

To make these notions more concrete, consider a highly stylized representation of the fair premium for a given policy or group of policies at the beginning of period t:

$$P_t^f = \delta_t L_t^f + \alpha_t P_t^f + \pi_t P_t^f. \tag{1}$$

P_t^f is the fair premium. L_t^f is the rational (optimal) forecast (i.e., conditional expectation given all available information) of nominal (undiscounted) claim costs (including loss adjustment expenses) for insured events during the coverage period. The parameter δ_t is the risk-adjusted discounted value of \$1 of L_t^f, which depends on riskless spot interest rates at time t for periods over which cash flows from the policy occur and any risk premia for systematic risk associated with claim costs. The parameter α_t is the known loading for underwriting and administrative expenses paid at the beginning of the period, and π_t is the fair pre-tax profit margin that is just sufficient to compensate shareholders for tax and agency costs of capital (and expected taxes on any underwriting profits), again assuming that the amount of capital invested is sufficient to produce a negligible probability of default by the insurer.[2]

Solving (1) for P_t^f gives:

$$P_t^f = \delta_t (1 - \alpha_t - \pi_t)^{-1} L_t^f \tag{2}$$

The rational forecasts of the loss ratio (L_t^f/P_t^f) and combined ratio (loss ratio plus underwriting expense ratio) at the beginning of period t are therefore:

[2] Cummins and Phillips (2000) provides detailed discussion of insurance pricing models elsewhere in this volume.

$$LR_t^f = \delta_t^{-1}(1-\alpha_t - \pi_t) \text{ and} \tag{3}$$

$$CR_t^f = \delta_t^{-1}(1-\alpha_t - \pi_t) + \alpha_t. \tag{4}$$

Borrowing terminology from the literature on financial price volatility, expressions (2)–(4) indicate that fair premiums, expected loss ratios, and expected combined ratios vary over time in relation to the fundamental determinants of prices. These *fundamentals* include predicted claim costs and underwriting expenses, riskless interest rates, any systematic risk of claim costs and associated market risk premia, and the tax and agency costs of holding capital to bond an insurer's promise to pay claims.[3] Expense and profit loadings and predicted claims payout patterns tend to vary slowly over time, and systematic (i.e., market) claim risk may be negligible for most types of insurance (see Cummins and Harrington, 1985). As a result, short-run variation in fair premiums will be caused largely by changes in predicted claim costs and interest rates. Correspondingly, this model predicts that changes in interest rates will be the primary cause of short-run variation in underwriting profit margins. Over longer periods, changes in capital structure that alter π and changes in technology that alter α will play a more material role according to this model.

Not surprisingly, there is abundant evidence that changes in claim costs, which should be highly correlated with insurer forecasts when policies are priced, explain much of the time series variation in premiums.[4] Examples include studies of premium growth in automobile insurance (e.g., Cummins and Tennyson, 1992), medical malpractice insurance (Danzon, 1985), and workers' compensation insurance (e.g., Danzon and Harrington, 1998).[5] Also consistent with the perfect markets model, numerous studies have documented the predicted inverse relationship between interest rates and loss ratios or combined ratios (Doherty and Kang, 1988; Fields and

[3] Capital shock models (discussed in Section 20.4) suggest that capital costs per unit might vary inversely with the total level of capital. Also, models incorporating default risk suggest that, all else equal, premiums will vary directly with the total level of insurer capital. Sommer (1996) presents evidence that prices vary across insurers in relation to insolvency risk, which of course depends on the amount of capital held. Choi and Thistle (1997), however, find no long-run relationship between aggregate underwriting profit margins and the ratio of capital to assets. Also see Phillips, Cummins, and Allen (1998).

[4] Of course, it also is well known that differences in predicted claim costs across regions and risk classes explains much of the cross-sectional variability of premium rates within a given time period (see e.g., Harrington and Niehaus, 1998).

[5] Evidence indicates that a material proportion of the growth in premiums and availability problems in the 1980s was caused by growth in claim cost forecasts and uncertainty of future liability claim costs rather than by cyclical influences (Tort Policy Working Group, 1986, and Clarke, et al. 1988; Harrington, 1988; Harrington and Litan, 1988). Basic theory and numerous studies argue that increased uncertainty would be expected to lead to increases in prices needed to cover expected future costs including the cost of capital (e.g., Danzon, 1984; Doherty and Garven, 1986, Clarke, et al., 1988; and Winter, 1988). Cummins and McDonald (1991) provide evidence of increased variance in liability insurance claim cost distributions during the early 1980s. Other research argues that increased uncertainty is likely to have increased adverse selection and that the introduction of claims-made coverage and the exclusion of pollution claims in basic liability coverage were efficient methods of separating low risk and high risk buyers (Priest, 1987; also see Trebilcock, 1987). See Harrington and Danzon (2000) in this volume for further discussion.

Venezian, 1989; Smith, 1989; Haley, 1993; Grace and Hotchkiss, 1995; Choi and Thistle, 1997; also see Harrington, 1988, and Harrington and Litan, 1988). Evidence also suggests that underwriting results vary in relation to changes in the estimated market price of risk, as is predicted if claim costs load on priced risk factors in the economy (see Cagle, 1992).[6] In addition, premium levels appear to vary predictably in relation to changes in income tax treatment of insurers (see Bradford and Logue, 1996).

To be sure, even skeptics concede that fundamentals explain at least part of the variation in premiums; the key question is how much. Before turning to a discussion of evidence that is more difficult to reconcile with the model, we first provide a simple framework for understanding this evidence.

20.3 UNEXPLAINED / PREDICTABLE VARIATION IN UNDERWRITING RESULTS

Empirical Framework

Given the perfect markets framework, unexplained premium volatility can be represented as variation of actual premiums around fair premiums. Letting u_t denote any component in premiums that cannot be explained by fundamentals in period t, the actual premium can be written as:

$$P_t = P_t^f + u_t, \tag{5}$$

where, as before, P_t^f is the rational forecast of costs (see equation 2). The perfect markets model implies that u_t should be serially uncorrelated and uncorrelated with any information available at the beginning of period t, including P_t^f and past profitability. The variance of u also should be comparatively small. Under these conditions:

$$\mathrm{Var}(P_t) \cong \mathrm{Var}(P_t^f) \tag{6}$$

The hypothesis that variation in premiums is fully explained by variation in fair premiums is surely false, given real world frictions. The interesting questions are whether premiums deviate materially from levels predicted by this model, and, if so, the causes of the deviations. Depending inter alia on the sign of any non-zero covariance between u_t and current and lagged values of P_t^f and any other prior information, unexplained variation in premiums could either increase or decrease premium volatility.

Measuring and testing for unexplained volatility presents several formidable chal-

[6] Mei and Saunders (1994) provide evidence of predictable variation in risk premia for insurance stocks.

lenges. Perhaps most important, expectations and the "true" fair premium model and its parameters are unobservable to researchers. Like tests of market efficiency in financial markets, tests of the perfect markets model of insurance prices using premium data or data on loss ratios or combined ratios are necessarily tests of a joint hypothesis—that premiums are determined primarily by fundamentals and that the assumed model of fair premiums is correct.

Because data on average premiums per exposure generally are not available to researchers, most empirical analyses of volatility in insurance markets use data on loss ratios or combined ratios to control for scale effects and abstract in part from the effects of changes in claim cost forecasts over time. These underwriting profit measures reflect realized claim costs that are reported by insurers, specifically, updated forecasts of incurred losses as of the time those losses are reported. Most studies have necessarily relied on "calendar-year" data in order to obtain enough time series observations for meaningful analysis. Calendar-year losses reflect loss forecasts for accidents during the given year and revisions in loss forecasts for prior years' accidents.

To illustrate the implications of using reported losses (see Cummins and Outreville, 1987, and below for further discussion), the reported combined ratio (CR^r) can be written as the combined ratio predicted by the perfect market model (CR^f) plus two error terms:

$$CR_t^r = CR_t^f + \varepsilon_t + \phi_t, \tag{6}$$

where

$$\varepsilon_t = \frac{L_t^r - L_t^f}{P_t} \quad \text{and} \quad \phi_t = CR_t^m - CR_t^f .$$

The first error, ε, is the difference between reported losses and the rational forecast of losses (L_t^f) as a proportion of premiums. The second error, ϕ, is the difference between the expected combined ratio using L_t^f and market-determined parameters, which we denote CR_t^m, and CR_t^f (see equation 4).[7]

The perfect markets models predicts that ϕ_t is uncorrelated with prior information and that Var(ϕ) is comparatively small. Note that large variation in the rational loss forecast error, ε_t, clearly will produce large variation in reported combined ratios—even if the perfect market model holds. In addition, serial correlation between *reported* combined ratios (or loss ratios) and any other prior information could reflect accounting effects and reporting bias, such as managerial smoothing of reported losses (see Cummins and Outreville, 1987; also see Weiss, 1985, and Petroni, 1992). Serial

[7] For example, market prices could cause π (conditional on L_t^f) to differ from the value implied by the perfect markets model, which would cause CR_t^m to differ from CR_t^f.

correlation in reported underwriting profit measures also might reflect adaptive but rational updating of loss forecasts, rather than unexplained variation in premiums.

Time Series Evidence of Second-Order Autoregression in Underwriting Results

As noted in the introduction, casual observation suggests that insurance premiums are not readily explained by the perfect markets model (e.g., see Figures 1 and 2). Moreover, numerous studies document empirical regularities in underwriting profit measures that are not easily reconciled with the model's predictions. In particular, like many economic time series, numerous studies document that property-liability insurance underwriting results follow a second-order autoregressive process.[8]

This subsection briefly describes time series studies that for the most part do not attempt to explain the causes of second-order autoregression, in contrast to studies that test the predictions of alternative models, such as the capital shock model (see below). We note, however, that the distinction between these avenues of inquiry is not sharp, given that shock models predict correlation between current and past underwriting results. Following this brief description, we provide illustrative evidence of second-order autoregression in underwriting margins and describe analyses that have considered whether underwriting profit measures have unit roots and are cointegrated with interest rates and macroeconomic factors.

Time series studies of underwriting results, like many analyses of the business cycle and of long-term predictability of returns on financial assets, are inherently limited by the comparatively small number of annual observations. In addition, the types of business sold and regulatory environment in the property-liability insurance industry have changed substantially during the latter half of this century, raising serious questions about the stability of the process generating underwriting profits and the efficacy of extending the time series backwards. While some quarterly data are available since the early 1970s (see Cummins and Harrington, 1985), these data may be of limited value in analyzing long-term predictability (see, for example, the general discussion by Enders, 1995; but also see Grace and Hotchkiss, 1995, who employ quarterly data).

As a result of these problems, many studies of volatility in insurance underwriting results employ fairly crude models and statistical methods, especially studies that pre-date developments in modern time series methods. The focus of time series studies on levels or differences in underwriting profit measures, ignoring possible conditional heteroscedasticity, can be explained at least in part by these problems. The estimation of ARCH and GARCH models with annual data over several decades may be unlikely to provide material insight.[9] When considering the following evidence, it is useful to

[8] Berger (1988) shows that if industry supply depends on surplus and current profits depend on lagged premiums and quantity, then premiums follow a second-order autoregressive process.

[9] Fung, et al. (1998) estimate ARCH/GARCH in mean models of changes in by line premiums for the period 1946–1989.

keep in perspective the date that particular studies were conducted and that weak data limit the potential returns from increased methodological sophistication.

Consistent with traditional conjecture, several studies using data prior to the mid 1980s provide statistical evidence that loss ratios and reported underwriting profit margins (e.g., one minus the combined ratio) exhibit second-order autoregression that implies a cyclical period of about six years (see Venezian, 1985; Cummins and Outreville, 1987; and Doherty and Kang, 1988).[10] Statistical analysis also suggests cyclical underwriting results in a number of other countries (Cummins and Outreville, 1987; Lamm-Tennant and Weiss, 1997; Chen, Wang, and Lee, 1999) and different turning points / cyclical periods for different lines of insurance (Venezian, 1985; Fields and Venezian, 1989; Lamm-Tennant and Weiss, 1997).[11]

Studies also suggest that underwriting results remain cyclical after controlling for the expected effects of changes in interest rates (see Fields and Venezian, 1989, and Smith, 1989; also see Winter, 1991a).[12] These results imply that historical cycles in reported underwriting margins cannot simply be explained by the expected effect of changes in interest rates, i.e., that operating profits including investment income also are cyclical. Cagle (1993) presents some evidence of cyclical variation in underwriting results after controlling for variation in the estimated market price of risk (see, e.g., Ferson and Harvey, 1991).

As suggested above, empirical regularities in reported underwriting results could largely or even exclusively be caused by financial reporting procedures and lags in price changes due to regulation. Cummins and Outreville (1987) provide a lucid discussion of this issue. They show conditions under which accounting and regulatory lags could generate a cycle in underwriting margins without either excessive price-cutting during soft markets or sharp reductions in supply following reductions in surplus.[13] However, like other studies, their empirical analysis of underwriting profits cannot distinguish the extent to which correlation in profit measures over time is due to accounting issues and regulatory lags, as opposed to pricing that materially violates the perfect markets model.

In addition, evidence suggests that underwriting expense ratios (ratios of underwriting expenses to written premiums) have varied cyclically after controlling for trend and changes in interest rates (e.g., Ellis, 1988; Cagle, 1993). Cyclical variation in premiums would imply cyclical variation in expense ratios, provided that some expenses are fixed in the short run. As a result, this evidence suggests that pre-

[10] A few studies (e.g., Doherty and Kang, 1988; Grace and Hotchkiss, 1995) also use spectral analysis.

[11] Higgins and Thistle (1997) provide evidence of structural shifts in underwriting returns. Cassidy, Hardigree, and Hogan (1996) present evidence of second order auto regression in health insurance underwriting results.

[12] Other studies analyze the effect of changes in interest rates on fair premiums for commercial liability insurance during the early and mid-1980s (see Harrington, 1988; also see Harrington and Litan, 1988).

[13] The authors note, however, that regulatory lag and financial reporting procedures are unlikely to explain large price fluctuations in the commercial liability insurance market in the mid-1980s.

dictability in reported underwriting results is not fully explained by accounting and reporting lags.

Analogous to Cummins and Outreville, Doherty and Kang (1988) argue that cyclical patterns in underwriting results reflect slow but presumably rational adjustment of premiums to changes in expected claim costs and interest rates. Their empirical work, however, does not clearly distinguish this hypothesis from the alternative of material deviations from the perfect markets model due, for example, to possible suboptimal forecasting.[14]

Illustrative Evidence

Table 1 presents estimates of second-order autoregressive models of aggregate combined ratios for the U.S. property-liability insurance industry using data for the period 1955–96 and for consecutive (over-lapping) 25-year subperiods during this time. Results are shown for two equations each period. The first equation includes a time trend (TIME); the second includes a time trend and the average yield on 5-year (constant maturity) U.S. Treasury Bonds during the year (YIELD; also see Figure 1).[15]

Like earlier studies, the results generally suggest that combined ratios follow a second-order autoregressive process that is consistent with a cycle. The estimated period of the cycle (see Venezian, 1985) is 6.2 years for 1955–1979 and ranges from 7.1 to 9.6 years for the later and longer subperiods. There is no obvious trend in the estimated cyclical period over time. As predicted by the perfect markets model, the coefficient on YIELD is positive and significant for the last 25-year subperiod (1970–94) and for the 40 and 42 year subperiods. The low t values for the coefficients on YIELD for the earlier 25-year subperiods could reflect inability of the data to distinguish the effects of YIELD and TIME.[16]

Using data for 1972–96 (the most recent 25-year period with available data), Table 2 presents estimates of second-order autoregressive models of (1) the combined

[14] The causes of lags in adjustment are not explored in this work. Also see Tennyson (1993).

[15] Augmented Dickey-Fuller tests (see Enders, 1995) including intercept and trend generally reject the null hypothesis of a unit root for both the combined ratio and interest rate series (as well as the gross margin and the ratio of net premiums written to GDP, see below), and suggest that the series were trend stationary during these periods. Box-Pierce and Box-Ljung statistics generally indicate that the residuals in the models reported in Tables 1 and 3 are white noise (two lags were included). Qualitatively similar results were obtained using yields on 1-year treasuries. Unit root tests suggested that longer-term bond yields were non-stationary. We included a dummy variable for 1992 in the combined ratio models that included this year to control for the effects of Hurricane Andrew on the loss ratio. The implications are not sensitive to the inclusion of this dummy. We emphasize, however, that our purpose is illustrative. Apart from these and a few other robustness checks, we have not investigated the sensitivity of the results of alternative specifications, such as alternative lag structures and the use of first differences. Also see our discussion below of studies that fail to reject the null hypothesis of a unit root (presumably without including a trend variable in the testing equation) and then consider whether underwriting margins are cointegrated with other variables.

[16] When TIME is omitted, the coefficient on YIELD becomes significant in the earlier subperiods. However, the evidence that the series are trend stationary makes interpretation of the models without a trend problematic. Similar results to those reported are obtained when YIELD is interacted with a proxy for the length of the claims tail (i.e., the "funds generation coefficient," calculated as the predicted value of a linear trend model of the ratio of loss and unearned premium reserves to earned premiums).

Table 1

Estimates of Second-Order Autoregressive Models of Industry Combined Ratio
$CR_t = \beta_0 + \beta_1 CR_{t-1} + \beta_2 CR_{t-2} + \beta_3 TIME_t + \beta_4 YIELD_t + v_t$

Sample	Constant	CR_{t-1}	CR_{t-2}	$TIME_t$	$YIELD_t$	Adj. R^2	Period
1955–79	84.18	0.94	−0.80	0.12		0.71	6.2
	(7.27)	(7.37)	(6.23)	(2.48)			
	83.75	0.94	−0.79	0.11	0.05	0.70	6.2
	(6.50)	(7.12)	(5.58)	(0.69)	(0.09)		
1960–84	39.16	1.30	−0.71	0.17		0.77	9.2
	(2.34)	(6.80)	(3.31)	(2.08)			
	34.55	1.21	−0.58	−0.05	0.58	0.77	9.6
	(2.05)	(6.02)	(2.53)	(0.28)	(1.27)		
1965–89	52.84	1.16	−0.71	0.29		0.82	7.8
	(4.51)	(7.53)	(4.57)	(3.29)			
	46.53	1.09	−0.59	0.19	0.33	0.82	8.1
	(3.46)	(6.35)	(2.97)	(1.44)	(0.96)		
1970–94	59.33	0.86	−0.46	0.29		0.69	7.1
	(3.44)	(4.62)	(2.41)	(2.04)			
	44.78	0.73	−0.26	0.22	0.90	0.79	8.2
	(3.04)	(4.70)	(1.56)	(1.87)	(3.33)		
1955–94	54.19	0.88	−0.44	0.17		0.76	7.4
	(4.53)	(6.28)	(3.11)	(2.78)			
	44.28	0.84	−0.32	0.04	0.54	0.79	8.7
	(3.71)	(6.34)	(2.22)	(0.55)	(2.41)		
1955–96	51.62	0.89	−0.42	0.14		0.75	7.7
	(4.45)	(6.46)	(3.04)	(2.57)			
	44.53	0.84	−0.31	0.05	0.54	0.79	8.7
	(4.02)	(6.50)	(2.32)	(0.72)	(2.77)		

Note: Dependent variable is CR_t = loss ratio (adjusted for dividends) plus expense ratio (in percent). $TIME_t$ = time trend. $YIELD_t$ = average percentage yield on 5-year treasury bonds. Period is estimated period of cycle (in years). Absolute t-ratios in parentheses below coefficient estimates. 1970–94, 1955–94, and 1955–96 sample periods include a dummy variable for 1992 (Hurricane Andrew). Sources: *Best's Aggregates & Averages, Property-Casualty, United States*, 1997 (A.M. Best Company) and Federal Reserve Bank of St. Louis FRED data system.

ratio, (2) the gross underwriting margin, defined as 100 percent minus the percentage underwriting expense ratio, and (3) the ratio of net premiums written to GDP (see also Figure 2). The gross margin measures the margin available in premiums to fund predicted claim, tax, and agency costs, and it will reflect any economic profit (or loss). Because neither the gross margin nor the ratio of net premiums written to GDP reflect reported claim costs, any cycle in or interest rate sensitivity of these variables cannot be attributed to bias or lags associated with loss reporting.

Consistent with previous analyses of expense ratios (Cagle, 1993; also see Gron, 1994a), the estimates of the gross margin equations provide strong evidence of second-order autoregression. Results for the ratio of net premiums written to GDP also indicate second-order autoregression. The coefficient on YIELD is not

Table 2

Estimates of Second-Order Autoregressive Models of Industry Combined Ratio, Gross Margin, and Ratio of Net Premiums Written to Gross Domestic Product
$Y_t = \beta_0 + \beta_1 Y_{t-1} + \beta_2 Y_{t-2} + \beta_3 TIME_t + \beta_4 YIELD_t + v_t$

Y_t	Constant	Y_{t-1}	Y_{t-2}	$TIME_t$	$YIELD_t$	Adj. R^2	Period
$CR_t = LR_t + ER_t$	50.62	0.88	−0.37	0.12		0.64	8.2
	(3.02)	(4.78)	(1.96)	(0.90)			
	42.39	0.73	−0.23	0.17	0.90	0.76	9.1
	(3.07)	(4.73)	(1.42)	(1.53)	(3.39)		
$GM_t = 100 - ER_t$	35.49	1.25	−0.74	0.29		0.79	8.3
	(4.38)	(8.45)	(4.99)	(2.03)			
	35.47	1.25	−0.74	0.03	0.00	0.78	8.3
	(4.27)	(7.55)	(4.47)	(1.94)	(0.04)		
NPW_t/GDP_t	0.28	1.27	−0.71	0.01		0.94	8.8
	(3.79)	(8.01)	(4.37)	(3.17)			
	0.30	1.23	−0.67	0.01	−0.00	0.94	8.7
	(3.82)	(7.42)	(3.99)	(3.08)	(0.88)		

Note: CR_t = combined ratio (in percent), LR_t = loss ratio (adjusted for dividends), ER_t = expense ratio, GM_t = gross margin, NPW_t/GDP_t = net premiums written divided by gross domestic product (in percent). $TIME_t$ = time trend. $YIELD_t$ = average percentage yield on 5-year treasury bonds. Period is estimated period of cycle (in years). Absolute t-ratios in parentheses below coefficient estimates. Combined ratio model includes a dummy variable for 1992 (Hurricane Andrew). Sources: *Best's Aggregates & Averages, Property-Casualty, United States*, 1997 (A.M. Best Company), Federal Reserve Bank of St. Louis FRED data system, and *Statistical Abstract of the United States*.

significantly negative for either series, in contrast to the prediction of the perfect markets model.[17] These results also contrast with those for the combined ratio, where the coefficient on YIELD is positive and significant as predicted (recall that the combined ratio is an inverse profitability measure). A possible negative relationship between GDP growth and interest rates might obscure the predicted negative effect of interest rates on net premiums written. However, this possibility cannot explain the lack of a relationship between the gross margin and YIELD. Of course, it is not clear which, if any, of these results are spurious (e.g., the strong interest rate sensitivity of the combined ratio, which reflects reported losses, or the lack of interest rate sensitivity of the gross margin and ratio of net premiums written to gross national product, which do not).

What can be made of these results and those of similar studies? Persons predisposed towards the perfect markets model might argue that the generally strong evidence of second-order autoregression and the fragile relationship with interest rates could reflect the small sample period, aggregations bias, structural instability due, for example, to changes in regulation, possible omitted variable or data snooping bias,

[17] When the time trend is omitted, the coefficients are negative but with absolute t-ratios less than one.

and so on. Variation in the estimates for different models and subperiods suggests some fragility in the results. Even so, absent specific details on the causes of any bias, the evidence of second-order autoregression in all three series must be considered anomalous from the perspective of the perfect markets model. This result is by and large consistent with the decades old story about periodic hard and soft markets. Because there is no reason to expect that shocks are predictable, the evidence of *second-order autoregression* in combined ratios or the other variables also is not readily explained by shock models.[18]

Unit Roots and Cointegration

Several comparatively recent time series studies have considered the short and long-run relation between underwriting margins, interest rates, and other macroeconomic variables using cointegration analysis and error correction models. Each of these studies fails to reject the hypothesis of a unit root in underwriting margins and the other series examined, presumably without allowing for trend in the underlying series (as we did). They then assume that the series are difference stationary.[19] Haley (1993) presents evidence that underwriting profit margins and interest rates are negatively related and cointegrated. He also provides evidence of a short-run relation between interest rates and underwriting margins using error correction models.[20] Grace and Hotchkiss (1995) provide evidence of cointegration between quarterly combined ratios and short-term interest rates, the consumer price index, and real GDP. Choi and Thistle (1997) provide evidence that underwriting profit margins are cointegrated with annual Treasury bond yields but not with the ratio of capital to assets.

20.4 CAPITAL SHOCKS AND CAPACITY CONSTRAINTS

Common aspects of capital shock models of underwriting cycles are that (1) industry supply depends on the amount of insurer capital and (2) that industry supply is upward sloping in the short run because the stock of capital is costly to increase due to the costs of raising new capital.[21] These features imply that shocks to capital (e.g., catastrophes or unexpected changes in liability claim costs) affect the price and

[18] Winter's model (see below), for example, implies first-order autoregression, although he suggests that overlapping policy periods might explain second-order autoregression within the context of his model.

[19] Note that our augmented Dickey-Fuller tests that include and intercept and trend (trend was significant) might cast doubt on the assumption that the series have a unit root and are difference stationary. Fung et al. (1998) estimate a VAR model of by line premiums in differences after finding, perhaps not surprisingly, that premiums in levels are non-stationary.

[20] Subsequent analysis of by-line underwriting results (Haley, 1995) suggests cointegration between underwriting margins (weighted by the proportion of total premiums represented by the line each year) and interest rates for some but not all lines.

[21] All of the capital shock models are built on the assumption that external capital is costlier than internal capital. This notion is usually justified using the logic of Myers and Majluf (1984) where managers are better informed than investors and that transaction costs make raising new capital costly.

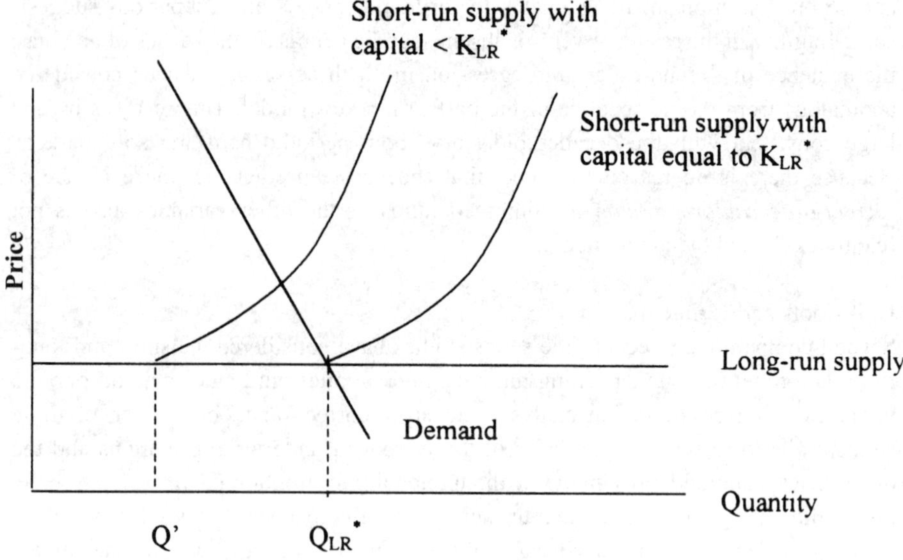

Figure 3 Industry Supply with Capital Shocks

quantity of insurance supplied in the short run.[22] Holding industry demand fixed, a backward shift in supply due to a capital shock causes price to increase and quantity to decrease, which roughly describes the hard phase of the cycle. The soft phase—low prices and high availability—either is not addressed by these models or is explained by periods of excess capital that is not paid out to shareholders because of capital exit costs. After providing an overview of the capital shock models, the empirical evidence is summarized.

The Basic Story

The main theoretical contributions to the literature on the relationship between cycles and insurer capital are Winter (1988, 1991, 1994), Gron (1994a), Cummins and Danzon (1997), Cagle and Harrington (1995), and Doherty and Garven (1995). While the assumptions and specific objectives of these papers differ on some dimensions, the main message is similar: shocks to capital can cause price increases and quantity reductions consistent with a hard market.

To illustrate the basic story, we focus on the determination of three endogenous variables in a competitive market: price, quantity, and insurer capital. Figure 3 illustrates the key ideas for a representative insurer. The horizontal axis measures quantity of coverage as the total value of its expected claim costs. The vertical axis measures the price of coverage as the difference between the premium and the

[22] Similar effects are highlighted in recent macro-finance literature. See, for example, Greenwald and Stiglitz (1993), Bernake and Lown (1991), and Prowse (1997).

expected claim cost per unit of coverage. The price of coverage therefore is the premium loading per dollar of expected claim costs, i.e., the excess amount paid for each dollar of expected claim costs. For simplicity, we ignore the time value of money and administrative costs (underwriting and claims-processing costs). Given the latter assumption, the only input into production of insurance is financial capital.

All capital shock models incorporate the idea that insolvency risk depends on the amount of insurer capital because of uncertainty in claim costs (due to correlation across policyholders) or uncertainty in investment returns (due for example to uncertainty in interest rates). Although not all models consider the issue, we assume that in the long run insurers choose an optimal amount of capital, which equates the marginal costs and benefits of capital.[23] By reducing insolvency risk, additional capital benefits insurers by (1) increasing the demand for coverage by consumers who are averse to insolvency risk (Cummins and Danzon, 1997), and/or (2) reducing the likelihood that insurers lose franchise value (Cagle and Harrington, 1995; also see Pauly, 1984; and Munch and Smallwood, 1982).[24] The costs of insurer capital include double taxation of investment returns on capital and agency costs (Winter, 1994; Cagle and Harrington, 1995).[25] The cost per dollar of capital equals s. The long-run cost of supplying coverage therefore equals the total capital cost per-unit of coverage.[26] Instead of modeling insurer choice of capital based on costs and benefits, some models simply assume that insurer capital must satisfy a regulatory constraint on the probability of bankruptcy (Gron, 1994a and b, and Winter, 1994).

Assuming that the optimal level of capital is a fixed proportion of output, the long-run supply curve is perfectly elastic at the cost per unit of coverage of the optimal long run level of insurer capital (see Figure 3). Exogenously imposing a downward sloping demand curve in Figure 3, the long run equilibrium corresponds to an output level equal to Q^*_{LR}, a level of insurer capital of K^*_{LR}, and a price (premium loading per unit of coverage) equal to the capital costs per unit of coverage, sK^*_{LR}/Q^*_{LR}.

In the capital shock models, short run equilibrium differs from the long run equilibrium because capital adjustment costs cause capital to be a fixed (or at least sticky) factor of production in the short run. Consequently, the short run supply curve is upward sloping. To illustrate, suppose that the representative insurer finds itself with capital equal to the long run optimum, K^*_{LR}, in Figure 3, which corresponds to a long-run output level of Q^*_{LR}, and that capital cannot be adjusted. In order to induce

[23] While the optimal amount of capital per unit of coverage is likely to decline with the number of units of coverage over some range given the greater diversification of claim costs that can be achieved by writing additional coverage, for simplicity, it is common to assume that demand for coverage (at any price) greatly exceeds the point at which such economies of scale are material.

[24] These benefits of holding capital hold over multiple periods, although most models analyze a single period. Thus, to the extent that capital protects insurer franchise value against future shocks or increases consumer demand following future shocks, insurers have greater incentives to hold capital.

[25] As discussed below, the cost of new capital in Cummins and Danzon (1997) is that it bails out old claimants without increasing the premiums paid by these claimants.

[26] The costs of holding capital should be distinguished from the cost of adjusting capital, which are central to short-run analyses of prices and quantities.

the insurer to supply output beyond the long-run equilibrium, the price of coverage would have to increase above the long-run equilibrium price. If insurers increased output and kept price equal to the long-run equilibrium price, then insolvency risk would increase above the optimum level, which would imply a higher cost of selling coverage (e.g., there would be an increased likelihood that the insurer would lose part of its franchise value). Thus, there is an additional cost of increasing output beyond Q^*_{LR}, holding capital fixed at K^*_{LR}. Greater increases beyond Q^*_{LR} imply greater increases in costs. Thus, the short-run supply curve is upward sloping.

The location of the short-run supply curve depends on the amount of insurer capital. If insurer capital were depleted below the long-run equilibrium, then the short run supply curve would be upward sloping starting below Q^*_{LR}. Figure 3 illustrates the case where capital is depleted to the point where the insurer's capital corresponds to a long run equilibrium output level of Q'.

This framework can now be used to motivate how hard markets could develop. A shock to capital in the form of unexpected claim payments on existing policies or a reduction in the value of assets would deplete insurers' capital and shift back the short run supply curve. Holding demand constant, the short run equilibrium price would increase and the short run equilibrium quantity of coverage would decrease, thus producing the hard phase of the cycle.

The higher prices and lower quantities then help to replenish insurer capital and gradually the supply curve shifts back, which lowers price and increases quantity. Insurers also could replenish capital by issuing new debt and equity securities, but raising new capital is costly because of issuance costs and potential underpricing costs. Thus, the short run supply curve is "bounded" by these costs. That is, if price rose sufficiently above the long run equilibrium price, insurers would likely raise new capital, which would shift out the supply curve and cause prices to fall and quantities to increase. Insurers therefore would be more likely to raise new capital following large negative shocks to capital.

Although most models focus on negative shocks to capital (an exception is Doherty and Garven, 1995), it is useful to consider whether positive shocks to capital can explain the soft phase of the underwriting cycle (prices below long run equilibrium prices).[27] Just as there are costs of raising new capital there also are costs of paying out capital (see e.g., Winter, 1994). Insurers can dispose of excess capital by increasing dividends or stock repurchases. Dividend payments, however, can impose tax costs on owners and stock repurchases involve transaction costs. To the extent that these costs induce insurers to hold excess capital, the price of coverage can fall below long run equilibrium levels. Selling policies for less than the long run equilibrium price could be less costly than either paying out the capital or having it less than fully utilized in supporting additional output.

[27] Some authors suggest that capital is gradually restored following negative shocks that cause a hard market, and that prices eventually fall to long-run equilibrium values until another negative capital shock occurs. Accordingly, the soft phase of the underwriting cycle is characterized by prices equal to long-run equilibrium values not by prices below long-run equilibrium values (see e.g., Gron 1994a,b).

In summary, the main predictions from these models are (1) insurance prices are negatively related to insurer capital, (2) the quantity of coverage falls following negative shocks to capital, but coverage is not rationed, and (3) capital infusions (payouts) take place during periods of high (low) insurance prices.

Discussion of Specific Models

Industry Models. Although the insurance cycle is a dynamic phenomenon, most of the capital shock papers employ static models like the one outlined above. The dynamic aspects of the market are then explained by periodic exogenous shocks. An exception is Winter (1994), which models the dynamics of the insurance market in a discrete time equilibrium model. The evolution of insurer capital is explicitly modeled and insurers optimally choose to add or dispose of capital each period, as well as the quantity of coverage to offer.[28] Unlike most other papers, Winter explicitly models the capital adjustment costs (the costs of adding and distributing capital). However, he does not model the optimal level of capital based on the costs and benefits of holding capital. Instead, insurers must hold an amount of costly capital that satisfies the constraint that the probability of insolvency is zero. This constraint, along with the capital adjustment costs, gives rise to an upward sloping short run supply curve. That is, in order for insurers to increase supply beyond the point where existing capital ensures a zero probability of insolvency, price must increase so that the additional revenue from the higher price satisfies the insolvency constraint.

In addition to showing that insurance prices vary inversely with insurer capital and that new additions of capital occur during hard markets, Winter's model also implies that market-to-book ratios are a declining function of insurer capital. Intuitively, as capital becomes scarce, its value within the insurer increases. This suggests that stock market reactions to unexpected losses are less than dollar-for-dollar.[29]

Cagle and Harrington (1995) examine the extent to which the cost of a capital shock may be passed on to consumers in the form of higher prices. In their model,

[28] Relatively little work has been done on dynamic capital structure models in the general finance literature. Fischer, Heinkel, and Zechner (1989) develop a dynamic model of capital structure incorporating adjustment costs. However, unlike the insurance capital shock models, firms' investment decisions are held constant. As in Winter (1994), firms wait to adjust their leverage ratio until it reaches a critical low and high level. They derive and test predictions about how the optimal leverage ratio range varies with parameters measuring bankruptcy cost, tax shields from debt, and risk of the firm's underlying assets. See Mauer and Triantis (1994), Kumar (1998), Goldstein, Ju, and Leland (1998) for other dynamic models of capital structure.

[29] As noted earlier, Winter's model predicts a first order process for prices, not a second order process. He suggests, however, that a higher order process would result from the model if the assumption of single period contracts were replaced with the more realistic assumption of overlapping contracts. Winter (1991b) extends the basic capital shock story by examining the effect of regulation that restricts an insurer's premium to surplus ratio to be below a certain level. This regulatory constraint can further exacerbate the reduction in short-run supply following a capital shock if demand is inelastic. Intuitively, as prices rise in response to the capital shock, inelastic demand implies that premium revenue will increase, which in combination with the reduction in capital causes more insurers to bump up against the regulatory constraint, which in turn causes supply to shift back even more. This story is clever, although there is little evidence that implicit or explicit regulatory constraints in practice are binding for many insurers during hard markets.

insurers choose an optimal level of capital based on the cost of holding capital and the benefits of protecting franchise value. They derive comparative statics for the upper bound effect on price of a shock to capital, assuming that demand is perfectly inelastic and that additional capital cannot be raised. In this best case scenario (for insurers), they show that the entire cost of the shock is not passed on to policyholders. Intuitively, the supply curve is not sufficiently responsive to a decrease in capital to cause prices to increase sufficiently to offset completely the capital shock. The reason for this is that higher prices help to replenish capital, which dampens the effect of the capital shock on supply.

Firm Level Models. The basic idea of the industry level models has also been developed in models of individual insurers. These models do not assume a perfectly competitive market and thus prices can vary across insurers. In addition to the implication that insurance prices rise in response to industry-wide capital shocks, firm level models provide predictions about firm-specific shocks and cross-sectional predictions about industry-wide shocks.

Doherty and Garven (1995) consider the effects of interest rate changes in the context of capital shock models. A change in interest rates can influence capital by changing the value of insurer assets and liabilities. Depending on whether the duration of assets exceeds the duration of liabilities and the sign of the interest rate change, interest rate changes influence the value of an insurer's capital and thus can cause short-run effects similar to those outlined above. In addition, the level of interest rates influences the long-run equilibrium price of coverage—higher interest rates cause the fair premium to decline, all else equal. Thus, they predict that interest rate changes will cause firm-specific capital shocks, as well as alter the long run equilibrium price of insurance. They therefore predict that there will be cross-sectional differences in insurers' price response to interest rate changes, depending on the insurer's exposure to interest rate risk (surplus duration) and its costs of raising capital (mutual versus stock).

Cummins and Danzon (1997) also consider firm specific effects of shocks. They consider an insurer that enters a period with existing liabilities and a stock of capital. The insurer chooses the amount of new capital to raise and the price for new policies. Demand for coverage depends both on price and quality (insolvency risk). The benefit of additional capital is an increase in consumer demand for new policies, but the cost of additional capital is that the old policyholders (existing liabilities) have less insolvency risk, but pay no additional premiums. In essence, capital infusions can bail out old claimants (also see Myers, 1977). Thus, unlike other models that either impose explicit capital adjustment costs (Winter, 1994) or assume capital is fixed in the short run (Gron, 1994a, and Cagle and Harrington, 1995), Cummins and Danzon impose a specific capital market imperfection (or product market imperfection, depending on the semantics you prefer) by assuming contracts with old policyholders cannot be adjusted to reflect changes in default risk.

Another important aspect of Cummins and Danzon's analysis is the explicit modeling of the response of demand to insolvency risk.[30] If price is measured as the premium per policy or per dollar of expected *promised* claim costs, as opposed to per dollar of expected claim costs (where the expectation incorporates default risk), then price would be expected to move inversely with insolvency risk, all else equal. The analogy to risky debt is helpful—as default risk increases, a bond's price would be expected to fall, holding the promised payment constant. Consequently, in response to a capital shock that increased insolvency risk, price could very well fall. In part because of this effect, Cummins and Danzon's model does not provide an unambiguous prediction concerning the effect of a shock on price. Similarly, their model does not provide an unambiguous prediction concerning the response of capital to a negative shock. In their model, insurers face a trade-off with respect to raising additional capital. Additional capital will transfer wealth to old policyholders, but will also increase demand by new policyholders.

Although not specific to insurers, Froot and Stein (1998) present a model that provides some interesting predictions about the effect of capital shocks to insurers. In their model, firms are faced with the possibility of a shock that will deplete internal funds. Due to the costs of raising external capital, the realization of the shock will cause the firm to pass up profitable investment opportunities (also see Froot, Scharfstein, and Stein, 1993). The firm can manage this risk by (1) holding capital ex ante, which is costly due to tax and agency costs, (2) engaging in costly hedging (reinsurance) transactions, and (3) adjusting their exposure through their investment policies. Their model implies that insurer pricing depends on their capital. Consequently, capital shocks should affect pricing across lines of business, regardless of the source of the shock.[31]

Empirical Evidence on Capital Shock Models

The capital shock models have motivated considerable empirical research. The most important prediction of most of these models is that insurance prices are negatively related to insurer capital. As discussed earlier, a problem encountered by empiricists is that the ex ante price of insurance is not observable because expected losses are unobservable. Thus, most studies examining the relation between price and capital use some variant of premiums relative to realized losses as a measure of price.[32] Table 3 summarizes some of the empirical evidence on the capital shock models. In the following pages, we provide some additional detail of selected papers listed in Table 3 to provide an overview of how the capital shock models have been tested.

[30] As noted earlier, Winter (1994) avoids this issue by imposing a zero probability of insolvency constraint, and Gron (1994a) assumes that there is regulatory constraint on the probability of insolvency. Cagle and Harrington (1995) consider demand responses to capital shocks and show that such responses diminish the ability of insurers to recoup losses from price increases following capital shocks.

[31] Also see the model and discussion in Gron and Winton, 1999.

[32] A number of studies (e.g., Shelor, Anderson, and Cross, 1992; Anghazo and Narayanan, 1996) analyze insurer stock price responses to large unexpected claim costs. In principal, analysis of stock returns around

Table 3
Evidence on Capital Shock Models

Study	Data	Main Results
Industry Aggregate Time Series Studies		
Winter (1994)	'48–'88	Difference between premiums and prediction of the present value of future losses is negatively related to insurer capital
Gron (1994a)	'49–'90	Changes in premiums minus underwriting expenses (the "price payment margin" or PPM) are negatively related to lagged capital. Negative capital shocks influence PPM more than positive capital shocks. Capital growth is positively related to contemporaneous PPM.
Niehaus and Terry (1993)	'46–'88	Premiums are related to lagged capital
Choi and Thistle (1997)	'26–'93	Surplus is not a determinant of profits in the short run or long run
Higgins and Thistle (1997)	'34–'93	Underwriting profits follow an AR(1) process when capital is high and AR(2) process when capital is low
Insurer Panel Data		
Cummins and Danzon (1997)	'80–'88	Capital flows are positively related to price changes and loss shocks
Doherty and Garven (1995)	'76–'88	Sensitivity of insurer underwriting returns to interest rates (speed of adjustment) is negatively related to surplus duration (capital shock from the interest rate change)
Guo and Winter (1997)	'90–'95	Ratio of capital to premiums is positively related to past profitability
Aggregate Line-Specific Data		
Froot and O'Connell (1997)	catastrophe reinsurance	Prices increase following capital shocks even for catastrophes and regions not affected by the shock
Yuengert (1991)	Six lines, '84–'89	Prices are positively related to capital and negatively deviations of capital from its average level
Gron (1994b)	Four lines, '52–'86	Underwriting profits are negatively related to capital for auto physical damage, homeowners, auto liability, but not other liability
Froot and O'Connell (1996)	catastrophe reinsurance	Low estimates for the price elasticity of supply
Other Evidence		
Gron and Lucas (1994)	Insurer financing decisions '70–'93	Payout ratios fall following shocks; equity issues increase following shocks, but most additional capital is small relative to size of capital shocks
Gron (1995b)	Agent commissions '55–'85	Commission rates decline during hard markets

Aggregate Time Series Studies. Winter (1994) calculates an "economic loss ratio" for year t as the present value of an estimate of actual future claims arising from policies sold in year t divided by premiums in year t. The economic loss ratio is regressed on the lagged values of insurer capital relative to its previous five-year average and interest rates. Consistent with the prediction of the capital shock models that higher prices (lower expected loss ratios) occur when capital is low, the coefficients on the lagged capital variables are positive and statistically significant in most of his specifications.[33]

Gron (1994a) uses both the difference between premiums and underwriting expenses and the ratio of premiums to underwriting expenses as dependent variables. To control for the present value of claim costs, she includes variables for the expected inflation rate and interest rates. GNP is used to control for demand. Consistent with capital shock models, the results indicate that changes in the margin between premiums and underwriting expenses are negatively related to lagged values of capital relative to its long-run equilibrium value, where the latter variable is measured as capital relative its 5-year average, 3-year average, or GNP.

Aggregate Line Specific Studies. Gron (1994b) examines aggregate time series data for four lines of business: auto physical damage, auto liability, homeowners' multiple peril, and other liability. Unlike her time-series study of aggregate industry data (1994a), she examines the determinants of the underwriting profit margin, defined as earned premiums minus incurred losses, divided by earned premiums. After controlling for expected inflation, unexpected inflation, changes in expected inflation, and changes in discount rates, she finds that deviations of relative capacity (surplus to GNP) from its normal level are negatively related to underwriting profits in all four lines, which is consistent with the notion that prices increase when capacity (insurer capital) is reduced.

Panel Data Studies. The model developed by Cummins and Danzon (1997) emphasizes that price and capital are jointly determined. They therefore estimate a two-equation system using insurer level data, where price depends on lagged capital (as a measure of financial quality) and additions to capital depend on the change in price. Their results indicate that insurers with more capital charge higher prices, which is consistent with the risky debt notion of insurance policies. In addition, they find that price is inversely related to deviations of capital from normal levels, which lends support to the capital shock models. The capital equation results support the notion

sudden events could provide evidence of capacity effects on prices if the stock price response could be compared to the direct losses from the shock. Because the full magnitude of losses becomes known slowly over time, it is difficult, however, to construct a powerful test. Any changes in demand or price regulation due to the shock could also confound the results.

[33] During the 1980s, however, the correlation between domestic insurer capital and the economic loss ratio was negative. Winter argues that the 1980s can be explained in part by the omission of reinsurance capacity from the capital variables.

that insurers have an optimal capital structure and that capital is more likely to be raised following an increase in price.

Doherty and Garven (1995) use panel data to estimate the sensitivity of insurer underwriting returns to interest rate changes. They then regress these sensitivity measures on measures of surplus duration and proxies for the cost of raising capital (e.g., privately-owned and mutual companies are assumed to have higher costs of raising capital). They find that the interest rate sensitivity coefficient from the first pass regression is negatively related to surplus duration. This finding suggests that if interest rates increase, thus causing the long-run equilibrium underwriting return to decrease, insurers with a high surplus duration and therefore a large decrease in capital from the interest rate increase will adjust less rapidly to the lower equilibrium price. Thus, capital shocks caused by interest rate fluctuations influence price adjustment. They also find that privately-owned insurers adjust more slowly to interest rate changes, which is consistent with these insurers having greater capital adjustment costs.

Froot and O'Connell (1997) test the extent to which shocks in one insurance market influence pricing in other markets. In particular, they present evidence that catastrophe reinsurance prices changed across the board in response to shocks caused by specific types of catastrophes (e.g., a hurricane) or by catastrophes in specific regions. This evidence suggests that insurance prices vary inversely with insurer capital in the short run.

Shocks and Optimal Sharing of Correlated Risk

In a study that is closely related to the capital shock literature, Doherty and Posey (1997) develop a model that results in rationing of coverage (also see the discussion in Winter (1991a, 1994)). Following Dionne and Doherty (1997) and Marshall (1974), their model pursues the idea that the risk associated with correlated losses optimally should be shared between insurers and policyholders based on their relative costs of bearing risk (risk aversion for consumers and presumably capital costs for insurers). The ideal policy (ignoring moral hazard, adverse selection, and transaction costs) would pay all policyholder-specific losses, but would share losses that are economy-wide. Price increases following systematic losses would be consistent with such a sharing rule. The ideal contract is not feasible, however, because stock insurers have an incentive to falsely attribute losses to systematic events. Doherty and Posey therefore suggest that insurers can signal that aggregate losses occurred by selling less coverage than would be optimal at the higher price. In essence, by rationing coverage, insurers forego profits, which credibly signals that systematic losses occurred. The main predictions of this model are that premium revenue is negatively related to the magnitude of losses in the previous period and that the price response for mutuals will be less than for stocks given the reduced incentive for mutuals to dissemble. Their analysis of panel data for general liability insurers during the 1980s support these predictions.

20.5 PRICE CUTTING AND SOFT MARKETS

The traditional view of underwriting cycles by insurance industry analysts emphasizes fluctuations in capacity to write coverage as a result of changes in surplus and insurer expectations of profitability on new business (see Stewart, 1984; also see Berger, 1988). The essence of this explanation is that supply expands when expectations of profits are favorable, that competition then drives prices down to the point where underwriting losses deplete surplus, and that supply ultimately contracts in response to unfavorable profit expectations or to avert financial collapse. Price increases then replenish surplus until price-cutting ensues again.

The traditional explanation of supply contractions is largely consistent with shock models. The apparent missing link in this story, however, is why competition in soft markets ultimately leads to inadequate rates. Compared to the wave of research on shock models, there has been relatively little rigorous analysis of this issue. Instead, the traditional explanation of cycles has been appropriately challenged by researchers because it fails to explain how and why competition would cause rational insurers to cut prices to the point where premiums and anticipated investment income are insufficient to finance rational forecasts of claim costs and ensure a low probability of insurer default.[34] Thus, it could be that the data and evidence on predictability are soft (pun intended), rather than insurance prices during soft market periods.

Assuming that there is something to explain, what might explain soft markets culminating in inadequate rates? Winter's model implies that hard markets that follow large shocks tend to be preceded by periods of excess capacity and soft prices. However, as suggested earlier, shocks should be unpredictable. Neither Winter's model nor other shock stories can tightly explain second-order autoregression in profits.

Alternatively, it has been suggested that a tendency towards inadequate prices might arise from differences in insurer expectations concerning the magnitude of future loss costs (McGee, 1986, and Harrington, 1988; also see the comments in Stewart, 1984), from differences in insurer incentives for safe and sound operation (Harrington, 1988), or both.[35] Harrington and Danzon (1994) develop and test hypotheses based on this intuition and the large literatures on optimal bidding and moral hazard within the framework of alleged underpricing of commercial general liability insurance during the early 1980s. In the Harrington and Danzon analysis, some firms may price below cost because of moral hazard that results from limited liability and risk-insensitive guaranty programs. Others may price below cost due to heterogeneous information concerning future claim costs that results in low loss forecasts relative to rational forecasts accompanied by winners' curse effects. In

[34] Similarly, popular explanations of "cash flow underwriting" usually imply that insurers are irrational in that they reduce rates too much in response to increases in interest rates.

[35] McGee (1986) speculated that insurers with optimistic loss forecasts may cause prices to fall below the level implied by industry average forecasts. Winter (1988, 1991a) mentions the possibility of heterogeneous information and winner's curse effects.

response to underpricing by some firms, other firms may cut prices to preserve market share and thus avoid loss of quasi-rents from investments in tangible and intangible capital.

Harrington and Danzon use cross-section data from the early 1980s to test whether moral hazard and/or heterogeneous information contributed to differences in general liability insurance prices and premium growth rates among firms. Loss forecast revisions are used as a proxy for inadequate prices.[36] Estimation of reduced form equations for loss forecast revisions and premium growth and a structural model to test for a positive relation between premium growth and forecast revisions provides some evidence that is consistent with the moral hazard hypothesis.[37] An implication of this analysis is that increased market or regulatory discipline against low priced insurers with high default risk would reduce price volatility.

20.6 REGULATORY INFLUENCES

Delays in the rate approval process under prior approval rate regulation could influence or even cause cyclical fluctuations in underwriting results (Cummins and Outreville, 1987). Many studies analyze whether rate regulation affects cyclical movements in statewide loss ratios (see, e.g., Witt and Miller, 1981; Outreville, 1990; Tennyson, 1993; Harrington, 1984).[38] Most of these studies consider the hypothesis that regulatory lag amplifies cyclical movements in underwriting results. The basic story is that regulatory lag increases loss ratios in hard markets by delaying rate increases and reduces loss ratios in soft markets by delaying rate reductions. Alternatively, rate regulation could conceivably damp cycles by preventing excessive price-cutting in soft markets. Other research argues that rate regulation may have little effect on loss ratios for many commercial lines due to widespread use of schedule rating and other procedures that provide insurers with substantial flexibility in pricing even when rates are regulated (Stewart, 1987).

Empirical analyses of the effects of rate regulation on variability of loss ratios over time generally employ auto insurance data prior to the mid-1980s. Some studies provide evidence that rate regulation amplifies movements in loss ratios (e.g., Witt

[36] Loss forecast revisions will reflect moral hazard induced prices assuming that low price firms deliberately understate initial reported loss forecasts to hide inadequate prices from regulators and other interested parties, but that positive forecast errors materialize as paid claims accumulate. In addition, if prices vary due to differences in loss forecasts at the time of sale, less-informed firms should experience relatively greater upward forecast revisions over time as information accumulates.

[37] Specifically, forecast revisions and premium growth were generally positively and significantly related to the amount of liabilities ceded to reinsurers, consistent with the moral hazard hypothesis that reinsurance was used to conceal low prices and excessive growth. In addition, they find that mutual insurers generally had significantly lower forecast revisions and premium growth than stock insurers, which they argue is consistent with mutuals being less prone to low pricing due to moral hazard.

[38] Note that our focus here is on rate regulation and volatility, as opposed to the literature that suggests chronic effects of rate regulation on rate levels.

and Miller, 1981; Outreville, 1990), and, using cross-country data, that rate regulation increases the period of cycles (Lamm-Tennant and Weiss, 1997). Tennyson (1993) provides evidence that dependence of current inverse loss ratios for automobile insurance on lagged values is significantly larger in states with prior approval regulation. On the other hand, comparisons of average commercial lines loss ratios over time in states with prior approval and competitive rating laws suggest little effect of type of rating law (Stewart, 1987).

Another issue that has received attention is whether solvency regulation affects premium volatility. As noted earlier, explicit or implicit regulatory constraints on the maximum permissible ratio of premiums to surplus could amplify cycles (Winter, 1991b). This could occur if premium increases in hard markets and associated increases in the ratio of premiums to surplus were to cause some insurers to reduce output further, thus producing higher prices, in order to meet regulatory constraints on the maximum permissible ratio. Whether such constraints lead to undesirable reductions in output for enough firms to have a material effect on prices is arguable.

Finally, some authors discuss whether cooperative pricing activities in conjunction with the insurance industry's limited exemption from federal antitrust law might aggravate hard markets (e.g., Abraham, 1988; also see Angoff, 1988, for allegations of price fixing, and Ayres and Siegelman, 1989).[39] The McCarran-Ferguson Act exemption applies to the extent that these activities are regulated by the states or unless boycott, coercion, and intimidation are involved.[40] Other studies argue that these effects are difficult to reconcile with the industry's competitive structure, with the modern operation of advisory organizations, or both (e.g., Clarke, et al., 1988; Winter, 1988; Harrington and Litan, 1988; Harrington, 1990; also see Danzon, 1992, Gron, 1995, and Lacey, 1988).

In addition, analysis suggests that the activities of advisory organizations in auto insurance are (1) inconsistent with cartel behavior and (2) likely to be procompetitive (e.g., Danzon, 1983 and 1992). In most commercial insurance lines, independent rate filings, percentage deviations from ISO advisory rates or loss costs, and individual risk rating provide substantial flexibility in pricing. It also is argued that cooperative ratemaking activities for commercial lines are likely to enhance economic efficiency rather than amplify cyclical fluctuations or otherwise harm consumers (see Winter, 1988, and Harrington, 1990). If these activities reduce the likelihood of widespread underpricing in soft markets, they also may reduce premium volatility. In any case, the weight of the evidence suggests that price fixing is an unlikely cause of or contributing factor in hard markets.

[39] Two forms of cooperative activity have been subject to substantial controversy in recent years: the cooperative development of policy forms (see Ayres and Siegelman, 1989) and the development of advisory rates or prospective loss costs by advisory organizations such as the Insurance Services Office (ISO). For example, it is argued that advisory rates or loss costs stimulate price-cutting during soft markets and permit collusion to raise rates above costs during hard markets (Angoff, 1988).

[40] Many states have similar exemptions from state antitrust statutes.

20.7 CONCLUSIONS

There is no reasonable doubt that variation in insurance premiums over time and across buyers is largely attributable to variation in "fundamentals." However, there is substantial evidence that there is more to the story; i.e., that there sometimes is material variation in premiums that cannot be explained by the perfect markets model. The predictions of capital shock models are intuitively plausible, and there is some evidence consistent with their predictions. We know less about whether and why prices tend to fall too low during soft markets.

Additional theoretical work on capital shock models is needed to explore the relationship between costly external capital and capital structure decisions and pricing prior to any shock. Additional empirical work could provide evidence of the duration of any shock-induced price increases and whether costly external capital can explain both hard and soft markets. Unfortunately, it might be difficult to provide convincing evidence with respect to these issues using time series data because of the relatively small number of usable observations and the serious potential for data snooping bias. These problems suggest the need for more analyses that make creative use of cross-sectional (or panel) data.

20.8 REFERENCES

Abraham, Kenneth S. (1988). "The Causes of the Insurance Crisis," in Walter Olson, ed., *New Directions in Liability Law*, New York: The Academy of Political Science.

Angbazo, Lazarus A. and Ranga Narayaran (1996). "Catastrophic Shocks in the Property-Liability Insurance Industry: Evidence on Regulatory and Contagion Effects," *Journal of Risk and Insurance* 63, 619–637.

Angoff, Jay (1988). "Insurance Against Competition: How the McCarran-Ferguson Act Raises Prices and Profits in the Property-Casualty Insurance Industry," *Yale Journal on Regulation* 5, 397–415.

Ayres, Ian and Peter Siegelman (1989). "The Economics of the Insurance Antitrust Suits: Toward and Exclusionary Theory," *Tulane Law Review* 63, 971–997.

Bagwell, Laurie and John Shoven (1989). "Cash Distributions to Shareholders," *Journal of Economic Perspectives* 3, 129–141.

Berger, Lawrence A. (1988). "A Model Of The Underwriting Cycle In The Property/Liability Insurance Industry," *Journal Of Risk and Insurance* 50, 298–306.

Berger, Larry A., Cummins, J. David and Tennyson, Sharon (1992). "Reinsurance and The Liability Insurance Crisis," *Journal Of Risk and Uncertainty* 5, 253–272.

Bradford, David F. and Kyle D. Logue (1996). "The Effects of Tax-Law Changes on Prices in the Property-Casualty Insurance Industry," Working paper 5652, National Bureau of Economic Research, Inc.

Cagle, Julie (1993). "Premium Volatility in Liability Insurance Markets," unpublished doctoral dissertation, University of South Carolina.

Cagle, Julie and Scott Harrington (1995). "Insurance Supply with Capacity Constraints and Endogenous Insolvency Risk," *Journal of Risk and Uncertainty* 11, 219–232.

Cassidy, Steven M., Donald W. Hardigree and Arthur M.B. Hogan (1996). "Underwriting Cycles in Health Insurance," *Journal of Insurance Regulation* 14, 504–514.

Chen, Renbao, Kie A. Wong and Hong C. Lee (1999). "Underwriting Cycles in Asia," *Journal of Risk and Insurance* 66, 29–47.

Choi, Seungmook and Paul Thistle (1997). "A Structural Approach to Underwriting Cycles in the Property-Liability Insurance Industry," working paper, Western Michigan University.

Clarke, Richard N., Warren-Boulton, Frederick, Smith, David K. and Simon, Marilyn J. (1988). "Sources Of The Crisis In Liability Insurance: An Empirical Analysis," *Yale Journal On Regulation* 5, 367–395.

Cummins, J. David and Danzon, Patricia M. (1997). "Price, Financial Quality, and Capital Flows in Insurance Markets," *Journal of Financial Intermediation* 6, 3–38.

Cummins, J. David and Francois Outreville (1987). "An International Analysis Of Underwriting Cycles In Property-Liability Insurance," *Journal Of Risk and Insurance* 54, 246–262.

Cummins, J. David and James B. McDonald (1991). "Risk Probability Distributions and Liability Insurance Pricing," in J. David Cummins, J. David, Scott Harrington and Robert Klein, eds., *Cycles and Crises in Property/Casualty Insurance: Causes and Implications for Public Policy*, Kansas City, Mo.: NAIC, 1991.

Cummins, J. David and Richard A. Phillips (2000). "Applications of Financial Pricing Models in Property-Liability Insurance," in this book.

Cummins, J. David and Scott Harrington (1985). "Property-Liability Insurance Rate Regulation: Estimation of Underwriting Betas Using Quarterly Profit Data," *Journal of Risk and Insurance* 52, 16–43.

Cummins, J. David, Scott Harrington and Robert Klein, eds. (1991). *Cycles and Crises in Property/Casualty Insurance: Causes and Implications for Public Policy*, Kansas City, Mo.: NAIC, 1991.

Cummins, J. David and Sharon Tennyson (1992). "Controlling Automobile Insurance Costs," *Journal of Economic Perspectives* 6, 95–115.

Danzon, Patricia (1983). "Rating Bureaus In U.S. Property-Liability Insurance Markets: Anti Or Pro-Competitive?" *Geneva Papers On Risk and Insurance* 8, 371–402.

Danzon, Patricia (1985). *Medical Malpractice: Theory, Evidence and Public Policy*. Cambridge, Mass: Harvard University Press.

Doherty, Neil A. and Georges Dionne (1993). "Insurance with Undiversifiable Risk: Contract Structure and Organizational Form of Insurance Firms," *Journal of Risk and Uncertainty* 6, 187–203.

Doherty, Neil and James Garven (1986). "Price Regulation In Property-Liability Insurance: A Contingent Claims Analysis," *Journal Of Finance* 41, 1031–1050.

Doherty, Neil A. and James Garven (1995). "Insurance Cycles: Interest Rates and the Capacity Constraint Model," *Journal of Business* 68, 383–404.

Doherty, Neil and Han Bin Kang (1988). "Price Instability For A Financial Intermediary: Interest Rates and Insurance Price Cycles," *Journal of Banking and Finance* 12, 199–214.

Doherty, Neil A. and Lisa Posey (1993). "Asymmetric Information and Availability Crises in Insurance Markets: Theory and Evidence," working paper, University of Pennsylvania.

Ellis, Peter M. (1988). "The Aggregate Expense Ratio Limit in the Domestic Property-Casualty Industry, Department of Business Administration," Utah State University.

Enders, Walter (1995). *Applied Time Series Econometrics*, New York: John Wiley and Sons.

Ferson, Wayne E. and Campbell, Harvey R. (1991). "The Variation Of Economic Risk Premiums," *Journal Of Political Economy* 99, 385–415.

Fields, Joseph and Emilio Venezian (1989). "Profit Cycles In Property-Liability Insurance: A Disaggregated Approach," *Journal of Risk and Insurance* 56, 312–319.

Finsinger, Jorg and Pauly, Mark V. (1984). "Reserve Levels and Reserve Requirements For Profit Maximizing Insurance Firms." In G. Bamberg and K. Spremann eds., *Risk and Capital*, Berlin: Springer-Verlag; reprinted in J. David Cummins and Scott E. Harrington, *Fair Rate of Return in Property-Liability Insurance*, Boston: Kluwer, 1986.

Froot, Kenneth, David Scharfstein and Jeremy Stein (1993). "Risk Management: Coordinating Corporate Investment and Financing Policies," *Journal of Finance* 48, 1629–1658.

Froot, Kenneth and Jeremy Stein (1998). "Risk Management, Capital Budgeting, and Capital Structure Policy for Financial Institutions: An Integrated Approach," *Journal of Financial Economics* 47, 55–82.

Froot, Kenneth and Paul O'Connell (1997). "The Pricing of U.S. Catastrophe Reinsurance," working paper 6043, National Bureau of Economic Research.

Fung, Hung-Gay, Gene Lai, Gary A. Patterson and Robert C. Witt (1998). "Underwriting Cycles in Property-Liability Insurance: An Empirical Analysis of Industry and By-Line Data," *Journal of Risk and Insurance* 65, 539–562.

Goldstein, Robert, Nengjiu Ju and Hayne Leland (1998). "Endogenous Bankruptcy, Endogenous Restructuring and Dynamic Capital Structure," working paper, Fisher College of Business, Ohio State University.

Greenwald, Bruce and Joseph Stiglitz (1993). "Financial Market Imperfections and Business Cycles," *Quarterly Journal of Economics* 108, 77–114.

Grace, Martin and Julie Hothkiss (••). "External Impacts on the Property-Liability Insurance Cycle," *Journal of Risk and Insurance* 62, 738–754.

Gron, Anne (1994a). "Evidence of Capacity Constraints in Insurance Markets," *Journal of Law and Economics* 37, 349–377.

Gron, Anne (1994b). "Capacity Constraints and Cycles in Property-Casualty Insurance Markets," *RAND Journal of Economics* 25, 110–127.

Gron, Anne (1995). "Collusion, Costs or Capacity? Evaluating Theories of Insurance Cycles," working paper, Northwestern University.

Gron, Anne and Deborah Lucas (1995). "External Financing and Insurance Cycles," working paper, Northwestern University.

Haley, Joseph (1993). "A Cointegration Analysis of the Relationship Between Underwriting Margins and Interest Rates: 1930–1989," *Journal of Risk and Insurance* 60, 480–493.

Haley, Joseph (1995). "A By-Line Cointegration Analysis of Underwriting Margins and Interest Rates in the Property-Liability Insurance Industry," *Journal of Risk and Insurance* 62, 755–763.

Harrington, Scott E. (1984). "The Impact of Rate Regulation on Prices and Underwriting Results in the Property-Liability Insurance Industry: A Survey," *Journal of Risk and Insurance* 51, 577–623.

Harrington, Scott E. (1988). "Prices and Profits in The Liability Insurance Market," in Robert Litan and Clifford Winston, eds., *Liability: Perspectives and Policy*, Washington, D.C.: The Brookings Institution.

Harrington, Scott E. (1989). "Fact vs. Fiction On Advisory Rates," *Best's Review, Property-Liability* 90, 56–60, 119.

Harrington, Scott E. (1990). "The Liability Insurance Market: Volatility in Prices and in The Availability of Coverage," in Peter Schuck, ed., *Tort Law and The Public Interest: Competition, Innovation, and Consumer Welfare, New York:* W.W. Norton.

Harrington, Scott E. and Robert E. Litan (1988). "Causes Of The Liability Insurance Crisis," *Science* 239, 737–741.

Harrington, Scott E. and Greg Niehaus (1998). "Race, Redlining, and Automobile Insurance Prices," *Journal of Business*, July.

Harrington, Scott E. and Patricia Danzon (1994). "Price Cutting in Liability Insurance Markets," *Journal of Business* 67, 511–538.

Harrington, Scott E. and Patricia Danzon (2000). "The Economics of Liability Insurance," in this book.

Higgins, Matthew and Paul Thistle (1997). "Capacity Constraints and the Dynamics of Underwriting Profits," working paper, Western Michigan University.

Kaplan, Seven and Luigi Zingales (1997). "Do Investment-Cash Flow Sensitivities Provide Useful Measures of Financing Constraints?" *Quarterly Journal of Economics* 112, 169–215.

Kumar, Praveen (1998). "Strategic Uncertainty, Learning, and Dynamic Financial and Investment Policy," working paper, University of Houston.

Lacey, Nelson (1988). "The Competitiveness of the Property-Casualty Insurance Industry: A Look at Market Equity Values and Premium Prices," *Yale Journal on Regulation* 5, 501–516.

Lamm-Tennant, Joan and Mary A. Weiss (1997). "International Insurance Cycles: Rational Expectations / International Intervention," *Journal of Risk and Insurance* 64, 415–439.

Marshall, John (1976). "Insurance Theory: Reserves Versus Mutuality," *Economic Inquiry*, 476–492.

Mauer, David C. and Alexander J. Triantis (1994). "Interactions of Corporate Financing and Investment Decisions: A Dynamic Framework," *Journal of Finance* 49, 1253–1278.

McGee, Robert (1986). "The Cycle In Property-Casualty Insurance," *Federal Reserve Bank Of New York Quarterly Review*, 22–30.

Mei, Jianping and Anthony Saunders (1994). "The Time Variation of Risk Premiums on Insurer Stocks," *Journal of Risk and Insurance* 61, 12–32.

Munch, Patricia and Dennis Smallwood (1982)." Theory Of Solvency Regulation In The Property and Casualty Industry," in Gary Fromm, ed., *Studies In Public Regulation*, Cambridge, Mass.: MIT Press.

Myers, Stewart C. (1977). "Determinants of Corporate Borrowing," *Journal of Financial Economics* 5, 147–175.

Myers, Stewart C. and Richard A. Cohn (1986). "A Discounted Cash Flow Approach To Property-Liability Insurance Rate Regulation," in J. David Cummins and Scott E. Harrington, eds., *Fair Rate Of Return In Property-Liability Insurance*. Boston: Kluwer.

Myers, Stewart C. and N. Majluf (1984). "Corporate Financing and Investment Decisions When Firms Have Information that Investors Do Not," *Journal of Financial Economics* 11, 187–221.

Niehaus, Greg and Andy Terry (1993). "Evidence on the Time Series Properties of Insurance Premiums and Causes of the Underwriting Cycle: New Support for the Capital Market Imperfection Hypothesis," *Journal of Risk and Insurance* 60, 466–479.

Outreville, Francois J. (1990). "Underwriting Cycles and Rate Regulation in Automobile Insruance Markets," *Journal of Insurance Regulation* 8, 274–286.

Petroni, Kathy R. (1992). "Optimistic Reporting In The Property-Casualty Insurance Industry," *Journal Of Accounting and Economics* 15, 485–508.

Phillips, Richard D., J. David Cummins and Franklin Allen (1998). "Financial Pricing of Insurance in the Multiple-Line Insurance Company," *Journal of Risk and Insurance* 65, 597–636.

Priest, George (1987). "The Current Insurance Crisis and Modern Tort Law," *Yale Law Journal* 96, 1521–1590.

Shelor, Roger M., Dwight C. Anderson and Mark L. Cross (1992). "Gaining from Loss: Property-Liability Insurer Stock Returns in the Aftermath of the 1989 California Earthquake," *Journal of Risk and Insurance* 5, 476–488.

Smith, Michael (1989). "Investment Returns and Yields To Holders Of Insurance," *Journal Of Business* 62, 81–98.

Sommer, David W. (1996). "The Impact of Firm Risk on Property-Liability Insurance Prices," *Journal of Risk and Insurance* 63, 501–514.

Stewart, Barbara D. (1984). "Profit Cycles In Property-Liability Insurance," in John D. Long, ed., *Issues In Insurance*, Malvern, Pa.: American Institute For Property and Liability Underwriters.

Stewart, Richard E. (1987). *Remembering A Stable Future: Why Flex Rating Cannot Work*. New York: Insurance Services Office and Insurance Information Institute.

Tennyson, Sharon L. (1993). "Regulatory Lag in Automobile Insurance," *Journal of Risk and Insurance* 60, 36–58.

Tort Policy Working Group (1986). "Report of the Tort Policy Working Group on the Causes, Extent, and Policy Implications of the Current Crisis in Insurance Availability and Affordability," Washington, D.C.: U.S. Department Of Justice.

Trebilcock, Michael J. (1987). "The Insurance-Deterrence Dilemma of Modern Tort Law," *San Diego Law Review*.

Venezian, Emilio (1985). "Ratemaking Methods and Profit Cycles in Property and Liability Insurance," *Journal of Risk and Insurance* 52, 477–500.

Weiss, Mary (1985). "A Multivariate Analysis of Loss Reserving Estimates in Property-Liability Insurers," *Journal Of Risk and Insurance* 52, 199–221.

Winter, Ralph A. (1988). "The Liability Crisis and The Dynamics of Competitive Insurance Markets," *Yale Journal On Regulation* 5, 455–499.

Winter, Ralph A. (1991a). "The Liability Insurance Market," *Journal of Economic Perspectives* 5, 15–136.

Winter, Ralph A. (1991b). "Solvency Regulation and the Insurance Cycle," *Economic Inquiry* 29, 458–471.

Winter, Ralph A. (1994). "The Dynamics Of Competitive Insurance Markets," *Journal Of Financial Intermediation* 3, 379–415.

Yuengert, Andrew (1991). "Excess Capacity in the Property/Casualty Industry," working paper, Federal Reserve Bank of New York.

Part VII
Industrial Organization of Insurance Markets

21 Organizational Forms Within the Insurance Industry: Theory and Evidence*

David Mayers

University of California

Clifford W. Smith, Jr.

University of Rochester

Abstract

Organizational forms within the insurance industry include stock companies, mutuals, reciprocals, and Lloyds. We focus on the association between the choice of organizational form and the firm's contracting costs, arguing that different organizational forms reduce contracting costs in specific dimensions. This suggests that differing costs of controlling particular incentive conflicts among the parties of the insurance firm lead to the efficiency of alternative organizational forms across lines of insurance. We analyze the incentives of individuals performing the three major functions within the insurance firm—the executive function, the owner function, and the customer function. We review evidence from the insurance industry that directly examines the product-specialization hypothesis. We then examine evidence on corporate policy choices by the alternative organizational forms: executive compensation policy, board composition, distribution system choice, reinsurance purchases, and the use of participating policies. Finally, we review evidence of the relative efficiency of the alternative organizational forms.

Keywords: Insurance, organizational form, executive compensation.
JEL Classification Numbers: G22; L22; D23.

21.1 INTRODUCTION

The range of organizational forms within the insurance industry is perhaps the broadest of any major industry. Included are stock companies that employ the standard cor-

* We thank the Bradley Policy Research Center at the Simon School for financial support.

porate form, mutuals and reciprocals that are more like cooperatives where customers are the owners of the firm, and Lloyds associations that offer insurance contracts by syndicates of individual underwriters.

Coase (1960) indicates that with no contracting costs, the organizational form of the insurance supplier (the assignment of property rights within the firm) will have no effect on real activity choices. But where contracting is costly, differing incentives among the parties to a contract generate costs. Relevant contracting costs take a variety of forms—the direct costs incurred in attempting to control incentive conflicts (for example, negotiation, administration, information, and litigation costs) as well as the opportunity cost that remains after appropriate control steps are taken, since it generally is not optimal to exercise complete control.

We examine the association between the choice of organizational form and the firm's contracting costs. We argue that different organizational forms reduce contracting costs in specific dimensions. This suggests that differing costs of controlling particular incentive conflicts among the parties of the insurance firm lead to the efficiency of alternative organizational forms in specific activities.

An important aspect of our analysis is its focus on the contracting costs associated with managerial discretion. Required managerial discretion should be lower in lines of insurance for which more loss data are available (Mayers and Smith, 1981), variance is lower (Fama and Jensen, 1983; Lamm-Tennant and Starks, 1992; and Doherty and Dionne, 1993), screening is less valuable (Hansmann, 1985, and Smith and Stutzer, 1990), and claims are expected to be adjudicated within a more stable legal environment (Mayers and Smith, 1988). Generally, the more discretion managers are authorized to exercise, the greater the potential for the managers to operate in their own interests. Since required managerial discretion varies across lines of insurance, and the costs of controlling managerial discretion vary across organizational forms, the organizational form most appropriate for particular lines of insurance also will vary. Recent empirical analyses provides tests of these hypotheses.

In Section 21.2, we analyze the incentives of individuals performing the three major functions within the insurance firm—the management function, the owner function, and the customer function. This section presents our theory of alternative organizational forms within the insurance industry. In Section 21.3, we review evidence from the insurance industry that directly examines the product-specialization hypothesis. We examine evidence on corporate policy choices by the alternative organizational forms in Section 21.4. In Section 21.5 we review the evidence that pertains to the relative efficiency of the alternative organizational forms. Section 21.6 contains our conclusions.

21.2 ALTERNATIVE ORGANIZATIONAL FORMS

We first examine the costs and benefits of the alternative organizational forms in order to better understand the nature of their respective comparative advantages. Different organizational forms create different incentives for the various contracting parties; variation in costs of controlling the resulting incentive problems imply that different forms are efficient in different circumstances. For instance, contracting costs are related to factors such as the degree of managerial discretion required in setting rates in a given line of insurance. Generally, the more discretion managers are authorized to exercise, the greater is the potential for those managers to operate in their self-interest at the expense of other parties to the firm. Alternative organizational forms thus provide control mechanisms that to varying degrees limit the ability of particular parties to operate in an opportunistic manner.

There are three important functions within each organizational form. The first is the manager function; managers are the decision makers—the executives that establish corporate strategy and decide how the firm will be organized and financed. Second is the owner function; owners provide capital and bear risk by owning claims to the residual income stream of the organization. Third is the customer function; policyholders pay premiums in return for a promise that they will receive stipulated indemnity payments from the insurance firm in the event that they incur specified losses. Figure 1 illustrates how the alternative organizational forms differ in the manner in which they combine these three functions.

Common Stock Companies. The distinguishing characteristic of the common stock insurance company is the potentially complete separation of the manager, owner, and customer functions. Separation allows specialization in these activities—this lowers costs. Thus, the unrestricted common stock of the insurance company allows efficiencies in riskbearing through specialization that are complemented by the benefits of managerial specialization. For example, managerial talent may be chosen in a common stock insurance company without strong consideration of a manager's wealth or willingness to bear risk.

Yet separation of the manager and owner functions means that managers of a stock company do not bear the full wealth effects of their actions. This leads to an important incentive problem. Managers generally have interests that diverge from those of owners.

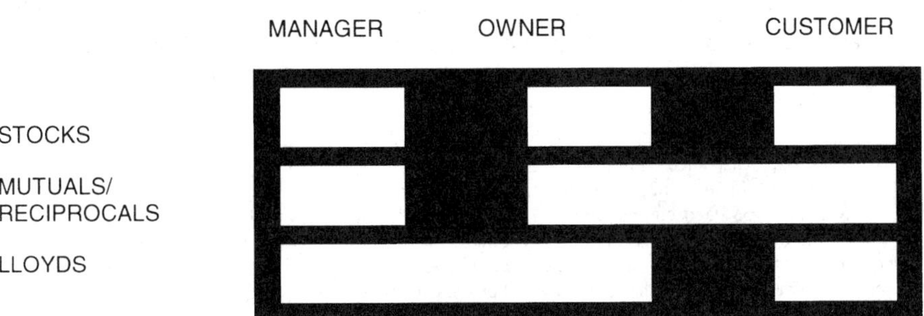

Figure 1 Organizational Forms Within the Insurance Industry and the Assignment of Manager, Owner, and Customer Functions

This incentive conflict between stockholders and managers is controlled in stock companies in several ways: (1) Insurance industry regulatory bodies and rating agencies monitor managers. (2) The executives are appointed by a stockholder-elected board of directors. (3) Most firms complement an external managerial labor market with an internal market through which executives compete. (4) Restrictions in the corporate charter limit managerial actions. (5) Executives are monitored in capital markets by stock analysts, institutional investors, and other large stockholders.[1] (6) The manager's compensation package can include incentive provisions which tie the manager's compensation to the performance of the firm's stock.[2] (7) An alternative management team can wrest control from the firm's current managers through an outside takeover if the firm is run inefficiently.[3] Yet these control devices neither separately nor collectively are perfect; unresolved conflicts between owners and managers generally remain.

In some stock insurance companies, managers also are major stockholders. Merging the manager and owner functions reduces control costs that arise if they are separate. The more complete the merger of owner and manager functions, the greater the internalization of the wealth consequences of the manager's decisions. Hence, closely-held stocks should have a comparative advantage in writing insurance where discretion is important.

Because stockholders and policyholders are separate parties, problems arise in stock insurance companies that are like the incentive problems between stockholders and bondholders in industrial corporations.[4] Thus, stockholders potentially gain from changing the firm's dividend, financing, and investment policies after insurance contracts are sold. For example, if customers buy policies expecting the firm to maintain its dividend payments at their current level, equity value would increase at policyholder expense if the firm increases its dividends financed by asset sales.[5]

In competitive markets, potential customers recognize these incentives. Rationally priced insurance reflects an unbiased forecast of these potential costs. Therefore, by limiting opportunities for expropriation by owners, the demand price for the company's policies increases. Potentially important mechanisms to limit such expropriation include: (1) loss of reputational capital and the consequent expected lower future demand prices for the company's policies, (2) state insurance guaranty funds,[6] (3) charter restrictions on assets in which the firm can invest, (4) charter restrictions and regulatory limitations on the dividends that can be paid to stockholders, and (5)

[1] See Brickley, Lease and Smith (1988, 1994).
[2] See Smith and Watts (1982, 1992) and Gaver and Gaver (1993).
[3] See Manne (1965), Jensen and Ruback (1983), and Jarrell, Brickley and Netter (1988).
[4] For example, both bondholders and policyholders own fixed payment claims. The difference is that for the bondholder the fixed promised payment (think of a zero coupon bond) is across states of the world for a given date, whereas for policyholders the fixed promised payment (think of a whole life policy) is across dates for a given state of the world.
[5] See Smith and Warner (1979).
[6] See Lee, Mayers and Smith (1997).

issuance of participating policies. Nonetheless, these control mechanisms fail to completely resolve the conflict between stockholders and policyholders.

Mutual Companies. In a mutual insurance company, the policyholders are both customers and owners—these functions are merged. Yet the rights of a policyholder in a mutual are more limited than the combination of stockholder and policyholder rights in a common stock firm. For example, ownership rights are limited through the company charter, policy provisions, and regulation in ways that are not imposed on stockholders of common stock firms. Importantly, ownership rights of the mutual policyholders are not transferable.[7] But by eliminating stockholders with their separate and sometimes conflicting interests, potential conflicts between owners and customers over dividend, financing, and investment policies are internalized. This is the major benefit of the mutual organizational form.

These benefits from control of the customer-owner conflict, however, are offset by less effective control of the owner-manager conflict. Specifically, inalienability of ownership rights in mutuals limits the mechanisms by which owner-manager conflicts can be controlled in at least three ways: (1) Without traded shares mutual managers are not monitored in capital markets by stock analysts, institutional investors, or block holders. (2) Stock-based compensation plans which can control aspects of the owner-manager conflict are infeasible without alienable shares. (3) A potentially significant factor in controlling management of a stock company is the threat of a hostile takeover (in which a tender offer is made directly to the firm's owners for their shares); such offers are impossible in a mutual. This more restricted corporate-control technology is thus a cost of the mutual organizational form.

The potential advantage of mutuals over stocks in controlling incentive problems between customers and owners is offset by exacerbated incentive problems between owners and managers. If the costs of controlling management in mutual insurers is higher than in stock firms, mutuals should have a comparative advantage in lines of insurance requiring less managerial discretion (for example, in lines of insurance for which there is extensive loss data).

Other aspects of coverage are important as well. For example, hold discretion constant but consider lines where the effective life of the policies is longer. Even small changes in dividend, financing, or investment policies can cumulate to have a material impact on the riskiness of the promised payoffs under this policy. Hence, mutuals should have a comparative advantage in such lines. For example, in 1993 mutuals generated \$36.5 billion of premium income in ordinary life compared to \$35.6 billion by stocks. However, across all property-liability lines, mutuals only generated \$63.3 billion compared to \$162.7 billion by stocks.

Finally, some mutuals own subsidiaries that are established as common-stock

[7] Hetherington (1969), Anderson (1973), and Kreider (1972) debate the implications of these restrictions for policyholder control of mutuals.

companies. The problems of controlling the managers in such a mutual-owned stock company are similar to that of a mutual; the owners of a mutual-owned stock company are ultimately the policyholders of the parent mutual. This implies that mutual-owned stock companies should have a comparative advantage in the same activities as mutuals.

Reciprocal Associations. Although reciprocal insurance associations appear similar to mutuals (in that the customer and owner functions appear to be merged) there are potentially important differences. A reciprocal is unincorporated with no stated capital; mutuals are incorporated with both stated capital and surplus. In a reciprocal, the policyholders appoint an individual or a corporation as an attorney-in-fact to operate the company, while in a mutual policyholders elect a board of directors to manage the company.

Further, the reciprocal provides cooperative insurance in which individual subscribers assume their liability as individuals.[8] A separate account generally is established for each subscriber, and subscribers can be required to accumulate reserves (typically equal to between two and five annual premiums) before becoming eligible to receive underwriting earnings. Not all reciprocals operate on a separate-accounts basis; the subscriber agreement sometimes simply provides for dividends at the discretion of the attorney-in-fact. Where reserves are fully allocated, the sum of the individual reserve accounts plus the current premiums represent the funds held by the reciprocal. However, generally the reciprocal maintains additional surplus. For example, Norgaard (1964) indicates that unallocated surplus existed in thirty-nine out of forty-four reciprocals in his sample. Beyond reserves, reciprocals sometimes retain the option to levy an (limited) assessment.

The manager of a reciprocal, the attorney-in-fact, is usually appointed by the policyholders with an advisory committee, that has control responsibility, representing the members of the association.[9] Some reciprocals, however, are organized and initially financed by corporate attorneys-in-fact who provide a "guaranty surplus," usually in the form of an interest-bearing note. In these cases, the structure of the reciprocal is like that of a closely-held stock company, with the manager and owner functions effectively residing with the corporate attorney-in-fact.

Even though the management function can be quite similar to that in a common stock insurance company, the insurance policies tend to differ; reciprocals more fre-

[8] Reinmuth (1967, pg. 32) states, "Those reciprocals operating on a separate account basis usually provide in the subscriber's agreement for the accumulation of a 'contingency surplus' by withholding a stated percentage of each subscriber's deposit premium or 'savings' which will not be available on withdrawal."

[9] This is really an oversimplification. The management of a reciprocal is appointed by policyholders through the subscriber's agreement or power of attorney. Thus, whether a subscriber has voting rights depends on the terms of the subscriber's agreement. The job of management can in fact be proprietary. If it is, the subscriber usually has the right to vote for an advisory committee, which may or may not have the right to replace the manager. For further discussion see Reinmuth (1967, pg. 15–16).

quently issue what amounts to participating, assessable policies. Thus, depending on the structure of the reciprocal, the owner-manager control problems can be similar to that of either a mutual insurance company or a closely-held stock insurance company.

This owner-manager control problem potentially is more severe in a reciprocal than in either closely held stocks or mutuals because individual subscribers may be required to leave reserves at risk. Of course, the policyholders' option to withdraw this capital also is a potentially important disciplining mechanism. While policyholders of stock or mutual insurance companies also can withdraw patronage as a disciplining device, this mechanism should be more effective for reciprocal subscribers if their subscriber agreement stipulates the (limited) return of surplus. Reinmuth (1967, pg. 32) reports, "Those reciprocals operating on a separate account basis usually provide in the subscriber's agreement for the accumulation of a "contingency surplus" by withholding a stated percentage of each subscriber's deposit premium or 'savings' which will not be available on withdrawal."

Another control device that reciprocal policyholders have is the potential to discipline management by forced dissolution of the association through the courts.[10] This apparently is accomplished more easily for reciprocals than for mutuals due to the courts interpretation of the nature of an association as opposed to a mutual corporation. In this regard, Reinmuth suggests that the reciprocal can be considered a "trust for a purpose."

In sum, it is difficult to classify the managerial-control problems of reciprocals. The managerial-control problems can vary from reciprocal to reciprocal and can be similar to that of a mutual insurance company or that of a closely-held stock insurance company. Only the rather weak statement that managerial discretion in a reciprocal should be somewhere in between that of these two alternative organizational forms appears appropriate.

Lloyds Associations. In a Lloyds, syndicates of members typically underwrite policies; members are then personally responsible for that portion of the risk underwritten. Thus, since individual underwriters are the insurers, this organizational form merges the manager and owner functions. By merging the functions, incentive problems between managers and owners are controlled. However this benefit comes with potentially substantial costs. Merging the manager and owner functions reduces gains from specialization as well as raising expected costs of opportunistic actions with respect to policyholders.

Underwriting through syndicates also raises problems of controlling intra-

[10] As reported by Reinmuth, (1967, pg. 36): "It would appear that the subscribers of a reciprocal have the power to request a court of equity to dissolve the exchange. In McAlexander v. Waldscriber it was held that a court of equity, at the suit of a subscriber, had the power to appoint a receiver for a reciprocal insurance 'fund,' upon allegations that the fund was being mismanaged and dissipated by the attorney-in-fact. The receiver was directed to manage, disburse and liquidate the 'fund' so as to do justice to all parties in interest under their contract. In Irwin v. Missouri Valley Bridge and Iron company, a case involving a similar set of facts, the court reached a similar conclusion."

syndicate conflicts. Typically, members have relatively specialized roles within the syndicate; in some cases the organization looks like a partnership with general partners making most decisions and limited partners primarily supplying capital. And while syndicate managers historically were also underwriters, there has been a shift to syndicates run by professional managers. In general, the costs of controlling intra-syndicate conflicts are reduced through: (1) mutual monitoring, which controls potential problems among syndicate members as well as problems between owners and policyholders (since syndicate members have few liability limitations included in the contracts, they have incentives to monitor syndicate decisions); (2) restrictions on membership through net-worth requirements, mandatory audits, and constraints on the size of commitments in relation to the capital individual members may undertake; (3) the central guarantee fund posted by the members, which acts like a bond; (4) stable syndicates, implying a form of long-run implicit contract. (The differential application of these control mechanisms helps explain reputational difference between London and American Lloyds.)

Thus there are costs and benefits of the Lloyds organizational form. Because the benefits largely stem from controlling the incentive conflicts between managers and owners, Mayers and Smith (1981) argue that Lloyds associations should have a comparative advantage in writing insurance where managerial discretion in rate setting is important—for example, in insuring against unusual hazards.[11]

21.3 MANAGERIAL DISCRETION AND ALTERNATIVE ORGANIZATIONAL FORMS

Because control mechanisms differ across organizational forms, the discretion authorized management also should differ. Moreover, variation in managerial decision-making authority implies that different organizational forms have a comparative advantage in different activities. Mayers and Smith (1981) argue that mutuals should have a comparative advantage in activities which require lower managerial discretion, while stocks should have a comparative advantage in activities which require higher discretion.

Mayers and Smith (1988) test this managerial-discretion hypothesis employing cross-sectional data from the property liability insurance industry; they document variation in product specialization across organizational forms. Their evidence is consistent with the managerial-discretion hypothesis; it suggests that Lloyds operate in

[11] One case in which risks changed frequently and managerial discretion was important is marine insurance in the early nineteenth century. Wright and Fayle (1928) report the adjustment of rates by an underwriter at Lloyd's of London. "Take, for example, the year of Trafalgar, and the routes specially affected by movements of hostile fleets. For homeward voyages from the West Indies, the average rate on 76 risk accepted by Mr. Janson during the first quarter of the year was 8½ per cent. The arrival of Villeneuve's fleet in the West Indies, sent it up to 13½ per cent, and thence to 15 per cent and over. It touched 16 per cent when he was making for the Channel, but fell to 11 per cent after his indecisive actions with Calder and his return to Cadiz."

the highest discretion lines, followed by stocks and reciprocals, with mutuals in the lowest discretion lines. They also find that stocks operate on a geographically less concentrated basis than Lloyds, mutuals, or reciprocals.

Lamm-Tennant and Starks (1993) test the managerial-discretion hypothesis by examining insurer activity choices using panel data. They measure underwriting risk by the variance of the loss ratio. Their evidence indicates that, compared to mutual insurers, stocks write more business in lines with higher underwriting risk. Kleffner and Doherty (1996) examine underwriting of catastrophic earthquake insurance. They find that stock insurers underwrite more earthquake insurance than mutuals.[12] If managerial-discretion requirements are greater when underwriting risks are higher, these studies support the managerial-discretion hypothesis.

Yet taxes and regulation vary across organizational forms as well as across states in which the firms do business. For example, minimum capital requirements and tax rules vary between mutual and stock companies. Thus, it is unclear how much of the variation documented by Mayers and Smith, Lamm-Tennant and Starks, or Kleffner and Doherty is attributable to the control-related arguments of the managerial-discretion hypothesis.

To help solve this identification problem, Mayers and Smith (1994) focus just on common-stock insurers, their sample varies widely in ownership structure; at one extreme, the equity is owned by a mutual insurer; at the other, by a single individual or family. By focusing on variation among stock insurers, they better control for potential effects of taxes and regulation. And by distinguishing among closely-held, widely-held, and mutual-owned stock companies, they exploit more texture in organization form than previous studies, thereby providing a richer understanding of this industry. They argue that the analysis of managerial-control problems within mutuals also applies to stock companies owned by mutuals, and that the incentives associated with Lloyds are similar to those for closely held stock companies. Their evidence indicates that an insurer's activity choices, its product lines, are strongly related to ownership structure; in particular, the activities of stocks owned by mutuals are more like those of mutuals and those of closely held stocks are more like those of Lloyds. The activities of widely held stocks fall in between. Hence this evidence is consistent with the hypothesis that different organizational forms have comparative advantage in different lines of insurance.

21.4 CORPORATE POLICY CHOICES AND ORGANIZATIONAL FORM

Milgrom and Roberts (1995) examine complementarities among inputs to explain corporate choices of organizational structure, technology, and strategy. The standard def-

[12] Kleffner and Doherty (1996) suggest organizational form is important because of stock companies' more ready access to capital.

inition of complementarity in economics states that two inputs to a production process are complements if a decrease in the price of one causes an increase in the use of the other. But Milgrom and Roberts use this term not just in its traditional sense of a relation between pairs of inputs, but also in a broader sense as a relation among groups of activities. They introduce a broader definition: several activities are *strategic complements* if doing more of one activity increases the marginal profitability of each of the other activities. If the activities can be expressed as differentiable functions, this corresponds to positive mixed partial derivatives of the payoff function—the marginal returns to one activity are increasing in the levels of other activities. Yet their analysis emphasizes that continuity, differentiability, and convexity of the payoff functions are not necessary—only an ability to order the various activities is required.

This framework is particularly useful here where we want to examine executive compensation packages, distribution systems, board composition, risk-taking, and insurance contracts across the various organizational forms. The key idea in the Milgrom and Roberts analysis is that if choosing a particular organizational form changes payoffs from using a particular distribution system, then organizational form and distribution systems are strategic complements.

Executive Compensation and Organizational Form. If mutuals have a comparative advantage in business activities requiring less managerial discretion, then the value of the marginal product of executives of mutual companies should be lower than that of stock-company executives. Therefore, given competitive markets for managers, mutual executives should be paid less and receive less incentive compensation than stock-company executives. But managers of a mutual are not subjected to the same disciplining forces from the market for corporate control as are managers of a widely-held stock company. If mutual managers more successfully insulate themselves from competitive market forces than do the managers of widely-held stocks, mutual managers' compensation is potentially higher.

To test these hypotheses Mayers and Smith (1992) examine stock and mutual chief executive officer compensation within the life insurance industry. Their evidence is consistent with the managerial-discretion hypothesis—the compensation of mutual CEOs is significantly lower than that of stock CEOs and the compensation of mutual CEOs is significantly less responsive to firm performance than that of stock CEOs.

Nonetheless, it is possible that mutual CEOs are entrenched and hence extract more total compensation than comparable stock CEOs—not in salary, but through excessive perquisite consumption. Mayers and Smith examine this possibility by exploiting details of the ownership structure of insurance firms. Insurance company subsidiaries can be owned either by a stock or a mutual parent. If subsidiaries have a comparative advantage in business activities similar to those of their parents, then compensation among CEOs of mutuals' subsidiaries also should be lower than that of CEOs of stock-company subsidiaries. However, perquisite consumption by subsidiary

CEOs should exhibit less variation than that by parent company CEOs so long as control systems between parents and subsidiaries are similar for both mutual and stock parents. Mayers and Smith find that, consistent with the managerial-discretion hypothesis, the compensation of mutual-subsidiary CEOs is significantly lower than that of stock-subsidiary CEOs.

Further evidence on managerial entrenchment among mutual executives is provided by Bohn (1995). He examines CEO turnover for a sample of 93 stock and 168 mutual insurance firms from 1984–1992. Inconsistent with the hypothesis that mutual managers are entrenched, he finds that the unconditional probability of CEO turnover is higher in mutuals than stocks (8.3% per annum compared to 6%). In addition, he reports that the probability of CEO turnover is related to firm performance both for stocks and mutuals.

Board Composition and Organizational Form. Variation in organizational form within the insurance industry affords an opportunity to test hypotheses about the role of board composition within the technology for corporate control. The inalienability of mutual ownership claims restricts corporate-control mechanisms like the external takeover market, capital-market monitoring, and stock-based incentive compensation. These limitations increase the importance of monitoring by outside directors. If these alternate mechanisms are substitutes, mutuals should use more outside directors than stocks. Alternatively, if mutual managers are entrenched, they might use few outside directors to avoid the bother.

Mayers, Shivdasani and Smith (1997) examine the composition of the board of directors for 345 life insurance companies. Their evidence indicates that mutuals employ a significantly larger fraction of outside directors than do stock companies. This result appears robust; it obtains both in the unadjusted data as well as after controlling for differences in firm size, operating policy, and ownership concentration. Moreover, neither variation in board size nor state laws regulating board composition can explain these results.

They also examine changes in board composition around changes in organizational form. For a sample of 27 life insurance firms that switch from stock to mutual form, they find a significant increase in the use of outside board members. For a sample of 50 property-liability insurers that switch from mutual to stock charter, they find a significant reduction in the use of outside directors. Board size is unchanged in both samples. This consistency between their cross-sectional and time-series evidence helps ensure that their cross-sectional results are not attributable to uncontrolled differences in business operations between stocks and mutuals. Thus, the Mayers, Shivdasani, and Smith evidence supports the hypothesis that outside directors are an important control mechanism.

Distribution System Choice and Organizational Form. The insurance industry employs a variety of distribution systems: insurance contracts are sold through direct writers, exclusive agents, independent agents, and brokers. In the direct-writer system, the sales agent is an employee of the insurance firm. An exclusive agent also represents a single insurer, yet is not technically the firm's employee. An independent agent represents more than one insurance company. Finally, a broker represents the customer and negotiates with multiple insurers. Thus, exclusive agents and direct writers are more closely tied contractually to the insurer than are independent agents, while brokers' interests are more closely aligned with those of their customers than are other agents. These relations are illustrated in Table 2.

Mayers, and Smith (1981) argue that the use of independent agents (and brokers) better bonds the insurer's promise to provide services to the policyholder and helps control potential expropriative behavior by the insurer. Thus, the independent-agency system is more valuable for organizational forms where these incentive problems are more severe. Independent agents have a comparative advantage because their knowledge makes them effective in influencing claim settlements and because a threat to switch their business to an alternate insurer is credible.

If the use of independent agents more effectively bonds against policyholder expropriation, the value of an independent-agency system will be higher where the opportunities for expropriation are greater. This should occur in companies with organizational forms that permit more managerial discretion. Therefore, independent agents should be used more frequently by Lloyds and closely-held stocks because the value of bonding against opportunistic behavior should be higher for these organizational forms. Conversely, independent agents should be used less frequently by mutuals and mutual-owned stocks because the value of such bonding is lower.

To test this hypothesis Kim, Mayers, and Smith (1996) examine a large sample

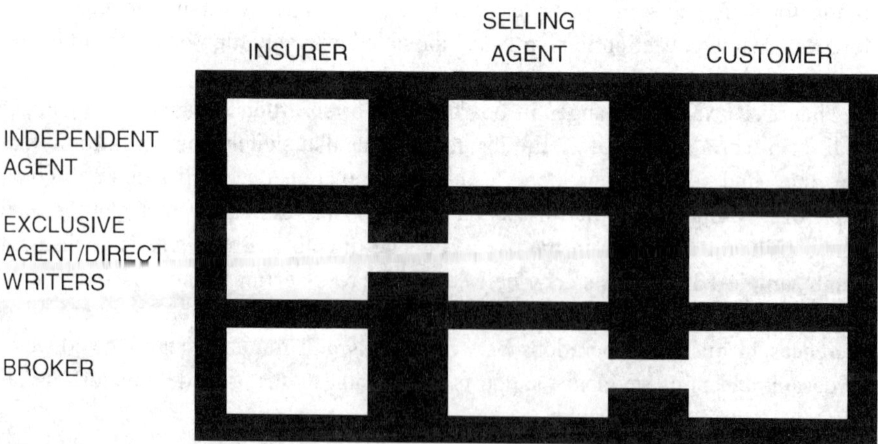

Figure 2 Distribution System Within the Insurance Industry and the Relations Among Insurer Selling Agent and Customer Functions

of property-liability insurance companies. Their evidence is consistent with the managerial-discretion hypothesis. The independent-agency system is more prevalent among Lloyds associations and closely-held stock companies, followed in order by widely held stocks, mutuals, mutual-owned stocks, reciprocals, and association-owned stocks. These results obtain either from examining the number of firms employing a particular distribution system, or from examining average direct business written by the firms using alternative distribution systems. Thus, for example, more Lloyds associations use the independent-agency system; moreover, the average independent-agency Lloyds writes more business than the average exclusive agent Lloyds.

Risktaking and Organizational Form: Reinsurance. Incentives for risktaking vary with organizational form. Within the insurance industry, reinsurance purchases—like traditional insurance purchases by industrial corporations—are a mechanism that can be used to limit risktaking. A reinsurance contract is an insurance policy purchased by one insurance company, the ceding company, from another, the reinsurer.

Risk aversion is the primary motive for insurance purchases by individuals; moreover risk aversion can partially explain the demand for insurance by closely-held corporations and partnerships. But risk aversion provides a deficient explanation for insurance purchases by widely held corporations. The corporate form is itself a contractual structure with significant risk-management capabilities. Since the corporation's owners, its stockholders, can hold well-diversified portfolios of financial claims, idiosyncratic losses can be managed through diversification. Thus, instead of risk aversion, corporate insurance purchases should be driven by the structure of the tax code, costs of financial distress (including potential investment-incentive effects of a corporation's capital structure), the corporation's ownership structure, comparative advantages in real service production, and the composition of corporate managers' compensation packages (see Mayers and Smith 1982, 1987).

Mayers and Smith (1990) analyze reinsurance purchases for a sample of 1,276 property-liability insurance companies. Their sample includes firms across a broad range of organizational forms—stocks, mutuals, Lloyd's, and reciprocals. Moreover, they distinguish among stocks that are widely held, closely held, owned by a single family, owned by a mutual, and owned by an association. Their evidence suggests organizational form matters. Generally, the less diversified the owners' portfolios (the more concentrated is ownership), the greater the reinsurance purchases. Thus Lloyd's reinsure most, while widely held stocks reinsure least. Moreover, subsidiary and group relations affect the demand for reinsurance. Subsidiaries and group members reinsure more (although their data do not allow distinguishing between intra-group transactions and reinsurance transactions with external reinsurance companies). They also provide evidence that size, credit standing, and geographic concentration reduce the demand for reinsurance, as well as weak evidence that line-of-business concentration reduces reinsurance demand.

Risktaking and Organizational Form: Guaranty Funds. Lee, Mayers and Smith (1997) examine the impact of establishing post-assessment guaranty funds on property-liability insurance company risktaking. They investigate insurers' portfolio-composition changes that occur around the time these state guaranty-fund laws are enacted. Merton (1977) argues that guaranty funds are like put options granted to the insurance firms. To maximize the value of this option, insurers should increase the riskiness of their underlying activities. Yet proponents of guaranty funds have argued that structure of the funds establish incentives for competitors to monitor. The more effective additional monitoring, the smaller any increase in risktaking.

Lee, Mayers and Smith find that property-liability insurers shift their asset portfolios around the date of guaranty-fund enactments, increasing their holdings of stocks and reducing their holdings of bonds and other assets. Their evidence thus is inconsistent with the hypothesis that the structure of the guaranty funds provides sufficient incentives to reduce risktaking in the industry through effective monitoring, either by competing insurance firms or regulators. Rather, their evidence is consistent with the hypothesis that because the firm's assessment does not vary with its asset risk, the structure of guaranty funds provides an incentive for increased risktaking in insurers' investment activities.

The incentives for increased risktaking differ across organizational forms. For example, when they investigate the asset adjustments for stock and mutual insurers separately, they find that the shift to riskier assets following fund enactment occurs only for stock insurers, supporting the hypothesis that stock insurers have stronger incentives to increase investment risk. This helps explain the observed higher insolvency rates among stocks than mutuals in the period since 1969. They also find increased risktaking by stock companies that are owned by mutuals. This suggests that the bundling of owner and customer claims in a mutual is the important factor controlling incentives for excessive risktaking.

This evidence has potentially important implications for survivorship of the mutual form of organization. While the mutual form imposes costs in the form of lost specialization in risk-bearing and limited corporate governance/control mechanisms, this evidence suggests that merging owner and customer functions controls conflicts of interest over investment policy. Fama and Jensen (1983) argue that mutuals survive because the redeemable claims they offer are a substitute for the control systems of stock companies. Yet stock insurers offer claims with redeemability features virtually identical to those offered by mutuals. Thus, redeemable claims are not unique to mutuals. Moreover, mutual life companies (the dominant organizational form in this line) offer whole life policies with significant "lock in" terms. This suggests that claim redeemability is not necessary for the survival of mutuals. The reduced incentives for risktaking which Lee, Mayers and Smith document are specific to mutuals and, as argued in Mayers and Smith (1981), provide an important benefit contributing to the efficiency and survival of the mutual form of organization.

Insurance Contracts and Organizational Form. Another way to control the policyholder-stockholder conflict is to issue participating policies (Mayers and Smith, 1981, and Garven and Pottier, 1995). A participating policy gives the policyholder a claim on a fraction of the insurance firm's accounting earnings. This acts somewhat like a convertibility provision in a corporate bond contract, except that the policyholder has a claim to only current accounting earnings, whereas the convertible bondholder has a claim to the capitalized value of the economic cash flows (Smith and Warner, 1979 and Mikkelson, 1981). Thus, to the extent that the firm's capitalized cash flows and accounting earnings are positively related, any gain to stockholders from transferring resources to themselves after the sale of the policy is reduced by issuing participating policies.

Thus, participating policies offer stocks a way to control the policyholder-stockholder problem that is similar to the way mutuals control the problem. This would suggest participating policies would be most important in stock companies. In fact, participating policies were first offered, in the United States, by a stock company.[13] But they are now more prevalent in mutuals than in stocks. Garven and Pottier, for a sample of 475 stock life insurers and 109 mutual life insurers in 1991, show that 12.5% of the stock company business was through participating policies, whereas 94.2% of the mutuals' business was through participating policies. In dollar amounts the mutuals had $4,159 million of participating insurance in force and $255 million of non-participating insurance in force. The numbers are practically reversed for the stock companies.

In a participating policy, higher premiums are charged at the beginning of the period and policy dividends are returned at the end of the period. If the company experiences a shock to surplus during the period, the dividend is reduced. Since mutuals have less effective access to capital markets than stocks, participating policies are more valuable to mutuals in allowing them to better absorb such shocks. In effect, economic leverage is less volatile if the insurer issues participating policies. Thus, issuing such policies can help control a form of the underinvestment problem discussed by Myers (1977).

Moreover, an important cost of the mutual organizational form is less effective control of the owner-manager conflict. One facet of the owner-manager conflict is the managerial-discretion problem labeled the free-cash-flow problem by Jensen (1986). Jensen defines free cash flow as cash in excess of that required to fund all positive net present value projects. If managerial perquisites are positively related to firm size, managers with free cash flow have an incentive to undertake projects that have zero or negative net present value in order to make the firm larger.

Jensen argues that debt reduces the agency costs of free cash flow by reducing

[13] In 1836, the Girard Life Insurance Annuity and Trust Co. Issued the first participating policy in the United States. A circular issued that year says, "The income of the company will be apportioned between the stockholders and the assured for life, an advantage given in America by this company alone." (Stalson, 1942, p. 94)

the cash available for spending at the discretion of managers. Thus, industrial firms that have large free cash flow should be more highly leveraged to control this problem. Similarly, mutual insurance companies can control this managerial-discretion problem by issuing participating policies (Wells, Cox, and Gaver, 1995). These policies require the firm to pay dividends that are based on accounting earnings, thus reducing the cash available for unprofitable projects.

The control function of participating policies should be more important in organizations that generate large cash flows but have low growth prospects. Wells, Cox, and Gaver (1995) argue that large cash flow and low growth prospects to a large degree characterizes the life insurance industry. Since they expect a more severe owner-manager conflict in mutuals, they examine the relation between organizational form and free cash flow. Their results support the joint hypothesis that the managerial-discretion problem is greater in mutuals and that participating policies provide less than complete control—they find that mutual insurers have a greater level of free cash flow than stock insurers.

21.5 ORGANIZATIONAL FORM AND EFFICIENCY

Several authors have examined the relative efficiency of stock versus mutual or reciprocal organizational forms. For example, Spiller (1972) argues that management exploits its position in a mutual to gain personally at the expense of the firm's other claimholders. Frech (1980) concludes the "examination of the actual property rights structure of mutual insurers indicates that their owners do not have full property rights. Thus they are expected to perform less efficiently then stock insurers, and that expectation is borne out." Reinmuth (1967) in a study analyzing reciprocals, determines that they also are inefficient. Thus, each of these cross-sectional studies conclude that mutuals and reciprocals are less efficient than stocks.

In contrast to these studies, the analysis in Mayers and Smith (1981) assumes the efficiency of the mutual form of organization in explaining the observed distribution of organizational forms including both stock and mutual firms. Schwert's (1981) analysis suggests that a more powerful test of the hypothesis that mutuals are potentially efficient would focus on time-series evidence from firms that switch organizational form from stock to mutual, that is, that mutualize, or from mutual to stock, that is, that demutualize. To test the implications of the different theories of the efficiency of mutuals, Mayers and Smith (1986) analyze the impact of the change in organizational form from stock to mutual on the three major groups of claimholders—managers, owners, and customers. They examine the changes in stock prices, premium income, and management turnover that accompany mutualization for a sample of 30 life insurance firms.

Mayers and Smith examine returns to stockholders, as well as changes in premium income, product mix, policy lapse rates, and management turnover. They conclude that for their sample of firms which change from a stock to a mutual organizational form, that on average the change is efficiency-enhancing. Their evidence indicates that growth in premium income does not fall, policy lapse rates do not rise, stockholders receive a substantial premium for their stock, management turnover declines, and there is no material change in product mix. Thus, no group of claimholders systematically loses in this sample of firms that chooses to go through the mutualization process. And if mutuals were inefficient—if the firm were less valuable after the change in organizational form—then at least one of these groups would have to lose. These results also are consistent with rational voting behavior, since stockholders, policyholders, and managers all have effective vetoes of the mutualization plan.

The Mayers and Smith evidence should be contrasted with that of Spiller, Frech, and Reinmuth who conclude that mutuals and reciprocals are inefficient. We believe that this difference in results occurs because the Mayers and Smith time-series examination of changes in organizational form picks up both the additional costs of mutuals associated with less effective control of managers as well as the additional benefits associated with more effective control of the owner-customer conflict. Cross-sectional tests cannot easily measure these additional benefits.

21.6 CONCLUSIONS

Gregor Mendel is generally regarded as the father of modern genetics. Yet this monk's scientific work concentrated on breeding edible peas in the garden behind his monastery. From peas—dwarfed, tall, smooth, wrinkled, green, yellow—he was to derive the basic laws which make modern genetics the most exact of the biological sciences.

In a sense, the insurance industry offers a laboratory for the study of organizational forms that is like Mendel's garden. Insurance firms exhibit rich variation in their choices of ownership structure, executive compensation, board composition, distribution system, risktaking activities, and contract structure. Yet this variation occurs within a single industry. This makes the analysis of this variation more controlled and the likelihood of omitted-variables problems lower. And while this industry is important in itself, it offers a potentially invaluable springboard for a richer understanding of organizational forms in other industries across the economy.

21.7 REFERENCES

Anderson, B.M. (1973). "Policyholder Control of a Mutual Life Insurance Company," *Cleveland State Law Review* 22, 439–449.

Bohn, J.G. (1995). "Management Turnover and Succession in the Insurance Industry," Working Paper, Harvard University.

Brickley, J.A., R.C. Lease and C.W. Smith, Jr. (1988). "Ownership Structure and Voting on Antitakeover Amendments," *Journal of Financial Economics* 20, 1/2, 267–291.

Brickley, J.A., R.C. Lease and C.W. Smith, Jr. (1994). "Corporate Voting: Evidence from Charter Amendment Proposals," *Journal of Corporate Finance* 1, 1, 5–31.

Coase, R. (1960). "The Problem of Social Cost," *Journal of Law and Economics* 3, 1–44.

Doherty, N.A. and G. Dionne (1993). "Insurance With Undiversifiable Risk: Contract Structure and Organizational Forms of Insurance Firms," *Journal of Risk and Uncertainty* 6, 2, 187–203.

Fama, E.F. and M.C. Jensen (1983). "Agency Problems and Residual Claims," *Journal of Law and Economics* 26, 327–349.

Frech, H.E., III (1980). "Health Insurance: Private, Mutuals or Government," *Economics of Nonproprietary Organizations Research in Law and Economics*, Suppl. 1. Greenwich, Conn.: JAI Press, Inc., 61–73.

Garven, J.R. and S.W. Pottier (1995). " Incentive Contracting and the Role of Participation Rights in Stock Insurers," *Journal of Risk and Insurance* 62, 253–270.

Gaver, J.J. and K.M. Gaver (1993). "Additional Evidence on the Association Between the Investment Opportunity Set and Corporate Finance, Dividend and Compensation Policies," Journal of Accounting and Economics, 125–160.

Hansmann, H. (1985). "The Organization of Insurance Companies: Mutual versus Stock," *Journal of Law, Economics, and Organization* 1, 125–154.

Hetherington, J.A.C. (1969). "Fact v. Fiction: Who Owns Mutual Insurance Companies?" *Wisconsin Law Review* 4, 1068–1103.

Jarrell, G., J. Brickley and J. Netter (1988). "The Market for Corporate Control: The Empirical Evidence Since," *Journal of Economic Perspectives* 2, 49–68.

Jensen, M. (1986). "Agency Cost of Free Cash Flow, Corporate Finance and Takeovers," *American Economic Review* 76, 323–339.

Jensen, M. and R. Ruback (1983). "The Market for Corporate Control: The Scientific Evidence," *Journal of Financial Economics* 11, 5–50.

Kim, W.J., Mayers, D. and C.W. Smith (1996). "On the Choice of Insurance Distribution Systems," *Journal of Risk and Insurance* 63, 207–227.

Kleffner, A.E. and N.A. Doherty (1996). "Costly Risk and the Supply of Catastrophic Insurance," *Journal of Risk and Insurance* 63, 657–671.

Kreider, G.P. (1972). "Who Owns the Mutuals? Proposals for Reform of Membership Rights in Mutual Insurance and Banking Companies," *Cincinnati Law Review* 41, 275–311.

Lamm-Tennant, J. and L.T. Starks, (1993). "Stock versus Mutual Ownership Structures: The Risk Implications," *Journal of Business* 66, 29–46.

Lee, S.J., D. Mayers and C.W. Smith, Jr. (1977). "Guaranty Finds and Risk-Taking Behavior: Evidence for the Insurance Industry," *Journal of Financial Economics* forthcoming.

Manne, H.G. (1965). "Mergers and the Market for Corporate Control," *Journal of Political Economy* 73, 110–120.

Mayers, D., A. Shivdasani and C.W. Smith, Jr. (1997). "Board Composition in the Life Insurance Industry," *Journal of Business* 70, 33–63.

Mayers, D. and C.W. Smith, Jr. (1981). "Contractual Provisions, Organizational Structure, and Conflict Control in Insurance Markets," *Journal of Business* 54, 3, 407–434.

Mayers, D. and C.W. Smith, Jr. (1982). "On the Corporate Demand for Insurance," *Journal of Business* 55, 2, 281–296.

Mayers, D. and C.W. Smith, Jr. (1986). "Ownership Structure and Control: The Mutualization of Stock Life Insurance Companies," *Journal of Financial Economics* 16, 73–98.

Mayers, D. and C.W. Smith, Jr. (1987). "Corporate Insurance and the Underinvestment Problem," *Journal of Risk and Insurance* LIV, 1, 45–54.

Mayers, D. and C.W. Smith, Jr. (1988). "Ownership Structure Across Lines of Property Casualty Insurance," *Journal of Law and Economics* 31, 351–378.

Mayers, D. and C.W. Smith, Jr. (1990). "On the Corporate Demand for Insurance: Evidence from the Reinsurance Market," *Journal of Business* 63, 19–40.

Mayers, D. and C.W. Smith, Jr. (1992). "Executive Compensation in the Life Insurance Industry," *Journal of Business* 65, 51–74.

Mayers, D. and C.W. Smith, Jr. (1994). "Managerial Discretion, Regulation, and Stock Insurer Ownership Structure," *The Journal of Risk and Insurance* 61, 4, 638–655.

Merton, R.C (1977). "An Analytic Derivation of the Cost of Deposit Insurance and Loan Guarantees: On Application of Modern Option Pricing Theory," *Journal of Banking and Finance* 1, 3–11.

Mikkelson, W.H. (1981). "Convertible Calls and Security Returns," *Journal of Financial Economics* 9, 237–264.

Milgrom, P. and J. Roberts (1995). "Complementarities and Fit: Strategy, Structure, and Organizational Change," *Journal of Accounting and Economics* 19, 179–208.

Myers, S. (1977). "Determinants of Corporate Borrowing," *Journal of Financial Economics* 5, 147–175.

Norgaard, R.L. (1964). "What is a Reciprocal?" *Journal of Risk and Insurance* 31, 51.

Reinmuth, D.F. (1967). The Regulation of Reciprocal Insurance Exchanges, Homewood, Ill,: Richard D. Irwin, Inc.

Schwert, G.W. (1981). "Using Financial Data to Measure Effects of Regulation," *The Journal of Law and Economics* 24, 121–158.

Smith, C.W., Jr. and J.B. Warner (1979). "On Financial Contracting: An Analysis of Bond Covenants," *Journal of Financial Economics* 7, 117–161.

Smith, C.W., Jr. and R. Watts (1982). "Incentive And Tax Effects of Executive Compensation Plans," *Australian Journal of Management* 7, 139–157.

Smith, C.W., Jr. and R. Watts (1992). "The Investment Opportunity Set and Corporate Financing Dividend and Compensation Policies," *Journal of Financial Economics* 32, 263–292.

Smith, B.D. and M.J. Stutzer (1990). "Adverse Selection, Aggregate Uncertainty, and the Role for Mutual Insurance Contracts," *Journal of Business* 63, 4, 493–510.

Spiller, R. (1972). "Ownership and Performance: Stock and Mutual Life Insurance Companies," *Journal of Risk and Insurance* 34, 17–25.

Wells, B.P., L. Cox and K.M. Gaver (1995). "Free Cash Flow in the Life Insurance Industry," *Journal of Risk and Insurance* 62, 50–64.

Wright, C. and D.E. Fayle (1928). "A History of Lloyd's," London: Macmilla.

22 Insurance Distribution Systems

Laureen Regan
Temple University

Sharon Tennyson
Cornell University

Abstract
This chapter details the use of different insurance distribution systems in practice, analyzes key issues in distribution system use based on economic theories of the organization of the firm, and discusses public policy and regulatory issues related to insurance distribution. The chapter focuses on what we believe to be the three major economic issues in insurance distribution: the choice of distribution system(s) by an insurer; the nature of insurer-agent relationships, including compensation structure and resale price maintenance; and regulatory oversight of insurance distribution activities, including regulation of entry and of information disclosure to consumers.

Keywords: Insurance firms, organizational form, regulation.
JEL Numbers: G22, L20, G28

22.1 INTRODUCTION

Firms in the insurance industry vary along many dimensions, including product distribution systems. A wide variety of distribution methods are used in the industry. Insurance distribution systems span the spectrum from the use of a professional employee sales force, to contracting with independent sales representatives, to direct response methods such as mail and telephone solicitation. The ongoing competitive and technological revolution in the financial services industries has resulted in greater segmentation of distribution by product market, and greater use of multiple distribution methods by firms, including the establishment of marketing relationships and alliances with non-insurance concerns.

The purpose of this chapter is to detail the use of insurance distribution systems in practice, to understand their use from a theoretical perspective and to discuss public policy and regulatory issues related to insurance distribution. Two points about the chapter are worth noting in advance. First, because much of the academic literature on insurance distribution has focused on the United States, and because we have greater access to databases on that country, most of the detailed discussion of insurance institutions in this chapter will refer to the U.S. marketplace. We make reference to insurance distribution in other countries where the data are available, but refer the reader to other sources for details on these markets.[1] The second noteworthy point is that the academic literature on insurance distribution is quite narrowly focused. There are many interesting and important issues that have received little or no attention in the literature. The approach taken in this chapter is therefore to discuss not only the state of knowledge from existing literature, but also to raise questions arising from economic theory regarding areas that need further research.

We focus our discussion on what we believe to be the three major economic issues in insurance distribution. The first is distribution system choice. Due to the variety of distribution systems employed in the industry, the differences in contractual relationships across them, and the recent market share gains of nontraditional distribution systems, an important area of research is the optimal choice of distribution system. Much of the existing research on property-liability insurance distribution has examined aspects of this question. This will continue to be an important question for both property-liability and life insurers, as the use of multiple distribution systems becomes increasingly common.

Closely linked to this question are others regarding the nature of the insurer-agent relationship. One particular area of interest is the structure of agent compensation. The differences in agent compensation structure across different distribution systems have received attention in property-liability insurance. Questions also surround the incentive effects of commission compensation schemes with regard to agent service and information provision, and, in the life insurance industry, unethical practices such as unnecessary policy replacement (often known as *twisting*). Compensation structure is also related to agent incentives to offer price discounts via commission rebating, a practice outlawed in all U.S. states until recently.

The final issue that we explore is regulatory oversight of insurance distribution activities. Life insurance sellers in many countries recently have come under criticism for misleading sales practices or high-pressure tactics. Agents have been alleged to exaggerate the benefits of their policies or fail to reveal key elements of risk to policyholders. In response to these and similar concerns, information disclosure regulation for both life and property-liability insurance sellers has been strengthened significantly in several countries, and is being considered in others. As new regulatory systems are designed, questions intensify regarding the need for such regulation, the appropriate regulatory mechanism, and the effectiveness and results of regulations.

[1] Much of our information on markets outside of the United States is drawn from Skipper, 1998, Nuttney, 1994, Hoschka, 1994, and Finsinger and Pauly, 1986.

The organization of the chapter is as follows. Section 22.2 provides background information on the different distribution systems employed in the insurance industry. Section 22.3 summarizes the state of knowledge from theoretical and empirical studies of distribution system choice by insurance firms. Section 22.4 discusses issues surrounding commission compensation and commission rebating in insurance retailing. Section 22.5 describes the regulation of insurance distribution and the potential economic rationales for this regulation. Section 22.6 concludes with a discussion of recent trends in insurance markets and their implications for insurance distribution.

22.2 BACKGROUND

Product distribution channels in the insurance industry can be classified into five types: (1) mass marketing or direct selling; (2) employee sales representatives; (3) non-employee sales agents who sell for a single company; (4) non-employee agents who sell for more than one company; and (5) brokers. Mass marketing methods are those that do not involve a sales intermediary, such as mass mailings, television or radio solicitations, and increasingly, the internet. Employee sales representatives constitute a dedicated sales force under the direct employ of a single insurer. Non-employee agents are independent from the insurer, and are typically small businesses or franchisees with a well-specified contractual relationship with a single insurer; these sales agents are often called exclusive agents. Agents with non-exclusive sales relationships are independent businesses with contractual agreements to sell the products of more than one insurer; these agents are often called independent agents. Brokers too are independent businesses who may sell the products of more than one insurer. However, unlike exclusive or independent agents, brokers have no formal contractual relationships with insurance firms and hence represent the insurance purchaser as a client. This distinction means that a broker cannot commit an insurer to provide insurance without the insurer's specific approval of the policy, whereas many independent sales agents can bind the insurer to offer a policy. In practice, however, the multiple representation opportunities of independent agents and brokers makes these systems very similar.

Because the life and property-liability insurance industries developed separately, distribution systems in life insurance and property-liability insurance differ significantly.[2] Changes in regulation and in market forces have brought greater integration of life insurance and property-liability insurance sales, as insurance firms combine and insurance agencies expand their product offerings. Nonetheless, there remain differences in the market penetration of competing distribution systems in property-liability insurance and life insurance. The contractual relationships between agents

[2] For example, in the United States, regulations prohibited an insurance firm from selling both property-liability and life insurance until the 1940s (Huebner, Black and Webb, pg. 648).

and insurers, and the functions of agents, also differ across the property-liability and life insurance industries. Some of these differences have implications for the economic issues surrounding distribution system use in the two industries. For these reasons, it is useful to characterize property-liability and life insurance distribution systems separately.

22.2.1 Property-Liability Insurance

Property-liability insurance is sold primarily by professional agents. Independent agents (including brokers) and agents tied to a specific insurance firm (whether via employment or exclusive contract) together account for the vast majority of the direct premium revenues of the industry throughout most of the world (Skipper, 1998).

22.2.1.1 Market Shares

The 1995 U.S. market shares of insurers using independent agency, brokerage or *direct writing* (exclusive agents, employee agents or direct marketing) distribution methods are reported in Table 1. The table reports the shares of direct premium revenue by these three major distribution systems for property-liability insurance overall, and for selected lines of property-liability insurance. The data are constructed from premiums reported at the individual firm level, and each firm is catalogued according to its primary distribution system.[3] Note that since some companies use more than one distribution method, the table does not provide an exact apportionment of premiums by distribution system. However, this problem is minimized by reporting at the individual firm level rather than by consolidated insurance firms (known as *groups*), because individual firms within groups may use different distribution methods.[4]

The table documents that independent agency companies have the largest market share overall, with 49.7 percent of premium volume; direct writer firms closely follow, with a 43.4 percent overall market share. Firms that distribute primarily through brokers achieve a 6.4 percent market share. There are significant variations in market shares across line of insurance, however. Independent agency firms dominate the commercial insurance lines, especially commercial multiperil and ocean marine, where they capture over three-quarters of the market. Broker distributors also achieve their greatest market penetration in the commercial lines, most notably in general liability and ocean marine insurance. Direct writer companies dominate in the personal insurance lines, controlling about 60 percent of both the automobile and homeowners insurance markets.

These dramatic differences in market shares by line of insurance preview the market share dynamics shown in Table 2. Independent agency was the earliest method

[3] The classifications are taken from A.M. Best Company's *Key Rating Guide*.

[4] Market share figures do not add to 100 percent, as there are small shares of premium volume written by firms using other primary distribution systems (general agents or mass marketing), which are not reported here.

Table 1
Market Shares by Distribution System U.S. Property-Liability Insurance, 1995

Line of Business	Independent Agency	Broker	Direct Writing
Private Passenger Automobile			
Physical Damage	35.6	1.0	62.6
Liability	39.8	2.7	57.0
Homeowners Multiperil	37.4	0.3	62.0
Commercial Multiperil	80.5	1.8	17.4
Workers Compensation	70.4	9.0	20.2
General Liability	62.0	26.2	11.5
Fire	52.7	14.3	31.8
Ocean Marine	76.4	19.4	4.0
Inland Marine	62.1	14.6	22.5
Boiler and Machinery	68.5	2.7	28.8
Allied Lines	71.0	5.9	20.7
Total	49.7	6.4	43.4

of distributing property-liability insurance in the United States, and remained by far the predominant system until the latter half of this century. Over the past three decades, however, the share of insurance sold through the independent agency system has declined significantly. This trend is documented in Table 2, which shows the change in U.S. market shares of direct writer insurers (where this category combines exclusive agency, employee agency and direct marketing) for the major lines of property-liability insurance between 1980 and 1997. Independent agency insurers experienced a 10.1 percent decrease in market share over this period, which is equivalent to a loss of 2.71 billion dollars in premium revenue for 1997. Consistent with the data in Table 1, we observe that the largest market share gains of the direct writing firms are generally in personal insurance, particularly homeowners. Market share gains have also occurred in some commercial insurance lines, especially fire and allied lines insurance. However, independent agency has made market share advances in some commercial lines during this time period, notably boiler and machinery, workers compensation and general liability.

22.2.1.2 Insurer-Agent Relationships

An important distinction between insurer-agent relationships across the different property-liability insurance distribution systems in the United States lies in which party owns the policy "expirations" or customer list. Under independent agency and broker distribution, the ownership rights to the customer list accrue to the agent. This means that the insurance firm cannot contact the customer for policy renewal or for the sale of additional products, without doing so through the agent. With exclusive

Table 2
Trends in Direct Writer Market Shares U.S. Property-Liability Insurance

Line of Business	1980 Share (percent)	1997 Share (percent)	Change
Private Passenger Automobile			
Physical Damage	60.9	69.2	+8.3
Liability	60.5	67.8	+7.3
Homeowners Multiperil	45.0	63.3	+18.3
Commercial Multiperil	12.2	19.1	+6.9
Workers Compensation	22.1	19.8	−2.3
General Liability	17.8	15.6	−2.2
Fire	24.4	37.0	+12.6
Ocean Marine	9.8	13.0	+3.2
Inland Marine	22.8	27.0	+4.2
Boiler and Machinery	33.2	25.9	−7.3
Allied Lines	20.6	30.5	+9.9

agency contracts or employee agents the insurance firm retains ownership of the customer list.

Compensation systems for the independent agents also tend to differ from those of the tied agents. Independent agents (including brokers) are generally compensated wholly by commissions. The commission rate varies across insurance products, with new policies and renewal policies often receiving the same commission rate. Many insurers also pay profit-contingent commissions to independent agents, based upon premium volume and the loss ratio of the business sold for the insurer. Exclusive agents are also generally paid by commission. Commission rates tend to be lower than those for the independent agent, and commission rates for renewal policies are lower than those for new business. There is also some evidence that exclusive agents are less likely to receive profit-contingent commissions than independent agents (Regan and Tennyson, 1996). However, other forms of compensation or company benefits, including participation in retirement plans, may be afforded exclusive agents. Employee sales agents tend to be compensated at least partially by salary rather than commission, and many are compensated wholly by salary and bonus schemes rather than commissions.

The provision of agent training and support by insurers using exclusive agents or employee sales forces tends to be greater than that provided to independent agents. Exclusive agency insurers often treat new agents as employees during a specified training period. The agent becomes an independent contractor paid on a commission basis only after this period (Rejda, 1998). Exclusive agency insurers also advertise more heavily than the independent agency firms, who may rely more on agent marketing efforts (Regan, 1997).

Customer service functions such as billing and claims processing are performed by the insurance company under the exclusive or employee agency system. Traditionally, the independent agent himself provided most of these services for his customers. In recent times, insurers using independent agents have begun to provide these services more centrally.[5] Starting in the mid-1980s many independent agency insurers moved claims handling, premium collection, policy issuance and communication functions away from the agent to insurer-controlled service centers. Another type of restructuring is the provision of customer service functions in combinations of independent agencies rather than at the individual agency level. Under the insurer service center model commission payments to agents are reduced to reflect the reduction in agent service activities. Under the agent service center model each agent pays fees to the center to support the service provision, and insurers generally must agree to the servicing arrangements.

22.2.2 Life Insurance

As in property-liability insurance, distribution via professional agents is the dominant form of life insurance sales. In most countries, including the United States, Canada, Germany and Japan, the majority of life insurance agents are either employees or exclusive agents who sell the products of only one company. However, there are countries such as the United Kingdom where brokers and financial service advisors are more prevalent. Mass-marketing companies are making significant inroads in some countries, and the sale of life insurance products through banks is also gaining acceptance. The latter trend is particularly true in European countries, most notably France, where bank sales represent over 50 percent of life insurance premiums.[6]

The differences across life insurance distribution systems in the United States are less pronounced than those in property-liability insurance. Importantly, in life insurance there are no differences regarding ownership of policy renewals, with the insurance company typically retaining ownership under all systems. However, there are differences in the degree of vertical control of the distribution system. Insurers may operate an exclusive agency system in which independent contractors are contractually bound to sell the products of only one insurer. This is commonly called the career agency system, where the insurer invests heavily in recruiting and training a dedicated sales force. The career agency force may be directly managed by the insurer through a branch office network, or through non-employee managing general agents who operate with the authority of the insurer. Insurers may also be represented by independent agents or brokers with non-exclusive representation contracts. In this case, the insurer's control of the distribution channel is much looser, and the insurer does not invest in agency building.

[5] See Anderson, Ross, and Weitz, 1998, for a discussion of the creation of more vertically integrated relationships between independent insurance agents and insurers.

[6] These data are from Skipper, 1998.

22.2.2.1 Market Shares

U.S. life insurance market shares by distribution system are presented in Table 3. The table shows the share of total premiums generated by each distribution system for each major product category in 1995. The data are constructed from reports at the individual firm level, and each firm is catalogued by its primary distribution system. It should be noted that although most firms do have a primary distribution system, it is relatively rare for a life insurance firm to use a single distribution method for all products and markets (Carr, 1997). Hence, the market shares reported here are only an approximation of true premium shares by distribution system.

The table shows that the most prevalent method of distribution is the career (exclusive) agency system. Career agency firms have a 78 percent market share overall; non-career (independent) agency distributors obtain a 16.4 percent market share, and mass marketing insurers take the remaining 5.6 percent. Market shares for life insurance products are even more skewed toward career agency, especially in ordinary and group life, which account for the bulk of life insurance premiums. However, annuity sales account for the majority of total life insurance and annuity revenues (62 percent using 1995 data), and both independent agency insurers and mass-marketers obtain greater market shares for annuity products. The independent agency market share in individual annuities is 31.6 percent, and in group annuities it is 22.1 percent. Mass marketers achieve a 12.7 percent share of the individual annuities market and a 9.0 percent share of the group annuities market.

Total premium volume represents premiums collected in a particular year, irrespective of when the original policy was sold. Due to the long term nature of most policies in this industry, market shares by total premium volume will thus overstate the share of current sales for a distribution system experiencing market share declines, and understate the share of current sales for a distribution system experiencing market share gains. To provide better evidence on market shares of current sales, and to

Table 3

Market Shares by Distribution System U.S. Life Insurance, 1995 Total Premium Volume

Line of Business	Career Agency (percent)	Independent Agency (percent)	Mass Marketer (percent)
Ordinary Life Insurance	89.5	7.6	2.9
Group Life Insurance	85.3	9.6	5.1
Credit Life Insurance	65.5	5.1	29.5
Industrial Life Insurance	96.8	2.4	0.8
Individual Annuities	55.7	31.6	12.7
Group Annuities	68.9	22.1	9.0
Total	78.0	16.4	5.6

provide some insight into market share gainers and losers, Table 4 presents the market shares of each distribution system using new premium volume rather than total premium volume. New premiums are those arising from the sales of new policies in the reported year.

Table 4 shows that, relative to the share of total premiums, independent sales agents achieve a greater share of new annuity premiums, especially group annuities. In group annuities, the independent agents' share of new premiums is 62.1 percent, although its share of total premiums is only 22.1 percent. In group annuities this increase comes solely at the expense of the career agency system, with the market share of mass marketers also slightly higher than their share of total premiums. Both the career agency and independent agency systems achieve higher shares of new premiums than of total premiums in the individual annuity market, with mass marketers experiencing a decrease. The market shares of new premiums and total premiums in life insurance lines are relatively constant for all distribution systems, except for group life and credit life, where mass marketer shares of new premiums are higher. This increase comes primarily at the expense of the independent agency system. Taken together, these findings indicate that market shares for annuities are more fluid than market shares in life insurance products, with the career agency system losing significant market share to the independent agency and mass marketing distribution systems.

22.2.2.2 Insurer-Agent Relationships

In the United States, life insurance agents with ties to a single insurer are organized under branch offices or managing general agents of the insurance company. Under the branch office system, the selling agents report to the regional office, and agent recruitment, training and oversight are often provided at this level of the organization. Under the general agency system the managing general agent is an independent contractor

Table 4

Market Shares by Distribution System U.S. Life Insurance, 1995 New Premiums Only

Line of Business	Career Agency (percent)	Independent Agency (percent)	Mass Marketer (percent)
Ordinary Life Insurance	90.9	7.0	2.1
Group Life Insurance	85.9	7.0	7.1
Credit Life Insurance	63.9	3.9	32.2
Industrial Life Insurance	98.7	1.3	0.0
Individual Annuities	58.9	36.2	4.9
Group Annuities	26.3	62.1	11.6
Total	69.8	24.0	6.2

who invests his own capital, and is charged with building a full-time career agency sales force for a single insurer. The managing general agent typically is not engaged in personal selling, but is paid an override on the commissions of the producing agents. As in property-liability insurance, company-provided training and other evidence of committed relationships with agents are relatively higher under these tied agency systems than under other agency systems.

Independent agency in life insurance takes two primary forms, known respectively as personal producing general agency and brokerage. Unlike managing general agents, the principal goal of the personal producing general agent is to sell insurance. Although the personal producing general agent may have a primary relationship with a specific insurer, the personal producing agent, and the selling agents appointed by the personal producing general agent, may sell the products of more than one company. Like brokerage in property-liability insurance, life insurance brokers represent the products of more than one insurer. Typically, the insurer fills the role of product manufacturer, providing products for life insurance sales outlets that may be developed by other organizations. For example, many brokerage insurers distribute their products through the independent agency forces of property-liability insurers, or through securities dealers or banks. Brokers are appointed by the insurer as authorized representatives, and are compensated solely on a commission basis.

Under all distribution systems in life insurance, agent compensation is largely via commissions. Life insurance commission schemes tend to be weighted heavily toward motivating sales of new policies, rather than rewarding renewals or profitability. A large fraction of the first year premium paid by the consumer is often devoted to the sales commission, with a much smaller percentage of annual renewal premiums (sometimes for up to 10 years) also being paid as commission. A recent survey of life insurer business practices in the United States reveals first year commission rates for individual life insurance ranging from 50 percent to 120 percent of the first year premium. These rates did not vary systematically across the distribution system employed (Wharton Financial Institutions Center, 1997).

22.3 DIRECT WRITING VERSUS INDEPENDENT AGENCY

There is a large academic literature focused on questions regarding which of the general methods of distributing insurance products is more efficient. The vast majority of these studies have been undertaken in property-liability insurance rather than life insurance. This is probably due to the greater differences in organizational relationships between firms and agents under the property-liability systems. Moreover, the historical development of property-liability distribution systems in relation to the regulation of rates in this industry has made these differences starkly apparent.

Comparative studies of insurance distribution systems typically group the various systems into two main categories, based upon the degree of vertical control of the sales force. The two broad categories analyzed are "direct writer" and "independent agency". The direct writer category encompasses mass marketing, the use of employee sales agents, and exclusive agents. The independent agency category encompasses both the independent agency system of marketing and the use of insurance brokers.

There are two distinct bodies of literature on insurers' choice of distribution systems. The first, a largely empirical literature, compares the relative costs or profitability of the two distribution systems. These studies have consistently found that property-liability insurers using the independent agency system have higher costs than those using direct writing. The second literature attempts to interpret or explain the coexistence of the two systems in light of these observed cost differences. Early papers in this literature viewed the continued existence of independent agency as viable only in the short run; more recent papers argue that distribution system coexistence is a long run equilibrium. We begin with a summary of the findings of the cost and profit estimation literature, and then discuss the theoretical explanations for distribution system coexistence.

22.3.1 Cost and Profit Comparisons

A number of prominent studies compare the average costs of property-liability insurance distribution systems. Most of these studies use data on insurance firms or groups to estimate a regression model of insurer average variable costs, incorporating a dummy variable to distinguish firms with different distribution systems. Under the assumption that insurers offer homogeneous products and use identical production technologies, a coefficient estimate on the dummy variable which is significantly different from zero implies average cost differences across the two distribution systems.[7]

The first such analysis is by Joskow (1973), in his study of the industrial organization of the property-liability insurance industry. Joskow measures costs as the ratio of underwriting expenses to premiums (the expense ratio), and estimates linear models of the expense ratio as a function of total premium volume, reinsurance use, ownership form (stock or mutual) and distribution system. Using data on 157 fire and automobile insurance groups for 1970–1971, Joskow estimates that the expense ratios of insurers using direct writing are approximately 11 percent lower than those of insurers using independent agency.

More recent studies examine cost differences for later time periods, and incorporate model specification and data refinements to Joskow's basic analysis. Cummins and Vanderhei (1979) examine a total variable cost measure as well as the underwriting expense ratio. Total variable costs include loss adjustment expenses (costs of claims settlement) in addition to underwriting expenses. If independent agency firms are more likely to perform loss adjustment at the agent level, the costs of claim

[7] See Braeutigam and Pauly, 1986, for a critique of this methodology when insurance products are not homogeneous.

settlement will appear as part of underwriting expenses for independent agency firms but not for direct writing firms. This accounting difference could produce apparent differences in costs if measured by the expense ratio. These authors also estimate log-linear models of costs premised on a Cobb-Douglas production function. Barrese and Nelson (1992) refine the distinctions between direct writer and independent agency insurers by incorporating a continuous variable defined to be the percentage of an insurance group's premiums obtained from independent agents, and by adding an additional dummy variable for groups using direct mail methods or salaried employee distributors. They also experiment with using incurred losses as the insurer's output measure rather than premium revenue.

Even with these refinements, both sets of authors find results that are consistent with Joskow's. Direct writers are found to have lower average costs both overall and for automobile physical damage insurance separately, and the results hold under both linear and log-linear model specifications. These studies also find no significant decline in the direct writer cost advantage over time. Cummins and Vanderhei use data for the time period 1968–1979, and Barrese and Nelson use data for the period 1978–1990; neither study finds evidence that the cost difference across distribution systems is smaller in the later years of their respective sample periods.

Regan (1999) extends this type of analysis to a much larger sample of firms, and analyzes a larger variety of property-liability insurance lines. In regression models of underwriting expense ratios for personal automobile liability, personal automobile physical damage, homeowners multi-peril, commercial multi-peril, workers compensation and general liability insurance for 260 firms in 1990, Regan finds that direct writer cost advantages differ significantly across lines. Direct writers' expense ratios are significantly lower than those of independent agency firms in homeowners and commercial multi-peril insurance, but not in the other lines of insurance examined. Consistent with previous studies, however, her results show that direct writers have significantly lower expense ratios when all lines of business are combined.

Rather than testing for differences in expense ratios, Berger, Cummins and Weiss (1997) use frontier efficiency analysis to examine differences in both cost and profit efficiency across property-liability insurance distribution systems.[8] Their estimation methodology improves over previous studies by allowing for efficiency differences across individual firms rather than simple intercept shifts between direct writer and independent agency firms on average, and by estimating a multi-product cost function derived from economic theory. Consistent with the results from earlier studies, these authors find that independent agency insurers are significantly less cost efficient than direct writers. However, they find no significant differences in profit efficiency across the two distribution systems.[9] The authors interpret this finding to indicate that

[8] See Chapter 26 by Cummins and Weiss of this volume for an in depth discussion of this methodology.

[9] An earlier study by Cather, Gustavson and Trieschmann, 1985, compared the mean accounting profitability levels of 68 insurance groups for each year in the time period 1975 to 1982, and also found little evidence of profitability differences across firms using different distribution systems.

product quality or service differences underlay distribution system coexistence, reasoning that such differences will be manifested in costs but not in profits.

Several other studies have hypothesized that the higher expense ratios of independent agency insurers may reflect greater service or quality provision.[10] Etgar (1976) looks for direct evidence of quality or service differences across distribution systems by comparing the services provided by 116 personal lines agents operating in the state of California. Using data from a survey of agent practices, the study reveals that independent agents intervene in claims settlement significantly more often than exclusive agents, but finds no other significant difference in service provision. A larger survey of independent agency operations is undertaken by Cummins and Weisbart (1977), obtaining responses from nearly 700 personal lines agents in three different states. While this study finds that independent agents are significantly more likely to provide claims assistance and to review coverages more frequently than tied agents, in other areas independent agents provide less service than tied agents.

To surmount the difficulties associated with comparing multiple measures of service, and to capture service provision by the insurance company as well as its agents, Doerpinghaus (1991) measures customer service indirectly by examining consumer complaints to regulators. She posits that better customer service will lead to fewer complaints, and thus tests the hypothesis that independent agency insurers receive fewer complaints than tied agency insurers. Her empirical analysis uses data from three state insurance departments regarding consumer complaints about individual insurance firms. Regressions of each firm's rate of complaints on firm characteristics plus an indicator variable for the firm's distribution system produce no evidence of significant differences in complaint rates across the two systems. A follow-up study by Barrese, Doerpinghaus and Nelson (1995) uses complaint data from five states, a richer empirical model and tobit estimation methods rather than ordinary least squares. This study finds that independent agency insurers receive fewer complaints when the data from all five states are pooled, and in two of five individual states studied. This provides evidence of greater satisfaction on the part of independent agency customers, and hence is not inconsistent with superior service or quality provision by independent agency insurers.[11]

On balance, however, existing studies present mixed evidence of superior service provision by independent agency insurers or their agents. The focus of many of these studies on personal insurance lines may provide a partial explanation. Recall that independent agency insurers have lost significant market share in the personal

[10] Venezia, Galai and Shapira (1996) develop a theoretical model which shows that tied and independent agency insurers may coexist in equilibrium when independent agents provide greater assistance in claims processing. Under the additional assumption that consumers have private information about their risk types, it is shown that higher risk consumers will choose independent agency insurers, which will in turn offer higher prices and lower deductibles in equilibrium.

[11] Of course, if consumer complaints are made only when service fails to live up to expectations, there is the possibility that selection bias in the distribution system clienteles will affect these results. For example, if shopping with a particular distribution system is correlated with service expectations or innate tendencies to file complaints, the study results may be compromised.

lines over time. If independent agency firms enjoy a competitive advantage in service provision, but personal insurance lines are not service-intensive, this could explain both the lack of independent agent service advantages found in these studies, and the lower independent agency market share in these lines. A difficulty of interpretation arises, however, because these studies do not relate differences in service provision to the costs incurred by insurers or their agents. As a consequence, one cannot determine whether any observed differences in service provision are the source of the cost differences between the two distribution systems. This remains an open question.

The one unquestioned conclusion arising from this literature is that in property-liability insurance direct writers have lower underwriting costs on average than independent agency insurers. This cost difference has persisted over time, although it is not large, and is even insignificant, in some lines of insurance. The cost difference does not, however, translate into differences in profitability. While these findings appear to suggest that service, quality or product differences are the most likely reasons that the two distribution systems coexist, they do not rule out other possibilities. For example, even if independent agency insurers survive in the market only because of regulations that protect them from competition, direct writers could experience only normal profits if their excess profits are competed away via advertising or other non-price competition. As a second example, if consumers fail to purchase from low-cost providers due to search costs or switching costs, independent agency firms could earn supra-normal profits despite having higher costs than direct writers.

More generally, the coexistence of a high-cost and a low-cost distribution system in the industry could be simply a short run phenomenon, or it could be a long-run equilibrium. Recall that independent agency was the original distribution system in the industry, and direct writing developed later. Hence, the observed use of independent agency could be a temporary phase in the evolution of the industry. Alternatively, there may exist conditions under which independent agency is optimal for firms and consumers, despite its higher costs. Under these circumstances independent agency will continue to exist in long run equilibrium. Both of these views have been put forward in the literature, with the latter gaining greater prevalence over time. We review the arguments and evidence for each below.

22.3.2 Slow Adjustment Theories

Joskow (1973) advances a regulatory protection hypothesis for the continued existence of independent agency insurers. This hypothesis is based on the observation that, at the time of his study, direct writers had both lower market shares and higher price-cost margins in automobile insurance markets in which rates were regulated than in those that were not. Joskow argues that the direct writers are a low cost oligopoly protected by entry barriers, and their failure to take over the market is profit-maximizing behavior in the face of short run capacity constraints and price floors created by rate regulation.

At the time of Joskow's study, insurance rates were regulated in all states except California, Illinois and New York. Joskow's conjecture became a testable hypothesis when a larger number of states deregulated insurance rates in the 1970s. Since that time, several studies have examined the impact of rate regulation on the market shares of direct writers. Most of these studies use regression models of state-wide market shares of direct writers, and test for regulatory effects by including a dummy variable for regulated states.[12] The evidence is somewhat mixed, but generally supports the hypothesis that direct writers have lower market shares in regulated markets. Contrary to Joskow's findings, however, the more recent evidence also suggests that rate regulation creates price or profit ceilings rather than price floors.

These results have several possible interpretations. First, it is possible that rate regulation reduces price competition and thereby increases the market shares of higher cost independent agency firms. Note that if rate regulation imposes price ceilings, the price advantage of low cost firms will be lower and hence their market share may be lower (Pauly, Kunreuther and Kleindorfer, 1986). Alternatively, it may be that low cost direct writer firms choose to lower their market shares in regulated states. This could occur if regulation limits firms' profits, and low cost firms can earn supra-normal profits in unregulated states (Suponcic and Tennyson, 1998). Finally, it is possible that the differences in market shares of direct writers in regulated and unregulated states are due to omitted effects that are simply correlated with rate regulation.

Analyzing state level data for the late 1970s, Pauly, Kleindorfer and Kunreuther (1986) find that the effect of regulation on direct writer market shares is greatly diminished when the 1969 market share is included in regressions as a control variable. Given that virtually all states regulated rates in 1969, this finding suggests that unobservable differences in state environments (and not regulation) are the primary determinants of direct writer market shares. Consistent with this, Regan and Tennyson (1996) find no effects of regulation on direct writer automobile insurance market shares in the 1980s once the correlation between direct writer market shares across lines of business in a state is accounted for. Similarly, using data from 1971 to 1983, Gron (1995) finds no significant effect of rate regulation on direct writer market shares when variables representing the political influence of insurance agents are included in regression models. She argues that it is the political actions of agents, rather than reduced price competition, that reduces direct writer shares under rate regulation.

An analysis of market shares by Grabowski, Viscusi and Evans (1989) suggests a different interpretation. These authors find that, in states which deregulated automobile insurance rates in the 1970s, direct writer market shares increased significantly.

[12] See, for example, Pauly, Kleindorfer and Kunreuther, 1986; Grabowski, Viscusi and Evans, 1989; Gron, 1995.

This suggests that regulation had some direct effects, at least in these states. In addition, for the late 1980s, Suponcic and Tennyson (1998) find that the growth in direct writer market shares is slower in several of the most stringently rate-regulated states, and that this effect is greatest for the lowest-cost direct writer firms. Both sets of results are consistent with the view that low cost firms choose to reduce their market shares in regulated environments.

It is important to note, however, that by the 1990s there is little difference in direct writer market shares in regulated and unregulated states on average. For example, in 1995 direct writing firms averaged a 67.1 percent market share in regulated automobile insurance markets compared with an average 68.1 percent share in unregulated markets (Cummins, Phillips and Tennyson, 1999). Moreover, as noted earlier, independent agency insurers continue to dominate in some commercial lines of property-liability insurance, in which rates tend to be less heavily regulated. Thus on the whole, although it appears that rate regulation may have slowed direct writers' growth in automobile insurance markets, the continued existence of the independent agency system does not stem from rate regulation.

Of course, market imperfections not created by regulation could sustain high cost firms in the short run. Several deviations from perfect competition have been documented in insurance markets. Information about insurance prices and quality may spread only slowly among consumers, who tend to obtain this information from family and friends (Berger, Kleindorfer and Kunreuther, 1989). Seog (1999) finds that there are conditions under which a slow learning process could prevent consumers from moving to a lower cost distribution system, even in the long run. Costs associated with finding price information could also allow high cost firms to survive in the market, as costly search will imply that not all consumers identify the lowest cost firm. Dahlby and West (1986) present evidence that price dispersion in automobile insurance markets is consistent with costly price search, and Mathewson and Winter (1983) find evidence consistent with costly search in life insurance markets. Switching costs, due for example to imperfect rating models, could also lead to some consumers using high cost firms in equilibrium. Schlesinger and von-der-Schulenberg (1992) find that consumers are imperfectly informed about insurance prices, and that consumers switch insurers only for large price reductions. This pattern is consistent with both search and switching costs.

While market imperfections could lead to the slow evolution of the industry toward the use of direct writing, little direct evidence has been presented in the literature to gauge their importance for distribution system market shares. More importantly, the idea that market failures sustain an inefficient distribution system fails to address the question of why firms would continue with the inefficient system. It has been argued that contractual constraints prevent independent agency insurers from changing systems, and agent ownership of the customer list is surely a significant barrier to change. However, some insurers have partially changed their distribution systems or instituted multiple distribution systems through divestitures, acquisitions or new subsidiaries. The changes in insurer-agent relationships discussed earlier in the chapter also imply that independent agency is now less distinct from direct writing than in the past. Despite this, the fact that independent agency continues to serve nearly half the total market, and over 70 percent of the commercial market, casts doubt on the idea that there is no efficiency basis for its existence. A number of recent studies have examined the coexistence of independent agency and direct writing from this perspective.

22.3.3 Equilibrium Coexistence Theories

The economic theory of the firm maintains that the organizational choices of firms will be made in an optimizing manner, just as are the operating decisions of ongoing firms.[13] Under this theory, organizational form is chosen to minimize both the production and agency or transaction costs associated with incomplete information. This implies that when more than one organizational form is observed in an industry, there must exist differences in firms' operating or contracting environments which lead them to efficiently choose different organizational forms.

Within this theoretical framework, the relevant question is the identity of the key factors that determine the efficiency of one organizational form over others. Two general classes of arguments have been applied to the choice of insurance distribution system using this perspective. The first focuses on incentive conflicts between an insurer and its sales agents or its customers, and the second focuses on consumer search costs in markets for insurance.

22.3.3.1 Incentive Conflicts

Marvel (1982) theorizes that direct writing protects the promotional efforts of the insurance firm. Suppose, for example, that customers are attracted to a sales agent by an insurance firm's promotions for its specific product. If the agent sells other insurers' products as well, he may have a financial incentive to switch customers to the product of a non-advertising firm, to avoid paying a share of promotion costs passed on by the advertising firm. The customer may have an incentive to switch to this product as well, due to its lower price. This potential for free-riding will reduce the level of advertising expenditures chosen by each insurance firm dealing with an independent agent. The prediction of this theory is therefore that when insurer-level advertising is the most efficient way to increase product sales, direct writing will be used because it preserves the incentive to invest in advertising.

Marvel provides empirical support for this theory by demonstrating that independent agency insurers spend relatively less on advertising than direct writers. Evidence consistent with the theory is also provided by the observation that independent

[13] Important early works taking this perspective include Alchian and Demsetz, 1972; Jensen and Meckling, 1976, Williamson, 1979; and Fama, 1980. See Holmstrom and Tirole, 1990, for a complete review of the theoretical literature.

agency is more prevalent in commercial insurance lines where, presumably, brand advertising is less important than in personal lines. Marvel also interprets the higher commission rates of independent agents as payment for greater agent level promotional effort.

Grossman and Hart (1986) make an argument regarding investment incentives that is similar to Marvel's, but allow for moral hazard on the part of both the insurance firm and the agent. In this setting efficiency requires that ownership rights to productive assets must be given to the party whose investments most greatly affect the value of those assets, because ownership increases investment incentives. The key productive asset in insurance sales is the customer list, and hence ownership of the customer list will optimally be assigned to that party (insurer or agent) whose investments are most important to the value of the list. Firm ownership of the list will be preferred when the list size is the most important determinant of profitability, and hence the insurer's brand investments are most important. Agent ownership will be preferred when customer persistency is the most important determinant of profitability, and hence the agent's services are most important. This reasoning implies that independent agency will be used when agent services are relatively important to insurer profitability. Like Marvel's, this theory is also consistent with the prevalence of independent agency in commercial insurance (if agent services are important in building the client list in these lines), and higher commission payments to independent agents (because of agent efforts in building the client list).

Sass and Gisser (1989) theorize that direct writing reduces the costs associated with an agent's sales effort being divided among competing brands. Direct writing lowers the agent's opportunity cost of sales effort devoted to a given firm's product, which allows the firm to pay a lower commission rate per policy. The only limitations to the use of direct writing under this theory are firm and market size. In order for a firm to attract tied agents, the firm must be able to offer the agent a larger sales volume to overcome the lower commission rate.

To provide evidence for their theory, Sass and Gisser estimate a probit model of the probability that an insurance group is a direct writer. Using data on 116 property-liability insurance groups from 1974, they find that firm size and insurance market density are positively correlated with the use of direct writing. This is consistent with the view that direct writing is limited by the size of the market. In regression models of insurer commission payments, the authors also find direct writers pay lower commission rates, even after controlling for advertising expenditures and line of business specialization. This is inconsistent with the view that tied agents' commission rates are lower only due to implicit charges for insurers' advertising.

Regan and Tennyson (1996) present an alternative model of agent effort differences across distribution systems. They argue that independent agency provides agents with greater incentives to exert (unverifiable) effort in risk selection and classification. The incentive differences across independent agency and direct writing arise because the independent agent can extract a share of the residual profits from his efforts, through his ability to place desirable risks with other firms. Tied agents with no such leverage must be compensated directly for their risk assessment efforts, even if these efforts do not lead to higher profits. Under this theory, the total cost of independent agent compensation will be greater as a result of profit sharing and commission competition across insurers. However, the marginal cost of compensating an independent agent for information gathering effort will be lower. Independent agency will thus be more efficient only when subjective information provided by the agent is important to profitable underwriting. When applicants can be sorted using verifiable information or standardized classification algorithms, direct writing will be preferred due to its lower cost.

Regan and Tennyson estimate regression models of state level market shares of direct writers using panel data for 1980–1987. Consistent with their views of the role of independent agents in risk assessment, these regressions show that direct writer shares are lower in markets where risk exposures are relatively heterogeneous and complex, and thus more difficult to classify using standardized tools. In regression models of insurer commission payments, the authors also find that independent agency insurers pay a larger proportion of agent commissions on a profit-contingent basis. This is consistent with their theory, since profit-contingent-commissions reward an agent for distinguishing profitable from unprofitable business.

Kim, Mayers and Smith (1996) focus on potential incentive conflicts between the insurer and consumer as the prime determinant of distribution system choice. They argue that independent agents should be more effective at monitoring and preventing opportunistic behavior by insurers, due to the agent's ownership of the customer list and his relationship with several insurers. Hence, independent agency should be used when agent monitoring of the insurer is important to consumers. Because policyholders are the ultimate owners of the firm under the mutual form of organization, stock insurers may require more monitoring on policyholders' behalf. This theory thus predicts a relationship between ownership form and distribution system, with independent agency used by stock firms and direct writing used by mutual firms.

Using data on 1,480 individual insurance firms from 1981, Kim, Mayers and Smith estimate logistic regression models of distribution system use which show a positive and significant relationship between direct writing and the mutual form of ownership. These results hold even after controlling for firm characteristics such as size, advertising, geographic concentration and line of business concentration. The authors also find evidence consistent with Marvel's (1982) predictions regarding differences in advertising intensity across distribution systems, and with Sass and Gisser's (1989) predictions regarding differences in firm size across distribution systems.

Regan (1997) proposes a more general transactions costs theory to determine distribution system choice. Transactions costs theory posits that the integration of functions within a firm is more likely when the costs of market transactions are high. Regan argues that integration (direct writing) is more likely when relationship-specific investments are important, and non-integration (independent agency) confers advantages when products are complex or the environment is uncertain. The need for relationship-specific investments favors integration because of the potential for ex-post opportunism under market exchange (Williamson, 1979). Regan hypothesizes that independent agency is preferred when products are complex because of the greater need for agents to intervene in insurer/customer conflicts and the need for agent participation in risk assessment (Regan and Tennyson, 1996). Independent agency is preferred in uncertain environments because the agent's greater ability to diversify risk across insurers lowers the compensation that agents require for risk bearing.

Regan (1997) estimates logit models of the probability that an insurer is a direct writer using data on 149 insurance groups from 1990. Consistent with the findings of Kim, Mayers and Smith (1996) she finds that direct writing is positively associated with the mutual form of ownership. She also finds that direct writing is positively related to insurer advertising and technology investments, and associated with lower risk and lower product complexity. These findings are consistent with her hypothesis relating distribution system use to transactions costs. Her findings are also consistent with the arguments of Marvel (1982) regarding advertising and those of Regan and Tennyson (1996) regarding product complexity.[14]

22.3.3.2 Search Costs

There is a small strand of literature focusing on costly consumer search as the reason for the equilibrium coexistence of independent agency and direct writers. What distinguishes this literature from the literature arguing that costly search preserves an inefficient distribution system is the assumption that the distribution systems differ materially in ways other than costs. This literature notes that the search for information about insurance prices and products is part of the purchase process, and that direct writer and independent agency distribution systems differ with respect to how consumers can search for information. Under direct writing, each individual insurer must be contacted for price and product information. Under independent agency, the agent may serve as an intermediary between the consumer and multiple insurers. This difference in search processes provides a rationale for firms and consumers of differing characteristics to choose different distribution systems.

Posey and Yavas (1995) present the first formal analysis of this type. These authors model the insurance purchase transaction as requiring two-sided search, due to differences in risk characteristics across consumers and product differentiation across insurers. Independent agents act as middlemen in facilitating these matches. Shopping with an independent agent guarantees a match in a single search, while shopping in the direct writer sector requires sequential search. The model assumes that

[14] Regan and Tzeng (1999) provide additional evidence on the relationship between insurance distribution system and ownership form. This study explicitly treats the choice of distribution system and ownership structure as jointly determined, to control for the fact that common exogenous factors may influence both choices. The findings confirm the view that stock ownership and independent agency distribution are likely to be observed together.

price is exogenously set at the zero-profit level, and the only element in the search process is for appropriate coverage. Under fairly general conditions, the authors are able to derive coexistence equilibria in this model. In most of these equilibria, consumers with high costs of search choose the independent agency system.

Posey and Tennyson (1998) analyze distribution system coexistence under pure price search. Similar to Posey and Yavas, these authors assume that shopping in the independent agency sector entails nonsequential search, while shopping in the direct writer sector entails sequential search. However, in this model it is assumed that products are homogeneous and prices are determined endogenously. Under certain conditions regarding the relative distributions of production and search costs, they find that both distribution systems may exist in equilibrium. The constructed equilibrium is one in which low production cost producers and low search cost consumers utilize the direct writer sector, while high cost producers and high search cost consumers utilize independent agency.

The search-based models of distribution system choice have not been extensively tested. Posey and Tennyson (1998) show that price levels and price variances for independent agency and direct writers in automobile insurance are consistent with the predictions of a price search model. However, more direct evidence relating consumer search costs to distribution system choice is needed to test the relevance of these models.

22.3.3.3 Open Issues

The theories of equilibrium coexistence of direct writer and independent agency distribution systems yield predictions consistent with a number of features observed in the property-liability insurance industry. This congruence of theoretical predictions and observed phenomena provides support for the general view that distribution system choices have an efficiency basis. The more detailed empirical evidence discussed in the previous section also makes clear that there are substantial differences in organization, product specialization and agent compensation across firms using different distribution systems. However, given the similarities in predictions derived from the alternative theories, obtaining empirical support for one theory to the exclusion of others has proven difficult. The empirical evidence thus far suggests that many factors play a role in determining distribution system choice, and leaves open the question of their relative importance. Other studies that could advance our understanding of this question include examination of the distribution system choices of new entrants to the industry, analysis of the relative success of firms using the same distribution system, and analysis of distribution system use in relation to consumer shopping behaviors.

Two other topic areas that have not received much study may also shed further light on the determinants of distribution system use. The first of these is the choice of distribution systems by life insurance firms. Many of the conditions argued to be at work in the choice of distribution system by property-liability insurers should exist in the life insurance industry as well. Carr, Cummins, and Regan (1999) present a transaction cost analysis of distribution system choice in life insurance.[15] Consistent with traditional transaction cost reasoning, they find that tied agency is more prevalent among life insurance firms that sell complex products.[16] Further, after controlling for product specialization and other firm characteristics, the authors find no significant differences in overall cost efficiency across life insurance distribution systems.[17]

These findings are quite distinct from the findings of studies in property-liability insurance. One intriguing explanation is that life insurance firms have optimally aligned distribution systems with product characteristics and markets, and are thus in equilibrium. Another interesting possibility is that the findings in property-liability insurance are driven primarily by the differences in client list ownership across distribution systems, which do not occur in life insurance. A final potential explanation is that there are measurement difficulties in the life insurance industry, due to the use of multiple distribution systems within a single firm (Carr, 1997), or due to omitted factors such as bank alliances or other marketing relationships. Further research into this question would be useful.

Another open question in the literature is the vertical separation between insurers and agents. The primary focus of the theoretical arguments has been on comparisons of the direct writer and independent agency distribution systems. Yet both of these systems most often involve vertical separation of the agent from the insurer; relatively few insurers utilize an employee sales force. The more natural question arising from the economics literature on transactions or contracting costs is the choice of internal versus external sales forces. Several studies have documented that insurers using an employee sales force or mass marketing have lower costs than other insurers (Barrese and Nelson, 1992; Regan, 1993; Carr, Cummins and Regan, 1999). Research examining why vertical separation is so common in insurance, and the determinants of this organizational choice, would increase our understanding of distribution system use in the industry.

22.4 AGENT COMPENSATION AND RESALE PRICE MAINTENANCE

Due to both competitive and regulatory concerns, the nature of insurance agent compensation has come under increasing scrutiny within the industry and among policy

[15] Grossman and Hart (1986) present evidence of specialization in term life insurance by independent agency insurers. However, their arguments regarding why independent agency is optimal for term life insurance rely on differences in client list ownership across the different distribution systems. In life insurance there are no such differences, with the insurance firm typically retaining ownership of policy renewals.

[16] Group insurance programs and individual whole life insurance were classified by the authors as relatively more complex than other products, such as individual term life or credit insurance.

[17] Efficiency is measured using data envelopment techniques, which decompose cost efficiency into technical and allocative efficiency. The authors find that both independent agency and tied agency insurers are less technically efficient than mass marketing insurers.

makers. Insurance agents are most commonly compensated via commissions based on premium revenues sold. Concerns center on the effects of such commission payments on agent sales and service incentives in general, and on unethical sales practices in particular.

Closely linked to the question of agent compensation is that of resale price maintenance. Resale price maintenance restrictions in the insurance industry prevent sales agents from reducing policy prices below those stated by the insurer, with agent commissions embedded in the retail price. While *per se* illegal in most industries in the United States since 1975 (Ippolito and Overstreet, 1996), this restrictive practice is not only legal but required in the insurance industry, due to state laws in effect since the 1940s. Because of the overwhelming use of commission-based compensation in insurance, these state laws are worded as "anti-rebating" laws, which prohibit agents from rebating any portion of their sales commission to the customer. A common justification for these laws is to discourage agents from needlessly replacing policies as a way of increasing commission income. Because of this link with agent compensation and incentive issues, we discuss resale price maintenance in conjunction with other issues regarding commission compensation.

22.4.1 Commission Compensation

22.4.1.1 Compensation and Incentives

Economic theories of optimal contract design lend insight into the use of commission compensation for sales agents. The perspective of these theories is that sales agents are self-interested, and hence must be encouraged to behave in ways that further the interest of the firm. It is further assumed that agents have private information about their efforts, abilities or market conditions related to sales, and that outcomes for the firm (sales or profits) are only stochastically related to agent inputs (effort or ability). The information asymmetry between the employer and the sales agent and the stochastic nature of output precludes the use of direct monitoring and enforcement of agent behaviors by the employer. In this environment, the compensation system can provide financial incentives to motivate the agent to act in the interest of the firm.

The simplest form of commission plan is to pay commissions only. Such a plan is the least costly way to motivate a risk-neutral agent to act in the interest of the firm, by directly aligning the agent's compensation with the employer's payoffs. For risk-averse agents, commission plans that involve some fixed (salary) component are preferable. Although the straight commission system provides the best incentives, the need to compensate a risk-averse agent for bearing income risk makes this form of compensation ultimately more costly. From this perspective, payment of salary plus commission reflects a trade-off between providing work incentives and sharing risk with the agent (Basu et al, 1985).

Other theoretical perspectives also predict that optimal agent compensation schemes may involve some salary component. Marketing and organization theorists point out that straight commission schemes are poor instruments for building long term relationships (John and Weitz, 1989). Transactions cost theory notes that commission compensation does not provide agents with incentives to invest in firm-specific human capital (Anderson, 1985). These arguments imply that commission-only compensation will be preferred only when the sales force is readily replaceable; otherwise the optimal compensation scheme will also involve a salary component. In this view, the optimal weighting of salary and commission compensation reflects a trade-off between effort incentives and relationship-building.

These theoretical predictions about the merits of salary versus commission compensation appear to be borne out in the insurance industry. For example, the compensation of independent agents is often solely commission-based whereas tied agents often receive some additional fixed compensation. Some employee agents are compensated through salary and bonuses only. These differences are consistent both with the greater earnings diversification opportunities of independent agents (risk issues) and their weaker links to a specific insurer (relationship issues).

The heavy reliance on commission compensation in life insurance has recently come into question. Consistent with the theories discussed above, one specific issue cited by life insurers considering compensation system changes is the inability to form long term relationships with agents. Life insurers currently experience an average annual turnover rate for agents of approximately 26%, and an average four year retention rate of new agents of only 18% (Hoesly, 1996). Insurers' concern about the cost of this turnover suggests that the existing compensation structure may be inappropriate in the current environment for life insurance products.

22.4.1.2 Unethical Agent Behavior

It has been argued that commission compensation does not control, and may exacerbate, conflicts of interest between sales agents and consumers (Kurland, 1995, 1996). Of particular concern in the insurance industry is the agent's incentives regarding disclosure and information provision, and choice of policy or product to sell (Howe et al, 1994). For example, an agent might recommend a particular insurer's product because it generates a higher commission rather than because it is the best match for the consumer. These concerns should be especially salient in circumstances in which part of the value-enhancing input of the agent is to provide consumer information and aid in the choice of product. It is therefore not surprising that concerns about the effects of commissions on agent sales practices are particularly strong in the life insurance industry.

Whether commission compensation does in fact encourage unethical behaviors is uncertain, as research into the effects of commission compensation on sales agent behavior is scarce. Kurland (1996) surveyed insurance agents regarding their predicted actions in scenarios that involved ethical dilemmas. Contrary to her hypothesis, she finds that the percentage of annual earnings from commissions does not affect insurance agents' ethical intentions toward consumers. A study by Howe, et al. (1994) may provide indirect evidence regarding the effect of compensation method on ethical behavior. This study finds that agents with higher customer orientation (as opposed to sales orientation) exhibit higher ethical standards in sales practices. If commission compensation encourages greater sales orientation, this finding suggests a link between commission-based compensation and unethical practices.[18]

The general marketing literature on sales practices provides suggestive evidence of a link between commission compensation and sales practices. Agents in more competitive environments are more likely to approve of unethical solutions to problems, and the operating environment is found to affect agents' perceptions of acceptable sales practices. However, this literature concludes that there is no direct effect of compensation practices on agent ethics. Rather, a complex set of factors which include the compensation system, management practices, perceived corporate codes of ethics, competitive pressures and the agent's personal ethics affect the ethical behavior of sales agents.

22.4.1.3 Alternative Compensation Systems

An often-suggested alternative to commission compensation for life insurance agents is consumer-paid fees provided to the agent (either with or without salary compensation from the insurer). Largely because of concerns about unethical agent behavior, regulatory commissions in several countries have considered mandating fee-based compensation for financial service sellers. Some U.S. states prohibit financial service agents from receiving both fees and commissions on the same transaction (Lefenfeld, 1996). The hypothesized benefit of fee-based systems is that agents compensated by fees would have no incentive to offer biased advice regarding the merits of purchase, or the relative merits of alternative products.

To highlight the issues in determining whether consumers would be better served under the alternative systems, Gravelle (1993, 1994) undertakes a theoretical welfare analysis of commission-based versus fee-based compensation systems in a life insurance market. Consistent with current public policy concerns, Gravelle assumes that agents play an important informational role in the market. The insurance market is assumed to be competitive, but agents hold a monopoly in providing consumers information about the benefits of life insurance.

In this model, all agents have a financial incentive to exaggerate the benefits of life insurance to consumers if compensated by sales commissions from the insurer. However, even dishonest agents have some social value, because they may contact consumers whose *true* benefit from life insurance exceeds the purchase price. Replacing sales commissions with fees paid by consumers may or may not improve social

[18] Eastman, et al (1996) find that the professional ethics of insurance agents are lower than their personal ethics, but do not study the relationship between compensation methods and ethical beliefs.

welfare. The quality of advice will be greater under the fee-based system (that is, agent dishonesty will be less), as generally argued. However, the fee will be set at the monopoly level, and hence too few consumers will become informed and will potentially make purchasing errors. This latter finding depends of course on the assumption that agents have a monopoly in information provision, which is questionable in the current market environment.[19] Nonetheless, Gravelle's analysis demonstrates that the relative merits of compensation systems depend not only on agent actions, but on the equilibrium prices for products and services, availability of product variety and services, and the number of agents and insurers that enter the market under alternative compensation schemes.

Another alternative to the current life insurance compensation system is to offer a more level commission structure, reducing first-year sales commissions and raising renewal-year commissions. Puelz and Snow (1995) demonstrate theoretically that high first-year commissions are optimal if agent efforts in attracting new customers are more productive than agent efforts in attracting renewal customers. However, their analysis does not consider effects that this commission scheme may have on the non-sales behavior of agents. In addition to concerns about service and information provision, it has been argued that large first year commissions engender incentives for "twisting". Policy twisting is said to occur when an agent convinces a consumer to replace an existing policy with one of no greater benefit, in order to generate commission income for the agent. While we are aware of no empirical studies of the effects of commission structure on the prevalence of twisting, it is apparent that higher first year commissions will increase agents' incentives to replace rather than renew policies.

22.4.2 Resale Price Maintenance

In the abstract, an insurance firm can be viewed as an upstream supplier of a product to an insurance agent, who adds some value to the product and sells it in the retail market. The insurer chooses the wholesale price for the product by specifying the premium for the consumer and the sales commission for the insurance agent. In the absence of legal or contractual restrictions, the agent could alter the retail price of the policy by either offering a rebate of part of his commission to the consumer, or charging a separate service fee. Resale price maintenance restrictions prevent the agent from influencing the retail price in this way. In the insurance industry these restrictions operate as a price floor, prohibiting agents from rebating commissions to consumers. Resale price maintenance restrictions have received the most attention in the life insurance industry, where agent first-year commissions are high and hence there exists significant potential for rebating.

[19] In Gravelle's model there is also no competition between agents. Consumers are contacted by at most one agent and cannot seek out advice from other agents.

22.4.2.1 Economic Issues

While there are no existing studies of the rationale for resale price maintenance in the insurance industry, economic theory identifies two possibilities: resale price restrictions may support price collusion or other anti-competitive practices, or may represent a solution to some principal-agent problem (Katz, 1990; Ippolito, 1988).

Collusion theories focus on the anti-competitive effects of reducing retail market price differences. One argument is that removing uncertainty about prices at the retail level increases the monitoring ability of a price-setting cartel. Thus, if industry conditions are otherwise conducive, anti-rebating agreements can help maintain price collusion by inhibiting secret chiseling on price agreements. Short of collusion, resale price restraints may reduce price competition by reducing consumer search, since price dispersion will be lower in a market with no retail price competition. Resale price restraints may also facilitate price discrimination, which can increase insurer profits. Uniform prices charged to all customers is a form of price discrimination if the marginal cost of product provision differs across customers, for example due to different levels of service demand (Caves, 1980).

Principal-agent theories focus on how resale price restraints may change the behavior of retail sellers in ways that benefit the producer. One argument is that price floors encourage service provision. Resale price floors prevent consumers from shopping at a full-price outlet to obtain pre-sale services, but purchasing from a discount seller. If the price floor involves a high retailer profit margin, competition among retail sellers will take the form of service competition and advertising, thereby building markets and brand reputations for upstream producers (Katz, 1990).

A similar argument refers to quality provision by the retail seller when consumers cannot distinguish product quality from retailer quality. If the level of retailer quality or service can be specified and periodically monitored by the upstream producer, the retail price floor will serve to increase the retailer's costs of dismissal for inadequate quality provision (Telser, 1960). This provides direct financial incentives for quality or service provision by the agent.

These latter theories of resale price are related to insurer arguments for resale price maintenance in the life insurance industry. It is often argued that the complexity of many life insurance products necessitates that agents provide services in the form of information provision. It has also been argued that rebating may undermine customer persistency. A customer who will purchase only if offered a rebate has a lower valuation of the product, or of the services provided by the agent, than the customer who purchases at full price. If low-valuation customers are more likely to cash in their policies early, insurers may not recover the fixed costs of selling and underwriting on these policies. Under this argument, insurers' expectations of losing money on such customers could explain resale price restrictions.

The history of the anti-rebating laws in the United States life insurance industry offers some corroboration of this perspective on the issue. Stalson's classic book on the history of life insurance distribution makes clear that agent rebating was viewed as a problem by life insurers as early as the 1860s, and was something that insurers and agents unsuccessfully tried to deal with via informal agreements (Stalson, 1951). While the precise reasons for industry opposition to rebating are not made clear in that text, it appears that the practice created problems associated with the twisting of policies. High commission levels and the ability to rebate commissions to policyholders heighten the agent's incentives to engage in this policy turnover. In addition, if first year commissions exceed the first year policy premium it is possible for an agent to collude with consumers (those not interested in maintaining the policy) against the insurance company for financial gain. Stalson notes that in the heavy rebating era of the late 1800s competition for agents led to some first year commissions in excess of 200 percent of the first year premium, so this scenario is a possibility.

New York was the first state to outlaw rebating in 1889, and 21 other states quickly followed. However, rebating continued, and in fact intensified in the ensuing ten years. With the 1906 New York state Armstrong Commission review of the insurance industry, New York and other state legislatures enacted stricter laws which made not only giving a rebate, but also receiving a rebate, illegal. These laws were incorporated into the National Association of Insurance Commissioner's 1945 Unfair Trade Practices Model Act. Supported by the industry, the stated rationale of the legislation is to protect consumers from "unfair discrimination" and to prevent "destructive price competition".

These concerns provide a weak justification for resale price restrictions in the current regulatory environment. Solvency regulation, guaranty funds, and direct restrictions on discriminatory pricing are other tools to meet these objectives. Moreover, the public interest arguments for anti-rebating laws are strongest within the prevailing compensation system that pays life insurance agents a large first year commission. Changes to the commission structure would be a more direct way to reduce agents' incentives to twist policies or to offer discriminatory rebates.

At best, the effect of resale price maintenance agreements on consumer welfare is ambiguous. Even if resale price maintenance fosters agent service, it will enforce a uniform level of quality provision that may be greater than that desired by some consumers. For example, life insurance buyers who do not need as much information as others are forced via resale price maintenance to pay the high-information price. Resale price maintenance will also lessen price differences at the retail level. Given the empirical evidence on costly price search in insurance markets (Mathewson and Winter, 1983; Dahlby and West, 1986), this will reduce consumer search with negative implications for consumer welfare.

22.4.2.2 Recent Developments

Empirical research on the impact of resale price restraints in insurance markets is needed to more fully understand the issues surrounding their use. Recent events provide some opportunity for such study. In 1986 the state of Florida repealed its anti-rebating law after it was declared unconstitutional by the state Supreme Court. California repealed its law in 1988 with the passage of Proposition 103, which contained a provision overturning rebating restrictions. No other state has yet followed suit, and anti-rebating laws have survived constitutional challenges in several states.

Trade press accounts note that the effects of rebating have been modest in the two states that have allowed it. It is argued that there are several reasons for this. First, in both states insurers are allowed to refuse to deal with discounting agents. Second, Florida has put restrictions on rebating practices to assure that the market abuses seen in the earlier rebating era are not revisited. Important provisions of the law include the requirement that agents prominently display their rebate schedules, and offer equivalent discounts to all customers. Although this provision has not been explicitly written into California law, the state's strong anti-discrimination laws may make agents and insurers feel that this restriction would apply. Thus, in order to offer rebates an agent must operate solely as a discount agent or broker. This may lower agent participation in rebating.

Although limited, the experiences of California and Florida provide at least some basis for empirical explorations of the impact of rebating. Russell (1997) uses state-level data on life insurance surrender activity for the period 1960–1992 to examine the effect of rebating on policy replacements. The study develops a regression model of surrender activity which includes a dummy variable equal to one in the states and years for which rebating is allowed. In all model specifications employed, the estimated coefficient on the rebating dummy variable is positive and significant, indicating that state surrender activity is higher when rebating is allowed. Interpretation of this positive correlation is difficult because there are no data available to determine whether the policies surrendered were replaced with other policies, and there are a very small number of observations in the data for which rebating activity was allowed. Nonetheless, these results warrant further research into the question.

22.5 THE REGULATION OF INSURANCE DISTRIBUTION

The regulation of insurance distribution is extensive in virtually all countries with developed markets for these services.[20] Insurance distribution is regulated in two distinct ways: the set of market participants is restricted, and the marketing practices of insurers and their intermediaries are regulated. Entry restrictions take the form of licensing requirements for insurers, agents and brokers, and regulations that prohibit insurance sales by certain types of firms (e.g., banks) or methods (e.g., direct mail). Market conduct regulations take such forms as requiring dissemination of certain

[20] These policies and regulations tend to be similar in intent to those directed toward marketing practices in other financial services industries.

types of information, and prohibiting misrepresentation and false advertising. Regulations are often directed at both insurance companies and insurance agents or brokers, but insurance companies also are typically held responsible for the actions of their representatives.

22.5.1 Entry Regulation

22.5.1.1 Major Regulations

Entry restrictions for insurance producers and sellers exist in virtually all countries, but the focus and extent of these restrictions varies greatly. Until recently in the United States, the Glass-Steagall Act prohibited commercial banks from entering other financial services industries, including insurance. However, exceptions had always been allowed for certain state-chartered banks, and banks serving very small markets. Further, banks are very active in the credit life and mortgage insurance markets. Even before repeal of the Act, court and regulatory rulings allowed some banks to own insurance subsidiaries and to engage in insurance distribution. Bank alliances with insurance companies are becoming increasingly common, and banks are becoming a significant distributor of annuities in the United States.

In most European countries there have historically been fewer restrictions on bank involvement in insurance. While all European Union countries prohibit banks from engaging directly in the production of insurance, most allow banks to own insurance subsidiaries and to distribute insurance products (Hoschka, 1994). The formation of insurance subsidiaries by banks is growing, and insurance distribution at bank branches is quite common in some countries. Strong restrictions on banks selling insurance remain in other countries such as Japan, however. Until recently, Japan also prohibited other insurance distribution systems such as direct selling and brokerage (Skipper, 1998).

In most countries both insurance companies and sales agents much be licensed. Licensing requirements for insurers generally include financial standards and ethical standards for company officers. In the United States, licensing is done at the state level and firms must be licensed in all states in which they do business on an admitted basis. Each company has a primary state of domicile, however, and it is this state that takes primary responsibility for regulatory oversight. In the E.U., the single market directives require insurers to be licensed only in their home country rather in each country in which they intend to sell insurance. The home country retains responsibility for solvency oversight of the insurer.

Licensing requirements for agents and brokers typically entail meeting certain ethical standards and passing a written test, but standards vary greatly across jurisdictions and often the requirements are minimal. Moreover, in many countries the licensing requirements apply only to independent agents, financial advisors and brokers; employee sales agents often need not be licensed. However, due to the growing complexity of insurance products, the move toward price and entry deregulation in many markets, and to recent problems with marketing practices in some countries, professional standards for insurance intermediaries are receiving increased attention in many countries.

The standardization of agent licensing requirements and licensing reciprocity across jurisdictions is another important issue across the individual states of the U.S. and across countries, especially those of the European Union. Not only do licensing requirements vary, but agents often must be licensed in each jurisdiction in which they sell. These barriers to agents operating across borders are eroding, however. In the U.S., a 1998 NAIC Model licensing reciprocity agreement would require participating states to eliminate countersignature[21] laws, and allow producers licensed in good standing in a participating state to be eligible for streamlined licensing in any other participating state. Uniform licensing and education requirements are also being developed. Similar developments are occurring in the E.U., and in 1996 a proposal to harmonize agent licensing and regulation was forwarded (Skipper, 1998).

22.5.1.2 Economic Issues

Legal restrictions on the entry of banks into insurance are rationalized by concerns about the stability of the financial system and about detrimental effects of market power in financial services delivery. While both of these concerns have some theoretical and historical foundations, it is not clear that prohibiting entry is a necessary response to the potential problems. In countries that allow banks to enter insurance, laws still prohibit direct ownership and funds co-mingling at banks and insurance firms. This reduces the risk that banks will use insurance assets to meet liquidity needs, and makes regulatory monitoring easier. Empirical studies also suggest that the overall risk of a combined banking-insurance entity could be lower than that of either one separately (Santomero, 1993).

Market power in financial services provision is a serious concern as bank markets are becoming increasingly concentrated. However, an alternative to entry restrictions is to mitigate abuses by market conduct regulation. Moreover, allowing greater entry into insurance markets should foster competition in those markets and spur efficiency-enhancing innovations. Thus, while many complex regulatory issues remain to be resolved, allowing bank-insurance combinations may be economically sound.

Licensing requirements for agents are often justified as protecting consumers from incompetent or dishonest practitioners, and often are imposed with the support of the regulated industry or profession. The efficiency argument for industry support is that incompetent or dishonest sellers create negative externalities for other sellers by undermining industry reputation. However, there is also a political argument for industry support based on the fact that licensing requirements act as barriers to entry into the market. The requirements are sufficiently lenient that this argument seems weak in most markets. However, differenceing in licensing requirements across states

[21] In the United States, agents may sell insurance in states in which they are not licensed, but must obtain a countersignature from a licensed agent, who also shares in the commission.

or countries do limit entry, thereby protecting resident agents and insurers from competition. In addition, differential licensing requirements for independent versus tied agents may increase the costs of distribution through independent agents or brokers relative to other systems.

Even if licensing does not serve to raise entry barriers and limit competition, there is the additional question of whether licensing requirements provide any benefits to consumers. Studies of the impact of licensing restrictions in industries other than insurance tend to show no significant quality improvements obtained from licensing. Benefits from licensing insurance agents may be particularly low, since imposing liability on insurance companies for the actions of their agents may give sufficient incentives for companies to choose honest agents and provide adequate training. Although differences in agent licensing requirements across jurisdictions and changes in requirements over time make it possible to examine its effects empirically, to our knowledge this has not been studied.

22.5.2 Conduct Regulation

22.5.2.1 Major Regulations

Market conduct in distribution is a major focus of regulatory oversight in insurance. Virtually all countries have legislation in place to regulate insurance company and agent practices in the marketing of insurance. For example, the 1945 Unfair Trade Practices Model Act of the National Association of Insurance Commissioners (NAIC) defines and prohibits: the misrepresentation of policy benefits, terms and conditions, dividends or premiums, and the financial condition of the insurer; false, misleading or deceptive advertising about the business of insurance or the business of a specific insurer; agent misrepresentations on insurance applications in order to get a fee or commission; and agent misrepresentation of himself as a financial advisor.[22] This legislation has been adopted in whole or in part by all U.S. states.

Additional legislation has been adopted in many U.S. states to specify in more detail the allowable marketing practices of companies and agents offering life insurance and accident and health insurance. Advertising regulations adopted by some states move beyond general proscriptions against certain types of practices to provide detailed instructions regarding elements of policies that must be disclosed in advertising materials. Virtually all states have also adopted legislation regulating the activities of insurance agents with respect to the replacement of life insurance and annuities. This legislation requires agents to fully inform the buyer of changes in terms and conditions of insurance under the new policy, and to have the buyer sign a statement indicating knowledge that a replacement policy is being issued. The agent must include a statement on the policy application that indicates whether a policy is being

[22] Commission rebating is also prohibited in the Act.

replaced, and the buyer must be given a free-look period to compare the replacement policy with the existing policy.[23]

Another aspect of life insurance regulation is rules regarding illustrations of projections of death benefits and cash values. All states have regulations specifying the nature and content of materials that must be disclosed to potential purchasers, including allowable methods to calculate the yields of different types of policies. Sellers are also required to provide Buyers Guides and other comparative information on forms approved by the state commissioner.

The NAIC recently developed more stringent rules on illustrations for whole life, universal and term life products in the United States, designed to prevent exaggerations and to ensure that consumers understand the hypothetical nature of the projections. Even more stringent disclosure rules have been introduced in several other countries, including the United Kingdom, New Zealand and Australia. New rules in force in the U.K. since 1995 institute more realism in life insurance illustrations, require agents to document that they gave the "best advice" to each insurance applicant, and require agents to fully disclose their relationships with insurance firms and the compensation that they receive from any sale.

The weakest link in market conduct regulation is discovery and enforcement. In the United States, each state insurance commissioner has broad powers to investigate insurer and agent practices, to issue cease and desist orders and to invoke fines or revoke licenses if violations of the law are found. In other countries enforcement authority may be shared between state or provincial and federal regulatory agencies, and in some other countries enforcement authority lies with industry self-regulatory bodies. A significant problem is that investigations are costly and are most effective at the level of the individual agent; this implies that abuses may go on for a long time without being discovered. Another impediment is the lack of information sharing and coordination across jurisdictions, a growing concern among the U.S. states and the individual members of the European Union. This latter problem may be mitigated somewhat in the U.S. as the NAIC implements its producer information database. This database aims to collect and disseminate information about licensed agents in every state, including licensing status and disciplinary actions.

22.5.2.2 Economic Issues

Economic efficiency rationales for government intervention into sales and distribution practices are generally couched in terms of information problems, especially information asymmetries between sellers and buyers.[24] A central information problem

[23] Replacement of a policy with one that does not significantly increase insurance or other benefits is costly to the consumer because of the high levels of commission that go to agents at the time of sale. Other detrimental effects may include higher premium rates because the consumer is older, loss of cash value in the policy, and new incontestability and suicide clauses imposed in the new policy.

[24] These issues are discussed extensively in Ippolito, 1988.

that consumers face in insurance markets is judging product quality. The quality characteristics of an insurance policy are difficult to ascertain due to the complexity of the contract, the contingent nature of many of the services provided (e.g., claims handling and payments), and the fact that many services are provided over time (e.g., investments). This implies that quality is difficult to ascertain in advance of purchase, and may continue to be even after significant experience with the product.[25] Under this circumstance insurance sellers may have a financial incentive to charge a high price but to provide low quality. From this perspective, government regulations that prevent false or misleading advertising and that mandate full disclosure of relevant policy features may improve consumers' ability to estimate product quality at the point of purchase. Disclosure of relationships and commissions can be justified as making consumers aware of potentially biased incentives of the selling agent.

Arguments against disclosure regulation are often couched in terms of market responses to these problems. One argument is that firms have reputational incentives to maintain faith in their products and thus to provide high quality products. However, this mechanism may work imperfectly in markets for personal insurance because of consumers' limited opportunities to observe many aspects of quality. Moreover, the nature of insurance policies and their pricing is such that information may be difficult to compare across consumers. This may reduce the information content of negative consumer experiences, and hence mitigate adverse effects on reputation.

Another argument is that insurers have an incentive to provide information that is valued by consumers, because the consumer can be charged for it by the bundling of insurance products with information. This may be the case, for example, with sales through a professional agent. In this circumstance high quality producers have an incentive to inform consumers about quality. However, to the extent consumers may obtain information about insurance and then use this to purchase elsewhere, the incentive to provide information is reduced. Thus, if a significant fraction of information provision in the insurance sale is of a general educational nature, information may be under-provided in the unregulated market.

If individual insurance companies have insufficient incentive to provide quality information to consumers, other market entities may arise to provide this information. For example, consumer publications may provide general information and quality comparisons. However, because information of this sort is not proprietary, there will still be free riding problems and hence likely under-provision of the information. Similarly, an industry cooperative association may provide educational materials that would benefit the sales of all companies, but would not have the correct incentives to provide company-specific information or comparative information across companies.

[25] At least as significant for consumers is the possibility that product quality may change after the purchase is made. Even if quality can be determined at the time of purchase, it may vary over time and hence continuous monitoring is required. This problem may be mitigated by solvency regulation and regulation of other insurer practices.

Given the nature of information problems in insurance markets, it is not clear that the market alone will provide sufficient information to insurance consumers. Hence, government intervention could improve the working of the market. The optimal form of intervention and the benefits of current regulatory measures are uncertain, however. It is possible that detailed regulations on information provision do not improve consumer decision making. Additional information may not be processed efficiently by the consumer, and large amounts of information may even exacerbate information-processing problems. The appropriate level of detail in the regulatory standards is also uncertain given the costs of compliance to insurance companies.

There also may be unintended side effects of disclosure regulation that can harm consumers. For example, the "best advice" requirements in the U.K. have been argued to lead to a move away from independent agency, since this form of distribution carries a greater disclosure burden. If independent agency distribution enhances price and quality comparisons, then the net effect of the rules could be to increase consumer search costs and reduce consumer information. Additional research is needed to evaluate the necessity of regulation and the best methods of achieving regulatory objectives.

22.6 CONCLUDING REMARKS

The deregulation and increasing integration of financial services markets, technological progress and changing demographics have resulted in a vast expansion of financial products and providers in direct competition with the insurance industry. For property and liability risks, the development of inexpensive hedging methods that are substitutes for insurance products has reduced the share of business risks covered by traditional insurance to less than 50 percent as of 1996. Even medium size businesses increasingly make use of self-insurance, captives and risk retention groups. The alternative risk transfer market has seen growth averaging six percent per year since the mid-1980s, about twice the growth rate in the commercial insurance market (Andre and Sudowsky, 1997).

In the life insurance market, demographic shifts, longer life expectancies in retirement, and reductions in benefits from government retirement plans have reduced the demand for traditional life insurance products and increased demand for annuities and other financial planning products. Sales of ordinary life insurance continue to decline each year, while annuity sales increase at a rapid rate (Hoesly, 1996). This shift in product demand has increased insurers' competition from banks and investment houses, which are licensed to sell investment products and tend to have lower distribution costs.

At the same time, in both property-liability and life insurance markets technological progress and competition have resulted in increasing standardization of the simpler insurance products. For these products there is an increasing emphasis on low-cost distribution, and non-traditional methods of reaching customers are an important area of growth in this sector. Direct response selling has attracted interest from even the more traditional insurers, as communication technology advances, including the internet, make direct response more cost-effective. Insurers are also focusing on worksite marketing programs for simple products. These programs differ from the traditional group insurance programs in that customers pay their own premiums and insurers use individual underwriting. The aim of this marketing approach is simply expense reductions through administrative and marketing cost savings. These new distribution methods have been most effective for products such as automobile, homeowners, credit and term life insurance, standardized products for which price is seen as an important factor in the buying decision. These forces have put considerable stress on traditional insurance distribution systems, and produced pressure for innovation.

Two important trends are becoming visible in insurance marketing relationships: the use of multiple distribution systems within a single firm, and increased specialization of the roles of different distribution systems. The industry is moving away from a set of fixed relationships between insurer and agent based upon company traditions, toward a more flexible system in which the distribution method is determined by the product and the customer base. Professional agents are increasingly focused on the sale of complex, service-oriented products such as commercial insurance or other hedging instruments in property-liability markets, or estate and accumulation products in life insurance markets. Low-cost direct response alternatives are becoming more common for standardized insurance products. Some industry analysts predict that the tied agency system will be the ultimate loser in this shift, as it has neither the advantages of independent advice and service provided by brokers, nor the low costs of the direct selling alternatives (Nuttney, 1995).

The increasing polarization of distribution systems by product and market is in keeping with economic theories of the firm that predict organizational structures will be chosen to minimize both operating costs and transactions or agency costs. While existing academic studies of distribution system choice have focused primarily on the choice between an independent or a tied agency force, current market trends distinguish more clearly between fully integrated distribution without the use of professional agents versus the agency system of distribution itself. This appears to be due to both technological and competitive changes in insurance markets.

As the professional agent's role becomes more specialized, and as increasing numbers of insurance products are being sold without the benefit of agent advice, market conduct and disclosure regulation will become increasingly important in the industry. Professional certification and regulatory monitoring of agents must receive more attention in the service-oriented sectors of the industry. Consistent with approaches in other financial services industries, disclosure issues will likely become the key enforcement tool for standardized insurance products sold via direct marketing. Issues surrounding resale price maintenance and the potential for agent discounting should become less important, as price sensitive products are increasingly sold through alternative means.

22.7 REFERENCES

Alchian, Armen and Harold Demsetz (1972). "Production, Information Costs and Economic Organization." *American Economic Review* 62, 777–795.

Anderson, Erin (1985). "The Salesperson as Outside Agent or Employee: A Transaction Cost Analysis." *Marketing Science* 4, 234–254.

Anderson, E., W.T. Ross, Jr. and Barton Weitz (1998). "Commitment and its Consequences in the American Agency System of Selling Insurance." *Journal of Risk and Insurance* 65, 637–669.

Andre, John E. and Rich Sodowsky (1997). "Considering the Alternative Markets." *Best's Review. P/C* May, 42–46.

Barrese, James, Helen I. Doerpinghaus and Jack M. Nelson (1995). "Do Independent Agent Insurers Provide Superior Service? The Insurance Marketing Puzzle." *Journal of Risk and Insurance* 62, 297–308.

Barrese, James and Jack M. Nelson (1992). "Independent and Exclusive Agency Insurers: A Reexamination of the Cost Differential." *Journal of Risk and Insurance* 59, 375–397.

Basu, A.K., Rajiv Lal, V. Srinivasan and Richard Staelin (1986). "Sales Compensation Plans: An Agency Theoretic Perspective." *Marketing Science* 4, 267–291.

Berger, Allen N., J. David Cummins and Mary A. Weiss (1997). "The Coexistence of Multiple Distribution Systems for Financial Services: The Case of Property-Liability Insurance." *Journal of Business* 70, 515–546.

Berger, Lawrence, Paul Kleindorfer and Howard Kunreuther (1989). "A Dynamic Model of the Transmission of Price Information in Auto Insurance Markets." *Journal of Risk and Insurance* 56, 17–33.

Bernheim, Douglas and Michael Whinston (1985). "Common Marketing Agency as a Device for Facilitating Collusion." *Rand Journal of Economics* 16, 269–281.

Braeutigam, Ronald and Mark V. Pauly (1986). "Cost Function Estimation and Quality Bias: The Regulated Automobile Insurance Industry." *Rand Journal of Economics* 17, 606–617.

Carr, Roderick A. (1997). "Strategic Choices, Firm Efficiency, and Competiveness in the U.S. Life Insurance Industry." Ph.D. Dissertation, The Wharton School, University of Pennsylvania, Phila. PA.

Carr, Roderick A., J. David Commins and Laureen Regan (1999). "Efficiency and Competitiveness in the U.S. Life Insurance Industry: Corporate, Product, and Distribution Strategies" in J.D. Cummins and A. Santomero eds., *Changes in the Life Insurance Industry: Efficiency, Technology, and Risk Management*, Kluwer Academic Publishers.

Cather, David, Sandra Gustavson and James Trieschmann (1985). "Profitability Analysis of Property-Liability Insurers Using Alternative Distribution Systems." *Journal of Risk and Insurance* 52, 321–332.

Caves, Richard E. (1986). "Vertical Restraints in Manufacturer-Distributor Relations: Incidence and Economic Effects." In R.E. Grieson, ed., Antitrust and Regulation. Lexington: Lexington Books.

Crosby, Lawrence A., Kenneth R. Evans and Richard S. Jacobs (1991). "Effects of Life Insurance Price Rebating on Simulated Sales Encounters." *Journal of Risk and Insurance* 58, 583–615.

Cummins, J. David and Jack VanDerhei (1979). "A Note on the Relative Efficiency of Property-Liability Insurance Distribution Systems." *Bell Journal of Economics* 10, 709–719.

Cummins, J. David and Stephen Weisbart (1977). *The Impact of Consumer Services on Independent Insurance Agency Performance*. Glenmont, New York: IMA Education and Research Foundation.

Dahlby, Bev and Douglas West (1986). "Price Search in an Automobile Insurance Market." *Journal of Political Economy* 94, 418–438.

Darby, Michael and Edi Karni (1979). "Free Competition and the Optimal Amount of Fraud." *Journal of Law and Economics* 22, 67–88.

Doerpinghaus, Helen I. (1991). "An Analysis of Complaint Data in the Automobile Insurance Industry." *Journal of Risk and Insurance* 58, 122, 120–127.

Eastman, Kevin L, Jacqueline K. Eastman and Alan D. Eastman (1996). "The Ethics of Insurance Professionals: Comparison of Personal versus Professional Ethics." *Journal of Business Ethics* 15, 951–962.

Etgar, Michael (1976). "Service Performance of Insurance Distribution." *Journal of Risk and Insurance* 43, 487–499.

Fama, Eugene (1980). "Agency Problems and the Theory of the Firm." *Journal of Political Economy* 88, 288–307.

Fields, Joseph A. and Neil Murphy (1989). "An Analysis of Efficiency in the Delivery of Financial Services: The Case of Life Insurance Agencies." *Journal of Financial Services Research* 2, 323–356.

Finsinger, Jorg and Mark V. Pauly, eds. (1986). *The Economics of Insurance Regulation: A Cross-National Study*. New York: St. Martin's Press.

Finsinger, Jorg and F.A. Schmid (1992). "Prices, Distribution Channels and Regulatory Intervention in European Insurance Markets." Working paper. University of Vienna.

Gaunt, Larry D., Neuman A. Williams and Everett D. Randall (1990a). *Commercial Liability Underwriting, Volume II*. Malvern: Insurance Institute of America.

Grabowski, Henry, W. Kip Viscusi and William N. Evans (1989). "The Effects of Regulation on the Price and Availability of Automobile Insurance." *Journal of Risk and Insurance* 56, 275–299.

Gravelle, Hugh (1994). "Remunerating Information Providers: Commissions versus Fees in Life Insurance." *Journal of Risk and Insurance* 61, 425–457.

Gravelle, Hugh (1993). "Product Price and Advice Quality: Implications of the Commission System in Life Assurance." *Geneva Papers on Risk and Insurance Theory* 16, 3–19.

Gron, Anne (1995). "Regulation and Insurer Competition: Did Insurers Use Rate Regulation to Reduce Competition?" *Journal of Risk and Uncertainty* 11, 87–111.

Grossman, Sanford and Oliver Hart (1986). "The Costs and Benefits of Ownership: A Theory of Vertical and Lateral Integration." *Journal of Political Economy* 94, 691–719.

Harrington, Scott E. (1982). "Operating Expenses for Agency and Nonagency Life Insurers: Further Evidence." *Journal of Risk and Insurance* 49, 229–255.

Hoesly, Michelle L. (1996). "Life Insurance Distribution: The Future is Not What it Used to Be", *Journal of the American Society of CLU and ChFC* 50, 88–100.

Holmstrom, Bengt R. and Jean Tirole (1990). "The Theory of the Firm." in R. Schmalensee and R. Willig, eds., *Handbook of Industrial Organization*. Amsterdam: Elsevier Science Publishers.

Hoschka, Tobias C. (1994). *Bancassurance in Europe*. New York: St. Martin's Press.

Howe, Vince, Douglas K. Hoffman and Donald W. Hardigree (1994). "The Relationship between Ethical and Customer-oriented Service Provider Behaviors." *Journal of Business Ethics* 13, 497–506.

Ippolito, Pauline M. and Thomas R. Overstreet Jr. (1996). "Resale Price Maintenance: An Economic Assessment of the Federal Trade Commission's Case against the Corning Glass Works." *Journal of Law and Economics* 39, 285–328.

Ippolito, Pauline M. (1988). "The Economics of Information in Consumer Markets: What do we Know? What do we need to Know?" In E.S. Maynes, ed., *The Frontier of Research in the Consumer Interest*. Columbia: American Council on Consumer Interests.

Jensen, Michael C. and William H. Meckling (1976). "Theory of the Firm: Managerial Behavior, Agency Costs and Ownership Structure." *Journal of Financial Economics* 3, 305–360.

John, George and Barton Weitz (1989). "Salesforce Compensation: An Empirical Investigation of Factors Related to the Use of Salary Versus Incentive Compensation." *Journal of Marketing Research* 26, 1–14.

Joskow, Paul (1973). "Cartels, Competition and Regulation in the Property-Liability Insurance Industry" *Bell Journal of Economics and Management Science* 4, 375–427.

Katz, Michael L. (1990). "Vertical Contractual Relations." In R. Schmalensee and R. Willig, eds., *Handbook of Industrial Organization*. Amsterdam: Elsevier Science Publishers.

Kim, Won-Joong, David Mayers and Clifford Smith (1996). "On the Choice of Insurance Distribution Systems." *Journal of Risk and Insurance* 63, 207–227.

Kurland, Nancy B. (1996). "Sales Agents and Clients: Ethics, Incentives and a Modified Theory of Planned Behavior." *Human Relations* 49, 51–74.

Kurland, Nancy B. (1995). "Ethics, Incentives and Conflicts of Interest: A Practical Solution." *Journal of Business Ethics* 14, 465–475.

Lefenfeld, Mark S. (1996). "Fee based Compensation Replaces Shrinking Income." *Best's Review* 96, 68.

Lewis, Tracy and David Sappington (1989). "Inflexible Rules in Incentive Problems." *American Economic Review* 79, 69–84.

Martimort, David (1996). "Exclusive Dealing, Common Agency, and Multiprincipals Incentive Theory." *Rand Journal of Economics* 27, 1–31.

Marvel, Howard (1982). "Exclusive Dealing." *Journal of Law and Economics* 25, 1–25.

Mathewson, Frank (1983). "Information, Search and Price Variability of Individual Life Insurance Contracts." *Journal of Industrial Economics* 32, 131–148.

Morgan, Glenn et al (1994). "Bancassurance in Britain and France: Innovating Strategies in the Financial Services." *The Geneva Papers on Risk and Insurance* 19, 178–195.

Nuttney, Andrew (1995). *The Marketing and Distribution of European Insurance*. Financial Times Management Reports. London: Pearson Professional Ltd.

Pauly, Mark, Paul Kleindorfer and Howard Kunreuther (1986). "Regulation and Quality Competition in the U.S. Insurance Market." In Finsinger, Jorg and Mark Pauly, eds., *The Economics of Insurance Regulation*. New York: St. Martin's Press 65–107.

Posey, Lisa L. and Sharon Tennyson (1998). "The Coexistence of Distribution Systems under Price Search: Theory and some Evidence from Insurance." *Journal of Economic Behavior and Organization* 35, 95–115.

Posey, Lisa L. and Abdullah Yavas (1995). "A Search Model of Marketing Systems in Property-Liability Insurance." *Journal of Risk and Insurance* 62, 666–689.

Pritchett, S. Travis and Benjamin Y. Brewster, Jr. (1979). "Comparison of Ordinary Operating Expense Ratios for Agency and Non-Agency Insurers." *Journal of Risk and Insurance* 46, 61–74.

Puelz, Robert and Arthur Snow (1991). "Efficient Contracting in a Market for Life Insurance Agents with Asymmetric Information." *Journal of Risk and Insurance* 58, 729–736.

Regan, Laureen (1999). "Expense Ratios Across Insurance Distribution Systems: An Analysis by Line of Business." *Risk Management and Insurance Review* 2.

Regan, Laureen (1997). "Vertical Integration in the Property-Liability Insurance Industry: A Transactions Cost Approach". *Journal of Risk and Insurance* 64, 41–62.

Regan, Laureen (1993). "Vertical Integration in the Property-Liability Industry", Ph.D. Dissertation, The Wharton School, University of Pennsylvania, Phila.PA.

Regan, Laureen and Sharon Tennyson (1996). "Agent Discretion and the Choice of Insurance Distribution System." *Journal of Law and Economics* 39, 637–666.

Regan, Laureen and Larry Tzeng (1999). "Vertical Integration and Ownership Form in the Property-Liability Insurance Industry." *Journal of Risk and Insurance* 66, 253–274.

Rejda, George E. (1998). *Principles of Risk Management and Insurance*. 6th edition. Reading: Addison-Wesley Educational Publishers Inc.

Russell, David T. (1997). *An Empirical Analysis of Life Insurance Policyholder Surrender Activity*. Unpublished Ph.D. dissertation, University of Pennsylvania.

Santomero, Anthony M. (1993). "Banking and Insurance: A Banking Industry Perspective." In J.D. Cummins and J. Lamm-Tennant, eds., *Financial Management of Life Insurance Companies*. Norwell: Kluwer Academic Publishers.

Sass, Tim and Misha Gisser (1989). "Agency Costs, Firm Size and Exclusive Dealing." *Journal of Law and Economics* 32, 381–400.

Schlesinger, Harris and Mathias von-der Schulenburg (1991). "Search costs, Switching costs and Product Heterogeneity in an Insurance Market." *Journal of Risk and Insurance* 58, 109–120.

Seog, Sun Hung (1999). "The Coexistence of Distribution Systems when Consumers are not Informed." *The Geneva Papers on Risk and Insurance Theory*, forthcoming.

Skipper, Harold D., ed. (1998). *International Risk and Insurance: An Environmental-Managerial Approach.* Boston: Irwin-McGraw-Hill Publishers.

Stalson, Owen J. (1949). *Marketing Life Insurance: Its History in America.* Cambridge: Harvard University Press.

Suponcic, Susan J. and Sharon Tennyson (1998). "Rate Regulation and the Industrial Organization of Automobile Insurance." In D. Bradford, ed., *The Economics of Property-Casualty Insurance*. University of Chicago Press.

Telser, Lester (1960). "Why Should Manufacturers Want Fair Trade?" *Journal of Law and Economics* 3, 86–105.

Tennyson, Sharon (1997). "The Impact of Rate Regulation on State Automobile Insurance Markets." *Journal of Insurance Regulation* 15, 502–523.

Venezia, Itzhak, Dan Galai and Zur Shapira (1996). "Exclusive Vs. Independent Agents: A Separating Equilibrium Approach." Working paper #9-96, Anderson School of Management, UCLA.

Webb, Bernard, J.J. Launie, W.P. Rokes and N.A. Baglini (1984). *Insurance Company Operations*. (Volume 1). Malvern: American Institute for Property and Liability Underwriters.

Weiss, Mary A. (1986). "Analysis of Productivity at the Firm Level: An Application to Life Insurers." *Journal of Risk and Insurance* 53, 49–84.

Williamson, Oliver E. (1990). "Transaction Cost Economics." In R. Schmalensee and R. Willig, eds., *Handbook of Industrial Organization*. Amsterdam: Elsevier Science Publishers.

Williamson, Oliver E. (1979). "Transaction-Cost Economics: The Governance of Contractual Relations." *The Journal of Law and Economics* 22, 233–261.

23 The Retention Capacity of Insurance Markets in Developing Countries*

J. François Outreville

Office of the United Nations

Abstract

In the past, many developing countries have considered financial institutions locally incorporated or even State-owned monopolies, an essential element of their economic and political independence. At the same time, structural, financial and technical constraints such as the small size of the markets and the lack of sufficient experience have limited the retention capacity of these markets. Reliance on foreign reinsurance has remained an important policy issue. The purpose of this cross-sectional study of developing countries is to present some empirical tests of the relationship between insurance development and socio-economic characteristics of these countries.

Keywords: Retention capacity, developing countries, insurance markets.
JEL Classification Numbers: G22, G28.

"Indeed, if it is agreed that differences in government policies are responsible for much of the variation in economic performance among nations, it must be a research topic of the uppermost priority to try to establish which institutional circumstances are conductive to various types of policies." J.E. Stiglitz, "Economics of Information and the Theory of Economic Development," NBER, 1985, Working-paper no. 1, p. 566.

23.1 INTRODUCTION

The developing countries are not only consumers but also suppliers of insurance services. In domestic markets, the supply of insurance services generally consists of services provided by national companies, with local and/or foreign capital, as well as

* The views expressed in this paper do not necessarily reflect those of the United Nations.

by foreign companies and agencies or branches. The insurers can reinsure their own operations with domestic or foreign reinsurers when the risks they cover are considered to be excessive in relation to their capacity. It may therefore be said that domestic and imported insurance and reinsurance services are the two components of the total supply of insurance services.

Insurance, like other financial services, has grown in quantitative importance as part of the general development of financial institutions and markets. Studies of total premium volume for non-life insurance demonstrate the high-income elasticity of the demand for insurance in developing countries [Beenstock et al. (1988), Outreville (1990)]. However, the demand remains insufficient in many developing countries and mainly focuses on low expense coverages such as automobile insurance or on high risk coverage such as transport insurance or insurance for large plants, leaving the insurance companies with an unbalanced portfolio of risks. As a result, insurers in most developing countries have to rely heavily on international insurance and reinsurance services.

The protectionism which has developed in most countries should be viewed as a decision to produce internal insurance services, as opposed to importing these services. Public enterprises were considered a macroeconomic tool and as such used by governments to produce not only insurance services but also social and macroeconomic outputs. Today, almost all developing countries have a local insurance industry providing coverage for the domestic risks. However, if their reliance on foreign insurers has decreased markedly for some lines of business during the last twenty years, reliance on foreign reinsurance services has increased. Structural, financial and technical constraints such as undercapitalization, the small size of markets and the lack of sufficient experience and know-how limit the reinsurance capacity of these markets. In principle, and all other things being equal, as the volume of business increases in line with economic growth in these countries, it might be expected that the capacity will automatically be enhanced and the present dependence on reinsurance will decrease.

The decision to produce internal insurance as opposed to importing external insurance and reinsurance services was also viewed against the background of the critical shortage of foreign exchange affecting most developing countries.[1] It is, however, almost impossible to assess the volume of trade in insurance services. Systematic analysis of the balance of payments is virtually useless unless it takes into account the net present value of inflows and outflows over a full business cycle.

Empirical evidence in the literature suggests that the developing countries rather have a supply-leading causality pattern of development than a demand-following pattern [Jung (1986), Dee (1986)]. Many governments have indeed established new financial institutions under what has been termed a "supply-leading approach" to financial development and have considered locally incorporated insurance institutions

[1] For another argumentation see Launie (1973).

or even State-owned monopolies an essential element of their economic and political independence.[2] The trend toward liberalization of services should not overcome the main national policy objective of the developing countries.

The purpose of this paper is to investigate empirically which factors may be affecting the aggregate retention capacity of these markets in a cross-sectional analysis. The research is based on data published by the United Nations Conference on Trade and Development (UNCTAD, 1994) in a survey of insurance and reinsurance operations in developing countries. The data base for the analysis is limited to countries for which the overall retention ratio is available for years 1988 to 1990. It remains, at the present time, the only set of data available for most of the developing countries and providing detailed information by line of business, loss ratios, retention ratios and information on market structure.

The next two sections examine the economic importance of insurance markets in developing countries and the retention capacity of these markets. The retention capacity is defined as the total premium volume of business retained at the country level by the market for its own net account.[3] Two approaches which have been suggested in the literature are examined in the following sections: i) the structure of providers in a market determines the capacity and there is a justification for political intervention; ii) resources' endowment in a country influence the capacity and more attention shall be paid to development factors. Because of the shortcoming of these two approaches and rather than assess which model determines the most the behavior of the retention ratio, an alternative proposal combining all factors is developed and tested empirically in the last section.

23.2 MEASURING THE ECONOMIC IMPORTANCE OF INSURANCE MARKET IN DEVELOPING COUNTRIES

Insurance is of primordial importance in domestic economies and internationally. The role of insurance in the development process is difficult to assess but there is some evidence that the promotion of insurance programmes might have a particularly significant impact on the level of personal saving in many developing countries (UNCTAD, 1982). However, the insurance industry remains small in developing countries as measured by the market share of world insurance premiums (Table 1).

[2] According to this view, called "supply-leading", the financial sector precedes and induces real growth. On the contrary in the "demand-following" pattern, the real side of the economy develops, its demands for financial services materialize and are met passively from the financial side. As the process of real growth occurs, the supply-leading impetus gradually becomes less important, and the demand-following financial response becomes dominant (Patrick, 1966, p. 177).

[3] The retention capacity is referring to the following variable: $(Pd + Pa - Pc)/Pd$ where Pd, Pa, Pc represents, respectively, premiums written in the country, reinsurance assumed, and premiums ceded outside the country. Countries having a reinsurance company operating locally (see appendix 1) may be assuming insurance business from abroad. The retention capacity is the net result of all insurance and reinsurance transactions.

Table 1
Market Share of The World Insurance Premiums

Market	1995	1990
North America	30.85	37.91
Europe	29.78	33.93
Japan	29.73	20.53
South Korea	2.80	2.02
Asia (others)	2.76	2.08
Oceania	1.47	1.77
Latin America	1.44	0.70
Africa	1.17	1.06
Total	100.00	100.00

Source: Sigma (April 1992 and April 1997).

The economic significance of the insurance industry in a country is commonly evaluated by means of the ratio of premiums to the gross domestic product (GDP). Although this measure of insurance penetration does not give a complete picture of the insurance output because of the considerable variation in premiums rates between different countries, it has the advantage of not being influenced by currency factors (see appendix 1).

The relationship between insurance premiums written per capita and GDP per capita is hypothesized to be a nonlinear relationship [Beenstock et al. (1988), Outreville (1990)]. Graphic analysis makes it possible to verify that the adjustment appears to be relatively satisfactory bearing in mind the diversity of the countries considered, the disturbing influence of exchange rates and the probable imperfections in the statistical data (Figure 1).

Income elasticity has been calculated in several studies and the results are very close to each other. Beenstock et al. (1988) found an income elasticity of 1.37 and Outreville (1990) found an elasticity of 1.34 for a cross-section of developing countries. Outreville (1996) found an elasticity of 1.31 for Latin and Central American countries alone. Grace and Skipper (1991) found that the income elasticity for developing countries was lower than the income elasticity for developed countries suggesting that as countries progress economically, non-life insurance becomes relatively more important.

In fact, individual country experiences are too heterogeneous to accord neatly with any very simple generalization and very little is known about the demand and supply relationship in these countries (Grace and Skipper, 1991). Some societies have achieved high levels of human development at modest levels of per capita income. Other societies have failed to translate their comparatively high income levels

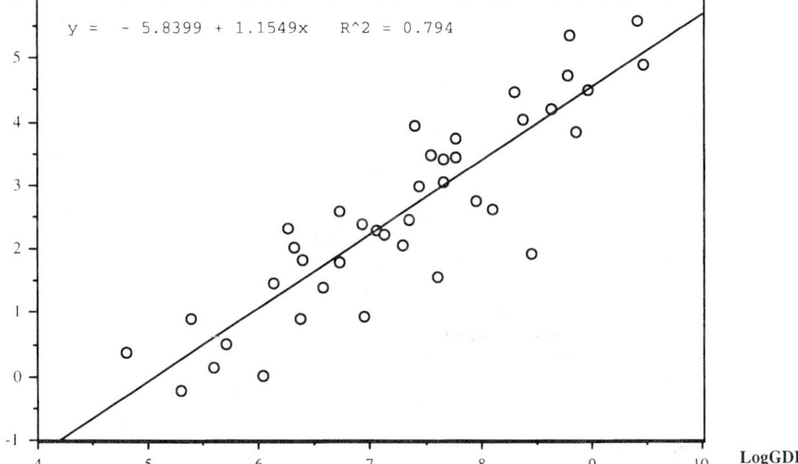

Figure 1 The Relationship Between Insurance Development and Economic Development

and rapid economic growth into commensurate levels of human development.[4] Unlike the situation with the banking sector, the linkages between insurance and economic development are poorly investigated. Studies by King and Levine (1993), Levine (1996) and Outreville (1999) have shown that various measures of financial development are strongly associated with various measures of economic growth and efficiency.[5]

The United Nations Development Programme (UNDP) published in 1990 a first Human Development Report providing indicators on human development. Human development is a process of enlarging people's choice. The most critical ones are to lead to a long and healthy life, to be educated and to enjoy a decent standard of living. Human development is measured by UNDP as a comprehensive index—called the human development index (HDI)—reflecting life expectancy, literacy and command over the resources to enjoy a decent standard of living. Figure 2 shows the relationship between the level of financial development and the human development index for the countries considered.

[4] Aristotle warned against judging societies merely by such things as income and wealth.

[5] In insurance, Outreville (1991) investigated the links between insurance development and financial development and found significant relationships between the size of the insurance market and several measures of financial development.

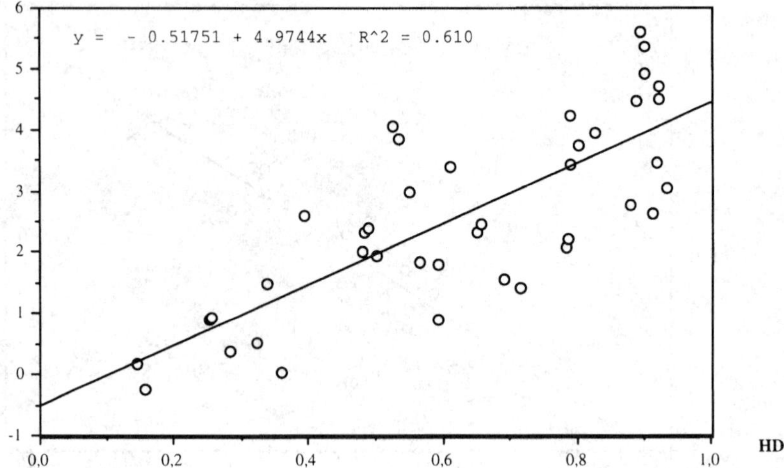

Figure 2 The Relationship Between Insurance Development and Human Resources Development

23.3 THE RETENTION CAPACITY OF DEVELOPING COUNTRIES' MARKETS

The problem of reinsurance planning at the level of a company is solved essentially according to the individual requirements of the company, the nature of the business, its volume and its territorial distribution in each class of business, the type and size of the risks to be covered, the capacity of the aggregate insurance portfolio, the financial strength of the company, the possibilities of placing its business and its past experience, know-how and future expectations.

One of the important reasons why reinsurance is taken out abroad is obviously to make up the shortage of capacity of the internal market. The aggregate retention capacity of the internal market remains very low and there are an important number of countries where it rarely reaches a global volume of more than half the total volume of business transacted by insurers (see Table 2). However, it is worth knowing that the protectionism which has developed in almost all countries has rarely been dictated by these technical considerations (UNCTAD, 1973).

The sizes and quantities of risks normally vary from one company to another and also from one country to another. The portfolio of a company operating in a small and highly fragmented market will inevitably be very different from that of a company enjoying a complete monopoly, and their respective retention capacities and reinsurance needs will also differ.

Table 2
Retention Capacity in Selected Developing Countries

Year	Sample size	Average retention	Number of countries with retention <50%
1988	62 countries	66.4	16
1989	50 countries	66.5	10

Source: UNCTAD (1994).
Note: The retention capacity is the ratio of net premiums written to gross premiums written at the aggregate level of the country.

The problem of optimal reinsurance has only received limited attention in financial economics or insurance literature (Doherty and Tinic, 1981; Mayers and Smith, 1982; Blazenco, 1986; Garven, 1987; Garven and Loubergé, 1996). Previous empirical research by Mayers and Smith (1990) documents that factors such as ownership structure, firm size, geographic concentration and line-of-business concentration influence the demand for reinsurance. At a country level, some of these variables remain important cross-sectionally as verified by Outreville (1995).

23.4 MARKET STRUCTURE AND THE RETENTION CAPACITY

Structural characteristics of the market for financial institutions play a major role in determining the allocational efficiency of the demand and supply of financial services. If the objective is to retain in the country as much insurance business as is technically possible—with due regard to the stability of the insurance concerns—market structure is the first aspect to be considered. The problem of reinsurance in many developing countries is that these structures have rarely been established according to given retention requirements.

As shown in Outreville (1991), the size of the insurance sector is significantly related to the level of development and size of the financial sector of the economy. The purpose of this section is to verify if the retention capacity of a market is affected by the size and the ownership structure or nature of the market, i.e., type of competition, restriction to competition. The following general equation is proposed:

$$\text{Retention Capacity} = f\,\{\text{Size of the market, Financial development, Market structure, Local reinsurance}\}$$

The retention capacity of a market is measured as the ratio of net property-liability insurance premiums written to gross premiums written. It seems plausible to assume that the retention capacity of a market is directly related to its absolute size.

Table 3
Estimates of the Relationship Between the Retention Capacity and Market Structure Variables

	(1)	(2)
Intercept	58.65	61.46
Size (Total premiums)	0.070	0.070
	(1.90)	(1.92)
M2/GDP	0.06	—
	(0.57)	
MONOP	17.40	17.35
	(2.97)	(2.99)
NATION	–5.98	–6.96
	(1.00)	(1.23)
LOCALRE	1.65	1.46
	(0.37)	(0.33)
R2	0.33	0.32
F	3.32	4.15

The size of the market is calculated by the total amount of gross premiums written in a country.[6]

Financial development is proxied by the ratio of the broad definition of money to GDP(M2/GDP) and defined by Feldman and Gang (1990) as financial deepening.[7]

Two dummy variables are used to evaluate the market structure; one variable indicates if the market is a monopolistic one or not (MONOP), and the other variable indicates if the market is competitive but restricted to national companies (NATION). The third alternative is a market fully open to international competitors. The appropriate variable to be tested in this context would be a measure of the concentration ratio. It is not available for most of the countries in our sample. Finally, a third dummy variable indicates the presence of a locally incorporated reinsurance company (LOCALRE).

The equation is estimated cross-sectionally with 40 developing countries of the sample (Appendix 1). Economic and financial variables are taken from the International Financial Statistics published by the IMF. Since the dependant variable is a ratio and the predetermined variables are assumed to be uncorrelated with the disturbance term, the OLS method is applied to estimate the impact coefficients of the equation.

The results are presented in Table 3. As expected, the retention capacity of a

[6] Retention is a function of the financial capacity of a firm which itself relates to the amount of business written. At the aggregate level the retention capacity of a market shall be related to the size of the market.

[7] This is the simplest indicator which measures the degree of monetization of the economy. This measure however, does not consider the full extent of financial intermediation. M2 is often taken as a proxy for the size of the financial sector because of the lack of data on other financial assets. Liu and Woo (1994) suggested the ratio of broad money to narrow money (M2/M1) as an alternative measure.

market increases with the size of the market and the level of financial development. However, only the estimated coefficient for the size variable is significant. Monopolistic companies enjoy a larger and more diversified portfolio. On average, the retention capacity of these markets is significantly higher as expected.

On the other hand, in markets restricted to foreign competition, the presence of many firms selling essentially identical products is not necessarily conducive to efficiency and profitability. In many developing countries, the insurance market is characterized by the existence of too large a number of small domestic companies with small retention limits. It is no coincidence that a few developing countries with a high concentration of the insurance business in few companies have been more successful in expanding business and retaining premiums.

Some developing countries have instituted compulsory reinsurance cessions to local reinsurance organizations. The efficacy of compulsory internal reinsurance cessions is a highly contentious issue. Although the sign of the variable is positive as expected, it is not significant. As advocated by Eden and Kahane (1990), the large, international reinsurers possess an advantage not available to local reinsurers: they are more diversified.

23.5 COMPARATIVE ADVANTAGE AND THE RETENTION CAPACITY

In recent years there has been a noticeable increase in attention paid to the factors responsible for the development and distribution of international financial services. Kindleberger (1974, 1985) listed a number of plausible factors and also pointed to the difficulties of reaching quantitative evaluations.

The analyses in quantitative studies are at a level of aggregation which deals with total financial activity. Indeed empirical work has frequently lumped together banking, insurance, real estate and other financial services, and certainly no attempt has been made to explain different activities with the exception of banking activities [Ball and Tschoegl (1982), Hultman and McGee (1989)].

The comparative advantage of some of the financial institutions of developed countries have provided a strong global network for the supply of international financial services (Moshirian, 1993). Historically connected with the pattern of international trade, insurance and reinsurance services are considered part of the financial services which are essential for adequate risk coverage.

A number of researchers have argued that there should be a similarity in the patterns of trade in goods and services Arndt (1988). In service industries including insurance the work of Sapir and Lutz (1981) confirms this similarity.[8]

An approach to testing the Heckscher-Ohlin-Vanek (HOV) theory to explain the

[8] See also Bhagwati (1987).

patterns of international trade in the context of inter-country differences in factor endowments is provided in Leamer (1974, 1984), Leamer and Bowen (1981) and Balassa (1979, 1986). The influence of scale economies on the volume of trade has also been recognized in the literature since Krugman's seminal paper in 1979.[9]

Trade in insurance services in developing countries shall be viewed as a component of total supply of insurance services and often make up for the shortage of internal services. Factor endowments of a country may explain the need for international insurance services. The purpose of this section is to verify if the determinants of comparative advantage in financial services also explain the production of insurance services in developing countries as measured by the retention capacity of these markets.

Following Moshirian (1994), a model of sources of comparative advantage of international financial services is proposed in the general following form:

Retention capacity$_i = a_0 + a_1 ES_i + a_2 CL_i + a_3 RE_i$
i = country subscript
and the variables
ES = scale variable
CL = capital-labour ratio
RE = resource endowment variable

The economy of scale factor is usually measured by the per capita gross domestic product (GDP). The GDP variable used by Sapir and Lutz (1981) for insurance services is not statistically significant for all their estimations. As an alternative approach, the size of the market is approximated by the measure of financial development suggested by Feldman and Gang (1990).

Following Leamer (1974) and Balassa (1979), the capital stock of each country is calculated by the country's gross domestic investment and divided by the labour force figure to obtain an estimate of the capital-labour ratio for each country.

The human capital endowment is one of the sources of comparative advantage for financial services. A standard approach is to treat human capital, or the average years of schooling of the labour force, as an ordinary input in the production function. The recent work of Makiw, Romer and Weil (1992) is in the tradition. Following Baldwin (1971) the percentage of the labour force with tertiary level education is used as a proxy variable for human capital endowment.[10]

[9] The monopolistic competition trade model is summarized in Helpman and Krugman (1995). Empirically the HOV theorem performs poorly and, by implication, so do increasing returns to scale and imperfect-competition models that yield the HOV theorem [Bowen et al. (1987), Trefler (1995)].

[10] As an alternative Benhabib and Spiegel (1994) propose a measure of physical capital and human capital to examine cross-country evidence of physical and human capital stocks on the determinants of the capacity of nations to adopt, implement and innovate new technologies.

Table 4
Estimates of the Equation for Reinsurance

Intercept	ES	CL	RE	R2/F
(1) 55.17	+1.44	+2.01	+0.47	0.26
	[0.51]	[1.97]	[2.17]	4.01
(2) 60.29	+0.11	+2.86	+0.46	0.27
	[0.84]	[2.16]	[2.14]	4.21

Note: The t values are shown in parentheses. The equation is estimated with a constant. The dependent variable is the retention capacity calculated as the ratio of net premiums written to gross premiums written. The size variable (ES) is the ratio of the premium volume to GDP in equation (1) and the ratio M2/GDP in equation (2).

Since the predetermined variables and stochastic disturbances appear on the right-hand side of the equation, and the predetermined variables are assumed to be uncorrelated with the disturbance term, the ordinary least squares method can be applied to estimate the impact coefficients of the equation. Several equations have been estimated to test for alternative proxies for the variables and the regression results are presented in Table 4. The Park test has been used to verify the assumption of homoscedasticity by regressing the residuals obtained from the regression on the size variable (Gujarati, 1988). There is no statistically significant relationship between the variables.

23.6 A CONSOLIDATED MODEL EXPLAINING THE RETENTION CAPACITY

Premiums written in a country do not seem to provide an answer for economies of scale in reinsurance services. This was also the case in Sapir and Lutz (1981) and Moshirian (1994) found no significant relationship with the size variable. The alternative measure of financial development is not significant either. This result surprisingly differs from the previous result and shall be attributed to the multicollinearity that appears to be present between the variables in the model.

It may be argued that the level of financial development is determined endogenously and belongs to a general interdependent system of simultaneous equations. The application of the ordinary least squares method leads to inconsistent estimates. An alternative approach is to regress the measure of financial development on the GDP, the average inflation rate, the resource endowment variable, and the dummy variable associated to a monopolistic market, and use residuals of the estimation procedure as an adjusted measure of financial development (FD*).[11] This variable also may be an appropriate measure of monetization in inflation prone countries.[12]

It has been argued by Gupta (1990) that the inclusion of sociopolitical variables in general and the factors of political violence in particular, changes the traditional model of economic growth. While investment in human capital is part of the income-increasing force, factors causing political instability, on the other hand, are part of the income-retarding force. The index (PI) published in Romer (1993) is used in this study. Following Barro (1991) he measures political instability as the mean number of revolutions and coups per year.[13]

Garven (1993) argues that not only the portfolio and financial leverage factors have an influence on reinsurance, but also the tax status of corporations, in an international framework, should be a relevant factor in determining the demand for reinsurance. Garven and Loubergé (1996) show that within an option-pricing framework, reinsurance is used to allocate tax shields to those firms that have the greatest capacity for utilizing them, in much the same manner as leasing companies share tax shield benefits with lessees in leasing markets. Insurers in low-tax countries will tend to provide reinsurance cover to insurers in high-tax countries. This may explain, at least partly, why captive reinsurance companies are located in low-tax domiciles.

The estimates including market structure variables and the index of political stability are presented in Table 5. Simple correlation coefficients are presented in column 1. If we regress each of the explanatory variables on all the remaining variables, the correlation coefficients of these auxiliary regressions (column 2) give a measure of the degree of multicollinearity. However, this measure, as well as other measures, suffers from the lack of a clear definition of what constitutes a "high" degree of multicollinearity.

Insurance retention in high-tax countries is lower as anticipated but the estimated coefficient is not significant in the multiple regression analysis. An alternative measure using taxes on international trade and transactions as measured by the International Monetary Fund is not significant either.

Some developing countries have instituted compulsory reinsurance cessions to local reinsurance organizations. It has also been observed that consumers display a bias toward domestically produced goods and services (Armington, 1969) and the HOV theorem is dominated by a model allowing for home bias and neutral technology differences (Trefler, 1995). The efficacy of compulsory internal reinsurance

[11] Liu and Woo (1994) suggest as a proxy for the degree of financial sophistication the ratio of the long-term to short-term financial assets value. Money supply (M1) is used as the short-term financial assets value. The ratio M2/M1 was included but not found significant.

[12] Studies suggest that changes due to disinflation and deregulation have had a smaller effect on M2 than on M1 growth and that the relationship between M2 growth and inflation has remained fairly stable [Bernanke and Blinder (1988) and Reichenstein and Elliott (1987)].

[13] It is worth noting that his results suggest that political instability is strongly associated with inflation and monetary instability.

Table 5
Estimates of the Regressions

	Bivariate regression	Auxiliary regression	Multiple regression	
	Correlation Coefficient	Correlation Coefficient	Coefficient	t-value
FD*	0.19	0.27	0.14	1.14
CL	0.39	0.36	2.49	2.03
RE	0.40	0.52	0.52	2.35
PI index	−0.17	0.34	−11.18	1.58
Monop	0.38	0.09	14.91	2.71
LocalRe	0.09	0.31	—	—
Taxes	−0.19	0.35	—	—
			$R^2 = 0.44$	
			F = 5.22	

cessions is a highly contentious issue. Although the sign of the variable is positive as expected, it is not significant when considered in the multiple regression analysis.

Political instability (PI index) affects negatively the reinsurance capacity of developing countries. Column 3 in Table 5 presents the results of the multiple regression analysis when the variables for local reinsurance and corporate taxes are excluded.

23.7 DISCUSSION

While in the past decades practically all developing countries have established national insurance companies to meet their own insurance needs, their reliance on foreign insurance and reinsurance markets is still high. The small size of the markets, the imbalance nature of the insurance portfolios and certainly the lack of sufficient experience and know-how are among the main reasons for this situation.

This paper has also analyzed the relationship between the retention capacity and structural factors affecting these markets. The empirical results, based on a cross-sectional analysis of 40 developing countries, indicate that, the size of the market, the level of financial development and the competitive structure of the market are relevant factors explaining the retention capacity. Human capital endowment and the capital-labour ratio are also significant factors explaining the retention capacity of insurance markets in developing countries.

The importance attributed to the existence of a local market and to the building up of a retention capacity have often been dictated by political considerations rather than by technical reasons. If it is true that the developing countries have a supply-leading causality pattern to development, then more attention should be paid to factors such as the level of financial development and the market structure of suppliers.

Many inefficiencies may be less a function of ownership than of government regulation and market structure. Adequate regulation of an industry requires so much information that establishing effective regulation of privatized firms may prove more demanding of the state's administrative capabilities than operating a state-owned monopolistic institution. The proper sequencing of privatization and liberalization is emerging as a critical issue for policy-makers (Hemming and Manson, 1988)(Van De Walle, 1989).

Acquiring a long-term competitive position in insurance services depends on the development of human capital, on the level of development in the rest of the economy and on improvements in the financial strength of the insurance carriers. It is unrealistic to presuppose that the developing countries will be able to gain access to developed countries' markets. The increased participation of companies from developing countries in sharing arrangements or pools with experienced and large companies from developed countries could help in transferring the necessary technological and human resources know-how which developing countries need for building competitive insurance firms.

APPENDIX 1: LIST OF COUNTRIES

Country	Insurance Penetration (%GDP)	Retention Ratio	Local Reinsurance	Monopolistic Market
Algeria	1.48	93.1	yes	yes
Argentina	1.04	74.9	yes	no
Bahamas	2.58	77.0	yes	no
Barbados	3.42	61.1	no	no
Chad	0.35	57.6	no	no
Chile	1.14	50.5	yes	no
Costa Rica	1.94	80.8	yes	yes
Cote d'Ivoire	1.55	70.6	no	no
Cyprus	1.41	80.8	no	no
El Salvador	0.84	44.5	no	no
Ethiopia	1.18	84.3	no	yes
Fiji	1.20	60.3	yes	no
Gabon	1.81	76.1	yes	no
Ghana	0.28	68.7	yes	no
Guatemala	0.67	62.6	no	no
Honduras	0.65	50.4	no	no
Indonesia	0.66	55.0	yes	no
Jamaica	3.45	54.3	no	no
Korea, Rep. of	1.43	93.4	yes	no
Malawi	1.52	78.6	yes	no
Malaysia	2.02	58.5	yes	no
Mali	0.50	71.0	no	no
Malta	2.10	86.3	no	no
Mauritius	1.60	51.5	no	no
Mexico	0.70	73.6	yes	no
Morocco	1.21	65.4	yes	no
Nigeria	0.55	49.9	yes	no
Oman	0.86	59.8	no	no
Paraguay	0.74	50.4	no	no
Philippines	0.61	77.0	yes	no
Seychelles	1.62	61.6	no	yes
Singapore	1.37	77.4	yes	no
Solomon Islands	1.30	41.0	no	no
Sudan	0.64	32.9	yes	no
Syria	0.32	76.1	no	yes
Thailand	0.66	63.4	yes	no
Togo	1.07	61.7	no	no
Trinidad & Tobago	2.40	52.7	yes	no
Tunisia	0.91	64.1	yes	no
Zambia	2.01	83.9	no	yes

Source: UNCTAD (1994).

APPENDIX 2: DATA SOURCES

Insurance data	UNCTAD	Statistical Survey on Insurance in Developing Countries
GDP, inflation, population Gross Domestic Investment	UNCTAD	Handbook of International Trade and Development Statistics
Education, labor force	UNDP	Human Development Report
Currency exchange rates, M1,M2	IMF	International Financial Statistics
Corporate tax rates	IMF	Government Finance Statistics

APPENDIX 3: CORRELATION MATRIX

	CL	RE	M2/GDP	Inflation	GDP	Politics	LocalRE	Monopoly	Corp. Tax
CL	1.0								
RE	0.25	1.0							
M2/GDP	0.62	0.15	1.0						
Inflation	−0.30	−0.01	−0.23	1.0					
GDP	0.16	0.57	−0.05	0.003	1.0				
Politics	−0.27	0.41	−0.21	0.12	0.20	1.0			
LocalRE	0.04	0.26	−0.03	−0.05	0.46	0.12	1.0		
Monopoly	−0.05	0.05	0.14	0.46	−0.12	−0.02	−0.33	1.0	
Corp. Taxes	−0.10	−0.33	−0.02	0.19	0.11	0.18	0.33	0.04	1.0

23.8 REFERENCES

Armington, P.S. (1969). "A Theory of Demand for Products Distinguished by Place of Production," *International Monetary Fund Staff Papers*, 16, 1, 159–178.

Arndt, H.W. (1988). "Comparative Advantage in Trade in Financial Services," *Banca Nazionale Del Lavaro Quarterly Review*, 41, 164, 61–78.

Balassa, B. (1979). "The Changing Pattern of Comparative Advantage in Manufactured Goods," *Review of Economics and Statistics*, 56, 2, 259–266.

Balassa, B. (1986). "Comparative Advantage in Manufactured Goods: A Reappraisal," *Review of Economics and Statistics*, 68, 2, 315–319.

Baldwin, R.E. (1971). "Determinants of the Commodity Structure of US Trade," *American Economic Review*, 61, 1, 126–146.

Ball, C. and A. Tschoegl (1982). "The Decision to Establish a Foreign Bank Branch or Subsidiary: An Application of Binary Classification Procedures," *Journal of Financial and Quantitative Analysis*, 17, 411–424.

Barro, R.J. (1991). "Economic Growth in a Cross-Section of Countries," *Quarterly Journal of Economics*, 106, 407–443.

Beenstock, M., Dickinson, G. and Khajuria, S. (1988). "The Relationship Between Property and Liability Insurance Premiums and Income," *Journal of Risk and Insurance*, 55, 259–272.

Benhabib, J. and M.M. Spiegel (1994). "The Role of Human Capital in Economic Development: Evidence from Aggregate Cross-Country Data," *Journal of Monetary Economics*, 34, 143–173.

Bernanke, B.S. and A.S. Blinder (1988). "Credit, Money and Aggregate Demand," *American Economic Review*, 78, 435–439.

Bhagwati, J. (1987). "International Trade in Services and its Relevance for Economic Development," in O. Giarini (Ed.) *The Emerging Service Economy*, Oxford: Pergamon Press.

Blazenco, G. (1986). "The Economics of Reinsurance," *Journal of Risk and Insurance*, 53, 258–277.

Bowen, H.P., Leamer, E.E. and L. Sveikauskas (1987). "Multicountry, Multifactor Tests of the Factor Abundance Theory," *American Economic Review*, 77, 5, 791–809.

Dee, P.S. (1986). *Financial Markets and Economic Development: The Economics and Politics of Korean Financial Reforms*, Kieler Studies, Universitat Kiel, Institut fur Weltwirtshaft.

Doherty, N.A. and S.M. Tinic (1981). "Reinsurance Under Conditions of Capital Market Equilibrium: A Note," *Journal of Finance*, 36, 949–952.

Eden Y. and Y. Kahane (1990). "Moral Hazard and Insurance Market Structure," in H. Loubergé (Ed.) *Risk, Information and Insurance*, Kluwer Academic Publishers, Boston.

Feldman, D.H. and I.N. Gang (1990). "Financial Development and the Price of Services," *Economic Development and Cultural Change*, 38, 2, 341–352.

Garven, J.R. (1987). "On the Application of Finance Theory to the Insurance Firm," *Journal of Financial Services Research*, 1, 57–76.

Garven, J.R. (1993). "The Demand for Reinsurance: Theory and Empirical Tests," Working Paper, The University of Texas at Austin.

Garven, J.R. and H. Loubergé (1996). "Reinsurance, Taxes and Efficiency: A Contingent Claims Model of Insurance Market Equilibrium," *Journal of Financial Intermediation*, 5, 1, 74–93.

Grace, M.F. and H.D. Skipper, Jr. (1991). "An Analysis of the Demand and Supply Determinants for Non-Life Insurance Internationally," Working-Paper 91–5, Center for Risk Management and Insurance Research, Georgia State University.

Gujarati, D.N. (1988). *Basic Econometrics*, New-York: McGraw-Hill, 2nd ed.

Gupta, D.K. (1990). *The Economics of Political Violence*, New-York: Praeger Pub.

Helpman, E. and P. Krugman (1985). *Market Structure and Foreign Trade: Increase Returns, Imperfect Competition, and the International Economy*, Cambridge, MA: MIT Press.

Hemming, R. and A. Manson (1988). "Is Privatization the Answer?," *Finance and Development*, 25, 3, 31–33.

Hultman, C.W. and L.R. McGee (1989). "Factors Affecting the Foreign Banking Presence in the US," *Journal of Banking and Finance*, 13, 383–396.

Jung, W.S. (1986). "Financial Development and Economic Growth: International Evidence," *Economic Development and Cultural Change*, 34, 333–346.

Kindleberger, C. (1974). "The Formation of Financial Centers: A Study in Comparative Economic History," *Princeton Studies in International Finance*, 36, Princeton, NJ: Princeton University Press.

Kindleberger, C. (1985). "The Functioning of Financial Centers: Britain in the 19th Century, The United States since 1945," in W. Ethier and R. Manston, eds., *Markets and Capital Movements*, Princeton, NJ: Princeton University Press.

King, R.G. and R. Levine (1993). "Finance and Growth: Shumpeter might be Right," *Quarterly Journal of Economics*, 108, 3, 717–737.

Krugman, P. (1979). "Increasing Returns, Monopolistic Competition, and International Trade," *Journal of International Economics*, 9, 469–479.

Launie, J.J. (1973). "The Balance of Payments Implications of Reinsurance for Emerging Countries," *Best's Review*, P/L Insurance ed.

Leamer, E.E. (1974). "The Commodity Composition of International Trade in Manufactures: An Empirical Analysis," *Oxford Economic Papers*, 26, 350–374.

Leamer, E.E. (1984). *Sources of International Comparative Advantage: Theory and Evidence*, Cambridge, MA: MIT Press.

Leamer, E.E. and H. Bowen (1981). "Cross-Section Tests of the Heckscher-Ohlin Theorem: Comment," *American Economic Review*, 71, 1040–1043.

Levine, R. (1996). "Foreign Banks, Finance Development, and Economic Growth," in C.E. Barfield (Ed.), *International Financial Markets*, Washington, D.C.: AEI Press.

Liu, L.Y. and W.T. Woo (1994). "Saving Behavior under Imperfect Financial Markets and the Current Account Consequences," *The Economic Journal*, 104, 512–527.

Makiw, G., D. Romer and D. Weil (1992). "A Contribution to the Empirics of Economic Growth," *Quarterly Journal of Economics*, 106, 407–437.

Mayers, D. and C.W. Smith (1982). "On the Corporate Demand for Insurance," *Journal of Business*, 55, 281–296.

Mayers, D. and C.W. Smith (1990). "On the Corporate Demand for Insurance: Evidence from the Reinsurance Market," *Journal of Business*, 63, 19–40.

Moshirian, F. (1993). "Determinants of International Financial Services," *Journal of Banking and Finance*, 17, 7–18.

Moshirian, F. (1994). "What Determines the Supply of International Financial Services," *Journal of Banking and Finance*, 18, 495–504.

Outreville, J.F. (1990). "The Economic Significance of Insurance Markets in Developing Countries," *Journal of Risk and Insurance*, 57, 487–498.

Outreville, J.F. (1991). "The Relationship Between Insurance, Financial Development, and Market Structure in Developing Countries," *UNCTAD Review*, 3, 53–69.

Outreville, J.F. (1995). "Reinsurance in Developing Countries," *Journal of Reinsurance*, 2, 3, 42–51.

Outreville, J.F. (1996). "Insurance in Central-America," *The World Economy*, 19, 5, 575–593.

Outreville, J.F. (1999). "A Note on Financial Development, Human Capital and Political Instability, forthcoming in *UNCTAD Discussion Papers*.

Patrick, H. (1966). "Financial Development and Economic Growth in Underdeveloped Countries," *Economic Development and Cultural Change*, 14, 174–189.

Reichenstein, W. and J.W. Elliott (1987). "A Comparison of Models of Long-Term Inflationary Expectations," *Journal of Monetary Economics*, 19, 405–425.

Romer, D. (1993). "Openness and Inflation: Theory and Evidence," *The Quarterly Journal of Economics*, 108, 869–903.

Sapir, A. and E. Lutz (1981). "Trade in Services: Economic Determinants and Development-Related Issues," *World Bank Staff Working Paper*, 410.

Trefler, D. (1995). "The Case of the Missing Trade and Other Mysteries," *American Economic Review*, 85, 5, 1029–1046.

UNCTAD (1973). *Reinsurance Problems in Developing Countries*, New-York: United Nations.

UNCTAD (1980). *Methods Used for Increasing the Local Retention of Insurance Business*, TD/B/C3/160, Geneva.

UNCTAD (1982). *The Promotion of Life Insurance in Developing Countries*, TD.B.C.3/177, Geneva: United Nations.

UNCTAD (1994). *Statistical Survey on Insurance and Reinsurance Operations in Developing Countries*, New-York: United Nations.

Van De Walle, N. (1989). "Privatization in Developing Countries: A Review of the Issues," *World Development*, 17, 5, 601–615.

24 Analyzing Firm Performance in the Insurance Industry Using Frontier Efficiency and Productivity Methods

J. David Cummins

University of Pennsylvania

Mary A. Weiss

Temple University

Abstract

Frontier efficiency and productivity methodologies have become the state-of-the-art for measuring the performance of firms and other organizations. Traditional theory assumes that all firms minimize costs and maximize profits and that firms that do not succeed in attaining these objectives do not survive. The frontier approach reflects the recognition that some firms will be less successful than others in minimizing costs or maximizing profits and that such firms may be able to survive for some period of time. Modern efficiency methodologies measure firm performance relative to "best practice" cost, revenue, or profit frontiers consisting of the dominant firms in the industry. This chapter explains modern frontier methodologies, discusses input and output measurement for insurers, and reviews the most significant studies utilizing frontier methodologies to analyze the insurance industry. These studies not only measure efficiency but also identify firm characteristics that are associated with efficiency and analyze classic industrial organization topics such as economies of scale and scope. Efficiency and productivity measurement is useful in testing economic hypotheses, informing regulators about firm performance, providing information to management, and comparing performance across countries. It is hoped that this chapter will encourage more economists to use these methodologies in testing hypotheses and measuring performance in insurance and other industries.

Keywords: Insurance, insurance companies, efficiency, productivity, frontier methodologies, economies of scale, economies of scope.

JEL Classifications Numbers: G2, G22, G34, D2, D24.

24.1 INTRODUCTION

An important development in modern economics has been the emergence of frontier methodologies for estimating efficiency and productivity. The theory underlying this development, originated by Farrell (1957), represents a departure from the traditional micro-economic theory of the firm. Traditional theory assumes that all firms minimize costs and maximize profits and that firms that do not succeed in attaining these objectives are not of interest because they will not survive. Farrell's contribution was to create a framework to analyze firms that do not succeed in optimization and, as a result, are not fully efficient.[1] Farrell's work suggested that efficiency could be evaluated by comparing firms to "best practice" efficient frontiers formed by the dominant firms in an industry. However, it took nearly twenty years following Farrell's initial theoretical contribution for empiricists to develop methodologies to estimate efficiency. The most important contributions were the development of stochastic efficient frontiers by Aigner, Lovell, and Schmidt (1977), Battese and Corra (1977), and Meeusen and van den Broeck (1977) and the development of non-parametric mathematical programming frontiers by Charnes, Cooper, and Rhodes (1978). Since that time, the growth in efficiency research has been explosive. Berger and Humphrey (1997) identify 130 studies in the financial institutions field alone.

The development of modern frontier efficiency methodologies has significant implications for insurance economics. Numerous studies are conducted that require the comparison of insurance firms relative to other firms in the industry. Traditionally, this has been done using conventional financial ratios such as the return on equity, return on assets, expense to premium ratios, etc. With the rapid evolution of frontier efficiency and productivity methodologies, the conventional methods are rapidly becoming obsolete.[2] Frontier efficiency measures dominate traditional techniques in terms of developing meaningful and reliable measures of firm performance. They summarize firm performance in a single statistic that controls for differences among firms in a sophisticated multidimensional framework that has its roots in economic theory. The objective of this chapter is to provide the foundations for insurance economists to use in adapting their research to incorporate the frontier efficiency approach. We do this by describing and analyzing the principal methodologies that have been developed for measuring frontier efficiency and productivity, defining the input and output concepts required to apply the methodologies to insurance firms, and review-

[1] Some additional modifications of the classic micro-economic assumptions also are needed to explain why such firms may survive over significant periods of time. These additional considerations are beyond the scope of the present chapter. However, evidence of inefficient firms surviving over significant periods of time has been observed in both banking (e.g., Berger and Humphrey 1991, 1992b, Berger 1993) and insurance (e.g., Cummins and Weiss 1993, Berger, Cummins, and Weiss 1997).

[2] An intermediate methodological development between financial ratios and frontier methods that can be used for some purposes consists of the (non-frontier) total factor productivity indices or index numbers. This approach also is briefly discussed in this chapter, but our main focus is on frontier efficiency and productivity methods.

ing the empirical literature on efficiency and productivity measurement in the insurance industry.

Most efficiency analyses to date in insurance and elsewhere have focused on production and cost efficiency. More recently, researchers have begun to estimate revenue and profit frontiers. Perhaps the most basic frontier is the production frontier, which is estimated based on the assumption that the firm is minimizing input use conditional on output levels.[3] Production frontiers can be estimated even if data on input and output prices are unavailable. If data on input prices are available, it is possible to estimate the cost frontier, usually based on the assumption that the firm is minimizing costs conditional on output levels and input prices. Ultimately, of course, the firm also can optimize by choosing its level of output and/or output mix. Revenue frontiers are estimated assuming that the firm maximizes revenues by choosing its output quantities holding constant input quantities and output prices. In profit efficiency analysis, the firm maximizes by choosing both its inputs and outputs, contingent only on input and output prices.[4] Finally, sophisticated methods such as Malmquist analysis have recently been developed for measuring changes in total factor productivity.

Frontier efficiency methods are useful in a variety of contexts. One important use is for testing economic hypotheses. For example, both agency theory and transactions cost economics generate predictions about the likely success of firms with different characteristics in attaining objectives such as cost minimization or profit maximization under various economic conditions. Firm characteristics that are likely to be important include organizational form, distribution systems, corporate governance, and vertical integration. Frontier methodologies have been used to analyze a wide range of such hypotheses.[5]

A second important application of frontier methodologies is to provide guidance to regulators regarding the appropriate response to problems and developments in an industry or the overall economy. For example, both the banking and insurance industries are experiencing a wave of mergers and acquisitions. Frontier methodologies can be used to determine whether consolidation is likely to be beneficial or detrimental in terms of the price and quality of services provided to consumers. The efficiency of insurer operations also is an important regulatory issue, as in the debate over the price of automobile insurance.

[3] This definition applies to an *input-oriented* frontier. It is also possible to develop output-oriented measures of efficiency by maximizing outputs conditional on inputs. Most efficiency analysis to date in insurance and other financial services industries have been input-oriented, and most of our discussion in the paper assumes an input-orientation.

[4] This discussion applies to *standard* cost, revenue, and profit efficiency analysis. Non-standard functions also are used for some purposes such as studying revenue or profit scope economies (see Berger, et al. 1997 for further discussion of the non-standard case). Frontier analysis is typically conducted under the assumption that the industry is competitive. However, it is also possible to test the hypothesis of competitiveness and to measure efficiency for non-competitive industries. One departure from the usual competitive assumptions is provided by a public entity such as a public utility or government agency. Such institutions have been widely studied using frontier methodologies. For examples, several chapters in Charnes, et al. (1994) deal with public entities.

[5] Berger and Humphrey (1997) provide a review of applications to financial institutions.

A third application of frontier methodologies is to compare economic performance across countries. For example, Färe, et al. (1994) compare the evolution of productivity in industrialized nations. Weiss (1991b) compares productivity in the property-liability insurance industries of the U.S. and four European countries, and recent studies have also compared banking efficiency in the U.S. and various European nations (e.g., Pastor, Pérez, and Quesada 1997).

A fourth application is to inform management about the effects of new strategies and technologies. Although firms currently employ a variety of benchmarking techniques, frontier analysis can provide more meaningful information than conventional ratio and survey analysis, which often overwhelms the manager with masses of statistics that are difficult to summarize conveniently. Frontier analysis can be used not only to track the evolution of a firm's productivity and efficiency over time but also to compare the performance of departments, divisions, or branches within the firm.

This chapter is organized as follows. Section 24.2 discusses the concepts of efficiency and productivity, whereas section 24.3 provides an overview of the estimation of efficiency and productivity. Section 24.4 discusses the measurement of inputs and outputs as well as some additional methodological issues and problems. Section 24.5 provides a review of the efficiency literature in insurance, and section 24.6 concludes.

24.2 THE CONCEPTS OF EFFICIENCY AND PRODUCTIVITY

This section provides an introduction to the economic concepts of efficiency and productivity to provide background for the discussion of estimation methodologies in section 24.3. In the interests of brevity, the discussion in this section focuses primarily on production and cost frontiers.

The *efficiency* of a firm is defined by reference to the observed and optimal values of its vector of inputs and outputs. Conditioning on a specific output vector, a firm is considered fully efficient if its actual input usage equals optimal input usage and is inefficient if actual input usage exceeds optimal input usage. *Total factor productivity* is defined as an index of total quantity of outputs produced divided by an index of total inputs consumed in the production process (Grosskopf 1993). Total factor productivity is a generalization of single factor productivity concepts such as labor productivity, where productivity is defined as total output divided by a single input.[6] Productivity and efficiency are related. Productivity at any given time is determined by the optimal production technology available for use in producing outputs as well as the efficiency with which firms employ the technology. The remainder of this

[6] Single factor productivity indices are considered to be uninformative by economists because they take into account only one input, such as labor, and omit other important inputs, such as capital.

section elaborates upon these concepts. We first discuss efficiency and then turn to a discussion of productivity.

24.2.1 Economic Efficiency

The concept of economic efficiency flows directly from the microeconomic theory of the firm. Perhaps the most basic concept is that of the *production frontier*, which indicates the minimum inputs required to produce any given level of output for a firm operating with full efficiency. A production frontier for a firm with one input and one output is shown in Figure 1. The production frontier in Figure 1 is characterized by *constant returns to scale* (CRS) for levels of input usage from 0 to point *c* on the horizontal axis and *decreasing returns to scale* (DRS) for levels of input greater than

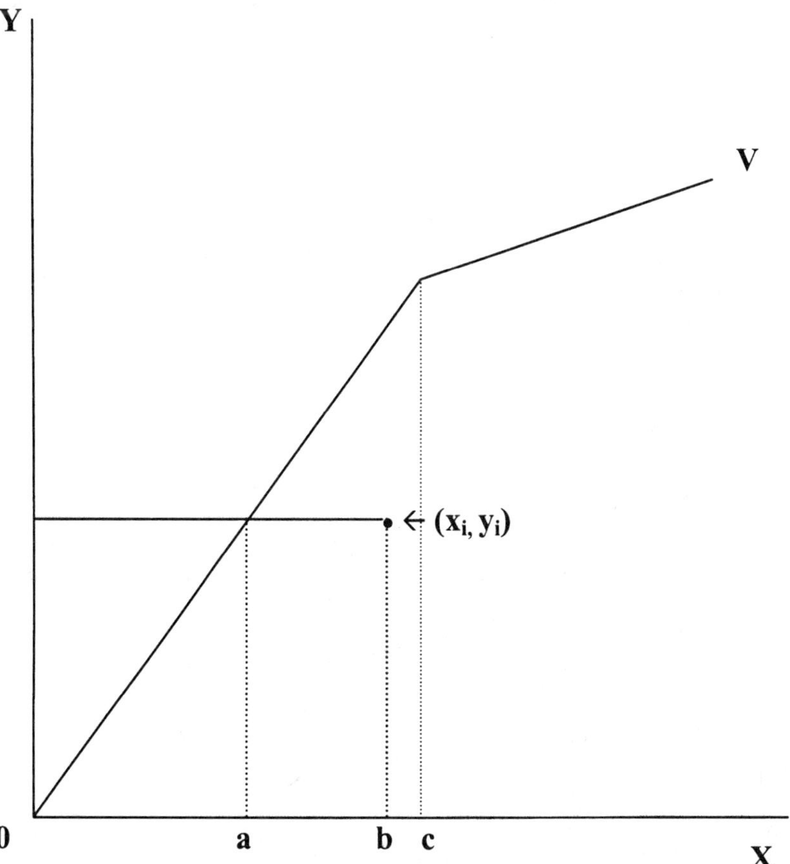

Figure 1 Production Frontier for the Single Input-Single Output Firm

$0c$. Thus, Figure 1 portrays a *non-increasing returns to scale* (NIRS) production frontier.

In Figure 1, firm i is operating at point (x_i, y_i). This firm could operate more efficiently by moving to the frontier, i.e., by adopting the state-of-the-art technology. The firm's level of *technical efficiency* is given by the ratio $0a/0b$, which is the reciprocal of its distance from the frontier, $0b/0a$.

If the firm has more than one input, inefficiency can also result from the firm's not using the cost minimizing combination of inputs. This type of inefficiency, known as *allocative inefficiency*, is shown in Figure 2, which illustrates Farrell's (1957) technical and allocative efficiency concepts. The diagram shows an isoquant for a firm with one output and two inputs, x_1 and x_2. The isoquant QQ′ in Figure 2 represents the various combinations of the two inputs required to produce a fixed amount of the single output using the best available technology. Thus, firms operating on the isoquant are considered to be technically efficient. The optimal operating point is represented by the tangency (point D) between the isoquant QQ′ and the isocost line ww′.

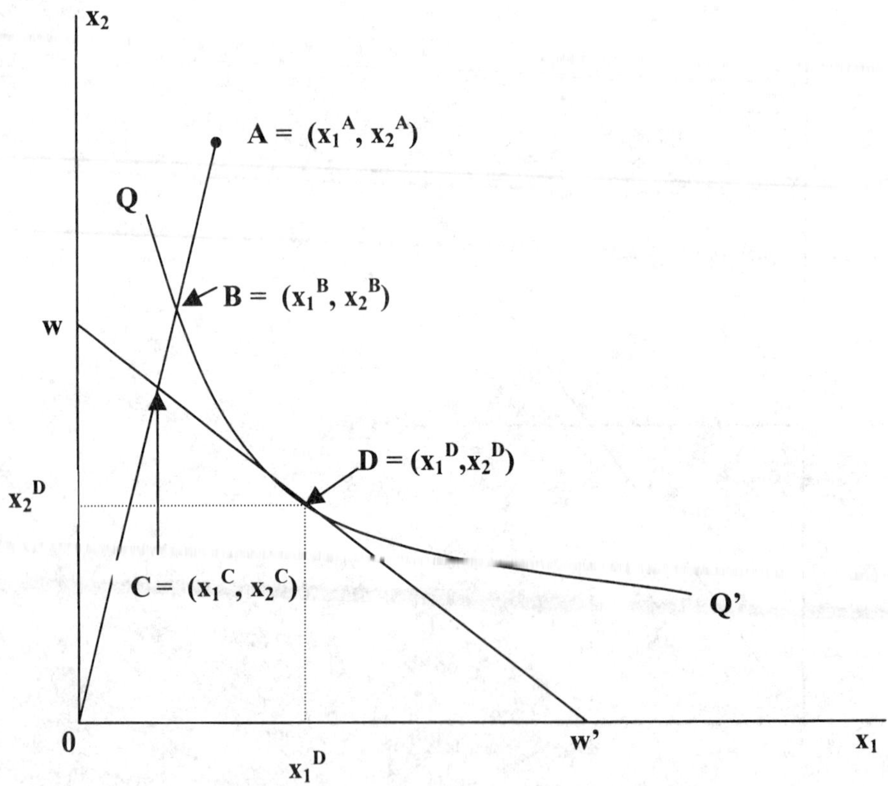

Figure 2 Farrell Technical and Allocative Efficiency

A firm operating at this point is considered to be fully *cost efficient*. The firm operating at point $A = (x_1^A, x_2^A)$ exhibits both technical and allocative inefficiency. It is technically inefficient because it is not operating on the best-technology isoquant. The measure of Farrell technical efficiency is the ratio $0B/0A$, i.e., the proportion by which it could radially reduce its input usage by adopting the best technology. However, this firm is also allocatively inefficient because it is not using its inputs in the correct proportions. Specifically, it is using too much of input 2 and not enough of input 1. The measure of allocative efficiency is thus the ratio $0C/0B$. Cost efficiency is then defined as follows:

$$\text{Cost Inefficiency} = \text{Technical Efficiency} * \text{Allocative Efficiency}$$
$$= (0B/0A) * (0C/0B) = 0C/0A$$

Technical efficiency can be decomposed into *pure technical efficiency* and *scale efficiency*. These concepts are illustrated in Figure 3, which shows two production frontiers for the single input-single output case. Frontier V^C represents a constant returns to scale (CRS) frontier, while frontier V^V is a *variable returns to scale* (VRS) frontier. A VRS frontier has regions characterized by increasing, decreasing, and

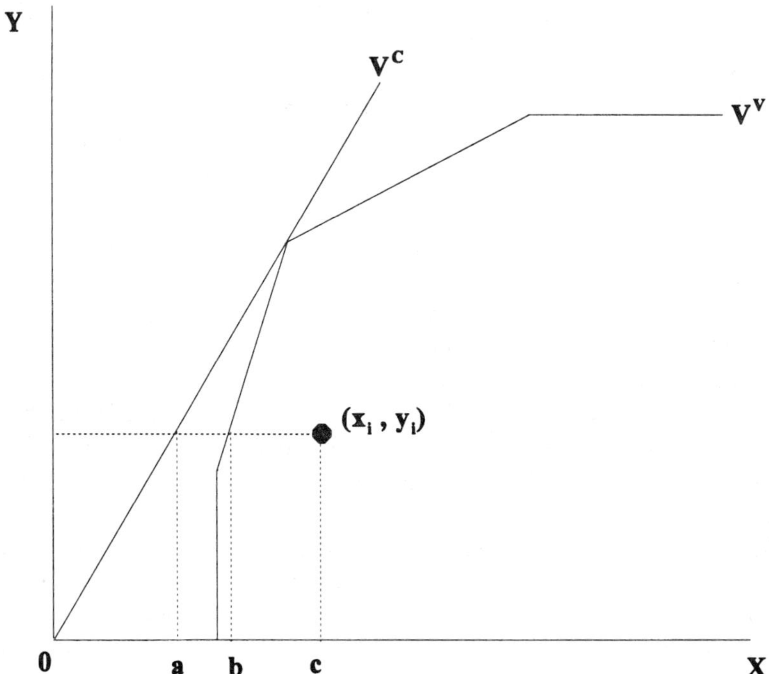

Figure 3 Pure Technical and Scale Efficiency

constant returns to scale, with the constant returns to scale segment of V^V consisting of a single point.

It is socially and economically optimal for firms to operate at constant returns to scale, providing the motivation for separating pure technical and scale efficiency. Consider firm i, operating at point (x_i, y_i) in Figure 3. Pure technical efficiency is measured relative to the VRS frontier and equals $0b/0c$. This is the proportion by which the firm could reduce its input usage by adopting the best technology represented by the VRS frontier. However, a firm operating on the VRS frontier at firm *i*'s output level is also scale inefficient because it is not operating on the CRS frontier. Its scale efficiency is measured by the ratio $0a/0b$. Thus, we can define:

$$\begin{aligned}\text{Technical Efficiency} &= \text{Pure Technical Efficiency} * \text{Scale Efficiency}\\ &= (0b/0c) * (0a/0b) = 0a/0c\end{aligned}$$

24.2.2 Total Factor Productivity

The production frontier also can be used to illustrate changes in total factor productivity, i.e., total factor productivity growth. Total factor productivity growth is defined as the change in output net of the change in input usage, i.e., total factor productivity growth occurs when more output can be produced per unit of inputs consumed, where output production and input usage are defined using appropriate aggregation techniques. Total factor productivity growth has two major components—technical change and efficiency change. Technical change is represented by a shift in the production frontier, and efficiency change is represented by an index of a firm's efficiency relative to the present and past frontiers. If the firm is fully efficient, i.e., operating on the production frontier, which is the usual assumption in micro-economics, then productivity growth and technical change are identical. However, if the firm is not operating on the frontier, i.e., is inefficient, then productivity growth can occur due to both improvements in efficiency and shifts in the production frontier. Of course, it is also possible for productivity to decline either because a firm becomes less efficient or the frontier shifts adversely (technical regress).

To illustrate the concept of total factor productivity growth, consider Figure 4, which shows constant returns to scale production frontiers for periods t and $t + 1$ (V^t and V^{t+1}, respectively) for the single input-single output firm. The frontier for period $t + 1$ lies to the left of the frontier for period t. This implies that productivity gains have been achieved between periods t and $t + 1$ because of technical change, i.e., a shift in the frontier. For a firm operating with full efficiency (i.e., on the frontier in both periods t and $t + 1$), technical change and total factor productivity change are identical. However, inefficient firms can also achieve total factor productivity gains by improving their efficiency. To see this, consider an inefficient firm operating at point (x_i^t, y_i^t) in period t and at point (x_i^{t+1}, y_i^{t+1}) in period $t + 1$. This firm has become more efficient between periods t and $t + 1$ because it is operating closer to the frontier in period $t + 1$ than in period t. In fact, in period $t + 1$, the firm is operating at a

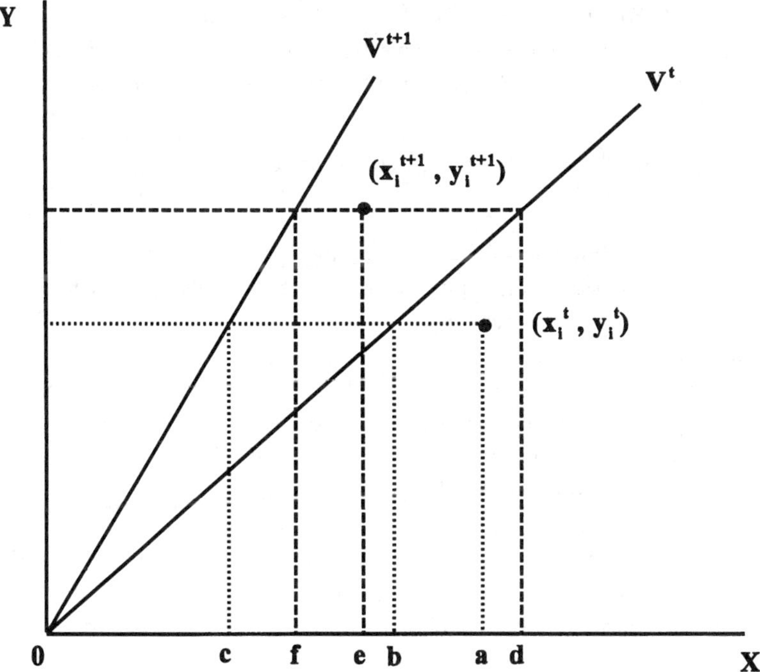

$$\text{Technical Efficiency Change} = \frac{D^t(x^t, y^t)}{D^{t+1}(x^{t+1}, y^{t+1})} = \frac{0a/0b}{0e/0f}.$$

$$\text{Technical Change} = \left[\left(\frac{D^{t+1}(x^{t+1}, y^{t+1})}{D^t(x^{t+1}, y^{t+1})}\right)\left(\frac{D^{t+1}(x^t, y^t)}{D^t(x^t, y^t)}\right)\right]^{\frac{1}{2}}$$

$$= \left[\left(\frac{0e/0f}{0e/0d}\right)\left(\frac{0a/0c}{0a/0b}\right)\right]^{\frac{1}{2}}$$

Figure 4 Productivity and Efficiency Change

level of output that would have been infeasible in period t, i.e., it has also taken advantage of technical change to move its operating point to the left of the production frontier for period t. Thus, the firm has achieved total factor productivity growth by improving its technology and by becoming more efficient.[7]

This discussion can be formalized by reference to the input distance function introduced by Shephard (1970). Suppose producers use input vector $x = (x_1, x_2, \ldots x_k) \in \mathbb{R}_+^k$ to produce output vector $y = (y_1, y_2, \ldots y_n) \in \mathbb{R}_+^k$. A production technology which transforms inputs into outputs can be modeled by an input correspondence

[7] The type of inefficiency considered here is *technical efficiency*, i.e., firms on the frontier are using the most efficient available technology, while those to the right of the frontier are not using this technology. It is also possible to develop similar concepts for cost and other types of efficiency.

$y \rightarrow V(y) \subseteq \mathbb{R}^k_+$. For any $y \in \mathbb{R}^n_{++}$, $V(y)$ denotes the subset of *all* input vectors $x \in \mathbb{R}^k_+$ which yield at least y. $V(y)$ is assumed to satisfy certain axioms (see Färe, Grosskopf, and Lovell 1985, and Färe 1988). The input oriented distance function is defined by

$$D(x, y) = \sup\left\{\theta : \left(\frac{x}{\theta}, y\right) \in V(y)\right\} = (\inf\{\theta : (\theta x, y) \in V(y)\})^{-1} \tag{1}$$

The input distance function is the same as the reciprocal of the minimum equi-proportional contraction of the input vector x, given outputs y, i.e., Farrell's (1957) measure of input technical efficiency.

To illustrate the distance function, consider the firm operating at point (x_i^t, y_i^t) in Figure 4. The distance function value for this firm is given by $D^t(x_i^t, y_i^t) = 0a/0b$, where superscripts on D indicate the time period of the frontier from which the distance is computed. Distance functions can be used to compare the firm's efficiencies in periods t and $t + 1$. In Figure 4, $D^{t+1}(x_i^{t+1}, y_i^{t+1}) = 0e/0f < D^t(x_i^t, y_i^t) = 0a/0b$, i.e., the firm is closer to the frontier in period $t + 1$ than in period t.

The distance function representation also can be used to define the *Malmquist index* of total factor productivity. If our interest is in determining whether productivity change has occurred between periods t and $t + 1$, we could use either the period t frontier or the period $t + 1$ frontier as our point of reference. With respect to the period t frontier, an input-oriented Malmquist productivity index can be defined as:

$$M^t = \frac{D^t(x^t, y^t)}{D^t(x^{t+1}, y^{t+1})} \tag{2}$$

The input-oriented Malmquist index with respect to the period $t + 1$ frontier is:

$$M^{t+1} = \frac{D^{t+1}(x^t, y^t)}{D^{t+1}(x^{t+1}, y^{t+1})} \tag{3}$$

To avoid arbitrarily choosing one frontier to compute the index, the usual approach is to take the geometric mean, yielding the following *Malmquist index of total factor productivity* (Grosskopf 1993):

$$M(x^{t+1}, y^{t+1}, x^t, y^t) = \left[\frac{D^t(x^t, y^t)}{D^t(x^{t+1}, y^{t+1})} \frac{D^{t+1}(x^t, y^t)}{D^{t+1}(x^{t+1}, y^{t+1})}\right]^{1/2} \tag{4}$$

This expression can be factored into two components, representing *efficiency change*, i.e., the change in Farrell technical efficiency between the two periods, and *technical change*, i.e., the shift in the frontier between the two periods. The decomposition is illustrated in Figure 4. Efficiency change is the ratio of the distance from the frontier in period t to the distance in period $t + 1$, i.e., $D^t(x_i^t, y_i^t)/D^{t+1}(x_i^{t+1}, y_i^{t+1}) = [(0a/0b)/(0e/0f)]$. If technical efficiency has improved between year t and year $t + 1$, i.e., if the firm is closer to the frontier in period $t + 1$ than in period t, the ratio will be greater than 1. Technical change is measured by comparing the input-output bundle in period $t + 1$ to both the period $t + 1$ and period t technologies, and likewise for the input-output bundle in year t. Technical change is then computed as follows:

$$\text{Technical Change} = \left[\frac{D^{t+1}(x^{t+1}, y^{t+1})}{D^t(x^{t+1}, y^{t+1})}\frac{D^{t+1}(x^t, y^t)}{D^t(x^t, y^t)}\right]^{1/2} = \left[\left(\frac{0e/0f}{0e/0d}\right)\left(\frac{0a/0c}{0a/0b}\right)\right]^{1/2} \quad (5)$$

Intuitively, if favorable technical change has occurred, the frontier will have moved to the left, and both output bundles will be further from the period $t + 1$ frontier than they are from the period t frontier. Thus, a ratio greater than 1 indicates favorable technical change. The product of technical efficiency change and technical change is total factor productivity change.

24.3 METHODOLOGIES FOR ESTIMATING EFFICIENCY AND PRODUCTIVITY

This section discusses the principal methodologies that have been developed to measure efficiency and productivity, emphasizing frontier approaches. We first discuss the two major classes of efficiency estimation methodologies—the *econometric (parametric) approach* and the *mathematical programming (nonparametric)* approach. The section concludes with a discussion of total factor productivity measurement.

24.3.1 Econometric Frontier Efficiency Models

The estimation techniques used in nearly all econometric analyses of efficiency are *stochastic frontier* models (Greene 1993). Stochastic frontier models were originated by Aigner, Lovell, and Schmidt (1977), Battese and Corra (1977), and Meeusen and van den Broeck (1977). The technique can be conceptualized in two stages: (1) the estimation of an appropriate function, such as a production, cost, revenue, or profit function, using an econometric method such as ordinary least squares, non-linear least squares, or maximum likelihood, and (2) the separation of the estimated regression error terms into components, usually a two-sided random error component and a one-sided inefficiency component. This produces an estimate of efficiency for every firm in the estimation sample. The technique allows firms to operate away from the efficient frontier due to random error ("bad luck") as well as inefficiency. The bad luck component of the error is filtered out in estimating inefficiency.

As the preceding discussion suggests, the two most important decisions that must be made in applying the econometric frontier efficiency methodology are the choice of functional form and the approach to use in separating the random and inefficiency components of the error term. This section first discusses the functional forms and then turns to a discussion of specifying and estimating the error term.

Functional Form. Ideally, researchers would be able to determine the exact form of the production function for the firms being analyzed. This is, in fact, possible for some physical production processes such as manufacturing chemicals or refining oil. However, in most industries, and especially in the service sector, the exact functional form is not known. In the past, this led economists to use various approximations such as the well-known Cobb-Douglas and constant elasticity of substitution (CES) production functions. One of the most important developments that facilitated the development of stochastic frontier models was the introduction of the translog production function by Christensen, Jorgenson, and Lau (1973). They reasoned that even though the functional form may be unknown, any function satisfying rather weak regularity conditions can be expanded as a single or multi-variate Taylor series. They proposed the use of a second-order Taylor expansion in natural logarithms as an approximation of the unknown production function. A directly analogous derivation leads to the translog cost function. The translog has an advantage over earlier functional forms in that it allows returns to scale to change with output or input proportions so that the estimated cost curve can take on the familiar U-shape. The quadratic feature of the translog is also a potential disadvantage, as explained below.

A general expression of a cost function is $C = f(y, w, t)$, where C is total cost, y is output, w is input price, and t is time. In most applications, y and w are vectors. The *cost frontier* is defined as the minimum total cost function, i.e., the function that gives the minimum attainable cost for each level of output. The cost frontier is denoted $C^F = C^F(y, w, t)$. The translog cost function is

$$\ln C_{st} = \Bigg[\alpha_0 + \sum_{i=1}^{N} \alpha_{yi} \ln y_{sit} + \frac{1}{2} \sum_{i=1}^{N} \sum_{k=1}^{N} \alpha_{yik} \ln y_{sit} \ln y_{skt} + \sum_{j=1}^{M} \alpha_{wj} \ln w_{sjt} + \frac{1}{2} \sum_{j=1}^{M} \sum_{f=1}^{M} \alpha_{wjf} \ln w_{sjt} \ln w_{sft} + \sum_{i=1}^{N} \sum_{j=1}^{M} \alpha_{yiwj} \ln y_{sit} \ln w_{sjt} \Bigg] + v_{st} + \varepsilon_{st} \tag{6}$$

where $s = \{1, \ldots, S\}$, $i = \{1, \ldots, N\}$, and $j = \{1, \ldots, M\}$ index firms, outputs, and inputs, respectively, C_{st} = observed total costs for firm s in year $t = \Sigma_j w_{sjt} x_{sjt}$, y_{sit} = amount of output i produced by firm s in year t, w_{sjt} = price of input j to firm s in year t, ε_{st} = a random error term, and v_{st} = an inefficiency error term. The estimation is usually conducted as a system of equations consisting of the cost function and the first-order conditions for cost minimization:

$$\frac{\partial \ln C_{st}}{\partial \ln w_{sjt}} = \frac{w_{sjt} x_{sjt}}{C_{st}} = \left[\alpha_{wj} + \sum_{f=1}^{M} \alpha_{wjf} \ln w_{sft} + \sum_{i=1}^{N} \alpha_{yiwj} \ln y_{sit} \right] + \omega_{sjt} \tag{7}$$

where x_{sjt} = quantity of input j used by firm s in year t, and ω_{sjt} = a random error term. Linear homogeneity and symmetry restrictions are imposed in the estimation.

Firms are assumed to share a common cost function given by the bracketed expression in equation (6). The stochastic nature of the frontier is modeled by adding a two-sided random error term, ε_{st}, to the cost equation. The realizations of these random errors differ across firms, but the errors are assumed to be independent, identically distributed, and beyond the control of individual firms. Hence, ε_{st} is not indicative of inefficiency. Inefficiency is captured by the additional error term in equation (6), v_{st}. Because inefficiency can only increase (not reduce) costs, v_{st} is a one-sided error term, $v_{st} \geq 0$, or more generally $v_{st} \geq \zeta$, where ζ = a non-negative parameter. The input shares are assumed to have a functional component common to all firms (the bracketed expression in (7)) and a random component captured by the two-sided error term ω_{sjt}, where $\Sigma_j \omega_{sjt} = 0$.

While the translog has been widely used in econometric efficiency studies, it has some limitations that have led some researchers to seek alternative forms for the cost function. One limitation is that the translog does not naturally allow any of the independent variables to be equal to zero. Although this is not a problem with regard to input prices, it can be a limitation for outputs if more than one output is present and some firms do not produce all outputs. This is especially problematical in studying economies of scope, where zeros for some outputs are required to obtain meaningful results.

When zero outputs are present, one approach is to salvage the translog using somewhat ad hoc techniques such as setting all zero outputs to a small positive number or adding 1 to the value of all outputs (not just the output involving the zeros). The approach of setting zero outputs to a small positive number has been shown to be unsatisfactory in studies of scope economies because quite different estimates of scope economies can be obtained, depending upon how close the number is to zero (e.g., Röller, 1990).

Because of the limitations of the ad hoc techniques, for many purposes it is advisable to use an alternative functional form. We discuss three alternatives that show up relatively often in the financial services literature.[8] The simplest is the Fuss normalized quadratic, which replaces the logged values of outputs and input prices in equation (6) with the unlogged values of the variables (Morrison and Berndt 1981). Homogeneity is imposed by dividing all variables by one of the input prices. A limitation of this form is that the results are not completely invariant to which input is chosen for normalization. An alternative is the generalized translog cost function,

[8] For further discussion of the importance of functional form and some additional alternatives see Gagné and Ouellette (1998) and Terrell (1995).

obtained by transforming the output variables using a Box-Cox transformation (Caves, Christensen, and Tretheway 1980). I.e., the $\ln(y_{sit})$ in equation (6) are replaced by the Box-Cox transformed variate defined as $y_{sit}^{(\phi)} = (y_{sit}^{\phi} - 1)/\phi$, $\phi \neq 0$. The Box-Cox model is the same as the translog if $\phi = 0$; and thus fails to improve on the translog if ϕ is near 0.

Another functional form that seems ideally suited to the analysis of scope economies is the *composite function* (Pulley and Braunstein 1992). This functional form consists of a quadratic component for outputs, linked through interaction terms with a log-quadratic component for input prices. The resulting functional form can be estimated linearly, log-linearly or using a Box-Cox transformation. This functional form has been used by Berger, Cummins, and Weiss (1999) to analyze economies of scope in the insurance industry, considering firms that specialize in either life or property-liability insurance along with those that write both types of insurance.

A limitation of quadratic cost functions such as the translog is that they force the cost function to be U-shaped. This may be a problem if, for example, the actual cost curve exhibits constant returns to scale after output reaches the level where firms are no longer operating in the range of increasing returns to scale. The problem arises because the translog was developed as a local approximation to the true underlying cost function and thus may give misleading results when used globally. This problem cannot be solved by extending the Taylor series expansion to include higher-order terms because the resulting function is still a local approximation. Several approaches have been proposed for solving this problem. A particularly promising approach is the use of the Fourier flexible functional form, first proposed by Gallant (1982). This form arises from the expansion of the unknown true cost function as a Fourier series. The usual procedure is to append the Fourier (sine and cosine) terms to a standard translog, giving an extremely flexible function that will not force the estimated cost function to have a region characterized by decreasing returns to scale. The Fourier flexible form is a global approximation because the sine and cosine terms are mutually orthogonal over the $[0, 2\pi]$ interval, so that each additional term can make the approximating function closer to the true path of the data wherever it is needed.[9] A disadvantage of this functional form is that the number of Fourier terms can become very large, increasing the number of parameters and causing degrees of freedom problems. Consequently, the method cannot be used for small data sets.[10]

McAllister and McManus (1993) find the Fourier form to be superior to the translog in estimating bank cost functions. In the only insurance application of the function to date, Berger, Cummins, and Weiss (1997) find that the Fourier terms in

[9] The orthogonality is perfect only if the data are evenly distributed over the $[0, 2\pi]$ interval, but in most applications that have been reported, the Fourier terms lead to a significant improvement in the fit of the model (Berger and Mester 1997).

[10] The recommended number of parameters is $N^{(2/3)}$ where N is the number of observations. For example, Berger, Cummins, and Weiss (1997) had 4720 observations and 492 parameters including translog and first, second, and third-order Fourier terms. For relatively large data sets such as theirs and the even larger data sets used in many banking studies, the number of parameters is not a serious problem because the number of parameters as a proportion of the total number of observations is declining in N.

their cost and profit function models add significant explanatory power to the translog. However, the results of their hypothesis tests were the same under the translog and the Fourier functional forms.

Separating Inefficiency and Random Error. There are two principal methods for separating the random and inefficiency components of the error term—(1) making distributional assumptions about the error terms and (2) averaging estimated residuals over time to "average out" the random component of the error (the "distribution free" approach). The general procedure for estimating efficiency under the first approach is to jointly estimate the parameters of the cost function (6) and the parameters of the assumed distributions of the error terms using maximum likelihood, where the form of the likelihood function is determined by the distributional assumptions. The usual distributional assumptions are normal distributions for ε_{st} and ω_{sjt} (see equations (6) and (7)) and a truncated normal, exponential, or gamma distribution for v_{st}.[11] Efficiency is then estimated by separating the random and inefficiency components of the residuals $z_{st} = \varepsilon_{st} + v_{st}$ from the maximum likelihood estimation. The separation technique involves finding the conditional probability distribution of v_{st} given z_{st} and finding the conditional expectation $E(\exp(-v_{st})|z_{st})$ (see Greene 1993), providing an estimate of the ratio of frontier costs to actual costs for each firm in the sample.

The *distribution free* method developed by Schmidt and Sickles (1984) and Berger (1993) provides an alternative to the distributional assumption approach when several years of data are available. The cost function is estimated for the entire data period, either year by year or by pooling the data for all years. In the absence of distributional assumptions, least squares estimation (ordinary, non-linear, etc.) must be used rather than maximum likelihood estimation. The residuals from the cost function estimation constitute a vector of random error terms for each firm, $z_s = \{z_{s1}, z_{s2}, \ldots, z_{sT}\}$, $s = 1, 2, \ldots, S$. The error term z_{st} is specified here as $z_{st} = \varepsilon_{st} + v_s$, i.e., the inefficiency component is assumed to be the same for all years. No distributional assumptions are required for ε_{st} or v_s. Rather, an estimate of the efficiency is extracted by averaging the estimated overall error, $z_{st} = v_s + \varepsilon_{st}$, over the sample period on the assumption that the random error ε_{st} will average out over time. Cost efficiency is then estimated for each firm as:

$$E[v_s|z_{s1} \ldots z_{sT}] = \exp(\min_S(\bar{z}_s) - \bar{z}_s) \tag{8}$$

where $\bar{z}_s$ denotes the average over the sample period of the residuals z_{st} for firm s, and $\min_S(\bar{z}_s)$ is the minimum average error term for the firms in the sample. In addition to avoiding distributional assumptions, this method is also easier to implement than the distributional approach because it does not require the use of maximum likelihood methods.

[11] For specificity, this discussion focuses on the translog, but a similar approach would apply for the other functional forms discussed above.

The distributional assumptions approach has been criticized for confounding efficiency estimates with the choice of inappropriate probability distributions. However, Cummins and Zi (1998) show that the efficiency rankings of firms in their sample of U.S. life insurers are robust to the distributions assumed for the error terms. Further research is needed to determine whether this finding can be extrapolated to other data sets. The distribution free method is not susceptible to errors stemming from incorrect distributional assumptions. However, it may give misleading results if the inefficiency component of the error term is not constant over time or if the number of available data years is not sufficient to average out the random error.

24.3.2 Mathematical Programming Methods

The mathematical programming (non-parametric) approaches to estimating efficiency represent an empirical implementation of Shepard's distance function methodology discussed in section 2. The implementation that is used most frequently is *data envelopment analysis* (*DEA*), which was originated by Charnes, Cooper, and Rhodes (1978). The method can be used to estimate production, cost, revenue, and profit frontiers and provides a particularly convenient way for decomposing efficiency into its components.[12] E.g., cost efficiency can be conveniently decomposed into pure technical, scale, and allocative efficiency. DEA imposes somewhat less structure on the optimization problem than the econometric approach. The method is non-parametric, and neither functional form nor error term assumptions are required. Intuitively, the method involves searching for a convex combination of firms in the industry that dominate a given firm. These firms constitute the given firm's *reference set.* If the reference set consists only of the firm itself, it is considered self-efficient and has an efficiency score of 1.0. However, if a dominating set can be found consisting of other firms, the firm's efficiency is less than 1.0. The implication is that the firm's outputs could be produced more cheaply (in the case of cost efficiency) by the "best practice" firms in the industry. In this section, we focus primarily on DEA, but we conclude the section with a discussion of the free disposal hull (FDH) methodology, which departs from DEA by dropping the convexity requirement.

DEA efficiency is estimated by solving linear programming problems. For example, technical efficiency is estimated by solving the following problem, for each firm, $s = 1, 2, \ldots S$, in each year of the sample period (time superscripts are suppressed):

$$(D(y_s, x_s))^{-1} = T(y_s, x_s) = \min \theta_s \tag{9}$$

Subject to $Y\lambda_s \geq y_s$, $X\lambda_s \leq \theta_s x_s$, and $\lambda_s \geq 0$,

[12] Profit frontiers pose a somewhat different problem than the other types of DEA frontiers. See Färe, Grosskopf, and Lovell (1994), pp. 212–217.

where Y is an $N \times S$ output matrix and X a $M \times S$ input matrix for all firms in the sample, y_s is a $N \times 1$ output vector and x_s an $M \times 1$ input vector for firm s, and λ_s is an $S \times 1$ intensity vector for firm s (the inequalities are interpreted as applying to each row of the relevant matrix). The constraint $\lambda_s \geq 0$ imposes constant returns to scale. The firms for which the elements of λ_s are non-zero constitute the firm s's reference set.

Technical efficiency is separated into pure technical and scale efficiency by reestimating problem (9) with the additional constraint $\sum_{s=1}^{S} \lambda_s = 1$ for a variable returns to scale (VRS) frontier (this step estimates pure technical efficiency), and again with the constraint $\sum_{s=1}^{S} \lambda_s \leq 1$ for a non-increasing returns to scale (NIRS) frontier. Pure technical efficiency is defined as the distance from the variable returns to scale frontier (see Figure 3), and the relationship $TE(x_s, y_s) = PT(x_s, y_s)\, SE(x_s, y_s)$ can be used to separate pure technical and scale efficiency, where $SE(x_s, y_s)$ represents scale efficiency and $PT(x_s, y_s)$ pure technical efficiency. Thus, if $TE = PT$, i.e., the CRS and VRS technical efficiency estimates are equal, then $SE(x_s, y_s) = 1$ and CRS is indicated. If $SE \neq 1$ and the NIRS efficiency measure $= PT$, DRS is present; whereas if $SE \neq 1$ and the NIRS efficiency measure $\neq PT$, then IRS is indicated (Aly, et al. 1990).

A two-step procedure is used to estimate DEA cost efficiency. The first step is to solve the following problem for each firm $s = 1, 2, \ldots, S$:

$$\underset{x_s}{Min}\; w_s^T x_s \tag{10}$$

Subject to: $Y\lambda_s \geq y_i$, $i = 1, 2, \ldots, N$, $X\lambda_s \leq x_j$, $j = 1, 2, \ldots, M$, and $\lambda_s \geq 0$.

where T stands for vector transpose. The solution vector x_s^* is the cost-minimizing input vector for the input price vector w_s and the output vector y_s. The second step is to calculate firm s's cost efficiency as the ratio $\eta_s = w_s^T x_s^* / w_s^T x_s$, i.e., the ratio of frontier costs to actual costs. Thus, cost efficiency satisfies the inequality, $0 < \eta_s \leq 1$, with a score of 1 indicating that the firm is fully cost efficient.

Revenue efficiency is estimated similarly to cost efficiency. However, in this case we adopt an output-oriented rather than an input-oriented approach and maximize revenues rather than minimizing costs. The setup of the problem is suggested by Lovell (1993). Specifically, the following problem is solved for each firm in each year of the sample period:

$$\underset{y_s}{Max} \sum_{i=1}^{N} p_{si}\, y_{si} \tag{11}$$

Subject to: $Y\lambda_s \geq y_i$, $i = 1, 2, \ldots, N$, $X\lambda_s \leq x_j$, $j = 1, 2, \ldots, M$, and $\lambda_s \geq 0$.

The solution vector y_s^* is the revenue maximizing output vector for the output price vector p_s and the input vector x_s. Revenue efficiency is then measured by the ratio $\kappa_s = p_s^T y_s / p_s^T y_s^* \leq 1$. Linear programming is used to solve the problem defined in (11).

All of the DEA methods discussed so far impose the condition that the efficient frontier be a convex set. While this generally seems to be a reasonable assumption, there is no necessary mathematical or economic reason why it should always hold in practice. Deprins, Simar, and Tulkens (1984) criticize the DEA methodology for imposing the convexity assumption, contending that it leads to a poor fit to some observed data sets because it does not allow for local non-convexities. Intuitively, the convexity assumption allows a firm to be dominated by a convex combination of other firms even if there is no firm actually operating with the input-output vector of the "virtual" firm created by the convex combination.

Deprins, Simar, and Tulkens (1984) propose the elimination of the convexity assumption, leading to the *free disposal hull (FDH)* estimation technique. The FDH name comes from its retention of another major assumption of DEA, free disposability, which implies, for example, that outputs do not decrease if some inputs are increased (strong disposability of inputs). The FDH method allows the frontier to have local non-convexities. It has been shown to envelop the data more closely than DEA, and FDH efficiencies tend to be considerably higher than those for DEA with many more self-efficient firms (Vanden Eeckaut, Tulkens, and Jamar 1993, Cummins and Zi 1998). However, it is not at all clear that the increase in goodness of fit is economically meaningful, i.e., the frontier may indeed be convex for some industries. More research is clearly needed to resolve the convexity issue.

24.3.3 Pros and Cons: Econometrics Versus Mathematical Programming

The choice of methodology for estimating efficient frontiers has generated controversy in the literature, with some researchers arguing for the econometric approach (e.g., Berger 1993, Greene 1993) and others for the mathematical programming approach (e.g., Seiford and Thrall 1990, Charnes, et al. 1994, chapter 1). The primary advantage of the econometric approach is that it allows firms to be off the frontier due to random error as well as inefficiency and, consequently, does not count purely random error as inefficiency. The primary disadvantage of the econometric approach is that it requires the specification of a functional form such as the translog to estimate the frontier and, as well, requires distributional assumptions in order to recover the efficiency estimates. The choice of an inappropriate functional form or distributional assumptions for the error terms potentially confounds the efficiency estimates with specification error.[13] It is also more difficult to decompose efficiency into its components with an econometric model than with DEA.

A principal advantage of the mathematical programming approach is that it is

[13] Gagné and Ouellette (1998) provide evidence on the importance of the choice of functional form and data quality when using econometric methodologies.

non-parametric and thus avoids specification error because it is not necessary to specify a functional form or distributional assumptions. However, in most applications of the methodology, any departure from the frontier is measured as inefficiency, i.e., random error or bad luck is not separated out. Another advantage of DEA is that it solves the optimization problem separately for each decision making unit (DMU) and thus optimizes over individual units (Charnes, et al. 1994, pp. 4–5). Econometric models, on the other hand, optimize over the sample as a whole, and the estimated function is assumed to apply to all units in the sample, with all of the differences among firms captured through the estimated residuals. Thus, DEA can produce estimates of important quantities such as economies of scale that apply to specific units of observations (firms), whereas econometric estimates of scale economies are based on the same parameter estimates for all units.

DEA is at a disadvantage if the outputs of firms in a given sample are characterized by significant heterogeneity, e.g., if there are significant quality differences among firms. Because DEA involves the selection of a reference set for each firm in the sample, with heterogeneity it is possible that the firms in a given firm's reference set are not producing comparable outputs. For example, a high quality firm may appear to be dominated by a set of low quality firms. Heterogeneity may be a less serious problem in econometrics because an "average frontier" is being estimated and because the error terms can absorb some of the effect of heterogeneity. It is important, however, to utilize samples of firms with outputs that are as homogeneous as possible in both methodologies.

How important is the choice of an efficiency estimation methodology? Some clues are provided by the few studies that have applied a range of estimation methodologies to the same data set. Cummins and Zi (1998) apply a variety of econometric and mathematical programming techniques to estimate the cost efficiency of U.S. life insurers and find that econometric efficiency estimates are robust to the choice of distributional assumptions for the error term.[14] The rank correlations among efficiency scores for the econometric methods are typically above 0.95. The rank correlations between the econometric and mathematical programming efficiency estimates are lower (around 0.67). They also find that the convexity assumption makes a significant difference in the mathematical programming approach. The rank correlations for cost efficiencies between DEA and FDH averaged about 0.6, and the rank correlations between FDH and the econometric methods also averaged about 0.6. The choice of whether to impose the convexity assumption in mathematical programming may be as important as the choice between econometrics and mathematical programming. More research is clearly needed to analyze the consistency among the various methodologies as well as the economic significance of the alternative efficiency scores.

The advantages and disadvantages of the econometric and the mathematical programming approaches provide some guidance as to the choice of a methodology for specific data sets. For example, if the data are known to be noisy due to reporting

[14] For a similar analysis of the banking industry see Bauer, et al. (1998).

errors, etc., the econometric approach might be expected to yield more accurate results because of its ability to filter out random error. However, if the noise is in the independent variables of the econometric model rather than the dependent variable, then the model will be subject to errors-in-variables bias, with unknown impact on the efficiency estimates. Additionally, the disadvantage of counting random error as part of inefficiency in DEA can be partially obviated by conducting ex post regressions with efficiency scores as dependent variables and firm characteristics as independent variables—a procedure that is often convenient for hypothesis testing (e.g., see Cummins, Weiss, and Zi 1999). Because efficiency is used as the dependent variable, the ex post regressions partially correct for the inclusion of random error in the efficiencies without causing errors-in-variables bias.

Mathematical programming is likely to be advisable if the objective is to study the performance of specific units of observation, because the optimization is conducted separately for each unit. Mathematical programming may be the only alternative for problems involving small numbers of observation units. Because the method is not statistical, it is possible to estimate DEA efficiency in very small samples, as long as the number of inputs and outputs is not very large. For moderate sample sizes, DEA may give more reliable estimates than econometrics even for larger numbers of inputs and outputs. Of course, it should be borne in mind that any efficiency estimation only provides an indication of "best practices," i.e., the true frontier can never be estimated with real data. With a small sample, there are fewer observations to form the dominating sets and hence efficiency is likely to be overestimated.

In summary, it is difficult to give clear guidelines about whether econometrics or mathematical programming is likely to give more accurate results for specific samples. However, the econometric and mathematical programming methods have advantages and disadvantages that can make a difference in specific situations. Probably the best approach is the one recommended by Cummins and Zi (1998)—use at least one econometric methodology and at least one mathematical programming methodology. This approach is likely to pay dividends in terms of obtaining meaningful and useful results.

As the methodologies continue to evolve, it is likely that the major limitations of the methods will be overcome and a type of convergence will be achieved. For example, recent papers have begun to develop stochastic mathematical programming models (Land, Lovell, and Thore 1993) as well as providing the underlying statistical theory for the mathematical programming (e.g., Grosskopf 1996).

24.3.4 Measuring Total Factor Productivity

Because the primary purpose of this paper is to discuss frontier efficiency methods, we provide only a brief overview of total factor productivity measurement, focusing on non-frontier productivity indices (index numbers) and the more recently developed fronitier-based Malmquist approach. The index number approach to total factor productivity originated with Tinbergen in 1942 (Kendrick and Vaccara 1980). The Malmquist method is credited to Caves, Christensen, and Diewert (1982), for the theory, and to Färe, Grosskopf, Lindgren, and Roos (1994), for the empirical methodology.

Under the index number approach, total factor productivity (TFP) growth is defined as the difference between output and input growth. Productivity indices are often used to gauge the performance of national economies, and indices are also sometimes used to condense the number of outputs and/or inputs for a multi-output or multi-input firm. The challenge in developing productivity indices is to summarize in a single number the performance of an operating unit producing multiple outputs with multiple inputs. To use this approach, data for output and input quantities and prices are required. No parameters are estimated, but the index formula itself usually is derived from an assumed functional form for cost or production.

The most popular non-frontier index by far is the *Divisia index* of total factor productivity (Diewert 1981). The Divisia index of TFP growth can be derived from a translog aggregator (flexible) function exhibiting constant returns to scale and profit maximizing competitive behavior. When used to measure TFP, productivity growth is assumed to be Hicks neutral.[15] An alternative index, the *"exact" index* may be used if non-constant returns to scale are known to exist. In cases where these assumptions are not reasonable, ex post regression analysis may be used to isolate the effect of such factors as size and regulation. To define the Divisia index, we first define the production function $y(t) = F[x(t), t] = A(t)f[x(t)]$, where $y(t)$ = the output at time t, $x(t)$ = the vector of inputs, and $A(t)$ = a cumulative shift factor for the production function at time t. Then the Divisia index of total factor productivity growth is defined as:[16]

$$\frac{\dot{A}(t)}{A(t)} = \frac{\dot{y}(t)}{y(t)} - \sum_{j=1}^{M} s_j(t)\frac{\dot{x}_j(t)}{x_j(t)} \tag{12}$$

where $w_j(t)$ = price of the jth input, $s_j(t)$ = the jth input share = $w_j(t)x_j(t)/\sum_{j=1}^{M} w_j(t)x_j(t)$, A dot over a symbol indicates a time derivative. Hicks neutrality allows us to separate the shift factor $A(t)$ from the function $f[x(t)]$ and thus to conveniently measure productivity growth.

The index approach is used typically in cases where direct econometric estimation of a cost or production function is infeasible because the functional form for cost or production is not known and/or a sufficient number of observations to estimate the parameters in flexible functional forms are not available. This approach is sometimes

[15] Hicks neutrality means that the ratio of the marginal products of capital and labor for any ratio of capital and labor input is independent of time.

[16] For simplicity, we use only one output. However, the Divisia index can be defined for multiple outputs.

used in analyzing national accounting data, such as insurance gross product originating because it is easy to compute (i.e., no estimation is conducted) (e.g., Bernstein 1997).

As discussed above, Malmquist indices also can be used to measure total factor productivity growth. The approach is to compute the distance of each decision making unit's operating point in period t to the frontier in periods t and $t + 1$ as well as the distance of its $t + 1$ operating point from both frontiers and then to compute the index using equation (4). Malmquist indices are estimated by solving linear programming problems similar to (9). For example, for firm s, the distance of the time t input-output bundle (x_s^t, y_s^t) from the time $t + 1$ frontier, i.e., $D^{t+1}(x_s^t, y_s^t)$, can be obtained by solving the following problem:

$$(D^{t+1}(x_s^t, y_s^t))^{-1} = \min \theta_s \tag{13}$$

$$\text{Subject to: } Y^{t+1}\lambda_s \geq y_s^t, \quad X^{t+1}\lambda_s \leq \theta_s x_s^t, \quad \text{and } \lambda_s \geq 0$$

where Y^{t+1} is the $N \times S$ output matrix for all sample firms at time $t + 1$, y_s^t is the $N \times 1$ output vector for firm s at time t, X^{t+1} is the $M \times S$ input matrix for all sample firms at time $t + 1$, x_s^t is the $M \times 1$ input vector for firm i at time t, and λ_s is the intensity vector for firm s. The Malmquist approach has the advantage of lending itself to the decomposition of total factor productivity growth into technical change (shifts in the frontier) and efficiency change (movement of operating units closer to or further from the frontier over time).

24.4 DEFINING OUTPUTS AND INPUTS

An important step in efficiency analysis is the definition of inputs and outputs and their prices. Indeed, the results can be misleading or meaningless if these quantities are poorly defined. This problem is especially acute in the service sector, where many outputs are intangible and many prices are implicit. Defining inputs also must be done with care in studies of the U.S. insurance industry, where data on the number of hours worked and number of employees, are not available in public sources. In spite of the challenges, researchers have devised measures of inputs, outputs, and prices that produce economically meaningful results. This section discusses the concepts and definitions of outputs, inputs, and their prices.

24.4.1 Outputs and Output Prices

Measuring Financial Services Output. Insurers are analogous to other financial firms in that their outputs consist primarily of services, many of which are intangible. Three principal approaches have been used to measure outputs in financial services—the asset (intermediation) approach, the user-cost approach, and the value-added approach (see Berger and Humphrey 1992b). The asset approach treats financial firms as pure financial intermediaries, borrowing funds from one set of decision makers, transforming the resulting liabilities into assets, and paying out interest to cover the time value of funds used. The asset approach would be inappropriate for property-liability insurers because they provide many services in addition to financial intermediation. In fact, the intermediation function is somewhat incidental to property-liability insurers, arising out of the contract enforcement costs that would be incurred if premiums were not paid in advance of covered loss events. This is true to a lesser extent for life insurers, where intermediation is the most important function. However, ignoring insurance outputs is likely to overlook important distinctions among insurers and thus give less accurate results than if a wider range of outputs were used. Accordingly, the asset approach also is not likely to be optimal for either property-liability (*P*/*L*) or life insurers.

The user-cost method determines whether a financial product is an input or output on the basis of its net contribution to the revenues of the financial institution (Hancock 1985). If the financial returns on an asset exceed the opportunity cost of funds or if the financial costs of a liability are less than the opportunity costs, then the product is considered to be a financial output. Otherwise, it is classified as a financial input. This method is theoretically sound but requires precise data on product revenues and opportunity costs, which are difficult to estimate.[17] This approach is especially problematical for the insurance industry because insurance policies bundle together many services, which are priced implicitly.

The third approach to measuring output—the value-added approach—is the most appropriate method for studying insurance efficiency. The value-added approach considers all asset and liability categories to have some output characteristics rather than distinguishing inputs from outputs in a mutually exclusive way. The categories having significant value-added, as judged using operating cost allocations, are employed as important outputs. Others are treated as unimportant outputs, intermediate products, or inputs, depending on their other characteristics. The following discussion focuses solely on the value-added approach.

Services Provided by Insurers. Since insurance outputs are mostly intangible, it is necessary to find suitable proxies for the volume of services provided by insurers. This section discusses the principal services provided, and subsequent sections deal with insurance output measurement.

Insurers provide three principal services:

[17] Efforts to apply the user cost method in banking found that the classifications of inputs and outputs were not robust to the choice of opportunity cost estimates nor were they robust over time (see Berger and Humphrey 1992b).

- ***Risk-pooling and risk-bearing.*** Insurance provides a mechanism for consumers and businesses exposed to insurable contingencies to engage in risk reduction through pooling. Insurers collect premiums from their customers and redistribute most of the funds to those policyholders who sustain losses. The actuarial, underwriting, and related expenses incurred in operating the risk pool are a major component of value added in insurance. Policyholders may also have their risks reduced because insurers hold capital to cushion unexpected loss and investment shocks. Again, this creates value-added by increasing economic security.
- ***"Real" financial services relating to insured losses.*** Insurers provide a variety of real services for policyholders. In life insurance, these services include financial planning and counseling for individuals and pension and benefit plan administration for businesses. In property-liability insurance, real services include risk surveys, the design of coverage programs, and recommendations regarding deductibles and policy limits. Insurers also provide loss prevention services.
- ***Intermediation.*** Insurers issue debt contracts (insurance policies and annuities) and invest the funds until they are withdrawn by policyholders (in the case of life insurers) or are needed to pay claims. In life insurance, interest credits are made directly to policyholder accounts to reflect investment income; whereas, in property-liability insurance, policyholders receive a discount in the premiums they pay to compensate for the opportunity cost of the funds held by the insurer. The net interest margin between the rate of return earned on assets and the rate credited to policyholders represents the value-added of the intermediation function.

Insurance expense data presented in Table 1 helps us to identify the main sources of value-added. In 1996, about 41 (30) percent of operating expenses for life insurers (property-liability insurers) were for agents' commissions. Agents perform real

Table 1
Expense Analysis: US Life and Property-Liability Insurers

Expense Item	Life	Property-Liability
Commissions and Brokerage	40.9%	30.0%
Claims Adjustment	1.0%	14.7%
Employee Salaries & Benefits	27.8%	29.3%
Advertising	1.0%	0.9%
Postage, Telecommunications, etc.	2.3%	2.1%
Equipment	2.8%	3.4%
Real Estate and Rent Items	3.3%	3.1%
All Other	20.1%	16.5%
Total Expenses (in Billions)*	$80	$107

Note: All data are for 1996.
Source: *Best's Aggregates and Averages* 1997, NAIC life data tapes, 1996.

services such as financial counseling and giving advice on coverages and deductibles. They also collect underwriting information and expand the size of the insurer's risk pool. About 28 (29) percent of total expenses are for personnel costs for functions other than sales and claims settlement. These expenditures are for the underwriters, actuaries, and administrators that operate the insurance risk pool. For property-liability insurers, a substantial share of expenses (15 percent) goes for claims settlement services, which include such real services as providing a legal defense against liability suits. Investment expenses account for 9 (2) percent of total expenses for life (property-liability) insurers. These expenses along with the net interest margin between what insurers earn on their investments and what they credit to policyholders, is a measure of the value added by the intermediation function. A rough idea of the magnitude of the net interest margin can be obtained by observing that a 50 basis point margin on invested assets would be equivalent to 14 (10) percent of total expenses for life (property-liability) insurers. Thus, intermediation is also an important output for insurers.

Defining Insurance Output: Theoretical Foundations. Before turning to the specification of the variables used to represent insurer outputs in efficiency estimation, we briefly consider the concept of insurance output from a theoretical perspective. The provision of real services poses no conceptual hurdles that need to be explored here. However, it is useful to explore the concept of the value-added from the risk-pooling/risk-bearing function in the context of the theory of insurance economics. The treatment of the intermediation function also requires some discussion.

In terms of insurance economics, the value-added from risk-pooling is measured by the Pratt-Arrow concept of the *insurance premium*. The result is stated succinctly by Arrow (1971, p. 95):

> Consider an individual faced with a random outcome Y and offered the alternative of a certain income, Y_0. A risk averter would be willing to accept a value of Y_0 less than the mean value, $E(Y)$, of the random income; the difference may be thought of as an insurance premium.

Stated more precisely, the insurance premium (value-added) is the amount which makes the individual just indifferent between retaining and insuring the risk, i.e., the insurance premium π is the solution to:

$$U(W - \mu_L - \pi) = \int U(W - L) f(L) dL \tag{14}$$

where $U(W)$ = utility function, with $U' > 0$, $U'' < 0$
W = initial wealth (non-stochastic),
L = the loss (stochastic), with $L \geq 0$,
$f(L)$ = the probability of loss distribution, and $\mu_L = E(L)$.

Thus, the value added by the insurance transaction is the maximum amount over and above the expected loss the policyholder is willing to pay, i.e., π. After all, the consumer clearly has the option of going uninsured and having risky wealth with expected value $(W - \mu_L)$. It is the additional amount he/she is willing to pay over and above the expected loss that constitutes the value of the insurance.

In a competitive market, the full amount of consumer welfare gain from insurance may not be observed, i.e., the market may be able to provide the insurance for a loading less than π. It is not possible to measure the unobservable consumers' surplus that results. However, it should be clear that the amount paid in addition to the expected value is the measurable value-added by risk-pooling.

Although we have used the term insurance premium in this discussion to be consistent with Arrow (1971), in the remainder of the paper we refer to π as the *loading* in order to avoid confusion with the standard terminology in the insurance literature, where the term *premium* is used to mean the total amount paid by the policyholder for insurance, i.e., the expected loss plus the loading.

Because premiums are usually paid in advance of loss payments, it is necessary to appropriately account for investment income when measuring insurance output, output prices, revenues and profits. The correct approach for incorporating investment income can be illustrated by a simple one-period, two-date model of the insurance firm. The insurer is assumed to commit equity capital of S to the insurance enterprise at time 0. Premiums in the amount P are paid at time zero, and the premiums and equity are invested at rate of return r. Losses are paid at the end of the period (time 1). To avoid unnecessarily complicating the analysis, we assume that there are no taxes.[18]

The first concept to illustrate is the price of insurance, which corresponds to π in equation (12). Following the approach in Myers and Cohn (1987) and Cummins (1990), the premium is:

$$P = \frac{L(1+e) + S\rho}{1+r} \tag{15}$$

where L = the expected loss,
e = insurer expenses expressed as a proportion of the expected loss, and
ρ = the risk premium received by equity holders for bearing insurance risk.

The quantity of insurer output is proxied by the present value of losses incurred, i.e., output $= L/(1+r)$. This is appropriate because the purpose of insurance is to redistribute funds from those members of the pool who do not have a loss to those who do suffer a loss. Thus, L is the total amount redistributed by the insurer and proxies for the amount of pooling conducted. Insurer revenues are equal to total premiums

[18] Myers and Cohn (1987) and Cummins (1990) generalize the model to incorporate taxes.

received plus investment income earned, i.e., revenues = $P + r(P + S)$; and value-added is defined as revenues minus loss payments and the interest earned on equity, or

$$\text{Value Added} = P + r(P + S) - rS - L = eL + \rho S \tag{16}$$

It is necessary to subtract out the investment income on equity because this amount will be earned by equity holders in any case. Equity holders have the option of writing no insurance and thus operating as a mutual fund so that merely investing the equity carries no opportunity costs associated with operating an insurance business. The additional costs resulting from placing the money at risk in the insurance business are reflected in the risk premium ρ. The total value-added, $eL + \rho S$, thus equals the insurers expenses plus the owners' profit for bearing insurance risk. The price of insurance is defined as the value-added per dollar of output:

$$\text{Price} = \frac{P - PV(L)}{PV(L)} = \frac{P - \dfrac{L}{1+r}}{\dfrac{L}{1+r}} = e + \frac{S}{L}\rho \tag{17}$$

This result can easily be generalized to incorporate the intermediation function. This is done by discounting at a rate $r_P < r$ to obtain the premium, where $(1 + r) = (1 + r_P)(1 + m)$ and m = the net interest margin received by the insurer for performing the intermediation function. Continuing to use r as the investment income rate, it is easily shown that the value-added becomes:

$$V = m[L(1+e) + rS] + [eL + rS] \tag{18}$$

which equals the value added from intermediation plus the value added by risk-pooling.[19]

Defining Insurance Output In Practice. Some efficiency studies have used premiums to measure output. This is inappropriate, however, because premiums represent price times the quantity of output not output (Yuengert 1993). As he points out, "sys-

[19] It is hoped that this discussion will clear up some confusion in the literature about insurance price and output. For example, Armknecht and Ginsburg (1992) define insurance price as $(P - L)/L$, which in our notation equals $[e + (S/L)\rho - r]/(1 + r)$, i.e., in their formulation investment income on policyholder funds is part of the price. This is not correct because the policyholder could invest these funds in any event and thus there is no opportunity cost associated with having the funds invested instead by the insurer except in the case where the insurer earns a net interest margin from intermediation. The type of fallacious reasoning that the Armknecht-Ginsburg definition can lead to is exemplified by Lipsey (1992), who, in commenting on their paper observes that "a rise in investment earnings by casualty insurance companies does make it cheaper to insurer your car."

tematic differences in price across large and small firms may lead to misleading inferences about average costs if premiums are used as an output proxy" (Yuengert 1993, p. 489). Thus, it is important to develop measures that are consistent with the preceding discussion.

For property-liability insurers, it is possible to develop practical measures of price and output that correspond closely to the theoretical measures discussed above. Specifically, the present value of real losses incurred can be used as a reasonable proxy for output.[20] Estimates of the payout proportions can be obtained by applying the Internal Revenue Service or Taylor separation methods to data from Schedule *P* of the regulatory annual statement that provides information on reserve runoffs (see Cummins 1990); and discounting can be performed using U.S. Treasury yield curves. Because the various lines of business offered by insurers have different risk and payout characteristics, it is usually appropriate to use several output measures, grouping together lines with similar characteristics. Output prices can then be obtained using the formula: $(P - PV(L))/PV(L)$, where $PV(\cdot)$ is the present value operator.

For life insurers, it is not possible to obtain meaningful present values based on publicly available data because of the complexity of life insurance products and limitations on the types of information reported by life companies. The approach used in some of the most recent papers is to define output as incurred benefits plus additions to reserves (Berger, et al. 1999, Cummins, Tennyson, and Weiss 1999, Meador, Ryan and Schellhorn 1997). Incurred benefits represent payments received by policyholders in the current year and are useful proxies for the risk-pooling and risk-bearing functions because they measure the amount of funds pooled by insurers and redistributed as benefits. The funds received by insurers that are not needed for benefit payments and expenses are added to policyholder reserves. Additions to reserve thus should be highly correlated with the intermediation output. Both incurred benefits and additions to reserves are correlated with real services provided by insurers, such as financial planning. Because the major products offered by life insurers differ in the types of contingent events that are covered and in the relative importance of the risk-pooling, intermediation, and real services, it is necessary to define several types of output, representing the major lines of insurance. In keeping with the value-added

[20] A potential disadvantage of using losses as an output proxy is that losses are a random variable, i.e., are observed with error. This has the potential of creating errors-in-variables bias in the estimated econometric functions and of introducing error that is picked up as inefficiency by DEA. In econometric models this problem might be dealt with by using instrumental variables estimation. An alternative that would apply to both the econometrics and DEA would be to use a measure of expected losses equal to premiums earned multiplied by the average loss ratio for the appropriate line(s) of business over a period of *n* years prior to the year of analysis. As such a measure has not been used in any extant insurance efficiency studies, further research is needed to determine the effect of using this type of variable on the efficiency scores, as well as to determine which of the available output proxies is most economically meaningful. In the case of extreme randomness in losses, it is conceivable that using premiums might create less bias in the analysis than a loss-based proxy. Further research also should be conducted on the impact of using losses versus premiums as the output proxy. The loss randomness problem is less serious for life insurers because life insurance benefit payments are highly predictable, i.e., characterized by less random error than property-liability insurance losses.

approach to output measurement, the price of each insurance output is defined as the sum of premiums and investment income minus output for the line divided by output (investment income is reported by line in insurance accounting statements).

A promising avenue for future research is to use physical measures to proxy for insurance outputs in life insurance. Life insurers are required to report the number of claims paid and incurred as well as the number of policies issued and in force and the amount of insurance written and in force. Using these physical measures can control more precisely for differences among companies. For example, expenses differ among companies as a function of average policy sizes and the proportion of new business to existing business (Weiss 1986), but the usual measures of life insurance output do not control for such differences.

24.4.2 Inputs and Input Prices

Insurer inputs can be classified into three principal groups: labor, business services and materials, and capital. For some applications it also may make sense to split labor into agent labor and all other (mostly home office) labor because the two types of labor have different prices and are used in different proportions by firms in the industry (e.g., some firms use direct marketing in whole or in part, while others rely heavily on agents). In addition, there are at least three types of capital that can be considered—physical capital, debt capital, and equity capital. However, it is rare for insurance efficiency studies to utilize more than four inputs. Because physical capital expenditures are a small proportion of the total (see Table 1), they are often lumped together with business services and materials.

Because physical measures of input quantities are not publicly available for insurers, the approach taken in most insurance efficiency studies is to impute the quantity of physical inputs by dividing the relevant insurer expense item by a corresponding price index, wage rate, or other type of deflator. e.g., the quantity of labor is equal to the total expenditures on labor, from the regulatory annual statement, divided by the wage rate, i.e.:

$$Q_{Lt} = \frac{X_{Lt}^c}{w_{Lt}^c} \tag{19}$$

where Q_{Lt} = quantity of labor,
w_{Lt}^c = current dollar hourly wages, and
X_{Lt}^c = current dollar expenditures on labor.

The price of labor is then obtained as:

$$w_{Lt} = \frac{w_{Lt}^c}{p_t} \tag{20}$$

where w_{Lt} = constant dollar wage rate, and
p_t = the consumer price index (CPI).

Multiplying Q_{Lt} by w_{Lt} then gives constant dollar labor expense $X_{lt} = X^c_{Lt}/p_t$.

The wage rate for administrative labor is usually measured for life insurers using U.S. Department of Labor (DOL) data on average weekly wages for Standard Industrial Classification (SIC) class 6311, life insurance companies, and for property-liability insurers using DOL data on SIC class 6331, property-liability companies. Because wages vary significantly by state, the ideal administrative wage rate would be a weighted average based on the amount of work performed in various locations. However, to do this accurately would require data on the locations and relative sizes of the insurer's processing operations, which are not publicly available. Two approximations that are often used for administrative labor are the wage rate for the state in which the company maintains its home office and a weighted average wage rate using the proportions of premiums written by state as weights. Neither measure is completely satisfactory. Most insurers either conduct their operations from a single home office or rely on regional (not state) offices. The limited research available on the administrative wage variable suggests that neither the efficiency scores nor the efficiency rankings are significantly affected by the definition of this variable (e.g., Cummins, Tennyson, and Weiss 1999). Our view is that it makes more sense to use the wage rate for the state where the home office is located rather than the premium-weighted-average wage rate.

The price of agent labor is measured using U.S. Department of Labor data on average weekly wages for SIC class 6411, insurance agents. A weighted average wage variable is often used, with weights equal to the proportion of an insurer's premiums written in each state. The weighted average approach is more appropriate for agent labor than for home office labor because most agency services are provided at the local level, whereas most of the other tasks performed by insurance company employees take place at the home office or in regional offices.

If prices were available for materials and business services, the quantity of this input would be:

$$Q_{Mt} = \frac{X^c_{Mt}}{w^c_{Mt}} \tag{21}$$

where Q_{Mt} = quantity of materials and business services,
w^c_{Mt} = price of one unit of materials and business services, and
X^c_{Mt} = current dollar expenditures on materials and business services.

The price of materials and business services is typically not available. Instead, a price index is used, defined as: $p_{Mt} = w^c_{Mt}/w^c_{M0}$, where w^c_{M0} = the price of materials and business services in a base period ($t = 0$). Then the quantity is obtained as:

$$Q_{Mt} = \frac{X^c_{Mt}}{w^c_{Mt}/w^c_{M0}} = \frac{X^c_{Mt}}{p_{Mt}} \tag{22}$$

and the price is defined as

$$w_{Mt} = \frac{w^c_{Mt}}{w^c_{M0}\,p_t} \tag{23}$$

Multiplying price times quantity yields constant dollar expenditures on materials and business services, i.e., $X_{Mt} = Q_{Mt}w_{Mt} = X^c_{Mt}/p_t$. A price index often used for the materials category is the business services deflator from the U.S. Department of Commerce, Bureau of Economic Analysis.

Early studies of the efficiency of financial institutions tended to include physical capital as an input but ignored financial equity capital. However, a number of the more recent financial institutions studies have recognized financial equity capital as an input (e.g., McAllister and McManus 1993, Hermalin and Wallace 1994, Berger, Cummins, and Weiss 1997, Berger and Mester 1997, Hughes and Mester 1998). This is a departure from traditional production theory, where physical capital and labor are the primary inputs in the production function. The inclusion of equity capital is justified under the modern theory of the firm where a firm's technology is viewed as including all of the contractual relationships that comprise the firm as well as physical technology choices such as computer and communications systems. Among the important contractual relationships are implicit and explicit contracts with the suppliers of the firm's financial capital.

Financial equity capital is also viewed as an important input under the financial theory of insurance pricing, where insurance is viewed as risky debt (e.g., Cummins and Danzon 1997). Under this theory, insurance prices are discounted in the market to reflect the expected costs of insurer default. Better capitalized insurers should receive higher prices for their products than riskier insurers, other things equal, because more capital implies a higher probability that losses will be paid if higher than anticipated. If the ultimate output of the insurance firm is economic security, equity capital is a necessary input to bring the firm as close as possible to the typical insurance demand theory assumption that claims are paid with certainty (see the discussion above of the utility-theory rationale for defining insurance output).[21] Financial equity capital is quantitatively quite important for insurers. E.g., the equity capital-to-asset ratios for life-health and property-liability insurers are 6.9 and 32.8

[21] Another rationale for the recognition of equity capital is that capital constitutes a constraint on the firm imposed by regulation. This was the approach taken in Weiss 1990. However, subsequent work has convinced us that it is better to treat capital as an input rather than a constraint, especially in view of the fact that most insurers, at least in the U.S., hold much more capital than is required by risk-based capital regulations (Cummins, Grace, and Phillips 1999).

percent, respectively.[22] Accordingly, failure to recognize the cost of equity capital is likely to distort the results of efficiency estimation.

The recognition of financial debt capital as an input is a less recent development than the recognition of financial equity in view of the fact that numerous banking studies have used deposits (the most important source of debt capital for banks) as an input. The rationale for the use of debt capital is that insurers raise debt capital by issuing insurance and annuity policies and then "intermediate" this capital into invested assets. Debt capital is not always used as an input in insurance or banking studies because reserves for insurers and deposits for banks have some characteristics of both inputs and outputs. Additional research is needed to determine the sensitivity of the estimated efficiency scores to the use of debt capital as an input.

Because the data for all extant insurance efficiency studies comes from regulatory annual statements, the quantity of equity capital is usually defined as statutory policyholders surplus, deflated to constant dollars using the CPI. In property-liability insurance studies this is sometimes adjusted by an estimate of the equity in the unearned premium reserves and other statutory balance sheet categories such as non-admitted assets whose treatment under statutory accounting principals (SAP) is not consistent with generally accepted accounting principles (GAAP). Adjustment for prepaid expenses are not possible for life insurers based on statutory data because of the complexity of the pre-paid expense calculations in life insurance. A possibility for future research would be to conduct the analysis using GAAP accounting statements.

To measure the cost of equity capital, it would be desirable to use the market value expected return on equity (ROE). However, few insurers are publicly traded so using market ROE greatly restricts the sample size. Consequently, book value measures usually are used. One approach is to use the average book ROE (net income divided by policyholders surplus) for the three or five years prior to the year of analysis. A problem with this approach is that it reduces the number of years for which efficiencies can be calculated by requiring at least three years prior to the start of the first year of efficiency analysis to compute average ROE. Another problem is that realized ROE can be negative, whereas the ex ante ROE must be positive. An alternative approach to ROE estimation is to estimate a regression equation with realized ROE as the dependent variable and variables such as leverage, business mix, and asset mix as independent variables.

A method that avoids the theoretical problem of negative ROE values but does not provide for much variability in costs of capital among insurers is to base the cost of capital on the financial ratings assigned by the A.M. Best Company, the leading financial rating firm for insurers. Cummins, Tennyson, and Weiss (1999) (CTW) adopt a three-tier approach to measuring the cost of capital based on Best's fifteen tier rating system that ranges from A ++ for the strongest insurers to *F* for insurers in liquidation. The three tiers consist of the four ratings in the "A" range, the four ratings in

[22] The source for these ratios is the Federal Reserve Flow of Funds Accounts.

the "B" range, and all other rating categories. Based on an examination of the cost of equity capital for traded life insurers, a cost of capital of 12 percent is assigned to the top tier, 15 percent for the middle tier, and 18 percent for insurers in the lowest quality-tier. CTW also conduct their analysis using the insurers' average return on book equity over the three years prior to each sample year. Although the use of the alternative cost of capital measure did not materially affect the results, it seems clear that more research is needed on the cost of capital issue.

The debt capital of insurers consists primarily of funds borrowed from policyholders. For life insurers, debt capital includes the aggregate reserve for life policies and contracts, the aggregate reserve for accident and health policies, the liability for premium and other deposit funds, and other reserve items. For property-liability insurers, reserves consist of loss reserves and unearned premium reserves. Insurers may borrow money through their holding companies, especially if they are publicly traded, but the amount of borrowed funds appearing on the statutory annual statements is trivial in comparison with reserves and thus is generally lumped together with reserves. Debt capital is deflated to constant dollars using the CPI.

The interest payment made to policyholders for the use of policyholder-supplied debt capital (i.e., the cost of this type of debt capital) is implicit in the premium and in the dividend payments made by insurers to policyholders. The cost of policyholder-supplied debt capital is estimated as the ratio of total expected investment income minus expected investment income attributed to equity capital divided by average policyholder-supplied debt capital (Berger, Cummins, and Weiss 1997). Expected investment income attributable to equity capital equals the expected rate of investment return multiplied by average equity capital for the year. This is based on the Myers and Cohn (1987) argument that investors will not supply capital to an insurer unless they receive a market return equal to the amount they could receive by investing in an asset portfolio that replicates the insurer's portfolio plus a risk premium for any additional costs associated with committing capital to the insurance business.

24.5 A SURVEY OF INSURANCE EFFICIENCY RESEARCH

This section provides a comprehensive survey of the research on productivity and efficiency in the insurance industry, focusing on studies that utilize modern frontier efficiency methodologies.

24.5.1 Outputs and Inputs

The outputs used in the extant insurance efficiency studies are summarized in Table 2. The life insurance studies are discussed first, followed by property-liability. While some of the earlier life insurance studies used premiums as an output measure (e.g., Fecher, 1993, Gardner and Grace, 1993), most of the more recent studies have used

Table 2
Output Definitions in Insurance Efficiency Studies

Study	Output Volume	Output Price	Lines of Insurance
Berger, Cummins, Weiss, and Zi (1999)	Real PV of Expected Losses	—	P/L Personal
	Expected Benefits + Additions to Reserves (Deflated by year)	—	P/L Commercial
		—	Life Personal
		—	Life Commercial
	Real Invested Assets	—	P/L
		—	Life
Cummins, Tennyson, and Weiss (1999)	Expected Benefits + Additions to Reserves (Deflated by year)	(Real Premiums-Real Investment Income-Output)/Output	Individual Life Individual Annuities Group Life Group Annuities Accident & Health
Cummins and Rubio-Misas (1998)	Losses Incurred	—	Life
		—	P/L
	Reserves	—	Primary Market
		—	Reinsurance
	Invested Assets	—	
Cummins, Turchetti and Weiss (1997)	Real Expected Losses	—	Auto Property Auto Liability Other Long-Tail Other Short-Tail
	Benefits Incurred + Changes in Reserves	—	Life
Fukuyama (1997)	Real Insurance Reserves	—	—
	Real Loans	—	—
Cummins, Weiss, and Zi (1999)	Real Invested Assets	—	—
	Real PV of Expected Losses	—	Short-Tail Personal Short-Tail Commercial Long-Tail Personal Long-Tail Commercial

Cummins and Zi (1998)	Real Additions to Reserves	—	—
	Real Incurred Benefits	—	Individual Life Group Life Individual Annuities Group Annuities Accident & Health
Berger, Cummins, and Weiss (1997)	Total Real Invested Assets	Expected ROR on Invested Assets (Real Premium—Real PV Expected Losses)/Real PV Expected Losses	—
	Real PV of Expected Losses		Short-Tail Personal Short-Tail Commercial Long-Tail Personal Long-Tail Commercial
Meador, Ryan and Schellhorn (1997)	Real Additions to Reserves	—	—
	Real Incurred Benefits	—	Individual Life Group Life Individual Annuities Group Annuities Accident & Health
Bernstein (1997) alternative price measures similar to this tested too vary by treatment of inv. income and consideration of reins	Number of Policies (or Certificates)	(Premium + Investment Income – Change in Reserves)/Number of Policies (or Certificates)	Individual Insurance Individual Annuities Group Life Group Annuities
Kim and Grace (1995)	Total Investment Expenses	—	—
	Earned Claim Payments + Changes in Reserves	—	Individual Life Individual Annuity Group Life Group Annuity Group Health
Grace (1995)	Not Given	—	—

Table 2
(Continued)

Study	Output Volume	Output Price	Lines of Insurance
Cummins and Weiss (1993	All Policyholder Reserves (real)	—	—
	Extrapolated Loss Adjustment Expenses	—	—
	Real PV of Expected Losses	—	Short-Tail Personal Short-Tail Commercial Long-Tail Personal Long-Tail Commercial
Yuengert (1993)	Reserves	—	Accident & Health
	Additions to Reserves	—	Individual Life Group Life Individual Annuity Group Annuity Deposit Funds Other
Gardner and Grace (1993)	Dollar Amount of Securities Investment	—	—
	Premiums	—	Individual Life Group Life Individual Annuity Group Annuity Group Accident & Health
Fecher et al. (1993)	Gross Premiums	—	Life Civil Liability Fire & Property Accident and Health Motor Non-Motor (nonlife)

Weiss 1991	All Policyholder Reserves Expected Losses/Claims Cost Index	Three month T bill rate (Premiums-Expected Losses)/(Expected losses/ Claims Cost Index)	— Long-tail, Competitive States Long-Tail, Regulated States Short-Tail, Competitive States Short-Tail, Regulated States
Weiss (1991b)	All Policyholder Funds (Real) Real Expected Losses	Overall ROR on Assets (Country) (Premium-Expected Losses)/Real Expected Losses	— Motor Marine Fire Accident Liability Other
Weiss (1990)	Real Policyholder Reserves (Expected Losses)/Claims Cost Index	— —	— Workers Compensation, Competitive State Auto Liability (net of AIP). Competitive State General Liab. and Med. Mal., Competitive States Assigned Risk Plan, Competitive States All other, Competitive States Long-Tail in Regulated States Assigned Risk Plan, Regulated Stat All other, Regulated States
Weiss (1986)	Number of Policies Constant Dollar Insurance In Force "Real" Premium	Price allocations based on LOMA Functional Cost Reports	Individual Life—New Issue Individual Life—Renewal, Non Term Individual Life—Reneral, Term Individual Accident & Health Group
Kellner and Mathewson (1983)	Number of Policies (or number in group)	Premiums	Individual Life Group Life Individual Annuities Group Annuities

Note: P/L = property-liability, PV = present value, LOMA = Life Office Management Association.

more appropriate output measures, such as incurred benefits and changes in reserves. This measure is used by Cummins, Tennyson, and Weiss (1999), Cummins and Zi (1998), Meador, Ryan, and Schellhorn (1997), and Kim and Grace (1995). Yuengert (1993) uses additions to reserves but does not include incurred benefits. Fukuyama (1997), following an intermediation approach, uses reserves and loans as his output measures. Another group of authors uses physical output measures such as numbers of policies or insurance in force (Bernstein 1997, Weiss 1986, Kellner and Mathewson 1983). We are aware of no research that compares the use of monetary and physical output proxies in measuring insurer output.

Nearly all property-liability insurance studies use either the present value of losses or losses as an output measure, usually broken down into four or more lines of insurance. Berger, Cummins and Weiss (1997), Cummins, Weiss, and Zi (1999), and Cummins and Weiss (1993) use present values, whereas the other *P*/*L* studies use undiscounted losses. Some papers use assets to measure the intermediation function, while others use reserves. Only one study (Fecher, et al. 1993) uses premiums as output for *P*/*L* insurers.

There is even more uniformity in the choice of inputs for insurance efficiency studies than there is for the choice of outputs (see Table 3). Virtually every study uses labor and capital as well as a third category called business services or materials. About one-fourth of the studies distinguish between home office and agent labor. The studies are about evenly split between the use of physical and financial capital, and two studies use both physical and financial capital. A considerable amount of agreement also exists about the types of wage and price indices that are used to represent prices of the inputs.

24.5.2 Average Efficiency Scores

The results of the insurance industry efficiency studies are summarized in Table 4. The majority of the studies focus on the U.S., but analyses also have been conducted for France, Italy, Japan, and Spain. Two of the sixteen studies summarized in Table 4 use both econometric and mathematical programming methodologies. Of the remaining fourteen studies, nine employ econometric techniques and five use mathematical programming. The mathematical programming technique used almost exclusively has been DEA. Only one study utilized the FDH approach, even though the relaxation of the convexity assumption is potentially quite important. It would be useful to have additional research comparing DEA and FDH. The single study that made such a comparison for insurers found that the FDH efficiency scores tended to correlate somewhat better than the DEA scores with conventional performance measures such as return on equity, whereas both types of mathematical programming scores correlated somewhat better with the conventional measures than did the econometric scores (Cummins and Zi 1998).

The extant insurance applications have mainly focused on cost and technical effi-

Table 3
Inputs Used in Insurance Efficiency Research

Study	Input Type	Input Volume	Input Price
Berger, Cummins, Weiss, and Zi (1999)	Labor—Life	Real Dollar Wage/Input Price	Real Avg. Weekly Wages SIC 6311
	Labor—P/L	Real Dollar Wage/Input Price	Real Avg. Weekly Wages SIC 6331
	Business Services	All Non Labor Expenses/Input Price	Real Avg Weekly Wages SIC 7300
	Debt Capital—Life	Real Insurance Reserves	Fixed Netput
	Debt Capital—P/L	Real Insurance Reserves	Fixed Netput
	Financial Capital-Life	Real Equity Capital (Surplus)	Fixed Netput
	Financial Capital-P/L	Real Equity Capital (Surplus)	Fixed Netput
Cummins, Tennyson, and Weiss (1999)	Home Office Labor	Real Dollar Wage/Input Price	Real Avg. Weekly Wages SIC 6311—Home Office
	Agent Labor	Real Dollar Wage/Input Price	Real Avg. Weekly Wages SIC 6411—Prem Weighted State Average
	Business Services	Real Intermediate Expenses/Input Price	Real Avg Weekly Wages SIC 7300
	Financial Capital	Real Equity Capital (Surplus)	Based on A.M. Best Rating
Cummins and Rubio-Misas (1998)	Labor	Real Peseta Labor Expenditures	Real Avg. Monthly Wages, Spanish Insurance Sector
	Business Services	Real Peseta Business Services	Spanish Business Services Deflator
	Debt Capital	Real Peseta Financial (Non-insurance) Debt Capital	1-Year Spanish Treasury Bill Rate
	Equity Capital	Real Peseta Financial Equity Capital	Rate of Return on Madrid Stock Exchange
Cummins, Turchetti and Weiss (1997)	Home Office Labor	Total Adm. and Mgr Labor Expense/Input Price	Weighted Avg Salary and Rental Deflator
	Agent Labor	Total Acquisition Expenses/Input Price	Business Services Price Deflator
	Fixed Capital	Total Fixed Capital Asset/Input Price	Weighted Avg. Computer and Real Estate Deflator
	Financial Capital	Fin. Capital (Surplus) net of Fixed Capital/Deflator	GDP Deflator

Table 3
(Continued)

Study	Input Type	Input Volume	Input Price
Fukuyama (1997)	Home Office Labor	Office and Internal Workers	
	Agent Labor	Tied Agents and Sales Representatives	
	Fixed Capital	Real Value of Bank Premises and Real Estate	
Cummins, Weiss, and Zi (1999)	Labor	Total Labor Expense/Input Price	Real Avg. Weekly Wages SIC 6331
	Business Services	All Non Labor Expenses/Input Price	Real Avg Weekly Wages SIC 7300—Deflator
	Debt Capital	Real Loss Reserves and Unearned Premium Reserves	Inv. Income Attributed to PH/Input quantity
	Equity Capital	Equity Capital (Surplus)	Expected net income/Avg Input quantity
Cummins and Zi (1998)	Labor	Total Labor Expense/Input Price	Real Avg Weekly Wages SIC 6311
	Materials	All Non Labor Expenses/Input Price	Premium Weighted State Average Composite Index of Expenses (from US Dept of Commerce)
	Financial Capital	Real Equity Capital (Surplus)	3 Year avg net income/equity capital
Berger, Cummins, and Weiss (1997)	Labor	Total Labor Expense/Input Price	Real Avg. Weekly Wages SIC 6331—Prem Weighted State Average
	Business Services	All Non Labor Expense/Input Price	Real Avg. Weekly Wages SIC 7300—Prem Weighted State Average
	Debt Capital	Real Loss Reserves and Unearned Premium Reserves	
	Equity Capital	Real Equity Capital (Surplus)	
Meador, Ryan, and Schellhorn (1997)	Labor		Premium weighted Statewide Avg. Ins. Salary
	Physical Capital		Physical Capital Expenses/Physical Capital Assets
	Materials		Misc. Reported Costs (Non-Variant by firm)

Bernstein (1997) tests also variants of inputs listed	Labor	Total Labor Expenses/Labor Deflator	Labor Price Index Constructed for Life Insurers
	Buildings Capital	Buildings Capital Cost/Buildings Capital Price Index	Buildings Capital Price Index
	Machinery Capital	Machine Capital Cost/Machine Price Capital Index	Machine Price Capital Index
	Materials	Total Material Costs/Input Price	Materials Price Deflator (Published)
Gardner and Grace (1997)	Labor		Premium weighted Statewide Avg. Ins. Salary
	Physical Capital		Physical Capital Expenses/Physical Capital Assets
	Materials		Premium Weighted State Average Composite Index of Expenses (from US Dept of Commerce)
Kim and Grace (1995)	Labor		Weighted Avg Employee and Agent Wages
	Physical Capital		Physical Capital Expense/Physical Capital
	Materials		Adm. + Other Misc. Expenses
Grace (1995)	Labor—Life		Weighted Avg Employee and Agent Wages
	Physical Capital		Physical Capital Expense/Physical Capital
	Materials		Adm. + Other Misc. Expenses
	Labor—P/L		Deflator for Ins Wages—SIC 6331
	Business Services		Deflator for Business Services—SIC 7300
	Financial Capital		Net Income/Capital
Cummins and Weiss (1993)	Labor		Deflator for Ins Wages—SIC 6331
	Business Services		Deflator for Business Services—SIC 7300
	Financial Capital		Net Income/Capital
Yuengert (1993)	Labor		Avg Annual Pay by State of Home Office
	Physical Capital		Avg. Replacement Cost of Nonresidential Cap. in Home Office State

Table 3
(Continued)

Study	Input Type	Input Volume	Input Price
Gardner and Grace (1993)	Labor		Weighted Avg Employee and Agent Wages
	Physical Capital		Physical Capital Expense/Physical Capital
	Materials		Adm. + Other Misc. Expenses
Fecher et al. (1993)	Labor	Labor costs including agents	
	Other Outlays	Outlays such as equip. and supplies	
Grace and Timme (1992)	Labor		Premium Weighted Statewide Avg. Fin. Services Salary
	Physical Capital		Physical Capital Expenses/Physical Capital Assets
	Materials		Miscellaneous Expenses
Weiss (1991)	Labor		National Avg Wage Deflator for SIC 6331
	Materials		Weighted Expense Deflator for Other Non Labor Expenses
	Financial Capital		Net Income/Financial Capital
Weiss (1990)	Labor		National Avg Wage Deflator for SIC 6331
	Materials		Weighted Expense Deflator for Other Non Labor Expenses
	Financial Capital		Cost of Capital for Beta = 1
Weiss (1986)	Supervisor Labor	Number of Hours Paid For	Sup. Labor Expense/Input Quantity
	Other Labor	Number of Hours Paid For	Oth. Labor Expense/Input Quantity
	Agent Labor	Number of Agents	Agent Commission/Input Quantity
	Materials	Intermediate Expense/Input Price	Weighted Expense Deflator
	Home Office Capital	Liab. * (Target Liab/Surplus)	ROR on Stock or Aa bond rate
	Field Office Capital	Field Office Rent/Input Price	Rent Deflator
Kellner and Mathewson (1983)	Agents Input		No factor price
	Advertising		No factor price

Note: P/L = property-liability.

Table 4
Insurance Efficiency Studies—Average Efficiencies

Author(s)	Country	Method	Analysis Type	Type of Instituion	Sample Period	No. of Units/Yr	Average Efficiency Per Year	Note
Berger, Cummins, Weiss, and Zi (1999)	U.S.	DFA	Cost	Life	1988–1992	111	0.337	Joint—Life & P/L firms
		DFA	Revenue	Life	1988–1992	111	0.245	Joint—Life & P/L firms
		DFA	Profit	Life	1988–1992	111	0.182	Joint—Life & P/L firms
		DFA	Cost	Life	1988–1992	293	0.567	Life only
		DFA	Revenue	Life	1988–1992	293	0.395	Life only
		DFA	Profit	Life	1988–1992	293	0.264	Life only
		DFA	Cost	P/L	1988–1992	111	0.505	Joint—Life & P/L firms
		DFA	Revenue	P/L	1988–1992	111	0.547	Joint—Life & P/L firms
		DFA	Profit	P/L	1988–1992	111	0.275	Joint—Life & P/L firms
		DFA	Cost	P/L	1988–1992	280	0.759	P/L only
		DFA	Revenue	P/L	1988–1992	280	0.546	P/L only
		DFA	Profit	P/L	1988–1992	280	0.271	P/L only
Cummins, Tennyson, and Weiss (1999)	U.S.	DEA	Technical	Life	1988–1995	735	0.569	Life only
		DEA	Cost	Life	1988–1995	735	0.358	Life only
		DEA	Scale	Life	1988–1995	735	0.895	Life only
		DEA	Revenue	Life	1988–1995	732	0.337	Life only
Cummins and Rubio-Misas (1998)	Spain	DEA	Pure Technical	Life & P/L	1989–1996	110	0.664	Joint—Life & P/L firms
		DEA	Scale	Life & P/L	1989–1996	110	0.483	Joint—Life & P/L firms
		DEA	Allocative	Life & P/L	1989–1996	110	0.799	Joint—Life & P/L firms
		DEA	Cost	Life & P/L	1989–1996	110	0.256	Joint—Life & P/L firms
Berger, Cummins, and Weiss (1997)	U.S.	DFA	Cost	P/L	1981–1990	472	0.387	Fourier flexible form
		DFA	Profit	P/L	1981–1990	472	0.315	
Cummins and Zi (1998)	U.S.	SFA	Cost	Life	1988–1992	455	0.698	Group data
		DFA	Cost	Life	1988–1992	455	0.455	Group data
		DEA	Cost	Life	1988–1992	455	0.460	Group data
		FDH	Cost	Life	1988–1992	455	0.910	Group data

Table 4
(Continued)

Author(s)	Country	Method	Analysis Type	Type of Institution	Sample Period	No. of Units/Yr	Average Efficiency Per Year	Note
Cummins, Weiss,	U.S.	DEA	Technical	P/L	1981–1990	417	0.869	Pooled frontier results
and Zi (1999)		DEA	Cost	P/L	1981–1990	417	0.600	
Meador, Ryan, and Schellhorn (1997)	U.S.	DFA	Cost	Life	1990–1995	358	0.416	Translog cost function
Kim and Grace (1995)	U.S.	DFA	Cost	Life	1988–1992	248	Not given	Hybrid Box-Cox function
Grace (1995)	U.S.	SFA	Cost	Life	1988	1113	0.757	Truncated normal cost function
		SFA	Cost	P/L	1988	1591	0.486	
Cummins and Weiss	U.S.	SFA	Cost	P/L	1980–1988	261	0.860	
(1993)			Scale	P/L	1980–1988	261	Mixed	
Gardner and Grace (1993)	U.S.	SFA	Cost	Life	1985–1990	561	0.420	
Yuengert (1993)	U.S.	SFA	Cost	Life	1989	757	.35–.5	Normal-half normal, ML
Weiss (1991)	U.S.	SFA	Profit	P/L	1980–1984	100	.67–.82	Generalized Leontief function
Fecher et al. (1993)	France	DEA	Technical	Life	1984–1989	84	0.330	
		SFA	Cost	Life	1984–1989	84	0.500	
		DEA	Technical	P/L	1984–1989	243	0.521	
		SFA	Cost	P/L	1984–1989	243	0.412	
Fukuyama (1997)	Japan	DEA	Technical	Life	1988–1993	25	0.794	Compares mutuals and stocks
		DEA	Scale	Life	1988–1993	25	0.918	
Cummins, Turchetti,	Italy	DEA	Technical	Life & P/L	1986–1993	94	0.682	Survivors sample
and Weiss (1997)		DEA	Technical	Life & P/L	1986–1993	161	0.517	Industry sample

Note: Averages of reported scores shown for some studies. DEA = data envelopment analysis; FDH = free disposal hull; SFA = stochastic frontier approach; DFA = distribution free method P/L = property-liability.

ciency. Thirteen of the sixteen studies summarized in Table 4 estimate cost efficiency, and six studies estimate technical efficiency. Three studies consider profit efficiency, and two report revenue efficiency results. As efficiency analysis evolves, the trend will be towards the estimation of both technical/cost efficiency and revenue/profit efficiency. One reason for this is that estimating only cost or technical efficiency misses the "big picture" question, i.e., whether the firm characteristics under analysis have an impact on the bottom line.

A related reason for investigating revenue/profit efficiency as well as technical/cost efficiency is that looking at the latter types of efficiency alone can produce misleading conclusions. For example, numerous researchers have found that independent agency insurers have higher expense ratios than direct writing insurers and interpreted the results as implying that independent agency firms are less efficient. Berger, Cummins, and Weiss (BCW) (1997) argue that this inference is incorrect. Their cost efficiency estimates confirm that independent agency firms have higher costs than direct writers. However, BCW provide evidence that the higher costs of independent agents are due to product quality differences, arguing that consumers are willing to pay for the higher quality so that the higher costs of independent agency firms are offset by additional revenues. The net result is that there are no significant differences in profit efficiency among insurers using the two distribution systems. Estimating both cost and profit efficiency thus provides a general technique to control for unmeasured differences in the quality of services provided.

The average cost efficiency estimates for life insurers are reasonably consistent across studies. Of the seven U.S. studies that report averages, four report average cost efficiencies between 0.35 and 0.5, a fifth (Cummins and Zi 1998) reports scores in this range for some methodologies, and a sixth (Berger, Cummins, Weiss, and Zi 1999) reports scores in this range for the life insurance operations of firms that produce both life and property-liability insurance. Higher scores were reported by Cummins and Zi (1998) for their econometric models (excepting DFA) and FDH, by Grace (1995), using econometrics, and by Berger, Cummins, Weiss, and Zi (1999) for insurers specializing in life insurance. DEA scores are generally expected to be lower than econometric scores, because DEA measures all departures from the frontier as inefficiency, whereas the econometric approach allows for random error. However, this expectation is not always borne out in practice, i.e., DEA gives lower efficiency scores than the econometric approach for some data sets (see, for example, Ferrier and Lovell 1990 for U.S. banks, and Fecher, et al. 1993 for French property-liability insurers) probably because the efficiency scores also are expected to reflect the appropriateness of the methodologies for the data. E.g., the use of an inappropriate functional form or distributional assumption could result in econometric efficiencies that are lower than DEA efficiencies. The higher scores for FDH than for DEA also are expected given the relaxation of the convexity condition.

The *P/L* efficiency scores are less consistent across studies. The averages for U.S. studies range from 0.39 to 0.86, while Fecher, et al. (1993) find average cost efficiency of 0.41 for French P/L insurers. The dispersion of scores within the industry are generally relatively high in insurance relative to banking, perhaps suggesting that insurers have been somewhat sheltered from competition, at least in the past.

24.5.3 Economies of Scale and Scope

Table 5 summarizes the results of scale and scope studies that use modern frontier efficiency techniques, with the exception of Kellner and Mathewson (1983) and Grace and Timme (1992), which are included because they have received a significant amount of attention in the literature. In considering the results, it is important to keep in mind that DEA solves the optimization problem for each insurer and thus provides a unit-specific estimate of scale economies. However, the econometric approach estimates a single function that applies to all insurers in the sample and thus provides less specific information about economies of scale. In addition, the use of cost functions such as the translog and quadratic force the estimated models to have regions of increasing, constant, and decreasing returns to scale. DEA does not suffer from this potential problem because it does not require the specification of a functional form.

Economies of scale are present if the unit costs of production decline as firm size (output volume) increases. The two DEA studies of U.S. life insurers summarized in Table 5 both find that most life insurers with less than $1 billion in assets are operating with increasing returns to scale and that the majority of larger firms are operating with decreasing returns to scale (Cummins, Tennyson and Weiss (CTW) 1999, Cummins and Zi 1998). However, these studies find a number of firms that operate with constant returns to scale even in the largest size categories.

Using an econometric model, Grace and Timme (1992) find that increasing returns to scale disappear for the largest quartile of stock insurers but that increasing returns are present for all quartiles of mutuals. They do not report quartile boundaries, but based on the Cummins-Tennyson-Weiss study, the largest size quartile begins at roughly $1 billion. Thus, Grace and Timme's results are consistent with CTW in terms of the region in which returns to scale disappear. Yuengert (1993), on the other hand, also using an econometric model, finds that returns to scale do not disappear until around $15 billion in assets. Based on the CTW asset size distribution, $15 billion is approximately the 98th percentile.

The CTW study used scale economy estimates primarily as an explanatory variable, and scale economy results were not presented in their article. Because scale economies is an important topic and CTW estimated the most detailed set of results currently available, we present their scale economy results for U.S. life insurers in Table 6. The Cummins-Zi (1998) results are also reproduced in the table for purposes of comparison. The table shows the percentage of firms operating in the segments of the DEA frontier characterized by increasing, constant, and decreasing returns to scale in each of ten asset size categories. There is a very definite inverse relationship

Table 5
Scale and Scope Economies In the Insurance Industry

Author	Country	Method	Analysis Type	Type of Institution	Sample Period	No of Units/Yr	Result	Notes
Berger, Cummins, Weiss, and Zi (1999)	U.S.	DFA	Scope	Life & P/L	1988–1992	684	Positive cost economies (.248), negative revenue economies (–.195), positive profit economies (.036)	Composite Functional Form New scope methodology Cost and revenue economies significant at 1 percent level
Meador, Ryan, and Schellhorn (1998)	U.S.	DFA	Diversification vs. Focus	Life	1990–1995	321	Firms diversified across multiple products are more efficient than focused firms	Translog cost function
Cummins, Tennyson, and Weiss (1999)	U.S.	DEA	Scale	Life	1988–1995	735	IRS to $1 billion assets, then DRS CRS for some firms of all sizes	
Cummins and Rubio-Misas (1998)	Spain	DEA	Scale	Life & P/L	1989–1996	110	57% IRS, 20% CRS, 23% DRS (1996)	

Table 5
(Continued)

Author	Country	Method	Analysis Type	Type of Institution	Sample Period	No of Units/Yr	Result	Notes
Cummins and Zi (1998)	U.S.	Multiple	Scale	Life	1988–1992	445	IRS to $1 billion assets, then DRS CRS for a few firms of all sizes	
Yuengert (1993)	U.S.	Multiple	Scale	Life	1989	757	IRS up to $15 billion assets; then CRS	
		Multiple	Scope	Life	1989	757	No support	
Grace and Timme (1992)	U.S.	FIML	Scale	Life	1987	423	Increasing to constant in largest quartile (S); increasing all quartiles (M)	Hybrid translog cost function
		FIML	Scope	Life	1987	423	No clear support	Hybrid translog cost function
Kellner and Mathewson (1983)	Canada	ML	Scale	Life	1961, 66, 71, 76	All Canada	Constant returns to scale	No input prices, Hybrid translog
		ML	Scope	Life	1961, 66, 71, 76	All Canada	Some support in 61, 66, 71, none in 76	No input prices, Hybrid translog

Note: Averages of reported scores shown for some studies. P/L = property-liability.
Key:
- ML Maximum Likelihood Technique
- FIML Full Information Maximum Likelihood Technique
- Multiple More than one method
- DFA Distribution Free
- S Stock insurers
- M Mutual insurers.

Table 6

Scale Economies in the U.S. Life Insurance Industry

Year	<30M	30M–50M	50M–100M	100M–300M	300M–1B	1B–2.5B	2.5B–5B	5B–10B	10B–15B	>15B	All Firms
1995*											
%IRS	76.6%	61.4%	55.4%	43.6%	19.0%	8.5%	4.9%	2.9%	0.0%	0.0%	37.1%
%CRS	19.1%	19.3%	18.5%	20.5%	24.6%	29.3%	22.0%	28.6%	18.8%	21.7%	22.3%
%DRS	4.3%	19.3%	26.2%	35.9%	56.3%	62.2%	73.2%	68.6%	81.3%	78.3%	40.6%
1994*											
%IRS	71.5%	59.4%	56.6%	40.9%	25.9%	14.5%	4.3%	0.0%	0.0%	0.0%	39.7%
%CRS	21.2%	18.8%	18.4%	24.8%	22.2%	27.6%	19.6%	23.3%	21.4%	28.6%	22.4%
%DRS	7.3%	21.9%	25.0%	34.3%	51.9%	57.9%	76.1%	76.7%	78.6%	71.4%	38.0%
1993*											
%IRS	78.9%	66.0%	63.5%	51.0%	36.0%	6.9%	0.0%	0.0%	0.0%	0.0%	45.4%
%CRS	15.6%	19.1%	10.8%	7.3%	15.3%	20.7%	11.4%	14.3%	30.0%	31.6%	14.9%
%DRS	5.5%	14.9%	25.7%	41.7%	48.6%	72.4%	88.6%	85.7%	70.0%	68.4%	39.7%
1992*											
%IRS	80.5%	78.0%	71.4%	50.5%	20.6%	0.0%	0.0%	0.0%	0.0%	0.0%	45.2%
%CRS	14.6%	12.0%	10.0%	14.0%	28.4%	20.4%	8.8%	12.5%	37.5%	37.5%	17.3%
%DRS	4.9%	10.0%	18.6%	35.5%	51.0%	79.6%	91.2%	87.5%	62.5%	62.5%	37.5%
1991*											
%IRS	41.5%	39.2%	38.8%	35.4%	23.6%	6.0%	0.0%	0.0%	0.0%	0.0%	30.4%
%CRS	7.9%	10.3%	10.1%	6.7%	15.8%	16.9%	18.8%	6.3%	12.5%	22.7%	11.1%
%DRS	50.6%	50.5%	51.1%	57.9%	60.6%	77.1%	81.3%	93.8%	87.5%	77.3%	58.5%
1990*											
%IRS	67.7%	57.7%	31.3%	10.1%	3.8%	0.0%	0.0%	0.0%	0.0%	0.0%	26.7%
%CRS	23.1%	30.8%	38.8%	34.3%	21.9%	23.0%	22.2%	40.0%	33.3%	18.2%	27.7%
%DRS	9.2%	11.5%	29.9%	55.6%	74.3%	77.0%	77.8%	60.0%	66.7%	81.8%	45.5%
Cummins & Zi (1998)**											
%IRS	94.7%	94.1%	85.2%	84.1%	54.7%	16.7%	11.1%	4.2%	0.0%		62.9%
%CRS	5.3%	3.9%	5.6%	2.4%	9.4%	7.1%	7.4%	8.3%	15.4%		6.3%
%DRS	0.0%	2.0%	9.3%	13.4%	35.9%	76.2%	81.5%	87.5%	84.6%		30.8%

Key: M stands for millions of constant dollars, B stands for billions of constant dollars, IRS = increasing returns to scale, CRS = constant returns to scale, DRS = decreasing returns to scale.

* Results based on Cummins, Tennyson, Weiss (1998) study but not published in their paper.

** Cummins and Zi's last size category is >10 billion. The Cummins and Zi results are 5-year averages for 1988–1992.

between asset size and the percentage of firms operating with IRS and a corresponding direct relationship between size and the proportion of firms operating with DRS. Interestingly, however, a significant proportion of the largest firms manage to operate with CRS. A useful topic for future research would be to investigate the characteristics of the large CRS firms to identify the "best practices" that enable this group of firms to avoid DRS.

These results are important because of the consolidation that is taking place in the life insurance industry. If scale economies disappear at about $1 billion, then it is difficult to justify mergers within the top quartile of the life insurers on cost economy grounds; and if firms with more than $1 billion tend to encounter DRS rather than CRS, mergers and acquisitions in this size range become even more difficult to justify. More research is clearly needed to resolve this issue; and more research is needed on scale economies in the property-liability insurance industry, which is also undergoing consolidation.

The issue of scope economies is also important because of the increasing prevalence of cross-industry mergers involving life insurers, property-liability insurers, and other financial institutions. Because scope economies are studied less frequently than scale economies, it is useful to define the concept. For simplicity, we focus on the case of firms that produce at most two outputs. Cost scope economies are defined as follows:

$$S_C^T = \frac{C(y_1, 0; w_1) + C(0, y_2; w_2) - C(y_1, y_2; w_1, w_2)}{C(y_1, y_2; w_1, w_2)} \tag{24}$$

where S_C^T = cost scope economies; $C_J(\bullet)$ = the cost function; y_1, y_2 = outputs; and w_1, w_2 = input prices. If $S_C^T > 0$, *cost scope economies* are present, i.e., it is more costly for specialist firms to produce the two outputs separately than for a joint firm to produce both outputs; and if $S_C^T < 0$, *cost scope diseconomies* are present, i.e., separate production is more efficient than joint production. Whereas scale economies result from spreading fixed costs over higher output volume, scope cost economies arise due to *production complementarities*, i.e., the joint use of some or all inputs. For example, a firm that writes both life and property-liability insurance needs to develop only one prospect list, which can be used in producing both types of insurance. Executive talent and brand names are other resources that can give rise to production complementarities.

Revenue scope economies are defined as follows:

$$S_R^T = \frac{R(y_1, y_2; w_1, w_2) - R(y_1, 0; w_1) - R(0, y_2; w_2)}{R(y_1, y_2; w_1, w_2)} \tag{25}$$

If $S_R^T > 0$, *revenue scope economies* are present and a joint producing firm will earn higher revenues by producing outputs y_1 and y_2 than would be earned by specialist firms producing these outputs; and if $S_R^T < 0$, *revenue scope diseconomies* are present, and specialists earn more than joint producers. Revenue scope economies arise due to *consumption complementarities*, e.g., customers may be willing to pay more to a joint producer because of the value of convenience or lower search costs that arise from buying more than one product from the same producer. Revenue scope diseconomies could arise if specialists provide higher quality products than joint producers, for example, because they are better able to tailor products to customers' specific needs. Profit scope economies are defined analogously to revenue scope economies and represent the net effects of production and consumption complementarities.[23]

There have been only a few studies of cost scope economies and only one study of revenue and profit scope economies in the insurance industry. Neither Yuengert (1993) nor Grace and Timme (1992) find evidence of cost scope economies in the U.S. life insurance industry. Kellner and Mathewson (1983) find some evidence of cost scope economies for Canadian life insurers in the earlier years of their sample period but not for their most recent year. Their study is dated, however, ending in 1976. Although not strictly speaking a scope economies study, Meador, Ryan, and Schellhorn (1998) find that firms that are diversified across multiple product lines are more efficient than those following a more focused strategy.

Berger, et al. (1999) provide the only extant study of scope economies across the life and property-liability (*P/L*) segments of the U.S. insurance industry and also the only insurance study to estimate revenue and profit as well as cost scope economies. They analyze firms that produce both life and *P/L* insurance as well as life insurance specialists and *P/L* specialists. They test the *conglomeration hypothesis,* which holds that operating a broad range of businesses leads to cost scope economies through sharing inputs in joint production and/or revenue scope economies through providing "one-stop shopping" to consumers who are willing to pay for the extra convenience. The competing hypothesis is the *strategic focus hypothesis*, which holds that firms can maximize value by focusing on core businesses and core competencies. Under this hypothesis, conglomeration is viewed as reflecting agency problems and managerial opportunism.

Berger, et al. (1999) find evidence of statistically significant cost scope economies for firms at the first size quartile, the median, and the third size quartile. At the first size quartile and the median, they find significant revenue diseconomies of scope that wipe out the cost economies, leading to zero profit economies of scope. However, there are no revenue economies or diseconomies for firms at the third size quartile so that cost scope economies translate into profit scope economies for these firms. Thus, the overall conclusion is that profit scope economies are more likely to be realized

[23] Berger, et al. (1999) develop an alternative to the traditional scope economy measures shown as equations (24) and (25). They estimate separate functions for joint producers and specialists in order to allow for differences in technology between joint producing and specializing firms. For their data set, the new approach gives significantly different scope estimates than the traditional approach.

for large insurers. They also find evidence that insurers with vertically integrated marketing systems such as exclusive agents are more likely to realize profit scope economies than firms using non-integrated systems such as independent agents.

24.5.4 Total Factor Productivity Growth

Several papers explore the issue of total factor productivity (TFP) growth in the insurance industry. Measuring TFP growth is important to gauge the effects of changing industry structure such as the wave of mergers and acquisitions currently underway in the U.S. insurance industry. It is also important to measure the effects of changes in management practices and the introduction of new technologies. The two principal approaches to measuring TFP growth are non-frontier TFP indices and the Malmquist index method.

The results of TFP studies in the insurance industry are summarized in Table 7. Three studies have utilized the non-frontier index approach, five have utilized the Malmquist approach, and one used an econometric approach. Cummins, Tennyson, and Weiss (1999) find productivity growth of 4.1 percent per year in the U.S. life insurance industry for the period 1991–1994, while Cummins, Weiss, and Zi (1999) find virtually no growth in productivity in the U.S. property-liability insurance industry for the period 1981–1990. It is possible that advances in technology have led to higher productivity gains for the property-liability insurance industry during the 1990s, and this would be an interesting topic for future research.

Malmquist index analyses of Japanese life insurers (Fukuyama, 1997) and Italian life and property-liability insurers (Cummins, Turchetti, and Weiss, 1996) show efficiency gains that are considerably higher than in the U.S. Fukuyama reports TFP gains of about 19 percent for Japanese life insurers over the period 1988–1993. Cummins, Turchetti, and Weiss find that firms which were in the Italian market for the entire period 1986–1993 showed TFP gains of about 3.4 percent per year but that when firms that entered or exited are included in the sample, efficiency gains are about 19 percent per year. Cummins and Rubio-Misas find that Spanish stock insurers improved total factor productivity by about 3 percent per year over the period 1989–1996, while Spanish mutuals experienced TFP regress of 3.5 percent per year over the same period. The non-frontier index methodology studies tend to show more modest efficiency gains for insurers in the U.S., Canada, Japan, and three European countries.

24.5.5 Other Economic Hypotheses

Efficiency analysis has been used to investigate a number of economic hypotheses and issues in addition to economies of scale and scope and total factor productivity (see Table 8). One important issue is the effect of organizational form on performance. The two major hypotheses about organizational form are the *expense preference* hypothesis (Mester 1991) and the *managerial discretion* hypothesis (Mayers and

Table 7
Total Factor Productivity in the Insurance Industry

Author	Country	Method (Index)	Analysis Type	Type of Instituion	Sample Period	No. of Units/Yr	TE Change Per Year	Technical Change Per Year	Malmquist Index Per Year
Cummins, Tennyson, and Weiss (1999)[1]	U.S.	Malmquist	Technical	Life	1991–1994	535	1.066	0.990	1.041
Cummins and Rubio-Misas (1998)	Spain	Malmquist	TFP Growth	Life & P/L	1989–1996	117	1.030 Stock 0.991 Mutual	0.999 Stock 0.973 Mutual	1.029 Stock 0.965 Mutual
Cummins, Weiss, and Zi (1999)[2]	U.S.	Malmquist	Technical	P/L	1981–1990	417	0.997	1.005	1.002
Fukuyama (1997)[3]	Japan	Malmquist	Technical	Life	1988–1993	25	1.035	1.164	1.189
Cummins, Turchetti and Weiss (1996)[4]	Italy[5]	Malmquist	Technical	Life & P/L	1986–1993	94	0.999	1.035	1.034
	Italy[6]	Malmquist	Technical	Life & P/L	1986–1993	161	1.060	1.120	1.187
Bernstein (1997)	Canada	Divisia	TFP Growth	Life	1979–1989	12	Approx. 2% growth per year		
		Divisia	Tech. Component	Life	1979–1989	12	More important than scale		
		Divisia	Scale Component	Life	1979–1989	12	Slightly increasing		
Weiss (1991)	Five[7]	Divisia	TFP Growth	P/L	1975–1987	5	W. Ger, France, & Switz highest growth		
		Multilateral	Relative TFP			5	U.S. and Germany highest TFP growth		
Weiss (1990)	U.S.	Cost Funct	TFP Growth	P/L	1980–1984	100	TFP growth 1% per year		
Weiss (1986)	U.S.	Divisia	TFP Growth	Life	1976–1980	2	Some TFP decline; illustrates method		
		Exact	TFP Growth	Life	1976–1980	2	Similar to Divisia		

Note: Averages of reported scores shown for some studies.
Key: DEA = Data Envelopment Analysis, P/L = property-liability insurers, TE = technical efficiency.
Divisia Index and Exact Index [Diewert (1981)]
Multilateral Index Multilateral Index [Caves, Christensen, and Diewert (1982)]
Cost Funct Cost Function estimated, parameters analyzed (normally distributed error term)
[1] Compares merged and nonmerged firms. [2] Compares mutuals and stocks. [3] Compares mutuals and stocks. [4] Determinants of efficiency identified. [5] Sample consists of firms present for all years of the sample period. [6] Sample consists of maximum number of firms in each year. [7] Countries are U.S., Japan, France, Switzerland, Germany.

Table 8
Other Economic Issues and Hypotheses

Author	Country	Type of Institution	Issue/Hypothesis	Findings
Berger, Cummins, Weiss and Zi (1999)	U.S.	Life & P/L	New methodology to measure scope economies Conglomeration versus Strategic Focus	Traditional method to measure scope misleading Conglomeration benefits for large, personal, lines, vertically integrated, profit efficient firms Strategic Focus benefits for small, commercial lines, non vertically integrated, profit efficient firms
Cummins, Tennyson, and Weiss (1999)	U.S.	Life	Efficiency of merger/acquisition targets Returns to scale and acquisitions Financial strength and acquisitions Group affiliation and acquisitions	Target firm efficiency gains > for non-targets Acquirers prefer IRS and CRS firms Vulnerable firms more likely to be acquired. Unaffiliated firms less likely to be acquired
Cummins, Weiss, and Zi (1999)	U.S.	P/L	Organizational form	Stocks and mutuals have different technologies (supports managerial discretion hypothesis) Mutuals less successful at minimizing costs (also supports expense preference hypothesis)
Cummins and Rubio-Misas (1998)	Spain	Life & P/L	Introduction of European Economic Union's Third Generation Directives	Cost efficiency declined following introduction of Directives

Cummins and Zi (1998)	U.S.	Life	Organizational form	Stocks and mutuals equally efficient
Fukuyama (1997)	Japan	Life	Organizational form	Stocks and mutuals have identical technologies Performance differs by org form under different economic conditions
Carr (1997)	U.S.	Life	Management strategies	Career agency firms more efficient than brokers Technology improves efficiency
Gardner and Grace (1993)	U.S.	Life	Organizational form External monitoring	Stocks and mutuals equally efficient Stringently regulated firms are more efficient
Berger, Cummins and Weiss (1997)	U.S.	P/L	Insurance distribution systems	Independent agents less cost efficient but equally profit efficient as direct writers
Cummins, Turchetti, and Weiss (1996)	Italy	Life/P-L	Insurance distribution systems	Direct writers less efficient than ind agents* New entrants more efficient than incumbent firms Telemarketing not more efficient than agents
Fecher et al. (1993)	France	Life/P-L	Organizational form	Stock life insurers more efficient than mutuals Mutual P/L insurers more efficient than stocks
Weiss (1990)	U.S.	P/L	Rate regulation	Regulated rates > competitive rates, 1980–84 Some cost subsidization among lines, especially in regulated states

Note: Averages of reported scores shown for some studies, P/L = property-liability, ind agents = independent agents.

*Direct writers and independent agents have different relationships with insurers in comparison with the U.S. so the Italian and U.S. results not directly comparable.

Smith 1988). These non-mutually exclusive hypotheses are based on the agency theoretic observation that the mutual organizational form provides weaker mechanisms for owners to control managers than the stock organizational form. The expense preference hypothesis holds that mutuals will be less efficient than stocks because managers will behave opportunistically, engaging in higher perquisite consumption than stock managers. The managerial discretion hypothesis posits that mutuals will be more successful in lines of business and other activities that involve relatively low managerial discretion such as lines with good actuarial tables. The hypothesis predicts that stocks are more likely to succeed in lines where managers need more discretion such as complex commercial coverages. The managerial discretion hypothesis implies that stocks and mutuals will use different technologies, where technology is defined as including the contractual relationships that comprise the firm, as well as physical technology choices. Stocks and mutuals are predicted to be sorted into market segments where they are relatively successful in dealing with various types of agency costs, and efficiency differences between the two firm types are not necessarily predicted.

An analysis of the efficiency of U.S. mutual and stock property-liability insurers is presented in Cummins, Weiss, and Zi (CWZ) (1999). They estimate a pooled frontier, including both organizational forms, and separate frontiers for mutuals and stocks. Hypothesis tests show that stocks and mutuals are using different technologies, supporting the managerial discretion hypothesis. They also perform a *cross-frontier* analysis, computing efficiencies of mutuals (stocks) against a reference set consisting of all stock (mutual) firms. If the distance of mutuals (stocks) from the stock (mutual) frontier is greater than the distance from their own frontier, the implication is that the stock technology dominates the mutual technology. CWZ find that the stock technology dominates the mutual technology for producing stock output vectors, and that the mutual technology dominates the stock technology for producing mutual output vectors. This supports the managerial discretion hypothesis prediction that firms are sorted into market segments where they have comparative advantages. However, in the cross-frontier *cost* efficiency analysis, they find that the stock cost frontier dominates the mutual cost frontier, implying that mutuals are less successful in minimizing costs. Thus, the paper also supports the expense preference hypothesis. Efficiency analysis thus enables researchers to come to a much richer understanding of firm performance than the conventional approach of using a single dummy variable to differentiate between stocks and mutuals.

Another analysis of organizational form is provided by Fukuyama's (1997) study of Japanese life insurers. He finds that the Japanese stock and mutual insurers have identical technologies. Neither organizational form is clearly dominant in terms of efficiency, but the organizational forms tend to perform differently relative to one another depending on the economic conditions.

The effects of organizational form on the efficiency of U.S. life insurers have been analyzed by Gardner and Grace (1993) and Cummins and Zi (1998). Neither study finds significant efficiency differences between stocks and mutuals. However, it would be interesting to conduct a cross-frontier analysis to determine if a more sophisticated approach would find differences in efficiency by organizational form. Fecher, et al. (1993) analyze French life and non-life insurers. They find that stock life insurers have higher average efficiency scores than mutuals, but mutual non-life insurers have higher efficiencies than stocks.

The effect of insurance distribution systems on efficiency has been studied by Cummins, Turchetti, and Weiss (CTcW) (1996) and Berger, Cummins, and Weiss (BCW) (1997). CTcW find significant efficiency differences between direct writing and independent agency firms in their sample of Italian insurers. BCW shed additional light on this time-honored area of empirical investigation, as discussed above, finding that the higher costs of U.S. independent agency firms are due to unmeasured differences in service intensity that are compensated for by higher revenues.

Another application of efficiency analysis in insurance is to analyze the efficiency effects of mergers and acquisitions (M&A) (Cummins, Tennyson, and Weiss 1999). CTW analyze the efficiency effects of mergers and acquisitions in the U.S. life insurance industry, covering the period 1988–1995. They find that acquisition targets tend to show significantly larger efficiency gains between the post and pre-acquisition periods than a control group of firms not involved in M&A activity. They further find that acquirers tend to acquire target firms that are operating with non-decreasing returns to scale. Weiss (1990) and Carr (1997) use productivity and efficiency estimates to investigate the effects on firm performance of regulation and management strategies, respectively, providing additional evidence of the versatility of efficiency analysis.

Finally, Cummins and Rubio-Mises (1998) evaluate changes in the efficiency of Spanish insurers following the introduction of the European Union's (EU) Third Generation Directives in July 1994. The Third Generation Directives created a single-license system, whereby an insurer licensed in one EU country can do business in all EU countries without obtaining additional licenses or being regulated by host countries. The Directives also freed insurers from price regulation and removed other impediments to competition. The Directives were expected to increase competition in European insurance markets. Cummins and Rubio-Misas (1998) find that efficiency declined following the introduction of the Directives, primarily due to allocative inefficiency. They interpret this result as implying that insurers either made mistakes in adjusting to the new environment or had to incur non-recurring costs in order to adjust to deregulation.

24.6 SUMMARY AND CONCLUSIONS

Modern frontier efficiency and productivity methodologies are rapidly becoming the dominant approach to measuring firm performance using accounting data. These methodologies estimate "best practice" efficient technical, cost, revenue, and profit frontiers based on DMU-level data. Frontier efficiency methods have been applied to analyze a wide range of industries and public entities in many different nations. Frontier methodologies can also be used to analyze growth in total factor productivity.

The two primary methods for estimating efficient frontiers are the econometric approach and the mathematical programming approach. Because each has advantages and disadvantages, it is advisable to estimate efficiency using more than one method. The econometric approach involves estimating a cost, revenue, or profit function, while the mathematical programming approach is a non-parametric approach implemented using linear programming. The mathematical programming approach provides a particularly convenient method for decomposing cost efficiency into pure technical, scale, and allocative efficiency.

There are many important applications of frontier efficiency methods. One important application is the measurement of scale and scope economies. Measuring scale and scope economies is particularly important when industry structure is changing rapidly due to mergers, acquisitions, insolvencies, or other factors. Another important application is to measure the growth in total factor productivity (TFP). TFP growth can then be analyzed for correlations with various macro and micro-economic conditions to determine the drivers of productivity in an industry or economy. Frontier efficiency analysis also is useful in testing hypotheses about firm or industry structure, such as the effects of organizational form and product distribution systems, leading to a richer understanding of the issues than conventional approaches.

Another use of efficiency analysis is in comparing performance of departments, divisions, or profit centers within a firm. Mathematical programming is particularly useful for this purpose because it is not as demanding in terms of degrees of freedom as the econometric approach and performs the optimization separately for each decision making unit. Regulators also can benefit from efficiency analysis. The Federal Reserve has used efficiency analysis to study the effects of bank branching, mega-mergers, and other elements of banking industry structure. This type of analysis could be used in insurance to study industry consolidation, expense and rate regulation, and solvency regulation. Efficiency and productivity analysis also has been used in cross-national comparisons of efficiency of firms and other institutions.

An important trend in the literature is to estimate profit and/or revenue efficiency in addition to technical and cost efficiency. Technical and cost efficiency are useful in studying the efficiency effects of firm characteristics and of new policies, strategies, and technologies. However, the ultimate test of any organizational feature is its impact on the bottom line, i.e., ultimately on profit. It is clearly possible to introduce a new strategy or technique in one area of the firm that improves cost efficiency which never finds its way to the bottom line due to inefficiencies in other sectors of the firm. The only way to tell whether a program has met with ultimate success is to measure its effects on profit efficiency.

A wide range of under-researched insurance topics provide fruitful avenues for future research. Economies of scale in the property-liability insurance industry has received little attention using modern frontier efficiency methods. Organizational form in the life insurance industry could be investigated using the cross-frontier approach to provide further tests of the expense preference and managerial discretion hypotheses. Analyzing the efficiency of life insurance distribution systems using cost and profit functions could determine whether unmeasured product quality differences exist in the life insurance industry. The effects of consolidation on efficiency in the property-liability insurance industry also would be an interesting topic. A further example of potential future research would be an analysis of corporate governance on efficiency in the insurance industry. Finally, frontier methods will be very useful in studying economies of scope across the financial services industry as mergers and acquisitions involving insurers, banks, mutual fund companies, securities dealers, and other types of financial services firms become more widespread.

24.7 REFERENCES

Aigner, D., K. Lovell and P. Schmidt (1977). "Formulation and Estimation of Stochastic Frontier Production Function Models," *Journal of Econometrics* 6, 21–37.

Aly, H.Y., R. Grabowski, C. Pasurka and N. Rangan (1990). "Technical, Scale, and Allocative Efficiencies in U.S. Banking: An Empirical Investigation," *Review of Economics and Statistics* 72, 211–218.

Armknecht, P.A. and D.H. Ginsburg (1992). "Improvements in Measuring Price Changes In Consumer Services," in Z. Griliches, ed., *Output Measurement in the Service Sectors*, National Bureau of Economic Research, Studies in Income and Wealth, Vol. 56, University of Chicago Press (Chicago, IL), 109–156.

Arrow, Kenneth, (1971). *Essays in the Theory of Risk Bearing* (Chicago: Markham Publishing Company).

Battese, G. and G. Corra (1977). "Estimation of Production Frontier Models With Application to the Pastoral Zone of Eastern Australia," *Australian Journal of Agricultural Economics* 21, 167–179.

Bauer, Paul W., Allen N. Berger, Gary D. Ferrier and David B. Humphrey (1998). "Consistency Conditions for Regulatory Analysis of Financial Institutions: A Comparison of Frontier Efficiency Methods," *Journal of Economics and Business* 50, 85–114.

Berger, Allen N. (1993). "'Distribution-Free' Estimates of Efficiency in the U.S. Banking Industry and Tests of the Standard Distributional Assumptions," *Journal of Productivity Analysis* 4, 261–292.

Berger, Allen N., J. David Cummins and Mary A. Weiss (1997). "The Coexistence of Multiple Distribution Systems for Financial Services: The Case of Property-Liability Insurance," *Journal of Business* 70, 515–546.

Berger, Allen N., J. David Cummins, Mary A. Weiss and Hongmin Zi. (1999). "Conglomeration Versus Strategic Focus: Evidence from the Insurance Industry," Forthcoming in *Journal of Financial Intermediation*.

Berger, Allen N. and David B. Humphrey (1991). "The Dominance of Inefficiencies over Scale and Product Mix Economies in Banking," *Journal of Monetary Economics* 28, 117–148.

Berger, Allen N. and David B. Humphrey (1992a). "Megamergers in Banking and the Use of Cost Efficiency as an Antitrust Defense," *Antitrust Bulletin* 37, 541–600.

Berger, Allen N. and David B. Humphrey (1992b). "Measurement and Efficiency Issues in Commercial Banking," in Z. Griliches, ed., *Output Measurement in the Service Sectors*, National Bureau of Economic Research, Studies in Income and Wealth, Vol. 56, University of Chicago Press (Chicago, IL), 245–279.

Berger, Allen N. and David B. Humphrey (1997). "Efficiency of Financial Institutions: International Survey and Directions for Future Research," *European Journal of Operational Research* 98, 175–212.

Berger, Allen N. and Loretta J. Mester (1997). "Inside the Black Box: What Explains Differences in the Efficiencies of Financial Institutions?" *Journal of Banking & Finance* 21 (7), 895–947.

Bernstein, J.I. (1997). "Total Factor Productivity Growth in the Canadian Life Insurance Industry: 1979–1989," CSLS Conference on Service Centre Productivity and the Productivity Paradox, April 11–12, Ottawa, Canada.

Carr, Roderick M. (1997). "Strategic Choices, Firm Efficiency and Competitiveness in the US Life Insurance Industry," Doctoral Dissertation, Wharton School, University of Pennsylvania, Philadelphia.

Caves, D., L. Christensen and W.E. Diewert (1982). "The Economic Theory of Index Numbers and the Measurement of Input, Output, and Productivity," *Econometrica* 50 (6), 1393–1414.

Caves, Douglas W., Laurits R. Christensen and Michael W. Tretheway, (1980). "Flexible Cost Functions for Multiproduct Firms," *Review of Economics and Statistics* 62, 477–481.

Charnes, Abraham, William Cooper, Arie Y. Lewin and Lawrence M. Seiford (1994). *Data Envelopment Analysis: Theory, Methodology, and Applications* (Norwell, MA: Kluwer Academic Publishers).

Charnes, Abraham, William Cooper and Edwardo Rhodes (1978). "Measuring the Efficiency of Decision Making Units," *European Journal of Operational Research* 2, 429–444.

Christensen, Laurits R, Dale W. Jorgenson and Lawrence J. Lau (1973). "Transcendental Logarithmic Production Frontiers," *Review of Economics and Statistics* 55, 28–45.

Clark, Jeffrey A. (1996). "Economic Cost, Scale Efficiency and Competitive Viability in Banking," *Journal of Money, Credit, and Banking* 28, 25–31.

Cowing, Thomas G. and Rodney E. Stevenson (1981). *Productivity Measurement in Regulated Industries* (New York: Academic Press).

Cummins, J. David (1990). "Multi-Period Discounted Cash Flow Ratemaking Models in Property-Liability Insurance," *Journal of Risk and Insurance* 57, 79–109.

Cummins, J. David, Martin F. Grace and Richard D. Phillips (1999). "Regulatory Solvency Prediction in Property-liability Insurance: Risk-based Capital, Audit Ratios, And Cash Flow Simulation," *Journal of Risk and Insurance* 66, 417–458.

Cummins, J. David (1999). "Efficiency in the U.S. Life Insurance Industry: Are Insurers Minimizing Costs and Maximizing Revenues?" in J.D. Cummins and A.M. Santomero, eds., *Changes in the Life Insurance Industry: Efficiency, Technology, and Risk Management*. (Norwell, MA: Kluwer Academic Publishers).

Cummins, J. David and Patricia M. Danzon (1997). "Price Shocks and Capital Flows in Liability Insurance." *Journal of Financial Intermediation* 6, 3–38.

Cummins, J. David and Maria Rubio-Misas (1998). "Deregulation and Consolidation In The Spanish Insurance Industry: Efficiency Effects," working paper, Wharton Financial Institutions Center, Philadelphia.

Cummins, J. David, Sharon Tennyson and Mary A. Weiss (1999). "Consolidation and Efficiency in the U.S. Life Insurance Industry," *Journal of Banking and Finance* 23, 325–357.

Cummins, J. David, Giuseppe Turchetti and Mary A. Weiss (1997). "Productivity and Technical Efficiency in the Italian Insurance Industry," working paper, Wharton Financial Institutions Center, University of Pennsylvania, Philadelphia.

Cummins, J. David and Mary A. Weiss (1993). "Measuring Cost Efficiency in the Property-Liability Insurance Industry," *Journal of Banking and Finance* 17, 463–481.

Cummins, J. David, Mary A. Weiss and Hongmin Zi. (1999). "Organizational Form and Efficiency: An Analysis of Stock and Mutual Property-Liability Insurers," *Management Science* 45, 1254–1269.

Cummins, J. David and Hongmin Zi. (1998). "Measuring Economic Efficiency of the US Life Insurance Industry: Econometric and Mathematical Programming Techniques,"*Journal of Productivity Analysis* 10, 131–15.

Deprins, E., L. Simar and H. Tulkens (1984). "Measuring Labor Efficiency in Post Offices," in M. Marchand, P. Pestieau and H. Tulkens, eds., *The Performance of Public Enterprises: Concepts and Measurement* (Amsterdam, North Holland).

Diewert, W. Erwin (1995)."Functional Form Problems in Modeling Insurance and Gambling," *Geneva Papers on Risk and Insurance Theory* 20, 135–150.

Diewert, W. Erwin (1981). "The Theory of Total Factor Productivity Measurement in Regulated Industries," in T.G. Cowing and R. Stevenson (eds.) *Productivity Measurement in Regulated Industries.* (New York: Academic Press).

Färe, R., S. Grosskopf, B. Linrgren and P. Roos (1994). "Productivity Developments in Swedish Hospitals: A Malmquist Output Index Approach," in A. Charnes, W. Cooper, A.Y. Lewin and L.M. Seiford, eds., *Data Envelopment Analysis: Theory, Methodology, and Applications* (Norwell, MA: Kluwer Academic Publishers).

Färe, R., S. Grosskopf, M. Norris and Z. Zhang (1994). "Productivity Growth, Technical Progress, and Efficiency Change in Industrialized Countries," *American Economic Review* 1994, 66–83.

Färe, R. (1988). *Fundamentals of Production Theory* (New York: Springer-Verlag).

Färe, R., S. Grosskopf and C.A.K. Lovell (1994). *Production Frontiers* (New York: Cambridge University Press).

Färe, R., S. Grosskopf and C.A.K. Lovell (1985). *The Measurement of Efficiency of Production.* (Boston: Kluwer-Nijhoff).

Farrell, M.J. (1957). "The Measurement of Productive Efficiency," *Journal of the Royal Statistical Society* A 120, 253–281.

Fecher, F., D. Kessler, S. Perelman and P. Pestieau (1993). "Productive Performance of the French Insurance Industry," *Journal of Productivity Analysis* 4, 77–93.

Ferrier, G.D. and C.A.K. Lovell (1990). "Measuring Cost Efficiency in Banking: Econometric and Linear Programming Evidence," *Journal of Econometrics* 46, 229–245.

Fukuyama, Hirofumi (1997). "Investigating Productive Efficiency and Productivity Changes of Japanese Life Insurance Companies," *Pacific-Basin Finance Journal* 122.

Gagné Robert and Piere Ouellette (1998). "On the Choice of Functional Forms: Summary of a Monte Carlo Experiment," *Journal of Business & Economic Statistics* 16, 118–124.

Gallant, A.R. (1982). "Unbiased Determination of Production Technologies," *Journal of Econometrics* 20, 285–323.

Gardner, L. and M. Grace (1993). "X-Efficiency in the U.S. Life Insurance Industry," *Journal of Banking and Finance* 17, 497–510.

Gardner, L. and M. Grace (1997). "Cost Differences Between Mutual and Stock Life Insurance Companies," Working paper, Center for Risk Management and Insurance Research, College of Business Administration, Georgia State University, Atlanta, GA.

Grace, Martin F. (1995). "Firm Efficiency and Insolvency: An Investigation of the US Insurance Industry," Working paper, Center for Risk Management and Insurance Research, College of Business Administration, Georgia State University, Atlanta, GA.

Grace, Martin F. and Stephen G. Timme (1992). "An Examination of Cost Economies in the United States Life Insurance Industry," *Journal of Risk and Insurance* 59, 72–103.

Greene, W.H. (1993). "The Econometric Approach To Efficiency Analysis," in H.O. Fried, C.A.K. Lovell, and S.S. Schmidt, eds., *The Measurement of Productive Efficiency* (New York: Oxford University Press).

Grosskopf, Shawna (1993). "Efficiency and Productivity," in H.O. Fried, C.A.K. Lovell and S.S. Schmidt, eds., *The Measurement of Productive Effiiency* (New York: Oxford University Press).

Grosskopf, Shawna (1996). "Statistical Inference and Nonparametric Efficiency: A Selective Survey," *Journal of Productivity Analysis* 7, 161–176.

Halpern, P.J. and G.F. Mathewson (1975). "Economies of Scale in Financial Institutions: A General Model Applied to Insurance," *Journal of Monetary Economics* 1 (2), 203–220.

Hancock, Diana (1985). "The Financial Firm: Production With Monetary and Nonmonetary Goods," *Journal of Political Economy* 93, 859–880.

Hermalin, Benjamin E. and Nancy E. Wallace (1994). "The Determinants of Efficiency and Solvency in Savings and Loans," *RAND Journal of Economics* 25, 361–381.

Hornstein, A. and E.C. Prescott (1991). "Measures of the Insurance Sector Output," *Geneva Papers on Risk and Inurance* 16, 191–206.

Hughes, Joseph P. and Loretta J. Mester (1998). "Bank Capitalization and Cost: Evidence of Scale Economies in Risk Management and Signaling," *Review of Economics and Statistics* 80, 313–325.

Kellner, S. and F.G. Mathewson (1983). "Entry, Size Distribution, Scale, and Scope Economies in the Life Insurance Industry," *Journal of Business* 56, 25–44.

Kendrick, John W. and Beatrice N. Vaccara (1980). *New Developments in Productivity Measurement and Analysis* (Chicago: University of Chicago Press).

Kim, Hunsoo and Martin F. Grace (1995). "Potential Ex Post Efficiency Gains of Insurance Company Mergers," Working paper, Center for Risk Management and Insurance Research, College of Business Administration, Georgia State University, Atlanta, GA.

Land, Kenneth C., C.A. Knox Lovell and Sten Thore (1993). "Chance-Constrained Data Envelopment Analysis," *Managerial and Decision Economics* 14, 541–554.

Lipsey, Robert E. (1992). "Comment on Armknecht and Ginsburg," in Z. Griliches, ed., *Output Measurement in the Service Sectors*, National Bureau of Economic Research, Studies in Income and Wealth, Vol. 56, University of Chicago Press (Chicago, IL), 156–157.

Lovell, C.A.K. (1993). "Production Frontiers and Productive Efficiency," in H.O. Fried, C.A.K. Lovell and S.S. Schmidt, eds., *The Measurement of Productive Efficiency* (New York: Oxford University Press).

Mayers, David and Clifford W. Smith, Jr. (1988). "Ownership Structure Across Lines of Property-Casualty Insurance," *Journal of Law and Economics* 31, 351–378.

McAllister, P.H. and D. McManus (1993). "Resolving the Scale Efficiency Puzzle in Banking," *Journal of Banking and Finance* 17, 389–406.

Meador, Joseph W., Harley E. Ryan, Jr. and Carolin D. Schellhorn (1998). "Product Focus Versus Diversification: Estimates of X-Efficiency for the U.S. Life Insurance Industry," working paper, Northeastern University, Boston, MA.

Meeusen, W. and J. van den Broeck (1977). "Efficiency Estimation from Cobb-Douglas Production Functions with Composed Error," *International Economic Review* 18, 435–444.

Mester, L.J. (1991). "Agency Costs Among Savings and Loans," *Journal of Financial Intermediation* 1, 257–278.

Morrison, C.J. and E.R. Berndt (1981). "Short-Run Labor Productivity in a Dynamic Model," *Journal of Econometrics* 16, 339–365.

Myers, Stewart and Richard Cohn (1987). "Insurance Rate Regulation and the Capital Asset Pricing Model." In J.D. Cummins and S.E. Harrington, eds., *Fair Rate of Return In Property-Liability Insurance* (Norwell, MA: Kluwer Academic Publishers).

Pastor, José M., Francisco Pérez and Javier Quesada (1997). "Efficiency Analysis in Banking Firms: An International Comparison," *European Journal of Operational Research* 98, 395–407.

Pulley, L.B. and Y. Braunstein (1992). "A Composite Cost Function for Multiproduct Firms With an Application To Economies of Scope in Banking," *Review of Economics and Statistics* 74, 221–230.

Röller, L.H. (1990). "Proper Quadratic Cost Functions With an Application To the Bell System," *Review of Economics and Statistics* 72, 202–210.

Schmidt, P. and R.C. Sickles (1984). "Production Frontiers and Panel Data," *Journal of Business and Economic Statistics* 2, 299–326.

Seiford, L.M. and R.M. Thrall (1990). "Recent Developments in DEA: The Mathematical Programming Approach to Frontier Analysis," *Journal of Econometrics* 46, 7–38.

Shephard, R.W. (1970). *Theory of Cost and Production Functions* (Princeton, NJ: Princeton University Press).

Sherwood, Mark (1997). "Output of the Property and Casualty Insurance Industry," Paper presented at the CSLS Conference on Service Centre Productivity and the Productivity Paradox, April 11–12, Ottawa, Canada.

Terrell, Dek. (1995). "Flexibility and Regularity Properties of the Asymptotically Ideal Production Model," *Econometric Reviews* 14, 1–17.

Vanden Eeckaut, Philippe, Henry Tulkens and Marie-Astrid Jamar (1993). "Cost Efficiency in Belgian Municipalities," in H.O. Fried, C.A.K. Lovell and S.S. Schmidt, eds., *The Measurement of Productive Efficiency* (New York: Oxford University Press).

Weiss, Mary A. (1986). "Analysis of Productivity at the Firm level: An Application to Life Insurers," *Journal of Risk and Insurance* 53, 49–83.

Weiss, Mary A. (1987). "Macroeconomic Insurance Output Estimation," *Journal of Risk and Insurance* 54, 582–593.

Weiss, Mary A. (1989). "Analysis of Productivity at the Firm Level: An Application to Life Insurers: Author's Reply," *Journal of Risk and Insurance* 56, 341–346.

Weiss, Mary A. (1990). "Productivity Growth and Regulation of *P/L* Insurance: 1980–1984," *Journal of Productivity Analysis* 2, 15–38.

Weiss, Mary A. (1991a). "Efficiency in the Property-Liability Insurance Industry," *Journal of Risk and Insurance* 58, 452–479.

Weiss, Mary A. (1991b). "International *P/L* Insurance Output, Input and Productivity Comparisons," *Geneva Papers on Risk and Insurance Theory* 16, 179–200.

Yuengert, A. (1993). "The Measurement of Efficiency in Life Insurance: Estimates of a Mixed Normal-Gamma Error Model," *Journal of Banking and Finance* 17, 483–96.

25 Dealing with the Insurance Business in the Economic Accounts*

Tarek M. Harchaoui

Statistics Canada

Abstract

This chapter synthetizes and extends the treatment of the insurance business in the system of national accounts, with a focus on the measurement of the production activity. The framework begins with an overall discussion, at the macroeconomic level, on the past and current approaches on the measure of the insurance business production activity in the system of national accounts. But this macroeconomic approach of the insurance business turns out to be limited in many important respects. In extending the framework, I adopt a more disaggregated approach, making a strong case on the need to understand the behaviour and to measure the activities of the insurance business at the level of the line of business. This approach, overlooked by the existing economic literature, provides many insights in terms of the delineation of insurers' lines of business, the measurement of their activities and their interaction within an integrated input-output framework. As a by product, the chapter also discusses issues related to the regional breakdown of insurers' activities and the unduplicated measure of the insurance firm's output.

Keywords: Output, producing units, technology.
JEL Classification Numbers: C8, L8, M4, G22.

25.1 INTRODUCTION

Insurance companies have historically been an important player of the "four pillars" of developed countries' financial services sector, offering financial protection, investment products and reinsurance services. Banks (concentrating on lending to businesses, collecting households and business deposits, and offering payment services through these deposits), trust and mortgage loan companies (concentrating on fidu-

* I am indebted to John R. Baldwin, Georges Dionne, Revé Durand and four anonymous referees for their valuable and decisive comments made on an earlier draft. Any remaining errors are mine alone and the views expressed in this paper should not be attributed to Statistics Canada.

ciary services and mortgage lending to households), and securities dealers (focussing on the underwriting and marketing of investment products) were considered the other pillars in the financial services sector.[1]

The recent years have witnessed a gradual merging of the four pillars, with much greater overlap of business lines. These developments stemmed from many factors, including globalization of financial markets, technological innovation, changing demographics, rising household wealth, and adjustments within the financial sector to shifting business prospects. Changes in the environment have been a major factor in the legislative and regulatory revisions that have widened the powers of financial institutions and placed financial groups in direct competition with each other.

Structural change in some major countries' financial system in the 1980s and early 1990s was similar in many other industrialized countries. As one would expect, such forces have significantly affected the financial sector in general and the insurance business in particular. Their product lines have broadened considerably beyond the core business of financial protection. Therefore, one of roles of economists concerned with organizing economic data into meaningful formats is to ask periodically whether existing data sets of accounts adequately describe important economic trends and are useful to public and private policymakers. This is one of the objectives of this chapter.

The other goal of this chapter is to provide an overall picture of the treatment of insurance in the SNA at the micro and macro levels. The chapter discusses the previous and actual treatments of insurance in the system of national accounts (SNA) framework and discusses some of the ways in which the framework is applied, depending on specific country requirements. It then introduces the main categories for national accounting which draw upon the records of businesses, and the accounting rules to be followed when recording the various entries. The chapter then describes the activities of the producing units and their classification required for a program of economic statistics. The chapter also investigates the behaviour and activities of insurers' lines of business and the transactions that take place between them within an integrated input-output framework. In particular, this chapter looks at the link between the line of business and the enterprise from the standpoint of a complete production account statement.

25.2 INSURANCE IN THE SYSTEM OF NATIONAL ACCOUNTS: A MACROECONOMIC APPROACH

25.2.1 Background

The System of National Accounts (SNA) is implemented at different levels of aggregations: at the level of the institutional sectors and at the level of the economy.

[1] The co-operative credit movement is sometimes cited as a "fifth pillar," offering banking and other financial services to households. Other financial institutions include pension funds, mutual funds, finance companies and leasing companies.

Although traditionally described as a SNA, for analytical purposes the SNA is also to be implemented at lower levels of aggregation. In order to understand the workings of the economy of some specific industries, it is essential to be able to observe and analyse the economic interactions taking place between different producing units. Certain key aggregate statistics, such as gross domestic product (GDP), that are widely used as indicators of the economic activity at the level of the economy, are also defined at the level of these units.

As emphasized by Bloem (1990, section 3), national economic accounts retain in general two distinct types or statistical reporting units: a) the establishment, yielding industrially homogeneous production and related data, and b) the enterprise, yielding financial and related data on a consolidated basis for the unit's total constituent establishments. (The enterprise can also yield industrially heterogeneous production data on a consolidated basis). Also, national accounts construct input-output tables reflecting aggregation and allocation of establishment-based data and flow-of-funds tables and sectoral balance sheets, reflecting aggregation of enterprise-based data.

At the higher level of aggregation, there are institutional units which a) are centres of decision-making for all aspects of economic activity and b) owns assets and incur liabilities on their own behalf. The institutional units are grouped together to form institutional sectors.

The institutional units involved in insurance are pre-eminently insurance corporations. In principle it is possible for another type of enterprise to carry out insurance as a non-principal activity, but usually the legal regulations surrounding the conduct of insurance mean that a separate set of accounts covering all aspects of the insurance activity must be kept and thus in the SNA a separate institutional unit, classified to the insurance corporations and pension funds sub-sector, is identifiable. According to Skipper (1993, 116), in many countries, including the US, regulation prevents insurers from undertaking activities not reasonably related to insurance. However, insurers that wish to engage in other activities, except banking, are allowed to do so through holding companies.

The activity of insurance is intended to provide individuals and institutional units exposed to certain risks with financial protection against the consequences of occurrence of specified events. It is also a form of financial intermediation in which funds are collected from policyholders and invested mainly in financial assets which are held as technical reserves to meet future claims arising from occurrence of the events specified in the insurance policies.

Is there any rational classification of the insurance business? The buyers of insurance are either private persons or business firms and their motivation for buying insurance may differ from one case to another. Borch (1981) provided an interesting classification of the insurance business into three parts:

i) *Life insurance*, i.e., annuities and ordinary life insurance with payment at death;
ii) *Business insurance*, the insurance bought by businessmen, covering commercial risks of all kinds;

iii) *Household insurance*, bought by the ordinary consumer as protection against the risks in everyday life.

Three reasons at least underline the delineation of these three classes of insurance:

i) Each class seems to require its own special types of theoretical analysis;
ii) In the market each class of insurance faces different types of competition;
iii) The government, through its regulatory authority, often takes different attitudes to these three classes of insurance.

Because of what are perceived as substantial operational and product differences, insurance regulation generally requires legally separate companies for the transaction of the life and non-life business and, hence, the maintenance of a separate set of consolidated accounts for each type of business. Unlike the approach proposed by Borch (1981), the latter corresponds exactly to the needs of the SNA's sectoring.

Accordingly, the SNA defines two classes of insurance businesses in terms of the services they provide. Life insurers sell life insurance and annuities, manage pension funds and sell accident and sickness insurance. Non-life insurers offer a wide range of financial protection on all kinds of assets (automobile, property, liability insurance etc.). Insurance businesses provide financial protection by spreading the risk among the other insureds and, if necessary, with other insurers by means of reinsurance. If, for example, an insurer found that there was only one particular policy of a kind being insured by him, then there might wish to share the risk with other insurers by paying a premium to them.[2] Despite the similarity of the activity of life and non-life insurance (see section 25.3.3 below), there are significant differences in terms of the characteristics of the product which lead to different types of treatement in the SNA.

25.2.2 Measurement of the Output

There are two *non exclusive* approaches to the measurement of output: gross output and value added. Gross output can be measured either by the value of services produced, or by the sum of income payments and other costs. Business purchases on current account from other businesses are subtracted from gross output to arrive at value-added, or gross product originating, an unduplicated measure of economic activity.

1. Nominal Output

As emphasized by Ruggles (1983b, 67) and many others, in the insurance business, much like banking, the problem of specifying the output of the business is complicated by the two factors which are not shared by goods producing industries. These

[2] Reinsurance is a process by which the reinsurer (the first party) in consideration of a premium agrees to indemnify the reinsured (the second party) against a risk insured by the reinsured under a policy in favour of the insured (a third party).

are: i) the consumer's expenditures on insurance premiums are for a bundle of services plus transfers; ii) the prices and the values of the service portion are not separated from the transfer portion. For example, premiums paid for life insurance are paid partly to cover the value of services produced by the insurance company and partly to accumulate a financial asset (cash value) in the policyholder's name, and partly to pay for claims. The non-life insurance business provides a similar example—premiums cover both the value of services produced and, on an actuarial basis, claims paid out (which are not a measure of production but of transfers). In both cases, the policyholder does not know the split between payment for service and the transfer component—these are not priced separately. As a result, the output of the insurance business must be specified and their prices imputed.[3]

a) What Do Insurers Do?

The interest of economists in insurance is probably as old as economics itself. In his *Wealth of Nations*, (Book I, Chapter 10) Adam Smith (1776) writes that "*premiums must be sufficient to compensate the common losses, to pay the expense of management, and to afford such a profit as might have been drawn from an equal capital employed in any common trade*". This is a remarkable insight as to how insurance premiums should be determined. As for the peculiarity of the insurance business itself, Adam Smith writes (Book V, Chapter 1): "*The trade of insurance gives great security to the fortunes of private people, and by dividing among a great many that loss which would ruin an individual, makes it fall light and easy upon the whole society. In order to give this security, however, it is necessary that the insurers should have a very large capital.*" More than 100 years later, Alfred Marshall defines in his *Principles* (1890) the premiums as the price one has to pay to get rid of the "evils of uncertainty." He also noted that businessmen paid insurance premiums "*which they know are calculated on a scale sufficiently above the true actuarial value of the risk to pay the companies' great expenses of advertising and working, and yet to yield a surplus of net profits*".

The passages quoted above show that, although more than 200 years ago classical and neo classical economists had a good understanding of insurance, they have not addressed the issue of the value of insurance services. As it will be shown later, measuring the output of this business represents one of the building blocks of the SNA.

Insurers are engaged in the pooling of risk. Insured persons or businesses pay a premium to insurance carriers to perform this function. In addition, there is an associated function of providing annuities and managing pension funds. All of these activities involve investment of the policyholders funds. These two activities—underwriting insurance and investing funds—are reflected in two accounts—an underwriting account and investment account. From the point of view of the insurer much

[3] Other ways of measuring output are described by Sherwood (1999).

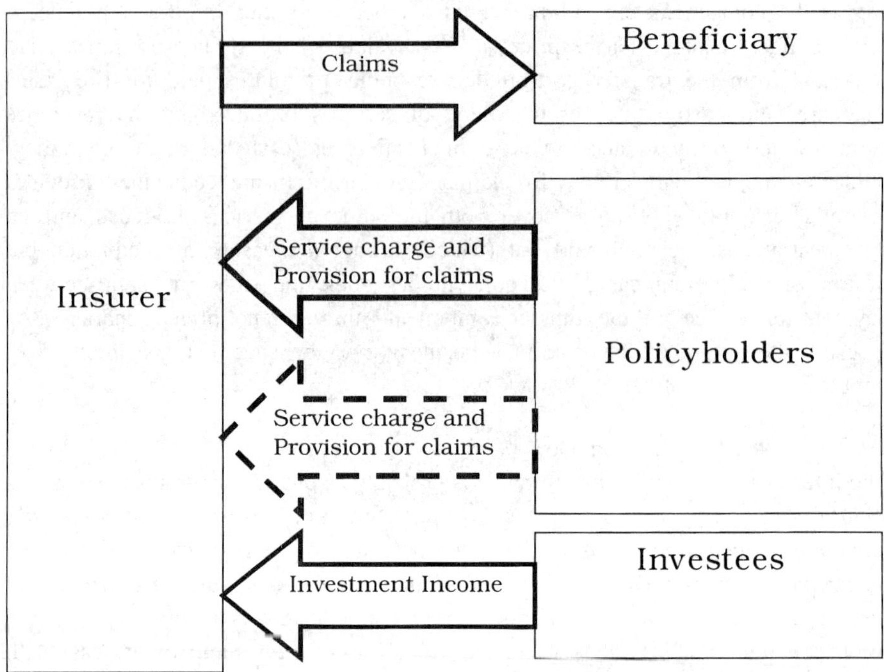

Figure 1 Service and Payment Flows Involved by the Insurance Business

of the income is derived from capital gains and investment income which are not traditionally considered income from the production of goods and services in the SNA. Rather they are considered as transfers.

The various payment flows that take place between the insurer, the policyholders and any other third party are illustrated in Figure 1. There is a flow of premiums between the insured and the insurer. The premium received should be considered as consisting of two parts—an amount placed in reserve to pay future claims and the remainder used to cover expenses including a return to shareholders of the insurer (service charge). The payment for future claims is a transfer to the insurer. The reserves are used to generate investment income which is used to cover expenses and claims. Between the insurer and the insured there is a barter arrangement in which the insured barters the investment income on the reserves to pay future claims to lower the overall payment for service charges and claims. There is a flow of investment income between the investee and the insurer. This investment income is a transfer between the investee and the insurer. The right to retain the investment funds represents the barter arrangement with the insured. There is a payment in respect of claims incurred in the current period between the insured and the insurer.

b) Gross Output under the 1968 SNA

Under the 1968 SNA (United Nations 1968), the gross output of insurance firms is not equal to premiums received. A large part of premium income is paid out as claims, hence the bulk of funds flowing through the insurance business are treated as transfers. By the conventions of the SNA, the gross output of the insurance business is equal to premiums less claims paid. GDP is therefore premiums less claims less intermediate expense, or equivalently, labour compensation plus surplus.

Gross Output = Premiums – Claims
GDP = Gross Output – Intermediated Expense.

But not everyone agrees with the SNA's approach to the measurement of insurance output. Ruggles (1983b), who claims that there are several inconsistencies in the way the treatment of the insurance in the SNA, proposed the use of premiums as a measure of output. Diewert (1995) seems also to agree with this way of measuring the output. Claims are considered to be part of transactions that affect the capital account and not the current account. Ruggles' understanding of the current treatment of the insurance in the SNA is clearly summarized in the following paragraph (p. 68):

> *"It is apparent that the present national income accounting treatment of insurance transactions would be quite inappropriate for the accounts of the individual transactor. If this treatment were used, business suffering no loss would record the cost of insurance as the premiums actually paid, but for those having a loss the cost in insurance would equal 'net premiums,' that is, premiums paid less claims received, and could be sizable negative flow; at the same time the fire or casualty loss would appear as a large increase in capital consumption allowance. These distortions are due in part to the failure of the national income accounts to achieve a proper separation of current transactions from capital transactions, and in part to a willingness to deal with consolidated accounts for all businesses as a group."*

This claim is partly true. The production (or current account under Ruggles' own terminology) account of the insurance business, based on the majority of items included in the income statement, certainly considers claims as part of the production account. They constitute the largest component of the operating expenses of the business, but unlike the other expenses, they belong neither to the category of intermediate expenses not to the primary expenses. They merely represent payout, much like dividends and experience rating refunds, that are transferred back to the consumer.

c) Gross Output under the 1993 SNA

It is not uncommon for underwriting gain and the corresponding value-added to be negative as intermediate expense (which includes commissions paid to brokers and agents of all kinds) represents one of the most important element of total expenses.

The profitability of the insurance business is preserved by net receipts of investment income which, until recently, were not included in the SNA measure of the gross output of the business. The new SNA (United Nations 1993a) recommends that investment income be added to the current measurement of gross output to arrive at measure of value added that is non negative.[4] The proposed approach has been proposed almost ten years ago by Weiss (1987) and Schiltz (1987) and it has been used by the US Bureau of Economic Analysis for life insurance services for many years (see Ruggles 1983a).

The rational behind this proposed treatment is the following: insurance companies usually perform two activities. First, they are enaged in a 'pure insurance' activity, i.e., they sell insurance policies for a premium P on which they pay a claim C with expected value. If the premium and claim payments are coincident in time (say, the periods), the companies' gross output in an expected value sense is $P_s - C_s$. The second activity performed by insurance companies is financial intermediation, which arises from the fact that premiums P_t are paid at time in advance of claims C_s, which are paid at time $s(t < s)$. Essentially, the problem of negative underwriting gain is caused by the error of comparing dollars of one period (P_t is valued at time t) with dollars of another period (C_s is valued at time s).

The expression $P_t(1 + r)$, where r is the (certainty equivalent) interest rate, represents premium revenue properly expressed in dollars of the same time period in which claims are paid. Clearly, the new SNA recommends that the financial intermediation activity of insurance companies be made explicit via an imputation equal to $P_t \cdot r$, the investment income, to be added to interest receipts, premium income and interest payments.

d) The SNA Approach in Practice

In an elegant multisectoral framework, Hartwick (1997) proposed a measure of value added of the insurance business that departs significantly from the new SNA. His concept of value added (payment to the primary inputs adjusted for the risk premium demanded by shareholders) corresponds roughly to the new SNA concept of gross output (premiums *minus* claims *plus* investment income)(see his equation (16), p. 15). However, this result constitutes a major departure from the SNA conventions, as it considers intermediate expenses as part of the value added. The same ambiguity in the treatment of intermediate expenses can also be found in Cummins and Weiss (1998) where all expenses are supposed to be part of value added (see their eq. (14)).[5] Intermediate expenses composed of commissions of all kinds paid to non employees

[4] Changes in actuarial reserves are not considered in this chapter for the sake of simplicity.

[5] *"The total value-added, (. . .), thus equals the insurers expenses plus the owners' profit charge for bearing insurance risk."* (p. 26).

and purchased goods and services can be as high as 30 percent of gross output. Thus, ignoring them may be grossly in error.

Although the new SNA approach to the measurement of output is still in its infancy, it has been successfully applied in areas such the analysis of costs structures of the insurance business (Bernstein 1992) and productivity measurement (Bernstein and Geehan 1988; Bernstein 1997 and Harchaoui 1997). Analyses of productivity are, however, only as good as the real output measure on which they are based. Unfortunately, the estimates of real output and, accordingly, productivity based on national accounts estimates are extremely poor. In some instances, the real output of insurance in national accounts is no more than an index of factor inputs, with the result that productivity change is, by definition, zero. In other instances like in Canada, the deflation leads to volatile estimates of labour productivity (see Lal 1990).

Griliches (1992) has suggested that an important source of the differential in productivity growth between goods and services is measurement error. He argued that problems in defining service-sector outputs and identifying price versus quality changes, as well as paucity of data on services, have resulted in underestimation of service-sector output. One of the most serious problem that face statistical agencies is the measurement of meaningful price series for financial services industries. For example, of the finance, insurance and real estate subsector, commercial banking is the only industry for which the US Bureau of Labor Statistics publishes a productivity measure (see Dean and Kunze 1992, 85).

Real output is generally measured in either of two way: by deflating current dollar values with an aggregate price index or by projecting base year values using an index of quantities (in which case real output is the ratio of current period quantities multiplied by base year prices divided by base year values). Either approach requires the specification of output in terms which clearly separates quantities from prices. The second approach has been applied by Weiss (1987). The first approach requires the construction of a consistent time series on prices indices.

With the exception of Jensen and Morrisey (1990), there has been no attempt to measure the problem of quality change in the insurance business using the hedonic approach which turned out to be particularly useful in many areas where prices do not measure the pure price change. Reece (1993) has developed an ad hoc measure of life insurance price indices that builds on the availability of series on number of policies by product line. The idea, which has been applied by Bernstein (1999) and Harchaoui (1997) to the measurement of the real output of the Canadian life insurance business, consists of the following steps:

a) for every product line i calculate the (average) nominal price:

$$p_i = \frac{V_i}{N_i}$$

where
V_i = nominal gross output of the product line i;
N_i = number of policy of the product line i;

b) construct a superlative index where the weights are based on the face value of the policy i, that is

$$\ln p_t - \ln p_{t-1} = \sum_{i=1}^{n} \overline{\omega}_{i,t} (\ln p_{i,t} - \ln p_{i,t-1})$$

$$\text{where } \overline{\omega}_{i,t} = \frac{1}{2}(\omega_{i,t} + \omega_{i,t-1}) \text{ and } \omega_{i,t} = \frac{V_{i,t}}{V_t}.$$

2. *Nominal Value-added*

National economic accountants take the value-added approach of output and construct from them a set of accounts showing production and distribution. The inception of the concept of value-added in national accounts goes back to Fabricant (1940) in his early work on US national accounts:

> *"The ideal index of the net physical output of an industry would measure the changes in the aggregate value of net output attributable exclusively to changes in the physical quantities of the final products and to changes in the quantities of the materials and other commodities consumed in the fabrication of the final products . . ."*

The nominal value-added of industries represents the value which industries add to commodities that they processed. That value is equal to the primary input costs of the industries, taken generally to be the cost of their labour and capital services. The primary input costs are to be contrasted with the intermediate input costs, that is the costs of goods and services purchased by industries from *upstream* supplying industries.

The nominal notion of value-added in terms of costs and sales may be closely associated with the idea of a real production process. Industries may be seen as jointly contributing, by using their capital and labour resources, to the production of the commodities delivered to final demand. In that production framework, each industry is viewed as contributing only partly to the production of some final demand commodity (ies). The contributions of each industry to all final demand commodities may consequently be seen as its contribution to the final output of the economy or as its real value-added.

3. *Double Deflation*

Measured growth rates for insurance industries are generally lower than the rates obtained for manufacturing industries. However, as emphasized by Bernstein and

Geehan (1988) in the Canadian context, this finding is suspect, because of the difficulties in using official statistics to measure real output of insurance industries. In the SNA the process of eliminating price change from a time series to lay bare the underlying real movements in production is known as deflation. The removal of price change from current price value series series is an attempt to provide a proxy for the sum of the real quantities embodied in the series. Aggregating physical commodities of differing nature (eggs and automobiles) is clearly an impractical proposition. Employing an underlying principle that involves holding prices of commodities fixed at some selected base year, and from that period forward valuing production in the prices of that base year, yields values for diverse products that are both proportional to real production and additive.

A large variety of different methods have been devised by countries to estimate real value added of insurance industries. Double deflation, one of the method which has been proposed to measure the real industry value-added, involves the deflation of the gross output of commodities and the deflation of intermediate inputs (see David 1962; David and Sato 1966). That subtraction is closely linked to the Laspeyres index number formula. Consequently, in the application, double deflation is generally based on a fixed base year Laspeyres index number formula. The base year applies to a delimited number of years before being moved forward. Then either the whole historical series are entirely based on that new base year (historical series are re-based on the new set of relative prices) or historical series are statistically linked to the new estimates while still based on the set of the past relative prices of their previous base year.[6]

Other methods of estimating real value-added have also been proposed in the past such as the single deflation method (see Hill 1971 for an overview), yet double deflation remains by far the most commonly used amongst OECD countries for the financial sector (see OECD 1998).

Despite its popularity, the double deflation approach has been at the centre of several criticism by the economic literature, including Sims (1969), Sato (1976) and Bruno (1978), as it does provide a meaningful measure of real output only under stringent assumptions. Other contributions, such as Denny and May (1977, 1978), have shown that for the Canadian manufacturing industries the double deflation' underlying assumptions are unlikely to be satisfied in the real world. Diewert (1978) finds that these conditions are unlikely to be satisfied empirically, in particular, because of the rapid relative price increase of energy following the 1973 oil shock. The second oil shock followed by the changes in the prices of computers prevented the conditions to be satisfied in recent years either. Durand (1994) proposed an alternative approach to double deflation which displays better theoretical properties. The new approach does not rest on the stringent assumptions of double deflation. In particular, it does

[6] The historical growth rates of industries' value added are preserved and the series are projected backward from the new base year on that basis while the following years are established on the basis of the relative prices of the new base year.

not rest on the separability condition between intermediate and primary inputs. Empirically, the proposed approach does not have the major defects of double deflation, including negative real value-added when nominal value-added is positive or real value-added higher than gross output. The real GDP estimates obtained under this approach displays less volatility than the standard estimates obtained under the double deflation approach, particularly for the industries where output is hard to measure.

25.3 A MICROECONOMIC APPROACH OF THE INSURANCE BUSINESS IN THE SYSTEM OF NATIONAL ACCOUNTS

25.3.1 Background

In many developed countries, insurance firms correspond largely to institutions which are governed by regulations. Institutions are legally constituted but usually belong to enterprises that are involved in activities in addition to those usually reserved to those institutions. The boundaries created by regulation may not correspond to the way a business organizes its operations. Furthermore, in recent years the institutions have been expanding their activities into areas previously reserved to other institutions. This creates two related problems. An industry based on institutions may contain a number of unrelated activities. Secondly, like activities are not grouped within the same industry if industry classes are based on institutions.

This section has two related goals:

a) To propose a delineation of the insurance business along the various producing units. In this business data are usually collected at the level of the institution, accordingly, there is very little experience with the organization of operating units. It is necessary to decide which of these units are technical units (or profit centres) and which are auxiliary units (cost centres). Technical units must have an industrial class into which to place them. Support units, depending on the conceptual approach, do not necessarily have to be classified to their own industry; they may be classified to the major industrial activity of the business. An additional problem is that the organization of activities and products into organizational units may vary from one business to another. Therefore, it is necessary to propose a general framework that encompasses the major characteristics of the business.

   Collecting the data at the level of the various producing units offers two kinds of advantages. From an operational perspective, there will be a consistency in the unit of observation across the business sector, as the data will be collected at the level of the producing unit from all kinds of industries, including those traditionally regulated. From the analytical perspective, the move away from the institutional framework is merely driven by the fact that a broad range of issues simply cannot be addressed without microdata on producing units and the firms that own them. As emphasized by McGuckin (1995), for many problems, the producing unit is a sensible unit of analysis. For example, from the standpoint of the production decision, the choice of inputs for use in output creation is often made at the plant level. Although the firm is the ultimate decision maker and thus the preferred unit of analysis for many problems, producing units have very different behavioural patterns, even when owned by the same firms. Thus producing units data are also necessary to understand the behaviour of the firm. The behaviour of one producing unit is not completely differentiated from other simply by the identity of its owner. Producing units data are also necessary to estimate the marginal impact of some event—for example, a purchase or divestiture of assets—on the firm. Focusing on the production relationship, one can see that their establishments are the primary purchasers of inputs. Even though primary resource-allocation decisions are often made at the firm level, producing unit data are useful in analysis of technical change because technical change is characterized by changes in the production relationship.

b) To analyse how the company-establishment problem, which has a long history in the national economic accounting literature, can be overcome in the particular context of the insurance business. The problem is of key importance in a paper by Sigel (1955) together with comments of Jaszi (1955). Their discussion is concerned with the technical issues of relating establishment-based input-output tables to a company-based flow-of-funds accounting system. This theme and others also turn up in the Report of a Conference on the Proposals for Revision of the United Nations of National Accounts (see Tice 1967). Copeland's (1957) classic challenge to Leontief to show how the input-output system could be synthetized with money-flows certainly implies respect for the company-establishment problem. A particularly clear statement of the problem, in a more general setting, appears later in Jaszi (1971): production and related statistics are best reported on the basis of industrially homogeneous units, the individual establishment; financial and related statistics come naturally from the (heterogeneous) legal entity responsible for and controlling their constituent establishments. More recently the company-establishment problem is the centre of attention in the debate between Ruggles and Ruggles (1982a, b) and a number of commentators concerning a proposed Integrated Economic Accounts for the United States.

25.3.2 Dealing with the Insurance Business at the Producing Unit Level

1. The Literature on Multiunit Firms

The modern multiunit business firm is one of the most prominent and significant innovations in the organization of production of recent years. For most of the two previous centuries, firms were organized as traditional single-unit firms. These firms operated in a local or regional market, produced a single product line, and were owned and managed by a single individual or a partnership. During the last two decades of the nineteenth century, the multiunit business firm emerged and began to displace the single-unit firm in a number of industries. The multiunit firm operated plants in many regions, produced various product lines, and were controlled by a hierarchy of managers. During the twentieth century, the predominance of multiunit firms grew domestically and internationally in the form of multinational firms.

For economists, the analysis of the rise of the modern multiunit firm, and of firm size in general, is based on transaction cost theory of the firm. This theory, originating from Coase (1937), revived and popularized by the works of Williamson (1975, 1985), Alchian and Demsetz (1972), and Klein, Crawford and Alchian (1972), argues that firms internalize production because they incur greater transaction costs when they use markets. The analysis of the rise of multiunit firm has been influenced by the works of Chandler (1977, 1990), who combined the elements of the traditional industrial organization literature and the transaction cost literature to explain the rise of the modern business firm. Chandler (1990, 17–18) argued that firm size is determined by transaction costs, but that these costs are, in turn, linked to technology:

> *"Transaction cost economies are, of course, closely related to those of scale and scope. The economies of scale and those of scope within a single unit of production or distribution permit that unit to expand the output of goods and services, which in turn, increases proportionately the number of recurring commercial transactions and contractual relations the enterprise may carry on with other operating units."*

Although the modern multiunit enterprises have been heralded by Chandler (1977, 1990) and others as a major and important phase of organizational change, and a significant source of growth, the prevalence of the multiunit firm engaged in financial services has been neglected by the economic literature. Bohman (1979), one of the few attempts that looked inside the insurance firm's black box, developed a framework that captures the transactions that take place between the two funds that compose the insurance firm—the insurance fund and surplus fund. But these two funds are not considered as producing units with the result that measurement of production was overlooked in his contribution. In the next section, we extend Bohman's framework along the following lines: a) the insurance firm is separated into various lines of business on the basis of the concept of production; the production of the various lines of business is measured and the transactions flows that take place between them are outlined; b) we show how the production account of each of these lines of business can be used to arrived at the production at the enterprise level; c) finally, the delineation of the different lines of business is assessed.

2. *Implementing the Multiunit Concept in the Insurance Business*

a) Framework

The insurance industry is in general dominated by large multi-product and multi-activity institutions. The large institutions, which operate a network in many regions, are generally engaged in direct insurance, reinsurance and investment activities. However, these activities often take place in separate organisations of the institution. What makes these institutions insurers is that they are primarily involved in financial protection and diversification of risks although increasingly they are also engaged in all kinds of financial activities. They may have both domestic and foreign clients for any of these services provided by these activities. As multi-regions imply, most of the dealings with clients are through a network of agents, brokers and claims adjusters. For other customers seeking for reinsurance and investment services, the dealings may be through the head office where the bulk of the decisions take place.

As previously indicated, there is nowhere a tradition of dealing with the insurance business at the level of producing units and this holds true for the whole financial sector. Therefore, this section, based on the work of Harchaoui (1998) for the Canadian banking industry, provides not only background material but also a framework for a proposed delineation of the insurance business at the level of the line of business. But what precisely constitute a line of business (or producing unit) reporting and its motivation? Large diversified insurance corporations are motivated to break down their operations into units of manageable size. The existence of such units creates a need on the part of the corporate management to know and appraise the performance of the units. The organization of corporation along producing units (or lines of business) has become increasingly popular and dominant in recent years (Reece and Cool 1978).

The particular context assumed here is the large multi-establishment multi-industry corporation whose industrial origins, strategy and structure are so well described in Williamson (1981). What are the natural organizational units of the large multiproduct and multiactivity enterprise featuring decentralized decision-making? There are essentially three (see Kaplan 1982, chapter 13): Cost centers are units that are responsible for satisfying externally given demands subject to a cost-minimizing efficiency standard. The cost of materials used and labour employed are controlled, but production sales revenue may not even be known. Revenue centers are units organized with the goal of attaining certain sales targets or market shares. These units may set the prices and choose product-mix, but are not directly concerned with cost of materials or labour employed in production. When output is difficult to measure and not necessarily related to inputs, then the organizational unit becomes a cost centre (e.g., general and administrative service departments). The cost centre is reminiscent of the national economic accountants' ancillary unit. The unit typically serves other (internal) units of the enterprise. If the management of an operating unit is given responsibility both for obtaining required inputs and for choosing and selling well-measured outputs, then this particular unit is know as a profit centre. Thus a profit centre combines the tasks of the standard cost centre and revenue centre.

For our purpose, a producing unit will refer to a business unit which combines the scope of the profit centre with at least the units' working capital and physical asset base. A producing unit is conceptually capable of reporting all the production-related information of an establishment. Producing units reports *per se* usually contain industrially-specified production (or operating revenue) data and the various costs of materials used and labour employed are detailed. On the other hand, the production statement tends to be complete in the sense that intermediate service input expenses charged are accounted for (these are mostly corporate overhead and indirect expenses charged to individual units). There certainly are common cost allocation problems to be resolved in producing unit reporting, but these problems are handled internally by corporate management accountants in a position of full information. In addition, the producing unit's gross operating surplus may be further refined by explicitly deducting depreciation.

b) Delineation of the Units

Recent decades have seen trends towards greater complexity and multiform legal structures of the institutions participating in the economic process. A number of factors have played a role in this respect. First of all, in many countries there is a trend towards formation of larger and larger units. Mergers led to large conglomerations of enterprises which often had a variety of activities. The roots of this development were, among other things, the need to spread risks, a wish for additional financial possibilities and the desire for product differentiation. Secondly, this desire for product differentiation led to enterprises turning their attention to various production processes and entering new markets.

While there are variations in structure among the major insurers, the internal organization of insurers is usually composed of two major divisions each performing various activities—head office operations and branch or field operations. The head office may be structured along vice-presidential lines on a activity basis. The direct insurance vice-president usually has actuarial, agency, advertising, sales promotion and field force supervision under his direction. The financial vice-president is usually responsible for investment operations, the management of the portfolio of the company's or various clients' assets. The reinsurance vice-president performs essentially functions that allow the insurance company to increase its underwriting capacity through reinsurance assumed and/or reduce it through reinsurance ceded and retrocession. The administrative vice-president is usually responsible for internal audit, controllership, banking and accountancy functions and general service departments of the corporation. Among the other units that potentially could be auxiliary units because they provide support services to the principal activities of insurance are investment, general and administrative services where one can finds human resources, advertising, promotion and public relations etc.

Branch or field operations may be carried out by a branch office system or a general agency and broker system. The branch office system consists of branch managers, known as agents, who are sales experts directing agents who market their product line of one insurance company only. In contrast, a broker runs his own office,

Table 1
Delineating the Units of the Insurance Business

Type of Unit or Account	Highest Level Unit	Activity
Core Business Lines	Direct Insurance	Underwriting insurance policies; Retail Network: Agents, Brokers and Claims Adjusters
	Reinsurance	Reinsurance ceded; reinsurance assumed; retrocession
	Investment	Portfolio management
Support Business Lines	General Administrative and Corporate Services	Finance Human Resources Computer Services General Administration: Legal Services, Public Affairs and Treasury Other Corporate Services

pays his own expenses and may represent one or more insurance companies and carry life and non life product lines. Berger, Cummins and Weiss (1997) and Cummins and Weiss (1998) treat direct insurance, investment and branch operations as services and not as lines of business. This is incorrect for two reasons: a) there are clearly identifiable inputs that operate within each of these lines of business and b) each of these lines of business sells for profit different kinds of services.[7]

The internal organization of a typical insurance form is mainly important in delineating and valuing flows and perhaps in determining industrial classification (more on that below). If, for example, a unit supports direct insurance exclusively, then the only flows of services should be to direct insurance. In addition, its industrial classification should be the same as the direct insurance units. In general, the delineating of flows has two aspects: the delineation of flows to ultimate customers and the delineation of internal flows between units in the same enterprises.

3. The Production Account at the Level of the Line of Business

Consider an economy with two regions A and B and an insurance firm which operates with three producing units: direct insurance, investment and reinsurance. Assume that the head office of the firm is located in the region A, where all the decisions related to direct insurance and reinsurance take place; the network of the firm which provides retails services to consumers is located in both regions.

[7] Direct insurance sells financial protection for various kinds of assets; reinsurance provides diversification of risks on various kinds of financial protection; investment provides various kinds of investment advices to different clients.

a) Direct Insurance Activity with a Regional Network of Agents
Measurement of output can be derived from the income statement. The basic identity underlying the income statement is profit before income tax which is equal to its revenue less its costs. In the income statement shown in Table 2, operating revenue comes from premiums and from investment income earned on interest and dividends-paying securities (including gains (net of losses) on sales on fixed assets and securities). Operating expenses includes insurance claims paid, wages and salaries, purchased goods and services and investment service fees (for the sake of simplicity, policyholder dividends, depreciation and amortization, indirect business taxes and home office overhead are assumed equal to zero).

Rearranged and modified, the income statement provides the production account, which records the production attributable to the firm in terms of services produced and the income payments and other costs arising in the production. The derivation of the production accounts is described in two steps: 1) The rearrangement of the business accounting statements into the T-account form and 2) the modification of the T-accounts to obtain economic accounts that measure production. The production account shows, on the right side, the value of the firm's production in terms of services produced and, on the left, the value added by the firm in terms of income payments to primary inputs.

To the extent that all the decisions related to the insurance business take place at the head office, located in region A, it then makes sense to attribute all the value of output to that region. Indeed, the network located in the two regions are essentially

Table 2
Income Statement of an Insurance Firm

	Direct premiums earned	1,000
Plus:	Investment income	100
Equals:	Operating revenue	1,100
Less:	Operating expenses	750
	Insurance claims paid	500
	Wages and salaries (total)	75
	• Head office (province A)	25
	• Network (province A)	25
	• Network (province B)	25
	Purchased goods and services (total)	125
	• Head office (province A)	105
	• Network (province A)	10
	• Network (province B)	10
	Investment service fees	50
Equals:	Profit before income tax	350

Table 3 The Production Account of the Direct Insurance Activity is Assumed to Take Place only in Region A

Uses		Sources	
Wages and salaries	75	Gross Output	600
Profit before income tax	350	*Equals:*	
		Direct premiums	1,000
		Plus	
		Investment income	100
		Less	
		Insurance claims incurred	500
		Less:	
		Purchased goods and services	125
		Less:	
		Investment Service Fees	50
Charges against output	425	Value Added	425

cost centres whose *raison d'être* is to support direct insurance activity. Under this assumption, the production account of direct insurance is shown in Table 3.

The problem with the above assumption is that all the insurance production will be assigned to one region. In some countries where regions constitute an important level of decisions and where the regional breakdown of output represents an important tool for policy makers, this assumption is clearly unrealistic. Therefore, one needs to assume that production is attributed to the region where the inputs are expensed. In other words, the network itself generates retail services for which it receives an explicit service charge. Assume that the head office pays $45 in terms of commissions to each network for services rendered (we assume that the commissions, which represent 9% of premiums, are equally distributed between the network A and B).[8] Under this new scenario, as shown in Table 4, we will have three production accounts: two for the region A (one for the direct insurance activity and another for the network located in that region) and one for the network located in region B.

b) Introducing Reinsurance and Investment Activities

Let us now introduce the reinsurance and investment activities, the other two major activities of insurers very often neglected by the economic litterature. Essentially, reinsurance activity undertakes the following operations: It assumes reinsurance of a third

[8] In practice, if this information is not available, one may use the commissions rate that insurers offer to independent brokers.

Table 4a The Production Account of Direct Insurance Located at the Head Office in Region A

Uses		Sources	
Wages and salaries	25	Gross Output	600
Profit before income tax	330	*Equals:*	
		Direct premiums	1,000
		Plus	
		Investment income	100
		Less	
		Insurance claims incurred	500
		Less:	
		Purchased goods and services	105
		Less:	
		Investment service fees	50
		Less	
		Commissions to agents	90
Charges against output	355	Value Added	355

Table 4b
The Production Account of the Network Located in Region A

Uses		Sources	
Wages and salaries	25	Gross Output (commissions)	45
Profit before income tax	10	*Less*	
		Purchased goods and services	10
Charges against output	35	Value Added	35

Table 4c
The Production Account of the Network Located in Region B

Uses		Sources	
Wages and salaries	25	Gross Output (commissions)	45
Profit before income tax	10	*Less*	
		Purchased goods and services	10
Charges against output	35	Value Added	35

party located in a foreign country (in which case, we are dealing with exports of reinsurance services) and cedes reinsurance on behalf of direct insurance activity. The following flows involve reinsurance activity:

- Premiums, claims and investment income associated with reinsurance assumed, respectively, \$300, \$150 and \$30;
- Reinsurance activity cedes a portion of the direct insurance activity to a third party: \$100 of premiums ceded; \$50 of claims ceded and \$10 of investment income. The reinsurance activity incurs the following expenses: wages and salaries for \$70, purchased goods and services for \$50, investment service fees for \$10.

Using this information, the production account of reinsurance activity is displayed in Table 5 which shows the value of reinsurance services provided by this activity. The demand side of this market is represented by direct insurance activity and the foreign sector. Owing to a lack of the required price of reinsurance services, the measurement of the elasticity of supply and demand of reinsurance services constitutes a major gap in our understanding of the reinsurance market. An important attempt has been made recently by Froot and O'Connell (1997) who concluded that in the market of catastrophic reinsurance services, the supply is by far more elastic than the demand side.

An important aspect of the reinsurance market is its international scope. As stressed by Wasow (1986), international trade in insurance occurs in good part through reinsurance, as residents do not directly purchase insurance abroad nor do non-

Table 5
The Production Account of Reinsurance Activity Located in Region

Uses		Sources	
Wages and salaries	70	Gross Output (reinsurance assumed)	180
Profit before income tax	110	*Equals:*	
		Premiums assumed	300
		Plus	
		Investment income	30
		Less	
		Insurance claims incurred	150
		Gross Output (reinsurance ceded)	60
		Less:	
		Purchased goods and services	50
		Less:	
		Investment Service Fees	10
Charges against output	180	Value Added	180

Table 6
The Production Account of Investment Located in Region A

Uses		Sources	
Wages and salaries	20	Gross Output (Service fees)	100
Profit before income tax	60	• Direct Insurance	50
		• Reinsurance	10
		• External Client	40
		Less:	
		Purchased goods and services	20
Charges against output	80	Value Added	80

residents travel to a foreign country to buy insurance. Carter and Dickinson (1992) and United Nations (1993b) indicate that the reinsurance activity has been historically less subjected to the constraints affecting delivery of insurance and the regulatory barriers to international transactions observed in life and non-life industries. Consequently, the most important developments in international insurance transactions have taken place in the reinsurance industry.

As for the investment activity, the following transactions are recorded in its production account shown in Table 6:

- In terms of revenue, the investment activity charges a service fee to direct insurance and reinsurance activities for a total of $60 ($50 for direct insurance and $10 for reinsurance); it also charges $40 to a client for the management of his (or her) pension fund.
- It pays $20 for wages and salaries, $20 for purchased goods and services.

In reality, the measurement of investment activity's output is not always that easy. In fact, the output of this activity is one the hardest to measure as it transforms liabilities (policyholders' deposits) into earning assets (loans through different financial instruments). The measurement of the investment unit output is hindered by the inapplicability of standard national income accounting procedures.[9] Here the experience gained in the area of measurement of banking output may be useful.

The role of the investment unit as a financial intermediary suggests that deposits

[9] Specifically, the use of standard national accounting procedure to measure the output (gross output or value added) originating in financial intermediation would yield a figure that would be too low without the addition of an imputed value of financial services rendered (see Berger and Humphrey 1992; Fixler and Zieschang 1991). To illustrate, suppose that the GDP for the investment unit was calculated simply by summing wages, profits and net interests (where net interests are interest earned on loans and interest paid to the direct insurance for funds loaned). A characteristic of the investment unit is that interest received typically exceeds interest paid; it typically pays below market interest rates on liabilities. The interest rate differential serves as an implicit payment for services rendered. Without the explicit addition of the value of these implicit payments the GDP for investment would be understated.

accounts should be considered as inputs since the unit acquire these funds in order to acquire earning assets. But as Sealey and Lindley (1977) recognized, deposits are not inputs in the same sense as labour and capital; they are in effect a technical output of the unit. Nevertheless, because deposits are used to produce earning assets, Sealey and Lindley argued that earning assets should be viewed as the final output of financial intermediaries. The problem with this view is that it misses the importance of the financial services attached to deposit accounts.

Until recently, the striking feature of the input-output issue was the absence of a mechanism that determines inputs and outputs. Hancock (1985) established such a mechanism through the application of the user cost of money concept developed in Barnett (1980). The user cost of money is analogous to the user cost of capital and measures the net benefit of a particular way of holding money. In general, the user cost measures the economic cost of providing the financial services attached to investment unit output. Accordingly, the user costs are the signals by which the investment unit allocates resources to provide the financial services and therefore qualify as service process. Because the user costs can be either positive or negative, the prices are defined in terms of the absolute value of the user costs. The variability in the sign of the user cost creates a way to determine input-output status endogeneously. A positive user cost indicates that the financial service is an input while a negative user cost indicates that the financial service is an output. With the the measure of investment unit output the user cost of the assets is given by $u = \frac{(\rho - h)}{(1+\rho)}$ while the user cost for the liability is given by $u = \frac{(h-\rho)}{(1+\rho)}$, where u denotes the user cost of the asset (liability), ρ is the investment unit's opportunity cost and h the holding cost or revenue for the financial good.

To provide some of the intuition underlying the expression for the user cost, consider the case where the only concerns of the investment unit are the interest rate and the opportunity cost of capital. Suppose that the unit has only bonds with a face value of V^0 in period 0. If the investment unit's holding of bonds remains fixed the value of its holdings in period 1 is $V^0(1 + \pi)$ where π is the interest rate on bonds. The investment unit decides between selling bonds in period 0 and holding them until period 1. The user cost in effect is the difference between the two alternatives, that is

$$\text{Net Return} = V^0 - \left[V^0 \frac{(1+\pi)}{(1+\rho)}\right] = V^0 \frac{(\rho - \pi)}{1+\rho}$$

and thus the user cost per bond dollar is simply $\frac{(\rho-\pi)}{(1+\rho)}$. Similar reasoning would apply to the derivation of the user cost for a liability. Observe that in this example the sign of the user cost is determined by the difference between the two rates of return. Since the investment unit would maintain its bonds holdings only if π was greater

Table 7
Modified Production Account of Direct Insurance Located at the Head Office in Region A

Uses		Sources	
Wages and salaries	25	Gross Output	600
Profit before income tax	270	*Equals:*	
		Direct premiums	1,000
		Plus	
		Investment income	100
		Less	
		Insurance claims incurred	500
		Less:	
		Purchased goods and services	105
		Less	
		Commissions to agents	90
		Less	
		Purchased reinsurance services (Premiums *minus* Claims *plus* Investment Income of reinsurance ceded)	60
		Less	
		Investment Service Fees	50
Charges against output	295	Value Added	295

then ρ it follows that the user cost for bonds should be negative and they are therefore classified as a financial output; that is, the purchase of bonds by the investment unit (making a loan) is a financial output.

The production account of direct insurance activity, which now should record the flows of services purchased from reinsurance and investment activities, is shown in Table 7.

4. *Integrating all the Lines of Business*

a) The Consolidated Production Account

In constructing national economic accounts, it is necessary to add together corresponding accounts belonging to two or more transactors and, occasionally, to add together two or more accounts belonging to the same transactor. In the aggregate account, an entry may occur twice, either once on each side of the account, or twice—with opposite signs—on the same side. If such entries are netted out, the aggregate account is a consolidation; if these cancellations are not made, the aggregate account is a combined account.

Production account of the insurance firm (Table 8) is obtained by adding together the production account shown for all producing units in Tables 4–7. The account is

Table 8
Production Account of the Insurance Firm

Uses		Sources	
Wages and salaries	165	Gross Output (direct insurance)	600
Profit before income tax	460	*Equals:*	
		Direct premiums	1,000
		Plus	
		Investment income	100
		Less	
		Insurance claims incurred	500
		Gross Output (reinsurance assumed)	180
		Equals:	
		Premiums	300
		Plus	
		Investment income	30
		Less	
		Insurance claims incurred	150
		Gross Output (Investment)	40
		Less:	
		Purchased goods and services	195
		• Direct Insurance	105
		• Reinsurance	50
		• Investment	20
		• Agency	20
Charges against output	625	Value Added	625

prepared on a consolidated basis. The entries for a transaction between two producing units cancel, leaving only transactions between the producing unit and units outside the firm. These entries are: direct insurance (–$90 for commissions) and agency (+$90); direct insurance (–$60 for reinsurance ceded) and reinsurance (+$60); direct insurance (–$50 for purchase of investment services) and investment (+$50) and reinsurance (–$10 for purchase of investment services) and investment (+$10).

It is important to note that the sum of value added generated by the different lines of business (see Tables 4b–7) is equal to the value added calculated at the consolidated level of the insurance firm (Table 8). Therefore, given this property of additivity, the sum of value added generated by the different lines of business constitutes a sufficient statistics to estimate an unduplicated measure of production activity at the level of consolidation (i.e., the insurance firm).

b) Input-Output Accounting

Information on the flows of goods and services that make up the production relationships between insurance industries and the rest of the economy is missing from the income and expenditures accounts (IEA), but is provided by the input-output (I-

O) accounting. I-O accounting can be viewed as a deconsolidation, along detailed industry lines, of the subsectoral production account of Table 7, with a separate production account presented for each industry. Both IEA and I-O accounts present GDP in terms of final product flows (final demand, using I-O terminology) and in terms of charges against GDP (value added, using I-O terminology). The distinctive feature of the I-O accounts is the presentation of detailed information for each industry on the consumption of purchased materials and services that canceled in arriving at an unduplicated measure of production for the business sector. This detailed information is presented in a matrix—an I-O table.

In the I-O table, each column records the gross output of an industry and the inputs used by that industry in production; that is,

Gross Industry Output = Consumption of Purchased Goods and Services
+ Value Added.

Each row records the gross output of a good or services (commodity in I-O terminology), the consumption of the commodity by producing industries, and the final demand for the commodity, where final demand consists of sales of the commodity to final users, the change in inventories of the commodity held by both the producing and consuming industries, less imports of the commodity; that is,

Gross Commodity Output = Consumption by Producing Industries
+ Sales to Final Users
+ Change in Inventories
– Imports.

To illustrate the derivation of the I-O Account, Tables 9–13 present production accounts for the four hypothetical insurance industries—agency and brokerage, direct insurance, reinsurance and investment—and the rest of the business sector that make up the whole business sector. Unlike the production accounts derived above, these accounts record production on a gross basis; that is consumption has not been subtracted from both sides. Also, these accounts provide a breakdown of purchased goods and services shown in Tables 4b–7 in terms of services transacted between the insurance lines of business and goods and services purchased outside the insurance firm. For the rest of the economy, Table 13 presents a single consolidated production account.

Several features of the illustration in Tables 9–13 should be noted: a) each industry produces a single commodity and that commodity is not produced by any other industry; b) the commodities produced by agency, direct insurance, reinsurance and investment industries are services, therefore, they are not inventoried; the commodity produced by the rest of the business sector is inventoriable; c) producing units in each industry purchase inputs from other units in the same industry.

Table 9
Agency Industry

Uses		Sources	
Consumption		Sales of agency services	
Intermediate expenses		To producers	
Agency services		Agency industry	0
Direct insurance services	10	Direct insurance industry	90
Reinsurance services		Reinsurance industry	0
Investment services		Investment industry	0
Other goods and services	10	Rest of the economy	0
Less: Change in raw materials inventories		To final users	0
Agency services		Change in work-in-process and finished goods Inventories	0
Direct insurance services		*Less:* Imports of agency services	0
Reinsurance services			
Investment services			
Goods and services			
Value added	70		
Charges against gross output	90	Gross output	90

Table 10
Direct Insurance Industry

Uses		Sources	
Consumption		Sales of direct insurance services	
Intermediate expenses		To producers	
Agency services	90	Agency industry	10
Direct insurance services	10	Direct insurance industry	10
Reinsurance services	60	Reinsurance industry	10
Investment services	50	Investment industry	10
Other goods and services	95	Rest of the economy	160
Less: Change in raw materials inventories		To final users	400
Agency services	0	Change in work-in-process and	
Direct insurance services	0	finished goods Inventories	0
Reinsurance services	0	*Less:* Imports of direct insurance services	0
Investment services	0		
Goods and services	0		
Value added	295		
Charges against gross output	600	Gross output	600

Table 11
Reinsurance Industry

Uses		Sources	
Consumption		Sales of reinsurance services	
Intermediate expenses		To producers	
Agency services	0	Agency industry	0
Direct insurance services	10	Direct insurance industry	60
Reinsurance services	0	Reinsurance industry	
Investment services	10	Investment industry	
Goods and services	40	Rest of the economy	
Less: Change in raw materials inventories		To final users	180
Agency services	0	Change in work-in-process and finished goods Inventories	0
Direct insurance services	0		
Reinsurance services	0	*Less:* Imports of reinsurance services	0
Investment services	0		
Other goods and services	0		
Value added	180		
Charges against gross output	240	Gross output	240

Table 12
Investment Industry

Uses		Sources	
Consumption		Sales of investment services	
Intermediate expenses		To producers	
Agency services	0	Agency industry	0
Direct insurance services	10	Direct insurance industry	50
Reinsurance services	0	Reinsurance industry	10
Investment services	0	Investment industry	0
Goods and services	10	Rest of the economy	40
Less: Change in raw materials inventories		To final users	0
Agency services	0	Change in work-in-process and finished goods Inventories	0
Direct insurance services	0		
Reinsurance services	0	*Less:* Imports of investment services	0
Investment services	0		
Other goods and services	0		
Value added	80		
Charges against gross output	100	Gross output	100

Table 13
Rest of the Economy

Uses		Sources	
Consumption		Sales of goods and services	
Intermediate expenses		To producers	
Agency services	0	Agency industry	10
Direct insurance services	160	Direct insurance industry	95
Reinsurance services	0	Reinsurance industry	40
Investment services	40	Investment industry	10
Goods and services	10	Rest of the economy	10
Less: Change in raw materials inventories		To final users	100
Agency services	0		
Direct insurance services	0	Change in work-in-process and	
Reinsurance services	0	finished goods Inventories	20
Investment services	0	*Less:* Imports of goods and	10
Other goods and services	0	services	
Value added	65		
Charges against gross output	275	Gross output	275

Table 14 illustrates the construction of the I-O table from the information contained in Tables 9–13. The first five columns on the left side of the matrix record the consumption of intermediate inputs, as well as value-added, by the producing industries. For each industry, consumption is derived from the left side of the industry's production account in Tables 9–13 as the purchase of the commodity less the change in raw material inventory. Value added is also taken from the left side of the industry production account. Three columns, further to the right, record the components of final demand. Sales to final users are obtained from the right side of the production accounts in Tables 9–13.

25.3.3 Assessing the Delineation of Insurance Producing Units

a) Set Up

So far I have delineated the insurance firm now as a set of integrated producing units performing different activities. The question is how meaningful are these activities. Following Clarke (1989), I investigate how well the proposed delineation of the insurance business separates groups of insurance firms into economically distinct activities. The maintained hypothesis is that there are input shares that are more similar among producing units that occupy the same industry than among units that are in more remotely connected industries.

The delineation of insurance industries is said to be significant if, and only if, the production units of an industry react the same way to any exogenous shock

Table 14
Input-Output Table

Distribution of output / Composition inputs	Producers						Final demand				Gross commodity output
	Agency	Direct Insurance	Reinsurance	Investment	Rest of the economy	Total intermediate use	Sales to final users	Change in inventories	Imports	Total of final demand	
Agency services	0	90	0	0	0	90	0	0	0	0	90
Direct insurance services	10	0	10	10	150	200	400	0	0	400	600
Reinsurance services	0	60	0	0	0	60	180	0	0	180	240
Investment services	0	50	10	0	40	100	0	0	0	0	100
Goods and other services	10	95	40	10	10	165	100	20	–10	110	275
Total intermediate inputs	20	305	60	20	210	635	......	......	......	......	......
Value added	70	295	180	80	65						690
Gross industry output	90	600	240	100	275	......	680	20	–10	690	......

(industry-wide or economy-wide). For this to be true, the production units of this industry must have similar technologies. However, the similarities diminish within coarser industrial groups. To test this proposition, I use a variation of the diversification concept developed by Gollop and Monahan (1991), which allows me to quantify the extent to which an industry's production units have similar technologies.

The properties of a technology are captured in parameters defining the relationships among inputs, outputs and costs. Identical cost function parameters across producing units suggest homogeneous technologies while different parameters specify heterogeneous technologies. Identifying and measuring these parameters is the key to designing a statistical measure that can be used to assess the delineation of the insurance business. It turns out that, under reasonable assumptions, the information required for identifying these technology parameters can be extracted from data commonly available in industrial accounts. To show this, consider the following cost function of a production unit *i* defined in (1)

$$G_j(w, Q, R, t), \tag{1}$$

where *w*, *Q*, and *R* represent, respectively, vectors of input prices, output, and any other input peculiar to the activity of the production unit;[10] G_j represents the minimal cost incurred by the production unit *j* in order to produce a vector of output *Q* under given market conditions, and any idiosyncratic aspect represented by *w* and *R*, respectively. The simplest parameterization of this cost function is to assume that it has the Cobb-Douglas form

$$\ln C_j = \sum_f^J \beta_{j,f} \ln w_{j,f} + \sum_\kappa^I \lambda_{j,\kappa} \ln Q_{j,\kappa} + \sum_\tau^M \alpha_{j,\tau} \ln R_{j,\tau}. \tag{2}$$

Assuming competitive (input and output) markets, the Cobb-Douglas parameters $\beta_{j,f}$ and $\alpha_{j,\tau}$ associated with the inputs are equal to the corresponding revenue shares (using Shephard lemma)

$$\begin{aligned}
\beta_{j,f} &\equiv \frac{\partial \ln C_j}{\partial \ln w_{j,f}} = \frac{w_{j,f} \cdot X_{j,f}}{V_j} = s_{j,f} \\
\alpha_{j,\tau} &\equiv \frac{\partial \ln C_j}{\partial \ln R_{j,\tau}} = \frac{z_{j,\tau} \cdot R_{j,\tau}}{V_j} = \omega_{j,\tau} \\
\lambda_{j,\kappa} &\equiv \frac{\partial \ln C_j}{\partial \ln Q_{j,\kappa}} = \frac{p_{j,\kappa} \cdot Q_{j,\tau}}{V_j} = \vartheta_{j,\kappa}
\end{aligned} \tag{3}$$

so that $\sum_f^J s_{j,f} + \sum_\tau^M \omega_{j,\tau} = 1$ where

[10] The variable *R* could represent reinsurance ceded for direct insurance production unit.

$w_{j,f}$ = the price of the input f,
$z_{j,\tau}$ = the (shadow) price of the input τ,
$X_{j,f}$ = the quantity of the input f used by the $j-th$ production unit,
$R_{j,\tau}$ = any other input τ used by the $j-th$ production unit,
V_j = the nominal output produced by the $j-th$ production unit,
Q_j = the quantity of output produced by the $j-th$ production unit,
$\alpha_{j,\tau}$ = the (shadow) revenue service share of any of the $\tau-th$ inputs in the total nominal output of the $j-th$ production unit,
$\lambda_{j,\kappa}$ = the revenue share of the $\kappa-th$ output in the total nominal output of the $j-th$ production unit.

If one considers another producing unit, say h, which performs the same activity and uses a Cobb-Douglas technology, this technology will correspond to parameters $\beta_{h,f}$, $\alpha_{h,\tau}$ and, accordingly, to input shares $s_{h,f}$, $\omega_{h,\tau}$. If both production units have the same technology, then one may expect to obtain $s_{j,f} = s_{h,f}$ and $\omega_{i,\tau} = \omega_{h,\tau}$. Otherwise, none of these equalities would hold. Differences in input cost shares and output shares among producing units, which, therefore, quantify differences among parameter technologies, can be used to calibrate the extent of heterogeneity among producing units within an industry. The heterogeneity index Δ has the following form

$$\Delta = \sum_{j}^{J} \mu_j \Delta_j, \tag{4}$$

with

$$\mu_i = \frac{V_j}{\sum_j V_j}, \tag{5}$$

and

$$\Delta_j = \sum_h \mu_h = \left(\frac{\sum_j |s_{j,f} - s_{h,j}|}{2} + \frac{\sum_\tau |\omega_{j,\tau} - \omega_{h,\tau}|}{2} \right). \tag{6}$$

The symbol $|\cdot|$ refers to the absolute value. Dividing by two prevents double counting and ensures that the index Δ is bounded in the zero-one interval, $0 \leq \Delta \leq 1$. As differences among the parameters increase, Δ increases. As the differences decrease, the index Δ approaches zero. It turns out that the heterogeneity index is simply a weighted sum over differences in cost function parameters describing the technology structures employed by producing units within an industry, where the weights μ_j and μ_h are defined as the shares of the $j-th$ and $h-th$ producing units in the industry's nominal output. For any given difference in the input shares of the $j-th$ and $h-th$ producing units, the overall effect on industry Δ is determined by the relative importance of the $j - th$ and $h - th$ producing units. Therefore, input differences between large producing units have more impact on Δ than do input differences between small establishments. The share variables μ_j and μ_h insure this result.

b) Empirical Results

Once the delineation has been completed, the issue is whether production units in each industry operate under the same technology or not. This question is crucial since firms specialized in the same product line can use a different technology or different input mix. This, in turn, means that they will not react identically to a common shock. For this purpose, the heterogeneity index appears to be helpful. It enables us to examine whether or not there is a large dispersion in the technology of production units that are members of the same industry by using information on the input shares of each of them. This index also indicates whether or not the industrial classification is becoming more accurate by progressive refinements to the structure of the classification. For example, does it suggest that the heterogeneity in the technology of producing units substantially decreases as we move from a classification based on institutions to another based on producing units? If so, this implies that it is likely that the production units that are members of the institutions display different technologies.

Table 15 summarizes the application of the heterogeneity index Δ at the different level of refinement for both life and non-life insurance using data from the Office of Superintendent of Financial Institution, the regulator of the insurance business in Canada. Although the results are based on 1994 data, they do seem to be fairly stable over time. The level of the heterogeneity index for the whole insurance subsector is fairly high at 0.88. Making the distinction between life and nonlife insurance industries at the institutional level (i.e., the insurance firm) somehow reduces, albeit not dramatically, the level of heterogeneity. Although the level of heterogeneity still remains high for both types of insurance, life insurance industry displays a slightly

Table 15

Heterogeneity Index Applied to Insurance Industries

Insurance	88
Life Insurance	85
Agency	33
Direct insurance	64
Reinsurance	79
Investment	45
Non-Life Insurance	93
Agency	42
Direct insurance	66
Reinsurance	48
Investment	74

lower level of heterogeneity than non-life insurance industry (0.85 versus 0.93). Separating the insurance firm into distinct lines of business implies a significant decrease of the level of heterogeneity for both life and non-life insurance businesses. In both instances, agency industry display the lowest level of heterogeneity in comparison with other industries. Owing to the small number of producing units accounted for in the sample in comparison with other insurance industries, reinsurance and investment industries display a relatively high level of heterogeneity, respectively, for life insurance and non life insurance. Despite the refinement made to the insurance business through these four industries, the direct insurance industry still shows a high level of heterogeneity for both life and non-life insurance businesses. This tends to suggest that a further refinement can be implemented in this particular industry through the distinction between multiproduct and monoproduct producing units.[11] Finally, it is important to note that the level of the heterogeneity index is not significantly different between pairs of the same industry that belong to life and non-life insurance. This clearly suggest that, on the basis of the technology, the distinction between life and non-life insurance businesses is irrelevant. What is more relevant, however, is the delineation of the various lines of business which happen to display the same technology across the type of insurance.

In most cases, the results indicate that heterogeneity in technology tends to increase when n-digit level of refinement is coarsened into $(n-1)$-digit level refinement. These results suggest that the delineation of the insurance business proposed in this paper is quite robust as a method to separate insurers' production units into very refined groups based on similar technologies. Since the latter level is the one that most economists view as being close to economic industries, the proposed approach turns out to be successful at delineating economic industries.

25.4 CONCLUDING REMARKS

This chapter reviews and extends the measurement framework of the insurance business at both macro and micro levels. The main results of this framework are easily summarized. First, the SNA consists of a coherent, consistent set of macroeconomic accounts and tables designed for a variety of analytical and policy purpose. Nevertheless, certain key aggregates of the system, such as industry GDP, have acquired an identity of their own and are widely used by users of all kinds as summary, global indicators of economic and welfare. Movements of such aggregates, and their associated price and volume measures, are used to evaluate the performance of the economy and industries. The first part of the chapter applies illustrates this framework using the insurance sub-sector as an example.

[11] The new North Americain Industrial Classification System for the Canadian insurance business actually does introduce this distinction between multiproduct and monoproduct producing units. See Statistics Canada (1997).

Second, although the SNA was born in the world of macroeconomics, its roots have been in the data relating to individual decision-making units in the economy. Since its inception, both the complexity of the economic system and the concern with new analytical problems have increased. Currently, governments are faced with the need to evaluate both the macro and micro aspects of their policies in many areas. The national accounts alone are not sufficient for this task. Both the need and technical feasibility of linking the macro framework with micro data have increased.[12]

The second contribution of this paper is to unravel the behaviour of the various activities performed by insurance firms, with a special focus on the interactions between the various production units, their output and the characterization of their behavioural functions. The need to go beyond the concept of insurance firm builds on the tradition initiated by Coase. Just recently, in his Alfred Nobel Memorial Prize in Economic Sciences' lecture, Coase (1992, 714) emphasized once again the need to go beyond the traditional "black box" concept of firms:

> *"What is studied (in the mainstream theory of firm) is a system which lives in the minds of economists but not on earth. The firm in mainstream economic theory has often been described as a 'black box.' And so it is. This is very extraordinary given that most resources in a modern economic system are employed within firms, with how these resources are used depended on administrative decisions and not directly on the operation of a market. Consequently, the efficiency of the economic system depends to a very considerable extent on how these organizations conduct their affairs, particularly, of course, the modern corporation."*

On the other hand, the practical reasons that motivate this option are numerous. In North America, like in many other developed continents, the financial services business corresponds exclusively to regulated institutions, legally constituted, and often members of enterprises with a wide variety of activities. The concept of institutional entity is far from unambiguous and that the motives for legal structures are often other than purely organizational. They are often associated with tax-legislation and regulation, rather than reflecting economic reality. It is questionable whether the chosen legal structure corresponds with the way in which economic agents perceive reality themselves. It is even very likely that their view of economic reality is a very different one.

At least three areas of the analysis of the insurance business remain fertile ground for further research. First, I suggest that the analysis of the insurance production structures at the level of the line of business should be listed to the top of the agenda in

[12] The UN SNA (1993) states explicitly its position concerning the relation of the macro accounts to micro data: *"Nevertheless, as a general objective, the concepts, definitions and classifications used in economic accounting should, so far as possible, be the same at both a micro and macro level of facilitate the interface between the two kinds of data."* (p. 12).

applied econometrics and determine which production units drive the economic performance of the insurance firm. While many studies documented the fact that the life insurance industry shifted from financial protection services to investment products (see Poterba (1997)), no contribution has ever tried to determine the difference in the economic performance between financial protection (direct insurance) and financial intermediation (investment activity).

The other remaining areas for further research concern the economic performance of the investment activity and reinsurance. This last item includes issues such as the turbulence in the insurance business in terms of entry-exit, concentration by product line, pricing and a cross country comparison in the structures, conduct and economic performance of insurers lines of business.

25.5 REFERENCES

Alchian, A. and H. Demsetz (1972). "Production, Information Costs, and Economic Organization," *American Economic Review* 62, 777–95.

Barnett, W.A. (1980). Economic Monetary Aggregates: An Application of Index Number and Aggregation Theory, Annals of Applied Econometrics, (supplement to the *Journal Econometrics*), 14, 11–48.

Berger, A.N. and D.B. Humphrey (1992). "Measurement and Efficiency Issues in Commercial Banking," 245–300, in Griliches, Z. (ed.): *Output Measurement in the Service Sectors*, National Bureau of Economic Research Conference on Research in Income and Wealth, 56, The University of Chicago Press.

Berger, A.N., Cummins, J.D. and M.A. Weiss (1997). "The Coexistence of Multiple Distribution Systems for Financial Services: The Case of Property-Liability Insurance," *Journal of Business* 70, 515–46.

Bernstein, J.I. and R. Geehan (1988). *The Insurance Industry in Canada,* Fraser Institute, Vancouver.

Bernstein, J.I. (1992). "Information Spillovers, Margins, Scale and Scope: With an Application to Canadian Life Insurance," *Scandinavian Journal of Insurance*, 94 (Supplement), 95–105.

Bernstein, J.I. (1999). "Total Factor Productivity Growth in the Canadian Life Insurance Industry: 1979–1989," *Canadian Journal of Economics* (Special Issue on Service Sector Productivity and the Productivity Paradox) 32, 500–17.

Bloem, A.M. (1990). "Units in National Accounts and the Basic System of Economic Statistics," *Review of Income and Wealth* 36, 275–88.

Bohman, H. (1979). "A Mathematical Model of Insurance Business and How it May Be Used?," *The Geneva Papers on Risk and Insurance*, 11, 34–8.

Borch, K. (1981). "The Three Market of Private Insurance," *Geneva Papers on Risk and Insurance*, 20, 7–31.

Bruno, M. (1978). "Duality, Intermediate Inputs and Value-Added," in M. Fuss and D. McFadden (eds.): *Production Economics: A Dual Approach to Theory and Application*, 2, 3–16, North-Holland.

Carter, R.L. and G.M. Dickinson (1992). *Obstacles to the Liberalization of Trade in Insurance*, Harvester for the Trade Policy Research Centre, London.

Chandler, A. (1977). *The Visible Hand*, Cambridge: Belknap Press.

Chandler, A. (1990). *Scale and Scope*, Cambridge: Belknap Press.

Clarke, R.N. (1989). "SICs as Delineators of Economic Markets," *Journal of Business* 62, 17–31.

Coase, R.H. (1992). "The Institutional Structure of Production," *American Economic Review* 82, 713–19.

Coase, R.H. (1937). "The Nature of Firm," *Economica 4*, 386–405.

Copeland, M.A. (1957). "The Feasibility of a Standard Comprehensive System of Social Accounts," in *Problems in the International Comparison of Economic Accounts*, Studies in Income and Wealth, 20, National Bureau of Economic Research, New York.

Cummins, J.D. and M.A. Weiss (1998). "Analyzing Firm Performance in the Insurance Industry Using Frontier Efficiency Methods," 45p., The Wharton School, Discussion Paper 98–22.

David, P. and K. Sato (1962). "The Meaning and Measurement of the Real Value-Added Index," *Review of Economics and Statistics* 58, 434–42.

David, P. (1962). "The Deflation of Value-Added," *Review of Economics and Statistics* 44, 148–55.

Denny, M. and D. May. (1977). "The Existence of a Real Value-Added Function in the Canadian Manufacturing Sector," *Journal of Econometrics* 5, 55–69.

Denny, M. and D. May. (1978). "Homotheticity and Real Value-Added in Canadian Manufacturing," in M. Fuss and D. McFadden (eds.): *Production Economics: A Dual Approach to Theory and Application*, 2, 53–70, North-Holland.

Dean, E.R. and K. Kunze (1992). "Productivity Measurement in Services Industries," in Griliches, Z. (ed.)(with the assistance of Berndt, E.R., Bresnahan, T.F. and Manser M.E.: *Output Measurement in the Service Sectors*, 73–101, The University of Chicago Press.

Diewert, W.E. (1978). "Hicks' Aggregation Theorem and the Existence of a Real Value-Added Function," in M. Fuss and D. McFadden (eds.): *Production Economics: A Dual Approach to Theory and Application*, 2, 17–52, North-Holland.

Diewert, W.E. (1995). "Functional Form Problems in Modeling Insurance and Gambling," *The Geneva Papers on Risk and Insurance Theory*, 20, 135–50.

Durand, R. (1994). "An Alternative to Double Deflation for Measuring Real Industry Value-Added," *Review of Income and Wealth* 16, 221–35.

Fabricant, S. (1940). *The Output of Manufacturing Industries, 1899–1937*, National Bureau of Economic Research, New York.

Fixler, D.J. and K.D.Zieschang (1991). "Measuring the Nominal Value of Financial Services in the National Income Accounts," *Economic Inquiry* 29, 53–68.

Froot, K.A. and P.G. O'Connell (1997). "On the Pricing of Intermediated Risks: Theory and Application to Catastrophe Reinsurance," National Bureau of Economic Research, WP 6011.

Gollop, F. and M. Monahan (1991). "A Generalized Index of Diversification: Trends in U.S. Manufacturing," *Review of Economics and Statistics* LXIII, 318–30.

Griliches, Z. (1992). "Services Industries," in Griliches, Z. (ed.) (with the assistance of Berndt, E.R., Bresnahan, T.F. and Manser M.E.: *Output Measurement in the Service Sectors*, 11–34, The University of Chicago Press.

Hancock, D. (1985). "The Financial Firm: Production with Monetary and Non-Monetary Goods," *Journal of Political Economy*, 96, 859–80.

Harchaoui, T.M. (1997). "Measuring the Productivity of the Insurance Business at the Firm Level," 25 p., Paper presented at the CSLS Conference on Service Sector Productivity, April 11–12, 1997, Ottawa.

Harchaoui, T.M. (1998). "Dealing with Deposit Taking Institutions at the Level of the Line of Business: Delination, Data Collection and Analysis," 25 p., mimeo.

Hartwick, J.M. (1997). "On Insurance Firms in the National Accounts, Mimeo, Queen's University," 20 p.

Hill, T.P. (1971). *The Measurement of Real product: A Theoretical and Empirical Analysis of the Growth Rates for Different Industries and Countries*, OECD, Paris.

Jaszi, G. (1955). "Comment on Papers by Sigel and Liebling," in *Input-Output Analysis: An Appraisal*, Studies in Income and Wealth, 18, National Bureau of Economic Research, New York.

Jaszi, G. (1971). "An Economic Accountant's Ledger," *Survey of Current Business*, Anniversary Issue, 51(7), Part II.

Jensen, G.A. and M.A. Morrisey (1990). "Group Health Insurance: A Hedonic Price Approach," *Review of Economic and Statistics* 74, 39–44.

Kaplan, R.S. (1982). *Advanced Management Accounting*, Prentice-Hall Inc., New Jersey.

Klein, B., Crawford, R. and A. Alchian (1978). "*Vertical Integration, Appropriable Rents, and the Competitive Contracting* Process," *Journal of Law and Economics* 21, 297–326.

Lal, K. (1990). "Services Industries in the Business Sector of the Canadian Economy," *Review of Income and Wealth* 36, 83–94.

Marshall (1890). *Principles of Economics*, London.

McGuckin, R.H. (1995). "Establishment Microdata for Economic Research and Policy Analysis: Looking Beyond the Aggregates," *Journal of Business and Economic Statistics* 13, 121–6.

OECD (1998). *Services: Statistics on Value Added and Employment*, 327 p., Paris.

Poterba, J. (1997). "The History of Annuities in the United States," NBER Working Paper Series, WP #6001, 50 p.

Reece, J.S. and W.R. Cool (1978). "Measuring Investment Centre Performance," *Harvard Business Review*.

Reece, W.S. (1993). "Output Price Indexes for the U.S. Life Insurance Industry," *Journal of Risk and Insurance* 22, 104–17.

Ruggles, R. and N.D. Ruggles (1982a). "Integrated Economic Accounts for the United States, 1947–1980," *Survey of Current Business* 62.

Ruggles, R. and N.D. Ruggles (1982b). "Integrated Economic Accounts: Reply," *Survey of Current Business* 62.

Ruggles, N.D. and R. Ruggles (1983a). "The Treatment of Pensions and Insurance in National Accounts," *Review of Income and Wealth*, 4, 371–404.

Ruggles, R. (1983b). "The United States National Income Accounts, 1947–1977," in Foss, M.F. (ed.): *The US National Income and Product Accounts*, Income and Wealth Conference Volume, National Bureau Economic Research, New York.

Sato, K. (1976). "The Meaning and Measurement of the Real Value-Added Index," *Review of Economics and Statistics* 58, 434–42.

Schiltz, M.T. (1987). "A New Method of Assessment of the Insurance Service Production," *Review of Income and Wealth* 4, 431–7.

Sealey, C.W. and J. Lindley (1977). "Inputs, Outputs, and a Theory of Production and Cost at Depository Financial Institutions," *Journal of Finance* 32, 1251–66.

Sherwood, M.K. (1999). "Output of the Property and Casualty Insurance Industry," *Canadian Journal of Economics* (Special Issue on Service Sector Productivity and the Productivity Paradox) 32, 518–46.

Sigel, S.J. (1955). "A Comparison of the Structures of Three Social Accounting Systems," in *Input-Output Analysis: An Appraisal*, Studies in Income and Wealth, 18, National Bureau of Economic Research, New York.

Sims, C.A. (1969). "Theoretical Basis for a Double Deflated Index of Real Value-Added," *Review of Economics and Statistics* 51, 470–1.

Skipper, H.D. (1993). Insurers Solvency Regulation in the United States, in OECD (1993). *Policy Issues in Insurance*, 75–146, OECD, Paris.

Smith, A. (1776). *The Wealth of Nations*, Edimburgh.

Statistics Canada (1997). *The North American Industrial Classification System, Canada 1997*, 12–501 XPE, Ottawa.

Tice, H.S. (1967). "Report of a Conference on the Proposals for revision of the United Nations System of National Accounts," *Review of Income and Wealth* 18, 243–52.

United Nations (1968). *A System of National Accounts*, Studies in Methods, Series F., No. 2, Rev. 3, New York: United Nations.

United Nations (1993a). *System of National Accounts*, Inter-Secretariat Working Group of National Accounts, New York: United Nations.

United Nations (1993b). *International Tradibility in Insurance Services: Implications for Foreign Direct Investment in Insurance Services*, Transnational Corporations and Management Division, Department of Economic and Social Development, New York.

Weiss, M.A. (1987). "Macroeconomic Insurance Output Estimation," *Journal of Risk and Insurance* 53, 582–93.

Wasow, B, (1986). "Insurance and the Balance of Payments," in B. Wasow and R.D. Hill (eds.): *The Insurance Industry in Economic Development*, New York University Press, New York.

Williamson, O.E. (1975). *Markets and Hierarchies*, New York, Free Press.

Williamson, O.E. (1981). "The Modern Corporation: Origins, Evolution, Attributes," *Journal of Economic Literature*, 12, 144–212.

Williamson, O.E. (1985). *The Economic Institutions of Capitalism*, New York, Free Press.

Part VIII
Life Insurance, Pensions and Economic Security

26 Developments in Pensions*

Olivia S. Mitchell

University of Pennsylvania

Abstract

In both developed and developing countries, many elderly depend on government and employment-based pensions. Yet the pension institution faces difficult challenges, even as a rapidly growing aging population turns to it for retirement support. One development is that defined contribution plans have become very popular, sometimes at the expense of defined benefit pensions. This changes the risks and rewards for plan sponsors and participants, as well as government regulators charged with pension oversight. Expenses associated with pension management have also come under scrutiny, imposing new performance pressures on trustees and other pension stakeholders. Finally, it is now becoming clear that far-reaching reforms will be required to restore government social security programs to solvency. As a result, pension plans will require the attention of insurance experts for the foreseeable future.

Keywords: Benefit pensions, aging population, pension management, reform, social security, solvency.

JEL Classification Numbers: G23, H55, J14, J32, G22.

26.1 INTRODUCTION

The world's population is aging rapidly: in 2030, over one third of the developed world's people will be older than age 60, and many developing nations will find their population does not lag far behind (Chand and Jaeger 1996). What does the global aging trend portend for public and private pension systems on which people rely for old-age support? This chapter explores recent developments in pension plan form and function, in order to assess how well pension institutions are suited to meet global demands for retirement income into the foreseeable future.

We organize the chapter around four central questions regarding the way pension institutions work and their impacts in labor and capital markets:

* Research support for this study was provided by the Wharton School and the Pension Research Council. The author is solely responsible for opinions contained herein.

- How do pensions influence the risks workers confront in retirement?
- What explains the global trend toward defined contribution pension plans?
- What other factors influence the market for pensions?
- How can pension performance be judged?

In what follows, we review the key empirical and theoretical lessons offered by recent literature on these questions. But it is useful to first define the concept of a pension, which we take here to mean a financial contract promising to deliver regular income payments to the retired elderly.[1] A pension promise may be supplied by a variety of different entities including employers, insurers, unions, governments, and other institutions offering financial services.

The nature of the pension contract depends on whether the plan is a defined benefit (DB) or a defined contribution (DC) pension. What distinguishes a DC from a DB plan is that in the former, the sponsor promises to deposit a specified contribution into the plan periodically (e.g., per week, month, or sometimes year).[2] In the US, common DC formulas promise contribution rates of 6–8% (combining both employer and employee contributions). These monies are then invested, often at the participant's direction, in stocks, bonds, or other financial instruments. At retirement, the DC plan participant may convert his accumulation into an annuity payable from retirement until death (or the death of the spouse, if a joint and survivor benefit is selected). It is also usual to allow the DC participant to take some or all of his pension accrual in the form of a lump sum. This sum may then be spent immediately, or invested individually and then drawn down based on anticipated life expectancy (this is the "programmed withdrawal" or "minimum distribution" notion consistent with US tax law).

By contrast, a DB plan commonly fashions the pension promise by defining a benefit formula that determines a participant's eventual retirement payments. For instance, a formula for a retirement benefit amount (B) might be:

$$B_t \mid A, R = b(\text{YRS}, \text{FAP}, A)^*\text{YRS}^*\text{FAP},$$

where the dependence of the benefit on t, A and R shows that the amount paid in year t depends on the worker's retirement age (A) as well as the year of his retirement (R); YRS refers to the employee's years of service with the pension sponsor as of retirement; FAP refers to a final average pay computation; and b(·) is some function transforming the worker's age at retirement, service, and pay into a benefit amount. This function can be smooth (e.g., 1% of pay per year of service) but more commonly is nonlinear, granting higher benefits for longer years of service or for pay earned above some threshold (Fields and Mitchell 1984; Stock and Wise 1990). In the case of a

[1] This discussion draws on published and unpublished research by Mitchell (1998a and b, 1997a and b); Gustman et al. (1994), Gustman and Mitchell (1992), and other items listed in the references.

[2] For an excellent discussion of pension financing and benefits see McGill et al. (1996).

funded DB plan, the plan sponsor is expected to contribute to the plan in an orderly fashion according to actuarial standards, so the needed funds are available when the worker retires. Generally a defined benefit pension is payable in the form of an annuity, though occasionally a firm will permit a lump sum cash-out equal to the discounted present value of the future benefit.

Contributions flowing into pension accounts of both the DB and DC variety are typically sheltered from income tax, and investment earnings built up inside the pension fund also tend to accumulate on a pre-tax basis. When this is so, the pension plan is said to be "tax qualified"—where contributions and within-plan build-ups are not subject to tax until retirement.[3] The tax-deferral feature of pensions is particularly valuable to workers in a high marginal tax bracket, and when the plan is funded—i.e., when it has assets to back pension liabilities. Oftentimes pension assets are segregated from the sponsoring employer's own assets, held in trust on the participants' behalf. In this case, a DC plan's assets are by definition equal to plan liabilities, since participants have full claim on what is deposited in the plan via contributions, and also on investment earnings. By contrast in the DB case, plan participants own the promised benefit, but the plan may not be fully backed by sufficient assets to pay future benefits. When this occurs, current contributions may be used to support current retirees, at least in part. This type of DB plan would be characterized as underfunded; in the most extreme case where no assets at all are set aside, the plan is known as a "pay as you go" pension.

Pension systems, like many other institutions entrusted with peoples' financial wellbeing, are generally subject to a wide range of legislative and regulatory oversight. One social goal sometimes expressed by pension regulators is to ensure that participants have a reasonable chance of receiving promised benefits. In this instance, plans tend to be treated as though they were institutions akin to insurers, with solvency and disclosure regulations imposed. Another goal often emphasized by policymakers is the provision of social insurance, which explains the redistributive element of many government-supplied pension programs (Kotlikoff 1987). Thus some pension systems pay higher proportional benefits to poor retirees and conversely, offer a lower replacement rate to the rich. Most government-run social security systems offering retirement pensions are rather redistributive in this way.

Considering public and private pension systems as a whole, these financial institutions represent the main source of old-age support for most elderly in industrial countries. Summary statistics on *private* pension fund accumulated assets appear in Table 1 for several developed nations. Of the countries listed, Switzerland has the most well-developed funded private system, with pension assets amounting to US$40,000 per person; the second-best funded is in Netherlands with per capita pension assets of $20,000. Several countries follow, with around $15,000 per person including the US and the UK. Because Germany uses a "book reserve" system rather

[3] For a comparative discussion of pension tax treatment see Dilnot (1996).

Table 1
Selected Public and Private Pension System Characteristics

Country	Population (M)	Private Pension Assets $USb	State Pension Benefit		Financing of State Pension Payroll Tax %
			% of GDP	as % of Av.Pay	
United States	263	4,258	60	43	12.4
Japan	125	1,321	29	54	16.5
United Kingdom	58	879	81	33	13.6–19.4
Netherlands	16	327	83	33	15.85
Canada	30	320	62	34	4.6
Switzerland	7	280	90	37	8.4
Australia	18	192	55	25	na
Germany	82	140	7	53	20.3
……					
Singapore	3	47	57	40	40
Chile	14	25	39	na	na

Source: Dresdner Bank (1997) 17. Information for 1995 except for Australia (1996). Data for Japan and Germany exclude book reserves; Dutch data exclude insurer reserves, Canada data include only RPP trust agreements and RRSPs. na signifies not applicable.

than setting aside assets in pension trust, its funded status is among the lowest of the OECD.[4]

The importance of *public* pension systems is also reflected in Table 1, where it is noted that the German public retirement system provides a high replacement rate (benefits equal to half of average wages), and the plan taxes earners at a high rate to support these payments. What these figures do not show is the unfunded obligation behind the cash flows pertinent to the government programs. For example, the US Old-Age, Survivors, and Disability (OASDI) program—the agency that pays social security old-age benefits—faces an unfunded obligation of approximately $9 trillion. Filling this gap over the next 75 years will require a benefit cut of about 25% per year, or a tax increase of approximately the same measure (Quinn and Mitchell 1996). A different way to assess the challenges faced by public pension systems is to note that the present value of pension liabilities in the major industrial countries averages around 100–200% of GDP, with estimates ranging even higher for Italy (202%), Germany (236%) and France (259%). Remedying this deficit would require additional taxes valued at 1–4% of GDP annually in perpetuity to achieve solvency of the current unfunded systems, or taxes worth 4–8% of GDP to make a transition to a fully funded system.[5]

[4] German and other European pension systems are described in detail in Bodie et al. (1996) and Davis (1996).

[5] These estimates are taken from Chand and Jaeger (1996).

26.2 HOW DO PENSIONS INFLUENCE THE RISKS WORKERS CONFRONT IN RETIREMENT?

The simple life cycle saving model posits that a rational and well-informed worker would forecast the future and save enough to smooth consumption over time. In a certainty world, the individual will save enough while earning so as to smooth real consumption over his lifetime. For example, one might assume the worker enters employment at age 20, works until retirement at 65 earning a steady real income, and saves some fraction of it for retirement. Assuming that he earns a constant real rate of interest his retirement consumption path could be configured so that at death the retirement fund was completely depleted (abstracting from bequests).

In this framework, the ratio of consumption to earnings must equal the ratio of years of work to total years of work and retirement (Bodie et al 1996). As constructed, there are 45 years of work and 15 years of retirement, so the replacement rate (the ratio of consumption/earnings) is equal to 45/60 or 75%, derived as follows:

Work Years * (Earnings – Consumption) = Retirement years * Consumption
Work Years * Earnings = (Work Years + Retirement years) * Consumption
Replacement rate = Consumption/Earnings
= Work Years/(Work Years + Retirement Years)

In this framework the function of a pension is to help the worker meet his saving target during the earning years, so that he has adequate saving to meet retirement consumption needs. Depending on the institutional setting, this need may be fulfilled by a government pension (often termed social security), and/or an employer or union-sponsored pension. Social security taxes are generally paid by both the worker and his employer; job-based or corporate pensions also usually require both worker contributions and contributions from the employer (or union). Economists generally recognize that employer contributions to both public and private pensions represent employee compensation foregone in the amount devoted to the pension (Gruber 1997). Remaining or residual saving needs must be met with private asset accumulation, as in housing stock, bank accounts, or investments in the broader capital market.

The power of this simple life cycle framework is its clarity in highlighting the factors that determine retirement saving needs. In particular, the rational economic man's saving profile is seen to depend on his life expectancy, his work and retirement pattern, his real earnings profile, the anticipated returns on his public and private pension savings, the tax structure he faces, and how he wishes to make provision for a surviving spouse and children. But implementing the plan of action in practice is difficult, by virtue of the fact that the real world is fraught with risk. This is, workers must form and constantly update forecasts of anticipated trajectories of the uncertain components of the lifetime budget constraint—real earnings, public and private pension benefits, investment returns, healthcare needs and insurance. Also workers must attempt to make these decisions subject to substantial uncertainty regarding health capacity, preferences for work versus leisure, and personal factors including marital status. And of course, in retirement, both constraints and preferences are likely to change through time in sometimes unpredictable ways as health deteriorates, asset values evolve, and family relationships change. In addition, the retirement problem is complicated in practice by the interactions between workers, their plan sponsors, and the economic and legal environment in which the pension systems are set.

In illustrating the role of uncertainty in the retirement setting, it is useful to identify the four main risks confronting a life-cycle saver when he makes retirement saving decisions and plans.[6] These are *individual risk, plan sponsor risk, country risk, and global risk.* Focusing on the first, older people of course face an uncertain life expectancy. This *individual risk* then prompts concern about the chances of one outliving one's own retirement saving. Pensions play a key role in protecting against this risk, because they offer a mechanism for people to share longevity risk with a group of fellow-employees—a relatively diverse risk pool formed for purposes other than obtaining this insurance. Of course an insurer can also pool mortality across a large number of purchasers, but the retail market for individually-purchased annuities is skewed by adverse selection because people who buy individual annuities are likely to live much longer than the population average.[7] For this reason, a firm-based or occupational pension plan can afford workers a valuable precommitment device, namely access to a group survival risk pool early in life. The precommitment is useful since the buy-in occurs before workers' health and mortality risks become known. A related issue is that some perceive their pension as a self-control device, by which employees are helped to automatically deduct from their pay a regular amount that is then saved rather than spent.[8] The pension institution therefore helps enforce the worker's resolve to follow a saving plan that he otherwise might find difficult to implement if left to his own devices each pay period.

Another way in which pensions help protect workers against individual risk has to do with unexpected earnings fluctuations, such as those caused by job loss or disability. If one were to experience a sudden work incapacity, retirement saving might fall below one's plan and retirement consumption would decline below one's hoped-for living standard. This kind of risk, sometimes known as "replacement rate risk", can be protected against to the extent that the pension benefit formula is redistributive and guarantees a minimum benefit. These are commonly found in defined benefit pensions, when the benefit formula offers a subsidized benefit in the event of disability or sudden earnings declines.[9]

[6] More detail is available in Mitchell (1997b); see also Diamond and Mirrlees (1985) and Bodie (1992).

[7] For a recent analysis of the risk-pooling aspects of annuities see Mitchell, Poterba, Warshawsky, and Brown (1999).

[8] Thaler and Shefrin (1991) take this view of pensions as a self-control mechanism.

[9] Studies that model the disability aspect of pensions include Diamond and Sheshinsky (1995) and Ippolito (1986).

While pensions can help mitigate these potent individual risks, they in turn expose employees covered by a firm-based pension to risk associated with the plan sponsor. One such *plan sponsor risk* occurs in both DC and DB plans, if a pension fiduciary absconds with the monies, mis-directs investments, or permits too much to be spent on administrative costs. Protection against such behavior often motivates government regulation governing pension asset allocation, investment practices, and self-dealing, as with the US Employee Retirement Income Security Act (ERISA) of 1974; related rules in the United Kingdom were adopted after the Maxwell pension scandal (Bodie et al. 1996).

A closely-linked concern that workers face regarding their pension is the chance of being discharged prior to gaining a legal right to the benefit. Before ERISA's passage in 1974, US companies would sometimes vest pension-covered workers only at retirement; this meant that employees changing jobs prior to that date lost their pension accumulations despite years of contributions (Sass 1997). This risk of loosing a pension accrual was in fact partly offset by a higher cash wage, confirming that pensions represent deferred compensation (Montgomery et al. 1992). Nevertheless many governments today require that a pension-covered worker vests after a fixed period of years, which means that he maintains a claim on the benefit accrued to date in his original firm even if he changes jobs after that (in the US, vesting in the private sector now is required after 5 years of full-time employment at a firm offering a pension plan). The value of vesting is less than it might seem at first, however, since the DB pension promise is often not indexed to inflation for those leaving the firm. Thus a young worker changing employers will have earned a *nominal* benefit, rather than one protected against inflation up to and after retirement. Defined contribution pension plans suffer less from this problem, inasmuch as they often permit vested participants to take their assets as a lump sum when they change jobs by rolling over the funds into a tax-deferred personal account (e.g., an Individual Retirement Account) which they manage themselves. Of course having a self-managed pension does not by any means guarantee that the retirement pension is a *real* benefit.

Yet another type of plan sponsor risk arises only in DB pensions, and it is a risk associated with underfunded plan terminations. This occurs when the employer offering the plan declares bankruptcy, and has insufficient assets to cover promised pension benefits. Such underfunded plan terminations are rare in practice in the US, but when they happen they highlight the fact that a DB pension with insufficient assets imposes bankruptcy risk on participating employees. Several notorious historical cases including the mid-1960's bankruptcy of the US Studebaker automobile firm showed how pension benefits can be threatened when pension assets are inadequate to meet promised benefits (Sass 1997). Transferring bankruptcy risk in this way may be economically useful, according to Ippolito (1985), if it in effect turns employees into shareholders interested in the long-term success of the firm. On the other hand, having an underfunded pension can greatly increase the risk of old-age economic insecurity.

An alternative way to protect against the risk of plan sponsor bankruptcy is to have a pension solvency guarantee system. The US federal agency known as the Pension Benefit Guaranty Corporation acts to protect vested nominal benefits, in exchange for a risk-related insurance premium charged to all with DB pensions. This federal institution now has several billion dollars in assets and is working to assess its future liability for pension sponsor bankruptcies (Bodie and Merton, 1993; Ippolito 1989). A similar system was adopted in Ontario but the model has not spread elsewhere in Canada. Further, since there is an unchanged nominal ceiling on the maximum insured benefit, the Ontario termination insurance system is diminishing in importance over time (Pesando 1996). In Germany, by contrast, DB pension insurance takes the form of a pay-as-you-go solvency fund into which all corporations with DB pensions pay an annual fee (Ahrend 1996). Thus far, these insurance systems have worked relatively smoothly, but it is not known how they would perform in a serious and persistent market economic downturn.

A worker saving via a pension also faces a host of *country-specific risks* exposing him to potential economic insecurity in old age. These include macroeconomic risks associated with inflation and recession, and also country-specific fluctuations in capital markets (Feldstein 1983). Often these economic problems generate political risks produced by changes in a nation's legal and regulatory system, and they are extremely difficult to predict. Yet because pension participants invest for the long term, changes in real and financial conditions can have a potent effect on the risk and return characteristics of pension assets. Some point to DB pensions as a means to protect against local capital market risk, since a plan sponsor bases a DB pension promise on service and pay rather than investment returns. Hence it is often alleged that the firm bears most of the investment risk in the pension, rather than his firm. By comparison a worker with a defined contribution pension tends to be exposed to capital market risks more directly.[10] If a country's economic and political environment does not promise long-term stability and good returns, people will tend to seek international portfolio diversification to protect against such country risks (Davis 1996).

Another country risk concerning workers in recent years is the threat of insolvency in the national social security system (Merton et al. 1987). Many government-run old-age programs in the developed world will become too expensive to sustain over the next two to three decades, and in some cases the day of reckoning will arrive much sooner (James and Vittas 1996). Employer pensions may be able to offset this risk to some extent, for instance by integrating privately-paid benefits with government-provided retirement payouts. However workers concerned about the

[10] It is possible to design a DC pension plan that could offer a minimum benefit (cf Bodie 1990). Also it is at least imaginable that if investment performance were poor, unionized firms would be induced to make additional contributions; in this instance, the employers would undoubtedly place this increased cost on the bargaining table in the next round of collective bargaining and seek to extract an appropriate concession.

long-run benefit levels payable by eroding public programs may also seek other assets in which to invest, including foreign assets.

The final type of risk concerning people seeking to save for retirement is *global risk*, a concern highlighted by the global financial crisis of recent times. Additional future global risks include the chance of world-wide climatic change, economic depression, war, or far-flung epidemics. Unfortunately little can be done privately to protect against the negative financial consequences of such potentially catastrophic crises, since even a well-funded pension system invested in a diversified international portfolio cannot protect against risks affecting all economies and workers at the same time. Some protection can be afforded if risk-averse cohorts spread global shocks through time and across generations. This, it has been argued, is one explanation for the adoption of the huge unfunded government-sponsored social security system around the time of the Great Depression (Pestieau 1995). By promising a defined benefit system transferring income from workers to the retired generation, this program redistributed some of the pain of the Depression from the then-old to future taxpayers (Geanakoplos et al. 1999).

26.3 WHAT EXPLAINS THE GLOBAL TREND TOWARD DEFINED CONTRIBUTION PENSION PLANS?

Whereas years ago the modal pension in the developed world was of the defined benefit variety, today defined contribution plans are becoming more the norm in the US, Canada, and some European nations. In addition, much recent pension growth in developing countries has also been of the DC variety. In the United States, for instance, the fastest-growing plan type is the popular 401(k) vehicle, named after the section of the tax code permitting employers to create this type of DC pension as a tax-qualified vehicle. As illustrated in Table 2, DB pensions are now fewer in number than DC plans in the US, include only about half the total participants, and control

Table 2
Private Employer-Sponsored Defined Benefit and Defined Contribution Pensions in the United States

	Total	DB plans	DC plans
Number of plans:	702,097	12%	87%
Number of participants:	83.9M	48%	52%
Assets:	$2.3B	54%	46%
Contributions received:	$154M	34%	66%
Benefits paid:	$156M	51%	49%

Source: Mitchell (1998b).

Table 3
Administrative Costs in Private US Defined Benefit and Defined Contribution Pension Plans

I. Annual Administrative Costs for a Corporate Defined Benefit Pension Plan:
$850/yr/participant for small plan (15 lives) *versus*
$56/yr/participant for large plan (10,000 lives)

II. The Defined Benefit/Defined Contribution Cost Ratio Has Risen Over Time:

Year	*Small Plan (15 lives)*	*Large Plan (10,000 lives)*
1981	142%	91%
1996	216%	139%

Source: Mitchell and Scheiber (1998).
Note: Money management costs are excluded from these computations.

about half the total asset pool.[11] This picture results from impressive growth in the DC pension environment over the past several decades. For example, asset holdings in both pension types have grown substantially, but the rate of expansion has been much faster for DC than for DB plans in the United States. Likewise, the rate of growth in DC participants has far exceeded that in DB plans. In many other countries, the plans growing the fastest have also been in the DC arena, in part due to the trend toward privatization of social security about which more will be said below.

Why have defined contribution pensions grown so quickly in both relative and absolute terms in recent years? One explanation is that some employers are reluctant to launch new DB pensions because of relatively high and rising expenses.[12] For instance, Table 3 shows that DB plans in the US became relatively more costly to administer over time than did DC plans, particularly in small firms. The estimated per-participant cost for a DB plan is thus measured at $850 per year per employee in a small company, 216 times than the DC cost (money management costs are not included in this calculation). Scale economies are important, so that a large firm with 10,000 employees faces a per-participant cost of only about $60 per year, still 139 times that in a DC plan. Some of the costs are administrative in nature due to record-keeping requirements, reporting and disclosure to the government, actuarial fees associated with funding computations, and the expenses associated with the mandatory pension insurance. Clearly cost differentials can explain some of the trend favoring defined contribution pensions over time.[13]

Another reason that defined contribution pension have grown is that they are appealing to both employers and employees alike. In some instances, DC plans afford participants the opportunity to select how much to invest in their pension (up to a

[11] For more discussion of private pensions see Gordon et al. (1997). The figures on private pensions do not include public sector pension plans, which have approximately 16 million participants and more than $1 trillion in assets; see Mitchell and Carr (1996).

[12] An analysis of administrative costs appears in Mitchell (1998a).

[13] For a full discussion of this question see Gustman et al. (1994).

legal limit) and permit participants the chance to manage their own investments within the plan. In the US, a 401(k) participant must have a choice of at least three funds to choose from (a stock index fund, a bond fund, and usually a money market); additional options are becoming the norm as money managers offer alliances with fund families and a wide range of institutional investors. Employees who invest in such plans are often "rewarded" for participation with an employer match for some of their contributions, anywhere from 20 to 100%. Since the employer match vests only after 5 years, this pattern rewards longer-staying employees. The typical sum invested in a 401(k) plan currently is currently about 6% of pay, and about half of all offering companies match employee contributions at some level. Participation rates have risen quite dramatically in the last decade, with over 75% of all eligible workers contributing something to their plans.

Several policy questions loom large on the pension horizon regarding these DC plans, some specific to the 401(k) environment and others to DC plans more generally. One issue is that pension participants have increasingly been given access to their funds prior to retirement, a pattern that will surely erode eventual retirement benefits. For instance, 401(k) plans commonly offer loans against pension assets to active workers experiencing financial hardship, and lump-sum cash-outs are commonly paid to workers leaving the sponsoring firm. Under these circumstances, some participants will spend their funds rather than roll the money into another tax-protected pension account.[14] An interesting development in the US is that many *defined benefit* plans are now permitting vested workers to take a lump-sum if they leave prior to retirement, a development that also elicits consternation in some pension circles.

A different policy concern is whether enough money is being deposited into DC pension accounts during the earning years. It is extraordinarily expensive to fund an annuity that pays a reasonable pension annuity for 15–20 retirement years (and perhaps even longer, as life expectancies continue to rise). Yet combined employee/employer contribution rates to DC plans are low, around 6% of pay in US 401(k) plans to a limit of less than $10,000 per year. In the UK, traditional company-based DB pension plans cost around 15.25% of pay, but a 50-year old worker in a DC plan contributes only 9.9% of pay (in the personal pension DC account; Blake 1997). Such a low rate of contributions may deeply disappoint participants reaching retirement age when the time comes. Of course, many workers who now have DC pensions might have had no employment-based pension at all, if the only feasible model were the defined benefit plan of the past. And research suggests that 401(k) plans have added to net retirement saving as compared to what it would have been without these pension innovations.[15]

A further issue has to do with the way in which pension systems are designed and governed, especially those DB pensions created by state and local governments to provide retirement benefits to teachers, uniformed officers, and other civil ser-

[14] This practice is subject to regulation; for instance in Canada all pension funds that receive tax preferences must be paid out in the form of annuities (or like streams).

[15] A summary of the recent literature appears in Disney (1996).

vants.[16] These public plans are managed differently than are their private counterparts in the US at least, mainly because corporate pensions must meet fiduciary standards codified in the Employee Retirement Income Security Act (ERISA). By contrast public plans are subject to less stringent and less uniform regulation. As a result, public plan governance has been subject to political pressure influencing funding decisions and the choice of actuarial assumptions. In particular, research shows that pension liability measures respond to local fiscal stress, and investments are frequently subject to non-financial criteria. Also political appointees and *ex officio* board members tend to dominate decision-making, frequently with many public pension directors chosen to represent the interests of plan participants. Perhaps because of this different governance structure, public pension plans often direct their investments toward "in-state" projects, a practice associated with diminished rates of investment return. In general, though, public sector pensions in the US are relatively well funded, partly because their asset allocations have changed dramatically over time: by the mid 1990's over 40% of public plan assets were held in stock, up from 3% in 1960 (Mitchell and Smith 1994; Mitchell and Carr, 1997).

Another area just beginning to engage public interest concerns the payout or decumulation phase of the pension system. This has to do with retirement annuities—insurance products that offer protection against the risk that someone could outlive his saving. These annuities are of utmost importance for older people considering how to draw down their assets over the retirement period. The problem in the US, and in many Latin American nations that have privatized their pension system in recent years, is that retirees are often allowed to access all or most of their pension assets rather than being required to annuitize their benefits. This breakdown in the annuity market may produce increasing adverse selection, a development that should be carefully monitored (Mitchell, Poterba, Warshawsky, and Brown 1999).

Having described how *private* pension systems have migrated toward the DC model in the last decade or two, we also should point to the strong appeal of DC pensions in the *public* pension arena.[17] Specifically, several Latin American nations have followed Chile's 1981 termination of its national underfunded social security system and replacement with a privately-managed defined-contribution pension structure. The Chilean model operates a system of mandatory DC pensions called AFPs (Asociaciones de Fondos de Pensiones), backstopped by a minimum retirement benefit guaranteed by the government. These individual account plans are paid for from a mandatory payroll tax set at 10% of pay (an additional 3% is charged for health and survivors insurance and administrative costs).

Key design features of the Chilean and other similar Latin American DC national pension schemes are sketched in Table 4. The Chilean AFP system now holds about $40B and real returns have been substantial (about 12% real per year) over the last

[16] See Mitchell and Carr (1997); Hsin and Mitchell (1994); and Mitchell and Hsin (1997a and b).

[17] See Barreto and Mitchell (1997), Demirguc-Kunt and Swarz (1996), and Mitchell and Barreto (1997) for analysis of global pension privatization patterns.

Table 4
Key Features of Several Latin American Pension Reform Programs

	Chile	Peru	Argentina	Colombia	Uruguay	Mexico
Structure	Mandatory	Mandatory	Mandatory	Mandatory	Mandatory	Mandatory
1st Pillar	Public	Public	Public	Public	Public	Public
2nd Pillar	Private Only	Optional Pub/Priv.	Optional Pub/Priv.	Optional Pub/Priv.	Optional Pub/Priv.	Private Only
Financing						
E'r payroll tax	0%	0%	0%	10%/7.5%	NA/0%	0%
E'ee payroll tax	10%	11% or 10%	11% both	3.5% or 2.5%	NA/0%–7.5%	6.5%
Other Gen'l Rev.	Yes	Yes	Yes	Yes	Yes	Yes
Benefits						
Ret. Age (m/f)	65/60	65	65/60	62/57	60	65
1st Pillar: %Pay	25%	NA	28%	55%	NA	40%
2nd Pillar: Payout	Lump-ProgWD-Annuity	ProgWD-Annuity	ProgWD-Annuity	ProgWD-Annuity	Annuity	Annuity-ProgWD
Regulatory Structure						
Fees Regul.	Yes	No	No	NA	No	No
Int'l Invst. OK	Yes	Yes	Yes	NA	No	Yes
Min. ROR Req.	Yes	Yes	Yes	NA	Yes	No
Transition Costs						
% of GDP	100–80%	27%	NA	87%	NA	80%
Recog. Bond	Yes	Yes	No	Yes	No	No
Performance						
Fund (US$)	$28B	$900M	$4.5B	$50M	$25.6M	$3.9B
Fund (%GDP)	41% ('94)	1.5% ('96)	0.7% ('95)	NA	NA	NA
Recent ROR (%)	12.5% ('82–95)	15.5% ('94–95)	19.9%('95–96)	15.5% ('96)	NA	NA
AFP's (No.)	15	6	21	9	6	25
Affiliates (No.)	5.5M	1.5M	5.5M	2.1M	0.5M	11.2M

Source: Mitchell and Barreto (1998).
Note: NA signifies not available. ProgWD signifies programmed withdrawal. E'r signifies employer; E'ee means employee.

decade and a half. DC pensions are also becoming popular in Europe of late, encouraged by the UK's example which permits workers to opt out of both public and company pensions by establishing their own personal pensions of the DC variety (Holzmann 1997a, b). Eastern European nations are following suit, and this model is even being discussed in China. On the other hand, critics of the DC movement point out several inefficiencies in these new plans. For example, obtaining the pension contributions is costly in Chile, as are administrative costs associated with having over several thousand agents inducing plan participants to switch funds every year. In addition, money managers in these DC plans have typically not been able to diversify their holdings internationally, raising questions about the system's vulnerability to domestic market shocks. Here and in other nations adopting the DC structure, critics have also worried that government guarantees of minimum retirement benefits may end up being quite expensive (Pennacchi 1999).

26.4 WHAT OTHER FACTORS INFLUENCE THE MARKET FOR PENSIONS?

Thus far we have emphasized how pensions protect the employee against one set of risks while exposing him to others. In this section we note other factors driving the demand for and supply of pensions, including the economic and regulatory environment in which the plans are operating.[18]

26.4.1 The Demand for and Supply of Pensions

Above we argued that the main reason that employees demand pensions is that they help them pool the risks associated with not saving enough for retirement and outliving their assets in old age. The life cycle saving model recognizes that employment-based pensions are one leg of the so-called "three legged stool" supporting retirement, with the other two legs consisting of government pensions (e.g., social security), and private or individual support (e.g., personal assets, family transfers).[19] Pensions in fact are quite important in protecting retiree wellbeing, as demonstrated in the Health and Retirement Study (HRS), a nationally representative sample of older Americans age 51–61 in 1992.[20] Here the median older household has about one-fifth of its retirement assets in a company pension, two-fifths of its wealth in expected social security payments, and the rest in housing wealth and financial assets. Unfortunately for many this is simply not enough: though the median household has about US$325,000 in

[18] Further discussion of the factors influencing the demand for and supply of pensions appears in Mitchell (1998a); Gustman et al. (1994); and Quinn et al. (1990).

[19] This discussion draws on Mitchell (1998b).

[20] The Health and Retirement Study (HRS), covering people age 51–61 and their spouses of any age, first surveyed in 1992 and reinterviewed every two years thereafter (see www.umich.edu/~hrswww/)

Table 5
Wealth by Decile of Older US Households

Wealth Decile	Current Wealth	Projected Wealth at Age 62	Projected Wealth at Age 65
1	$ 39,470	$ 43,804	$ 49,031
2	97,452	109,578	121,123
3	156,288	182,494	202,946
4	219,797	256,636	283,184
5	**287,692**	**338,153**	**372,701**
6	364,802	429,253	471,308
7	459,858	543,397	595,408
8	590,079	699,681	763,756
9	804,934	944,894	1,030,054
10	1,764,414	2,117,052	2,362,963
Mean	$478,313	$566,431	$625,066
— Housing	65,940	76,410	80,507
— Financial	175,974	205,653	228,133
— Soc. Security	119,793	128,712	142,018
— Pension	116,606	155,656	174,408
Median 10%	$325,157	$382,678	$420,537
— Housing	59,746	71,097	75,047
— Financial	66,530	71,004	71,175
— Soc. Security	133,606	143,864	160,824
— Pension	65,275	96,713	113,491

Source: Moore and Mitchell (2000).

total assets, a sum projected to grow to $380,000 by age 62, this is inadequate to produce a smooth consumption into retirement. Rather, an additional 16% of annual income would have to be saved *per year* above and beyond normal asset appreciation, in order to preclude consumption shortfalls after retirement (Table 5).

There remains the puzzling question of why people fail to save more for retirement—and particularly in their pensions—since in most countries, tax law favors pensions in the retirement saving portfolio. That is, a middle or upper-income earner can reduce his lifetime tax bill substantially by accumulating compensation in a tax-deferred pension account. The size of the pension tax subsidy can be quite substantial—on the order of 15% of lifetime tax in the US, for instance (Ippolito 1986). There is controversy, however, about the how strongly pension saving patterns respond to these subsidies, with estimated tax price elasticities ranging from –0.8 to –0.3 (Gustman et al. 1994). More critically, there is as yet no empirical study unraveling how pension tax deferrals affect lifetime pension saving, substitution between pension and other saving, and total lifetime retirement accumulation and decumulation patterns.

One probable explanation for why people save less than they should in their pensions is financial illiteracy. Many Americans have no understanding of simple compound interest, and cannot explain the risk-return tradeoff (Bernheim 1998). Recent discussions of "mis-selling" of personal pensions in the UK indicate that ill-informed workers in that nation had a difficult time determining which pension options are best (Blake and Orszag 1997). Corporate human resource and personnel managers are often loath to offer investment advice since they may be held liable for poor investment outcomes. And financial professionals are also in frequent disagreement, giving wildly different prescriptions to workers seeking investment advice; further they tend to overlook or ignore important differences in peoples' human capital and other assets, when giving investment advice.[21]

Another explanation for why workers save less than they should in their pensions is that a pension plan is subject to agency problems under a variety of circumstances (Bodie 1990). For instance, an employer providing workers with a deferred match in the company 401(k) plan can structure the pension to attract and retain people with a low discount rate, which in effect pays desirable low-turnover employees more than those who quit.[22] Knowing this, workers would decide how much and whether to participate in the plan after weighing the pension tax deferral against the chance of foregoing the accrual when leaving the firm. A different way in which employers use pensions as a personnel device is to backload the DB benefit formula. This has the effect of deferring most of the pension accrual until late in the worker's career, thus inducing him not to quit until the "right" age, and then retire after that.[23] However increased workforce mobility means that fewer employees expect to remain with any one firm over their entire worklives, eroding the appeal of a defined benefit promise rather seriously.

A different type of agency problem pertains particularly to the DB context, where modern corporate managers have increasingly seen the DB pension as component of the sponsoring company's extended balance sheet, rather than as a trust operated independently. This integrated perspective suggests that pension funding and asset allocation decisions will be evaluated insofar as they improve the firm's overall corporate financial picture, rather than just the workers' retirement income security (Bulow 1982; Bodie 1992). One question hotly contested in the literature is whether stockholders' interests have come to outweigh employees' interests, particularly in the decision to terminate an overfunded pension. For instance, during the latter half of the 1980's, some 2.3 American workers in about 2,000 plans found their defined benefit pensions terminated; this action produced approximately $20 billion dollars in pension

[21] For a review of various investment advisers' suggestions see Mitchell and Moore (1999).

[22] A discussion of how pensions are used to attract, retain, and then retire workers appears in Ippolito (1997) and Kotlikoff and Wise (1987). Luzadis and Mitchell (1991) show how pensions are adapted by firms to offset government prohibition of mandatory retirement.

[23] See Lazear (1979 and 1983); a substantial body of literature surveyed in Hutchens (1989) and more recently by Lumsdaine (1997) confirms the importance of these patterns in practice.

reversions to corporate management (Gustman et al. 1994). Nevertheless, only a tiny fraction of the pension assets that could have been attached by managers was in fact taken, and event studies show that company share prices are not sensitive to termination of an overfunded pension (Alderson and Vanderhei 1991; Petersen 1992).

26.4.2 The Role of the Economic and Regulatory Environment

Pensions in many countries are mandated, while in others they are offered voluntarily when both the employer and employee desire the financial services of a pension plan. In the US, for example, providing a company pension is not mandatory, though as many of half of all workers in the private sector are expected to retire with a company-sponsored pension. Not only is the decision to supply a pension plan voluntary; so too is the choice over plan type and the level of benefits or contributions is up to the employer and sometimes the union as well, in the case of a multi-employer plan. Nevertheless, in every country the entity that issues a pension promise is typically subject to extensive government legislation and oversight. The general goal of these efforts is to ensure that contributions are made in a regular manner, and that promised benefits are delivered. For example, in the US, the ERISA law requires a corporate DB pension to fund retirees' promised life annuities by setting aside enough to cover accruing future liabilities, and it insures bankrupt plan sponsors in the event of an underfunded termination.

Related to this point is the powerful influence of the tax environment as it favors—or penalizes—pension saving. As noted earlier, US research on tax preferences afforded Individual Retirement Accounts (IRA's) and 401(k) plans indicates that workers are somewhat sensitive to pension saving incentives. Confirming this conclusion is evidence from Australia: when tax preferences for pension contributions and pension earnings were drastically reduced, pension saving declined (and tax-protected life annuity purchases soared; Edey and Simon 1996). Unfortunately, while we know that tax policy matters, it is rarely simple to determine how it works. For instance, investing a marginal dollar in a pension plan, versus one's house, a tax-free municipal bond, or an insurance annuity, can have quite different tax consequences given today's tax schedule, assuming one remains alive. An entirely different payout menu would apply if the asset passed into an estate at death. Furthermore tax rates and coverage change frequently through time, making it extraordinarily difficult to forecast future payout patterns sensibly. So other than concluding that "taxes matter", how they matter deserves a great more detail in future work.

It is also clear that both mandatory and voluntary pensions are predicated on having a strong financial system (Mitchell 1997b). For example, the Latin nations with a mandatory pension have discovered that a reliable banking system is needed to ensure that collections are handled promptly and efficiently. A well-developed market for government bonds is also instrumental when instituting a funded pension system, so that the promised benefits can be delivered with some degree of certainty. Whether having a domestic stock market is central to a pension system is the subject of some debate, though experts generally agree that investors of all kinds (including pension savers) do better when there is better information about asset risk and return characteristics. Hence a country seeking to build a strong pension system would find that it is useful to adopt, and enforce, internationally-accepted accounting and rating standards.

A final institution that pensions lean on heavily is the insurance industry (Mitchell 1997b). Since pensions' main function is to help insure against outliving one's assets, it is imperative to have a well-functioning insurance market that can accurately price and manage such risk. In developed nations this is a challenge—particularly as life expectancies rise—but it is even more difficult in developing countries where mortality and morbidity data are unavailable and unreliable. Often, too, the insurance business is held as a government monopoly or is poorly regulated when competition is permitted. In addition insurers tend to be prohibited from investing in anything but domestic assets, leaving them vulnerable to inflation and other country risks. As a result, insurance company mismanagement and bankruptcies undermine workers' belief in pensions. For this reason, creating and maintaining a strong insurance industry is critical for a believable retirement system.

26.5 HOW CAN PENSION PERFORMANCE BE JUDGED?

Today's workers—tomorrow's retirees—clearly expect pensions to play a central role in their retirement wellbeing. Whether reality will meet expectations depends in large part on how well the pension plans are managed. In this section we take up the question of how to judge pension performance, and outline the most important factors enhancing pension performance along with those that most deeply threaten pension plans' ability to deliver retirement income.

A pension system has one main objective—namely, to generate ample and reliable retirement payouts for retirees—but there are four ancillary functions that contribute to that ultimate goal. These interim goals are to collect contributions, manage the funds, handle recordkeeping, and pay benefits.[24] Looking across pension systems, there is much variation in the efficiency with which the four functions are carried out.

Focusing first on the *fund collection* step, a determinant of pension contributions has to do with how efficiently these contributions are gathered by the firm or by the government, depending on the extant pension structure. In Mexico, for instance, employers must deposit workers' mandated contributions at a central financial clearing house no more than seven days after the funds are withheld. This approach, which relies on the central tax authority to collect the funds, is anticipated to be less costly

[24] This discussion draws on Mitchell and Sunden (1994).

than the Chilean system where thousands of individual tax agents are deployed monthly to gather the funds from individual workers. Unfortunately, efficiency in collecting the funds has not yet been the focus of much detailed analysis, but it is clear that the more such costs are constrained, the more retirement saving will be generated (Mitchell 1997a). In addition, more efficient collection is likely to increase pension participation and reduce evasion, particularly in public pension plans (Manchester 1998). Of course, when pension/social security payroll taxes are high and loosely linked with eventual benefits, the lower the incentive to report earnings and remain in the "formal" sector.

An area that pension experts have written more widely on pertains to *investment performance* in pension assets. Of course, if a pension scheme is unfunded, the goal of money management tends to simply be to ensure that there are few leakages of cash between the collection of contributions and the payment of benefits. This is not a trivial job, of course, since it requires careful record-keeping and accountability—management techniques that are often in short supply. By contrast, when a pension system has assets to invest, the money management task becomes much more critical, requiring that investment decisions be made over time. Pension systems around the world have reported widely divergent investment experiences in recent years; the World Bank's survey of global pension systems concluded that privately-managed funds had positive returns but public funds reported substantially negative real returns during the 1980's (James and Vittas 1996).

A pension fiduciary, the person or institution charged with managing a pension plan, is generally obligated to make investment decisions in such a way as to balance risk and return while meeting liquidity requirements. In practice however, there are wide differences in how this obligation is translated to practice. In the US, for example, ERISA regulations requires a corporate defined benefit pension manager to invest according to the so-called "prudent man rule", keeping prominent the pension participant's best interests (Logue and Rader 1997). A similar rule regulates many public sector pension managers as well (Mitchell and Carr 1997). This requires the DB plan manager to meet investment performance criteria similar to those followed by other pension investors, balancing risk/return criteria set by his pension Board.

Though ERISA was legislated almost twenty-five years ago, interpreting the prudent man rule remains controversial today—particularly since trustees are held personally liable for investments determined to be in conflict with the principle. In practice this debate translates into analysis of the most appropriate benchmarks for evaluating investment performance in a defined benefit environment. Those who argue for efficient capital markets suggest that pension money managers should not try to beat the market, but rather should invest passively with indexed portfolios and low levels of annual turnover. Opponents point out that research and analysis pays off for less liquid holdings such as real estate and global investment opportunities. In any event, defined benefit plans have substantially altered their investment holdings over time: equity investments have grown from 45% of the portfolio to 57%, and bonds

Table 6
Asset Breakdown by Plan Type: US Private Defined Benefit and Defined Contribution Pensions

Asset Category	Def. Benefit		Def. Contribution	
	1983	1996	1983	1996
Equity	45%	57%	27%	60%
Bonds	27	33	22	30
Other	28	10	51	10

Source: Mitchell (1998b).

grew from 27 to 33% (cash and real estate fractions diminished; see Table 6). Interest in international holdings has also grown in the last half-dozen years, with non-US stock now at around 10% of the private plan portfolio.

Not only are pension fiduciaries concerned about investment performance in DB plans—increasingly DC sponsors and participants are also asking questions about money management expenses so as to be able to assess net rather than gross return performance. Of course, in a DC pension, participants select their own asset mix from among the investment options provided by the employer. This worries policymakers, however, since workers who may be financially illiterate must make individual investment choices regarding their own pension holdings. In the US for instance, many Americans rely on unsophisticated sources for financial advice (friends and relatives) and lack a basic understanding of stock-market risk, bond prices and returns, and simple compound interest (Bernheim 1998). More recently, however, defined contribution participants have begun to alter their asset allocations substantially over the last decade, moving increasingly into equities and away from guaranteed insurance contracts. This is particularly true of younger workers who invest 70–80% of their 401(k) portfolios in equities, a strategy in keeping with advice often offered by financial planners (Mitchell and Moore 1999). Also employers offering defined contribution pensions have found that offering their workers educational courses regarding financial preparedness for retirement raises the likelihood that workers will join in the plan, and may influence their asset allocation decisions (Mitchell and Scheiber, 1998). This in turn raises another concern, however, since parties offering financial advice in the US can be subject to legal suits should the investments turn sour. An important case on this point is currently wending its way through the court system, where 401(k) participants allege that their employer, a major computer systems manufacturer, offered an investment option that later proved to be worth less than anticipated. This case challenges many corporations' assumptions that giving workers investment options freed the sponsor from capital market risk in a defined contribution pension.

Table 7

Mutual Fund Expense Ratios by Fund Type
(Funds with assets > given levels)

Type of Fund	Dollar Wt'd Average Expense Ratio		
	Average (%)	Lowest Quartile (%)	Highest Quartile (%)
Equity Index (A > \$100M)	0.324	0.150	1.640
Money Market (A > \$1B)	0.613	0.150	1.000
Fixed Income (A > \$1B)	0.876	0.280	2.000
Growth (A > \$500M)	1.043	0.500	2.460
Growth & Income (A > \$500M)	0.834	0.390	1.840
Balanced (A > \$250M)	0.895	0.350	1.910
Global (A > \$250M)	1.250	0.840	1.380

Source: Mitchell (1998).
Expense ratio is % of assets devoted to fund administrative expenses annually.

Table 8

College Retirement Equity Fund (CREF) Administrative Expenses

Type of Fund	Total Expenses (%)	Investment Advisory Fees (%)	Administrative Expenses (%)	Distribution Expenses (%)
Equity Index	0.32	0.08	0.21	0.03
Stock Account	0.34	0.10	0.21	0.03
Growth	0.42	0.18	0.21	0.03
Global equities	0.41	0.17	0.21	0.03
Social choice	0.33	0.09	0.21	0.03
Money market	0.29	0.05	0.21	0.03
Bond market	0.30	0.06	0.21	0.03

Source: Mitchell (1998).

Employer liability is limited to the selection and offering of diverse investment options, but that in turn raises the question of which funds should be offered and whether cost should be a criterion in the fund selection. Administrative costs vary widely across funds, as illustrated in Table 7; one of the lowest-cost funds is depicted in Table 8 which shows the pattern of charges of the largest US defined contribution pension, the College Retirement Equity Fund (CREF). Money management expenses in many other countries are substantially higher though some offer fewer services (Mitchell 1998). Related to the topic of pension plan performance is the issue of plan efficiency, a topic but little studied to date. Public sector pension plans appear to operate at only 65% of potential efficiency, mainly because of the many small funds that fail to take advantage of scale economies.[25]

The third function of a pension plan is *recordkeeping*, a necessary if seemingly mundane area that concerns both DC and DB participants alike. In the DB environment, it is essential to track contributions by year as well as the participants' age, years of service, and employment status, since usually these affect the worker's coverage status and eventual benefit eligibility and payment amount. Without a credible recordkeeping system, workers may avoid paying pension contributions and/or defraud the system at the point of filing for benefits. Indeed pension fraud is a serious problem in developing countries lacking a good personnel management system, and national computerization has been an inevitable element of the move toward social security privatization. Many governments have also established investment restrictions and rate of return standards, so here too, new forms of recordkeeping are needed. Perhaps one of the most positive aspects of this process has been the development of interest in internationally accepted accounting and actuarial standards, making it necessary to mark assets to market and calculate DB pension liabilities in readily understandable ways.

The ultimate objective of a pension system is, of course, the payment of benefits, and *benefit payout performance* has several aspects. One area to be monitored is how quickly and accurately the pension system establishes beneficiary eligibility and payments, while at the same time controlling fraud. Several European nations have permitted large numbers of beneficiaries to file for early retirement via disability pensions, a practice that is now being seen as an expensive way to subsidize unemployment. Another issue with regard to benefit payout is whether the system has accurately predicted actuarial risks, and provided for these in a cost-effective manner. Many developing countries lack adequate mortality and morbidity data, making it extremely difficult to predict life expectancy and disability claims patterns. Benefit payout performance also involves the pension system's ability to continue preserving real benefit value into the future, and to do so while withstanding shocks (e.g., inflation, unemployment). Finally, pension systems are often judged according to equity standards—guaranteeing some minimum consumption level, ensuring at least a proportion of active workers' pay, paying each cohort relatively similar benefits, etc.

26.6 LOOKING AHEAD

This is a time of substantial change and opportunity in the global pension arena. New types of retirement systems are springing up to meet emerging economic and demographic challenges; many of these will enhance retirement security for the future. In

[25] Evidence on this point appears in Hsin and Mitchell (1994), and Mitchell and Hsin (1997 a and b).

our view, three factors will exert a potent influence on future retirement wealth accumulation and decumulation patterns. First, it seems likely that growth in defined contribution plans will continue, away from defined benefit pensions. This will make pension portability easier, but it will also place more responsibility on workers' shoulders—instead of their employers' and the government's—for retirement saving. Second, there will be increasing attention to expenses associated with pension plan activities and services, with an eye to implementing cost-cutting and efficiency measures. This will place new cost and performance pressure on the investment community, pension trustees, government and private pension managers, along with other stakeholders in the pension arena. Third, additional reforms will be required to bring government social security programs into solvency. These reforms will doubtless include paring down regular retirement benefits, raising the retirement age, limiting access to disability benefits, and increasing taxes. Each of these developments implies that individuals and their families will have to learn to save more, if they are to meet retirement consumption targets.[26]

The global move to defined contribution pensions offers much promise and some risk. The most important beneficial effect of the mandatory defined contribution model is that it reduces workers and retirees' exposure to political risk (Mitchell and Zeldes 1996). Many young people today do not believe they will receive benefits from their soon-to-be insolvent government-run defined benefit programs. As a result, this uncertainty threatens the system's security, compounding the uncertainty. A funded DC approach, by contrast, reduces government's need to periodically change social security benefits and taxes in response to solvency pressures. Of course, other factors must also be attended to when evaluating the global trend toward defined contribution plans. DB pensions can pool many different risks ranging from income loss due to disability and economic insecurity due to longevity. Nevertheless some of these risks are also covered by the mandatory national DC plans adopted in Latin America, Eastern Europe, and elsewhere. While DC plans in many cases remain exposed to country risk and global shocks, the defined contribution pension model is a popular choice for workers of the new millenium.

26.7 REFERENCES

Ahrend, Peter (1996). "Pension Financial Security in Germany," In *Securing Employer-Based Pensions: An International Perspective*, Eds. Z. Bodie and O.S. Mitchell. Philadelphia, PA: Pension Research Council and University of Pennsylvania Press.

[26] In the present analysis we do not describe potential solutions to the so-called "transition problem" or the unfunded liability burdening many nations' pay-as-you-go social security programs. Some argue that privatizing social security—i.e., instituting funded individual defined contribution accounts allowing investment diversification—would be useful so as to ease this burden. It can be demonstrated that this would not necessarily make everyone better off, though after an initial set of workers who would pay more, subsequent generations could be in better conditions (Geanakoplos, Mitchell, and Zeldes, 1999).

Alderson, Michael and Jack Vanderhei (1991). "Disturbing the Balance in Corporate Pension Policy: The Case of Excess Asset Reversion Legislation". *Benefits Quarterly*, Third Quarter.

Barreto, Flavio A. and Olivia S. Mitchell (1997). "Privatizing Latin American Retirement Systems". *Benefits Quarterly*, 13 (3), 83–85.

Bernheim, B. Douglas (1998). "Financial Illiteracy, Education and Retirement Saving", In *Living with Defined Contribution Pensions*. O.S. Mitchell and S. Schieber, eds. Pension Research Council and University of Pennsylvania Press.

Blake, David (1997). "Pension Choices and Pensions Policy in the UK". In *The Economics of Pensions: Principles, Policies, and International Experience*. S. Valdes-Prieto, ed. Cambridge University Press: New York.

Blake, David and J. Michael Orszag (1997). *Towards a Universal Funded Second Pension*. Special Report submitted to the 1997 UK Pensions Review, Pensions Institute Birkbeck College, University of London.

Bodie, Zvi (1992). "Pensions". *New Palgrave Dictionary of Money and Finance*. Newman, P., M. Milgate and P. Newman, eds. New York, NY Stockton Press, 130–133.

Bodie, Zvi (1990). "Pensions As Retirement Income Insurance." *Journal of Economic Literature*, 28 (1), 28–49.

Bodie, Zvi and Robert C. Merton (1993). "Pension Benefit Guarantees in the United States: A Functional Analysis." In *The Future of Pensions in the United States*, Ed. R. Schmitt. Philadelphia, PA: Pension Research Council and University of Pennsylvania Press, 194–234.

Bodie, Zvi, Olivia S. Mitchell and John Turner, Eds. (1996). *Securing Employer-Provided Pensions: An International Perspective*. Pension Research Council. Philadelphia, PA: University of Pennsylvania Press.

Bulow, Jeremy I. (1982). "What Are Corporate Pension Liabilities?" *Quarterly Journal of Economics* 97 (3), 435–452.

Chand, Sheetal and Albert Jaeger (1996). "Aging Populations and Public Pension Schemes". IMF Occasional Paper 147, Washington D.C.

Davis, E. Philip (1996) "An International Comparison of the Financing of Occupational Pensions" In *Securing Employer-Based Pensions: An International Perspective*, Eds. Z. Bodie and O.S. Mitchell. Philadelphia, PA: Pension Research Council and University of Pennsylvania Press.

Demirguc-Kunt, Asli and Anita Schwarz (1996). "Taking Stock of Pension Reforms Around the World". Paper presented at EDI Conference on "*Pension Systems: From Crisis to Reform*", EDI, World Bank, Washington, D.C.

Diamond, Peter A. and James A. Mirrlees (1985). "Insurance Aspects of Pensions." In *Pensions, Labor, and Individual Choice*. David A. Wise, ed. Chicago: The University of Chicago Press, 317–356.

Diamond, Peter A. and E. Sheshinsky (1995). "Economic Aspects of Optimal Disability Benefits", *Journal of Public Economics*, 1–23.

Dilnot, Andrew (1996). "The Taxation of Private Pensions". In *Securing Employer-Provided Pensions: An International Perspective*. Z. Bodie, O.S. Mitchell and J. Turner, Eds. Pension Research Council. Philadelphia, PA: University of Pennsylvania Press.

Disney, Richard (1996). *Can We Afford to Grow Older?* MIT Press: Cambridge, MA.

Edey, Malcolm and John Simon (1996). "Australia's Retirement Income System". NBER Working paper 5799.

Dresdner Bank (1997). *Pension Fund Systems in the World*. Economic Research Unit. Frankfurt/Main: Dresdner Bank.

Feldstein, Martin (1983). "Should Private Pensions Be Indexed?," In *Financial Aspects of the United States Pension System*. Z. Bodie and J.B. Shoven, eds. Chicago: The University of Chicago Press, 211–230.

Fields, Gary S. and Olivia S. Mitchell (1984). *Retirement, Pensions and Social Security*. Cambridge: MIT Press.

Geanakoplos, John, Olivia S. Mitchell and Stephen Zeldes. (1999). "Social Security Money's Worth".

In *Prospects for Social Security Reform*. O.S. Mitchell, R. Myers and H Young, eds. Pension Research Council. Philadelphia, PA: University of Pennsylvania Press, 79–151.

Gordon, Michael, Olivia S. Mitchell and Marc Twinney, Eds. (1997). *Positioning Pensions for the 21st Century*. Pension Research Council. Philadelphia, PA: University of Pennsylvania Press.

Gruber, Jonathan (1997). "The Incidence of Payroll Taxation: Evidence from Chile", *American Economic Review*.

Gustman, Alan L. and Olivia S. Mitchell (1992). "Pensions and the Labor Market: Behavior and Data Requirements", In *Pensions and the U.S. Economy: The Need for Good Data*. Z. Bodie and A. Munnell, eds, Philadelphia, Pa: Pension Research Council, 39–87.

Gustman, Alan L., Olivia S. Mitchell and Thomas L. Steinmeier (1994). "The Role of Pensions in the Labor Market" *Industrial and Labor Relations Review* 47 (3), 417–438.

Holzmann, Robert (1997a). "Starting Over in Pensions: The Challenges Facing Central and Eastern Europe", World Bank Working Paper. Washington, D.C.

Holzmann, Robert (1997b). "On the Economic Benefits and Fiscal Requirements of Moving from Unfunded to Funded Pensions", American Institute for Contemporary German Studies Research Report no. 4, Johns Hopkins University. Baltimore, Md.

Hsin, Ping-Lung and Olivia S. Mitchell (1994). "The Political Economy of Public Pensions: Pension Funding, Governance, and Fiscal Stress". *Revista de Analisis Economico*, Special Issue on Pension Systems and Reform. Edited by P. Arrau and K. Schmidt-Hebbel. 9 (1), 151–168.

Hutchens, Robert (1989). "Seniority, Wages, and Productivity: A Turbulent Decade." *Journal of Economic Perspectives*. 3 (4), 49–64.

Ippolito, Richard (1985). "The Labor Contract and True Economic Pension Liabilities." *American Economic Review*. 75 (5), 1031–1043.

Ippolito, Richard (1997). *Pension Plans and Employee Performance*. Chicago: University of Chicago Press.

Ippolito, Richard (1986). *Pensions, Economics and Public Policy*. Pension Research Council. Homewood, Illinois: Dow Jones-Irwin.

Ippolito, Richard (1989). *The Economics of Pension Insurance*. Pension Research Council. Homewood, Illinois: Dow Jones-Irwin.

James, Estelle and Dmitri Vittas (1996). "Mandatory Savings Schemes: Are They an Answer to the Old Age Security Problem?" In *Securing Employer-Based Pensions: An International Perspective*, Z. Bodie and O. Mitchell, eds. Philadelphia, PA: Pension Research Council and University of Pennsylvania Press.

Kotlikoff, Laurence J. (1987). "Justifying Public Provision of Social Security". *Journal of the American Public Policy Association and Management* 6 (4), 674–689.

Kotlikoff, Laurence J. and David A.Wise (1987). "The Incentive Effects of Private Pension Plans," In *Issues in Pension Economics*. Z. Bodie, J. Shoven and D.A. Wise, eds. Chicago: University of Chicago Press, 283–336.

Lazear, Edward P. (1979). "Why Is There Mandatory Retirement." *Journal of Political Economy*, 87 (6), 1261–1284.

Lazear, Edward P. (1983). "Pensions as Severance Pay." In *Financial Aspects of the United States Pension System*. Z. Bodie, J. Shoven and D. Wise eds. Chicago: The University of Chicago Press, 57–85.

Logue, Dennis E. and Jack S. Rader (1997). *Managing Pension Plans: A Comprehensive Guide*. Harvard Business School Press.

Lumsdaine, R. (1997). "Factors Affecting Labor Supply Decisions and Retirement Income". In *Assessing Knowledge of Retirement Behavior*. Eds. E. Hanushek and N. Maritato. National Academy Press.

Luzadis, Rebecca A. and Olivia S. Mitchell (1991). "Explaining Pension Dynamics." *Journal of Human Resources*. 26 (4), 679–703.

Manchester, Joyce (1998). "Taxing Issues for Social Security". In *Living with Defined Contribution Pensions*. O.S. Mitchell and S. Schieber, eds. Pension Research Council, University of Pennsylvania Press.

McGill, Dan, Kyle Brown, John Haley and Sylvester Scheiber (1996). *Fundamentals of Private Pension Plans.* 7e. University of Pennsylvania Press.

Merton, Robert; Zvi Bodie and Alan J.Marcus (1987). "Pension Plan Integration As Insurance Against Social Security Risk." In *Issues In Pension Economics*. J. Shoven and D. Wise, eds. Chicago: University of Chicago Press, 147–169.

Mitchell, Olivia S. (1998a). "Administrative Costs of Public and Private Pension Plans". In *Social Security Privatization.* M. Feldstein, ed. University of Chicago: Chicago, Il.

Mitchell, Olivia S. (1997a). "An Evaluation of Pension System Administrative Costs in Mexico". Working Paper, Pension Research Council, Wharton School.

Mitchell, Olivia S. (1997b). "Building an Environment for Pension Reform in Developing Countries". Pension Research Council Working Paper, The Wharton School.

Mitchell, Olivia S. (1998b). "International Models for Pension Reform". Presentation before the Social Security Committee, House of Commons, UK Parliament.

Mitchell, Olivia S. and Flavio Barreto (1997). "After Chile What?: Second Round Pension Reforms in Latin America". *Revista de Analisis Economico.*

Mitchell, Olivia S. and Rod Carr (1996). "State and Local Pension Plans". In *Handbook of Employee Benefits*. Jerry Rosenbloom, ed. Chicago, IL: Irwin, 1207–1222.

Mitchell, Olivia S. and Ping-Lung Hsin (1997a). "Managing Public Sector Pensions". In *Public Policy Toward Pensions*. J. Shoven and S. Schieber, eds. Twentieth Century Fund: New York.

Mitchell, Olivia S. and Ping-Lung Hsin (1997b). "Public Sector Pension Governance and Performance". In *The Economics of Pensions: Principles, Policies, and International Experience.* Salvador Valdes Prieto, ed. Cambridge: Cambridge Univ. Press.

Mitchell, Olivia S. and James Moore. (1999). "Retirement Wealth Accumulation and Decumulation: New Developments and Outstanding Opportunities". *Journal of Risk and Insurance*: 65 (3), 173–193.

Mitchell, Olivia S., Jim Poterba, Mark Warshawsky and Jeff Brown. (1999). "New Evidence on the Money's Worth of Individual Annuities". *American Economic Review*, 299–318.

Mitchell, Olivia S. and Sylvester Schieber, Eds. (1998). *Living with Defined Contribution Pensions*, Pension Research Council. Philadelphia, PA. University of Pennsylvania Press.

Mitchell, Olivia S. and Robert Smith (1994). "Public Sector Pension Funding". *Review of Economics and Statistics,* 278–290.

Mitchell, Olivia S. and Annika Sunden (1994). "An Examination of Social Security Administration Costs in the United States". Pension Research Council Working Paper. Wharton School.

Mitchell, Olivia S. and Steven Zeldes (1996). "A Framework for Analyzing Social Security Privatization". *American Economic Review Papers and Proceedings*. 86 (2), 363–367.

Montgomery, Edward, Kathryn Shaw and Mary Ellen Benedict (1992). "Pensions and Wages: an Hedonic Price Theory Approach." *International Economic Review*. 33 (1), 111–128.

Moore, James and Olivia S. Mitchell. (2000). "Projected Retirement Wealth and Saving Adequacy in the Health & Retirement Study". In *Forecasting Retirement Needs and Retirement Wealth*. O. Mitchell, B. Hammond and A. Rappaport, eds. Pension Research Council. Philadelphia, PA: University of Pennsylvania Press, 68–94.

Pennacchi, George. (1999). "Government Guarantees for Old Age Income". In *Prospects for Social Security Reform*. O.S. Mitchell, R. Myers and H. Young, Eds. Pension Research Council and University of Pennsylvania Press, 221–242.

Pesando, James (1996). "The Government's Role in Insuring Pensions," In *Securing Employer-Based Pensions: An International Perspective*. Z. Bodie and O.S. Mitchell, eds. Philadelphia, PA: Pension Research Council and University of Pennsylvania Press.

Pestieau, P. (1995). "Social Protection and Private Insurance: Reassessing the Role of Public Sector vs Private Sector in Insurance". *18th Annual Lecture of the Geneva Association.*

Petersen, Mitchell A. (1992). "Pension Reversions and Worker Stockholder Wealth." *Quarterly Journal of Economics* 107 (3), 1033–1056.

Quinn, Joseph F., Richard V. Burkhauser and Daniel A. Myers (1990). *Passing The Torch: The Influence of Economic Incentives on Work and Retirement*. Kalamazoo: W.E. Upjohn Institute.

Sass, Steven (1997). *The Promise of Private Pensions: The First Hundred Years*. Cambridge, MA: Harvard University Press.

Stock, James H. and David A. Wise (1990). "Pensions, The Option Value Of Work, and Retirement." *Econometrica*. 58 (5), 1151–1180.

Sundaresan, Suresh and Fernando Zapatero (1997). "Valuation, Optimal Asset Allocation, and Retirement incentives of Pension Plans". *Review of Financial Studies*. Fall 10 (3), 631–660.

Thaler, Richard and H.M. Shefrin (1981). "Pensions, Savings and Temptation." Graduate School of Business and Public Administration Working Paper No. 81-26. Cornell University.

27 Life Insurance*

Bertrand Villeneuve

CEA and Université de Toulouse

Abstract

This survey reviews the micro-economic foundations of the analysis of life insurance markets. The first part outlines a simple theory of insurance needs based on the life-cycle hypothesis. The second part builds on contract theory to expose the main issues in life insurance design within a unified framework. We investigate how much flexibility is desirable. Flexibility is needed to accommodate changing tastes and objectives, but it also gives way to opportunistic behaviors from the part of the insurers and the insured. Many typical features of actual life insurance contracts can be considered the equilibrium outcome of this trade-off.

Keywords: Life insurance, life cycle, flexibility, insurance contracts.
JEL Classification Numbers: G22, D91, D82.

27.1 INTRODUCTION

Life insurance serves to guarantee a periodic revenue or a capital to dependents of the policyholder (the spouse, or the children, sometimes the parents or any other person) in case of his death, or to himself, in case he survives. Life insurance economics is undoubtedly a question of applied theory and most useful ideas originated in other fields: savings theory or contract theory flourished well before their interests for insurance were perceived. Rather than trying to be complete and fair with respect to the valuable studies in saving theory, contract theory, the economics of the family, and standard insurance theory, we cite essentially papers that have reinterpreted these ideas and applied them to life insurance particularities. We will not always follow this line, especially when certain such transfers have not yet been effected. This survey will therefore give a personal view of the state of the art and will suggest certain extensions that remain to be formalized.

We start by providing in section 27.2.1 a description of insurance supply or *insurance possibilities*. The theory of contingent claims has improved the understanding

* Many thanks to Helmuth Cremer, Georges Dionne, Jeff Myron and the anonymous referees. All errors and imprecisions are my responsibility.

of life insurance contracts as bundles of elementary assets whose costs for the insurer are rather easy to measure. With this actuarial view, we come up with a production set which will serve as a basis for further investigation.

We want to build a consistent *theory of life insurance needs*. Needs are determined of course by the policyholder's tastes and the stage of the life-cycle that is considered, but also by his economic conditions, the structure of his family, etc. In section 27.2.2, we discuss the factors affecting the portfolio choice between ordinary savings, life insurance, and life annuities in an ideal financial environment. We give some indications on the so-called bequest motive, which is often a blackbox in insurance and saving models. This section being more formalized than the others, the reader may want to skip certain technicalities.

In the last part (section 27.3), this survey provides ultimately a basis for a *theory of life insurance contracts*. Markets do not work as perfectly as suggested by the theoretical benchmark described in the first two sections. In practice the contracts offered to the consumers are limited to a few typical structures; explaining these features and the stability of this selection is the role assigned to the economic theory of insurance. The main limitations to the implementation of first-best contracts are the parties' inability to commit, asymmetric information before signing, and asymmetric information emerging during the life of the contract. The existence of options (extension of coverage, renewability, surrender values, etc.) needs a particular and thorough treatment. In any case, an understanding of each party's objective is an imperative condition for characterizing incentive compatible contracts: indeed, the actuaries must be aware of self-selection effects (i.e., actuarial non-neutrality) in choices between the offered options. We have to clarify and model under which circumstances they would be exercised.

Starting from the fact that life insurance contracts are incomplete, we propose in section 27.3.1 some clarification of the reasons for the existence of options in contracts. This latter fact appears to be linked to renegotiation possibilities that kill intertemporal insurance to some extent, and to the fact that essential information (shocks in tastes to be short) may not be observable by both parties, which explains why a degree of discretion at some points is desirable.

Section 27.3.2 discusses the importance of adverse selection (and moral hazard) in life insurance markets. These markets are interesting in two respects: the first is that there exist relatively close substitutes to life insurance, which is only part of a balanced saving portfolio; the second is that it is almost impossible to ensure exclusivity, policyholders being typically able to secretly hold as many contracts as they want. The modeling of markets and the power of public regulation are deeply affected by these particularities.

The conclusion in section 27.4 gives a series of modest reflections on the value of theory for designing life insurance contracts.

Two important limitations of this study must be mentioned. The first one concerns the literature on investment policy, a topic that has not been related to well-structured insurance demand models. Some intuition on the effect of financial uncertainty on saving strategies (precautionary saving, risk premia on securities, structure of the portfolio, etc.) may be found in several other contributions to this handbook. Though strictly speaking, our study cannot be orthogonal to these concerns, we think that a complete model of the effects of risk to life has to be built first in a simpler framework.

The second limitation concerns the effect of taxes on insurance demand. At first sight, taxes simply distort prices of the contingent claims that insurance contracts bundle. This simple picture is rarely valid. In general, the tax system gathers non-linear benefits and penalties. Insurance supply is also affected by the efforts of actuaries to find and sell fiscal niches. Moreover, a serious analysis of taxes on life insurance would require a clear notion of the aim of the public authority. This last requirement is the most disappointing. A mere description of actual practices is definitely not within the scope of this survey.

27.2 POSSIBILITIES AND NEEDS IN LIFE INSURANCE

27.2.1 Life Insurance Possibilities

The purpose of this section is to present a simple description of the technical and financial constraints that are imposed on life insurance contracts. Though we acknowledge that probabilities are tightly connected to statistical observations, probabilities are seen in the sequel primarily as a measure of information, notably because this modern view will enable us to explore the evolution of information over time. The minimal requirement is that insurance contracts must be measurable, at each date, with respect to the available information. This preliminary remark makes sense for three reasons.

The first reason is that in financial markets, there is an almost continuous flow of information and the funds invested by the insurance company are managed so as to accommodate with maximal foresight the movements of the rates of return of the various possible assets. This aspect of insurance contracts is particularly worthy of mention for long term arrangements where benefits are typically somehow linked to financial performance.

The second reason is that time allows for some learning of policyholders' abilities and preferences. Often for the best: the contract will take into account essential changes in the policyholder's objective. But, even in the case of symmetric evolution of knowledge, if commitments on both parts are not total, the contractual relationship may be disrupted in certain contingencies, e.g., if the policyholder proves too risky. Though legal restrictions moderate this threat, there exists serious obstacles to the sustainability of most desirable long term contracts.

The third reason that makes a powerful information structure indispensable is that in the standard modelling, informational asymmetries are not due to someone being wrong, but rather on different precisions in the information possessed by the parties. Modeling how parties interpret each other's actions requires a well-suited formal setting. For example, a question that can be addressed with this methodology is the effect of prohibiting the use for contract design of certain pieces of information (anti-discriminatory laws) in spite of their objective relevance.

The Production Set

Actuarial Approach. A life insurance contract is a financial agreement between an insurer and a policyholder, signed at a date t_0, specifying monetary transfers at certain dates $\{t_0 + d, \ldots, t_0 + d + m\}$ where d is a delay and m the maximal duration ($0 \leq d < +\infty$ and $0 \leq m$). We work with discrete time throughout the paper. The flows either go from the policyholder to the insurer or the other way around. We denote by $p_t^i(s)$ a payment at date t from the insurer to beneficiary i ($i = 1 \ldots n$), conditionally upon the arrival of state of the world $s \in I_t$ where I_t is the information set at date t (an element of I_t contains all the available information, and $\{I_t\}_{t \geq t_0}$ is a filtration to capture the fact that information is more and more accurate). A negative $p_t^i(s)$ is interpreted as a "premium" or contribution, a positive $p_t^i(s)$ as an "indemnity" or benefit.

The two substantial elements in this definition are that payments are contingent on a potentially very rich algebra of events, and that they are assigned to named persons (the beneficiaries).

In practice, payments contingent upon survival or death can be explicitly specified quite simply in contracts, nevertheless, all contingencies are not listed in details, or are used in a crude manner: for example, financial performance is often utilized under the form of some simple sharing rule.

Non-anonymity is the major difference with purely financial assets. For obvious moral hazard reasons, there is a legal prohibition on betting on other people's lives. This is not a neutral limitation: if, for example, your income is highly dependent on the survival of your associate, you cannot hedge against that eventuality without his agreement. In other words he has to agree to purchase life insurance with you as beneficiary, possibly in exchange of some compensation.

The production set is defined by the following standard economic principle: expected profits must be positive. Formally:

$$\sum_{t=t_0}^{t=t_0+d+m} \left(\sum_{s \in I_t} a_t(s) \cdot \sum_{i=1}^{i=n} p_t^i(s) \right) \leq 0 \tag{1}$$

where $a_t(s)$ represents the cost (at date t_0) of one unit at date t in state s. In an economy with complete markets, the $a_t(s)$ represent the prices of the Arrow–Debreu assets; otherwise, they represent marginal value for shareholders and may contain the shadow cost of liquidity constraints or reserve regulation. In any case, discount factors (interest rates, probabilities, risk premia, etc.) are embodied in the $a_t(s)$. To simplify, I_t can be structured as $F_t \times M_t$, where F_t represents states of financial markets and M_t is a list of indicators of who is alive and who is dead. If one assumes that mortality is independent of interest rates, then for all $f, f' \in F_t$ and for all $m, m' \in M_t$: $\Pr\{f|m\} = \Pr\{f|m'\}$ and $\Pr\{m|f\} = \Pr\{m|f'\}$. We can write for all $s = (f, m): a_t(s) = \phi_t(f) \cdot \mu_t(m)$.

The aim of this last factorization is to show that insurers' technical ability, summarized by the $a_t(s)$, comes from two independent expertises: actuarial estimates ϕ_t, and asset management μ_t; these two dimensions are of course complementary for assessing the global performance of a given insurer. The reader should retain for the moment that (essentially) the technical dimension of insurance boils down to a single constraint. The determination of the optimal contracts under this constraint requires of course also a good understanding of policyholders tastes.

To illustrate the non-triviality of the actuarial dimension, one should keep in mind that life expectancy has increased steadily in developed countries during the last fifty years. Insurers have to extrapolate somehow the past trend when using mortality tables, since actual mortality tables are not applicable directly to younger customers. Mullin and Philipson (1997) developed methods to estimate the mortality rates implicit in competitive prices of life insurance policies, in other words, the anticipation of the market on the evolution of longevity for the current generations. They claimed that the increase of longevity is expected (by insurers) to follow at least the same pace as observed recently.

Incentive Compatibility. In principle, in a world of symmetric verifiable information and full rationality, decisions nodes are useless in contracts since the optimal plan was completely specified ex ante and continuations are mechanically determined by the observation of the state of the world. Leaving aside for methodological reasons bounded rationality problems, there are two essential assumptions behind this view of contracts. The first is that parties are committed to the complete implementation of the contract. The second is that no information relevant to the optimal continuation can emerge asymmetrically during the life of the contract (not to speak of asymmetries at the time the contract is signed).

Under a more realistic view, it may be optimal, under identified informational constraints, to leave the policyholder choose an option at certain dates, his choice being determined by his current interest.

Accordingly, we have to add decisions by agents in the definition of the states. Typically, insurance policies contain renewal options, without medical examination, for a limited number of additional periods; they also specify surrender values, that is, the money the policyholder can get if he dismisses the contract. Another common option, though not always seen as such, is due to the legal requirement that if the insured stops paying his contributions, the insurance company can only reduce the benefits in proportion to the missing contributions, the contract being totally kept in force.

The difficulty now is that it becomes indispensable to ensure consistency of the contracts in the sense that probabilities put on the decision tree have to be compatible with actual behavior of the party taking decisions. Now we are leaving the comfortable realm of purely statistical evaluation of contracts: technical ability cannot be disentangled from the ability to understand behavior. The exact nature of the restrictions imposed by incentive compatibility will be explored in the third part of this survey.

Taxes. We will not deal with the important question of tax rules applied to life insurance. However, the reader must keep in mind that these rules are an important determinant of life insurance yields. We just mention the fact that the tax system in this matter is often intended to give incentives to financing old-age incomes (typically, contributions are deductible from the taxable income), while trying to ensure that they are not used for other purposes (by putting penalties on "premature" withdrawals).

Our choice is to give an extensive pure theory of life insurance, i.e., to offer a theory of needs in life insurance, a theory of production, and a theory of the impact of asymmetric information. Though in practice, taxes do not have a marginal effects in life insurance (it is even often stated that most of life insurance demand is tax-driven), we think that taxes are of secondary importance for understanding life insurance. Once the theory is clear, the effect of taxes becomes a relatively easy problem, conceptually at least.

It should be mentioned in passing that the rational foundations of the fiscal doctrine in life insurance has not been seriously studied by public economists.

Typical Life Insurance Contracts

We give indications of the principal characteristics encountered in practice. Basically, life insurance contracts serve to guarantee a revenue to dependents of the policyholder (the spouse, or the children, sometimes the parents or any other person) in case of his death, or to himself, in case he survives. The benefits may depend on who is alive in the household in a potentially sophisticated way.

In the following, we shall insist on survival/death of the policyholder and beneficiaries in the definition of a state of the world. Depending on how these states are utilized, we can outline the broad categories of insurance contracts. Here we follow (approximately) the classification and definitions proposed by Huebner and Black (1976).

Life Insurance. A term policy in life insurance is a contract that furnishes life insurance protection for a limited number of years (m is typically 5–20 years), payments to beneficiaries being effected only if death occurs during the stipulated term, and nothing being paid in case of survival. Instead of specifying a duration of coverage, whole-life insurance contracts provide payment in case of death to the beneficiary whenever it happens ($m = +\infty \ldots$).

Life Annuities. A life annuity may be defined as a periodic payment made during the duration of a designated life. A life annuity may be either whole or temporary (the payments contingent upon survival being then terminated after a fixed period). Typically, pensions are annuities.

Endowment Insurance. Endowment insurance provides the payment of the face value of the policy upon the death of the insured during the fixed term of years, and also the payment of the full face value at the end of the term if the insured is living. We recognize a sort of mix of term life insurance (the first part) and a term (with a single payment) annuity.

Miscellany. Contracts where benefits in case of death of the insured are annuities for the beneficiary are common: pension benefits for widows, minimum income until adulthood or until a child's college graduation, settlement for a handicapped child.[1] Disability insurance can be linked to life insurance for the reason that the breadwinner needs in fact coverage against permanent income losses, not against death per se.[2] In practice, contracts have a finite duration since they are conditioned upon a finite number of lives. There may be a delay ($d > 0$) between the signature of the contract and the first transfer.

Indices and Rates of Return

Market conditions and macroeconomic factors play a role in the evolution of contributions and benefits over time. Using a correction for (anticipated or random) inflation is a way of securing stable purchasing power for, e.g., a life annuity. The beneficiary may prefer a variable payment, adjusted for the financial performances of his fund, notably if he is relatively little risk averse so as to prefer to bear some residual risk in exchange for a share of possible high gains in financial markets; he may prefer a less risky (but less profitable on average) agreement. These sorts of arrangements are known as variable payments. What index is used, and how payments are index-linked, are contractual agreements.

Several papers calculate the rate of return implicit in life insurance and life annuities. These studies intend to isolate loadings due to commissions and administrative costs, corrections due to adverse selection, and financial performance corrected for taxes.[3] The calculated financial return can be compared to the returns of other types of assets.

[1] See, e.g., Gustavson and Trieschmann (1988).

[2] See Cox, Gustavson and Stam (1991) for empirical evidence on demand of these insurances.

[3] In this section, the reader must be aware that our selection of papers is extremely short. The papers retained here are chosen because they associate an economic reflection on the methodology to the calculations. Purely actuarial studies (published or unpublished) on similar issues abound.

Babbel (1985) proposed a simple index of life insurance costs (the consumer's viewpoint is taken; costs are the contributions paid above the actuarial benefits). His estimates suggest that consumers are sensitive to costs, and tend to diminish their purchases when they increase, which is, as Babbel claimed, a point in favor of economic theory and against the popular view among salesmen that "life insurance is sold, not bought."

Winter (1982) discussed the theoretical possibility of an index (a single number) facilitating the comparisons between life insurance policies for heterogenous consumers. Though he proposed a reasonable solution to that problem, he also made clear why the quest for an indisputable index is hopeless. The notion of rate of return makes no exception to his critique: an index based only on the $a_t(s)$—see our definition of contracts—may be right for assessing the purely technical ability of the insurers. However, the allocation of benefits across contingencies (the payments $p_t^i(s)$), however crucial they might be for policyholders, would not be captured.[4]

Despite these caveats, simplifying computations are useful. Warshawsky (1985), for example, defended the idea that the decline in life insurance savings from the mid 1950s to 1981 (life insurance has boomed since that paper was written) is largely imputable to the lower rate of return on the investment part of cash-value policies. Obviously, the complex structure of these contracts makes this assertion relatively delicate to establish, but Warshawsky subjected his calculations to a sensitivity analysis by screening a large set of plausible scenarios. Warshawsky (1988) in his study of annuity markets in the United States over 1919–1984 estimated that the loading factor ranged from 10 cents to 29 cents per dollar of actuarial present value.[5] The major cause of the evolution would be the tendency on the part of the insurers to use assets whose yields are significantly lower than that of the reference portfolio (namely, U.S. government bonds). The aggravation of adverse selection also seems to have a non-negligible impact on the loading factor. Mitchell *et al.* (1997) defend the view that costs have declined. The period covered by their study includes more recent years.

27.2.2 Life Insurance Needs

The aim of this section is to provide a relatively simple theory of *needs* in life insurance, i.e., demand in an ideal world where markets would be complete and competitive. The model is compatible with most views and formal studies of life insurance demand. We adopt this terminology (needs) to grasp the multidimensional aspect of life insurance contracts that "demand" would not suggest. To start with, we offer an analysis of the life-cycle theory and of the so-called bequest motive.

[4] Using a bounded rationality approach, Puelz (1991) proposes a practical strategy for selecting a life insurance policy.

[5] See also Poterba (1997).

The Life-cycle Hypothesis

Suppose the individual knows the date of his death. The allocation of his wealth over time may be assumed to derive from the maximization of the following inter-temporal objective (the Fisherian model after Fisher (1930), to retain Yaari's (1965) terminology):[6]

$$\sum_{t=1}^{t=T} U_t(c_t) + V_{T+1}(b_{T+1}) \tag{2}$$

where $U_t(\cdot)$ is the period t felicity derived from current consumption c_t, and $V_{T+1}(b_{T+1})$ is the value of bequest b_{T+1} left at date $T + 1$.[7]

We retain a discrete approach mainly because it facilitates the introduction of imperfect markets and the analysis of long term contracts. The drawback is that calculations in the simplest cases become less compact than with continuous time modeling.[8]

When the horizon is random, one can assume that the individual maximizes expected utility with respect to the distribution of T, $\bar{T}$ being the upper limit of the support

$$E_T\left\{\sum_{t=1}^{t=\bar{T}} U_t(c_t) + V_{T+1}(b_{T+1})\right\}. \tag{3}$$

The main restriction embodied in this objective function is the additive separability over time and states of the world: the marginal rate of substitution between two consumptions is independent of the other consumptions. Still, this formulation allows for time dependent utilities: it is consistent with the frequent assumption that future utility is discounted, and with an evolution of risk aversion over time. Rearranging we get

$$\sum_{t=1}^{t=\bar{T}} \{q_t U_t(c_t) + (q_{t-1} - q_t)V_t(b_t)\} + q_{\bar{T}} V_{\bar{T}+1}(b_{\bar{T}+1}) \tag{4}$$

where q_t denotes the probability of living at least until period t; in particular $q_t > q_{t+1}$, $q_0 = 1$ and $q_{\bar{T}+1} = 0$, and the mortality rate at the end of period t is $1 - \frac{q_{t+1}}{q_t}$. Compared to the certainty case, future consumption is further discounted by the survival probability; moreover, in all periods where death is probable, the bequest has a value.

[6] See also Fischer (1973) or Karni and Zilcha (1986).

[7] We could also enrich the model by giving value to inter-vivos transfers at other dates.

[8] For examples of this last category, see, e.g., Yaari (1965) and Pissarides (1980) where perfect markets are assumed.

In the objective above, the value of bequests is not built on primitives, and a rationale for particular specifications or properties is rarely even mentioned in studies interested in saving-consumption choice. Still a literature has developed an analytical description of the bequest motive, notably in view of deriving testable implications of the theory.

The first point is that we know little about the specification of $V_t(\cdot)$ as compared to $U_t(\cdot)$, and about how it should evolve period after period. Life insurance being after all only a financial tool for controlling inter-personal transfers, references to the theory of transfers (bequest, gifts, inter-vivos transfers) are necessary. The reader interested in this literature could for example refer to Bernheim, Shleifer and Summers (1985), Hurd (1987, 1989) and Ando, Guiso and Terlizzese (1993), the latter providing a Probit estimation of the determinants of life insurance demand. Abel and Warshawsky (1988) presented a useful discussion and implementation of how bequest motives could be specified and calculated, starting from simple principles.

Lewis (1989) extended Yaari's model by exploring explicitly how the bequest motive should be formed when it is intended to take into account the direct utilities of the dependents to be protected. In particular, he calculated theoretically and tested empirically the impact of the number of beneficiaries on life insurance demand. To this end, he modelled the way beneficiaries respond to the protection they receive. In some cases, their incomes may be sufficiently high relatively to that of the potential policyholder for life insurance to be unnecessary.[9]

Fitzgerald (1987) and Bernheim (1991) used information on the levels of pensions to explore the effects of social security (treated as exogenous) on life insurance demand. Given that insurance is crowded out on the one hand, and that increased pensions increase actual wealth on the other hand, the net effect is ambiguous a priori. Fitzgerald's data confirm that the impact of marginal pension differs according to who is the principal beneficiary (husband or wife) of the supplement. Bernheim's project is more focussed on the estimation of bequest motives. His estimates support the view that the differences in insurance purchases (whether people buy life insurance or annuities, or neither) are significantly determined by the differences in the generosity of the pension benefits: the better the pensions, the larger the bequests; the lower the pensions, the larger the propensity to cover oneself with private annuities.

Auerbach and Kotlikoff (1986, 1991) questioned whether women are well-covered by the life-insurance plans of their husbands. The normative standpoint is that a sound protection should allocate savings and insurance in view of maximizing a weighted sum of the spouses' utilities, taking into account their survival probabilities. The 1986 paper examined the case of the elderly and the 1991 one explored and found confirmation of the inadequacy of insurance coverage of younger households, who, given that a large part of their lifetime resources is tied up in human wealth, were supposedly more in need of protection. Fitzgerald (1989) proposed, with the help of a structural econometric model, to study the dependency on age of the relative

[9] With our notations, it amounts to say that the marginal utility $V_t'(0)$ may be low.

(expected or actual) economic well-being of widows according to whether the husband lives or not. He suggested that, because economies of scales in households are not very large, the standard-of-living falls after death of the husband are not as dramatic as previously reported, and is even contradicted in certain groups.

Most authors find convenient to let the market be the only institution where insurance is available, and to assume that there is a single decision-maker (or at least a leader) involved in purchase decisions. Nevertheless a few papers have scrutinized the insurance demand of households in imperfect contexts. Despite their interest, they have unfortunately not yet given rise to econometric applications.

Kotlikoff and Spivak (1981) viewed the family as an institution able to replace inefficient annuity markets. They assumed that markets are incomplete: there exist no life insurance or annuity markets; members of the household can only save. In a single agent household, savings would be lost in case of death in the sense that they provide no utility to the decision-maker; here, savings are mutually bequeathed, and they are lost only in case of simultaneous deaths, an event of relatively low probability. Kotlikoff and Spivak proved that this risk sharing arrangement over few household members is sufficient to approximate first-best allocations very closely.

Browning (1994) insisted on the strategic issue. The difference here with standard individualistic models is that each household member has access to life insurance markets (in fact life annuities) and savings, but they act non-cooperatively. The source of inefficiency is that consumption being in the model a purely public good, each household member free-rides the other's savings. The consequence is that one member only (typically the husband) will subscribe life annuities. Though indisputably a caricature, this alternative approach (as compared to the single decision-maker tradition) is original and deserves attention and development.

Empirical studies like Arrondel and Masson (1994), Sachko Gandolfi and Miners (1996) or Goldsmith (1983) document the determinants of household demand. Typically, wealth, income, the number of children have significant positive effects. Arrondel and Masson also show that professions where human wealth (expected future income from labor) is relatively large are more likely to demand life insurance.

Constraints

An Image of Financial Markets. Let us define additional control and state variables:

A_t and L_t: the face value (i.e., the benefit) of, respectively, short term annuities and short term life insurance, to be paid to the beneficiary at date t in the corresponding contingency;

R_t^A and R_t^L: the gross rate of return of, respectively, annuities and life insurance received at date t; contributions $\frac{A_t}{R_t^A}$ and $\frac{L_t}{R_t^L}$ are paid at date $t-1$; taxes are ignored throughout, but may be included in the rates of return;

R_t: the gross rate of return on saving;

W_t^A and W_t^L: the disposable wealth of the agent at the beginning of period t if he is alive (respectively if he is just dead);

Y_t: the exogenous income (wage or pension) which is conditional on the consumer being alive;

$W_t^A + Y_t - c_t - \frac{A_{t+1}}{R_t^A} - \frac{L_{t+1}}{R_t^L}$: short term saving at the end of period t.

The constraints to respect are the following:

$$A_t \geq 0 \tag{5}$$

$$L_t \geq 0 \tag{6}$$

(5) and (6) are short-sale constraints. They need an explanation. Saving and insurance leave three assets for two states of the world. In terms of *benefits*, one unit of ordinary saving is replicable by simultaneously purchasing one unit of life insurance and one unit of life annuities for the same period. If the *costs* were the same, (5) and (6) would be purely arbitrary and would only serve to fix a terminology: for example, if $A_t > L_t$, we could apply the convention that the agent "saves and purchases annuities". But in practice, insurance prices are loaded and the equivalence is not true. Intuitively, high mortality individuals tend to buy life insurance whereas low mortality individuals tend to buy annuities; in consequence, actual purchases provide some information to the insurers on the consumer's riskiness that is taken into account in the prices charged. Short-sale constraints represent how markets deal with adverse selection: by setting (simplified) non-linear prices. Technically, short-sale constraints prevent the arbitrage argument to work, as a consequence, all three assets are needed.

Most papers assume either that insurance is available at an actuarial price (the interest rate corrected for mortality) or that it is not available at all, which leads to comparisons of the profiles of consumption in the two contexts.[10] When insurance is actuarial, we find: $R_t^A = \frac{q_t}{q_{t+1}} R_t$ and $R_t^L = \frac{q_t}{q_t - q_{t+1}} R_t$. For example in Fischer (1973), assuming perfect markets amounts to imposing $\frac{1}{R_t^A} + \frac{1}{R_t^L} = \frac{1}{R_t}$, which explains why he finds negative purchases of life insurance (i.e., implicit positive purchases of annuities) in his examples.

Loading factors decrease insurance yields; they are principally due to administrative costs, to adverse selection, and to fiscal regimes. Another factor that may enlarge the gap between *average* market returns and life insurance returns is that life insurance funds are backed by a larger proportion of low return (presumably less risky)

[10] Yaari (1965), Fischer (1973), Levhari and Mirman (1977), Pissarides (1980).

assets in general (Friedman and Warshawsky (1990)). Papers where both imperfect markets (life insurance and annuities) are modelled at the same time are scarce. For a simple theoretical example and an empirical application, see Bernheim (1991). It is proved in Moffet (1979a,b) or Villeneuve (1996) that if $\frac{1}{R_t^A}+\frac{1}{R_t^L}>\frac{1}{R_t}$, then the agent never purchases life insurance and annuities at the same time for the same term: else it would be cheaper to cut life insurance and annuity benefits by an arbitrary quantity and to compensate it exactly by an increase of savings.[11]

We impose that the agent's disposable wealth be always non-negative

$$W_t^A \geq 0 \tag{7}$$

$$W_t^L \geq 0 \tag{8}$$

Such borrowing constraints are discussed at length by Yaari (1965). (8) simply says that negative net wealth cannot be inherited. It should be possible in principle to overcome (7) if the agent were able to publicly commit to a contingent borrowing plan for the future. In the absence of such a commitment, the policyholder would be able to play a sort of "Ponzi game", i.e., a strategy of unbounded rolling debt.[12] In response to this threat, the liquidity constraint, though very conservative, is in practice easily implemented. Another practical useful interpretation of the choice between insurance and savings is the following: if the individual borrows money, he must provide a guarantee under the form of life insurance. This is the standard practice for mortgage loans.

$$W_{t+1}^A = R_t\left(W_t^A + Y_t - c_t - \frac{A_{t+1}}{R_t^A} - \frac{L_{t+1}}{R_t^L}\right) + A_{t+1} \tag{9}$$

$$W_{t+1}^L = R_t\left(W_t^A + Y_t - c_t - \frac{A_{t+1}}{R_t^A} - \frac{L_{t+1}}{R_t^L}\right) + L_{t+1} \tag{10}$$

[11] If $\frac{1}{R_t^A}+\frac{1}{R_t^L}<\frac{1}{R_t}$, the individual would never have interest to detain ordinary assets: his portfolio would be entirely composed of insurance. But, except if insurance if heavily subsidized, insurance companies would not be able to sustain such yields: the inequality says that no financial assets could match these liabilities.

[12] Assume that, each period, the individual is able to borrow on the promise he would reimburse, with the payment of a certain interest adjusted for mortality risk, *only if he lives*. Without control, the individual would borrow, period after period, unbounded quantities of money, first to pay back the previous loan, and second to finance consumption. With an infinite support of life duration (and even if the probability of staying alive is extremely low), we typically enter into the Ponzi game problem, well-known in public finance. When the support of life duration is bounded, a consistency problem appears at the upper bound date, when the individual becomes certain to die: no insurance company will lend money and the individual is bankrupt. It is not clear that this is sufficient to impose discipline to the agent: punishment being necessarily limited, the Ponzi game problem remains an issue.

$$b_{t+1} = W_{t+1}^L \tag{11}$$

(9) and (10) give the laws of motion of conditional wealth: they express the dependency of incomes in case of survival and in case of death at date $t + 1$ on the portfolio choice at date t. (11) reminds that in case of death, the entire wealth, composed of savings and life insurance, is left to the beneficiaries.

Remark that it is assumed that no information is revealed over time except the date of death at the exact moment when it occurs. If the policyholder were to learn progressively his survival law, then the initial objective should be an expectation over the possible upcoming information too. If this information is observed by both parties (insurers and the policyholder) and if insurance prices depend on it, this would increase the number of necessary state variables and insurance markets. Fortunately, the dynamics of consumption would not be affected seriously since complete markets would provide insurance against these shocks. In general however, the equivalence between the optimal long term contract (agreed upon at period zero) and the optimal choice of short term contract would disappear. See Babbel and Ohtsuka (1989), and section 27.3.

Regimes. Because of the uncertainty, we introduced additional state variables (conditional wealth) to the standard life-cycle model. Classically, under complete markets, they can be eliminated so as to give a single inter-temporal budget constraint where the present value of consumption equals the present value of income. Here, we have to determine, as a first step, non-binding constraints in order to reduce the complexity of the program.

The sub-optimality of simultaneous purchases of life insurance and annuities opens the possibility of different regimes at different periods of the life-cycle: the individual may want to purchase life insurance at certain dates and life annuities at others. At each period t, the individual saves or borrows, but concerning insurance, he purchases either annuities or life insurance, or neither. For example, a man below fifty will be covered by life insurance; above seventy, by life annuities. It is possible in practice that he seems to have both (e.g., a pension plus life insurance). However, his net position will presumably be as we say.

The consequence of the existence of these three regimes is that it is not possible a priori to write a unique constraint, since part of the individual decision is the qualitative choice of the contingent assets he needs. Confronted with this difficulty, several papers have supposed, or set conditions ensuring, that a certain regime is systematically in force (Abel (1986)), or have limited the conclusions regarding the temporal evolution of the structure and quantity of saving to a certain regime.[13]

To simplify the rest of the exposition, we write the relevant budget constraint within a regime *as if* it were prevailing throughout the individual's life-cycle: either

[13] Yaari (1965), Fischer (1973), Levhari and Mirman (1977).

the individual is a permanent annuitant (regime A), or he is always covered by life-insurance (regime L), or he holds neither (regime N). The difference between regime N and the other two is that then it is not possible to eliminate wealth variables (W_t^A, W_t^L) to build a single budget constraint: there is only one control variable (saving) per period for two arguments in the utility.

In contrast, in regime A, where annuities demand is always non-negative, a single constraint can be used:

$$\sum_{t=0}^{t=\bar{T}}\left\{\left(Y_t - c_t - \frac{R_{t-1}^A - R_{t-1}}{R_{t-1}} b_t\right)\prod_{s=t}^{s=\bar{T}} R_s^A\right\} = 0. \tag{12}$$

In regime L, where life insurance demand is always non-negative:

$$\sum_{t=0}^{t=\bar{T}}\left\{\left(Y_t - c_t - \frac{R_{t-1}}{R_{t-1}^L - R_{t-1}} b_t\right)\prod_{s=t}^{s=\bar{T}} \frac{R_s R_s^L}{R_s^L - R_s}\right\} = 0, \tag{13}$$

When prices are fair, the notion of regime, as said before, is only semantic, and we find in all cases:

$$\sum_{t=0}^{t=\bar{T}}\left\{(q_t Y_t - q_t c_t - (q_{t-1} - q_t) b_t)\prod_{s=t}^{s=\bar{T}} R_s\right\} = 0 \tag{14}$$

In all cases, we see that what matters is the present value of income discounted (implicitly in (12) and (13) or explicitly in (14)) by the survival probability (future incomes are conditional on living); the correction also applies to consumption and bequests.

Portfolio Choice

Within each regime, the Euler condition indicates the forces driving the short-run evolution of saving and insurance purchases. (Calculations are not detailed; hints are given in the appendix.)

In case A (annuities every period)

$$\frac{U'_{t+1}(c_{t+1})}{U'_t(c_t)} = \frac{1}{R_t^A}\frac{q_t}{q_{t+1}}, \tag{15}$$

$$\frac{V'_t(b_t)}{U'_t(c_t)} = \frac{R_{t-1}^A - R_{t-1}}{R_{t-1}}\frac{q_t}{q_{t-1} - q_t}. \tag{16}$$

In case L (life insurance every period)

$$\frac{U'_{t+1}(c_{t+1})}{U'_t(c_t)} = \left(\frac{1}{R_t} - \frac{1}{R_t^L}\right)\frac{q_t}{q_{t+1}}, \tag{17}$$

$$\frac{V'_t(b_t)}{U'_t(c_t)} = \frac{R_{t-1}}{R_{t-1}^L - R_{t-1}}\frac{q_t}{q_{t-1} - q_t}. \tag{18}$$

In any case we see that the variations of consumption depend positively upon the interest rate and negatively upon mortality. The sensitivity to these two effects is proportional to the elasticity of substitution between periods. For example, when $U_{t+1}(\cdot) = \beta U_t(\cdot)$, (15) can be approximated by

$$\frac{c_{t+1} - c_t}{c_t} \simeq \frac{1 - \dfrac{q_t}{\beta R_t^A q_{t+1}}}{\left(-\dfrac{c_t U''_t(c_t)}{U'_t(c_t)}\right)}, \tag{19}$$

We recover the usual result that consumption profiles depend directly on the comparison of interest rates with the discount factor.[14]

Consider the case where the individual purchases annuities throughout his life. When insurance markets are perfect, the first order conditions above are simplified and the marginal rate of substitution of consumption between two periods becomes equal to the interest rate, exactly as without uncertainty. Expected utility over states and additivity over time have the advantage, already noticed by Yaari, that weights attached to felicities (partial utilities) on the one hand, and prices on the other hand, are proportional. Except for the effects of risk-free interest rates and taxes, programmed consumption is extremely smooth.

In the periods when the individual is more risk averse (because of old age, or because dependents are more in need of protection), consumption and bequests tend to be less sensitive to price incentives and are therefore more likely to be protected by an insurance contract. On the role of risk aversion (or resistance to inter-temporal substitutability), see for example Karni and Zilcha (1986) or Hu (1986).

When the rate of return on annuities increases in a given period, contingent consumption that period becomes cheaper; the utility being additively separable, the income effect works in the same direction as the substitution effect to increase current consumption. Still, the increase in the rate of return of insurance decreases the value of incomes earned after that period (this is a well-known paradoxical property of lifetime earnings); the consequence of that particular effect is a decrease of insurance

[14] Again, Yaari (1965), Hakanson (1969), Fischer (1973), Levhari and Mirman (1977), Pissarides (1980).

demand. The net effect is ambiguous. The same indeterminacy occurs for life insurance: budget constraint (13) shows the depreciation of the present value of earnings Y_s for $s \geq t + 1$ provoked by an increase in life insurance returns R_t^L.[15] Fischer (1973) noticed this "inferior good" nature of insurance in his particular specification without market imperfections. Predictions are complicated by regime switches, though the effects above give some clues on when switches are likely to occur.

Other things equal, it is clear that an increase in mortality probabilities a given period should decrease the demand for annuities that period. Predictions however depend on whether the survival law is shifted so as to increase the weight of future, or past, consumptions. For example, Levhari and Mirman (1977) questioned whether changes in lifetime uncertainty should increase or decrease the rate of consumption. Using a stochastic ordering measuring dispersion lifetime, they point out two opposite (and paradoxical) effects: on the one hand, more uncertainty shortens the horizon (death at young ages becomes more probable), which increases the rate of consumption; on the other hand, longer lives also become relatively more probable, preserving wealth for those eventualities plays in favor of a decreased initial consumption. They conclude that the first effect dominates with Cobb-Douglas utility functions provided that, for a given discount factor, the interest rates are not too large. The approach, though interesting, remains difficult to generalize.[16] We should note in passing that there exists a limited literature examining the consistency of beliefs on mortality and economic behavior, in the framework of life-cycle theory. See for example Hamermesh (1985), or Hurd and McGarry (1995) for more details on the distribution of beliefs and their relationship to portfolio choice.

Friedman and Warshawsky (1990) explained that the average American pensioner should stop purchasing short term annuities between age 60 and 70, his constant pension (or publicly provided annuities) becoming larger than his free demand for annuities. Yagi and Nishigaki (1993) insisted on the fact that within the Fisherian model itself, optimal long term annuities should not be constant but rather declining over time in real value.

Leung (1994) gave a clue for these results. He showed, keeping the same assumptions as in Yaari, that there always exists an age, strictly before the upper limit, from which the individual consumes all his current income. Moreover, he proved, on the basis of simulations, that this constrained period is not negligible. According to Leung, this prediction contradicts empirical evidence since the elderly are conservative in the use of their assets. This remark is close in spirit to the disconnection between the prediction that wealth should exhibit a hump-shape over the life-cycle and the empirical finding that the elderly do not dissave in reality. To reconcile theory and evidence,

[15] The reader must be careful that the present value in that reasoning is taken in terms of first period disposable income.

[16] Kessler and Lin (1989) examined the comparative statics of a choice between cash and annuities in individual retirement accounts by varying the survival law. They show that the third derivative of the cumulative survival probability distribution plays a role.

Attanasio and Hoynes (1995) attempt to correct for the selectivity biases due to differential mortality across wealth groups (richer people living longer, dissaving is apparently slow since richer individuals become relatively more numerous). It seems that dissaving at old age calculated that way is more important than previously claimed, which gives new evidence in favor of the life-cycle hypothesis.

Life Insurance and Social Security

We leave aside the debate on the potential macroeconomic inefficiency of pay-as-you go systems to concentrate our attention on the specific effects on insurance markets. See also Mitchell (this volume). Pensions are publicly provided annuities, mandated either directly by the State or by the employer. The development of social security is recognized by Abel (1986, 1988) or Eckstein, Eichenbaum and Peled (1985) as a likely cause of the decline of *annuity demand* in the developed countries since World War II.

There is no doubt that social security crowds out life annuities. Microeconometric studies like Rejda and Schmidt (1984), Rejda, Schmidt and McNamara (1987), Fitzgerald (1987) or Bernheim (1991) confirm the negative effect of public pensions (or similar programs) on annuity demand and/or private pensions. Concerning life insurance, the intuition is not clear: on the one hand pensions should decrease noninsurance saving and enhance purchase of life insurance; on the other hand, most pension programs cover spouses after the death of the beneficiary. This *life insurance* element of pensions, frequently ignored by analysts, renders the net effect ambiguous.

A study on aggregate data by Browne and Kim (1993) suggests that income and life expectancy being taken into account, the quality of social security still has a positive impact on life insurance premium volume per capita (life insurance and annuities are not separated). However, the state of the art is far from testing the microeconomic life-cycle model presented in this survey.

27.3 A CONTRACT THEORY OF LIFE INSURANCE

Section 27.1 set up the technical constraints that contracts should meet; section 27.2 gave the effect of tastes on the structures of ideal contracts, thereby offering a theory of needs of life insurance. We now show that informational constraints play a major role in the functioning of life insurance.

In principle, long term contracts have the major merit that they are the only and sufficient means of taking advantage of all insurance possibilities. If information pertaining to the cost for the insurer and the value for the individual of life insurance contracts were always kept symmetric, then maximizing expected inter-temporal utility of the individual under a unique purely technical constraint would give smooth consumption paths along the life-cycle and across states, and straightforward continuations period after period. There should remain no ambiguity: a long term contract must not be a "stationary" contract paying a fixed amount whatever the conditions. On the contrary, well-conceived contracts take into account the passage of time: tastes change, notably those dictated by the composition of the household, new information (the arrival of which being anticipated as a possibility, and probabilized) may arise, for example on health conditions or future income.

A long term contract under symmetric information must not leave any choice to either the individual or the insurer: discretion is undesirable. Yet, we have to find explanations for the features observed in real contracts, all somehow linked to the fact that the informational situation is frequently not idyllic. Options in contracts may be desirable trade-offs between insurance needs and incentive compatibility.

We can classify the main types of imperfections as follows: 1. Incompleteness, namely (a) limited commitment, and (b) incomplete contracts (certain continuations are too complicated to write explicitly); 2. Asymmetric information (a) before signing, and (b) appearing over time.

We will take up each in turn.

27.3.1 Incompleteness

Limited Commitment

It is well recognized in insurance theory that long term contracts provide insurance against the risk of becoming a high risk, specifically against the risk of seeing future insurance applications rejected, or accepted only at high price. Therefore, the best insurance contract should be taken very early, even before any party becomes "advantaged" in terms of information.

Babbel and Ohtsuka (1989) applied these ideas to explain why policyholders should continue to hold whole life insurance, though, if prices are considered naively, this strategy seems dominated by a combination of successive term contracts and saving. The argument runs as follows: future health conditions being random, the average term contracts might turn inaccessible to certain individuals; consequently, the "dominant" strategy would be not implementable and the arbitrage argument does not work.

Cochrane (1995), in an article dedicated to health insurance organization, offered an interesting reflection on the various channels through which commitment could be escaped, stressing the importance of regulation. There, information over health is improved symmetrically over time. The main problem is that, if competition were unregulated, lucky persons would like to switch to an other insurer proposing better prices; this would break the cross-subsidies implicit in the first-best arrangement. He proposes a solution to overcome the market failure: insurance contracts last one period only (long-term commitment is not forced); insurers are free to charge the price they want to their clients, and markets are competitive; people have personal accounts to which their insurers pay severance payments when they are denied average price insurance; this money is given to the unlucky to finance their higher premia. This payment is intended to compensate exactly for the discrimination these people suffer. Basically, Cochrane shows that the desirable cross-subsidies are *exactly* implementable by this minimal new institution preserving competition and incentives.

In practice, in life insurance as well as in health insurance, asymmetries of information are multi-dimensional and the motivations of the agents are so diverse that the implementability of the first-best is not warranted (insuring taste shocks is considerably more difficult than probability shocks). The proposal however goes in the right direction and is capable of correcting a non-negligible part of the undesirable effects of discrimination.

The diffusion of group insurance seems to be a second-best response of certain communities in a world where the absence of commitment affects welfare significantly. These insurance programs are efficient in terms of coverage of long term risk since they are not discriminatory in general, and tax incentives plus economies of scale are substantial. However, group insurance may be efficient within the group, but different groups may be treated very differently, not to speak of people who are not eligible to these programs. The appropriate public policy at the highest level is not totally clear in this context.

Incomplete Contracts

Optimal contracts should take into account an enormous quantity of detailed information. In practice, we do not observe a high degree of complexity in the way, e.g., incomes are utilized. Contracts are incomplete in the sense that a contract may become sub-optimal in terms of its dependency on income given some new information coming up: if his future incomes are from a certain date on expected to follow a certain path that was unlikely ex ante (inheritance, wage rise), the insured may want to reallocate his contributions and benefits in a way that significantly differs from that the contract would pursue. This creates situations where renegotiation becomes desirable, i.e., where mutually advantageous arrangements could be found. Other examples could be found in the way the composition of the family (birth, divorce) can affect the desirable continuation of the contracts.

Incomplete commitment interacts in an important way with incomplete contracts. The problem of mortgages renegotiation is well-known in the finance literature: a decrease in the interest rate may induce premature repayments financed by cheaper new mortgages. In life insurance, a cause of premature termination of a contract would be an increase in interest rates, new contracts becoming more attractive.

In order to limit the effects of renegotiation, and given that more complete contracts cannot reasonably be conceived, it may be optimal to circumvent, within certain limits, this problem by setting penalties for premature termination. We are not aware of any formal literature drawing conclusions on the constrained best contracts.

27.3.2 Asymmetric Information

Asymmetric Information Before Signing

Empirical Evidence. Adverse selection in life insurance markets is a well-known phenomenon, one known by actuaries before it became popular in economic theory after Akerlof (1970) or Pauly (1974). This asymmetry of information may be due to the inobservability of certain mortality factors (health, life-style) or a consequence of legal restrictions on the use of certain observable information (sex). It should be clear that the asymmetric information we are talking about is the residual (small or large) after classification has taken place.

In life insurance econometrics, testing the adverse selection hypothesis presents methodological problems similar to, and perhaps worse than, those encountered in automobile insurance (on this, see e.g., Chiappori (this volume)). Policyholders are submitted to medical examinations leading to the exclusion of certain categories, and to complex pricing. These two factors give rise to selection and self-selection biases that are extremely difficult to correct. Applicants themselves are self-selected, due to the fear (or simply the certitude) of denial by those who would show tangible signs of higher mortality.[17] Among applicants, new policyholders tend to be healthier on average than the population (lower mortality). The econometrician has to be careful that he might have less data available than the insurers. If this is the case, spurious regressions could bias the interpretations. See also Dionne, Gouriéroux and Vanasse (1999).

Even if observed, the classification techniques used by the actuaries should not be taken for granted. The insurance industry has been perhaps excessively conservative in risk selection. We see in Cummins *et alii* (1982) that the degree of sophistication of scoring methods can be pushed extremely far, and the statistician may wonder whether the corrective factors that are applied to premia are reliable. The series of statistical models from which their were estimated are not likely to be consistent which each other. Overall, major identification problems are obvious.

There is one modest way to escape this difficulty: working on insurance contracts offered without medical examination, like annuities where age is the only parameter that is used. Indeed testing for adverse selection is relatively easy in this market: it suffices to calculate the mortality experienced, age by age, by policyholders and to compare these with mortality tables, and to relate the differences to the quantities purchased.[18] In this case basically, adverse selection can be proved because classical antidotes are hardly used (selection, non-linear pricing, etc.). However, one cannot draw valuable conclusions from this on the degree of sophistication that insurers are *able* to reach in general.

[17] Attanasio and Hoynes (1995) showed on micro data that there is a positive correlation between survival prospects and saving. This phenomenon is presumably not negligible for life insurance applicants.
[18] See Philippe (1987) for a study of this type.

The classical paper of Rothschild and Stiglitz (1976), adapted for life insurance or annuities, has given rise to several direct applications.[19] Beliveau (1984) illustrated this view with a reduced form analysis of adverse selection. Her estimates support the hypothesis that people demanding more life insurance are charged a higher price, a result in accordance with Rothschild's and Stiglitz's prediction. However, given that she observes very few variables (presumably fewer than the insurers), it is not clear that there was really asymmetric information.

Cawley and Philipson (1996) also started from the assumption that life insurance contracts were designed according to Rothschild's and Stiglitz' premises and predictions. They tested whether larger coverages were charged larger prices per dollar, and the answer is no. To us, the main interest of that study is that it shows the shortcomings of standard theory as a description of life insurance markets. Indeed, they have extrapolated the conclusions of the classical static model to a situation where several of its assumptions are not met (heterogeneity on probabilities only, one-shot game, exclusivity, no saving, no loadings, etc.). All these hypotheses being tested at the same time, one cannot conclude that adverse selection, rather than any other assumption, is rejected.

When efficiency and regulatory problems arise, models suitable for finer descriptions are required. We now see papers addressing the most remarkable particularities of life insurance markets.

Quantities. The number of periods involved changes completely the notion of quantity (is it the face value? the duration of the contract?) and the notion of exclusivity (do we have exclusivity—one insurer at once—each period only, or also over the lifetime of the insured?). These factors inflating the dimension of the space of contracts over which the insurers design their strategies, the elaboration of simple robust empirical methods becomes an utopia.

Townley and Boadway (1988) made an original contribution to the description of life annuity markets. Offers consist of constant term annuities at a given price per unit of income. People can purchase as many annuities as desired but they have to choose the term (choice takes place at retirement time and no supplementary annuity can be purchased afterwards). The term will be used for self-selection: indeed, the marginal rate of substitution between the duration and the quantity of annuities is dependent on the type of the individual. A standard single-crossing argument à la Mirrlees suggests that sorting agents by type is possible: as expected, short-lived people tend to give relatively less value to long terms than long-lived people. However, the shapes of the indifference curves are difficult to characterize, which makes the problem slightly different from Rothschild's and Stiglitz'. Now, pooling contracts are not excluded. The normative part of the analysis is less convincing for game theoretic

[19] Carlson and Lord (1986) stressed an unsurprising consequence of prohibiting discrimination between men and women: it creates a problem of adverse selection. Rea (1987) explained how that problem could be circumvented (not solved) by offering menus of contracts à la Rothschild and Stiglitz.

reasons. Forcing linear prices, they assumed implicitly that *instantaneous exclusivity* was not possible (see the discussion in the following). But this interpretation is at odds with the fact that one term only is possible, since the individual could after all request different terms of different insurers. Their bounds on the insurers' strategy space is hard to justify as an equilibrium outcome of a well-specified game.

In a related paper (where the contracts permitted are the same), Townley (1990) shows that, in equilibrium, in a world of adverse selection, whole life insurance with non-linear prices is inefficient (rationing terms is more efficient). Moreover, most simple public interventions (uniform compulsory plan, forcing linear prices) cannot guarantee efficiency gains. This is the origin of the "policy dilemma": public policy in that field can only be redistributive (rather than Pareto improving). Theoretically, the case is clear: the fact that contracts *and* policy tools are incomplete is a systematic obstacle to the elimination of ambiguity.

Non-Exclusivity and Unobservable Savings. As we have seen in the life-cycle model of demand, life insurance is only part of a portfolio. Ordinary savings being a substitute to life insurance, insurers are forced to keep their prices relatively low even in a situation where competition is weak. Moreover, the threat of arbitrage opportunities limits their ability to propose effective non-linear prices. The papers we cite now are based on the particularities of asymmetric information in life insurance.

Exclusive insurance contracts and unobservable savings. In Eichenbaum and Peled (1987), agents have no bequest motives (they don't give value to their assets in case of death), therefore a replication argument shows that annuities are the dominant asset (strictly dominant if yields are calculated on the basis of a strictly *positive* mortality) compared to ordinary saving. However, mortality being private information, the equilibrium menu of annuity contracts must take into account the fact that the low mortality type (= high cost risk) can combine the contract assigned to the other type *plus savings* to bypass incentives taken naively. The consequence of this additional incentive constraint (compared to the exclusivity case in Rothschild and Stiglitz) is that the high mortality type (= low cost risk) is more drastically rationed as far as annuities are concerned.

Moreover, the only people that save (in addition to purchasing annuities) in equilibrium are the high mortality people, i.e., those who are least in need of second period income! The authors show that in an overlapping generation model, this characterizes an inefficient level of saving. They also show that a mandatory annuity program which is actuarially fair on average results in an equilibrium without involuntary bequests (proceeds of savings in case the agent dies at the end of the first period) that Pareto-dominates the *laissez-faire* equilibrium. This conclusion is related to the known result that a small amount of mandatory insurance is welfare-enhancing when the Rothschild-Stiglitz equilibrium is inefficient.

Non-exclusivity. If policyholders can purchase several insurance contracts, and this is unobservable by insurers, finding non-linear pricing equilibria in pure strategies is possible when endogenous communication between firms is allowed (Jaynes, 1978). However, without exclusivity and communication, linear pricing is *not* theoretically well-founded: in any linear equilibrium, there exist non-linear deviations that kill the equilibrium. At best, linear pricing may be seen as a self-restriction of the strategy space by the insurance industry. This restriction is convenient for applied theory, and is taken for simplicity in the following studies.

Prior to the approach offered by Rothschild and Stiglitz (1976), Pauly (1974) studied linear price equilibria in insurance under adverse selection. His conclusions fit particularly well life insurance, one of the rare instances where linear prices is a reasonable assumption. The equilibrium price is higher that the average fair price since higher risk people purchase more insurance, and are thereby statistically over-represented in clienteles.

With similar assumptions on the functioning of markets, Abel (1986) explored the effect of Social security on capital accumulation in an overlapping generations model. Consumers save by purchasing life annuities in a private market: differing by their survival probabilities, they differ by their insurance demands. Given that private markets are subject to adverse selection, whereas the public sector can propose a uniform level of pensions (i.e., compulsory annuities), the issue is to find the effect of increasing pensions on total wealth. Ambiguity comes from the fact that mandatory pensions force saving on high mortality people (a positive effect on total saving), while it aggravates the adverse selection problem by raising the equilibrium price in the private market (a negative effect on total saving). Overall, the effect of public pensions remains ambiguous, except when they pass from zero to a small positive level (saving decreases). Abel supposed for simplicity that all individuals participated in the annuity markets, and accordingly, he did not model life insurance. Villeneuve (1996) developed Abel's model in view of examining systematically the effect of public pensions on the functioning of life insurance *and* life annuity markets at the same time. It is proved that typically, if public pensions were to decrease, one should observe an alleviation of adverse selection in annuity market as well as an increased participation. However, the social welfare generated by the reform would be *generically* negative. Factors not modelled in the paper (incentives to work, endogenous growth, etc.) could attenuate this strong conclusion.

Brugiavini (1993) started with a set-up similar to Abel's, abandoning the overlapping generations in order to study annuities markets more in details. She assumed that the consumers live three periods and have no bequest motive. In the first period (when people are young), they only know the average mortality rate. In the second period they learn privately their probability of dying before the third period (old age). Markets are complete in all periods and prices are endogenous so as to adjust to the actual mortality of policyholders. Brugiavini proves that no transactions will be observed in equilibrium in the second period, though intuitively low mortality people should demand supplementary insurance. We recognize the idea that if markets were complete before the arrival of asymmetric information, then a first-best allocation is attained and no additional transaction can take place (Laffont (1985)). A practical interpretation of this result can be seen as a variety of the classical argument in favor of redistributive taxation: public intervention mimics what ex ante markets that did not exist would have achieved.

Power and Townley (1993) studied similar questions with numerical simulations. The main limitation is that annuity markets are constrained to offer only whole life annuities at a certain age, there is no bequest motive (therefore annuities are given exaggerated importance in the model), and the distribution of information that individuals are supposed to have on their own riskiness is rather arbitrary. The simulations are interesting in that they show the complexity of the redistribution due to the pension system and insurance markets.

Fraud and Moral Hazard. Moral hazard is also an interesting hypothesis in life insurance. Intuitively, if people care for their dependents' welfare, i.e., if they value the money they give them, then life insurance can diminish (even if very little) their incentives to live since transfers are no longer conditional upon the donator being alive. Symmetrically, an improvement of the standard-of-living (through annuities) gives an incentive to invest in goods that favor good health (see Ehrlich and Chuma (1990)). Starting from this idea, Davies and Kuhn (1992) explored the effect of Social security on longevity. Whether the impact of insurance is considerable compared to the other determinants of the "willingness to live" is not evident.

The case of suicide is particular. People *determined* to commit suicide may want to protect their dependents by purchasing generous life insurance. However, this should be seen not as moral hazard but rather as adverse selection: moral hazard would be the case where somebody would renounce to suicide if insurance were not available. It seems to us that adverse selection hypothesis is more likely than moral hazard. In any case, traditionally, suicides are eliminated as causes of death that are covered by life insurance during the first years of the policy. This rationing of benefits finds an easy explanation in both theories.

A case of fraud was quite famous in France in the 80's. A man subscribed life insurance policies on his head at several companies; he simulated a mortal automobile accident where his body (in fact the body of a tramp he had murdered) was unrecognizable; his wife received the money; he took plastic surgery and changed his identity. The fraud was suspected when it was found that the same person had paid insurance premia that were disproportionate to his standard of living.

There is no formal literature on these topics. The general literature on fraud and moral hazard in insurance may interest the reader for application.

Asymmetric Information Appearing Over Time

In structuring a long term contract, it would be useful to detail all events that may arise in one's life and which are not neutral to decision-making. Health is an obvious example: when life conditions change, optimal consumption plans are modified. However health is inherently hard to assess without possible dispute; nevertheless, a non-flexible contract is generally inefficient. Because of this inobservability of the crucial factor, the optimal compromise is to leave the individual with a certain degree of discretion regarding the continuation of the contract.[20]

From the point of view of efficiency, the ideal options in contracts are those which are motivated only by changes in tastes or economic conditions that are neutral in terms of survival probability. The information that is asymmetric concerns only one party's objective. Now assume that a young worker subscribes to whole life insurance. We can imagine at least three reasons why he could prefer to liquidate his contract for cash after a while. The first case is when the motivation for life insurance disappears: he divorces, or his children are doing better than expected, his spouse finds a better paid job, etc. The second case could be that he has suffered important wealth losses and is in need of cash. The third case could be that his health proves to be better than average and he tries to obtain a better contract with the cash.

At first sight, only the last issue leads to a selection bias in the technical characteristics of the clientele. It is clear, however, that options free of adverse selection are almost impossible. Whatever the primary observable motivation for the exercise of the option, the information that the individual has on his riskiness will play a role at the margin in his decision, and actuarial neutrality is unlikely. Discretion becomes a compromise, in a context where contracts are incomplete, between benefits of flexibility and the costs of adverse incentives. Whether adverse selection is serious or negligible becomes a matter of experience or judgment.

27.4 CONCLUSION

As they grow older, people caring for their future or for the future of their family become very responsive to the evolution of their life prospects, and, as a result, insurers are extremely cautious with the aged clientele. Life insurance is a sector where risk classification was pushed very far (Cummins *et alii*, 1982). One may wonder whether insurers have gone too far, by discriminating between groups of people who were unaware of their differences.[21] We observe that certain individuals with identified chronic diseases have difficulty in obtaining insurance, though in principle an actuarial price could be proposed and accepted. In any case, there is a tendency now to impose simplified medical questionnaires. Clearly, the practical need for risk selection is mainly associated with individual purchases, where the mere fact of demanding insurance is a signal to the insurers. The development of group insurance has changed the picture in two essential respects.

First, life insurance being more attractive when offered to groups, we can predict as an immediate consequence that individual life insurance contracts will tend to be

[20] Technically, the fact that the MRS of consumptions at different periods is affected by the type of the agent can be used efficiently for self-selection.

[21] Villeneuve (1998, 1999) models insurance markets where individuals are ignorant of their risk relatively to insurers. The consequences are contrasted with those of adverse selection.

demanded by less representative people and we can expect a decline in life insurance technical (i.e., due to pure mutualization) returns on these contracts.

Second, given the costs of classification, pricing in group insurance is often very simplified (costless observables like sex may not be used); but, despite the costs of diversifying offers (actuaries have to relate individual data to costs, and to optimize the offers given incentives), flexibility is needed to accommodate the variety of the clientele's objectives (a certain degree of discretion has to be left to the agent all over the duration of the contract).

Indeed, options are intended to leave people express their differences. The trade-off between flexible contracts (and adverse selection) and rigid contracts (and inadequacy with current needs) is subtle. The classical non-linear pricing methods have to be used; moreover, the intertemporal dimension increases the separating possibilities:[22] differences in risk aversions (a typically unobservable data) may be exploited by leaving people choose the index used for index-linked contracts. More generally, the multiple dimensions of life insurance should be arranged so as to accommodate the multiple dimensions of symmetric and asymmetric information.[23] In practice, once the initial choice in a menu is made, contracts will leave some discretion to the policyholder at certain points in the future, as we discussed in the text. This is a difficult balance. On the one hand, when policyholders take advantage of acceptable motivations for such changes, they cannot be indifferent to new information relevant for expected costs on the continuation of the contract; on the other hand, an individual may cumulate several reasons for changing his contributions and benefits, and this should be left possible to some extent.

APPENDIX

In case N, we can solve:

$$W_{t+1}^A = R_t(W_t^A + Y_t - c_t) \tag{20}$$

but there remain one constraint on b_t for each t that cannot be eliminated.

In case A, we know that L_t is always equal to zero. We first eliminate A_{t+1} in the following equations:

$$\begin{cases} W_{t+1}^A = R_t\left(W_t^A + Y_t - c_t - \dfrac{A_{t+1}}{R_t^A}\right) + A_{t+1} \\ b_{t+1} = R_t\left(W_t^A + Y_t - c_t - \dfrac{A_{t+1}}{R_t^A}\right) \end{cases} \tag{21}$$

[22] Venezia (1991).
[23] Laffont and Rochet (1988).

and then we solve the derived equation:

$$W_{t+1}^{A} = R_t(W_t^A + Y_t - c_t) - \frac{R_t^A - R_t}{R_t} b_{t+1} \tag{22}$$

In case L, we first eliminate L_{t+1}:

$$\begin{cases} W_{t+1}^{A} = R_t\left(W_t^A + Y_t - c_t - \dfrac{L_{t+1}}{R_t^L}\right) \\ b_{t+1} = R_t\left(W_t^A + Y_t - c_t - \dfrac{L_{t+1}}{R_t^L}\right) + L_{t+1} \end{cases} \tag{23}$$

and then we solve:

$$W_{t+1}^{A} = \frac{R_t R_t^L}{R_t^L - R_t}(W_t^A + Y_t - c_t) - \frac{R_t}{R_t^L - R_t} b_{t+1} \tag{24}$$

27.5 REFERENCES

Abel, Andrew B. (1986). "Capital Accumulation and Uncertain Lifetimes with Adverse Selection," *Econometrica*, 54, 1079–1097.

Abel, Andrew B. and Mark Warshawsky (1988). "Specification of the Joy of Giving: Insights from Altruism," *Review of Economics and Statistics*, 70, 145–149.

Akerlof, George A. (1970). "The Market for 'Lemons': Quality Uncertainty and the Market Mechanism," *Quarterly Journal of Economics*, 84, 488–500.

Ando, Alberto, Luigi Guiso and Daniele Terlizzese (1993). "Dissaving by the Elderly, Transfer Motives, and Liquidity Constraints," NBER Working Paper No. 4569, Cambridge.

Arrondel, Luc and André Masson (1994). "L'assurance-vie et le motif de précaution dans les choix patrimoniaux des ménages," Chaire d'économie et d'économétrie de l'assurance, Paris.

Attanasio, Orazio P. and Hilary W. Hoynes (1995). "Differential Mortality and Wealth Accumulation," NBER Working Paper No. 5126, Cambridge.

Auerbach, Alan J. and Laurence J. Kotlikoff (1986). "Life Insurance of the Elderly: Its Adequacy and Determinants," in Gary Burtless (ed.): Work, Health, and Income Among the Elderly, The Brookings Institution, Washington.

Auerbach, Alan J. and Laurence J. Kotlikoff (1991). "The Adequacy of Life Insurance Purchase" *Journal of Financial Intermediation*, 1, 215–241.

Babbel, David F. (1985). "The Price Elasticity of Demand for Whole Life Insurance," *Journal of Finance*, 40, 225–239.

Babbel, David F. and Eisaku Ohtsuka (1989). "Aspects of Optimal Multiperiod Life Insurance," *Journal of Risk and Insurance*, 56, 460–481.

Beliveau, Barbara C. (1984). "Theoretical and Empirical Aspects of Implicit Information in the Market for Life Insurance," *Journal of Risk and Insurance*, 51, 286–307.

Bernheim, B. Douglas, Andrei Shleifer and Lawrence H. Summers (1985). "The Strategic Bequest Motive," *Journal of Political Economy*, 93, 1045–1076.

Bernheim, B. Douglas (1991). "How Strong are Bequest Motives? Evidence Based on Estimates of the Demand for Life Insurance and Annuities," *Journal of Political Economy*, 90, 899–927.

Browne, Mark J. and Kihong Kim (1993). "An International Analysis of Life Insurance Demand," *Journal of Risk and Insurance*, 60, 616–634.

Browning, Martin (1994). "The Saving Behavior of a Two-Person Household," typescript.

Brugiavini, Agar (1993). "Uncertainty Resolution and the Timing of Annuity Purchases," *Journal of Public Economics*, 50, 31–61.

Carlson, Severin and Blair Lord (1986). "Unisex Retirement Benefits and the Market for Annuity 'Lemons'," *Journal of Risk and Insurance*, 53, 408–418.

Cawley, John and Tomas Philipson (1996). "An Empirical Examination of Information Barriers to Trade in Insurance," typescript.

Chiappori, Pierre André (2000). Asymmetric Information in Automobile Insurance: an Overview, this book.

Cochrane, John H. (1995). "Time-Consistent Health Insurance," *Journal of Political Economy*, 103, 445–473.

Cox, Larry A., Sandra G. Gustavson and Antonie Stam (1991). "Disability and Life Insurance in the Individual Insurance Portfolio," *Journal of Risk and Insurance,* 58, 128–137.

Cummins, J. David, B.D. Smith, R.N. Vance and J.L. Vanderel (ed.) (1982). "Risk Classification in Life Insurance," Kluwer Academic Publishers, Boston.

Davies, James B. and Peter Kuhn (1992). "Social Security, Longevity, and Moral Hazard," *Journal of Public Economics*, 49, 91–106.

Deaton, Angus S. (1992). Understanding Consumption, Clarendon Press, Oxford.

Dionne, Georges, Christian Gouriéroux and Charles Vanasse (1998). "Evidence of Adverse Selection in Automobile Insurance Markets," in Automobile Insurance: Road Safety, New Drivers, Risks, Insurance Fraud and Regulation (G. Dionne and Claire Laberge-Nadeau, eds.), Kluwer, Academic Publishers, Boston.

Eckstein, Zvi, Martin Eichenbaum and Dan Peled (1985). "Uncertain Lifetimes and the Welfare Enhancing Properties of Annuity Markets and Social Security," *Journal of Public Economics*, 26, 303–326.

Eichenbaum, Martin S. and Dan Peled (1987). "Capital Accumulation and Annuities in an Adverse Selection Economy," *Journal of Political Economy*, 95, 334–354.

Ehrlich, Isaac and Hiroyuki Chuma (1990). "A Model of the Demand for Longevity and Value of Life Extension," *Journal of Political Economy*, 98, 761–782.

Fischer, Stanley (1973). "A Life Cycle Model of Life Insurance Purchases," *International Economic Review*, 14, 132–152.

Fisher, Irving (1930). The Theory of Interest, Macmillan, New York.

Fitzgerald, John M. (1987). "The Effects of Social Security on Life Insurance Demand by Married Couples," *Journal of Risk and Insurance*, 54, 86–99.

Fitzgerald, John M. (1989). "The Taste for Bequests and Well-Being of Widows: A Model of Life Insurance Demand by Married Couples," *Review of Economics and Statistics*, 71, 206–214.

Friedman, Benjamin M. and Mark J. Warshawsky (1990). "The Cost of Annuities: Implications for Saving Behavior and Bequests," *Quarterly Journal of Economics*, 105, 135–154.

Goldsmith, Art (1983). "Household Life Cycle Protection: Human Capital Versus Life Insurance," *Journal of Risk and Insurance*, 50, 473–486.

Gustavson, Sandra G. and James S. Trieschmann (1988). "Universal Life Insurance as an Alternative to the Joint and Survivor Annuity," *Journal of Risk and Insurance*, 55, 529–538.

Hakanson, Nils H. (1969). "Optimal Investment and Consumption Strategies Under Risk for a Class of Utility Functions," *International Economic Review*, 10, 443–466.

Hamermesh, Daniel S. (1985). "Expectations, Life Expectancy, and Economic Behavior," *Quarterly Journal of Economics*, 100, 389–408.

Hu, Sheng Cheng (1986). "Uncertain Life Span, Risk Aversion, and the Demand for Pension Annuities," *Southern Economic Journal*, 52, 933–947.

Huebner, S.S. and Kenneth Black Jr. (1976). Life Insurance, 9th edition, Prentice Hall, New Jersey.

Hurd, Michael D. (1987). "Savings of the Elderly and Desired Bequests," *American Economic Review*, 77, 298–312.

Hurd, Michael D. (1989). "Mortality Risk and Bequests," *Econometrica*, 57, 779–813.

Hurd, Michael D. and Kathleen McGarry (1995). "Evaluation of Subjective Probability Distributions in the Health and Retirement Study," *Journal of Human Resources*, 30, S268–S292.

Jaynes, Gerald D. (1978). "Equilibria in Monopolistically Competitive Insurance Markets," *Journal of Economic Theory*, 19, 394–422.

Karni, Edi and Itzhak Zilcha (1986). "Risk Aversion in the Theory of Life Insurance: The Fisherian Model," *Journal of Risk and Insurance*, 53, 606–620.

Kessler, Denis and Tang Lin (1989). "Rente Viagère ou Capital?," Paper presented at the 16th Seminar of the European Group of Risk and Insurance Economists, Jouy-en-Josas.

Kotlikoff, Laurence J. and Avia Spivak (1981). "The Family as an Incomplete Annuities Market," *Journal of Political Economy*, 89, 372–391.

Laffont, Jean-Jacques (1985). "On the Welfare Analysis of Rational Expectations Equilibria with Asymmetric Information," *Econometrica*, 53, 1–29.

Laffont, Jean-Jacques and Jean-Charles Rochet (1988). "Stock Market Portfolio and the Segmentation of the Insurance Market," *Scandinavian Journal of Economics*, 90, 435–446.

Leung, Siu Fai (1994). "Uncertain Lifetime, the Theory of the Consumer, and the Life Cycle Hypothesis," *Econometrica*, 62, 1233–1239.

Levhari, David and Leonard J. Mirman (1977). "Savings and Consumption with an Uncertain Horizon," *Journal of Political Economy*, 85, 265–281.

Lewis, Frank D. (1989). "Dependents and the Demand for Life Insurance," *American Economic Review*, 79, 452–467.

Life Insurance Fact Book (various issues), American Council of Life Insurance, Washington.

Mitchell, Olivia S., James M. Poterba and Mark J. Warshawsky (1997). "New Evidence on Money Worth of Individual Annuities," NBER Working Paper No 6002, Cambridge.

Mitchell, Olivia S. (2000). Developments in Pensions, this book.

Moffet, Denis (1979a). "An Analysis of the Demand for Life Insurance: Mathematical Foundations," *Journal of Risk and Insurance*, 46, 87–98.

Moffet, Denis (1979b). "An Analysis of the Demand for Life Insurance: The Consumer's Problem," *Journal of Risk and Insurance*, 46, 99–112.

Mullin, Charles and Tomas Philipson (1997). "The Future of Old-age Longevity: Competitive Pricing of Mortality Contingent Claims," NBER Working Paper No. 6042, Cambridge.

Pauly, Mark V. (1974). "Overinsurance and Public Provision of Insurance: The Roles of Moral Hazard and Adverse Selection," *Quarterly Journal of Economics*, 88, 44–54.

Philippe, Jean-Marie (1987). "Analyse du risque technique sur un portefeuille de rentiers," ISUP, Mémoire d'actuariat.

Pissarides, C.A. (1980). "The Wealth-age Relation with Life Insurance," *Economica*, 47, 451–457.

Poterba, James M. (1997). "The History of Annuities in the United States," NBER Working Paper No 6001, Cambridge.

Power, Simon and Peter G.C. Townley (1993). "The Impact of Government Social Security Payments on the Annuity Market," *Insurance: Mathematics and Economics*, 12, 47–56.

Puelz, Robert (1991). "A Process for Selecting a Life Insurance Contract," *Journal of Risk and Insurance*, 58, 138–146.

Rea, Samuel A. Jr. (1987). "The Market Response to the Elimination of Sex-Based Annuities," *Southern Economic Journal*, 54, 55–63.

Rejda, George E. and James R. Schmidt (1984). "The Impact of the Social Security and ERISA on Private Pension Contributions," *Journal of Risk and Insurance*, 51, 640–651.

Rejda, George E., James R. Schmidt and Michael J. McNamara (1987). "The Impact of Social Security Tax Contributions on Group Life Insurance Premiums," *Journal of Risk and Insurance*, 54, 712–720.

Rothschild, Michael and Joseph Stiglitz (1976). "Equilibrium in Competitive Insurance Markets: An Essay on the Economics of Imperfect Information," *Quarterly Journal of Economics*, 90, 629–649.

Sachko Gandolfi, Anna and Laurence Miners (1996). "Gender-Based Differences in Life Insurance Ownership," *Journal of Risk and Insurance*, 63, 683–693.

Townley, Peter G.C. and Robin W. Boadway (1988). "Social Security and the Failure of Annuity Markets," *Journal of Public Economics*, 35, 75–96.

Townley, Peter G.C. (1990). "Life-insured Annuities: Market Failure and Policy Dilemma," *Canadian Journal of Economics*, 23, 546–562.

Venezia, Itzhak (1991). "Tie-in Arrangements of Life Insurance and Savings: an Economic Rationale," *Journal of Risk and Insurance*, 58, 383–396.

Villeneuve, Bertrand (1996). "Mandatory Insurance and Intensity of Adverse Selection," CREST Working Paper No 9606, Paris.

Villeneuve, Bertrand (1998). "The Insurers as the Informed Party: A Solution to Three Insurance Puzzles," IDEI Working Paper, University of Toulouse.

Villeneuve, Bertrand (2000). "The Consequences for the Monopolistic Insurance Firm of Evaluating Risk Better than Customers: The Adverse Selection Hypothesis Reversed," forthcoming in the Geneva Papers on Risk and Insurance Theory.

Warshawsky, Mark (1985). "Life Insurance Savings and the After-tax Life Insurance Rate of Return," *Journal of Risk and Insurance*, 52, 585–606.

Warshawsky, Mark (1988). "Private Annuity Markets in the United States: 1919–1984," *Journal of Risk and Insurance*, 55, 518–528.

Winter, Ralph (1982). "On the Choice of an Index of Disclosure in the Life Insurance Market: An Axiomatic Approach," *Journal of Risk and Insurance*, 49, 513–538.

Yaari, Menahem E. (1965). "Uncertain Lifetime, Life Insurance, and the Theory of the Consumer," *Review of Economic Studies*, 32, 137–150.

Yagi, Tadashi and Yasuyuki Nishigaki (1993). "The Inefficiency of Private Constant Annuities," *Journal of Risk and Insurance*, 60, 385–412.

28 The Division of Labor Between Private and Social Insurance*

Peter Zweifel

University of Zurich

Abstract

This contribution reviews two types of reasons for the existence and growth of social insurance, viz. possible enhancements of efficiency and public choice reasons related to the interests of governments and politicians. Empirical evidence suggests these latter reasons to be important in explaining the existing division of labor between private and social insurance. However, this division is being challenged in several ways; its modification may therefore result in improved efficiency. Viewing the several lines of private and social insurance as elements of a portfolio, one can indeed conclude that individuals in the United States and Germany at present are subject to excess asset variance. A few proposals for improving the interplay between private and social insurance are formulated, which tend to accord a more important role to the private component.

Keywords: Private insurance, social insurance, public choice, portfolio choice.
JEL Classification Numbres: D72, D81, G11, G22, H23, H55.

28.1 INTRODUCTION AND OVERVIEW

Most of the teaching of the economics of insurance is couched in terms of an individual who is free to decide the amount of coverage he or she desires. This is a fair description of reality as far as insurance purchased by companies and property insurance (e.g., fire, theft) purchased by households is concerned. However, almost all individuals (at least in industrial countries) are mandated to purchase a good deal of coverage provided by social insurance. While the domain of social insurance is delimited differently between countries, it typically covers provision for old age, disability, workmen's compensation, sick leave pay, health care, long-term care, unemployment,

* This work has profited greatly from suggestions and criticisms by Roland Eisen (Frankfurt/Main, Germany) and Friedrich Schneider (Linz, Austria), Michael Breuer (Zurich, Switzerland), and two anonymous referees.

Table 1
Social and Private Insurance compared to the GDP, Several Countries

Country	Social insurance in %			Private insurance in %		
	1980	1984	1990	1984	1990	1990*
France	27.0	30.2	28.0	4.3	5.9	3.1
Germany	30.1	29.5	27.6	5.9	5.8	2.2
Great Britain	25.7	28.3	26.2	7.1	9.7	6.2
Italy	24.4	28.4	28.1	2.4	2.6	0.7
Netherlands	39.6	39.4	39.8	5.6	8.1	4.2
Spain	15.7	17.7	18.4	1.9	3.3	0.9

* life insurance only.
Sources: Yfantopoulos, J. (1991), Financing of social security in the E.C., in: Pieters, D. (ed.), Social Security in Europe, Miscellanea of the Erasmus Programme of Studies Relating to Social Security in the European Communities, Brussels: Bruylant, pp. 217–237; Sigma of Swiss Re, several editions.

and health.[1] Thus, it is in the domain of personal insurance where private and social insurance are close substitutes and where the division of labor between the two is at issue. Accordingly, this contribution focuses on personal insurance.

As a matter of fact, in personal insurance premiums paid to social insurance schemes typically outweigh those paid to private companies by at least a factor of three. In Germany for example, contributions to social insurance added up to almost 28 percent of Gross Domestic Product (GDP) in 1990, compared to 5.8 percent for private insurance (see Table 1). If one focuses on private life insurance (last column of Table 1), thus excluding e.g., motor and homeowner insurance where social insurance is not present as a rule, this percentage drops to 2.2 percent, making social insurance loom 12 times as large as its private counterpart. And even in the important insurance market of Great Britain, social insurance accounts for three times more premiums than does private insurance.

While the division of labor between private and social insurance is heavily in favor of the social component, it is not immutable. During the later 1980s, the share of social insurance fell while that of private insurance increased in several countries. In Spain (and other countries of Southern Europe not shown), social insurance is still expanding, albeit at a lower relative rate than its much smaller private counterpart.

These observations raise four important and interesting issues.

(1) What are the factors determining the division of labor between private and social insurance?
(2) What are the challenges confronting the existing division of labor?

[1] Following Atkinson (1991), no attempt will be made here to formally define social insurance. However, "social security" is understood as the component of social insurance whose benefits are retirement pensions, possibly combined with widows' pensions.

(3) How can a given division of labor be judged in terms of efficiency?
(4) Is there scope for an efficiency-enhancing change of the existing division of labor?

This contribution is organized around these issues. Its first part deals with the reasons that may give rise to social insurance, distinguishing between efficiency and public choice explanations. The second part is devoted to exogenous changes that may render the existing division of labor between private and social insurance inefficient. In the third part, a simple test for measuring the performance of the present division of labor is proposed. Finally, some efficiency-enhancing reforms and their chances of realization in the light of public choice theory are discussed. The standard of reference used throughout is the Pareto criterion in the guise of an expected utility possibility frontier. It is only on that frontier that the opportunity cost of pursuing a distributional objective can be correctly measured. However, distributional issues are already reflected in the discussion of topic (1), where political decision makers with their interest in gaining votes enter the picture. They surface again in topic (4), where obstacles to potential Pareto improvements are expounded.

28.2 FACTORS DETERMINING THE DIVISION OF LABOR BETWEEN PRIVATE AND SOCIAL INSURANCE

There seem to be two groups of factors determining the division of labor between private and social insurance. Traditionally, the literature has emphasized efficiency gains that may be achieved through (some degree of) compulsory social insurance [see Aarts (1997) for a recent survey]. It is doubtful, however, that efficiency reasons should result in a structure of premium payments so much biased in favor of social insurance, as shown in Table 1.

The second group of factors relate to the interests of political decision makers. In a democracy, politicians must win votes (often the majority). One way to achieve this is to structure public expenditures (among them, the benefits of social insurance) in a way as to win the support of pivotal voter groups.

28.2.1 Efficiency Reasons for a Division of Labor

Mandatory insurance can result in a Pareto improvement for three reasons. One argument is based on the assumption that rich individuals are characterized by a certain degree of altruism towards poor ones. This invites free riding by others, which can be countered by compulsion. The second argument relates to asymmetric information problems in insurance markets. In particular, "bad" risks impose a degree of externality on the "good" ones, which may be internalized to some extent by mandatory insurance. The third argument states that insurance exhibits increasing returns to scale, which make social insurance a natural monopoly. However, increasing returns to scale (as suggested by early research) have been shown to be incompatible with the structure and development of the North American insurance industry (Kellner and Matthewson, 1983). More recent studies [e.g., Fecher, Perelman, and Pestieau (1991)] fail to find evidence of increasing returns to scale precisely among French public insurers (which do not exactly match social insurers). Moreover, historically social insurance did not come about because a private insurance company, profiting from returns to scale, became dominant. These considerations speak against the natural monopoly argument, which therefore will not be pursued any further.

28.2.1.1 Altruism as a Reason for Mandatory Insurance Coverage

The following argument is adapted from Pauly (1971, ch. 2). Let there be a poor individual P whose marginal willingness to pay for insurance ($MWTP_P$) falls short of the marginal cost (MC) of providing coverage (see Figure 1). Let there also be a rich person R that is concerned about the distress suffered by poor individual P in the event of an insurable loss (if the poverty of P were permanent, a simple gift rather than granting access to insurance would be the natural solution). Due to this utility externality, R has a marginal willingness to pay for insurance coverage to be enjoyed by P, which presumably decreases with the amount of coverage provided (see $MWTP_{R,P}$ in Figure 1). Insurance being a normal good, R's marginal willingness to pay for his own coverage is higher throughout, given e.g., by $MWTP_{R,R}$. For simplicity, let the marginal cost of providing insurance coverage be constant and independent of the individual insured (MC).

Vertical aggregation of $MWTP_P$ and $MWTP_{R,P}$ results in P's augmented willing-

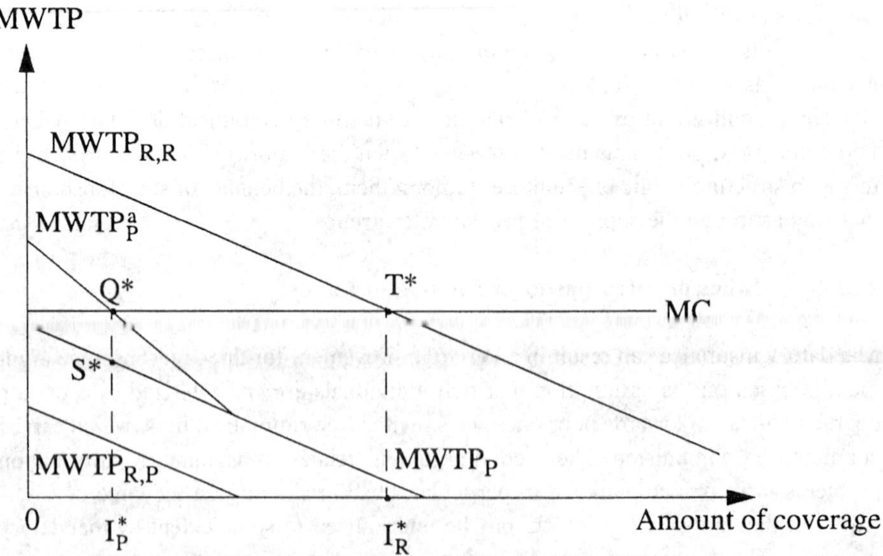

Figure 1 Positive Utility Externality due to Insurance of the Poor

ness to pay, $MWTP_P^a$. Equating this with marginal cost MC determines the optimal solution, indicated by point Q*, with the premium subsidy amounting to S*Q*. The rich individual buys coverage I_R^*; the allocation $\{I_P^*, I_R^*\}$ is efficient (i.e., Pareto optimal) because each individual's MWTP equals MC.

Such a solution is unlikely to come about in a voluntary way, however. Other rich individuals, contemplating to buy insurance coverage on behalf of poor individual P, would be unwilling to disclose their willingness to pay, hoping for R to step in. Knowing this, R will shy away from disclosing his willingness to pay as well. In order to reap the external benefits of P's having insurance, the rich members of the community may agree to create a mandatory insurance scheme for the poor, to be paid for by compulsory contributions. Since neither $MWTP_P$ nor $MWTP_{R,P}$ are known, I_P^* is unknown also for a particular individual. This paves the way for uniform coverage with its concomitant loss of efficiency (possible savings in transaction costs are considered in section 28.2.1.3). It should also be noted that efficiency considerations do not require that the insurance be provided by the government; only its finance involves tax money.

Conclusion 1. Altruism in conjunction with free riding may serve to explain the existence of mandatory insurance for the poor. Neither uniformity of benefits nor provision by the government follow from efficiency considerations.

28.2.1.2 Adverse Selection as a Reason for Mandatory Insurance Coverage

Under conditions of adverse selection, mandatory social insurance again serves to internalize an externality. But this time, the source of the externality is not a poor individual but a bad risk that cannot be identified as such by the insurer. The insurer knows that a pooling contract (with a premium calculated according to the average loss probability) can always be challenged by a competitor who offers better conditions to good risks. Therefore, he wants to have a contract designed for the good risks that cannot be contaminated by the bad ones. However, this means he can only offer limited coverage to the good risks. In this situation, the good risks can obtain more total coverage by having some coverage mandated for everyone.

The illustration of the argument in Figure 2 follows Dahlby (1981), building on Rothschild and Stiglitz (1976). In the contingent claims (c_1, c_2)-space, let the two risk types have the same endowment point Q. A risk neutral insurer, charging the fair premium, is able to exchange wealth from the loss-free state (c_1) to the loss state (c_2) along the line $\pi_1^g/(1-\pi_1^g)$ for the good risk, with π_1 denoting the probability of no loss occurring. The bad risks are characterized by a $\pi_1^b < \pi_1^g$, and therefore, their relevant insurance line runs flatter. Moreover, the slope of their indifference curve is given by $dc_2/dc_1 = -[\pi_1^b \partial U/\partial c_1]/[(1-\pi_1^b)\partial U/\partial c_2]$, i.e., the ratio of probability-weighted marginal utilities. Since $c_1 = c_2$ on the security line (implying $\partial U/\partial c_1 = \partial U/\partial c_2$), this slope becomes $\pi_1^b/(1-\pi_1^b)$. Equality of slopes indicates that the optimum must lie on the security line, such as H* for the bad risks (L* for the good risks). If recognized as

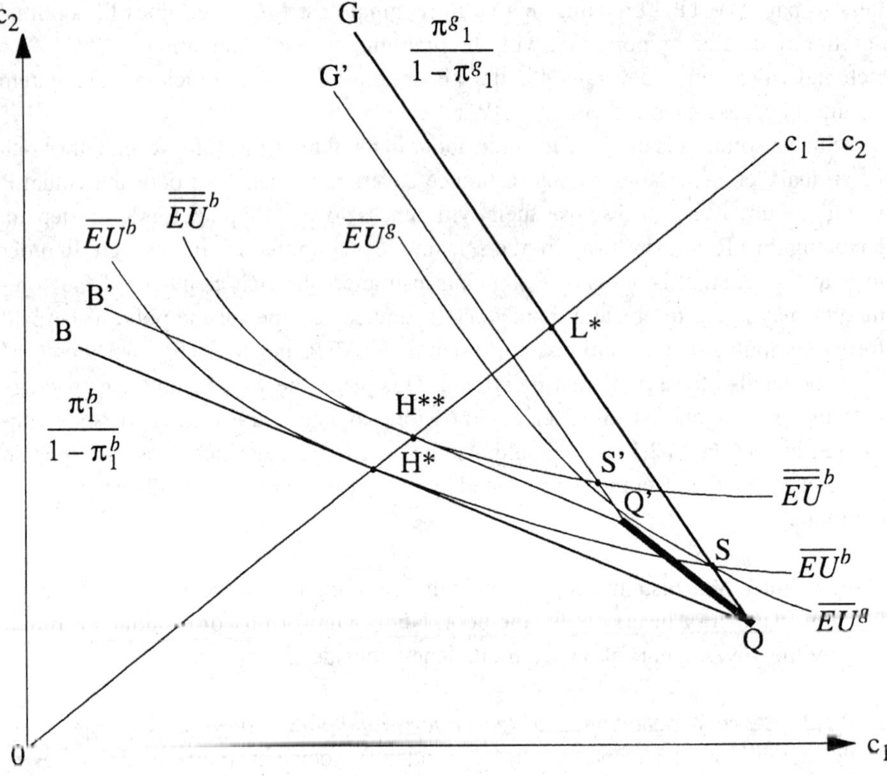

Figure 2 Pareto Improvement Under Adverse Selection

such, the bad risks therefore are offered a contract at rather unfavorable terms which however still induces them to buy full coverage.

The insurer may actually determine point H* in a trial and error process, offering a high-premium contract and observing some individuals buying full coverage nevertheless. Again by trial and error, he may determine the point S of Figure 2, where another group (the good risks) buys a policy featuring only very partial coverage but at a favorable premium. At the same time, the bad risks will not want to give up their full coverage (point H*) in favor of the other insurance policy (point S), where their indifference curve $\overline{EU}^b$, showing constant expected utility, passes. Therefore, under certain conditions the contract pair {H*, S} may constitute a separating equilibrium. The problem is that the good risks, being rationed at point S, would be attracted by a contract that offers more coverage at slightly less favorable terms than QG. Thus, a competitor conceivably could undermine the stability of the separating contract.

Now let there be a mandatory scheme which can be administered by regulated private insurers. They would have to calculate a uniform risk premium on the basis of the share of good and bad risks in the population, assumed to be 50 percent each for simplicity. Thus, the scheme can offer e.g., QQ′ units of coverage at an averaged premium without jeopardizing its financial stability. Starting from Q′, a private insurer may now search for another separating equilibrium, this time characterized by points {H**, S′}. For the bad risks, mandated coverage results in an unambiguous improvement. Along QQ′ they profit from the low probability of loss characterizing the good risks, permitting them to obtain full coverage (point H**) at a reduced total contribution. However, in the example of Figure 2, the good risks profit from the mandatory scheme, too. For point S′ indicates a higher level of expected utility, since it lies above $\overline{EU}^g$ passing through the initial separating contract S. Thus, in this particular case, the fact that the private insurer rations coverage starting from Q′ rather than Q is sufficiently beneficial to the good risk to outweigh the loss caused by having to pay a contribution to mandatory insurance that also reflects the presence of bad risks. It should be noted, however, that the equilibrium {H**, S′} can again be challenged by an alternative offering more coverage at slightly less favorable terms than Q′G′.

Conclusion 2. Adverse selection problems can be alleviated by partial mandatory insurance, resulting in a Pareto improvement for both good and bad risks, provided the separating equilibrium in the private insurance market is not challenged.

In a more recent contribution, social insurance (in particular social security) serves as an efficiency-enhancing complement to banks rather than private insurance, on the presumption that banks are unable to distinguish between good and bad credit risks (Reichlin and Siconolfi, 1996).

28.2.1.3 Risk-specific Transaction Cost as a Reason for Mandatory Insurance Coverage

The following argument is a variation on Newhouse (1996), who notes that the policy concern is not so much the inability of the good risks to purchase full coverage but the inability of the bad risks to obtain the amount of insurance they desire. In fact, bad risks often fail to obtain coverage at all.[2] One reason for this phenomenon may be that insurers, while able to recognize bad risks, do not know their precise probability of loss.[3] Thus, they not only attach a high probability of loss $\pi_2^b = (1 - \pi_1^b)$ to bad risks but also a great deal of uncertainty to its estimate. Due to the marked skewness of the loss distribution in many lines, π_2 is difficult to estimate in the domain of large losses, caused by bad risks. It is in this domain, however, that estimation error causes the risk of insolvency to increase. Managerial risk aversion, limited diversifi-

[2] In the model of Newhouse, transaction costs arise because devising a policy that attracts good risks is costly. In the resulting pooling equilibrium, the bad risks obtain a positive amount of coverage. However, in U.S. private health insurance, sizable parts of the population are uninsured.

[3] Another reason may be that the Rothschild-Stiglitz formulation is not sufficiently specific about the structure of moves in the insurance market. In the three-stage-game of Hellwig (1987), for example, insurers make initial contract offers, individuals select a contract, but the company can reject the application.

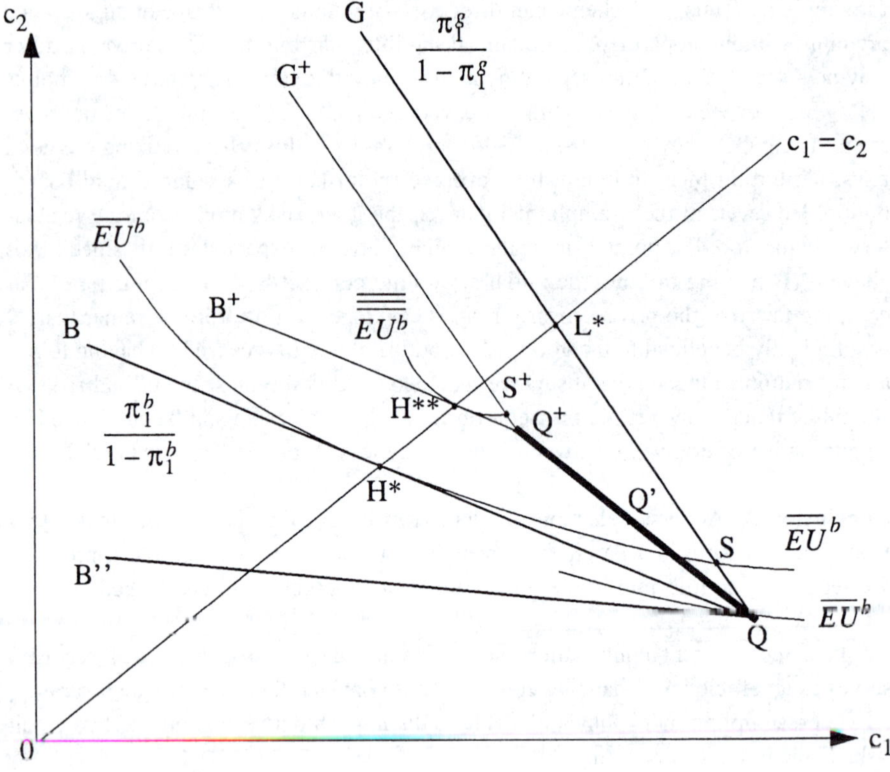

Figure 3 Risk-Specific Transaction Cost and Pareto Improvement

cation of the risk portfolio, or public regulation therefore makes insurers add a safety loading to any policy that might attract bad risks.

In Figure 3, the premium for the good risks is assumed for simplicity to be without such a safety loading. Therefore, their insurance line QG has slope $\pi_1^g/(1 - \pi_1^g)$, precisely as in Figure 2. The bad risks are offered a contract containing a proportional loading in excess of the fair premium; rather than being offered contracts along QB as in Figure 2, they face the still flatter (i.e., unfavorable) insurance line QB″. Under these conditions, the bad risk shown does not opt for full coverage at point H* anymore but settles for no insurance at all (endowment point Q, yielding expected utility $\overline{EU}^b$). However, this also means that no separating contract along QG can be launched exclusively for the good risks because the bad risks would have every incentive to buy it. For example, contract S (which did not dominate H* absent a risk-specific safety loading) now dominates Q. In this situation, there is great scope for Pareto improvement through mandatory social insurance because a governmental scheme cannot become insolvent, allowing the uniform contribution to be calculated without a loading for the bad risk. Its premium calculation thus results in the rather favorable insurance line QQ′ (taken over from Figure 2). However, Q′ is unlikely to become the new point of departure for separating contracts. The losses to be covered are still large for a private insurer, who therefore would continue to charge a safety loading for (suspected) bad risks.

By increasing mandatory coverage to QQ^+, the losses to be covered by the private insurer become smaller, permitting him to reduce the loading. For simplicity, let the loading become zero; thus, the insurance line Q^+B^+ shows the actuarially fair premium for bad risks. Accordingly, the bad risk can afford to buy full coverage (see point H**), while the good risk is offered a separating contract at S^+. Thus, under mandatory partial insurance, a separating equilibrium {H**, S^+} replaces the separating equilibrium {H*, S}. Point H**, indicating full coverage at a reduced premium, is certainly preferred to H* by the bad risks. Point S^+, indicating increased coverage but at a higher premium, may be preferred to S by the good risks. Note that since the slope of the indifference curve characterizing the good risks necessarily exceeds that of the pooled insurance line QQ^+, full mandated coverage can never be optimal for the good risks. Therefore, Pareto improvement may only occur as long as compulsory coverage remains partial.

Conclusion 3. Private insurers' inability to precisely estimate the probability of loss in the case of suspected bad risks may constitute an efficiency reason for mandatory insurance with partial coverage.

However, even leaving aside government's own interest in mandatory insurance (see section 28.2.2.1), there are several conditions that make a Pareto improvement due to mandated insurance coverage less likely. These conditions will be discussed in the context of risk-specific transaction cost (Figure 3) but also apply to adverse selection (Figure 2).

1. **Transaction cost of private insurance.** The more private insurance is loaded with transaction cost, the smaller the advantage for the good risks when purchasing private insurance beyond the compulsory amount. In Figure 3, the line Q^+G^+ would rotate counterclockwise around the new endowment point Q^+, possibly causing S^+ to rank lower than Q^+.
2. **Transaction cost of social insurance.** Although it is often argued that mandatory insurance avoids a great deal of transaction cost (especially in the guise of sales expense), it is not without such cost (see below). In Figure 3, it is now the segment QQ^+ that is rotated counterclockwise. Clearly, this hurts both risk types in a similar manner.
3. **Low share of good risks in the population.** If the bad risks dominate, the contribution to social insurance paid by the good risks becomes more and more loaded as it were. In Figure 3, the insurance line QQ^+ more and more approaches the line QB, causing the good risks to lose their advantage while the bad risks continue to profit from the scheme, although to a lesser extent.

28.2.1.4 Moral Hazard as a Qualification

While mandatory insurance mitigates or even solves the problems of adverse selection and risk-specific transaction cost, it is likely to exacerbate the other problem of asymmetric information, i.e., moral hazard effects (Stiglitz, 1983). Moral hazard can be controlled by putting a price on it in the guise of cost sharing or increased future premiums in response to current losses. During the life of a contract, the occurrence of losses generates information about likely moral hazard effects. Thus, at least in insurance lines characterized by a certain frequency of loss (such as health), experience-rating of premiums may be used in addition to cost sharing for limiting moral hazard.

However, use of either instrument would require a good deal of justification on the part of the social insurer. Note that lack of knowledge about marginal willingness to pay for insurance may lead to uniform benefits (section 28.2.1.2). This uniformity does not sit well with a differentiation on the contribution side.

On the other hand, a lack of premium differentiation certainly encourages moral hazard. Thus, the mere existence of the mandatory scheme serves to decrease the share of good risks and increase the share of bad risks in the population. This causes the good risks to possibly lose the Pareto improvement originally granted by compulsory insurance, while the bad risks still derive an (albeit reduced) advantage from the scheme, as argued in the preceding section.

28.2.1.5 Slow Adjustment to Exogenous Change as a Qualification

Industrial societies are undergoing major changes that require insurance products to be adapted (see section 28.3 below). Specifically, individuals are becoming less likely to be employed in the same firm, industry, and country during their work career. This has caused full portability of insurance benefits to become a major issue (in the case of the European Union, see e.g., Commission of the European Communities, 1992). Countries with generous social insurance schemes fear to be exploited by migrant workers who, after meeting minimal requirements for eligibility, claim benefits from their host country. On the other hand, since social insurance is financed by both employer and employee contributions in most countries, a change of employer gives rise to a conflict over whether portability of benefits extends to employer contributions. Moreover, in the case of international migration it has not been clear whether benefits of e.g., social health insurance can be claimed outside the country of origin.

Adjustment of social insurance to these pressures has been slow because it usually must pass parliament (or even a popular vote in the case of a direct democracy). These political processes are known for their sluggishness. Whereas social insurance is slow to adjust to change, private insurance must taylor its products to individual needs, at least if exposed to competition, which makes for a good deal of flexibility.

28.2.1.6 Efficiency Reasons for Social Insurance: Summary

Some degree of compulsory social insurance may improve Pareto efficiency because it helps to overcome externality problems, associated with free riding of potential donors, adverse selection, and risk-specific transaction cost in the private insurance market. Being mandatory and uniform in its benefits, social insurance also recommends itself in view of its low transaction cost. On the other hand, social insurance typically aggravates moral hazard effects, and it is slow to adjust to changes in the environment resulting in changed preferences of individuals with regard to insurance products. In the wake of restructuring and increased mobility, these disadvantages may well have increased importance in the future, calling for a modification in the division of labor between private and social insurance.

28.2.2 Public Choice Reasons for a Division of Labor

28.2.2.1 The Public Choice View of the Political Process

Starting in the early 1960s, a growing number of researchers applied economic analysis to explain the behavior of actors in the public domain, viz. voters, lobbies, members of parliament, government, and bureaucracies [Mueller (1989), Niskanen (1971), Olson (1965)]. Their basic tenet is that representatives of these groups pursue their own interests very much like consumers and entrepreneurs in the market domain. For example, members of government want to stay in power. To this end, they must win an election. An important way to secure votes is by redistributing income and wealth in favor of one's own constituencies. For politicians in general, an excellent justification for such redistribution emanates from the argument that people may care about the welfare of their fellow beings (see section 28.2.1.1 above). Thus, the public choice view does not deny that political decision makers can contribute to Pareto improvements (by enabling altruism to become effective, thus enhancing social cohesion). It merely argues that the necessity of gaining the votes of self-interested individuals causes them to also consider redistributional measures that do not have an altruistic motive.

Among the more visible instruments of redistribution are taxes and public expenditure. However, public regulation can also be quite effective as a means of redistribution. Thus, Fields et al. (1990) found that California's cap on automobile-insurance rates (Proposition 103) shifted wealth from owners of insurance companies (mainly non-Californian) to local consumers. In this particular instance, demand for and supply of regulation interacted as to make the bill pass the popular vote.

More generally, the division of labor between private and social insurance can be viewed as the equilibrium outcome of the interaction of demand and supply of public regulation (Peltzman, 1976). Demand for regulation may originate with consumers (e.g., the bad risks that do not obtain insurance coverage in the unregulated market). The supply side is governed by three groups of decision makers in the public domain, (1) politicians making up the government (or seeking to win the power to form the government), (2) members of the legislature, and (3) the heads of public bureaucracies.

Specifically, the introduction of social insurance can be interpreted as a particular outcome on the continuum of intensity of regulation. The actual performance of the insurance function by the government marks the high end of the intensity scale. However, the literature on insurance regulation has focused on the lower end of the scale, indicated by public regulation of private insurance [see Meier (1991)]. Whatever the existing intensity of regulation and hence division of labor between private and social insurance, the public choice view reminds one of the stakes government, legislature, and bureaucracy have in preserving the status quo, resisting the efficiency-enhancing changes to be discussed in section 28.5.

28.2.2.2 The Government's Interest in Social Insurance

Individuals pursuing their own interests in the political domain tend to select politicians for office with a view on the impact of their choice on their own economic well-being (Frey and Schneider, 1982). On the other hand, in a democracy politicians must gain a majority of votes to be able to form the government; this can be achieved by redistribution of income and wealth in favor of pivotal voter groups (Mueller, 1989).

This redistribution need not only occur by a shifting of the benefits of public expenditure and the burden of tax finance. The same purpose may also be served by social insurance. Indeed, majority voting per se has been shown to cause a tendency towards excessive social security programs (Browning, 1975). The median voter will support these programs because he can count on obtaining its benefits too. However, the special advantage of social insurance seems to be that the very idea of insurance is redistribution. In private insurance, redistribution is by chance, between those individuals who were lucky not to suffer a loss and those few unlucky ones who obtain benefits in order to be compensated for their loss. It is an easy matter to inject an element of systematic redistribution into insurance because losses still occur by chance, making the detection of net contributions difficult for the insured.[4]

In addition, social insurance protects not only the population but government itself. Without social insurance an economic slump would immediately spill over into the public budget, forcing changes that may not be compatible with the longer-run goal of re-election. Thus, social insurance acts as an automatic insulator, serving to protect the strategic budget from the vagaries of the economy.

Unfortunately, there is little empirical work on the contribution of social insurance to the chance of re-election of governments. There is an extensive literature on popularity functions, linking popularity surveys (which substitute for actual elections, which are a very rare event) to the unemployment rate and the inflation rate (Nannestad and Paldam, 1994). The investigation by Schneider (1986) adds social security and transfer payments (which together roughly match social insurance benefits) as part of total public expenditure to the equation, along with additional controlling variables. The results are presented in Table 2 below.

[4] This argument may provide a solution to the puzzle of why a desired income distribution is not simply achieved by nondistortionary income taxation (Pestieau, 1994).

Table 2
The Contribution of Social Insurance Payments to Government Popularity

Country Government Period of observation	Rate of inflation	Rate of unemployment	Social security and transfer payments, in percent of public expenditure
Australia Party in power 1970–1977 Monthly data	−0.38** (−2.69)	−1.32** (−4.65)	0.58** (4.43)
Germany (West) SPD/FDP-coalition 1970–1980 Quarterly data	−0.20** (−2.71)	−0.43** (−2.81)	0.48(*) (1.81)
USA Presidents Kennedy/Johnson Nixon I and II, Ford 1961–1976 Quarterly data	−2.61* (−2.41)	−3.64** (−2.88)	0.67* (2.36)

Taken from regressions containing additional explanatory variables.
**, *, (*): Levels of significance, 1 percent, 5 percent, and 10 percent. t ratios in parenthesis, OLS estimation.
Source: Schneider (1986).

In two of the three countries examined (Australia and USA), spending on social insurance does appear to make a contribution to the popularity of the government (or the president in the case of the United States). In Germany, the estimated coefficient, while having the predicted sign, does not quite attain conventional significant levels. The contribution of social insurance to popularity is comparable to more conventional influences (such as the rate of unemployment).[5]

While there does not seem to exist more recent research into the contribution of social insurance to government popularity, van Dalen and Swank (1996) seek to determine whether social security outlays are used as an instrument for securing re-election. Indeed, they find clear evidence that the Dutch government increased social security payments when it expected an election. They analyze government spending

[5] Taking the case of the United States as the example, the following elasticity comparison can be made. During the observation period, a unit change in the rate of unemployment would have amounted to one over roughly six percent, amounting to a relative change of approximately 17 percent. A unit change in the share of social security expenditure amounts to approximately one over 50 percent, or 2 percent. Thus, in order to make the regression coefficients comparable in terms of impulses of equal relative strength, the coefficient of the rate of employment has to be scaled down by a factor of 17/2 = 8.5. The coefficient pertaining to the rate of unemployment of −3.64 therefore has to be divided by 8.5, resulting in −0.43, which is comparable in absolute value to the coefficient of the social insurance benefits variable (0.67).

Table 3 Evidence on the Use of Social Insurance Expenditure for Re-election Purposes, The Netherlands

	Dependent variable: Government spending (% of GDP in logs)					
	Public goods			Quasi-public goods		Transfers
	Defense equation	Infra-structure equation	Public administration equation	Education equation	Health care equation	Social security equation
Share of old population	—	—	—	—	3.461**	3.521*
Share of young population	—	—	—	1.495**	–4.863**	4.245**
Unemployment rate	0.728	—	—	—	1.926**	3.143**
$ELEC_e$	0.065**	—	—	—	—	—
$ELEC_a$	0.010	—	—	—	—	—
$ELEC_{ca}$	—	0.102**	—	0.045**	—	—
$ELEC_{bea}$	—	—	0.091**	—	—	0.122**
AR	4	1	1	0	3	3
Sample period	1957–93	1954–93	1954–93	1953–93	1956–93	1957–92
Adj. R^2	0.983	0.951	0.982	0.989	0.998	0.994

Note: Variables not shown are income, price, population size, ideological orientation of the cabinet, and a trend. Estimated with OLS. The symbols ** denote significance at the 5% level and * significance at the 10% level. AR is the number of autoregressive terms, adj. R^2 is the adjusted coefficient of determination.
Source: Van Dalen and Swank (1996).

on public goods (such as defense), quasi-public goods (such as education) and social security transfers using annual data covering 35 years or more. They relate the GDP shares of these expenditures to GDP, relative prices, population size and structure, and ideological orientation of the cabinet. Of particular interest in the present context is the question of whether the structure of expenditure changes around election time [for a similar approach using Australian data, see Pommerehne and Schneider (1983). If so, this would provide evidence supporting the claim that government spending (and in particular transfers in favor of social insurance) are used as a means for winning an election.

The evidence is presented in Table 3. There the dummy variable $ELEC_e$ takes on the value of 1 if the current year is one of an expected election, and 0 otherwise. Likewise, $ELEC_{bea}$ marks the three years before, during, and after an expected election. The main results in the present context are the following:

- During the 1957 to 1992 period, the election effect amounted to an extra 13 percent of social insurance share in GDP, e.g., 17 rather than 15 percent of GDP

(estimated dummy coefficient 0.122; retransformation using the values 1 and 0 of the dummy variable yields $e^{0.122} - e^{0} = 0.129$).
- No other component of public expenditure appears to be used for re-election purposes to the same extent. Expenditure on infrastructure comes close, with a coefficient of 0.102. However, the significant positive coefficients pertaining to the population shares of the old and the young suggest that the Dutch government viewed social insurance expenditures as highly targeted and hence crucial for its purposes (which presumably is to stay in power).

Conclusion 4. There is evidence based on popularity functions and increases of relevant expenditure around election time which supports the view that governments use social insurance as an instrument for securing their re-election.

While the emphasis on re-election provides an excellent opportunity for empirical analysis, it may distract from the fact that a government continuously is called upon to balance several interests in society. Van Velthoven and van Winden (1985) distinguish four such interest groups, viz. state sector workers (which include politicians and bureaucrats), private sector workers, capital owners, and beneficiaries of social insurance. Using the assumption that the first group seeks a Nash bargaining solution under a budget constraint, they derive optimal levels of public employment, taxation, and social security benefits. Although they add a private sector, the model remains silent on the division of labor between private and social insurance because private insurance premiums are not singled out as an expenditure category. However, their analysis could conceivably be generalized in this direction.

28.2.2.3 The Interest of the Legislature in Social Insurance

In general terms, legislators seek to maximize their chance of re-election. This means they must allocate their effort and time in a way as to generate maximum political support (Ehrlich and Posner, 1974; Crain, 1979). For example, by preparing a bill in favor of mandated insurance, the legislator stands to gain not only the votes of consumers who are judged bad risks by private insurers but those of good risks as well, in keeping with the argument developed in section 28.2.1.2 above. Even the private insurance industry may be in favor of such a proposal if the benefits due to the enhancement of demand for its products outweigh the costs in terms of regulation that invariably comes with the mandate (limits on premiums and premium differentials, prohibition of risk selection).

A bill introducing social insurance to be administered by public agencies may still win political support from both risk groups due to the possible reduction of risk-specific transaction costs (see section 28.2.1.3). In addition, both members of government and legislators have an interest in expanding the domain of their authority, which is served by the creation of these agencies. The one group against such a move is the private insurance industry, which however cannot easily muster political support with voters. After all, only a minority of insureds receives benefits during a given year, while the majority just pays premiums. This leaves campaign contributions to legislators as a channel of influence, where the insurance industry has to compete with other lobbies, however.

28.2.2.4 The Interest of the Public Bureaucracy

Public bureaucracies need to be distinguished from the government because its heads do not face an election constraint in the same way as members of the government do. In return, their influence on the formulation of public policy is somewhat indirect in that both parliament and government rely heavily on their advice in the design of legislative proposals. Ever since Niskanen (1971), pay, prestige, and power have been proposed as important motives of leaders of bureaucracy [for a more recent account especially of the power dimension, see Boulding (1991)]. Social insurance is a very effective means for attaining these objectives. In fact, the provision of mandated insurance could be delegated to private suppliers. Overseeing the operations of private insurers who have to comply with usually rather detailed regulation already requires a good deal of manpower (Meier, 1991). However, employment in public agencies and hence status and power of their leaders is at its maximum when public officials take over the actual administration of a social insurance scheme. In all, the interests of bureaucracy are best served if the division of labor between private and social insurance is shifted in favor of the social component, likely beyond the point that would be deemed optimal from the individual insured's point of view.

There does not seem to be much systematic empirical analysis of the relationship between the private—social mix of insurance and the power of public bureaucracies. However, there is some circumstantial evidence. As noted above, the provision of mandated insurance can be delegated to private suppliers. This solution should be observed in countries where bureaucracies are held in check, e.g., by a marked federalist structure or direct voter influence on the political process through popular initiative and referendum. The United States and Switzerland are (two otherwise very different) countries meeting these criteria, and in both, provision for old age and health insurance is carried out by private companies or funds to a considerable degree (Folland, Goodman, and Stano, 1993, ch. 10; Cummins and Outreville, 1984; Zweifel, 1997).

28.2.2.5 Public Choice Reasons for Social Insurance: Summary

According to the public choice view, social insurance is the result of demand for and supply of regulation meeting in the political arena. While demand originates with consumers/voters dissatisfied with private insurance, supply is under the control of government, the legislature, and the public bureaucracy. To these groups, social insurance is a very effective means for securing re-election and status and power, respectively. Increasing the intensity of regulation (i.e., shifting the division of labor away from private to social insurance) thus carries low marginal costs in terms of votes lost (and may have a net benefit to the heads of public bureaucracy). The predicted regulatory equilibrium therefore involves a great deal of social insurance in a democracy.

28.3 THE FOUR CHALLENGES CONFRONTING THE EXISTING DIVISION OF LABOR

The existing division of labor between private and social insurance has mainly involved during the two decades of fast economic growth following the second World War. Under the then prevailing circumstances, it may well have been appropriate. However, at the beginning of the 21st century, several developments challenge the status quo. Some of them are of domestic origin, related to the demographic transition in industrial countries. Others originate in the world economy, having to do with accelerated technological change in international division of labor. In the following, two of each type are singled out for discussion.

28.3.1 Domestic Challenges

There seem to be two major challenges to existing insurance arrangements in industrial countries, viz. population aging and the increased number of single-person households.

28.3.1.1 Population Aging

Industrial countries will be confronted with an increase in their dependency rate starting in 2000 at the latest (see Table 4). In Germany for example, one hundred active persons will have to support no less than 42 aged persons, compared to 23 at the present. This development exerts a marked pressure of adjustment (Pestieau, 1994, p. 89). This can be seen by envisaging the extreme counter-example of a population without any social insurance at all. The following adjustments may be predicted: (1) Increased savings during active life to provide for old age; (2) increased purchase of private pension insurance, disability insurance, and health insurance; (3) deferral of retirement. Social insurance, having defined uniform benefit plans, typically imposes increased contributions [which is equivalent to response (2)], a move that is welcomed not only by the retired population but also by those approaching retirement, who expect to receive more benefits in present value than their contributions. However, viewed over the entire life cycle, the median voter is predicted to opt for less social security and more private saving [see Boadway and Wildasin (1989)].[6] Similar problems confront social health insurance, where present working cohorts have an incentive to opt out because they have to finance an increased number of aged through their

[6] Their analysis is couched in terms of a change in population growth, which however affects the dependency rate. In the present context, this rate increases (which is equivalent to a slower rate of population growth in their model).

Table 4 Aging of the Population as Indicated by the Dependency Rate[a]

Country	1987	1990	2000	2020	2050
FR Germany	21.6	22.4	25.5	35.0	41.6
France	20.2	21.1	24.1	31.1	37.6
Great Britain	23.2	24.0	24.4	28.1	30.0
Italy	19.6	20.8	24.6	30.0	37.9
Spain	18.8	19.8	22.9	25.3	38.7

[a] Dependency rate defined as: number of aged 65^{+} /number of aged 15–64.
Source: Weber, Leienbach and Dohle (1994), p. 188.

Table 5 Share of One-person Households in Selected Industrial Countries (in Percent)

	around 1960	around 1980	around 1990
FR Germany	20	30	33
France	20	24	28
Great Britain	11	22	27
Netherlands	12	22	29
Sweden	20	33	36
U.S.A.	13	23	25

Source: Roussel (1986); for 1990: Eurostat (1993), Statistical Abstract of Sweden (1991), Demographic Yearbook 1990, UN, New York 1992.

contributions in the future (von der Schulenburg, 1989). These arguments suggest that the division of labor between private and social insurance has to be modified (see sections 28.4 and 28.5).

28.3.1.2 *Increase of Single-person Households*

Historically, the family provided its members with a great deal of protection against adverse events. This function has been increasingly taken over by social insurance (Kotlikoff and Spivak, 1981). As evidenced in Table 5, dramatic changes in household composition are occurring in major industrial countries. Specifically, the share of one-person households has increased markedly since 1960, resulting in a doubling in the United States and even more than that in Great Britain and the Netherlands. While this development may be due to aged females surviving their spouses, the surge of divorce rates has also raised the share of one-person households at working age.

The following thought experiment may serve to illustrate the importance of this demographic change. Suppose that the probability of falling ill is 0.2 for two individuals living together in a household and that they are willing to provide some care for each other. Thus, they will have to rely on formal medical care only if both are sick, which occurs with 0.04 probability. By way of contrast, the head of a one-person household will use medical services with probability 0.2. Similar arguments may apply to other lines of social insurance, such as unemployment, disability, and pensions as long as household members are willing to share benefits to some extent.

This change of household composition requires an adjustment of contribution rates and benefits. If these adjustments occur across the board, in keeping with the uniformity typically governing social insurance (see section 28.2.1.1), they may entail unintended cross-subsidizations. Since competitive private insurance tends to weed out cross-subsidization, individuals may wish to adjust the private-social mix in insurance.

28.3.2 International Challenges

28.3.2.1 Accelerated Technological Change

Triggered mainly by a marked fall in the cost of processing and transmitting information, technological change has accelerated recently. This has important implications for both private and social insurance.

- **Unemployment:** The acceleration of technological change has caused acquired skills to depreciate at an increased rate. For affected workers, productivity falls short of the asking wage, with unemployment as a consequence. Social insurers would be in a unique position to make benefits conditional on (re)training effort by the unemployed. However, the political process has been slow to respond beyond adjusting benefits and contribution rates. This sluggishness (see section 28.2.1.5) by itself speaks in favor of a changed division of labor between private and social insurance. However, Barr (1992, pp. 765–767) advances serious doubts that private insurance would provide a solution. He argues that incentives to engage in risk selection would be overwhelming, resulting in a "no-insurance" equilibrium for the bad risks, as in section 28.2.1.3.
- **Provision for old age:** Accelerated technological change results in an increased rate of depreciation of existing stock of human capital. Thus, many a worker losing his job not too far from retirement age will not deem an investment in human capital worthwhile anymore, causing him to become a "worse" risk. Once again, the risk composition of the insured population changes, with unintended cross-subsidization as a likely consequence. Those charged with the cost of the subsidy will redirect their demand from social to private insurance.
- **Health care:** Here, technological change seems to be of the product innovation

rather than process innovation type, with the consequence that it is usually cost increasing rather than cost reducing (Zweifel and Breyer, 1997, ch. 11). Managers of social health insurance are challenged to decide which of the newly available medical technologies are to be included in their (uniform) benefit plans. Their private counterparts could be expected to develop differentiated plans such that the additional benefits justify the increased premiums in view of their several groups of clients. Thus, the existing division of labor comes under pressure once more.

28.3.2.2 Opening up to International Competition

Up to the present, national social insurance schemes have not been exposed to international competition: (1) Individuals cannot choose the social insurance scheme they want to adhere to, and (2) they traditionally had to claim the benefits in the home country of the scheme. Restriction (2) has been lifted at least within the European Union, where full portability of social insurance benefits is the rule of the law, pursuant Ordnance (EEC) No. 1408/71, reaffirmed by the European Court of Justice on 3 May 1990. Lifting restriction (1) might well be in the individual's interest too. As evidenced in Table 6, take-home pay is roughly similar in France, Great Britain, and Italy. At the same time, employee benefits in Great Britain fall far short of the other two countries (mainly due to increased reliance on tax finance). Depending on his income and the progressiveness of the tax schedule, a particular individual may well prefer the British over the French or Italian solution.

Of course, Table 6 also points to a great deal of scope for international competition from the point of multinational enterprise. While its prime concern is total labor cost (relative to productivity), the share taken by employee benefits does have a certain importance. To the extent that employee benefits are imposed by social insurance, they

Table 6
Hourly Labor Cost in Manufacturing in Selected Industrial Countries (USD, 1993)

Country	Total (1)	Paid wage (2)	Employee benefits (3)	Share of employee benefits (3)/(1)
FR Germany	25.8	14.2	11.6	0.45
France	17.2	8.9	8.3	0.48
Great Britain	13.4	9.5	3.9	0.29
Italy	16.4	8.2	8.2	0.50
Japan	22.6	12.9	9.7	0.43
Spain	12.3	6.8	5.5	0.46
Portugal	4.7	2.6	2.1	0.45
U.S.A.	16.8	11.8	5.0	0.30

Source: Institut der deutschen Wirtschaft (Institute of the German Economy), 1994.

constitute a component of labor cost beyond control by the enterprise. For example, France and the United States look comparable in terms of total hourly labor cost (col. 1). However in France, a full 48 percent of that total is (in the main) exogenously determined by the provisions of social insurance. In the United States, this share is a mere 30 percent, leaving a considerable amount of maneuver to the employer for influencing total labor cost. Thus, multinational firms and their employees will be in favor of a shift toward more private insurance, where coverage can be easily extended to any country of residence.

Conclusion 5. Both the domestic and international challenges considered suggest a new division of labor between social and private insurance.

28.4 IMPROVING THE DIVISION OF LABOR BETWEEN PRIVATE AND SOCIAL INSURANCE

28.4.1 Proposed Criteria

Before engaging in discussion about possible improvement, it is necessary to define the criteria by which any change should be judged. The proposed criteria are the following, to be justified below: social adequacy, efficiency, flexibility, and transparency [for a more comprehensive list, see Barr (1992)].

- **Social adequacy:** Given that access to insurance creates a positive externality in society (see section 28.2.2.1 above), every member of society should have access to insurance under all circumstances, including in particular unemployment and bad health. It should be noted, however, that this does not imply that the insurance mechanism as such must redistribute income and wealth in a way that is partially systematic rather than governed by chance. Access to insurance may very well be guaranteed through earmarked transfers.
- **Efficiency:** In general terms, private and social insurance should, in their combination, permit individuals to make the most out of their disposable resources. In section 28.4.3, this objective will be operationalized to mean that individuals should be on the efficient frontier of asset allocation, abstracting from the problem that some preferred points on this frontier may not be attainable because of the uniformity of social insurance. Efficiency then depends on the cost of insurance (in the main, insurers's administrative expense) on the one hand and expected future benefits on the other. The latter hinge on the development of productivity in the economy, which in turn depends on individual decisions with regard to consumption and saving and labor and leisure, respectively.

  As pointed out by Mitchell and Zeldes (1996) and Reid and Mitchell (1995), social security administration costs are only one-fourth of those for private pension systems in the United States. Similar ratios may be expected to hold in other branches of insurance and other countries.

With regard to household incentives to save, the review by Barr (1992, p. 773) confirms the earlier finding of Aaron (1982), suggesting that at least in the United States, there is little evidence of a systematic effect. Household work incentives may be little affected as long as in both old age provision and unemployment insurance, a close link between contributions and benefits is maintained (Diamond, 1977). However, Moffitt (1992) concludes in his review that the major U.S. welfare schemes do reduce labor supply.

- **Flexibility:** In view of the challenges impinging on existing insurance mechanisms (see section 28.3), individuals should have the opportunity to adjust in an attempt to catch up with their changing efficiency frontier (see section 28.4.3). Now social insurance parameters cannot be changed very easily. In a democracy at least, a majority of parliament (in direct democracy: of voters) must be found. This is a time consuming process. By contradistinction, private insurers (unless hindered by regulation) are able to develop and market a new product in short time.
- **Transparency:** Both private and social insurance are characterized by a good deal of small print. Even seemingly simple Pay-as-you-go (PAYG) social security systems become complex once benefits are tied to previous contributions, which moreover need to be scaled up according to some formula in order to let the retired participate in income growth. In addition, social insurance too stipulates the precise conditions under which benefits are paid, likely in an attempt to control moral hazard. However, in the domain of competitive private insurance, lack of transparency (as perceived by the consumer) creates profit opportunities for a company that launches a new, "simple-to-use" product—in return for a higher premium or rate of cost sharing, of course (Eisen, Müller, and Zweifel, 1993). By way of contrast, a public monopoly insurer lacks the incentives to react in such a way.

28.4.2 Choice of Conceptual Framework

Traditionally, the division of labor between private and social insurance has been regarded as purely political. Indeed, there are several features of social insurance that seem to set it apart from private insurance (Thompson, 1983, p. 1436):

- The connection between benefits and contributions is loose in social insurance;
- There are no contractual rights to benefits;
- Contributions are compulsory;
- There are no substantial financial reserves.

These divergencies have led to three competing conceptualizations of social insurance, viz. the tax-transfer model, the insurance model, and the welfare-annuity model.

- **Tax-transfer model:** Social insurance is simply a redistribution mechanism [Pechman, Aaron and Taussig (1968)]. Accordingly, there is no particular reason why its benefits should be related to contributions, which amount to a tax on labor income. Moreover, contributions should reflect current ability to pay while benefits should be distributed according to value judgments prevalent in society. Finally, under this model there is no apparent need to analyze the incentive effects of social insurance beyond the current period; life-cycle effects can be disregarded.
- **Insurance model:** According to this conceptualization, individuals compare the present value of benefits from and contributions to social insurance, taking into account that they are to some extent connected during a given period. Accordingly, emphasis is on life-cycle rather than current-period incentives. With regard to distributional issues, there is a trade-off between individual equity (calling for equality of life-time benefits and contributions) and social adequacy (Diamond, 1977; Viscusi, 1979).
- **Annuity-welfare model:** This conceptualization strikes a balance between the other two. It maintains that the social insurance mechanism has to serve redistributional objectives. Thus, benefits are decomposed into a social adequacy component and an individual equity component (which is defined by the equality of benefits and contributions in present value).[7] The redistributional component then could be treated like a separate tax-transfer program, while the remainder (the individual equity component) continues to be examined in a life-cycle context.

In the following, a variant of the insurance model will be adopted. This permits to judge both social and private insurance by the same standard of performance. In this way, the existing division of labor between the two modes of insurance can be evaluated for all branches of insurance simultaneously.

28.4.3 Efficient Asset Allocation as the Standard of Performance

An insurance arrangement, private or social, can be viewed as an asset position of the individual. This view, pioneered by Doherty (1985), is becoming increasingly popular as banks and insurers begin to offer combined products. In the domain of private insur-

[7] By the same token, one might also decompose the contribution side into an actuarial component (reflecting the risk-based contribution) and a redistributional component.

ance, a policy may be viewed as a financial instrument having an expected rate of return (μ) and variance of return (σ^2). This holds not only for policies with a savings component such as whole life insurance. Since the benefit side of any insurance policy is stochastic, its return is a stochastic quantity too inspite of possibly deterministic premium flows.

However, exactly the same argument holds for all lines of social insurance. This is most visible in the case of public pensions, where a comparison between contributions paid and benefits received in present value can be expressed in a rate of return. Although most public pension plans have defined benefits, they continue to have a positive variance of return for at least three reasons.

- Benefits are triggered by events that are not fully under the control of the individual, such as early retirement caused by bad health.
- To the extent that benefits are in nominal terms, the rate of inflation injects an element of volatility into public plans.
- Benefits may be scaled downward by political decree, and details of the benefit formula can usually be changed by administrative fiat, causing future pensions to be subject to a good deal of political risk.

These features characterize other lines of social insurance as well, which may therefore be viewed as financial instruments of a certain volatility.

In Figure 4, the line EE′ symbolizes the efficient frontier of an insurance portfolio, freely choosen by a fully informed individual. Its shape is the more strongly concave the more the returns on the elements of the portfolio are positively correlated. Depending on his or her degree of risk aversion, the depicted individual would opt for a preferred combination of expected return and volatility such as point C**, yielding an expected utility of $\overline{\overline{EU}}$. The creation of mandatory social insurance has two effects. First, the individual is offered a new portfolio not available before, symbolized by the frontier E_sE_s'. It has three features. (1) Fixed contributions and uniform benefits usually do not leave much of a choice. Accordingly, E_sE_s' covers a limited range of $\{\mu, \sigma^2\}$ -combinations. (2) The minimum variance portfolio of social insurance (given by point E_s') probably has smaller volatility than its counterpart that could have been achieved without social insurance (point E′), although the risks mentioned above may cast some doubt on this proposition. (3) At least in the neighborhood of the minimum variance portfolio, social and private insurance do not differ systematically in their expected rates of return (cf. points E_s', E′ and E_p' in terms of μ). Of course, the frontier E_sE_s' may lie much higher for those who profit from redistribution in social insurance; conversely, it runs lower for those who finance this redistribution.

The second effect is that the efficient frontier pertaining to private insurance shifts inward, to E_pE_p'. With parts of the individual's resources tied up in social insurance, some private insurance products (requiring large upfront payments e.g.) are now out

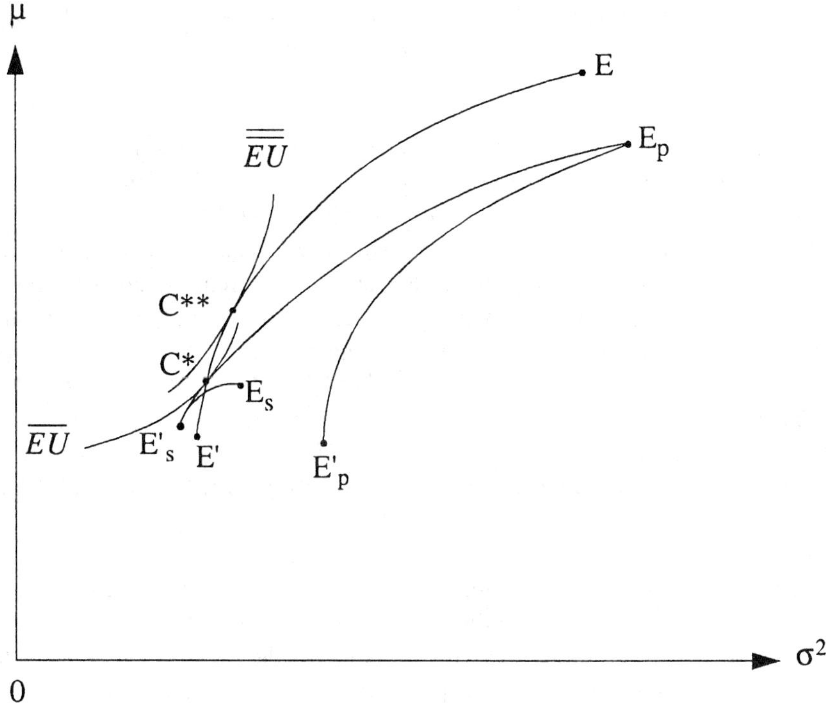

Figure 4 Private and Social Insurance as Portfolio Components

of reach. The combined efficiency frontier E_pE_s' is the envelope of all the frontiers derived from combining some portfolio contained in E_sE_s' with some other portfolio from E_pE_p' [see Doherty (1985), Ch. 6]. On the whole, the combined efficiency frontier E_pE_s' is likely to reflect an efficiency loss relative to EE′, for the following reasons:

1. **Imperfect pooling:** In social insurance even more than in private insurance, many risks cannot be combined to be covered under one policy. This prevents social insurers from a full pooling of their risks. The efficient frontier applicable to social insurance thus runs lower and more strongly concave, such as E_sE_s' in Figure 4. The frontier may even shrink to a single point if there is no choice element left.
2. **Restricted investments:** Social insurers typically must invest their reserves in a very narrow selection of assets, mainly government bonds. This has the same two effects (inward shift, increased concavity) on the individual's efficiency frontier as imperfect pooling.
3. **Lack of currency diversification:** Benefits of and contributions to social insurance are invariably denominated in the national currency, thus obviating individual choice of currency in the interest of risk diversification. For example, a

Canadian worker cannot enroll in a Canadian social insurance program whose benefits would be paid in U.S. Dollars. This once more serves to increase the concavity of E_sE_s'.

The individual can now pool the asset positions offered by social insurance (E_sE_s) and private insurance (E_pE_p) to reach the combined frontier E_pE_s'. In Figure 4, the optimum allocation C* has a reduced expected utility level $\overline{EU}$.

Of course, social insurance can also have efficiency-enhancing effects. Apart from those mentioned in section 2.1, individuals may be away from the efficient frontier to begin with, due e.g., to lack of information. Moreover, a strongly risk-averse individual would rank C* (with social insurance) higher than C** (no social insurance) in Figure 4.

Finally, social insurance may be a vehicle of paternalism on the part of the policy maker, who may decide that an optimum such as C** in Figure 4 is too risky. To the extent that social insurance indeed offers a low-volatility portfolio such as E_sE_s', the final allocation may be less risky (such as C*). However, as long as individuals are free to purchase private insurance (let alone other financial assets), they might actually increase the total amount of volatility in their portfolio by simply purchasing high-risk products such as private health insurance with high deductibles.

The issue to be addressed at this point is whether the existing division of labor between private and social insurance helps individuals to approach the efficiency frontier E′E′. In the investigation sketched in the following subsection, expected rates of return μ of different lines of both private and social insurance will be disregarded. This can be justified at least to some extent. As to private insurance, its products must have roughly the same μ as any other financial instrument. As to social insurance, at least its pay-as-you-go schemes have a "biological rate of return" given by the growth of the labor force (Samuelson, 1958). This rate may exceed or fall below the real rate of return on financial assets; there is no particular reason for the difference to go either way [see Zweifel (2000) for some evidence]. Therefore, the division of labor between private and social insurance can be studied approximately in terms of its effect on asset volatility.

28.4.4 Some Empirical Evidence

Payments by different lines of insurance may be viewed as part of an individual's assets. They are stochastic for two reasons. First, insurance benefits must be triggered by a hazardous event. Second, however, they may be more generous or more scanty than expected, depending on the insurer's interpretation of small print. Now if expected payments are chosen by the individual as to minimize final asset volatility, the second, unexpected component becomes decisive.[8] Indeed, across insurance lines,

[8] Insurance contributions are neglected in the argument because they typically are non stochastic ("There are three certain things in life, death, taxes, and insurance premiums").

unexpected deviations from expected benefits should be uncorrelated if final asset volatility would otherwise be reduced to zero and negatively correlated if it would otherwise still be positive [see Zweifel (2000) for a formula].

At the aggregate level, the unexpected component of insurance payments may be approximated by trend deviations. In an exploratory study, Zweifel and Eisen (1996) tested whether these trend deviations are positively or negatively correlated in the case of Germany and Switzerland [for the United States, see Zweifel (2000)]. The results for German private insurance are given in part A and those for their U.S. counterparts in part B of Table 7.

Positive correlations prevail in Germany, with the only exception of private disability insurance (PDI), which shows some (not significant) negative correlations with trend deviations in the remaining lines of private insurance. As a whole, then, private insurance in Germany does not seem to contribute much to decreasing volatility in individual assets.

In the United States, private insurance may be claimed to make a much more marked contribution to the reduction of asset volatility. Among the three personal lines distinguished, trend deviations are uncorrelated or even negatively correlated.

Table 8 displays the results of the correlation test with regard to social insurance. In Germany, positive values abound once more. In the United States, Workers Compensation appears to fill unexpected gaps left by Old Age and Survivors, while Medicare hospital benefits step in to make up shortfalls in Workmans Compensation.

Therefore, presumably through its piecemeal historic development, German social insurance does not serve to dampen asset volatility. However, the insurance mechanism as a whole may still perform well if shortfalls in social insurance benefits were made up by generous payments by private insurance. Unfortunately, the evi-

Table 7

Correlations of Trend Deviations in the Benefits of Private Insurance

	A: Germany 1975–1993				B: United States, 1974–1992			
	PLI	PHI	PDI	PGI	PLI	PHI	PDI	PGI
PLI	1				1			
PHI	0.37	1			0.28	1		
PDI	–0.19	–0.41	1		0.41	0.11	1	
PGI	0.54*	0.76*	–0.40	1	n.a.	n.a.	n.a.	1

PLI: Private life insurance.
PHI: Private health insurance.
PDI: Private disability insurance.
PGI: Private general liability insurance.
*: Correlation coefficient significantly different from zero (5% significance level or better).

Table 8

Correlations of Trend Deviations in Benefits of Social Insurance

	Germany, 1975–1993					United States, 1974–1992						
	OAS	WC	DI	UI	HI	OAS	WC	DI	UI	MCH	MCS	MA
OAS	1					1						
WC	0.91*	1				−0.64*	1					
DI	0.91*	1	1			−0.41	0.77*	1				
UI	0.76*	0.83*	0.83*	1		0.02	0.24	0.70*	1			
HI: MCH	n.a.	n.a.	n.a.	n.a.		0.82*	−0.65*	−0.21	0.28	1		
HI: MCS	0.45	0.67*	0.67*	0.65*	1	−0.29	0.31	0.16	0.29	−0.31	1	
HI: MA	n.a.	n.a.	n.a.	n.a.	n.a.	−0.55*	0.84*	0.93*	0.63*	−0.40	0.33	1

OAS: Old age and survivors insurance.
WC: Workers compensation (Germany: Accident insurance).
DI: Disability insurance (Germany: Accident insurance).
UI: Unemployment insurance.
HI: Health insurance (U.S.: divided into MCH Medicare hospital, MCS Medicare supplementary, MA Medicaid).

dence presented in Zweifel and Eisen (1996) and Zweifel (2000) does not support this view, in particular for Germany.

Conclusion 6. An analysis of correlations between trend deviations of aggregate private and social insurance payments suggests that in Germany (but less so in the United States) the insurance mechanism as a whole causes individuals' asset volatility to be unnecessarily high.

Of course, conclusion 6 is extremely preliminary. Correlation of insurance benefits might well be negative at the individual level, with a common stochastic shock transforming it into positive at the aggregate level. For example, in an economic downswing, not only does the number of beneficiaries of unemployment insurance rise but also the number of beneficiaries for old age provision due to early retirement. In order to shed more light on this issue, life cycle observations are needed which show the impulses impinging on the individual as well as the payments of the different lines of insurance (both private and social) over time. In this way, the contribution of the insurance mechanism to the reduction total asset volatility could be assessed.

28.5 SUGGESTIONS FOR AN IMPROVED DIVISION OF LABOR BETWEEN PRIVATE AND SOCIAL INSURANCE

28.5.1 Three Proposals

The following three proposals are designed to enable individuals to better reach the efficiency frontier for their assets, among which figure their private and social insurance provisions. These are the abolishment of separation of lines in insurance, design of umbrella policies and provisions having the stop-loss property, and hedging of domestic risks having positive correlation on international insurance markets.

- **Abolishment of separation of lines:** As long as insurers have to hold reserves for their lines of business separately, they cannot profit from risk diversification to the greatest amount possible. Historically, public regulation of insurance sought to build "firewalls" between life and nonlife insurance in order to prevent cross-subsidization of premiums in favor of nonlife business, using up reserves accumulated in life business. Until recently, there was no way of distinguishing cross-subsidization from efficient use of pooled reserves. Ever since Kahane and Nye (1975), however, it is possible to establish whether a company with a particular collection of assets and liability lies on the efficient frontier.

  For the consumer, an integration of lines would mean additional benefits for the same amount of contributions. This is also true of social insurance, where the separation of lines is imposed by the different agencies involved, such as the Social Security Administration and the Medicare Administration in the United States. Cross-subsidization often occurs in a haphazard manner, with politicians doing away with the deficit of one program by taking away any surplus from another program.
- **Creation of umbrella policies:** With the separation of lines abolished, it should become possible for private insurers to create umbrella policies with a common stop-loss feature. This would be a clear gain for risk-averse consumers. For as long as there is less than full coverage in several policies (replacement rate less than 100 percent in Workers Compensation, copayments in health insurance), consumers face the risk of an accumulation of such limitations. As shown by Arrow (1963), risk-averse individuals prefer to have full coverage beyond a deductible, i.e., a stop-loss contract. Such a contract could make them pay e.g., 5,000 Dollars out-of-pocket regardless of the cause of the loss. Beyond this common deductible, coverage should be complete unless moral hazard effects are an important consideration, in which case some amount of coinsurance may have to be imposed (in particular in health insurance).
- **Hedging of risks on international markets:** Consumers demand a great deal of (actuarially fair) insurance coverage if their assets prior to insurance are positively correlated (Doherty and Schlesinger, 1983). The three assets in question are health, wealth, and wisdom (with the latter symbolizing skills of value in the labor market). These three assets are likely to be positively correlated. For example, without insurance a spell of bad health entails a loss of wealth too because of the cost of medical care and the loss of labor income. Likewise, a loss of value of one's skills ("wisdom") easily results in health problems, especially if associated with unemployment.

  Insurers avoid covering positively correlated risks under one policy (unless they sufficiently save on administrative expense by doing so). However, with the growing internationalization of insurance markets, positively correlated risk portfolios in one country can be hedged using positively correlated risks in some other country. For example, a portfolio in Germany, consisting of policies covering health and old age, could be matched with a similarly composed portfolio in a Pacific Rim country where demographic aging will occur much later.

Clearly, such internationalization is not compatible with national compulsory pools designed to include the bad risks on uniform terms. However, the subsidization solution presented in section 28.2.1.1 may be applied. Through a subsidy, the willingness to pay of the bad risks is increased to the level of their marginal cost of insurance, which now equals the insurer's opportunity cost of complementing its risk portfolio in the country considered rather than somewhere else. This means that the possible efficiency gain from forced pooling (see section 28.2.1.3) would have to be given up; on the other hand, the risk-specific transaction costs (which are the cause of these gains) also lose importance in view of the improved hedging possibilities available to international insurers.

28.5.2 Implications for the Division of Labor between Private and Social Insurance

There is reason to believe that the three reform steps outlined in the preceding section can be achieved better by private rather than social insurance. Social insurance typically consists of separate programs each with its specific eligibility conditions and restrictions on benefits. The creation of umbrella policies would therefore call for an integration of these programs, along with the agencies running them. Whether such an integration into one large administration is in the consumers' interest has to be strongly doubted. Finally, social insurers cannot easily hedge risks on international markets. Based on their very mission, they must insure domestic but not foreign persons. Moreover, they may be constrained to hold their assets in domestic currency.

On balance, these reform steps suggest an enlarged role of private actors. The implications of increased privatization have been expounded by Mitchell and Zeldes (1996). They advocate two-pillar solution for old age provision, with the first pillar guaranteeing a minimum pension for retirees who contributed to the existing system. The second pillar would be a fully funded, individual, defined-contribution account, held by individuals with financial institutions of their choice. The transition to such a predominantly funded system would entail losses of promised benefits to current retirees, who however could obtain special government bonds for compensation.

In a simulation for Germany, Börsch-Schupan (1997) calculates the burden of a transition to a fully funded social security system. For the cohorts born between 1946 and 1964, the average worker would have to save an additional 190 DM per month (130 USD at 1997 exchange rates), which has to be compared with the

1,100 DM monthly he contributes under the current PAYG system. In return, cohorts born after 1964 would increasingly profit from the transition to a funded system, with the difference amounting to almost 1,000 DM (600 USD monthly) for those born after 2010.

Conclusion 7. Three reforms that would enable individuals to come closer to the efficiency frontier are abolishing the separation of lines, creation of umbrella policies, and international hedging of risks. They tend to favor private over social insurance in the division of labor between the two.

28.5.3 Obstacles to Reform

The public choice considerations expanded in section 28.2.2 above lead to the prediction that demanders and suppliers of regulation will resist any movement away from the prevailing equilibrium, unless they themselves experience a change in the costs or benefits of regulation. Evidently, the proposals outlined in the preceding section amount to a reduction in the intensity of regulation. Accordingly, objections will be voiced by some consumer groups, some members of government, the legislature, and public bureaucracies [for an analogous argument in the case of deregulation of telecommunications, see Knieps and Schneider (1990)].

- **Resistance from consumers.** A majority of consumers will get more security for their money if the proposals are realized. However, a private insurer will charge risk-based premiums because group insurance with its inherent cross-subsidization is not compatible with the creation of umbrella policies and integration across several lines of business in insurance. Risk-based premiums will make some individuals pay very high contributions even for minimum coverage of their health, old age, and unemployment risks. For these individuals, public welfare will have to step in, enabling them to buy a reduced amount of mandated insurance coverage from the provider of their choice.
- **Resistance from the government.** By changing the division of labor in favor of private insurance, the government partially renounces to a powerful instrument available for securing its success in re-election (see section 28.2.2.2). However, the challenges described in section 28.3 jeopardize the financial equilibrium of social insurance, whose deficits must be covered out of the public purse. This deprives the government of the means for financing other public expenditure, with negative effects on the chance of re-election. Thus, there is a trade-off involved which may cause the government to adopt a privatization policy.
- **Resistance from the legislature.** Legislators must also consider a trade-off in terms of political support. On the one hand, consumers who lose the cross-subsidization inherent in social insurance without being fully compensated by public welfare payments may turn to a competitor at election time. On the other

hand, private insurers are able to provide campaign contributions, which will help to make up for the lost votes.

- **Resistance from the public bureaucracy.** The agencies administering the social insurance programs are probably the major losers in a privatization program. Through their regular contacts with their clientele (which includes almost a country's entire population at present), they can easily inform about the drawbacks of privatization. Moreover, they can provide slightly biased expert opinion to legislators and members of government. Their resistance may well constitute the most formidable obstacle to a change in the mix of private and social insurance.

Nevertheless, it seems that the heyday of uniform national solutions for covering the essential risks with regard to health, wealth, and wisdom is over. In order to improve the overall performance of insurance mechanisms, mandatory coverage in the domain of social insurance may be reduced to low levels in order to grant individuals having additional insurance needs full flexibility of choice in contracting for supplementary coverage. This coverage might well be provided by private insurers, who increasingly have an opportunity to hedge their risk portfolios internationally. Through this modification of the division of labor between social and private insurance, individuals may be helped in their effort to manage their assets over the life cycle.

28.6 REFERENCES

Aaron, A.J. (1982). "Economic Effect of Social Security," Washington DC: The Brookings Institution.

Aarts, L.J.M. (1997). "Private provision of social security," in: P.R. de Jong and T.R. Marmor (eds.), Social Policy and the Labour Market, Aldershot: Ashgate, 41–62.

Arrow, K.J. (1963). "Uncertainty and the welfare economics of medical care," *American Economic Review*, 53, 941–973.

Atkinson, A.B. (1991). "Social insurance. The 15th annual lecture of the Geneva association," *Geneva Papers on Risk and Insurance Theory*, 16(2), 113–131.

Barr, N. (1992). "Economic theory and the welfare state: a survey and interpretation," *Journal of Economic Literature*, XXX (2), 741–803.

Boulding, K.E. (1991). "Three Faces of Power," Newbury Park CA: Sage.

Browning, E.K. (1975). "Why the social insurance budget is too large in democratic society," *Economic Inquiry* 13, 373–388.

Boadway, R. and Wildasin, D. (1989). "Voting models of social security determination," in: B.A. Gustavson and N.A. Klevmarken (eds.), The Political Economy of Social Security, Amsterdam: North-Holland, 29–50.

Börsch-Schupan, A. (1997). "Privatization of social security in Europe, Working paper 97-022," University of Mannheim (Germany), Mimeo.

Commission of the European Communities (1992). "Social security for persons moving within the Community, Social Europe, 3/92," Luxembourg: Office for Official Publications of the EC.

Crain, M. (1979). "Cost and output in the legislative firm," *Journal of Legal Studies* 8(3), 607–621.

Cummins, J.D. and Outreville, J.F. (1984). "The portfolio behavior of pension funds in the US: an econometric analysis of changes since the new regulation of 1974," *Applied Economics*, 16, 687–701.

Dahlby, D.G. (1981). "Adverse selection and Pareto improvements through compulsory insurance," *Public Choice* 37(3), 547–568.

Diamond, P. (1977). "A framework for social security analysis," *Journal of Public Economics* 8(3), 275–298.

Doherty, N. (1985). "Corporate Risk Management," New York: Mcgraw-Hill.

Doherty, N. and Schlesinger, H. (1983). "Optimal insurance in incomplete markets," *Journal of Political Economy* 91, 1045–1054.

Ehrlich, I. and Posner, R.A. (1974). "An economic analysis of legal rulemaking," *Legal Studies*, 3(1), 257–286.

Eisen R., Müller, W. and Zweifel (1993). "Entrepreneurial insurance." A new paradigm for deregulated markets, *The Geneva Papers on Risk and Insurance* (Issues and Practice), 66, 3–56.

Fecher, E., Perelman, S.D. and Pestieau, P. (1991). "Scale economies and performance in the French insurance industry," *Geneva Papers on Risk and Insurance* (Issues and Practice) 60, 315–326.

Fields, J.A., Ghosh, C., Kidwell, D.S. and Klein, L.A. (1990). "Wealth effects of regulatory reform. The reaction of California's Proposition 103," *Journal of Financial Economics*, 28, 233–250.

Folland, S., Goodman, A.C. and Stano, M. (1993). "The Economics of Health and Health Care." New York: Macmillan Publishing.

Frey, B.S. and Schneider, F. (1982). "Political-economic models in competition with alternative models: Who predicts better?" *European Journal of Political Research* 10, 241–254.

Hellwig, M. (1987). "Some recent developments in the theory of competition in markets with adverse selection," *European Economic Review* 31, 319–325.

Kahane, Y. and Nye, D.J. (1975). "A portfolio approach to the property-liability insurance industry," *Journal of Risk and Insurance*, 42(4), 579–598.

Kellner, S. and Matthewson, G.F. (1983). "Entry, size, distribution, scale and scope economies in the life insurance industry," *Journal of Business*, 56(1), 25–44.

Knieps, G. and Schneider, F. (1990). "Politico-Economic Aspects of Deregulation in the Telecommunication Sector," London: Institute of Economic Affairs.

Kotlikoff, L.J. and Spivak, A. (1981). "The family as an incomplete annuity's market," *Journal of Political Economy* 89, 372–391.

Meier, K.J. (1991). "The politics of insurance regulation," *Journal of Risk and Insurance* 58(4), 700–713.

Mitchell, O.S. and Zeldes, S.P. (1996). "Social security privatization: A structure for analysis," *American Economic Review* 86(2), 363–367.

Moffitt, R.A. (1992). "Incentive effects of the U.S. welfare system: a review," *Journal of Economic Literature*, 30(1), 1–61.

Mueller, D.C. (1989). Public Choice II, Cambridge: Cambridge University Press.

Nannestad, P. and Paldam, M. (1994). "The WP-function: a survey of the literature on vote and popularity functions after 25 years," Public Choice, 79(3–4), 213–245.

Niskanen, W.A. (1971). "Bureaucracy and Representative Government," Aldine: Chicago.

Newhouse, J.P. (1996). "Reimbursing health plans and health providers; efficiency in production versus selection," *Journal of Economic Literature* XXXIV, 1236–1263.

Olson, M. (1965). "The Logic of Collective Action. Cambridge." Cambridge University Press.

Pauly, M.V. (1971). "Medical Care at Public Expense." A Study in Applied Welfare Economics, New York: Praeger.

Pechman, J.A., Aaron, H.J. and Taussig, M.K. (1968). "Social Security: Perspectives for Reform," Washington D.C: Brookings Institution.

Peltzman, S. (1976). "Toward a more general theory of regulation," *Journal of Law and Economics* 19(2), 211–240.

Pestieau, P. (1994). "Social protection and private insurance: Reassessing the role of public sector versus private sector and insurance," *The Geneva Papers on Risk and Insurance Theory* (19), 81–92.

Pommerehne, W.W. and Schneider, F. (1983). "Does government in a representative democracy follow a majority of voters' preferences?" An empirical examination, in: H. Hanusch (ed.), Anatomy of Government Deficit, Heidelberg: Springer, 61–84.

Reichlin, P. and Siconolfi, P. (1996). "The role of social security in an economy with asymmetric information and financial intermediaries," *Journal of Public Economics* 60, 153–175.

Reid, G. and Mitchell, O.S. (1995). "Social Security Administration Lessons in America and the Caribbean." World Bank Report 14066, Washington DC.

Rothschild, M. and Stiglitz, J.E. (1976). "Equilibrium in competitive insurance markets: An essay on the economics of imperfect information," *Quarterly Journal of Economics*, 225–243.

Roussel, L. (1986). "Evolution récente de la structure des ménages dans quelques pays industriels," Population 41(6), 913–934.

Schneider, F. (1986). "The influence of political institutions on social security policies: A public choice view," in: J.-M. von der Schulenburg (ed.), Essays in Social Security Economics, Berlin: Springer, 13–31.

Samuelson, P.A. (1958). "An exact consumption-loan model of interest with or without the social contrivance of money," *Journal of Political Economy* 66(6), 467–482.

Stiglitz, J.E. (1983). "Risk, incentives and insurance: The pure theory of moral hazard," *Geneva Papers on Risk and Insurance* 8, 4–33.

Thompson, L.H. (1983). "The social security reform debate," *Journal of Economic Literature*, XXI, 1425–1467.

Van Dalen, H.P. and Swank, O.A. (1996). "Government spending cycles: Ideological or opportunistic?," *Public Choice* 89, 183–200.

Van Velthoven, B. and Van Winden, F. (1985). "Towards a political-economic theory of social security," *European Economic Review* 27, 263–289.

Viscusi, W.K. (1979). "Welfare of the Elderly: An Economic Analysis and Policy Prescription," New York: John Wiley and Sons.

von der Schulenburg, J.-M. (1989). "Gesundheitswesen (Krankenversicherung) und demographische Evolution (Health care, health insurance and demographic evolution)," in: H.C. Recktenwald (ed.), Der Rückgang der Geburten—Folgen auf längere Sicht, Düsseldorf: Verlag Wirtschaft und Finanzen, 279–297, cited in Zweifel and Breger (1997), ch. 9.

Weber, A. and Leienbach, V. and Dohle, A. (1994). "Soziale Sicherung in West-Mittel- und Osteuropa," Teil I (Social Insurance in Western, Central and Eastern Europe), Baden-Baden (Germany): Nomos.

Yfantopoulos, J. (1991). "Financing of social security in the E.C.," in: D. Pieters (ed.), Social Security in Europe, Miscellanea of the Erasmus Programme of Studies Relating to Social Security in the European Communities, Brussels: Bruyland, 217–237.

Zweifel, P. and Breyer, F. (1997). "Health Economics," New York: Oxford University Press.

Zweifel, P. and Eisen, R.E. (1996). Optimal combination of insurance products," in: International Insurance Society (ed.), Seminar proceedings, Amsterdam, 145–159.

Zweifel, P. (1997). "Swiss health policy," in: P. Bacchetta and W. Wasserfallen (eds.), Economic Policy in Switzerland, London: Macmillan Press, ch. 7.

Zweifel, P. (2000), "Criteria for the future division of labor between private and social insurance," *Journal of Health Care Finance*, 26(3), 38–55.

INDEX